THE OXFORD HANDBOOK OF

ENVIRONMENTAL CRIMINOLOGY

THE OXFORD HANDBOOKS IN CRIMINOLOGY AND CRIMINAL JUSTICE

General Editor: Michael Tonry

The Oxford Handbooks in Criminology and Criminal Justice offer authoritative, comprehensive, and critical overviews of the state of the art of criminology and criminal justice. Each volume focuses on a major area of each discipline, is edited by a distinguished group of specialists, and contains specially commissioned, original essays from leading international scholars in their respective fields. Guided by the general editorship of Michael Tonry, the series will provide an invaluable reference for scholars, students, and policy makers seeking to understand a wide range of research and policies in criminology and criminal justice.

Other titles in this series:

OFFENDER DECISION MAKING
Wim Bernasco, Jean-Louis van Gelder, and Henk Elffers

SEX OFFENCES AND SEX OFFENDERS
Teela Sanders

THE HISTORY OF CRIME AND CRIMINAL JUSTICE
Paul Knepper and Anja Johansen

WHITE-COLLAR CRIME
Shanna R. Van Slyke, Michael L. Benson, and Francis T. Cullen

ORGANIZED CRIME
Letizia Paoli

CRIMINOLOGICAL THEORY
Francis T. Cullen and Pamela Wilcox

THE OXFORD HANDBOOK OF

ENVIRONMENTAL CRIMINOLOGY

Edited by

GERBEN J. N. BRUINSMA

and

SHANE D. JOHNSON

OXFORD
UNIVERSITY PRESS

OXFORD
UNIVERSITY PRESS

Oxford University Press is a department of the University of Oxford. It furthers the University's objective of excellence in research, scholarship, and education by publishing worldwide. Oxford is a registered trade mark of Oxford University Press in the UK and certain other countries.

Published in the United States of America by Oxford University Press
198 Madison Avenue, New York, NY 10016, United States of America.

Library of Congress Cataloging-in-Publication Data
Names: Bruinsma, Gerben J. N., editor. | Johnson, Shane D., 1971– editor.
Title: The Oxford Handbook of Environmental Criminology /
edited by Gerben J. N. Bruinsma, Shane D. Johnson.
Description: New York, NY : Oxford University Press, [2018]
Identifiers: LCCN 2017022094 | ISBN 9780190279707 (hardcover) |
ISBN 9780190279714 (updf)
Subjects: LCSH: Offenses against the environment. | Criminology.
Classification: LCC HV6401 .O94 2018 | DDC 364.1/45—dc23
LC record available at https://lccn.loc.gov/2017022094

1 3 5 7 9 8 6 4 2

Printed by Sheridan Books, Inc., United States of America

Dedicated to our late parents,
who did not have the opportunity to attend university but who encouraged us to.

Contents

PART II METHODS OF RESEARCH IN ENVIRONMENTAL CRIMINOLOGY

PART III EVERYDAY URBAN CRIME: EMPIRICAL EXAMPLES AND REVIEWS OF RESEARCH

Neighborhoods and Communities

Routine Activity Convergence

Foreword

Edwin Sutherland long ago characterized criminology's subject as the making, the breaking, and the enforcement of criminal laws. That may be the best definition anyone will ever offer, and for sure it is the most succinct. However, its emphasis on law "breaking" risks putting too much focus on individuals' wrongful acts, and not enough on the circumstances in which they occur.

Individuals do break laws, but they do it more often in some times, places, and circumstances than in others. This has been known since the earliest systematic efforts to document and explain crime patterns were made by French statisticians early in the nineteenth century. They showed that crimes occurred not randomly but in patterns that are now commonly recognized: more often in some cities and regions than in others; more in urban than in rural areas; more on some days, at some times of day, and in some seasons than in others. Those early statisticians attempted to find out whether the differences could be explained by demographic characteristics of populations. They could not. Something made crime more likely in some times and places than in others. Context, of course, isn't the only explanation for why crimes occur. Emotion, self-control, alcohol, and greed self-evidently matter, among many other things, in individual cases. Explanations of crime need to attend not only to the characteristics of offenders but also to the contexts in which crimes occur.

Continuous efforts have been made since the middle of the nineteenth century to investigate the influence on lawbreaking of individuals' personal characteristics. Relative attention to biological, psychological, and social factors has varied over time, but the importance of individual differences has never fallen from view.

Interest in contextual influences has, to the contrary, waxed and waned. One high point, probably known at least by name to any scholar involved in crime research in the past century, was work by "Chicago school" sociologists in the 1920s, 1930s, and 1940s that sought to understand changes and continuities over time in crime patterns in Chicago neighborhoods. There have been low points, including in the late nineteenth and early twentieth centuries and for several decades in the middle of the twentieth.

Interest in contextual influences has roared back since the 1970s, generating new theories, research designs, research questions, and crime prevention strategies. New specialties including geographical, areal, ecological, and environmental Criminology, and the criminology of place have emerged, merged, divided, and evolved. The contextual focus, depending on what is being studied, has included communities, neighborhoods, police precincts, census districts, blocks, streets, street segments, intersections, and addresses. The resulting literature is huge, diverse, sophisticated, and mostly quantitative.

The *Oxford Handbook of Environmental Criminology* takes stock. The introduction, by itself worth the price of admission, provides a wide-ranging overview of historical and contemporary efforts to document, understand, and explain community and contextual influences. Taken as a whole, the Handbook's 39 articles provide the most ambitious, comprehensive, and imaginative source of knowledge about its subject in existence. The book is likely for many years to retain that status. Authors come from many countries and diverse disciplines. They include many senior scholars who as youngsters brought the study of community and other contextual influences on crime back to life in the 1970s and 1980s, and many of the less senior folk who are now doing the most exciting cutting-edge work.

Michael Tonry
December 2016

Acknowledgments

The editors want to thank all the contributors for delivering their chapters. When we sent out our invitations, hardly any of the invitees declined our request. Their willingness to demonstrate their expertise makes this volume a special one in the Oxford Handbook series, and a great pleasure for the editors. We are also grateful to Michael Tonry, series editor, who wrote the foreword of the volume. We owe much to Eon Kim for completing the journal search on environmental topics. Finally, we want to acknowledge our external reviewers Stijn Ruiter (Netherlands Institute for the Study of Crime and Law Enforcement), Martin Andresen (Simon Fraser University), Mike Townsley (Griffith University), Dietrich Oberwittler (University of Freiburg), Robert Svensson (Malmö University), and Gianluca Stringhini (University College London) for improving many of our chapters.

List of Contributors

Martin A. Andresen is Professor of Criminology and Director of the Institute for Canadian Urban Research Studies at Simon Fraser University. His current research interests are in spatial crime analysis, crime and place, geography of crime, environmental criminology, applied spatial statistics, and geographical information analysis.

Christopher J. Bates is a PhD student in the Department of Criminology, Law and Society at the University of California, Irvine. His research interest focuses on neighborhoods and how physical design environments influence well-being. He has published in the *Journal of Child Psychology and Psychiatry*.

Peter Baudains is a former researcher at the Department of Security and Crime Science, University College London. His interests lie in the application of mathematical modeling to problems in crime and security. He is now working as a data scientist in the fraud detection industry.

Wim Bernasco is a senior researcher at the Netherlands Institute for the Study of Crime and Law Enforcement and a Professor in the Department of Spatial Economics at the Vrije Universiteit Amsterdam. His research interests include offender travel behavior, target selection, and situational causes of offending and victimization.

Daniel Birks is a member of the Griffith Criminology Institute, Griffith University, Brisbane, Australia. He holds degrees in artificial intelligence, computer science, cognitive science, and criminology. His research interests are broadly based in the fields of environmental criminology, crime analysis, and computational methods.

Anthony Bottoms is Emeritus Wolfson Professor of Criminology at the University of Cambridge and Honorary Professor of Criminology at the University of Sheffield. He is a fellow of the British Academy, and received a knighthood in the Queen's Birthday Honours of 2001. He has also received awards from both the American Society of Criminology and the European Society of Criminology.

Kate Bowers is a Professor in Crime Science at the University College London Department of Security and Crime Science. She has worked in the field of crime science for over 20 years and has published more than 100 papers, books, and book chapters in environmental criminology and crime science. Her most recent research has focused on developing advanced methods for crime analysis (including innovative data sets), and improving the evidence base for crime prevention.

Nicholas Branic is a PhD student at the University of California, Irvine, and a member of the Irvine Laboratory for the Study of Space and Crime directed by Dr. Charis Kubrin and Dr. John Hipp. His research interests include the community context of crime, neighborhood change, social inequalities, and research methods.

Patricia L. Brantingham is Professor of Criminology, RCMP University Chair of Computational Criminology, and Associate Director of the Institute for Canadian Urban Research Studies at Simon Fraser University. Her current research interests are in computational criminology, pattern theory, environmental criminology, crime prevention through environmental design (CPTED), criminal justice planning, and policy evaluations.

Paul J. Brantingham is a professor of criminology, RCMP University Chair of Crime Analysis, and Associate Director of the Institute for Canadian Urban Research Studies at Simon Fraser University. His current research interests are in computational criminology, pattern theory, environmental criminology, ecology of crime, crime analysis, historical criminology, and comparative criminal justice.

Gerben J. N. Bruinsma is the former Director and nowadays Senior Researcher of the Netherlands Institute for the Study of Crime and Law Enforcement in Amsterdam, and Professor Emeritus of Environmental Criminology at the Department of Criminal Law and Criminology of the Faculty of Law of the Vrije Universiteit Amsterdam. His current interests are environmental, theoretical, and historical criminology.

Ian Brunton-Smith is Professor of Criminology and Quantitative Methods in the Department of Sociology at the University of Surrey. His current research interests include the role of context effect in shaping social outcomes, the spatial patterning of crimes, and the impacts of prison on prisoners.

Vania Ceccato is Associate Professor at Royal Institute of Technology (KTH), Stockholm, Sweden, and coordinator of the national network for crime prevention ***SafePlaces*** (Säkraplatser). In Brazil, she is affiliated with São Paulo State University (Unesp) and University of Campinas (Unicamp). Ceccato's research is on transit safety, housing and community safety, rural crime, and gender and intersectionality in safety issues.

James A. Cheshire is a Senior Lecturer in Quantitative Human Geography in the Department of Geography of University College London, London.

Timothy Coupe works at the Institute of Criminology of Cambridge University, Cambridge. His research interests are policing, crime detection and investigation, and burglary.

Francis T. Cullen is Distinguished Research Professor Emeritus and a Senior Research Associate in the School of Criminal Justice at the University of Cincinnati. He is author of *Environmental Corrections*. His current research focuses on the organization of criminological knowledge and on rehabilitation as a correctional policy. He is a past president of both the American Society of Criminology and the Academy of Criminal Justice Sciences.

Toby Davies is a Lecturer in the Department of Security & Crime Science at University College London. His research is concerned with the application of quantitative methods to the modelling of crime, with particular emphasis on the application of spatio-temporal analysis and network science.

John E. Eck is Professor of Criminal Justice at the University of Cincinnati. His research and writing focuses on police effectiveness and on the study and prevention of crime at high-crime places.

Graham Farrell is a Professor in the Centre for Criminal Justice Studies at the School of Law, University of Leeds. He has published 15 books and over 100 research papers, mostly in the area of crime science, particularly situational crime prevention and crime analysis, repeat victimization, policing, and illicit drug control. He has published widely on the security hypothesis that identified the role of security in the international crime drop.

Marcus Felson is Professor at Texas State University and recipient of the Honoris Causa from the Universidad Miguel Hernandez in Spain. He originated the routine activity approach to crime rate analysis and is author of *Crime and Nature* and coauthor of *Crime and Everyday Life* and *Opportunity Makes the Thief*. He has extended the routine activity theory to many topics, including white-collar crime, corruption, organized crime, and juvenile gangs.

Elizabeth R. Groff is an Associate Professor in the Criminal Justice Department at Temple University. Her research interests include place-based criminology, modeling geographical influences on human activity, the role of technology in police organizations, and the development of innovative methodologies using geographic information systems, agent-based simulation models, and randomized controlled field experiments.

Rob T. Guerette is an Associate Professor of Criminal Justice in the Steven J. Green School of International and Public Affairs at Florida International University. He currently serves as the Director of the International Crime and Justice doctoral program. His research interests include situational crime prevention, problem- and community-based policing, transnational crime, and program and policy evaluation. He received his PhD from Rutgers University.

Wim Hardyns is Lecturer in Criminology in the Department of Criminology, Criminal Law and Social Law at Ghent University. He has been a member of the Institute of International Research on Criminal Policy since 2015. His current interests are crime mapping and statistics, environmental criminology, crime prevention, new security technologies, big data, radicalization, and terrorism.

John R. Hipp is a Professor in the Departments of Criminology, Law and Society, and Sociology at the University of California, Irvine. His research interests focus on how neighborhoods change over time, how that change both affects and is affected by neighborhood crime, and the role networks and institutions play in that change.

Evelien M. Hoeben recently received her PhD from the Netherlands Institute for the Study of Crime and Law Enforcement and VU University Amsterdam. She currently works as an Assistant Professor at the School of Criminal Justice at the State University of New York at Albany. Her research interests include peer influences on adolescent behavior, group dynamics, and situational explanations for deviance.

Dainis Ignatans is a Lecturer in Criminology at the University of Huddersfield. His current research interests revolve around statistical examination of repeat victimization patterns as well as exploration of crime committed against, by, and within diverse immigrant communities.

Helen Innes is a Research Associate at Cardiff University specializing in the secondary analysis of large social surveys. Most recently, she has been working with the Metropolitan Police Service on a field experiment examining the efficacy of crime prevention communications, as part of a larger project developing a theory of behavioral crime prevention.

Martin Innes is Director of the Police Science Institute and Crime and Security Research Institute, both at Cardiff University. His most recent book is *Signal Crimes*, published by Oxford University Press. His current research interests are in counterterrorism policing, the implications of open source communications technologies for social reactions to crime, and innovations in policing.

Shane D. Johnson is Professor and Director of the Dawes Centre for Future Crime at University College London. His current research interests include understanding the changing nature of crime, and the application of multidisciplinary approaches to urban crime problems.

J. Bryan Kinney is Associate Professor, School of Criminology, at Simon Fraser University and Director of the Institute for Canadian Urban Research Studies Laboratory. Kinney is a specialist in crime analysis and crime prevention and in the use of computer analysis. His current research interests also include public safety in northern, rural, remote communities, and historical reactions to crime and deviance.

Edward R. Kleemans is Full Professor at the School of Criminology, Faculty of Law, Vrije Universiteit Amsterdam. His research interests include organized crime, drug trafficking, human smuggling, human trafficking, cybercrime, fraud, money laundering, social organization, and the interaction between offenders and the criminal justice system.

Charis E. Kubrin is Professor of Criminology, Law and Society and (by courtesy) Sociology at the University of California, Irvine. Kubrin's research focuses on neighborhood correlates of crime, with an emphasis on race and violent crime. In addition to her work in peer-reviewed journals, Kubrin is coauthor of *Researching Theories of Crime* *and Deviance* (Oxford University Press 2008) and coeditor of *Introduction to Criminal Justice* (Stanford University Press, 2013).

Teresa C. Kulig is a doctoral student in the School of Criminal Justice at the University of Cincinnati. Her recent writings have appeared in *Justice Quarterly*, the *Journal of Criminal Justice Education*, and *Victims and Offenders*. Her research interests include testing theories of victimization, human trafficking and child exploitation, correctional treatment, and the organization of criminological knowledge through meta-analysis.

Brian Lawton is an Assistant Professor in the Department of Criminal Justice at the John Jay College of Criminal Justice. His areas of research include environmental criminology and spatial analyses.

Fernando Miró Llinares is Professor of Criminal Law and criminology, director of the CRIMINA Research Center for the Study and Prevention of Crime, and Dean of the Faculty of Law and Social Sciences at Miguel Hernández University in Spain. Author of more than 80 publications, he has particular interests in applying crime theories to cybercrime, and in environmental criminology, modern criminal law, and new technologies in crime.

Tamara D. Madensen is an Associate Professor and Graduate Director in the Department of Criminal Justice at the University of Nevada, Las Vegas. She is the Associate Director of UNLV's Center for Crime and Public Policy and manages the associated Crowd Management Research Council. Her current research interests are place management, crime opportunity structures, and crowd dynamics and violence.

Andrew Newton is an Associate Professor of Criminology in the Department of Criminology, University of Leicester. He has a multidisciplinary background in criminology, geography, and urban studies. His research interests include crime and place, policy analysis, and evaluation; investigating and explaining crime patterns; crime, technology, and society; and crime and the built environment.

Lieven J. R. Pauwels is Professor of Criminology at Ghent University, Department of Criminology, Criminal Law and Social Law and Director of the Institute for International Research on Criminal Policy. He is interested in the integration of developmental, ecological, and situational theories, measurement problems in quantitative criminology, and the philosophy of science.

Ken Pease is a chartered forensic psychologist and Visiting Professor of Crime Science at the Jill Dando Institute, University College London, and at Loughborough University. His current interests are the use of Bayesian statistics in evaluating police work, and the renewed relevance of personal construct theory in the digital age.

Danielle M. Reynald is a Senior Lecturer and Criminologist at the School of Criminology and Criminal Justice at Griffith University and the Griffith Criminology Institute in Brisbane, Australia. Her main research interests include the role of guardianship in crime prevention and control, crime prevention through environmental design, and offender decision making.

D. Kim Rossmo is the University Chair and the Director of the Center for Geospatial Intelligence and Investigation in the School of Criminal Justice at Texas State University. He was formerly the Detective Inspector in charge of the Vancouver Police Department's Geographic Profiling Section, the Director of Research for the Police Foundation, and a management consultant with the Bureau of Alcohol, Tobacco, Firearms and Explosives.

Reka Solymosi is a Lecturer in Quantitative Criminology at the University of Manchester in the United Kingdom. Before that she was a data analyst researching issues around transport crime and policing at Transport for London. Her main interests are crowdsourced data collection, transport crime, and perception of crime and place.

Justin Song is a Research Assistant in the Institute for Canadian Urban Research Studies as well as technical staff in the Department of Geography at Simon Fraser University. His current research interests are spatial analysis of crime, geovisualization, and geographic information systems.

Valerie Spicer is a Postdoctoral Fellow conducting research with the Institute of Canadian Urban Research Studies at Simon Fraser University. Her research interests include environmental criminology, fear of crime, and big-data crime analysis techniques. She is an 18-year member of the Vancouver Police Department and currently deployed as an operational sergeant in Vancouver's downtown core.

Lucia Summers is an Assistant Professor in the School of Criminal Justice at Texas State University, San Marcos. Her research interests include the spatiotemporal patterns of crime, offender spatial decision-making, and situational crime prevention. Lucia received her PhD in criminology from University College London in 2012.

Kristin Swartz is an Assistant Professor in the Department of Criminal Justice at the University of Louisville. Her research focuses on how offending and victimization is shaped by context, with a special focus on cultural effects in the contexts of schools, communities, and correctional institutions.

Sema A. Taheri is a doctoral candidate in the School of Criminology and Criminal Justice at Northeastern University and a Senior Research Fellow at Measures for Justice. Her research interests include translational criminology and evidence-based criminal justice innovation.

Ralph B. Taylor is a Professor of Criminal Justice and member of the Center for Security and Crime Science at Temple University. His research has been funded by the National Science Foundation, the National Institute of Mental Health, the National Institute of Justice, and others. His 2015 volume *Community Criminology* (New York University Press) confronts four challenges currently bedeviling work on spatial, temporal, and spatiotemporal ecologies of crime.

Cody W. Telep is an Assistant Professor in the School of Criminology and Criminal Justice at Arizona State University. His current interests include evidence-based policing, police legitimacy, and experimental methodologies.

Nick Tilley is a Professor in the Department of Security and Crime Science at University College London and an Adjunct Professor at the Griffith Criminology Institute in Brisbane. His main research interests lie in evaluation methodology, policing, situational crime prevention, and the international crime drop.

George E. Tita is a Professor in the Department of Criminology, Law and Society and the Director of the Masters of Public Policy Program at the University of California, Irvine. His current interests include studying systems that generate crime patterns, social network analysis of crime, and the study of illegal firearms markets.

Lisa Tompson is a Lecturer in the Department of Security and Crime Science of University College London. Her research interests are spatiotemporal crime patterns and embedding evidence into police practice. She is a former police crime analyst.

Michael Tonry is McKnight Presidential Professor of Criminal Law and Policy and Director, Institute on Crime and Public Policy, University of Minnesota. He edits *Crime and Justice: A Review of Research* and writes on a topics including criminal justice policy, punishment theory, comparative criminal justice, race and crime, and sentencing.

Michael Townsley is an Associate Professor and Head of the School of Criminology and Criminal Justice, Griffith University. He is best known for demonstrating that burglary risk is infectious, a concept underpinning much of predictive policing and crime-forecasting methods. More broadly, his research interests focus on diagnosing crime problems in order to reduce, prevent, or alleviate their occurrence.

Andromachi Tseloni is Professor of Quantitative Criminology and leads the Quantitative and Spatial Criminology Research Group at Nottingham Trent University. She is currently Treasurer of the British Society of Criminology and member of the Nottingham Crime and Drugs Partnership Board. Her research revolves around crime victimization and inequalities; the "crime drop"; crime perceptions; social capital; and cross-national comparisons.

Faisal Umar is a Lecturer at the Department of Urban and Regional Planning, Ahmadu Bello University, Zaria, Nigeria. He received his PhD in Geographic Information Science at University College London. His current research concerned with how Euro-American theories of urban crime could be applied in the context of developing countries such as Nigeria. Other research interests revolve around the broader field of Urban Planning/Studies much of which involves the application of geographic information system (GIS) techniques in the analysis of urban datasets.

Matthew Valasik is an Assistant Professor of Sociology and Criminology in the Department of Sociology at Louisiana State University. His primary interests are the sociospatial dynamics of gang behavior and problem-oriented policing strategies (e.g., gang units, civil gang injunctions) used by law enforcement.

Frank M. Weerman is Senior Researcher of the Netherlands Institute for the Study of Crime and Law Enforcement in Amsterdam, and Professor of Youth Criminology at the Erasmus University, Rotterdam, the Netherlands. His research interests focus on explanation of juvenile delinquency, in particular on the role of peers, groups, and contexts.

David Weisburd is Distinguished Professor of Criminology, Law and Society at George Mason University in Virginia. He also holds an appointment as the Walter E. Meyer Professor of Law and Criminal Justice at the Hebrew University of Jerusalem. Professor Weisburd was the recipient of the Stockholm Prize in Criminology in 2010, and the Sutherland Award from the American Society of Criminology in 2014.

Brandon C. Welsh is a Professor of Criminology and Director of the Cambridge-Somerville Youth Study at Northeastern University. He is also the Royal Netherlands Academy of Arts and Sciences Visiting Professor and Senior Research Fellow at the Netherlands Institute for the Study of Crime and Law Enforcement in Amsterdam. His research focuses on the prevention of delinquency and crime and evidence-based social policy

Pamela Wilcox is a Professor in the School of Criminal Justice and Fellow of the Graduate School at University of Cincinnati. Her research focuses on understanding the opportunity for crime and victimization in school and community contexts. She is past chair of the Crime, Law, and Deviance section of the American Sociological Association and former Executive Counselor for the American Society of Criminology.

Mats Wilhelmsson is the former Director of Center for Banking and Finance and now the Vice Dean at the School of Architecture and Built Environment at Royal Institute of Technology, Sweden. He is also Professor in Applied Financial Economics, and his research is focused on housing and urban economics.

Richard Wortley has been Director of the University College London Jill Dando Institute since 2010. His research interests center on the role that immediate environments play in criminal behavior and how that behavior can be altered through situational crime prevention. His research has focused particularly on the situational prevention of child sexual abuse.

Kathryn Wuschke is an Assistant Professor at Portland State University and a member of the Institute for Canadian Urban Research Studies at Simon Fraser University, Vancouver. Her research focuses on spatial crime analysis, with particular focus on the impact of land use and urban development on local patterns of crime.

THE OXFORD HANDBOOK OF

ENVIRONMENTAL CRIMINOLOGY

CHAPTER 1

ENVIRONMENTAL CRIMINOLOGY

Scope, History, and State of the Art

GERBEN J. N. BRUINSMA AND SHANE D. JOHNSON

1.1 Purpose of the Volume

The purpose of this *Oxford Handbook of Environmental Criminology* is to provide researchers, teachers, students, and practitioners with the latest state-of-the-art knowledge of environmental criminology from around the world. The Handbook serves as a source for information on the core theoretical and empirical issues on how and why the physical and social environment influences the emergence of crime and how crime can affect the environment. By bringing together some of the best-known scholars, the Handbook reflects the diversity in research and theory that has been developed all over the Western world, not only in the United States but also in Europe, Australia, and Canada. The book covers most topics as intellectual challenges in criminology, asking why and how the physical environment has an impact on individual and group behavior (and vice versa). Environments can be seen as constellations of factors that shape the spatial distribution of offenders and the crimes they commit. They present specific criminal opportunities for individuals, for co-offenders, and for groups of criminals. Their configuration may facilitate the organization of criminal activities and, last but not least, provide opportunities to make criminal profits. In this Handbook, the editors have not limited themselves to traditional criminological research. Changes in the environment, global connectivity, and technology provide new criminal opportunities, or ways of committing existing crimes in different ways. Through the various contributions in this book, we ask whether theories of environmental criminology inform our understanding of these new problems. Similarly, we ask whether theories of environmental criminology offer insight into crimes committed in countries other than those for which the theories were initially conceived to explain observed patterns. For example, scholars are starting to take an interest in crimes committed in non-Western countries, such as China and West Africa, in which there are cultural differences that might lead to different spatial patterns in urban offending.

The aim of this chapter is to provide the reader with a background to the field of enquiry and to articulate the rationale for assembling the chapters contained within this volume. The chapter is organized as follows. In the next section, we discuss what environmental criminology is about and how its boundaries have been demarcated by scholars over the course of time. Some students of criminology mistakenly associate environmental criminology with the study of environmental crimes such as pollution, or the impact of toxic waste on the environment. These forms of crime are important and may be studied from an environmental criminology perspective, but they are not the focus of investigation and in no way define it. In section 1.3, we describe briefly the history of environmental criminology from its beginning in the early 19th century through to the present day. We distinguish four important periods in which environmental criminology flourished and scholars made significant progress in research. In section 1.4 we briefly introduce the key theoretical perspectives in environmental criminology and describe the core propositions of the field. For those new to the field in particular, this fourth section is intended to provide a useful background to help situate the theoretical and empirical chapters that are presented in this volume. In section 1.5 we demonstrate the growing importance of environmental criminology in mainstream criminology, documenting the growth in the number of articles published in top-ranked criminology journals. We close this chapter by outlining the volume and by explaining the kind of decisions the editors took when compiling it.

1.2 What Is Environmental Criminology?

Students enrolled in courses in general criminology at universities are typically taught that mainstream criminology is about the criminal behavior of individuals, co-offenders, groups, and organizations or institutions, or about the criminal justice system. Essentially, this is correct when criminologists want to explain why individuals commit crime or refrain from deviant behavior, or how judges sentence those convicted of crime. In such enquiry, criminologists try to find out (for example) what individual characteristics of people may influence the likelihood of criminal behavior, and their work is inspired by various theories of crime causation (Cullen & Wilcox, 2010, 2013). These criminologists are also interested in variation in the risk of victimization across groups of society, examining, for instance, the effects of gender, age, or social class. Such a focus considers what we call the *social* distribution of crime, victimization, or offenders across a society or societies. In studies of this kind, criminologists want to find out whether men commit more or less crimes than women, or older people less than adolescents, and so on. They may also be interested in questions such as whether men are more likely to become victims of crime than are women. The focus in such work is thus on people, and what disposes them to be more likely to be offenders or victims.

In contrast, criminologists active in the field of environmental criminology are particularly interested in the crime event. They are interested in the *spatial* distribution of crime, victimization, or offenders in society. They want to know whether there are differences in the distribution of crime, victimization, or perpetrators across cities, neighborhoods, or smaller units of analysis, such as street segments—and, if this is the case, how and why this is so. The physical and social characteristics of these spaces are seen as having the potential to explain differences in the distribution of crime. This is a perspective distinct from those that locate the genesis of crime in terms of the individual dispositions of offenders and for which opportunities for crime would be seen as ubiquitous in the environment. Put more explicitly, environmental criminologists see variation in the environment as shaping the likelihood that crime will actually occur as well as where it might do so. As the chapters in this book will attest, such variation might be explained in different ways, ranging from the number of police officers patrolling a location, to the social composition of a neighborhood, to the physical layout of the street network, to the way in which facilities are managed.

1.2.1 Ecological Origins

Over time, environmental criminology research has appeared under a variety of names, including ecological, geographical, and spatial criminology and cartography (the science of making maps). The older and commonly used name "ecological" originated from biology and was first used in 1878 by the philosopher and biologist Ernst Haeckel. We will briefly discuss this perspective as a way of framing what follows. The word *oikos*—from which the word "ecology" derives—literally means household or place of residence. In his work, Haeckel reserved the concept to describe the way in which various kinds of plants cluster across the landscape and apparently seem to form a community (mostly temporarily) until new plants invade the area. Sometimes such "invasions" happen in harmony, sometimes in conflict as species compete for limited available resources. The field of ecology flourished for a long time in biology, stimulated in part by Charles Darwin's popular concept of evolution.

By the beginning of the 20th century, Darwin's concept of evolution had been transformed to address social or human evolution. Burgess (1916) wrote, for instance, about the function of socialization from the perspective of social evolution, in which he made a connection between geography, heredity, and socialization. The importance of the geographical aspect lay in the impact that the physical environment could have on human beings. To elaborate, Darwin's ideas on evolution were at that time seen as a continuous process of the adaptation of organisms, plants, and animals to their (changing) environments. Through this process some species—that are maladapted to the new environment—disappear, while others survive. The basic assumption of ecology is "that adaptation is a collective rather than an individual process.... Such an approach is confined to properties and conditions that cannot be distributed to individuals" (Hawley, 1986, p. 126). From this perspective, a shortage of space (for example) leads inevitably to competition for the best locations. In ecology, these kinds of dynamic processes are central to understanding the system of interest.

Also important is the concept of communities. In the case of humans, these are groups of people living together in a certain area who are connected to each other by the soil (habitat). In those days (The 19th and early 20th century), scientists believed that people who resemble each other in many respects, who share the same history, who experience similar sentiments, and who feel themselves tied to their soil would form a community (Boyd & Richerson, 1985). Members of a community are likely to speak the same language, share a religion, have the same ethnic background, or be active in a particular economic sector. These similarities may develop into a shared system of attitudes, morality, and behavior norms for all, further connecting those who are part of a community. Communities can collaborate with other communities (symbiosis) or compete for the same space.

McKenzie (1924) elaborated on the ecological basis of a community. Humans are not solitary creatures. They cannot live without other humans. He stated that human ecology is fundamentally interested in the effect of geographical location, both in time and space, upon human institutions and behavior: "These spatial relationships of human beings are the products of competition and selection, and are continuously in a process of change as new factors enter to disturb the competitive relations or to facilitate mobility" (McKenzie, 1924, p. 288). In his view, humans differ from plants and animal communities since they can choose their own area and can transform it in accordance with their wishes (e.g., building roads, houses, canals, and so on). Communities are dynamic by nature, and continuously change. A city or a neighborhood is always moving to a new status quo. This dynamic is a characteristic of many cities, such as Chicago. In fact, as we shall see throughout this book, Chicago is one of the most researched cities in the world from this perspective (Sampson, 2012). One of the reasons for this is that Chicago experienced a large influx of immigrants at the end of the 19th century (Thomas, 1971 [1921]), which led to widespread change of the kind McKenzie described. These ideas and the transformation of Chicago were discussed by McKenzie and others in the famous book of Robert Park and Ernest Burgess entitled *The City* (1967 [1925]). As we shall see in the next section, the book detailed the fundamental principles of the "Chicago school" of thinking, which occupy a prominent place in urban criminology and sociology to this day. Ecology was in this vision elaborated as the physical dynamic expansion of a city and its consequences for the residents. As will be discussed, in the case of Chicago and other US cities, the influx of migrants into, and the way migrants settled in, cities were according to predicted patterns of ecology.

Bronfenbrenner gave a further boost to the application of the ecological perspective in his seminal study on the social development of children, noting

> the resilience, versatility, and promise of the species Homo sapiens as evidenced by its capacity to adapt to, tolerate, and especially create the ecologies in which it lives

> and grows. Seen in different contexts, human nature, which I had previously thought of as a singular noun, became plural and pluralistic; for the different environments were producing discernible differences, not only across but also within societies, in talent, temperament, human relations, and particularly in the ways in which the culture, or subculture, brought up its next generation. (Bronfenbrenner, 1979, p. xiii)

One of his key findings was that the development of children can never be validly researched without studying their natural ecological setting.

With similar implications, but more explicit about the influence of *both* the social and physical environment on human behavior, Morris suggested that "Human or social ecology is concerned with the relationships which exist between people who share a common habitat or local territory and which are distinctly related to the character of the territory itself; it is a study of social structure in relation to the local environment" (1957, p. 1). In his vision ecology should concern itself with the study of (1) specific features of the physical space; (2) the social relations between residents or people who temporarily stay there; and (3) the interaction between the physical and social environment and its impact on human thinking and behavior. The spatial setting is a place or location where people interact and communicate.

The name *environmental* criminology was coined by C. Ray Jeffery (1971, p. 279), and made popular by Paul and Patricia Brantingham (1981). According to Brantingham and Brantingham the incidence of criminal behavior can best be understood as a joint event of offenders, targets, and laws at a particular space and time. Their crime pattern theory is based on that assumption (Brantingham & Brantingham, 2008, 1991, 1993; see also their chapter in this volume). With his colleague Paul Wiles, Anthony Bottoms described environmental criminology as "the study of crime, criminality, and victimization as they relate, first, to particular places and, secondly, to the way individuals and organizations shape their activities spatially, and in so doing are in turn influenced by place-based or spatial factors" (Bottoms & Wiles, 2002, p. 620). The authors also emphasized the idea that criminologists should carefully distinguish between places where crimes are committed (crime events) and places where offenders reside, resulting in two leading questions of environmental criminology: (1) the explanation of the spatial distribution of crimes (locations where crimes are committed), and (2) the spatial distribution of offenders (where they live). For a similar reason, Anthony Bottoms preferred a few years later the term *socio-spatial perspective* in criminology (Bottoms, 2007) to stress the interaction between the spatial and social aspects of crime.

This focus differentiates environmental criminology from mainstream criminology, which is more concerned with what disposes individuals to offend. A distinct characteristic of environmental criminology, then, is that the unit of analysis is not the individual, but the crime event and the environment in which it occurs. This is typically related to spaces—locations, street segments, neighborhoods, or larger urban or rural areas—and most of the chapters in this book are concerned with this type of environment. But environments can be more broadly defined to include other forms of ecosystems in which crime may occur. For example, while not a physical space per se, cyberspace creates an environment or settings in which crime can occur (see Miró Llinares & Johnson in this volume), while systems of management for places such as bars create an ecological system that can make crime more or less likely (see Eck & Madensen in this volume). The key point of departure from other forms of criminology is that the environment is seen as shaping opportunities for offending, and consequently changes to it can influence these opportunities even if the dispositions of offenders remain unaffected.

Given the focus on crime events, another distinct feature of environmental criminology is that it is crime specific. That is, the environment is seen as providing choice-structuring properties (Cornish & Clarke, 1986) that make specific forms of crime—rather than some amorphous behavior referred to as "offending"—more or less likely at a particular location at a particular time. For example, the conditions that make residential burglary more likely (e.g., housing density, physical security) are not necessarily the same conditions that afford opportunities for sexual offenses or violence against the person. Particular environments and ecological conditions (which can change over the course of a day or year; see Tompson & Coupe and Newton in this volume) are thus believed to be conducive to particular types of crime, and understanding these environments is seen as fundamental to the research enterprise.

While the focus of environmental criminology is not the individual, a person is studied *in relation to the environment*. For example, a growing literature (discussed in Summers & Guerette, Bernasco, and Rossmo in this volume) examines how and why offenders decide to commit crimes at particular locations but not others (Bernasco, Block, & Ruiter, 2013; Townsley et al., 2015). In such cases, consideration is given to characteristics of the offenders as well as the locations at which they do and do not offend.

To help demarcate environmental criminology further, it is important to determine what we want to know. What questions occupy environmental criminologists? We want to venture our thoughts on two topics: (1) the number and nature of criminal actions in particular environments, and (2) the factors that influence humans and their behavior in particular environments. One assumption—which has much empirical support—associated with the first question is that crime clusters rather than occurring randomly in the environment: "Because criminal behaviour is dependent on situational factors, crime is patterned according to the location of criminogenic environments. Crime will be concentrated around crime opportunities and other environmental features that facilitate criminal activity" (Wortley & Mazerolle, 2008, p. 1). About the behavior of humans, it is assumed that "Criminal behaviour is significantly influenced by the nature of the immediate environment in which it occurs" (Wortley & Mazerolle, 2008, p. 1). As discussed above, to date most of the environmental criminology literature has focused on crime at physical locations. In the case of physical spaces, it is important to define the boundaries of what a location is (Taylor, 2015; Weisburd et al., 2016; Weisburd, Groff, & Yang, 2012). For theoretical and methodological reasons, it cannot be too large, because it is the space that offenders can observe through their senses:

> Small units of analysis are also better on theoretical grounds because they more closely approximate behavior-settings. Individuals' actions and development are

> only influenced by the environments they can access with their senses and the part of the environment which individuals can access with their senses is, arguably, generally small. Small units are also better from a methodological point of view because smaller units are more likely to be homogeneous in terms of environmental characteristics. (Oberwittler & Wikström, 2009, p. 57)

To conclude this section, we note that environmental criminology was in part motivated by developments in the field of ecology and our understanding of how changes to the environment can influence behavior across species. Environmental criminology is thus about the study of (1) the how and why of the *spatial concentration* of crime, victims, or offenders as a consequence of the physical and social characteristics of spaces, and their interaction, and (2) the how and why of the physical and social characteristics of locations that influence offenders' decision-making regarding possible specific crimes at specific places.

1.3 A Brief History of Environmental Criminology

Environmental criminology has a long historical tradition in criminology (for more details we refer to Beirne, 1987, 1994; Brantingham & Brantingham, 1981; Bruinsma & Weisburd, 2014a, 2014b; Weisburd, Bruinsma, & Bernasco, 2009). Its history can be divided into four periods during which scientific progress has particularly been achieved: (1) its beginning in Europe in the 19th century; (2) the heyday of the Chicago school of neighborhood research in the first half of the 20th century; (3) spatial research in Canada, Europe, and the United States from the 1980s; and (4) a more international focus on the study of crime in smaller spaces in the 21st century.

Criminology as a scientific enterprise started early in the 19th century in France. The first studies of the spatial distribution of criminals and crime were carried out after the French government published in 1825 the *Comptes Générales de l'Administration de la Justice Criminelle en France*, which involved the presentation of all kinds of data relating to crime and the prison system. Mathematicians and statisticians—criminology was not established as a scientific discipline at that time—examined the variability of crime across areas. Among the very first geographical criminologists was Baron Charles Dupont, who spoke for the first time about statistics concerning the morality of people and the nation at a meeting of the Conservatoire des Arts et Métiers in November 1826 (Beirne, 1987). As a cartographer, in 1816 he published tables on the "distribution of illiterates" across the regions of France. During the meeting of the Conservatoire, he promised to publish a map on crime and criminals soon. However, the Belgian Edouard Ducpétiaux was the first to publish a table containing such statistics (reproduced as Table 1.1), for England and Wales (Ducpétiaux, 1827). He observed remarkable differences between regions and countries and concluded that the morality of nations differed (Ducpétiaux, 1827, pp. 11–12).

Table 1.1 The Very First Spatial Analyses of Crime Rates by Ducpétiaux (1827) Showing Variation across England and Wales

Counties where the ratio of the number of defendants to the population is greatest	Counties where the ratio of the number of defendants to the population is smallest
Middlesex (London), 1 in 465	Wales, 1 in 4,285
Warwick, 1 in 650	Cumberland, 1 in 4,300
Lancaster, 1 in 650	Cornwall, 1 in 3,860
Surrey, 1 in 755	Durham, 1 in 2,990
Essex, 1 in 785	Northumberland, 1 in 2,716
Wilts, 1 in 861	Derby, 1 in 2,430
Chester, 1 in 1,106	Montmouth, 1 in 2,410

Bulletin Férussac, May 1825 and June 1826

In 1829, the first geographical map of crime of France was published. Michel-André Guerry and the Venetian cartographer Adriano Balbi published on one large sheet three maps showing the distribution of crime in France during the years 1825–1827 (Balbi & Guerry, 1829). Now commonplace, this was a novelty in a new field of science that made use of the cartographic method to present statistical material. They concluded from their work that (1) in certain regions of France (as defined by administrative *départements*) that had higher numbers of personal crimes (violent crimes), there was less property crime; (2) that the area north of Orléans and Lyon showed the highest rate of property crimes in France; and (3) the highest numbers of property and personal crimes were observed in urban areas, especially in the capital of Paris. Later, when Guerry became head of the Crime Statistics Unit of the Ministry of Justice, he continued his work on mapping crime. In 1833, his influential *Essai sur la Statistique Morale de la France* was published (Guerry, 1833). Inspired by the reform movement of the 19th century,[1] Guerry examined whether poverty and population density might be associated with higher crime rates (an example of one the maps Guerry produced is provided in chapter 12 by Brantingham et al. in this volume). He observed, however, an empirical complexity. The affluent *départements* in the north were found to experience higher property crime rates than were the poor *départements* in the south of France. He concluded that the level of poverty was not the direct cause of crime. Similarly, his data suggested that population density was not a cause of crime. The Belgian astronomer and mathematician Adolphe Quételet (who developed the idea of the normal distribution) examined in 1828 the French *Comptes Générales* in a lecture for the Academy of Science to demonstrate how crime rates vary across the seasons of the year (1984 [1831]). He demonstrated that the monthly volume of violent crime was highest in June. He also examined crime data in each arrondissement (administrative districts in Paris) and concluded that most crimes were committed in the arrondissements where the "inferior" classes lived (Quételet, 1984 [1831], p. 30).

The studies by Guerry soon became the subject of a heated debate between proponents and opponents of the reform movement, especially in England. French and English statisticians and mathematicians collaborated with each other in those days and had joint meetings to discuss mathematical issues related to crime. From 1838 onward, members of the Statistical Society of London regularly published papers on the topic of crime in the *Journal of the Royal Statistical Society*. In August 1835, William Greg gave a lecture on the spatial distribution of population density, fertility, education, and crime in the Lower Lands (Netherlands) to the British Association for the Advancement of Science, which was subsequently published by Ridgway and Sons (Greg, 1835). He compared crime rates for property crimes, violent crimes, and serious crimes like rape, murder, and manslaughter in the Netherlands with those of England and France and found major variations across these three countries: the lowest rates were observed in the Netherlands, while the highest were apparent in France (Greg, 1835, p. 15). Rawson R. Rawson, then secretary of the Statistical Society, correlated area-level population variables such as age and sex with crime as well as variation in climactic conditions. His study focused in particular on whether variation in climate and ethnicity might explain the variation observed, and used data for the districts (administrative and political regions of counties) of England and Wales, which represented smaller units of analysis than had previously been employed (Rawson, 1839). He discussed the variability in crime across the districts and concluded that climate and differences in ethnicity across the population could not be causes of crime.

After 1870 interest in geographic and statistical analyses diminished among French and English academics. According to Paul and Patricia Brantingham (1981, p. 12) the studies conducted in the 19th century on the spatial distribution of crime in Europe revealed the following important insights: (1) crime rates vary substantially across geographical areas; (2) these variations are found at different levels of aggregation; (3) these variations persist over (long) periods of time; (4) high crime rates are highly correlated with the presence of other social problems like poverty, alcoholism, high population density, and illiteracy, and, lastly, (5) locations with high number of crimes correlate with the presence of attractive targets and potential victims.

After the turn of the 20th century, the locus of research on crime and the environment shifted to the United States, and in particular to the city of Chicago. In the 1920s a group of sociologists at the University of Chicago took the initiative to undertake new research on urban problems, which centered in part, on crime (Beirne & Messerschmidt, 1991; Browning, Cagney, & Morris, 2014; Bulmer, 1984; Burgess & Bogue, 1964; Faris, 1967; Harvey, 1987; Short, 2002). They also moved the focus of spatial research from broad comparisons across large geographic areas to more careful comparisons within cities. Interestingly, at least until 1933, the Chicago school scholars were either not aware of or ignored the work of 19th-century environmental researchers in Europe (Elmer, 1933; Levin & Lindesmith, 1937). A group of American sociologists, among them, Robert Park, William Thomas, Louis Wirth, Ernest Burgess, Clifford Shaw, and Henry McKay took a leadership role in environmental criminology (Vold, Bernard, & Snipes, 2002). William Thomas contributed to environmental criminology by introducing the important concept of *social disorganization*, referring to "a decrease of the influence of existing social rules of behavior upon individual members of the group" (Thomas, 1966, p. 3). The concept naturally focused on neighborhoods or communities, and it was Robert Park (1864–1944), recruited by Thomas, who was the initiator of this important shift in focus from countries and large areas to cities and their neighborhoods (Park & Burgess, 1967 [1925]). Drawing from an inventory of price changes in housing values and other real estate in Chicago neighborhoods, Park's younger colleague, Ernest Burgess, presented a concentric zone model of the distribution of social problems and crime for cities (especially for Chicago) (Burgess, 1967 [1925]). Burgess suggested that Chicago included five concentric zones, each containing various neighborhoods, four of them situated around the Loop (the business center of the city). Clifford Shaw was one of the first Chicago sociologists to carry out extensive empirical research on the spatial distribution of crime informed by Burgess's zone model (Shaw et al., 1929). This study can be seen as a landmark in the history of environmental criminology because of its detailed data collection, advanced methods, and innovation in statistical methodology. Based on the concentric zone model of Burgess, the authors studied the distribution of truancy of young people, juvenile delinquents, and adult offenders in Chicago. Assisted by the then young researchers Henry McKay, Frederick Zorbaugh, and Leonard Cottrell, Shaw took natural (ecological) areas as units of analyses (Abbott, 1997) but in more detail than ever before in studies of this kind. Shaw and his colleagues introduced new units of analyses. First, they introduced *point maps* by plotting the home address of thousands of offenders on a map of Chicago. Second, they combined offender address data with census data to calculate *delinquency rate maps* of square-mile areas. And finally, they constructed *radial maps* and *zone maps*, which displayed delinquency rates at regular distances from the city center (Snodgrass, 1976).

In 1942, Clifford Shaw and Henry McKay published their magnum opus, *Juvenile Delinquency and Urban Areas*, in which they presented their geographical and etiological analyses of crime rates not only in the city of Chicago, but also partly for the cities of Philadelphia, Boston, Cincinnati, Cleveland, and Richmond. As in their study of 1929 (Shaw & McKay, 1942), they employed point maps, rate maps, radial maps, and zone maps to examine the concentrations of crime and offenders across the city of Chicago, and used data for a period of up to 60 years. Across all cities studied, they found similar patterns in the geographical distribution of crime. Areas closer to the business centers of cities had higher crime rates that were associated with poverty, higher population mobility, weak social structures, and the dilapidation of houses.

In the 1950s and 1960s interest in criminological research inspired by the Chicago school diminished. This was partly due to criticisms of the empirical methods, data, and theory used (Lander, 1954; Robinson, 1950), and partly because of a redirection of mainstream criminology that focused on individual criminality, itself stimulated by the rise of the (population) survey, and the introduction of the self-report method in criminology (Nye, 1958).

In the 1980s there was a revival of work concerned with environmental criminology in several countries around the world. This third period of environmental criminology represented a resurrection of the field. It was during this period that the Canadian criminologists Paul and Patricia Brantingham (1981) produced their landmark edited volume on environmental criminology. This collection included essays on how burglars elicit information from the environment regarding territoriality (Brown and Altman), the impact of crime on real estate prices (Eldon Miller), and how the surveillance provided by public and employees influences criminal opportunity (Mayhew). It included empirical studies on the importance of using appropriate denominators in the construction of crime rates (Harries), and factors that influence the distance offenders travel to commit crime (Rhodes and Conly). Perhaps most importantly, this volume included the Brantinghams' own chapter, "Notes on the Geometry of Crime." In this work they elaborated on their crime site selection model (Brantingham & Brantingham, 1978). The major contribution of this new chapter was to make this previously a-spatial model explicitly spatial. The ideas set forward in this chapter became the authors' highly influential crime pattern theory, which sought to explain how targets come to the attention of individual offenders, how that awareness influences where they offend, and how the collective activity patterns of offenders affect the distribution of crime events over time and across places (Brantingham & Brantingham, 2008, 1981). This work represents one of the many important contributions the Brantinghams have made to the discipline.

Around this time, Ralph Taylor initiated a line of research in Philadelphia for which the micro-level physical environment and its influence on an individual's behavior was the focus (Taylor, 1987, 2015). Among other topics, his colleague George Rengert introduced spatial research on burglars in Philadelphia and how the police respond to them (Rengert, 1981, 1991). He introduced the idea of the spatial choice model, and a statistical implementation of it. This work represented a departure from earlier studies that examined how far offenders traveled to commit crime, by estimating what it was about the areas (other than distance that would have to be traveled) offenders selected in which to commit crime that differed from those that they did not select. This study was an important precursor to the more recent studies discussed in Bernasco's chapter in this volume. Later, Rengert (1996) published his classic study on the spatial distribution of drug dealing on streets.

The built environment was also the inspiration for approaches to crime reduction. Jeffery (1971) suggested that the key to crime control was through the design of the physical environment by reducing the presence of opportunities. In the extreme, environmental characteristics could be argued to determine crime levels. Continuing this theme, Oscar Newman described how architectural solutions could help to reduce crime in neighborhoods (Newman, 1972). His defensible space thesis suggested that the architecture of the environment demarcated the spaces that residents feel responsibility for, and in which the presence or actions of offenders are most likely to be challenged. Key to his approach was the construction or perception of territorial boundaries (defensible spaces) that would maximize the effects of the natural surveillance created by the presence of residents, or those who felt responsible for a particular space.

Inspired by Hawley's (1950) work on human ecology, Lawrence Cohen and Marcus Felson (1979) developed the routine activity theory, arguing that the emphasis placed on individual motivation in existing criminological theory failed to recognize the importance of other elements of the crime equation. In particular, they argued that people's routine activities (including offenders) influence directly the likelihood that an offender will encounter a suitable target in the absence of a guardian who might otherwise prevent a crime from taking place. According to this perspective, absent such convergence, crime will not occur, and changes to patterns of convergence will affect crime rates, irrespective of the nature of criminal motivations. The routine-activities perspective they presented established the spatial and temporal context of criminal events as an important focus of study and provided a framework for much of the research that followed.

In 1982 James Q. Wilson and George Kelling published a newspaper article in which they outlined the first version of the broken windows theory (Wilson & Kelling, 1982). They argued that social incivilities (e.g., loitering, graffiti, public drinking, and prostitution) and physical incivilities (e.g., vacant lots, trash, and abandoned buildings) cause residents and workers in a neighborhood to be fearful (Welsh, Braga, & Bruinsma, 2015). According to the theory, fear causes stable families to move out of the neighborhood and the remaining residents to isolate themselves and avoid others. Anonymity increases and the level of informal social control decreases. The lack of control and disorder leads to a cascade that attracts more potential offenders to the area, which in turn increases serious criminal behavior.

In the United States in particular, part of the revival in urban neighborhood research was inspired by the works of Jane Jacobs (1961), Ruth Kornhauser (1978), and a volume initiated by Al Reiss and Michael Tonry (1986) in which a new generation of young scholars (Wes Skogan, Robert Sampson, Douglas Smith, Robert Bursik, Ralph Taylor, Stephen Gottfredson, Lawrence Sherman, and the British scholar Anthony Bottoms) presented new urban studies. Robert Sampson focused on the community, arguing that social cohesion within communities and the (shared) expectations of community members combine to influence the level and effectiveness of informal social control on crime and social disorder (Raudenbush & Sampson, 1999; Sampson, 2010; Sampson, Morenoff, & Earls, 1999; Sampson, Raudenbush, & Earls, 1997). Skogan brought new insights not only to our understanding of the interaction of community characteristics and policing (Skogan, 1987), but also more generally to the changes in urban processes that led to the emergence of crime and disorder in urban communities (Skogan, 1990). Bursik (Bursik, 1986; Bursik & Webb, 1982) revisited crime rates in Chicago neighborhoods over time and challenged earlier views of the stability of crime within neighborhoods and communities, arguing that stability in crime patterns was a result of long-term stability in the social characteristics of places, and that instability in such patterns would also lead to instability in crime rates.

In the United Kingdom two schools of thought emerged. One was inspired by the empirical tradition in spatial studies. Studies were carried out in Glasgow, Liverpool, London, and Poplar to examine the spatial distribution of crime (Baldwin, 1975; Morris, 1957). Antony Bottoms established a line of research in Sheffield on the geographic distribution of crime and victimization (Baldwin & Bottoms, 1976), and later continued this work with Paul Wiles (Bottoms, 2007; Bottoms & Wiles, 1992, 2002). Bottoms made a sharp distinction between the neighborhoods where residents live and the places where crimes are committed and revealed distinct processes of clustering (Bottoms & Wiles, 1986).

The second school of thought was initiated by Ron Clarke and colleagues at the UK Home Office Research Unit, and had crime prevention as its guiding principle (Clarke, 1980). The approach was underpinned by the rational choice perspective, developed with his colleague Derek Cornish (Clarke & Felson, 1993; Cornish & Clarke, 1986, 2008). Combining insights from a variety of disciplines, the fundamental principle of the perspective was that offenders are rational actors who consider the perceived risk, effort, and reward of action alternatives, but do so using imperfect information. At the center of these scholars' crime equation was opportunity, or an offender's perception of it. Critically, they sought to devise ways to change crime opportunities, rather than to reform the offenders themselves. This approach, which suggested that "opportunity makes the thief" (Felson & Clarke, 1998), was in sharp contrast to the traditional view at that time that offenders simply took advantage of a very large number of potential opportunities that were ubiquitous in the environment. Importantly, and as discussed in by Welsh and Taheri (this volume), across a series of case studies, evaluations of "situational crime prevention" have shown that reducing criminal opportunities in very specific contexts can lead to crime reduction (for a recent review, see Bowers & Johnson, 2016). Moreover, Farrell and colleagues have argued that changes to the physical security of homes (Farrell et al., 2011) and vehicles (Tilley, Tseloni, & Farrell, 2011)—a form of situational crime prevention that reduces opportunity—most likely explain the substantial drop in the frequency of these crimes observed in the UK over the last twenty years.

In the 1980s Patricia Brantingham and Paul Brantingham (1981) established a long-lasting line of research in Vancouver, Canada, focusing on topics of environmental criminology. As discussed, a major contribution was the development of their "crime pattern theory," which sought to explain how people's routine activities would influence the spatial distribution of crime (see chapter 12). Crime pattern theory focuses directly upon microspaces, asking how targets come to the attention of individual offenders, how that awareness influences where they offend, and how the collective activity patterns of offenders affects the distribution of crime events over time and across places (Brantingham & Brantingham, 1981, 2008). Like Cohen and Felson, Brantingham and Brantingham took routine human social and economic activities as a critical feature of the crime equation, but in this case the role of places was explicitly emphasized as providing a "backcloth" for human activity and behavior that would shape the opportunities for crime of which offenders became aware. According to their theory, crime is more likely to occur when there is an intersection between a suitable crime opportunity and an offender's awareness space.

In the 21st century the focus of research in environmental criminology has shifted more and more to the study of microplaces. Recent studies point to the potential theoretical and practical benefits of focusing research on micro crime places. A number of them, for example, suggest that there is a very significant clustering of crime at places, irrespective of the specific unit of analysis examined (Oberwittler & Wikström, 2009; Roncek, 1981; Weisburd, Bernasco, & Bruinsma, 2009). Clarke and Eck (2005) refer to this as the 80-20 rule of Pareto, while Weisburd describes this pattern and its apparent persistence over time as the Law of Crime Concentration (Weisburd, 2015). In one of the pioneering studies in this area, Sherman, Gartin, and Buerger (1989) found that only 3.5 percent of the addresses in Minneapolis produced 50 percent of all calls to the police. Fifteen years later in a study in Seattle, Washington, Weisburd et al. (2004) reported that between 4 and 5 percent of street segments in the city accounted for 50 percent of crime incidents each year over a 14-year period (Weisburd, 2015; Weisburd et al., 2012, 2016). As discussed in chapter 25 of this volume (Telep & Weisburd), similar patterns have been observed in many cities around the world.

Environmental criminology has developed progressively over the last two decades through innovative research and the development of theory that has been informed by cross-disciplinary ideas. Early research was hampered by the level of resolution at which data were available, but the availability of official statistical data at lower levels of aggregation, and technologies such as GPS and Google Street View in recent years have made progression in empirical research (Van Gelder & Van Daele, 2014), and the systematic testing of theoretical expectations ever more possible (for a discussion, see chapter 11 by Solymosi & Bowers).

1.4 Key Perspectives in Environmental Criminology

A key issue in environmental criminology is why certain places, streets, neighborhoods, areas, cities, or countries have more crimes than others. There is an excess of empirical research that confirms that crime is not randomly distributed but instead clusters at all levels of aggregation (Bottoms, 2007; Brantingham & Brantingham, 1991; Taylor, 2015; Weisburd, Bernasco, & Bruinsma, 2009; Weisburd et al., 2016). Countries differ in crime rates per 100,000 residents (Aebi et al., 2010); within countries rural and urban areas differ in crime concentrations (Clinard, 1942; Johnson, 1992; Rephann, 1999); between cities there is considerable variation in crime rates (Clinard, 1978; Eisner & Wikström, 1999; Sampson, 1986a); and the same is true across neighborhoods (Bruinsma et al., 2013; Shaw et al., 1929; Wikström, 1991), street segments (Groff, Weisburd, & Yang, 2010; Johnson & Bowers, 2010; Weisburd, 2015; Weisburd et al., 2012), facilities (Bowers, 2014; Wilcox & Eck, 2011), and homes (Tseloni, 2006; Tseloni et al., 2004). These differences are important because they provide insight into what types of causal mechanisms might explain crime and why such patterns form.

After two centuries of research, a great number of potential explanations and perspectives have been developed in the field of environmental criminology. We have rational choice theory (Cornish & Clarke, 2008, 1986); opportunity theory (Clarke, 1980; Felson & Clarke, 1998; Wilcox, Land, & Hunt, 2003); situational theories (Wortley, 2008); routine activity theory (Cohen & Felson, 1979; Felson, 2008); defensible space theory (Newman, 1972; Reynald & Elffers, 2009); environmental design theory (Mawby, 1977); crime pattern theory (Brantingham & Brantingham, 1984, 2008); hotspot theory (Sherman, Gartin, & Buerger, 1989); target selection theory (Brantingham & Brantingham, 2013); guardianship theory (Reynald, 2011); place management theory (Madensen & Eck, 2013); egohood theory (Hipp, 2007; Hipp & Boessen, 2013); offender mobility theory (Bernasco, 2010; Rengert, 2004; Ruiter, 2016; Tittle & Paternoster, 1988); foraging theory (inspired by behavioral ecology) (Bernasco, 2009; Johnson, 2014; Johnson & Bowers, 2004); ecological disadvantage theory (St. Jean, 2007); broken windows theory (Welsh et al., 2015; Wilson & Kelling, 1982); social disorganization theory in various versions (Bursik, 1984, 1998; Kornhauser, 1978; Kubrin & Weitzer, 2003); collective efficacy theory (Sampson, 2010, 2012); the theory of dangerous places (Graham & Clarke, 2001; Roncek, 1981); the epidemic model of crime-prone neighborhoods (Weatherburn & Lind, 2006); and the theory of deviant places (Stark, 1987). There is no shortage of explanations in environmental criminology.[2]

We cannot describe and discuss them all, and it is not our aspiration to do so, as many are discussed in more detail in the chapters of this volume, but discussing some of the key ideas together is necessary to provide a starting point for the volume. Accordingly, the most popular contemporary theories—crime pattern theory (CPT), routine activity theory (RAT), social disorganization theory (SDT), and rational choice perspective (RCP)—will now be discussed. Each of these has already been briefly outlined before, so our intention here is to elaborate on the theories to emphasize common ground and points of departure.

The last of these is not a specific theory of environmental criminology, but a decision-making framework often incorporated into the other theories. Rational choice theory originated in the 18th century (Bruinsma, 2017) and has been presented in a variety of forms across disciplines. Becker (1968) was the first to discuss it in relation to crime, but it is the rational choice perspective (RCP) as defined by Cornish and Clarke (1986) that informs studies of environmental criminology. According to RCP, individuals will commit a crime if they perceive the rewards of criminal action to outweigh the associated costs and effort involved. Rewards can be material or psychological, while costs and effort include the risk of apprehension and the time taken to travel to a crime location, respectively. Unlike in other theories of rational choice, decision-making is assumed to be imperfect due to offenders having only partial information about crime opportunities and because they employ rules of thumb when making choices, rather than deliberating on objective data on the true state of the world. While the RCP does consider some of the factors that influence whether an offender will desist from crime, it is the focus on (crime) event-level decision-making that has most informed studies of environmental criminology. The nature of the crime is in this theory always situationally specific. Certain settings are more attractive because the relative rewards are assessed to be higher than other settings. It is a so-called empty theory: the researcher must imagine and search for valid measurements of costs and rewards to study a particular behavior in a specific setting.

RAT was originally presented as a macro-level theory to explain why crime increased—rather than decreasing as would have been predicted by prevailing wisdom—during a period of social improvement in the United States (Cohen & Felson, 1979). However, these days it is more commonly used to explain why there is more crime at some locations than others (Felson, 2008). According to RAT, criminal behavior can be situated within routine daily life activities, which determine the ebb and flow of people at particular locations at particular times: "These routines deliver temptations and controls and thus organize the type and the amount of crime in society" (Felson, 1994, p. 42). From this perspective, crime is more likely to occur when two elements converge in the absence of the third: (1) the presence of motivated offenders; (2) the availability of suitable targets; and (3) the absence of capable guardians. Targets are available in various shapes and sizes; some are suitable (in that an offender can exploit them), while others are not. Targets can be static or mobile. The presence of capable guardians discourages offending, according to RAT, and guardians are not limited to police officers or guards, but may be anyone or anything that may deter a crime. In her work, Reynald (2011) has elaborated on the concept of guardianship, further developing guardians' influence, from being merely present or not, to a more continuous role of effectiveness, ranging from not present, to present, to monitoring and intervening (Reynald, 2011; see more in chapter 30 by Reynald in this volume). The focus of RAT is not directed at explaining what dispositional factors motivate offenders. Indeed, the presence of offenders and their motivation is assumed to be constant. Instead, the focus of the theory is about how variation in people's routine activities shapes the likelihood that the elements necessary for a crime to occur (defined above) will converge.

According to CPT (Brantingham & Brantingham, 1984, 2008; see, for more details, chapter 12 by Brantingham, Brantingham, Song, and Spicer in this volume), through their routine activities (such as going to school or work, shopping, or leisure activities) people get to know the spaces through which they move, learning over time both their physical and social characteristics. In doing so, they develop an *awareness space* (varying from small to large) of their environment and—in the case of offenders—of the criminal opportunities it provides. Awareness reduces uncertainty, and hence from a rational choice perspective, according to the theory, it is when offenders encounter suitable opportunities within their awareness spaces that they are most likely to offend. Not all opportunities will be suitable. Moreover, judgments of suitability are believed to be subjective, as offenders will rarely (if ever) have access to perfect information (Brantingham & Brantingham, 2013). According to CPT, key features of urban form structure people's activity spaces and hence the opportunities of which they will become aware and may exploit. In spatial terms, it is a micro-level theory concerned with exactly where (e.g., individual buildings or street segments) and when crimes are most likely.

SDT is the one of the oldest theories of environmental criminology and was developed, as we have seen in this chapter, as part of the activity of the Chicago school of sociology and criminology in the first part of the 20th century. In the case of this theory, the unit of analysis is not small spaces, but neighborhoods intended to represent the communities people live in. There are several versions of SDT (Bruinsma et al., 2013; Kubrin & Weitzer, 2003), all of which assume that rates of crime and the concentration of offenders will be higher in socially disorganized neighborhoods. The classic version, originally articulated in the 1920s, suggests that social disorganization is the outcome of three structural area characteristics: low socioeconomic status, high residential mobility, and ethnic heterogeneity (Shaw & McKay, 1969 [1942]; Shaw et al., 1929). These characteristics were argued to weaken the resistance of residents to unconventional behavioral norms. The weakening of traditional institutions was said to be responsible for the emergence of competing value systems in neighborhoods: unconventional behavioral norms "invaded" disorganized communities and challenged conventional moral values. Moreover, it was assumed that in (ethnically) heterogeneous communities, institutional participation would be lower and informal control obstructed because inhabitants of such areas would be unable to communicate effectively with each other. Residential mobility was believed to have detrimental effects on a community because inhabitants would not reside there long enough to develop informal control and a system of shared values.

Bourdieu, Coleman, and Putnam inspired urban research by supplying an explanatory framework for the relation between social capital and the presence of social problems (Bourdieu, 1986; Coleman, 1988, 1990; Granovetter, 1973; Putnam, 1995, 2001). They emphasized the importance of social ties as a way of connecting communities of individuals. Putnam introduced the term "social capital," which he defined as the connections among individuals that facilitate coordination and cooperation for mutual benefit (Putnam, 1995). According to this perspective, a community's social capital will increase as *trust, reciprocity*, and *formal networks between residents* (civic engagement or organizational participation) are embedded more deeply into the social relationships of a community. Social capital is a community characteristic that is seen as a collective good. Social capital at the macro level refers to *shared norms and values* that are beneficial for a community, while social capital at the micro level refers to *social relationships* that are beneficial for the individual.

The most influential contemporary theory of social disorganization is the collective efficacy theory of Sampson (and his colleagues), which is built on the theory of social capital (Sampson, 2010; Sampson et al., 1997, 1999). Collective efficacy theory stresses the importance of a community being able to solve commonly identified problems, such as crime and safety. Collective efficacy is defined by Sampson as "the process of activating or converting social ties among neighborhood residents in order to achieve collective goals, such as public order or the control of crime" (Sampson, 2010, p. 802). The theory aims to explain the nonrandom distribution of crime across urban spaces and why neighborhood characteristics such as poverty and residential mobility are positively related to crime. It elaborates mostly upon social capital theory, and Sampson's and his colleagues' work has involved the development of empirical measures to estimate components of social cohesion, such as trust, reciprocity, and generational change (Sampson, 1986b). The introduction of the concept of social cohesion creates the theoretical and empirical link between "social trust" on the one hand and "informal social control" on the other. According to the theory, social and mutual trust in a community is an essential condition for fostering informal social control in the community, and thus the willingness to intervene for the common good.

Despite their differences, theories of environmental criminology have much in common. Some of the themes common to a number of perspectives include the following:

(1) Crime is not randomly distributed in space or time.
(2) Daily routines influence what people have to do throughout the day, creating rhythms of activities.
(3) Routine activities and urban form interact to shape the places people (including offenders) visit and become aware of.
(4) Anyone can act in the capacity of a guardian, but whether they do so and how capable they are will vary. Different theories suggest different factors influence this behavior.
(5) The mix of targets, offenders, and potential guardians varies by the time of the day, and by the social and physical characteristics of the location.
(6) Opportunities for offending are likely to differ in space and time for different crime types.
(7) Offenders do not commit crime somewhere in general, but engage in some form of decision-making process (however brief) and take advantage of specific crime opportunities at particular locations and times.
(8) Changes to the environment—as a result of natural variation or intervention—can influence levels of crime.
(9) Until recently, environmental criminologists have largely ignored the characteristics of potential offenders, focusing instead on the complex interactions between people's routine activities and the physical and social features of environments that make crime more or less likely.

The chapters assembled for this volume are intended to more fully explain the perspectives discussed above, to highlight or introduce areas of controversy, and to illustrate how researchers study these assumptions empirically. In some chapters, the emphasis is placed on physical features of the environment, while in others the social features of spaces are of more concern.

1.5 The Growing Importance of Environmental Criminology

In this subsection, we examine the growth in interest in environmental criminology. There are various ways of doing this, but here we do so by examining changes over time in the frequency with which papers with a focus on environmental criminology have been published in the top peer-reviewed criminology journals. This provides an indication of the quantity of work produced and, importantly, its acceptance in the most influential scholarly journals. Given the effort involved, it was not possible to survey all journals over all time. Instead, we sampled the top five journals over the 15-year period 2000–2015. Journals were selected on the basis of the five-year impact factors associated with them in 2015. The top five journals identified were *Criminology, Journal of Research in Crime and Delinquency, Journal of Experimental Criminology, Justice Quarterly*, and the *Journal of Quantitative Criminology*. We acknowledge that alternative approaches to the selection of journals exist, but assume that the reader will see the logic of our approach.

A total of 1,924 articles were published in these journals over this interval. To code them, all titles, abstracts, and keywords were read, and if there was insufficient information to code them on this basis, the full article read. Articles were coded by one researcher,[3] but inter-rater exercises were completed over the course of the task to ensure that the coding was reliable and that there was no coder drift.

As already highlighted, a key distinction between studies of environmental criminology and mainstream criminology is that the former generally focus on the crime event and in particular when and where it happens. Consequently, articles were first coded on the basis of the unit of analysis employed in the study, with the categories used being place/space, individuals, or other (e.g., papers concerned with the effects of sentencing at the national level). Figure 1.1 shows the trend over time for the publication of articles for which the unit of analysis was space or place. It shows the count of articles published each year, indexed to (i.e., divided by) the count of articles published in 2000, and

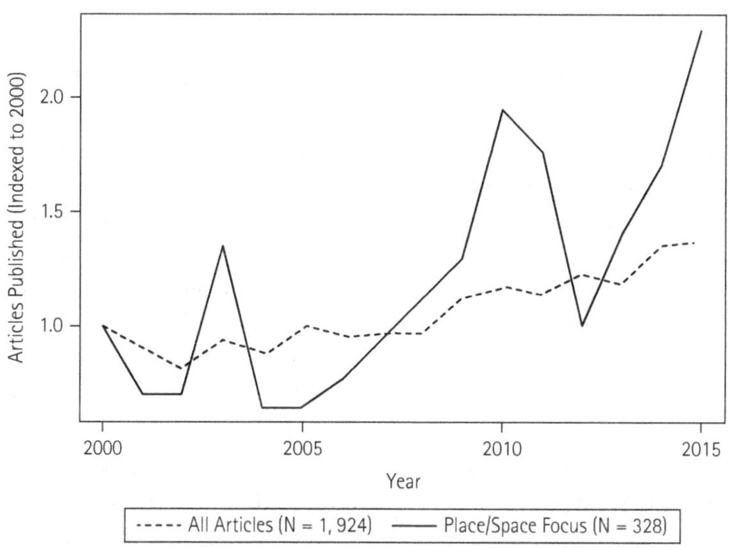

FIGURE 1.1 Yearly publication of articles in the top five peer-reviewed criminology journals indexed to the year 2000

demonstrates an increase over time in the number of published articles that focused on spatial patterns of crime. Relative to the year 2000, there was an approximately twofold increase in the number of articles published for which the unit of analysis was space or place. For the purposes of comparison, Figure 1.1 also shows the trend in the total number of articles published in the top five journals. This too increased, but at a much slower rate, suggesting an increase in the popularity of studies concerned with crime at places or the geography of crime. It is worth noting that the first issue of the *Journal of Experimental Criminology* was published in 2005, which explains some of the increase in the overall number of articles published across the five journals. It also worth noting that few articles concerned with spatial patterns of crime were published in this journal.

In addition to examining patterns in the aggregate, we examined changes in the rate at which articles were published with a particular theoretical focus. Articles were coded as to whether their primary focus was social disorganization theory, the rational choice perspective, routine activity theory, crime pattern theory, or some combination. In absolute terms, growth was observed for publications concerned with all theories. However, the largest increases were observed for the routine activity and crime pattern theories. For example, in the first five years (2000–2004) of the interval shown, an average of 0.8 articles per year focused on crime pattern theory. However, in the last five years (2011–2015) this increased to 6.4 articles per year. For routine activity theory, the equivalent rates were 8.8 and 14.8 per year. In short, it would appear that interest in environmental criminology—at least in the top criminology journals—is increasing.

1.6 Outline of the Volume

This volume has four parts and comprises 39 chapters, including this first introductory chapter. The first part, "Reflections on Theoretical Issues," is dedicated to theory in environmental criminology. Our approach to this part is intentionally different from that taken in traditional handbooks. Typically, scholars are invited to present and discuss their own theory in single chapters. Instead, for this handbook we invited well-known leading criminologists to write about important theoretical topics in environmental criminology: (1) social spatial influences such as social disorganization (Wilcox & Swartz); (2) how we get to causal clarity on physical environment-crime dynamics; (Taylor); (3) the individual perspective, specifically how individuals make use of space and the physical and social environments to commit crimes (Summers & Guerette). Additionally, we invited highly respected scholars to write chapters on the following provocative questions: do we really need the collective process to understand why crime occurs and offenders commit crime? (Groff); do we really need high offender neighborhoods to explain crime patterns? (Bottoms); why might social disorganization theory be redundant in environmental criminology? (Felson). Lastly, we invited two relative outsiders to evaluate the existing body of theory in environmental criminology (Cullen & Kulig). Our hope was that the authors would deliver chapters that provided a review of the state of the art concerning existing theory and associated developments, and that critically appraised the literature and challenged thinking in the field. We are delighted with what the authors produced, and this part provides a solid introduction to the field, its strengths, and its limitations.

The second part concerns the methodological approaches used in environmental criminology. This part has seven chapters. We have not included chapters on the general methods employed in criminology or the social sciences, but instead focus on important methodological issues in environmental criminology. The first chapter concerns a fundamental issue: what is the appropriate unit of analysis? This question can be deceptively difficult to answer, as the likelihood of crime at particular places can be influenced by factors that operate at a variety of different spatial scales. Moreover, the selection of the wrong unit of analysis can lead to errors of statistical inference, and so the choice of unit is paramount. Lawton discusses the theoretical and practical considerations researchers face when conducting research on crime and place, and provides empirical examples to illustrate issues concretely. Andresen's chapter builds on these issues and discusses how spatial data are analyzed by researchers using (for example) geographical information systems (GIS) and spatial statistics. In their chapter, Solymosi and Bowers discuss more recent developments in methods of data collection, considering (for example) the use of data collected through mobile phone applications, social media, Google street view, and CCTV recording of public space. They go on to illustrate the potential that such data have to inform research in environmental criminology. In their chapter, Brantingham, Brantingham, Song, and Spicer discuss techniques of visualization in environmental criminology and how these have progressed over time. In doing so, they also discuss recent advances in the testing and development of crime pattern theory. The two following chapters are on data collection in environmental criminological research.

Tseloni, Tilley, and Farrell discuss the strengths and limitations of the use of sample surveys in environmental criminology. In addition to these more traditional approaches, researchers increasingly apply observational methods in the study of small places or streets to audit characteristics of the physical environment—such as the kinds of buildings, roads, evidence of graffiti, and so on—or of the social environment—such as the presence of guardians, drunken people, or drug addicts. Brunton-Smith discusses the development of such methods of systematic social observation at places. The part is closed by a chapter on computer simulations. As discussed by Birks, the complexity of human interaction can make it difficult to collect the data necessary to test many of our theories. In his chapter, he considers how a different approach to theory testing, agent-based computer simulation modeling, can be helpful in this respect.

The third part, "Everyday Urban Crime: Empirical Examples and Reviews of Research," contains 17 chapters that represent a mixture of reviews of how empirical research has progressed on particular topics in the last 30 years, and novel empirical studies on specific issues in environmental criminology. Five chapters focus on neighborhood social processes and communities. The first reviews studies of social disorganization in European neighborhoods (Pauwels, Bruinsma, Weerman & Hardyns), while the second uses primary data collected in Nigeria to test the applicability of social disorganization theory in the developing world (Umar, Johnson, & Cheshire). In their chapter, Branic and Kubrin study gated communities in the United States and how they impact on neighborhood rates of violence and property crime in California. Hipp and Bates consider the problem of defining neighborhoods as discrete areas and use the concept of egohoods (which offer an alternative way of defining neighborhoods) to examine how neighborhood dynamics influence levels of crime. Informed by the broken windows theory of neighborhood crime, Innes and Innes consider how some crimes trigger signals in the environment that influence people's perception of safety, and how these influence different types of people.

The next sub-part focuses on the influence of the built environment on crime. In the first of four chapters, the extent to which variation in land uses is related to crime rates is the subject of Wuschke and Kinney's empirical study of property crime and crimes against the person in Canada. In his chapter, Newton reviews international research on how larger nodes of human activity influence levels of crime, considering in particular the influence of parks, stadiums, and transit stations. Ceccato and Wilhelmsson also examine accessibility, but in their chapter examine how rates of burglary affect real estate properties in Sweden. In doing so, they examine how crime affects the environment, rather than the other way around. Davies and Bowers close this sub-part with their chapter on how and why patterns of crime are shaped by the configuration of urban form. A key determinant of this configuration is the street network, which not only provides a convenient representation of space but also affects behavior.

Telep and Weisburd's chapter opens a sub-part on crime at specific places (as opposed to neighborhoods). They present an update of their work on the concentration of crime at places, reviewing empirical research to demonstrate the universality of this law. Weerman, Hoeben, Bernasco, Pauwels, and Bruinsma present Dutch data, including systematic observations of physical and social disorder in small spaces to characterize criminogenic settings. These data, collected using a direct research methodology, represent a considerable improvement over that collected via the kinds of survey questions that have been used in the past to test crime causation theories. Eck and Madensen write about place managers and how the decisions they make and their activity can deter potential offenders from committing crimes at specific locations. In their chapter on crime concentration, Ignatans and Pease distinguish between hot dots, hotspots and hot flushes to illustrate how and why theory can and should inform operational policing and the distribution of resources to reduce crime harm.

Under the umbrella of our subtitle, "Routine Activity Convergence," Tompson and Coupe show how crime risk varies across the seasons and over the course of the day, and how such patterns vary spatially. Crime not only clusters in space, but in time. Their findings are motivated by and discussed in relation to routine activity theory. The next chapter of this sub-part considers the role of a different set of actors in the crime equation—guardians (Reynald) and how they can deter potential offenders from committing crimes at specific locations. Bernasco presents an overview of the existing literature on the location choices of offenders, discusses different approaches to analysis, and summarizes findings to date.

Part III, on everyday urban crime, closes with a contribution from Welsh and Taheri, who take stock of how knowledge of environmental criminology has informed strategies or interventions intended to reduce crime. This is particularly true of work that has a situational crime prevention focus, but, as will be evident from the text of most chapters of this book, extends to other avenues of enquiry.

Part IV is dedicated to the application of environmental criminology to "Special Crimes and Circumstances." Criminology is concerned with a considerable variety of criminal behaviors, the nature of which have changed and continue to change. They are influenced by developments in technology, changes in urban form, changes in transportation infrastructure, social change, and so on. The chapters in this part demonstrate how environmental criminology has contributed to our understanding of the commission of crimes that are either not immediately connected to a specific physical location, or that might appear to be beyond the reach of environmental criminologists. For example, in their chapter, Baudains and Johnson examine offender decision-making during the 2011 London riots. They show that even for the extreme circumstances of a riot, offender spatial decision-making, far from being random, is consistent with theories of environmental criminology. Rossmo discusses and provides illustrations of geographic profiling, a technique motivated by crime pattern theory that is used to identify the likely activity nodes of offenders based on the locations of their crimes. In this chapter, he considers the application of the technique to terrorism and discusses how it can help law enforcement and intelligence agencies to prioritize and manage information in large-scale investigations. Wortley makes clear how in the case of child sexual abuse, the focus of research has generally been directed toward understanding the psychology of the offender, but that studying situational dynamics can contribute to understanding and preventing this serious form of offending.

Organized crime is partly transnational, partly very local. In contrast to transnational organized crime, as Valasik and Tita observe in their chapter, US gangs have a strong connection to neighborhoods and spaces, expressing "their territory" in competition with other gangs and law enforcement agencies. Kleemans in his chapter points out that, in some respects, space plays little role in international organized crime and that social networks (social embeddedness) are much more important. In this way, his chapter presents a challenge to environmental criminology.

Not all crimes that have recently emerged are bound to specific locations. The Internet has made it possible for existing crimes to be committed in new ways, and provides opportunities for new forms of offending. In their chapter, Miró Llinares and Johnson discuss how cybercrime can be studied from the perspective of environmental criminology and the challenges this type of offending presents for such enquiry. In the final chapter of the book, Townsley examines spatial patterns of maritime piracy and shows that attacks occur at locations when three conditions are met: suitable targets are accessible, there is a suitable land base (i.e. port) for supplies and disposal of plunder, and there is a lack of enforcement (guardianship) at sea. In the spirit of situational crime prevention, he then goes on to discuss the impact of different crime prevention strategies on this type of crime, providing a fitting end to this volume.

Notes

1. In France and England, the reform movement focused its policy on public health and education for the poor.
2. We have not mentioned here the kinds of theories that aim at explaining crime rate differences between countries.
3. We would like to thank Eon Kim for her sterling work in completing this mammoth task.

References

Abbott, A. (1997). Of time and space: The contemporary relevance of the Chicago school. *Social Forces* 75(4), 1149–1182.

Aebi, M. F., Aubusson de Cavarlay, B., Barclay, G., Gruszczyńska, B., Harrendorf, S., Heiskanen, M., et al. (2010). *European Sourcebook of Crime and Criminal Justice Statistics—2010*. The Hague: Boom Juridische uitgevers.

Balbi, A., & Guerry, A.-M. (1829). *Statistique Comparée de l'Etat de l'Instruction et du Nombre des Crimes dans les divers Arrondissements des Académies et des Cours Royales de France*. Paris: Unknown publisher.

Baldwin, J. (1975). British areal studies of crime: An assessment. *British Journal of Criminology* 15(3), 211–227.

Baldwin, J., & Bottoms, A. E. (1976). *The Urban Criminal*. London: Tavistock.

Becker, G. S. (1968). Crime and punishment: An economic approach. *Journal of Political Economy* 76, 169–217.

Beirne, P. (1987). Adolphe Quételet and the origins of positivist criminology. *American Journal of Sociology* 92(5), 1140–1169.

Beirne, P. (Ed.). (1994). *The Origins and Growth of Criminology: Essays in Intellectual History, 1760–1945*. Aldershot: Dartmouth.

Beirne, P., & Messerschmidt, J. (1991). *Criminology*. San Diego: Harcourt Brace Jovanovich.

Bernasco, W. (2009). Foraging strategies of homo criminalis: Lessons from behavioral ecology. *Crime Patterns and Analysis* 2, 5–16.

Bernasco, W. (2010). A sentimental journey to crime: Effects of residential history on crime location choice. *Criminology* 48, 389–416.

Bernasco, W., Block, R., & Ruiter, S. (2013). Go where the money is: Modeling street robbers' location choices. *Journal of Economic Geography* 13(1), 119–143.

Bottoms, A. E. (2007). Place, space, crime, and disorder. In M. Maguire, R. Morgan, & R. Reiner (Eds.), *The Oxford Handbook of Criminology* (pp. 528–574). Oxford: Oxford University Press.

Bottoms, A. E., & Wiles, P. (1986). Housing tenure and residential crime careers in Britain. In A. J. Reiss & M. Tonry (Eds.), *Communities and Crime* (pp. 101–163). Chicago: University of Chicago Press.

Bottoms, A. E., & Wiles, P. (1992). Explanations of crime and place. In D. J. Evans, N. R. Fyfe, & D. T. Herbert (Eds.), *Crime, Policing and Place: Essays in Environmental Criminology* (pp. 11–35). London: Routledge.

Bottoms, A. E., & Wiles, P. (2002). Environmental criminology. In M. Maguire, R. Morgan, & R. Reiner (Eds.), *The Oxford Handbook of Criminology*, 3rd ed. (pp. 620–656). Oxford: Oxford University Press.

Bourdieu, P. (1986). The forms of capital. In J. G. Richardson (Ed.), *Handbook of Theory and Research for the Sociology of Education* (pp. 241–258). New York: Greenwood Press.

Bowers, K. J. (2014). Risky facilities: Crime radiators or crime absorbers? A comparison of internal and external levels of theft. *Journal of Quantitative Criminology 30*(3), 389–414.

Bowers, K. J., & Johnson, S. D. (2016). Situational prevention. In D. Weisburd & D. P. Farrington (Eds.), *What Works in Crime Prevention and Rehabilitation* (pp. 111–135). New York: Springer.

Boyd, R., & Richerson, P. J. (1985). *Culture and the Evolutionary Process*. Chicago: University of Chicago Press.

Brantingham, P. J., & Brantingham, P. L. (1978). A theoretical model of crime site selection. In M. D. Krohn & R. L. Akers (Eds.), *Crime, Law and Sanctions* (pp. 105–118). Beverly Hills, CA: Sage.

Brantingham, P. J., & Brantingham, P. L. (Eds.). (1981). *Environmental Criminology*. Beverly Hills, CA: Sage.

Brantingham, P. J., & Brantingham, P. L. (1984). *Patterns in Crime*. New York: Macmillan.

Brantingham, P. J., & Brantingham, P. L. (Eds.). (1991). *Environmental Criminology*. Prospect Heights, IL: Waveland.

Brantingham, P. J., & Brantingham, P. L. (2008). Crime pattern theory. In R. Wortley & L. Mazarolle (Eds.), *Environmental Criminology and Crime Analysis* (pp. 78–94). Devon: Willan.

Brantingham, P. J., & Brantingham, P. L. (2013). The theory of target selection. In F. T. Cullen & P. Wilcox (Eds.), *The Oxford Handbook of Criminological Theory* (pp. 535–553). New York: Oxford University Press.

Brantingham, P. L., & Brantingham, P. J. (1993). Environment, routine, and situation: Toward a pattern theory of crime. In R. V. Clarke & M. Felson (Eds.), *Routine Activity and Rational Choice* (pp. 259–294), vol. 5 of *Advances in Criminological Theory*. New Brunswick, NJ: Transaction.

Bronfenbrenner, U. (1979). *The Ecology of Human Development: Experiments by Nature and Design*. Cambridge, MA: Harvard University Press.

Browning, C. R., Cagney, K. A., & Morris, K. (2014). The early Chicago school of sociology. In G. J. N. Bruinsma & D. Weisburd (Eds.), *The Encyclopedia of Criminology and Criminal Justice* (pp. 1233–1242). New York: Springer.

Bruinsma, G. J. N. (2017). The emergence of deterrence theory in the Age of Enlightenment. In F. T. Cullen, D. S. Nagin, & C. L. Cohen (Eds.), *Deterrence, Choice, and Crime: Contemporary Perspectives*. New Brunswick, NJ: Transaction Publishers (in press).

Bruinsma, G. J. N., Pauwels, L., Weerman, F. M., & Bernasco, W. (2013). Social disorganization, social capital and collective efficacy and the distribution of crime and criminals: An empirical test of the relevance of six American neighborhood theories for a Dutch city. *British Journal of Criminology 53*(5), 942–963.

Bruinsma, G. J. N., & Weisburd, D. (2014a). History of geographic criminology I: The 19th century. In G. J. N. Bruinsma & D. Weisburd (Eds.), *The Encyclopedia of Criminology and Criminal Justice* (pp. 2159–2163). New York: Springer.

Bruinsma, G. J. N., & Weisburd, D. (2014b). History of geographic criminology II: The 20th century. In G. J. N. Bruinsma & D. Weisburd (Eds.), *The Encyclopedia of Criminology and Criminal Justice* (pp. 2164–2172). New York: Springer.

Bulmer, M. (1984). *The Chicago School of Sociology: Institutionalization, Diversity, and the Rise of Sociological Research*. Chicago: University of Chicago Press.

Burgess, E. W. (1916). Origination as a function of organisation. PhD diss., University of Chicago.

Burgess, E. W. (1967 [1925]). The growth of the city: An introduction to a research project. In R. E. Park & E. W. Burgess (Eds.), *The City: Suggestions for the Investigation of Human Behaviour in the Urban Environment* (pp. 47–62). Chicago: University of Chicago Press.

Burgess, E. W., & Bogue, D. J. (1964). Research in urban society: A long view. In E. W. Burgess & D. J. Bogue (Eds.), *Contributions to Urban Sociology* (pp. 1–14). Chicago: University of Chicago Press.

Bursik, R. J. (1984). Urban dynamics and ecological studies of delinquency. *Social Forces 63*, 393–413.

Bursik, R. J. (1986). Ecological stability and the dynamics of delinquency. In A. J. Reiss Jr & M. Tonry (Eds.), *Communities and Crime* (pp. 35–66). Chicago: University of Chicago Press.

Bursik, R. J. (1998). Social disorganization and theories of crime and delinquency: Problems and prospects. In S. Henry & W. Einstadter (Eds.), *The Criminology Theory Reader* (pp. 156–172). New York: New York University Press.

Bursik, R. J., & Webb, J. (1982). Community change and patterns of delinquency. *American Journal of Sociology 88*, 24–42.

Clarke, R. V. (1980). Situational crime prevention: Theory and practice. *British Journal of Criminology 20*, 136–137.

Clarke, R. V., & Eck, J. E. (2005). *Crime Analysis for Problem Solvers in 60 Small Steps*. Washington, DC: US Department of Justice, Office of Community Oriented Policing.

Clarke, R. V., & Felson, M. (Eds.). (1993). *Routine Activity and Rational Choice. Advances in Criminological Theory*, vol. 5. New Brunswick, NJ: Transaction Books.

Clinard, M. B. (1942). The process of urbanization and criminal behaviour. *American Journal of Sociology 48*(2), 202–213.

Clinard, M. B. (1978). *Cities with Little Crime: The Case of Switzerland*. Cambridge: Cambridge University Press.

Cohen, L., & Felson, M. (1979). Social change and crime rate trends: A routine activity approach. *American Sociological Review 44*(4), 588–608.

Coleman, J. S. (1988). Social capital in the creation of human capital. *American Journal of Sociology 94* (Supplement), S95–S120.

Coleman, J. S. (1990). *Foundations of Social Theory*. Cambridge, MA: Belknap Press of Harvard University Press.

Cornish, D. B., & Clarke, R. V. (Eds.). (1986). *The Reasoning Criminal: Rational Choice Perspectives on Offending*. New York: Springer-Verlag.

Cornish, D. B., & Clarke, R. V. (2008). The rational choice perspective. In R. Wortley & L. Mazarolle (Eds.), *Environmental Criminology and Crime Analysis* (pp. 21–47). Devon: Willan.

Cullen, F. T., & Wilcox, P. (Eds.). (2010). *Encyclopedia of Criminological Theory*. Thousand Oaks, CA: Sage.

Cullen, F. T., & Wilcox, P. (Eds.). (2013). *Oxford Handbook of Criminological Theory*. New York: Oxford University Press.

Ducpétiaux, E. (1827). *De la Justice de prévoyance, et particulierement de l'influence de la misere et de l'aisance, de l'ignorance et de l'instruction sur le nombre des crimes*. Brussels: J.J. de Cautaerts.

Eisner, M., & Wikström, P.-O. H. (1999). Violent crime in the urban community: A comparison of Stockholm and Basel. *European Journal on Criminal Policy and Research 7*(4), 427–442.

Elmer, M. C. (1933). Century-old ecological studies in France. *American Journal of Sociology* 39(1), 63–70.

Faris, R. E. L. (1967). *Chicago Sociology, 1920–1932*. San Francisco: Chandler.

Farrell, G., Tilley, N., Tseloni, A., & Mailley, J. (2011). The crime drop and the security hypothesis. *Journal of Research in Crime and Delinquency 48*(2), 147–175.

Felson, M. (1994). *Crime and Everyday Life: Insight and Implications for Society*. Thousand Oaks, CA: Pine Forge Press.

Felson, M. (2008). Routine activity approach. In R. Wortley & L. Mazarolle (Eds.), *Environmental Criminology and Crime Analysis* (pp. 70–77). Devon: Willan.

Felson, M., & Clarke, R. V. (1998). *Opportunity Makes the Thief: Practical Theory for Crime Prevention*. London: Home Office.

Graham, P., & Clarke, J. (2001). Dangerous places: Crime and the city. In J. Muncie & E. McLaughlin (Eds.), *The Problem of Crime* (pp. 151–190). London: Sage.

Granovetter, M. S. (1973). The strength of weak ties. *American Journal of Sociology 78*(6), 1360–1380.

Greg, W. R. (1835). *Social Statistics of the Netherlands*. London: Ridgway, Harrison and Crosfield.

Groff, E. R., Weisburd, D., & Yang, S. M. (2010). Is it important to examine crime trends at a local "micro" level? A longitudinal analysis of street to street variability in crime trajectories. *Journal of Quantitative Criminology 26*, 7–32.

Guerry, A.-M. (1833). *Essai sur la Statistique Morale de la France*. Paris: Crochard.

Harvey, L. (1987). *Myths of the Chicago School of Sociology*. Hong Kong: Avebury.

Hawley, A. (1950). *Human Ecology: A Theory of Community Structure*. New York: Ronald.

Hawley, A. H. (1986). *Human Ecology: A Theoretical Essay*. Chicago: University of Chicago Press.

Hipp, J. R. (2007). Block, tract, and level of aggregation: Neighborhood structure and crime and disorder as a case in point. *American Sociological Review 72*(5), 659–680.

Hipp, J. R., & Boessen, A. (2013). Egohoods as waves washing across the city: A new measure of "neighborhoods." *Criminology 51*(2), 287–327.

Jacobs, J. (1961). *The Death and Life of Great American Cities*. New York: Vintage Books.

Jeffery, C. R. (1971). *Crime Prevention through Environmental Design* Beverly Hills, CA: Sage.

Johnson, E. A. (1992). Cities don't cause crime: Urban-rural differences in late nineteenth- and early twentieth-century German criminality. *Social Science History 16*(1), 129–176.

Johnson, S. D. (2014). How do offenders choose where to offend? Perspectives from animal foraging. *Legal and Criminological Psychology 19*(2), 193–210.

Johnson, S. D., & Bowers, K. J. (2004). The stability of space-time clusters of burglary. *British Journal of Criminology 44*(1), 55–65.

Johnson, S. D., & Bowers, K. J. (2010). Permeability and burglary risk: Are cul-de-sacs safer?. *Journal of Quantitative Criminology 26*(1), 89–111.

Kornhauser, R. R. (1978). *Social Sources of Delinquency: An Appraisal of Analytic Models*. Chicago: University of Chicago Press.

Kubrin, C. E., & Weitzer, R. (2003). New directions in social disorganization theory. *Journal of Research in Crime and Delinquency 40*(4), 374–402.

Lander, B. (1954). *Toward an Understanding of Juvenile Delinquency*. New York: Columbia University Press.

Levin, Y., & Lindesmith, A. (1937). English ecology and criminology of the past century. *Journal of Criminal Law and Criminology 27*, 810–816.

Madensen, T. D., & Eck, J. E. (2013). Crime places and place management. In F. T. Cullen & P. Wilcox (Eds.), *Oxford Handbook of Criminological Theory* (pp. 554–578). New York: Oxford University Press.

Mawby, R. I. (1977). Defensible space: A theoretical and empirical appraisal. *Urban Studies 14*, 169–179.

McKenzie, R. D. (1924). The ecological approach to the study of the human community. *American Journal of Sociology 30*(3), 287–301.

Morris, T. (1957). *The Criminal Area: A Study in Social Ecology*. London: Routledge & Kegan Paul.

Newman, O. (1972). *Defensible Space: Crime Prevention through Urban Design*. New York: Macmillan.

Nye, F. I. (1958). *Family Relationships and Delinquent Behavior*. New York: Wiley & Sons.

Oberwittler, D., & Wikström, P.-O. H. (2009). Why small is better: Advancing the study of the role of behavioral contexts in crime causation. In D. Weisburd, W. Bernasco, & G. J. N. Bruinsma (Eds.), *Putting Crime in Its Place: Units of Analysis in Geographic Criminology* (pp. 35–59). New York: Springer.

Park, R. E., & Burgess, E. W. (1967 [1925]). *The City: Suggestions for Investigation of Human Behavior in the Urban Environment*. Chicago: University of Chicago Press.

Putnam, R. D. (1995). Bowling alone: America's declining social capital. *Journal of Democracy 6*(1), 65–78.

Putnam, R. D. (2001). *Bowling Alone: The Collapse and Revival of American Community*. New York: Simon & Schuster.

Quételet, A. (1984 [1831]). *Research on the propensity for crime at different ages*. Translated by S. F. Sylvester. Cincinnati: Anderson.

Raudenbush, S. W., & Sampson, R. J. (1999). Ecometrics: Towards a science of assessing ecological settings, with appliance to the systematic social observations of neighbourhoods. *Sociological Methodology 29*, 1–41.

Rawson, R. W. (1839). An inquiry into the statistics of crime in England and Wales. *Journal of the Statistical Society of London 2*, 316–344.

Reiss, A. J., & Tonry, M. (Eds.). (1986). *Communities and Crime*. Chicago: University of Chicago Press.

Rengert, G. F. (1981). Burglary in Philadelphia: A critique of an opportunity structure model. In P. L. Brantingham & P. J. Brantingham (Eds.), *Environmental Criminology* (pp. 189–201). Prospect Heights: Waveland Press.

Rengert, G. F. (1991). *Burglary in Philadelphia: A Critique of an Opportunity Structure Model*. Waveland: Prospect Heights.

Rengert, G. F. (1996). *The Geography of Illegal Drugs*. Boulder, CO: Westview Press.

Rengert, G. F. (2004). The journey to crime. In G. J. N. Bruinsma, H. Elffers, & J. W. de Keijser (Eds.), *Punishment, Places and Perpetrators: Developments in Criminology and Criminal Justice Research* (pp. 169–181). Devon: Willan.

Rephann, T. J. (1999). Links between rural development and crime. *Papers in Regional Science 78*, 365–386.

Reynald, D. M. (2011). *Guarding against Crime: A Theoretical and Empirical Elaboration of the Routine Activity Concept*. London: Ashgate.

Reynald, D. M., & Elffers, H. (2009). The future of Newman's defensible space theory: Linking defensible space and the routine activities of place. *European Journal of Criminology 6*(1), 45–60.

Robinson, W. S. (1950). Ecological correlations and the behavior of individuals. *American Sociological Review* 15(3), 351–357.

Roncek, D. W. (1981). Dangerous places: Crime and residential environment. *Social Forces* 60(1), 74–96.

Ruiter, S. (2016). Crime location choice: State-of-the-art and avenues for future research. In W. Bernasco, H. E. Elffers, & J.-L. Van Gelder (Eds.), *Oxford Handbook of Offender Decision Making*. Oxford: Oxford University Press.

Sampson, R. J. (1986a). Crime in cities: The effects of formal and informal social control. In A. J. J. Reiss and M. Tonry (Eds.), *Communities and Crime* (pp. 271–311). Chicago: University of Chicago Press.

Sampson, R. J. (Ed.). (1986b). *Neighborhood Family Structure and the Risk of Personal Victimization*. New York: Springer.

Sampson, R. J. (2010). Collective efficacy theory. In F. T. Cullen & P. Wilcox (Eds.), *Encyclopedia of Criminological Theory* (pp. 802–812). Thousand Oaks, CA: Sage.

Sampson, R. J. (2012). *Great American City: Chicago and the Enduring Neighborhood Effect*. Chicago: University of Chicago Press.

Sampson, R. J., Morenoff, J. D., & Earls, F. (1999). Beyond social capital: Spatial dynamics of collective efficacy for children. *American Sociological Review* 64(5), 633–660.

Sampson, R. J., Raudenbush, S. W., & Earls, F. (1997). Neighbourhoods and violent crime: A multilevel study of collective efficacy. *Science* 277, 918–924.

Shaw, C. R., & McKay, H. D. (1942). *Juvenile Delinquency and Urban Areas*. Chicago: University of Chicago Press.

Shaw, C. R., & McKay, H. D. (1969 [1942]). *Juvenile Delinquency and Urban Areas: A Study of Rates of Delinquency in Relation to Differential Characteristics of Local Communities in American Cities*. Chicago: University of Chicago Press.

Shaw, C. R., Zorbaugh, F. M., McKay, H. D., & Cottrell, L. S. (1929). *Delinquency Areas: A Study of the Geographic Distribution of School Truants, Juvenile Delinquents, and Adult Offenders in Chicago*. Chicago: University of Chicago Press.

Sherman, L. W., Buerger, M. E., & Gartin, P. R. (1989). *Repeat Call Address Policing: The Minneapolis RECAP Experiment*. Washington, DC: Crime Control Institute.

Sherman, L. W., Gartin, P. R., & Buerger, M. E. (1989). Hot spots of predatory crime: Routine activities and the criminology of place. *Criminology* 27(1), 27–56.

Short, J. F., Jr. (2002). Criminology, the Chicago school, and sociological theory. *Crime, Law and Social Change* 37, 107–115.

Skogan, W. G. (1987). Disorder and community decline. Center for Urban Affairs and Policy Research, Northwestern University.

Skogan, W. G. (1990). *Disorder and Decline: Crime and the Spiral of Decay in American Neighborhoods*. New York: Free Press.

Snodgrass, J. D. (1976). Clifford R. Shaw and Henry D. McKay: Chicago criminologists. *British Journal of Criminology* 16, 1–19.

St. Jean, P. K. B. (2007). *Pockets of Crime: Broken Windows, Collective Efficacy, and the Criminal Point of View*. Chicago: University of Chicago Press.

Stark, R. (1987). Deviant places: A theory of the ecology of crime. *Criminology* 25(4), 893–910.

Taylor, R. B. (1987). Toward an environmental psychology of disorder: Delinquency, crime, and fear of crime. In D. Stokols & I. Altman (Eds.), *Handbook of Environmental Psychology* (pp. 951–986). New York: John Wiley & Sons.

Taylor, R. B. (2015). *Community Criminology: Fundamentals of Spatial and Temporal Scaling, Ecological Indicators, and Selectivity Bias*. New York: New York University Press.
Thomas, W. I. (1966). *On Social Organization and Social Personality: Selected Papers*. Edited by M. Janovitz. Chicago: University of Chicago Press.
Thomas, W. I. (1971 [1921]). The immigrant community. In *The Social Fabric of the Metropolis: Contributions of the Chicago School of Urban Sociology* (pp. 120–130). Chicago: University of Chicago Press.
Tilley, N., Tseloni, A., & Farrell, G. (2011). Income disparities of burglary risk security availability during the crime drop. *British Journal of Criminology* 51(2), 296–313.
Tittle, C. R., & Paternoster, R. (1988). Geographic mobility and criminal behaviour. *Journal of Research in Crime and Delinquency* 25(3), 301–343.
Townsley, M., Birks, D., Bernasco, W., Ruiter, S., Johnson, S. D., White, G., et al. (2015). Burglar target selection: A cross-national comparison. *Journal of Research in Crime and Delinquency* 52(1), 3–31.
Tseloni, A. (2006). Multilevel modelling of the number of property crimes: Household and area effects. *Journal of the Royal Statistical Society: Series A (Statistics in Society)* 169(2), 205–233.
Tseloni, A., Wittebrood, K., Farrell, G., & Pease, K. (2004). Burglary victimization in England and Wales, the United States and the Netherlands: A cross-national comparative test of routine activities and lifestyle theories. *British Journal of Criminology* 44(1), 66–91.
Van Gelder, J.-L., & Van Daele, S. (2014). Innovative data collection methods in criminological research: Editorial introduction. *Crime Science* 3(6), 1–4.
Vold, G. B., Bernard, T. J., & Snipes, J. B. (2002). *Theoretical Criminology*. 5th ed. New York: Oxford University Press.
Weatherburn, D., & Lind, B. (2006). *Delinquent-Prone Communities*. Cambridge: Cambridge University Press.
Weisburd, D. (2015). The 2014 Sutherland Address: The law of crime concentrations and the criminology of place. *Criminology* 53(2), 133–157.
Weisburd, D., Bernasco, W., & Bruinsma, G. J. N. (Eds.). (2009). *Putting Crime in Its Place: Units of Analysis in Geographic Criminology*. New York: Springer.
Weisburd, D., Bruinsma, G. J. N., & Bernasco, W. (2009). Units of analysis in geographic criminology: Historical development, critical issues, and open questions. In D. Weisburd, W. Bernasco, & G. J. N. Bruinsma (Eds.), *Putting Crime in Its Place: Units of Analysis in Geographic Criminology* (pp. 3–31). New York: Springer.
Weisburd, D., Bushway, S., Lum, C., & Yang, S.-M. (2004). Trajectories of crime at places: A longitudinal study of street segments in the city of Seattle. *Criminology* 42(2), 283–321.
Weisburd, D., Eck, J. E., Braga, A., Telep, C., Cave, B., Bowers, K. J., et al. (2016). *Place Matters: Criminology for the 21st Century*. Cambridge: Cambridge University Press.
Weisburd, D., Groff, E. R., & Yang, S.-M. (2012). *The Criminology of Place: Street Segments and Our Understanding of the Crime Problem*. New York: Oxford University Press.
Welsh, B. C., Braga, A. A., & Bruinsma, G. J. N. (2015). Re-imagining broken windows. *Journal of Research in Crime and Delinquency* 52(4), 447–463.
Wikström, P.-O. H. (1991). *Urban Crime, Criminals, and Victims: The Swedish Experience in an Anglo-American Comparative Perspective*. New York: Springer-Verlag.
Wilcox, P., & Eck, J. E. (2011). Criminology of the unpopular. *Criminology and Public Policy* 10(2), 473–482.

Wilcox, P., Land, K. C., & Hunt, S. A. (2003). *Criminal Circumstance: A Dynamic Multicontextual Criminal Opportunity Theory*. New York: Aldine de Gruyter.

Wilson, J. Q., & Kelling, G. (1982). Broken windows: The police and neighbourhood safety. *Atlantic Monthly* 249(3), 29–38.

Wortley, R. (2008). Situational precipitators of crime. In R. Wortley & L. Mazarolle (Eds.), *Environmental Criminology and Crime Analysis* (pp. 48–69). Devon: Willan.

Wortley, R., & Mazerolle, L. (Eds.). (2008). *Environmental Criminology and Crime Analysis*. Devon: Willan.

PART I

REFLECTIONS ON THEORETICAL ISSUES

CHAPTER 2

SOCIAL SPATIAL INFLUENCES

PAMELA WILCOX AND KRISTIN SWARTZ

2.1 Introduction

Although the study of the social ecology of crime has a long history (see Chapter 1), its contemporary form represents a particularly stark paradigm shift from older studies of social spatial influences. Specifically, contemporary forms of environmental criminology de-emphasize neighborhood-level origins of criminality and focus instead on understanding opportunity for crime events, typically at subneighborhood units of analysis (Sherman, Gartin, and Buerger 1989; Weisburd et al. 2004; Groff, Weisburd, and Yang 2010; Braga, Hureau, and Papachristos 2011). While contemporary environmental criminology and its microspatial focus is the overwhelming focus of this book, the purpose of this chapter is to review the older, more macrospatial tradition of community- or neighborhood-based theory and research, as this line of inquiry is a vital part of contemporary environmental criminology's intellectual ancestry.

Though "neighborhood" is variably defined, studies in the community tradition typically focus on units such as census tracts or block groups, police districts, political wards, or locally demarcated areas defined on the basis of within-area homogeneity and/or natural barriers. Regardless of the precise unit used, the assumption in this community criminology literature is that the neighborhood unit approximates an "urban village" (e.g., see Boessen and Hipp 2015). In order to understand cross-neighborhood variation in measures of offending behavior or incident rates, community criminology emphasizes community-level concepts such as social disorganization, systemic control, collective efficacy, concentrated disadvantage, street culture, and legal cynicism (e.g., Sampson and Groves 1989; Bursik and Grasmick 1993; Sampson, Raudenbush, and Earls 1997; Anderson 1999; Warner 2003; Kirk and Papachristos 2011; Sampson 2012). Other neighborhood-level work is theoretically more aligned with contemporary environmental criminology and therefore uses the concept of *crime opportunity* as the primary explanatory construct for understanding community variation in crime events.

This review of neighborhood-focused theory and research is provided over the course of five major sections. In Section 2.1, we discuss the relationship between neighborhood social disorganization and crime according to early Chicago school scholars. In the following sections, we address more recent ideas on social spatial influence, with emphasis on various social-structural and social-cultural neighborhood processes. More specifically, Section 2.2 highlights the role of neighborhood-based systemic control on community rates of crime, while Section 2.3 discusses the influence of community-based collective efficacy. In Section 2.4, we turn our attention to the influences of ecologically rooted cognitive landscapes, street culture, and legal cynicism. Finally, Section 2.5 discusses the various ways in which neighborhoods provide "crime opportunity contexts"—and it is in this section that the overlap and compatibility between community-focused criminology and contemporary environmental criminology is most explicit. The main conclusions of the chapter can be summarized as follows:

- Work emerging from the Chicago school in the early part of the 20th century firmly established the idea that crime was due to types of places as opposed to types of people. In particular, socially disorganized places affected aggregate rates of crime and the behavior of individuals within these spaces.
- Following Kornhauser's influential appraisal of prevailing theories of delinquency, the predominant model of neighborhood influence became that of "systemic control." From this perspective, systems of friendship and kinship ties are seen as the core of community life, providing effective socialization and informal social control against crime. While initial empirical research was supportive, subsequent research revealed that the relationship between social ties and crime was not so simple. Evidence currently suggests that dense and frequent ties are not always necessary or sufficient for effective social control of crime, though ties to extracommunity agents seem quite important.
- In the late 1990s, collective efficacy theory emerged as an alternative explanation for neighborhood influence. According to collective efficacy theory, social cohesion and trust, combined with a willingness to intervene for the common good, is the key social influence affecting crime. Many studies support the role of collective efficacy in explaining neighborhood-based crime events, but there is less solid evidence that collective efficacy explains variation in rates of offending among neighborhood residents.
- The 1990s also marked an emphasis on concentrated disadvantage (and accompanying racial inequality) in deindustrialized inner-city communities, with implications for community culture. Concentrated disadvantage is theorized to impact cultural norms regarding deviance in a variety of ways: (1) it promotes cognitive landscapes that tolerate deviance; (2) it leads to the development of a street code; and (3) it generates legal cynicism.

- An alternative approach to understanding neighborhood social influence views neighborhood processes like cohesion, collective efficacy, or informal control as impacting available crime opportunities since they can disrupt crime events by handling potential offenders, guarding potential targets or victims, and/or managing potential crime places.

2.2 The Early Chicago School: Neighborhood Social Disorganization and Crime

Though notable studies of the spatial distribution of crime date back to the 1800s (Guerry 1883; Quételet 1969 [1842]), it was Chicago school scholarship during the early part of the 20th century that served to fully articulate a social ecological perspective in criminology—in particular, a *community criminology*. Upon establishment in 1892, the faculty and graduate students at University of Chicago's Department of Sociology collectively engaged in theory and research aimed at understanding behavior in its social and physical environmental context. Importantly, these scholars studied the community in which they worked in order to understand contextual influence. In Chicago, they observed rapid growth and change in the forms of urbanization and immigration, both of which were fueled by industrialization.

Specifically, industry expanded greatly in the central part of the city during the early 1900s, bringing more residents to the urban core. Ernest Burgess (1925, 1926) posited a concentric zone theory in order to explain the specific pattern of growth observed in the city. The model suggested that the city developed through a series of concentric rings, or "zones," and Burgess noted five zones in Chicago. The city center was Zone I (aka "the Loop"), and it was comprised of business and industry. Zones III, IV, and V were primarily residential zones. They varied in terms of distance to the city center and age and expense of the housing stock. Among the zones dominated by residences, Zone III was closest to the city center; it had the oldest and most modest residences. In contrast, Zone V was furthest away, providing the most recently developed housing and accompanying amenities.

Zone II sat between Zone I's central business/industry district and the predominantly working-class residences comprising Zone III. Zone II was referred to as the "Zone in Transition," as it was "in the throes of change from residence to business and industry" (Shaw and McKay 1969 [1942], p. 18). The housing that once predominated in Zone II was often owned by those speculating that continued industrial expansion would cause business and industry to overflow from Zone I and "invade" Zone II. Since it was believed that housing structures in Zone II would ultimately be destroyed, owners had little incentive to keep up their property. Thus, they rented it to those that could afford no better alternative—typically, poor immigrants who had come to the industrializing city in search for work and a better life. Various immigrant groups would predominate in the area until they assimilated and were able to move to better housing in zones further from the inner city. However, the assimilating groups moving out of Zone II were simply replaced by successive waves of newly arriving immigrant groups (of different nationalities than the previous wave of immigrants) in need of cheap, first-settlement housing. Due to this pattern of movement, the residential population in Zone II in the early part of the 20th century was consistently poor, ethnically heterogeneous, and transient (Shaw and McKay 1969 [1942]). Accounts provided by Chicago school scholars suggest that other conditions in Zone II were problematic. Pollution, noise, and physical deterioration were apparent at every turn; disease was rampant; families, schools, and other institutions were weak; and gangs thrived. In short, Zone II was a "ghetto" or "slum" area (e.g., Thomas and Znaniecki 1920; Thrasher 1927; Shaw 1929, 1930; Shaw and McKay 1942).

Clifford Shaw and Henry McKay arguably provided the work that most famously linked the character of the slum to crime and other social ills (e.g., Shaw 1929; Shaw and McKay 1942). With Burgess's notion of the city's concentric development in mind, Shaw and McKay mapped the homes of juvenile delinquents in the city of Chicago over the course of multiple decades in the early part of 20th century. Regardless of the specific time period analyzed, the areas immediately surrounding the central business district (i.e., Zone II, or the Zone in Transition) consistently had the highest rates of juvenile delinquency. Shaw and McKay concluded that the reasons could not be due to person-level factors because the residential composition was continually changing due to the pattern of immigration and assimilation described above. They argued instead that there must be something about the *place* that was the causal force. McKay (1962, p. 50) summarizes this important position in a late-career review of his work with Shaw:

> In Chicago . . . the same areas have continued to be characterized by high rates of delinquents over a 60-year period, notwithstanding repeated change in the ethnic and racial composition of the population. This evidence leads to the question: what are the characteristics of the areas which produce the most delinquents?

In an attempt to address this question, Shaw and McKay's work highlighted the idea that high rates of poverty, ethnic heterogeneity, and instability among the residential population in Zone II fostered *social disorganization*. In turn, social disorganization provided fertile soil for the production of delinquents. Though Shaw and McKay were often inexplicit about the definition of "social disorganization" in their work, they implied that they were drawing upon other Chicago school scholars who described social disorganization as institutional breakdown such that there is "a decrease of the influence of existing social rules of behavior upon individual members of the group" (Thomas and Znaniecki 1920, p. 2). Shaw and McKay suggested that social disorganization fostered criminal behavior among an area's inhabitants for several reasons. First, with little institutional basis for articulating, upholding, and achieving shared community values, community youth were strained and community-based social control of youth was attenuated (see, e.g., Shaw and McKay 1969 [1942], pp. 183–185). In turn, weak control (premised on conventional values) allowed for the emergence of a value system supportive of crime as a competing way of life. This "oppositional subculture" could then be transmitted across generations, leading to ongoing high rates of crime in disorganized areas (see, e.g., Shaw and McKay 1969 [1942], pp. 170–174).

2.3 A Reconceptualized Social Disorganization: Neighborhood Systemic Control and Crime

While Shaw and McKay's social disorganization theory enjoyed a brief mid-century period of prominence in criminology, it fairly quickly fell by the wayside. However, with Ruth Rosner Kornhauser's (1978) insightful and compelling appraisal of analytic models of crime, a rebirth of social disorganization theory occurred in the 1980s in the form of a "systemic model" of neighborhood-level informal social control.

2.3.1 Building a Systemic Model of Neighborhood Control

In her transformative 1978 book, *Social Sources of Delinquency*, Kornhauser argued that the theory proposed by Shaw and McKay was "mixed" and logically inconsistent. In particular, she claimed that the theoretical assumptions underlying processes of strain, social control, and cultural deviance contradicted one another (i.e., assumptions regarding motivation and value consensus, in particular). Furthermore, she rejected the existence of deviant subcultures. With such criticism in mind, Kornhauser advocated a reconceptualized social disorganization theory that was stripped of elements of strain and cultural deviance, and she articulated, instead, a "pure" control theory (i.e., no longer a mixed model). According to her suggested conceptualization of social disorganization theory, the structural characteristics of poverty, racial/ethnic heterogeneity, and residential mobility influenced crime through weakened informal social control.

Precipitated by Kornhauser's appraisal, subsequent scholarship in the social disorganization tradition sought to clarify the mediating mechanism of informal social control. A popular approach in this regard was to draw from the systemic model of community attachment within the sociology literature (e.g., Kasarda and Janowitz 1974). This model viewed the community as a "complex system of friendship and kinship networks and formal and informal associational ties rooted in family life and on-going socialization processes" (Kasarda and Janowitz 1974, p. 329). Borrowing from this systemic perspective on community, neighborhood-level informal social control of crime was increasingly viewed as emerging from *friendship, kinship*, and *associational ties* among residents (e.g., Sampson 1988; Sampson and Groves 1989; Bursik and Grasmick 1993). Thus, the systemic model within the social disorganization tradition suggests that neighborhood-level density of friendship, kinship, and associational ties enhances informal social control, thus lowering crime rates.

Using data from the British Crime Survey on 238 electoral wards that were meant to represent "local communities" (p. 783), Sampson and Groves (1989) provided a landmark test of the systemic model of social disorganization theory by incorporating neighborhood social structural characteristics believed to foster disorganization, measures of systemic control, and various measures of community crime. Sampson and Groves (1989) measured the neighborhood structural deficits in terms of low SES, ethnic heterogeneity, residential mobility, family disruption, and urbanization. They measured weakened systemic control as sparse local friendship networks, low organizational participation, and unsupervised teenage peer groups. Neighborhood crime was measured as various crime-specific rates of offending and victimization, self-reported by residents. Their empirical analysis revealed that communities characterized by few friendship networks, unsupervised teenage peer groups, and low levels of organizational participation suffered higher rates of offending and victimization (Sampson and Groves 1989). Further, these factors mediated a large proportion of the effects of low SES, residential mobility, ethnic heterogeneity, and family disruption on crime (Sampson and Groves 1989). In short, Sampson and Groves's study provided strong initial support for the systemic control model, and it set the stage for further tests by a new generation of scholars interested in community influence on crime (e.g., Bellair 1997; Warner and Wilcox Rountree 1997; Wilcox Rountree and Warner 1999; Vélez 2001; Warner 2003). That said, the measures of systemic control (i.e., social ties) were not related to all measures of crime, nor did they completely mediate the effects of the structural characteristics on crime (see also Veysey and Messner 1999; Lowenkamp, Cullen, and Pratt 2003). The next section discusses literature that reveals more clearly the limits of social ties in controlling crime.

2.3.2 Questioning the Systemic Model

Several studies have indicated that strong or frequent ties are not necessary for effective informal social control, as implied by the systemic model. For example, using data from a victimization study based on a sample of 60 police beats (used to approximate neighborhoods), from three different US cities, Bellair (1997) analyzed the effects of various measures of social ties on community rates of victimization. He found that a measure that included *both* frequent *and infrequent* interaction among residents—"getting together once a year or more"—showed the strongest relationship with crime. Recent work by Bruinsma, Pauwels, Weerman, and Bernasco (2013) on 86 Dutch neighborhoods in The Hague also questions the link between ties and crime control; they reported null effects of friendship networks on neighborhood offense and offender rates.

Other work has demonstrated that the effect of social ties on crime is conditioned by the context in which the ties function. For example, in a study of 100 Seattle, Washington, census tracts, Warner and Wilcox Rountree (1997) found that the effect of social ties was conditional on the racial composition of the neighborhoods. Specifically, social ties had a significant negative effect on violent crime rates in predominantly white neighborhoods, whereas the effect was nonsignificant in neighborhoods that were racially heterogeneous or predominantly minority. In a related study of the same 100 Seattle census tracts, Wilcox Rountree and Warner (1999) examined the conditionality of social ties based on gender. Their analysis revealed that the extent of social ties was rather similar among females and males within the neighborhoods examined. However, the effect of the prevalence of social ties among men was not associated with community rates of violence, whereas the prevalence of ties reported by women was significantly and negatively related to violence. That said, the ability for females' ties to reduce violence was attenuated as the percentage of female-headed households in the neighborhood increased. The authors suggested that though neighborhood density of male ties did not significantly affect violence directly, male presence remained important for effective control via females' ties.

Qualitative work has also helped us recognize the complexity of the ties-crime relationship. Pattillo's (1998) research within a middle-class black neighborhood revealed that strong social ties might not effectively control crime if criminal networks are interwoven into the community's overall system of ties. Pattillo observed that criminal networks in such instances were often tolerated (i.e., not controlled), as law-abiding residents were reluctant to bring legal trouble upon those with whom they were socially connected. Venkatesh's (1997) ethnographic research in a disadvantaged public-housing development also suggested that the controlling capacity of social ties might be compromised if illicit networks are interwoven. He observed that community gang members used revenues from drug dealing to provide valuable services to the development that had otherwise been neglected by citywide public agencies. Thus, though the gang was involved in destructive actions (i.e., violence) that destabilized the community, residents also recognized that members performed positive functions that actually contributed to social organization. Accordingly, residents were somewhat ambivalent about the gang, once again suggesting that the extent to which social ties serve to enhance informal social control of crime is tenuous when there is an intertwining of conventional and criminal residents within the social network.

Overall, a number of studies reveal that friendship and kinship ties are not always related to neighborhood crime in a manner predicted by the systemic model. Perhaps the notion of systemic control, especially that stemming from neighborhood-based friendship and kinship ties, is outdated vis-à-vis the realities of contemporary community life. Robert Sampson has been at the forefront of synthesizing the research evidence regarding systemic control to date and challenging the systemic model's implicit assumption that healthy neighborhoods are idyllic urban villages with pervasive interpersonal ties connecting residents. Sampson (2002, pp. 219–220) states, "such ideal typical neighborhoods . . . bear little resemblance to contemporary cities where weak ties prevail over strong ties and social interaction among residents is characterized by increasing instrumentality . . .. Social ties thus present a challenge for thinking about crime. Most neighbors are acquaintances or strangers rather than friends." At the same time, despite infrequent interaction and relatively weak interpersonal ties, many communities seem to effectively control crime (e.g., Bellair 1997). Moreover, even when dense personal ties are present in neighborhoods, they might not control crime as theorized. Instead, they might actually *impede* effective social control because "networks connect not just do-gooders but the underbelly of social life, from drug dealers to gang members to crooked politicians" (Sampson 2012, p. 151; see also Venkatesh 1997; Pattillo 1998). As discussed next, several scholars suggest that the unreliability of the systemic model might be remedied by de-emphasizing private ties (i.e., intimate ties among family and friends) and parochial ties (i.e., participation in neighborhood organizations) and emphasizing instead public ties linking community members to extracommunity agents (e.g., see Bursik and Grasmick 1993; Triplett, Gainey, and Sun 2003).

2.3.3 Contemporary Systemic Control: Public Ties and New Parochialism

A relatively new body of work examines the importance of public ties to community crime. Again, public ties refer to a community's links to external resources, including police, other public officials, or business leaders (Bursik and Grasmick 1993). This line of inquiry supports the impact of community-level public ties on crime and victimization. For example, Vélez's (2001) study of 60 police beats across three US cities found that higher levels of public social control in the form of residents' ties to government and police significantly reduced burglary, assault, and mugging victimization rates. This was especially true in the most disadvantaged neighborhoods. Later, Vélez, Lyons, and Boursaw (2012) studied the effects of public control in the form of access to extracommunity economic resources across 118 Seattle, Washington, census tracts. Specifically, they found that neighborhood-level infusion of home mortgage loans reduced subsequent violent crime rates. Similarly, Ramey and Shrider (2014) found a significant negative relationship between Neighborhood Matching Funds resources and rates of crime in the same Seattle neighborhoods ($N = 118$ census tracts).

Such findings are supported and extended in a recent version of the systemic model referred to by Carr (2003) as "new parochialism." New parochialism involves an interconnectedness or partnership between neighborhood groups and public/extracommunity resources. Carr suggests that new parochialism is a common way to achieve effective control in contemporary communities—such as the Beltway neighborhood in Chicago that he studied—where traditional private and parochial ties are lacking. This type of systemic control relies on residents and/or resident-based organizations, but it also requires the assistance from formal agencies or public officials (see also Carr 2012).

2.4 Neighborhood-Based Collective Efficacy and Crime

Response to disenchantment with the utility of social ties (especially interpersonal ties) in accounting for neighborhood crime has followed several different paths. First, as discussed above, some scholars have widened the focus of the systemic-control model by emphasizing public ties and private/parochial-public partnerships. However, another path has involved the development of *collective efficacy theory* (Sampson, Raudenbush, and Earls 1997; Morenoff, Sampson, and Raudenbush 2001; Sampson 2002, 2006, 2012). This theory accepts the systemic model's underlying premise—that variation in community-level social control explains varying crime rates. However, it rejects systems of ties as the central constructs in understanding community crime, and it promotes instead the construct of collective efficacy. Collective efficacy, according to Sampson (2012, p. 152), "draws together two fundamental mechanisms—*social cohesion* (the 'collectivity' part of the concept) and *shared expectations for control* (the 'efficacy' part of the concept)" (see also, Sampson Raudenbush, and Earls 1997; Sampson 2002, 2006). According to collective efficacy theory, communities need not have dense interpersonal ties for effective community control. Instead, strong social control emerges in contexts where (1) there is some level of social cohesion *rooted in working trust and mutual support* (i.e., based on a sense of "we" rather than strong friendships); and (2) shared expectations for action when community well-being is at stake. Thus, collective efficacy theory serves to "elevate the 'agentic' aspect of social life over a perspective centered mainly on the accumulation of stocks of social resources as found in ties and memberships" (Sampson 2006, p. 153).

As originally formulated, collective efficacy is presumed to emerge in communities experiencing economic advantage, few immigrant residents, and a stable resident population (Sampson, Raudenbush, and Earls 1997). Conversely, the theory posited that neighborhoods characterized by concentrated disadvantage, large immigrant populations, and residential instability would suffer weak collective efficacy. In turn, communities with strong collective efficacy were expected to enjoy low rates of crime, while neighborhoods with weak collective efficacy were theorized to be plagued by higher levels of crime. It should be noted that since the theory's original formulation, the effect of immigrant concentration on collective efficacy and crime has been debated, with mixed results emerging in empirical tests. In fact, more recent formulations of the theory have removed immigrant concentration (Sampson 2006).

The heart of collective efficacy theory is thus formed by the causal pathways linking (1) concentrated (dis)advantage and residential (in)stability to collective efficacy, and (2) collective efficacy to crime. However, other important linkages are specified. For example, private and parochial ties are theorized to exert indirect effects on crime. In particular, collective efficacy theory suggests that friendship networks and levels of organizational participation affect crime indirectly, through their more immediate effects on collective efficacy. Thus, private and institutional ties may foster the development of collective efficacy (which affects crime), but they themselves are not independently related to crime (e.g., see Morenoff, Sampson, and Raudenbush 2001). Additionally, collective efficacy theory recognizes the potential endogeneity of collective efficacy in relation to crime. In other words, while the theory is primarily interested in the causal effect of collective efficacy on crime, it does specify that there is probable reciprocity regarding this relationship, with previous levels of crime likely influencing a community's level of collective efficacy (Sampson, Raudenbush, and Earls 1997; Morenoff, Sampson, and Raudenbush 2001). Finally, collective efficacy theory embraces the notion of neighborhood spatial interdependence—neighborhoods are viewed as functionally interwoven as opposed to islands unto themselves (see Morenoff, Sampson, and Raudenbush 2001, in particular). Therefore, crime in adjacent neighborhoods is expected to affect crime in focal neighborhoods, net of focal neighborhood characteristics. Furthermore, crime in adjacent neighborhoods is expected to moderate effects of focal neighborhood characteristics, including collective efficacy, on focal neighborhood crime.

Initial tests of these theoretical linkages relied upon data from the Project on Human Development in Chicago Neighborhoods (PHDCN). For example, in their seminal piece introducing collective efficacy theory to the field, Sampson, Raudenbush, and Earls (1997) showed that concentrated disadvantage and immigrant concentration were negatively related to neighborhood-level collective efficacy in Chicago neighborhoods, whereas residential stability was positively related to collective efficacy. In turn, collective efficacy was negatively related to three different measures of community violence: resident-perceived violence, resident-reported rates of victimization, and official homicide counts. The effects of collective efficacy were net of prior neighborhood levels of crime, thus controlling for the possible endogeneity of collective efficacy with respect to crime. Additionally, checks for discriminant validity indicated that the effects of collective efficacy on crime were stronger than were the effects of measures tapping into systems of ties/networks—measures such as friendship networks, organizational participation, and neighborhood services. In fact, those systemic measures were themselves not related to crime; collective efficacy was shown to have the more proximal effects (see also Morenoff, Sampson, and Raudenbush 2001).

Following Sampson, Raudenbush, and Earls's influential study, subsequent research using the PHDCN provides additional support for collective efficacy's effect on various community crime measures, particularly those tapping rates of neighborhood-based crime events (e.g., Sampson and Raudenbush 1999; Morenoff, Sampson, and Raudenbush 2001; Browning 2002; Kirk and Papachristos 2011; Morenoff et al. 2001). Further, there is mounting evidence that collective efficacy affects neighborhood crime or victimization events in a variety of countries, including Sweden (Sampson and Wikström 2007) Australia (Mazerolle, Wickes, and McBroom 2010), and those in South America (Chouhy 2016). International support for collective efficacy theory has also extended to China. For example, Jiang, Land, and Wang (2013) found that higher levels of collective efficacy were significantly and negatively associated with perceived neighborhood property crime in Guangzhou, China. In another study, Zhang, Messner, and

Liu (2007) found that neighborhood collective efficacy was associated with a lower risk of burglary in Tianjin, China.

Collective efficacy research conducted in several other countries has been less supportive. For example, the study by Bruinsma, Pauwels, Weerman, and Bernasco (2013)—mentioned earlier with respect to the null effects of friendship ties—also found that collective efficacy was unrelated to offense or offender rates across neighborhoods in The Hague, Netherlands. In addition, a Malaysian study by Hedayati Marzbali et al. (2014) found that higher perceived collective efficacy was actually positively associated with victimization likelihood. Such findings indicate that collective efficacy may not influence crime in the same manner in all countries and suggest that researchers should continue to assess the applicability of the theory in a variety of national contexts (see Bruinsma and Johnson, this volume).

In addition to evidence of collective efficacy's null effects in some contexts, there is also evidence that its effects can be bolstered or attenuated, depending on levels of collective efficacy and crime in adjacent areas (Morenoff, Sampson, and Raudenbush 2001). Additionally, there is evidence that the effects of collective efficacy may be conditional on neighborhood-level social ties and accompanying reciprocal exchange. Browning, Dietz, and Feinberg (2004) describe this latter effect as one of "negotiated coexistence," whereby the regulatory impact of collective efficacy is attenuated in contexts of strong social ties that provide social capital for offenders (see also Browning 2009).

Finally, despite the considerable support of collective efficacy theory, it is noteworthy that most support to date stems from studies estimating its effects on neighborhood-based crime events (e.g., homicide counts, reports of victimization in the neighborhood, neighborhood perception of crime) as opposed to rates of delinquency among neighborhood residents (e.g., arrests among residents, residents' self-reported criminal behavior). Thus, an important caveat is that collective efficacy theory has fared somewhat poorly in terms of explaining antisocial behavior of residents (but see Maimon and Browning 2010). For example, Sampson, Morenoff, and Raudenbush (2005) reported a null effect of collective efficacy on self-reported violence among 18- to 25-year-olds, and Kirk (2008) showed a null effect of collective efficacy on individual offending, as measured by arrest. Such findings have raised the question as to whether collective efficacy theory is better viewed as a situational theory of neighborhood-based control of crime events, as opposed to a theory of neighborhood-based control of criminality among residents (Kirk 2009; Sampson 2006). Kirk (2009, pp. 484–485) summarizes this debate as follows:

> It is vital to ask what exactly is the causal mechanism underlying collective efficacy? Is collective efficacy simply a form of group intervention to redress a problem, or does collective efficacy more broadly involve the collective socialization of youths (i.e., toward prosocial behavior)? Is collective efficacy a theory of crime rates, individual human development, or both? . . . With the former, collective efficacy inhibits crime in a given neighborhood regardless of where the would-be criminal resides, whereas in the latter, collective efficacy in an individual's neighborhood of residence influences his or her behavior even when he or she leaves the confines of the neighborhood.

In sum, research to date supports situational effects of collective efficacy in that it is consistently related to neighborhood-based crime events (e.g., homicide counts, victimization in the neighborhood, neighborhood perception of crime), whereas extant research less conclusively supports enduring effects of collective efficacy on residents' criminal offending. Such evidence has led some scholars to propose integration of collective efficacy theory, as well as other control-based theories in the social disorganization tradition, with situational theories (i.e., contemporary environmental criminology) in order to form a more general, multilevel opportunity theory of crime events (e.g., Wilcox, Land, and Hunt 2003; Wilcox, Gialopsos, and Land 2013). We return to this issue in Section 2.6, "Neighborhood and Crime Opportunity," but we move next to discussion of social-cultural influences on community crime.

2.5 Neighborhood Culture and Crime

Perhaps due Kornhauser's (1978) rejection of cultural deviance theory, the role of culture in understanding community crime was neglected for decades. However, in the middle to late 1990s, cultural research began to gain traction within community criminology once more. A number of these perspectives are faithful to Kornhauser's view of community influence as one of control—treating attenuated mainstream culture, alongside weakened social structure, as yet another source of ineffective informal social control. Collective efficacy theory, discussed above, perhaps marked this movement toward reincorporating cultural attenuation into community crime models. Its linking of efficacy to shared values and shared expectations regarding rules of behavior offered a cultural dimension to community influence that was absent from the systemic model's concept of social ties. Other lines of inquiry, discussed below, have more explicitly addressed cultural attenuation.

2.5.1 Concentrated Disadvantage and "Cognitive Landscapes"

With his seminal work *The Truly Disadvantaged*, William Julius Wilson (1987) contributed greatly to the community crime tradition by describing the idea of *concentrated disadvantage*—a unique type of poverty experienced in inner-city sections of deindustrialized US cities, different from the urban poverty observed by Shaw and McKay during the early 1900s. Ultimately, Wilson suggested that deindustrialization, and its associated factors, created an inner city characterized by extreme disadvantage and isolation from mainstream society. Such conditions fueled a cultural disorganization that tolerated "ghetto behaviors," including crime.

To provide more detail, Wilson described the large employment void created by the deindustrialization that hit cities built on a strong manufacturing base (e.g., northeastern and midwestern Rust Belt cities), especially between 1970 and 1980. As industrial jobs vacated these cities, so did the residents with enough resources to follow the jobs. The out-migration was not only economically but racially patterned, leaving behind the poorest and predominantly black segment of the inner-city population (i.e., white flight). With fewer jobs that supplied a living wage available in these transforming inner cities, unemployment among the black men in their populations soared. Wilson suggested that such unemployment hindered black male "marriageability," and thus fueled a large increase in black female-headed households and a rate of poverty among inner-city households that was far more severe and pervasive than in the industrial era. In the deindustrialized inner city, more households were impoverished, and the poverty appeared more concentrated—in other words, poor households were increasingly living among many other poor households, as neighborhoods became *truly disadvantaged*. In short, residents in deindustrialized inner-city neighborhoods had become socially and culturally isolated from "mainstream" or middle-class society. Wilson suggested that this isolation meant there were few "social buffers" to attenuate the effects of disadvantage—there were few residents left who could infuse resources into the community or provide cultural models for a mainstream way of life.

Due to this isolation, residents in these communities were thought to acquire adaptations to their constraints and blocked opportunities, resulting in cultural disorganization. Sampson and Wilson (1995) described this cultural disorganization by way of *cognitive landscapes*, or "ecologically structured norms" that set the standards or expectations for behavior relevant to the disadvantaged situational context (Sampson and Wilson 1995, p. 50; see also Sampson and Bartusch 1998). For example, in neighborhoods characterized by extreme disadvantage, a set of norms tolerant of disorder, crime, and drugs might exist. Such behaviors are tolerated because mainstream behaviors, though valued, are not particularly useful or relevant given the setting. In short, a disadvantaged context provides cognitive landscapes whereby unconventional behaviors are not internalized as "good" or "right," but are accepted as a situationally realistic way of life (Sampson and Wilson 1995; Warner 2003). In turn, the attenuation of mainstream cultural values loosens control, and crime concentrates in this social-spatial setting.

2.5.2 Street Codes and Crime

Elijah Anderson's seminal ethnographic work *Code of the Street: Decency, Violence, and the Moral Life of the Inner City*, has been extremely influential in the renewed interest in culture within community criminology. Anderson (1999) argued that crime, especially violence among young males, is heavily influenced by an emergent cultural code—the "code of the street"—that encourages violence in certain situations. He proposed that some inner-city residents adapt to structural deprivations by developing and adhering to this street code. Anderson described this street code as consisting of a set of informal rules that dictate the interpersonal behavior between residents, especially in public spaces. Because structural deprivation makes achieving status and respect through mainstream channels unlikely, the code establishes a new set of standards for status and respect. Further, many of the rules within the street code counter mainstream values, often promoting the use of violence. In particular, public displays of physical toughness are valued, and violent retaliation to insults and other forms of disrespect is an expected response.

Anderson implied that the effect of the street code would function at multiple levels of analysis. At the individual level, Anderson described residents as having a personal level of adherence to the code. Individual-level variation in the internalization of street values was especially illustrated in Anderson's discussion of the "street" versus "decent" orientation. According to Anderson, street individuals more fully internalize the street values, and they are thus more violent. In contrast, decent individuals do not internalize the values. However, they use the street code situationally for survival. Thus, in the case of decent individuals, neighborhood culture in the form of the street code can influence individuals' behavior above and beyond their own values. Here, the code is operating as an emergent sociocultural property of the neighborhood collective, influencing residents' behavior in certain urban public spaces regardless of whether its values are internalized.

Since the publication of Anderson's work, researchers have examined the effects of individual adherence to the code of the street as well as the contextual effect of a neighborhood-level code. For example, Stewart and Simons (2006) found support for the posited link between "street" orientation and violent delinquency. In a subsequent multilevel study, Stewart and Simons (2010) showed that neighborhood-level street culture *and* the individual adherence to the code were significant predictors of violent delinquency. For adolescents residing in neighborhoods where the code was prevalent, their likelihood of being involved in violence increased by 14%; those adolescents who adhered to the code themselves had a 25% increased likelihood of being involved in violence. Stewart and Simons (2010) also found a significant positive cross-level interaction between adolescents' adherence to the code and neighborhood street culture—indicating that violence was most likely among those with strong individual-level adherence to the code *and* strong neighborhood-level street cultures. In short, some evidence suggests that street codes can exert contextual influences, net of individual value differences, thus helping account for spatial variation in violence.

Related to the various ways that street codes affect crime, as implied by Anderson, other community crime scholars have emphasized two distinct positions regarding cultural influence: (1) "culture as values" and (2) "culture as performance," or "culture-in-action" (e.g., Sampson and Bean 2006). From the culture-as-values perspective, culture comes from values that are transmitted to individuals through social interactions and, in turn, internalized. Therefore, values espoused by a community culture are thought to be internalized by individual residents, and it is these individual values that ultimately guide individual behavior. In this way "community culture" essentially becomes "individual culture," making the two indistinguishable. This is the sort of view of cultural influence that was so resoundingly rejected by Kornhauser (1978) but seemingly apparent in Anderson's (1999) description of street-oriented individuals.

On the other hand, the culture-in-action perspective proposes that culture is not deeply embedded within us but rather is a social process that occurs through everyday social interaction (Swidler 1986, p. 277; Sampson and Bean 2006; Lamont and Small 2008; Berg and Stewart 2013; Kirk and Papachristos 2015; Matsueda 2015). Akin to Sampson and Wilson's (1995) discussion of cognitive landscapes and Anderson's (1999) description of code-switching among decent youth, the culture-in-action perspective refers to culture as a toolkit or repertoire of situationally specific behavioral responses. In other words, culture is thought to provide tools that enable individuals embedded in social contexts to actively choose behaviors that are situationally appropriate, rather than simply serving as a mechanism that always produces behavior reaffirming a particular value orientation. Thus, even if individuals hold cultural "values" that promote convention or violence, their actions may not always follow those values based on the specific situation. From this view, community culture and individual culture are *not* one and the same. Rather, community culture is expected to influence individual behavior above and beyond individual values, thus helping explain community-level spatial patterns of crime.

2.5.3 Legal Cynicism

One of the specific cultural frames or lenses in which individuals perceive the world around them and choose situationally specific action is referred to as legal cynicism. Legal cynicism invokes a view that the police are illegitimate, nonresponsive to residents' needs and calls for assistance, and unable to adequately provide public safety (Kirk and Papachristos 2011). While mentioned in the work of Anderson (1999), legal cynicism has been more fully developed theoretically in the work of Kirk and Papachristos (2011, 2015). They specify that legal cynicism is not an attribute of an individual, but is a cultural frame that varies across neighborhoods, restraining or limiting residents' available responses in threatening situations. Due to legal cynicism, residents perceive that it is necessary to take the law into their own hands and resolve disputes without police, often resulting in use of violence. Here, breaking the law and resorting to violence is not a representation of internalized values that promote law violations but rather a behavioral response of necessity based on a cultural frame. This view of legal cynicism helps solve the paradox of how research indicates that most individuals—including criminals—do not morally support or promote using violence. However, because of the perception that these individuals cannot depend on law enforcement to provide protection, they often choose to respond to threats with violence (Kirk and Papachristos 2011, 2015; Papachristos, Meares, and Fagan 2012). In brief, legal cynicism is yet another social process that helps explain community-level crime patterns.

Kirk and Papachristos (2011) empirically examined the effects of legal cynicism using data from the PHDCN. They found that neighborhood structural characteristics such as concentrated disadvantage and residential mobility predicted legal cynicism. Second, while individuals' attitudes toward deviance were unrelated to homicide (thus, opposing a culture-as-values perspective), legal cynicism was positively related to neighborhood homicides, controlling for social structural characteristics such as concentrated disadvantage.

While structural conditions (most specifically, concentrated disadvantage) appear to be associated with legal cynicism, Kirk and Papachristos also propose that this cultural frame is likely to persist should structural conditions change. They suggest that the pattern of mass incarceration and prisoner reentry in the United States is one of the most viable explanations for the persistence of legal cynicism. More specifically, there are large numbers of prisoners taken from and returning to communities each year, yet not all communities experience this out- and in-migration of residents due to incarceration equally. In fact, a relatively small number of communities absorb the brunt of this out- and in-migration. Kirk and Papachristos suggest that the sheer number of prisoners leaving and then later re-entering some neighborhoods helps feed the legal cynicism already in existence; such communities would be hard-pressed to perceive criminal justice as equitable. Additionally, insofar as convicted criminals are more distrustful of police and the legal system, cynicism is likely to be reproduced through cultural transmission within social networks with high concentrations of former prisoners.

2.6 Neighborhood and Crime Opportunity

A final approach to understanding social spatial influences on crime at the neighborhood level rests on the concept of crime opportunity. Here, neighborhoods are viewed as potential markets for crime, with their social conditions providing greater or lesser supplies of crime opportunities. In particular, weak informal social control is thought to provide a large supply of opportunities, thus suggesting an overlap between the concepts of "informal social control" and "crime opportunity" (Wilcox, Land, and Hunt 2003).

It is important to consider this overlap more fully because theories of control and opportunity are typically viewed as competing. Social control has historically been treated as a concept aimed at understanding *criminality*—why some people are more inclined than others to commit crime (Hirschi 1986). The control perspective assumes that individuals who have weak constraints are more likely to offend. Aggregate-level control theories—including most of the community criminology perspectives discussed above—assume that structurally and culturally disorganized contexts produce weak controls and, thereby, more offenders. Hence, in a traditional sense, these are theories of the spatial patterning of delinquents and criminals (Shaw and McKay 1942). In contrast, the crime opportunity concept emerges from contemporary forms of environmental criminology, and it is aimed at understanding the patterning of *crime events*. Though opportunity for crime events is thought to be "situational," there is nonetheless recognition that it exists at multiple spatial scales, including at places, along streets, and in neighborhoods (see Wilcox, Gialopsos, and Land 2013 for recent review). Most relevant to this chapter, a neighborhood-level opportunity theory assumes that structurally and culturally disorganized communities produce greater opportunities for crime events, as they are larger-scale places that allow the convergence of motivated offenders and suitable, inadequately guarded targets (e.g., Sampson and Wooldredge 1987; Wilcox, Land, and Hunt 2003).

Despite the theoretical distinction between control and opportunity perspectives of neighborhood criminality and neighborhood crime, respectively, empirical tests of aggregate-level control theories often rely upon models of neighborhood-based crime events. For example, these theories are often tested using outcome measures such as crime counts and neighborhood-based victimization events, with results showing strong support for the effects of key control-theory concepts on crime events (e.g., Sampson, Raudenbush, and Earls 1997; Morenoff, Sampson, and Raudenbush 2001; Vélez 2001). Thus, the distinction between neighborhood-based control and neighborhood-based opportunity appears confounded.

However, Marcus Felson provides an avenue for understanding how weak social control can produce not only high numbers of offenders but also ample opportunity for crime events. Felson (1994, 1995) accomplishes this by describing two distinct stages of social control. In the first stage, bonds are created between an individual and society. The relative strength versus weakness of the bond establishes criminality. For example, individuals form varying degrees of attachments to intimate others and commitments to conventional ideals, both of which serve to control criminal propensity. Considering stage 1 control at a macro level, neighborhoods are variably successful at producing youth with strong bonds. For example, neighborhoods with weak institutional ties likely lack the ability to provide youth with a clear sense of valued goals, paths to achieving goals, or effective socialization (Kornhauser 1978, p. 73). Hence, they are likely to produce higher proportions of youth with weak attachments and commitments and, in turn, higher rates of juvenile delinquency among the youth population.

However, Felson describes a second stage of control that impacts whether *crime events* transpire. In this second stage, the issue is whether agents of control detect, intervene, and/or engage in other deterrent efforts when rules are being broken. At the neighborhood level, this stage of control translates into aggregate levels of resident-based supervisory and intervention behavior—or, the extent to which residents provide eyes on the street (supervising youth, in particular) and act to disrupt misbehavior when it is observed. This sort of control overlaps substantially with handling, guardianship, and place management behavior that is so key to understanding opportunities for crime events (Felson 1995). In short, stage 2 control at the neighborhood level minimizes the opportunity for neighborhood-based crime events by providing situational constraints that disrupt the convergence of offenders and targets/victims within community spaces. Thus, community-level control theories are potentially relevant for understanding *both* community-level criminality and community crime events.

Regarding their relevance for understanding crime events, several scholars have integrated concepts from neighborhood-level control theories with individual-level perspectives on opportunity to form a broader, multilevel perspective on crime-event opportunity. For example, several studies have shown that indicators of neighborhood social disorganization, in conjunction with individual-level routine activities, are important for understanding opportunities for victimization (e.g., Sampson and Wooldredge 1987; Miethe and McDowall 1993; Wilcox Rountree, Land, and Miethe 1994). Other literature shows that offenders' search/selection of targets involves multilevel, sequential decisions in which offenders assess crime opportunities at progressively smaller units of analysis—for instance, first selecting opportunistic neighborhoods (i.e., those with plentiful targets and perceived weak cohesion/control) and then selecting opportunistic places or people within neighborhoods (e.g., Taylor and Gottfredson 1986; Brantingham and Brantingham 1993; Wright and Decker 1994, 1997; Bernasco and Luykx 2003; Bernasco and Nieuwbeerta 2005; Bernasco and Block 2009). In sum, weak resident-based informal social control, stemming from structural or cultural disorganization, has potential implications for both community-level patterning of criminality and community-level opportunity for crime events, as suggested by the work reviewed here. However, it is worth noting that those working in the community-control tradition and those working in the situational opportunity tradition have not universally embraced concepts from the other, and there is still important debate about the relevance and utility that each perspective has for the other (c.f., see Braga and Clarke 2014; Weisburd, Groff, and Yang 2012).

2.7 Conclusion

Shaw and McKay's classical neighborhood social disorganization theory was a "mixed model" in that it emphasized processes of resident-based control *and* cultural transmission of deviant values in order to understand spatial patterns of crime. Subsequently, Kornhauser rejected the cultural transmission component of Shaw and McKay's theoretical ideas and articulated social disorganization theory anew as one based on informal social control alone. Her suggested reconceptualization of the theory reinvigorated community-focused criminology, leading to several offshoots of social disorganization theory, including (1) the development and testing of systemic models of crime control, emphasizing effects of social ties; (2) the emergence of collective efficacy theory as an alternative explanation for community-level control of crime; and (3) the eventual reintegration of cultural disorganization into community crime models via processes of cognitive landscapes, street codes, and legal cynicism. Finally, aligned with contemporary environmental criminology's emphasis on crime opportunity at microspatial levels of analysis, some neighborhood-level research views community-based control as affecting the degree to which potential offenders are handled, potential victims are guarded, and potential crime places are managed at the spatial scale of neighborhood.

REFERENCES

Anderson, Elijah. 1999. *Code of the Streets: Decency, Violence, and the Moral Life of the Inner City*. New York: Norton.

Bellair, Paul. 1997. "Social Interaction and Community Crime: Examining the Importance of Neighbor Networks." *Criminology* 35: 677–703.

Berg, Mark T., and Eric A. Stewart. 2013. "Street Culture and Crime." In *The Oxford Handbook of Criminological Theory*, edited by Francis T. Cullen and Pamela Wilcox, 370–388. New York: Oxford University Press.

Bernasco, Wim, and Richard Block. 2009. "Where Offenders Choose to Attack: A Discrete Choice Model of Robberies in Chicago." *Criminology* 47: 93–130.

Bernasco, Wim, and Floor Luykx. 2003. "Effects of Attractiveness, Opportunity and Accessibility to Burglars on Residential Burglary Rates of Urban Neighborhoods." *Criminology* 41: 981–1002.

Bernasco, Wim, and Paul Nieuwbeerta. 2005. "How Do Residential Burglars Select Target Areas?" *British Journal of Criminology* 45: 296–315.

Boessen, Adam, and John R. Hipp. 2015. "Close-Ups and the Scale of Ecology: Land Use and the Geography of Social Context and Crime." *Criminology* 53: 399–426.

Braga, Anthony A., and Ronald V. Clarke. 2014. "Explaining High-Risk Concentrations of Crime in the City: Social Disorganization, Crime Opportunities, and Important Next Steps." *Journal of Research in Crime and Delinquency* 51: 480–498.

Braga, Anthony A., David M. Hureau, and Andrew V. Papachristos. 2011. "The Relevance of Micro Places to Citywide Robbery Trends: A Longitudinal Analysis of Robbery Incidents at Street Corners and Block Faces in Boston." *Journal of Research in Crime and Delinquency* 48: 7–32.

Brantingham, Patricia L., and Paul J. Brantingham. 1993. "Nodes, Paths, and Edges: Considerations on the Complexity of Crime and the Physical Environment." *Journal of Environmental Psychology* 13: 3–28.

Browning, Christopher R. 2002. "The Span of Collective Efficacy: Extending Social Disorganization Theory to Partner Violence." *Journal of Marriage and Family* 64: 833–850.

Browning, Christopher R. 2009. "Illuminating the Downside to Social Capital: Negotiated Coexistence, Property Crime, and Disorder in Urban Neighborhoods. *American Behavioral Scientist* 52: 1556–1578.

Browning, Christopher R., Robert D. Dietz, and Seth L. Feinberg. 2004. "The Paradox of Social Organization: Networks, Collective Efficacy, and Violent Crime in Urban Neighborhoods. *Social Forces* 83: 503–534.

Bruinsma, Gerben J. N., Lieven J. R. Pauwels, Frank M. Weerman, and Wim Bernasco. 2013. "Social Disorganization, Social Capital, Collective Efficacy, and the Spatial Distribution of Crime and Offenders: An Empirical Test of Six Neighbourhood Models for a Dutch City." *British Journal of Criminology* 53: 942–963.

Burgess, Ernest W. 1926. *The Urban Community*. Chicago: University of Chicago Press.

Burgess, Ernest W. 1967 [1925]. "The Growth of the City: An Introduction to a Research Project." In *The City*, edited by Robert E. Park, Ernest W. Burgess, and Roderick Duncan McKenzie, pp. 47–62. Chicago: University of Chicago Press.

Bursik, Robert J., Jr., and Harold G. Grasmick. 1993. *Neighborhoods and Delinquency: The Dimensions of Effective Community Control*. New York: Macmillan.

Carr, Patrick J. 2003. "The New Parochialism: The Implications of the Beltway Case for Arguments Concerning Informal Social Control." *American Journal of Sociology* 108: 1249–1291.

Carr, Patrick J. 2012. "Citizens, Community and Crime Control: The Problems and Prospects for Negotiated Order. *Criminology and Criminal Justice* 12: 297–412.

Chouhy, Cecilia. 2016. *Collective Efficacy and Community Crime Rates: A Cross-National Test of Rival Models.* Unpublished Ph.D. dissertation, University of Cincinnati.

Felson, Marcus. 1994. *Crime and Everyday Life: Insight and Implications for Society.* Thousand Oaks, CA: Pine Forge Press.

Felson, Marcus. 1995. "Those Who Discourage Crime." In *Crime and Place*, edited by John E. Eck and David Weisburd, pp. 53–66, vol. 4 of *Crime Prevention Studies.* Monsey, NY: Criminal Justice Press.

Groff, Elizabeth R., David Weisburd, and Sue-Ming Yang. 2010. "Is It Important to Examine Crime Trends at a Local 'Micro'" Level? A Longitudinal Analysis of Street to Street Variability in Crime Trajectories." *Journal of Quantitative Criminology* 26: 7–32.

Guerry, André-Michel. 1883. *Essai sur la Statistique Morale de la France.* Paris: Crochard.

Hedayati Marzbali, Massoomeh, Alrin Abdullah, Nordin Abd Razak, and Mohammad Javad Maghsoodi Tilaki. 2014. "Examining Social Cohesion and Victimization in a Malaysian Multiethnic Neighborhood." *International Journal of Law, Crime and Justice* 42: 384–405.

Hirschi, Travis. 1986. "On the Compatibility of Rational Choice and Social Control Theories of Crime." In *The Reasoning Criminal: Rational Choice Perspectives on Offending*, edited by Ronald V. Clarke and Derek B. Cornish, pp. 105–118. New York: Springer-Verlag.

Jiang, Shanhe, Kenneth C. Land, and Jin Wang. 2013. "Social Ties, Collective Efficacy, and Perceived Neighborhood Property Crime in Guangzhou, China." *Asian Criminology* 8: 207–223.

Kasarda, John D., and Morris Janowitz. 1974. "Community Attachment in Mass Society." *American Sociological Review* 39: 328–339.

Kirk, David S. 2008. "The Neighborhood Context of Racial and Ethnic Disparities in Arrest." *Demography* 45: 55–77.

Kirk, David S. 2009. "Unraveling the Contextual Effects on Student Suspension and Juvenile Arrest: The Independent and Interdependent Influences of School, Neighborhood, and Family Social Context." *Criminology* 47: 479–520.

Kirk, David S., and Andrew V. Papachristos. 2011. "Cultural Mechanisms and the Persistence of Neighborhood Violence." *American Journal of Sociology* 116: 1190–1233.

Kirk, David S., and Andrew V. Papachristos. 2015. "Concentrated Disadvantage and the Persistence of Legal Cynicism." In *Challenging Criminological Theory: The Legacy of Ruth Rosner Kornhauser*, edited by Francis T. Cullen, Pamela Wilcox, Robert J. Sampson, and Brendan D. Dooley, pp. 259–274, vol. 19 of *Advances in Criminological Theory.* New Brunswick, NJ: Transaction.

Kornhauser, Ruth Rosner. 1978. *Social Sources of Delinquency.* Chicago: University of Chicago Press.

Lamont, Michèle, and Mario Luis Small. 2008. "How Culture Matters: Enriching Our Understanding of Poverty." In *The Colors of Poverty: Why Racial and Ethnic Disparities Persist*, edited by Ann Chih Lin and David R. Harris, pp. 76–102. New York: Russell Sage.

Lowenkamp, Christopher T., Francis T. Cullen, and Travis C. Pratt. 2003. "Replicating Sampson and Groves's Test of Social Disorganization Theory: Revisiting a Criminological Classic." *Journal of Research in Crime and Delinquency* 40: 351–373.

Maimon, David, and Christopher R. Browning. 2010. "Unstructured Socializing, Collective Efficacy, and Violent Behavior among Urban Youth." *Criminology* 48: 443–474.

Matsueda, Ross L. 2015. "Social Structure, Culture, and Crime: Assessing Kornhauser's Challenge to Criminology. In *Challenging Criminological Theory: The Legacy of Ruth Rosner Kornhauser*, edited by Francis T. Cullen, Pamela Wilcox, Robert J. Sampson, and Brendan Dooley, pp. 117–143, vol. 19 of *Advances in Criminological Theory*. New Brunswick, NJ: Transaction.

Mazerolle, Lorraine, Rebecca Wickes, and James McBroom. 2010. "Community Variations in Violence: The Role of Social Ties and Collective Efficacy in Comparative Context." *Journal of Research in Crime and Delinquency* 47: 3–30.

McKay, Henry D. 1962. "Social Influence on Adolescent Behavior." *Journal of the American Medical Association* 182: 643–649.

Miethe, Terance D., and David McDowall. 1993. "Contextual Effects in Models of Criminal Victimization." *Social Forces* 71: 741–759.

Morenoff, Jeffrey D., Robert J. Sampson, and Stephen W. Raudenbush. 2001. "Neighborhood Inequality, Collective Efficacy, and the Spatial Dynamics of Urban Violence." *Criminology* 39: 517–560.

Papachristos, Andrew V., Tracey L. Meares, and Jeffrey Fagan. 2012. "Why Do Criminals Obey the Law? The Influence of Legitimacy and Social Networks on Active Gun Offenders." *Journal of Criminal Law and Criminology* 102: 397–440.

Pattillo, Mary E. 1998. "Sweet Mothers and Gangbangers: Managing Crime in a Middle Class Neighborhood." *Social Forces* 76: 747–774.

Ramey, David M., and Emily A. Shrider. 2014. "New Parochialism, Sources of Community Investment, and the Control of Street Crime." *Criminology and Public Policy* 13: 193–216.

Quételet, Adolphe. 1969 [1842]. *A Treatise on Man and the Development of His Facilities*. Edinburgh: William and Robert Chambers.

Sampson, Robert J. 1988. "Local Friendship Ties and Community Attachment in Mass Society: A Multilevel Systemic Model." *American Sociological Review* 53: 766–779.

Sampson, Robert J. 2002. "Transcending Tradition: New Direction in Community Research, Chicago Style." *Criminology* 40: 213–230.

Sampson, Robert J. 2006. "Collective Efficacy Theory: Lessons Learned and Directions for Future Research." In *Taking Stock: The Status of Criminological Theory*, edited by Francis T. Cullen, John Paul Wright, and Kristie R. Blevins, pp. 149–167, vol. 11 of *Advances in Criminological Theory*. New Brunswick, NJ: Transaction.

Sampson, Robert J. 2012. *Great American City: Chicago and the Enduring Neighborhood Effect*. Chicago: University of Chicago Press.

Sampson, Robert J., and Dawn Jeglum Bartusch. 1998. "Legal Cynicism and (Subcultural?) Tolerance of Deviance: The Neighborhood Context of Social Differences." *Law and Society Review* 32: 777–804.

Sampson, Robert J., and Lydia Bean. 2006. "Cultural Mechanisms and Killing Fields: A Revised Theory of Community-Level Racial Inequality." In *The Many Colors of Crime: Inequalities of Race, Ethnicity, and Crime in America*, edited by Ruth D. Peterson, Lauren J. Krivo, and John Hagan, pp. 8–36. New York: New York University Press.

Sampson, Robert J., and W. Byron Groves. 1989. "Community Structure and Crime: Testing Social Disorganization Theory." *American Journal of Sociology* 94: 774–802.

Sampson, Robert J., Jeffrey D. Morenoff, and Stephen W. Raudenbush. 2005. "Social Anatomy of Racial and Ethnic Disparities in Violence." *American Journal of Public Health* 95: 224–232.

Sampson, Robert J., and Stephen W. Raudenbush. 1999. "Systematic Social Observation of Public Spaces: A New Look at Disorder in Urban Neighborhoods." *American Journal of Sociology* 105: 603–651.

Sampson, Robert J., Stephen W. Raudenbush, and Felton J. Earls. 1997. "Neighborhoods and Violent Crime: A Multilevel Study of Collective Efficacy." *Science* 277: 918–924.

Sampson, Robert J., and Per-Olof Wikström. 2008. "The Social Order of Violence in Chicago and Stockholm Neighborhoods: A Comparative Inquiry." In *Order, Conflict, and Violence,* edited by Stathis N. Kalyvas, Ian Shapiro, and Tarek Masoud, pp. 97–119. New York: Cambridge University Press.

Sampson, Robert J., and William Julius Wilson. 1995. "Toward a Theory of Race, Crime, and Inequality." In *Crime and Inequality,* edited by John Hagan and Ruth D. Peterson, pp. 37–54. Stanford, CA: Stanford University Press.

Sampson, Robert J., and John D. Wooldredge. 1987. "Linking the Micro- and Macro-Level Dimensions of Lifestyle-Routine Activity and Opportunity Models of Predatory Victimization." *Journal of Quantitative Criminology* 3: 371–393.

Shaw, Clifford R. 1929. *Delinquency Areas: A Study of the Geographic Distribution of School Truancy, Juvenile Delinquency, and Adult Offenders in Chicago.* Chicago: University of Chicago Press.

Shaw, Clifford R. 1966 [1930]. *The Jack Roller: A Delinquent Boy's Own Story.* Chicago: University of Chicago Press.

Shaw, Clifford R., and Henry D. McKay. 1969 [1942]. *Juvenile Delinquency and Urban Areas.* Chicago: University of Chicago Press.

Sherman, Lawrence W., Patrick R. Gartin, and Michael E. Buerger. 1989. "Hot Spots of Predatory Crime: Routine Activities and the Criminology of Place." *Criminology* 27: 27–55.

Stewart, Eric A., and Ronald L. Simons. 2006. "Structure and Culture in African American Adolescent Violence: A Partial Test of the 'Code of the Street' Thesis." *Justice Quarterly* 23: 1–33.

Stewart, Eric A., and Ronald L. Simons. 2010. "Race, Code of the Street, and Violent Delinquency: A Multilevel Investigation of Neighborhood Street Culture and Individual Norms of Violence." *Criminology* 48: 569–605.

Swidler, Ann. 1986. "Culture in Action: Symbols and Strategies." *American Sociological Review* 51: 273–286.

Taylor, Ralph B., and Stephen Gottfredson. 1986. "Environmental Design, Crime, and Prevention: An Examination of Community Dynamics." In *Communities and Crime,* edited by Albert J. Reiss Jr. and Michael Tonry, 387–416, vol. 8 of *Crime and Justice.* Chicago: University of Chicago Press.

Thomas, William I., and Florian Znaniecki. 1920. *The Polish Peasant in Europe and America: Monograph of an Immigrant Group.* Vol. 4, *Disorganization and Reorganization in Poland.* Boston: Gorham Press.

Thrasher, Frederic M. 1927. *The Gang: A Study of 1,313 Gangs in Chicago.* Chicago: University of Chicago Press.

Triplett, Ruth A., Randy R. Gainey, and Ivan Y. Sun. 2003. "Institutional Strength, Social Control, and Neighborhood Crime Rates." *Theoretical Criminology* 7: 439–467.

Vélez, María B. 2001. "The Role of Public Social Control in Urban Neighborhoods. A Multilevel Analysis of Victimization Risk." *Criminology* 39: 837–864.

Vélez, María B., Christopher C. Lyons, and Blake Boursaw. 2012. "Neighborhood Housing Investments and Violent Crime in Seattle, 1981–2007." *Criminology* 50: 1025–1056.

Venkatesh, Sudhir A. 1997. "The Social Organization of Street Gang Activity in an Urban Ghetto." *American Journal of Sociology* 103: 82–111.

Veysey, Bonita M., and Steven F. Messner. 1999. "Further Testing of Social Disorganization Theory: An Elaboration of Sampson and Groves's 'Community Structure and Crime.'" *Journal of Research in Crime and Delinquency* 36: 156–174.

Warner, Barbara D. 2003. "The Role of Attenuated Culture in Social Disorganization Theory." *Criminology* 41: 73–97.

Warner, Barbara D., and Pamela Wilcox Rountree. 1997. "Local Social Ties in a Community and Crime Model: Questioning the Systemic Nature of Informal Social Control." *Social Problems* 44: 520–536.

Weisburd, David, Shawn Bushway, Cynthia Lum, and Sue-Ming Yang. 2004. "Trajectories of Crime at Places: A Longitudinal Study of Street Segments in the City of Seattle." *Criminology* 42: 283–321.

Weisburd, David, Elizabeth R. Groff, and Sue-Ming Yang. 2012. *The Criminology of Place: Street Segments and Our Understanding of the Crime Problem.* New York: Oxford University Press.

Wilcox, Pamela, Brooke Miller Gialopsos, and Kenneth C. Land. 2013. "Multilevel Criminal Opportunity." In *The Oxford Handbook of Criminological Theory*, edited by Francis T. Cullen and Pamela Wilcox, 579–601. New York: Oxford University Press.

Wilcox, Pamela, Kenneth C. Land, and Scott A. Hunt. 2003. *Criminal Circumstance: A Dynamic, Multi-contextual Criminal Opportunity Theory.* New York: Aldine de Gruyter.

Wilcox Rountree, Pamela, Kenneth C. Land, and Terance D. Meithe. 1994. "Macro-Micro Integration in the Study of Victimization: A Hierarchical Logistic Model Analysis across Seattle Neighborhoods." *Criminology* 32: 387–414.

Wilcox Rountree, Pamela, and Barbara D. Warner. 1999. "Social Ties and Crime: Is the Relationship Gendered?" *Criminology* 37: 401 425.

Wilson, William Julius. 1987. *The Truly Disadvantaged: The Inner City, the Underclass, and Public Policy.* Chicago: University of Chicago Press.

Wright, Richard T., and Scott H. Decker. 1994. *Burglars on the Job: Street Life and Residential Break-Ins.* Boston: Northeastern University Press.

Wright, Richard T., and Scott H. Decker. 1997. *Armed Robbers in Action: Stickups and Street Culture.* Boston: Northeastern University Press.

Zhang, Lening, Steven F. Messner, and Jianhong Liu. 2007. "A Multilevel Analysis of the Risk of Household Burglary in the City of Tianjin, China." *British Journal of Criminology* 47: 918–937.

CHAPTER 3

HOW DO WE GET TO CAUSAL CLARITY ON PHYSICAL ENVIRONMENT-CRIME DYNAMICS?

RALPH B. TAYLOR

3.1 Introduction: Organization and Slant of the Chapter

Section 3.1 describes the focus of the current chapter, relates it to past reviews of scholarship in this area, and highlights the crucial question of causality. Section 3.2 reminds readers of important metalessons from founding scholars. These are the giants upon whose shoulders current scholars stand. Section 3.3 introduces key stumbling blocks in community criminology that must be addressed before scholarship can advance on the crucial causality question. Environmental criminology in a deep sense represents a field within a broader field of community criminology. Section 3.4 highlights just a few of the most important recent works in four select areas within the physical environment-crime scholarship: space syntax, facilities and land use, accessibility/permeability, and crime prevention through environmental design (CPTED) / defensible space. Scholarship in each of these areas has yet to address adequately several of the community criminology stumbling blocks outlined in Section 3.3. Section 3.5 sketches one possible avenue for future research that can address these concerns.

3.1.1 What Is In and What Is Out

Research and theorizing about the crime impacts of the physical environment, at spatial scales from individual parcels, dwelling units, and facilities, up to subcity or subjurisdiction neighborhoods, merit scrutiny in the current chapter. Questions about how successfully recent research has specified and documented causal impacts of physical environment features, alone or in combination with cultural, social, or structural features, receive particularly close inspection.

Four conditions bound the scope of the chapter. First, matters reviewed in detail in previous publications on physical environment that the first author here authored or coauthored, are not considered here. These include the origins and evolution of defensible space (Taylor, Gottfredson, and Brower 1980), meso-level built environment and implications for offender movement patterns (Taylor and Gottfredson 1986), models of resident or regular user dynamics and potential offender interpretations of environment features and behavior traces (Taylor 1987), calls for integrating different crime/design perspectives (Taylor and Harrell 1996), spatial scaling and questions around hotspots (Taylor 1998), concerns about the dynamics of the incivilities thesis (Taylor 1999, 2001), the causal claims specifically of CPTED (Taylor 2005), and public transportation, street network, and boundary land use links to crime at the jurisdiction level (Groff et al. 2014).

Second, links between physical environment and noncrime outcomes like fear of crime (Taylor 2002), perceived risk, behavioral avoidance; and other aspects of person-environment transactions such as perceived problems (incivilities), territorial behaviors or cognitions, sense of community, residential satisfaction (Robinson et al. 2003), or other person-place bonds are excluded as outcomes of interest. These processes merit attention if and only if strong claims can be made that they mediate or moderate environment-crime relationships. Despite considerable research, those claims remain in question.

Third, topic coverage is by design selective. Discussion considers only a handful of current subtopics within this broad field. Further, within each of these subtopics this chapter does not attempt a comprehensive summary of what has been learned. Rather it considers just a few of the most current findings and does so through the lens of specific stumbling blocks recently highlighted in community criminology (Taylor 2015). Community criminology addresses the causes and consequences of crime levels and patterns at the subcity neighborhood geographic scale, and smaller geographic scales. Relationships at each geographic scale, and across different geographic scales (e.g., impacts of neighborhoods on street blocks), and impacts of levels and patterns at these scales on individuals and groups are all of interest. How does this link to environmental criminology? Paul Cozens (2011b) routinely cites Bottoms and Wiles's (1997: 305) definition of the latter. "Environmental criminology is defined as 'the study of crime criminality and victimization as they related first, to particular places, and secondly, to the way that individuals and organizations shape their activities by place-based or spatial factors.'" Given this definition, environmental criminology focuses on community criminology dynamics that intertwine with crime- or victimization-linked spatial factors relevant to individuals or organizations. Accordingly, environmental criminology represents place-linked dynamics operating within the smaller geographic scales considered within community criminology.

Fourth, impacts of crime on physical environment, an equally important and policy-relevant and in some ways more intriguing set of questions (Taylor 1995), are ignored.

That said, these impacts need to be separated out when longitudinal ecological dynamics are considered.

3.1.2 What's the Angle?

The perspective adopted here is deliberately critical, but with a specific goal in mind. The agenda here is not to scorn current and recent research. Clearly, enormous progress is evident in this domain of scholarship, in both theoretical and practical realms, as well as in the quality of many of the empirical studies. Researchers *have* come a long way since the 1960s or 1970s. At the same time, researchers have shied away from key critical issues for too long, and these gaps impede theoretical and practical progress in this area. The critical stance here seeks to inspire those just beginning in the field today, the graduate student or beginning assistant professor squinting in the sunlight at his or her Kindle on some greensward someplace or while being jostled by commuters on a bus somewhere. The message is: ask the big questions and think about how to get there. What skills do you need or does your research team need? What do you need to think hard about? How do we bring theoretical clarity, accuracy, and precision to this area of scholarship? What new analytic and conceptual approaches might shed light on some of the recurrent tough questions in this arena of scholarship? Toward that end, a closing section comments on two possible avenues of scholarship.

3.1.3 The Goal

Environmental criminology is simultaneously and equally a theoretical and practical area within criminology. Consequently, whether we are talking about physical environment causal impacts on crime or the reverse, the goal is both to understand, on the conceptual side, and to predict and prevent, on the practical side. The ultimate goal on the conceptual side, leaving aside new street blocks and new communities laid down wholesale, is figuring out what physical environment shifts have what impacts on what offending and/or victimization patterns. This makes it a matter of marginal impacts.

3.1.4 The Challenge

To restate what is already well known by all beginning graduate students, we must move beyond correlation to causation (Hope 2008a, 2008b). When we are talking about features of the physical environment, features that have been in place for some time, and at different geographic scales, that people are exposed to for different durations, during different periods of life or times of day, this is no simple task. At the same time, this is the crux of the matter.

3.2 Taking Heed from Our Forefathers and Foremothers

Crucial challenges confronting the field today are not new. Leading scholars in environmental criminology, and their predecessors in other fields that helped spawn the current approaches, laid down key ideas that are all too often forgotten. Just a handful of the most cogent, given the current focus, appear here.

3.2.1 Jane Jacobs

The late Jane Jacobs promoted specific design solutions in a specific context. For example, she thought more "eyes on the street" would make urban street blocks safer. This could be accomplished by having first-floor commercial land uses on predominantly residential, but short-length, street blocks in dense urban neighborhoods (Fowler 1992). She also advocated other design ideas that Oscar Newman later adopted into defensible space. But, as importantly, Jacobs (1961: 26) explicitly warned us against overgeneralizing from one type of community to another: "I hope no reader will try to transfer my observations into guides as to what goes on in towns, or little cities, or in suburbs which are still suburban." Further, the urban design solutions she promoted would not be appropriate practically or ideologically in suburban communities (Hummon 1985). So at bottom the extent to which her most widely promoted idea, mixed use on short, predominantly residential street blocks (Fowler 1987, 1992), would be appropriate across a range of communities, remains an open question, despite strong census tract crime connections for part of her proposal (Browning et al. 2010). She warns us against overgeneralizing.

3.2.2 Kevin Lynch

The late Kevin Lynch cautioned against a static perspective. Succinctly and cogently, he stated, "Environments change" (Lynch 1972: 3). Sometimes cities are remade wholesale, as San Francisco was after the 1906 earthquake and fire. But as crucially, physical features are constantly shifting: houses deteriorate and become vacant and maybe later become vacant lots or new construction, for example. It is these shifts, whether planned or unplanned, whether smaller scale or larger scale, that represent the core conceptual concern for this area of scholarship. If we close off streets to vehicle traffic (Atlas and LeBlanc 1994) or gate alleyways (Armitage, Monchuk, and Rogerson 2011; Bowers, Johnson, and Hirschfield 2004), or just slow down traffic speeds (Craik and Appleyard 1980; Appleyard 1981), how is crime changed and via what attitudinal, cognitive, behavioral, or emotional mediating dynamics involving offenders, potential offenders, regular users, space managers, and/or residents?

3.2.3 Hal Proshansky

The late Hal Proshansky, one of the founding fathers of environmental psychology, described the field as "concerned with establishing empirical and theoretical relationships between the behavior and experience of the individual and his [/her] built environment" (Proshansky 1976: 305). A case can be made that the portion of environmental criminology concerned with individual-level behaviors like offending and individual-level experiences like being victimized lie within this field. Proshansky (1976) laid down five methodological axioms. Given the topics to be addressed below, the most relevant of these is what he called "the content orientation of environmental psychology" (Proshansky 1976: 307). "In the attempt to establish . . . relationships" between individual experiences and behaviors and the built environment, "we have to identify what physical settings are involved, what purposes they are being used for, and what specific kinds of behavior and experiences they elicit in the person. In other words, the actual character of a physical setting . . . and broader environmental context, is important" (Proshansky 1976: 307). This warns us strongly against highly abstract representations of environment, a point to which I return later. Key questions are what are people doing in the location, what are they using it for, and how do they see it?

3.2.4 Patricia and Paul Brantingham

The acknowledged founding mother/father duo Patricia and Paul Brantingham discerned almost four decades ago that relationships between physical environment and crime shift at different spatial scales (Brantingham, Dyreson, and Brantinghm 1976). This is not just a statistical, analytical, or methodological artifact; it represents a conceptual and empirical reality that needs attention (Taylor 1998). The field has recently recognized the importance of this source of variation (Weisburd, Bruinsma, and Bernasco 2009). But, in this author's view, the proposed resolution by focusing on just one range within a much broader range of spatial scales, which is what place criminology does, has significant limitations (Taylor 2015: 124–129). The field should be wary of narrowing its view on these questions. In short, place criminology is not the answer.

3.2.5 Amos Hawley

Hawley's (1950) perspective on human ecology has been widely criticized for decades (Bursik and Grasmick 1993). Nevertheless, three key points he highlighted must be remembered. "The community may be conceived as a series of layers or strata" (Hawley 1950: 209). Further, at any spatial layer, there are interdependencies. "The relationship in which individuals are linked together to form communal units occurs also as between such units" (Hawley 1950: 220). There are interdependencies within the same layer of community, as well as dependencies from higher-level layers to lower-level layers, and vice versa. Third, and more broadly, this creates a broader functioning ecosystem (Bursik 1986). Roles or niches served by individual communities arise because of their relative positions within that broader ecosystem. And, as will be discussed below, those roles can change. Hawley's points underscore the importance of paying attention to crime-relevant dynamics across a *range* of layers of community, from the parcel to the street block and up to subcity neighborhoods (Suttles 1972).

3.3 Some Stumbling Blocks in Brief

If community criminology is to advance beyond knowing things we have known for close to a century (Burt 1925; McKenzie 1921b, 1921a), scholars will need to squarely face four stumbling blocks. Those four impediments are spatial scaling, temporal scaling, ecological construct validation, and selection dynamics (Taylor 2015). Conceptual and practical progress will prove limited until scholars take up these challenges. Those four concerns are briefly sketched below.

Each of these impediments is complex in that each *simultaneously* involves questions of theory, methods, and analysis. These are problems of *both* "conceptualization and measurement," and it is their hybrid nature that in part explains why they "have [for] far too long been neglected" (Blalock 1979: 882). If these are to be solved, teams of scholars with expertise in all three domains will need to work together.

3.3.1 Spatial Scaling

"Spatial scaling addresses both what shifts theoretically when examining variables and processes at different geographic scales, and how variables and processes connect across different spatial scales" (Taylor 2015: 7). Hannan (1991) drew sociologists' attention to these matters, but to date community criminologists have overlooked them.

Graduate students imbibe warnings about avoiding the ecological fallacy or the individual fallacy. But they receive less instruction about how to think about how the same variable means different things at different spatial scales or how processes connecting variables at different spatial scales might represent related *but distinct* dynamics. This is not just a question of selecting the "right" level of aggregation or disaggregation for the data. It is a matter of thinking hard about how crime or victimization when compiled in different ways represents different things theoretically, as do the causes to which it is linked when those causes too are organized at different levels. A street block burglary count represents different dynamics and has different prevention implications than a burglary count at the level of a Chicago natural area.

3.3.2 Temporal Scaling

"Temporal scaling is about how long it takes for variables to shift significantly or to change other variables significantly. In community criminology, the two issues are the temporal interval required for significant change to accumulate on an ecological predictor or outcome and the period required for a single-level or multi-level ecological process to 'cycle'" (Taylor 2015: 7). Abbott (2001) drew sociologists' attention to these matters, but community criminologists have overlooked them to date.

How long will it take a change in physical environment to demonstrate an impact on a crime rate? Will it depend on the physical change in question? The crime in question? The broader community or cultural context?

Some physical environment changes, like alley gating or road closures, one might expect to have relatively immediate impacts on crime because the spatial behavior of potential offenders is, presumably, directly affected. Other physical alterations like Newman-esque restrictions on the number of entrances into a neighborhood (Newman 1996) might—or might not—take longer to affect potential offenders' behaviors, depending on the latter's activity spaces, search spaces, journeys to crime, and residential locations. The key point is that many theories in community criminology, and in environmental criminology, lack specificity about timing (Taylor 2015: 154–158).

Meshing concerns about temporal dynamics with a Hawley/Bursik perspective on ecological change creates an even more severe problem. The short version can be stated simply: any cross-sectional analysis is extremely unlikely to illuminate causal dynamics (Taylor 2015: 158–162). At any point in time, any ecological indicator contains two components: a component reflecting ongoing ecological continuity, and a component reflecting recent ecological discontinuities (Bursik 1986). Cross-sectional analyses simply cannot pull these two components apart for any one indicator. Therefore, all links in all cross-sectional models are inherently nonrecursive, with dynamics going in both directions. Instrumental variables cannot fix this problem. The implications for numerous studies about physical environment and crime prove sobering. Put bluntly, cross-sectional ecological work on crime and physical environment cannot shed light on causal dynamics. This may sound like a harsh conclusion, but it follows inevitably if we accept the Hawley/Bursik perspective on ecological continuity and discontinuity.

3.3.3 Ecological Construct Validation

Researchers investigating connections between physical environment and crime extract a dizzying array of physical environment indicators, via an equally dizzying array of physical environment indicators. Although the instruments, data extraction protocols, and measurement properties of these various indicators may be clear, the meaning of them is not. There is a problem of ecological construct validation with a good number of environment indicators. In many instances, "key indicators are plagued by semantic ambiguity," meaning the indicator-construct linkages are unclear (Taylor 2015: 205). This is a problem of ecological construct validation. It can be addressed in different ways, including Messick's unified perspective on construct validation (Messick 1995), but the field has yet to clear up these matters. In brief, Messick's (1995) approach suggests moving away from restricted investigations of multimethod convergent and discriminant validities, although these are indeed useful, and considering a broader range of empirical evidence.

3.3.4 Selection Dynamics

"Selection effects refer to selectivity bias . . . [the latter] can be created when some unidentified individual-level features, which correlate with the outcome, also correlate with entering or exiting a specific spatial context" (Taylor 2015: 225). Selection is a huge problem in many areas of research, including work on establishing neighborhood effects (Sampson, Morenoff, and Gannon-Rowley 2002; Tienda 1991). It is a potentially sizable problem for some areas of physical environment/crime research.

3.3.5 And . . . There Is an Outcome Problem: Radical Operationalism and Crime Rates

This last concern is not a problem per se but just a feature of how researchers think about spatially located crime or victimization data. There are two points (Taylor 2015: 33–66). First, researchers ignore varying levels of intrusion by agents of criminal justice agencies into different neighborhoods and street blocks, and the implications of these dynamics for generating crime data. Researchers overlook important roles of exposure differentials of residents or regular users across different settings or communities. In addition, there are numerous factors affecting localized dynamics that can affect whether a victimization is reported or a crime is discovered or overlooked. This approach is tantamount to a radical operationalism perspective on the key outcomes in this area. The point here is not that crime statistics are biased or represent undercounts. Rather the point is that crime counts are outcomes of complex, spatially, organizationally, and socially dependent processes involving many agents.

3.4 Selected Current Research Streams Meet the Stumbling Blocks

Attention turns to a small number of current active research areas. For each, just a few recent studies are noted on the presumption that they are emblematic of the best work in the area. Then research is critiqued in light of the theory/analysis/measurement stumbling blocks in community criminology just introduced.

3.4.1 Space Syntax

Graph theory-based models of complex social behaviors have had varying degrees of popularity since Kurt Lewin developed topological field theory in the 1930s (Lewin 1966, 1951, 1938). Topological graph theory has returned to place-based studies of social behavior in the last 20 years with space syntax models (Banfa 2003; Hillier and Shu 2000). For example, one of the processes relevant to space syntax "refers to the effects of the emergent spatial geometry on movement patterns" (Hillier 2012: 14–15). "In urban systems, configuration is the primary generator of pedestrian patterns" (Hillier et al. 1993: 31). The configuration of the urban grid generates "natural movement," which "is the proportion of urban pedestrian movement determined by the grid configuration itself. Natural movement, although not always quantitatively the largest component of movement in urban spaces, is so much the most pervasive type of movement in urban areas that without it most spaces will be empty for most of the time. It is also the most consistent" (Hillier et al. 1993): 32).

In space syntax studies, different configurational properties of the urban street grid get measured. For example the "connectivity" of a node where lines representing street segments meet captures "how many other nodes are directly accessible from it" (Hillier et al. 1993: 25). In short, there are three basic ideas with space syntax theory: first, the configuration of a street network or grid in an urban area is a primary determinant of how pedestrians move through that network. Second, that configuration generates properties of particular line segments, or nodes where line segments meet, and those properties such as connectivity can be quantified using topological graph theory. Third, those properties, because they have implications for pedestrian traffic, may shape the activity and awareness spaces of potential offenders, thereby creating implications for crime (Chang 2011).

Davies and Johnson (2015) sought to advance the space syntax scholarship by deriving a grid-based property of street blocks keyed to the concept of journeys: the betweenness of street segments. This feature "measures the frequency with which street segments feature in the shortest paths . . . for journeys though the [street] network" (Davies and Johnson 2015: 482). "The value for every segment depends entirely on its role in the [street] network as a whole" (Davies and Johnson 2015: 493). Further, for each street block the researcher can vary the radius of the surrounding network considered, thereby permitting an approximation to "journeys through the network that represent 'local' trips" (Davies and Johnson 2015: 493).

The link to crime comes through the behavioral geography assumptions of crime pattern theory: "betweenness is particularly pertinent to the study of crime through the prism of pattern theory, since it approximates exactly those journeys through the network which would be expected to shape awareness spaces" (Davies and Johnson 2015: 493). And, indeed, Davies and Johnson (2015) do find some indicators of betweenness do link as anticipated to burglary levels.

Summing up on the best of the space syntax / crime work suggests the following. Focusing measurement of graph-based, space-syntax-derived features of street blocks on journey-based concepts such as betweenness represents an advance in the space syntax / crime work. The link to behavioral geography and awareness spaces becomes clearer. Further, it aligns the work in this area more closely with the third principle of microecology, "Block life is conditioned by features of adjoining blocks" (Taylor 1997: 134). Here the feature of adjoining street blocks is the number of paths they create leading to or away from the street block in question. Third, the methodological and analytic sophistication of work in this area has advanced enormously in just the past decade.

These advances notwithstanding, several features of work in this area prompt concern. Of the stumbling blocks mentioned earlier, two are especially worrying: ecological construct validation and temporal scaling.

Regarding the former, regardless of how precisely grid-based attributes of street blocks or whole neighborhoods are captured, the scores still represent highly abstract indicators derived not from the environments and settings themselves but from *maps* of those places. Yes, scores on those attributes have implications for offender spatial behavior and thus offender awareness spaces. But they also may have implications for other groups, such as residents or law-abiding users or those street blocks. How are the awareness spaces and surveillance activities of nonoffenders affected? Does heavier foot traffic mean nonoffenders pay less attention to other passersby? And what happens when we lose sight of documented (Roberts et al. 2014) intra-street block variations in foot traffic?

Further, what are the implications for land use patterns? Street blocks with more nonresidential land use draw more foot traffic (Taylor, Shumaker, and Gottfredson 1985) and more nonresidential land uses affect physical deterioration (Taylor et al. 1995) and resident-based informal control dynamics (Kurtz, Koons, and Taylor 1998). Are offenders responding directly to the increased likelihood that a street block higher on betweenness makes them more familiar with potential targets, or are they responding to spatial behavior and anticipated reactions of other users of the locale? We just don't know. In Abbott's (2001) terminology, there is a lot of semantic ambiguity associated with space syntax indicators such as betweenness.

How could this be cleared up? Here is what is needed. Researchers working in multiple cities, and in multiple neighborhoods in each city, could identify street blocks with varying scores on betweenness and, for each level of betweenness, burglary scores that are either significantly above or significantly below the crime level predicted by betweenness, after taking other structural and land use factors into account. Once selection is made, researchers conduct on-site behavioral observations to derive use patterns for each street block at different times of day, different weeks, and different seasons. They conduct interviews with residents, regular users of the street block, and proprietors of facilities on the street blocks. Interviews with potential offenders who are shown videos of the various streetscapes help clarify the offender perspective. Once all this is put together, we will have a decent idea of what varying levels of attributes such as betweenness *mean*, because betweenness can be translated to specific features of street block behavioral profiles, and perceptions and expectations of different user groups, in specific contexts (Proshansky 1976).

Turning to the second matter, one of the questions emerging from a consideration of temporal scaling is this: how long does it take for a change in a key predictor to affect a sizable change in a key outcome? Given the Hawley/Bursik perspective on ongoing ecological continuity and ecological discontinuity, *causal* questions can only be answered through studies where physical environment features shift over time. This creates a particular problem for space syntax studies, where the attribute in question derives from the position of the street block relative to the broader street network. Entire portions of an urban street grid cannot be altered barring some type of cataclysmic event.

There are, nonetheless, natural experiments creating short-term differences in betweenness that researchers might be able to capture. Temporary patterns of street closures provide one potential way to gauge impacts on crime and mediating dynamics (Atlas and LeBlanc 1994; Lasley 1996). This matter is discussed at more length in the section on permeability.

3.4.2 Facilities and Land Use

Two streams of research address links between facilities and crime. One looks at impacts of individual facilities thought to qualify as crime generators or attractors. Another looks more broadly at impacts of land use mixes on crime rates.

The facilities work has succeeded in substantiating links between crime and specific facilities. Many different types of facilities link to crime, including "schools . . . parks/playgrounds . . . malls . . . fast-food restaurants . . . hotels . . . abandoned buildings . . . halfway houses . . . drug treatment centers . . . check-cashing stores . . . and public transportation stops among others" (Groff and Lockwood 2014: 281).

Perhaps the most widely studied and best understood type of facility is bars; see Groff and Lockwood (2014: Table 1) for a list of studies to date. Important features of the crime impact of this facility type include that it is spatially constrained (Groff and Lockwood 2014; Jennings et al. 2013; Ratcliffe 2012; Frisbie et al 1978). Ratcliffe (2012), for example, finds the violence impacts drop sharply once one is more than 85 feet away from the facility.

Crime-generating or crime-attracting facilities by definition can concentrate or increase pedestrian or vehicular traffic within an area. These concentration effects broadly link to both crime pattern theory (Brantingham and Brantingham 1991) and some version of routine activity theory (Felson 1995). That said, the field needs to advance beyond these amorphous appeals to these broad theoretical frames. How to do this?

Longitudinal studies examining what happens when *specific* facilities open or close are needed (Taylor 2015).[1] What happens to the streetscape when a new bar opens? How are regular users' or residents' views of street block life at different times of the day or days of the week affected? How do the patterns of who is on the street when shift? Is the issue the change in the volume of people on the street? Or is it the volume of drunk people on the street? Or is it infrequent but potentially violent altercations developing inside the facility but spilling out into the street? Or is it street robbers pulled by the higher volume of pedestrian traffic, sober or not, waiting for their prey a half block away or around the corner? Unless and until we have detailed studies examining the opening or closing of specific individual facilities in specific contexts, the needed theoretical sharpening of the relevant dynamics linking environment and crime is unlikely to occur.

Staying with bars, a second stream of scholarship in this area considers alcohol outlets, either in terms of the number of outlets or their density, as a property of a locale like a zip code or a census block group (Nielsen et al 2005; Zhu, Gorman, and Horel 2004; Gorman et al. 2001; White, Gainey, and Triplett 2015). This work proves extremely difficult to interpret theoretically given the spatial scaling mismatch. Work on specific outlets clarifies that the outlet-violence relationship is highly distance dependent (Groff and Lockwood 2014; Ratcliffe 2012). These are impacts that degrade quickly over distance. The shape of that distance function may vary across contexts, but at least one study finds the effect washes out in less than 100 feet. If so, then it makes little sense to think of alcohol outlet density as a uniform spatial attribute over a larger area like a census block group. In short, the point-based work in this area raises serious questions about how, or whether, the areal-based work can be interpreted meaningfully. According to at least some distance estimations, alcohol outlet impacts are confined to the sub-street block level. Only theories specifying dynamics at this spatial scale are appropriate. We are awaiting such theories specifying these dynamics.

The broader question of crime impacts of land use mixes in residential locales, whether those be strictly commercial land uses, or more broadly any type of nonresidential land use, has been contested since Jacobs (1961) highlighted the virtues of first-floor commercial uses on short and predominantly residential urban street blocks. Some works find expected connections with crime; some do not (Fowler 1992, 1987; Browning et al. 2010; Weisburd, Groff, and Yang 2012). Numerous cross-sectional, and therefore causally uninformative, works have been done at either the street block or the areal (e.g., census block group or census tract) level.

Clearly, nonresidential, commercial land uses concentrate pedestrian and/or vehicular traffic, thereby making individual parcels with a business, or groups of parcels such as found in a small commercial center, potential crime generators. "As they concentrate people, shopping centres also create potential for conflict and theft" (Kinney et al. 2008: 71). Although some shopping centers may concentrate crime, others may not (Kinney et al. 2008). Fast-food facilities may elevate crime on street blocks, but the impact may be spatially dependent.

But land use mix variables like percentage commercial or percentage nonresidential (Stucky and Ottensmann 2009), whether on a street block or in an area like a census block group or a grid square, are still extremely broad abstractions. We have some extremely limited evidence linking such variations to variations in resident-based informal control and surveillance dynamics (Kurtz, Koons, and Taylor 1998; Baum, Davis, and Aiello 1978). We also know that crime-generating or crime-attracting land uses elevate residents' perceptions of local problems (McCord et al. 2007). But systematic studies in a broad array of residential contexts clarifying how *changes* in these *specific types* of crime-generating or crime-attracting *facilities* affect resident, regular-user, and potential offender behaviors and cognitions remain elusive.

Researchers looking at this topic have made extremely general appeals to routine activity theory. Unless significant further theoretical specification within routine activity theory is undertaken, such appeals are not helpful, for two reasons. First, and as highlighted elsewhere, is the spatial and temporal mismatch issue (Eck 1995). To my knowledge, *no one* has addressed it. In addition, many researchers continue to work with variables that are only extraordinarily crude proxies for key constructs in routine activities.

That said, we are still a long way from understanding the meaning of the physical environment ecological indicators in question here, and how those meanings might prove context dependent. Eidson (2015) found that real offenders' views of the robbery potential of streetscapes with varying levels and types of commercial land uses depended in part on assumptions made about the social class of the area.

Progress could be made on this problem of ecological construct validation if researchers were to systematically link street block behavior profiles, at different times of day, days of the week, and seasons, across a wide array of street blocks in different neighborhood and city contexts, with degree of commercial mixing present in land uses on the street block. I know of one study that gathered systematic behavioral observation data in small commercial centers (McPherson, Silloway, and Frey 1983).[2] Hopefully there are more.

In sum, one point seems clear from the current work. Crime is worse quite close to bars or other types of alcohol outlets. Although important, this is something we have known since the 1970s (Frisbie et al 1978). Beyond that the work seems muddled by confusions arising from overlooking spatial scaling, and clarifying how the relevant dynamics shift at different geographic units. The point-based versus area-based work on alcohol outlets just does not join up. If we turn to broader land use classifications like commercial or even more broadly just nonresidential land use mixes, problems of ecological construct validation surface. We don't know what these attributes *mean* for on-the-street dynamics and how those meanings might prove context dependent.

3.4.3 Accessibility / Permeability / New Urbanism / Cul-de-Sacs

This topic concerns a closely linked cluster of issues. The cluster of issues has different facets, including permeability, walkability, and cul-de-sacs. It relates to but is distinct from spatial syntax-based street block features, which concentrate on street block functions as determined almost completely by the surrounding street network. Here the features of the street blocks themselves merit attention, as do, to a lesser extent, features of the adjoining street blocks. For a somewhat recent summary of studies on permeability and crime, see Johnson and Bowers (2010: Table 5). These ideas go back at least to Sir Ebenezer Howard's Garden City Movement in England in the 1890s and, along related lines in the United States, the neighborhood unit plans of the 1920s as city planners here took on auto traffic challenges (Dahir 1947; Lawhon 2009).

The new urbanism policy context, combined with urban health emphases on walkability, promotes the idea of readily accessible street blocks and street networks. "Internal accessibility, such as an excellent public transport system, road network, and walkability is vital for creating an attractive city.... Well designed streets will encourage people to use them, and make the outside experience pleasant and safe" (Mulliner and Maliene 2011: 148).

Unfortunately, the new urbanism framework, which wants streets which are *both* safe and accessible/open, is at odds with environmental criminology (Schneider and Kitchen 2007; Cozens 2008). Although there are exceptions, and different studies measure accessibility/openness in different ways, the bulk of the research argues that accessibility is associated with higher crime (Schneider and Kitchen 2007).

The least accessible type of street is the cul-de-sac. There are different types of cul-de-sacs, for example, "leaky" (Armitage 2007) versus not, sinuous versus straight. One strong study finds that this least accessible type of streetscape, especially if it is winding and does not have alternate exit points, seems to be the safest type of street form when burglary is considered (Johnson and Bowers 2010).

But even the best studies "leave unresolved the underlying explanatory mechanism(s)" (Johnson and Bowers 2010: 107). Broadly, whether the mechanism largely or solely involves offender spatial behavior and awareness spaces; or features of resident or regular user behavioral profiles, including keeping an eye on things; variations in household composition and stage of the life cycle (Hindelang, Gottfredson, and Garofalo 1979); or a combination, remains an open question. "Teasing apart the contribution of [various] ... explanations ... might ... necessitate the use of ethnographic methods, or possibly spatial econometric techniques" (Johnson and Bowers 2010: 107).

Closing off streets to vehicular traffic and *creating* cul-de-sacs appears capable, at least in some studies, and depending on the configuration of the closures, of creating crime reductions (Atlas and LeBlanc 1994; Matthews 1992; Lasley 1996). Studies in Miami Shores, Dayton (OH), Hartford (CT), Newark (NJ), and LA all provide some evidence. (The closely related set of studies on alley-gating also provides supportive evidence

[Bowers, Johnson, and Hirschfield 2004].) So observing impacts of physical environment changes on later crime changes is somewhat encouraging about causal impacts of physical environment changes. But there is a weakness in these studies. It appears that *none* of these studies to date have provided closely spaced longitudinal observations, subsequent to a physical environment change, of subsequent changes in residents' and regular users' cognitions and behaviors, street block behavioral profiles, potential offenders' views, and organizational activities related to the physical changes. Consequently, questions of specific causal processes and temporal scaling remain open. We don't know how these changes work. And we don't know how long it takes for a sizable design change to lead to a sizable change in the outcome. Further, at least one study (Lasley 1996) suggests offenders cleverly adapt to such design changes, using them to decrease their chances of police apprehension. Who is doing what, where, and when, after such physical changes are put in place, becomes essential for figuring out the relevant causal dynamics.

Such studies also would help with the problem of ecological construct validation. Research has yet to learn what these changes mean to different user groups, including potential offenders.

Johnson and Bowers (2010) also raise two potential selection problems. First, households with lifestyles that are less burglar friendly, like households with young children, may be siting themselves on cul-de-sacs. Further, potential offenders may be selecting areas at a broader spatial scale. Selection effects have caused concern in the neighborhood effects and physical environment literatures for some time (Sampson, Morenoff, and Gannon-Rowley 2002). No ready remedy surfaces for discounting this alternate explanatory frame (Taylor 2015).

In summing up, roughly speaking, low permeability, as reflected in low-access streets such as cul-de-sacs, continues to be associated with lower rates for some types of crimes, even after taking features of surrounding context into account. (Schneider and Kitchen's [2007: 47] conclusion aligns with mine but only specifically for burglary.) Although this is a consistent finding going back to the 1970s (Bevis and Nutter 1977), researchers have yet to clarify the specific behavioral and cognitive dynamics, among different groups including potential offenders, that are affected by low permeability, or changes in permeability as happens when cul-de-sacs are created. So we don't know how long it takes for significant crime prevention impacts to emerge, nor the relevant specific dynamics involving different groups. Further, since such impacts may be completely dependent on social and structural conditions (Ward et al. 2014), systematic studies across a range of contexts are needed to understand the conditioning of the relevant dynamics.

3.4.4 CPTED / Defensible Space / Guardianship / Territorial Functioning

Resident and regular user behaviors and attitudes occupy center stage in physical environment/crime models concerned either with territorial functioning, or the impacts of design features like defensible space components or CPTED components on resident- or regular user-based behavior patterns, surveillance, or informal control dynamics. Previous reviews of this theory, and critiques of the theory, and some relevant evidence, have been presented elsewhere (Taylor 2005; Taylor, Gottfredson, and Brower 1980; Merry 1981; Reynald 2009). Cozens's (2011a) remarks prove particularly incisive and wide ranging.

Three substantial problems have bedeviled work in this area, and continue to do so. CPTED has become an extraordinarily broad catch-all category of physical design elements, like how quickly someone can enter or exit a parking lot at a mall (Crowe 1991); security add-ons like private or public CCTV (Ratcliffe, Taniguchi, and Taylor 2009; Welsh and Farrington 2009); target hardening; and public infrastructure enhancements like improved street lighting. We have studies looking at the crime impacts of changes in a suite of CPTED features, or changes in individual components. The interested reader can start at the Problem Oriented Policing library database for situational crime prevention to view studies on the impacts of different features (http://www.popcenter.org/library/scp/). Searching on street lighting alone calls up 43 studies.

The problem is that because there are so many potentially relevant design elements, whose relevance varies depending on many features of context and the specific type of crime in question, policymakers and practitioners have no idea of the *comparative* benefit of one design component versus another in *specific* settings. For example, to reduce purse snatches in the parking lot adjacent to a medium-size mall in a mixed-income/mixed-race suburban location, should the mall owner put in better street lighting or redesign the parking lot exit flow?

A second enduring challenge, despite broad and widely held assertions that CPTED works, is that we don't know *how* it works. Again, questions of relevant causal dynamics remain unanswered.

There is the issue of our limited understanding of how specific aspects of defensible space and CPTED work and in what context they are likely to work most effectively. There remains a critical void in our understanding of how physical design manipulations suggested by defensible space and CPTED translates into crime preventive action by residents and other legitimate users of space (Reynald 2015: 81).

And, I would add, we don't know how the above unknown dynamics translate into impacts on potential offenders' expectations about ease of access, detection, and ease of exit (Taylor and Gottfredson 1986).

The third challenge, arising from the previous one, is confusion about temporal scaling. Again, as seen before in other areas, we don't know how long it takes for the design change to create intermediate changes that eventuate in crime reductions.

On a positive note, despite the long-standing and hard-to-resolve challenges in this arena, scholars are seeking to theoretically reinvigorate these conceptual frameworks. Recent efforts at theoretical cross-fertilization propose connections between defensible space features, territorial functioning, and different varieties of routine activity theory; for the latter, a focus on capable guardianship has been suggested (Reynald 2011; Hollis-Peel et al. 2011; Reynald 2010, 2009) (see chapter 30 by Reynald in this volume). Connections between micro- and meso-level person-place dynamics and the wider surround are drawing interest as well (Reynald 2009).

Reynald's (2009) conceptual linkage of Newman's milieu idea with routine activities is an example of the latter. "*If an area is highly accessible to outsiders, for example, and highly attractive because of the facilities located within it, this makes it much more difficult for residents to exert control over it*" (Reynald 2009: 40). This was exactly the relationship observed among residents at varying distances from small commercial centers in Minneapolis (Taylor 1997: Figures 1 and 2). Reynald's suggestion calls for studies connecting site-level and street block design features with assessments of residents' and regular users' territorial behaviors and cognitions, and with broader profiles of streetscape usage driven by specific facilities.

Hopefully these efforts will lead to stronger theoretical integration with sociological frames on neighborhood crime (Bursik and Grasmick 1993) and place-specific informal control dynamics (Hunter 2003, 1985), and, as importantly, ecological construct validation efforts for all the key indicators in question in these different theories.

A question closes the discussion of CPTED. Researchers and planners might want to carefully consider whether CPTED "is a [series of] physical design concept[s] or a concept generating desired social outcomes" (Lawhon 2009).[3] If it is the latter, then it is not clear how to validate indicators of the construct CPTED.

3.5 Forging Ahead

3.5.1 Given the Preceding

The selective review of just some of the key questions in physical environment in crime has highlighted the repeated relevance of two conceptual/analytic/methodological concerns: temporal scaling and ecological construct validation. Although mentioned explicitly only once by one of the studies noted, selection dynamics are routinely relevant. People are constantly deciding whether to turn here or there, what times of day to go to this place or that place, and of course, where to live and shop.

The review also has pointed out that cross-sectional work is noninformative from a causal perspective. This may sound like a harsh statement to some, but this conclusion *necessarily* follows if one accepts Hawley's and Bursik's characterizations of continuity and discontinuity of ecological parameters (Bursik 1986). Any single measure of ecology or crime inextricably confounds ongoing ecological continuity and recent ecological discontinuity into one indicator (Taylor 2015: 149–154). The two components cannot be separated. Longitudinal works gauging changes in both environment and crime are needed.

Further, studies of changes need to consider mediating and moderating dynamics (Baron and Kenny 1986). Mediating dynamics, behavioral, cognitive, and emotional, of regular users, residents (if applicable), and potential offenders all deserve attention. Constraining or facilitating factors at different geographic scales, whether this is called milieu or structural fabric, merit consideration (Ward et al. 2014; Reynald 2009). This author rejects architectural determinism, and strongly encourages readers to do likewise (Broady 1972).

Given that rejection, the cognitive and emotional processing of perceived environments, as well as mediating and moderating dynamics, all prove essential for understanding causal dynamics in this arena. Given the relevance of perceived settings, situational action theory deserves close attention as a fruitful theoretic frame (Wikström et al. 2012).

3.5.2 How Do We Forge Ahead?

It seems extremely unlikely to this author that the empirical data structures required by the aforementioned conceptual/analytic concerns are likely to be obtained by researchers. Despite the promises (O'Brien and Sampson 2015), it is unlikely this problem will be solved with big data. The temporal and spatial requirements of needed data, from different sources, are just unlikely to line up adequately.

This author recommends that beginning scholars immerse themselves deeply in computational criminology, more specifically, agent-based simulation models (ABMs) (Taylor 2015) (see chapter 15 by Birks in this volume). This mode of scholarship has proven enormously valuable in many social science areas, including environmental criminology (Birks, Townsley, and Stewart 2012; Berk et al. 2011 [1999]; Yang et al. 2011; Townsley and Birks 2008; Liu and Eck 2008; Berk 2008; Groff 2007a, 2007b; Wang 2005). The structure of the environmental criminological theories that are so often called upon in the environment-crime research area are framed in ways that make their testing quite compatible with ABMs (Johnson and Groff 2014).

The general strategy would be:

- Start with a specific crime outcome of interest, at a particular geographic scale. Create a focus on a specified subset of physical features, whether those be design-based, user-generated, or behavior traces.
- Decide initial levels, then the rate and level of changes on those physical features of interest. Use empirical research and specific theoretical frames as touchstones where possible for each of these decisions.
- Use empirical research and specific theoretical frames to outline the most relevant classes of agents and for each class of agents, the most relevant attributes.
- For each class of agents and for each relevant attribute, use empirical research and theoretical frames to gauge impacts of specific attributes on other specific attributes, and to estimate the time horizon of such impacts.
- Use empirical research and relevant theoretical frames to estimate impacts of physical environment changes on different attributes of different classes of agents.
- Run models, examine patterns of crime impacts.
- Test ecological validity of the model.
- Progressively elaborate the model.[4]

ABMs allow researchers to conduct experimental tests of changes in physical design features within the simulation itself. "The agent's 'lives' can be restarted and allowed to play out under different assumptions. This might be used to test different theories or even interventions" (Johnson and Groff 2014: 515).

Take for example the question of creating cul-de-sacs. ABMs situated in real street networks (Groff 2007a) could gauge impacts of experiments that create varying numbers or arrangements of cul-de-sacs to gauge the number and arrangement needed to create a significant reduction in drive-by shootings (Lasley 1996), for example.

At some point in the model development stage, such models should be situated in real geographies (Groff 2007a), whether those geographies be parcels on street blocks, street blocks in a street grid, or something different.

Such simulations, even though they represent methodologies radically different from those available to the forefathers and foremothers of research in this area, align with their concerns. Lynch would embrace the consideration of changes, especially changes at different rates, and how different types of agents might adapt to those. Along a related line, Hawley would be eager to learn how variations in the relative levels of ecological continuity versus ecological discontinuity on key community attributes might shift over time in response to agents' actions. Proshansky would support basing simulation dynamics on processes taking place in specific contexts. Jacobs might express interest in the rich interplay between different classes of agents modeled in a shared context. The Brantinghams already have embraced this approach (Brantingham 2011; Brantingham et al. 2008; Brantingham et al. 2005). Researchers can simultaneously embrace this new analytic approach while staying true to the important guiding lessons imparted by the founders in this field.

***

In the late 1960s and early 1970s empirical scholarship on environment and behavior, including crime and environment, unearthed many relationships. These gave policymakers and opinion makers hope that well-understood design guidelines might help create safer places. "How could we not want urban design to inoculate us against bad things, including crime?" (Schneider and Kitchen 2007: 52). Much more is known today about how to make some kinds of places safer. Such achievements are notable. At the same time, we are still a long ways away from fully understanding the relevant causal or even transactional (Werner et al. 1987) dynamics that connect physical environment and crime over time, for different types of individuals and groups, in different contexts. This author is not sure researchers are getting closer to such an understanding. Part of the problem, as outlined here, has been several overlooked stumbling blocks. Hopefully, in spite of always inadequate external funding sources, real-world complexities arising with multisite investigator teams, and pressures to publish as many pieces as possible in the shortest time, some significant cadre of scholars will take these stumbling blocks into account, and confront the challenge of directly investigating the dynamics underpinning these potential causal connections.

Acknowledgment

Charles Ries provided substantial and enormously helpful bibliographic assistance.

Notes

1. There is one census block group-level study of changing alcohol outlets on changing violent crime (White, Gainey, and Triplett 2015). Unfortunately, researchers appear to have applied an OLS regression model to a count outcome.
2. These behavioral observation data are available in a reconstructed file at ICPSR, DS2: Pedestrian Activity Data in the data set "Impact of Neighborhood Structure, Crime, and Physical Deterioration on Residents and Business Personnel in Minneapolis–St. Paul, 1970–1982" (ICPSR 2371).
3. This question adapts Lawhon's (2009) phrasing of a criticism of neighborhood unit planning into a question about CPTED. Given the number of disparate design elements involved in both, this is an important question to carefully consider.
4. The above represents an enormous oversimplification of the process of ABM development and testing. For more see Gilbert and Troitzsch (2005).

References

Abbott, Andrew. 2001. *Time Matters: On Theory and Method.* Chicago: University of Chicago Press.

Appleyard, Donald. 1981. *Livable Streets.* Berkeley: University of California Press.

Armitage, Rachel. 2007. "Sustainability versus Safety: Confusion, Conflict and Contradiction in Designing Out Crime." In *Imagination for Crime Prevention: Essays in Honour of Ken Pease*, edited by Graham Farrell, Kate J. Bowers, Shane D. Johnson, and Michael Townsley, 81–110. Monsey, NY: Criminal Justice Press.

Armitage, Rachel, Leanne Monchuk, and Michelle Rogerson. 2011. "It Looks Good, but What Is It Like to Live There: Exploring the Impact of Innovative Housing Design on Crime." *European Journal of Crime and Policy Research* 17:29–54. doi 10.1007/s10610-014-9257-3.

Atlas, Randall, and William LeBlanc. 1994. "Environmental Barriers to Crime." *Ergonomics in Design* October 1994:9–16.

Banfa, Sonit. 2003. "Space Syntax: A Brief Introduction to Its Logic and Analytical Techniques." *Environment and Behavior* 35 (1):17–29.

Baron, R. M., and D. A. Kenny. 1986. "The Moderator-Mediator Variable Distinction in Social Psychological Research: Conceptual, Strategic and Statistical Considerations." *Journal of Personality and Social Psychology* 51:1173–1182.

Baum, A., A. G. Davis, and J. R. Aiello. 1978. "Crowding and Neighborhood Mediation of Urban Density." *Journal of Population* 1:266–279.

Berk, Richard. 2008. "How You Can Tell If the Simulations in Computational Criminology Are Any Good." *Journal of Experimental Criminology* 4 (3):289–308. doi: 10.1007/s11292-008-9053-5.

Berk, Richard, Jason Bond, Rong Lu, Richard Turco, and Robert Weiss. 2011 [1999]. "Computer Simulations as Experiments: Using Program Evaluation Tools to Assess the Validity of Interventions in Virtual Worlds." Department of Statistics Papers, Department of Statistics, UCLA. Online: http://escholarship.org/uc/item/90m4686r.

Bevis, C., and J. B. Nutter. 1977. "Changing Street Layouts to Reduce Residential Burglary." Paper presented at the Annual Meeting of the American Society of Criminology, Atlanta, Georgia.

Birks, D., M. Townsley, and A. Stewart. 2012. "Generative Explanations of Crime: Using Simulation to Test Criminological Theory." *Criminology* 50 (1):221–254. doi: 10.1111/j.1745-9125.2011.00258.x.

Blalock, H. M., Jr. 1979. "The Presidential Address: Measurement and Conceptualization Problems. The Major Obstacle to Integrating Theory and Research." *American Sociological Review* 44 (6):881–894.

Bottoms, Anthony E., and Paul Wiles. 1997. "Environmental Criminology." In *The Oxford Handbook of Criminology*, 2nd ed., edited by Mike Maguire, Rod Morgan, and Robert Reiner, 305–59. Oxford: Oxford University Press.

Bowers, Kate J., Shane D. Johnson, and Alex F. G. Hirschfield. 2004. "Closing Off Opportunities for Crime: An Evaluation of Alley-Gating." *European Journal on Criminal Policy and Research* 10 (4):285–308. doi: 10.1007/s10610-005-5502-0.

Brantingham, Patricia L. 2011. "Computational Criminology." Paper presented at the Intelligence and Security Informatics Conference (EISIC), September 12–14.

Brantingham, Patricia L., Uwe Glasser, Piper Jackson, Bryan Kinney, and Mona Vajihollahi. 2008. "Mastermind: Computational Modeling and Simulation of Spatio-temporal Aspects of Crime in Urban Environments." In *Artificial Crime Analysis Systems: Using Computer Simulations and Geographic Information Systems*, edited by John E. Eck and Lin Liu, 252–280. Hershey, PA: Idea Group.

Brantingham, Patricia L., Uwe Glasser, Bryan Kinney, Suraj K. Singh, and Mona Vajihollahi. 2005. "A Computational Model for Simulating Spatial Aspects of Crime in Urban Environments." Paper presented at the IEEE International Conference on Systems, Man, and Cybernetics. Online: http://ieeexplore.ieee.org.libproxy.temple.edu/xpls/abs_all.jsp?arnumber=1571717&tag=1.

Brantingham, Paul J., and Patricia L. Brantingham. 1991. "Notes on the Geometry of Crime." In *Environmental Criminology*, edited by Paul J. Brantingham and Patricia L. Brantingham, 27–54. Prospect Heights, IL: Waveland Press.

Brantingham, Paul J., D. A. Dyreson, and Patricia L. Brantingham. 1976. "Crime Seen through a Cone of Resolution." *American Behavioral Scientist* 20:261–274.

Broady, Maurice. 1972. "Social Theory in Architectural Design." In *People and Buildings*, edited by Robert Gutman, 170–185. New York: Basic Books.

Browning, Christopher R., Reginald A. Byron, Catherine A. Calder, Lauren J. Krivo, Mei-Po Kwan, Jae-Yong Lee, and Ruth D. Peterson. 2010. "Commercial Density, Residential Concentration, and Crime: Land Use Patterns and Violence in Neighborhood Context." *Journal of Research in Crime and Delinquency* 47 (3):329–357. doi: 10.1177/0022427810365906.

Bursik, Robert J., Jr. 1986. "Ecological Stability and the Dynamics of Delinquency." In *Communities and crime*, edited by Albert J. Reiss and Michael Tonry, 35–66. Chicago: University of Chicago Press.

Bursik, Robert J., Jr., and Harold G. Grasmick. 1993. *Neighborhoods and Crime*. New York: Lexington Books.

Burt, Cyril. 1925. *The Young Delinquent*. London: University of London Press.

Chang, Dongkuk. 2011. "Social Crime or Spatial Crime." *Environment and Behavior* 43 (1):26–52.

Cozens, Paul Michael. 2011a. "Crime Prevention through Environmental Design." In *Environmental Criminology and Crime Analysis*, edited by Richard Wortley and Lorraine Mazerolle, 155–177. Portland, OR: Willan.

Cozens, Paul Michael. 2011b. "Urban Planning and Environmental Criminology: Towards a New Perspective for Safer Cities." *Planning Practice and Research* 26:481–508. doi: 10.1080/02697459.2011.582357.

Cozens, Paul Michael. 2008. "New Urbanism, Crime and the Suburbs: A Review of the Evidence." *Urban Policy and Research* 26 (4):429–444. doi: 10.1080/08111140802084759.

Craik, K. H., and D. Appleyard. 1980. "Streets of San Francisco: Brunswik's Lens Model Applied to Urban Inference and Assessment." *Journal of Social Issues* 36:72–85.

Crowe, Timothy D. 1991. *Crime Prevention through Environmental Design: Applications of Architectural Design and Space Management Concepts*. London: Butterworth-Heinemann.

Dahir, J. 1947. *The Neighborhood Unit Plan: Its Spread and Acceptance*. New York: Russell Sage Foundation.

Davies, Toby, and Shane D. Johnson. 2015. "Examining the Relationship between Road Structure and Burglary Risk via Quantitative Network Analysis." *Journal of Quantitative Criminology* 31:481–507.

Eck, John E. 1995. "Review Essay: Examining Routine Activity Theory." *Justice Quarterly* 12:783–797.

Eidson, Jillian L. 2015. "Offenders' and Non-offenders' Perceptions of Streetscapes." Paper presented at the Annual Meetings of the American Society of Criminology, November, Washington, DC.

Felson, M. 1995. "Those Who Discourage Crime." In *Crime and Place*, edited by John E. Eck and David Weisburd, 53–66, vol. 4 of *Crime Prevention Studies*. Monsey, NY: Criminal Justice Press.

Fowler, Edmund P. 1987. "Street Management and City Design." *Social Forces* 66 (2):365–389.

Fowler, Edmund P. 1992. *Building Cities That Work*. Montreal: McGill-Queens University Press.

Frisbie, Douglas W., Glenn Fishbine, Richard Hintz, Mitchell Joelson, and Julia Brown Nutter. 1978. *Crime in Minneapolis: Proposals for Prevention*. Minneapolis: Minnesota Crime Prevention Center.

Gilbert, Nigel, and Klaus G. Troitzsch. 2005. *Simulation for the Social Scientist*. 2nd ed. Berkshire, UK: Open University Press.

Gorman, D. M., P. W. Speer, P. J. Gruenewald, and E. W. Labouvie. 2001. "Spatial Dynamics of Alcohol Availability, Neighborhood Structure and Violent Crime." *Journal of Studies on Alcohol* 62 (5):628–636.

Groff, Elizabeth R. 2007a. "Simulation for Theory Testing and Experimentation: An Example Using Routine Activity Theory and Street Robbery." *Journal of Quantitative Criminology* 23 (2):75–103. doi: 10.1007/s10940-006-9021-z.

Groff, Elizabeth R. 2007b. "'Situating' Simulation to Model Human Spatio-temporal Interactions: An Example Using Crime Events." *Transactions in GIS* 11 (4):507–530.

Groff, Elizabeth R., and Brian Lockwood. 2014. "Criminogenic Facilities and Crime across Street Segments in Philadelphia." *Journal of Research in Crime and Delinquency* 51 (3):277–314.

Groff, Elizabeth R., Ralph B. Taylor, David Elesh, Lallen T. Johnson, and Jennifer McGovern. 2014. "Permeability across a Metropolitan Area: Conceptualizing and Operationalizing a Macro Level Crime Pattern Theory." *Environment and Planning A* 46 (1):129–152.

Hannan, Michael T. 1991. *Aggregation and Disaggregation in the Social Sciences*. Rev. ed. Lexington, MA: Lexington Books.

Hawley, Amos H. 1950. *Human Ecology: A Theory of Community Structure*. New York City: Ronald Press.

Hillier, Bill. 2004. "Can Streets Be Made Safe?" *Urban Design International* 9 (1):31–45.

Hillier, Bill. 2012. "Studying Cities to Learn about Minds." *Environment and Planning B: Planning and Design* 39:12–32.

Hillier, Bill, Alan Penn, Julienne Hanson, Tadeusz Grajewski, and Jianming Xu. 1993. "Natural Movement: Or, Configuration and Attraction in Urban Pedestrian Movement." *Environment and Planning B: Planning and Design* 20:29–66.

Hillier, Bill, and Simon Shu. 2000. "Crime and Urban Layout: The Need for Evidence." In *Secure Foundations: Key Issues in Crime Prevention, Crime Reduction and Community Safety*, edited by S. Ballintyne, K. Pease, and V. McLaren. London: IPPR.

Hindelang, Michael J., Michael Gottfredson, and James Garofalo. 1979. *A Theory of Personal Victimization*. Cambridge: Ballinger.

Hollis-Peel, Meghan E., Danielle M. Reynald, Maud van Bavel, Henk Elffers, and Brandon C. Welsh. 2011. "Guardianship for Crime Prevention: A Critical Review of the Literature." *Crime, Law and Social Change* 56 (1):53–70. doi: 10.1007/s10611-011-9309-2.

Hope, Tim. 2008a. "Dodgy Evidence—Fallacies and Facts of Crime Reduction: Part I." *Safer Communities* 7 (3):35–38.

Hope, Tim. 2008b. "Dodgy Evidence—Fallacies and Facts of Crime Reduction: Part Two." *Safer Communities* 7 (4):46–51.

Hummon, David M. 1985. "Urban Ideology as a Cultural System." *Journal of Cultural Geography* 5 (2):1–15.

Hunter, Albert. 1985. "Private, Parochial and Public Social Orders: The Problem of Crime and Incivility in Urban Communities." In *The Challenge of Social Control: Citizenship and Institution Building in Modern Society*, edited by Gerald D. Suttles and Mayer N. Zald, 230–242. Norwood, NJ: Ablex.

Hunter, Albert. 2003. "Social Control." In *Encyclopedia of Community*, edited by Karen Christensen and David Levinson, 1297–1302. Thousand Oaks, CA: Sage.

Jacobs, Jane 1961. *The Death and Life of Great American Cities*. New York: Vintage.

Jennings, Jacky M., Adam J. Milam, Amelia Greiner, Debra M. Furr-Holden, Frank C. Curriero, and Rachel J. Thornton. 2013. "Neighborhood Alcohol Outlets and the Association with Violent Crime in One Mid-Atlantic City." *Journal of Urban Health* 91 (1):62–71.

Johnson, Shane D., and Kate Bowers. 2010. "Permeability and Burglary Risk: Are Cul-de-Sacs Safer?" *Journal of Quantitative Criminology* 26 (1):89–111. doi: 10.1007/s10940-009-9084-8.

Johnson, Shane D., and Elizabeth R. Groff. 2014. "Strengthening Theoretical Testing in Criminology Using Agent-Based Modeling." *Journal of Research in Crime and Delinquency* 51 (4):509–525.

Kinney, J. Bryan, Patricia L. Brantingham, Kathryn Wuschke, Michael G. Kirk, and Paul J. Brantingham. 2008. "Crime Attractors, Generators and Detractors: Land Use and Urban Crime Opportunities." *Built Environment* 34 (1):62–74.

Kurtz, Ellen M., Barbara A. Koons, and Ralph B. Taylor. 1998. "Land Use, Physical Deterioration, Resident-Based Control, and Calls for Service on Urban Streetblocks." *Justice Quarterly* 15 (1):121–149.

Lasley, James R. 1996. "Using Traffic Barriers to 'Design Out' Crime: A Program Evaluation of LAPD's Operation Cul-de-Sac." Final Grant Report 96-IJ-CX-0009. Online: http://www.popcenter.org/library/scp/pdf/104-Lasley.pdf.

Lawhon, Larry Lloyd. 2009. "The Neighborhood Unit: Physical Design or Physical Determinism?" *Journal of Planning History* 8 (2):111–132. doi: 10.1177/1538513208327072.

Lewin, Kurt. 1938. *The Conceptual Representation and the Measurement of Psychological Forces*. Durham, NC: Duke University Press.

Lewin, Kurt. 1951. *Field Theory in Social Science: Selected Theoretical Papers*. Edited by Dorwin Cartwright. New York: Harper.

Lewin, Kurt. 1966. *Principles of Topological Psychology*. Edited and translated by Fritz Heider and Grace M. Heider. New York: McGraw-Hill.

Liu, Lin, and John E. Eck, eds. 2008. *Artificial Crime Analysis Systems: Using Computer Simulations and Geographic Information Systems*. Hershey, PA: Information Science Reference.

Lynch, Kevin. 1972. *What Time Is This Place?* Cambridge, MA: MIT Press.

Matthews, Roger. 1992. "Developing More Effective Strategies for Curbing Prostitution." In *Situational Crime Prevention: Successful Case Studies*, edited by Ronald V. Clarke, 74–82. New York: Harrow & Heston.

McCord, E. S., J. H. Ratcliffe, R. M. Garcia, and R. B. Taylor. 2007. "Nonresidential Crime Attractors and Generators Elevate Perceived Neighborhood Crime and Incivilities." *Journal of Research in Crime and Delinquency* 44 (3):295–320.

McKenzie, R. D. 1921a. "The Neighborhood: A Study of Local Life in the City of Columbus, Ohio. I." *American Journal of Sociology* 27 (2):145–168.

McKenzie, R. D. 1921b. "The Neighborhood: A Study of Local Life in the City of Columbus, Ohio. II." *American Journal of Sociology* 27 (3):344–363.

McPherson, M., G. Silloway, and D. L. Frey. 1983. *Crime, Fear, and Control in Neighborhood Commercial Centers*. Minneapolis: Minnesota Crime Prevention Center.

Merry, S. E. 1981. "Defensible Space Undefended: Social Factors in Crime Control through Environmental Design." *Urban Affairs Quarterly* 16:397–422.

Messick, S. 1995. "Validity of Psychological Assessment: Validation of Inferences from Persons' Responses and Performances as Scientific Inquiry into Score Meaning." *American Psychologist* 50 (9):741–749.

Mulliner, Emma, and Vida Maliene. 2011. "Editorial Review: An Introductory Review to the Special issue: Attractive Places to Live." *Urban Design International* 16:147–152.

Newman, O. 1996. *Creating Defensible Space*. Washington, DC: US Department of Housing and Urban Development, Office of Policy Development and Research.

Nielsen, Amie L., Ramiro Martinez Jr., and Matthew T. Lee. 2005. "Alcohol, Ethnicity, and Violence: The Role of Alcohol Availability for Latino and Black Aggravated Assaults and Robberies." *Sociological Quarterly* 46 (3):479–502.

O'Brien, Daniel Tumminelli, and Robert J. Sampson. 2015. "Public and Private Spheres of Neighborhood Disorder: Assessing Pathways to Violence Using Large-Scale Digital Records." *Journal of Research in Crime and Delinquency* 52 (4):486–510. doi: 10.1177/0022427815577835.

Proshansky, H. M. 1976. "Environmental Psychology and the Real World." *American Psychologist* 31:303–310.

Ratcliffe, Jerry H. 2012. "The Spatial Extent of Criminogenic Places: A Changepoint Regression of Violence around Bars." *Geographical Analysis* 44:302–320.

Ratcliffe, Jerry H., Travis Taniguchi, and Ralph B. Taylor. 2009. "The Crime Reduction Effects of Public CCTV Cameras: A Multi-method Spatial Approach." *Justice Quarterly* 26 (4):746–770. doi: 10.1080/07418820902873852.

Reynald, Danielle M. 2009. "The Future of Newman's Defensible Space Theory." *European Journal of Criminology* 6 (1):25–46.

Reynald, Danielle M. 2010. "Guardians on Guardianship: Factors Affecting the Willingness to Supervise, the Ability to Detect Potential Offenders, and the Willingness to Intervene." *Journal of Research in Crime and Delinquency* 47 (3):358–390. doi: 10.1177/0022427810365904.

Reynald, Danielle M. 2011. "Factors Associated with the Guardianship of Places: Assessing the Relative Importance of the Spatio-physical and Sociodemographic Contexts in Generating Opportunities for Capable Guardianship." *Journal of Research in Crime and Delinquency* 48 (1):110–142. doi: 10.1177/0022427810384138.

Reynald, Danielle M. 2015. "Environmental Design and Crime Events." *Journal of Contemporary Criminal Justice* 31 (1):71–89.

Roberts, David, Ralph B. Taylor, R. Marie Garcia, and Amber Perenzin. 2014. "Intra-streetblock Ordered Segmentation in a High Crime Urban Neighborhood." *Journal of Architectural and Planning Research* 31 (2):143–162.

Robinson, J., B. Lawton, R. B. Taylor, and D. D. Perkins. 2003. "Longitudinal Impacts of Incivilities: A Multilevel Analysis of Reactions to Crime and Block Satisfaction." *Journal of Quantitative Criminology* 19 (237–274).

Sampson, Robert J., Jeffrey D. Morenoff, and Thomas Gannon-Rowley. 2002. "Assessing 'Neighborhood Effects': Social Processes and New Directions in Research." *Annual Review of Sociology* 28:443–478.

Schneider, Richard H., and Ted Kitchen. 2007. *Crime Prevention and the Built Environment*. New York: Routledge.

Stucky, Thomas D., and John R. Ottensmann. 2009. "Land Use and Violent Crime." *Criminology* 47 (4):1223–1259.

Suttles, G. D. 1972. *The Social Construction of Communities*. Chicago: University of Chicago Press.

Taylor, Ralph B. 1987. "Toward an Environmental Psychology of Disorder." In *Handbook of Environmental Psychology*, edited by D. Stokols and I. Altman, 951–986. New York: Wiley.

Taylor, Ralph B. 1995. "Impact of Crime on Communities." *Annals of the American Academy of Political and Social Science* 539:28–45.

Taylor, Ralph B. 1997. "Social Order and Disorder of Streetblocks and Neighborhoods: Ecology, Microecology and the Systemic Model of Social Disorganization." *Journal of Research in Crime and Delinquency* 33:113–155.

Taylor, Ralph B. 1998. "Crime in Small Scale Places: What We Know, What We Can Do about It." In *Research and Evaluation Conference 1997*, 1–20. Washington, DC: National Institute of Justice.

Taylor, Ralph B. 1999. "The Incivilities Thesis: Theory, Measurement and Policy." In *Measuring What Matters*, edited by R. L. Langworthy, 65–88. Washington, DC: National Institute of Justice, Office of Community Oriented Policing Services.

Taylor, Ralph B. 2001. *Breaking Away from Broken Windows: Evidence from Baltimore Neighborhoods and the Nationwide Fight against Crime, Grime, Fear and Decline*. New York: Westview Press.

Taylor, Ralph B. 2002. "Physical Environment, Crime, Fear, and Resident-Based Control." In *Crime: Public Policies for Crime Control*, edited by James Q. Wilson & Joan Petersilia, 413–434. Oakland: Institute for Contemporary Studies.

Taylor, Ralph B. 2005. "Crime Prevention through Environmental Design: Yes, No, Maybe, Unknowable, and All of the Above." In *Handbook of Environmental Psychology*, edited by Robert Bechtel and Arzu Churchman, 413–426. New York: Wiley.

Taylor, Ralph B. 2015. *Community Criminology: Fundamentals of Spatial and Temporal Scaling, Ecological Indicators, and Selectivity Bias*. New York: New York University Press.

Taylor, Ralph B., and Stephen D. Gottfredson. 1986. "Environmental Design, Crime and Prevention: An Examination of Community Dynamics." In *Communities and Crime*, edited by Albert J. Reiss Jr. and Michael Tonry, 387–416. Chicago: University of Chicago Press.

Taylor, Ralph B., Stephen D. Gottfredson, and Sidney N. Brower. 1980. "The Defensibility of Defensible Space." In *Understanding Crime*, edited by Travis Hirschi and Michael Gottfredson, 53–71. Beverly Hills, CA: Sage.

Taylor, Ralph B., and Adele V. Harrell. 1996. *Physical Environment and Crime*. Washington, DC: National Institute of Justice.

Taylor, Ralph B., Barbara A. Koons, Ellen M. Kurtz, Jack R. Greene, and D. Perkins. 1995. "Streetblocks with More Nonresidential Landuse Have More Physical Deterioration: Evidence from Baltimore and Philadelphia." *Urban Affairs Review* 30:120–136.

Taylor, Ralph B., Sally A. Shumaker, and Stephen D. Gottfredson. 1985. "Neighborhood-Level Links between Physical Features and Local Sentiments: Deterioration, Fear of Crime, and Confidence." *Journal of Architectural Planning and Research* 2:261–275.

Tienda, M. 1991. "Poor People in Poor Places: Deciphering Neighborhood Effects on Poverty Outcomes." In *Macro-Micro Linkages in Sociology*, edited by Joan Huber, 244–262. Newbury Park, CA: Sage.

Townsley, Michael, and Daniel Birks. 2008. "Building Better Crime Simulations: Systematic Replication and the Introduction of Incremental Complexity." *Journal of Experimental Criminology* 4 (3):309–333. doi: 10.1007/s11292-008-9054-4.

Wang, Xuguang. 2005. "Spatial Adaptive Crime Event Simulation with RA/CA/ABM Computational Laboratory." PhD diss., University of Cincinnati.

Ward, J. T., M. R. Nobles, T. J. Youstin, and C. L. Cook. 2014. "Placing the Neighborhood Accessibility-Burglary Link in Social-Structural Context." *Crime and Delinquency* 60 (5):739–763. doi: 10.1177/0011128710364804.

Weisburd, David, Gerben J. N. Bruinsma, and Wim Bernasco. 2009. "Units of Analysis in Geographic Criminology: Historical Development, Critical Issues, and Open Questions." In *Putting Crime in Its Place: Units of Analysis in Geographic Criminology*, edited by David Weisburd, Wim Bernasco, and Gerben J. N. Bruinsma, 3–34. New York: Springer.

Weisburd, David, Elizabeth R. Groff, and Sue-Ming Yang. 2012. *The Criminology of Place: Street Segments and Our Understanding of the Crime Problem*. Oxford: Oxford University Press.

Welsh, Brandon C., and David P. Farrington. 2009. *Making Public Places Safer: Surveillance and Crime Prevention*. New York: Oxford University Press.

Werner, C. M., I. Altman, D. Oxley, and L. M. Haggard. 1987. "People, Place, and Time: A Transactional Analysis of Neighborhoods." In *Advances in Personal Relationships*, vol. 1, 243–275. Greenwich, CT: JAI Press.

White, Garland F., Randy R. Gainey, and Ruth A. Triplett. 2015. "Alcohol Outlets and Neighborhood Crime: A Longitudinal Analysis." *Crime and Delinquency* 61 (6):851–872. doi: 10.1177/0011128712466386.

Wikström, Per-Olof H., Dietrich Oberwittler, Kyle Treiber, and Beth Hardie. 2012. *Breaking Rules: The Social and Situational Dynamics of Young People's Urban Crime*. Oxford: Oxford University Press.

Yang, Yong, Ana V. Diez Roux, Amy H. Auchincloss, Daniel A. Rodriguez, and Daniel G. Brown. 2011. "A Spatial Agent-Based Model for the Simulation of Adults' Daily Walking within a City." *American Journal of Preventive Medicine* 40 (3):353–361. doi: http://dx.doi.org/10.1016/j.amepre.2010.11.017.

Zhu, L., D. M. Gorman, and S. Horel. 2004. "Alcohol Outlet Density and Violence: A Geospatial Analysis." *Alcohol and Alcoholism* 39 (4):369–375.

CHAPTER 4

THE INDIVIDUAL PERSPECTIVE

LUCIA SUMMERS AND ROB T. GUERETTE

4.1 Introduction

Environmental criminology is primarily interested in understanding how the physical, situational environment works to promote or inhibit offending. Less concerned with individual offender dispositions that are the focus of traditional criminology, the environmental perspective is instead interested in understanding individual situational decision-making and its resulting behavior patterns. Indeed, it is difficult to understand how the environment contributes to crime without understanding the individual perspective of potential offenders and victims. In other words, when environmental criminologists study the individual, it is not to determine why certain people may be at greater risk of engaging in crime behavior generally; rather, the focus is on understanding how and why offenders may choose to carry out specific crimes at a given point in time and why certain individuals, systems, or products become likely targets for crime. In doing so, environmental criminology treats motivations for offending as normative rather than defective, and assumes that much crime is the product of fundamental human needs and desires. Because of this, the potential for individuals to offend is assumed to be constantly present across any given population. It is therefore the intersection of individuals—both as potential offenders and victims—and offending opportunities within the situational landscape that is seen to play a larger, sometimes causal, role in determining the occurrence of crime.

Understanding how offenders find or come in contact with crime opportunities and how they perceive victim and target vulnerabilities is useful for explaining the influence of the environment on crime. At the same time, the nature of victim behaviors, product characteristics, and system procedures also inform the study of offending patterns.

The importance of understanding the manifestation of crime within the intersection of offenders, victims, and the environment serves to illuminate possibilities for preventing crime through the alteration of the situational landscape, a primary goal of environmental criminology.

In this chapter, we consider how offenders and victims make use of space and how variation in their patterns of movement influences the occurrence of crime. We examine examples of individual offender decision-making, such as how past experience informs future decisions (both legitimate and illegal), and how individual activity patterns can influence the broader social processes that take place within the environment. The first section starts with an exploration of the fundamental theoretical frameworks upon which environmental criminology is based. We then discuss how these frameworks inform various aspects of our endeavor to understand crime, the particular benefits of each theoretical approach, and how they complement and contrast with one another. Particular emphasis is placed on how potential offenders, victims, and others use space, and how this impacts crime patterns. Sections 4.2 and 4.3 discuss specific areas related to offender mobility, namely the journey to crime and displacement. We finish with some concluding thoughts about how the theories and empirical work presented have served to further our understanding of individual-level criminal behavior patterns within the environmental landscape.

4.2 Theoretical Foundations of Offenders and Victims in Place and Time

In explaining crime events, environmental criminology is most centrally grounded in three primary theories that offer to explain the occurrence and resulting patterns of crime events. These theories are the rational choice perspective, the routine activity approach, and crime pattern theory. A fourth theoretical and heuristic framework developed more recently, crime scripting, also extends our ability to understand the commission of crime within the situational environment. Together these theories and approaches aim to explain crime patterns at the macro, meso, and micro levels, and also serve as a basis for drawing predictions for future crime vulnerabilities and for developing sound prevention strategies. In all three of these respects, no one theory holds the ability to provide a complete understanding of crime within the environment. Rather, theories are commonly used together to provide a more complete portrait of how and why crime occurs across the situational landscape. Each theory offers a unique understanding and, where one perspective has a limitation, the other theories serve to fortify it (see Table 4.1).

Table 4.1 Overview of Primary Theoretical Frameworks in Environmental Criminology

Theory	Main concepts	Helps explain . . .	Less suited for explaining . . .
Rational choice perspective (RCP)	Offender choice Effort, risk, reward Choice-structuring properties Bounded rationality	Offenders' victim/target selection Nexus between offender & environment Why specific prevention tactics may work	Aggregate crime trends Offender mobility patterns
Routine activity approach (RAA)	Everyday activities Motivated offender Capable guardian Suitable target	Aggregate crime trends Ambient crime surges Crime within everyday life The basis for crime opportunity reduction strategies Victimization	Offender perceptions Offenders' mobility or target selection
Crime pattern theory (CPT)	Activity nodes, paths, edges Awareness space / cognitive map Crime generators Crime attractors	Offenders' activity spaces Offenders' victim/target selection Offenders' mobility patterns The nature of crime hotspots	Individual offender or victim perceptions Aggregate crime trends or shifts
Crime scripts (CS)	Levels: tracks, scripts, protoscripts, metascripts Preparation Preactivity Activity Postactivity	The sequence of crime How offenders carry out different crimes across place & target Offenders' victim/target selection "Pinch points" for interventions	Aggregated crime concentrations or trends Offender mobility patterns Offender or victim perceptions

4.2.1 Rational Choice Perspective

The rational choice perspective of offending (RCP; Clarke and Cornish 1985, 2001) is mostly recognized as an explanation for understanding how and why offenders decide to carry out crime. It is comprised of two types of decision models. The first is the criminal participation model, which focuses on an individual's decision to engage in crime generally as a means for satisfying one's needs and wants. This first model has received less attention from environmental criminologists, as it does not focus on the crime event. Instead, it mainly draws on the macro, sociological influences that may lead to criminality. These include differential opportunity structures, social learning, peer group influences, and social bonds, among others. The second RCP model, which is known as the crime event decision model, is devoted to understanding the factors that influence an offender's decision to engage in a *specific* criminal act at a *particular* place and time, and is therefore central to environmental criminology.

Regardless of whether an individual is making a decision to engage in crime more generally or in a specific criminal act, the RCP argues that assessments of the effort, risk, and rewards involved are made before arriving at a conclusion. Where the effort and risk outweigh the anticipated rewards, crime is less likely to occur. Likewise, where the perceived effort and risk are low relative to the anticipated reward, crime is much more likely. A central assumption in both decision models is the idea of free will and the ability of individuals to choose their behavior. The RCP is also in line with the utilitarian perspective of human behavior, which posits that individuals generally act to maximize pleasure and minimize pain. Thus, offenders act on opportunities to commit crime when it is perceived that the benefits outweigh the potential consequences of doing so. Importantly, the theory recognizes that offender choices are often rudimentary, as they can be carried out in haste, based on limited or imperfect information, and/or deliberated while impaired. This so-called "bounded rationality" highlights the practical realm of offender decision-making within the situational environment. It also helps to explain the occurrence of crime under seemingly irrational situations as perceived by outsiders.

The crime event decision model helps us to understand the nexus between offenders and the environment. It explains why some targets are victimized and others are not, and why some locations experience more crime than others. Because offenders perceive and assess anticipated effort, risks, and rewards for offending as they interact with the environmental landscape, the environment is said to contain *choice-structuring properties* that facilitate where and when crime will likely occur. Thus, crime vulnerabilities in the landscape will be commonly perceived by any given potential offender. It is this risk heterogeneity that sometimes gives rise to certain targets experiencing what is referred to as *repeat victimization* (Pease 1998; Polvi et al. 1991; also see Ignatans and Pease in this volume). For example, properties located on corner plots have been shown to be more attractive to offenders, due to easier access and exit (Cromwell, Olson, and Avery 1991).

Oftentimes, it is not just the originally victimized target itself that experiences an increased subsequent risk, but also similar targets (virtual repeats) and those nearby (near repeats). *Virtual repeat victimization* occurs when a target is chosen by an offender based on its similarity to a previously victimized target (Pease 1998; also see Summers 2010). An example of virtual repeat victimization is a shoplifter targeting stores from a given chain, as they have similar layouts (and hence similar associated benefits, risk, and effort), or a car thief pursuing a specific make and model over and over. Although sometimes similar targets are close to each other in space (e.g., residences with identical layouts), virtual repeat targets can be far away from each other, as it is the similar target characteristics that place them at increased risk, rather than their location. In contrast, *near repeat victimization* relates to the increase in risk that is experienced by the targets that are in close proximity of the originally victimized target (Johnson et al. 2007; Morgan 2001; Townsley, Homel, and Chaseling 2003). This risk increase is thought to occur because offenders become more familiar with the environment within which both the originally victimized target and nearby targets are located, which minimizes the associated risks and makes them aware of alternative crime opportunities (Bernasco 2008; Johnson, Summers, and Pease 2009). In either case, prior exposure is assumed to reduce the effort and risk for the offender in subsequent victimizations, thus making it more likely for him or her to offend against such targets in future.

The RCP also helps to frame understanding and the identification of crime prevention tactics, particularly those that involve some form of *situational crime prevention* (SCP; Clarke 1992, 1995; also see Welsh and Taheri in this volume). Situational prevention techniques mainly aim to either increase the perceived effort or risk of committing a particular offense, or reduce the anticipated rewards, thus tipping the offender decision-making toward desistance. Some authors have argued that SCP does not prevent crime, but rather displaces it to other places (spatial displacement), time periods (temporal), or targets, or that offenders adapt by using alternative methods (tactical), or engaging in different crime types (functional; Reppetto 1976). However, research has shown displacement is not inevitable and, when it occurs, it tends to be partial, rather than absolute (Bowers et al. 2011; Guerette and Bowers 2009; Hesseling 1994; Johnson, Guerette, and Bowers 2012). Indeed, recent reviews of the effectiveness of SCP have concluded that situational techniques appeared to be effective in around 75% of the evaluation studies considered (Guerette 2009; Johnson, Guerette, and Bowers 2012), even after controlling for any displacement effects (Guerette and Bowers 2009; for more on displacement, again see Welsh and Taheri in this volume).

Another criticism leveled at situational crime prevention, and the RCP more generally, is that these approaches are not relevant to violent crime, which is often an expressive and/or irrational act (e.g., Hayward 2007; Miethe et al. 1987; Trasler 1986; Tunnell 2002). An effective rebuttal to this suggestion was provided by Farrell (2010), who discussed how situational crime prevention can be successfully employed to deal with expressive crimes, including football hooliganism (Madensen and Eck 2008) and child sexual abuse (Wortley and Smallbone 2006; also see Smallbone, Marshall, and Wortley 2013). Further evidence supporting the effectiveness of SCP in preventing violent crime has emerged in regard to barroom violence (Graham 2009), drive-by gang-related shootings (Lasley 1998), sexual violence against women (see Leclerc et al. 2016), and prison-based violence (Wortley and Summers 2005), to name but a few examples.

However, while the RCP gives insight into individual offenders and how they interact with the situational environment, the theory is less suited for understanding aggregate crime trends and offender mobility patterns. The routine activity approach is stronger in this respect.

4.2.2 Routine Activity Approach

The routine activity approach (RAA; Cohen and Felson 1979) provides both a macro- and meso-level perspective on crime events and trends within a framework that identifies the necessary elements for crime events. The RAA is an ecological theory that specifies that, in order for crime to occur, three elements must coincide in time and space: the absence of a capable guardian; the presence of a suitable target; and the presence of a motivated offender. Absent any of these elements, crime is much less likely.

Like the rational choice perspective, the RAA views crime as normative. Thus, motivated offenders are simply those who have decided that engaging in crime is an acceptable way to satisfy one's needs and wants. What dictates whether or not crime will occur is tied less to the motivation of offenders than to the intersection of those individuals with suitable targets in time and place in the absence of capable guardianship (for a detailed discussion of guardianship, see Reynald's chapter in this volume). In the development of this theory, the authors argued that rising US crime trends in 1947–1974 were not the result of changes in the number or disposition of offenders, but rather the proliferation of suitable targets coupled with absentee guardianship in society. Following the same logic, decreasing crime trends in the 1990s and 2000s have been attributed to fewer crime opportunities within communities (Farrell et al. 2011).

The theory also argues that crime is a common part of everyday life. Sensational and extreme crime events that are frequently showcased in popular media are the exception compared to more common petty thefts and other crimes that occur on a daily basis and which largely go unreported. Accordingly, the convergence of motivated offenders with suitable targets usually takes place during the course of the normal daily activities of both offenders and victims. Because the theory also highlights the role of victim activities as a conduit for crime, it is often identified as a theory of victimization and has been used for explaining differential victimization rates.

It is also important to note here that, within various routine activities, different opportunities for specific crime types exist. Thus, the occurrence of crime will be regulated to some degree by the convergence of an offender who is motivated to commit a specific type of crime and the suitable context for that particular crime type. Not all places or times offer the same opportunities or provide the same availability of targets; nor do all offenders possess the same skill sets or knowledge of how to carry out all varieties of crime. Moreover, some crime targets are fixed (such as residences and businesses), while others are more transient and tend to move about (such as motor vehicles, cell phones, individuals, etc.). Other crime types, such as drug and prostitution markets, are strongly associated with specific locations within communities. These features therefore dictate the types and nature of crime patterns that will manifest across any given environmental landscape.

The RAA offers several contributions for understanding crime within the environment. First, as previously mentioned, the theory offers an explanation for increases and decreases in crime across society. On a more focused level, it also helps to understand ambient crime surges within particular areas, such as recreational and retail districts as well as entertainment and sporting venues. Second, because it highlights the normalcy of crime within everyday activities, it helps us to understand the processes by which offenders and victims converge and how offending opportunities become known to motivated offenders. The RAA also explains the processes that lead to victimization, that is, those routine activities that place suitable targets in time and place among likely offenders where capable guardianship is absent. Third, the framework identifies the importance of time as a necessary ingredient for the production of crime. Accordingly, it helps us to understand temporal patterns and variations in crime frequency. Finally, the RAA is useful for situational crime prevention, as it identifies possibilities for practitioners to implement prevention tactics that seek to establish or strengthen capable guardianship; remove, control access to, or minimize attractiveness of potential targets; or otherwise control motivated offenders. Yet, unlike the rational choice perspective, the theory does not offer explanations for offender and victim perceptions, nor does it fully explain offenders' mobility patterns or target selections, the latter of which are better understood by crime pattern theory.

4.2.3 Crime Pattern Theory

Crime pattern theory (CPT; Brantingham and Brantingham 1981, 1993) was developed to understand the spatial distribution and patterning of crime. Building on the rational choice perspective and the routine activity approach, CPT argues that crime occurs where crime opportunities overlap with offenders' awareness spaces. Within a crime opportunity surface, offenders are more likely to commit crime in areas they know and frequent, for two main reasons: (*a*) unless they know and frequent the area, they may not become aware of any crime opportunities present; and (*b*) a certain degree of familiarity is required for their risk of apprehension to be minimized. While the RAA specifies the need for temporal congruence, CPT focuses primarily on spatial overlap. Because of this, both theories work best together to better explain the occurrence of crime within a spatiotemporal context.

The term *awareness space* simply refers to the areas that are familiar to offenders. Crime pattern theory posits that the nature of offenders' everyday spatial behavior does not significantly deviate from the spatial behavior of the population at large (Brantingham and Brantingham 1981). For this reason, much can be learned by drawing from the human mobility and spatial cognition literature. Research in this area shows that aggregate mobility patterns are mostly made up of short, everyday trips relating to going to work or school, grocery shopping, and the like (see Toole et al. 2015). These short, everyday trips have been shown to display great regularity, both spatially and temporally (González, Hidalgo, and Barabási 2008; Lu et al. 2013; Schneider et al. 2013; Song et al. 2010; also see Bernasco in this volume), which helps in our efforts to understand and predict crime patterns.

Not only do individuals exhibit great regularity in the places they frequent, but also the *routes* taken to reach them (Toole et al. 2015). The process by which an individual selects a particular route from one location to another is known as *wayfinding* in the spatial cognition field (Golledge 1999). Wayfinding is directed and motivated by the principle of least resistance, especially for routine journeys (e.g., going to work, grocery shopping), and research has shown optimal routes are selected and adhered to after just a few trips (Rogers 1970).

It is through visiting these places repeatedly, and reaching them using those same routes, that mental maps—and awareness spaces—develop, through a process known as *route-based environmental learning* (Golledge 1999; also see Hanson 1984 and

MacEachren 1992). As the level of interaction with the physical environment expands, so does spatial knowledge. Mental maps, in turn, guide our choice of destinations and wayfinding, which makes the relationship between spatial knowledge and spatial behavior dynamic and reciprocal (Bovy and Stern 1990; Golledge 1999).

In line with this, CPT argues that an offender's awareness space exists around his or her *activity nodes*, which are the primary places that such an offender occupies in his or her daily activities (such as residence, place of work, and locations of recreation), and the *paths* that are regularly taken to travel from one activity node to another. The assumption is, therefore, that offenders, just like everyone else, develop their spatial knowledge via legitimate experience or use of space. In some cases, however, offenders have been reported to engage in spatial exploration, where an offender makes a decision to familiarize him- or herself with a yet-unknown area with the intention to commit crimes there in the future (Cromwell, Olson, and Avary 1991; also see Rengert and Wasilchick 2000).

While individuals' activity nodes are likely to be specific to the circumstances of those particular individuals (e.g., where they live, work, go to school, etc.), there are certain places that possess some degree of collective relevance and familiarity in that many people would choose to visit them. These may then be regarded as unique and common nodes, respectively. Obvious examples of common nodes are city centers and commercial business districts, which are known to contain large concentrations of retail and entertainment locations and are, therefore, likely to be frequented by the public at large. Oftentimes, common nodes become *crime generators*, which are defined as places that attract potential offenders and victims for purposes unrelated to crime yet generate opportunities for offending (Brantingham and Brantingham 1995; also, for a recent review of land use and crime, see Groff and Lockwood 2014). Where offenders travel to a specific place because they know that crime opportunities exist, the place becomes a *crime attractor*; examples of crime attractors include known street-level drug and prostitution markets.

The street and public transport network often influence where common nodes such as commercial premises are located, as business owners aim to place these at highly accessible locations so as to maximize their patronage (Peponis 2004; Hillier 2007). In a similar vein, the physical configuration of the street network can make some routes more likely to be chosen than others (e.g., if they allow the individual to reach a given destination more quickly or directly; Freeman 1977). From a CPT perspective, it is those paths that are more frequently used and therefore better known by offenders that are most vulnerable to crime, a hypothesis that has been substantiated by empirical research (e.g., Davis and Johnson 2015; Summers and Johnson 2016; also see Davies and Bowers in this volume).

From a RAA perspective, however, the heightened use of these paths means a greater availability of potential offenders and victims but also of potential guardians, which is why sometimes crime is likely to occur not on busy streets, but instead on more isolated nearby locations, in what have been referred to as *critical intensity zones* (Angel 1968). The likely scenario involves an offender identifying potential targets within a busy street and then following them until they reach an isolated location, where the risk of apprehension is likely to be smaller. This is much more efficient than trying to identify a suitable target on an isolated street, where fewer potential targets may come about and where the offender might also be conspicuous.

These critical intensity zones are also an example of what Brantingham and Brantingham (1993) referred to as "edges." Edges delimit areas that are qualitatively different and that tend to be associated with a heightened crime risk, through multiple mechanisms. For instance, in an edge separating a commercial busy street from a quieter residential area, it might be commonplace for nonresident shoppers to slightly permeate the neighborhood (e.g., when parking their vehicles), so that locals residing close to the main street are not as able to identify and challenge strangers as those living further away from it.

Crime pattern theory does a great deal to inform understanding of the mobility patterns of both offenders and victims. It provides a backcloth for understanding not only offenders' activity spaces but also victim and target selection within a given physical space. Like the rational choice perspective and the routine activity approach, CPT is a foundational theory of the situational crime prevention framework, as it helps us to identify locations where crime prevention tactics could be most useful. Crime pattern theory also helps to explain the circumstances responsible for high-crime places, information that can assist in the development of prevention tactics that are relevant to the nature of the problem.

4.2.4 Crime Scripts

Although situational prevention techniques can be developed based on the principles of increasing the effort and the risk associated with the commission of the crime, as well as minimizing the expected rewards, the appropriate techniques for each specific crime type can only be identified after the dynamics of the offense act are properly understood. Crime scripting (CS) was developed for this very purpose: to assist in better understanding the processes by which offenders carry out specific crime types (Cornish 1994). At its essence, CS recognizes that behavior patterns tend to be systematic. Crime scripts are usually based on past experiences and tend to be repeated as long as they continue to prove functional and effective. When behavior scripts encounter problems or inhibitors, adaptations and learning of new behavioral processes are undertaken (Tedeschi and Felson 1994). Several levels of crime script specificity have been identified, namely metascripts, protoscripts, scripts, and tracks. Metascripts and protoscripts are the most general and identify the type of crime, such as theft of property (metascript) and robbery (protoscript). Scripts and tracks relate to more specific levels of description, such as robbery from an individual (script) and subway muggings (tracks). Tracks are the most useful for behavioral sequencing and for identifying pinch points for prevention activities. Within crime scripts, certain components are identified, much as in theatrics. These include scenes, paths, actions, roles, props, and locations.

In terms of understanding the behavioral steps required to commit crime, four general steps have been identified, namely preparation, preactivity, activity, and postactivity (Tompson and Chainey 2011). These four steps are a more recent synthesis of Cornish's (1994) initial breakdown of nine steps.[1] Preparation is similar to staging, and refers to the activities involved when an offender is getting ready to engage in a specific crime type. For instance, for a convenience store robbery, obtaining a gun or knife and a mask to conceal the offender's identity are possible preparations. Preactivities are those processes that lead up to the actual event, such as traveling to an area and searching for a suitable convenience store, while the activity step relates to carrying out the crime itself. Postactivities are the offender's behaviors that take place after the commission of the crime, such as fleeing the area or disposing of the stolen goods.

The addition of the CS perspective to the three foundational theories of environmental criminology helps further our understanding of where and when crime occurs. Not only must offenders be aware of the availability of suitable crime targets (within their awareness space), but they also must possess the motivation and understanding of the relevant crime script in order to carry out the criminal act. Where some crime types are available but are not within the motivation or script knowledge base of the intersecting offender, crime is less likely. To put the idea more broadly, we can say that motivated offenders who intersect in time and place with suitable targets in the absence of capable guardianship, must also possess the knowledge of the crime script behaviors necessary to carry out the crime. The successful completion of past crime events increases the likelihood that offenders will repeatedly target the same or similar targets in the same or similar areas using the same or similar techniques (i.e., scripts), engaging in repeat and near repeat victimization.

4.3 The Offender's Journey to Crime

As discussed earlier, CPT argues that offenders commit crime within their awareness spaces, which are based on their activity nodes, the paths joining these nodes, and the areas around them. For most offenders—and individuals in general—the home is the main activity node, as this is the location where they usually start off and where they eventually return at the end of the day. This is supported by empirical human mobility research which shows that more than 50% of daily trips are home-base generated (Golledge 1999).

In general, the assumption is made that, the closer a place is to an individual's home, the more likely it is that such a place is known by such an individual. In this way, distance from the home is used as a proxy for familiarity, a key concept in CPT. Within the criminological literature, the distance between an offender's home and the location where he or she commits a crime is known as the *journey to crime* (JTC).

Distance is a measure of impedance (or effort), so the hypothesis that offenders are more likely to commit crime closer to their homes is consistent with the rational choice perspective, and with the least-effort principle (Zipf 1949) more generally. Support for this hypothesis has been forthcoming from studies that demonstrate that the distance between an offender's home and the locations where he or she commits crime are typically short (e.g., Rengert and Wasilchick 2000; Rossmo 2000). To elaborate, at least when JTCs are aggregated, the data suggest that the chances of an offender committing a crime at a particular location decrease exponentially as the distance of that location from his or her home increases. A buffer can sometimes be observed around the home location (see Figure 4.1), which has been interpreted as being the result of the offender avoiding the area immediately surrounding his or her home in an attempt to avoid recognition and potential consequent apprehension (Rossmo 1995). The relationship between criminal behavior and distance from the offender's home is "one of the most fundamental relationships in theoretical environmental criminology" (Rengert, Piquero, and Jones 1999, p. 429).

Although the JTC distance decay function has been argued to be a statistical artifact resulting from aggregating crime trips across offenders who have varying spatial ranges of criminal activity (Van Koppen and De Keijser 1997; Smith, Bond, and Townsley 2009), *prolific* offenders' JTCs have been shown to correspond to a distance decay distribution at the individual offender level (Townsley and Sidebottom 2010). In such cases, offenders appear to travel away from their homes in various directions, conforming to a radial structure with buffered distance decay; as one of the interviewed offenders in Summers, Johnson, and Rengert's (2010) study explained, "it'll be a mile that way, a mile that way, a mile that way, a mile that way in a circle . . . the police actually had a map of all my burglaries and it was just like that, a circle getting closer to the house."

However, individuals—unlike most nonhuman species—usually have more than one spatial anchor (Golledge 1999), which is consistent with the framework proposed by CPT. Secondary anchors may include previous residence locations (Bernasco 2010), the homes of significant others (Wiles and Costello 2000), and, for drug-using offenders, the places where they buy their drugs (Rengert 1996). Nevertheless, most empirical

FIGURE 4.1 Buffered distance decay function

studies focus on the offender's home as the sole anchor, as information regarding secondary bases is not usually forthcoming.

Journeys to crime are often said to be shorter for violence than for property crime (e.g., Phillips 1980; Rhodes and Conley 1981; for reviews of JTC research, see Rossmo 2000 and Groff and McEwen 2006). But the figures relating to violent crime JTCs should be interpreted with caution, as analyses often involve domestic violence offenses that are committed in the offender's own home. When these cases are excluded, the mean (or median) distances traveled are likely to be on a par with those for property crime. To illustrate, we draw on Van Patten and Delhauer's (2007) study of sexual homicide in Los Angeles County for the 25-year period 1980–2004 (107 offenses). The mean and median JTCs for all offenses were 43.68 and 0.79 miles, respectively; when the 21 homicides that took place at the offender's home were removed, these figures increased to 54.21 (mean) and 2.43 (median) miles.

Longer JTCs are sometimes observed when the offender is anticipating greater rewards (Morselli and Royer 2008; Vandeviver, Van Daele, and Vander Beken 2015). This has been described by Felson (2006) as *strategic foraging* and is consistent with the rational choice perspective, as the increased effort associated with traveling further distances would be compensated by the higher reward in the cost-benefit assessment the offender is thought to perform. Higher levels of effort—and consequent lower chances of crime occurring—may also be expected for trips requiring physical barriers such as rivers and motorways to be crossed (Clare, Fernandez, and Morgan 2009). Social barriers can also be influential. For instance, offenders have been shown to be more likely to commit offenses in areas with ethnic and socioeconomic profiles similar to their own (e.g., a white offender may favor a predominantly white area; Bernasco and Block 2009; Bernasco and Nieuwbeerta 2005; Carter and Hill 1979; Clare, Fernandez, and Morgan 2009; Reynald et al. 2008).

The findings regarding the JTC, the buffered distance decay, and the arguments of crime pattern theory more generally have led to the development of geographic profiling (Rossmo 2000). Geographic profiling is an investigative tool that analyzes the locations of crimes within a series to determine the most probable area of offender residence. A geoprofile, therefore, resembles a hotspot map but, rather than displaying crime density (i.e., where crime is most prevalent), it displays probability densities of offender residence (i.e., where the concerned offender is most likely to have his or her base), which are estimated based on where such an offender committed his or her crimes. Geographic profiles are used to prioritize suspects and tips, and/or to focus investigative efforts (e.g., door-to-door enquiries), and work best when used in conjunction with other investigative strategies (Rossmo 2014). The technique has been applied in criminal investigations of serial homicide, rape, robbery, arson, bombing, burglary, and even terrorism (see also Rossmo in this volume).

Some have argued that distance may not be a sufficient measure when explaining human movement, which is a shortcoming of JTC. As Toole et al. (2015) argue, what lies between an origin and a destination must influence how far the individual travels; in their own words, it would be unreasonable to expect "the same flow of people being estimated between two locations whether there is an entire city or an empty desert between them" (p. 26). This shortcoming led scholars to favor alternative models of human mobility, including the intervening opportunities model (which considers the opportunity surface; Stouffer 1940) and the radiation model (which estimates the probability of being "absorbed" before reaching the originally set destination; Simini et al. 2012). A study conducted by Elffers et al. (2008), however, concluded that controlling for intervening opportunities did not significantly enhance predictions of offender mobility.

A final consideration relates to the mobility of potential targets. When potential targets are mobile—such as individual persons or vehicles—the mobility of the victimized target also needs to be studied to fully understand the spatial distributions of crime observed. In the context of homicide, this has led to the development of a mobility triangle classification, which categorizes offenses based on the relative location of the crime site, the offender's home, and the victim's home (Groff and McEwen 2007; Tita and Griffiths 2005). Even for crime types involving stationary targets (e.g., residential burglary), the mobility of the victims—and other potential guardians—is relevant, as they will need to be absent for the crime to be committed (in most cases). Based on the RAA, most residential burglaries are expected to occur during the day on workdays (when most occupants are at work) and commercial burglaries at night (when the business is closed; see Felson and Eckert 2015).

4.4 Offender Mobility and Displacement

A common concern among those interested in efforts to prevent crime through opportunity reduction approaches is that of crime displacement. As was explained earlier, crime displacement is the relocation of crime following focused prevention efforts. Geographic or spatial displacement is the type that is most commonly thought of, but there are also other forms such as tactical, temporal, target, and crime type (the latter is also referred to as offense or functional displacement; Reppetto 1976). While it is known that sometimes displacement occurs, research has shown that it is not absolute and, oftentimes, it does not arise at all following sound prevention activities. Indeed, the opposite of displacement, diffusion of crime control benefits (Clarke and Weisburd, 1994), appears to be just as likely an outcome as the re-placement of crime (see Bowers et al. 2011; Guerette and Bowers 2009; Johnson, Guerette, and Bowers 2012).

Of more importance here is the theoretical understanding of when and where displacement is likely to occur and the explanation for why it does not. In a general sense, displacement is expected if opportunities for crime are evenly present across space and time. If, however, the presence of crime opportunities is heterogeneous, then displacement should be less likely. More specifically, there are three factors that work together to determine whether or not crime will displace in the aftermath of situational prevention efforts. These include the presence of other crime opportunities, offender familiarity, and offender motivation (for a more extended discussion, see Guerette 2009). Each of these three factors is grounded in the foundational theories discussed previously. Where opportunities for offending are shut down, offenders will be more likely to displace their crime activity if there are alternative similar crime targets in nearby areas. This is because areas close to the previous offending site are more likely to be known by offenders (i.e., fall within their awareness space) and accessing the new area will not require much more effort or risk than what was originally required. As already stated, spatial familiarity also implies lower risks for offenders, as they can more readily identify entry and exit points that will allow them to access and escape crime sites more effectively.

Displacement is more likely when offenders already have some familiarity with other crime targets, places, times, and tactics (Eck 1993). While this displacement may be more likely to occur in areas close to the previous offending location, it could also occur in areas further away insofar as they provide similar opportunities and offenders are familiar with their existence. The idea that areas close to previous offending sites are more likely to be familiar to offenders than areas further away has been termed familiarity decay (Eck 1993). Thus, the likelihood of displacement occurring decreases as the distance from the former crime site increases. Offenders will be less likely to offend outside of their awareness spaces, as this carries greater risks and requires more effort to learn of new locations, targets, and optimal times.

For other forms of displacement, such as target and tactical, offenders will be more likely to select other targets and use tactics that are similar to those that have been used before. In other words, they will be more likely to displace to targets and tactics that they are most familiar with, and least likely to select targets that are different from those they have targeted before or those which require different tactics or skill sets. Since most offenders learn how to commit crime from peer groups and other delinquent associations as well as from direct and indirect experiences (Cornish 1994), it is the offender's motivation level that will determine the likelihood of displacement when familiar alternative crime opportunities are limited.

When unfamiliar with alternative crime opportunities, the more common opportunistic offender will be more likely to desist, while highly motivated offenders will be more likely to develop new skill sets and to search for new crime opportunities. Highly motivated offenders, such as those with a drug addiction, will be more likely to select other crime types and targets that sustain their addiction. Career criminals will also be more likely to displace their criminal activity in comparison to opportunistic offenders. In a similar vein, instrumental offenders, or rather those motivated by monetary gain, will be more likely to displace to other crime targets that offer financial benefits compared to those offenders motivated by emotion (i.e., expressive offenders), given that emotional motivations tend to be highly contextual.

For some of the same reasons why displacement could occur, there are also many reasons why crime displacement will not occur. To extend the ideas already mentioned: displacement will not occur when an offender's knowledge is bounded as it relates to committing other varieties of crime outside existing skill sets. They are also less likely to offend in unfamiliar areas. When offending opportunities are removed through prevention activities, opportunistic offenders may desist, while highly motivated offenders require more time to develop new crime opportunities. Thus, in the short term at least, crime displacement would be limited.

Two additional factors inhibit crime displacement. First, some offenders are limited in the amount of time that they have to commit crime within their daily routines. Thus, when faced with blocked offending opportunities, they may be unable to displace their criminal behavior within their available time frame. Second, oftentimes, illicit markets are informally governed by opposing criminal groups such as gangs or pimps. When illicit markets are shut down, it is unlikely that offenders will relocate to other areas that are within other protected turf zones (Weisburd et al. 2006). In short, offenders' decisions whether to displace their criminal activity will be shaped by a number of circumstances found among other crime targets, types, times, and places (Cornish and Clarke 1987).

It should also be noted that much of the thinking on whether displacement will occur is tied to theoretical perspectives on the nature of offending. Dispositional theories of offending would suggest that displacement is highly likely since offenders are compelled to offend as a result of societal forces that have instilled "predispositions" or "propensities" for committing crime. Yet that view does not recognize the role and the influence that opportunities for crime play in the situational environment. According to theories of environmental criminology, because decisions on when, where, and how to commit crime are the product of reasoning and choice, offenders will choose not to displace their crime behavior when the risks and effort of committing new crimes are no longer worth the anticipated reward. Also because of this reasoning, when criminal opportunities are blocked, obtaining one's needs and desires through legitimate activities may become more appealing, resulting in desistance from crime.

In a similar way, these features also explain the presence of the diffusion of crime control benefits, which results in reductions of crime in areas surrounding places where the intervention was targeted (Clarke and Weisburd 1994). Diffusion is likely when offenders are uncertain of the scope of the intervention strategy that produces a perceived increased risk. This perception of heightened risk leads to discouragement since it offsets the certainty of reward from carrying out a particular crime in relation to the effort and risk (Clarke and Weisburd 1994).

4.5 Conclusion

The aim of this chapter was to consider how individuals perceive, make use of, and relate to their environment, and how this shapes spatial and temporal distributions of crime. Rather than concentrating on the environment per se, which is the focus of other chapters in this volume, the goal here was to emphasize the importance of understanding how individual offenders *interact* with an environment.

We described how the rational choice perspective posits that offenders do not commit crime anywhere or anytime, but instead make decisions as to how, where, and when to commit crime, based on a pseudorational assessment of the associated effort, risk, and anticipated rewards, which tend to vary across space and time. Routine activity theory argues individuals' daily activities shape the relative positioning in space and time of potential offenders, victims, and guardians, and how opportunities for crime arise when certain configurations are realized. Building on these two perspectives, crime pattern theory states that a given offender will commit crime only where such opportunities overlap with his or her awareness and/or activity space (where the effort and risk associated with the commission of the crime are potentially lower), and that such space exists around the offender's activity nodes (e.g., home, work, entertainment) and the paths that join them. Finally, crime scripts emphasize that offenders must also possess offense-specific procedural knowledge, which develops as they commit crime and more generally interact with their environment.

We have also borrowed concepts from general theories of human mobility, and applied these to criminal behavior. This was based on the environmental criminology premise that offenders are no different from the general population in how they relate to their environment. These theories, and the environmental criminology theories presented, provide sound explanations for phenomena such as repeat victimization and near repeats, offenders committing crime near their homes (i.e., the journey-to-crime literature), and how offenders' past experiences—both legitimate and illegal—shape their situational and spatial decision-making.

This chapter was primarily focused on the individual-level theories and perspectives that relate to understanding crime patterns in the situational environment. Rather than providing a comprehensive review of relevant empirical findings, the goal here was to articulate why crime can be expected to conform to certain spatiotemporal patterns, from the viewpoint of the individual offender. In doing so, our aim was to set the stage for subsequent chapters in the book that elaborate on the various topics that comprise the study of environmental criminology.

Note

1. Cornish's (1994) nine behavioral steps consisted of preparation, entry, precondition, instrumental precondition, instrumental initiation, instrumental actualization, doing, postcondition, and exit.

References

Angel, Shlomo. 1968. "Discouraging Crime through City Planning." Working Paper No. 75, Center for Planning and Development Research, University of California at Berkeley.

Bernasco, Wim. 2008. "Them Again? Same-Offender Involvement in Repeat and Near Repeat Burglaries." *European Journal of Criminology* 5(4): 411–431.

Bernasco, Wim. 2010. "A Sentimental Journey to Crime: Effects of Residential History on Crime Location Choice." *Criminology* 48(2): 389–416.

Bernasco, Wim, and Richard Block. 2009. "Where Offenders Choose to Attack: A Discrete Choice Model of Robberies in Chicago." *Criminology* 47(1): 93–130.

Bernasco, Wim, and Paul Nieuwbeerta. 2005. "How Do Residential Burglars Select Target Areas? A New Approach to the Analysis of Criminal Location Choice." *British Journal of Criminology* 44(3): 296–315.

Bovy, Piet H. L., and Eliahu Stern. 1990. *Route Choice: Wayfinding in Transport Networks*. Dordrecht: Kluwer Academic.

Bowers, Kate J., Shane D. Johnson, Rob T. Guerette, Lucia Summers, and Suzanne Poynton. 2011. "Spatial Displacement and Diffusion of Benefits among Geographically Focused Policing Initiatives: A Meta-analytical Review." *Journal of Experimental Criminology* 7(4): 347–374.

Brantingham, Patricia L., and Paul J. Brantingham. 1993. "Nodes, Paths and Edges: Considerations on the Complexity of Crime and the Physical Environment." *Journal of Environmental Psychology* 13(1): 3–28.

Brantingham, Patricia L., and Paul J. Brantingham. 1995. "Criminality of Place: Crime Generators and Crime Attractors." *European Journal on Criminal Policy and Research* 3(3): 5–26.

Brantingham, Paul J., and Patricia L. Brantingham. 1981. *Environmental Criminology*. Prospect Heights, IL: Waveland Press.

Carter, Ronald L., and Kim Q. Hill. 1979. *The Criminal's Image of the City*. New York: Pergamon Press.

Clare, Joseph, John Fernandez, and Frank Morgan. 2009. "Formal Evaluation of the Impact of Barriers and Connectors on Residential Burglars' Macro-Level Offending Location Choices." *Australian and New Zealand Journal of Criminology* 42(2): 139–158.

Clarke, Ronald V. (Ed.). 1992. *Situational Crime Prevention: Successful Case Studies*. New York: Harrow & Heston.

Clarke, Ronald V. 1995. "Situational Crime Prevention." In *Building a Safer Society: Strategic Approaches to Crime Prevention*, edited by Michael Tonry and David Farrington. Chicago: University of Chicago Press.

Clarke, Ronald V., and Derek B. Cornish. 1985. "Modeling Offenders' Decisions: A Framework for Research and Policy." In *Crime and Justice: An Annual Review of Research*, edited by Michael Tonry and Norval Morris. Chicago: University of Chicago Press.

Clarke, Ronald V., and Derek B. Cornish. 2001. "Rational Choice." In *Explaining Criminals and Crime: Essays in Contemporary Criminological Theory*, edited by Raymond Paternoster and Ronet Bachman. Oxford: Oxford University Press.

Clarke, Ronald V., and David Weisburd. 1994. "Diffusion of Crime Control Benefits: Observations on the Reverse of Displacement." In *Crime Prevention Studies*, vol. 2, edited by Ronald V. Clarke. Monsey, NY: Criminal Justice Press.

Cohen, Lawrence E., and Marcus Felson. 1979. "Social Change and Crime Rate Trends: A Routine Activity Approach." *American Sociological Review* 44(4): 588–608.

Cornish, Derek B. 1994. "The Procedural Analysis of Offending and Its Relevance for Situational Prevention." In *Crime Prevention Studies*, vol. 3, edited by Ronald V. Clarke. Monsey, NY: Criminal Justice Press.

Cornish, Derek B., and Ronald V. Clarke. 1987. "Understanding Crime Displacement: An Application of Rational Choice Theory." *Criminology* 25(4): 933–948.

Cromwell, Paul F., James N. Olson, and D'Aunn Wester Avary. (1991) *Breaking and Entering: An Ethnographic Analysis of Burglary*. Newbury Park, CA: Sage.

Davies, Toby, and Shane D. Johnson. 2015. "Examining the Relationship between Road Structure and Burglary Risk via Quantitative Network Analysis." *Journal of Quantitative Criminology* 31(3): 481–507.

Eck, John E. 1993. "The Threat of Crime Displacement." *Criminal Justice Abstracts* 25(3): 527–546.

Elffers, Henk, Danielle Reynald, Margit Averdijk, Wim Bernasco, and Richard Block. 2008. "Modelling Crime Flow between Neighbourhoods in Terms of Distance and of Intervening Opportunities." *Crime Prevention and Community Safety* 10(2): 85–96.

Farrell, Graham. 2010. "Situational Crime Prevention and Its Discontents: Rational Choice and Harm Reduction versus 'Cultural Criminology.'" *Social Policy and Administration* 44(1): 40–66.

Farrell, Graham, Nick Tilley, Andromachi Tseloni, and Jen Mailley. 2011. "The Crime Drop and the Security Hypothesis." *Journal of Research in Crime and Delinquency* 48(2): 147–175.

Felson, Marcus. 2006. *Crime and Human Nature*. Thousand Oaks, CA: Sage.

Felson, Marcus, and Mary Eckert. 2015. *Crime and Everyday Life*. 5th ed. Thousand Oaks, CA: Sage.

Freeman, Linton C. 1977. "A Set of Measures of Centrality Based upon Betweenness." *Sociometry* 40(1): 35–41.

Golledge, Reginald G. 1999. "Human Wayfinding and Cognitive Maps." In *Wayfinding Behavior: Cognitive Mapping and Other Spatial Processes*, edited by Reginald G. Golledge. Baltimore, MA: John Hopkins University Press.

González, Marta C., César A. Hidalgo, and Albert-László Barabási. 2008. "Understanding Individual Human Mobility Patterns." *Nature* 453(5): 779–782.

Graham, Kathryn. 2009. "They Fight Because We Let Them! Applying a Situational Crime Prevention Model to Barroom Violence." *Drug and Alcohol Review* 28(2): 103–109.

Groff, Elizabeth R., and Brian Lockwood. 2014. "Criminogenic Facilities and Crime across Street Segments in Philadelphia: Uncovering Evidence about the Spatial Extent of Facility Influence." *Journal of Research in Crime and Delinquency* 51(3): 277–314.

Groff, Elizabeth R., and Tom McEwen. 2006. *Exploring the Spatial Configuration of Places Related to Homicide Events*. Final Report. Washington, DC: National Institute of Justice.

Groff, Elizabeth R., and Tom McEwen. 2007. "Integrating Distance into Mobility Triangle Typologies." *Social Science Computer Review* 25(2): 210–238.

Guerette, Rob T. 2009. *Analyzing Crime Displacement and Diffusion*. Washington, DC: US Department of Justice, Office of Community Oriented Policing Services.

Guerette, Rob T., and Kate J. Bowers. 2009. "Assessing the Extent of Crime Displacement and Diffusion of Benefits: A Review of Situational Crime Prevention Evaluations." *Criminology* 47(4): 1331–1368.

Hanson, Susan. 1984. "Environmental Cognition and Travel Behavior." In *Geography and the Urban Environment: Cognitive Mapping and Spatial Behavior*, edited by T. David Herbert and Ron J. Johnston. Chicago: Aldine.

Hayward, Keith. 2007. "Situational Crime Prevention and Its Discontents: Rational Choice Theory versus the 'Culture of Now.'" *Social Policy and Administration* 41(3): 232–50.

Hesseling, René. 1994. "Displacement: A Review of the Empirical Literature." In *Crime Prevention Studies*, vol. 3, edited by Ronald V. Clarke. Monsey, NJ: Criminal Justice Press.

Hillier, Bill. 2007. *Space Is the Machine*. Cambridge: Cambridge University Press.

Johnson, Shane D., Wim Bernasco, Kate J. Bowers, Henk Elffers, Jerry Ratcliffe, George Rengert, and Michael Townsley. 2007. "Space-Time Patterns of Risk: A Cross National Assessment of Residential Burglary Victimization." *Journal of Quantitative Criminology* 23(3): 201–219.

Johnson, Shane D., Rob Guerette, and Kate J. Bowers. 2012. "Crime Displacement and Diffusion of Benefits." In *The Oxford Handbook of Crime Prevention*, edited by Brandon Welsh and David Farrington. Oxford: Oxford University Press.

Johnson, Shane D., Lucia Summers, and Ken Pease. 2009. "Offender as Forager? A Direct Test of the Boost Account of Victimization." *Journal of Quantitative Criminology* 25(2), 181–200.

Lasley, James. 1998. "'Designing Out' Gang Homicides and Street Assaults. National Institute of Justice Research in Brief. Washington, DC: US Department of Justice.

Leclerc, Benoit, Yi-Nung Chiu, Jesse Cale, and Alana Cook. 2016. "Sexual Violence against Women through the Lens of Environmental Criminology: Toward the Accumulation of Evidence-Based Knowledge and Crime Prevention." *European Journal on Criminal Policy and Research* 22(4): 593–617. doi 10.1007/s10610-015-9300-z.

Lu, Xin, Erik Wetter, Nita Bharti, Andrew J. Tatem, and Linus Bengtsson. 2013. "Approaching the Limit of Predictability in Human Mobility." *Scientific Reports* 3, article number 2923.

MacEachren, Alan M. 1992. "Application of Environmental Learning Theory to Spatial Knowledge Acquisition from Maps." *Annals of the Association of American Geographers* 82(2): 245–274.

Madensen, Tamara D., and John E. Eck. 2008. *Spectator Violence in Stadiums*. Problem-Oriented Guides for Police, Problem-Specific Guides Series No. 54. Washington, DC: US Department of Justice.

Miethe, Terance D., Mark C. Stafford, and J. Scott Long. 1987. "Social Differentiation in Criminal Victimization: A Test of Routine Activities/Lifestyle Theories." *American Sociological Review* 52(2): 184–194.

Morgan, Frank. 2001. "Repeat Burglary in a Perth Suburb: Indicator of Short-Term or Long-Term Risk." In *Repeat Victimization*, vol. 12 of *Crime Prevention Studies*, edited by Graham Farrell and Ken Pease. Monsey, NY: Criminal Justice Press.

Morselli, Carlo, and Marie-Noële Royer. 2008. "Criminal Mobility and Criminal Achievement." *Journal of Research in Crime and Delinquency* 45(1): 4–21.

Pease, Ken. 1998. *Repeat Victimization: Taking Stock*. London: Home Office.

Peponis, John. 2004. "Space Syntax." *Implications* (InformeDesign newsletter), 4(12): 1–4.

Phillips, Phillip D. 1980. "Characteristics and Typology of the Journey to Crime." In *Crime: A Spatial Perspective*, edited by Daniel E. Georges-Abeyie and Keith D. Harries. New York: Columbia University Press.

Polvi, Natalie, Terah Looman, Charlie Humphries, and Ken Pease. 1991. "The Time Course of Repeat Burglary Victimization." *British Journal of Criminology* 31(4): 411–414.

Rengert, George F. 1996. *The Geography of Illegal Drugs*. Boulder, CO: Westview Press.

Rengert, George F., Alex R. Piquero, and Peter R. Jones. 1999. "Distance Decay Reexamined." *Criminology* 37(2): 427–446.

Rengert, George F., and John Wasilchick. 2000. *Suburban Burglary: A Tale of Two Suburbs*. Springfield, IL: Charles Thomas.

Reppetto, Thomas A. 1976. "Crime Prevention and the Displacement Phenomenon." *Crime and Delinquency* 22(2): 166–177.

Reynald, Danielle, Margit Averdijk, Henk Elffers, and Wim Bernasco. 2008. "Do Social Barriers Affect Urban Crime Trips? The Effect of Ethnic and Economic Neighbourhood Compositions on the Flow of Crime in The Hague, the Netherlands." *Built Environment* 34(1): 21–31.

Rhodes, William M., and Catherine Conly. 1981. "Crime and Mobility: An Empirical Study." In *Environmental Criminology*, edited by Paul J. Brantingham and Patricia L. Brantingham. Prospect Heights, IL: Waveland Press.

Rogers, David S. 1970. "The Role of Search and Learning in Consumer Space Behavior: The Case of Urban Migrants." Master's thesis, Department of Geography, University of Wisconsin, Madison.

Rossmo, D. Kim. 1995. "Multivariate Spatial Profiles as a Tool in Crime Investigation." In *Crime Analysis through Computer Mapping*, edited by C. Rebecca Block, Margaret Dabdoub, and Suzane Fregly. Washington, DC: Police Executive Research Forum.

Rossmo, D. Kim. 2000. *Geographic Profiling*. Boca Raton, FL: CRC Press.

Rossmo, D. Kim. 2014. "Geographic Profiling." In *Encyclopedia of Criminology and Criminal Justice*, edited by Gerben Bruinsma and David Weisburd. New York: Springer.

Schneider, Christian M., Vitaly Belik, Thomas Couronné, Zbigniew Smoreda, and Marta C. González. 2013. "Unravelling Daily Human Mobility Motifs." *Journal of the Royal Society: Interface*, 10, article number 20130246.

Simini, Filippo, Marta C. González, Amos Maritan, and Albert-László Barabási. 2012. "A Universal Model for Mobility and Migration Patterns." *Nature* 484(7392): 96–100.

Smallbone, Stephen, William L. Marshall, and Richard Wortley. 2013. *Preventing Child Sexual Abuse: Evidence, Policy and Practice*. 2nd ed. London: Routledge.

Smith, William, John W. Bond, and Michael Townsley. 2009. "Determining How Journeys-to-Crime Vary: Measuring Inter-and Intra-offender Crime Trip Distributions." In *Putting Crime in Its Place*, edited by David Weisburd, Wim Bernasco, and Gerben J. N. Bruinsma. New York: Springer.

Song, Chaoming, Zehui Qu, Nicholas Blum, and Albert-László Barabási. 2010. "Limits of Predictability in Human Mobility." *Science*, 327(5968): 1018–1021.

Stouffer, Samuel A. 1940. "Intervening Opportunities: A Theory Relating Mobility and Distance." *American Sociological Review* 5(6): 845–867.

Summers, Lucia. 2010. "Virtual Repeats and Near Repeats." In *Encyclopaedia of Victimology and Crime Prevention*, edited by Bonnie S. Fisher and Steven P. Lab. London: Sage.

Summers, Lucia, and Shane D. Johnson. 2016. "Does the Configuration of the Street Network Influence Where Outdoor Serious Violence Takes Place? Using Space Syntax to Test Crime Pattern Theory." *Journal of Quantitative Criminology* 33(2): 397–420. doi:10.1007/s10940-016-9306-9.

Summers, Lucia, Shane D. Johnson, and George F. Rengert. 2010. "The Use of Maps in Offender Interviewing." In *Offenders on Offending: Learning about Crime from Criminals*, edited by Wim Bernasco. Cullompton, Devon, UK: Willan Publishing.

Tedeschi, James T., and Richard B. Felson 1994. *Violence, Aggression, and Coercive Actions*. Washington, DC: American Psychological Association.

Tita, George, and Elizabeth Griffiths. 2005. "Traveling to Violence: The Case for a Mobility-Based Spatial Typology of Homicide." *Journal of Research in Crime and Delinquency* 42(3): 275–308.

Tompson, Lisa, and Spencer Chainey. 2011. "Profiling Illegal Waste Activity: Using Crime Scripts as a Data Collection and Analytical Strategy." *European Journal of Criminal Policy and Research* 17(3): 179–201.

Toole, Jameson L., Yves-Alexandre de Montjoye, Marta C. González, and Alex (Sandy) Pentland. 2015. "Modeling and Understanding Intrinsic Characteristics of Human Mobility." In *Social Phenomena: From Data Analysis to Models*, edited by Bruno Gonçalves and Nicola Perra. Cham, Switzerland: Springer International.

Townsley, Michael, Ross Homel, and Janet Chaseling. 2003. "Infectious Burglaries: A Test of the Near Repeat Hypothesis." *British Journal of Criminology* 43(3): 615–633.

Townsley, Michael, and Aiden Sidebottom. 2010. "All Offenders Are Equal, but Some Are More Equal Than Others: Variation in Journeys to Crime between Offenders." *Criminology* 48(3): 897–917.

Trasler, Gordon. 1986. "Situational Crime Control and Rational Choice: A Critique." In *Situational Crime Prevention: From Theory into Practice*, edited by Kevin Heal and Gloria K. Laycock. London: HMSO.

Tunnell, Kenneth D. 2002. "The Impulsiveness and Routinization of Decision-Making." In *Rational Choice and Criminal Behavior: Recent Research and Future Challenges*, edited by Alex R. Piquero and Stephen G. Tibbetts. New York: Routledge.

Van Koppen, Peter J., and Jan W. De Keijser. 1997. "Desisting Distance Decay: On the Aggregation of Individual Crime Trips." *Criminology* 35(3): 505–515.

Van Patten, Isaac T., and Paul Q. Delhauer. 2007. "Sexual Homicide: A Spatial Analysis of 25 Years of Deaths in Los Angeles." *Journal of Forensic Sciences* 52(5): 1129–1141.

Vandeviver, Christophe, Stijn Van Daele, and Tom Vander Beken. 2015. "What Makes Long Crime Trips Worth Undertaking? Balancing Costs and Benefits in Burglars' Journey to Crime." *British Journal of Criminology* 55(2): 399–420.

Weisburd, David, Laura A. Wyckoff, Justin Ready, John E. Eck, Joshua C. Hinkle, and Frank Gajewski. 2006. "Does Crime Just Move around the Corner? A Controlled Study of Spatial Displacement and Diffusion of Crime Control Benefits." *Criminology* 44(3), 549–592.

Wiles, Paul, and Andrew Costello. 2000. *The "Road to Nowhere": The Evidence for Travelling Criminals.* Home Office Research Studies No. 207. London: Research, Development and Statistics Directorate, Home Office.

Wortley, Richard, and Stephen Smallbone. 2006. *Situational Prevention of Child Sexual Abuse.* Monsey, NY: Criminal Justice Press.

Wortley, Richard, and Lucia Summers. 2005. "Reducing Prison Disorder through Situational Crime Prevention: The Glen Parva Experience." In *Crime Science: New Approaches to Preventing and Detecting Crime*, edited by Melissa Smith and Nick Tilley. Cullompton, Devon, UK: Willan Publishing.

Zipf, George K. 1949. *Human Behavior and the Principle of Least Effort: An Introduction to Human Ecology*. Cambridge, MA: Addison-Wesley.

CHAPTER 5

DO WE REALLY NEED COLLECTIVE SOCIAL PROCESS TO UNDERSTAND WHY CRIME OCCURS AND OFFENDERS COMMIT CRIME?

ELIZABETH R. GROFF

5.1 Introduction

This chapter examines the potential role of social process in contributing to our understanding of why crime occurs where it does. It focuses on the role of social process in explaining crime that occurs at microplaces; in "small-scale social systems whose components include people and inanimate objects" (Wicker, 1987, p. 614) known as behavior settings (Barker, 1968). Behavior settings emphasize the situational and dynamic nature of interactions between the social and physical environment of the microplace as situated within a particular context. Investigating crime patterns so that we can reduce or prevent future crime is of primary interest here.

Because social science theories are predominantly verbal rather than mathematical or generative, terminology is important. But terminology becomes a source of confusion when it shifts over time (Taylor, 2002). Take, for example, the set of terms that were in use in the 1970s and 1980s to describe social processes such as the *willingness to intervene, territorial functioning, attachment to place, informal social control*, and *local social ties* and contrast them with those terms in current use such as *social capital* and *collective efficacy*. Theorists in the earlier period focused on the following main ideas: (1) residential stability encourages the establishment of informal social control and the willingness to intervene; (2) social ties and participation in local organizations strengthen informal social control, willingness to intervene, attachment to place, and territorial functioning

(Taylor, 2002). If these sound familiar, it is because the main ideas described here apply to both sets of terms. Taylor goes on to note that "this change in the labels for relevant constructs applied, even though the *specific indicators* are often the same or nearly the same" (Taylor, 2002, p. 787). A discussion of indicators and measurement follows later in the chapter.

Theories in environmental criminology (EC) use some of the terms associated with social process and many more of the ideas. With this issue in mind, the chapter begins with a brief introduction to social process and its operation at microplaces. Next, the chapter identifies instances where the inclusion of social process enhances current EC theory. The chapter concludes by discussing some of the challenges to the measurement of social process-related mechanisms hypothesized to affect crime events and suggesting a way forward.

5.2 What Is Social Process and How Does It Operate at Microplaces?

A social process consists of patterns of dynamic social interaction that are discernible, consistent, and occur over time (Bardis, 1979). Sociologists identify acculturation, accommodation, cooperation, competition, and conflict as the core social processes. A social process is more like a video in which the plot develops over the span of many scenes than a photograph that only captures a moment in time. Social interaction is a necessary component of social process, and it describes the way in which *individuals or groups* behave toward one another and reciprocally influence one another. When a social process involves more than one person acting to achieve shared goals, it is commonly referred to as a collective social process. Thus collective social processes typically involve action by groups of individuals. This chapter focuses on the social process of informal social control in interactions between individuals.[1] Individuals make their own decisions, but they do so in the context of their knowledge regarding social norms, a knowledge that is developed via the process of repeated interactions with others and is tied to particular settings. A separate section discusses territorial functioning because it identifies key mechanisms underpinning informal social control.

5.2.1 Informal Social Control

Social control has long been an important concept in criminology (Janowitz, 1975). It operates via the rewards and penalties, real or imagined, that accrue from either following or not following social norms (Kornhouser, 1978). Conceptually, social control exists along two dimensions: an internal-external dimension and a direct-indirect dimension. The internal-external dimension captures the locus of control, from either within the individual or triggered from outside. The direct-indirect dimension reflects whether the actions taken go toward limiting deviance or are a byproduct of relationships established for other reasons. Social control that is internal and direct comes from the acceptance of cultural values (i.e., an internal moral code). Internal indirect controls relate to stakes in conformity (Toby, 1957), and satisfying relationships strengthen their influence. External direct controls have to do with supervision and surveillance by others. The enforcement of role obligations by others based on the relevance of the rewards they offer and their place in network relationships describes external indirect controls (Kornhouser, 1978).

Greenberg, Rohe, and Williams (1981) identify three core elements of informal social control: *informal surveillance, movement-governing rules*, and *direct intervention*. Informal surveillance is the casual observation of street activity. It includes behaviors such as noticing who is on the street and paying attention to his or her activities. Movement-governing rules represent the perception of safe and unsafe areas (as gleaned from conversation with other residents and through personal experience) as translated into the spatial boundaries and paths of daily routine. Direct intervention refers to actions that go beyond observation or changing one's own behavior. It can take the form of offering help or delivering sanction—whichever is appropriate.

Informal social control arises from the distinct nature of social bonds present and varies depending on the size of the unit of analysis from private to parochial to public (Bursik & Grasmick, 1993; Hunter, 1985). Private bonds form between friends and family. Neighbors form parochial bonds based on face-to-face interactions. Typically, these "passive contacts" occur near their homes as they go about their daily life. Passive contacts are the foundation for the development of the neighboring role, which consists of being considerate and offering help (Keller, 1968; Mann, 1954). These are the bonds most closely associated with maintaining order in behavior settings (Taylor & Covington, 1988; Taylor, Gottfredson, & Brower, 1984). Proximity underlies the number and frequency of passive contacts and the subsequent development of "weak ties" (Granovetter, 1973). Over time, this cumulative exposure increases familiarity and the level of commitment to the neighbor role. It also stimulates familiarity with group norms and builds social cohesion. Because of the dynamics just mentioned, the parochial level of informal social control seems most relevant to understanding crime in behavior settings.

The previous perspectives focus on individual perceptions of social control, but informal social control also figures prominently in theories that explain neighborhood levels of crime and delinquency via the self-regulation of groups. *Systemic theory* and *collective efficacy* emphasize social dynamics within the context of social structure. Specifically, *systemic theory* (Berry & Kasarda, 1977; Bursik & Grasmick, 1993) focuses on "the degree to which a neighborhood can employ the *interactional networks* that tie together community residents to effectively regulate the nature of the activities within its boundaries" (Bursik, 2000, p. 92). The theory of *collective efficacy* focuses on the ability of neighborhood residents to achieve common goals. It identifies the basis for collective efficacy as *mutual trust* and the *willingness to intervene* on behalf of the common good (Sampson, Raudenbush, & Earls, 1997, p. 919). The *willingness to intervene* is largely dependent on *mutual trust* among members, which develops from the shared expectations for behavior that accrue over time (i.e., over the accumulated interactions and observations that are made). When the users of a place feel confident that they understand the standards for behavior, they are more likely to take action if they see a violation.

5.2.2 Human Territorial Functioning

Human territorial functioning (HTF) draws from a wide variety of perspectives to explain how informal social control develops (Taylor, 1988; Taylor et al., 1984). In Taylor's own words, it tackles "how and why people manage different kinds of spaces, and the consequences of that management or lack thereof" (Taylor, 1988, p. 4). HTF is relevant to this discussion because it explains the formation of behavior patterns associated with particular behavior settings. The *social legibility* of a behavior setting affects whether individual users feel confident that they understand the social norms and thus know how to behave. HTF is part of a feedback loop that both stems from and reinforces social norms. Routine maintenance and boundary marking by behavior-setting users set expectations for behavior. Setting users observe the setting's environmental conditions (presence of graffiti, trash on the street, and unkempt buildings) and social interactions (demeanor and tone, violence). These observations contribute to users' perception of the level of social control present. Spatially, HTF extends from the private level of homes and yards to the street in front and the alleyway behind homes.

Under HTF, the following elements are necessary for the effective exercise of informal social control in settings: *marking behaviors, actual territorial behaviors*, and *cognitions or attitudes* (Taylor, 1988). *Marking behaviors* consist of observable actions and the outcomes of those actions, such as exterior maintenance, beautification of home and/or yard, decoration, and so on. Nonresidents perceive such markers as indicating that residents are more likely to be vigilant and to take action to defend their property. For residents, marking behaviors also contribute to the formation of mutual trust through a shared investment in the behavior setting. *Territorial behaviors* consist of direct or indirect efforts to control the behavior of other setting users by communicating boundaries and controlling access. *Cognitions or attitudes* refer to individuals' perceptions of situations as either a problem that is out of their hands or something that they have the power to control. To an extent, *cognitions and attitudes* also relate to the social legibility of a behavior setting because they capture the ability of users to distinguish who belongs in a situation (Taylor, 1988). High *social legibility* translates into a higher confidence in taking action to control behavior. Finally, *cognitions* also include the amount of responsibility an individual feels for a setting. This feeling typically develops over time, and greater feelings of *attachment* are often associated with greater surveillance and greater *social legibility*.

The physical environment of a behavior setting—particularly land use, facilities, and traffic—influences the ability of HTF elements to regulate behavior. Nonresidential land use draws nonresidents to the setting and decreases *social legibility*. Because there are more outsiders on the street, residents feel less confident in determining which actions to take and less responsible for the location. Additionally, nonresidents such as business owners and employees are typically present for only part of the day. Higher traffic volume has similar effects on the ratio of residents to nonresidents and is associated with lower levels of interaction among residents and a reduced area over which residents perceive they have control (Appleyard, 1981; Appleyard & Lintell, 1972).

5.3 Is Social Process Already Part of EC Theories?

This preceding review of social process identifies mechanisms that are also relevant for EC. Indeed, several of these mechanisms appear within the three core theories of EC. The rational choice perspective (Clarke & Cornish, 1985) provides the theory for the decision to offend. Routine activity theory (Cohen & Felson, 1979) addresses the space-time convergence of the elements necessary for a crime to occur. Crime pattern theory (Brantingham & Brantingham, 1984, 1991 [1981]; Brantingham & Brantingham, 1993a) emphasizes offender behavior and the role of the built and social environment in structuring crime patterns. The next sections address where these theories integrate social processes. As a group, EC theories' focus is on how social process might influence individuals' decisions in particular behavior settings.

5.3.1 Rational Choice Perspective

The rational choice perspective views criminal acts as purposeful decisions made using "bounded rationality" (Clarke & Cornish, 1985). Under this perspective, criminal decision-making is a process that includes *involvement* decisions and *event* decisions. Each time individuals evaluate whether crime is a viable alternative for achieving their goals, they are making one of three types of *involvement* decisions: initiation, habituation, or desistance. An initiation decision occurs the first time someone makes a positive involvement decision. Subsequent involvement decisions are whether to continue (habituation) or to stop (desistance). These decisions take place in the context of social processes such as the individual's moral code and number and type of social ties, which contribute to an individual's social bonds. The *event* decision takes into account the particular circumstances of a situation in the calculation of risk and reward. Social process is evident in this stage also. Individuals consider the likelihood someone will challenge them in conjunction with their ability to blend in to make their assessment of the risk level in a situation. Criminally inclined individuals also consider the likelihood that other bystanders will react. The success or failure of an attempted crime then informs the individual's mental template for evaluating subsequent situations.

5.3.2 Routine Activity Theory

Much theoretical development has occurred within routine activity theory since its inception in 1979. The guardianship component has been the target of most of these extensions, and that is where the incorporation of informal social control took place. The original specification identified a lack of a capable guardian as one of the three elements necessary for a crime to occur (Cohen & Felson, 1979). Two notable extensions have elaborated guardianship by including informal social control via sets of mechanisms for discouraging crime, place managers (Eck, 1994, 1995) and intimate handlers (Felson, 1986, 1995). Additional work has elaborated general guardianship (Hollis, Felson, & Welsh, 2013; Leclerc & Reynald, 2015; Reynald, 2009, 2010, 2011, In press).

Felson's (1986, 1995) extension to routine activity theory describing the role of intimate *handlers* in discouraging crime incorporated social process via social control theory (Hirschi, 1969). Handlers discourage crime via their emotional connection to the potential offender (i.e., through their social bonds). Felson incorporated the four components of a social bond in the original theory (i.e., attachment, commitment, involvement, and belief) as a single concept, *handles*. "Just as a guardian supervises the suitable target, a handler supervises the likely offender. In both cases, direct physical contact serves to discourage crime from occurring. Thus, social control in society requires keeping suitable targets near capable guardians and likely offenders near intimate handlers" (Felson, 1995, p. 54).

Another elaboration on the guardianship element of routine activity theory came in the form of *place managers*, that is, people who have a formal relationship to a place. Felson lauds Eck's (1994) identification of place managers as a useful extension of routine activity theory because it specifies the operation of informal social control as it relates to the supervision of places by those who monitor them (Felson, 1995). According to Eck (1995, p. 70), all "people who have the authority to regulate who has access to property and the behavior of people who use the place" are place managers (see also Eck & Madensen, In press).

Felson proposes a matrix of crime discouragement that incorporates handlers and place managers and retains his original idea of general guardianship (Felson, 1995). He suggests four levels of responsibility that exist for guardians: *personal, assigned, diffuse*, and *general*. Owners, family, and friends take *personal* responsibility for their possessions, friends, and real property (such as home or store). Employees with a specific duty as part of their job description have an *assigned* responsibility for safeguarding clients, students, store goods, and so on. Examples of assigned responsibility are a jewelry store clerk who keeps an eye on a customer who is trying on rings, or a principal who calls out a student who is in the lunchroom instead of class. Employees who discourage criminal acts by virtue of their presence in situations rather than a specific job responsibility are exercising *diffuse* responsibility. The presence of a night janitor in an office park hallway discourages a potential burglar, but that is not part of the janitor's specific job responsibility. Bystanders whose mere presence discourages crime are exercising *general* responsibility regardless of their actions. For the purposes of his matrix, Felson assumed the benefit of crime discouragement based on general responsibility accrues "regardless of whether they show courage or a willingness to intervene" (Felson, 1995, p. 80). The matrix is a critical contribution because it provides an integrated framework for understanding and accounting for the myriad informal social control mechanisms that might discourage crime in particular behavior settings.

Recent elaborations on the concept of guardianship attempt to distinguish guardianship from informal social control. Leclerc and Reynald (2015) focus upon guardianship in public places as a micro-level process, centered on individual action and independent of collective social processes. They suggest guardianship operates in two dimensions—offender perception and guardian perception. Successful guardianship occurs when there is a guardian *available* and, due to that person's presence, offenders perceive that there is a greater risk of failing to complete the crime; consequently, they do not attempt the crime. The act of undertaking *supervision/monitoring* serves two functions. First, it allows the guardian to develop enhanced "awareness and contextual knowledge" of situations. Second, this greater contextual knowledge of situational norms provides the basis for intervention by potential guardians. Finally, there must be an *intervention* by the guardian (Leclerc & Reynald, 2015). As described above, collective social process is not relevant, but individual-level use of informal social control is relevant and exists in the social process of developing knowledge regarding the range of acceptable behaviors at a place.

In contrast, Hollis and colleagues (2013) focus on individuals as agents of guardianship and try to distinguish how guardianship at the individual level can exist even in the absence of informal social control. In their own words, "informal social control implies *intent* on the part of the controlling individuals, whereas guardianship does not involve an *intention* of the guardian to prevent deviant or criminal behavior" (Hollis et al., 2013, p. 72). A relevant question concerns whether it matters to the outcome of a situation whether an individual *intends* to deter a crime through mere presence or not. If the crime is deterred because of that individual's presence, then he or she acted as a general guardian (as defined by Felson, 1995). Of course, empirically, we lack rich, dynamic data that reveal the relative importance of situational factors and how potential offenders weigh them in the process of making an event decision. Whether or not the reader accepts the need for Hollis et al.'s proposed distinction, the relevance of guardianship continues to grow.

Leveraging guardianship is of particular interest today, when there is renewed emphasis on finding alternatives to arrest and incarceration. As Felson notes, "the main goal of discouragement is to prevent crime without arrests and punishment" (1995, p. 62). The matrix of crime discouragement seems a promising avenue for implementation of these ideas because it provides an integrated framework for understanding and empirically examining the various types of controllers and the potential informal social control mechanisms they employ in particular behavior settings.

5.3.3 Crime Pattern Theory

Crime pattern theory addresses the important role of the built and social environment in shaping human activity and how that affects where and when crime occurs (Brantingham & Brantingham, 1984, 1991 [1981]; Brantingham & Brantingham, 1981, 1993b). It identifies three elements that are important to understanding the routine activity of places: nodes, paths, and edges. All three of those elements have connections to social process. Nodes and paths are the basic building blocks of activity spaces. Nodes are locations where individuals accomplish the goals of everyday life (e.g., shopping, work, school among others). Paths are the routes taken between nodes. The transportation network determines travel routes and brings places to the attention of potential offenders. The configuration of facilities shapes choices for accomplishing particular activity goals (e.g., grocery shopping requires a grocery store) (Felson, 1987). The routine aspect of most human activity translates into varying levels of familiarity with microplaces depending on the frequency with which they are used. These features of the built environment also act to funnel human activity and increase the number of convergences of potential offenders and potential victims.

All individuals develop mental maps over the course of their daily activities, and these maps include routing information and facilities but also information regarding the social climate and safety of places. The mental maps that potential offenders develop over the course of their routine activities reflect individuals' perceptions of how well they will fit in at a particular place as well as the level of informal social control in places. With each successive crime committed, an offender adds to his or her knowledge of what works and updates his or her mental templates (crime templates, in CPT terminology) for evaluating subsequent situations. With each crime that comes to their attention, targets and bystanders also adjust their mental map of risky places.

Finally, edges are places in the urban backcloth where a noticeable change occurs, for example, the edge of a campus or park, or where land use transitions abruptly from commercial to residential. These places tend to have more crime. Drawing from social process, the Brantinghams (1993b) suggest the following mechanisms may be at work: the lack of comfort potential offenders feel in places with which they are not as familiar, the inability of territoriality to function effectively in areas with many outsiders, and the higher potential for conflict in heterogeneous places, especially those frequented by large numbers of people.

5.4 Summary of Social Process in EC Theory

This chapter discussed how the theories of EC weave in social process in the form of informal social control as perceived by individuals. It also demonstrated that the integration of social process has increased our understanding of why crime occurs in particular behavior settings, at particular times. However, collective social process (i.e., group-based action) is more difficult to identify in EC theories.

In answer to the question of whether social process is necessary for explaining crime, which was posed in the title, this review indicates social process as individual action has made important contributions to explaining crime patterns. Contributions to EC theory include intimate handlers, active guardianship, and place managers in routine activity theory, as well as better modeling of the initiation-desistance and event decisions of offenders in the rational choice perspective and of the effect of routine activities on familiarity with behavior settings. At the same time, most environmental criminologists neglect the fuzzier aspects of collective social process that are part of group-based action precisely because they are difficult to accurately measure and do not provide as clear a link to crime prevention strategies. However, their potential value is generally underexplored. Some scholars have attempted to operationalize collective social process in behavior settings (Weisburd, Groff, & Yang, 2012, 2014), which has stimulated some debate on the specific data used and whether it represents collective social process or not (Braga & Clarke, 2014). The value of collective social process for explaining crime patterns is an empirical question that remains in need of exploration and testing. It certainly seems premature to state that collective social process is not necessary.

Social processes play out at various scales from the micro level of behavior settings to the macro level of neighborhoods and beyond. This also means that social processes exist on a continuum of concreteness from the individual to the micro level of behavior settings to neighborhoods. These levels do not operate in isolation; rather there is significant interaction among them. Individuals make choices based on their internalized moral code. However, their level of concern about other people's reactions to their behavior influences their decision. Individuals use a variety of social and environmental cues to read and interpret the landscape of social norms. To the extent that multiple users interpret and respond to cues in the same way, there are shared norms. The label used to describe these activities does not change the fact they occur and that they may be important to understanding the pattern of crime events.

5.5 Thoughts on a Way Forward

From this review it is clear that social disorganization theories and EC theories conceptualize some of the same basic mechanisms in slightly different ways and emphasize different aspects. However, the importance of informal social control is commonly accepted. As Braga and Clarke note, "Informal social controls matter in crime prevention and control and there is some conceptual overlap in social disorganization and opportunity theories in the mechanisms through which informal social control can be achieved" (2014, p. 491). The next paragraphs discuss some suggestions for leveraging that overlap to strengthen EC theories and achieve a better understanding of crime in behavior settings.

Increase the conceptual clarity of theories in EC. There is certainly a need for conceptual clarity when discussing theory regardless of whether the theories fall under the rubric of EC or focus on collective process. At the same time, some scholars have expended a great deal of energy arguing why certain mechanisms fall into one theoretical box or another. A more productive model to follow is the evolution of the "capable guardianship" concept in routine activity theory traced earlier in this chapter. Today, the standard concept of guardianship includes handlers, place managers, and general guardians. However, there is still work to do to illuminate guardianship. Other mechanisms remain underinvestigated and provide the impetus for some of the suggestions that follow.

Improve measurement of theoretical constructs. In addition to the focus on conceptual clarity, we need more attention directed toward developing appropriate measures that capture the mechanisms of interest. Measures to capture the influence of parents, teachers, and other authority figures offer a good example. Would different situational measures be used if we called those actors "handlers" under routine activity theory or if we called them "agents of informal social control": under systemic theory? After all, some might argue that if the underlying measures are the same, the disagreements are down to theoretical attribution, which is of less interest to scholars who are focused on preventing crime.

Existing work offers examples of measurements developed to represent mechanisms. Researchers have developed and used several block environment instruments (Perkins et al., 1990; Perkins, Meeks, & Taylor, 1992; Taylor et al., 1984). In addition, there is more recent work on systematic social observation (Sampson & Raudenbush, 1999). All these efforts involved formulating questions that measure the mechanism underlying theoretical concepts. These and many other sources provide a rich stable of questions regarding HTF, community attachment, informal social control, and neighboring behavior, among other concepts. Reynald's (2011) work drew from and advanced these concepts by collecting information on resident guardianship behavior as well as asking about their attitudes and cataloging features of the built environment. Additionally, measures of attitudes and perceptions for individuals can be aggregated to the appropriate behavior setting, and provide information about the average levels of informal social control present (Taylor, 2002).

Leverage technology to illuminate human behavior in settings. New technologies offer access to a veritable firehose of data that may help shed light on interactions in behavior settings. Various video technologies offer one example. The use of Google Street View to code the physical and social environment is increasing (Hwang & Sampson, 2014; Odgers et al., 2012; Rundle et al., 2011). The recent availability of historical images has extended research capabilities to include the examination of change over time. CCTV is another potential source of data that has the advantage of capturing human behavior in public places. As the coverage of public streets by CCTV cameras increases, the potential to use prerecorded video rather than active data collection comes closer to reality. Other technology systems such as automated license plate readers (LPRs) could provide information regarding the numbers of cars on particular street segments (Lum et al., 2011). New sources of video technology continue to appear at a rapid rate and hold great promise for providing both quantitative and qualitative information about human behavior in particular settings.

5.6 Conclusion

In sum, this chapter has argued that theories in EC already include social process in the form of informal social control and various aspects of HTF. However, the inclusion of collective social process is underdeveloped and reflects the difficulty in developing measures of those processes. Future work needs to further develop those measures and include them in studies that also quantify EC mechanisms. As more data at more micro levels becomes available, robust empirical tests will be possible and an answer to the question of the relative value of collective social process can be provided. Until then, criminologists will be busy improving conceptual clarity, developing measures, and leveraging technology—all of which will further illuminate why crime happens in certain places and at certain times.

Note

1. This introduction is necessarily brief. For a more comprehensive review of informal social control, territorial functioning, and crime events see Groff (2015).

References

Appleyard, D. (1981). *Livable Streets*. Berkeley: University of California Press.

Appleyard, D., and M. Lintell. (1972). The Environmental Quality of City Streets: The Resident's Viewpoint. *Journal of the American Planning Association* 38(2), 84–101.

Bardis, P. D. (1979). Social Interaction and Social Processes. *Social Science* 54(3), 147–167.

Barker, R. G. (1968). *Ecological Psychology: Concepts and Methods for Studying the Environment of Human Behavior*. Stanford, CA: Stanford University Press.

Berry, B. J. L., and J. D. Kasarda. (1977). *Contemporary Urban Ecology*. New York: Macmillan.

Braga, A. A., and R. V. Clarke. (2014). Explaining High-Risk Concentrations of Crime in the City: Social Disorganization, Crime Opportunities, and Important Next Steps. *Journal of Research in Crime and Delinquency* 51(4), 480–498.

Brantingham, P. J., and P. L. Brantingham. (1984). *Patterns in Crime*. New York: Macmillan.

Brantingham, P. L., and P. J. Brantingham. (1981). Notes on the Geometry of Crime. In P. Brantingham and P. Brantingham (Eds.), *Environmental Criminology* (pp. 27–54). Prospect Heights, IL: Waveland Press. Reprinted in 1991.

Brantingham, P. J., and P. L. Brantingham. (1991 [1981]). *Environmental Criminology*. Prospect Heights, IL: Waveland Press.

Brantingham, P. L., and P. J. Brantingham. (1993a). Environment, Routine, and Situation: Toward a Pattern Theory of Crime. In R. V. Clarke and M. Felson (Eds.), *Routine Activity and Rational Choice* (vol. 5 of *Advances in Criminological Theory*, pp. 259–294). New Brunswick, NJ: Transaction.

Brantingham, P. L., and P. J. Brantingham. (1993b). Nodes, Paths and Edges: Considerations on the Complexity of Crime and the Physical Environment. *Journal of Environmental Psychology* 13, 3–28.

Bursik, R. J., Jr. (2000). The Systemic Theory of Neighborhood Crime Rates. In S. S. Simpson (Ed.), *Of Crime and Criminality: The Use of Theory in Everyday Life* (pp. 87–108). Thousand Oaks, CA: Sage.

Bursik, R. J., Jr., and H. G. Grasmick. (1993). *Neighborhoods and Crime: The Dimensions of Effective Community Control*. New York: Lexington Books.

Clarke, R. V., and D. B. Cornish. (1985). Modeling Offender's Decisions: A Framework for Research and Policy. In M. Tonry and N. Morris (Eds.), *Crime and Justice: An Annual Review of Research* (vol. 6: pp. 23–42). Chicago: University of Chicago Press.

Cohen, L. E., and M. Felson. (1979). Social Change and Crime Rate Trends: A Routine Activity Approach. *American Sociological Review* 44, 588–608.

Eck, J. E. (1994). "Drug Markets and Drug Places: A Case-Control Study of the Spatial Structure of Illicit Drug Dealing." PhD diss., University of Maryland.

Eck, J. E. (1995). A General Model of the Geography of Illicit Retail Marketplaces. In J. E. Eck and D. Weisburd (Eds.), *Crime and Place* (pp. 67–93). Monsey, NY: Willow Tree Press.

Eck, J. E., and T. Madensen. (In press). Place Management. In G. Bruinsma and S. D. Johnson (Eds.), *Handbook of Environmental Criminology*. New York: Oxford University Press.

Felson, M. (1986). Linking Criminal Choices, Routine Activities, Informal Control, and Criminal Outcomes. In D. B. Cornish and R. V. Clarke (Eds.), *The Reasoning Criminal: Rational Choice Perspectives on Offending* (pp. 119–128). New York: Springer-Verlag.

Felson, M. (1987). Routine Activities and Crime Prevention in the Developing Metropolis. *Criminology* 25(4), 911–931.

Felson, M. (1995). Those Who Discourage Crime. In J. E. Eck and D. Weisburd (Eds.), *Crime and Place* (pp. 53–66), vol. 4 of *Crime Prevention Studies*. Monsey, NY: Criminal Justice Press.

Granovetter, M. S. (1973). The Strength of Weak Ties. *American Journal of Sociology* 78(6), 1360–1380. doi:10.2307/2776392.

Greenberg, S. W., W. M. Rohe, and J. R. Williams. (1981). *Safe and Secure Neighborhoods: Physical Characteristics and Informal Territorial Control in High and Low Crime Neighborhoods: Final Report*. Washington DC. National Institute of Justice

Groff, E. R. (2015). Informal Social Control and Crime Events. *Journal of Contemporary Criminal Justice* 31(1), 90–106. doi:10.1177/1043986214552619.

Hirschi, T. (1969). *Causes of Delinquency*. Berkeley: University of California Press.

Hollis, M. E., M. Felson, and B. C. Welsh. (2013). The Capable Guardian in Routine Activities Theory: A Theoretical and Conceptual Reappraisal. *Crime Prevention and Community Safety* 15(1), 65–79. doi:10.1057/cpcs.2012.14.

Hunter, A. J. (1985). Private, Parochial and Public Social Orders: The Problem of Crime and Incivility in Urban Communities. In G. F. Suttles and M. N. Zald (Eds.), *The Challenge of Social Control: Citizenship and Institution Building in Modern Society* (pp. 230–242). Norwood: Ablex Publishing.

Hwang, J., and R. Sampson. (2014). Google Street View Shows That Gentrification in Chicago Has Largely Bypassed Poor Minority Neighborhoods, Reinforcing Urban Inequality. *LSE US Centre, United States Politics and Policy*. Blog entry: http://blogs.lse.ac.uk/usappblog/2014/07/09/google-street-view-shows-that-gentrification-in-chicago-has-largely-bypassed-poor-minority-neighborhoods-reinforcing-urban-inequality/.

Janowitz, M. (1975). Sociological Theory and Social Control. *American Journal of Sociology 81*(1), 82–108. doi:10.2307/2777055.

Keller, S. (1968). *The Urban Neighborhood: A Sociological Perspective*. New York: Random House.

Kornhouser, R. (1978). *Social Sources of Delinquency: An Appraisal of Analytic Models*. Chicago: University of Chicago Press.

Leclerc, B., and D. M. Reynald. (2015). When Scripts and Guardianship Unite: A Script Model to Facilitate Intervention of Capable Guardians in Public Settings. *Security Journal*, 1–14. doi:10.1057/sj.2015.8.

Lum, C., J. Hibdon, B. Cave, C. S. Koper, and L. Merola. (2011). License Plate Reader (LPR) Police Patrols in Crime Hot Spots: An Experimental Evaluation in Two Adjacent Jurisdictions. *Journal of Experimental Criminology 7*(4), 321–345.

Mann, P. H. (1954). The Concept of Neighborliness. *American Journal of Sociology 60*, 163–168.

Odgers, C. L., A. Caspi, C. J. Bates, R. J. Sampson, and T. E. Moffitt. (2012). Systematic Social Observation of Children's Neighborhoods Using Google Street View: A Reliable and Cost-Effective Method. *Journal of Child Psychology and Psychiatry 53*(10), 1009–1017.

Perkins, D. D., P. Florin, R. C. Rich, A. Wandersman, and D. M. Chavis (1990). Participation and the Social and Physical Environment of Residential Blocks: Crime and Community Context. *American Journal of Community Psychology 18*(1), 83–115. doi:10.1007/bf00922690.

Perkins, D. D., J. W. Meeks, and R. B. Taylor. (1992). The Physical Environment of Street Blocks and Resident Perceptions of Crime and Disorder: Implications for Theory and Measurement. *Journal of Environmental Psychology 12*(1), 21–34. doi:http://dx.doi.org/10.1016/S0272-4944(05)80294-4.

Reynald, D. M. (2009). Guardianship in Action: Developing a New Tool for Measurement. *Crime Prevention and Community Safety 11*(1), 1–20. doi:http://dx.doi.org/10.1057/cpcs.2008.19.

Reynald, D. M. (2010). Guardians on Guardianship: Factors Affecting the Willingness to Supervise, the Ability to Detect Potential Offenders, and the Willingness to Intervene. *Journal of Research in Crime and Delinquency 47*(3), 358–390. doi:10.1177/0022427810365904.

Reynald, D. M. (2011). Factors Associated with the Guardianship of Places: Assessing the Relative Importance of the Spatio-Physical and Sociodemographic Contexts in Generating Opportunities for Capable Guardianship. *Journal of Research in Crime and Delinquency 48*(1), 110–142. doi:10.1177/0022427810384138.

Reynald, D. M. (In press). Guardianship. In G. Bruinsma and S. D. Johnson (Eds.), *Encyclopedia of Environmental Criminology*. New York: Oxford University Press.

Rundle, A. G., M. D. Bader, C. A. Richards, K. M. Neckerman, and J. O. Teitler. (2011). Using Google Street View to Audit Neighborhood Environments. *American Journal of Preventive Medicine 40*(1), 94–100.

Sampson, R. J., and S. W. Raudenbush. (1999). Systematic Social Observation of Public Spaces: A New Look at Disorder in Urban Neighborhoods. *American Journal of Sociology 105*(3), 603–651.

Sampson, R. J., S. W. Raudenbush, and F. Earls. (1997). Neighborhoods and Violent Crime: A Multilevel Study of Collective Efficacy. *Science 277*, 918–924.

Taylor, R. B. (1988). *Human Territorial Functioning: An Empirical, Evolutional Perspective on Individual and Small Group Territorial Cognitions, Behaviors and Consequences.* Cambridge: Cambridge University Press.

Taylor, R. B. (2002). Fear of Crime, Social Ties, and Collective Efficacy: Maybe Masquerading Measurement, Maybe Déjà Vu All Over Again. *Justice Quarterly 19*(4), 773–792.

Taylor, R. B., and J. Covington. (1988). Neighborhood Changes in Ecology and Violence. *Criminology 26*(4), 553–589.

Taylor, R. B., S. D. Gottfredson, and S. Brower. (1984). Block Crime and Fear: Defensible Space, Local Social Ties, and Territorial Functioning. *Journal of Research in Crime and Delinquency 21*(4), 303–331.

Toby, J. (1957). Social Disorganization and Stake in Conformity: Complementary Factors in the Predatory Behavior of Hoodlums. *Journal of Criminal Law and Criminology 48*, 12.

Weisburd, D., E. Groff, and S.-M. Yang. (2012). *The Criminology of Place: Street Segments and Our Understanding of the Crime Problem.* Oxford: Oxford University Press.

Weisburd, D., E. R. Groff, and S.-M. Yang. (2014). The Importance of Both Opportunity and Social Disorganization Theory in a Future Research Agenda to Advance Criminological Theory and Crime Prevention at Places. *Journal of Research in Crime and Delinquency, 51*(4), 499–508.

Wicker, A. W. (1987). Behavior Settings Reconsidered: Temporal Stages, Resources, Internal Dynamics, Context. In D. Stokels and I. Altman (Eds.), *Handbook of Environmental Psychology* (pp. 613–653). New York: Wiley-Interscience.

CHAPTER 6

THE IMPORTANCE OF HIGH OFFENDER NEIGHBORHOODS WITHIN ENVIRONMENTAL CRIMINOLOGY

ANTHONY BOTTOMS

6.1 Introduction

Within the last fifty years, an important shift has taken place in the main focus of environmental criminology. As is universally acknowledged, the dominant influence in this field in the period between the two world wars was provided by scholars from the Chicago school of sociology, notably Clifford Shaw and Henry McKay (1942/1969), the principal empirical focus of whose work was the study of the location of residences of offenders, especially juvenile offenders ("delinquents"). Their research produced a consistent pattern of results both in Chicago and in other US cities, namely that the highest concentration of juvenile offenders was found in inner-city areas with high population turnover (described as the "zone of transition"); and these findings were explained through the concept of "social disorganization" (see fuller discussion below, also chapter 2 by Wilcox and Swartz in this volume). For thirty years after the Second World War, Shaw and McKay's work remained the principal influence within what was then called "the ecology of crime." The 1970s, however, saw the emergence of both routine activities theory (or "RAT"—see Cohen and Felson 1979) and opportunity theory (Mayhew et al. 1976; Clarke 1980), with the latter being soon linked to a rational choice perspective (Cornish and Clarke 1986). These two approaches had some differences, but also many similarities (Clarke and Felson 1993), and together they became the dominant forces within a new version of environmental criminology whose focus was significantly different from that of the Chicago school. As Wortley and Mazerolle

(2008, p. 2) put it in their introduction to a landmark overview of these developments, in this new approach

> *crime* is the object of interest. The offender is just one element of a criminal event, and how offenders come to be the way they are is of little immediate relevance. Instead, the focus is on the current dynamics of crime. . . . The aim of the environmental perspective is to prevent crime, not to cure offenders.

As regards locational issues, a consequence of this new approach was that the attention of researchers shifted from the study of *where offenders live* (as in the Chicago school) to *where offenses are committed*. This eventually led to a new focus on *microlocations* rather than *neighborhoods* as the principal unit of study. This shift occurred because there can be quite marked variations in offense rates even in streets that are close to one another; accordingly, the adoption of a neighborhood focus (as in the Chicago tradition) can mask important differences in crime frequencies at a microlocational level (Weisburd, Bernasco, and Bruinsma 2009).

This set of developments has brought about two further consequences. First, there has been a significant decline in a previous staple of criminological research, namely the study of high offender neighborhoods. Second, as David Weisburd and his colleagues have pointed out, in recent years "scholars who study the criminology of place have virtually ignored social disorganization theories in empirical analysis and theoretical discussion" (Weisburd, Groff, and Yang 2012, p. 43). Interestingly, however, Weisburd and colleagues have reacted in different ways to these two consequences. They view the "neglect of social disorganization in the study of the criminology of place" as a regrettable phenomenon attributable to scholarly competitiveness and a lack of interest in theoretical integration (pp. 43–44). In their major longitudinal study of the criminology of place in Seattle (focused on street segments as microlocations), they accordingly attempted to integrate insights from social disorganization theory with those from opportunity and routine activities theories. Yet offender areas as such (the main empirical focus of Shaw and McKay's work) are given no place in this landmark Seattle study.[1] A possible reason for this omission is hinted at in an earlier research report by these authors on juvenile crime in Seattle, in which the dependent variable was police data on "the location of crimes committed by juveniles." Explaining the choice of this variable, the authors comment that it "characterizes juvenile crime in terms of where it is committed and thus is measuring a different construct than the traditional measure of juvenile crime which *represents juvenile crime by offender residence location*" (Groff, Weisburd, and Morris 2009, p. 71; emphasis added).

Here, therefore, the study of "offender residence location" is apparently seen simply as an inferior way of characterizing the crime rate of an area. By contrast, earlier empirical studies of the geography of crime in major European cities (Baldwin and Bottoms 1976 in Sheffield, England; Wikström 1991 in Stockholm) viewed the study of offense locations and offender residence locations as different but complementary measures, which together provide a fuller understanding of crime in a city than can be gleaned from studying only one of these matters. The present chapter is written from this latter standpoint, the value of which has been powerfully restated in Ralph Taylor's (2015) recent incisive analysis of conceptual and methodological issues within what he calls "community criminology."[2] In particular, it is argued here that *the study of the geographical distribution of crimes is significantly enriched when it takes into account the location of offender residences, especially high offender-rate neighborhoods.*

The remainder of this chapter has two main sections and a conclusion. The first section seeks to explain why the study of high offender neighborhoods is vital to the study of the criminology of place, both in explanatory terms and as regards implications for crime prevention. The second and longer section shows that high offender neighborhoods are not all the same, and that the single concept of social disorganization is not adequate to explain these differences. The conclusion summarizes the argument of the chapter, and considers its implications for the important question of the optimum units of analysis in the study of environmental criminology.

6.2 Why High Offender Neighborhoods Matter When Studying Local Crime Rates

The "new" environmental criminology mentioned in the introduction is generally considered to have originated in three closely related, but distinct, theoretical approaches. Two of these ("opportunity/rational choice" and RAT) have had the most extensive impact on criminological thought in general, but in the present context the third approach is of special significance. This third theoretical strand derives from the work of Canadian criminologists Paul and Patricia Brantingham, and is now referred to as "crime pattern theory" (for a brief overview see Brantingham and Brantingham 2008; see also chapter 4 by Summers and Guerette in this volume). Whereas most research using the opportunity approach and RAT has focused heavily on the offense rather than the offender, one of the major topics highlighted by crime pattern theory is the offender's *awareness space*.[3]

Beyond infancy, human beings have an "awareness space" that consists of the geographical locations with which they are familiar. Imagine, for example, a hypothetical adolescent (Jane): she is very familiar with the area around her home and her school, and the route between home and school; she is broadly aware but has a less detailed knowledge of the city center and the area where her best friend lives; but she has no awareness of residential areas in the city where she has no particular friends. Like most people, Jane feels much more confident in areas that she knows well (her awareness space) than in other areas; so, for example, when she begins flute lessons and has to find her way to the teacher's home in a strange part of the city, for the first few lessons she finds this to be an uncomfortable experience. In other words, awareness space arises out of an individual's routine activities, and can change as those activities change.

In a pathbreaking article, Patricia and Paul Brantingham (1981) postulated that offenders are just like everyone else, and therefore that they will feel much more comfortable committing crimes within their awareness space rather than in other areas. Combining this thought with the insights of opportunity theory, they proposed that crimes will be particularly likely to be committed where there is *an intersection between a suitable opportunity and an offender's awareness space*. This hypothesis is schematically illustrated in Figure 6.1 (reproduced from an early text by the Brantinghams in 1984), where it will also be noted that the offender's awareness space is postulated to consist primarily of areas around his or her home, workplace, and leisure outlets, and the routes linking these venues.

Of special interest in the present context is the suggestion that an offender's home area will always constitute an important part of his or her awareness space. If this is correct, and if the Brantinghams' general thesis (see above) is also substantiated, then—other things being equal—we would expect a disproportionate number of offenders' crimes to be committed fairly close to their home area. That is, in fact, precisely what empirical research studies have found—a phenomenon described in the literature as a "distance decay" relationship (that is, the greater the distance from the offender's home, the fewer crimes will be committed: see, e.g., Wiles and Costello 2000; Wikström et al. 2012, pp. 239–249).[4] An additional reason for the distance decay relationship, over and above familiarity, has also been established: this is the utilitarian principle of least effort—that is, why travel a significant distance if one can adequately achieve one's objective nearby?

The significance of the issue of distance decay for the study of crime locations has been recognized by a minority of contemporary environmental criminologists, notably those working with the concept of "discrete spatial choice" (see further chapter 31 by Wim Bernasco in this volume). This theoretical approach was first developed by

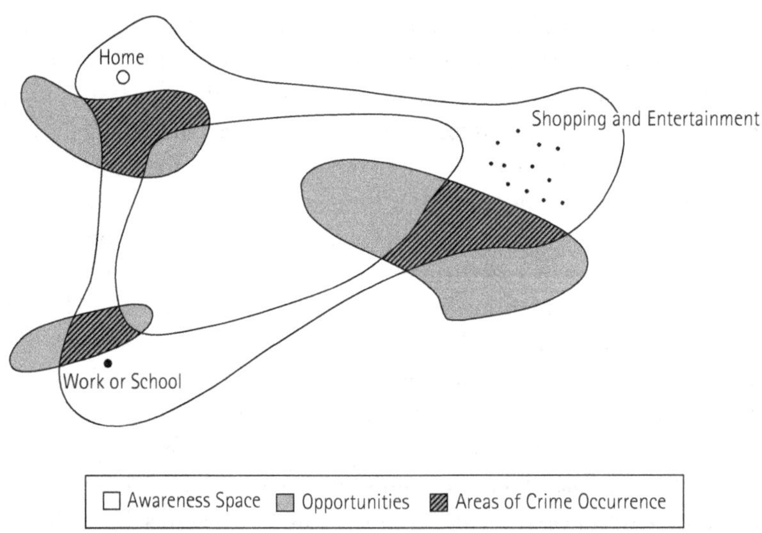

FIGURE 6.1 Brantinghams' model of intersection of opportunities with awareness space

Source: Brantingham and Brantingham 1984, p. 362.

Bernasco and Nieuwbeerta (2005), who attempted to overcome some of the limitations of prior research into crime locations by taking simultaneously into account three different matters, namely: (1) the attributes of alternative target locations; (2) the proximity of the target to the offender's home; and (3) individual differences (such as age) that might be relevant to target choice criteria. Several studies have subsequently confirmed the value of the discrete spatial choice approach. For example, in recent research on the locations of residential burglaries in cities in three different countries (Australia, Great Britain, and the Netherlands), it was found that "the likelihood an offender selects an area for burglary is positively influenced by proximity to their home, the proportion of easily accessible targets, and the total number of targets available"; also, in two of the three cities, juvenile offenders were significantly more influenced by the proximity of the target to home than were adult offenders (Townsley et al. 2015, pp. 3–4).

While such studies are illuminating, they do not fully explore the "awareness space" dimension of crime pattern theory. However, in a rigorous study in The Hague (Netherlands), Wim Bernasco (2010) demonstrated the relevance of a further aspect of offenders' awareness space, namely their familiarity with locations close to their former home(s). In this research, Bernasco examined the locations of four selected offenses (residential burglary, thefts from vehicles, robbery, and assault) and used an odds-ratio methodology to test the probability of an offense occurring in or near the offender's present or past home area, by comparison with neighborhoods that were matched with those areas on four control variables.[5] Two of the conclusions of this analysis are of particular importance in the present context:

> Offenders are more likely to commit an offense in the area where they currently live than in an area where they used to live, and are more likely to commit it in the latter than in an area where they have never lived. . . . Offenders are [also] more likely to commit an offense near an area where they live or used to live than in areas further away from their present or former residences. (2010, p. 412)[6]

Consider the implications of these results for the relationship between the offense rate of a neighborhood and its offender rate. Other things being equal, one may logically infer three important points from the results. First, a high offender-rate area will usually also be a high offense rate area, because many offenders will commit crimes close to home, and others who used to live in the area might return to find suitable targets in a neighborhood that is familiar to them. Second, if two low offender-rate areas have identical crime opportunity structures, but one is located adjacent to a high offender-rate area and the other is not, then the former area will usually have the higher crime rate.[7] Third, it is clear from the two preceding points that the geographical distribution of offense rates cannot be fully understood without taking into account the location of high offender areas.[8]

The maps shown in Figure 6.2 illustrate the first and third of these points from empirical research in Sheffield.[9] Figure 6.2(a) shows that the city has a striking east-west contrast in wealth—an affluent west and a deprived east. All criminologists know that convicted offenders come disproportionately from disadvantaged backgrounds, so it is

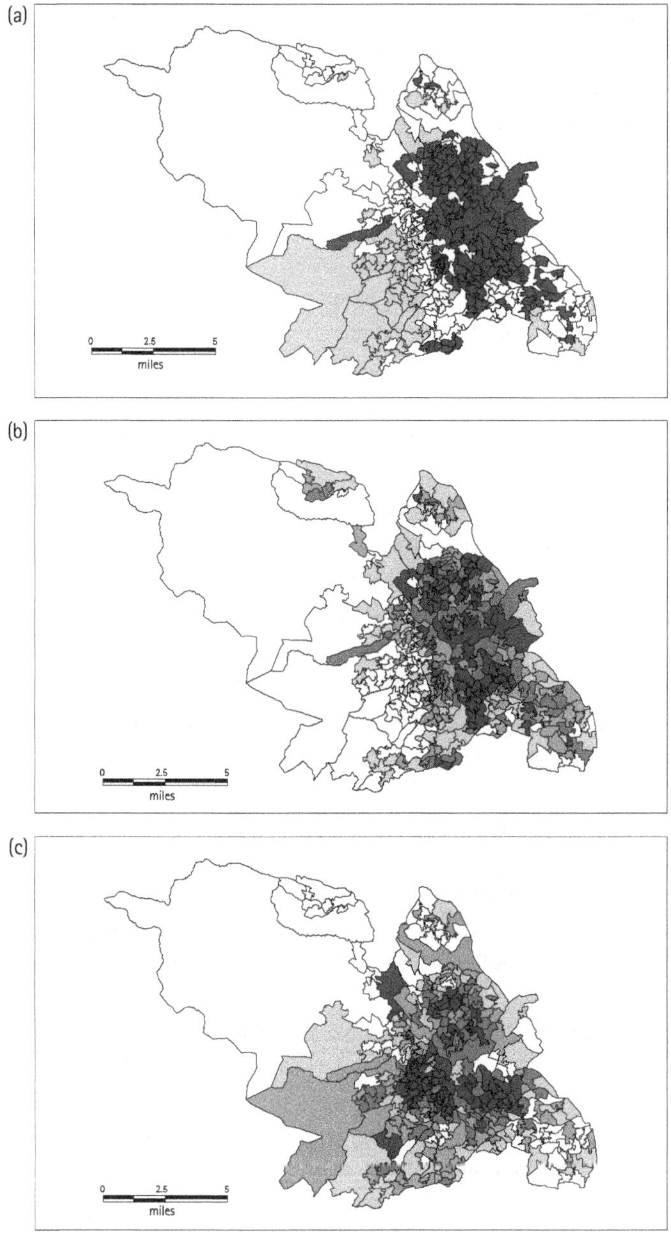

FIGURE 6.2 Deprivation, offender areas, and residential burglary in Sheffield (UK)
(a) Official Government Index of Multiple Deprivation 2005–2006
Key: Gray = among 25% most affluent areas in England; White = middle 50%; Black = among 25% most deprived areas in England.
(b) Offender Residences 2004–2006 (in quintiles, highest rate darkest)
(c) Recorded Crimes of Residential Burglary 2004–2006 (in quintiles, highest rate darkest)

Source: Bottoms 2012, p. 459.

no surprise to discover that offender residences in Sheffield are heavily concentrated in the east (Figure 6.2(b)). Given the relative proximity of some very affluent residential areas in the west of the city, a simple opportunity approach would suggest that offenders in Sheffield would be regularly traveling west when they choose to commit residential burglary. However, Figure 6.2(c) shows that this is not the case; while there is some movement across the city in pursuit of opportunities, the residential burglary rates in the poorer eastern parts of the city are in general significantly higher than those in the affluent west. Consistent with the Brantinghams' awareness space hypothesis (see above), an interview study of Sheffield offenders (including burglars) showed that they did not actively shun going to the middle-class western parts of the city; rather, "the offenders simply did not know [these areas] to any extent" (Wiles and Costello 2000, p. 32).

A consequence of this general line of argument is that, when conducting criminological analyses of residential areas of a city, we need to collect data on both their offense rate and their offender rate. This point has been particularly pressed by Wiles and Costello (2000), who further argue that both sets of information are vital when considering crime prevention programs for residential areas (see also the crime prevention handbook prepared by Shapland, Wiles, and Wilcox, 1994). Wiles and Costello illustrated their argument with an instructive contrast between two small areas in Sheffield (identified as areas E and F), the first of which was a high-offense/low-offender area, while the second was a high-offense/high-offender area (Wiles and Costello 2000, pp. 21–22, 47–48, 51, and 53). Area E was a moderately well-off residential area about a mile from the city center, with the houses clustered around what had recently become a desirable shopping area. It had few resident offenders, but seems to have become known to offenders from elsewhere because of their visits to the local shops; hence, detected offenders committing crimes in the area (against shops or in the surrounding residential streets) were on average 2.3 miles from home when the offense was committed. Area F was a cluster of three small and relatively deprived public sector housing areas in the north of the city, with high offender and offense rates; here, the offending was much more local, with the average distance from home of the crimes of recorded offenders being 0.8 miles. As Wiles and Costello suggest, in devising appropriate crime prevention strategies for these two areas, one will necessarily have to take account of the fact that in Area F "local offenders are largely driving the victimisation rate" (p. 48), whereas that is not the case in Area E.

6.3 Differences between High Offender-Rate Neighborhoods

As we have seen, within the Chicago school tradition social disorganization was the dominant theoretical explanation offered for the emergence of high offender-rate areas (especially high youth-delinquency areas). To understand how this explanation developed, it is necessary to recall some of the empirical findings of the Chicagoans' research, particularly the following:

(1) The highest youth offending rates were found in the "zone of transition," close to the central business district, with declining offender rates the further one moved outwards toward the suburbs.
(2) The zone of transition contained the cheapest housing in the city.
(3) At a time of high foreign immigration into the United States in the early twentieth century, most immigrant families found it economically easiest to make their first home in the zone of transition of their chosen city.
(4) As they became established in their new environment, many but not all immigrant families moved on, which meant that the inner-city area was indeed a zone of transitional living for many—and it also became multicultural as some people from successive waves of migration remained in the area.
(5) High youth-offender rates in the zone of transition were maintained over decades, notwithstanding successive waves of migration from different groups of foreign nationals.

The development of social disorganization theory from these observations has been well described by Finestone (1976, pp. 28–29):

> The same selective processes which made it relatively easy for the first generation of newcomers . . . to become aggregated in inner-city areas also permitted the location there of many illegitimate enterprises and deviant moral worlds. Such moral diversity within the inner city areas meant that it was difficult if not impossible for immigrant communities to insulate themselves from illegitimate and criminal enterprises and influences. In the face of many centrifugal pulls, the traditional institutions [of the immigrant groups], the family, the church and the community, became incapable of maintaining their solidarity. Their inability to organise effectively in defense of conventional values meant that they were unable to resist or limit the influence exercised upon their youth by the diverse value systems which became rooted in such areas.

Hence, when analyzed from the point of view of immigrant communities, Chicago school theorization postulated that, as Ruth Kornhauser (1978, p. 63) famously put the matter, "social disorganization exists in the first instance when the structure and culture of a community are incapable of implementing and expressing the values of its *own* residents." However, as Kornhauser (p. 62) also pointed out, this was not the only feature of Shaw and McKay's (1942/1969) theorization, because they also identified, as a contributor to the high youth-offender rate in the zone of transition, "the 'cultural transmission' of delinquency by the delinquent gang." Putting this another way, within the social context described by Finestone (above), those who organized "illegitimate and criminal enterprises" *were* able to "implement and express" their values—and to pass them on to others in a process of cultural transmission. Analytically, there is some tension, within this "mixed [theoretical] model," between the two different mechanisms in play—namely, weak community controls and cultural transmission of deviant norms (Kornhauser 1978, p. 68ff). How this tension plays out in specific empirical situations is a complex matter, one aspect of which will be discussed later.

In considering issues of this kind, it is perhaps helpful to note the suggestion of the sociologist Dennis Wrong (1994, ch. 6) that the "problem of disorder" within social groups can be seen as having two distinct ideal-typical forms, which he describes as "Hobbesian" and "Marxian." Wrong argues that Thomas Hobbes's (1651/1996) famously warring "state of nature" was essentially "pre-political and pre-social" (p. 160); Hobbes saw it as a conflict *between individuals* who, in a presocial context, were in competition for the necessities of life. By contrast, what Wrong calls the "Marxian" form of disorder is about *conflicts between coherent groups*, large or small.[10] As Wrong rightly states, this simple distinction has too rarely been noticed in scholarly discussions of the problem of social order, and this has sometimes led to a conflation of what can be very different kinds of situation (at the extremes, quasi-anarchy and long-term conflict between groups). Conceptually, the most important difference between these situations is one of norms: "Hobbesian" situations are characterized by a relative absence of clear social norms, whereas "Marxian" situations involve some degree of normative conflict between groups. From the perspective of compliance with laws, this difference is crucial: in "Hobbesian" situations there may be no clear norms to comply with, whereas in "Marxian" situations individuals will have to decide which of two very different sets of norms they wish to follow. As noted, however, these are ideal types, and specific empirical situations will not necessarily fit neatly into either category. Moreover, within a given local context, both kinds of situation might be discernible. It is even possible that something like this occurred within the Chicagoan "zone of transition"; that is, there was value conflict between leaders of immigrant groups and those in charge of illegal enterprises, but immigrant children growing up in this social context might have interpreted their situation as one in which there were no clear norms.

Shaw and McKay's concept of "social disorganization" has been remarkably resilient in criminological thought, notwithstanding that criticisms of it go back seventy-five years (see, for example, Wirth 1940). One feature of this resilience has been a tendency to assume that all high offender neighborhoods manifest "social disorganization,"[11] which in turn has led to the (frequently unexamined) view that all such neighborhoods are basically similar. There are, however, two difficulties with this stance. First, as Taylor (2015, pp. 207–210) and others have noted, within the criminological literature there has been significant ambiguity, and therefore inconsistency, in the way in which the concept "social disorganization" has been used. Second, whatever might have been the case in the 1930s, it is now clear from empirical studies that the social character of different high offender neighborhoods can vary in important ways. In what follows, some contrasting examples of high offender neighborhoods will be described and, among other things, these will be considered against the template of Wrong's ideal types.

6.4 Case Studies of Some High Offender Neighborhoods in England

To illustrate the diversity of high offender neighborhoods, data from the second stage of the Sheffield Urban Crime Study will first be considered. This study was conducted in the 1970s and 1980s in Sheffield, a city with a population of approximately half a million. The first stage of the study, briefly mentioned above, consisted of an overview analysis of police-recorded offense and offender data for the city (Baldwin and Bottoms 1976). In the second stage, attention was focused on seven small areas of the city (each with a population of ca. 2,000–3000), and the data collection was widened to include a survey of residents in all seven areas, and participant observation in most of them. The seven areas were carefully selected as being of varied characteristics, with the main criteria for selection being their housing type and their offender rate. Three of the seven areas were high offender-rate areas, and two of these were part of the then extensive range of public housing in the city.[12] Brief initial descriptions of these three areas follow:

- *Skyhigh* was a purpose-built public housing area, situated close to the city center, which consisted of some low-rise apartment blocks plus a large and dominant "sky-scraper" block. At the time of the research fieldwork, it was the least popular public housing development in the city, and therefore the one with the shortest average waiting time.[13]
- *Gardenia* was also a public housing area. However, it differed from Skyhigh in being located three miles from the city center, and in consisting predominantly of two-story semidetached houses. It had been built in the period between the two world wars, and its planners had deliberately incorporated a "garden city" element into its design. It was originally considered to be a select housing development, but it had "tipped" sometime in the 1940s, and at the time of the main fieldwork it had the shortest average waiting time in the city for a non-high-rise public sector estate (high-rise areas being generally more unpopular than areas of conventional housing).
- *Redlight* was a smallish housing area not far from the city center, and very close to the University of Sheffield. The majority of households in the area (about two-thirds) rented their property from a private landlord, but a significant minority were owner-occupiers. At the time of the main research fieldwork, considerable uncertainty hung over the area because, in the strategic plans of the local government authority, much of it was scheduled for demolition and redevelopment, although no date had been set for this. Socially, the area was widely known as the city's main prostitution district.

Table 6.1 provides some basic statistical data on these neighborhoods, relating to demography, residents' perceptions of the area, and offender and victimization rates.[14] These data can be read as a background to the analytic descriptions that follow, in which the varied characteristics of the three neighborhoods as high offender areas are

Table 6.1 Selected Indicators for Three High Offender Neighborhoods in Sheffield

	Skyhigh	Gardenia	Redlight
(a) Demography (from 1975 survey data; last row from public housing data, 1975)			
Mean household size	3.3	3.3	3.3 (3.5†)
% residents aged 16 or under	36	30	21 (28†)
% residents male	50	52	58 (57†)
% survey respondents single	17	16	44 (45†)
% survey respondents born in GB	94	98	76 (78†)
% households resident <2 yrs	27	19	46 (28†)
% households resident 10 yrs+	30	60	32 (43†)
% households in Social Class I/II	2	3	19†
% households in Social Class IV/V	50	39	39†
% households in rent arrears	25	16	n.a.
(b) Perceptions of area (from 1975 survey data)			
% who feel at home in area	46	80	62 (65†)
% would like to leave area	73	40	48 (48†)
(c) Official indicators of offending by residents of the neighborhoods (per 1,000 households per annum)			
General offender rate (indictable offenses, 1971)	82	130	157
% of detected indictable offenses in area committed by residents (1971)	74	62	39
Drug offenders (1974–76)	2	4	22
Prostitution: soliciting in area (1973)*	0	0	74
Television licence evasion (1971–73)	44	62	37
Domestic and neighbour-related disputes (1974)	54	80	50
(d) Victimization indicators (per annum, from 1975 survey data)††			
Victimizations for household offenses (per 100 households)**	67	58	79 (94†)
Victimizations for personal offenses (per 100 respondents)	24	5	40 (50†)

† = excludes student households
†† = includes only victimizations within the neighborhood
* = includes non-residents soliciting in area
** = excludes thefts of milk bottles and milk tokens from outside front doors (especially prevalent in Skyhigh)
Sources: (i) sections (a), (b) and (d): survey data derived from Tables 2-3, 7, 10 and 13 in Bottoms, Mawby and Walker (1987) 'rent arrears' in section (a) from Table 1 in that source; (ii) section (c): data derived from Mawby (1979), Tables 2.8, 2.12, and 8.11, row D.

delineated.[15] As a preliminary observation, it is important to note that while all three neighborhoods were high offender areas, there was a clear difference between them in the proportions of recorded offenses against individual residents (or households) that were committed by other residents (Table 6.1(c), row 2). In both Skyhigh and Gardenia, over 60 percent of such offenses were committed by other residents; in Redlight, the corresponding figure was less than 40 percent.[16] Such a difference is, of course, potentially of great significance in explaining the crimes committed in the areas.

The first neighborhood to be considered is Skyhigh, which—although it was by far the most recently constructed of the three areas—was the most unpopular with its residents. As Table 6.1(b) shows, less than half of survey respondents said that they felt at home in the neighborhood, and nearly three-quarters wanted to leave it. Survey and ethnographic data indicated that, while residents appreciated the internal arrangements of the apartments, and the proximity of the development to the city center, there was widespread disquiet about what is referred to in housing management literature as the "estate outside the dwelling." Thus, residents complained about "the elevators not working and the physical condition of the landings," and observation in the area showed that "litter blows everywhere, graffiti is ubiquitous, there are vandalized telephone boxes and a cacophony of noise" (Bottoms and Xanthos 1981, pp. 218–219). These are, of course, the "incivilities" soon afterward made famous in Wilson and Kelling's (1982) "broken windows" thesis. Moreover, the research showed that residents' dislike of the disorder in the public spaces of the area did indeed lead to the initial consequences predicted by Wilson and Kelling; that is, there was "a self-feeding effect, because people spend as little time as possible in the public areas, leaving them in effect unpoliced by normal informal community controls" (Bottoms and Xanthos 1981, pp. 221–222). There was, however, no evidence to support Wilson and Kelling's further prediction that major criminals would—as a consequence of the absence of community controls—find the area attractive and attempt to operate in it. Hence, crime in the area was mostly minor, consisting mainly of vandalism, thefts, and assaults; and as previously noted, it was predominantly committed by locals.

Given its design features and the level of incivilities, Skyhigh was widely regarded by its residents as an unsuitable area in which to bring up children, but ironically it had a higher proportion of children in its population than either of the other two high offender neighborhoods (Table 6.1(a)). Because of its unpopularity—widely known in the city as a whole—in general only those who were most desperate for housing applied for places in Skyhigh within the public housing allocation system. Such families were often poor,[17] and also tended to have more than their share of personal and social problems. Because of these problems, children were frequently "allowed to roam freely around the balconies and other communal areas" of Skyhigh. There was also little sense of community among the residents, so there was a general "unwillingness to control other people's children in the public spaces of the estate" (Bottoms and Xanthos 1981, p. 221)—a clear indicator of what criminologists would later come to describe as "low collective efficacy" among the residents.[18]

The incivilities so evident in Skyhigh (litter, graffiti, vandalism, noise, and unsupervised children) might be thought to be not very relevant to the present discussion, given that some of these matters are not illegal, and almost all of them are—taken by themselves—apparently minor. To take such a view would, however, be a mistake, because recent criminological research has demonstrated that minor physical and social incivilities, especially when frequently repeated (as on Skyhigh), can lead to profound insecurity among residents (see, for example, Innes and Weston 2010; also chapter 20 by Martin and Helen Innes in this volume). This is because they send a message that "my area is out of control," and this makes it much harder for residents to feel that ordinary daily routines can be accomplished without difficulty. This paradox was well expressed by one of Innes's research respondents: "Yes, it is daft, it is almost daft, but graffiti is the thing that sort of bothers me more, because it is in my face every day. I mean, obviously rape and murder are more horrendous crimes, but it is graffiti that I see" (Innes 2004, p. 348).

Was Skyhigh a "socially disorganized" area at the time of the research? Everything depends on definitions. It had poverty and a relatively high population turnover, both of which are often regarded as indicators of social disorganization; but it had no organized deviant enterprises of the kind regarded as key in Finestone's description of the Chicagoan "zone of transition" (see above). On the available evidence, however, a strong case can be made that Skyhigh at the time of the research constituted a good example of what Wrong described as a "Hobbesian" version of social disorder, in which there were few clear community norms. In this respect, as we shall see, it differed significantly from the next Sheffield neighborhood to be considered.

Gardenia was also a public housing estate, but as a high offender neighborhood it generated two remarkable survey results, both of which contrasted sharply with the comparable data for Skyhigh. First, Gardenia was in no sense an "area in transition," because 60 percent of its households had lived in the area for more than ten years. Second, as many as 80 percent of residents said that they felt at home in the area (Table 6.1(a)). But despite such findings, some residents hated the area, particularly fearing its potential effect on their children's future: one such mother said: "It's just unbearable here; I can't even let the children out of the door." Accordingly, in a research paper on the area we commented that "the paradox of Gardenia was that it could generate both loathing and affinity." We further argued that it was necessary to appreciate both of these emotional reactions to understand the area fully (Bottoms, Mawby, and Xanthos 1989, p. 63).

Criminologically, the most interesting feature of Gardenia was its criminal subculture. There was no formal or semiformal criminal organization, but—particularly in one part of the area—attitudes favorable to offending were not at all uncommon:

> Many or most members of the subculture (including women) were occasional offenders; some were career criminals, consistently seeking out opportunities for (usually medium-size) material gains through criminal activities; and all accepted that some activities (such as . . . mum buying a carpet "very cheaply" off someone in a pub) were part of the normal pattern of life. (Bottoms, Mawby, and Xanthos 1989, p. 57)

An interesting small manifestation of attitudes of this kind was that, among the three high offender-rate neighborhoods, Gardenia had the highest rate for the offense of television license evasion, notwithstanding that its residents were, on average, less poor than those of Skyhigh (Table 6.1(c)).[19]

Geographically, Gardenia was located on top of an escarpment, which meant that links to other parts of the city were restricted, and few except its residents visited it. Empirical research showed that the criminal subculture was especially located in the most isolated part of the area (the southeast), and within that subarea there were some remarkably complex intermarriages among families with long ties to the neighborhood (see the addendum in Bottoms, Mawby, and Xanthos 1989, pp. 75–79). Even outside this relatively limited group, however, many who had grown up in the area valued some of its family and social networks. As adults, they therefore often preferred to obtain houses in the neighborhood rather than to move to a less criminal area; Gardenia's poor reputation did not deter them (see earlier comments on "affinity"). Ironically, the relative unpopularity of Gardenia within the public housing system made such moves easier to achieve than would have been the case in some of the public sector's more select estates.

Among the values of Gardenia's subculture was that beyond a certain age children needed little supervision. For example, one mother from among the interlocking families in the southeast of the area said: "Five, six, seven, they're the worst ages. Before that you can make them fit in with you; after that they can look after themselves" (Bottoms, Mawby, and Xanthos 1989, p. 78). Thus, as in Skyhigh but for subtly different reasons, many children and adolescents roamed the area.

Gardenia's subculture was clearly the main reason for its high offender rate, and, consistently with this, a higher proportion of offenders in Gardenia than in the other two areas appeared repeatedly before the courts (compare Offender Rates A and B in Table 6.1(c)). Residents were aware that the southeast of the area was the main contributor to the neighborhood's high number of offenders, and also that—as in Skyhigh—crimes in Gardenia were mostly committed by local residents (Table 6.1(c)). Those who found this situation to be the most difficult—and who therefore hated continuing to live in the area (see above)—were families with children who had rather unwillingly accepted a house on the estate because they were desperate for housing, but whose values were very different from those of core members of the subculture. One such mother, living in southeast Gardenia, commented: "They're so rough down this end, we've had bricks through our window after John [her partner] complained about their noise, and I just don't like Kevin [her son] to mix with their kids, he'll get into their ways. Their language, you've never heard anything like it" (Bottoms, Mawby, and Xanthos 1989, p. 57).

Although Gardenia was a long-standing high offender-rate neighborhood, it did not display some of the classic features of "social disorganization." For example, it did not have high residential turnover (rather, the reverse), nor could it be said that that the socially dominant group in the area (the interlocking families in the southeast) were, in Kornhauser's (1978) words, prevented by "the structure and culture of a community" from "implementing and expressing the values of its own residents." On the other hand, there was some real normative conflict in the area, which is vividly illustrated in the example given above—and, as we see in that example, such conflicts could sometimes take a violent form.[20] In that sense, and despite the strong evidence of affinities in the area, some aspects of life in Gardenia could be described as close to the "group conflict" ("Marxian") model of social disorder as conceptualized by Dennis Wrong.

The third Sheffield high offender-rate neighborhood, Redlight, differed from the other two because it was not a public sector estate. Its particular location in the city (see above) also meant that it was much more often visited by nonresidents than was either Skyhigh (because of its high-rise character) or Gardenia (because of its geographical isolation). The footfall of nonresidents into the neighborhood was also, of course, increased by the fact that it was the main area in Sheffield where prostitutes chose to operate.

Physically, Redlight was a small and discrete neighborhood, tightly bounded by main roads, a public housing estate and a middle-class conservation area. It had a socially mixed population, including some long-stay residents—over 40 percent of its nonstudent households had lived in the area for over ten years (Table 6.1(a)). But more relevantly for present purposes, and as summarized in a housing-related report in the 1970s, Redlight contained a high proportion of privately rented furnished accommodation, at low rentals, and this meant that the area was attractive to "those who lack[ed] access to other sectors of the [housing] market"[21] and to "young and single people wanting a furnished place near to their work or study" (quoted in Bottoms and Wiles 1986, p. 141). Some of the houses in Redlight were large, having been built in the nineteenth century for affluent residents; these were now in multiple occupation, with several subtenants, who tended to be single persons. Thus, demographically, the neighborhood contained a relatively high proportion of short-term and single residents (Table 6.1(a)). It also contained a higher proportion of foreign-born residents than any other neighborhood in Sheffield at that time (Table 6.1(a)), again as a result of its position in the housing market as a low-price area of predominantly private rental housing. These various population characteristics are, of course, strongly reminiscent of the "interstitial social area," as classically described by Chicago school researchers. However, Redlight also had some unusual characteristics for a neighborhood of this type. Its proximity to the university meant that it was attractive as a source of rented accommodation to students,[22] and as a place to buy a "starter home" for young professionals who did not mind living in an area widely known as a "red-light" neighborhood. Together with the continued presence of some long-stay residents (see above), the latter point meant that Redlight had more residents from higher social groups (in the UK census classification, Social Classes I and II) than is normal for an interstitial area (Table 6.1(a)).

As in Gardenia, there was some important subarea differentiation within Redlight, as between an "inner core" of about four short streets, and the remainder of the area. "The longer-stay residents, the older residents . . . and those of higher socioeconomic status were more likely to live in the outer, peripheral parts"; by contrast "the inner core . . . had a higher proportion of the young, the unemployed, students and shorter stay residents" (Bottoms and Wiles 1986, p. 141). Not surprisingly, offender residences were concentrated in this inner core, and this subarea was also the center of the prostitution-related activities in the neighborhood (Mawby 1979, pp. 50 and 61).[23] It is possible (although this goes beyond the empirical research conducted) that some offenders were attracted to live in this subarea precisely because of its reputation as a high crime and prostitution location; and it is certain that those who wished to gain a secure foothold in the city's prostitution scene usually aspired to rent an apartment in this inner subarea of Redlight. Exactly as described by Finestone (see above), deviant enterprises had been initially easy to set up in Redlight because of the availability of cheap rental properties in the neighborhood; and once some prostitutes had established the area's reputation as a center of this trade, then other women wanted to work from the same location because they knew that potential clients could be found there.

As regards Redlight's more general crime pattern, at the time of the research study this neighborhood had "the highest recorded notifiable offender and offense rate of any residential district in the city" (Bottoms and Wiles 1986, p. 142; see also Table 6.1(c) and Table 6.1(d)). As previously noted, however, within Redlight—unlike the other two neighborhoods discussed—only a minority of the offenses occurring in the area were committed by residents (Table 6.1(c)), so the coupling of high offense and offender rates was less tight than in the other two neighborhoods.

In explaining this finding, it is obviously relevant that the existence of the prostitution activities brought a significant number of nonresidents to Redlight. Similarly, although to a lesser extent, the area was known as a location where drugs could be obtained, and some illegal drinking clubs ("shebeens") were run by members of immigrant communities. These "footfall" dimensions interacted (as predicted by the Brantinghams—see Figure 6.1) with various opportunities for crime in Redlight, of which two were of special importance. First, the area's proximity to the city center and the university meant that on-street parking was common, and so Redlight had a high rate of thefts from cars. Second, the multioccupied houses, in particular, offered opportunities for anonymous access, leading to burglaries and thefts. Together, these various matters meant that Redlight came within the category of what Brantingham and Brantingham (2008) have described as a "crime attractor area."

But if these factors help to explain Redlight's high offense rate, what drove its high offender rate? For technical reasons we can be less sure of the answer to this question in Redlight than in either Skyhigh or Gardenia,[24] but two matters were perhaps operative. First, although there were proportionately fewer children in Redlight than in the other two high offender neighborhoods (Table 6.1(a)), rates of juvenile delinquency were high, very likely for similar reasons as in the Chicagoan "zone of transition." Second, as noted above, the illegal enterprises in the area probably attracted some existing offenders (particularly young adult single males) to come and live there.

At the time of the main research fieldwork, Redlight—unlike the other two areas—was regularly visited by police, particularly the vice and drug squads. However, the policing of prostitution was not draconian, and seemed to be aimed mainly at "contain[ing] the activity within socially acceptable bounds" (Bottoms and Wiles 1986).[25] But in the late 1970s this broadly accommodative relationship between residents, prostitutes, and police gradually changed, following an important alteration in Redlight's housing status. New national legislation in 1974 created a fresh mechanism ("Housing Action Areas," or HAAs) whereby government improvement grants could be obtained for decaying privately rented inner-city areas. Redlight's position close to the university had led to its becoming "a focus for the attention of a number of middle-class professionals who wanted to improve it," and with their active assistance the neighborhood succeeded in gaining HAA status in 1978 (Bottoms and Wiles 1986, p. 144). This decision immediately removed the previous long-standing uncertainty over the area's future (see above). To cut a long story short, this in turn led to some gentrification of the area, and eventually (in the early 1980s) to a major local conflict between the "mainstream" residents and the prostitutes, involving also the police, the local government authority, and the city's magistrates (Bottoms and Wiles 1986, pp. 144–150). As in Gardenia, therefore, we see here an example of Wrong's "Marxian" type of disorder emerging in a high offender area. However, the conflict in Redlight took a more explicitly political form, and it was causally triggered by an important change in Redlight's housing status.

The short descriptive analyses provided above have shown that very different types of high offender neighborhoods can—and did—exist simultaneously in a single city. The social life of one of these areas was dominated by its high physical and social incivilities, while a second possessed a well-entrenched but not particularly organized criminal subculture. In the third neighborhood, although there were high rates of property and personal crime, the dominant criminological feature of the area was the daily presence of soliciting for prostitution, and this trade undoubtedly contributed to the fact that the majority of offenses in this area, unlike the other two, were committed by nonresidents. These divergences are striking, but they do not exhaust possible differences in the characteristics of high offender neighborhoods. To illustrate this, one further English example of a high offender-rate neighborhood will be described, after which some analytical implications of this diversity will be considered.

Sandra Walklate and Karen Evans (1999) studied two inner-city neighborhoods in Salford, Greater Manchester, and—as in the Sheffield study—discovered some significant differences between them. In the present context, one of these neighborhoods ("Oldtown") is of particular interest because, in contrast to all the Sheffield areas, the social life of much of this area was dominated by an organized criminal gang, known as the "Salford Firm," who "claim[ed] to control the area" (p. 7).

The neighborhood of Oldtown had two distinct parts: first, "Canalside," which contained "private luxury flats and housing developments alongside new commercial enterprises in an attractively landscaped waterside setting"; and second, across a four-lane roadway, a public housing area, "The Triangle," which was a "geographically bounded area which there is very little reason to enter unless you live there" (pp. 43–44). Similarly to Gardenia, The Triangle was a high offender-rate area that housed many long-stay residents, and it was here that members of the Salford Firm lived. As in Gardenia, members of this group could be described as belonging to a criminal subculture, but with the important difference that they were an organized group with an acknowledged leader (known as "Mr Big") and an articulated ideology.

One local community activist told Walklate and Evans that "everyone knows who this group is and what they are into at any particular time." In view of this, a given "exploit" (criminal act), although usually committed against people from outside The Triangle (see further below), became "known throughout the estate very quickly after [the] incident has occurred" (p. 7). This knowledge, however, had the consequence that "everyone is a potential grass" (p. 8—i.e., someone who could inform the police), so the Salford Firm set about generating strategies of intimidation to reduce grassing (pp. 90–92). In particular, there was an area of The Triangle "in which nearly all the local amenities were located," and which was therefore frequently visited by residents. In this location, the gang regularly inscribed graffiti naming individuals who they believed had "grassed"; and Walklate and Evans report that this practice was effective in producing "a public arena of shame" that intimidated residents and reinforced some "locally accepted norms and values" about the suspicion of authorities (pp. 91–92).[26] However, intimidation was not the only strategy adopted by members of the Salford Firm. They also tried to legitimate themselves by improving the lives of ordinary residents in Oldtown, and one spokesman for the Firm said that it aimed to "make [residents'] lives better where politicians and local activists have failed" (p. 128).[27] Among other things, this involved the informal policing of local criminal incidents by giving the culprits (mostly local youth) a "smacking" (p. 93). The researchers reported that these quasi-political claims by the Firm received some limited, but ambivalent, support from residents. For example, many residents believed that "the presence of the . . . Firm had kept 'hard drugs' off the estate" (p. 95), and it was acknowledged that in this and in some other ways the area had benefited from the gang's activities. However, residents also "expressed a sense of unease that this was the case"; so in the final analysis, the Firm had failed to win over "the hearts and minds of the majority on the estate" (p. 129).

Walklate and Evans present only minimal statistical data on crime and offending in Oldtown, but clearly the presence of the Salford Firm meant that The Triangle was a high offender neighborhood. What is of special interest in the present context is the apparently reductive effect of the Firm on the local *offense rate*. For most residents of The Triangle, the gang's "street justice" activities, together with its philosophy of committing crimes only against "outsiders," meant that the chances of victimization were not high, and indeed residents regularly said things like: "you're alright round here if you're local," or "Oldtown is a great area [to live in] if you . . . went to school and grew up with the local villains" (Walklate and Evans 1999, pp. 85, 83). As the researchers summarized the matter, a sense of belonging to the area was therefore "closely connected to the belief that you will be protected from being a victim of crime if you belong" (p. 84), although local people were well aware that this protection was only available to them "if they go along with the [gang's] rules" (pp. 128–129).[28] The dilemma that this created for many residents was, of course, the understandable ambivalence that they felt about going along with these rules (see above).

One striking example of this ambivalence links to some wider theoretical issues about social disorganization theory. The example concerns a man who had "grown up with the local villains" and therefore said that he had "no real problems" with living in The Triangle. However, when this man's teenage son "got into trouble whilst hanging around with the local gang," the father promptly took steps to move the boy out of Oldtown (Walklate and Evans 1999, p. 129). The case is of special interest because it seems to be a living example of the operation of the "mixed model" that Shaw and McKay developed in their Chicagoan studies (see previous discussion). The teenager's delinquency seems to have arisen initially because "the structure and culture of [the] community" in Oldtown did not express the values of the boy's parents, and therefore created a degree of Hobbesian-style normative uncertainty; but the boy then seems to have learned pro-offending values, and no doubt also techniques of offending, from specifically associating with a criminal gang. As part of her influential critique of Shaw and McKay's "mixed model," Ruth Kornhauser (1978) comments on this kind of situation as follows:

> If [as Shaw and McKay contend] the family, the school and all other institutions are carriers of conventional values, then the delinquent subculture, however well established, is dependent for recruits upon youth who are freed from ordinary controls because the community's institutions are ineffective. If the [criminal gang] can never transform the slum into a community organized to nourish and protect delinquent and criminal values, then it persists only as an unwanted incubus upon a supine community with weak social controls. (pp. 72–73)

Walklate and Evans's (1999) rich qualitative picture of social life in Oldtown suggests, however, that the phrase "unwanted incubus upon a supine community" greatly oversimplifies the complex normative and power dynamics that can be present when a community with many conventional values is living in the same area as a criminal gang that has the goal of exercising significant control over that area.

The existence of the Salford Firm, and the complex social practices that they put in place, meant that Oldtown, as a high offender neighborhood, was clearly different from any of the Sheffield neighborhoods. The case study of Oldtown therefore adds to the complexity of our understanding of high offender-rate neighborhoods, yet it also seems unlikely that the four area case studies presented in this subsection will exhaust the range of divergence in the social characteristics of high offender areas. If this is correct, it poses a significant theoretical challenge to environmental criminologists, some aspects of which must now be addressed.

6.5 Analytical Issues

Three main analytical issues arise from the preceding discussion. The first concerns the relationship between crimes, places, and offenders. The second raises questions concerning the links between analyses of crime in small neighborhoods and the wider sociopolitical contexts within which they are set; and the third concerns the concept of "social disorganization."

6.5.1 Crimes, Places, and Offenders

The "new" environmental criminology, in its various forms, often seems keen to declare that the study of offenders is not its primary concern. So, for example, in the quotation included in the introduction to this chapter, Wortley and Mazerolle (2008, p. 2) state with emphasis that "*crime* is the object of interest" and that the aim of scholars in this tradition is "to prevent crime, not to cure offenders." In a similar fashion, Weisburd, Groff, and Yang (2012, pp. 3–4) say that they offer a "radical reconceptualization of the crime problem" that breaks with traditional offender-focused approaches. Accordingly, they say that they begin "not . . . with the people that commit crime, but rather with the places where crime occurs"; and they claim that this new "criminology of place" will yield "significant new criminological insights that both advance theory and practical crime prevention."

There is of course a real point to moves of this kind. To give just one example, studies of criminal careers traditionally paid little or no attention to the specifics of the crimes committed by their research subjects, nor where they were committed (although for a recent and important exception, see Wikström et al. 2012). Also, preventive strategies aimed at specific types of crime in particular places have sometimes shown positive results, even though the strategy pays no attention to the characteristics of the offenders committing the crimes (see for example so-called alley-gating strategies in Britain: Sidebottom et al. 2016). Yet there remains a danger of, in the folksy saying, "throwing the baby out with the bathwater." Certainly we should not pursue an environmental criminology that pays no attention to offenses, but focusing on offenses does not necessarily mean that one should pay no attention to offenders. If we consider, for example, the three high offender-rate Sheffield neighborhoods described above, it would clearly be sensible to develop situational, non-offender-focused strategies to try to prevent the high rate of thefts from cars in Redlight (many of which were committed by nonresidents). But trying to tackle the long-standing victimization "hotspot" in southeast Gardenia without taking account of the high offender rate and the criminal subculture in that small area would make no sense; and nor would trying to tackle the high rate of vandalism in Skyhigh while ignoring that area's lack of community, and the consequent low collective efficacy that had helped to generate its high offender rate. In other words, local crime prevention strategies need to be both holistic and sensitive to the specific characteristics of that particular location; and this will sometimes mean taking account of the area's offender rate, and what seems to be driving it.

To put this another way, in the words of Ralph Taylor (2015, p. 143), although places may host crimes, they do not commit them. Furthermore, "if we want to learn about the causes of crime in communities, we need to know which individuals are committing which crime acts in what places, at what times, and why" (p. 144). The "new" environmental criminology has taught us much about "crime acts," and about crime prevention, that was not previously known. Perhaps in its early stages this movement needed, as a pragmatic matter, to assert that it was not very interested in offenders. But now that this mode of criminological thought is well established, there should be no difficulty in moving beyond this kind of tactical pragmatism, and adopting instead the more defensible and holistic approach proposed by Taylor. The "discrete spatial choice" studies (see above) have made a good start in this direction, but further work is clearly needed. (For a fuller argument along these lines, see Bottoms 2012.)

6.5.2 Wider Sociopolitical Contexts

A fully holistic approach to explanation, as proposed by Taylor (2015), will need to go beyond the integration of offense-based and offender-based perspectives. In an important late twentieth-century study in Chicago, Bursik and Grasmick (1993) found that many of Shaw and McKay's (1942/1969) insights remained relevant; however, they argued that there were "two aspects of community structure" which Shaw and McKay had "virtually ignored," yet which were of great importance in the study of neighborhoods and crime. These neglected matters were, first, "the networks [between] residents and local institutions" and, second, "the networks [between] local representatives of the neighborhood and external actors, institutions and agencies" (Bursik and Grasmick 1993, p. x). In short, the argument was that neighborhoods cannot be properly understood unless they are studied within the wider sociopolitical context, including the institutional and power-based contexts, within which they are set.

A rather similar message emerged from the earlier work of Taub, Taylor, and Dunham (1984), also in Chicago, that had focused on neighborhood change. These authors proposed that there are "three types of social and ecological pressures that interactively determine the pattern of change in urban neighborhoods"; these are "ecological facts," "corporate decisions," and "individual decisions" (p. 182).[29] Each of these can be seen at work in the four case studies presented in the previous subsection. "Ecological facts" included the fact that Redlight happened to be situated next to the university. "Individual decisions" were to be seen in all the Sheffield areas, as families in need of housing discovered that the most readily available housing was to be found in a high offender neighborhood, and then had to work out how they would live in such a neighborhood. "Corporate decisions," in a broad sense, were strikingly apparent in the institutional dominance of the Salford Firm over many aspects of the social life of Oldtown; they were also—though in a very different way—exemplified in the consequences of the granting of Housing Action Area status to Redlight.

A central issue within this wider sociopolitical context concerns the role of local housing markets—a topic that has been frequently alluded to in the three analytic case studies of Sheffield neighborhoods. (For a fuller discussion of the importance of housing markets within the Sheffield study, see Bottoms and Wiles 1986). As Robert Sampson (2009, p. 90) has rightly observed, "because housing markets act as a mechanism of allocation . . . , they . . . need to be better integrated into sociological and criminological theory." Their influence is apparent at many levels: obviously at the individual and corporate levels (see above), but also at the level of local government policies relating to land use, and—in such matters as the availability of public housing and grants to improve decaying private sector areas—potentially at national level also. This is a richly relevant topic in the study of neighborhoods, but one that mainstream environmental criminology has been slow to recognize (see further chapter 23 by Ceccato and Wilhelmsson in this volume).

6.5.3 "Social Disorganization"

It seems clear from the area case studies discussed above that the single concept of "social disorganization" cannot adequately explain offending in all the varied types of high offender neighborhood that have been described. As Walklate and Evans (1999, p. 6) put it after their work in Salford, "our work . . . suggests that . . . poorer, inner city neighbourhoods, far from being the disorganised neighbourhoods of popular imagination, may exhibit many and different community structures and patterns of local organisation and networks." This raises the question whether constructive alternative suggestions for future theorization can be identified.

A brief excursion into the history of criminological theory might be helpful in this regard. The great early American criminologist Edwin Sutherland had been happy to use the term "social disorganization" in the third edition of his textbook, published in 1939, but by the fourth edition, eight years later, he was less sure. In this fresh edition, he first asserted that when considering theories of criminal behavior "from the point of view of the community [or] nation" (as opposed to that of the individual) "one of the best explanations . . . is that a high crime rate is due to social disorganization." However, he immediately qualified this statement, saying (in the same paragraph) that "the term 'social disorganization' is not entirely satisfactory, and it seems preferable to substitute for it the term 'differential social organization' " (Sutherland 1947, p. 8). Gaylord and Galliher (1988) have helpfully shown that this shift in Sutherland's thinking was prompted by two rather different thoughts. First, he was influenced by the critique of Louis Wirth (1940) that the concept of "social disorganization" might carry an unfortunate evaluative connotation about poorer areas: " 'their' social organization is disorganized, while 'ours' is not." Second, Sutherland thought that the concept of differential social organization "better conveyed the idea that society is two-minded about crime—one part being organized for criminal activities, the other organized against them" (Gaylord and Galliher 1988, p. 142).

However, despite his careful and principled preference for the concept of "differential social organization," Sutherland did little to expound or develop this term, and—unlike "social disorganization"—it has disappeared from the common stock of concepts used by contemporary criminologists. One prominent criticism of the concept has appeared in successive editions of Vold's *Theoretical Criminology*:[30]

> Sutherland's theory . . . states that in a situation of differential social organization and normative conflict, differences in behavior, including criminal behaviors, arise because of differential associations. This is really only another way of saying that a person who associates with Methodists is likely to become a Methodist, a person who associates with Republicans is likely to become a Republican, and a person who associates with criminals is likely to become a criminal. (Bernard, Snipes, and Geroud 2010, p. 182)

It is certainly correct that Sutherland's concept of "differential social organization" was seen by him as the social dimension of his theory of differential association (on which see Cressey 1964). But there appears to be no necessary reason why the concept should be understood in this limited way—in which case, there may be significantly more to say about the nature and consequences of differential social organization than Bernard and colleagues suggest.

A helpful way of beginning to reinterpret Sutherland's concept is perhaps through the work of Neil MacCormick, a legal theorist who worked in close conjunction with criminologists at the University of Edinburgh. One of MacCormick's central claims, fully elaborated in some of his later work, is that systems of law are always versions of an "institutional normative order" (MacCormick 2007, p. 11). By this he meant, first, that laws *always embody norms*; and the normative concepts in play in a specific legal or social context are sometimes "dense and thickly concatenated" (MacCormick 2009, p. 190). But, second, in contemporary societies laws are set within a legal system, which manifests itself in *complex institutional forms* (police services, prosecutors, courts, and so on); and even social institutions that are not intrinsically part of the legal system (such as businesses or schools) are always connected to the law through contracts, regulatory systems, and so on.

In developing this kind of conceptual framework, we must not, of course, forget the most important contribution of environmental criminologists to the study of crime and compliance—namely the frequent relevance to behavior of the *situational context* of a given action or projected action, over and above its normative and institutional dimensions. A classic illustration of this point is Clarke and Mayhew's (1988) demonstration that the sharp drop in the suicide rate in Great Britain in the 1970s was not the result of any normative or institutional change, but could realistically be attributed only to the nationwide alteration in the nature of the gas supply (from toxic coal gas to nontoxic natural gas).

Environmental criminologists conduct social scientific studies of crime (or the lack of crime) in specific locations (neighborhoods or street segments), and this kind of research can reasonably be regarded as the study of manifestations of lawbreaking, or legal compliance, in those areas. If MacCormick's theoretical framework for the understanding of law, and the insights of environmental criminologists, are both correct—as I believe that they are—then research on the reasons for crime, or the absence of crime, in particular places must involve analyses of the potential influences of the *institutional frameworks*, *normative understandings*, and *specific situational features* that are to be found in these different locations. We have seen in this chapter that each of these matters can be of great significance in the study of high offender-rate areas. Thus, for example, Bursik and Grasmick's (1993) work rightly emphasized institutional influences on the social life of small areas, in contrast to the neglect of such matters by Shaw and McKay; and, among relevant institutional influences, the Sheffield research points to the substantial significance of housing markets in differentially (if indirectly) shaping the crime rates of neighborhoods. As for MacCormick's emphasis on normative matters, the case studies in this chapter have frequently illustrated Sutherland's claim that both procriminal and anticriminal norms can be seen in conflict in specific settings; this was most clearly evident in Oldtown, but could also be observed in Gardenia and—eventually—in the political struggle over prostitution in Redlight. These case studies all illustrate what Dennis Wrong called "Marxian" value conflicts; but we must not forget that "Hobbesian" situations, with their lack of clear norms, are also an important manifestation of MacCormick's emphasis on normative issues, and this was seen most clearly in the description of social life in Skyhigh. As for situational issues, these were of relevance both as regards the geographically isolated location of Gardenia and the high-rise design features of Skyhigh, although in neither case were these features the sole issues in play in those neighborhoods.

It can, therefore, reasonably be claimed that close attention to the institutional frameworks, normative understandings, and specific situational features of places is vital to the study of environmental criminology. It is also abundantly clear from the case studies in this chapter that such matters show substantial variation, *even among high offender-rate areas.* A revival of Sutherland's concept of "differential social organization," with special attention to the institutional, normative, and situational features of specific locations, would therefore seem to be a promising way forward for environmental criminology.

6.6 Conclusions

This chapter has, in agreement with the "new" environmental criminologists, fully embraced the importance of studying the places where crimes are committed. It has also, however, argued for the importance of *context* when studying local crime rates. In the first main section, it was contended that two potentially important contextual elements in the explanation of local crime rates are (1) the offender rate of the locality, and (2) the proximity of the locality to high offender-rate areas. In the second section of the chapter, it was demonstrated that high offender-rate areas can themselves differ significantly in both their social and their criminal characteristics, and therefore that an important element of the contextual understanding of crimes in such areas will be to delineate with precision what seems to be driving the high offender rate. It was further suggested that Sutherland's (1947, p. 8) concept of "differential social organization," reinterpreted as embracing the institutional frameworks, normative understandings, and specific situational features of places, provides a valuable framework for analyses of this kind.

As a concluding comment, we can usefully return to the strong preference, in contemporary environmental criminology, for studying local offense rates on a microlocational basis, for example, using street segments as a unit of analysis (Weisburd, Bernasco, and Bruinsma 2009; Weisburd, Groff, and Yang 2012). The case for this approach is, in its own terms, very strong. But does it need to be modified in light of the arguments in this chapter on the need also to take account of local offender rates?

The answer to this question is in the negative. It is true that the location of offender residences is a topic not usually best studied on a truly microlocational level—although as we have seen in the descriptions of both Gardenia and Redlight, important subarea differences in offender rates can be apparent even within relatively small neighborhoods. But it is not necessary, when studying crime rates in cities, to work with identical units of analysis for offense and offender rates—or indeed for other indicators, as a few existing studies in environmental criminology have already shown (e.g., Johnson and Bowers 2010; Davies and Johnson 2015). Southeast Gardenia had seven or eight streets, but it would be highly relevant to the study of offenses in any of these streets, even one with little crime, to know that the street was located in a subarea with a long-standing high offender rate, and a criminal subculture.[31] Context matters, and the offender rate of both the specific street and the surrounding streets is an important part of the context when studying microlocational crime rates.

NOTES

1. Some other papers in contemporary environmental criminology share Weisburd et al.'s (2012) approach of simultaneously examining "social" and "situational" factors at the street segment level, while also not explicitly addressing the location of offender residences: see, e.g., Johnson and Bowers (2010) and Davies and Johnson (2015). For contributions to environmental criminology that consider offender residence variables, see the discussion of the "discrete spatial choice" approach, below.
2. Taylor (2015, p. 29) generously describes the work of John Baldwin and myself in Sheffield as the first systematic investigation of the offense-offender rate distinction across a whole city. He also comments that, in the United States in the 1970s, the results of the study "startled other scholars" because—to a degree—they ran counter to the "earlier widely accepted" notion of the spatial congruence of offender and offense rates.
3. Of course, researchers pursuing rational choice and RAT approaches could in principle be interested in offenders. But rational choice researchers in criminology have tended to assume rational choice rather than to investigate it, and RAT-oriented scholars such as Marcus Felson have usually chosen to focus on the routine activities of general populations and potential victims rather than offenders.
4. Note, however that, while distance decay is an accurate description of the aggregate findings in "journey to crime" studies, recent research suggests that among persistent offenders there can be significant inter- and intra-offender variation in the extent of these "journeys" (Smith, Bond, and Townsley 2009).
5. The area variables used as controls were population size; percentage of single-person households; poverty; and degree of urbanization.
6. Wiles and Costello (2000) reported some similar results. These authors interviewed 70 offenders from Sheffield, and were able to analyze in detail the travel patterns relating to 90 burglaries and 72 offenses of taking cars. They found statistically significant relationships between the offense location and (1) the area currently lived in ($p < .001$), and (2) areas lived in at some previous time ($p < .01$).
7. Hence, for example, in Wikström's (1991, p. 227) Stockholm study, although residential burglary rates were often low in what were described as "problem areas" of the city, high victimization rates for this crime were found in districts near to "high offender rate areas in the outer city," as well as in districts near to parts of the inner city (where offender rates are generally high).
8. On this point, see also the argument by Bernasco and Nieuwbeerta (2005, p. 301 n. 4) that "ignoring the home locations of offenders" when studying crime locations is at the very least "questionable."

9. The subareas shown on these maps all have an approximately equal population. The large subarea in the northwest of the city is mostly moorland.
10. Wrong's terminology is retained here, although it is not optimal because Marxism primarily anticipates conflicts based on economic interests, whereas Wrong is referring (quite appropriately) to group conflicts arising for any reason.
11. This can, and sometimes has, led to an unfortunate (and indeed tautological) tendency to treat evidence of a high area-offender rate as evidence of social disorganization.
12. Public sector housing expanded rapidly in Britain after the Second World War as a result of the adoption of welfare state policies, and it became much more extensive than in the United States. By the mid-1970s, no fewer than 30 percent of households in England and Wales were in public housing, and in some cities, including Sheffield, the proportion was higher than this. As a result of various policy developments, the proportion has subsequently declined significantly.
13. The public sector housing allocation system operative in Sheffield at the time of the research is described fully in Bottoms and Xanthos (1981). As explained in that source, people seeking public sector housing were checked for eligibility and then (in the usual case) placed on the waiting list for an estate of their choice. However, "the waiting time for estates can vary enormously . . . from perhaps a few months . . . on the least popular high-rise developments to *over ten years* for the most popular and 'desirable' estates . . . .. This has the effect that those . . . who are most desperate for housing are informally steered [by housing officials] toward the least popular estates" (Bottoms and Xanthos, 1981, p. 210).
14. In an era before personal computers, all offender and offense rate data for these areas had to be extracted by hand from police files, so it is not possible to provide city-wide data as a comparison for the data in Table 6.1. However, in the original research study, each of the high offender-rate areas had a roughly matched comparison area of the same housing type, and two of these comparison areas (those for Skyhigh and Gardenia) were geographically adjacent to the high offender area. Using 1971 data, the official offender rates per 1,000 households for the three selected areas and their comparators were Skyhigh 82, comparison area 22; Gardenia 130, comparison area 32; Redlight 157, comparison area 22 (using for this purpose "Offender rate B in Table 6.1). For further data on the three selected areas and their comparators, see Bottoms, Mawby, and Walker (1987)
15. Fuller descriptions of the three neighborhoods can be found in the following sources: for Skyhigh, Bottoms and Xanthos (1981, especially at pp. 217–224—Skyhigh is there referred to as "CFH"); for Gardenia, Bottoms, Mawby, and Xanthos (1989); and for Redlight, Bottoms and Wiles (1986, especially at pp. 137–150). The results of the survey of residents in all the seven selected neighborhoods, including the three high offender areas, will be found in Bottoms, Mawby, and Walker (1987). Mawby (1979) contains an extensive discussion of various kinds of official data for all seven areas.
16. Of necessity, this comparison is restricted to detected offenses.
17. The population of Skyhigh was, on average, the poorest of any of the three high offender areas, and it had high levels of rent arrears (see Table 6.1(a)).
18. Collective efficacy has been defined as "the institutional ability to achieve what a group or community collectively wishes to achieve." Methodologically, it has been operationalized within neighborhood studies through survey items measuring two linked concepts: first, the willingness of residents to intervene for the common good in certain defined situations (such as children spray-painting graffiti on a building); and, second, the existence or otherwise of "conditions of cohesion and mutual trust among neighbors" (since "one is

unlikely to take action in a neighborhood context where the rules are unclear and people mistrust each other": Sampson and Raudenbush 1999, p. 612). For a fuller discussion of collective efficacy see Sampson (2006).

19. In the United Kingdom, public broadcasting is provided by the British Broadcasting Corporation, whose activities are financed by a license fee that must be paid annually by any household where there is a functioning television. Enforcement of license fee payments is the responsibility of a special agency (not the police), and nonpayment is a minor criminal offense.
20. Note also that Gardenia had, by comparison with the other two areas, a substantially higher rate of domestic and neighbor-related disputes to which the police were called (Table 6.1(c)).
21. In England at that time there were three main housing market sectors: the owner-occupied sector (usually accessible with the help of a mortgage); the public housing sector; and the private rental sector. The first required down payment of a capital sum, and the second required eligibility and a period on the waiting list (see note 13 above). The private rental sector was therefore the only realistic choice for those who did not meet either of these requirements.
22. In the household survey conducted as part of the Sheffield Urban Crime Study in 1975, 30 percent of households sampled in Redlight were student households (Bottoms, Mawby, and Walker 1987). In Table 6.1, survey-generated data relating to Redlight are shown separately for (1) all sampled households, and (2) nonstudent households only.
23. That is, the inner core was where most soliciting took place. Not all prostitutes actually lived in Redlight, although the more senior and well-established women tended to do so. Other women might rent a room in the area for "business" purposes, while at the low prestige end of the market some women were dependent on carrying out transactions in customers' cars.
24. This is because the participant observation in Redlight was focused exclusively on the soliciting and drugs activities in the area.
25. Thus, for example, in 1973 only 48 women working in Redlight (on average, one per week) were actually charged with soliciting (Mawby 1979, p. 59), although it should be noted that, in law, no one could be charged with soliciting unless she had previously received two cautions, and no doubt other women had been cautioned.
26. A spokesman for the Salford Firm explained to the researchers that there was a "code" in place in Oldtown. It was "right to inform the police" about certain things, such as a rape, child abuse, or the mugging of an old lady; but "if somebody goes and says 'so and so has done a ram raid' or 'so and so has done a post office,' then it's grassing, it's not acceptable": Walklate and Evans (1999), p. 93.
27. For example, the researchers report that "the local 'Mr Big' would even indulge in small acts of philanthropy," as on one occasion when he gave money to "a local family whose belongings had been destroyed in a house fire" (Walklate and Evans 1999, p. 128).
28. It needs to be added that the category "local" was not straightforward. For example, while Canalside was clearly part of Oldtown, people in that area felt that they were not accepted as "local" by the Firm, and that "their houses and cars were more likely to be vandalised or broken into as a result" (p.77). Also, managers of local firms throughout the neighborhood said they "were treated as though their businesses did not belong, and that they suffered much petty and some serious crime as a result"; this had led to "local shops [being] closed because of armed raids and shoplifting" (pp. 77, 80).

29. Taub, Taylor, and Dunham (1984, ch. 9) particularly emphasized the impact that corporate decisions can have on paths of neighborhood change, because a corporate actor has a significantly greater likelihood of influencing others' decisions than do individual actors. They offer an extended illustration of this point as regards the Hyde Park-Kenwood district of Chicago (pp. 96–102), where the University of Chicago intervened strategically in the local housing market, and also introduced a private police force and safety buses. The result was a significant stabilization of the neighborhood; it continued to have a high crime rate, but (very unusually for a high crime area) it also had rapidly appreciating property values (p. 24).
30. This paragraph was first included in the third edition of this classic textbook, edited by Thomas J. Bernard and published in 1986. It has remained unaltered through the sixth edition.
31. Not least because there is at least some evidence that offenders sometimes deliberately travel a short distance so as not to commit crimes against their immediate neighbors (referred to as a relatively immune "buffer zone").

References

Baldwin, John, and Anthony E. Bottoms. 1976. *The Urban Criminal: A Study in Sheffield.* London: Tavistock Publications.

Bernard, Thomas J., Jeffrey B. Snipes, and Alexander L. Gerould. 2010. *Vold's Theoretical Criminology.* 6th ed. New York: Oxford University Press.

Bernasco, Wim. 2010. "A Sentimental Journey to Crime: Effects of Residential History on Crime Location Choice." *Criminology* 48(2): 389–416.

Bernasco, Wim, and Paul Nieuwbeerta. 2005. "How Do Residential Burglars Select Targets? A New Approach to the Analysis of Criminal Location Choice." *British Journal of Criminology* 45(3): 296–315.

Bottoms, Anthony E. 2012. "Developing Socio-spatial Criminology." In *The Oxford Handbook of Criminology*, 5th ed., edited by Mike Maguire, Rod Morgan, and Robert Reiner. Oxford: Oxford University Press.

Bottoms, Anthony E., Rob I. Mawby, and Monica A. Walker. 1987. "A Localised Crime Survey in Contrasting Areas of a City." *British Journal of Criminology* 27(2): 125–154.

Bottoms, Anthony E., Rob I. Mawby, and Polii Xanthos. 1989. "A Tale of Two Estates." In *Crime and the City: Essays in Memory of John Barron Mays*, edited by David Downes. Basingstoke, Hampshire: Macmillan.

Bottoms, Anthony E., and Paul Wiles. 1986. "Housing Tenure and Community Crime Careers in Britain." In *Communities and Crime*, edited by Albert J. Reiss Jr., and Michael Tonry. Vol. 8 of *Crime and Justice: A Review of Research*, edited by Michael Tonry. Chicago: University of Chicago Press.

Bottoms, Anthony E., and Polii Xanthos. 1981. "Housing Policy and Crime in the British Public Sector." In *Environmental Criminology*, edited by Paul J. Brantingham and Patricia L. Brantingham. Beverly Hills, CA: Sage.

Brantingham, Patricia L., and Paul J. Brantingham. 1981. "Notes on the Geometry of Crime." In *Environmental Criminology*, edited by Paul J. Brantingham and Patricia L. Brantingham. Beverly Hills, CA: Sage.

Brantingham, Paul J., and Patricia L. Brantingham. 2008. "Crime Pattern Theory." In *Environmental Criminology and Crime Analysis,* edited by Richard Wortley and Lorraine Mazerolle. Cullompton, Devon, UK: Willan Publishing.

Bursik, Robert J., Jr., and Harold G. Grasmick. 1993. *Neighborhoods and Crime: The Dimensions of Effective Community Control.* New York: Lexington Books.

Clarke, Ronald V. 1980. "Situational Crime Prevention: Theory and Practice." *British Journal of Criminology* 20(2): 136–147.

Clarke, Ronald V., and Marcus Felson, eds. 1993. *Routine Activity and Rational Choice.* New Brunswick, NJ: Transaction.

Clarke, Ronald V., and Pat Mayhew. 1988. "The British Gas Suicide Story and Its Criminological Implications." In *Crime and Justice: A Review of Research*, vol. 10, edited by Michael Tonry and Norval Morris. Chicago: University of Chicago Press.

Cohen, Lawrence E., and Marcus Felson. 1979. "Social Change and Crime Rate Trends: A Routine Activity Approach." *American Sociological Review* 44(4): 588–608.

Cornish, Derek B., and Ronald V. Clarke, eds. 1986. *The Reasoning Criminal: Rational Choice Perspectives on Offending.* New York: Springer.

Cressey, Donald R. 1964. *Delinquency, Crime and Differential Association.* The Hague: Martinus Nijhoff.

Davies, Toby, and Shane D. Johnson. 2015. "Examining the Relationship between Road Structure and Burglary Risk via Quantitative Network Analysis." *Journal of Quantitative Criminology* 31(3): 481–507.

Finestone, Harold. 1976. "The Delinquent and Society: The Shaw and McKay Tradition." In *Delinquency, Crime and Society*, edited by James F. Short, Jr. Chicago: University of Chicago Press.

Gaylord, Mark S., and John F. Galliher. 1988. *The Criminology of Edwin Sutherland.* New Brunswick, NJ: Transaction.

Groff, Elizabeth R., David Weisburd, and Nancy A. Morris. 2012. "Where the Action Is at Places: Examining Spatio-temporal Patterns of Juvenile Crime at Places Using Trajectory Analysis." In *Putting Crime in Its Place: Units of Analysis in Geographic Criminology*, edited by David Weisburd, Wim Bernasco, and Gerben J. N. Bruinsma. New York: Springer.

Hobbes, Thomas. 1996. *Leviathan.* Edited by John C. A. Gaskin. Oxford: Oxford University Press. Originally published 1651.

Innes, Martin. 2004. "Signal Crimes and Signal Disorders: Notes on Crime as Communicative Action." *British Journal of Sociology* 55(3): 335–355.

Innes, Martin, and Nicola Weston. 2010. *Re-thinking the Policing of Anti-social Behaviour.* London: Her Majesty's Inspectorate of Constabulary.

Johnson, Shane D., and Kate J. Bowers. 2010. "Permeability and Burglary Risk: Are Cul-de-Sacs Safer?" *Journal of Quantitative Criminology* 26(1): 89–111.

Kornhauser, Ruth R. 1978. *Social Sources of Delinquency: An Appraisal of Analytic Models.* Chicago: University of Chicago Press.

MacCormick, Neil. 2007. *Institutions of Law: An Essay in Legal Theory.* Oxford: Oxford University Press.

MacCormick, Neil. 2009. "Concluding for Institutionalism." In *Law as Institutional Normative Order*, edited by Maksymilian Del Mar and Zenon Bankowski. Farnham, Surrey: Ashgate.

Mawby, Rob I. 1979. *Policing the City.* Farnborough, Hampshire: Saxon House.

Mayhew, Patricia, Ronald V. Clarke, Andrew Sturman, and Mike Hough. 1976. *Crime as Opportunity.* Home Office Research Study No. 34. London: Her Majesty's Stationery Office.

Sampson, Robert J. 2006. "Collective Efficacy Theory: Lessons Learned and Directions for Future Inquiry." In *Taking Stock: The Status of Criminological Theory*, edited by Francis T. Cullen, John Paul Wright, and Kristie R. Blevins. New Brunswick, NJ: Transaction.

Sampson, Robert J. 2009. "Analytic Approaches to Disorder." *British Journal of Sociology* 60(1): 83–93.

Sampson, Robert J., and Stephen W. Raudenbush. 1999. "Systematic Social Observation of Public Spaces: A New Look at Disorder and Crime." *American Journal of Sociology* 105(3): 603–651.

Shapland, Joanna M., Paul Wiles, and Paula Wilcox. 1994. *Targeted Crime Reduction for Local Areas: Principles and Methods*. Home Office Police Research Group Crime Prevention Handbook. London: Home Office.

Shaw, Clifford R., and Henry D. McKay. 1969. *Juvenile Delinquency and Urban Areas: A Study of Rates of Delinquency in Relation to Differential Characteristics of Local Communities in America Cities*. Revised ed. Chicago: University of Chicago Press. Original edition published 1942.

Sidebottom, Aiden, Lisa Tompson, Amy Thornton, Karen Bullock, Nick Tilley, Kate Bowers, and Shane D. Johnson. 2016. *Gating Alleys to Reduce Crime: A Meta-analysis and Realist Synthesis*. College of Policing What Works Crime Reduction Systematic Review Series No. 1. London: College of Policing.

Smith, William, John W. Bond, and Michael Townsley. 2009. "Determining How Journeys-to-Crime Vary: Measuring Inter- and Intra-offender Crime Trip Distributions." In *Putting Crime in Its Place: Units of Analysis in Geographic Criminology*, edited by David Weisburd, Wim Bernasco, and Gerben J. N. Bruinsma. New York: Springer.

Sutherland, Edwin H. 1947. *Principles of Criminology*. 4th ed. Chicago: J. B. Lippincott.

Taub, Richard P., D. Garth Taylor, and Jan D. Dunham. 1984. *Paths of Neighborhood Change: Race and Crime in Urban America*. Chicago: University of Chicago Press.

Taylor, Ralph B. 2015. *Community Criminology: Fundamentals of Spatial and Temporal Scaling, Ecological Indicators and Selectivity Bias*. New York: New York University Press.

Townsley, Michael, Daniel Birks, Wim Bernasco, Stijn Ruiter, Shane D. Johnson, Gentry White, and Scott Baum. 2015. "Burglar Target Selection: A Cross-National Comparison." *Journal of Research in Crime and Delinquency* 52(1): 3–31.

Walklate, Sandra, and Karen Evans. 1999. *Zero Tolerance or Community Tolerance? Managing Crime in High Crime Areas*. Aldershot, Hampshire: Ashgate.

Weisburd, David, Wim Bernasco, and Gerben J. N. Bruinsma, eds. 2009. "Putting Crime in Its Place." In *Putting Crime in Its Place: Units of Analysis in Geographic Criminology*, edited by David Weisburd, Wim Bernasco, and Gerben J. N. Bruinsma. New York: Springer.

Weisburd, David, Elizabeth R. Groff, and Sue Ming Yang. 2012. *The Criminology of Place: Street Segments and Our Understanding of the Crime Problem*. New York: Oxford University Press.

Wikström, Per-Olof H. 1991. *Urban Crime, Criminals and Victims: The Swedish Experience in an Anglo-American Comparative Perspective*. New York: Springer.

Wikström, Per-Olof H., Dietrich Oberwittler, Kyle Treiber, and Beth Hardie. 2012. *Breaking Rules: The Social and Situational Dynamics of Young People's Urban Crime*. Oxford: Oxford University Press.

Wiles, Paul, and Andrew Costello. 2000. *The "Road to Nowhere": The Evidence for Travelling Criminals*. Home Office Research Study No. 207. London: Research, Development and Statistics Directorate, Home Office.

Wilson, James Q., and George L. Kelling. 1982. "Broken Windows: The Police and Neighborhood Safety." *Atlantic Monthly*, March: 29–38.
Wirth, Louis. 1940. "Ideological Aspects of Social Disorganization." *American Sociological Review* 5(4): 472–482.
Wortley, Richard, and Lorraine Mazerolle. 2008. "Environmental Criminology and Crime Analysis: Situating the Theory, Analytic Approach and Application." In *Environmental Criminology and Crime Analysis*, edited by Richard Wortley and Lorraine Mazerolle. Cullompton, Devon, UK: Willan Publishing.
Wrong, Dennis H. 1994. *The Problem of Order: What Unites and Divides Society.* Cambridge, MA: Harvard University Press.

CHAPTER 7

FOUR IMAGES OF THE DELINQUENCY AREA

MARCUS FELSON

7.1 Introduction

Introductory students of criminology usually learn about "social disorganization theory," and graduate students are usually examined on that same theory. As they study for their exams they quickly discover that this theory is often vague, and is defined and measured in different ways. They may well realize that the theory has taken many forms over the eighty years since it was formulated by Shaw and McKay, along with their collaborators (Shaw et al., 1929; Shaw and McKay, 1942). My main purpose in this chapter is to sort out some of the ideas that are sometimes mixed together under the rubric of "social disorganization." I shall argue that

- Social disorganization is really not an independent variable or a theory;
- Rather, it is a composite *image* of the "delinquency area"—the part of town that also has very high crime rates; and
- This composite image can be disentangled and then clarified, allowing students to learn it and researchers to sharpen their findings.

I shall extract four distinct images of the delinquency area in the effort to clarify the topic, help people learn it, and assist researchers.

This would not be necessary if criminologists were already consistent in defining social disorganization theory or doing research on it. Indeed, several review articles note that social disorganization ideas and indicators are not consistent from study to study, producing considerable confusion (Bursik, 1984; Hipp and Steenbeek, 2016; Faris, 1955; Sampson and Groves, 1989; Sampson, Raudenbush, and Earls, 1997). What confuses professors also confuses many of our students, while interfering with the accumulation of consistent research findings.

A major rule of scientific research is that one is not supposed to mix up cause and effect. In statistical parlance, one should keep the independent and dependent variables separate. Yet research on social disorganization often mixes these up, thus interfering with research progress while making it harder for our students to figure out what's going on.[1] To illustrate how cause and effect are mixed up, consider this standard social disorganization hypothesis: *Low neighborhood cohesion causes crime to increase in the neighborhood.* The independent variable is "neighborhood cohesion" and the dependent variable is "crime in the neighborhood." Neighborhood cohesion is often measured with survey questions such as these:

How afraid are you to walk around at night?
Do you trust your neighbors?

Researchers then discover that local crime rates increase with fear of walking around at night and distrust of neighbors. They then combine these variables under the label "social cohesion," interpreting their research as proof that low cohesion produces more crime.

A more plausible explanation is that high crime rates make people afraid to walk around at night and suspicious of neighbors. In other words, the causation is the other way around. The confusion of independent and dependent variable is not merely a methodological issue, but rather reflects conceptual vagueness in presenting social disorganization as a theory. That brings us back to the original question that emerged in the era of the Chicago school.

7.2 The Early 20th-Century Research Context

Do not forget that social disorganization was really an ad hoc explanation, devised by Shaw and McKay to deal with the rough data they had on hand. In the first half of the 20th century, sociologists began to find statistical evidence that some places within a city tend to concentrate crime (Burgess, 1916). They asked themselves why. In the subsequent ten years, various members of the Chicago school contributed research on crime and related social problems (Bulmer, 1984). However, the Chicago school had no single theory and were not even a unified school of thought (Becker, 1999.) That helps explain why social disorganization was less a theory of crime than an amalgam of ideas addressing crime and social problem concentrations in urban space. The various professors were inventing modern sociology and criminology, improvising as they went along.

I should not be too harsh in judging Chicago sociologists for failing to sort out these ideas neatly. Their empirical tools were limited at the time, and so they depended on a substantial amount of speculation as they carried out empirical research. That was an era when numbers were added either by hand or by using crude adding machines and other desk calculators (Aspray et al., 1990). These machines worked slowly and required a roomful of students at desks, taking months or years to enter data and find minimal results that now take a few moments. It was not possible to do the mapping or statistical analysis that are normal with today's computers, so pins were pushed into the wall map and a photographer brought in when they were finally finished. Crude tools yield crude statistics, with little impetus to refine the theory in the absence of any means to test the refinements.

To illustrate that point, consider that Chicago's population in 1930 was just under 3.4 million, yet only 77 community areas could be analyzed in practice given the tools at hand. An average of just under 44,000 residents in each community area *were treated as a single data point*. You can see why theory and measurement were constrained and why they compared rather large parts of the city to each other. Thus social disorganization was a theory of the 1930s, addressing data then available. Given the tools at hand, Shaw and McKay made a remarkable contribution. They did so by naming the "delinquency area" and giving us an image of what it was like.

7.3 The "Delinquent Area"

Unlike cities in Europe and Latin America, American cities tend to have low-income areas inside, surrounding the central business district and within or near the industrial zones. Going outward from the center, income tends to rise, with suburban areas highest. However, near the center is a "zone of transition," wherein deterioration is common as factories close down and properties are abandoned. New low-income persons move into the zone of transition from countryside or other nations. As soon as people earn enough money, they flee to the next ring of the city if they can afford to do so, onward to the outer suburbs.

Abandoned near the center is the delinquency area, containing broken-down factories, warehouses, railroad yards, and dilapidated housing. Its residents are not homeowners and their rental status is not stable. Their ethnicity is diverse and their cultures are conflicting. Social disorganization theory offered an image of the delinquency area, mixing together these various physical and social phenomena. The statement that the high crime rate was *caused* by "social disorganization" was a useful stopgap theory based on what they knew at the time. But it was really a limited causal statement that the breakdown of people and buildings, concentrated in one part of a city, generates an elevated level of crime and delinquency. They were able to demonstrate the correlations among these variables, but not to tease apart a clear causal process. One would hope to refine that statement with better data and analysis tools. Yet such refinement is not guaranteed.

7.4 Modern Is Not Always Better

Modern tools permit us to investigate new and more precise ideas with more detailed measures. Unfortunately, the power of new computers and software does not automatically produce clarity and may even lead to intellectual entropy and confusion. This happens because I can now throw in so many independent variables and turn them over to the computer, giving us very confusing results. Statisticians remind us that, as the number of variables in the model increases, the fit of an equation generally worsens (Kenny and McCoach, 2009). Indeed, modern hardware and software allow us to compile a much longer list of social disorganization measures, undermining clarity even further. While least squares regression is designed to handle noise in the *dependent* variable, the same is not the case with noise in the *independent* variables (Babyak, 2004). That noise causes us to lose the signal if too many wrong variables are tossed into an equation by an unthoughtful researcher, or one who is trying to cover all the bases in the literature to date.

As measurement and computational tools improve, one must avoid using those tools to produce greater confusion through longer and bigger equations and tables growing for no good reason. Nor should one fall for the illusion that statistical tools are powerful enough to sort out conceptual confusion. The adage "garbage in, garbage out" applies not only to bad data but also to bad thinking. The emulsion of social disorganization ideas makes them intellectually alluring, but also renders them untestable. Not only do ideas require disaggregation, but the same is true of spatial data.

7.5 Progress Arrives

Those machines and software that can produce confusion also allow progress when used cautiously. That requires devising sharper concepts that can make greater sense of more diverse and voluminous data. Analysis over the past few decades has transformed what is known about how crime distributes over space (Roncek and Bell, 1981; Weisburd, Groff, and Yang, 2012). That progress has been obtained using data for specific blocks and for specific addresses. From block-level analyses, it is now evident that attributing high crime to whole chunks of a metropolis is false and obsolete. *The "high-crime side of town" contains a good majority of blocks that have no crime at all.* Indeed, crime is concentrated within a small number of blocks across a metropolis. In addition, analyses of specific addresses show that *only a small percentage of addresses account for the vast majority of crime.* That is true for the whole metropolis, but also for the low-income part of town.

These findings from block data challenge us to sharpen our understanding of delinquency zones, not only focusing on much smaller areas but also on more specific criminogenic processes. Accordingly, I have concluded that a composite image of the "delinquency area" is obsolete, based on current knowledge from block and address data. I conclude that it is necessary to disaggregate the different processes that can produce a high-crime neighborhood. The next section offers four distinct images of the delinquency area. These images have different implications about local crime and its control. Each image is suitable for articulation and measurement. Disentangling the four makes the social disorganization ideas less confusing by showing us alternative pathways to a high-crime zone.

7.6 Four Images of the Delinquent Area

Travis Hirschi (1989) taught us that crime images are important. He criticized "integrated theory" for mixing many images of the criminal, hence confusing students and researchers alike. He argued that oppositional images of crime facilitate empirical progress by giving us clear hypotheses. His argument applies not only to criminology, but also to the general progress of science. However, I have modified his intuition in one sense, allowing the possibility that multiple images of delinquency areas can operate in different parts of the same city. Additional empirical power offers us an incentive to sharpen our concepts and make distinctions that might have been premature if formulated in the past. I now have the tools available to improve measurement of both independent and dependent variables, providing that concepts are sharpened first.

Accordingly, I distinguish four very different images of the high-crime zone within a metropolitan area. These are presented in order of the pejorative implications for people residing in those zones, starting with the worst image:

(a) The *zone of criminality*, within which most residents are crime participants in one form or another
(b) The *zone of indifference*, where residents do not care about their neighborhood or neighbors
(c) The *zone of intimidation*, where residents care about crime and would like to help reduce it, but are intimidated by offenders
(d) The *zone of impracticality*, where are unable to see what offenders are doing at the time of the crime

The pejorative order is easily explained. A "zone of criminality" is an extremely negative image. The ultimate insult is to say that residents of a high-crime zone are almost all criminals. They are to blame for local crime because they are the ones doing it. The zone of indifference is slightly less insulting to residents. Even though they might not all be crime participants, they are seen as indifferent to the plight of their neighbors—as very bad citizens. The "collective efficacy" concept (Sampson, Raudenbush, and Earls, 1997) was not intended to be pejorative, but in effect it divides a metropolis into areas of good citizens and bad ones.[2] The zone of indifference has a better image than the zone of criminality, but not by much.

Next consider the zone of intimidation, where residents do not approve of crime and wish they could do something about it. They care. Yet they are intimidated by offenders, who have the upper hand, rendering good citizenship inoperable. Some citizens might also fear the police, providing a double threat if they intervene against a crime. Intimidation and fear prevent residents from thwarting crime. The zone of intimidation is largely populated by people who would *prefer* to be good citizens but cannot achieve that goal under adverse circumstances.

These first three zones allow room for overt crime to occur. In the zone of criminality, offenders might commit crimes openly with little fear that their criminal neighbors will summon police. In the zone of indifference, a dearth of good citizens allows criminals to operate in the open. In the zone of intimidation, citizen fear allows offenders to be overt through a different mechanism. The fourth type of high-crime zone differs from the others in qualitative terms.

7.7 The Zone of Impracticality

It is an illusion that good citizenship guarantees low crime rates. That only occurs if good citizens are *able to deliver guardianship in reality*. The absence of guardianship does not prove the absence of good citizenship.[3] People who care about their neighborhood might still be unable to supervise their block while away at work or out shopping. Nor can they protect those blocks that are out of sight when they are home. They might not be able to spot burglars entering the house two blocks away.

Guardianship is often impractical, even when citizens are motivated to provide it and would like to do so. Danielle Reynald's research (Reynald, 2009, 2011; Hollis-Peel, Reynald, and Welsh, 2012) illustrates this point with a simple but powerful experiment in which the researchers became quasi-intruders. She and her colleagues approached homes, walked in front, and looked around overtly. They observed the situational features at the time of their visit, checking off four queries, in this order:

1. Is anybody around? (If yes, proceed.)
2. Do they see me? (If yes, proceed.)
3. Do they say anything about my being there?[4] (If yes, proceed.)
4. Do they call the police?

Reynald then correlated these data with local crime rates. She found that the first query best predicts local crime rates. When the intruding researcher sees *nobody* around, crime rates tend to be high in the immediate area. Second most important was whether anybody saw the intruding researcher. Third most important was whether that person said anything, or questioned the researcher's presence. Least important was whether the resident called police.

The importance of *mere presence* offers a stark confirmation of routine activity thinking, and a sharp contrast to the approach taken by many criminologists studying social disorganization. Indeed, it tells us that a local block can have high crime rates without being a zone of criminality or a zone of indifference. If local residents are absent, or if the layout of the local area impairs visibility, guardianship is impractical. That condition does not require us to attribute any negative traits to most local residents or to assume they are bad citizens.

A zone of impracticality might be able to discourage overt crime, namely, crime that is carried out openly. Yet it remains highly vulnerable to covert crime, which can occur when residents are away or in places from which they cannot see a crime in progress. In contrast, zones of criminality, indifference, or intimidation might allow high levels of overt crime. That tells us to measure specific independent variables for all four concepts, but also to diversify our dependent variables to consider whether crime is overt and whether people have a chance to intervene against it.

7.8 Perspective

Do residents fail to intervene against crime because they are criminals? Because they are indifferent? Because they are afraid? Or because they are away from their neighborhood, or unable to see around the corner? How common are the four zones? These are empirical questions.

I would hypothesize that the frequency of these zones in real city blocks is directly proportional to the order in which they were presented. That is, the zone of criminality is rare, perhaps applying to a few of the worst blocks in the worst parts of the worst city, but not generally. The second rarest would be the zone of indifference, to which I return below.

When crime is overt, I would predict the zone of intimidation to be far more common than the zone of criminality or the zone of indifference. If this is correct, many social disorganization studies have looked at the wrong variables and offered the wrong interpretation, emphasizing indifference and a lack of citizen will. In contrast, I believe that people who would like to be good citizens are unable to fulfill their own wishes, fearing what will happen if they intervene.

A longtime principle of Chicago sociology states that familiarity among neighbors tends to inhibit crime. Perhaps that principle is reversed in some areas where offenders have the upper hand. With widespread recognition of neighbors, offenders can then intimidate anyone who interferes with their crimes. This reversal tells us to measure whether offenders have the upper hand and whether they can retaliate with impunity. This also reminds us to distinguish fear of crime in general from fear of retaliation against activist citizens.

I would further hypothesize that most high-crime blocks fit the last category, the zone of impracticality. In these locations, crime is largely covert, with guardianship not easily delivered at all times and places. Again, this does not derive from bad citizenship. Indeed, local citizens prevent crime when they can do so—that is, when they are present and aware it is happening. Yet they are often absent from the block, carrying out their daily routine activities, unable to witness or report crime. Or they are home but unable to monitor the entire local area. Thus crime risk can be high for *practical* reasons, not because of moral weakness or indifference.

Although I hypothesize that the "zone of indifference" is given too much credit by theorists, that hypothesis requires testing. Doing so requires sharpening up our concepts of "indifference." Does it mean that the local resident does not care about (*a*) any fellow human beings, (*b*) strangers in the neighborhood, (*c*) casual acquaintances, (*d*) anybody outside one's immediate family, (*e*) this neighborhood *as a collective unit*, or what? It is quite possible to have no interest in the specific neighborhood or block but still to care about other human beings. "Indifference" is an ambiguous term. If I sharpen up exactly what it means, I can them measure the mechanism by which it operates, if it operates at all. It is quite possible that people with warm hearts and empathy for others have nonetheless given up on the specific locality from which they cannot easily escape. Of course, this discussion may prove irrelevant if zones of indifference are vastly outnumbered by zones of intimidation and zones of impracticality.

I should also distinguish different types of crime as they distribute over space. Some high-crime zones may have little violence, while others may have quite a bit. Some high-crime zones may have substantial drug abuse but no open-air drug markets, while others might feature overt drug sales. Perhaps different types of crime create different risks for those who are considering an intervention against it. It is no longer justifiable to toss together all types of crime and all types of local involvement, relating these vaguely.

Scholars have long known that homeowners and long-term residents have a greater incentive to protect their local area and might be willing to take more risk in so doing. Does that prove that homeowners are more altruistic and socially responsible to the community? Or does it mean that property owners are more active against crime given their selfish stake in the neighborhood? This is an empirical question, and should not be built into the theory in advance. As a general rule, I would hypothesize that a mixture of altruism and self-interest is most likely to energize local action against crime.

More generally, one would hope that crime reduction can occur with minimal confrontation by police or citizens. Reynald's experiments show that sheer presence and visibility of others can greatly reduce crime risk. "Crime prevention through environmental design" (CPTED) offers many techniques for increasing visibility within a neighborhood (Zahm, 2005). When such techniques are applied, guardianship can be enhanced without requiring additional confrontation, and the dormant seeds of good citizenship can then begin to sprout.

Notes

1. In their critique of integrated theory, Gottfredson and Hirschi (1990) noted this problem, with one type of crime predicted by other types of crime-like variables. One could argue that social disorganization is in fact the earliest integrated theory, since it combines many urban problems in describing the delinquency area and suggesting how it got that way.

2. Why would scholars with very good intentions end up producing a negative image of citizens? I believe that the problem stems from mixing too many ideas together, and then using umbrella terms. Sometimes a more positive term hides an unintended negative image. The "absence of collective efficacy" is much worse in reality than its technical title indicates, and surely much worse than its authors intended. By separating out the various components of social disorganization I have a better chance to find the good in people and separate that from the bad.
3. Mixing indicators of good citizenship with indicators of guardianship tends to produce a correlation with crime. But it is not clear which mechanism produces that correlation. Social scientists prefer social explanations. That's why collective efficacy, altruism, citizenship, and community are much more appealing to social scientists than the simple ability to see what's going on and then act against it.
4. Example, "What the hell are you doing here?"

References

Aspray, William, Bromley, Allan G., Campbell-Kelly, Martin, Ceruzzi, Paul E., and Williams, Michael R. 1990. *Computing before Computers*. Ames: Iowa State University Press.

Babyak, Michael A. 2004. "What You See May Not Be What You Get: A Brief, Nontechnical Introduction to Overfitting in Regression-Type Models." *Psychosomatic Medicine* 66 (3): 411–421.

Becker, Howie. 1999. "The Chicago School, So-Called." *Qualitative Sociology* 22 (1): 3–12.

Bulmer, Martin. 1984. *The Chicago School of Sociology: Institutionalization, Diversity, and the Rise of Sociological Research*. Chicago: University of Chicago Press.

Burgess, Ernest W. 1916. "Juvenile Delinquency in a Small City." *Journal of Criminal Law and Criminology* 6 (5): 724–728.

Bursik, Robert J. 1984. "Urban Dynamics and Ecological Studies of Delinquency." *Social Forces* 63 (2): 393–413.

Faris, R. E. L. 1955. *Social Disorganization*. 2nd ed. New York: Ronald Press.

Gottfredson, Michael, and Hirschi, Travis. 1990. *A General Theory of Crime*. Stanford, CA: Stanford University Press.

Hipp, John R., and Steenbeek, Wouter. 2016. "Types of Crime and Types of Mechanisms: What Are the Consequences for Neighborhoods over Time?" *Crime and Delinquency* 62 (9): 1203–34.

Hirschi, Travis. 1989. "Exploring Alternatives to Integrated Theory." In *From Theoretical Integration in the Study of Deviance and Crime: Problems and Prospects*, edited by Messner, Steven F., Krohn, Marvin D., and Liska, Allen E., 37–49. Albany: SUNY Press.

Hollis-Peel, M. E., Reynald, D. M., and Welsh, B. C. 2012. "Guardianship and Crime: An International Comparative Study of Guardianship in Action." *Crime, Law and Social Change* 58 (1): 1–14.

Kenny, D. A., and McCoach, D. B. 2009. "Effect of the Number of Variables on Measures of Fit in Structural Equation Modeling." *Structural Equation Modeling* 10 (3): 333–351.

Reynald, D. M. 2009. "Guardianship in Action: Developing a New Tool for Measurement." *Crime Prevention and Community Safety* 11 (1): 1–20.

Reynald, D. M. 2011. "Factors Associated with the Guardianship of Places: Assessing the Relative Importance of the Spatio-physical and Sociodemographic Contexts in Generating

Opportunities for Capable Guardianship." *Journal of Research in Crime and Delinquency* 48 (1): 110–142.

Roncek, D. W., and Bell, R. 1981. "Bars, Blocks, and Crime." *Journal of Environmental Systems* 11 (1): 35–47.

Sampson, Robert J., and Groves, W. Byron. 1989. "Community Structure and Crime: Testing Social Disorganization Theory." *American Journal of Sociology* 94 (4): 774–802.

Sampson, Robert J., Raudenbush, Stephen W., and Earls, Felton. 1997. "Neighborhoods and Violent Crime: A Multilevel Study of Collective Efficacy." *Science* 277 (5328): 918–924.

Shaw, Clifford R., and McKay, Henry D. 1942. *Juvenile Delinquency in Urban Areas.* Chicago: University of Chicago Press.

Shaw, Clifford R., Zorbaugh, Harvey, McKay, Henry D., and Cottrell, Leonard S. 1929. *Delinquency Areas.* Chicago: University of Chicago Press.

Weisburd, David, Groff, Elizabeth, and Yang, Sue-Ming. 2012. *The Criminology of Place: Street Segments and Our Understanding of the Crime Problem.* Oxford: Oxford University Press.

Zahm, D. 2005. "Learning, Translating, and Implementing CPTED." *Journal of Architectural and Planning Research* 22 (4): 284–293.

CHAPTER 8

EVALUATING THEORIES OF ENVIRONMENTAL CRIMINOLOGY

Strengths and Weaknesses

FRANCIS T. CULLEN AND TERESA C. KULIG

8.1 Introduction

Environmental criminology, also increasingly known as "crime science" (Clarke 2010), has emerged as a vibrant and expanding criminological paradigm that directs theory, research, and practice (Cullen 2011a; Lilly, Cullen, and Ball 2015). Given its increasing diversity and growth, attempting to identify core strengths and weaknesses that transcend all variants of this perspective is a daunting challenge. Neither good nor bad points characterize all works that fall under the umbrella of environmental criminology (hereinafter "EC"). Still, it is useful to illuminate clear tendencies that characterize the scholarship in this area—again with the caveat that nuance and qualification can be found in individual writings.

In pointing out the strengths of environmental approaches, these are best understood as efforts to rectify omissions and narrow thinking that have long marked more traditional, mainstream theories found in all criminological texts (see, e.g., Lilly, Cullen, and Ball 2015). These works—most notably the Chicago school, anomie-strain theory, and control theory—had their origins in the early to mid-1900s and sought to situate the causes of crime in the then-changing fabric of American society (Cullen 2011a). In response, EC has illuminated fresh ways of thinking about crime. Here, we identify four strengths that flow from the paradigm shift offered by environmental approaches:

- EC shifted the focus from criminals to conventional people, thus enriching understanding of crime events and their prevention.

- EC challenged the view that some sort of "evil" condition generated the evil of crime.
- EC rejected the root-causes approach to crime, instead showing the benefits of a situational perspective.
- EC rejected the "nothing works" professional ideology of criminology in favor of practical solutions to reducing crime.

The weaknesses of EC seem to have two sources. They tend to involve either the premature dismissal of elements of mainstream theories that have value or the failure to develop ideas within their paradigm to the fullest degree. Four weaknesses can be identified. Again, these are limitations that some EC works clearly overcome. Still, they remain tendencies that warrant more systematic attention:

- EC has neglected the study of "motivated offenders," treating them as a given in the crime event.
- EC needs to develop a fuller understanding of the risk of victimization.
- EC relies on the concept of "informal social control," which is often ill-defined and its components left unspecified.
- EC neglects the role of inequality in the broader social environment.

8.2 Four Strengths

8.2.1 Focus on Conventional People

Criminology is dominated by a theoretical orientation aimed at explaining why some people break the law and others do not. In rejecting the multifactor, empirical approach of the Gluecks, Sutherland argued that to be a true science, the field had to develop a unifying general theory of crime (Laub and Sampson 1991; Cullen 2011a). General theories have been the holy grail of criminology as one scholar after another has endeavored to formulate such frameworks (see, e.g., Hirschi 1969; Gottfredson and Hirschi 1990; Moffitt 1993; Sampson and Laub 1993; Akers 1998; Agnew 2006; see also Lilly, Cullen, and Ball 2015). The ultimate goal has been to identify the origins of "criminality" or the "propensity" to offend. This task can only be achieved by probing the lives, minds, and bodies of those we call "criminals."

A strength of EC is that it challenged this near-exclusive focus on criminals, instead arguing that the key to understanding crime events—and how to prevent them—was to focus on *conventional* people, those who did not break the law. This conceptual reorientation was most fully accomplished in Cohen and Felson's (1979) classic statement of routine activity theory. In their model, offenders are reduced to an undifferentiated mass of "motivated offenders." Who they are or why they have become criminally motivated is not of much concern. Their existence is taken for granted, and the goal is for the rest of us to avoid intersecting with them in time and space without adequate protection. Two important insights flow from this view.

First, the subject matter of criminology is changed from explaining why people break the law—*criminality*—to explaining why *crime events* take place. Criminology is thus transformed into crime science (Clarke 2010). Cohen and Felson's genius lay in their realization that lots of criminals can exist but that they cannot actualize their propensity unless the opportunity exists to do so. Of course, they brilliantly divided the concept of opportunity into two components: attractive targets and capable guardianship.

Second and relatedly, Cohen and Felson's routine activity theory suggested that criminals had little to do with what made a target attractive and whether guardianship was present. Of course, offenders could search for targets that were attractive (e.g., portable goods) and for unguarded targets (e.g., empty houses). But in the end, *conventional people* had the capacity to make targets less attractive (e.g., security devices affixed to products displayed in a department store) or to increase guardianship (e.g., place manager at an apartment). Beyond routine activity theory, other variants of EC also emphasized how nonoffenders could act to minimize their victimization. For example, the physical design of a street block could harden targets (making them less attractive) and increase natural surveillance (and thus guardianship). Conventional citizens could also emigrate from where motivated offenders were concentrated, perhaps to affluent suburbs to reside in a home equipped with a burglar alarm and located in a gated community.

Thus, in the EC paradigm, conventional or "normal" people were moved from irrelevance to playing a central role in determining whether a crime event could occur. Crime was not an inevitability but, in a very real sense, "chosen" not only by offenders but also by their potential victims. Conventional people were, both literally and figuratively, the architects of their crime risk. They could take steps to avoid intersecting with offenders and to make their property and their bodies less vulnerable to victimization. In one way, this view could be criticized for "blaming the victim": those suffering a criminal incident could have taken steps to nullify their exposure to a motivated offender. But in another sense, this perspective was empowering, suggesting that crime events were not an inevitable price of modern society but rather were within our individual and collective discretion to prevent. This perspective's implications for reducing victimization are clear and will be discussed later.

8.2.2 Rejecting the Evil-Causes-Evil Fallacy

Starting with the positivist school of criminology and Lombroso, criminology has sought to identify *individual differences in criminality* (Matza 1964). To be sure, heated debate has occurred—and continues to occur—about what makes offenders different from "the rest of us." Criminological wars are waged over whether these differences are produced by traits emanating from offenders' bodies or psyches or by exposure to detrimental social conditions. Regardless, at some level, the project for scholars is to theorize what it is about criminals that makes them ply their trade. What makes them different?

For the most part, crime is typically linked to some defect or pathology found either within offenders or their social environment. It is generally assumed that criminal behavior is bad and that it must be caused by something bad in the lives of offenders. This might be a neuropsychological deficit, low self-control, structurally induced strain, or perhaps growing up in a disorganized neighborhood where criminal traditions are easily learned. Most theories implicitly argue that the extent of criminal involvement is due to a dose relationship: the more of a defect that people have (e.g., more strain experienced), the more crime in which they will be involved. Worse still, having a bunch of bad things in one's life (e.g., more strain and a lot less self-control) will create a crime-dose that will almost certainly result in high offending.

Most EC theories do not so much highlight and criticize this evil-causes-evil thesis as ignore it. Again, this can be traced to their focus on conventional people and their willingness to categorize all criminals as "motivated offenders." Still, when environmental criminologists suspend their disinterest in offenders, they tend to emphasize the normality of criminals and of the causes of crime—in three ways.

First, because they are interested in crime events, EC scholars are mainly concerned with how motivated offenders act at the point that a criminal victimization is possible. They are less concerned with why a particular offender arrived in a situation motivated to commit a crime and far more concerned with what choices these individuals are likely to make. For this reason, they emphasize not the pathology of offenders but their *rationality* (Cornish and Clarke 1986). They do not take the naive position that criminals are just like the rest of us, noting that their rationality is "bounded" in ways that encourage crime. But they then proceed to show that offenders' decisions are very similar to what our decisions would be—were we to find ourselves, that is, in the same situation and motivated to break the law. In short, in accomplishing crime events, many offenders' decision-making is not driven wildly by some underlying pathology but rather is shaped by the normal, rational desire to gain a profit and avoid detection. "Offenders are no different from anybody else," observe Clarke and Felson (2011, p. 247), "in that they are trying to benefit themselves by their actions—a premise that finds its most explicit expression in the rational choice perspective."

Second, when they embrace a mainstream theory, EC scholars tend to show a preference for control theories. In large part, this attraction can be traced to control theorists' view that all of us—offenders and conventional people alike—have the same human nature: we all seek easy, immediate gratification that serves our interests. What differentiates us is not our inherent differences but whether our impulse for gratification is somehow blocked. Control theorists ultimately locate these blocking factors or controls within the individual, produced either by social bonds (that can vary over time) or by self-control (a more permanent trait) (see Hirschi 1969; Gottfredson and Hirschi 1990). Environmental criminologists place the mechanisms blocking crime not within the person but within the situation or environment. It makes sense, for example, that offenders marked by low self-control will decide not to commit a crime if opportunity is not immediately apparent or if committing a crime would require a lot of effort. Similarly, some EC scholars have advised using "handlers" to work with potential offenders to dissuade them from breaking the law (Schaefer, Cullen, and Eck 2016).

Third, on a more macro level, EC scholars seek to unmask the evil-causes-evil thesis as a fallacy by demonstrating that good things in society can lead to the evil of crime. In large part, this occurs because crime is produced not only by motivated offenders but also by the availability of opportunities. Crime opportunities can be increased by bad circumstances, such as the lack of collective efficacy in a community due to concentrated disadvantage (Sampson 2012) or the inability of impoverished citizens to escape to safer communities in the suburbs. But as Cohen and Felson (1979) pointed out, crime opportunities can also be increased by good circumstances, such as affluence that increases the sale and ownership of goods that can be stolen or gender equality that brings women into situations outside the home that increases the risk of victimization. In concluding their classic article, they noted poignantly, "Rather than assuming that predatory crime is simply an indicator of social breakdown, one might take it as a byproduct of freedom and prosperity as they manifest themselves in the routine activities of everyday life" (1979, p. 605).

In short, EC challenges the positivist view of criminals as driven to crime by unique individual differences (Matza 1964). Instead, it brings attention to the ways in which offenders, as would any of us, make bounded rational choices in crime situations and are born with similar natures. EC also alerts us that crime is not only linked to societal evils but also to positive developments that have the unanticipated consequences of increasing available targets and of reducing guardianship. In this way, it enriches the narrower view of crime and crime causes found in traditional criminology.

8.2.3 Beyond Root Causes

In his controversial *Thinking About Crime*, James Q. Wilson (1975) offered his stinging critique of mainstream criminology's preference to identify the "root causes" of crime. In part, his challenge was substantive; it was not clear to him that the factors identified by sociological theories could be shown empirically to cause crime. But his more damning indictment was that extant criminological theories had no practical utility. Even if the criminogenic conditions advanced by such theories underlay criminal conduct, he doubted these so-called root causes were amenable to change by any known policy (see, however, Currie 1985). The very nature of root causes placed them far away from specific criminal acts—they were distal rather than situational—and the tightness with which they were woven into the fabric of society (e.g., community disorganization, structural inequality) made them virtually impossible to change, at least in the short run or by any politically feasible means. Instead of causal analysis, Wilson favored "policy analysis." For Wilson, as a political scientist, this meant using available government resources to reduce a problem as much as possible in the most practical way possible. His specific solution was to ignore social reform as a crime prevention policy and instead use imprisonment—specifically, selective incarceration of high-rate offenders—to lower the crime rate. He suggested that this policy could reduce crime 20%.

Wilson's rejection of sociological orthodoxy in criminology and embrace of incarceration as a preferred policy option was widely attacked. In retrospect, Wilson's endorsement of imprisonment proved unwise, given that the use of this policy option grew to massive proportions with disquieting outcomes (Pratt 2009; Clear and Frost 2014). Nonetheless, Wilson's general critique of root-causes thinking and his urging to criminologists to consider practical solutions to reducing criminal harms now appear prescient. Attempting to change distal and largely static causes of crime is a recipe for policy failure. Advocates get to decry social injustice, but little crime is knifed off and many people's lives are damaged.

EC has been far more successful than Wilson in arguing that manipulating proximate and dynamic causes of offending offers the best hope of reducing crime events. To be sure, their purposeful neglect of root causes has earned EC scholars pejorative labels, such as the claim that they engage in "administrative criminology" or the "criminology of everyday life" (Garland 2001; Matthews 2014; see Clarke and Felson 2011). But the powerful response of EC has been that their work has led to many people being spared preventable victimizations (Felson and Boba 2010). They do not receive accolades for preaching to the social justice choir, but they can be thanked for devoting their careers to identifying the mechanisms in crime-event situations that thwart offenders' decision to victimize.

Notably, by taking this perspective, EC shares much in common with the most successful paradigm of correctional rehabilitation: the risk-need-responsivity (RNR) model (Gendreau 1996; Andrews and Bonta 2010). As a correctional theory, the RNR model is interested not in explaining crime generally but in reducing reoffending in the time immediately ahead. Accordingly, its advocates ignore more distal root causes of crime and focus instead on proximate factors that characterize offenders in the current moments. They also identify "criminogenic needs" or risk factors shown empirically to lead to recidivism that are changeable (e.g., antisocial attitudes). They call these "dynamic risk factors" (as opposed to "static risk factors," such as age, that cannot be changed). This aspect of the approach—the importance of targeting dynamic risks or needs—is called the "need principle." They further recommend concentrating attention on high-risk offenders (the "risk principle") and using treatment modalities (e.g., cognitive-behavioral therapy) that are capable of changing, or are "responsive" to, the factors leading offenders into crime (the "responsivity principle"). EC scholars might well recognize how this model overlaps with their own recommendations to focus on proximate dynamic factors, on high-risk crime "hotspots," and on using "problem-oriented" interventions that are responsive to the crime events to be prevented. In a sense, the RNR model thus offers a general paradigm for crime prevention that may transcend EC, corrections, and other fields of prevention (Cullen 2011b).

Finally, unlike Wilson, EC offered approaches to crime prevention that tried to avoid excessive state intervention, including incarceration. In large part, this aversion to criminal justice solutions to crime is rooted in EC's belief that the key to preventing crime events lies not in catching criminals—whether that is to incapacitate or rehabilitate them—but in guiding conventional people in the methods they can employ to reduce crime opportunities and thus events. Relatedly, there is a preference to stop victimizations from ever occurring rather than dealing with the aftermath of a preventative incident. Even when EC scholars advocate for the use of police, they do so not as a means of rounding up bad people to lock them up for years on end. Rather, the very role of police as crime responders and crime fighters is transformed into that of "problem solvers" who work with the community to disrupt the situational elements that allow crime to flourish in certain locations. To its credit, the goal, and likely outcome, of EC is to lessen the need for imprisonment, an extreme form of intervention into the lives of offenders.

8.2.4 Rejecting "Nothing Works"

Beginning in the first stages of the 1970s, criminology embraced the notion that through the criminal justice system, the state can do nothing to reduce crime. This has been called the "nothing works doctrine" (Cullen and Gendreau 2001) and "impossibilism" (Matthews 2009). The idea that the state is impotent to stop crime was found most fully within corrections, especially following Martinson's (1974) work allegedly showing that "nothing works" in rehabilitation to reduce recidivism (Cullen and Gendreau 2001; cf. Andrews and Bonta 2010). But the same thinking pervaded policing (Sherman 1993). Most criminologists, it seemed, endorsed the position of labeling theorists that any negative societal intervention would prove ineffective, if not criminogenic.

EC has played a crucial role in combating the idea that it is "impossible" to reduce crime by embracing this goal and then identifying an array of effective prevention strategies (see, e.g., Eck 2002; Felson and Boba 2010). Opponents have used what have been called "knowledge destruction techniques" to undermine these findings—that is, voicing criticisms that have little substantive bases but call positive findings into question (see Gottfredson 1979; Andrews and Bonta 2010). As noted, one method is to claim that EC is a form of "administrative criminology," focusing on risk reduction favored by the state as opposed to unmaking the social injustices in need of broader reform. The intent is to taint the EC enterprise as morally suspect, suggesting that a narrow concern with sparing people harmful victimization comes at the steep cost of ignoring, if not accepting, criminogenic structural inequalities. Of course, critics never feel obliged to present data showing that their root-causes perspective can do as much as EC to reduce crime and, even if it did, why both approaches could not be complementary as opposed to oppositional. Another technique is to claim that apparent crime savings are not real because they result in the "displacement" of offending to neighboring areas. These critics, of course, do not demonstrate that these effects have actually occurred, but rather raise this possibility as a convenient way to delegitimize EC findings. In fact, research shows that the displacement critique is largely unfounded (Guerette and Bowers 2009; Madensen and Eck 2013).

In sum, EC theoretical models, with their effectively practical applications, have posed a healthy challenge to mainstream criminology. They have questioned the tendency to pathologize offenders and their circumstances, showed that crime is a normal feature of society that includes not only its bad side but also its positive side, revealed the need to focus on proximate and dynamic causes of crime, and rejected the dangerous notion that nothing can be done to make people safer. As with any perspective, however, EC has its weaknesses. In this regard, the following section will identify four weaknesses. The criticisms to be offered do not apply to all EC scholars; instead, they represent tendencies found in that literature that deserve more attention. Nonetheless, they are important because they potentially offer fresh avenues for future research within the EC paradigm.

8.3 Four Weaknesses

8.3.1 Neglect of Offenders

Beyond the time immediately before and during the crime event, EC does not pay much attention to offenders. Indeed, the very distinctiveness of EC is rooted in its departure from mainstream scholars' focus on explaining the criminality of offenders. Instead, they assert that it is more productive to redirect attention to the causal effects of opportunity in crime events. As noted, Cohen and Felson's (1979) use of the concept of "motivated offenders" embodied this lack of concern, treating criminals as a largely undifferentiated pool of victimizers to be avoided or thwarted. EC has shown a similar disinterest in corrections, seeing rehabilitation as a largely fruitless endeavor (Cullen et al. 2002; for an exception, see Schaefer, Cullen, and Eck 2016). When offenders have been studied, attention has more often been given not to how they became criminally motivated but rather to how they exercise choice in traveling to places where a crime victim might be selected (Brantingham and Brantingham 2013) or in assessing whether situational circumstances render a criminal act rational (Cornish and Clarke 1986). Again, when motivation occupies attention, it is either implicitly seen as a universal part of human nature (embracing the control theory view) or attributed to a rational response to situational inducements ("opportunity makes the criminal").

This limited interest in and view of crime causation has a cost: in short, EC undertheorizes offenders. It would be too much to expect EC to develop its own propensity-type theory, given this has been done with only modest success by the rest of the field (Weisburd and Piquero 2008). Still, more detailed studies of offenders might illuminate fresh ways of seeing how they become involved in crime events. For example, a developmental/life-course perspective might probe at what age youths come to recognize crime opportunities, including developing the cognitions that allow them to see a target as attractive. Similarly, it might be possible to probe how siblings and peers might be involved in this process. Or how might perceiving opportunity be linked to residing in a neighborhood where crime-specific skills can be modeled?

In fact, these types of questions might have been pursued previously had not EC scholars ignored the writings of Richard Cloward (1959; Cloward and Ohlin 1960) on "illegitimate means"—or his version of criminal opportunity. He conceptualized opportunity from the perspective of the offender, not from the perspective of conventional people (as is typically the case in EC). Cloward noted that opportunity or illegitimate means had two components. The first was the sheer opportunity to "discharge" a criminal role or act (1959, p. 168). Opportunity in this sense means whether the act can be completed or is impossible to complete. This conceptualization coincides with how opportunity is used by EC scholars. Thus, a target exists or it does not; capable guardianship exists or it does not. If there is no target and/or impenetrable guardianship, the opportunity does not exist. A criminal role cannot be discharged.

But Cloward then recognized another component of illegitimate means—or of "opportunity" more broadly understood—that has been largely ignored by EC scholars: the opportunity to learn the values and skills needed to undertake an offense. Essentially rejecting the idea of unlimited versatility in offending, Cloward drew upon the work of the Chicago school to note that not just anyone can simply become a professional thief (Sutherland 1937) or juvenile jack-roller (Shaw 1930). Access to criminal "learning structures—as could be true of access to the socialization and schooling needed for conventional occupational roles—is differentially available across the social structure" (Cloward 1959, p. 168).

In essence, Cloward was arguing that the opportunity to engage in a crime event did not involve just the sheer situational opportunity to undertake the act but also the socialization and human capital (cognitions and skills) needed to complete or discharge the act (see also Cullen 1984). Seeing opportunity as ubiquitous and crime as a simple act that requires little planning, EC scholars dismiss this kind of perspective as manifesting what Felson and Boba (2010, pp. 10–11) call the "ingenuity fallacy"—that is, suggesting that "most crimes are not ingenious" (see also Kornhauser 1978; Gottfredson and Hirschi 1990). However, as the "actor-center approach" of Steffensmeier and Ulmer (2015) shows, opportunity is not fixed at a simplistic level but varies in complexity along several crime-related dimensions (e.g., time, skillfulness, risk). And similar to Cloward (1959), they note that opportunity is differentially available across social contexts. The point is that only by focusing on offenders in detail can all features of opportunity become transparent. Future EC inquiries might profit from pursuing this topic.

8.3.2 Understanding the Risk of Victimization

At the core of EC is the proposition that potential victims engage in routines or lifestyles that place them at a greater or lesser risk of experiencing a crime event (see, e.g., Cohen and Felson 1979; Garofalo 1987; see also Pratt and Turanovic 2016). This simple, but important insight has not resulted in a systematic theory of victimization risk. Some important advances have been made, especially with the voluminous literature on the crime prevention strategies that can be employed to make targets less attractive and fortify guardianship. Still, more needs to be accomplished in this area, especially with regard to the individual-level factors that are related to risk exposure. This research should be undertaken along two lines of inquiry.

First, what causes individuals to place themselves at a higher risk of victimization? Routine activity theory emphasized that risk might well be due to positive developments, such as gender equality, that have led women to spend more time away from their residences, including in the evening hours, either at work or play. More recently, EC has moved away from the normalization of victims to emphasize how risk is produced by undesirable factors. Thus, literatures are growing that seek to link the pursuit of risky lifestyles to low self-control and to deviant or partying lifestyles (see Pratt et al. 2014). Why this is the case is less clear, however. For example, those with low self-control might act impulsively and not think in advance about how entering a social situation could entail risk. An alternative possibility is that possessing low self-control could cause individuals to act in bothersome ways to others, which in turn could result in their being bullied or otherwise attacked. Much work needs to be done to demonstrate what factors—and under what circumstances and to what degree—heighten exposure to victimization risk.

Second, the other side of the coin is the need to explain why some individuals are less exposed to risk. Some of these insulating factors can be involuntary in the sense that they are not actively chosen by people—such as which neighborhood one is born into. But in other instances, avoidance of risk can be seen as involving human agency—as a matter of taking specific steps to reduce vulnerability to victimization. Efforts to limit risk can involve personality traits that make individuals risk averse. It might involve being embedded in social networks where risky conduct (e.g., binge drinking when at a party) is discouraged and where participation in conventional structured activity is encouraged. It can also be related to increasing guardianship, such as seeking out escorts when walking at night or purchasing a gun or a dog to fend off potential intruders into one's residence. More work needs to be done to explain why different individuals take specific steps to avoid risk under certain circumstances.

8.3.3 Unclear Use of Informal Social Control

Although doing so is more common in community criminology (Kornhauser 1978; Cullen et al. 2015), EC scholars occasionally use the concept of "informal social control" to describe how neighborhood residents exert control over public spaces. When scholars employ the concept in this way, however, they fall into the same trap as other criminologists: nobody clearly defines what informal social control is or how precisely it works to limit crime events. Most scholars have a sense of what this concept means, but it mostly serves as a catch-all category to describe everything that citizens, rather than the state, do to try to stop offending from occurring. In studies, it is often measured by questions tapping the willingness of respondents to intervene in their neighborhood, such as upbraiding unruly teens or tamping down incivilities. Whether such intentions to exercise control would materialize into actions—such as in actual uncivil or threatening situations—or merely reflects a social desirability response to survey questions is rarely probed.

Thus, it is unclear whether the construct of informal social control has much utility. At the very least, EC scholars need to develop a theory of informal social control, unpacking its components and testing their effects on opportunity within crime events. For example, the willingness to intervene might involve surveillance, reporting incidents to the police or to juveniles' parents, personally confronting and scolding offenders, or the use of physical or lethal force. Similarly, informal social control might be an individual or collective act. And it might involve organization and planning or be a natural occurrence of activity patterns in an area. These thoughts are preliminary, but they demonstrate that the construct of informal social control is complex and in need of elaboration.

8.3.4 Neglect of the Role of Inequality

EC's laser-like focus on the proximate crime situation has often caused it to ignore the larger context in which crime events occur (for an exception, see Wilcox, Gialopsos, and Land 2013). Recently, some attention has been paid to how social disorganization—the key construct of Shaw and McKay's (1942) theory—might influence the nature of crime situations (see Weisburd, Groff, and Yang 2012; Wilcox and Land 2015). But perhaps because of their aversion to root-causes thinking, EC scholars have not paid adequate attention to the role of inequality in shaping key elements of opportunity. If anything, such constructs either do not come to mind or are seen as relevant only to the extent that they produce motivated offenders who then must be avoided (for an exception, see Cao and Maume 1993).

This omission needs to be rectified. Inequality matters because it pertains to the distribution of resources across the class structure. The capacity to avoid victimization likely has complex causes (as noted), but one of these most certainly is material resources. Thus, most directly, money can be used to purchase a security system or residence in a safe neighborhood. It can also be employed to design built environments to create an inviting public space that will be flooded by citizens providing mutual surveillance. Inequality is implicated as well in people's capacity to exert political power on government officials to "do something about" criminogenic places, such as unruly bars or crack houses close by—regardless of whether that involves increased police scrutiny, filing civil cases, revoking business licenses, or revising zoning regulations.

Admittedly, recognizing the concentration of crime in impoverished areas (Weisburd, Groff, and Yang 2012), governments now engage in what Rengert (1989) called "spatial justice" by investing crime control resources disproportionately in these communities. These supports potentially mitigate vulnerability to victimization that might be tied to a lack of private resources to purchase various forms of protection. Still, two potential problems exist. First, the prevention methods often are not based on EC principles, emphasizing instead an "enforcement" approach rather than a "situational" approach (Weisburd et al. 2016, p. 124). At the extreme, these strategies can involve mass imprisonment and aggressive policing tactics, which may have questionable crime-control benefits and generate community hostility (Weisburd and Braga 2006; Clear 2007; Pratt

2009). Second and related, privately purchased prevention involves consumer choice. By contrast, unless involving a measure of coproduction, government initiatives risk being imposed on community residents. Even if well intended, they still reflect the powerlessness of more impoverished citizens to exert collective efficacy and control their own destiny.

Ironically, critical criminology and EC are viewed as scholarly enemies—the former illuminating root causes and favoring broad social reforms and the latter illuminating causes of crime events and favoring situational crime prevention (or "administrative criminology"). In this case, however, a degree of theoretical integration might be mutually beneficial. A "critical opportunity theory" might be imagined in which the agenda is to show how the suffering of criminal harms is differentially distributed by people's capacity to avoid motivated offenders, make themselves less attractive targets, and access formidable guardianship.

8.4 Conclusion

Environmental criminology's theoretical perspectives, individually and collectively, have enriched criminology and provided one of the few practical avenues for reducing crime events and the harms they cause. EC advocates showed courage in forfeiting their membership in mainstream criminology in favor of thinking "outside the box." Their genius has been in their understanding that focusing on the actions of conventional people, not on offenders, and on the proximate features of crime events provided a paradigm-shattering way of studying and preventing crime. Still, no perspective, including EC, should be seen as sacrosanct or remain static. As suggested, EC might well be further enriched by giving more detailed attention to offenders, to what produces and protects against risk victimization, to the components of informal social control, and to contextual factors such as inequality.

References

Agnew, Robert. 2006. *Pressured into Crime: An Overview of General Strain Theory*. Los Angeles: Roxbury.

Akers, Ronald L. 1998. *Social Learning and Social Structure: A General Theory of Crime and Deviance*. Boston: Northeastern University Press.

Andrews, D. A., and James Bonta. 2010. *The Psychology of Criminal Conduct*. 5th ed. New Providence, NJ: Anderson/LexisNexis.

Brantingham, Paul J., and Patricia L. Brantingham. 2013. "The Theory of Target Search." In *The Oxford Handbook of Criminological Theory*, edited by Francis T. Cullen and Pamela Wilcox. New York: Oxford University Press.

Cao, Liqun, and David J. Maume, Jr. 1993. "Urbanization, Inequality, Lifestyle, and Robbery: A Comprehensive Model." *Sociological Focus* 26: 11–26.

Clarke, Ronald V. 2010. "Crime Science." In *The Sage Handbook of Criminological Theory*, edited by Eugene McLaughlin and Tim Newburn. London: Sage.

Clarke, Ronald V., and Marcus Felson. 2011. "The Origin of the Routine Activity Approach and Situational Crime Prevention." In *The Origins of American Criminology*, edited by Francis T. Cullen, Cheryl Lero Jonson, Andrew J. Myer, and Freda Adler. Vol. 16 of *Advances in Criminological Theory*. New Brunswick, NJ: Transaction.

Clear, Todd R. 2007. *Imprisoning Communities: How Mass Incarceration Makes Disadvantaged Neighborhoods Worse*. New York: Oxford University Press.

Clear, Todd R., and Natasha Frost. 2014. *The Punishment Imperative: The Rise and Failure of Mass Incarceration in America*. New York: New York University Press.

Cloward, Richard A. 1959. "Illegitimate Means, Anomie, and Deviant Behavior." *American Sociological Review* 24: 164–176.

Cloward, Richard A., and Lloyd E. Ohlin. 1960. *Delinquency and Opportunity: A Theory of Delinquent Gangs*. New York: Free Press.

Cohen, Lawrence W., and Marcus Felson. 1979. "Social Change and Crime Rate Trends: A Routine Activities Approach." *American Sociological Review* 44: 588–608.

Cornish, Derek B., and Ronald V. Clarke, eds. 1986. *The Reasoning Criminal: Rational Choice Perspectives on Offending*. New York: Springer-Verlag.

Cullen, Francis T. 1984. *Rethinking Crime and Deviance Theory: The Emergence of a Structuring Tradition*. Totowa, NJ: Rowman and Allanheld.

Cullen, Francis T. 2011a. "Beyond Adolescence-Limited Criminology: Choosing Our Future—the American Society of Criminology 2010 Sutherland Address." *Criminology* 49: 287–330.

Cullen, Francis T. 2011b. "Cincinnati and Beyond." Presentation to the 20th year anniversary of the Ph.D. Program, University of Cincinnati, May.

Cullen, Francis T., and Paul Gendreau. 2001. "From Nothing Works to What Works: Changing Professional Ideology in the 21st Century." *Prison Journal* 81: 313–338.

Cullen, Francis T., Travis C. Pratt, Sharon Levrant Miceli, and Melissa M. Moon. 2002. "Dangerous Liaison? Rational Choice Theory as the Basis for Correctional Intervention." In *Rational Choice and Criminal Behavior: Recent Research and Future Challenges*, edited by Alex R. Piquero and Stephen G. Tibbetts. New York: Routledge.

Cullen, Francis T., Pamela Wilcox, Robert J. Sampson, and Brendan D. Dooley, eds. 2015. *Challenging Criminological Theory: The Legacy of Ruth Rosner Kornhauser*. Vol. 19 of *Advances in Criminological Theory*. New Brunswick, NJ: Transaction.

Currie, Elliott. 1985. *Confronting Crime: An American Challenge*. New York: Pantheon.

Eck, John E. 2002. "Preventing Crime in Places." In *Evidence-Based Crime Prevention*, edited by Lawrence W. Sherman, David P. Farrington, Brandon C. Welsh, and Doris Layton MacKenzie. London: Routledge.

Felson, Marcus, and Rachel Boba. 2010. *Crime and Everyday Life*. 4th ed. Thousand Oaks, CA: Sage.

Garland, David. 2001. *The Culture of Control: Crime and Social Order in Contemporary Society*. Chicago: University of Chicago Press.

Garofalo, James. 1987. "Reassessing the Lifestyle Model of Criminal Victimization." In *Positive Criminology*, edited by Michael R. Gottfredson and Travis Hirschi. Newbury Park, CA: Sage.

Gendreau, Paul. 1996. "The Principles of Effective Intervention with Offenders." In *Choosing Correctional Options That Work: Defining the Demand and Evaluating the Supply*, edited by Alan T. Harland. Thousand Oaks, CA: Sage.

Gottfredson, Michael R. 1979. "Treatment Destruction Techniques." *Journal of Research in Crime and Delinquency* 16: 39–54.

Gottfredson, Michael R., and Travis Hirschi. 1990. *A General Theory of Crime.* Stanford, CA: Stanford University Press.

Guerette, Rob T., and Kate J. Bowers. 2009. "Assessing the Extent of Crime Displacement and Diffusion of Benefits: A Review of Situational Crime Prevention Evaluations." *Criminology* 47: 1331–1368.

Hirschi, Travis. 1969. *Causes of Delinquency.* Berkeley: University of California Press.

Kornhauser, Ruth Rosner. 1978. *Social Sources of Delinquency: An Appraisal of Analytic Models.* Chicago: University of Chicago Press.

Laub, John H., and Robert J. Sampson. 1991. "The Sutherland-Glueck Debate: On the Sociology of Criminological Knowledge." *American Journal of Sociology* 96: 1402–1440.

Lilly, J. Robert, Francis T. Cullen, and Richard A. Ball. 2015. *Criminological Theory: Context and Consequences.* 6th ed. Thousand Oaks, CA: Sage.

Madensen, Tamara D., and John E. Eck. 2013. "Crime Places and Place Management." In *The Oxford Handbook of Criminological Theory*, edited by Francis T. Cullen and Pamela Wilcox. New York: Oxford University Press.

Martinson, Robert. 1974. "What Works? Questions and Answers about Prison Reform." *Public Interest* 35: 22–54.

Matthews, Roger. 2009. "Beyond 'So What' Criminology: Rediscovering Realism." *Theoretical Criminology* 13: 341–362.

Matthews, Roger. 2014. *Realist Criminology*. Houndmills, UK: Palgrave Macmillan.

Matza, David. 1964. *Delinquency and Drift.* New York: John Wiley.

Moffitt, Terrie E. 1993. "Adolescence-Limited and Life-Course-Persistent Antisocial Behavior: A Developmental Taxonomy." *Psychological Review* 100: 674–701.

Pratt, Travis C. 2009. *Addicted to Incarceration: Corrections Policy and the Politics of Misinformation in the United States.* Thousand Oaks, CA: Sage.

Pratt, Travis C., and Jillian J. Turanovic. 2016. "Lifestyle and Routine Activity Theories Revisited: The Importance of 'Risk' to the Study of Victimization." *Victims and Offenders* 11: 335–354. doi: 10.1080/15564886.2015.1057351.

Pratt, Travis C., Jillian J. Turanovic, Kate A. Fox, and Kevin A. Wright. 2014. "Self-Control and Victimization: A Meta-analysis." *Criminology* 52: 87–116.

Rengert, George F. 1989. "Spatial Justice and Criminal Victimization." *Justice Quarterly* 6: 543–564.

Sampson, Robert J. 2012. *Great American City: Chicago and the Enduring Neighborhood Effect.* Chicago: University of Chicago Press.

Sampson, Robert J., and John H. Laub. 1993. *Crime in the Making: Pathways and Turning Points through Life.* Cambridge, MA: Harvard University Press.

Schaefer, Lacey, Francis T. Cullen, and John Eck. 2016. *Environmental Criminology: A New Paradigm for Supervising Offenders in the Community.* Thousand Oaks, CA: Sage.

Shaw, Clifford R. 1930. *The Jack-Roller: A Delinquent Boy's Own Story.* Chicago; University of Chicago Press.

Shaw, Clifford R., and Henry D. McKay. 1942. *Juvenile Delinquency and Urban Areas.* Chicago: University of Chicago Press.

Sherman, Lawrence W. 1993. "Why Crime Control Is Not Reactionary." In *Police Innovation and Control of the Police*, edited by David Weisburd and Craig Uchida. New York: Springer-Verlag.

Steffensmeier, Darrell J., and Jeffrey T. Ulmer. 2015. "Taking Criminal Opportunity Seriously: An Actor-Centered Approach." In *Challenging Criminological Theory: The Legacy of Ruth Rosner Kornhauser*, edited by Francis T. Cullen, Pamela Wilcox, Robert J. Sampson, and Brendan D. Dooley. Vol. 19 of *Advances in Criminological Theory*. New Brunswick, NJ: Transaction.

Sutherland, Edwin H. 1937. *The Professional Thief: By a Professional Thief.* Chicago: University of Chicago Press.

Weisburd, David, and Anthony A. Braga, eds. 2006. *Police Innovation: Contrasting Perspectives.* Cambridge: Cambridge University Press.

Weisburd, David, John E. Eck, Anthony A. Braga, Cody W. Telep, Breanne Cave et al. 2016. *Place Matters: Criminology for the Twenty-First Century*. New York: Cambridge University Press.

Weisburd, David, Elizabeth R. Groff, and Sue-Ming Yang. 2012. *The Criminology of Place: Street Segments and Our Understanding of the Crime Problem*. New York: Oxford University Press.

Weisburd, David, and Alex R. Piquero. 2008. "How Well Do Criminologists Explain Crime? Statistical Modeling in Published Studies." In *Crime and Justice: A Review of Research*, Vol. 37, edited by Michael Tonry. Chicago: University of Chicago Press.

Wilcox, Pamela, Brooke Miller Gialopsos, and Kenneth C. Land. 2013. "Multilevel Criminal Opportunity." In *The Oxford Handbook of Criminological Theory*, edited by Francis T. Cullen and Pamela Wilcox. New York: Oxford University Press.

Wilcox, Pamela, and Kenneth C. Land. 2015. "Social Disorganization and Criminal Opportunity." In *Challenging Criminological Theory: The Legacy of Ruth Rosner Kornhauser*, edited by Francis T. Cullen, Pamela Wilcox, Robert J. Sampson, and Brendan D. Dooley. Vol. 19 of *Advances in Criminological Theory*. New Brunswick, NJ: Transaction.

Wilson, James Q. 1975. *Thinking About Crime*. New York: Vintage.

PART II

METHODS OF RESEARCH IN ENVIRONMENTAL CRIMINOLOGY

CHAPTER 9

DECIDING ON THE "APPROPRIATE" UNIT OF ANALYSIS

Practical Considerations in Environmental Criminology

BRIAN LAWTON

The selection of units of analysis should be guided ideally by knowledge of the phenomenon under investigation. (Messner et al. 1999)

9.1 Introduction

One of the primary decisions of any research endeavor is to identify where the information necessary for successfully completing the study is going to come from. In traditional criminological research this is a relatively easy question to answer. When we want to know about victims, we study victims. When we want to know about agents of the criminal justice system, we speak to them directly. Unlike these prior examples, the study of environmental criminology, or crime at places, does not have such a straightforward gatekeeper to this information. Often the information collected will be applied to a geography through a process of aggregation, spatial joining, or decision-making on the part of the researchers themselves. These actions may raise concerns of the accuracy of the measures and generalizability of any findings.

Concerns about decision-making, on the part of the researcher, are further complicated by the fact that data at macro levels of analysis may not have been generated at that particular level of analysis. For example, while we may speak about neighborhood differences in regard to crime, we are in truth discussing data collected at an individual level that has been aggregated to a larger unit of analysis. To some extent this concern is compounded by the availability of individual data, and the multiple possible levels of aggregation that are provided by state and federal agencies for a variety of purposes. For example, the decision to conduct a neighborhood-level analysis of individual data is not the only option researchers have; they could easily examine the county, census tract, census block group, census block, or street segment level as an alternative.

These alternatives were selected as those most readily available through the US Census Bureau, and do not take into consideration other possible geographies, such as zip code tabulated areas, congressional districts, facilities, individual buildings, or geographies that may have been defined by a municipality (e.g., school catchment areas) or by service providers (e.g., police districts). This example is intended to illustrate the question, what is the appropriate unit of analysis for research?

In an attempt to address this question I start by considering the importance of the decision, followed by a series of concerns often associated with this decision-making process. I will highlight, using publicly available data from the Baltimore City Police Department, how changing units of analysis can suggest different ecological patterns. Finally, I close with a discussion of how these considerations may impact our findings.

9.2 Considering Different Units of Analysis

Prior research has demonstrated that criminal behavior is not randomly distributed (Brantingham and Brantingham 1999; Roncek 2000; Weisburd and Green 1995; Weisburd et al. 1992; Weisburd, Bernasco, and Bruinsma 2009; Johnson and Bowers 2010; Johnson 2010, to name a few). More specifically, there is a body of evidence to suggest that there are geographic, and temporal, patterns to criminal behavior (Andresen and Malleson 2015, 2011, 2013; Bernasco and Nieuwbeerta 2005; Jobes et al. 2004, Weisburd et al. 2004; Groff et al. 2009; Johnson and Bowers 2010; see also Telep and Weisburd in this volume). Understanding that criminal behavior is clustered makes the decision about which geographic units are employed to examine crime even more crucial. Tita and Greenbaum (2009) highlight important decisions that researchers must make in modeling crime. One of these is that they must choose a unit of analysis "that is consistent with the social processes believed to be driving the observed patterns" (p. 145).

The decision on which unit of analysis to utilize for a research study is not one made lightly. The consequences of this decision can have both ethical and statistical consequences (Maltz 2009). Statistically, units that are too small may have insufficient activity for analysis, and those that are too large may have insufficient variation. Ethically, the decision to aggregate or not to aggregate can have repercussions on the conclusions drawn from an analysis and the way in which these areas are characterized. Failure to account for this geographic variation can result in incorrect estimates, yielding inaccurate results on the basis of which decisions may be made (Messner et al. 1999).

9.3 Causes for Concern

One of the unique qualities of understanding the relationship between variables in the study of environmental criminology is that often our questions and conclusions run across different units of analysis. This is unlike a traditional criminological approach, where often only a single unit of analysis is employed.[1] For example, analyses measured at a single level are relatively straightforward in how they are understood and described. Measures are made of a group of individuals, and the relationship between these measures is used to draw a conclusion about the group studied and often to generalize findings to a larger group. In studies where the measures are taken across different units of analysis (i.e., environmental), the same type of conclusions can be made (within-unit analysis) without taking environmental identifiers into account; however, conclusions may also be drawn about the relationships between measures at different units of analysis (across-unit analysis) comparing individuals within different environments.

This latter type of examination and conclusion can be problematic if the relationship between the units of analysis is not well understood, and can lead to two distinct mistakes on the part of the researcher. They are the ecological fallacy and the atomistic fallacy; each one is the product of an incorrect conclusion drawn about the nature of the relationship of variables at different units of analysis or aggregation.

Ecological fallacy is a term coined by Selvin (1958) referring to a fallacy when conclusions are drawn about a microunit of analysis based only on data from the macrounit in which the microunits are nested. For example, individuals within high-crime neighborhoods are more likely to be criminals. Robinson (1950) brought this "paradox" to the forefront by demonstrating that the same data analyzed at two different levels of analysis, the individual and state, could lead to conflicting results.[2] Robinson's examination of a measure of percentage literate and percentage foreign born found a moderate negative correlation when measured at the state level, but a weak positive correlation when measured at the individual level. In sum, he argued that use of a macrounit measure was not valid for drawing conclusions about the microunits nested within.

The atomistic fallacy (Susser 1973), also known as the individualistic fallacy (Alker 1969), occurs when conclusions are drawn about the nature of the macrounit based on data collected on the microunits nested within. Here the concern is that researchers "try to generalize from individual behavior to collective relationships" (Alker 1969, p. 78). The awareness of these fallacies has generated interest in alternatives to traditional single-level analyses, and has emphasized the need to incorporate multilevel analyses or analyses that describe relationships between variables across multiple levels of analysis simultaneously.[3]

A third concern is how much impact the selection of a particular unit of analysis can have on the conclusions drawn in a research study. This concern, referred to as the modifiable areal unit problem (MAUP) refers to "a problem arising from the imposition of artificial units of spatial reporting on continuous geographical phenomena resulting in the generation of artificial spatial patterns" (Heywood et al. 1998, p. 8). The term *modifiable* refers to the choices that researchers can have in determining the appropriate unit of analysis; as that unit changes, the results themselves can change as well. Early research highlighted this problem (Openshaw 1984; Bailey and Gatrell 1995; Messner et al. 1999) and the impact that it can have on utilizing predefined geographic definitions.

Armhein (1995) identified two components to errors associated with MAUP, the "scale effect" and the "zonation effect."[4] The scale effect is the difference in number due to the number of possible aggregate units (e.g., neighborhood versus police district). The zonation effect is the variation surrounding the nested structure of the aggregate units (e.g., block groups that make up census tracts). Nakaya (2000) emphasizes that these larger aggregate units will be more stable due to the nested structure of the data and the higher number of cases making up the aggregate; however, this may mask meaningful variation that would be notable if a smaller unit of analysis was employed.

These concerns surrounding the selection of the appropriate level of analysis should not be considered as only methodological considerations. As we examine the evidence surrounding tests of spatial theory such as routine activity theory or crime pattern theory, it is easy to recognize that our ability to obtain support for these theories is likely contingent upon our selection of the appropriate level of analysis. Cohen and Felson (1979) introduced the "routine activity approach," which highlighted the intersection of motivated offenders, suitable targets, and a lack of capable guardians. If we take, for example, the question of suitable targets, we recognize that the selection of level of analysis may have an impact not only on the raw count of potential suitable targets, but on how a suitable target is operationalized. Cohen and Felson's original work used number of adults in the household to help explain burglary rates using the General Social Survey; Stack (1995) used county-level counts of residences. Is it fair then to suggest that similar or different findings across these levels of analysis provide comparable tests of the theory?

9.4 Example: Violent Crime in Baltimore City (2015)

In order to demonstrate the concerns previously discussed, data were obtained on violent crimes reported to the Baltimore City Police Department. The City of Baltimore currently uploads all Part 1 crimes to an online website in order to make the data readily available to the public (https://data.baltimorecity.gov/). Data on all Part 1 violent crimes were downloaded from this site, along with shapefile coverages of city-defined neighborhoods, police districts, and street segments. Additional coverages were obtained from the US Census Bureau's Tiger Files Project, specifically coverages of the county, census tracts, census block groups, and blocks that make up the city of Baltimore.

Individual-level violent[5] crime data were aggregated to each of these coverages to generate count-level measures. In order to compare across these areas, new estimates were calculated, controlling for the size of the geography in square miles.[6] Table 9.1 reports findings of the comparison across the coverages. For example, Baltimore has a total of nine police districts with an average size of nine square miles. This results in an average of approximately nineteen hundred violent crimes per district with about twenty-six hundred of those occurring in the top 10% of the police districts (*N* = 1), meaning that approximately the top 10% of the police districts account for 15% (15.13%) of the total violent crime.

Looking across the geographies, we see a pattern. With the exception of the city-defined neighborhoods, as the geography becomes smaller, we see a greater concentration of violent crimes. The top 10% of census tracts (*N* = 200) account for almost a quarter (23.4%) of the total violent crime. The top 10% of census block groups (*N* = 653) account for about 30% (29.66%) of the total violent crimes. Neighborhoods (*N* = 278) account for 37.68% of the total violent crime in the top 10% of violent crime neighborhoods. The top 10% of city blocks (*N* = 13,488) for violent crime account for 59% of the total violent crime, and the top 10% of the street segments (*N* = 24,992) account for almost 70% (69.48%) of the total violent crime.

Table 9.1 Baltimore City Violent Crime Count Comparisons and across High-Concentration Units (Top 10%)

	Number of areal units	Mean area (sq. miles)	Mean violent crime	Min.	Max.	Violent crimes in top 10% of areas	Percentage violent crimes in top 10% of areas
Police districts	9	9.03	1905.22	1,584	2,595	2,595	15.13
Census tracts	200	0.46	85.73	5	659	4,013	23.4
Neighborhoods	278	0.29	61.68	0	606	6,461	37.68
Census block groups	653	0.14	26.26	0	386	5,085	29.66
Blocks	13,488	0.006	1.27	0	68	10,148	59.18
Streets	24,992	0.067[a]	0.69	0	68	11,914	69.48

[a] Street length is reported in miles, not square miles.

This is in line with findings from a number of prior studies (Sherman et al. 1989; Weisburd et al. 1992, just to name two) showing a high concentration of crime in limited number of areas. In short, crime is not equally distributed across any of the areal units, but as the number of areal units increase, we see a higher concentration of violent crime. In short, the larger areal units mask a great deal of heterogeneity that becomes apparent in the smaller-sized units. Looking at Figure 9.1, we can see the visual representation of this concentration, noting the clustering in the neighborhoods in the center of the city, and an increased presence of violent crimes per square mile in neighborhoods in the northeast portion of the city. Comparing this to Figure 9.2 suggests a very different set of findings, when the emphasis is on the block group level of analysis. Here we do see a series of high violent crime areas in the center of the city, as well as the northwest and southeast. Finally, in Figure 9.3 we can see that by examining the census blocks we have high violent crimes areas across the city, including a concentration in the west and north that was not apparent with the other levels of analysis.

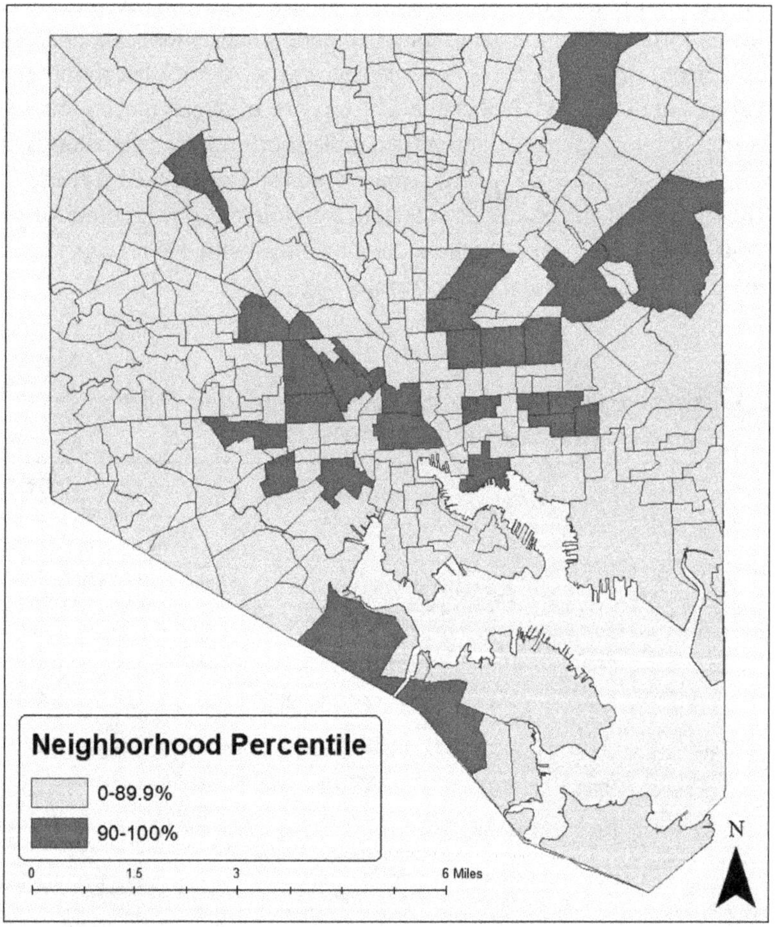

FIGURE 9.1 Neighborhoods in the top 10% for violent crime

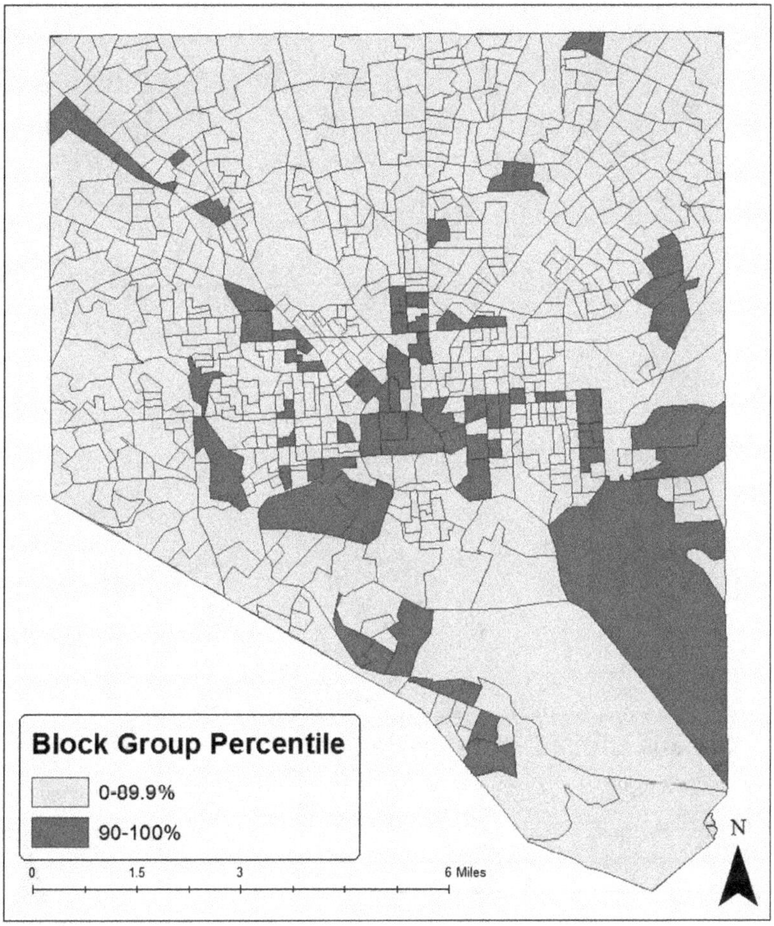

FIGURE 9.2 Blocks groups in the top 10% for violent crime

These examples are intended to illustrate concerns about findings drawn from an analysis conducted at a single level. Here we would have over- or underestimated the distribution of high violent crime areas based on the level of measurement that we had chosen in regard to addressing our research question. While the decision on which level to use will often by driven by data availability or theoretical focus, researchers have suggested more practical considerations. Oberwittler and Wikstrom (2009) support evidence demonstrating the homogeneity of smaller units, and conclude that "smaller is better" (p. 41) in regard to selecting a unit of analysis.

The emphasis on the smaller unit, while increasing the homogeneity of the units, does raise analytic concerns about the independence of the unit of analysis. While this should be observed regardless of the level of the unit of analysis, prior work (Bernasco et al. 2013) has demonstrated that examining small units of analysis has the potential to

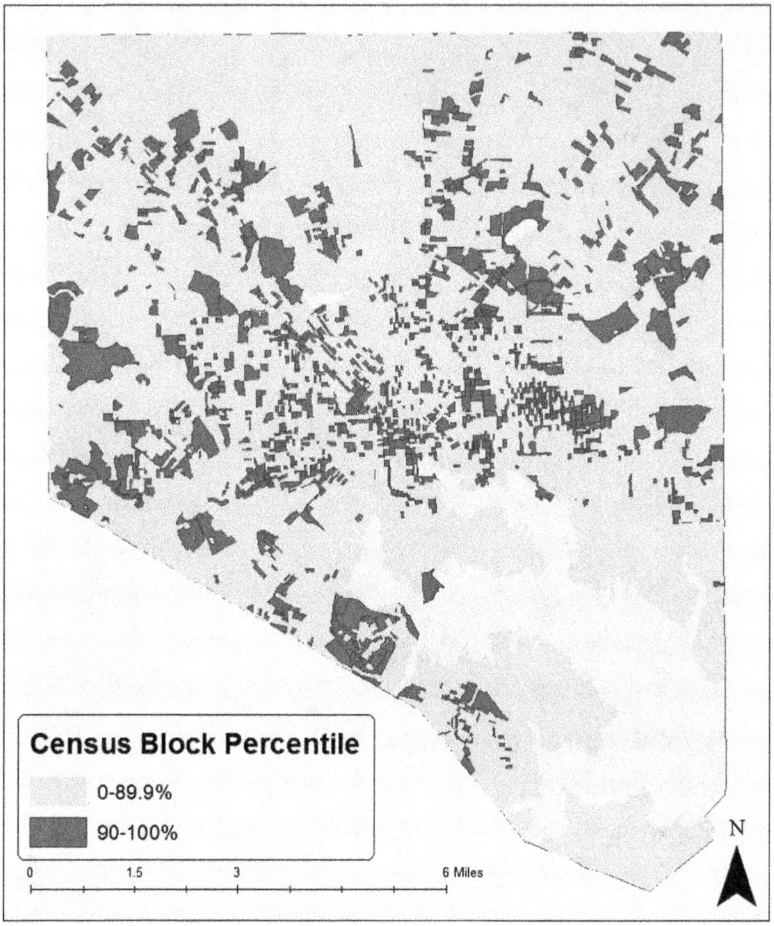

FIGURE 9.3 Census blocks in the top 10% for violent crime

produce spillover effects from adjacent units. In addition, when utilizing smaller units the researcher must be aware of the potential of having more units than cases to aggregate to them, and accordingly should consider using techniques and statistics to correct for this potential bias (see Bernasco and Steenbeek, 2016).

It is also important to note that these types of geographic units are not the only manner in which we demonstrate spatial patterns of crime or other behaviors. As noted in Table 9.1, researchers may choose to use the street segment or block face[7] as a catchment area for individual units. A body of research has demonstrated the utility of examining specific types of facilities (Eck et al. 2007) such as liquor license locations or other "risky" locations. Individual addresses have also been used to demonstrate the geographic concentration of crime (Sherman et al. 1989) and provided evidence for a focus on microunits.

9.5 Units for a Purpose

Which then is the ideal unit of analysis to employ? Oberwittler and Wikstrom (2009) lean toward the smaller unit of analysis; Nakaya (2000) points out that these smaller units may offer more variation, but will be less stable in regard to their estimates. Smith et al. (2009) state that the most appropriate unit will be the one that "minimizes the heterogeneity within groups of observations while attempting to maximize the heterogeneity between groups of observations" (p. 218). While these approaches offer valid reasons for their suggestions, it seems that there are three considerations in identifying the appropriate unit of analysis for an intended research study. First, there is *access to data*. It cannot be taken for granted that available data will allow for examination at multiple units of analysis. Data released from the US Census Bureau contains a Federal Information Processing Standard (FIPS) code that can be used to identify the geographic location of data across multiple units of analysis; this, however, is not the norm. Secondary data may have location identification masked, recoded for privacy concerns, or estimated to hundred-block addresses, raising concerns about the accuracy of their location on a map.

It cannot be assumed that because data are available that they are entirely appropriate for use by the researcher. For example, researchers and analysts often rely on geographies that have been defined for administrative purposes, rather than for a purpose in line with the goal of the research (Rengert and Lockwood 2009). These administrative purposes may have the goal of emphasizing spatial patterns within a particular geography, such as a city boundary, to the exclusion of what is going on outside of those areas, referred to as "edge effects." It brings to mind images of ancient maps where the unchartered areas were simply labeled as "Here be Dragons," suggesting that nothing good would come of looking in these areas. However, failure to observe what is occurring outside these borders may result in a misunderstanding of the nature of the ecological reality.

Agencies and institutions are not the only parties making an effort to develop their own geographies. More recently there has been an increasing utilization of participatory GIS where individuals play a part in identifying borders, boundaries, and points on a GIS map. The goal is to ensure that GIS maps are taking into account the experiences of individuals who utilize these geographic areas, and not limiting them to big-data representations of geographic areas (Mukherjee 2015; see also Solymosi and Bowers in this volume).

The second consideration is the *purpose* of the research effort. A researcher engaging in an atheoretical effort may choose the unit of analysis that lends itself to the most interesting findings. Theoretically driven research, however, should have a logical context to consider the interaction of individuals within their larger aggregation. From a criminological perspective, we would not expect the same process to impact individuals across neighborhoods as we might city blocks, or across a state.

The final concern in considering the most appropriate unit of analysis is that of the *skill set* of the researcher. The discussion up to this point has emphasized only the use of predefined geographies, giving no consideration to geographies that may be generated by researchers themselves, as well as through an automated process (Ratcliffe and McCullagh 1999; see also Umar, Johnson, and Cheshire in this volume). Researchers with experience may choose to engage in sensitivity analyses and run comparative analyses of the results across multiple units (Brantingham et al, 2009; Messner et al. 1999). They may choose to develop their own geographic boundaries (Rengert and Lockwood 2009) that may address issues around homogeneity of the variance and the distribution of values.

Skill set can also be applicable in consideration of what is to be done with the spatially enabled data. The necessary skill set of a researcher must be different if the goal is to employ a multilevel model approach (Johnson and Bowers 2010) to examine factors that operate at different geographic levels as compared to visually presenting a spatial distribution. While Esri products have increasingly included statistical testing functions in their software, they are not always intuitively understandable.

In short, there is no simple answer to our initial question of what is the most appropriate unit of analysis for research purposes. An argument could be made for aggregation to any logical and valid geographic unit of analysis. Concerns about the ecological fallacy and atomistic fallacy can only be addressed through a responsible effort on the part of the researcher to interpret statistics accurately, or to engage in multilevel analyses. Concerns about MAUP can never be completely ignored, but can be limited through efforts on the part of the researcher to conduct sensitivity analyses and to examine results across different levels of aggregation. Ultimately this suggests the simple fact that researchers need to be thoughtful in any decision they make in regard to their research:

> No single level of aggregation can constitute the "best" unit of analysis for studying the spatial or temporal patterns in crime. Data should be collected at the most detailed level possible and aggregated upward to fit the requisites of theory or the limitations of data unit aggregations of those elements . . . thought to be important. (Brantingham et al. 2009, p. 90)

Notes

1. This is not to suggest that nonenvironmental studies never use more than a single unit. For example, studies of group participation or dyads would be exceptions; however, it is more likely to be a cause for concern with an environmental study.
2. It is important to note here as well that Robinson was not the first to introduce this concept. Other scholars (Gehlke and Biehl 1934; Thorndike 1939) had also discussed this concern. However, Robinson's demonstration brought this concern to a wider audience.
3. See Andresen (in this volume) for a more detailed discussion of the modifiable areal unit problem and ecological fallacy.

4. The zonation effect has also been referred to as the "problem of aggregation" (Weisburd, Bruinsma, and Bernasco 2009).
5. Violent crimes consisted of aggravated assaults, common assaults, homicide, rape, robbery, and shootings ($N = 17{,}155$).
6. With the exception of the street segments, which were reported in miles.
7. There is some disagreement about whether "street segments" and "block face" are interchangeable terms. The street segment is generally characterized as the area of a street between two intersections, while the block face can be used to describe only one side of that street segment. In short, a street segment is made up of two block faces.

References

Alker, H.R. (1969). A typology of ecological fallacies. In M. Dogan and S. Rokkan (Eds.), *Quantitative Ecological Analysis in the Social Sciences* (pp. 69–86). Cambridge, Mass.: MIT Press.

Andresen, M. A., and Malleson, N. (2011). Testing the stability of crime patterns: Implications for theory and policy. *Journal of Research in Crime and Delinquency* 48, 58–82.

Andresen, M. A., and Malleson, N. (2013). Crime seasonality and its variations across space. *Applied Geography* 43, 25–35.

Andresen, M. A., and Malleson, N. (2015). Intra-week spatial-temporal patterns of crime. *Crime Science* 4, Article 12.

Armhein, C. (1995). Searching for the elusive aggregation effect: Evidence from statistical simulations. *Environment and Planning A* 27(1), 105–119.

Bailey, T. C., and Gatrell, A. C. (1995). *Interactive Spatial Data Analysis*. New York: Routledge Press.

Bernasco, W., Block, R., and Ruiter, S. (2013). Go where the money is: Modeling street robbers' location choices. *Journal of Economic Geography* 13, 119–143.

Bernasco, W., and Nieuwbeerta, P. (2005). How do residential burglars select target areas? *British Journal of Criminology* 45, 295–315.

Bernasco, W., and Steenbeek, W. (2016). More places than crimes: Implications for evaluating the law of crime concentration at place. *Journal of Quantitative Criminology*. Advance online publication. doi:10.1007/s10940-016-9342-7.

Brantingham, P. L., and Brantingham, P. J. (1999). Theoretical model of crime hot spot generation. *Studies on Crime and Crime Prevention* 8, 7–26.

Brantingham, P. L., Brantingham, P. J., Vajihollahi, M., and Wuschke, K. (2009). Crime analysis at multiple scales of aggregation: A topological approach. In David Weisburd, Wim Bernasco, and Gerben J. N. Bruinsma (Eds.), *Putting Crime in Its Place: Units of Analysis in Geographic Criminology* (pp. 87–107). New York: Springer.

Cohen, L., and Felson, M. (1979). Social change and crime rate trends: A Routine activity approach. *American Sociological Review* 44, 588–608.

Eck, J. E., Clarke, R. V., and Guerette, R. T. (2007). Risky facilities: Crime concentration in homogenous sets of establishments and facilities. In Graham Farrell, Kate J. Bowers, Shane D. Johnson, and Michael Townsley (eds.), *Imagination for Crime Prevention: Essays in Honour of Ken Pease* (pp. 225–264), vol. 21 of *Crime Prevention Studies*. Monsey, NY: Criminal Justice Press.

Gehlke, C. E., and Biehl, K. (1934). Certain effects of grouping upon the size of the correlation coefficient in census tract material. *Journal of the American Statistical Association* 29, 169–170.

Groff, E., Weisburd, D., and Morris, N. A. (2009). Where the action is at places: Examining spatio-temporal patterns of juvenile crime at places using trajectory analysis. In David Weisburd, Wim Bernasco, and Gerben J. N. Bruinsma (Eds.), *Putting Crime in Its Place: Units of Analysis in Geographic Criminology* (pp. 61–86). New York: Springer.

Heywood, D. I., Cornelius, S., and Carver, S. (1998). *An Introduction to Geographical Information Systems*. New York: Addison Wesley Longman.

Jobes, P. C., Barclay, E., Weinand, H., and Donnermeyer, J. F. (2004). A structural analysis of social disorganization and crime in rural communities in Australia. *Australian and New Zealand Journal of Criminology* 37(1), 114–140.

Johnson, S. D. (2010). A brief history of the analysis of crime concentration. *European Journal of Applied Mathematics* 21, 349–370.

Johnson, S. D., and Bowers, K. J. (2010). Permeability and burglary risk: Are cul-de-sacs safer? *Journal of Quantitative Criminology* 26, 89–111.

Maltz, M. D. (2009). Waves, particles, and crime. In David Weisburd, Wim Bernasco, and Gerben J. N. Bruinsma (Eds.), *Putting Crime in Its Place: Units of Analysis in Geographic Criminology* (pp. 123–142). New York: Springer.

Messner, S. F., Anselin, L., Baller, R., Hawkins, D. F., Deane, G., and Tolnay, S. E. (1999). The spatial patterning of county homicide rates: An application of exploratory spatial data analysis. *Journal of Quantitative Criminology* 15(4), 423–450.

Mukherjee, F. (2015). Public participatory GIS. *Geography Compass* 9(7), 384–394.

Nakaya, T. (2000) An information statistical approach to the modifiable areal unit problem in incidence rate maps. *Environment and Planning A* 32(1), 91–109.

Oberwittler, D., and Wikstrom, P.-O. H. (2009). Why small is better: Advancing the study of the role of behavioral contexts in crime causation. In David Weisburd, Wim Bernasco, and Gerben J. N. Bruinsma (Eds.), *Putting Crime in Its Place: Units of Analysis in Geographic Criminology* (pp. 35–59). New York: Springer.

Openshaw, S. (1984). The modifiable areal unit problem. *Concepts and Techniques in Modern Geography* 38, 41–53.

Ratcliffe, J. H., and McCullagh, M. J. (1999) Hotbeds of crime and the search for spatial accuracy. *Geographical Systems* 1(4), 385–398.

Rengert, G., and Lockwood, B. (2009). Geographic units of analysis and the analysis of crime. (2009). In David Weisburd, Wim Bernasco, and Gerben J. N. Bruinsma (Eds.), *Putting Crime in Its Place: Units of Analysis in Geographic Criminology* (pp. 109–122). New York: Springer.

Robinson, W. S. (1950). Ecological correlations and the behavior of individuals. *American Sociological Review* 15, 351–357.

Roncek, D. W. (2000). Schools and crime. In Victor Goldsmith, Philip G. McGuire, John H. Mollenkopf, and Timothy A. Ross (Eds.), *Analyzing Crime Patterns: Frontiers of Practice* (pp. 153–165). Thousand Oaks, CA: Sage.

Selvin, H. C. (1958). Durkheim's suicide and problems of empirical research. *American Journal of Sociology* 63, 607–619.

Sherman, L. W., Gartin, P. R., and Buerger, M. E. (1989). Hot spots of predatory crime: Routine activities and the criminology of place. *Criminology* 27, 27–55.

Smith, W., Bond, J. W, and Townsley, M. (2009). Determining how journeys-to-crime vary: Measuring inter- and intra-offender crime trip distributions. In David Weisburd, Wim

Bernasco, and Gerben J. N. Bruinsma (Eds.), *Putting Crime in Its Place: Units of Analysis in Geographic Criminology* (pp. 217–236). New York: Springer.

Stack, S. (1995). The Effects of temporary residences on burglary: A test of criminal opportunity theory. *Journal of Criminal Justice* 19, 197–214.

Susser, M. (1973). *Causal Thinking in the Health Sciences.* London: Oxford University Press.

Thorndike, E. L. (1939). On the fallacy of imputing the correlation found for groups to the individuals or smaller groups containing them. *American Journal of Psychology* 52, 122–124.

Tita, G. E., and Greenbaum, R. T. (2009). Crime, neighborhoods, and units of analysis: Putting space in its place. In David Weisburd, Wim Bernasco, and Gerben J. N. Bruinsma (Eds.), *Putting Crime in Its Place: Units of Analysis in Geographic Criminology* (pp. 145–170). New York: Springer.

Weisburd, D., Bernasco, W., and Bruinsma, G. J. N. (2009). *Putting Crime in Its Place: Units of Analysis in Geographic Criminology.* New York: Springer.

Weisburd, D., Bruinsma, G. J. N., and Bernasco, W. (2009). Units of analysis in geographic criminology: Historical development, critical issues and open questions. In David Weisburd, Wim Bernasco, and Gerben J. N. Bruinsma (Eds.), *Putting Crime in Its Place: Units of Analysis in Geographic Criminology* (pp. 3–31). New York: Springer.

Weisburd, D., Bushway, S., Lum, C., and Yang, S. M. (2004). Trajectories of crime at places: A longitudinal study of street segments in the city of Seattle. *Criminology* 42(2), 283–321.

Weisburd, D. W. and Green, L. (1995). Policing drug hot spots: The Jersey City DMA experiment. *Justice Quarterly* 12(4), 711–735.

Weisburd, G., Maher, L., and Sherman, L. (1992). Contrasting crime general and crime specific theory: The case of hot spots of crime. In Freda Adler and W. S. Laufer (Eds.), *New Directions in Criminological Theory* (pp. 45–70), vol. 4 of *Advances in Criminological Theory.* New Brunswick, NJ: Transaction.

CHAPTER 10

GIS AND SPATIAL ANALYSIS

MARTIN A. ANDRESEN

10.1 Introduction

Though the spatial analysis of crime had its beginnings in early 19th-century France with the work of Michel Guerry (1832, 1833) and Adolphe Quételet (1831, 1842) (see Weisburd et al. 2009 for a history of spatial criminology), environmental criminology came about when C. Ray Jeffery (1971) coined the term; Jeffery was calling for a new school of thought within criminology to better understand the environment within which crime occurs. This call for a new school of thought was in spite of the fact that crime had been mapped for close to 150 years and was an important component of social disorganization theory. Shaw and McKay (1942), for example, had many maps of juvenile delinquency and related factors in Chicago. As pointed out by Brantingham and Brantingham (1981), previous research in criminology has focused on one of three dimensions: the law, the offender, or the target. However, there is a fourth dimension of space-time that is the concern of environmental criminology and critical for understanding the environment within which crime occurs.

Because of the importance of the spatial-temporal dimension(s) within environmental criminology, the use and applications of geographic information systems (GIS) and spatial analysis are rather widespread. In this chapter I will cover some of the principles and advancements in the use of crime mapping and spatial analysis to study the spatial distribution of crime, primarily through the lens of environmental criminology. Books can be (and have been!) written on many of the topics covered here, so this discussion cannot be considered exhaustive, but an introduction to the issues of how GIS and spatial analysis are used in that regard.

10.2 What Are Crime Mapping and Spatial Analysis? And How Are They Done?

Simply put, crime mapping is the spatial representation of crime (in the context of criminal events) on a map. Consequently, in order to make such a representation, one must have geographic coordinates for each criminal event to place it on a map. This may come across as an obvious statement in this context, but it is an important factor in crime mapping for the accuracy of the information. For example, due to privacy concerns, a police agency may provide only the neighborhood within which a criminal event occurs. Or, more commonly, a police agency will provide X,Y coordinates or the 100-block (street segment) to locate where the criminal event occurred in order to provide some level of privacy. Though such information may be accurate, the degree of that accuracy may be deceptive.

Most often, X,Y coordinates are assumed to be as accurate geographic information as one can get. If this information was obtained using a global positioning system (GPS) unit, that may be the case. Though weather and receiver quality impact the accuracy of data, most high-quality GPS receivers are accurate within 3.5 meters, often within 1 meter.[1] Such accuracy, however, cannot be assumed with criminal event data. Did the police officer on scene bring the GPS receiver to the exact location of the criminal event, or is the GPS receiver located in the police vehicle that may be one or two properties away? If a researcher or practitioner is interested in general spatial crime patterns, such issues are not of much concern, but if an analysis is concerned with minute details such as land use or inside/outside location of the criminal event, such an analysis must proceed with caution. Additionally, the X,Y coordinates provided may represent the geocoded location of the criminal event: the coordinates where a GIS places the address on a road network.[2] The primary limitation of this method is that GIS geocoding procedures may assign geographic coordinates to a criminal event based on a linear interpolation in a street segment. That means that if a street segment has an address range from 101 to 199 and the address is 150, the GIS places that address in the center of the street segment. Though this will most often prove to be reasonably accurate, we must always use caution when interpreting the accuracy of spatially referenced data of any kind. For more details regarding geocoding (criminal event) data, see Ratcliffe (2001, 2004).

Once spatially referenced criminal event data are available, they need to be represented on a map. There are three primary ways in which spatially referenced data can be presented: points, lines, and areas. Most often, criminal event data are represented as points (dot maps) or areas (census tracts or neighborhoods, for example), but maps considering lines (street segments) are becoming more commonplace (see Curman et al. 2015 and Weisburd et al. 2012, for example). In this chapter, I show maps of points and areas because they are the most common in crime mapping.

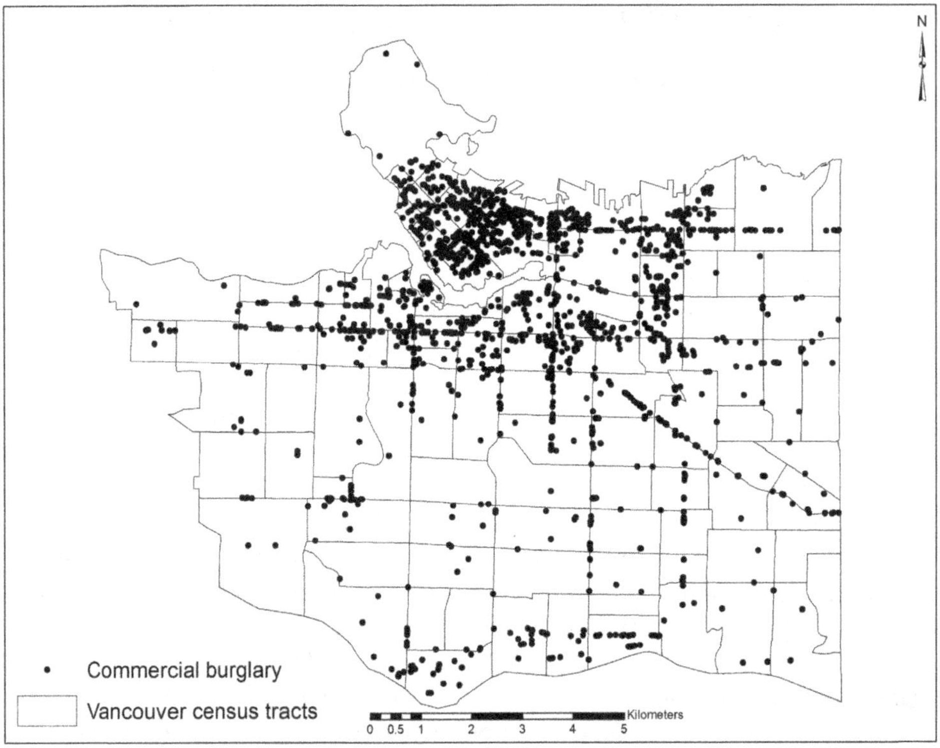

FIGURE 10.1 Commercial burglary, Vancouver, Canada, point data

Figure 10.1 shows a map of commercial burglary in Vancouver, British Columbia, Canada, in 2013. These data are represented as points, but were derived from 100-block (street segment) data. Consequently, no inference can be made at a spatial resolution smaller than the street segment; however, when viewed at the level of the city, this inaccuracy is unlikely to distort perceived patterns. As can be seen in Figure 10.1, 2013 commercial burglaries in Vancouver appear to be clustered, especially in the central-northern peninsula of the city, which contains the central business district. It is important to note that this is not a particularly interesting "result" because commercial land use in Vancouver is also clustered. This highlights the importance of understanding the context in which criminal event maps are made. Generally speaking, if point-level criminal event data are available, they should be used by the researcher because they will be the *most* spatially accurate. However, one difficulty with point-based maps is that if the phenomenon being mapped has a high volume in a particular area, it is difficult to see how many points are present because they are on top of each other. This can be addressed using a number of different visualization techniques, one of the more common being aggregating points within an area; another method is kernel density estimation, discussed further below.

Figure 10.2 shows commercial burglary counts within census tracts in Vancouver. The cluster of commercial burglaries in the central business district is still quite apparent, with most of the city's census tracts having very low counts of this crime for the year.

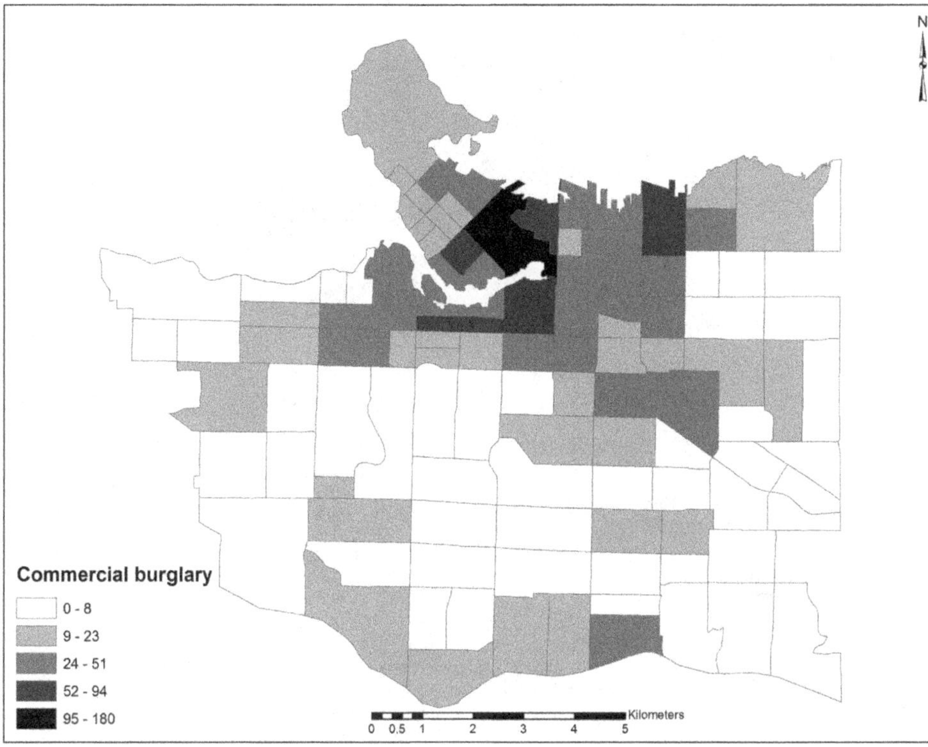

FIGURE 10.2 Commercial burglary, Vancouver, Canada, census tracts

Figure 10.3, on the other hand, shows the same commercial burglary data aggregated to dissemination areas; dissemination areas are similar in size to the census block group in the United States, most often with 400 to 700 persons. Though the same general spatial pattern is present, notable differences emerge when using this smaller spatial unit of analysis. This points to two related, but distinct, issues in spatial analysis: the ecological fallacy and the modifiable areal unit problem. The modifiable areal unit problem, discussed here, refers to changes in statistical results when the spatial units of analysis change. The ecological fallacy essentially means that what is true of the whole is not necessarily true of its parts; this is evident in Figures 10.2 and 10.3, with large areas in Figure 10.2 being represented differently in Figure 10.3. Each of these figures is discussed in further detail below.

10.3 Modifiable Areal Unit Problem and the Ecological Fallacy

The modifiable areal unit problem (MAUP) emerges because raw point-level data are aggregated into area-based units (see Brian Lawton's chapter in this volume, which also

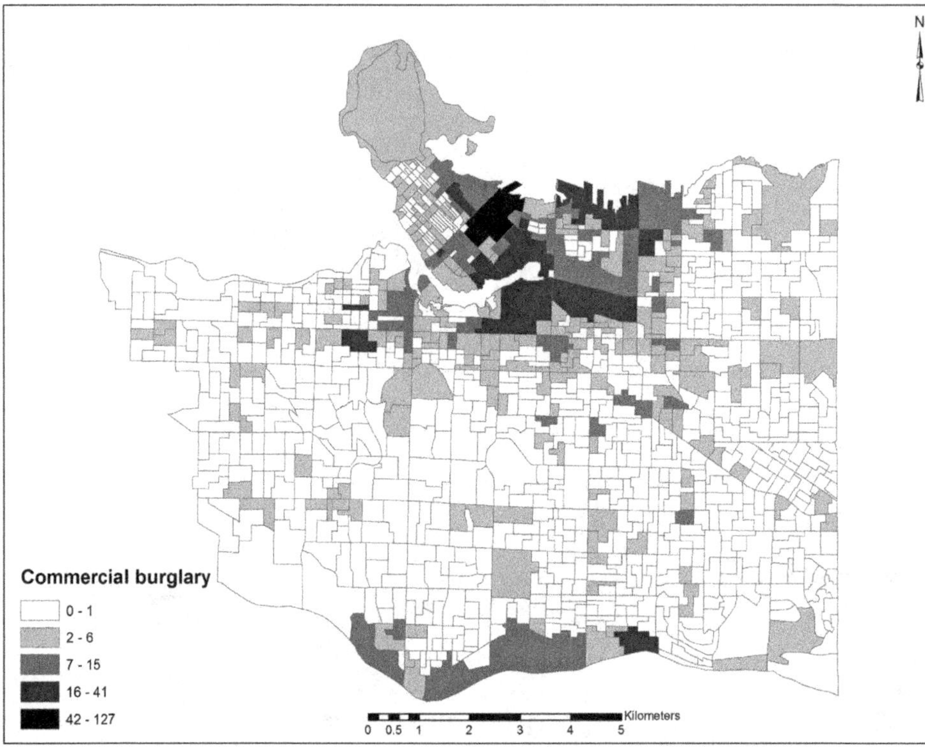

FIGURE 10.3 Commercial burglary, Vancouver, Canada, dissemination areas

discusses this issue). MAUP tends to be problematic because these area-based units do not have "natural" boundaries that make sense for the analysis at hand. Census-based boundaries, for example, are defined by roads and how many homes census workers can visit in a day. Though it is possible that these areas represent actual neighborhoods, many do not. In any case, these area-based units are modifiable because they can be redefined by arbitrarily changing their boundaries. The MAUP, though often attributed to Openshaw (1984a) for its identification, was noticed in statistical analysis as early as the work of Gehlke and Biehl (1934), who found that correlation coefficients increased in magnitude as the size of the area-based units increased.

The MAUP can emerge in one of two primary ways. The first is referred to the zoning problem and occurs when there is a spatial shift in currently defined boundaries. In this case, the size and shape of the areas do not change, they just represent different places. A clear example of the zoning problem would be if a grid of one-square-kilometer cells were shifted 500 meters in one direction. In this case, there would be a change in which point-level events would be aggregated to each cell, potentially altering statistical results.

The second, and more commonly referred to, version of the MAUP is the scale problem. With the scale problem, statistical results change when the size of the area-based units changes. A prime example of the potential for the scale problem is shown in Figure 10.2: because of the moderate changes when changing from census tracts to dissemination areas, any statistical analyses undertaken could produce different results. Of course, simply because there is the potential for a problem does not mean that a problem will emerge. The difficulty, however, is that, with two exceptions, there is no way to predict or correct problems associated with the MAUP. The first exception was identified by Gehlke and Biehl (1934), with the magnitude of correlation coefficients increasing with the size of the area-based units. The second exception is related to sample sizes and statistics; if the area-based units under analysis are smaller while representing the same overall area (i.e., there are more area-based units), you are more likely to find statistically significant results because you have a larger sample size.

Despite the fact that the problem with MAUP is only a potential, research has emerged that shows how problematic the MAUP can be. Openshaw (1984b) found that, through modifications considering the zooming problem alone, one can get correlation coefficients for the same two variables to range from −.99 to +.99. Not only can the magnitude be incorrect, but so can the estimated coefficient sign. Moreover, Fotheringham and Wong (1991) extended the work of Openshaw (1984b) and considered the MAUP in a multivariate (regression) context. The authors investigated the reliability of regression coefficients in the presence of the MAUP and, similar to Openshaw (1984b) in the context of correlation, found unreliability. With regard to the scale problem, Fotheringham and Wong (1991) were able to have the magnitude of regression coefficients change by a factor of nine when reducing the number of area-based units from 800 to 25, covering the same area. Though such a reduction in the number of area-based units representing one place may not appear to be realistic, in the maps of Vancouver in Figure 10.2, there are 993 dissemination areas, 106 census tracts, and 24 official neighborhoods. All of these area-based units have socioeconomic and sociodemographic data available. In other words, drastic changes in the number of area-based units are not merely an abstract methodological issue, but quite possible in actual research. In the end, Fotheringham and Wong (1991) were able to generate almost any result desired by changing the area-based units in a regression context. In fact, they showed that statistical results are even more unpredictable than found by Openshaw (1984b).

With such results in a sensitivity analysis investigating the MAUP, it is easy to become disenchanted with spatial analysis. However, it is important to continue doing such analyses to investigate spatial patterns in hopes of reducing crime. Within the criminological literature the impact of the MAUP has not proven to be as depressing. Wooldredge (2002) analyzed 1,932 individuals, 129 census tracts, and 48 official neighborhoods in Cincinnati in a regression context with over 30 variables. Overall he found that the differences were not qualitatively different most of the time. And Hipp (2007) spoke to the importance of considering the most natural area-based unit of analysis with regard to theoretical relationships. Specifically, the area used to represent a variable (or construct) may vary from variable to variable. In my own research that has considered multiple spatial units of analysis (usually census tracts and dissemination areas) I have not found any particularly interesting or disturbing changes in statistical results. Most often, with this possibility discussed above, dissemination area results tend to have more statistically significant variables, likely because of the larger sample size.

Overall, researchers and practitioners need to be aware of the MAUP and its potential impact on anything they study. If possible, it is advisable to use more than one spatial unit of analysis, particularly if one is attempting to inform policy. Because of the availability of so many forms of spatial analysis, not taking advantage of these statistical methods because of the MAUP would be worse than the possibility of being wrong.

The ecological fallacy is actually something that can be avoided by those who are careful with their inferences. The ecological fallacy is committed when a researcher interprets statistical results at a level finer than that at which the analysis was undertaken. For example, one commits the ecological fallacy if an analysis is undertaken at the neighborhood level and inferences are made on the individuals who live in those neighborhoods. In order words, it is assumed that what is true of the whole is true of all its parts. Though this must be true, on average—otherwise the statistical result at the neighborhood level would not have emerged—it is most certainly not true for all individuals within that neighborhood. Relatedly, the atomistic fallacy occurs when inference is incorrectly made in the other direction: what is true of the part is expected to be true of the whole. For the same reasoning as the ecological fallacy, such a relationship may be true in some cases but cannot be assumed to be true all of the time.

Robinson (1950) was the first to identify and analyze what we now call the ecological fallacy. He defined an ecological correlation as a statistic that included multiple subjects that could be divisible, a neighborhood, for example; an individual correlation is a statistic that involves subjects that cannot be divisible, such as individuals. Robinson (1950) was able to show the conditions within which individual correlations and ecological correlations were the same (no ecological fallacy), but he found this to be the exception, not the rule. Openshaw (1984b) found that the ecological fallacy was important for area-based census data, but the degree of the ecological fallacy depended upon the statistical analysis undertaken. Generally speaking, Openshaw (1984b) found that the differences between any ecological and individual correlations could not be known beforehand.

In some of my own research, when comparing the changes in spatial patterns over time, a colleague and I found that smaller area-based units that were contained within larger area-based units (dissemination areas within census tracts, for example) never had the same degree of change over time in more than 60% of cases (Andresen and Malleson 2013). In fact, in a small number of cases, the type of change found at the level of the census tract was not found for any of the dissemination areas within that census tract! Only when the dissemination areas were aggregated into a census tract did the identified change (marginally) occur.

As stated above, however, despite the problems associated with the ecological and atomistic fallacies, they are easy to avoid. Simply do not make any statistical inferences at levels different from the level used in your analysis: do not make inferences about people when you analyze neighborhoods, and vice versa. The ecological and atomistic fallacies are always a potential in any method of spatial analysis, but we can avoid them if we make statistical inference with care.

10.4 Methods of Spatial Analysis

There are a number of ways to conduct spatial analyses (of crime), and some are more "spatial" than others. The primary distinction is between statistical and visualization methods. However, there are a number of statistical methods that generate output that can be visualized. Each will be discussed below.

10.4.1 Kernel Density Estimation

I have already discussed and shown two visualization methods above: point-based and area-based maps. A "spatial analysis" could simply be the mapping of crime and comparing that map to some other phenomenon that varies spatially. However, one of the most common forms of spatial analysis in the context of visualization is the kernel density map. Kernel density estimation involves placing a grid over the entire study area and essentially counting the number of events that fall within a certain distance of each grid cell. Depending on the size of the grid cells and the distance being used, there will be a high or low degree of "double counting" of points. This is done for the purposes of smoothing data over the entire study area to avoid the high density of points (sometimes referred to as blobs!) that make inferences difficult. The difficulty with kernel density estimation is that it generates a value for each grid cell over the entire study area. Consequently, a kernel density map may show "crime" in an area that experienced no criminal events; however, the same is true for any area-based representation, such as those shown in Figure 10.2 and Figure 10.3.

The kernel density map for commercial burglary in Vancouver is shown in Figure 10.4. It should be clear that the representations of the greatest volumes of commercial burglary are in the same places as in the maps previously shown. Figure 10.4, however, is more visually appealing than the maps in Figures 10.1, 10.2, and 10.3 because of the smooth contours on the map, and it is not constrained by the boundaries used and, so, gives a more accurate picture of where crime clusters. One of the advantages of the area-based maps (Figures 10.2 and 10.3) is that risk can be measured by calculating a rate: the number of commercial burglaries per number of commercial establishments, if such data are available. These calculations cannot be made using point-based maps. However, if point-level data are available for the number of commercial establishments, a dual-kernel density map can be generated that considers both burglaries and establishments, providing an equivalent to a rate.

10.4.2 Journey to Crime

One of the simplest, and oldest, methods to spatially analyze crime is to measure the distance traveled by offenders to the crime site, often referred to as the journey to crime—sometimes "distance to crime" is preferred because some scholars say the "journey"

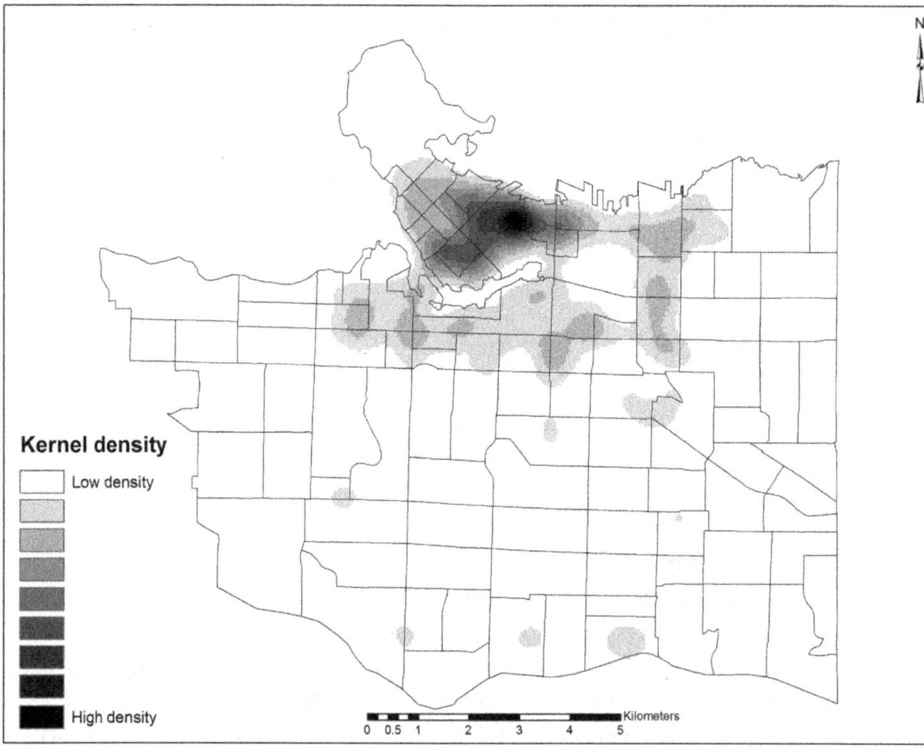

FIGURE 10.4 Commercial burglary, Vancouver, Canada, kernel density map

involves more than just the distance traveled. This literature on the journey to crime dates back at least 85 years (White 1932) and has found two general results: the journey to crime is short (most often less than two kilometers) and the journey to violent crime is shorter than the journey to property crime (see Townsley and Sidebottom 2010 for a review and Andresen et al. 2014 and Ackerman and Rossmo 2015 for some more recent analyses).

There are three primary methods by which one may calculate these distances. The first method is to calculate the "as the crow flies" distance. This is simply the linear distance between the home location of the offender and the criminal event location. Wiles and Costello (2000) used the location the offender slept the night before the crime as the origin of the journey to crime with similar results to those studies that always used the home location of the offender. Though it is possible that an offender may travel in a straight line to a criminal event location (walking down the street, for example), this is unlikely to occur in many contexts. The second is "Manhattan distance" and is measured as the distance along the two sides of a triangle with the hypotenuse representing the "as the crow flies" distance between the offender's home and the criminal event location. The Pythagorean theorem is used to calculate this distance and has been found to be representative of an area that has a Manhattan grid street network. The limitation of this method, though it is often superior to "as the crow flies," presents itself in more recent street networks in North America, particularly suburban neighborhoods, and older European cities that do not have a grid-based street network. Thus, the third method for calculating the journey to crime is using a network or route-finding algorithm. Such algorithms have to use assumptions (shortest distance, for example), but they will be more precise than either of the first two methods outside a grid-based street network and just as precise within a grid-based network.

Though it is possible to calculate the journey to crime using locations on a map, a ruler, and the scale, the advent of GIS and spatial analysis methods that go along with it make it possible to undertake research in this area that would not have been feasible only a little more than a decade ago—for example, Andresen et al. (2014) calculate the journeys to crime for over 80,000 criminal events. A GIS makes "as the crow flies" and Manhattan distance calculations relatively simple and quick. Moreover, the use of network analysis and route-finding algorithms within a GIS are relatively straightforward. What this does is allow for the use of larger and larger data sets that can then be parsed into specific research questions that could not be answered previously because of a lack of data or the computational power to do so. For example, Andresen et al. (2014) had enough criminal events to break down the journey to crime by 12 crime types and individual years of age from 8 to 68. The availability of these data and the ability to use a GIS make significant insights possible.

A related avenue of research that considers distances traveled is the mobility triangle literature that considers the interaction between the offender's journey to crime and the victim's journey to victimization. This literature goes back over 90 years (Burgess 1925) and has primarily been interested in identifying how close offenders and victims live to one another. Quite often, two of the three locations (offender's home, victim's home, and criminal event location) are in the same neighborhood (see Andresen et al. 2012 for a review). Distances, and subsequent areas, calculated for mobility triangles tend to be "as the crow flies" for simplicity in calculations. However, just as with the journey to crime, advances in GIS and spatial analysis allow for more nuanced insight into this strongly geographical phenomenon.

10.4.3 Spatial Autocorrelation and Spatial Regression

Moving beyond the conceptually simple calculations of distance and area (which can be complex from a computational perspective), I will now turn to more complex spatial analyses that are statistical in nature and refer to the spatial relationships between places. These spatial analyses assume spatial relationships exist (and they almost always do!), considering *spatial* autocorrelation: how similar are places within some context (crime, for example) to other places that are nearby? In other words, can we make predictions about one place based on the values of places that are nearby?

Before spatial autocorrelation can be calculated, the concept of *near* has to be better defined. Near can be measured based on distance, often in the case of point-based data, or based on contiguity. Areas are considered to be contiguous if they share a border: Rook's contiguity is present if two areas share a border of some length, and Queen's contiguity is present if two areas share a border even if it is at a corner. Queen's contiguity is most commonly used in environmental criminology (and the social sciences, more generally) because Rook's contiguity is considered rather strict—two neighborhoods would still be considered as contiguous if they met at an intersection diagonal from one another. Contiguity can also be ranked according to how near the areas actually are to one another. First-order contiguity means that two areas actually share a border, second-order contiguity means that two areas have one other area in between them that shares a border with each of them, and so on. More often than not, first-order Queen's contiguity is sufficient to account for spatial autocorrelation in the spatial statistical methods discussed below.

Once "near" has been specified, the degree of spatial autocorrelation can be measured. For simplicity, I will use areas (census tracts and dissemination areas) and first-order Queen's contiguity to measure spatial autocorrelation. Though there are two spatial statistics to measure the degree of spatial autocorrelation across a study area, Geary's (1954) *C* and Moran's (1950) *I*, Moran's *I* is far more commonly used because its interpretation is more "natural" and along the lines of more traditional correlation. Moran's *I* ranges from −1 (perfect negative spatial autocorrelation) to +1 (perfect positive spatial autocorrelation). Positive spatial autocorrelation means that near places have similar values with one another, and negative spatial autocorrelation means that near places have dissimilar values with one another—a black and white checkerboard is an example of perfect negative spatial autocorrelation. In most, but not all, criminological contexts, positive spatial autocorrelation is present.

With regard to the maps in Figure 10.2 and Figure 10.3, the Moran's *I* values are .51 (census tracts) and .36 (dissemination areas), with both being statistically significant. As such, at both the census tract and dissemination area levels there is positive spatial autocorrelation. Moreover, it is important to note that the Moran's *I* value for census tracts is greater than the Moran's *I* value for dissemination areas. This is consistent with the statements above regarding the MAUP: geographically larger areas have increases in the magnitudes of correlation coefficients.

The degree of spatial autocorrelation and whether it is positive or negative can sometimes be of interest on its own. However, most often, the presence of (positive) spatial autocorrelation is viewed as a nuisance because it poses difficulties for inferential statistics. One of the assumptions in classical regression is the independence of the residuals terms: knowing the value of one residual does not provide enough information to predict the value of the next residual term any better than a random guess. However, the presence of positive spatial autocorrelation in our variable(s) of interest most often leads to positive spatial autocorrelation in the residuals of a regression.[3] This means that knowing one residual's value can provide enough information to predict the value of the next residual's value better than a random guess. The assumption of independence is violated. This leads to one primary problem: in the presence of positive spatial autocorrelation, the underestimation of standard errors. As with any case of underestimating standard errors, statistical significance values appear to be higher, and one may consider a potential explanatory variable statistically significant when it is not—it is only statistically significant because of the positive spatial autocorrelation.

Spatial regression is a spatial statistical technique that was developed to address such an assumption violation. Spatial regression techniques filter out the spatial autocorrelation in order to identify the underlying theoretical relationships without those relationships being muddled by the presence of spatial autocorrelation. There are two primary forms of spatial regression: spatial lag models and spatial error models. A spatial lag model filters out the spatial autocorrelation only from the dependent variable, whereas a spatial error model filters out the spatial autocorrelation from both the dependent and independent variables. The choice of spatial regression model is identified using statistics (both GeoDa[4] and R[5] provide the statistics to make the appropriate model choice), but can be thought of as follows. If the spatial autocorrelation is only present in the dependent variable, there is no sense in filtering out any spatial autocorrelation from the independent variables; this implies a spatial lag model. However, if there is nothing to filter out, running a spatial error model when only a spatial lag model is necessary should not have any impact on the results. A spatial error model will be necessary when the nature of the spatial autocorrelation is different in the dependent and independent variables such that filtering out the spatial autocorrelation from one will not remove it from the other. Though the various statistical outputs should be used to identify the appropriate spatial regression model to be used, in my experience it makes little difference in the statistical results if a spatial lag model or a spatial error model is used.

10.4.4 Local Spatial Analysis

The methods of spatial analysis discussed thus far are classified as global spatial analysis methods. They are global in the sense that the statistics represent the study area globally, as a whole. For example, as mentioned above, commercial burglary in Vancouver has a statistically significant level of positive spatial autocorrelation for census tracts and dissemination areas. Also, in either a spatial lag or spatial error regression model, the estimated parameters represent the entire study area: a one-unit increase in an independent variable represents a β increase in dependent variable regardless of where you are in the city—it is an average representation for the city as a whole.

But are these global representations realistic? Positive spatial autocorrelation means that high-crime areas are close to high-crime areas and low-crime areas are close to low-crime areas. Is it not possible that there are places in Vancouver that do not have any clustering of crime, high or low? Is it not possible that there are low-crime areas that border high crime areas (negative spatial autocorrelation) and vice versa? In the context of a regression, is it reasonable to think that a one-unit change in one variable, say the unemployment rate, has the same impact of β in all areas of the city? Would going from 2% to 3% unemployment in a wealthy neighborhood of Vancouver have the same impact as going from 14% to 15% unemployment in a disadvantaged area of Vancouver? The first is a 50% relative change in an area that has very little unemployment, and the latter is a 7% change in an already disadvantaged area. One could argue that the first change would be significant but the second would hardly be noticed. Based on this brief discussion, it is easy to question the usefulness of global statistical analyses. Theoretical developments and social policy have to consider populations as a whole, but it is important to remember that they will not apply in all contexts, and we can empirically investigate *where* global relationships will hold and *where* they will not.

Local spatial analysis methods focus on understanding local spatial relationships rather than global spatial relationships. In one sense, they can be considered to be efforts to search for exceptions to the rule, with the corresponding global spatial relationship being the rule. The end result will be a (potentially) large number of spatial patterns to investigate and a better understanding of the nature of spatial patterns (of crime) across an area.

Fotheringham (1997) discussed three reasons why we should not expect global spatial relationships to hold when we consider local relationships—he referred to this as spatial nonstationarity. First, he stated that there will be variations by random chance. Though important to note, this is not particularly interesting. One could consider this along the lines of standard errors for regression coefficients. If regression coefficients only varied spatially within two standard deviations of the estimated parameter, that would not be particularly interesting. Second, some things may matter more in particular places than others. A prime example is situations similar to the effect of a 1% change in the unemployment rate in different socioeconomic status areas of the city. And finally, spatial nonstationarity may be found because of statistical misspecification. In other words, it may be found by accident because we failed to include all relevant variables (omitted variable bias), used an inappropriate statistical method (ordinary least squares instead of a count-based model), or included variables that are not measured properly. In other words, researcher error. Though this third reason is very important for any type of analysis, the second reason is of primary interest to most spatial/geographical scholars. Where do our expectations hold, and where do they not hold? Can we explain why our expectations hold here and not there? These are not only interesting questions to ask and answer, but critically important for understanding the spatial distribution of crime and, hopefully, reducing crime. Additionally, because local spatial statistics vary spatially, they can be mapped to help identify interesting spatial relationships.

Anselin's paper (1995) is probably the best-known piece of research regarding local spatial analysis. In this article, he outlines local indicators of spatial association (LISA), which represent a category of local spatial statistics that have a corresponding global spatial statistic: local Moran's *I* and Moran's *I*, for example. As stated above, Moran's *I* ranges from −1 (perfect negative spatial autocorrelation) to +1 (perfect positive spatial autocorrelation. Local Moran's *I* is measured the same way, but a (local) statistic is calculated for each spatial unit in the study area, instead of having one (global) statistic representing the entire study area. This allows for the identification of differing spatial autocorrelation for different places within the same study area. In addition to allowing for the presence of no statistically significant spatial autocorrelation, local Moran's *I* identifies four types of local clusters: High-High, High-Low, Low-High, and

Low-Low. High-High and Low-Low represent positive spatial autocorrelation, with the former being areas with high values (high crime in the current context) surrounded by areas with high values and the latter being areas with low values being surrounded by areas with low values—hotspots and coldspots. High-Low and Low-High represent areas with negative spatial autocorrelation: areas with high values surrounded by areas with low values and areas with low values surrounded by areas with high values, respectively. Though positive spatial autocorrelation is the norm for most sociodemographic and socioeconomic variables, particularly at the global level, negative spatial autocorrelation is often found in a handful of places at the local level.

Figure 10.5 shows the local Moran's *I* clusters for commercial burglary in Vancouver. It should be clear that the dominant form of local clustering is High-High in the eastern portion of the central business district peninsula, extending moderately to the south and to the east. Considering the crime maps already shown, particularly those in Figure 10.2 and Figure 10.3, such a set of local crime clusters should not be a surprise. However, there are two things to note. First, though Figures 10.2 and 10.3 identified a strip of higher-crime areas along the central southern border of the city, this does not emerge as a local crime cluster. In other words, commercial burglary is higher in that area, but not so high as to establish a cluster of commercial burglary activity. This also highlights the importance of testing for statistical significance rather than just visualizing spatial

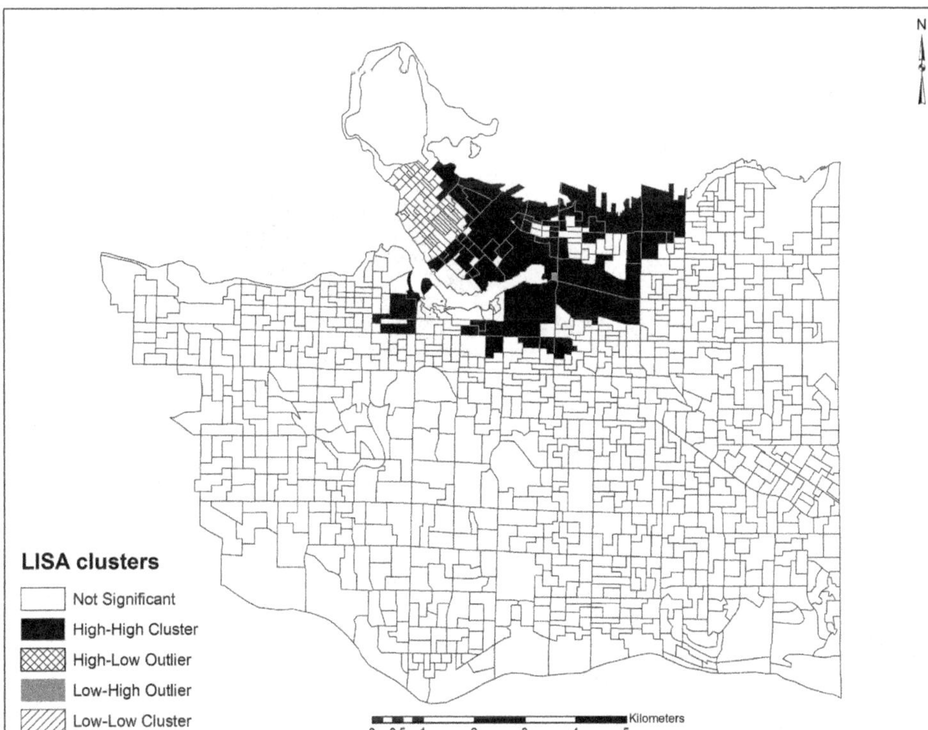

FIGURE 10.5 Commercial burglary, Vancouver, Canada, local Moran's *I*

patterns and assuming that the pattern matters. Second, though the area is small, there is a small dissemination area that exhibits negative spatial autocorrelation, Low-High, in the center of the High-High local crime clusters. Other research in Vancouver has shown a greater presence of local negative spatial autocorrelation (Andresen 2011), but this result shows that there are exceptions to the rule, and this may prove to be a more interesting result than finding that commercial burglary clusters in Vancouver. Is there something different about this dissemination area? Does it simply have no commercial land use, or is it able to repel commercial burglary in spite of having commercial land use and being surrounded by other places with statistically significant clustering of commercial burglary?

Another commonly used local spatial statistic is the Getis-Ord Gi* (Getis and Ord 1992; Ord and Getis 1995). The Getis-Ord Gi* statistic identifies clustering (positive spatial autocorrelation) through a comparison of the values for each local area and its surrounding areas. Unlike local Moran's *I*, the Getis-Ord Gi* statistic identifies only High-High and Low-Low local (crime) clusters. A map of the Getis-Ord Gi* statistics is shown in Figure 10.6. It should be clear that the statistical results for the Getis-Ord Gi* statistic and local Moran's *I* are very similar. Both local spatial statistics identify the eastern portion of the central business district as a High-High local crime cluster of commercial burglary that extends slightly east and south of the central business district.

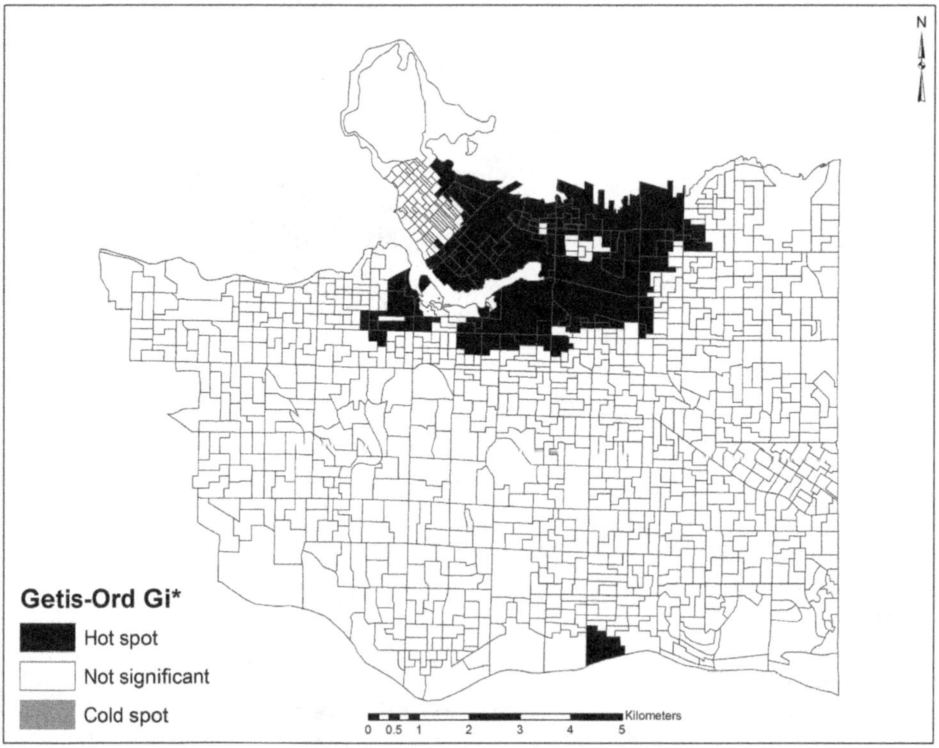

FIGURE 10.6 Commercial burglary, Vancouver, Canada, Getis-Ord Gi*

Both local spatial statistics also identify some degree of statistically insignificant clustering in the center of the larger High-High local crime cluster. The presence of this area is interesting in and of itself, and is not just an artifact of one (local) statistical method. However, the Getis-Ord Gi* statistic, unlike local Moran's *I*, does identify a local crime cluster (High-High) in that central southern strip of Vancouver.

Part of the reason for the differences in the Getis-Ord Gi* and local Moran's *I* results is quite simple: the default statistical significance level for local Moran's *I* is 95%, whereas Getis-Ord Gi* presents all results for 90%, 95%, and 99% statistical significance as a default. Of course, I could have presented the 95% statistical significance results for both local spatial statistics, but I did not in order to show that one does need to be careful when considering default program settings and then comparing statistical output. Regardless, using the same level of statistical significance does not meaningfully change the comparison of the local spatial statistical results. The Getis-Ord Gi* statistic is always more inclusive for High-High local crime clusters, but the results are qualitatively the same. Incidentally, at the 90% statistical significance level, local Moran's *I* does identify a local crime cluster in the central southern strip of Vancouver, but it is the dissemination area immediately to the west identified in Figure 10.6.

The last local spatial statistical method I will discuss here is geographically weighted regression. Geographically weighted regression was developed in an effort to identify local parameters in a regression context (Brunsdon et al. 1996; Fotheringham et al. 2002). Just as local measures of spatial autocorrelation provide a statistic for each spatial unit under analysis, so does geographically weighted regression, but for regression parameters. This allows for the investigation outlined above: does an independent variable matter to the same degree for all areas in the analysis? It is possible that the global regression coefficient is the same in all places, though unlikely; more realistic is that there will be a range of values with some areas not even achieving statistical significance. In fact, some criminological research has found that the signs on the coefficients switch from positive to negative, place to place (Cahill and Mulligan 2007).

A geographically weighted regression was performed using commercial burglary as the dependent variable and the residential population as the independent variable. Of course, there are a number of other variables that should be included in a more formal analysis of the spatial patterns of commercial burglary, but this analysis is for illustrative purposes. The estimated parameter in the global regression is 0.007; commercial burglary is a low count crime type, and the residential population is measured using individuals. The white areas on the map (Figure 10.7) represent dissemination areas that have a value of 0.007 +/− 2 standard errors. It should be clear that this represents a small portion of the city. The hatched areas all represent dissemination areas that have estimated parameters that are greater than the global parameter, with the gray and back areas having estimated parameters that are less than global parameter. Of particular interest are the black areas that represent the dissemination areas with estimated parameters that are less than zero. Not all of these dissemination areas have estimated parameters that are significantly different from zero, but the point is that a lot of the area of the

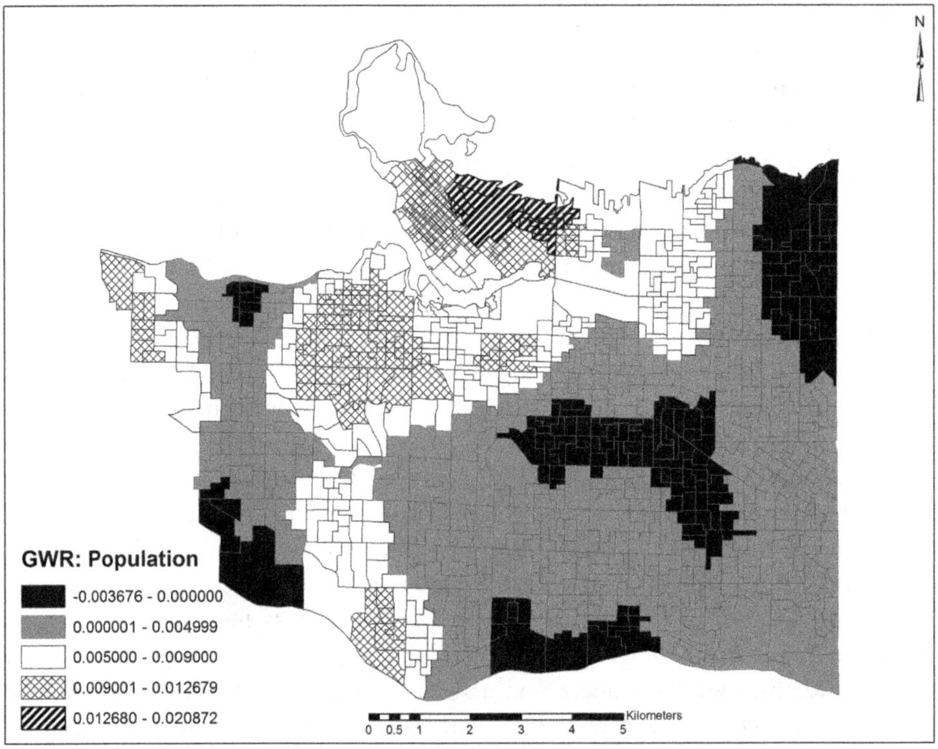

FIGURE 10.7 Commercial burglary, geographically weighted regression parameter estimates for residential population, Vancouver, Canada

city has results quite different from the global regression results. This set of results, yet again, shows the importance of considering spatial relationships, in general, and varying spatial relationships, specifically.

10.5 Where to Go from Here?

This chapter has discussed the importance of GIS and spatial analysis, generally and in the context of environmental criminology. Spatial data have been shown to present a new set of obstacles and limitations to overcome, but also a set of new opportunities to test theory, to develop crime-related policy, and simply to better understand the (spatial) patterns of crime. The question now is: where do we go from here?

Part of the answer is to keep doing what we have been doing. More spatially referenced data are becoming available all the time, and there are still many unanswered questions and replications that need to be done. If there is any work more pressing than others, I would argue for more environmental criminologists to undertake local spatial analysis methods. There is a fair bit of research in this area, but it is relatively infrequent in comparison to other forms of spatial analysis. Specifically, in the context of local crime clusters, there is very little research that investigates the properties of these clusters (see Andresen 2011 for an exception) that may prove to be particularly instructive. I am thinking specifically of better understanding negative local spatial autocorrelation. Another avenue of future research is the interaction of spatial and temporal analyses. This is not new to environmental criminology—see the chapter in this Handbook by Tseloni, Tilley, and Farrell that discusses near-repeat victimization, for example—but spatial-temporal statistical methods are relatively underutilized. Such methods identify clusters in both space and time (simultaneously) that occur and cannot be explained by random variation in the data.

Overall, this is an exciting time to be working in environmental criminology using GIS and (local) spatial analysis methods. The availability of spatially referenced data for both criminal events and explanatory variables is only increasing and providing more opportunities to test the nuances of the theories within environmental criminology and develop crime prevention policies.

Notes

1. http://www.gps.gov/systems/gps/performance/accuracy/.
2. A lot of crime data are now available with precise X,Y coordinates, but some crime data are still geocoded in this manner.
3. Spatial autocorrelation in the residuals often occurs when the analysis omits an important variable that varies spatially.
4. http://spatial.uchicago.edu/software.
5. https://www.r-project.org/.

References

Ackerman, J. M., and Rossmo, D. K. (2015). "How far to travel? A multilevel analysis of the residence-to-crime distance." *Journal of Quantitative Criminology* 31(2): 237–262.

Andresen, M. A. (2011). "Estimating the probability of local crime clusters: The impact of immediate spatial neighbors." *Journal of Criminal Justice* 39(5): 394–404.

Andresen, M. A., Felson, M., and Frank, R. (2012). "The geometry of offending and victimization." *Canadian Journal of Criminology and Criminal Justice* 54(4): 495–510.

Andresen, M. A., Frank, R., and Felson, M. (2014). "Age and the distance to crime." *Criminology and Criminal Justice* 14(3): 314–333.

Andresen, M. A., and Malleson, N. (2013). "Spatial heterogeneity in crime analysis." In *Crime Modeling and Mapping Using Geospatial Technologies*, edited by M. Leitner, pp. 3–23. New York: Springer.

Anselin, L. (1995). "Local indicators of spatial association—LISA." *Geographical Analysis* 27(2): 93–115.

Brantingham, P. J., and Brantingham. P. L. (1981). "Introduction: The dimensions of crime." In *Environmental Criminology*, edited by P. J. Brantingham and P. L. Brantingham, pp. 7–26. Prospect Heights IL, Waveland Press.

Brunsdon, C. F., Fotheringham, A. S., and Charlton, M. E. (1996). "Geographically weighted regression: A method for exploring spatial non-stationarity." *Geographical Analysis* 28(4): 281–298.

Burgess, E. W. (1925). "Can neighborhood work have a scientific basis?" In *The City: Suggestions for Investigation of Human Behavior in the Urban Environment*, edited by R. E. Park and E. W. Burgess, pp. 142–155. Chicago: University of Chicago Press.

Cahill, M., and Mulligan, G. (2007). "Using geographically weighted regression to explore local crime patterns." *Social Science Computer Review* 25(2): 174–193.

Curman, A. S. N., Andresen, M. A., and Brantingham, P. J. (2015). "Crime and place: A longitudinal examination of street segment patterns in Vancouver, BC." *Journal of Quantitative Criminology* 31(1): 127–147.

Fotheringham, A. S. (1997). "Trends in quantitative methods I: Stressing the local." *Progress in Human Geography* 21(1): 88–96.

Fotheringham, A. S., Brundson, C., and Charlton, M. (2002). *Geographically Weighted Regression: The Analysis of Spatially Varying Relationships*. Chichester, UK: John Wiley & Sons.

Fotheringham, A. S., and Wong, D. W. S. (1991). "The modifiable areal unit problem in multivariate statistical analysis." *Environment and Planning A* 23(7): 1025–1044.

Geary, R. C. (1954). "The contiguity ratio and statistical mapping." *Incorporated Statistician* 5(3): 115–145.

Gehlke, C. E., and Biehl, H. (1934). "Certain effects of grouping upon the size of the correlation coefficient in census tract material." *Journal of the American Statistical Association, Supplement* 29(185): 169–170.

Getis, A., and Ord, J. K. (1992). "The analysis of spatial association by use of distance statistics." *Geographical Analysis* 24(3): 189–206.

Guerry, A.-M. (1832). "La statistique compare de l'état de l'instruction et du nombre des crimes." *Revue Encyclopédique* 55: 414–424.

Guerry, A.-M. (1833). *Essai sur la Statistique Morale de la France*. Paris: Crochard.

Hipp, J. R. (2007). "Block, tract, and levels of aggregation: Neighborhood structure and crime and disorder as a case in point." *American Sociological Review* 72(5): 659–680.

Jeffery, C. R. (1971). *Crime Prevention through Environmental Design*. Beverly Hills, CA: Sage.

Moran, P. A. P. (1950). "Notes on continuous stochastic phenomena." *Biometrika* 37(1): 17–23.

Openshaw, S. (1984a). *The Modifiable Areal Unit Problem*. Concepts and Techniques in Modern Geography No. 38. Norwich: Geo Books.

Openshaw, S. (1984b). "Ecological fallacies and the analysis of areal census data." *Environment and Planning A* 16(1): 17–31.

Ord, J. K., and Getis, A. (1995). "Local spatial autocorrelation statistics: Distributional issues and an application." *Geographical Analysis* 27(4): 286–306.

Quételet, L. A. J. ([1831] 1984). *Research on the Propensity for Crime at Different Ages*. Translated by S. F. Sylvester. Cincinnati, OH: Anderson Publishing.

Quételet, L. A. J. (1842). *A Treatise on Man and the Development of His Faculties*. Edinburgh: W. and R. Chambers.

Ratcliffe, J. H. (2001). "On the accuracy of TIGER type geocoded address data in relation to cadastral and census areal units." *International Journal of Geographical Information Science* 15(5): 473–485.

Ratcliffe, J. H. (2004). "Geocoding crime and a first estimate of a minimum acceptable hit rate." *International Journal of Geographical Information Science* 18(1): 61–72.

Robinson, W. S. (1950). "Ecological correlations and the behavior of individuals." *American Sociological Review* 15(3): 351–357.

Shaw, C. R., and McKay, H. D. (1942). *Juvenile Delinquency and Urban Areas: A Study of Rates of Delinquency in Relation to Differential Characteristics of Local Communities in American Cities*. Chicago: University of Chicago Press.

Townsley, M., and Sidebottom, A. (2010). "All offenders are equal, but some are more equal than others: Variation in journeys to crime between offenders." *Criminology* 48(3): 897–917.

Weisburd, D., Bruinsma, G. J. N., and Bernasco, W. (2009). "Units of analysis in geographic criminology: Historical development, critical issues, and open questions." In *Putting Crime in Its Place: Units of Analysis in Geographic Criminology*, edited by D. Weisburd, W. Bernasco, and G. J. N. Bruinsma, pp. 3–31. New York: Springer.

Weisburd, D., Groff, E. R., and Yang, S.-M. (2012). *The Criminology of Place: Street Segments and Our Understanding of the Crime Problem*. New York: Oxford University Press.

White, R. C. (1932). "The relation of felonies to environmental factors in Indianapolis." *Social Forces* 10(4): 498–509.

Wiles, P., and Costello, A. (2000). *The "Road to Nowhere": The Evidence for Traveling Criminals*. Home Office Research Study No. 207. London: Research, Development and Statistics Directorate.

Wooldredge, J. (2002). "Examining the (ir)relevance of aggregation bias for multilevel studies of neighborhoods and crime with an example of comparing census tracts to official neighborhoods in Cincinnati." *Criminology* 40(3): 681–709.

CHAPTER 11

THE ROLE OF INNOVATIVE DATA COLLECTION METHODS IN ADVANCING CRIMINOLOGICAL UNDERSTANDING

REKA SOLYMOSI AND KATE BOWERS

11.1 Introduction

Environmental criminology emphasizes the importance of situational factors associated with increased risk in terms of crime opportunities. One branch of research in this field tries to strengthen scientific understanding of the link between exposure to risk and crime. To achieve this, we need information about how potential victims and potential offenders spend their time, and what places they visit as part of their daily activities. Routine activity theory (Felson & Cohen 1979) argues that individuals' risk of becoming a victim of crime varies with their activity patterns (and, similarly, the "risk" of potential offenders finding suitable opportunities to commit crimes varies with theirs). Some routine activities will result in greater exposure to risks than others. To identify what these are, we need data about what people do, where they perform these activities, and at what times. We also need data on victimization or whatever particular outcome variable we are interested in. To get a complete picture, however, we also need data that speak to people's perception of the environment, as what they are exposed to during their routine activities also varies in place and time. For example, some environments will provide more opportunities for people to experience fear of crime, or notice a "signal disorder" (see Innes 2004 and also Innes and Innes in this volume). To understand what it is about these environments that promote such perceptions, we also need data on what people do as they move about in place and time, and how their experiences vary.

One challenge with this type of research concerns data availability. It is a nontrivial task to gather data about the everyday activities of people or the particular "scene" (time and place) in which any significant event occurs. This chapter will lay out the potential role of novel data sets in addressing these gaps and then consider in more detail two of these new approaches. The first approach is to utilize advances in technology and sensing to develop bespoke surveys created with specific research studies in mind. The second approach is to make use of already available "big data" or "open-access data" sources on people's everyday interactions with the environment and combine multiple data sources to make inferences about routine activities and their link to perception of crime and place.

The chapter is organized as follows. Section 11.1 discusses traditional approaches to collecting data on people's routine activities and their levels of fear of crime and illustrates how these might fail to capture the dynamic nature of people's experiences. Section 11.2 discusses the promise of new data collection approaches, developed by the adoption of new technologies and innovations in data capture, which can help advance the study of routine activities, crime, and perception of place. Sections 11.3 and 11.4 detail empirical examples that can serve as guidelines for using these new approaches in environmental criminological research to situate perception of crime and place in environments within people's routine activities. Finally, Section 11.5 concludes by discussing the opportunities, but also the challenges and limitations of new approaches for measuring routine activities and other crime related constructs.

11.2 Previous Data Collection Approaches

The traditional way to collect data about people's routine activities is to use surveys, which collect activity pattern data from large quantities of people. These generally are retrospective, asking people to recall their activities over a specific period of time (usually 3, 6, or 12 months). They ask participants to reflect on this time and answer questions about their experiences concerning an outcome variable that is being measured, such as crime, or fear of crime. For example, in measuring fear of crime, national surveys such as the Crime Survey for England and Wales (CSEW) in the United Kingdom and the National Crime Victimization Survey (NCVS) in the United States ask a nationally representative sample about their levels of worry, while associating these experiences with some situational variables (for example: was it during the day or after dark?). While such surveys have many advantages, one issue is with their retrospective nature—people have to recall their activities over a long period of time, which can lead to overgeneralized answers, and potentially skewed results (Gray, Jackson, & Farrall 2008; Jackson & Gray 2009). Another issue is that these surveys are cross-sectional; they ask people about their experiences only once, resulting in a snapshot of their experiences, which consequently miss any variation that person might experience. Further discussion of the use of sample surveys can be found in the chapter by Tseloni, Tilley, and Farrell in this volume.

One way to address the issues with cross-sectional approaches is to collect information about people longitudinally, with time-use surveys. Participants of such surveys note down, in specific time intervals (for example every 10 minutes, or every hour) what they are doing, who they are with, and where they are. This allows for better understanding of variation in situational factors and individuals' activities. For example, by using such method, Wikstrom et al. (2010) demonstrated that there were clear associations between young people's activities and their exposure to criminogenic settings and, ultimately, their involvement in crime (mediated by the individual's "crime propensity"). A similar approach, but focused on people's emotions and perceptions rather than actions, is the experience sampling method (ESM). This method is popular in psychology research, as it provides an approach for gaining insight into not only what people are doing, but also their interpretations of or their emotional state in that situation (Christensen et al. 2003; Hektner, Schmidt, & Csikszentmihalyi 2007; Scollon, Kim-prieto, & Diener 2003). Like time-use surveys, ESM surveys can rely on prompts at certain predetermined intervals, but can also capture event-related prompts. This means participants may be instructed to fill out the questionnaire once every hour, or when a particular event takes place, for example, every time they experience feelings of worry about crime, or each time they use public transport (Solymosi, Bowers, & Fujiyama 2015).

These measurement approaches return more detailed and accurate data about everyday activities than do the cross-sectional approaches. However, they can be more taxing on the participant; therefore they tend to have smaller sample sizes, and greater attrition rates than large questionnaires. Because of the demand on participants, such studies are also difficult to sustain over a long period of time. Normally these studies are administered over short time-frames. For example, Wikstrom et al. (2010) used four days as their period of data collection, which is typical for these studies. However, employing advances in data capture might present a method to address this fault. The next section discusses some new data collection techniques that address issues raised here and therefore show a promise for the environmental criminologist.

11.2.1 The Promise of New Collection Techniques

As indicated, one issue with the above-mentioned techniques is that they require a lot of effort on behalf of the study participants. New technologies can assist in this respect. It is important to note here that technology is constantly changing, and new innovations enter the market every day, making what was novel last year outdated by the next. Therefore, the researcher must always be on the lookout for how emerging technologies can be utilized for research, and keep up with the ongoing development of large and often complex data sets being collected by, for, and about people and their everyday activities.

Large quantities of data are stored by businesses, government organizations, charities, and other bodies, which use them for a myriad of purposes. For example, online retailers track not only what customers bought, but also what else they looked at, to predict what books individual customers would like to read next (McAfee & Brynjolfsson 2012). One limitation of such data, raised by Boyd & Crawford (2012), is that although much enthusiasm around open data comes from its availability; it is not equally accessible to all. The concern over the openness of data is mirrored by Manovich (2011), who rightly points out that some data are owned by companies, who therefore have the advantage of processing their own data first. However, as we will explain in depth below, data provided by Volunteered Geographic Information (VGI) sources, within the ethos of crowdsourcing, should be freely available. As mentioned, crowdsourcing comes from the open-source movement and so provides data that people willingly put into the public domain. Although potentially useful large data sets can lie under the authority of private corporations that wish to hold it back, the focus of this chapter is to explore the use of openly available crowdsourced data for crime research.

The data that are openly available can be used by researchers to learn about people's behavior, and make inferences about exposure to risk by finding different patterns in people's daily routine activities. To demonstrate, various approaches to estimating ambient population to calculate risk have been explored using such data sources, for example through using data from smart ticketing systems to measure population flow through a transport network (Wang, Attanucci, & Wilson 2011). Further, the richness and detail of the data available through novel collection methods also allow for more in-depth exploration of such routine activities, and for research to move beyond questions about the "when" and "where" of activities, and to ask about the "who" and "what" as well. There are a number of techniques and methods that could usefully be applied to the study of crime, which we now review.

11.3 New Data Collection Techniques

In this section, we review some of the activity in a range of different fields and business pursuits and discuss the potential use of such methods and concepts in environmental criminology and crime science.

11.3.1 Crowdsourcing, Participatory Mapping, and Volunteered Geographic Information

Crowdsourcing involves harnessing the information and skills of large crowds of people into one collaborative project. Crowdsourcing originated in the open-source movement in software (Howe 2006); its definitions are rooted in online contexts, generally referring to it as an online, distributed problem-solving and production model (Brabham 2008,

p. 75). Some early examples of crowdsourced projects are Wikipedia—an encyclopedia where people write articles about topics they have knowledge on, which can be edited by others, pulling together the knowledge of many contributors to provide a reference source freely available to all; and the website Flickr, where people upload their photos and tag them with keywords that represent what the images are of. Then people visiting the site can search through these pictures using the assigned keywords, and immediately access the relevant photos of all contributors. What is novel about the mode of production of these projects is that it is not reliant on one person to work or collect data; instead, anyone can participate as much or as little as they are willing to, but the crowd's participation adds up to a complete output. So for example, if we wanted to search for images of the 2011 London riots, it is enough to enter these keywords into the Flickr search bar, and many images emerge that were taken by people present, who can serve as observers.

Participatory mapping refers to the practice of mapmaking by people with local knowledge who contribute to the creation of a map to represent the topic of their expertise. People contribute their skill and insight to collaboratively produce a representation of their (normally local) area by offering up their time to collect information that has a geographical component (Haklay 2013). For example, Open Street Map is a participatory open map where volunteers contribute information in order to map their local areas (Haklay & Weber 2008). In the last few decades, community-based participatory mapping has been used to better understand social problems (Balazs & Morello-Frosch 2013), and has gained respect for being both pragmatic but also aiming to highlight everyone's experiences in a space equally (Cornwall & Jewkes 1995). In certain cases, the "participatory approach explicitly challenges accepted conventions about who can legitimately create maps, using what process, and for what audience" (Kitchin 2002). For example, citizens involved with collecting data about noise pollution in their area can use that information as an evidence base when lobbying for interventions by local authorities (Becker et al. 2013).

Further, citizen involvement in mapping areas contributes to the categorization of places as pleasant or not by nonprofessionals (Becker et al. 2013). The output of crowdsourcing can have a direct influence on the world at large. For example, Yelp, a mobile application and website that allows users to rate and review restaurants in their area, has had a significant impact on restaurant revenue and market shares (Luca 2011), putting reviewing in the hands of all patrons, and not only professional critics.

Participatory methodologies not only extract information but also ask people to share local experience to achieve change. Crowdsourcing and advancements in technologies allow for larger-scale participation than previously possible, resulting in larger volumes of data that can facilitate more fine-grained analysis. For example, in Germany in 2012, scientists collaborated with 5,000 people to capture over 17,000 samples of mosquito, resulting in the discovery of an invasive species with implications for public health (Haklay 2013).

Overall, participatory methodologies not only extract information, but also ask people to share local experience to challenge current maps and understanding of the area, and through such challenge achieve change in the environment where they identify it to be important. This approach can help collect information about areas that official data sources might not be able to convey.

Online crowdsourcing has the potential to scale up participatory mapping, by encouraging people to submit volunteered geographic information (VGI) about their local areas, and combine these into one collective crowdsourced, spatially explicit data set about people's experiences and local expertise expanded over large areas using the Internet. Such crowdsourced VGI data can highlight new information for the researcher, but also collect data for the participants themselves to create useful outputs or data sources they can share and use to lobby for changes in their neighborhoods. For example, people might collect information on where cars are parked illegally, and use this to feed intelligence to their local policing team, who can then act on the matter. Even in itself, without requiring authoritative intervention, VGI can be used as a tool to improve people's access to services (Parker et al. 2013). For example, Wheelmap is a mobile platform where people voluntarily provide a traffic-light-scale rating of establishments in terms of their accessibility for wheelchair users on a publicly available map (Parker et al. 2013). By being both providers and consumers of content about the accessibility of venues, participants help improve each other's everyday lives.

Applying these principles to data collection about people's experiences with crime, such approaches could allow people to collect information on what matters to them, attaching a spatial and temporal component, in a way that can be fed back to their safer neighborhood or local policing teams. One such approach was tested in Wales where such community intelligence was fed back to inform neighborhood policing priorities (Innes et al. 2009). However, this information was collected using in-depth interviews and through community meetings, which limit the number of possible participants, and take up much time and resources. An *online* platform could collect such participatory mapping of perceived/experienced crime or antisocial behavior on a larger scale. It could serve to provide a forum for people to convey their own experiences, and let local authorities and other bodies (such as police or safer neighborhood authorities) know about their needs or request support or action taken for their benefit on a larger scale. Crime maps, which are produced based on official police recorded crime may underrepresent some types of crime due to the problems with reporting and recording crime (the "dark figure" of crime). Providing citizens with their own platform to report where they personally experience problems themselves in their everyday activities may supplement such maps, and encourage police and crime prevention practitioners to consider other hotspots (such as "unsafety" hotspots where people feel vulnerable) besides those based only on official data.

11.3.2 Big Data and Population Estimation

Also from the ethos of crowdsourcing and people's voluntary (and notably, sometimes involuntary) data production comes the idea of open data, large data sets that can be used to make inferences about people's behavior and routine activities. Such data in particular have been adopted into criminological studies for estimating ambient population. This is important to aid in calculating an accurate denominator for crime rates by estimating the number of crime opportunities present in a situation. A flurry of studies in the 1960s and 1970s drew attention to the importance of accurately estimating crime risk. A particular focus was on comparing opportunity-based versus population-based crime rates. Skogan (1976) concluded that "the most meaningful crime statistics are those which are related to the number of potential opportunities for victimization" (p. 173).

But measuring crime opportunities can be tricky. There is often a trade-off between how faithfully the data approximate the opportunity structure for the crime of interest and the practicalities of collecting such data. A recent development in this area has been to take advantage of new already available data sets to better approximate opportunities. For example, Lemieux and Felson (2012) used National Crime Victimization Survey and American Time Use Survey data to better estimate crime risk by place and type of facility; Chainey and Desyllas (2010) used purpose-collected pedestrian modeling data; and Kurland, Johnson, & Tilley (2014) used estimates of the ambient population measured using geographic information from a range of sources including remote sensing data to estimate meaningful denominators for crime rates. In a further study, Malleson and Andresen (2015) made use of crowd-sourced data from Twitter, in an attempt to create more accurate estimates of the population at risk for mobile crimes such as street robbery. What these studies share is an effort to take account of the dynamic nature of crime opportunities, and to gather data about the changes in these opportunities from big-data sources. However, it is possible to gain even more detail, and answer not only when and where, but also what and who, when mapping these routine activities in place and time.

11.3.3 Using Twitter Data to Examine Crime Problems

Twitter is social media platform, where people broadcast their thoughts into the abyss of the Internet in 140 characters or less. Twitter data are made freely available through its Application Programming Interfaces (APIs), which makes it one of the most popular open data sources for studies in social sciences (Leetaru et al. 2013). A small percentage of these messages (tweets) are geo-tagged, referencing the location where the person sent this tweet from (permission is necessary for this information to be captured). By analyzing the content of these tweets, researchers are able to make inferences about not only where and when people go, but also about these people's demographic information, their views, their interests, and how they all link together. For example, researchers at the Consumer Data Research Centre have been analyzing the geography of topics from geo-referenced tweets in London, grouping tweets based on the topic about which they were written (e.g., about sports, or transport, or containing mostly profanities) (Lansley 2015). They then used these classifications to look into where certain topics were overrepresented, and at what times. For example, they saw that tweets about train delays map nicely onto stations and rail lines that tend to have more delays, and that tweets about sports from a football stadium peaked at times when there was a football game being played at that venue (Lansley 2015).

This approach could be translated into crime prevention research by mapping fluctuations in crime-related tweets in both place and time. Even further in terms of reach, researchers have begun using geocoded tweets to perform next-place predictions and compare these with the occurrence of crimes, with the goal of aiding future research into automatic crime prediction (Wang & Gerber 2015). These approaches advance toward making use of the wealth of available data for crime research.

11.3.4 Sensing

Another approach for collecting data in a way alternative to questionnaires is to use sensors that extract information from people's physiology. Physiological measure capture provides a way for researchers to use biological signals to access data about people's interaction with their environment that cannot easily be observed using other approaches (Duarte, de Sá, & Carriço 2010). For example, in responding to fear-of-crime surveys, people may not remember or may not want to admit feeling afraid, or they may want to appeal to the interviewer (e.g., Sutton & Farrall 2004). While, as a consequence, they might lie about or exaggerate their feelings, their physiological reactions would reveal a different picture. Therefore, to correlate experiences of fear of crime with features of the environment, people's physiological reactions could be measured. The affective state of increased fear of crime is ordinarily (though not invariably) associated with certain physiological changes, including increased heart rate, rapid breathing, sweating, decreased salivation, and increased galvanic skin response (Warr 2000). To record such changes, sensors, such as an ambulatory device for measuring galvanic skin response (GSR), could be given to a group of participants, to identify where they encounter high-arousal areas that might be associated with feeling fear. In a study in Lisbon, Portugal, participants walked a predefined route wearing a wristband to measure skin conductance as an indicator or physiological arousal, to investigate the effects of different urban settings on peripheral-physiological changes (Hogertz 2010). The study found that peaks in physiological arousal as recorded by the GSR armband can be used to identify areas that evoke affective responses in participants, and these changes can be feasibly measured in real-time experiments. This could be applied, for example, to further fear-of-crime research, in which location of such affective peaks could be compared to fear-of-crime hotspots identified through other means of data collection.

11.4 GPS Tracking, Satellite Imagery, and Offender Tagging

There are many other emerging sources of data that are likely to extend our understanding of spatial and temporal distributions of crime that focus on activity patterns of actors other than residents—such as the police and offenders. To illustrate, research is currently investigating links between foot patrol police resourcing and crime reduction (see Hutt & Bowers forthcoming) and the supply-and-demand aspect of police vehicle movement (see Davies and Bowers 2016). Both of these research activities are based on information collected from police GPS devices and hence are able to measure resource distribution directly and accurately at the micro level. As with any other large-scale data set, using this source is not without its own challenges. Difficulties include dealing with the volume of information involved (to put this into context, the UK Metropolitan Police Force collect approximately 250 million Automatic Personnel Location Systems (APLS) records per annum) and assessing the real-world accuracy and the reliability of these data sets. From the offender perspective, similar data are becoming available on the patterns of parolees from electronic monitoring programs. For example, Rossmo et al. (2012) mapped the journey to crime of reoffending parolees using data from the Florida Department of Corrections' electronic monitoring program. They were also able to explore significant geographic features in relation to the parolees' journey choices.

Satellite imagery and three-dimensional photography also have potential for the use in research exploring crime patterns and in particular in mapping urban environments. For example, Wolfe and Mennis (2012) examined the relationship between remotely sensed vegetation coverage and rates of specific property crimes in Philadelphia. They found a relationship between vegetation and some crime types at the census level; more abundant vegetation was associated with lower levels of robbery, assault, and burglary. In another study, Rundle et al. (2011) assessed the viability of using Google Street View as an alternative to in-person audits of the environment. They found a high level of concordance between the recorded features of the urban environment between the two methods for approximately half the items investigated. Unsurprisingly, smaller features or those that vary over time were less likely to be consistently recorded. However, this research demonstrated that Street View can be used to conduct environmental audits.

This section has reviewed a number of different potential uses of new or innovative data sets in environmental criminology and potential ways to generate these. Hence there are exercises in both using existing data and primary data collection to capture new information. The next section illustrates two approaches to data collection about perception of crime and place using new approaches. The first gives the example of mobile phones and sensing (using a purpose-built phone app), and the second demonstrates the value of using existing crowdsourced VGI. These approaches are currently novel, and their application to environmental criminology research can lead to new insights into everyday activity patterns and experiences of crime. It is inevitable that the future will make these techniques commonplace, and even outdated, but it is important to be always looking out for emerging data and approaches to use for research.

11.4.1 Example 1: Using Innovation in Technology and Sensing to Collect Novel Data

As discussed earlier, fear of crime is a phenomenon that varies within people dynamically with changes in their routine activities. Experiences with fear of crime are situation-dependent, rather than a static state. In order to measure fear of crime in a way that reflects this, we utilized the sensors and convenience offered by the ubiquity of web-enabled smartphones among most sections of the UK population (see Solymosi et al. 2015). We applied the ESM approach outlined earlier to a mobile phone application that prompted users at repeated intervals to complete a questionnaire survey about how safe they felt at the time, while also using the phone's in-built sensors to record "metadata" about respondents, such as their location and the time of response. Such an approach provided many advantages over paper-based ESM approaches. The first advantage was that it made participation easier for the subjects of the study. Simply having to download an application onto their own mobile phones, people were not required to attend a meeting with the researcher to collect study materials. Similarly, as responses were sent electronically to a server that the researcher monitored, participants did not need to meet again with researchers. This is also an advantage for researchers in that even if a participant drops out midway in a study, the data collected up to that point has already been stored and can still be used for analysis. Another advantage to not requiring the participants to have separate study materials such as a paper survey or diary is the reduced likelihood of participants forgetting the survey or leaving it at home. Since people carry their mobile phones with them almost everywhere they go, the survey and reminders are more likely to be seen and requested actions completed (MacKerron 2012).

Another advantage to both researcher and participants is the use of sensors within the phone. In this case we used the internal clock and the GPS of each device to schedule reminders and to record exact spatial and temporal information to associate with people's responses. This is an advantage to participants as they are asked fewer questions; we could automatically detect where they were and what time it was, so unlike on a paper survey, we did not need to ask these questions explicitly. This is also an advantage to the researcher, as it eliminates issues with human error, such as people guessing what time it is, or approximating their location, or even providing their location in a way that is unusable to the researcher (for example, for location they could write "on the bus" or "at a friend's house," which would not be useful if we wanted to map their activities in geographical space). Of course it is important to consider *what* is being examined, and whether that can be automated, or if it requires the interpretation of the participant. For example, while the GPS will pinpoint geographically the location of the participant, if the research question requires the attribution of subjective meaning to the locations (such as "home" or "friend's house"), then the researcher will have to find a way to measure this, either by asking the participant directly with a question, of by finding ways to use the metadata, analysis, or further sensing to gather the additional details. In our case, we wanted to map where people feel safe and unsafe in geographical space, and therefore the GPS sensor was sufficient to gather the location information.

After an initial feasibility pilot (see Solymosi et al. 2015), we ran the study over a period of four months, during which 59 people took part, mapping their perception of safety. In interpreting the trends that follow, it should be noted that this in not necessarily a representative sample of any particular population, as it was an opportunity sample. The average age was 29 years, the youngest participants 19 years old, and the oldest participant 56. In terms of other characteristics, 53% of the respondents were male, 34% were white British and 31% white other, and the remaining third included Caribbean, Chinese, Indian, and other Asian background participants. Around a fifth of the sample (22%, or 13 people) had previously experienced personal victimization in the past 12 months.

Figure 11.1 shows the number of responses per participants. It is clear that participation varied, ranging from the submission of only one report ($N = 5$) up to 250 submissions over the four-month study period.

Figure 11.1 highlights the importance of gathering and storing data dynamically. If we had collected data only from those who contributed throughout the study, we would have collected data for significantly fewer participants and data points. What is novel about the mode of production of these projects is that it is not reliant on one person to work or collect data until they meet the expected requirements, but instead anyone can participate as much or as little as desired. Then, the crowd's participations add up to a complete output (Surowiecki 2005). This concept is known as participation inequality.

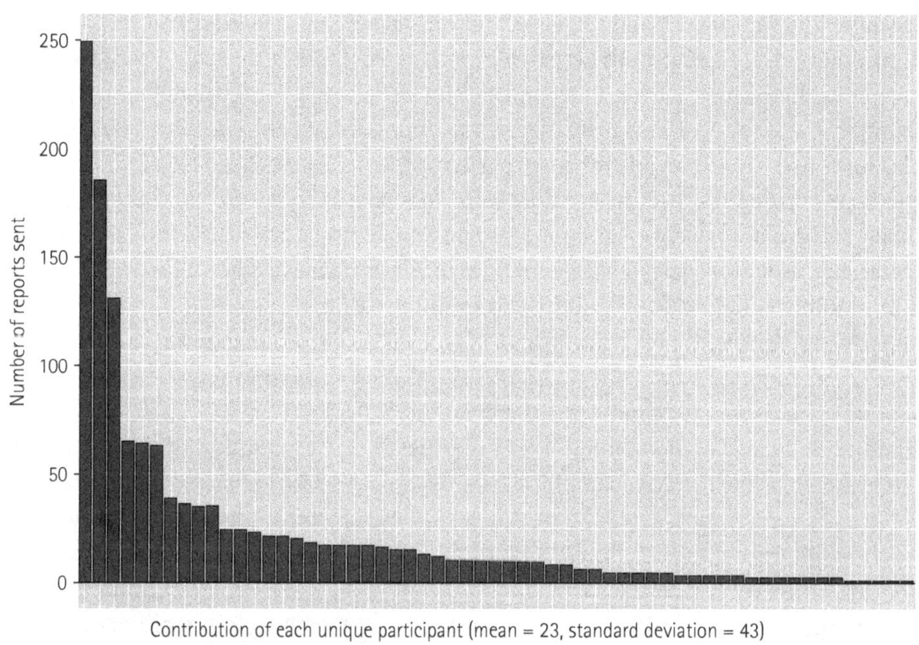

FIGURE 11.1 Number of responses sent by each participant

In economics and social sciences, such inequality in contributions is sometimes referred to as the Pareto principle, which states that approximately 80% of the observed effect comes from 20% of the units observed (Sanders 1987). The concept is also observed in environmental criminology research (Weisburd 2015). However, considering participation in crowdsourced projects, this discrepancy is even greater, as participation inequality has been noted to follow a 90-9-1 rule (Stewart et al. 2010), where, on the whole, about 90% of users are "outliers," people who read or observe but do not contribute to the project. Then there are 9% of users who contribute occasionally (contributors), and 1% of users to account for almost all the contributions (supercontributors). While this bespoke data collection project didn't have "consumers" of the information, these will be relevant to the crowdsourced data used in the next section. However, participation inequality is observed in both data sets.

The first step toward examining fear of crime as an everyday experience is to examine fluctuations in people's reported fear over time. As mentioned, of all 59 participants, five people submitted only one point during the entire duration of the study. For these people it is impossible to observe fluctuation in fear levels over time. For those who submitted at least two data points, 17 reported consistent levels of fear of crime over time, while the other 36 showed fluctuation in levels of fear over time. Further, the 17 who consistently reported the same level of fear all reported being "Not at all worried" about crime. So the only people who did not show fluctuation in worry were "Not at all worried." Those who did experience instances of worry moved in and out of this state, and were certainly not statically or consistently worried all the time. Notably, if this had been measured using cross-sectional surveys, some people would be recorded as statically "Very worried," whereas, based on our results, we can say that those people who did experience a fear of crime event were not necessarily always worried about crime. Instead, most of the time they were not at all worried about crime, and their levels of worry increased in certain situations at certain times, before returning to a baseline state of not at all worried (for an example, see Figure 11.2).

These data therefore allow us to explore within-person variation in fear of crime, and illustrate that it is a much more complex phenomenon than something that can

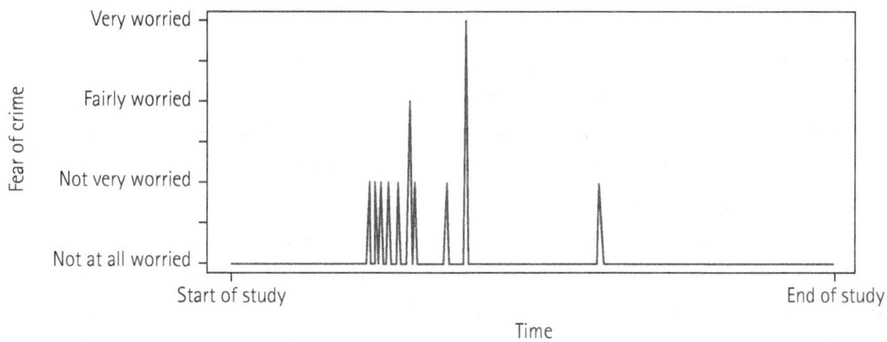

FIGURE 11.2 One participant's fear of crime over the duration of the experiment

be a static attribute of people (or neighborhoods). When measured by cross-sectional methods, we gain only a snapshot of this dynamic experience, losing the longitudinal variation in fear of crime over place and time. To illustrate the importance of longitudinal variation in fear with changing situations, we examined the personal characteristics that are associated with increased feelings of fear. Previous research into the topic has identified "social structure" variables (Smith 1987) such as age and gender (Lagrange & Ferraro 1989), and previous experience with victimization (Box, Hale, & Andrews 1988) as key predictive factors. Using the locational tracking data, we are able to introduce an important dynamic variable to this mix, which is whether or not people were within their own neighborhood when they reported their level of fear.

The outcome variable of interest is fear of crime measured as people describe their feelings of worry about crime at a particular moment in time. The resulting data is an ordinal variable that ranges from "Not at all worried" to "Very worried." One approach for analysis that accounts for the ordered nature of these data is to use a cumulative link model, to try to examine the effects of the measured variables on reported fear of crime. Cumulative link models provide the regression framework familiar from linear models while treating the response rightfully as categorical. While cumulative link models are not the only type of ordinal regression model, they are "by far the most popular class of ordinal regression models" (Christensen 2011, p. 3). Additionally, as discussed earlier, different participants sent different numbers of reports. Therefore, each report cannot be treated as independent, as this would bias results greatly toward representing the views of those who submit frequently, and would fail to consider the linked nature of the data. For the analysis of these data, therefore, repeated observations from the same participant must be considered as nested within each subject. Using a mixed model that includes both fixed and random effects is one method of accounting for this. The fixed effects are the ones that are known; in the case of the model here, these are gender (can be male or female), age (split into four groups), previous victimization (yes or no), whether the report was made after dark (yes or no), and whether it was inside the participant's home neighborhood (yes or no). The random effects are the participant-level effects that are not explicitly measured. There are lots of participants, with different propensities to experience fear of crime, which can be influenced by many variables that we have not included in this model. We do not want to know more about the difference between people in propensity for being worried about crime, but it is important to account for differences in the model. A mixed model allows for such random effects as well as the fixed effects (Agresti 2010). By using this approach, we can nest the responses within the individuals, accounting for personal biases that might affect fear of crime, characterizing idiosyncratic variation due to individual differences.

The results from this analysis are very interesting—none of the factors traditionally associated with increased fear (age or gender or previous victimization) showed a significant effect in the FOCApp data (Table 11.1). Instead, the only variables that have a measured effect are whether or not the report came from within a participant's home or work postcode area, or whether the report was made after dark or during daylight hours.

Table 11.1 Relationship between Person-Variables and Fear Measured by Mobile Phone App

	Estimate	*p*-value
Age	−0.04563	.4337
Gender (male)	−0.36436	.3866
Gender (transgender)	0.84289	.437
Within local area	−0.44208	.0127*
Experience of previous victimization	−0.31707	.0653

* Significant at $p < .05$.

This demonstrates that environmental variables have a strong role in predicting levels of fear.

In examining the role of the variables in more depth, we can examine the model condition number. The condition number measures how much of the output value can change for a small change in the input argument, and can be used to measure how sensitive a model is to change or errors in the input. The condition number of the Hessian for this model in Table 11.1 is 4173964.43. High numbers, for example, larger than 10^4 or 10^6, indicate that the model is ill-defined (Christensen 2011). This would indicate that the model can be simplified, that possibly some parameters are not identifiable, and that optimization of the model can be difficult (Christensen 2011). In this case, the condition number of the Hessian measure of fit does indicate a problem with the model.

If we remove all the personal variables and keep only the situational variables, then the condition number of Hessian drops to 29.74, which would not indicate a problem with the model. Conversely, if the situational variables are removed and the personal ones only remain, then the condition number of Hessian increases to 15011413.22. The best model, as indicated by the Hessian score, is the one with only the situational variables in it, and this new model is shown in Table 11.2.

The coefficient for darkness is positive, indicating that when it is dark, higher fear-of-crime reports increase, meaning that reporting in higher categories of fear is more likely in darkness. The coefficient for being in the home neighborhood, on the other hand, is negative, which means that when people are within their own neighborhood, reporting in higher categories is less likely than when they are outside of this area. This finding reinforces the need for a measurement of fear of crime that addresses people's entire activity spaces, not just their home or work neighborhoods.

These findings appear to indicate that situational factors are significant predictors of experiencing fear of crime as part of one's routine activities. However, none of the personal variables showed up as significant. Does this mean that individual variation in the propensity to experience fear of crime does not matter? In fact, the answer to this is no. As mentioned earlier, a random effect, for the "subject effect" (this means the effect of

Table 11.2 Model with Only Situational Predictor Variables

	Estimate	*p*-value
Dark (yes)	0.97	.00
Within local area (yes)	−0.91	.01

the participants) is also included. For random effects in a model, a likelihood ratio test can be used as a means to attain *p*-values. The likelihood is the probability of seeing the data collected given the model (Winter 2013). The logic of the likelihood ratio test is to compare the likelihood of two models with each other: the model without the random effect (this is the null model) against the model with the random effect.

Table 11.3 shows the results of the likelihood ratio test to compare the model with the random effect to a model without it. It returns a *p*-value of .001, indicating that the subject term is significant. Also, the Akaike information criterion (AIC) can be used here as well to assess whether the model with the subject effect is a better fit than the null model without. The model with the smaller AIC value is the preferred model, which in this case is the model with the subject effects included (Table 11.3). Overall it can be concluded that subject effects are important.

The results of the test of significant subject effects imply that subjects experience fear of crime differently. Two natural interpretations are that either a level of fear of crime of, for example, "Not very worried" means different things to different people, or the subjects actually experienced fear of crime differently as they move across different activity spaces. Possibly both effects play their part. This serves to illustrate that while situational factors were the only variables captured by the FOCApp data collection method that showed up as significantly influencing people's likelihood of experiencing fear of crime events, individual factors also play a significant part. This is reinforced by looking at the distribution of fear of crime reports within participants. This illustrates that while most participants report being "Not at all worried" most of the time, with other levels of worry as outliers, there are participants who report higher levels of worry. The distribution of responses varies between people. However, what these key factors are that influence people's propensity to feel worried about crime have not been captured in the data included here.

While these results present some interesting insight into how fear of crime varies across changes in situational context, due to the relatively small sample and the biases in the data discussed earlier, their generalizability remains questionable, and replications on a larger scale are necessary. Overall, in the study, as mentioned, most people felt unworried most of the time. Unfortunately this renders the data on fear events too sparse to attempt meaningful hotspot analysis, let alone spatiotemporal analysis. However it does provide a wealth of new insight into people's everyday experiences of fear of crime at such a microresolution of place, and raises many questions that could be answered by future, larger-scale research.

Table 11.3 Result of Likelihood Ratio Test

	AIC	*p*-value
Null model (no subject effect)	500.57	.001
Model with subject effect	465.89	

11.4.2 Example 2: Using Big Data to Make Inferences about Crime and Constructs

The second example illustrates how existing VGI / open access / big data can be used to make inferences about people's experiences with signal disorders (incidents or experiences they deem significant) during their routine activities. As discussed earlier, openly available crowdsourced data can be used to learn about spatiotemporal fluctuation in people's routine activities.

Our VGI data come from an online problem-reporting tool called FixMyStreet (hereon referred to as FMS), run by the not-for-profit organization mySociety, which aims to "invent and popularise digital tools that enable citizens to exert power over institutions and decision makers."[1] It created FMS to enable citizens to report potholes, broken streetlights, and other problems in their area as easily as possible, in order to get them fixed. Using the website, citizens are able to locate their problem on a map, choose a category for their report, give it a title, and provide a brief description. The report is logged with the time and date of reporting, and the name of the person submitting the report (unless the person chooses to remain anonymous). As of 2010, some local authorities have integrated the platform into their own website, indicating to citizens that their comments are noted and responded to by their local authority.

While such big data is available to view on the web page provided, this does not necessarily mean that it is in a form that is readily accessible to the researcher. In this case the data needed to be downloaded and compiled in such a way that they are available for analysis. One way to acquire such data is by carrying out a "scrape" of the site(s) where the data is presented. Web scraping refers to an application that processes the HTML of a web page to extract data for manipulation. In the case of FMS, we wrote a script that would open up each report, save the relevant information, close the report, and move on to the next one. This script iterated through the hundreds of thousands of reports made on FMS from 2010 to 2015, compiling the data in a format that was suitable for our research purposes. It is important to note here that this was done with the full permission of mySociety. Using this method, we collected five years' worth of reporting data that included the following for each report:

Latitude and longitude
Category of report

Time and date report was made
Name of person reporting (if given, "anonymous" if not)
Detailed description of the report

According to the signal crimes perspective, when people encounter signs of disorder, they interpret these as signs of the deterioration of social order, and these interpretations can lead to feeling of fear and worry about crime (Innes 2004, and the chapter by Innes and Innes in this volume). If we are able to map where people encounter these signals, we can identify where clean-up efforts could have the most impact in preventing people from encountering these signals and experiencing fear. But beyond that, by identifying where people are reporting these issues, we can gain insight into their routine activities, and make connections with crime and fear of crime. These data, comprising people's reports about their experiences reflects where and when people encountered signs of disorder in their environments. These signs of disorder are filtered through people's interpretations of them as problems, which sets them apart from measures of disorder collected through official observers (Solymosi et al. 2017).

One approach that appears particularly effective is to examine FMS reports that relate to *incivilities* in particular. Here we use the term "incivilities" synonymously with environmental antisocial behavior (enviro-ASB). Enviro-ASB includes any antisocial behavior act that is not aimed at an individual or group but targets the wider environment, for example, public spaces or buildings (Home Office 2013). Examples include litter, criminal damage, vandalism, and graffiti (Donoghue & Colover 2011). These are the issues that can be interpreted as signal disorders with potentially harmful consequences on health and well-being (Sampson & Raudenbush 2004). It is such instances of disorder that have been studied to assess their relationships with crime (e.g., broken windows theory [Wilson & Kelling 1982] and the fear of crime [Innes 2004]).

A major advantage of this crowdsourced open data is that information is available in much greater volume than the fear-of-crime data we collected with our bespoke application-based survey described in the last section. FMS data are available for the whole of the UK, for example, as well as other platforms in other countries. This gives us more scope to look for hotspots using these data and to potentially identify areas where people are more likely to encounter signal crimes, and therefore feel worried about crime. The spatial resolution with which we approach this can be varied, due to this increased scope. For example, on a macro level we can identify that in London 29.4% of FMS reports are incivilities, 10 percentage points higher than the national rate of 19.3%. This suggests that incivilities are more of a problem within London than in the UK overall. But due to the low spatial resolution of the data, we can zoom in further, and look at micro-level variation within the city.

Figure 11.3 demonstrates that different areas of central London are hotspots for different types of incivilities. Interestingly, mapping these data appears to reflect certain "activity hubs." Since these data reflect people's routine activities, they can also reflect when people are out and about on the street and *how* the area is used by the public. For example, the hotspot for litter is a major transport hub containing two large train

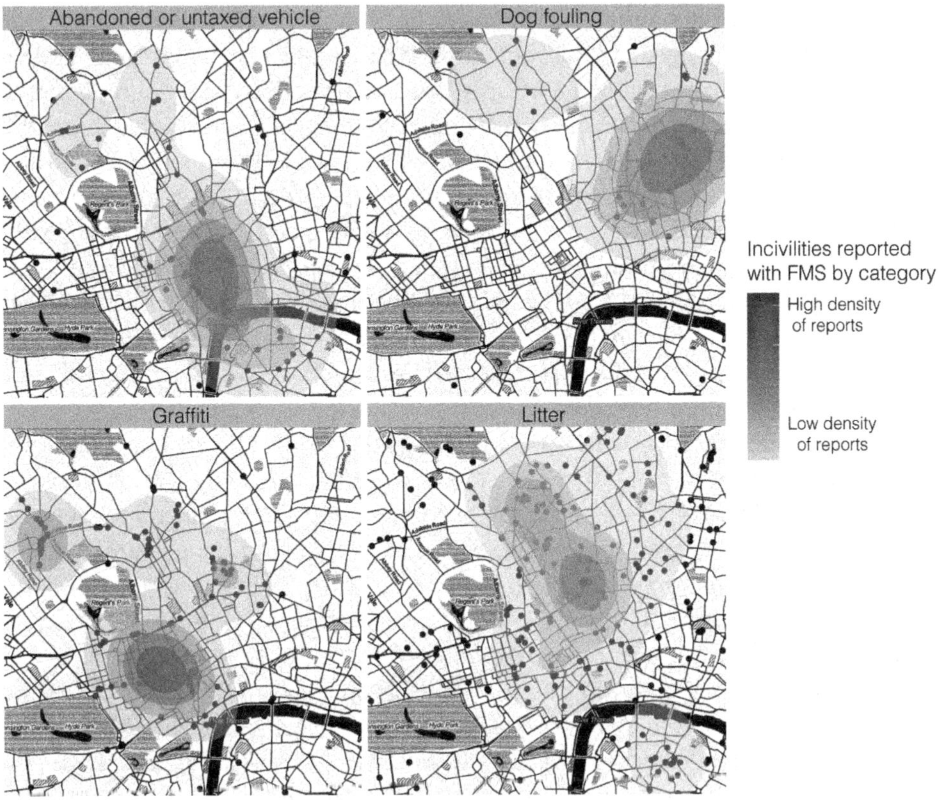

FIGURE 11.3 Hotspot map of different incivilities in central London (U.K.)

stations. Reports about dog fouling, however, are restricted almost entirely to the residential areas, and a mini-hotspot south of a popular dog-walking park. This seems to reflect concern when other's leave a "residue" of their routine activities, people rush through busy train stations, leaving their rubbish behind, and other people then come and encounter these issues. With dog fouling, people walk their dogs in the residential areas near their homes, and then leave behind their mess for their neighbors to come across and be upset by. This highlights the ability of such data not only to locate where these issues happen, but to show how certain spaces facilitate different routine activities that lend themselves to different types of "offenses," or different signals that people might encounter and use to make judgement about their environments.

There is a caveat to keep in mind with such data, however, when mapping these hotspots, which is illustrated well by the graffiti hotspots in Figure 11.2. On investigation, we found that all reports within this hotspot were made by a single individual. This illustrates a central issue with both the approaches in this chapter; that contributors ranging from those who participate only once, to supercontributors who might dominate the data. For example, in the FMS data, the top 10% of contributors submitted over half the reports (51%), while 73% contributed only one report. And, of course, for the reports left anonymously, we cannot know if they are coming from distinct individuals or not. The graffiti hotspot in Figure 11.2 is the work of one vigilant reporter, and therefore might require a different response than a hotspot that developed from distinct reporters. It might be that the person has higher expectations about the local area, or that the graffiti is actually harassing the person in some way. Accordingly, the intervention should also be specific to the source of the problem. For example, in this case, rather than something about the physical environment that lends itself to graffiti, which could be mediated by some physical environmental intervention, it might be important to investigate someone's potential personal victimization through these recorded instances of disorder. In any case, it is important to consider the fact that records collected via VGI/ESM approaches cannot be treated as independent observations, and should be considered nested within the content providers.

As well as using these data to tell us about when and where people encounter instances of disorder that they respond to, they can be also used to gain insight into the people doing the reporting. Much research in fear of crime has looked into differences between different demographic groups in their experiences of fear. One demographic variable that has an effect on people's perception of crime and safety and their neighborhoods is gender (Davenport 2010). If possible, it would be interesting to use the FMS data set to look further into these differences in perception of enviro-ASBs.

However, a challenge with using already available open data is that, unlike in studies where the researcher can design a bespoke questionnaire, the researcher does not have a say in what information gets collected. This is similar to the basic differences between primary and secondary data. Primary data are data collected for the specific research problem at hand, using procedures that fit the research problems best. On the other hand, material that has been collected for other research, or any other prior purpose, is referred to as secondary data (Hoop & Boeijie 2005). In the case of secondary data, the researcher must make do with what has already been collected, in whatever form it was collected.

In this case, for example, we might wish to look at gender differences in reporting behavior. Unfortunately, however, this information is not collected in the reports. However, one approach in using open data for research is to combine multiple available data sets in order to infer more than is directly communicated by one data source, and attempt to extract missing information by linking up with other data sets. For example, to study demographic differences in tweets, Longley, Adnan, and Lansley (2015) linked Twitter usernames with birth names and associated demographic information, using a database they created from credit card and birth certificate data. Using this database, kindly shared by our colleagues, in our current study we can assign a likely gender to each report, based on the name provided.

Overall, 66.8% of FMS reports were made anonymously or under an obvious pseudonym (e.g., "Concerned citizen," "Donald Duck"), but the remaining one-third left their name. Linking each name with a gender reveals that name-given reports are mainly made by men, composing 24.5% of all reports, and less frequently by women, who submitted only 8.6% of all reports. There are two potential reasons for this. On the one hand it is possible that men overall submit more FMS reports than women do, which would make this source of information heavily biased toward men's experiences. But it is also possible that when men make reports, they are more likely than women to leave their name. Future qualitative inquiry into this difference in FMS reporting behavior by gender would be useful in terms of adding to the literature around gender bias in such data sets.

Classification of people into men or women based on their names makes it possible to explore between-group differences in reporting disorder. A chi-square test comparing reporting of instances of disorder or reporting in nondisorder categories between genders (male, female, or unknown) reveals that there is a relationship between gender and reporting on particular topics. Reports about issues that fall within the category of enviro-ASB are made more by women, whereas men are more likely to report nonincivility issues (chi-square = 1614.343, df = 2, p-value < .001). Thus while there are fewer reports from females, these are more likely to be about incivilities than reports made by males. This finding is in line with results from ASB victims survey data from Innes (2014), who found that women, on average, attend more carefully to physical disorder signals.

Looking into differences in what is being reported between all possible categories of report (e.g., potholes, litter, broken streetlights) reveals a significant gender difference in reporting within these (chi-squared statistic = 4822.301, df = 58, p-value < .001) as well. Drilling down into the data suggests that men make more reports in categories related to driving (e.g., potholes and road problems), whereas women are more likely to report about categories related to walking (e.g., parks, dead animals, dog fouling, litter). There is great potential scope for exploring this further for researchers interested in the role of gender and the use of public space, and the implications for systematic differences in exposure to risk between different routine activities.

With the advent of other large data sets, potentially more meaningful or interesting groupings could be made beyond gender or static demographic characteristics. Instead, it could be possible to use information about people's routine activity to identify them as belonging to different types of activity patterns. For example, Phithakkitnukoon et al. (2010) use an analysis of mobile phone data, nearly one million records of location traces, to identify different profiles of people's work areas through finding similarity in daily activity patterns. In terms of applicability for environmental criminology, big-data sources such as smartcard data from travel, mobile phone data, supplemented by crowdsourced data such as FMS or other sources, could be used to create groups of different vulnerability to victimization based on activity patterns. This would allow profile-specific crime prevention advice, which may be more effective than blanket messages that may not apply to all.

Overall, while obviously subject to some limitations, such crowdsourced data about people's perceptions of problems in their environments can be used to identify differences in how people use and experience their environments on a large scale. Data can be used to scale up participatory mapping to determine not only when and where people are, but also what they are doing and how they are experiencing these places. Inferences can then be made about their experiences with crime and disorder, and further analysis can be carried out by linking up multiple data sets to answer our research questions relating to people, places, time, and crime.

11.5 Opportunities, Limitations, and Future Possibilities

The use of innovative data sets in crime-related research will inevitably bloom over the next decade. This should rightly happen, as these data sets offer great promise in advancing our understanding of crime problems. We assert that this is particularly true in research that examines micro-level relationships between crime and place. While recorded crime data and traditional sociodemographic and population data have offered many research opportunities, to study the micro-level interactions between what people do all day in what place and how they experience threats and perceive safety, the only truly valid source of data comes from tracking the people themselves in their environment.

The use of this type of data, however, also raises some research challenges. Our empirical examples demonstrated some of these; the potential "overinfluence" of supercontributors in VGI data sets, for example, needs to be addressed in analysis. Another issue was raised with the requirement that participants in studies that employ new technology be technology literate. Indeed, it is important to discuss these issues more generally, as a very important limitation of both crowdsourced data and data collected with new technologies is bias inherent in the sampling.

In the case of crowdsourced data, the sample is entirely self-selected and out of the researcher's hands, giving way for people more motivated to speak about the issue to voice their concerns, and leaving out those who do not participate so extensively, but might still be affected (Budhathoki 2010; Haklay 2010). This is something to keep in mind when drawing conclusions based on such data, as it introduces an inherent bias in the data. These biases typically raise concerns about sampling, and ultimately the generalizability of any findings that can be drawn from such data (Malleson & Andresen 2015). Longley (2012) also comments on this: "Self-selection is an enemy of robust and scientific generalization, and crowdsourced consultation exercises are likely to contain inherent bias" (2012, p. 2233).

Beyond self-selection issues in general, an entire body of work has explored the impacts of the "digital divide" (for an example, see Yu 2006), which refers to certain socioeconomic groups being overrepresented in data generated online (Malleson & Andresen 2015). Gender bias has been found, showing that men tend to participate in such activities more than women do. Further work on VGI participation has also shown a divide in participation along sociodemographic variables. Employed people, people between the ages of 20 and 50, and those with a college or university degree are most likely contributors (Budhathoki 2010; Haklay 2010). Looking into what contextual factors influence participation in Open Street Map, Mashhadi et al. (2013) find that socioeconomic factors such as population density, dynamic population, distance from city center, and levels of poverty play a role. These factors are important to keep in mind when reporting findings based on analysis of such data.

However, as discussed by Savage and Burrows (2007), the social sciences must embrace these new forms of data that, although messy, biased, and noisy, have the potential to describe social phenomena better than well-organized small surveys or even national censuses (Malleson & Andresen 2015). As detailed with examples in the previous sections, even with these limitations, crowdsourced data that are both up to date and specific to the problem at hand can provide insight in addition to the knowledge from established sources of data collected using traditional methods (Birkin et al. 2011). This in turn helps us to understand the relations between the events and the occurrences that come together in unique places and provides a framework for understanding how places change over different time periods (Longley 2012).

Sampling bias should be balanced against the potential of these new forms of data to address the many limitations with traditional surveying methods (Malleson & Andresen 2015). For example, data collected in new ways can actually sometimes be more reliable: "When data are collected passively while people do what they normally do anyway, the old biases associated with sampling and questionnaires disappear" (Mayer-Schonberger & Cukier 2013, p. 30). Further, this information also has the potential to complement traditional data by enhancing the overall picture of a particular crime phenomenon. For example, to explore the microregulation of violence, Levine et al. (2011) conducted a systematic behavioral analysis of footage from closed-circuit television surveillance of public spaces. Similarly, Lindegaard (2016) used video footage of bystander actions during robberies involving violence to supplement official data, which had the drawback of having been subject to police interpretations. Going back to the source footage allowed the researchers to systematically and directly measure in detail what bystanders do, to identify the consequences of these actions for themselves and others involved.

As with any empirical research, data accuracy is an important consideration. In many ways it is the geographical specificity of the data discussed above that is a considerable strength. However, the reader should consider the distinction between specificity and accuracy. In general, GPS location tools are fairly reliable, but not infallible. There is evidence, for example, that a major limitation to GPS is the inability for receivers to determine positions that are indoors, underground, under dense tree coverage, between large buildings in "urban canyons," or anywhere else a solid object obstructs the view of the sky (Zandbergen & Barbeau 2011). On the other hand, VGI, which presents users with a map instead of using GPS sensing, relies on users pinning incidents with spatial accuracy.

Temporal accuracy is another issue, as data sets that use sensing or satellite imagery such as Street View or ambient population estimation only reflect the exact state of affairs at the moment that the information was captured. Places change quickly, and this needs to be recognized in studies using "point in time" data sets. Temporal accuracy of VGI data sets relating to events is also of concern. Do people report events in real time? If they do not, what is the implication of using the time of report as the estimated time of the incident? We have encountered these issues with our research on perceptions of incivilities, and we report consideration of this potential bias in depth elsewhere (Solymosi et al. 2016).

From a methodological point of view, a frequently raised concern is that machine-learning approaches to data analysis, which trawl data for significant relationship, can be atheoretical. In particular, they can foster a lack of understanding of the micro-level processes that lead to the emergence of characteristics observed at higher levels (Snijders et al. 2012). Due to the challenges associated with analyzing large quantities of data, these approaches are most likely to be utilized on very large data sets. Other issues are that these automatic approaches do not address the validity of the data (there is sometimes a misconception that large amounts of data equate to reliable data sources, but this is not necessarily the case) and that they are subject to the multiple comparison problem (Ioannidis 2005), which states that repeated trawling exercises are more likely to get some significant results by chance alone. We would advise using machine-learning approaches with caution for these reasons. Alternative approaches, such as those offered by agent-based models or complexity science methods, have the advantage that they focus on understanding the system dynamics and hence have more capacity to assist with making predictions in changing environments.

The elephant in the room is ethical implications of the use and potential misuse of the types of data sets reported here. In our increasingly technology savvy society, the use of mobile phone apps, GPS tracking, and online participation is on the rise. It is conceivable and indeed likely that those who "volunteer" information are not aware that this might enable others to discover their individual actions and routines. Earlier we detailed an exercise where we combined two large data sets and were able to make inferences about individuals in terms of gender and apply that information to the reporting activity patterns from a different data set. Presumably, scraping data from many different information sources could enable researchers to build up fairly detailed pictures of the lives of distinct individuals. We therefore have an ethical duty as researchers to be sensitive to these possibilities. Individuals should always be informed of the type of data they are providing and the conditions for its use. For example, we made it very clear to users of the mobile phone app described earlier that a GPS location and time would be attached to their reports; we also made it clear that published results would never enable the identification of individuals.

The possibilities offered by the collection and analysis of innovative data sets will continue to grow. Geolocated Twitter data enables the mapping of a new social dimension onto space; we should soon be able to infer more about the nature of communities with distinct types of crime problem (see Kim et al. 2016). VGI data will help us pinpoint vulnerabilities in people's everyday lives that should ultimately help us protect high-risk groups. Better estimation of the ambient on-street population should assist with understanding the optimal conditions for offenses such as street robbery (see Tompson and Bowers 2015), and 360-degree digital camera shots should assist with micro-level assessment of the safety of current environmental design. Attaching physiological sensors to willing participants to examine physical reactions to situations will provide a new angle on methods of making people feel safe. Tracking police car movement should assist in locating communities that are less frequently visited than they should be (see Davies and Bowers 2016). The list goes on. There is no doubt that the increasing availability of new data sets will lead to fertile new research in environmental criminology and ultimately make people be and feel safer in their everyday lives.

Note

1. https://www.mysociety.org/about/. The organization's "About" page has changed since the quoted self-description was downloaded in 2015.

References

Agresti, A. (2010). *Analysis of Ordinal Categorical Data* (Vol. 656). Hoboken, NJ: John Wiley & Sons.

Balazs, C. L., & Morello-Frosch, R. (2013). The three Rs: How community-based participatory research strengthens the rigor, relevance, and reach of science. *Environmental Justice* 6(1), 9–16.

Becker, M., Caminiti, S., Fiorella, D., Francis, L., Gravino, P., Haklay, M. M., . . . & Servedio, V. D. (2013). Awareness and learning in participatory noise sensing. *PLoS One* 8(12), e81638.

Birkin, M., Malleson, N., Hudson-Smith, A., Gray, S., & Milton, R. (2011). Calibration of a spatial simulation model with volunteered geographical information. *International Journal of Geographical Information Science* 25(8), 1221–1239.

Box, S., Hale, C., & Andrews, G. (1988). Explaining fear of crime. *British Journal of Criminology* 28(3), 340–356.

Boyd, D., & Crawford, K. (2012). Critical questions for big data: Provocations for a cultural, technological, and scholarly phenomenon. *Information, Communication and Society* 15(5), 662–679.

Brabham, D. C. (2008). Crowdsourcing as a model for problem solving: An introduction and cases. *Convergence* 14(1), 75–90.

Budhathoki, N. R. (2010). Participants' motivations to contribute geographic information in an online community, 115. Retrieved from https://www.ideals.illinois.edu/bitstream/handle/2142/16956/1_Budhathoki_Nama.pdf?sequence=2.

Chainey, S., & Desyllas, J. (2010). Modelling pedestrian movement to measure on-street crime risk. In *Movement-Aware Applications for Sustainable Mobility: Technologies and Approaches*, edited by Mona Wachowicz (pp. 243–263). Hersey, PA: Information Science Reference.

Christensen, R. (2011). Analysis of ordinal data with cumulative link models: Estimation with the ordinal package. *R-Package Version*, 1–31. Retrieved from http://scholar.google.com/scholar?hl=en&btnG=Search&q=intitle:Analysis+of+ordinal+data+with+cumulative+link+models+—+estimation+with+the+R+-package+ordinal#0.

Christensen, T. C., Barrett, L. F., Bliss-Moreau, E., Lebo, K., & Kaschub, C. (2003). A practical guide to experience-sampling procedures. *Journal of Happiness Studies 4*, 53–78. Retrieved from http://link.springer.com/article/10.1023/A:1023609306024.

Cornwall, A., & Jewkes, R. (1995). What is participatory research?. *Social Science & Medicine 41*(12), 1667–1676.

Davenport, R. A. (2010). *Incivilities, crime and social order: The role of repeat experience* (Doctoral dissertation, University of Sheffield).

Davies, T., & Bowers, K (2016, in preparation). Patterns in the supply and demand of urban policing at the street segment level.

Donoghue, J., & Colover, S. (2011). Anti-social behaviour and the courts in England and Wales report of findings. *Economic and Social Research Council Report 44* (March), 1–34. Retrieved from https://s3-eu-west-1.amazonaws.com/esrc-files/outputs/kYmWQJcn_Um7jtvsu3gDig/ZTNpUorSnkeu5f4aKGtC6Q.pdf Accessed: 18 August 2017

Duarte, L., de Sá, M., & Carriço, L. (2010). Physiological data gathering in mobile environments. In *Ubicomp '10: Proceedings of the 12th ACM International Conference. Adjunct Papers on Ubiquitous Computing—* (pp. 405–406). New York: ACM Press. doi:10.1145/1864431.1864459.

Felson, M., & Cohen, E. L. (1979). Social change and crime rate trends: A routine activity approach. *American Sociological Review 44*(4), 588–608.

Gray, E., Jackson, J., & Farrall, S. (2008). Reassessing the fear of crime. *European Journal of Criminology 5*(3), 363–380. doi:10.1177/1477370808090834.

Haklay, M. (2010). How good is volunteered geographical information? A comparative study of OpenStreetMap and ordnance survey datasets. *Environment and Planning B: Planning and Design 37*(4), 682–703. doi:10.1068/b35097.

Haklay, M. (2013). Citizen science and volunteered geographic information: Overview and typology of participation. In *Crowdsourcing Geographic Knowledge: Volunteered Geographic Information (VGI) in Theory and Practice*, edited by D. Sui, S. Elwood, & M. Goodchild (pp. 105–122). New York: Springer.

Haklay, M., & Weber, P. (2008). OpenStreetMap: User-generated street maps. *IEEE Pervasive Computing 7*(4), 12–18.

Hektner, J. M., Schmidt, J. A., & Csikszentmihalyi, M. (2007). *Experience Sampling Method: Measuring the Quality of Everyday Life*. Thousand Oaks, CA: Sage.

Hogertz, C. (2010). Emotions of the urban pedestrian: sensory mapping. *Pedestrians' Quality Needs 31*.

Home Office. (2013). Anti-Social Behaviour, Crime and Policing Bill fact sheet: Environmental anti-social behaviour (part 4). London.

Howe, J. (2006). The rise of crowdsourcing. *Wired Magazine 14*(6), 1–4.

Hox, J. J., & Boeije, H. R. (2005). Data collection, primary vs. secondary. *Encyclopedia of Social Measurement*, editor-in-chief Kimberly Kempf-Leonard (vol. 1, pp. 593–599). New York: Elsevier Academic Press.

Hutt, O. & Bowers, K. (forthcoming). Data and evidence challenges facing place-based policing. *Policing*.

Innes, M. (2004). Signal crimes and signal disorders: Notes on deviance as communicative action. *British Journal of Sociology 55*(3), 335–55. doi:10.1111/j.1468-4446.2004.00023.x.

Innes, M. (2014). *Signal Crimes: Social Reactions to Crime, Disorder, and Control*. Oxford: Oxford University Press.

Innes, M., Abbott, L., Lowe, T., & Roberts, C. (2009). Seeing like a citizen: Field experiments in "community intelligence-led policing." *Police Practice and Research 10*(2), 99–114. doi:10.1080/15614260802264545.

Ioannidis, J. P. (2005). Why most published research findings are false. *PLoS Med 2*(8), e124.

Jackson, J., & Gray, E. (2009). Functional fear and public insecurities about crime. *British Journal of Criminology 50*(1), 1–22. doi:10.1093/bjc/azp059.

Kim, E., Bowers, K., and Johnson, S. D. (2017). Using geo-located Twitter data to measure community cohesion and social efficacy. Poster given at the 2017 Environmental Criminology and Crime Analysis Symposium, El Salvador.

Kitchin, R. (2002). Participatory mapping of disabled access. *Cartographic Perspectives 41*, 44–54.

Kurland, J., Johnson, S. D., & Tilley, N. (2014). Offenses around stadiums: A natural experiment on crime attraction and generation. *Journal of Research in Crime and Delinquency 51*(1), 5–28. doi:10.1177/0022427812471349.

Lagrange, R. L., & Ferraro, K. F. (1989). Assessing age and gender differences in perceived risk and fear of crime. *Criminology 27*(4), 697–720. doi:10.1111/j.1745-9125.1989.tb01051.x.

Lansley, G. (2015). Linking socio-economic and demographic characteristics to Twitter topics in London. In *XIX European Colloquium on Theoretical and Quantitative Geography*. Bari, Italy. Retrieved from http://discovery.ucl.ac.uk/1495415/

Leetaru, K., Wang, S., Cao, G., Padmanabhan, A., & Shook, E. (2013). Mapping the global Twitter heartbeat: The geography of Twitter. *First Monday 18*(5). Retrieved from http://firstmonday.org/ojs/index.php/fm/article/view/4366/3654

Lemieux, A. M., & Felson, M. (2012). Risk of violent crime victimization during major daily activities. *Violence and Victims 27*(5), 635–655. doi:10.1891/0886-6708.27.5.635.

Levine, M., Taylor, P. J., & Best, R. (2011). Third parties, violence, and conflict resolution the role of group size and collective action in the microregulation of violence. *Psychological Science 22*(3), 406–412.

Lindegaard, M. R. (2016). Violence, bystanders, and . . . action! Danish Research Grant. Retrieved from https://www.nscr.nl/en/danish-research-grant-for-violence-bystanders-and-action/.

Longley, P. A. (2012). Geodemographics and the practices of geographic information science. *International Journal of Geographical Information Science 26*(12), 2227–2237.

Longley, P. A., Adnan, M., & Lansley, G. (2015). The geotemporal demographics of Twitter usage. *Environment and Planning A, 47*(2), 465–484. doi:10.1068/a130122p.

Luca, M. (2011). Reviews, reputation, and revenue: The case of Yelp.com. Harvard Business School NOM Unit Working Paper, 12-016, September 16.

MacKerron, G. (2012). *Mappiness*. Department of Geography and Environment, London School of Economics and Political Science. Retrieved from http://eprints.lse.ac.uk/36319/1/Landscape_MacKerron.pdf.

Malleson, N., & Andresen, M. A. (2015). The impact of using social media data in crime rate calculations: Shifting hot spots and changing spatial patterns. *Cartography and Geographic Information Science 42*(2), 112–121.

Manovich, L. (2011). Trending: The promises and the challenges of big social data. *Debates in the Digital Humanities 2*, 460–475.

Mashhadi, A., Quattrone, G., & Capra, L. (2013). Putting ubiquitous crowd-sourcing into context. In *Proceedings of the 2013 Conference on Computer Supported Cooperative Work* (pp. 611–622). New York: ACM.

Mayer-Schonberger, V., and Cukier, K. (2013). *Big Data: A Revolution That Will Transform How We Live, Work and Think*. London: John Murray.

McAfee, A., & Brynjolfsson, E. (2012). Big data: The management revolution. *Harvard Business Review 90*(10). doi:10.1007/s12599-013-0249-5.

Parker, C. J., May, A., Mitchell, V., & Burrows, A. (2013). Capturing volunteered information for inclusive service design: Potential benefits and challenges. *The Design Journal 16*(2), 197–218.

Phithakkitnukoon, S., Horanont, T., Di Lorenzo, G., Shibasaki, R., & Ratti, C. (2010). Activity-aware map: Identifying human daily activity pattern using mobile phone data. In *International Workshop on Human Behavior Understanding* (pp. 14–25). New York: Springer.

Raudenbush, S. W., & Bryk, A. S. (2002). *Hierarchical Linear Models: Applications and Data Analysis Methods*. 2nd ed. Thousand Oaks, CA: Sage.

Rossmo, D. K., Lu, Y., and Fang, T. (2012). Spatial-temporal crime paths. In *Patterns, Prevention, and Geometry of Crime*, edited by M. A. Andresen and J. B. Kinney (pp. 16–42). New York: Routledge.

Rundle, A., Bader, M., Richards, C., Neckerman, K., and Teitler, J. (2011). Using Google Street View to audit neighborhood environments. *American Journal of Preventive Medicine 40*(1), 94–100.

Sampson, R. J., & Raudenbush, S. W. (2004). Seeing disorder: Neighborhood stigma and the social construction of "broken windows." *Social Psychology Quarterly 67*(4), 319–342. doi:10.1177/019027250406700401.

Sanders, R. (1987). The Pareto principle: Its use and abuse. *Journal of Services Marketing 1*(2), 37–40.

Savage, M., & Burrows, R. (2007). The coming crisis of empirical sociology. *Sociology 41*(5), 885–899.

Scollon, C. N., Kim-prieto, C. H. U., & Diener, E. D. (2003). Experience sampling: Promises and pitfalls, strengths and weaknesses. *Journal of Happiness Studies 4*(1), 5–34.

Skogan, W. G. (1976). Victimization surveys and criminal justice planning. *University of Cincinnati Law Review 45*, 167.

Smith, S. (1987). Fear of crime: Beyond a geography of deviance. *Progress in Human Geography 11*(1), 1–23. doi:10.1177/030913258701100101.

Snijders, C., Matzat, U., & Reips, U. D. (2012). "Big data": Big gaps of knowledge in the field of Internet science. *International Journal of Internet Science 7*(1), 1–5.

Solymosi, R., Bowers, K., & Fujiyama, T. (2015). Mapping fear of crime as a context-dependent everyday experience that varies in space and time. *Legal and Criminological Psychology, 20*(2), 193–211.

Solymosi, R., Fujiyama, T., & Bowers, K. (2017). Crowdsourcing subjective perceptions of neighbourhood disorder: interpreting bias in open data. *British Journal of Criminology 57*(6).

Stewart, O., Lubensky, D., & Huerta, J. M. (2010). Crowdsourcing participation inequality: A SCOUT model for the enterprise domain. In *Proceedings of the ACM SIGKDD Workshop on Human Computation* (pp. 30–33). New York: ACM.

Surowiecki, J. (2005). *The Wisdom of Crowds*. New York: Anchor.

Sutton, R. M., & Farrall, S. (2004). Gender, socially desirable responding and the fear of crime: Are women really more anxious about crime?. *British Journal of Criminology 45*(2), 212–224.

Tompson, L., and Bowers, K. (2015). Testing time-sensitive influences of weather on street robbery. *Crime Science 4*(8). doi:10.1186/s40163-015-0022-9.

Wang, M., & Gerber, M. S. (2015). Using Twitter for next-place prediction, with an application to crime prediction. In *2015 IEEE Symposium Series on Computational Intelligence* (pp. 941–948). IEEE, Cape Town, South Africa. doi:10.1109/SSCI.2015.138.

Wang, W., Attanucci, J., & Wilson, N. (2011). Bus Passenger origin-destination estimation and related analyses using automated data collection systems. *Journal of Public Transportation 14*(4), 131–150. doi:10.5038/2375-0901.14.4.7.

Warr, M. (2000). Fear of crime in the United States: Avenues for research and policy. *Criminal Justice 4*(5), 451–489. Retrieved from http://www.crime-reg.com/police/warr_fear_of_crime.pdf.

Weisburd, D. (2015). The law of crime concentration and the criminology of place. *Criminology 53*(2), 133–157.

Wikstrom, P.-O. H., Ceccato, V., Hardie, B., & Treiber, K. (2010). Activity fields and the dynamics of crime: Advancing knowledge about the role of the environment in crime causation. *Journal of Quantitative Criminology*, (February). doi:10.2307/23367577.

Wilson, J., & Kelling, G. (1982). Broken windows. *Atlantic Monthly*, March, pp. 1–9. Retrieved from http://www.lantm.lth.se/fileadmin/fastighetsvetenskap/utbildning/Fastighetsvaerderingssystem/BrokenWindowTheory.pdf.

Winter, B. (2013). A very basic tutorial for performing linear mixed effects analyses. arXiv preprint arXiv:1308.5499.

Wolfe, M., & Mennis, J. (2012). Does vegetation encourage or suppress urban crime? Evidence from Philadelphia, PA. *Landscape and Urban Planning* 108(2–4), 112–122,

Yu, L. (2006). Understanding information inequality: Making sense of the literature of the information and digital divides. *Journal of Librarianship and Information Science 38*(4), 229–252.

Zandbergen, P. A., & Barbeau, S. J. (2011). Positional accuracy of assisted GPS data from high-sensitivity GPS-enabled mobile phones. *Journal of Navigation 64*(03), 381–399. doi:10.1017/S0373463311000051.

CHAPTER 12

ADVANCES IN VISUALIZATION FOR THEORY TESTING IN ENVIRONMENTAL CRIMINOLOGY

PATRICIA L. BRANTINGHAM, PAUL J. BRANTINGHAM, JUSTIN SONG, AND VALERIE SPICER

12.1 Introduction

Environmental criminology focuses on both the socio-spatial-temporal environment in which crimes occur and on offender-target interactions in order to develop better understandings of the processes behind the distribution of criminal events in space-time and the choice of targets made by offenders. Understanding the criminal decision process, both conscious and quasi-automatic, includes study of the movement patterns both of individuals and of groups of people. Finding what elements of the environment attract people and what repels them is a goal of much research in the field.

The environment within which people move has many dimensions that influence or constrain decisions and actions by individuals and by groups. This complexity creates a challenge for theoreticians and researchers in presenting their research results in a way that conveys the dynamic spatiotemporal aspects of crime and actions by offenders in a clearly understandable way. There is an increasing need in environmental criminology to use scientific visualization to convey research results. A visual image can describe underlying patterns in a way that is intuitively more understandable than text and numeric tables. Research depends on well-framed questions, on careful data collection, and on both sensitive qualitative and mathematical and statistical analysis, but the process of describing results in science increasingly relies on the use of visualization techniques. The advent of modern information systems generating large and deep data sets (Big Data) provides researchers unparalleled possibilities for asking and answering questions about crime and the environment, and this will require new techniques and methods for presenting findings. Visualization will be key.

12.2 Visualization as a Key Tool in the History of Environmental Criminology

Data visualization has been a feature of scientific criminology from its origins in the 19th century. The earliest scientific work in criminology utilized cartographic techniques to illuminate numeric tables showing the distribution of crime and other social phenomena across the provinces of France (Guerry, 1833; Quételet, 1842) and the counties of England (Mayhew, 1950 [1861–62]; Guerry, 1864). See Figure 12.1 for Guerry's map of the variation in crimes against persons across the departments of France in the 1820s. Detailed address-level point pattern mapping was used to envision the patterns of crime in London in the 1890s (Booth, 1891), Chicago during the first third of the 20th century (Shaw et al., 1929; Reckless, 1933), in New York City during the Great Depression (Halpern et al., 1934), and in several other large American cities (Shaw & McKay, 1931).

Clifford Shaw used E. W. Burgess's zonal hypothesis for urban dynamics (1925) and the visualization of that theory, to organize and interpret detailed point map data about the patterns in crime and delinquency in Chicago and other American cities (Figure 12.2). Through this research, Shaw set an empirical basis for very large portions of American criminology through the remainder of the 20th century. The scientific dialogue has involved questions about whether the zonal model of the city applies to cities outside the United States (see, e.g., Morris, 1958; DeFleur, 1967; Jarvis, 1972; Engstad, 1975; Baldwin & Bottoms, 1976; Herbert, 1977) and whether Shaw and McKay fell prey to the ecological fallacy in drawing conclusions from their data (Robinson, 1950). The power of this visualization framed much of the empirical research on crime and delinquency over the next 50 years (see, e.g., Lander, 1950; Schmid, 1960a, 1960b; Scarr, 1973). Shaw and McKay's explanation for the zonal patterns they observed—social disorganization of neighborhood communities—has held a major place in theoretical criminology and provided the starting point for much development and dissent among scholars. Yet many of the implications of Burgess's urban model (1925) had not been well explored prior to the 1980s, largely because researchers had not found a way to visualize them (see Brantingham & Jeffery, 1981).

The key empirical conclusions drawn from the visualization of maps and models of the 19th-century cartographers and the 20th-century ecologists set the stage for development of environmental criminology. Four observations are particularly important.

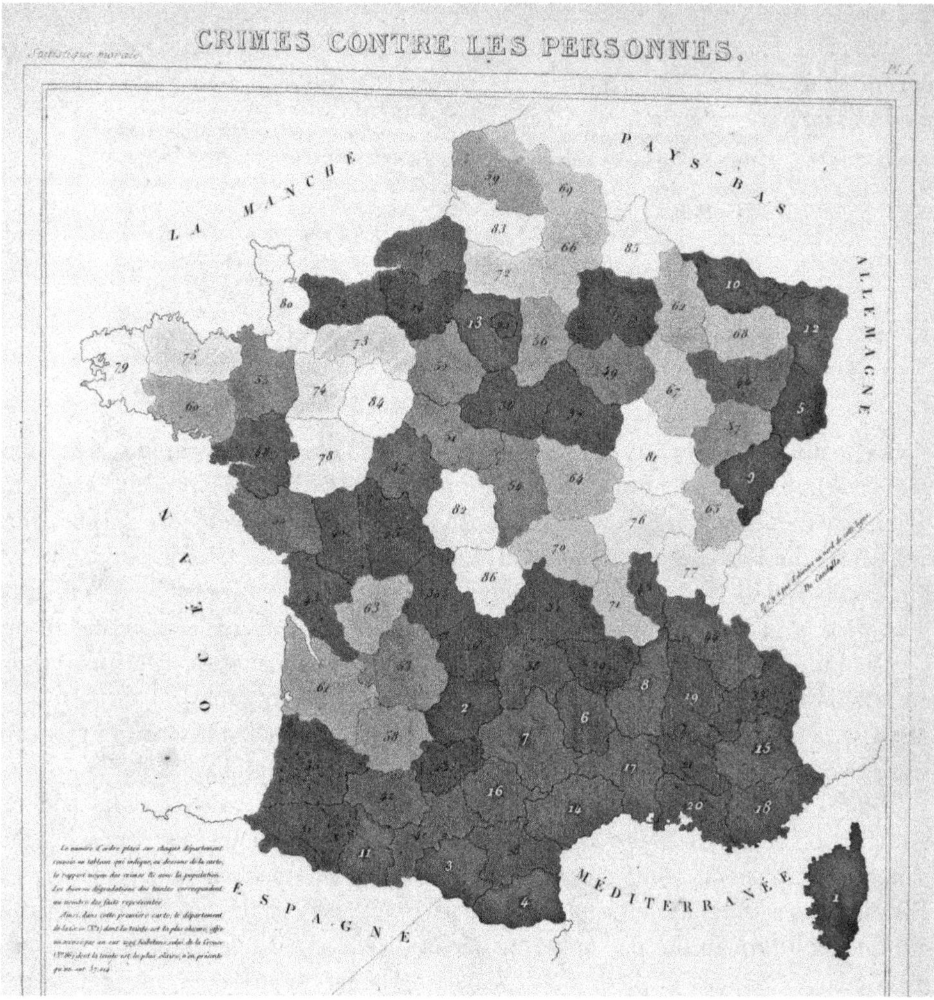

FIGURE 12.1 Crimes against persons

Source: Guerry, 1833.

First, crime is not random—it clusters in space and time. Second, those crime clusters are persistent—they reappear in the same patterns year after year and in country after country. Third, the character of the clusters of crime that can be observed is a function of scale. If scale matters, then the visualization of crime at different spatial and temporal scales is critical to both our understanding of crime and our ability to devise ways to reduce it. Fourth, crime clusters are produced by intersection of the physical and social environments with human activity and decision-making. Environmental criminology began to develop in the 1970s in pursuit of these conclusions.

That said, much of 20th-century criminology was focused on trying to explain why individuals develop a propensity for criminal action. Interestingly, other than Shaw and McKay and a few other Chicago school researchers, criminologists used few

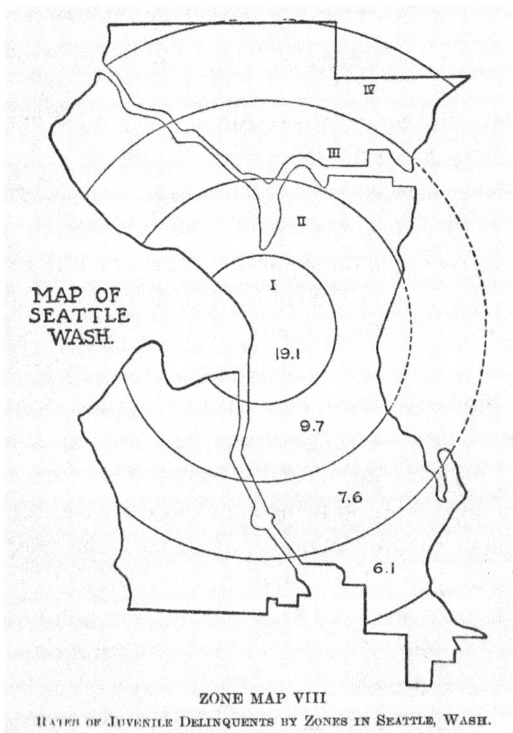

FIGURE 12.2 Zone map of delinquents' residences in Seattle (U.S.)

Source: Shaw & McKay, 1931.

visualizations of the theories they propounded or of their empirical findings until the 1970s. This shows most clearly in the examination of some iconic criminology text books of the mid-century. Edwin Sutherland's text *Principles of Criminology* dominated the American textbook market for more than 50 years and in the theory of *differential association* presented an explanation of criminal propensity acquired through social learning that continues to be influential. The fourth edition (1947) of the text, the first to contain a full statement of the theory of differential association and the last edition before Sutherland died in 1950, ran over 600 pages but contained no charts, diagrams, or maps of any kind. Focus was on the verbal description of the creation of criminal propensity and its control. George Vold's *Theoretical Criminology* (1958), a mid-century survey of criminological theories offering explanations of crime, criminality, and criminal propensity as well as descriptions of how those theories underwrote penal practice, provided no attempt to visualize any of the theories or data presented. The book contained no chart, diagram, or map of any kind. Herman Mannheim's two-volume textbook, *Comparative Criminology* (1965), presented a single Venn diagram illustrating the overlap between illegality and immorality. This was surprising because Mannheim's earlier study of juvenile delinquency in Cambridge had utilized address-level mapping to understand the distribution of delinquents across the city (1948). Criminologists cared so little for visualization of theory or data at mid-century that the *Journal of Criminal Law, Criminology and Police Science* declined to print Bullock's maps of the patterns of homicide in Houston (Bullock, 1955).

During the late 1960s and early 1970s researchers interested in the problem of *crime* (the criminal event itself), rather than the origin of *criminality* (the individual's propensity to commit crime), began to explore spatial and temporal patterns in criminal events. Geographers such as Keith Harries (1971, 1976), George Rengert (1972, 1975), and Gerald Pyle (1974, 1976) began to explore the spatial dynamics of crime. Criminologists such as C. R. Jeffery (1971), John Baldwin and Anthony Bottoms (1976), and Patricia and Paul Brantingham (1975a, 1975b, See also, Brantingham et al., 1976) began to focus on criminal events and the environments in which they occurred. Architects and urban planners began to explore the built environment (Newman, 1972) and the temporal dynamics of human land use (Angel, 1968) as ways to understand and reduce the number of criminal events occurring in those contexts and situations. Home Office researchers, led by Ronald Clarke, picked up on this growing body of theory and research and developed the idea of situational crime prevention (Clarke, 1980). The research field covered by these various but related approaches to studying crime soon became known as *environmental criminology* (Brantingham and Brantingham, 1981; Bottoms, 1994). The complex issues addressed in environmental criminology both call for and lend themselves to visualizations of theories and data.

From very early on, environmental criminologists saw that the clusters of criminal events were best understood as a cluster of decisions made at the endpoints of a series of movements of people, both offenders and victims or targets (Capone & Nichols, 1976; Brantingham & Brantingham, 1978; Cohen & Felson, 1979). Patterns in offenders' journeys to crime are shaped by and are very similar to the general movement patterns of the population at large. These patterns of movement involve some mix of both routine, repetitive decisions about when and where to go and occasional, unique, conscious decisions about journeys and destinations. The patterns of movement and decision have a dynamic characteristic. Environmental criminology, just like market geography, environmental psychology, landscape architecture, and urban studies, works on a premise that people move about in space and make decisions based in part on their surroundings. People also shape their surroundings to make it possible to modify their actions. Stated another way, surroundings may facilitate some actions, constrain others and can, in many cases, be modified or avoided.

Some of the early works that focus on human mobility and on how movement affects sequential decisions in target search are worth mentioning. In a more general sense, Alexander showed how the complexities of a city are all interconnected and shape urban users' perceptions and activities: visualizations would require the use of graphs (in the mathematical sense) and hypergraphs (1965a, 1965b). Kevin Lynch showed how the characteristics of urban neighborhoods shape activity choices (1960). Chapin showed how human activity patterns are shaped by the intersection of urban structure and the many different social characteristics of a city's population (1974). Criminologically, Burgess's crime mobility triangles (1925b) demonstrated the link between places, place use, and criminal choice. (See also Rand, 1986; Frank, Andresen & Felson, 2012.) Capone and Nichols (1976) showed the link between target type and the journey to crime for armed robbers. Cohen and Felson (1979) showed how changes in aggregate social routines can change the set of choices available to criminals in ways that affect the location and timing of criminal events. Beavon et al. (1994) showed how the structure of a city's road network shapes criminal target choice (see also Johnson and Bowers, 2010). Visualization provides a way to describe both the movements involved in crime and the decisions involved in making journeys to crime sites.

The environment contains elements that can create both pushes and pulls that impact how people move through it. A *push* is an environmental condition that provides impetus to move away from some specific location in space and time. A *pull* is an environmental condition that provides impetus to move toward some specific place or location. Some environmental elements, such as mass transportation hubs or major shopping centers or entertainment districts, pull people, including criminals, toward them. Some environmental conditions, such as difficult topography or high neighborhood efficacy or visible cultural differentials push people away from those locations toward others. These pushes and pulls create directionality of movement within the environment, with many people moving toward or away from places. Pushes and pulls inherent in the environment contribute to shaping all activity. Environmental criminology tracks the pushes and pulls that shape the activities of potential offenders and potential victims. Environmental pushes and pulls contribute to the development of regular activity nodes, regular paths between nodes and edges along the paths. Pushes and pulls also create areas that are avoided, both generally and by offenders and victims specifically. Overlapping of multiple individual paths, nodes, and edges results in functionally defined areas that are known by many people and help identify the potential areas where crimes might concentrate. The overlapping of routine paths, nodes, and edges also identifies areas in the environment that are known by only a few people as well as areas that are known by many. The cognitive spaces that surround people are not uniform. Paths are not necessarily straight lines. Activity nodes may be a building, a block, or an area of a city. Some of these activity nodes become crime attractors and crime generators, that is, the location of repeated crimes. For repeat offenders the pushes and pulls toward these crime attractors, over time, begin to shape future activity. What starts as an activity node for shopping or entertainment can become an activity node for crime after a series of crimes at or near the same location.

From a visualization perspective it is important to display the pushes and pulls within a city; the individual and aggregate nodes, paths, and edges that shape movement and mobility; the orientation of the directionality of offender and potential offender movement; the distribution of suitable targets for potential offenders with their relative risk; and the dynamic and temporal speed or rate of change in an environment.

The dynamic environment in which crimes occur is sometimes stable. At other times it changes, but very slowly. Sometimes the environment changes rapidly with sharp peaks and valleys altering the relationships between its elements. Words and tables of numbers often fail to convey the strength and direction of these relationships and the ways in which human activity must play out among them. Visualizations—maps, charts, diagrams—can often do a better job of communicating ideas and findings. This has proven particularly so in environmental criminology. The remainder of this chapter demonstrates contemporary visualization techniques in environmental criminology by working through some of its key concepts with associated visualizations. We first examine the idea of the environmental backcloth. We then examine target choice or search behavior theories. The chapter then moves into a more detailed exploration of current and new visualization techniques used to explain and convey: the power of crime attractors; the overarching influence of directionality in offender movements; the associated size and power of catchment areas around crime attractors; and a more detailed exploration of edge effects (or area permeability) in crime patterns and associated crime corridors and crime ridges. The chapter ends with a look to the future of visualization, particularly the future inherent in the increasing use of Internet connections and a requisite need for environmental criminology to integrate more firmly non-Euclidean or non-fixed-metric measures of distance and time into measures of nearness and linkages of people and places.

12.3 Environmental Backcloth

People exist within their surroundings. Our perception and cognition of what surrounds us is complex. Individual knowledge has uncountable dimensions, but conceptually it is perhaps best to think of it as existing at multiple scales of resolution with one's attention being focused on different levels by the requirements of short- and longer-term conditions. For example, you can be sitting in a chair at a table while working on a computer on the table. Your finest focus may be on keys on the keyboard or words on the screen of the monitor. At the same time, you pick up peripheral impressions of other physical objects on the table, the size and shape of the room. Cognitively you can place the room in the building in which it exists. You can place the building within its surrounds, be they apartments in a building, houses on a street, or buildings on a university campus or commercial offices in some part of a city. You are aware of other people nearby, sounds of other activities, and feelings of cold or warmth or light (see Alexander, 1965a, 1965b).

These and many more perceptions and bits of cognitive knowledge are always changing. When you are sitting at a specific desk for many days, over several months or years, many parts of the surrounds begin to enter into a generalized and often vague level of awareness. Your focus shifts from the local elements of your immediate surroundings to a wider awareness when an unexpected event occurs ("What made that loud noise?") or when occasion for asking spatiotemporal questions such as "Where should I eat lunch?" or "When does my next meeting start?" require it.

It is this ability to handle the uncountable range of scales and number of details and ways of perceiving and remembering what has occurred that is natural and essential to how people function. Egon Brunswik (1952) can be seen as one of the foundational leaders in the field of environmental psychology, a discipline that considers how people learn, make decisions, and function in their environments. Particular attention should be paid to his "Lens Model," where he conceptually presents and visualizes a structure for helping to identify which of the uncountable number of cues that exist in our surrounding environment are used for forming our cognitive knowledge of and specific actions within our surroundings. In a general sense, most people travel down infrequently used streets and suddenly notice that an old store or building is gone and wonder when the change occurred. But at the same time there may be a normal path routinely taken every day where a person sees a building being torn down and a new one built in the same location. In the latter situation, a person's memory of the street changes as the building is replaced. In the former, an older memory remains until something makes a person notice the change.

Overall, people have a memory of their immediate surrounds. However, what is in the immediate surrounds changes over the course of a day as they move through their routine daily activities. It helps to think of the immediate surrounds as a bubble space of expectations and observations that travels with a person during his or her daily movements. At the same time sharp events, general transmission of information, and conscious decisions change what is known about immediate surrounds. But movement and change in the surrounds are dynamic, not static.

Over the course of an individual's movements, immediate environmental surrounds change. In normal spatiotemporal movement, the immediate surrounds are contiguous and follow the movement pattern. This is what is frequently called an *activity space*. With normal visibility from a particular place, a person has a normal view angle of around 180 degrees without turning his or her head. This visibility can be interrupted by a building, hedge, or rapid change in topography. But add the *visibility space* to an activity space and you have *awareness space*. A good example of awareness space is seen in research using Space Syntax (Hillier and Hanson, 1984; Summers and Johnson, 2015). The currently available Space Syntax software presents visual images of the awareness space around streets and identified travel paths. This software provides a visual means to better understand activity and awareness space. The Bartlett Space Syntax Laboratory at University College London provides excellent examples of the visualization techniques derived from Space Syntax.

The previous examples describe someone working at a desk and traveling along a road. Another example could be a teenager on a normal school day. The teenager could be entering text through keys onto a smartphone. On the surface, this is similar to someone sitting at a desk and working on a computer, but the details of the object containing the keys and the structure of the screen changes the awareness space. The text that formed a document becomes text that communicates through social media ranging from WhatsApp, to Twitter, to Instagram, to a chat room associated with an online game. The immediate social surrounds of entering text into a computer device take on additional dimensions of communication links between individuals or groups on the Internet. The physical surrounds could be outside school, at home, or with friends, or anywhere where there is a Wi-Fi connection. The awareness space ranges across a cyber network.

In some application programs (apps), an individual can communicate with a large group and at the same time exchange text privately with individuals within the larger group. The physical surrounds can be many locations or can be a physical cluster of teenagers communicating through message apps with each other or with disparate groups. In this situation, the immediate surrounds on the Internet can change rapidly. Physical distance is replaced by Internet connections. Nodes are the interaction between individuals through linked connections. The teenager has a non-Internet activity space and awareness space that is expanded through an Internet activity space using specific apps with connectivity nodes and with relative strength of the frequency and the intensity of the interaction at the nodes. The activity space is formed through the process of using the apps, and the awareness space becomes the additional apps and links of which a user becomes aware while using the principal apps or through general app information exchange. Events can change an activity space through the introduction of additional people, an exchange of a common thread of knowledge, or the agreement of a group of people who do not physically know each other to meet at a common flash mob point for a street party, a protest, or a criminal contest such as automobile street racing. A similar example that helps explain these two types of activity spaces is the new private transportation capabilities realized through business applications such as Uber. Uber represents the merger of the physical awareness space with an Internet activity space.

These physical awareness spaces and activity spaces can be aggregated across the people within a physical area or over people who know each other in a physical area. A similar aggregation can occur in the Internet space. (Within computer science, nodes in distributed systems and peer-to-peer [P2P] links.) There are also computer network nodes, cloud computing end nodes and servers that are at the core of the computer network node links with others that are on the periphery. There can be traffic congestion on the links in the computer network. The user sees this as delay time in communication at busy activity times. This is much like the car and bus traffic jams that occur along major arteries and highways during a normal rush hour in a workday. The aggregation of individual physical activity spaces, seen in a temporal perspective, identifies likely traffic jam locations. Internet activity spaces identify high P2P links and heavily used server nodes with associated traffic jams generated from a temporal use pattern with peaks at the beginning of a workday, at lunch break, after school, and in the early evening.

Visualization becomes essential for understanding the environmental backcloth, both physical space and cyberspace, against which activities occur. The uncountable number of dimensions and scalar levels need to be reduced to numbers that are transferable to an image. What is physically a two-dimensional image can be converted to a three-dimensional object in a static image. With the use of color, saturation, hue, and shape, the number of dimensions can be expanded further. A series of static images or an animated image can illustrate temporal change. Exploration of the Internet awareness and activity spaces currently use network visualizations. When Internet spaces are combined with physical spaces, the result has been explored and visualized with hypergraphs (Cao et al., 2006; Brantingham & Brantingham, 2015). Effective visualization does require both skill and sensibility. Visualization is a critical theoretical tool because a visual cue can trigger the memory of concepts or classes of objects. For example, a visual map that shows crime along a commercial arterial road can trigger a memory of the characteristics of such strips and their commercial development. Similarly, a visual image that identifies large shopping malls or an entertainment district creates a personal image of something that means more than a line, an object, and a color. In state-of-the-art scientific visualization, actual digital images or digital streams of data can be attached to a surrogate map and accessed through zooming in on a location and a specification of attributes to be displayed. This is the experience of most people who use Google Maps, Google Earth, Microsoft Map, Wikimapia, or Nokia Maps. Similarly, animated visual images are used to display the results of simulations with associated formula, algorithms, and statistical tests. The visual presentation of the simulation provides more familiar and understandable information than what most people would understand by reading the code in an algorithm or simulation.

All of these visualization techniques require developing a fixed number of dimensions and using attributes associated to elements on each dimension. This understanding of visualization can be used to provide an image of the environmental backcloth in environmental criminology. A specific research project may focus on one or many layers and dimensions.

12.4 Dimensional Layers to the Environmental Backcloth

The dimension layers frequently used in environmental criminology (Figure 12.3) are

- A street network;
- Transit infrastructure (bridges, public transit, and private transit);
- Land uses (uses of land);
- Physical topography (bodies of water, mountains or steep hills, inaccessible areas); and
- Social and economic characteristics of resident and ambient population.

These dimensions are part of the study of urban morphology in urban studies. Urban morphology was developed as part of town and urban planning with reliance on the early work of Park, Burgess, and McKenzie (1925), M. R. G. Conzen (1960), and more recent complex systems work by Anas et al. (1998), and by Batty (2005, 2009).

12.4.1 Street Network

Understanding the environmental backcloth frequently starts with understanding the street network. The street network forms the backbone that shapes the city. It influences and is influenced by transit infrastructures and land uses or use of land, physical

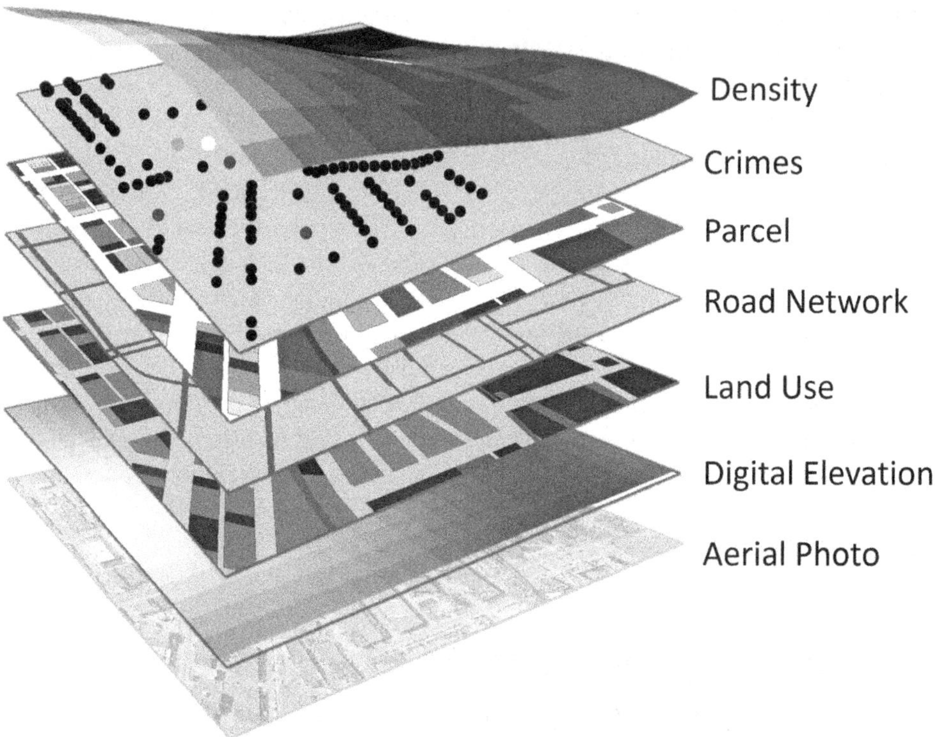

FIGURE 12.3 Environmental criminology dimension layers

topography, and socioeconomic conditions of areas and population. These street network dynamics will be covered in subsequent sections. The street network is the structural starting point for understanding crime distribution, human movement within the urban setting, and the pushes and pulls of the urban backcloth.

The street network is particularly important in understanding crime patterns. Crimes reported to and recorded by police using the actual street address where the crime occurred or the address of the nearest street intersection provide key information for visualizing the crime problem.

Street networks grow and evolve over time. Cities are born, age, gentrify in parts, change their economic role, but usually keep the spatial structure of older roads. In some ways, in a large city the structure of the roads can reveal the age of the city. Popular road structures have changed over time but left their imprint on cities. In older cities that have grown into modern cities, the central part of the city tends to have shorter street blocks. Most people were pedestrians in the early days of London, Paris, Rome, Amsterdam, Istanbul, and Cairo. In modern cities, people usually travel by vehicle when outside of the city center. Road segments on the growing edge of the city became longer as rapidity of travel made space less of a constraint (Burgess, 1925a; Brantingham & Jeffery, 1981). In more modern car-based cities, road networks are less dense. However, more recently urban planners have been trying to move people back to walking and biking in cities mostly dominated by cars. In many cities, this proves very difficult except in their older, denser parts. In many modern cities, there is a mixture of several older cities that have grown and merged together where several short-street segment areas are connected together with more limited links. Even in newer cities and metropolitan regions like Vancouver, Canada, there is an older city center with shorter street segments. Even in the newer parts, there are some commercial areas with denser street segments (Figure 12.4). The two old city centers in the Metro Vancouver area displayed in Figure 12.4 have on average shorter street segments, Vancouver with 87.6 meters and New Westminster with 98.7 meters, whereas a newer city center in the same region has on average a much longer street segment, 132.1 meters.

Graph theory and network analysis are the natural technique for exploring the urban morphology of street networks and dividing these networks into classes of structures. The work of the Brantinghams and colleagues (Brantingham and Brantingham, 1984, 1991, 2015; Frank et al., 2010; Park, Tsang, & Brantingham, 2012), as well as other scholars (Barthélemy and Flammini, 2008; Strano et al., 2013; Davies and Johnson, 2015) illustrates this approach.

There are several concepts in graph theory that should be mentioned. A graph, a network in a finite sense, is a mathematical object made up of nodes and links between nodes. In environmental criminology these links are often called *pathways*, representing routes between nodes used by individuals. Graphs are usually represented

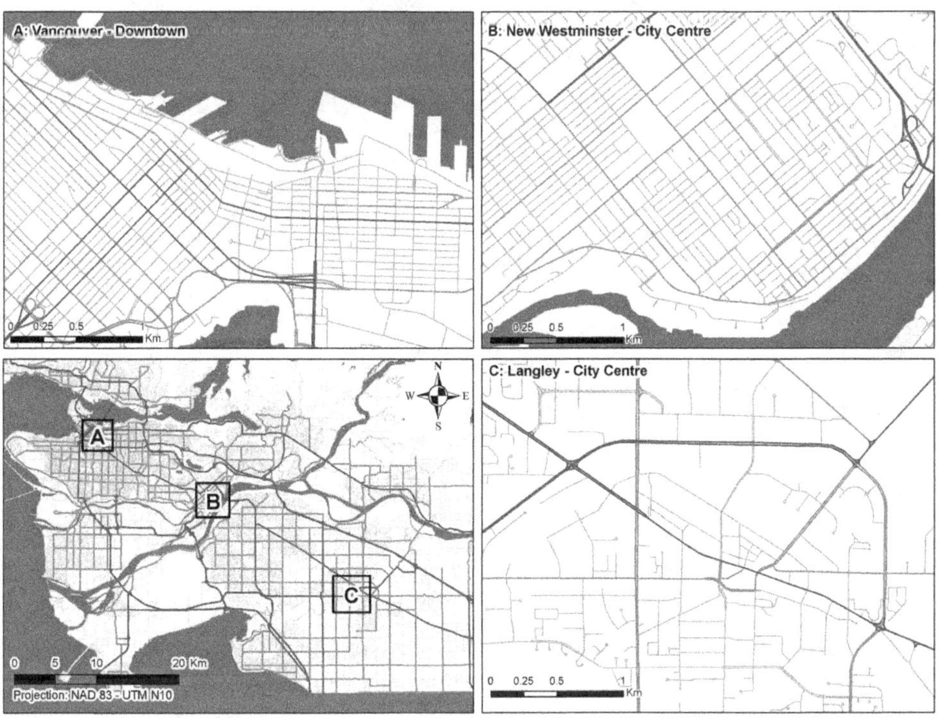

FIGURE 12.4 Metro Vancouver (Canada): Three city centers comparison

mathematically in a matrix where the cells of the matrix are either 0 or 1, representing no-adjacency or adjacency. The degree of a node represents the links to the node with the average degree the average of all nodes in an area. For a street network, the nodes are the intersections between streets; the links are the street segments linking two nodes. The degree for an intersection is the number of street segments coming together at an intersection. In a normal grid network, the degree of an intersection is four and the average degrees for a complete grid would be four as well. As seen in Figure 12.4, the likelihood of a complete grid decreases as the distance to the city center increases. In some parts of a street network, the network becomes like a tree, branching out into dead ends or cul-de-sacs.

Street segments usually fall into four categories: principal arterial streets, minor arterial streets, collector streets, and local roads. Highways form a higher level of road that moves through multiple urban subareas. These categories represent the volume of traffic carried and provide a rough index of mobility patterns. For the local residential roads, local accessibility to the area dominates. For highways and principal arteries, movement through an area is the goal of many people using these streets. Figure 12. 6 is a restatement of Figure 12.5 with street segments divided by their movement importance and degree of connectedness.

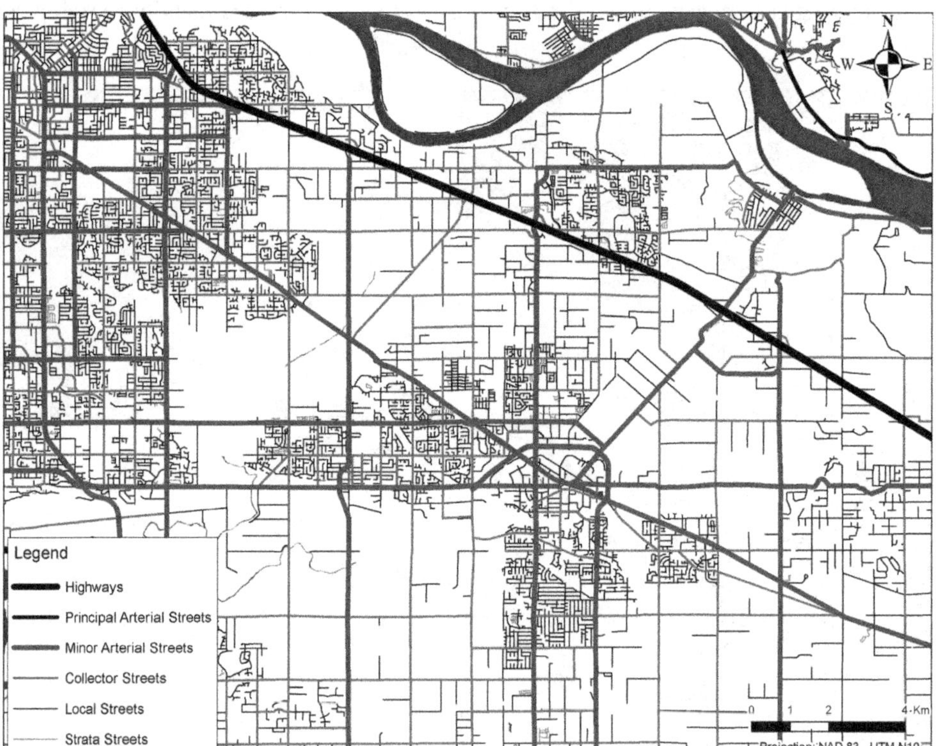

FIGURE 12.5 Categories of street segments

12.4.2 Transit Infrastructure

Transit infrastructure is core to urban morphology and to the way of life for people in urban areas. Rail transit has a long history, and in many ways we live with modern versions and survive with remnants of the original. It is best to view transit infrastructure as a way of moving people and commodities that is overlaid on a street network. It is also important to explore the impact on crime of lack of public transit in rural areas. For environmental criminologists it is best to think of entry and exit points along transit routes when visualizing crime patterns and awareness space.

A transit infrastructure may be below ground, above ground but disjoint from streets, or on streets as buses or trolleys. In all these situations, the surrounds that are best known by users of these services are the entry and exit points. With the daily flow of people, there are major entry and exit points associated with the primary origins and destinations of riders. Depending on where these are located on the transit network, these can be crowded locations with associated crime risks (Felson & Boivin, 2015; Block & Davis, 1996; Buckley, 1996; Brantingham, Brantingham, & Wong, 1991; Shellow, Romuladi, & Bartell, 1974).

12.4.3 Land Uses or Use of Land

Street networks are tied to the use of the land. Cities and rural areas have diverse individual structures, but there are one or more concentrations of sales of food and goods, areas that are identifiable as primarily used for housing arrangements, and other areas that are industrial or break-in-bulk points for major commodity transport (ports or rail hubs). Normally land use categories are divided into hundreds of subcategories, some of which only apply to a few cities. From an environmental criminology perspective, land use categories have a very important value. Many different types of crime concentrate in particular land uses: shoplifting; bar assaults; copper theft; residential burglary; and armed robbery, to mention a few. Some crimes appear in several types of land use, but may follow a different spatial and temporal pattern depending on the land uses. This will be covered in more detail later in the chapter, but at this point land use can be seen as forming the skeleton for activity spaces and awareness spaces. An area's land uses, with their associated densities, help identify likely home locations and activity nodes such as schools, work areas, and entertainment areas (Song et al., 2016; Kinney et al., 2008; McCord et al., 2007).

Figures 12.4, 12.5, and 12.6 provide the basis for many different activity spaces and awareness spaces. But within any environment, the street network, transit facilities, and land uses generate the pushes and the pulls that give impetus to movement patterns in a dynamic environment. Mobility within this environment contributes to shaping the concentration of people and the clustering of criminal events.

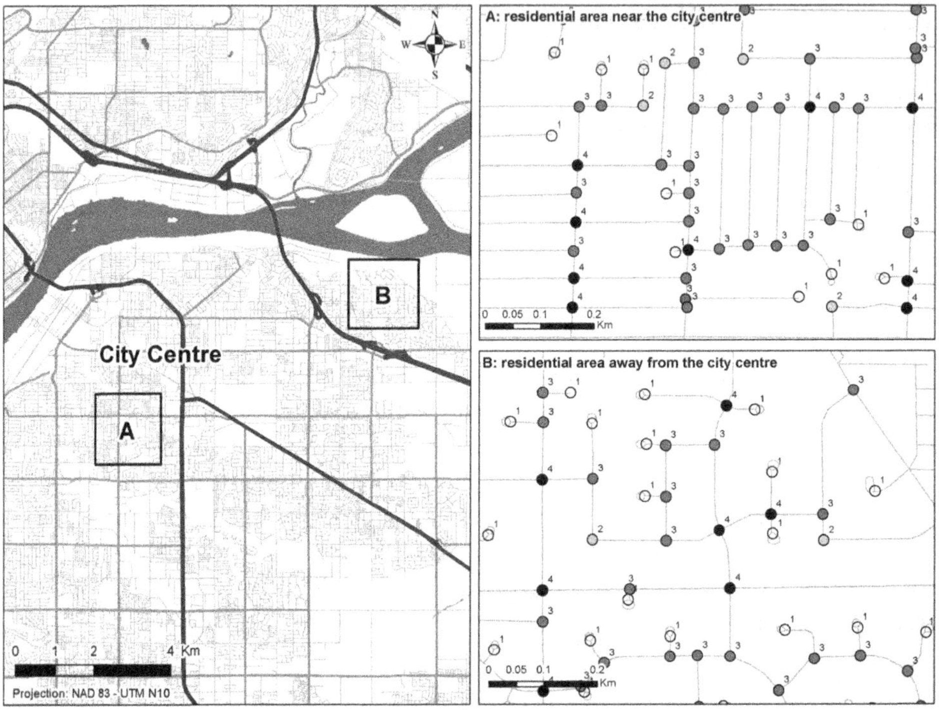

FIGURE 12.6 Degree of connected road segments

12.4.4 Physical Topography

Physical topography is presented here as a separate category, but the physical topography impacts on street networks, transit networks, and land uses. Commercial uses of land tend to be in highly accessible locations on a street network. The size of any cluster of commercial uses depends on the size of the easily accessible area and the mode of transit. City centers have commercial centers because these are usually the most accessible areas by foot, car, or train. Smaller commercial areas need only be accessible by smaller populations. Regional shopping centers frequently are situated on the outskirts of urban areas but are located so they are highly accessible by cars using highways or principal arteries or, in some cases, accessible to persons using major mass transit.

Shopping usually involves walking, so successful shopping areas are located on flat land. Residences, however, can exist on hillsides or in less accessible areas. Industry is usually located to be accessible by road and rail but to control its negative impact on other land uses. Baldwin & Bottoms's (1976) classic study of crime in Sheffield showed how the unique topography of the city—its division into multiple valleys separated by high escarpments—shaped both its patterns of land use and its patterns of crime.

Water is part of physical topography that influences streets and requires the building of bridges or the creation of ferries and water access. Water access and streets leading to bridges or ferries have a major impact on a city. Many readers will have experienced the island of Manhattan and the alterations in traffic flows and concentrations as people move to cross its water boundaries by bridge and tunnel. The canal system of Amsterdam has a similarly strong impact on whether two houses are functionally adjacent to one another or are merely visible across a canal's waterway. Water barriers more generally can have a profound effect on how a person travels from one part of the city to another and where an offender might choose to offend (Clare, Fernandez, & Morgan, 2009). Needless to say, all physical topography influences the pushes and pulls of a city and the associated activity spaces and awareness spaces.

12.4.5 Socioeconomic Characteristics

Within every environment where there are people, there is a mix of socioeconomic conditions. In some rural areas the variation may seem small; in other urban areas there is stark socioeconomic variation. This variation, tied to cultural and ethnic variation, creates the rest of the urban backcloth and results in an urban mosaic of great complexity. Each city is different, but from an environmental criminology perspective it is helpful to examine the differentiation between neighborhoods that have high levels of homogeneity and those that are very mixed on social, economic, and demographic characteristics. Neighborhoods are composed of consistent interior areas and boundary areas where one neighborhood type blends into another. Social and cultural differences create barriers between neighborhoods and limit the movement of offenders into neighborhoods that are different from their own (De Poot et al., 2005; Reynald et al., 2008). The boundary can be sharp or gradual, and the permeability of a neighborhood edge can vary greatly. In very homogeneous neighborhoods, there is a strong feeling of who belongs and who does not; this feeling decreases in less homogeneous neighborhoods. Along the edges of all neighborhoods, residents' and insiders' feelings of comfort and proprietary control decline and strangers are as comfortable as those who live there.

In commercial and entertainment areas, almost all users are strangers. These can be places that are part of the everyday experience for many people, but a lot of those people do not get to know each other. In these types of places, there are small groups of people that know each other, but they move about in larger groups of strangers. It should be noted that this is a phenomenon that has a scale element. In small rural areas there may be relative differences between people that are quite large, but they all know the names of one another. In large urban areas, people may be recognizable (they are leaving the same train stop at the same time every day), but their names are not known and they do not communicate. This is a step back to the Internet world, there are people who communicate through cyberspace and know an identity well, but never cross paths or recognize each other if they do. The actual crossing of paths and learning to recognize the other person creates the opportunity for a new class of events, some good and some criminal.

The environmental backcloth sets the stage for the visual description of criminal events. The next section of the chapter explores, visually, crime attractors, the issue of directionality in journeys to crime, and the catchment areas for attractors.

12.4.6 Crime Attractors

Within the environmental backcloth there are individual and aggregate crime attractors, that is, places that attract potential offenders. There are also crime generators that have such a high volume of people flowing through them that a number of potential offenders will find an easy opportunity to commit a crime.

In *Notes on the Geometry of Crime* (Brantingham and Brantingham, 1981) there are sequences of images that depict the process by which individuals and groups of co-offenders or aggregations of sole offenders who commit repeat offenses form crime patterns. These images show an individual forming a routine activity space and awareness space, followed by the identification of potentially suitable targets for that offender. Some of the potential targets fall within the awareness space of the potential offender. An even smaller number of potential targets fit a decision schema for suitable targets, and these become the likely pool of targets. In this section, the visualization images go on to show how multiple, independent individuals might have awareness spaces that overlap and with that a possible degree of overlap of suitable targets. The environmental backcloth helps shape individual activity spaces. When individuals living in the same general area work or go to school in the same areas, they are likely to travel on the same major arteries and stop at the same near-by commercial areas. If they all are potential offenders, they are likely to form some cluster of offenses. Restated more realistically, when you take a whole environment and look at the all of the people, there are likely to be several streets that stand out as heavily used streets and activity nodes that become attractors for many people (Curman, Andresen & Brantingham, 2015; Groff, Weisburd & Yang, 2010). Out of this group of all people there is a smaller group of potential offenders who develop some common travel paths and some common attractor nodes. Figure 12.7 is a visual representation of crime patterns expected from overlapping activity spaces. In this figure, crime hotspots are generated using the direction between offenders' home locations and their offence locations. These crime hotspots are then layered onto the street network. The overlapping activity nodes that stand out in this image are regional shopping centers that attract many people and many potential offenders. They are crime attractors but offer so many opportunities that they are crime generators as well.

Crime attractors are really hotspots with a reason for the labeling of those hotspots included in the name. Crime attractors are part of the pulls in the environmental backcloth that help shape crime patterns. There has been considerable evidence that a disproportionate amount of crime concentrates at or near these attractor locations (see, e.g., Block and Block, 1995; Eck, Clarke, and Guerette, 2007; Johnson and Bowers, 2010).]

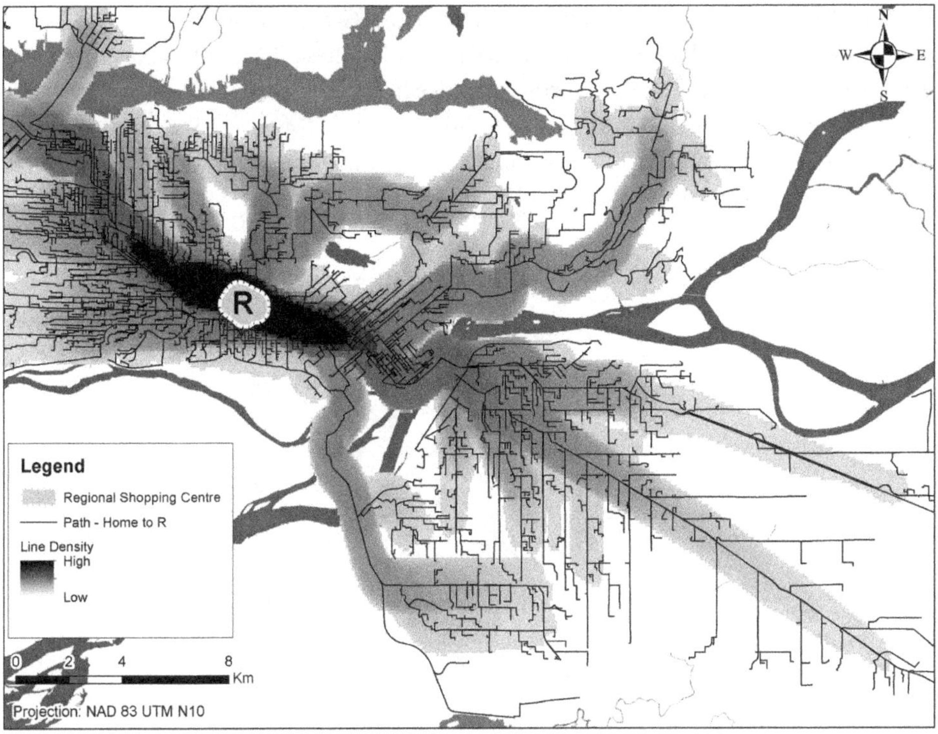

FIGURE 12.7 Regional shopping centers and offender pull

12.4.7 Directionality

Directionality is a term from geography that refers to an individual's orientation within an environment. For example, people will generally point in similar directions when asked to indicate where the center of the city is in a small city or when asked to point north or to point toward home. The ability to self-locate in the environment facilitates people finding their way or doing what is called *navigation*. Navigation apps in the mobile Internet world replace the need to self-locate and personally work out a way of moving between two points in novel space, but people still learn the directionality within their normal areas of routine activities, the directionality of landmarks within their activity space, and directionality of large topographic features. The modern work in directionality can be traced back to the fascinating work done by Kevin Lynch in his *Image of the City* (1960) where he explored the cognitive maps developed by individuals for cities where they lived. These individuals effectively learned to divide cities cognitively by areas they knew into paths, nodes, districts, edges, and landmarks, thus dictating how they navigated the city. Supportive views of structures and ways of learning about structures are found in the works of Piaget (1970) and the Bourbaki group (1966), to name a few from different disciplines. Wayfinding in a known environment in a spatiotemporal manner is related to moving between points or places. The pushes and pulls of a city have directionality that impacts wayfinding.

This directionality was initially described in the *Geometry of Crime* (1991) by the pathways between different nodal activity points. In these initial drawings, the paths were never straight, that is, the shortest distance between two points, but had an orientation *toward* an activity node. Figure 12.8 shows examples of how paths can change and still maintain an orientation or directionality. Figure 12.9 shows how this directionality would look on a street network.

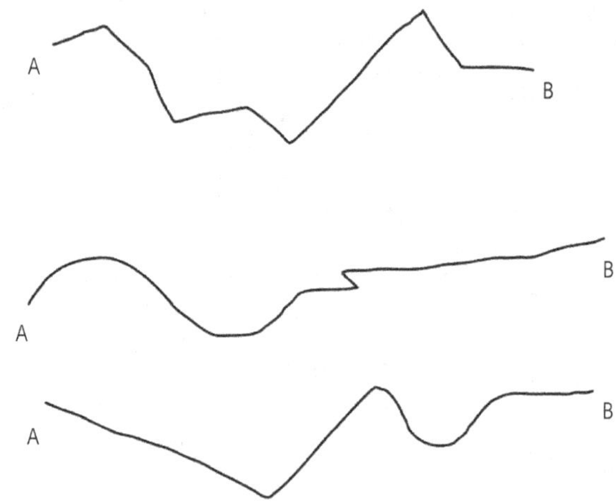

Three paths or routes between A and B

FIGURE 12.8 Different pathways

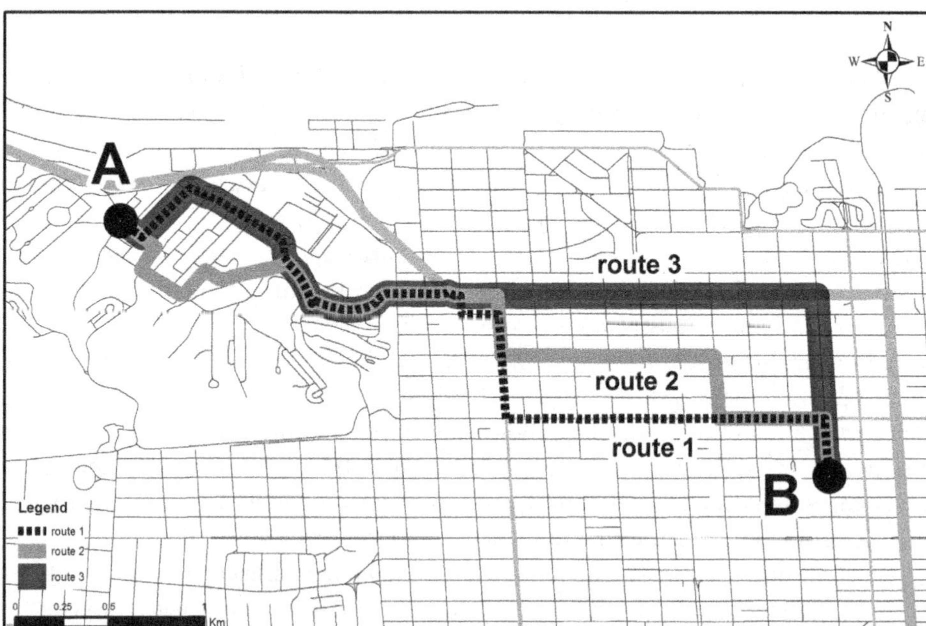

FIGURE 12.9 Pathways displayed on a map

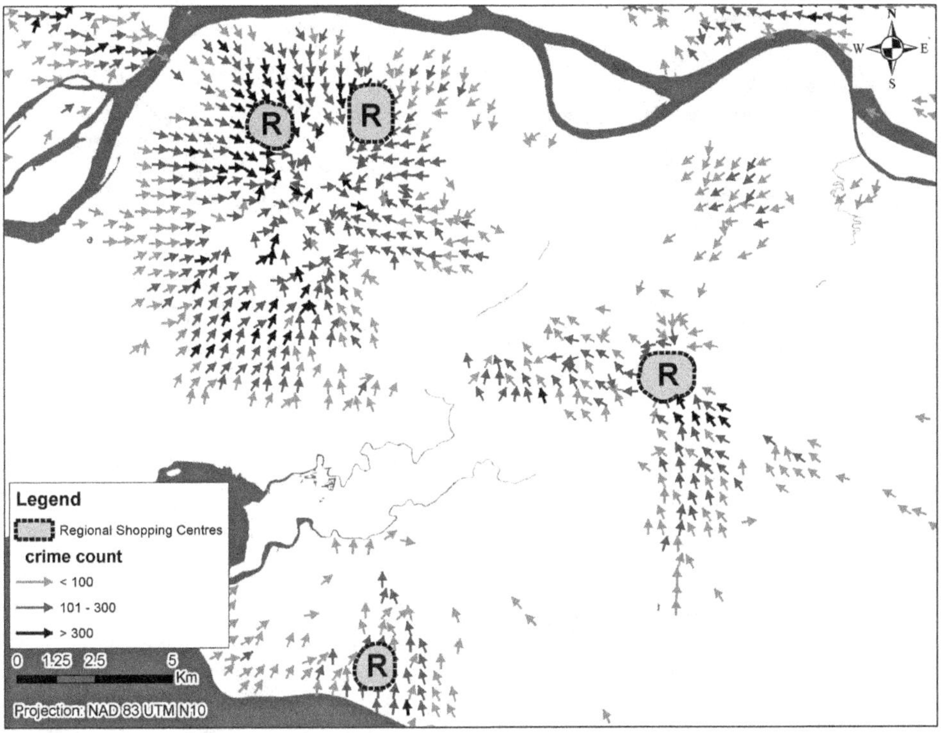

FIGURE 12.10 Shopping areas and directional pull of offenders

Directionality research has made rapid advances in environmental criminology with the work of Richard Frank. What Frank found in British Columbia was that, when taking the home location as a starting point, there are clear directionality decisions being made by repeat offenders as shown in their target choices. Overall around 50% of offenses occur within a 30-degree angle away from the home location (Frank, Andresen, & Brantingham, 2012, 2013). For very high repeat offenders, this can be divided into two very narrow directional angles.

When this tendency is added to the pull of crime attractors, a very strong pattern develops where many offenders are pulled from a range of locations toward the same attractor. Figure 12.10 shows the directional pull of several shopping centers in Metro Vancouver.

Figure 12.10 uses arrows to describe the direction in which offenders are moving from their home location to their crime location. Mathematically these directional vectors can be linked to preferred pathways, and algorithms developed to predict criminal navigation in a very precise manner.

12.4.8 Catchment Areas

Much of environmental criminology has parallels in marketing geography (or geo-marketing as it is sometimes called). In geo-marketing the interest is in determining the location of the client base likely to use a marketing location and the likely goods that

FIGURE 12.11 One-attractor and two-attractor diagrams

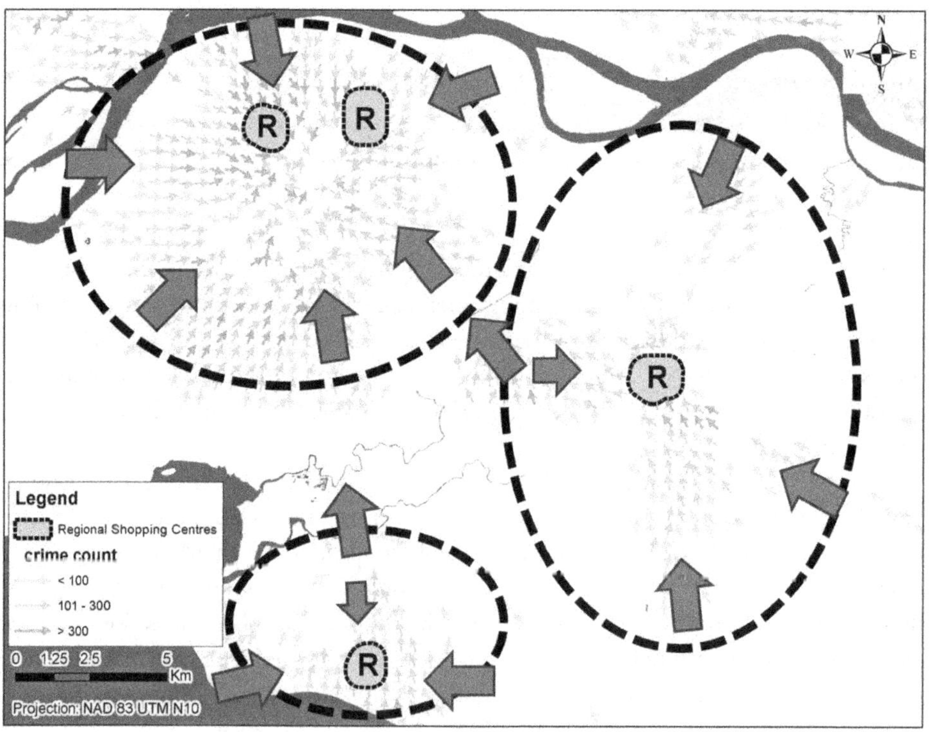

FIGURE 12.12 Crime catchment areas: offender pull

will be purchased. Geo-marketing frequently uses visualization techniques, considering travel times, number of stops in a shopping trip, and likelihood of returning. Geo-marketing on a visualization side uses point maps, circular and elliptical buffers, area maps, and kernel density functions.

One important part of geo-marketing is the idea of *catchment areas.* A catchment area is the geographic area from which a store gets most of its customers. It is a concept with promise for environmental criminology. Figure 12.11 provides examples of how a catchment area might work with one crime attractor or with multiple crime attractors.

As can be seen in this figure, there can be areas that feed more than one attractor. Figure 12.12 provides the visual images of the catchment areas for major commercial centers by identifying the concentration of known offenders. Several visualization techniques were used to show catchment areas. As with most ideas there are several ways of displaying the information.

12.5 Crime Patterns on the Environmental Backcloth

Crime attractors, directionality and catchment areas can be overlaid on the environmental backcloth making certain crime patterns more visible and understandable. This will be done in this section by looking at the street network, the hierarchy of types of streets, and the transit infrastructure and overlaying them with land use and physical topography. Social-economic factors will be discussed, but not included in this more general visualization. Visualization can become confusing when too many dimensions are introduced.

12.5.1 Edge Effect

The environmental backcloth is full of perceptual and physical edges, places where there is enough distinctiveness from one adjacent area to another that the change is noticeable. At an extreme, land bordering a river is an edge; houses directly behind a commercial strip or industrial area form a perceptual edge. Edges are everywhere. Residential areas have edges. Sometimes a change in type of residential building or a movement from residential to commercial use could produce an edge. Commercial areas have edges too. For some types of commercial area, like a strip mall, the entire mall is a perceptual edge.

Zoning and planning often work in tandem, making major roads the separator between different types of areas. Frequently a major road is a marker of a perceptual edge. Sometimes the major road is so large that it is an area that is an edge. This is certainly true of major highways. Edges can be characterized many ways. They can be physical barriers; or strong cognitive barriers making someone feel like they are crossing into new or different territory. Gangs use graffiti and symbols to mark the edge of their territories.

Edges are repeatedly found to have higher crime rates than the interiors of residential, commercial, or industrial areas. This may well be associated with how edges fall in areas where many diverse people may feel like they belong, or stated another way, there are no natural guardians. Edges do not belong to any one group, but to multiple and potentially different groups. As an example, most people feel comfortable walking very near their home if the surrounding homes are similar. On the other hand they feel more uncomfortable as they move into a completely different type of neighborhood where the visible cues indicate that the residents are not similar to the ones where they live or the cues make them feel like they stand out. Brantingham and Brantingham (1975b) found that the crime rate differences between the edges and the interior of neighborhoods varied by a factor of three. Justin Song and colleagues (Song, Spicer, & Brantingham, 2013; Song et al., 2016) found that this pattern repeated across Metro Vancouver by looking at the edges between single family residence neighborhoods and all other land uses. The edges were found to have considerably higher crime rates than the interiors of neighborhoods. The edge effect is strong, as shown by Figure 12.13.

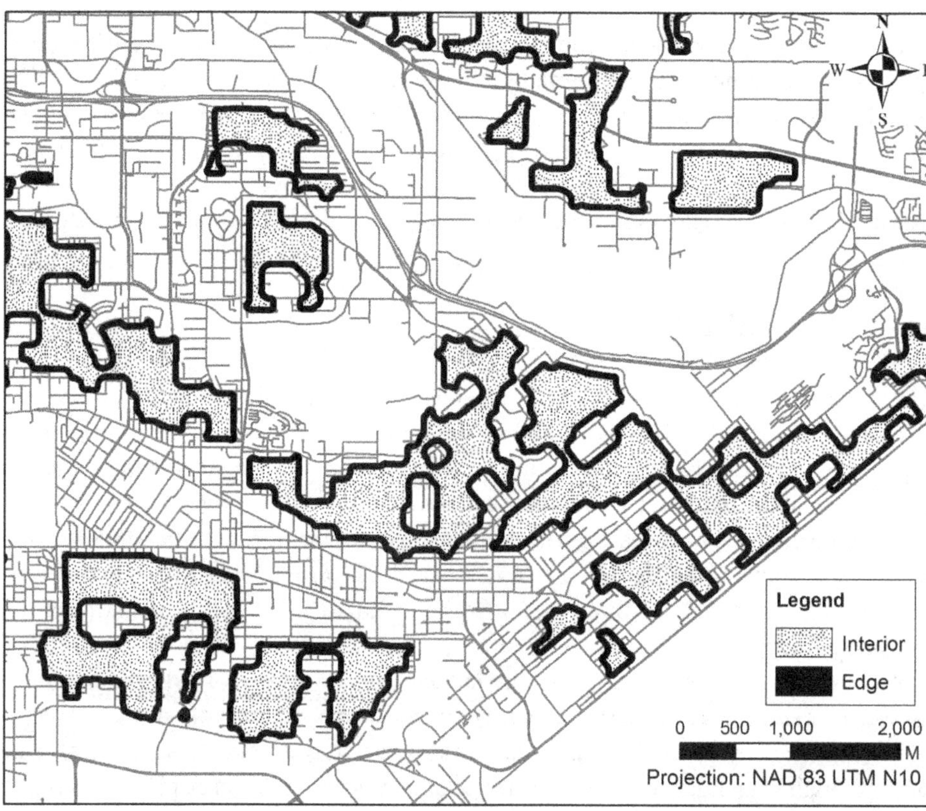

FIGURE 12.13 Edge effect and interior single-family residence

In Figure 12.13, large areas that contained single-family residences were parceled out and a small 30-meter buffer was created at the boundary between this type of land use and other forms of land use (multidwelling—commercial—industrial—park). Crime is substantially higher within this edge area where there is a distinctive transition in land use.

12.5.2 Crime Corridors

When aggregate crime patterns are explored, the major pushes and pulls of dynamic environments that influence crime are apparent on the backcloth of the environment. Certain parts of the environment stand out as high-crime locations. As noted before, crime is high in some limited locations within a city but low or close to nonexistent in others. The areas where offenders search for targets are limited (Bernasco, 2006; Bernasco & Nieuwbeerta, 2005; Bernasco, Johnson, & Ruiter, 2015). The decision process is not an optimization of target choice across the whole environment, but rather a target choice made along major routes or pathways where there are suitable targets.

Environmental criminological research finds that many street segments in a city have little or no crime (Groff, Weisburd, & Yang, 2012; Curman, Andresen, & Brantingham, 2015) and that street intersections with a small number of intersecting street segments (degrees in a graph theory) have less crime (Beavon et al., 1994; Davies and Johnson, 2015). Figure 12.14 shows the street network for a portion of Vancouver. Figure 12.15 shows the arterial roads. As can be seen from Figure 12.15, there are a limited number of arteries. This number is reduced even further if the principal high-traffic arteries are identified.

FIGURE 12.14 City of Vancouver (Canada) street network

A new visualization technique called *street profile analysis* has been developed for analyzing crime along these principal corridors. Unlike conventional crime-mapping techniques, the street profile technique utilizes a graph where the x-axis represents the street and the y-axis the volume of crime. The impact of major nodes and the directional mobility of people on arterial corridor streets become very evident through the visualization.

As an example of crime corridors, Broadway Avenue in Vancouver is one of the busiest arteries with an east-west express bus line that connects a Skytrain (metro line) from the suburban areas of greater Vancouver to highly accessed locations in the

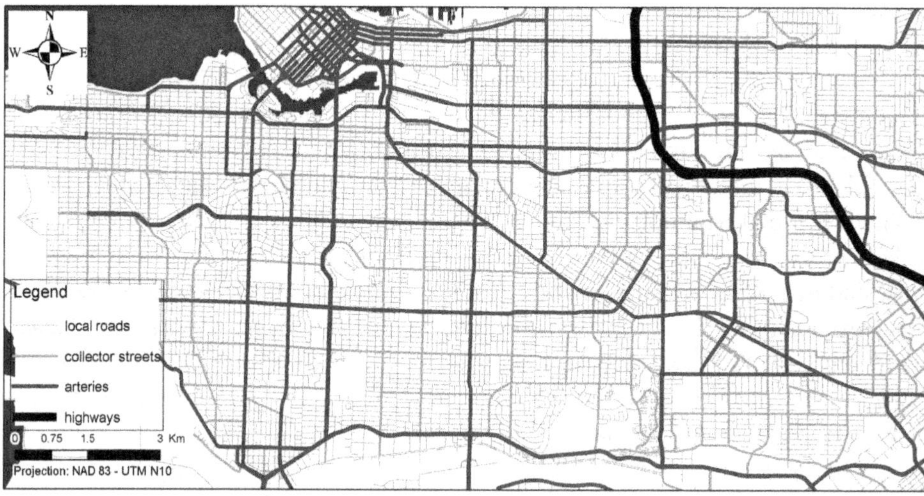

FIGURE 12.15 Arterial corridor streets

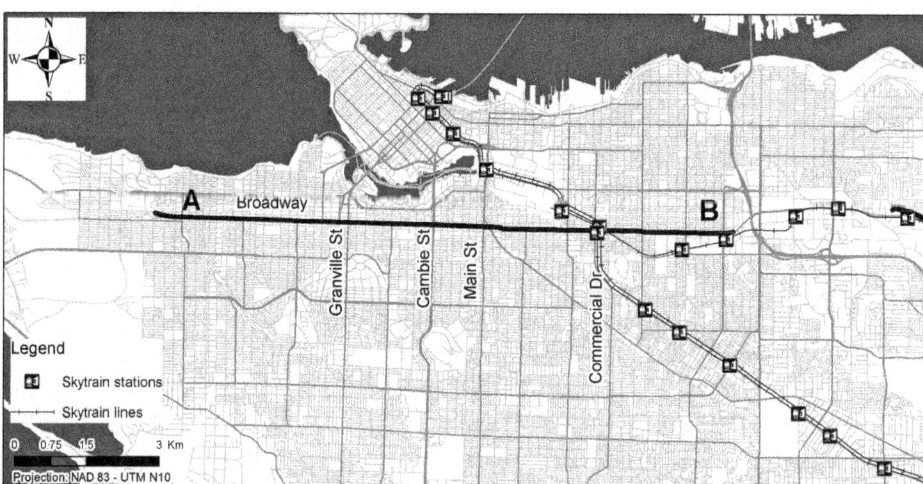

FIGURE 12.16 Broadway Avenue, Vancouver (Canada)

city, including City Hall, Vancouver General Hospital, and the University of British Columbia. This is combined with shopping centers, entertainment venues, and commercial strip development along this street. Figure 12.16 shows the location of Broadway in the city of Vancouver, and Figure 12.17 shows how crime rises and falls as one moves along this street. Crime is not uniform, but varies dependent on activity levels in a city, the pushes and pulls throughout the city, and the distribution of suitable targets that intersect aggregate awareness spaces.

Broadway is a major east-west corridor that intersects major north-south corridors and arteries that feed into other highly accessed locations, including downtown Vancouver, community colleges, regional shopping centers, and the Vancouver International Airport. As can be seen from Figure 12.17, crime increases at these intersections. The intersections have higher degrees of connectivity and are locations of commercial stores and government institutions. The major ones have heavy foot traffic as well as vehicle traffic. This is an ideal location for street-based person offenses, and indoor and outdoor property crime.

Figure 12.17 shows the volume of crime for three different years. This makes it possible to see the traces of a major change in the volume and flow of people and vehicles. This intersection at Broadway and Commercial is of particular interest because it contains the largest mass transportation hub in western Canada, and it grew significantly in the time period represented on this graph. In 1990 there was only one rapid train line going through this

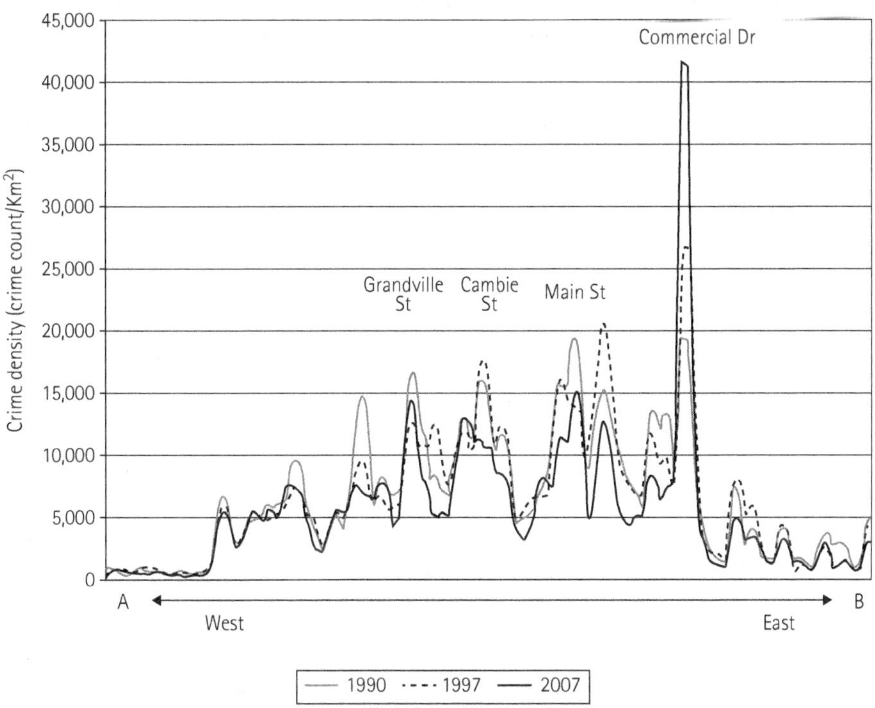

FIGURE 12.17 Street profile analysis, Broadway Avenue

location. In 2002, an extra line was added that ended at this station with an extension of one station added in 2006. Express bus lines connect this station to the rest of Vancouver.

12.5.3 Temporal Directionality

Temporal directionality can be understood in a number of ways and used to further describe the pushes and pulls in the environment. These variances can occur over a very small time period or a very long one. These variances can also be visualized in a sequential manner to show these differences. In Figure 12.18, the intersection that contains the high-crime mass transportation hub shown in Figure 12.17 is viewed at six different time periods, with the time stamp in the top-left corner of each image: the temporal directional pulls become evident.

Crime corridors analysis can be used on a network of streets using a 2.5-dimensional mapping technique where the x-y coordinates provide the map grid and the z-axis describes the volume of crime. These maps show how crime interacts with street types and land use. Figure 12.19 represents this type of visualization for the city of Surrey. As can be seen in this figure, crime is highest along certain corridors and much lower along others. Crime along these corridors peaks at or near high-activity commercial areas.

Crime corridor analysis using a combination of the street profile graph visualizations and 2.5-dimensional crime-mapping techniques is a way to bring crime onto the environmental backcloth in a visual way with special consideration given to road types and their associated high or low concentrations of activity and awareness spaces. It provides

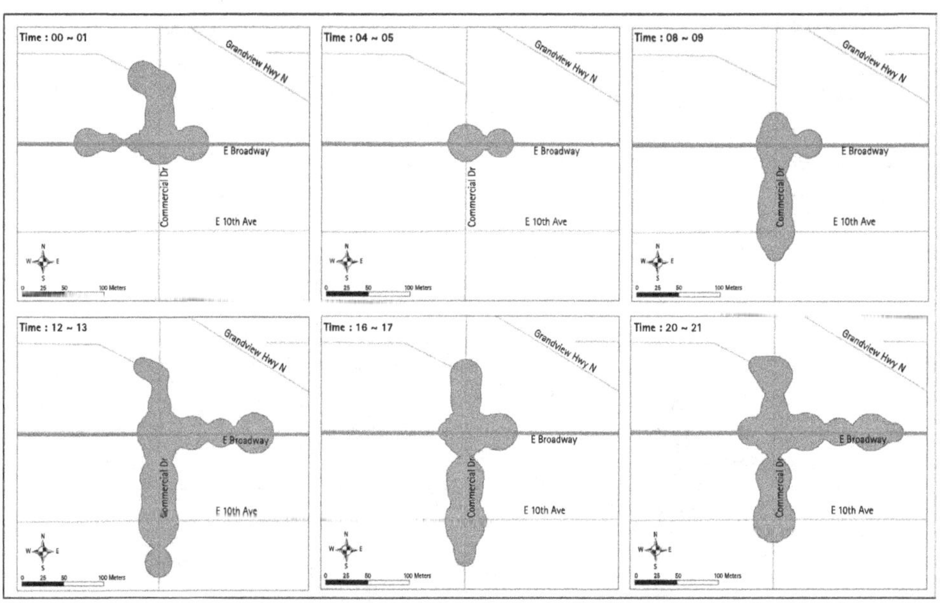

FIGURE 12.18 Temporal directionality at a mass transportation hub

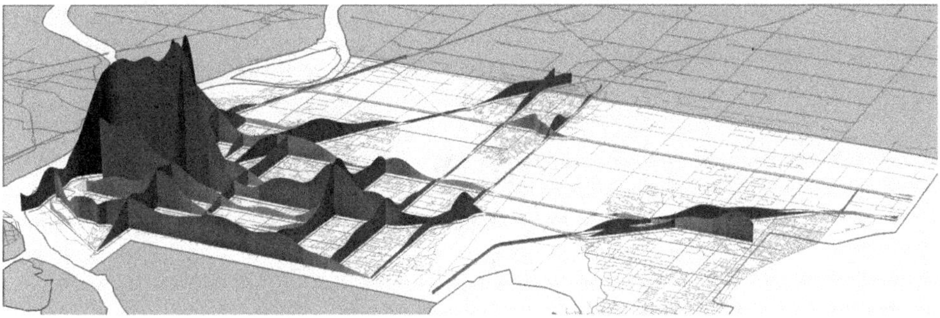

FIGURE 12.19 2.5-dimensional mapping visualization on the street network

the visual means to handle multiple dimensions and have a visual image trigger the memory of certain types of land uses and uses of land as well as differences in traffic volumes. The map identifies physical topography and, if modified, can identify edges as well. Crime corridor visualization presents a static image that provides a way to see the movement and mobility of people. Though a static image, it can begin to trigger a sense of time and the pushes and pulls of a city.

12.6 Additional Crime Patterns on the Environmental Backcloth

The visualization techniques shown in this chapter have additional uses. These uses exceed what is possible to discuss in a single chapter, but are worth mentioning. From an information perspective and using Big Data, it is possible to explore individual as well as aggregate patterns and co-offending patterns (Andresen and Felson, 2010, 2012) and particularly gang activity (Brantingham et al., 2012). The tools shown here can show how activity space expands as a gang grows in size; or the impact on a crime attractor with intervention strategies of the introduction of an additional potential crime attractor with overlapping catchment areas.

Near repeat analysis (Bowers and Johnson, 2004; Townsley et al., 2003) also becomes visually clearer when explored at many scales of aggregation. When repeat offenders are linked, it is possible to visualize the proportion of near repeats that are the result of returning repeat offenders and the proportion that may be co-offenders attracted to the same place. In particular, with the use of edges to neighborhoods, it is possible to visualize the distance of the push-pull of edges and the likelihood that offending in the interior of neighborhoods will be restricted to residents or associates of residents.

Visualizing the environmental backcloth is important when analyzing crime because simulations can show where people are moving (Felson & Boivin, 2015), being attracted to activity nodes, or moving about on a street network (Davies and Johnson, 2015). There is also value in virtual reality simulations to help explore the reasons for crime choices and fear of crime (Park et al., 2008).

12.7 Future of Visualization in Environmental Criminology

There is an important future for scientific visualization in environmental criminology. This becomes even more essential as we move into more action and interaction on the Internet. There is long tradition in criminology that uses the Euclidean concept of distance, but current patterns of human interaction and probable future interaction patterns require a more advanced, nonmetric sense of distance and a greater reliance on linkages and aspatial adjacency. As Cohen and Felson (1979) demonstrated, the change in the routine activities occasioned by the entry of women into the workforce in accelerating numbers had implications for the location and timing of many property crimes, so the changes in routine activities being pushed by the Internet are bound to change the patterns in crime. Graph theory as modeled through *graphs* (objects connected by vertices and nodes) and *hypergraphs* (subsets of graphs that connect through the edges) will become more important to our understanding of crime (Brantingham and Brantingham, 2015; Bichler and Malm, 2015; Davies and Johnson, 2015; Tayebi et al., 2014; Brantingham et al., 2012), and these usually require visualization to convey research results as well as concepts.

In this complex environment, research will continue to increase the use of simulated environments for visualizing crime patterns and conducting crime reduction experiments (Groff, 2007; Groff & Birks, 2008; Birks & Townsley, 2013; Birks, Townsley, & Stewart, 2012, 2013; Malleson and Brantingham, 2009; Malleson and Evans, 2013; Malleson, Evans, & Jenkins, 2009). By the time of the second edition of this Handbook, there are bound to be color images and visualizations using animation to capture four-dimensional patterns in associated online resources. As well, there will be an increased use of visual images where if you zoom in on a location you will be able to see other types of media: a 21st-century version of the text diaries and simple maps of Booth (1891) in his walks around London with constables, but providing much more effective communications of findings.

References

Alexander, C. (1965a). "A city is not a tree, part I." *Architectural Forum* 122(1): 58–62.

Alexander, C. (1965b). "A city is not a tree, part II." *Architectural Forum* 122(2): 58–62.

Anas A., Arnott R., and Small, K. A. (1998). "Urban spatial structure." *Journal of Economic Literature* 36: 1426–1464.

Andresen, M. A., and Felson, M. (2010). "The impact of co-offending." *British Journal of Criminology* 50(1): 66–81. doi:10.1093/bjc/azp043.

Andresen, M. A., and Felson, M. (2012). "Co-offending and the diversification of crime types." *International Journal of Offender Therapy and Comparative Criminology* 56(5): 811–829.

Angel, S. (1968). Discouraging crime through city planning. Working Paper No. 75, Center for Planning and Development Research, Berkeley, CA.

Baldwin, J., and Bottoms, A. E. (1976). *The Urban Criminal: A Study in Sheffield*. London: Tavistock Publications.

Barthélemy, M., and Flammini, A. (2008). "Modeling urban street patterns." *Physical Review Letters* 100 138702.

Batty, M. (2005). *Cities and Complexity: Understanding Cities with Cellular Automata, Agent-Based Models, and Fractals*. Cambridge, MA: MIT Press.

Batty, M. (2009). "Cities as Complex systems: Scaling, interaction, networks, dynamics and urban morphologies." In *The Encyclopedia of Complexity and System Science*, edited by R. A. Meyers. Berlin: Springer.

Beavon, D. J. K., Brantingham, P. L., and Brantingham, P. J. (1994). "The influence of street networks on the patterning of property offenses." In *Crime Prevention Studies*, vol. 2, edited by R. V. Clarke, pp. 115–148. Monsey, NY: Criminal Justice Press.

Bernasco, W. (2006). "Co-offending and the choice of target areas in burglary." *Journal of Investigative Psychology and Offender Profiling* 3(3): 139–155.

Bernasco, W., Johnson, S. D., and Ruiter, S. (2015). "Learning where to offend: Effects of past on future burglary locations." *Applied Geography* 60: 120–129.

Bernasco, W., and Nieuwbeerta, P. (2005). "How do residential burglars select target areas? A new approach to the analysis of criminal location choice." *British Journal of Criminology* 45(3): 296–315.

Bichler, G., and Malm, A. E. (2015). *Disrupting Criminal Networks: Network Analysis in Crime Prevention*. Boulder, CO: First Forum Press.

Birks, D., & Townsley, M. (2013). "Making crime simulation richer: Eight steps on the path to criminology's computational enlightenment". In *Eenvoud en verscheidenheid Liber amicorum voor Henk Elffers* (pp. 477–490). Amsterdam, Netherlands: NSCR.

Birks, D. J., Townsley, M., and Stewart, A. (2012). "Generative explanations of crime: Using simulation to test criminological theory." *Criminology* 50(1): 221–254.

Birks, D. J., Townsley, M., and Stewart, A. (2013). "Emergent patterns of interpersonal victimization: An agent-based approach." *Journal of Research in Crime and Delinquency*. Online first doi: 10.1177/0022427813487353.

Block, R. L., and Block, C. R. (1995). "Space, place and crime: Hot spot areas and hot places of liquor-related crime." In *Crime Prevention Studies*, vol. 4, *Crime and Place*, edited by J. E. Eck and D. Weisburd, pp. 145–184. Monsey, NY: Criminal Justice Press.

Block, R. L., and Davis, S. (1996). "The environs of rapid transit stations: A focus for street crime or just another risky place?" *Crime Prevention Studies*, vol. 6, *Preventing Mass Transit Crime*, ed. R. V. Clarke, pp. 237–257. Monsey, NY: Criminal Justice Press.

Booth, C. (1891). *Life and Labour of the People in London*. Vol. 1. London: Macmillan.

Bottoms, A. E. (1994). "Environmental Criminology." In *The Oxford Handbook of Criminology*, edited by M. Maguire, R. Morgan, and R. Reiner, pp. 585–656. Oxford: Clarendon Press.

Bourbaki, N. (1966). *Elements of Mathematics: General Topology*. Reading: Addison-Wesley.

Bowers, K. J., and Johnson, S. D. (2004). "Who commits near repeats? A test of the boost explanation." *Western Criminology Review* 5(3): 12–24.

Brantingham, P. J., and Brantingham, P. L. (1975a). "The spatial patterning of burglary." *Howard Journal of Penology and Crime Prevention* (14): 11–42.

Brantingham, P. J., and Brantingham, P. L. (1978). "A theoretical model of crime site selection." In *Crime, Law and Sanctions*, edited by M. D. Krohn and R. L. Akers, pp. 105–118. Beverly Hills, CA: Sage.

Brantingham, P. J., and Brantingham, P. L. (1977). "Housing patterns and burglary in a medium-sized American city." In *Criminal Justice Planning*, edited by J. Scott and S. Dinitz, pp. 63–74. New York: Praeger.

Brantingham, P. J., and Brantingham, P. L. (1981). *Environmental Criminology*. Beverly Hills, CA: Sage.

Brantingham, P. J., and Brantingham, P. L. (1984). *Patterns in Crime*. New York: Macmillan.

Brantingham P. J., Dyreson, D. A., and Brantingham, P. L. (1976). "Crime seen through a cone of resolution." *American Behavioral Scientist* 20: 261–273.

Brantingham, P. J., and Jeffery, C. R. (1981). "Afterword: Crime, space, and criminological theory." In *Environmental Criminology*, edited by P. J. Brantingham and P. L. Brantingham, pp. 227–238. Beverly Hills, CA: Sage.

Brantingham, P. L., and Brantingham, P. J. (1975b). "Residential burglary and urban form." *Urban Studies* 12: 273–284.

Brantingham, P. L., and Brantingham, P. J. (1981). "Notes on the geometry of crime." In *Environmental Criminology*, edited by P. J. Brantingham and P. L. Brantingham, pp. 27–54. Beverly Hills, CA: Sage.

Brantingham, P. L., and Brantingham, P. J. (2015). "Understanding crime with computational topology." In *The Criminal Act: The Role and Influence of Routine Activity Theory*, edited by M. A. Andresen and G. Farrell, pp. 131–145. New York: Palgrave Macmillan.

Brantingham P. L., Brantingham, P. J., Glässer U., and Tayebi, M. A. (2012). *An Analysis of RCMP "E" Division Data to Estimate Possible Criminal Organizations: Final Descriptive Report*. Ottawa: Public Safety Canada.

Brantingham, P. L., Brantingham, P. J., and Wong, P. (1991). "How public transit feeds private crime: Notes on the Vancouver 'Skytrain' experience." *Security Journal* 2: 91–95.

Brantingham P. L., Wuschke, K., Frank, R., and Brantingham, P. J. (2012). "Crime emergence and simulation modeling: Modeling crime space." In *When Crime Appears: The Role of Emergence*, edited by J. M. McGloin, C. Sullivan, and L. Kennedy, pp. 198–224. New York: Routledge.

Brunswik, E. (1952). *The Conceptual Framework of Psychology*. Chicago: University of Chicago Press.

Buckley, J. B. (1996). "Public transit and crime: A routine activities/ecological approach." Master's thesis, Simon Fraser University.

Bullock, H. A. (1955). "Urban homicide in theory and fact." *Journal of Criminal Law, Criminology and Police Science* 45: 565–575.

Burgess, E. W. (1925a). "The Growth of the City." In *The City*, edited by R. E. Park, E. W. Burgess, and R. D. McKenzie, pp. 47–62. Chicago: University of Chicago Press.

Burgess, E. W. (1925b). "Can neighborhood work have a scientific basis?" In *The City*, edited by R. E. Park, E. W. Burgess, and R. D. McKenzie, 142–155. Chicago: University of Chicago Press.

Cao, F., Ester, M., Qian, W., and Zhou, A. (2006). "Density-based clustering over an evolving data stream with noise." In *Proceedings of the Sixth SIAM International Conference on Data Mining*, edited by J. Ghosh, D. Lambert, D. Skillicorn, and J. Srivastava, pp. 328–339. Philadelphia, PA: Society for Industrial and Applied Mathematics.

Capone, D., and Nichols, W. (1976). "Urban structure and criminal mobility." *American Behavioral Scientist* 20: 199–201.

Chapin, F. S. (1974) Human Activity Patterns in the City: Things People Do in Time and Space. New York: Wiley.

Clare, J., Fernandez, J., and Morgan, F. (2009). "Formal evaluation of the impact of barriers and connectors on residential burglars' macro-level offending location choices." *Australian and New Zealand Journal of Criminology* 42(2): 139–158.

Clarke, R. V. G. (1980). "Situational crime prevention: Theory and practice." *British Journal of Criminology* 20: 136–147.

Cohen, L. E., and Felson, M. (1979). "Social change and crime rate trends: A routine activity approach." *American Sociological Review* 44: 588–608.

Conzen, M. R. G. (1960). *Alnwick, Northumberland: A Study in Town Plan Analysis.* London: Institute of British Geographers. 2nd ed., 1969.

Curman, A. S. N., Andresen, M. A., and Brantingham, P. J. (2015). "Crime and place: A longitudinal examination of street segment patterns in Vancouver, BC." *Journal of Quantitative Criminology.* 31: 127–147.

Davies, T., and Johnson, S. D. (2015). "Examining the relationship between road structure and burglary risk via quantitative network analysis." *Journal of Quantitative Criminology* 31: 481–507.

DeFleur, L. B. (1967). "Ecological variables in the cross-cultural study of delinquency." *Social Forces* 45: 556–570.

De Poot, C., Luykx, F., Elffers, H., and Dudink, C. (2005). "Hier wonen en daar plegen? Sociale grenzen en locatiekeuze" [Living here, offending there? On social boundaries and location choice]. *Tijdschrift voor Criminologie* 47(3): 255–268.

Eck, J. E., Clarke, R. V., and R. T. Guerette. (2007). "Risky facilities: Crime concentration in homogeneous sets of establishments and facilities." In *Imagination for Crime Prevention: Essays in Honor of Ken Pease*, edited by G. Farrell, K. Bowers, S. D. Johnson, and M. Townsley, pp. 225–264. Monsey, NY: Criminal Justice Press.

Engstad, P. A. (1975). "Environmental opportunities and the ecology of Crime." In *Crime in Canadian Society*, edited by R. A. Silverman and J. J. Teevan, pp. 193–211. Toronto: Butterworths.

Felson, M., and Boivin, R. (2015). "Daily crime flows within a city." *Crime Science* 4(1): 1–10.

Frank, R., Andresen, M. A., and Brantingham, P. L. (2013). "Visualizing the directional bias in property crime incidents for five Canadian municipalities." *Canadian Geographer* 57(1): 31–42.

Frank, R., Andresen, M. A., and Brantingham, P. L. (2012). "Criminal directionality and the structure of urban form." *Journal of Environmental Psychology* 32(1): 37–42.

Frank, R., Andresen, M. A., and Felson, M. (2012). "The geodiversity of crime: Evidence from British Columbia." *Applied Geography* 34: 180–188.

Frank, R., Park, A. J., Brantingham, P. L., Clare, J., Wuschke, K., & Vajihollahi, M. (2010). "Identifying high risk crime areas using topology." In C. C. Yang, D. Zeng, K. Wang, A. Sanfillippo, H. H. Tsang, M-Y. Day, U. Glasser, P. L. Brantingham, H. Chen (Eds.), *Proceedings of the 2010 IEEE International Conference on Intelligence and Security Informatics.* (Vancouver ed., Vol. 10.1109/ISI.2010.5484782, pp. 13–18). Vancouver, BC Canada: CPS/Elsevier

Groff, E. R. (2007). "Simulation for theory testing and experimentation: An example using routine activity theory and street robbery." *Journal of Quantitative Criminology* (23): 75–103.

Groff, E. R., and Birks, D. (2008). "Simulating crime prevention strategies: A look at the possibilities." *Policing: A Journal of Policy and Practice* 2 (2): 175–184.

Groff, E. R., Weisburd, D., and Yang, S.-M. (2010). "Is it important to examine crime trends at a local 'micro' level? A longitudinal analysis of block to block variability in crime trajectories." *Journal of Quantitative Criminology* 26: 7–32.

Guerry, A.-M. (1833). *Essai sur la statistique morale de la France*. Paris: Crochard.

Guerry, A.-M. (1864). *Statistique morale de l'Angleterre comparée avec la statistique morale de la France, d'après les comptes de l'administration de la justice criminelle en Angleterre et en France, etc.* Paris: J.-B. Baillière et fils.

Halpern, I. W., Stanislas, J. W., and Botein, B. (1934). *The Slum and Crime: A Statistical Study of the Distribution of Adult and Juvenile Delinquents in the Boroughs of Manhattan and Brooklyn, New York*. New York: New York City Housing Authority.

Harries, K. D. (1971). "The geography of American crime, 1968." *Journal of Geography* 70: 204–213.

Harries, K. D. (1976). "Cities and crime: A geographical model." *Criminology* 14: 369–386.

Herbert, D. T. (1977). "An areal and ecological analysis of delinquency residence: Cardiff 1966 and 1971." *Tijdschrift voor Economische en Sociale Geografie* 68: 83–99.

Hillier, B., and Hanson, J. (1984). *The Social Logic of Space*, Cambridge: Cambridge University Press.

Jarvis, G. K. (1972). "The ecological analysis of juvenile delinquency in a Canadian city." In *Deviant Behavior and Societal Reaction*, edited by C. L. Boydell, C. F. Grindstaff, and P. C. Whitehead, pp. 195–211. Toronto: Holt, Rinehart and Winston.

Jeffery, C. R. (1971). *Crime Prevention through Environmental Design*. Beverly Hills, CA: Sage.

Johnson, S. D., and Bowers, K. J. (2010). "Permeability and burglary risk: Are cul-de-sacs safer?" *Journal of Quantitative Criminology* 26: 89–111.

Kinney, J. B., Brantingham, P. L., Wuschke, K., Kirk, M. G., and Brantingham, P. J. (2008). "Crime attractors, generators and detractors: Land use and urban crime opportunities." *Built Environment* 34(1): 62–74.

Lander, B. (1954). *Towards an Understanding of Juvenile Delinquency*. New York: Columbia University Press.

Lynch, K. (1960). *The Image of the City*. Cambridge, MA: MIT Press.

Malleson, N., and Brantingham, P. L. (2009). "Prototype burglary simulations for crime reduction and forecasting." *Crime Patterns and Analysis* 2(1): 47–66.

Malleson, N., and Evans, A. (2013). "Agent-based models to predict crime at places." In *Encyclopedia of Criminology and Criminal Justice*, edited by G. J. N. Bruinsma and D. Weisburd, pp. 41–48. New York: Springer.

Malleson, N., Evans, A., and Jenkins, T. (2009). "An agent-based model of burglary." *Environment and Planning B: Planning and Design* 36: 1103–1123.

Mannheim, H. (1948). *Juvenile Delinquency in an English Middletown*. London: Kegan Paul, Trubner, Trench.

Mannheim, H. (1965). *Comparative Criminology: A Text Book*. 2 vols. London: Routledge & Kegan Paul.

Mayhew, H. (1950 [1861–62]). *London's underworld: Being selections from "Those that will not work"*. Vol. 4. of *London labour and the London poor*. Edited by P. Quennell. London: Spring Books.

McCord, E. S., Ratcliffe, J. H., Garcia, R. M., and Taylor, R. B. (2007). "Nonresidential crime attractors and generators elevate perceived neighborhood crime and incivilities." *Journal of Research in Crime and Delinquency* 44(3): 295–320.

Morris, T. (1958). *The Criminal Area: A Study in Social Ecology*. London: Routledge and Kegan Paul.

Newman, O. (1972). *Defensible Space: Crime Prevention through Urban Design*. New York: Macmillan.

Park, R. E., Burgess, E. W., and McKenzie, R. D. (1925). Chicago: University of Chicago Press.

Park, A. J., Calvert, T., Brantingham, P. L., and Brantingham, P. J. (2008). "The use of virtual and mixed reality environments for urban behavioural studies." *PsychNology* 6(2): 119–130.

Park, A. J., Tsang, H. H., and Brantingham, P. L. (2012). "Dynalink: A Framework for Dynamic Criminal Network Visualization." In *Proceedings of the European Intelligence and Security Informatics Conference, 2012*, pp. 217–224.

Piaget, J. (1970 [1968]). *Structuralism*. Translated and edited by C. Maschler. New York: Basic Books.

Pyle, G. F. (1974). "The spatial dynamics of crime." Research Paper No. 159. Department of Geography, University of Chicago.

Pyle, G. F. (1976). "Spatial aspects of crime in Cleveland, Ohio." *American Behavioral Scientist* 20: 175–198.

Quételet, L. A. J. (1842). *A Treatise on Man and the Development of His Faculties*. Edinburgh: W. and R. Chambers.

Rand, A. (1986). "Mobility Triangles." In *Metropolitan Crime Patterns*, edited by R. M. Figlio, S. Hakim, and G. F. Rengert, pp. 117–126. Monsey, NY: Criminal Justice Press.

Reckless, W. C. (1933). *Vice in Chicago*. Chicago: University of Chicago Press.

Rengert, G. F. (1972). "Spatial aspects of criminal behavior: A suggested approach." Paper presented to the Annual Meeting of the East Lakes Division, Association of American Geographers.

Rengert, G. F. (1975). "Journey to crime: An empirical analysis of spatially constrained female mobility." Paper presented to the Annual Meeting of the Association of American Geographers, Milwaukee.

Reynald, D., Averdijk, M., Elffers, H., and Bernasco, W. (2008). "Do social barriers affect urban crime trips? The effects of ethnic and economic neighbourhood compositions on the flow of crime in The Hague, the Netherlands." *Built Environment* 34(1): 21–31.

Robinson, W. S. (1950). "Ecological correlations and the behavior of individuals." *American Sociological Review* 15: 351–357.

Scarr, H. A. (1973). *Patterns in Burglary*. 2nd ed. Washington, DC: US Department of Justice.

Schmid, C. F. (1960a). "Urban crime areas, Part I." *American Sociological Review* 25: 527–543.

Schmid, C. F. (1960b). "Urban crime areas, Part II." *American Sociological Review* 25: 655–678.

Shaw, C. R., and McKay, H. D. (1931). *Social Factors in Juvenile Delinquency*. National Commission on Law Observance and Enforcement, Report on the Causes of Crime, Vol. 2. Washington, DC: Government Printing Office.

Shaw, C. R., Zorbaugh, F. M., McKay, H. D., and Cottrell, L. S. (1929). *Delinquency Areas: A Study of the Geographic Distribution of School Truants, Juvenile Delinquents, and Adult Offenders in Chicago*. Chicago: University of Chicago Press.

Shellow, R., Romualdi, J. P., and Bartel, E. W. (1974). "Crime in rapid transit systems: An analysis and a recommended security and surveillance system." *Transportation Research Record* 487: 1–12.

Song, J., Andresen, M. A., Brantingham, P. L., and Spicer, V. (2017). "Crime on the edges: Patterns of crime and land use change." *Cartography and Geographic Information Science*. 44 (1): 51–61.

Song, J., Spicer, V., and Brantingham, P. L. (2013). "The edge effect: Exploring high crime zones near residential neighborhoods." In *2013 IEEE International Conference on Intelligence and Security Informatics*, pp. 245–250. Seattle, Washington: IEEE.

Song J., Spicer, V., Brantingham, P. L., and Frank, R. (2013). "Crime ridges: Exploring the relationship between crime attractors and offender movement." In *2013 European Intelligence and Security Informatics Conference*, pp. 75–82. Uppsala, Sweden: IEEE.

Strano, E., Cardeillo, A., Porta, S., and Latora, V. (2013). "Urban street networks: A comparative analysis of ten European cities." *Environment and Planning B: Planning and Design* 40 (6): 1071–1086.

Summers, L., and Johnson, S. D (2015). "Using Space Syntax to inform crime prevention." In *Disrupting Criminal Networks: Network Analysis in Crime Prevention*, edited by G. Bichler and A. E. Malm, pp. 209–232. Boulder, CO: First Forum Press.

Sutherland, E. H. (1947). *Principles of Criminology.* 4th ed. Philadelphia, PA: Lippincott.

Tayebi, M., Ester, M., Glässer, U., and Brantingham, P. L. (2014). "Spatially embedded co-offence prediction using supervised learning." In *KDD 2014 Proceedings of the 20th ACD SIGKDD International conference on Knowledge and Data Mining*, pp. 1789–1798. New York, NY: Association for Computing Machinery (ACM).

Townsley, M., Homel, R., and Chaseling, J. (2003). "Infectious burglaries: A test of the near repeat hypothesis." *British Journal of Criminology* 43: 615–633.

Vold, G. (1950). *Theoretical Criminology*. New York: Oxford University Press.

Wuschke, K. (2016). "Planning for crime: Exploring the connections between urban space, development, and patterns of crime." PhD dissertation, Simon Fraser University.

CHAPTER 13

VICTIMIZATION SURVEYS IN ENVIRONMENTAL CRIMINOLOGY

ANDROMACHI TSELONI, NICK TILLEY, AND GRAHAM FARRELL

13.1 Introduction

Environmental criminologists have to make the best of more or less dodgy data that have generally been collected for purposes other than developing and testing relevant theory. Different data sets have different strengths and weaknesses. The most commonly used data on crime derive from police sources, but victimization surveys, the focus of this chapter, have also been used. National victimization surveys have existed since the 1970s. Examples of the earliest, most prominent, and analyzed ones include the National Crime Victimization Survey (NCVS) since 1976 in the United States, and the British Crime Survey (BCS) since 1982 in the UK. To our knowledge, the youngest national victimization survey in Europe is the Cadre de Vie et Sécurité (CVS) (Outline of life and security) since 2007 in France. Major national victimization surveys are being undertaken in other countries also. For example, Mexico has had a national household victimization survey since at least 2010, with a sample size of over 95,000 in 2014. Chile's national household victimization survey goes back further, to 2003. The above surveys aim to capture individuals' and households' crime experiences, attitudes, and perceptions. Others, such as the Commercial Victimization Survey (CVS) in the UK, focus on crime and security experienced by businesses. For a detailed account of the information provided in the BCS/CSEW (Crime Survey for England and Wales, the name of the BCS since 2012) please see Tilley and Tseloni (2016).

Police sources and victimization surveys do not, of course, exhaust the possibilities. Observational data, probation service data, photographic evidence, hospital and ambulance records, fire service data, business records, rubbish collection data, cleaning data, and so on, may all be used. And all have their shortcomings. This chapter's focus is on the uses and limitations specifically of victimization survey data. Some comparisons will be made with police data, in particular, given that both are widely drawn on for a variety of purposes and both have been used to estimate distributions and trends of a wide variety of crime types and to throw light on hypotheses that might explain those distributions and changes.

This chapter will give examples from the authors' work of ways in which victimization surveys have been used in environmental criminology to identify spatial distributions of crime and to test and refine hypotheses that speak to these distributions.

It needs to be made clear from the start that there are nonspatial patterns to crime events that form important parts of the broader field of environmental criminology to which much of our research has related but are not dealt with here. These patterns relate, in particular, to target-related crime concentrations, for example, those associated with vehicles. Much of our collaborative work has examined in detail ways in which victimization surveys help understand how and why crime has concentrated on insecure vehicles and how rates of vehicle theft have changed over time in response to the proliferation of security improvements (see Farrell et al. 2011; Farrell, Tseloni, and Tilley 2011).

Here, though, in accordance with our invitation to contribute to this volume, we focus on the contributions victimization surveys can make to understanding spatial distributions of crimes. Our focus is more particularly on how victimization surveys may throw light on ways in which individual activity patterns relevant to spatial distribution of crime may be illuminated with the use of victimization surveys. It may again be worth reminding the reader that some sources of spatial distribution may be little related to individual activity patterns but may relate instead to the accessibility and attractiveness of the potential target regardless of activities by potential victims, offenders, guardians, or handlers. Again some of our previous work has spoken to sources of spatial patterns that do not invoke individual activity patterns, but instead features of potential targets. Much of our work on domestic burglary patterns and trends is relevant here (see Tilley et al. 2011; Tilley et al. 2015; Tseloni et al. 2017).

The next section of our chapter makes some initial remarks on the variations in victimization surveys, which clearly affect what can be concluded from them with what confidence about differing forms of spatial contribution.

13.2 Victimization Surveys

National victimization surveys were established to throw light on the "dark figure" of crime and also to gauge the public's attitudes to crime and to criminal justice. Not all crimes are reported and of those reported not all are recorded. Moreover, the mismatch between crimes actually occurring and crimes recorded varies by place, time, and crime type. Victimization surveys were established to provide a more accurate fix on crime patterns and trends than is possible with recorded crime data.

Victimization surveys were not initiated to inform environmental criminology. Indeed in a volume marking the 25th anniversary of the first British Crime Survey, which also refers to other victimization surveys, attention to their relevance to environmental criminology is quite sparse (Hough and Maxfield 2007). There is, for example, only one cited reference to the Brantinghams, and that relates to fear of crime rather than to their work on crime patterns and their sources (Ditton and Farrall 2007, p. 224).

Victimization surveys vary widely, and their attributes clearly influence the contribution they can make to environmental criminology and in particular what they can tell us about the spatial distribution of crimes. Here are some key differences.

- Surveys can target different victim populations, for example, young people, adults, households, and businesses and hence contribute to identifying the distribution of the kinds of crime affecting each of them.
- Surveys can be pitched at an international, national, or neighborhood level and can speak to spatial distributions across varying geographic resolutions.
- Surveys can be one-off exercises, include regular sweeps of cross sections of the target population, or include panels asked more than once about their crime experiences, all of which influence what can be learned about changing distributions of crimes.
- Victimization surveys collect different data, and clearly the nature of the questions asked influences what can be concluded about the distribution of incidents.
- Victimization surveys can be conducted face to face or by telephone or by post or by Internet or be computer assisted, which both influence response rates and hence risks of bias in the findings and also the possibility of fieldworkers collecting ancillary observational data as they administer the questionnaire.
- Sample sizes vary widely affecting the level at which statistically significant variations in crime rate can be identified by any spatial indicators used.
- Sampling frames and sampling techniques vary across victimization surveys.
- Techniques for trying to ensure that all incidents are recalled that fall within the reference period vary.
- Victimization surveys are conducted by different bodies with different purposes, which influence the quality of the data, the questions asked, and the scope there may be for environmental criminologists to influence the questions asked.
- The coding practices used in victimization surveys vary, influencing the forms of analysis that then become possible for the environmental criminologist interested in crime distribution.

13.3 Examples of the Use of Victimization Surveys in Environmental Criminology

This chapter will provide three examples showing how national victimization surveys have been used to develop, test, and refine hypotheses drawn from environmental criminology that relate to spatial distributions of various crimes, which link back to individual activity patterns.

13.3.1 Number of Victimizations and Routine Activities

National victimization surveys have routinely been analyzed for testing the lifestyle and routine activities theory (RAT), which was developed around the same time as the NCVS (Hindeland, Gottfredson, and Garofalo 1978; Cohen and Felson 1979). Such tests rely on information collected by the interviewers that pertains to both direct and indirect measurements of crime exposure. Direct measurements include information about respondents' and their households' activities away from home. Sociodemographic and economic attributes of respondents, such as gender, marital status, or number of cars in the household, and other survey-derived data are routine activities proxies. For example, Osborn and Tseloni (1998) used the number of calls the interviewer had to make until successfully contacting the respondent as a proxy for time the house is left empty or time away from home. This section reviews some of our work testing RAT.

Tseloni and Pease showed that using public transport at any rate in the United States, spending evenings out daily, and/or going shopping daily—particularly, if the daily shopper is male or single—exposes North Americans to significantly more personal crimes than when they do not undertake these activities (Tseloni 2000; Tseloni and Pease 2004). Similarly, English and Welsh frequent pubgoers (three or more times per week and, especially, those living with children) and regular (at least once per week) clubgoers, particularly males, suffer roughly twice as many personal crimes as those visiting pubs and clubs less often (Tseloni and Pease 2015).

The previous evidence derived from similar statistical analyses of two national victimization surveys, the 1994 NCVS in the United States and the 2000 BCS in England and Wales. As perhaps noticed, survey indicators of respondents' lifestyle and routine activities differ between the two data sets. This discordance is to a certain extent expected and reflects cultural and lifestyle variations even between two countries so similar with regards to language, prevailing ethnic group and culture, and linked history. What is arguably unexpected is that, despite these theoretical concepts' operationalization dissimilarities, the above findings agree in providing qualified rather than full support to the lifestyle and routine activities theory.

As discussed in this and the following paragraphs, the NCVS and the BCS differ in many more ways than just their lifestyle and routine activities indicators. Tseloni et al. (2004) draw on data from victimization surveys in England and Wales (the 1994 sweep of the BCS), in the United States (the 1994 sweep of the NCVS), and in the Netherlands (the 1993 sweep of the PM) to test cross-nationally hypotheses relating to burglary incidence variations drawn from routine activities and lifestyle theory.

The sample size and methods used in the surveys differed. The 1993 PM sample was 50,704 individuals aged 15 or over, drawn from the sampling frame of national telephone numbers, and the questionnaire was administered using computer-assisted telephone interviewing, or CATI. The 1994 BCS sample consisted of 14,520 respondents aged 16 or over, drawn from the postcode address file (sampling frame), while the questionnaire was administered using computer-assisted personal interviewing, or CAPI. The 1994 NCVS uses a rotating panel design of those aged 16 and over, with addresses drawn from the address list of the decennial census, using alternately face-to-face interviews and CATI for administering the questionnaires. Likewise, the data collected from the surveys varied across the three countries, as did the methods to select individual respondent from the household (nearest birthday for PM, selection tables for the BCS, and, to answer questions for household crime, apparently most knowledgeable household member at least 18 years old for the NCVS).

Tseloni et al. abstract from the three victimization surveys those coded responses to questions that would predict differences in vulnerability to domestic burglary on the basis of lifestyle and routine activity theory. They focus not only on variations in prevalence (risk of being a victim over the reference period), but also variations in incidence, to include risks of repeat incidents over the reference period. The four risk factors they took from routine activities theory included "target exposure, absence of capable guardianship, attractiveness and proximity to potential offenders" (Tseloni et al. 2004, p. 73). Each was operationalized using victimization survey data, as shown in Table 13.1, with adjustments made for the different questions asked in each of the three victimization surveys.

In their analysis Tseloni et al. produce negative binomial models of burglary rates for each country. For the most part the findings accord with what would be expected from routine activities theory in the sense that they help explain risk variations. A recent work that examines equity and justice in relation to the crime drop found that households that leave their home empty for three to five hours on a weekday have experienced lower than national levels of burglary falls between 1993 and 2008/2009 (Hunter and Tseloni 2016).

Table 13.1 Routine Activity Theory Victimization Survey Indicators

Element of routine activity theory	Indicator	Variable
Target exposure	Residence type	Detached/semidetached Terraced/row Flat/apartment Other
Social guardianship/ occupancy	Household composition	Number of adults in household Includes children Lone adult
	Marital status	Married Divorced Separated Widowed Single
	Employment status	Full time Part time Homemaker Retired Sick/disabled Unemployed
Social guardianship	Lifestyle indicators	Hours house left empty Evenings out per week Time shopping
Physical guardianship	Physical security	Participation in neighbourhood watch Presence of security measures (including locks, lights on when house empty, lights on timer/external lights, burglar alarm/dog)
Target attractiveness	Income	Average income High income Low income
	Most recent educational level	Primary school Middle school High school University degree
	Cars	None One Two Three Four of more
Proximity to potential offenders	Type of area	Urban Nonurban Level of urbanization
	Population	Population of area of residence

13.3.2 Travel to Victimization Patterns

Crime pattern theory has focused mainly on offender routines and their associated awareness spaces to explain crime patterns (for an overview please see Chapter 16 by Wim Bernasco in this volume). This has led to a fairly substantial literature on offender travel-to-crime-commission patterns (see Hodgkinson and Tilley 2007 for a review of this). Complementing this, Hodgkinson and Tilley focus on travel-to-victimization patterns. They conjecture that risks of personal crimes are liable to increase at the intersection of offender awareness spaces and victim unawareness spaces. Those who are in unfamiliar surroundings will be less sensitive to the crime risks they face and hence more vulnerable than in areas that they frequent routinely. The high risks of theft faced by tourists accord with this.

Hodgkinson and Tilley took the 2002–2003 sweep of the British Crime Survey to provide a partial test of this hypothesis. The British Crime Survey asked victims two questions that speak to this hypothesis: first, whether the offense occurred within or outside England and Wales and second, whether victims were within or beyond 15-minute walk from their homes at the time of the incident. Hodgkinson and Tilley found that of the 4,240 incidents that occurred beyond a 15-minute walk from the respondent's home, 4 percent took place outside England and Wales.[1] The proportion of all incidents occurring beyond 15-minute walk from the respondent's home varied widely by crime type, as shown in Table 13.2.

Unsurprisingly only small percentages of household and burglary theft occurred beyond a 15-minute walk from the victim's home. These presumably relate, for example, to second homes that have been burgled. What is interesting is the preponderance of acquisitive personal crimes that occur at a distance from home. Although the victim may be familiar with the area (for example, if it is close to an activity node or route between nodes), distance from home is used as a rough indicator or probability of unawareness of crime risk. The pattern of victimization accords with expectations. Of course, absent controls for other differences of those victimized that might be associated both with higher risks of personal crime and being beyond a 15-minute walk from home (for example, age) and absent any measure of proportions of time spent within and beyond the 15-minute walk from home, these findings are at best suggestive. They do, however, accord with theoretical expectations of spatial distributions of victimization risks and also accord with findings for the crime risks encountered by tourists.

13.3.3 Place and Crime

Environmental criminology is equally concerned with individuals' routine activities and place characteristics. Influential studies drawing on the early sweeps of the BCS tested the extent of, and criminological theories explaining, area crime differences

Table 13.2 Type of Offense by Whether or Not It Occurs within 15 Minutes of Where the Victim Lives

Type of crime	Total offenses	Percent occurring beyond 15 minutes of where the victim lives
Snatch with stealth (including attempts)	408	72.8
Personal theft (excluding snatch with stealth)	730	70.8
Robbery (including attempts)	157	49.0
Common assault (including attempts)	668	42.8
Wounding (including sexual)	283	41.7
Threats	851	39.1
Theft from vehicles	1,440	32.2
Theft of vehicle	337	28.5
Attempted theft of vehicle	622	25.7
Bike theft	1,384	20.8
Vehicle vandalism	431	20.2
Other vandalism	992	8.3
Burglary in dwelling	864	5.7
Burglary in outhouse	468	4.3
Other household theft	965	3.4

Note: Unweighted data.

(Trickett et al. 1992; Sampson and Wooldredge 1987). These early studies inspired a body of research that seeks to address how area and place characteristics, including neighborhood cohesion, affect the geographical distribution of crime. These have been examined on their own or in conjunction with individuals' routine activities and target attractiveness. Pioneering work on individual and area determinants of crime based on victimization survey data originated roughly at the same period in Canada (Kennedy and Forde 1990) and the United States (Smith and Jarjoura 1988). Examples of this body of research drawing on the BCS are overviewed in this section.

Trickett et al. (1992) analyzed the very first BCS, 1982, and examined the distribution of crime across area deciles in England and Wales. They found that (*a*) crime prevalence (the percentage of victims in the surveyed population) and incidence (the percentage of crimes in the surveyed population) rates vary widely across areas; (*b*) the greatest differences appear to exist with regards to crime incidence rates rather than prevalence rates; and, as a result, (*c*) crime concentration (the mean number of crimes per victim) is distinctively higher (while the number of victims lower) in high-crime areas compared to low-crime areas than would be expected were crime to be randomly distributed. In other words crime rates are disproportionally higher in high-crime areas, with this difference mostly made up by more crimes per victim rather than more victims, that is, a disproportionally higher crime concentration (Trickett et al. 1992).

This analysis was replicated employing the 2000 BCS and more recently all the sweeps between 1982 and 2012/2013 (Kershaw and Tseloni 2005; Ignatans and Pease 2015). The originally found pattern of highly inequitable area crime distribution has persisted during the lifetime (accompanied by a number of methodological changes) of the BCS. If anything, it has become more inequitable after the crime drop both nationally and internationally (Ignatans and Pease 2015, 2016). Enough has been said, however, about crime concentration and issues of distributional justice, which are discussed in detail elsewhere. The study by Trickett et al. (1992) was the first step for developing spatial investigations of crime patterns based on victimization survey data.

How is area defined within survey data? "Area" in victimization surveys is the geocoded sampling point of the survey. In the 1982–1988 BCS these were based on electoral wards and since the 1992 BCS on postcode sectors of roughly 2,000 delivery points. There is, however, considerable variation in the number of selected households and interviews per sampling point. For example, the number of households per sampling point in the 2000 BCS is between 4 and 29 (Tseloni 2006, p. 208). The Trickett et al. (1992) study, therefore, has been criticized for portraying a very rough picture of the crime distribution: it relies on small area observations of crimes that were reported by the sample of respondents in that area. Crime is both rare and concentrated. Therefore, sample-based observed crime rates entail sampling errors, which are particularly large in less populated areas and/or those with high nonresponse (Lynn and Elliot 2000; Kershaw and Tseloni 2005; Osborn, Trickett, and Elder 1992). In fact Lynn and Elliot (2000) suggest that area-level crime inferences based on the BCS have some validity across area quartiles (rather than deciles) according to estimated (rather than observed) crime rates from hierarchical models. But more on this later. Despite this criticism, the study reported by Trickett et al. (1992) was influential and its findings remain consistent across replications.

A natural step forward from Trickett et al. (1992) is to identify the area characteristics that are associated with high crime rates. The theoretical underpinnings of this work directly relate to the Chicago school of social disorganization (Park 1936) and the current strands of environmental criminology (Brantingham and Brantingham 1991) and collective efficacy theory (Sampson 2006). Various data sources have furnished area information for explaining victimization survey-based crime rates:

- Victimization surveys via area aggregated responses, whereby individuals' answers are summed up within each area (Sampson and Wooldredge 1987; Sampson and Groves 1989; Tseloni et al. 2010)
- Local authority and other administrative data, including, for example, health, local economic, and deprivation profiles (Nilsson and Estrada 2007)
- Decennial census data (Osborn, Trickett, and Elder 1992; Kershaw and Tseloni 2005; Tseloni 2007)

- Social surveys as distinct from victimization surveys (Goudriaan, Wittebrood, and Nieuwbeerta 2006)
- Observational data on neighborhoods (Lens 2017)

Data from any of the above sources, except the first, would have to be added to victimization survey data. As already mentioned, surveys have a sample (and retain the geocoded record) of private addresses of the general population. Area characteristics taken from local authority / administrative data, the census, and other social surveys are merged with the victimization survey data via the surveys' unique geocoded sample point. This serves as a common data record across sources. Victimization surveys do not, however, have a geocoded record of the location of any crime incident reported during the interview. Therefore an investigation into area determinants of victimization survey-based crime rates is meaningful only if the victim's address and incident location coincide or are within the same sampling point. This explains why the bulk of this work focusses on property or household crimes (the terms are used interchangeably in the UK), such as burglary, household theft, criminal damage, and their aggregate, including also motor-vehicle theft (of/from) that occurred within a 15-minute walk from the victim's residence. A 15-minute walk rule is also used for examining area or neighborhood effects on personal crimes.

Each source has its own advantages and disadvantages. Local authority, other administrative, and census data tell us about the service infrastructure, overall sociodemographic and perhaps health profile of the resident population, and some statistics on areas' buildings, such as vacant properties. They provide an immensely rich set of factual information free from sampling errors. This is because administrative data refer to the entirety of the resident population and, in some instances, such as school records, the population who routinely visit the area. They fall short, however, of delineating residents' relations with one another, their sense of belonging in the area, or visual clues of area's safety and desirability, such as rubbish and graffiti. Social surveys and observational neighborhood data are best suited to examine these facets of community life and its physical environment.

A growing body of research is concerned with social capital, community cohesion, and collective efficacy, all of which are thought to improve quality of life in general and, among other specific outcomes, reduce crime (Bourdieu 1986; Putnam 1993; Sampson 2006; Sampson, Raudenbush, and Earls 1997). Information, therefore, on social capital measures is collected in social, including victimization, surveys. Indeed, the 1982 BCS had some friendship networks and support information that was readily used to revive, test, and expand the social disorganization theory (Sampson and Wooldredge 1987; Sampson and Groves 1989). Observational data on the physical environment and community relations as observed by outsiders are an additional source of neighborhood characteristics. They have the potential to reflect closely the environmental clues delineated by criminological theory. Both sources, however, have limitations with respect to the amount of information they can offer—they can only inform on what they had originally been designed and, equally important, costed to capture.

Social capital questions have been included sparingly and on an ad hoc basis in the BCS/CSEW. A rough list of these questions over the BCS/CSEW lifetime is given below:

- Do neighbors help each other?
- Would neighbors intervene if graffiti, fighting, or rudeness? / Ask someone to pick up litter.
- Or intervene with misbehavior
- Neighborhood cohesion / Close community / Get on well
- Do neighbors help each other? / Look out for each other?
- Influence on local decisions
- Would neighbors participate if asked to solve local issue?
- Involved in civil action
- Volunteering including for neighbors
- Do you trust neighbors? / Know people? / Would wallet get returned?
- Like living here
- Close friends / Relatives in the area
- Borrow money at short notice
- Find somewhere to stay the night at short notice

Researchers have employed them even more sparingly, if at all (Sampson and Wooldredge 1987; Walby and Allen 2004). It is possible, as mentioned, to aggregate answers to these (or any) questions of victimization surveys within areas in an attempt to tap community effects on crime. When doing so, researchers should keep a number of pitfalls in mind, especially when analyzing aggregate responses alongside individual ones (Osborn, Trickett, and Elder 1992):

(a) Sample aggregates within areas do not represent the area population unless appropriate weights are in place; therefore the estimated, especially unweighted, area effects thus produced are biased.[2]

(b) From the above it follows that census or local authority / administrative data on population profile are superior to survey-based ones and should be used, whenever possible, to explain area crime variation. Further data from other sources provide independent information to victimization surveys. This information is also uncorrelated with individual respondents' routine activities and target attractiveness.

Undoubtedly the most informative examinations of victimization data focus on how individuals' routine activities alongside areas' environmental conditions and also their interactions influence victimization risk and frequency (Trickett, Osborn, and Ellingworth 1995; Osborn and Tseloni 1998). These refer to different levels of crime predictors, the individual (micro) and the area (macro or meso, if a higher level of aggregation exists); hence such analyses are called multilevel. Further, to account for the hierarchy in survey data, whereby addresses (and therefore respondents and their households) are clustered at sampling points (in other words, selected from each already selected point) (Flatley 2014), multilevel analyses employ in principle hierarchical statistical methodology. To our knowledge, Rountree, Land, and Miethe (1994) pioneered victimization survey hierarchical analyses of individual and area predictors of crime more than 20 years ago.

Hierarchical models allow examination of (*a*) individual and area (i.e., multilevel), and their interactions' effects on crime; (*b*) any random variation of these effects at each level of analysis; and (*c*) the remaining unexplained variation of crime attributed to each level of analysis (Tseloni 2000; Tseloni 2006; Tseloni and Pease 2015). Therefore they offer unrivaled disaggregation of crime rates with respect to very finely—including their environment—defined targets and invaluable insights for theory testing and crime prevention. In our opinion they should be the backbone of any practical crime prevention advice (Pease and Tseloni 2014). It is important to know to what extent the at-risk population groups are so because of their own attributes (be it routine activities, target attractiveness, or a combination) or the structure of their place of residence. In the former case the at-risk population groups carry that risk wherever they reside and therefore crime preventive interventions should aim to help these people/households. In the latter, risky areas should be the focus of renewal interventions, and vulnerable groups should be encouraged and supported, not avoid living in these areas. The flipside question is whether areas have high crime rates because of who lives there or due to the areas' own attributes. The former cause is called the "composition" and the latter the "context" effect.

Is crime a "composition" or "context" problem? The answer depends on the particular crime type, population group, and area examined. Two population groups that have inspired various, including crime prevention, policy initiatives and/or fed policy rhetoric are social renters (another term for residents of public housing) and lone parents (commonly called single parents) (Fletcher-Morgan and Leyland 2010). The following evidence of these groups' crime vulnerability draws on hierarchical analyses of the 2000 BCS. Social renters experience between double and 10 times the national average household crimes depending on their area of residence (Tseloni 2006, p. 226). With regards to personal crimes they experience 40 percent more such crimes than owner-occupiers regardless of where they live (Tseloni and Pease 2015, p. 17). Turning our attention to the second group, on average lone parents experience more crimes than others. This positive association between lone parenthood and property victimization, however, varies considerably across areas. Lone parents face up to 28 times more property crimes than non-lone parents of otherwise similar profile in the highest crime areas. By contrast, they face national average property crime rates in the safest areas (Tseloni 2006). Lone parents, specifically divorced or separated with children, experience roughly five times more personal crimes than others (Tseloni and Pease 2015, p. 19). With regards to the starting question of this paragraph, the above four examples demonstrate the following: Social renters are highly vulnerable to victimization by either crime type wherever they live (composition). With regards to property crime the area they live also matters considerably (composition and context). Lone parents are vulnerable by property crime only in high-crime areas (context). By contrast, area does not matter with regards to high personal crime victimization frequency experienced by those divorced/separated with children (composition). This knowledge can be used to inform crime prevention interventions, as mentioned in the previous paragraph.

To conclude this section, knowing the interplay between individual and area predictors—or, to use a quested favored by the team and instigated by one of us, "Who and in what context?"—avoids wasting efforts and money on "one size fits all" policies. However, the criminological community has been slow in adopting hierarchical statistical modeling analyses of victimization survey data. Running the risk of falling into the composition or context trap ourselves, this is no surprise given that the criminological community has made little use of victimization survey data anyway, regardless of methodology.

13.4 Benefits and Limitations of Victimization Surveys in Environmental Criminology

This is not to say, of course that recorded crime data are of no value: for homicide and theft of vehicles they furnish relatively strong data, a least at a national level, given that homicides are normally discovered and victims clearly cannot be surveyed and that theft of vehicles is reported and recorded at a very high rate due to requirements for crime numbers in the event of the need for an insurance claim. Key events have led to sudden changes in recorded crime numbers; for example, in Britain the development of a National Crime Recording Standard, which was actively monitored by the Audit Commission, led to some increase in crime. However, in the short term, recorded crime data can be quite reliable indicators of crime levels, and for some analytic purposes it may reasonably be assumed that any biases following reporting and recording practices will not unduly influence conclusions. Moreover, police data can be drawn on in relation to offenders, at least in relation to those crimes that are cleared up. Although victimization surveys can, as shown below, make come inferences about offenders, they provide little direct information on them.

Notwithstanding their own limitations, however, for the most part victimization surveys provide a better estimate of the rates of crime that are included in the survey than recorded crime figures in relation to the populations from which the sample is drawn, provided that the survey has been conducted in a competent manner. They can also provide some suggestive evidence relating to offenders. Many tend to have rather little to say directly on individual activity patterns albeit that some do include relevant questions.

Recorded crime data are notoriously subject to errors. Not all crimes are reported, and of those reported, many are not recorded. Moreover, there is no reason to believe that shortfalls in reporting and recording are random. The reporting and recording rates of crime vary by country, crime type, police service, and community. The risk for environmental criminology is obvious. Patterns in recorded crime may as easily reflect patterns of reporting and recording as they do patterns of crime event.

Victimization surveys were developed to try to make good major weaknesses in recorded crime data. They were able to quantify the numbers of crimes that are omitted from recorded crime data. International victimization surveys adopt the same methods in different jurisdictions and hence allow comparisons between countries. National crime victimization surveys, where sample sizes are big enough, can be used to compare crime rates by area within countries.

Victimization surveys are weaker in relation to relatively rare crimes where sample sizes are insufficient to yield meaningful findings. National sample surveys are able to say little about patterns in microareas, for example, street networks, although this may be possible with very local surveys (see Umar et al. in this volume). Data on the timing of incidents is even less reliably collected through surveys than through recorded crime data unless diaries based on memorable dates within the reference period are employed. Nonresponse is a further problem. Early BCS/CSEW, for example, sweeps enjoyed very high response rates, but these have fallen slightly recently. Moreover, response rates where the target population comprises businesses have been lower than response rates where the target population comprises households or individuals. Many victimization surveys have been confined to those above a certain age and hence omit crimes targeting the young. Sample frames can omit highly vulnerable populations, such as the homeless and transient. Sample frames also normally omit visitors to a country, who may be vulnerable.

In answering questions about their experiences of crimes, well-designed surveys try hard to avoid errors that spring from respondents failing to assign crimes to the period about which they are being asked to recall, but there are clearly dangers of both including crimes that fall outside the reference period or omitting those that do. Well-designed surveys also try to obtain sufficient detail of crime incidents to make sure that they are allocated to the correct crime category, where everyday language might place them in the wrong one. But again, there is inevitably some scope for error here (Table 13.3).

Table 13.3 Victimization Surveys and Recorded Crime as Data Sources for Environmental Criminology

Types of information	Victimization survey	Recorded crime
Time of incident	Incidents during reference period	Report time and data stamped Earliest and latest time
Information on offenders	Little—victim views	Data on arrestees
Comprehensiveness	For those sampled, all crimes covered in survey	All recorded crimes
Repeat incidents	In principle all, in practice capped	Those recorded, depends on reporting and recording levels
Location of incident	General information on attributes of location Geocoded sampling point of residence	Geocoded
Environment of incident	Observations of fieldworker and/or as covered by survey instrument	Not directly recorded
Geographical concentration of incidents	By specific area for crime at or near home	By specific area
Target attractiveness	Often information on security for targets and nontargets and precautionary activities of victims and nonvictims	Sometimes security of some targets
Routine activities of victims and nonvictims / awareness spaces	As covered by survey instrument, often same information on victims and nonvictims	Generally no information, although sometimes some information on victims
Routine activities of likely offenders / awareness spaces	Generally no information as perceived by victims (drugs and alcohol influence)	Generally no information
Routine activities of guardians	As covered by survey instrument, often some information	Generally no information
Routine activities of handlers	As covered by survey instrument, often some information	Generally no information
Change over time	For repeated sweeps good trend data	Uncertain, depends on consistency of reporting and recording

13.5 Why Is More Use Not Made of Victimization Surveys in Environmental Criminology?

Victimization surveys can be technically complex to use. The 2013–2014 Crime Survey for England and Wales questionnaire (ONS, 2014), for example, ran to over 260 pages, including all modules, some of which were only asked of subsets of respondents. The technical guidance runs to 84 pages (ONS, 2015). The availability of the questionnaires and the technical support documents help avoid errors, of course, but they are testament to the difficulties faced by the crime scientist hoping to use the data.

There are some changes in repeated surveys from sweep to sweep, making trend identification quite difficult. The crime surveys in different countries vary in more or less subtle ways, making comparisons for many findings difficult. The survey is undertaken to meet multiple needs, most of them administrative, meaning that when used for purposes not originally envisaged, key questions are not asked or are asked in ways that make compromise some analyses of the data.

The CSEW survey now includes questions relating to traditional crimes such as domestic burglary and theft of and from cars. There is a separate exercise to collect data on the crimes experienced by 10- to 15-year-olds. It also has questions on domestic violence, sexual offenses, cybercrime, mobile phone crime, and fraud. There are sections on respondents' own offending and on their drinking and illicit drug taking. It also includes questions relating to experiences of the criminal justice system and views on how it is functioning. It contains background questions on household composition, employment, leisure activities, driving habits, and respondent's age, sex, and ethnicity. There are suites of questions relating to precautionary behavior, household security, and vehicle security measures. The sample size and selection methods are set to allow meaningful analysis of crime patterns nationally (while representativeness by police force area was limited to the 2004/2005 BCS/CSEW). The sample choice methods mean ordinarily that it is essential to work with weighted data.

This is to say that the CSEW (or other victimization surveys in other jurisdictions and relating to businesses as well as to individuals and households) may be a potential treasure trove for environmental criminologists in their efforts to test their hypotheses, but it is not for the faint-hearted. For ourselves, building on previous work with the CSEW, at the time of writing we are undertaking research on routine activities and violent crime and have a further grant to examine patterns of experience of antisocial behavior. In our research endeavors we have benefited from advice from advisory group members who are involved in administering the CSEW. Notwithstanding the extensive experience of some members of the research team, this advice has been invaluable and helped us avoid errors. It is also the case that research assistants who have come to work with us have been inducted into the complexities of the CSEW. Although the data are freely available to researchers to download and to use, in practice doing so without a helping hand from someone who has already made use of the survey would be difficult and would risk serious errors.

13.6 Conclusion

Environmental criminologists have dedicated much attention to the analysis of patterns of activity of detected offenders and the locations of crimes reported to the police, but less so on patterns identified in victimization surveys. In this chapter, analyses of the settings or conditions that affect victimization risk and frequency have been presented for various types of crime. The benefits and limitations of using victimization or population surveys in environmental criminology have also been discussed. Crime surveys are expensive and complex to run. They are also complex to use properly. They are insufficiently and inadequately drawn on, despite comprising the most robust data available on most types of crime.

Notes

1. Unfortunately, no further questions are asked in these cases. This means that the survey misses all crimes committed against visitors to England and Wales and also omits details of crimes experienced by residents when they are abroad. What was the case in 2002/2003 continued at least to 2014/2015.
2. It is inevitable that measures of neighborhood and community characteristics from social surveys entail sampling errors. These, however, should be minimal in high-quality surveys, while testing the internal validity of individual responses arguably offers a safety benchmark.

References

Bourdieu, Pierre. 1986. "The forms of capital." In *Handbook for Theory and Research for the Sociology of Education*, edited by J. G. Richardson, pp. 241–258. New York: Greenwood.

Brantingham, Paul J., and Patricia Brantingham. 1991. *Environmental Criminology*. Prospect Heights, IL: Waveland.

Cohen, Lawrence E., and Michael Felson. 1979. "Social change and crime rates trends: A routine activity approach." *American Sociological Review* 44: 588–608.

Ditton, Jason, and Stephen Farrall. 2007. "The British Crime Survey and the fear of crime." In *Surveying Crime in the 21st Century*, edited by Michael Hough and Michael Maxfield, pp. 223–241. Vol. 22 of *Crime Prevention Studies*. Monsey, NY: Criminal Justice Press.

Farrell, Graham, Andromachi Tseloni, Jennifer Mailley, and Nick Tilley. 2011. "The crime drop and the security hypothesis." *Journal of Research in Crime and Delinquency* 48(2): 147–175,

Farrell, Graham, Andromachi Tseloni, and Nick Tilley. 2011. "The effectiveness of vehicle security devices and their role in the crime drop." *Criminology and Criminal Justice* 11(1): 21–35.

Flatley, John. 2014. "British Crime Survey." In *Encyclopedia of Criminology and Criminal Justice*, edited by Gerben Bruinsma and David Weisburd, pp. 194–203. New York: Springer.

Fletcher-Morgan, Charlotte, and Kate Leyland. 2010. "Making people more responsible: The Blair governments' programme for changing citizens' behaviour." *Political studies* 58(3): 427–449.

Goudriaan, Heike, Karin Wittebrood, and Paul Nieuwbeerta. 2006. "Neighbourhood characteristics and reporting crime." *British Journal of Criminology* 46(4): 719–742.

Hindelang, Michael J., Michael R. Gottfredson, and James Garofalo. 1978. *Victims of Personal Crime: An Empirical Foundation for a Theory of Personal Victimisation*. Cambridge, MA: Ballinger.

Hodgkinson, Sarah, and Nick Tilley. 2007. "Travel-to-crime: Homing in on the victim." *International Review of Victimology* 14: 281–298.

Hough, Michael, and Michael Maxfield, eds. 2007. *Surveying Crime in the 21st Century*. Vol. 22 of *Crime Prevention Studies*. Monsey, NY: Criminal Justice Press.

Hunter, James, and Andromachi Tseloni. 2016. "Equity, justice and the crime drop: The case of burglary in England and Wales." *Crime Science* 5(3). Open access: http://www.crimescience-journal.com/content/5/1/3.

Ignatans, Dainis, and Ken Pease. 2015. "Distributive justice and the crime drop." In *The Criminal Act: Festschrift for Marcus Felson*, edited by M. Andresen and Graham Farrell, pp. 77–87. London: Palgrave Macmillan.

Ignatans, Dainis, and Ken Pease. 2016. "The global crime drop and changes in the distribution of victimisation." *Crime Science* 5(11). doi: 10.1186/s40163-016-0059-4.

Kennedy, L. W., and D. R. Forde. 1990; "Routine activities and crime: An analysis of victimisation in Canada." *Criminology* 28: 137–152.

Kershaw, Chris, and Andromachi Tseloni. 2005. "Predicting crime rates, fear and disorder based on area information: Evidence from the 2000 British Crime Survey." *International Review of Victimology* 12: 293–311.

Lens, Michael C. 2017. "Measuring the geography of opportunity." *Progress in Human Geography* 41(1). doi:10.1177/0309132515618104.

Lynn, Peter, and David Elliot. 2000. *The British Crime Survey: A Review of Methodology*. London: National Centre for Social Research.

Nilsson, Anders, and Felipe Estrada. 2007. "Risky neighbourhood or individuals at risk? The significance of neighbourhood conditions for violent victimisation in residential areas." *Journal of Scandinavian Studies in Criminology and Crime Prevention* 8: 2–21.

Office for National Statistics (ONS). 2014. *The 2013/14 Crime Survey for England and Wales Technical Report*. London: TNS.

Office for National Statistics (ONS). 2015. *Crime Survey for England and Wales, 2013–2014* [data collection]. 2nd ed. UK Data Service. SN: 7619. doi:10.5255/UKDA-SN-7619-2.

Osborn, Denise R., Alan Trickett, and Robert Elder. 1992. "Area characteristics and regional variates as determinants of area property crime levels." *Journal of Quantitative Criminology* 8: 265–285.

Osborn, Denise R., and Andromachi Tseloni. 1998. "The distribution of household property crimes." *Journal of Quantitative Criminology* 14: 307–330.

Park, Robert E. 1936. "Human Ecology." *American Journal of Sociology* 42: 1–15.

Pease, Ken, and Andromachi Tseloni. 2014. *Using Modelling to Predict and Prevent Victimization*. Springer Brief Criminology Series. New York: Springer.

Putnam, Robert D. 1993. "The prosperous community: Social capital and public life." *American Prospect* 13: 35–42.

Rountree, Pamela W., Kenneth C. Land, and Terence D. Miethe. 1994 "Macro-micro integration in the study of victimization: A hierarchical logistic model analysis across Seattle neighborhoods." *Criminology* 32: 387–414.

Sampson, Robert J. 2006. Collective efficacy theory: Lessons learnt and directions for future inquiry. In *Taking Stock: The Status of Criminological Theory, Advances in Criminological Theory*, edited by F. T. Cullen, J. P. Wright, and L. Blevins, pp. 149–167. Vol. 15. New Brunswick, NJ: Transaction Publishers.

Sampson, Robert J., and Byron W. Groves. 1989. "Community structure and crime: Testing social disorganization theory." *American Journal of Sociology* 94: 774–802.

Sampson, Robert J., Stephen W. Raudenbush, and Felton Earls. 1997. "Neighborhoods and violent crime: A multilevel study of collective efficacy." *Science* 227: 918–924.

Sampson, Robert J., and John D. Wooldredge. 1987. "Linking the micro- and macro-level dimensions of lifestyle-routine activity and opportunity models of predatory victimization." *Journal of Quantitative Criminology* 3: 371–393.

Smith, Douglas A., and Roger Jarjoura. 1989. "Household characteristics, neighborhood composition and victimization risk." *Social Forces* 68: 621–640.

Tilley, Nick, and Andromachi Tseloni. 2016. "Choosing and Using Statistical Sources in Criminology: What Can the Crime Survey for England and Wales Tell Us?" *Legal Information Management* 16(2): 78–90. doi: 10.1017/S1472669616000219.

Tilley, Nick, Graham Farrell, Louise Grove, Rebecca Thompson, and Andromachi Tseloni. 2015. "Do burglar alarms increase burglary risk? A counterintuitive finding and possible explanations." *Crime Prevention and Community Safety* 17(1): 1–19.

Tilley, Nick, Andromachi Tseloni, and Graham Farrell. 2011. "Income disparities of burglary risk: Security availability during the crime drop." *British Journal of Criminology* 51(2): 296–313.

Trickett, Alan, Denise R. Osborn, and Dan Ellingworth. 1995. "Property crime victimization: The roles of individual and area influences." *International Review of Victimology* 3: 273–295.

Trickett, Alan, Denise R. Osborn, Julie Seymour, and Ken Pease. 1992. "What is different about high crime areas?" *British Journal of Criminology* 32: 81–89.

Tseloni, Andromachi. 2000. "Personal criminal victimization in the U.S.: Fixed and random effects of individual and household characteristics." *Journal of Quantitative Criminology* 16: 415–442.

Tseloni, Andromachi. 2006. "Multilevel modelling of the number of property crimes: Household and area effects." *Journal of the Royal Statistical Society Series A—Statistics in Society* 169(2): 205–233.

Tseloni, Andromachi. 2007. "Fear of crime, perceived disorders and property crime: A multivariate analysis at the area level." In *Imagination for Crime Prevention: Essays in Honor of Ken Pease*, edited by Graham Farrell, Kate Bowers, Shane D. Johnson, and Michael Townsley, pp. 163–185. Vol. 21 of *Crime Prevention Studies*. Monsey, NY: Criminal Justice Press.

Tseloni, Andromachi, Ioannis Ntzoufras, Anna Nicolaou, and Ken Pease. 2010. "Concentration of personal and household crimes in England and Wales." *European Journal of Applied Mathematics* 21: 325–348.

Tseloni, Andromachi, and Ken Pease. 2004. "Repeat personal victimisation: Random effects, event dependence and unexplained heterogeneity." *British Journal of Criminology* 44(6): 931–945.

Tseloni, Andromachi, and Ken Pease. 2015. "Area and individual differences in personal crime victimization incidence: The role of individual, lifestyle / routine activities and contextual predictors." *International Review of Victimology* 21(1): 3–29.

Tseloni, Andromachi, Rebecca Thompson, Louise Grove, Nick Tilley, and Graham Farrell. 2017. "The effectiveness of burglary security devices." *Security Journal* 30(2), 646–664. doi: 10.1057/sj.2014.30.

Tseloni, Andromachi, Karin Wittebrood, Graham Farrell, and Ken Pease. 2004. "Burglary victimisation in England and Wales, the United States and the Netherlands." *British Journal of Criminology* 44: 66–91.

Walby, Sylvia, and Jonathan Allen. 2004. *Domestic Violence, Sexual Assault and Stalking: Findings from the British Crime Survey*. Home Office Research Study 276. Home Office Research, Development and Statistics Directorate. London: Home Office.

CHAPTER 14

SYSTEMATIC SOCIAL OBSERVATION

IAN BRUNTON-SMITH

> Many aspects of social life can be measured only through systematic social observation. This is true of much of the ebb and flow of life in time and space. (Reiss, 1971: 6)

14.1 Introduction

Systematic social observation (SSO) is the application of rigorous, replicable, and generalizable approaches from survey methodology to field observation (ethnography). With its roots in early symbolic interactionism in the late 1920s and 1930s—where the emphasis was on participant observation to study social interactions (e.g., Thomas et al., 1933; Whyte, 1943; Barker and Wright, 1955)—SSO provides researchers with independent, robust, and quantifiable data about the forms of social interactions most commonly obtained through qualitative inquiry. Introduced to criminology by Reiss (1968, 1971) in his detailed analyses of violence in police-citizen encounters, it was the work of Taylor and colleagues in Baltimore city that first demonstrated how SSO approaches could also be used to measure qualities of the urban environment including physical disorder, social incivilities, and housing quality (Taylor, Gottfredson, and Brower, 1984; Taylor, Shumaker, and Gottfredson, 1985). They showed that SSO could provide researchers with independent assessments of the urban environment that were considerably more detailed than available administrative sources like the census and land registry data. SSO was further cemented in the methodological toolbox of environmental criminologists by the work of Sampson and colleagues as part of the Project on Human Development in Chicago Neighborhoods (PHCDN). In particular, with the development of ecometrics—the science of measurement applied to ecological settings—researchers now had a robust methodological foundation from which to judge the quality of ecological measures, and make corrections for measurement error (Raudenbush and Sampson, 1999).

More recently, SSO for ecological assessment has evolved again. Data about the environment around survey respondents' houses is now routinely collected by interviewers during the fieldwork process, and this information is now being incorporated in research (Brunton-Smith and Sturgis, 2011). While questions remain about the quality of this data (Andresen et al., 2013; West, 2013; Casas-Cordero et al., 2013), this represents an extremely cost-effective source of SSO data for researchers. Perhaps more interestingly, the rapid growth of the online mapping tool Google Street View now provides an unprecedented amount of recorded observational data on environments across the globe that researchers are only just beginning to engage with (e.g., Badland et al., 2010; Clarke et al., 2010; Odgers et al., 2012). Methodological challenges with this data remain; however, Google Street View unquestionably represents an exciting opportunity for the widespread and routine adoption of SSO in studies of ecological settings.

This chapter proceeds as follows. First, section 14.1 provides a general overview of the SSO approach, drawing on the initial insights of Reiss (1971), as well as the work of Mastrofski et al. (2010). Section 14.2 describes the application of SSO approaches to environmental settings, from the original studies of Taylor and colleagues (Taylor, Gottfredson, and Brower, 1984; Taylor, Shumaker, and Gottfredson, 1985; Perkins et al., 1993; Perkins and Taylor, 1996; Taylor, 2001), to more recent work by Sampson and Raudenbush (1999; see also Raudenbush and Sampson, 1999). The ecometric approach first proposed by Raudenbush and Sampson (1999) is discussed in section 14.3, demonstrating how the science of SSO and the science of ecological analysis were intimately related. Finally, section 14.4 discusses current developments in SSO for environmental analysis. This focuses specifically on three areas: interviewer observational data routinely collected as part of larger social surveys; participant-generated observations using space-time budgets; and Google Street View as a repository for environmental audit data. Developments in crowdsourced SSO data like Mapilliary are also briefly discussed.

14.2 What Is Systematic Social Observation?

Systematic social observation represents a meeting point between the in-depth observational work championed by ethnographers and the large-scale, systematic, and generalizable approaches of quantitative social science. Recognizing the benefits of an observational approach for many research questions, the key innovation is in the incorporation of a rigorous and replicable methodology to ensure observations are representative of the population under study, and that observations are independent of those being observed. When coupled with an approach to data collection that emphasizes minimization (and quantification) of individual observer inaccuracies, this enables researchers to produce an accurate picture of a range of research outcomes previously beyond the reach of quantitative social science.

Despite a few examples of large-scale social observation in the early part of the 20th century (e.g., Madge, 1939), it is the work of Albert Reiss that is largely credited with the adoption of systematic observation approaches in criminology (Mastrofski et al., 1998; Sampson and Raudenbush, 1999). As Reiss states:

> By systematic observation, I mean only that observation and recording are done according to explicit procedures which permit replication and that rules are followed which permit the use of the logic of scientific inference. The means of observation and recording, whether a person or some form of technology, must be independent of that which is observed and the effects of observing and measuring must be measurable. (Reiss, 1971: 4)

Applied to the study of policing, Reiss used a group of 36 trained observers to record the behavior of police and citizens during a sample of interactions (Reiss, 1968). Observers used a detailed quantitative checklist to record specific details about the interactions, allowing Reiss to quantify the extent of violence in these interactions, as well as details of police misconduct and racial bias. From this work, Reiss (1971) subsequently laid out the fundamental approach of SSO and highlighted particular advantages for researchers (see Mastrofski, Parks, and McCluskey, 2010, for a useful summary). Reiss argued that there was considerable merit to promoting a systematized approach to observation of social phenomena, with some research questions only answerable using this type of strategy. Specifically, he advocated an approach to observation that was amenable to statistical manipulation and inference. This involved the use of multiple observers to collect systematic observational data on clearly defined phenomena of interest, with the observed phenomena assumed to be a representative subset from the underlying population of interest. Of particular importance was the selection of an appropriate sample of observations taken from a properly defined sampling frame (e.g., registers of eligible observations from which to select a sample for direct observation), and ensuring that observer assessments were reliable and could be appropriately quantified.

Drawing on the principles of statistical inference, sampling frames for SSO should reflect the population under study (Reiss, 1971). Units of observation should then be selected from the sampling frame using standard sampling procedures (Kish, 1965). This ensures that selected observations will be representative of the underlying population of interest, and means the collected data is amenable to the full complement of statistical procedures familiar to quantitative researchers. This makes SSO a flexible framework for analysis, with the specific features of the scenario under study guiding the final sample design (Reiss, 1971). For example, when considering relatively rare events like shoplifting, it may be more appropriate to fix the location and conduct more intensive periods of observation, rather than simply randomly sampling locations (see Buckle and Farrington, 1984, 1994, for examples of this approach).

The validity of SSO is underpinned by the assumption that the observations under study are independent of the observers. This means that different observers would make the same assessments of the same event. This *inter-rater reliability* can be maximized prior to data collection through appropriate training. For example, Mastrofski et al. (1998) describe a prestudy phase of observer calibration, where observers rate the same stimuli, differences between observers are noted and discussed, and consensus is reached. Careful design of the observation instrument is also crucial, with clear instructions for observers about what to observe and how to record it. This ensures that the phenomena under study can be appropriately quantified and included in statistical analyses. Those undertaking SSO generally also assign some events to multiple observers, enabling reliability to be assessed after data collection. Here the interest is in the levels of agreement between observers, over and above agreement expected by chance (as measured by Kappa, or other reliability statistics).

Building on Reiss's influential work, a number of criminologists and social scientists have since adopted SSO to measure phenomena including shoplifting (Buckle and Farrington, 1994), police procedures (Mastrofski et al., 1998), and discriminatory policing (Waddington, Stenson, and Don, 2004). Researchers have also adapted the SSO procedures to measure features of the urban environment (e.g., Taylor, Gottfredson, and Brower, 1984; Sampson and Raudenbush, 1999; Steenbeek and Kreis, 2015) and it is to these studies that we now turn.

14.3 Systematic Social Observation of Urban Spaces

Early work using SSO demonstrated that it could be an effective tool for measuring the types of social phenomena that were previously beyond the reach of quantitative approaches. But it was not until the pathbreaking work of Ralph Taylor and colleagues that SSO was adopted as a tool for audit of the local environment. This subsequently formed the blueprint for Sampson and Raudenbush's (1999) examination of the extent of disorder in Chicago neighborhoods as part of the PHDCN.

14.3.1 Crime in Baltimore: The Work of Taylor and Colleagues

In conjunction with survey data and administrative records from the US census, Taylor and colleagues demonstrated in a series of studies that the principles of SSO could be used to generate robust measures of area characteristics including physical disorder and housing conditions, as well as social incivilities (see, e.g., Taylor, Gottfredson, and Brower, 1984; Taylor, Shumaker, and Gottfredson, 1985; Perkins et al., 1993; Perkins and Taylor, 1996; Taylor, 2001). This approach, they argued, had several benefits over existing ecological analyses, ensuring more robust estimates of the impact of the urban environment (but see also Taylor, 2015, for a detailed critique of existing empirical assessments of the links between communities and crime).

Focusing on the city of Baltimore, Taylor and colleagues adopted a number of related strategies to effectively audit the local environment. This included requiring observers to photograph and rate the area immediately around sampled households for defensible space features (surveillance opportunities, real and symbolic barriers) and the garden at each property (Taylor, Gottfredson, and Brower, 1984). Subsequent research (Taylor, Shumaker, and Gottfredson, 1985) generated more detail about physical features of the local environment, including housing layout, whether the house was set back from the street, street length, street width, traffic volume, instances and types of nonresidential land use, graffiti, litter, people hanging out, vacant lots, and vacant buildings. Perkins et al. (1993) extended the original research with the Block Booster Environmental Inventory, capturing physical signs of social disorder, territorial symbols (signs and stickers, dogs, home-personalization, beautification efforts) and features of the built environment (see also Perkins and Taylor, 1996).

This work was notable for the rigorous approaches adopted to assess the reliability of these ecological measures, with multiple raters routinely observing the same location to assess inter-rater reliabilities, and extensive training used to ensure accurate measurement. They demonstrate reasonably good inter-rater reliability, suggesting that observers have the capacity to accurately assess distinct features of the environment. Physical features of the environment, and patterns of residential use, were found to be the most reliably measured, while less frequent social incivilities like drug were less well measured because they were generally too sporadic and time-of-day dependent (a finding later echoed by Sampson and Raudenbush, 1999).

These observational assessments of ecological settings were combined with survey data and administrative data about the structural character of local environments. Over the course of several studies, Taylor and colleagues went on to demonstrate that these independently rated, neighborhood-level physical and social incivilities correlated strongly with resident perceptions of disorder and fear of crime (Taylor, Shumaker, and Gottfredson, 1985), and that they were influential in shaping levels of crime (Taylor, 2001).

Several benefits of the SSO approach to ecological assessment were highlighted in this original work. Traditional approaches to ecological analysis generally relied on respondent assessments of the urban environment, which may be "contaminated by residents' fear of crime and other emotions about their community" (Perkins et al., 1993: 32). In contrast, independent assessments of the area are not likely to be influenced by residents' personal subjectivities. The SSO measures were also not subject to common method bias, ensuring that any observed associations with outcomes of interest were the result of true associations between differences in environmental context and individual outcomes. Data from SSO could also be used to validate individual assessments of local areas, and check the reliability of administrative records.

Other ecological analyses have capitalized on the increasing availability of administrative records about the local environment to capture ecological differences (e.g., Box, Hale, and Andrews, 1988; Brunton-Smith and Sturgis, 2011; Tseloni, 2006). While this data is not susceptible to shared-method bias, researchers are restricted to a fairly simple set of neighborhood measures—covering, for example, disadvantage, population density, population turnover, and ethnic composition. More nuanced neighborhood measures like low-level disorder cannot be reliably obtained from census data or other administrative records. In contrast, with the appropriate collection instrument, SSO has been effectively deployed to assess a range of environmental characteristics.

14.3.2 The Project on Human Development in Chicago Neighborhoods: The Work of Sampson and Colleagues

Informed by this earlier work, Sampson and Raudenbush (1999) have provided the most extensive SSO of the local environment to date (see also Raudenbush and Sampson, 1999). As part of the PHDCN, between June and October 1995 Sampson and colleagues conducted a detailed SSO of the extent of disorder (both physical and social) as well as the condition of local buildings in the Chicago area. This study was notable for the considerable scope of the SSO, with more than 23,800 separate face blocks (one side of a street block between two intersections) across 196 census tracts in 80 Chicago neighborhoods audited during the data collection period. The audit tool itself was also extensive, recording information on land use, traffic, the physical condition of buildings, and evidence of physical disorder within each street block.

To achieve such extensive coverage of Chicago streets, a team of researchers drove down each sampled street block at five kilometers per hour, with two observers carefully noting the condition of each street segment. A video recorder was also used, enabling the research team to independently verify the accuracy of the data generated by the trained observers. The video recordings also enabled the collection of more fine-grained detail about each face block, including additional information about the physical condition of the block, housing characteristics, presence of businesses, and social interactions. A high level of reliability was noted between observers, and also when comparing the observers with the video-recorded data. However, not all features of the local environment were measured with the same level of accuracy, with social incivilities measured less accurately than physical disorder and features of the physical environment. This, Sampson and Raudenbush argued, was a reflection of the comparative rarity of these events in Chicago streets during the data collection period, which may have been further compounded by the requirement to restrict data collection to daylight hours to ensure visibility (when many forms of social incivility like drug taking may be more likely to occur after dark). As a result, they note that while SSO can "tap aspects of the social and physical environment that survey respondents have difficulty describing accurately," they are less useful for capturing features of the urban environment like social cohesion, where resident perspectives are crucial (Raudenbush and Sampson, 1999: 11).

These street-level counts were subsequently aggregated to broader spatial scales, including census tracts and neighborhood clusters. Using them as measures of the ecological environment, Sampson and Raudenbush (1999) showed that they were related to a number of important social outcomes, including poverty, victimization, and population instability. In contrast to the prevailing ideas of the time, they also showed that disorder and perceptions of crime were less closely related than previous research had suggested, a finding they attribute to the earlier reliance on survey data from the same respondents.

14.3.3 More Recent SSO in Ecological Settings

The work of Ralph Taylor and Robert Samson demonstrated that SSO could be applied robustly to ecological settings, cementing SSO in the toolbox of environmental criminology. Detailed environmental audits now include the Irvine-Minnesota Inventory (Day et al., 2006), the Pedestrian Environment Data Scan (PEDS, Clifton, Livi Smith, and Rodriguez, 2007), the Maryland Inventory of Urban Design Qualities (MIUDQ, Ewing et al., 2005, 2006), and the New York Housing and Vacancy Survey (US Bureau of the Census, 2011). Other researchers have adopted similar strategies to explore other features of the urban environment. For example, Waddington, Stenson, and Don (2004) repeatedly drove down streets in two English cities to obtain estimates of the population use of space. This generated a total of 24,608 sightings of pedestrians, with data collated on the observable characteristics of the "available population" in each area. This information was used to demonstrate that the available population more closely represented the profile of those subject to police stop and search than would be expected if resident population figures were used. More recently, Steenbeek and Kreis (2015) have used SSO data as the basis for defining a new set of "natural areas of disorder" in the city of Amsterdam (524). Using observational data on signs of disorder from nearly 2,000 geographic locations (a maximum of 300 meters apart), they demonstrate that disorder clusters in space, but that these clusters have almost no correspondence with administrative boundaries. Earlier assessments of the spatial patterning of disorder that have relied on census geographies may, therefore, be misrepresenting the true extent of variation in disorder across areas.

Researchers have also begun to demonstrate how more qualitative insights about the character of particular streets generated using SSO can be combined with quantitative assessments of differential crime-risk (Rudes et al., 2014; Ready et al., 2014). Specifically, these researchers have conducted SSO in streets that have been empirically identified as crime hotspots, using the SSO data to assess how well their crime-risk models reflect the social reality of these streets, acting as an important cross-validation tool. They also demonstrate that this can be used to generate additional insights about the role of specific community features that might be missed by adopting a purely model-based approach to assessing crime risk.

14.4 Ecometrics: A Science for Observation of Ecological Settings

The work of Sampson and Raudenbush was notable, not just for the extensive nature of their SSO in Chicago, but also because they set out a detailed methodological framework for assessing the robustness of ecological assessments—ecometrics. Applying insights from psychometrics—the scientific assessment of the measurement of individual psychological properties—to the assessment of environmental context, ecometrics provided researchers with a statistically principled approach to utilize the data collected from environmental audits. Although not restricted to data obtained by SSO, it is in the context of SSO (where issues of reliability are critical, and where data may oftentimes be sparse) that the benefits of an ecometric approach have been demonstrated most clearly.

Raudenbush and Sampson (1999) used insights from item response theory (IRT) and factor analysis to generate measurement scales from the collected observational data in each sampled street segment. For example, when Raudenbush and Sampson were considering the presence of disorder, items measuring the presence of different forms of disorder were combined into a single scale, with IRT correctly accounting for the seriousness and rarity of each included disorderly activity. The patterning of multiple sources of disorder could also be examined, enabling more meaningful distinctions between social and physical disorder to be made. Ecological measures could then be generated at relevant spatial scales (census tract and neighborhood cluster) based on the combination of scores for all streets within a given cluster. Generalizability theory then provided a framework for accounting for measurement error associated with these ecological assessments, with multilevel models (Raudenbush and Bryk, 2002) used to take account of multiple sources of error simultaneously (between measurements from the same rater, between ratings from the same census tract, and between tracts within the same neighborhood). Account could also be straightforwardly taken of known sources of error by including these in the measurement model (e.g., time of audit to account for time-of-day effects).

This work has provided researchers with a general framework for generating appropriate and robust estimates of ecological characteristics from SSO data. Notably, Raudenbush and Sampson (1999) show that even when there is a high degree of variability between street segments about the presence of particular ecological attributes, as long as data is collected from a reasonable number of segments within a broader area, data can still be used to produce measures of ecological characteristics at the broader spatial scale that display a high level of reliability. This means that researchers can use SSO to produce robust estimates of ecological characteristics.

Verbistky-Savitz and Raudenbush (2009) have recently shown how researchers can further improve the estimates of ecological characteristics by taking into account spatial autocorrelation (that areas in close proximity to one another tend to be more similar to one another). Furthermore, Bayesian methods (Gomez-Rubio et al., 2010) may be used to generate robust ecological estimates for areas that were not included in the original SSO sample frame, by borrowing strength from similar areas in close proximity that were included.

14.5 Current Developments in the Use of Ecological SSO

SSO is still used comparatively rarely to robustly measure features of ecological settings. This is likely to reflect, in part, the high costs involved in conducting a detailed observational assessment of the urban environment. This means it is generally prohibitively expensive for most researchers. However, more recent developments are providing researchers with exciting new opportunities to incorporate elements of SSO within their research. Three developments are particularly noteworthy: the routine collection of interviewer observation data in social surveys; the space-time budget approach; and the introduction and rapid expansion of Google Street View. Crowdsourced data may represent a fourth valuable development in SSO. However, currently these approaches remain in their infancy.

14.5.1 Interviewer Observations in Social Surveys

Many large-scale social surveys now routinely collect observational data as part of the data collection process (e.g., the Crime Survey of England and Wales; the UK Household Longitudinal Survey). Interviewers are required to rate the immediate environment surrounding each sampled household, with information collated about the condition of houses, the extent of graffiti and rubbish in the area, along with any evidence of vandalism. This observational data is primarily used to generate weights for survey nonresponse, with features of the local environment like the condition of housing known correlates of nonresponse. However, in addition to its use for nonresponse adjustment, researchers are now increasingly utilizing this information as a form of SSO. For example, Brunton-Smith and Sturgis (2011) used interviewer ratings of the extent of signs of graffiti, litter, and vandalism in the area surrounding each sampled house as an objective sign of low-level disorder. This was demonstrated to be a reliable measure of the presence of neighborhood disorder, and was subsequently linked to residents' perceptions of crime. Crucially, like more traditional SSO, these measures are independent of the respondent-level data and are systematically collected at each household, enabling stronger conclusions to be made about their contribution to residents' perceptions.

Comparatively little evidence is currently available about the quality of these interviewer observations. Ratings are made at all sampled households; therefore there is good reason to believe that the collected information is representative of the broader environment. Interviewers also receive direct instruction in observation methods as part of fieldwork training. But unlike approaches used in more traditional SSO, no attempts are made to ensure that all data is collected during a similar time window, and the amount of information collected is often limited in comparison to the extensive audits undertaken as part of the PHDCN.

A small number of studies have begun to more directly assess the measurement properties of interviewer SSO data (Andresen et al., 2013; West, 2013; Casas-Cordero et al., 2013). Comparing interviewer assessments to known population values, West (2013) found accuracy levels of around 70%–80% when considering interviewer observations of personal characteristics, suggesting interviewers are reasonably adept at forming accurate judgements about people. No similar data was available about their ability to judge features of the broader spatial environment; therefore it remains unclear whether interviewers will be able to rate the environment with similar accuracy.

Casas-Cordero et al. (2013) focus specifically on the levels of agreement between multiple interviewers about the presence of particular environmental features. They identify a good level of prima facie similarity between multiple interviewer ratings of the same place (correlations of .66 to .99). However, more robust Cohen's kappa assessments tended to be moderate to low, and notably lower than the estimates reported in studies using specialized observers. Andresen et al. (2013) also find moderate reliability estimates in their study, although they do show that reliability generally improved if assessments took place closer together in time.

What is clear is that routine observational data collected as part of the interview protocol represents a potentially interesting source of ecological SSO data. The widespread nature of this data is of obvious benefit to researchers, and the comparatively low marginal cost to data agencies makes it a potentially sustainable source of SSO data. However, current evidence suggests a need for more rigorous training of interviewers to improve accuracy and maximize reliability.

14.5.2 Space-Time Budgets

Space-time budgets represent another novel source of SSO data, with ecological data generated from respondent self-reported activity rather than relying on independent auditor assessments. This approach combines time-use surveys—requiring individuals to carefully record how they have spent their time (either retrospectively or in real-time as part of a time-use diary)—with geocoded locational data to produce fine-grained details about the activities occurring in particular ecological settings at particular times throughout the day and night (Hoeben et al., 2014).

Time-use surveys are now a well-established strategy for recording individual activity in a given time period that have yielded important insights in a range of areas (Andorka, 1987; Belli et al., 2009; Pentland et al., 1999). Wikström and Butterworth (2006; see also Wikström et al., 2012) adapted this approach specifically for ecological settings, building on earlier criminological studies that had started to incorporate spatial information alongside individual activity data (see, e.g., Basta et al., 2010; Rengert and Wasilchick, 2000). Developed as part of the Peterborough Youth Study (Wikström and Butterworth, 2006) and the Peterborough Adolescent and Young Adult Development Study (Wikström et al., 2012), the space-time budget approach required young people to retrospectively record hourly measures of their activities. When recording their activities, they paid particular attention to *where they were spending their time* and *who else was present* (Hoeben et al., 2014). This individual data could then be aggregated up to meaningful geographic and temporal units to generate detailed pictures of specific criminogenic settings. Using this data, Wikström and colleagues developed situational action theory, providing important new insights into the ways that young people use the local areas and how patterns of criminal activity are directly related to young people's use of particular spaces (for a full account of situational action theory see Wikström, 2014). The space-time budget approach has since been replicated in the Netherlands, Sweden, and Ljubljana, providing further information about how delinquent activity is structured in space (Averdijk and Bernasco, 2015; Bernasco et al., 2013; Hoeben et al., 2014).

Work has also been done to assess the validity of data obtained from space-time budgets, comparing estimated activity patterns to external data sources (Hoeben et al., 2014). In general this has shown a moderate to high level of correspondence between self-reported activities derived from space-time budgets and other sources of data, suggesting this approach has the potential to complement more traditional forms of SSO based on independent assessments of local areas.

14.5.3 Google Street View

Perhaps the most exciting single development in the opportunities for conducting SSO is the rapid and expansive growth of Google Street View. Google has sent vehicles with 360-degree cameras down a large proportion of the world's streets, recording photographic evidence at approximately 10-meter or 20-meter intervals (Clarke et al., 2010). Adopting an approach that closely echoes the work of Sampson and colleagues in Chicago, researchers are now able to access a vast archive of documentary pictorial evidence. These images have been directly integrated into Google Maps (and Google Earth), enabling researchers to take a "virtual walkthough" of streets in diverse sites across multiple cities. This makes it possible to conduct detailed environmental audits at almost no cost to the researcher (Anguelov et al., 2010; Badland et al., 2010; Clarke et al., 2010; Curtis, Duval-Diop, and Novak, 2010; Odgers et al., 2012; Rundle et al., 2011;

Vargo, Stone, and Glanz, 2012; Wilson et al., 2012). One particularly promising aspect of Google Street View for SSO is the possibility of researchers conducting comparative research across different sites (Bader et al., 2015). Whereas existing SSOs have generally adopted inconsistent measurement practices, making direct comparison across sites untenable (Brownson et al., 2009), Google Street View has adopted a consistent data collection approach, and has unparalleled geographic reach. This makes it an ideal tool for comparative research.

The use of Google Street View as a social audit tool is becoming increasingly prevalent (see, e.g., Bader and Ailshire, 2014; Odgers et al., 2012; Brownson et al., 2009; Clarke et al., 2010). Initial evidence suggests that it can be a reliable (and cost-effective) alternative to more direct SSO of physical spaces (Clarke et al., 2010; Odgers et al., 2012). This allows researchers to cover a sufficient number of streets to undertake quantitative comparisons. Furthermore, in some instances the most up-to-date photos can be compared with previous archived images (accessed from Google history and collected since 2009). This can allow researchers to also identify signs of recent neighborhood change, introducing a much-needed temporal dimension to existing ecological SSO.

Clarke et al. (2010) compared data obtained from a virtual walkthough of Google Street View to data from in person observations obtained using an identical audit instrument of the same streets four to five years earlier. They found that Google Street View was able to generate reliable indicators for a range of ecological measures including recreational facilities, physical features of the local environment (e.g., trees and waterways), and general land use, with a good level of agreement with the earlier assessments. However, they note caution in the use of Google Street View for attempting to gather information about environmental features that are less frequently observed (e.g., the presence of pharmacies), or require more fine-grained detail (e.g., signs of litter or broken glass) with the resolution and movement restrictions inherent in Google Street View limiting the ability to code this data accurately (for similar results see Bader and Ailshire, 2014). The temporal distance between the virtual and in-person audits will, however, likely contribute to the larger disagreements over these types of measure.

Odgers et al. (2012) also assess the potential of Google Street View. Using data from over 1,000 neighborhoods in England, they focus specifically on inter-rater reliability and discriminant validity by linking virtual SSO data to independent measures of deprivation, individual survey data on disorder, and separate assessments of antisocial behavior. Virtual SSO data was collected on a range of street-level features, including signs of disorder and evidence of physical decay. They report high levels of observed agreement between raters about the presence of disorder, physical decay, and assessments of street safety in a sample of 120 streets that were each observed by four independent raters. They also note that "negative neighborhood features, including SSO-rated disorder and decay and dangerousness corresponded with local resident reports, demonstrated a graded relationship with census-defined indices of socioeconomic status, and predicted higher levels of antisocial behavior among local children" (Odgers et al., 2012: 1009). This leads them to conclude that Google Street View is both a reliable and cost-effective strategy for undertaking SSO. In a recent experiment, Yang and Pao (2015) provide a direct examination of the extent that people are able to accurately rate the disorderly content of photographic images. Looking specifically at participant reaction times and certainty of rating (as assessed by mouse cursor movements), they asked a sample of 241 students and 120 police officers to assess the levels of disorder in a random sample of photos, with each photo varying in the extent of physical and social signs of disorder. They confirmed that people are able to make consistent ratings of physical disorder when viewing photographs of local areas. But these judgments were also informed by the social characteristics of any people present within the space being rated, with existing negative cultural stereotypes leading to more judgments of disorderliness.

Hwang and Sampson (2014) recently used Google Street View to assess gentrification across Chicago. Designed as a follow-up to in-person observations conducted in 2002, they systematically observed and coded Google images from a sample of 2,709 street blocks, looking specifically for signs of gentrification. Signs of gentrification covered the "structural mix" of the area (the combined condition of older and newer properties), visible beautification efforts in the area, and the lack of disorder and decay. They then compared the measures obtained from their virtual audit to other, more objective measures of neighborhood gentrification (the presence of green roofs, and Starbucks coffeehouses), demonstrating a high level of correspondence between both sets of measures. They go on to show that the pace of gentrification was negatively association with concentration of black and Latinos, and that resident perceptions of disorder generally deter gentrification (although the same is not true for observed signs of disorder).

However, Bader and Ailshire (2014) note several limitations of Google Street View that prevent it from completely replacing more traditional approaches to SSO. In particular, they note the problem of image obstructions (e.g., parked cars and foliage) that can obscure raters' view of the side of the road, leading them to judge that approximately 40% of sampled segments were not "street viewable." They also argue that while virtual SSO can offer unprecedented geographic breadth, the depth of measures available from in-person audits are beyond Google Street View (e.g., noise, social incivilities, and aggressive dogs). According, it should be considered as another tool in the arsenal of researchers interested in ecological analyses, rather than a direct replacement for standard SSO. Images from Google Street View are also restricted to daytime photos. While this largely matches existing SSO, it does preclude the use of Google for examining features of the nighttime economy, or the sorts of low-level environmental disorders that are most common at night.

The recent success of virtual audits has led researchers to develop integrated auditing tools that are designed to directly interface with Google Street View—CANVAS (Bader et al., 2015) and FASTVIEW (Griew et al., 2013)—enabling users to more efficiently rate local areas on a range of different attributes. These allow researchers to input coordinate data for sampled streets, or to sample streets within particular geographic areas directly from within Google Earth. Criteria including proximity to specific geographic features can be used to refine the selection of viable study areas, and the tools also enable automatic generation of new sampled streets when Google Street View data is unavailable. Sampled streets can be collated and linked to specific environmental audit forms, ensuring audit records are correctly matched to geographic areas. Researchers can also adapt existing audit tools for specific purposes, focusing on particular features of the urban environment. Taken together, this provides researchers with a flexible set of tools with which to construct their own virtual SSO using Google Street View.

14.5.4 Crowdsourced/User-Generated SSO Data

Efforts are also being made to use crowdsourced photographic data to provide more detailed visual information about local areas (see www.mapillary.com). Individuals can upload geocoded street-level photographs to a central data repository, with more than 50 million photographs currently stored (at the time of writing). It is then possible to explore this visual data in a fashion similar to Google Street View. While still under development, this represents another potentially valuable source of visual information that could feature in future virtual SSO, covering areas not routinely covered by Google Street View. However, the user-generated nature of the content is likely to lead to substantial gaps in coverage, and there is no way to ensure that visual data is recorded in a consistent manner.

Geocoded data from smartphones represents another source of potentially valuable SSO data that may be used to assess how people make use of different environments (Blumenstock, Cadamuro, and On, 2015; Deville et al., 2014). While lacking the fine level of granularity available from more traditional approaches to ecological SSO, this data is being persuasively used to demonstrate dynamic population flows across urban areas (Deville et al., 2014). As these sources of data are more routinely harvested and made available for academic research, we might reasonably anticipate a further evolution in the use of ecological SSO in the next decade. A more detailed discussion of other novel methods of data collection (including open data, big data, and data from mobile devices) is provided by Solymosi and Bowers in chapter 11 in this volume.

14.6 Conclusion

This chapter has demonstrated how the techniques of SSO first pioneered in the work of Reiss (1968) were successfully redeployed in the investigation of ecological settings. This has provided researchers with a robust methodological approach for the collection of observational data about local areas, allowing them to more accurately measure the sorts of intangible qualities of the local environment that are not straightforwardly captured in official data sources. Importantly, researchers have also been furnished with a suitable methodology for collating this data—ecometrics—ensuring reliable conclusions can be drawn about the various influences that features of the local environment have on the experiences of residents.

Existing evidence suggests that SSO is capable of generating high-quality measures of many characteristics of the local neighborhood environment, including signs of physical disorder, land use and the character of local housing, and major physical features in the area. However, SSO may be less effective at capturing rarer events in the local environment, including signs of social disorder, and offending behavior. Accordingly, while SSO is clearly an important resource for researchers, this should be used in conjunction with other sources of information about local areas.

Until recently, however, the substantial time and financial resources required to conduct large-scale SSO in ecological settings has meant that, with few exceptions, ecological SSOs have been rare. With the advent of Google Street View these barriers have been removed, with SSO now a realistic option for many research problems. This has also created new opportunities for the establishment of comparative SSO projects in diverse ecological settings. Interviewer-collected observational data represents another valuable source of SSO data for environmental criminology, with survey agencies now regularly publishing paradata collected by interviewers about the environment surrounding respondent houses. Crowdsourced SSO data represents another potentially valuable source of observational data that may be mined by future researchers wishing to better measure some features of the urban environment. However, currently no evidence exists on the validity of this type of data.

Taken together, these developments suggest that this an exciting time for research into the impact of ecological settings using SSO.

References

Andorka, R. (1987). Time budgets and their uses. *Annual Review of Sociology* 13(1): 149–164.

Andresen, E. M., Malmstrom, T. K., Schootman, M., Wolinsky, F. D., Miller, J. P., and Miller, D. K. (2013). Observer ratings of neighborhoods: Comparison of two methods. *BMC Public Health* 13: 1024.

Anguelov, D., Dulong, C., Filip, D., Frueh, C., Lafon, S., Lyon, R., Ogale, A., Vincent, L., and Weaver, J. (2010). Google Street View: Capturing the world at street level. *Computer* 43(6): 32–38.

Averdijk, M., and Bernasco, W. (2015). Testing the situational explanation of victimization among adolescents. *Journal of Research in Crime and Delinquency* 52(2): 141–180.

Bader, M. D. M., and Ailshire, J. A. (2014). Creating measures of theoretically relevant neighborhood attributes at multiple spatial scales. *Sociological Methodology* 44(1): 322–368.

Bader, M. D. M., Mooney, S. J., Lee, Y. J., Sheehan, D., Neckerman, K. M., Rundle, A. G., and Teitler, J. O. (2015). Development and deployment of the Computer Assisted Neighborhood Visual Assessment System (CANVAS) to measure health-related neighborhood conditions. *Health and Place* 31: 163–172.

Badland, H. M., Opit, S., Witten, K., Kearns, R. A., and Mavoa, S. (2010). Can virtual streetscape audits reliably replace physical streetscape audits? *Journal of Urban Health* 87(6): 1007–1016.

Barker R. G., and Wright, H. F. (1955). *The Midwest and Its Children*. Evanston, IL: Row, Peterson.

Basta, L. A., Richmond, T. S., and Wiebe, D. J. (2010). Neighbourhoods, daily activities, and measuring health risks experienced in urban environments. *Social Science and Medicine* 71(11): 1943–1950.

Belli, R. F., Stafford, F. P., and Alwin, D. F. (2009). *Calendar and Time Diary: Methods in Life Course Research.* Los Angeles: Sage.

Bernasco, W., Ruiter, S., Bruinsma, G. J. N., Pauwels, L., and Weerman, F. M. (2013). Situational causes of offending: A fixed-effects analysis of space-time budget data. *Criminology* 51(4): 895–926.

Box, S., Hale, C., and Andrews, G. (1988). Explaining fear of crime. *British Journal of Criminology* 28, 340–356.

Brownson, R. C., Hoehner, C. M., Day, K., Forsyth, A., and Sallis, J. F. (2009). Measuring the built environment for physical activity: State of the science. *American Journal of Preventative Medicine* 36(4, Supplement 1): S99–S123.

Brunton-Smith, I., and Sturgis, P. (2011). Do neighborhoods generate fear of crime? An empirical test using the British Crime Survey. *Criminology* 49(2): 331–369.

Buckle, A., and Farrington, D. P. (1984). An observational study of shoplifting. *British Journal of Criminology* 24(1): 63–73.

Buckle, A., and Farrington, D. P. (1994). Measuring shoplifting by systematic observation: A replication study. *Psychology, Crime and Law* 1(2): 133–141.

Casas-Cordero, C., Kreuter, F., Wang, Y., and Babey, S. (2013). Assessing the measurement error properties of interviewer observations of neighbourhood characteristics. *Journal of the Royal Statistical Society: Series A (Statistics in Society)* 176(1): 211–225.

Clarke, P., Ailshire, J., Melendez, R., Bader, M., and Morenoff, J. (2010). Using Google Earth to conduct a neighborhood audit: Reliability of a virtual audit instrument. *Health and Place* 16:1224–1229.

Clifton, K. J., Livi Smith, A. D., and Rodriguez, D. (2007). The development and testing of an audit for the pedestrian environment. *Landscape Urban Planning* 80(1–2): 95–110.

Curtis, A., Duval-Diop, D., and Novak, J. (2010). Identifying spatial patterns of recovery and abandonment in the post-Katrina Holy Cross neighborhood of New Orleans. *Cartography and Geographic Information Science* 37: 45–56.

Day, K., Boarnet, M., Alfonzo, M., and Forsyth, A. (2006). The Irvine-Minnesota inventory to measure built environments: Development. *American Journal of Preventative Medicine* 30(2): 144–152.

Deville, P., Linard, C., Martin, S., Gilbert, M., Stevens, F. R., Gaughan, A. E., Blondel, V. D., and Tatem, A. J. (2014). Dynamic population mapping using mobile phone data. *Proceedings of the National Academy of Science* 111(45): 15888–15893.

Evanston, I. L., Blumenstock, J., Cadamuro, G., and On, R. (2015). Predicting poverty and wealth from mobile phone metadata. *Science* 350(6264): 1073–1076.

Ewing, R., Clement, O., Handy, S., Brownson, R. C., and Winston, E. (2005). *Identifying and Measuring Urban Design Qualities Related to Walkability—Final Report.* Princeton, NJ: Robert Wood Johnson Foundation.

Ewing, R., Handy, S., Brownson, R. C., Clemente, O., and Winston, E. (2006). Identifying and measuring urban design qualities related to walkability. *Journal of Physical Activity and Health* 3: S223–S240.

Gomez-Rubio, V., Best, N., Li, G., and Clarke, P. (2010). Bayesian statistics for small area estimation. Imperial College London.

Griew, P., Hillsdon, M., Foster, C., Coombes, E., Jones, A., and Wilkinson, P. (2013). Developing and testing a street audit tool using Google Street View to measure environmental supportiveness for physical activity. *International Journal of Behavioral Nutrition and Physical Activity* 10: 103.

Hoeben, E. M., Bernasco, W., Weerman, F., Pauwels, L., and van Halem, S. (2014). The space-time budget method in criminological research. *Crime Science* 3(12): 1–15.

Hwang, J., and Sampson, R. (2014). Divergent pathways of gentrification: Racial inequality and the social order of renewal in Chicago neighborhoods. *American Sociological Review* 79(4): 726–751.

Kish, L. (1965). *Survey Sampling*. New York: Wiley.

Madge, C. (1939). *Britain by Mass Observation*. Harmondsworth: Penguin.

Mastrofski, S. D., Parks, R. B., and McCluskey, J. D. (2010). Systematic social observation in criminology. In Piquero, A. R., and Weisburd, D. (Eds.), *Handbook of Quantitative Criminology*. New York: Springer, pp. 225–247.

Mastrofski, S. D., Parks, R. B., Reiss, A. J., Jr., Worden, R. E., DeJong, C., Snipes, J. B., and Terrill, W. (1998). Systematic observation of public police: Applying field research methods to policy issues. NCJ 172859. National Institute of Justice, Washington, DC

Odgers, C. L., Caspi, A., Bates, C. J., Sampson, R. J., and Moffitt, T. E. (2012). Systematic social observation of children's neighborhoods using Google Street View: A reliable and cost-effective method. *Journal of Child Psychology and Psychiatry* 53: 1009–1017.

Pentland, W. E., Harvey, A. S., Lawton, M. P., and McColl, M. A. (1999). *Time Use Research in the Social Sciences*. New York: Kluwer Academic Publishers.

Perkins, D. D., and Taylor, R. B. (1996). Ecological assessments of community disorder: Their relationship to fear of crime and theoretical implications. *American Journal of Community Psychology* 24:63–107

Perkins D. D., Wandersman A., Rich, R. C., and Taylor, R. B. (1993). The physical environment of street crime: Defensible space, territoriality and incivilities. *Journal of Environmental Psychology* 13:29–49

Raudenbush, S. W., and Bryk, A. S. (2002). *Hierarchical Linear Models: Applications and Data Analysis Methods*. 2nd ed. Thousand Oaks, CA: Sage.

Raudenbush, S. W., and Sampson, R. J. (1999). Toward a science of assessing ecological settings, with applications to the systematic social observation of neighborhoods. *Sociological Methodology* 29: 1–41.

Ready, J., Weisburd, D., Lawton, B., Haviland, A., Cave, B., and Nelson, M. (2014). Systematic social and physical observations at crime hot spots in Baltimore, MD: Methodology and baseline findings. Paper presented at American Society of Criminology conference.

Reiss, A. J., Jr. (1968). Police brutality—answer to key questions. *Transaction* 5:10–19.

Reiss, A. J., Jr. (1971). Systematic observation of natural social phenomena. *Sociological Methodology* 3: 3–33.

Rengert, G. F., and Wasilchick, J. (2000). *Suburban Burglary: A Tale of Two Suburbs*. 2nd ed. Springfield: Charles C. Thomas.

Rudes, D., Ready, J., Lawton, B., and Weisburd, D. (2014). Tempered hope: Spatial meaning in predatory, drug, and mixed hot spots. Paper presented at American Society of Criminology conference.

Rundle, A. G., Bader, M. D. M., Richards, C. A., Neckerman, K. M., and Teitler, J. O. (2011). Using Google Street View to audit neighborhood environments. *American Journal of Preventative Medicine* 40(1): 94–100.

Sampson, R., and Raudenbush, S. (1999). Systematic social observation of public spaces: A new look at disorder in urban neighborhoods. *American Journal of Sociology* 105(3): 603–651.

Steenbeek, W., and Kreis, S. (2015). Where broken windows should be fixed: Toward identification of areas at the tipping point. *Journal of Research in Crime and Delinquency* 52: 511–533.

Taylor, R. B. (2001). *Breaking Away from Broken Windows: Baltimore Neighborhoods and the Nationwide Fight against Crime, Grime, Fear, and Decline*. Boulder, CO: Westview Press.

Taylor, R. B. (2015). *Community Criminology: Fundamentals of Spatial and Temporal Scaling, Ecological Indicators and Selectivity Bias*. New York: New York University Press.

Taylor, R. B., Gottfredson, S. D., and Brower, S. (1984). Block crime and fear: Defensible space, local social ties, and territorial functioning. *Journal of Research in Crime and Delinquency* 21: 303–331.

Taylor, R. B., Shumaker, S., and Gottfredson, S. D. (1985). Neighborhood-level links between physical features and local sentiments: Deterioration of fear of crime and confidence. *Journal of Architectural and Planning Research* 21: 261–265.

Thomas, D. S., Loomis, A. M., and Arrington, R. E. (1933). *Observational Studies of Social Behavior*. New Haven: Institute of Human Relations, Yale University.

Tseloni, A. (2006). Multilevel modelling of the number of property crimes: Household and area effects. *Journal of the Royal Statistical Society: Series A (Statistics in Society)* 169(2): 205–233.

US Bureau of the Census (2011). New York City Housing and Vacancy Survey (NYCHVS).

Vargo, J., Stone, B., and Glanz, K. (2012). Google walkability: A new tool for local planning and public health research? *Journal of Physical Activity and Health* 9: 689–697.

Verbitsky Savitz, N., and Raudenbush, S. W. (2009). Exploiting spatial dependence to improve measurement of neighborhood social processes. *Sociological Methodology* 39: 151–183.

Waddington, P. A. J., Stenson, K., and Don, D. (2004). In proportion, race and police stop and search. *British Journal of Criminology* 44: 889–914.

West, B. T. (2013). An examination of the quality and utility of interviewer observations in the National Survey for Family Growth. *Journal of the Royal Statistical Society: Series A (Statistics in Society)* 176(1): 211–225.

Wikström, P-O. H. (2014). Why crime happens: A situational action theory. In G. Manzo (Ed.), *Analytical Sociology: Actions and Networks*. Hoboken, NJ: John Wiley and Sons, pp. 74–94.

Wikström, P-O. H., and Butterworth, D. A. (2006). *Adolescent Crime: Individual Differences and Lifestyles*. Cullompton, Devon, UK: Willan Publishing.

Wikström, P-O. H., Oberwittler, D., Treiber, K., and Hardie, B. (2012). *Breaking Rules: The Social and Situational Dynamics of Young People's Urban Crime*. New York: Oxford University Press.

Whyte, W. F. (1943). *Street Corner Society: The Social Structure of an Italian Slum*. Chicago: University of Chicago Press.

Wilson, J. S., Kelly, C. M., Schootman, M., Baker, E. A., Banerjee, A., Clennin, M., and Miller, D. K. (2012). Assessing the built environment using omnidirectional imagery. *American Journal of Preventative Medicine* 42(2): 193–199.

Yang, S-M., and Pao, C-C. (2015). Do we "see" the same thing? An experimental look into the black box of disorder perception. *Journal of Research in Crime and Delinquency* 52(4): 534–566.

CHAPTER 15

COMPUTER SIMULATIONS

Agent-Focused Environmental Criminology

DANIEL BIRKS

15.1 Introduction

Environmental criminology seeks to understand crime opportunities, events, patterns, and the proximal circumstances that influence their occurrence (Brantingham and Brantingham 1991). Over the last four decades, this rationale has supported a diverse range of research, generating essential knowledge, and—all importantly—leveraging it to reduce crime through techniques such as situational crime prevention, problem-oriented policing, and crime prevention through environmental design. Yet, for a range of reasons, empirical research in the field of environmental criminology can sometimes be practically infeasible, prohibitively expensive, or ethically questionable.

Consider, for instance, how we might quantify the role that the transport network plays in influencing the spatial distribution of crime events—a quandary that underpins a rich vein of environmental criminology. Application of the scientific apparatus desirable for robust research in this area—the experimental study—is largely infeasible. We simply cannot systematically manipulate transport networks and observe resulting distributions of crime. As a result, studies of road structure and crime risk must rely on nonexperimental methods, which in turn, are encumbered by a range of widely acknowledged weaknesses. Similarly, while environmental criminology's oft-cited opportunity theories propose intuitive individual-level accounts of cognition, action, and interaction among potential victims, offenders, crime preventers, and the environments they inhabit, our ability to systematically observe these behaviors in situ is severely restricted.

In a range of disciplines computational models support theoretical and empirical efforts by allowing researchers to construct simulations of real-world systems. The computational model, much like its written or mathematical equivalent, seeks to provide an abbreviated, yet useful, version of some more complex reality, in this case, by encoding an abstraction of the target system as a computer program (Gilbert and Troitzsch 2005). Simulating key structures and behaviors of the target system, the computational model seeks to provide a synthetic equivalent that is easier to both observe and control than its real-world counterpart. Studying this model, researchers investigate under what circumstances particular system outcomes come about, and estimate how changes to particular system components might impact on future states of the system. In this way, the computational model, and the analyses it enables, provides a laboratory of sorts (Dibble 2006), where simulated experiments can be conducted free from the constraints of empirical enquiry, and in which hypotheses concerning complex real-world systems can prototyped, tested, and refined.

Figure 15.1—recreated from Gilbert and Troitzsch (2005)—depicts the underlying logic of the simulation method. We begin by identifying a target system we hope to better understand. Through abstraction, we develop a computational model of that system. Using this model, computer simulations are conducted. Each simulation represents a particular instantiation of the computational model whereby the model is run, such that its components repeatedly act and interact according to some modeled behavior. This process creates simulated data, which are then compared to empirical data concerning the target system. Doing so, we are able to assess model validity by ascertaining if the model is capable of generating outputs similar to those observed of the real world. Once a model is sufficiently validated, it can be used to better understand how previous system states might have come about, and how changes to the system might generate novel states.

Computational models have proved useful in a wide range of domains, especially where logistical constraints limit the applicability of empirical approaches—for example, in understanding evolutionary processes that operate over deep time, in identifying useful organic compounds from vast numbers of potential structures, or in manipulating complex supply chains to estimate increases in efficiency without risk of destabilizing an existing system. While computational models such as these have supported the natural sciences for some time, over the last three decades social scientists have productively applied them to better understand societal systems.

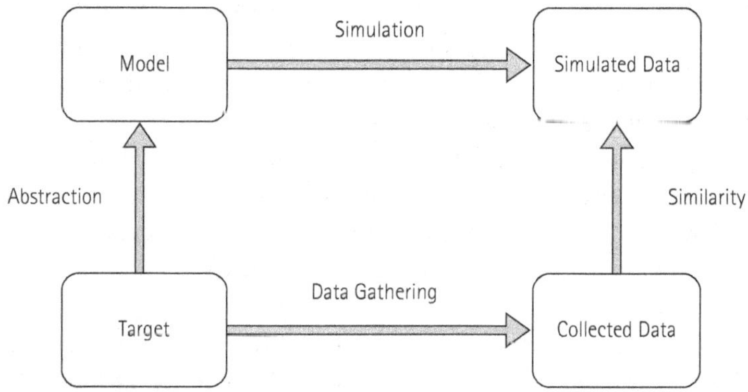

FIGURE 15.1 The logic of simulation as a method

Source: Gilbert and Troitzsch 2005.

Simulation models can take several forms. System dynamics models, for instance, are system-oriented and allow researchers to model the stocks and flow of information/materials through a complex system that is typically characterized by feedback loops. Using system dynamics models, researchers typically focus on replicating the key causal structure of the system to best understand it, and in some cases redesign it to be more effective. Conversely, discrete event simulations are process-oriented and consider how, usually homogenous, micro-level entities proceed through a system of prescribed discrete processes. Here, the researcher typically deals with manipulating not the structure of the system but those internal processes that make it up. In recent years the field of computational social science has been dominated by another approach—the individual- or agent-based computational model (ABM). As its name suggests, an ABM is the individual-oriented, explicitly modeling of a complex system through those individual agents that make it up—for example, people, peer groups, companies, or nations. In this case, the researcher seeks to examine the complex system by manipulating the nature and behavior of those individual entities and observing resulting system outcomes.

ABMs explore how the decisions, actions, and interactions of autonomous, heterogeneous individuals influence aggregate system outcomes. In the social sciences ABMs are thus well placed to explore how the choices people make on a day-to-day basis translate into observable societal phenomena such as wealth distributions, patterns of segregation, or rates of crime. As a result of rapid increases in the availability of computational resources to run them, and empirical data to calibrate and validate them, ABMs have provided broad insights in a range of research areas, including economics (Tesfatsion 2002), anthropology (Dean et al. 2000), epidemiology (Segovia-Juarez, Ganguli, and Kirschner 2004), geography (Valbuena et al. 2010), and criminology (Birks, Townsley, and Stewart 2012).

This chapter aims to provide the reader with a primer in the simulation method and in particular the application of ABMs in the field of environmental criminology. It begins by discussing the rationale behind the ABM approach. Subsequently, it summarizes fundamental processes involved in designing, constructing, verifying, calibrating, validating, and utilizing ABMs. The chapter concludes by discussing some of the overarching strengths and limitations of the approach, and by discussing several avenues of research that might aid in furthering the use of ABMs within the field of environmental criminology.

15.2 Agent-Based Environmental Criminology

An individual- or agent-based model is a type of computational model that seeks to explicitly model the multiple autonomous agents (individuals or groups) that comprise some target system with the intention of exploring how their action and interaction impact on the outcomes of the system as a whole. ABMs are particularly useful for studying complex adaptive systems where nonlinear relations between system properties dictate that analytical solutions are difficult to derive or require unrealistic assumptions in order to manage mathematical tractability (Epstein and Axtell 1996). To illustrate, an ABM might be applied to study the spread of disease. Here, the interrelationship between spatial and social proximity plays a key role in mediating the interactions, and subsequent transmission, among heterogeneous populations. These processes introduce complex dynamics that are difficult to incorporate into equation-based accounts that are often aspatial and assume population homogeneity and uniform mixing. ABMs thus provide a natural platform for modeling human systems (Bonabeau 2002; Hedström 2005) where the interactions of people impact on societal outcomes in rich and complex ways. By modeling the individual members of a society as autonomous agents, ABMs offer the ideal means to represent key properties of societal systems, including autonomy, heterogeneity, localized interaction, and feedback-driven processes. By modeling individual-level actions and interactions, ABMs are also capable of providing accounts of emergent—and sometimes counterintuitive—phenomena, such as Schelling's landmark research on the relationship between individual neighborhood preferences and aggregate patterns of segregation (Schelling 1971).

Within the social sciences, agent-based social simulation (ABSS) (Davidsson 2002) aim to construct artificial societies by modeling the behavior of large numbers of heterogeneous autonomous agents. Modeling these individual agents, their cognition, action, and interaction, ABSS seeks to understand social phenomena from the *bottom up*; assessing the societal outcomes that result from the decentralized individual-level interaction of multiple heterogeneous actors. Doing so, ABMs depart from traditional *top-down* analytic strategies that observe aggregate-level associations and in turn attempt to infer individual-level interactions capable of explaining them (Epstein 1999).

This *bottom-up* approach is well aligned with environmental criminology's depiction of crime events as the output of numerous interactions between potential offenders, victims, crime preventers, and the environments they inhabit. It is these interactions that influence where and when crime occurs, by whom it is perpetrated, and who experiences it. Yet, for the most part, such interactions remain largely unobserved, with only their outputs—crime—(somewhat) routinely observed. Accordingly, traditional analytical approaches within environmental criminology often assess the relationship between area-level indicators (affluence, number of public transport hubs, etc.) and crime. This is understandable. It seems unlikely (and undesirable) that the spatial and temporal activity patterns of all people be systematically observed. Similarly, the decision calculus employed by offenders in the evaluation of criminal opportunities can only be partially revealed through methods that are associated with a range of unwelcome weaknesses. This list of things we propose as significant in explaining crime events, yet cannot systematically observe, is considerable—offender perceptions of risk/reward/effort across multiple contexts, victim and offender cognitive maps, reinforcement processes, current and historic activity nodes, and so on. The primary consequence of this paucity of micro-level crime event data is that rigorous theoretical testing in the field of environmental criminology is difficult to undertake (Eck 1995). And, by extension, interventions that seek to reduce crime by preventing or disrupting individual-level interactions are difficult to most effectively design.

It is for these reasons that ABMs are becoming popular among environmental criminologists, with a range of scholars constructing models in a hope of better understanding crime events, patterns, and the mechanisms that underlie them. Conducting agent-based environmental criminology, we construct synthetic environments and populate them with artificial populations of potential victims, offenders, and/or crime preventers who interact with one another and commit, prevent, or respond to virtual crimes. By manipulating the characteristics and behaviors of these virtual populations to reflect our theories or state-of-the-art empirical knowledge, we utilize these models of crime events to better understand why particular crime problems might occur, and in some circumstances, how they might be most effectively prevented or disrupted.

By comparing simulated and empirical data, the veracity of encoded assumptions can be assessed. Thus, the ABM offers the environmental criminologist the means to assess the explanatory capacity of crime event theory (Groff 2007; Birks et al. 2012). Moreover, where models produce plausible outcomes, simulations can explore what approaches might be used in reducing crime by manipulating crime event mechanisms (Groff and Birks 2008; Malleson and Brantingham 2009; Bosse and Gerritsen 2010; Birks 2017). Over the last decade ABMs have been applied to explore a range of crime problems, including residential burglary (Birks, Donkin, and Wellsmith 2008; Malleson et al. 2012; Birks, Townsley, and Stewart 2012), interpersonal victimization (Groff 2007, 2008; Wang, Liu, and Eck 2008; Birks, Townsley, and Stewart 2014), maritime piracy (Marchione, Johnson, and Wilson 2014), and wildlife poaching (Hill, Johnson, and Borrion 2014), to name but a few.

To provide the reader with a better understanding of this approach, the following sections of this chapter outline core processes involved in the application of ABMs; model specification, design, construction, verification, calibration, validation, and experimentation. This description is supported throughout by illustrative examples concerning the design and development of two existing ABMs. The first, SimRobbery, applies agent-based modeling for explanatory purposes and aims to assess if several propositions derived from the routine activity approach (Felson 2008), rational choice perspective (Cornish and Clarke 2008), and crime pattern theory (Brantingham and Brantingham 2008) are sufficient to explain common empirical patterns of interpersonal victimization. The second, SimDespatch, utilizes agent-based modeling in a predictive capacity and aims to provide a platform for estimating the effectiveness of varying police call and despatch strategies. While presentation of the results of simulation experiments carried out using these models is beyond the scope of this volume, interested readers are directed to Birks, Townsley, and Stewart (2014) in the case of the former, and Birks and Townsley (2018) for the latter, where a range of simulation experiments using these models are conducted and analyzed in detail. Importantly, these examples are purposefully divergent in their goals—the former in supporting theoretical testing and foundational understanding of observed crime patterns; the latter in demonstrating how ABM can be applied to support real-world policy decisions of those who seek to respond to crime.

15.3 Building ABM in Environmental Criminology

15.3.1 Phase 1: Model/Problem Specification

Consider we have a research quandary—a desire to understand some particular observed crime phenomena, or the need to assess how we best respond to a particular crime problem. One analytical approach we might consider is the computational model. Before we do so, however, we must assess whether the construction of such a model will be useful and achievable. Like all analytical methods, the simulation approach is suitable for some problems and not suitable for others. Thus, the initial phase in the application of ABM is simply to ask ourselves, what is the system of interest? What is the research question concerning it? And in what ways will the construction of an ABM of that system aid in answering our questions?

In the cases where we might consider construction of a computational model it is typical that (1) the problem might be well described as some property of a system of interacting components (this is often the case in environmental criminology); and that (2) empirical study of that system is prohibitively expensive, logistically infeasible, or ethically unsound (Birks and Elffers 2014). After ascertaining that a computational model may support our study, the next task is to evaluate if development of the model is feasible. To address this question, we broadly aim to evaluate what theoretical and empirical sources of knowledge exist concerning the target system. Accordingly, sometimes the utility of simulating a particular system is clear, but during this phase it becomes clear that doing so will be very difficult. There are a wide range of (often interrelated) reasons why this may be the case—but typically these relate to one of the following: (1) there is general paucity of theory concerning the system being studied; (2) where theory exists, it is overly vague and not sufficiently explicit to be translated into model constructs; (3) there are no empirical data available describing the outcome of some process proposed by theory; and (4) there are large numbers of known significant parameters for which no estimates exist. Note that while empirical estimates for all parameters are likely unattainable, and may be the rationale for the model, if no data are available for model calibration, its insights may be appropriately limited, especially if one seeks to generalize from model outcomes to the real world.

To reiterate then, the first task in considering the simulation approach is to consider (*a*) what the construction of a simulation will bring to understanding the problem; and (*b*) whether the construction of such a model is practically feasible. Only if we answer yes to both these questions should we proceed. To briefly illustrate this phase, I now summarize the problem specification associated with our example models, SimRobbery and SimDespatch.

SimRobbery: Our first example model aims to answer the question *Are key propositions of environmental criminology sufficient to explain commonly observed patterns of interpersonal victimization?* Research consistently demonstrates that opportunistic interpersonal victimization is spatially concentrated (Block and Davis 1996; Braga, Hureau, and Papachristos 2011), disproportionately experienced by a small number of repeat victims (Farrell and Bouloukos 2001; Mukherjee and Carcach 1998), and perpetrated by offenders who operate close to home (LeBeau 1987; Wright and Decker 1997). The routine activity approach, rational choice perspective, and crime pattern theory provide explicit individual-level descriptions for why these phenomena occur. However, difficulties associated with observing crime events limit our ability to link these individual-level behaviors to observable crime patterns, and in turn, test our theoretical depictions of the crime event. To solve this problem we propose construction of a spatially explicit model of victims' and offenders' activities, where key agent behaviors are derived from the opportunity theories. In constructing this model we aim to assess if formalized theoretical propositions are capable of generating patterns of crime that resemble those consistently observed empirical regularities of interpersonal victimization.

SimDespatch: Our second example model seeks to address the question *How do police most effectively despatch resources to respond to calls for service?* A core activity of any policing agency relates to prioritizing and responding to ongoing requests for service. Clearly there is a diverse range of potential response strategies that might be implemented by a policing agency—allocated resources, despatch configurations, patrol strategies, and so on. Similarly, numerous metrics of strategy effectiveness might be assessed—response rates, response times, resourcing requirements, and so on. Unfortunately, logistical and ethical constraints severely limit our ability to evaluate large numbers of strategies, yet it is not immediately clear how some facets of a response strategy will impact on effectiveness. To solve this problem, we propose construction of a spatially explicit model of calls for service and response vehicles operating under various configurations. Using this model we seek to estimate the effectiveness of a large number of strategies rapidly, cheaply, and ethically.

15.3.2 Phase 2: Model Design

Once we have ascertained that an ABM may support our understanding, the next phase is design of the model itself. Reality is a rich and complex domain and all models that seek to better understand it rely on abstraction. In this phase it is the goal of the researcher to establish what should and should not be included in the model. Here it may be alluring to incorporate vast amounts of detail into a model. However, such models can prove exceedingly time consuming to construct, typically require considerable amounts of calibration, and ultimately may lack generalizability. Moreover, one should be mindful that very complex models can become as difficult to interpret as the systems they seek to describe. Conversely, very abstract models may be simple to construct but may limit inferences to real-world phenomena. Ultimately, our goal is to produce a model that represents the target system at a level of complexity commensurate with its intended purpose, and without compromising utility or generalizability. This, as you will imagine, is not a simple task.

An important criterion to consider in the design of any model is intended use. Broadly speaking, ABMs can serve two non-mutually exclusive, yet fundamentally different, purposes—to *explain* and to *predict*. Explanatory ABMs typically deal in theoretical proposition and hypotheses and seek to better understand how particular outcomes can and cannot come about. Doing so, they aim to provide an apparatus around which previous observations are better understood. Explanatory ABMs are typically quite abstract in nature and may ignore some components of a system in order to reveal generalizable insights into fundamental processes involved with another. This dictates that sometimes it can be difficult to ascertain how directly applicable their insights are to real-world systems. Conversely, predictive ABMs aim to estimate future observations given some particular configuration of initial conditions. The predictive ABM often seeks to generate applied insights that might inform policy or practice, and as a result often requires explicit understanding of the processes being modeled and associated empirical data through which the model can be closely calibrated and validated. In contrast to explanatory ABMs, the inclusion of large quantities of empirical calibration data can dictate that predictive ABMs offer limited generalizability and run the risk of overfitting to a particular scenario.

Thus, the choice of the type of model one creates is directly related to both the research question and the viability of empirical data available concerning the system to be modeled. Often, in practical terms, the latter—availability of empirical data describing the system—can have a direct impact on both model type and complexity. In domains where empirical data are limited, explanatory models are exploratory in nature and aim for simplicity, parsimony, and generalizability. Conversely, where copious and accurate data are available concerning the system of interest, predictive models can be constructed that focus on specificity and predictive accuracy, but at the same time may sacrifice generalizability.

Specification of a model, regardless of purpose, requires that researchers select the structural (what pieces) and behavioral (what the pieces do) components of the target system to be modeled. While the former may be a relatively simple task, the latter often requires theoretical perspectives to be selected and embedded within model constructs. This process, commonly referred to as *theory formalization*, typically involves translating verbal models into algorithmic formalization, to subsequently be endowed among a virtual population. This process of theory formalization is almost always an enlightening one, and can often generate considerable debate concerning the systems of interest, and/or highlight weakness/inconsistencies in theoretical propositions previously well accepted by those involved in the model design.

While there is no definitive method through which model design should be carried out, if we consider those ABMs that might be applied by environmental criminologists, model design will typically include answering the following questions:

- What is the target system?
- What theories/empirical data can inform simulation of the target system?
- What is known / somewhat known / unknown about the target system?
- What types of entities, actors need to be modeled to describe the system?
- What characteristics define actors?
- What mechanisms of cognition, action, and interaction do system actors exhibit?
- In what type of an environment should actors interact—spatial/aspatial, abstract / real world?
- What characteristics define this environment?
- What types of outcomes will the model produce?
- What components of the model will be manipulable to support experimentation?
- What types of experiments should be run to address the overarching research question?

To further illustrate this process we return to our example models.

SimRobbery: SimRobbery explores how individual-level mechanisms of movement, target selection, and learning proposed by the routine activity approach, rational choice perspective, and crime pattern theory impact on patterns of interpersonal victimization. To address this question the model simulates the spatiotemporal interactions of victims and offenders (see Figure 15.2). Following the theories it seeks to explore, all actors undertake spatially structured activities derived from assertions of the routine activity approach and crime pattern theory. Simulated offenders employ a target selection calculus derived from assertions of the rational choice perspective that allows them to evaluate potential targets, and a learning behavior inspired by crime pattern theory's awareness space construct that allows them to learn about their local environment. These behaviors can be individually enabled and disabled (in this case enabling a counterfactual behavior), thus allowing experiments to be performed that assess the impact of each on model outcomes. Simulated data generated by the model describe crime events that result when offenders encounter, select, and victimize suitable victims. Following an explanatory approach, simulations take place in an abstract environment that is easily manipulated to increase generalizability across multiple environmental contexts. Simulated experiments evaluate (and compare) the presence of three well-understood empirical regularities of crime under all combinations of simulated behavior—spatial clustering, repeat victimization, and distance-to-crime distributions.

SimDespatch: SimDespatch simulates (1) a series of spatiotemporally referenced calls for service and (2) a population of virtual responders tasked with responding to those calls in a spatially referenced environment (see Figure 15.3). Calls for service are defined by a location in the environment, a time at which the call was received,

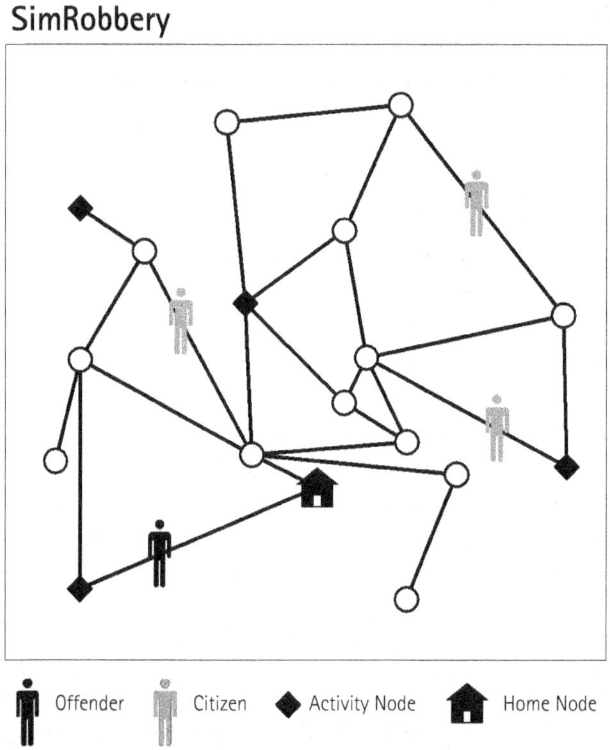

FIGURE 15.2 Conceptual design of SimRobbery

and an amount of time required to resolve an incident. Simulated responders navigate the environment according to a response strategy defined by the following parameters: number of response vehicles, call prioritization strategy (i.e., how responders choose which event to respond to), and patrol strategy (i.e., what responders do when they are not responding). The outcomes of the model are a series of measures of strategy effectiveness, which include min/max/mean response times, responder fuel consumption, and proportion of time spent responding (efficiency). Experiments will be performed that compare the effectiveness of different response strategies across these measures.

15.3.3 Phase 3: Model Development

The next phase is development of the computational model. This involves translating the model design discussed above into an ABM by writing a computer program. While ABMs can be developed from scratch using almost all modern programing languages, a range of purpose-built ABM frameworks exist. These frameworks provide prebuilt functions and objects that allow for rapid development of ABMs and often also include

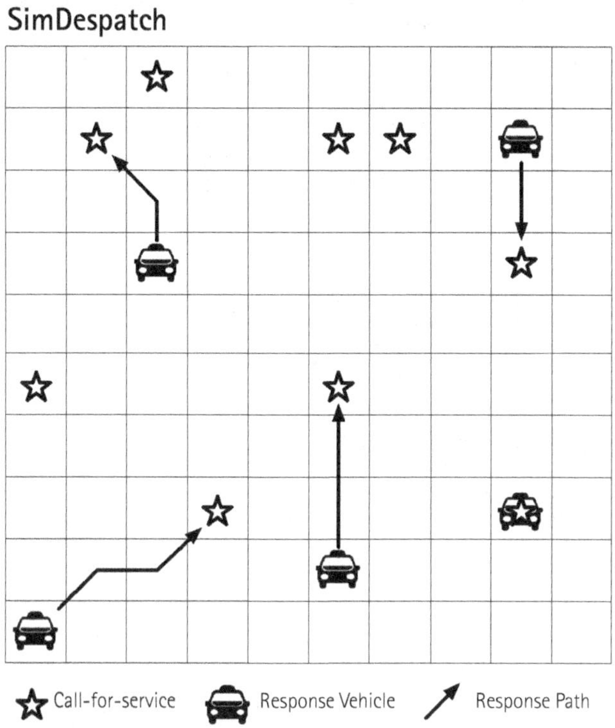

FIGURE 15.3 SimDespatch models

a custom development environment that provides tools for model testing, debugging, and the running of large numbers of simulation experiments. Examples of commonly used frameworks include Netlogo (Wilensky 1999), Repast (North et al. 2005), MASON (Luke et al. 2005), and Swarm (Minar et al. 1996).

The two key components of any ABM are a population of one or more agents and a synthetic environment within which these agents are situated, act, and interact. Agents represent the individual actors to be modeled. Within environmental criminology these typically represent people such as offenders, citizens, police officers, response vehicles, and so on. An agent is an autonomous, goal-directed program that is made up of (1) a series of characteristics that describe its persistent features, for example, home location, age, maximum speed; (2) a series of state variables that reflect its current internal state, for example, current location/speed, current motivation, cognitive map; and (3) a series of behaviors that allow agents to perceive, reason, and act within the simulation, and in turn, alter those characteristics, states, and the world around them. It is through these behaviors that agents are bestowed with decision calculi inspired by theory or previous knowledge.

To illustrate, drawing on propositions of the routine activity approach, Figure 15.4 depicts two conceptualizations of a simple offending behavior that agents enact to ascertain whether or not to offend. In the first version—Figure 15.4A—agents simply choose

(a)

(b)

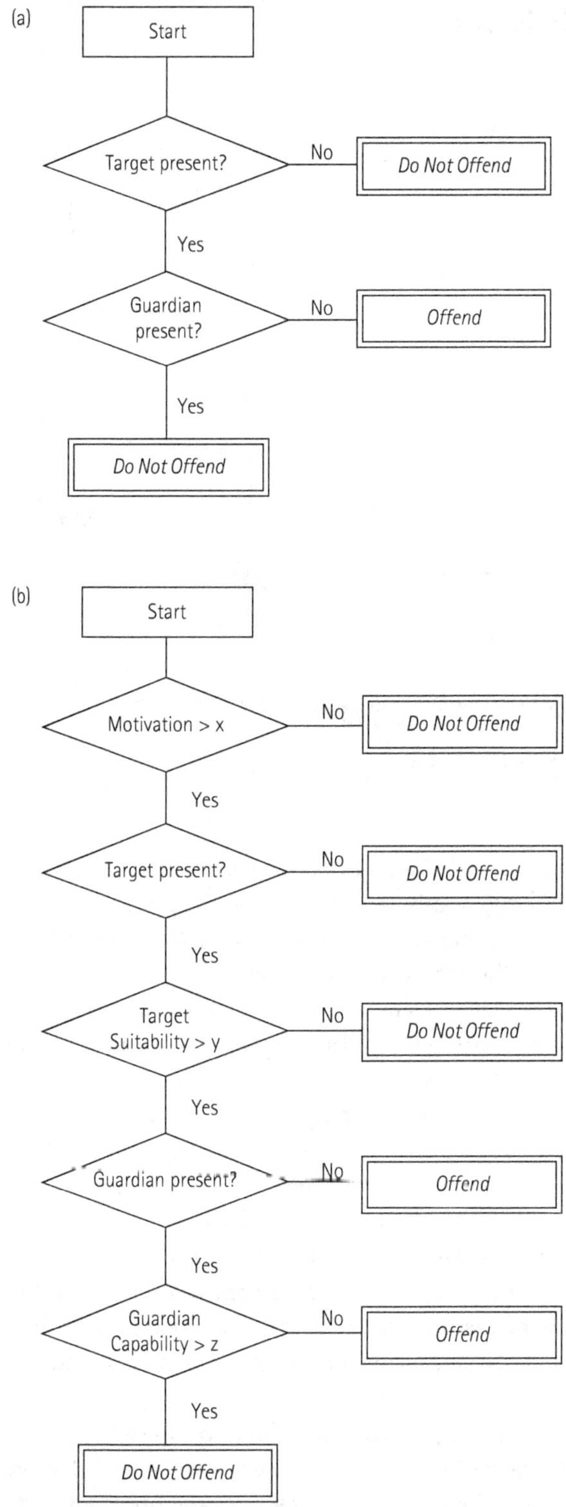

FIGURE 15.4A-B Example offending agent behaviors derived from the routine activity approach

to offend if there is a target present at their current location but no other (guardian) agent. In the second slightly more complex formalization—Figure 15.4B—agents also assess their current motivation, the target suitability, and guardian capability against some critical threshold values (which may or may not be agent-specific) before deciding whether or not to engage in crime.

Agent calculi can be represented in a wide variety of ways, from simple condition-action rule systems (Gilbert and Terna 2000) such as those described above, to complex, cognitively inspired models of reasoning (Rao and Georgeff 1991). In this sense there is no definitive architecture for modeling agent decision-making, and selection is typically defined by the behavior being examined and the scope of the model in which it is examined. While details are beyond the scope of this chapter, readers are directed to Balke and Gilbert (2014), where a range of agent architectures are reviewed.

The second key component of the ABM is the environment. This is the virtual world in which agents are situated, and subsequently act and interact with one another as a simulation is carried out. A simulated environment may represent a physical space where proximity relates to the Euclidian distance between agents, or some abstract construct where proximity instead indicates some aspatial property such as social cohesion, norm compatibility, and so forth. Again, the choice of environmental abstraction depends greatly on the system to be modeled. If we are to construct a model that seeks to better understand the emergence of co-offending networks, we might represent offender agents interacting in a social space where demographics, historical social ties, and offending histories influence the formation of social networks. Conversely, in considering patterns of nighttime economy violence, we might explicitly model an entertainment precinct, the bars and nightclubs located within it, and populations of patrons who move from bar to bar consuming alcohol and interacting with one another.

ABMs applied in the field of environmental criminology typically (although not exclusively) simulate spatially referenced spaces where agents physically navigate and interact with one another as a result of proximity. Such environments, much like the models they are part of, may be created at varying levels of complexity, from simple abstract lattices akin to a checkerboard, to complex environments digitized from GIS data describing real-world places. Again, selection of environment complexity should be closely tied to model design and a desire to maximize model utility with regard to intended purpose (Elffers and Van Baal 2008).

Finally, in the development of an ABM it is commonplace for the developer to create a series of manipulable model components that allow model configurations to be systematically manipulated. It is these switches that aid in conducting simulation experiments. Examples might include multiple versions of the same behavior enacted by an agent—each exploring a different hypothesis (Epstein and Axtell 1996)—for instance, comparing both offending behaviors depicted in Figure 15.4. Thus, we develop two revisions of the offending behavior and run the model under each configuration, in turn assessing the impact of that particular configuration on simulated crime. Similarly, in constructing predictive ABMs that seek to provide decision support, these switches might allow us to select from multiple response strategies in order to observe projected outcomes under a series of different policies or practices.

15.3.3.1 *SimRobbery*

Environment: We construct an urban environment around which agents undertake day-to-day routine activities. In order to maximize generalizability, we conceive a rudimentary street network made up of nodes and edges that attempts to capture the "funneling effect" of the real street network (Groff 2007, p. 522) but is easily manipulated.

Agents: We simulate two distinct types of agents—offenders and citizens. Offender agents represent individuals who may actively engage in criminal activity. Citizen agents represent everyday citizens who may be targeted by offender agents.

Characteristics and State Variables: Both citizen and offender agents are allotted a series of environmental nodes that represent their home node and four other commonly visited routine activity nodes. These are selected at random from the environment when a simulation is initialized. In addition, offender agents store a characteristic related to their criminal motivation. Citizen agents also store a target suitability characteristic that defines how attractive as crime targets they are to prospective offender agents. Both citizen and offender agents store state variables that include current location, current destination, and Euclidian distance to home. In addition, offender agents store a mental map of the environment that is built up through a learning behavior and subsequently used in the offending behavior, and a record of the crimes they have committed in a particular simulation.

Behaviors: Both victim and offender agents are bestowed with a spatial activity behavior that seeks to formalize propositions of the routine activity approach, crime pattern theory, and human geography concerning routinized, anchor-based movement patterns. This behavior allows all agents to plan activities such that an agent begins the simulation at home and then traverses the street network, moving between routine activity nodes. In addition, offender agents also act according to three further behaviors. First, a target selection behavior derived from the rational choice perspective allows offender agents to perceive the target suitability of citizen agents they encounter on the street. Second, a learning behavior derived from the awareness space construct described by crime pattern theory allows offender agents to build up an increased knowledge of locations they visit repeatedly. Third, combining behaviors of movement, target selection, and learning, offender agents also enact an offending behavior that probabilistically determines the likelihood a crime will occur when an offender agent converges with a citizen agent. This behavior incorporates measures of the offender agent's motivation; the potential victim's target utility; and the offender's awareness of the location in which the convergence occurred. In line with theory, as these three factors increase, so does the likelihood crime will occur.

Finally, in order to facilitate a series of simulation experiments, the three theoretically derived offender behaviors of movement, target selection, and learning offer both experimental and control states. The former provide the behavior described above. The latter represent the absence of a proposed mechanism (and thus a counterfactual)—such that in the respective control states agents do not follow a spatially structured routine; consider all targets equally viable; and do not learn about their environment.

15.3.3.2 *SimDespatch*

Environment: We construct a simple two-dimensional Euclidian lattice in which call-for-service events occur and responder agents respond to them. Each simulation cycle, we probabilistically generate a number of spatiotemporally clustered calls for service and distribute them across the lattice.

Agents: We create a single agent type—the responder agent. Responder agents represent police vehicles tasked to respond to call-for-service events. Responder agents store the following state variables: (1) their current location in environment; (2) their current destination; (3) a flag describing whether they are currently responding; and (4) a measure of the total fuel they have consumed in the given simulation.

Behaviors: Responder agents operate according to three primary behaviors. The first movement behavior allows them to respond to call-for-service events allocated to them. This behavior simply allows the responder to traverse the simulation environment by moving across the lattice. It is assumed that, in doing so, responders take the shortest route from their current location to reach their allocated call-for-service event. In addition, it is assumed that each move consumes a single unit of fuel. Once a responder reaches a call-for-service, it remains at the location of the call for the allotted number of cycles associated with that event. The second and third behaviors represent characteristics of a given response strategy and are thus manipulable by the experimenter in order to assess the effectiveness of different response strategies.

The first of these behaviors relates to how calls are allocated to responders. Two configurations of this behavior are available. The first simply allocates call-for-service events to responder agents using a traditional queuing system such that calls for service are allocated to free responder agents in the order they are received. The second configuration allocates call-for-service events to responders based on their location. In this configuration available responders are allocated to the nearest active call-for-service event irrespective of when the call was received.

The second response strategy behavior describes how responder agents should act in the event that they are currently not responding to a call-for-service event. This patrol behavior seeks to explore the impact that different patrol strategies have on responder effectiveness and resource consumption. The patrol strategy can be set in four configurations. In the first, responder agents simply remain static after responding to an event until they are allocated a new event. In the second, responders randomly traverse the environment until allocated an event to respond to. In the third, responders currently not responding move to the location that has historically received the most number of call-for-service events. Finally, in the fourth configuration responder agents move to the location within ten cells of their current location that has historically received the most number of call-for-service events.

15.3.4 Phase 4: Model Verification, Calibration, and Validation

Once a model is constructed, it should be verified, calibrated, and validated. Model verification seeks to establish whether the computational model developed in phase 3 is an appropriate translation of the conceptual model designed in phase 2 (Moss, Edmonds, and Wallis 1997). Model verification is, in essence, equivalent to assessing model internal validity and is a crucial part of the ABM process. Model implementation problems come in two key forms—(1) errors in the model programming that mean that the program does not execute in the way the developer intended it to; and (2) artifacts that result from seemingly insignificant choices made in the development of a model that turn out to have unpredicted impacts on model behavior (Galán et al. 2009). Because the systems we seek to model are typically complex, identifying errors and artifacts can be very difficult. This is because one may interpret an observed model outcome to be the result of accurately modeled behavior and not an error or artifact somewhere in the implementation of the model. Such problems can have significant impacts on model outcomes, and in turn compromise inferences drawn from the model (Edmonds and Hales 2003).

Here, like others (Gilbert and Troitzsch 2005), I support an approach of incremental model complexity (Townsley and Birks 2008) and use of extensive unit testing—a commonly used software-testing paradigm. Unit tests attempt to examine individual model components in a series of isolated test scenarios. In each test we examine the behavior of the model component being tested and compare it to that defined in the model design, known outcomes, and our common-sense expectations. This process is typically iterative in nature, with unit tests first being devised to examine the simplest of scenarios (a single agent or behavior operating, fixed parameters, a simplified environment, etc.) and slowly scaling up to more complex circumstances (multiple agents interacting, multiple behaviors, more complex environments, etc.). Most importantly, one should not overlook the significant resources required in attempting to ensure a model is doing what one thinks it is doing, and in turn that its outcomes are indeed the result of the assumptions one seeks to explore.

After verification, depending on the form of the model, calibration may be undertaken. Model calibration involves using existing data to ensure model components most effectively represent what is known of the target system (Hedström 2005). Calibration data can come from a range of sources and may include detailed empirical analyses, statistical estimates, or simply common-sense approximations. To illustrate, we might calibrate the number of agents in a model to reflect population estimates for a similar-sized location in the real world, use self-report data to calibrate the proportion of agents deemed to be criminally active, or calibrate the length of a simulation cycle to represent some unit of real time based on assumptions concerning the speed of modeled actors and the size of the simulated environment. Importantly, one should remain mindful of the quality of data used to calibrate different components of a given model. It is often good practice to probe constructs calibrated from the less robust of these sources and explore the impact on model outcomes of altering parameters within reasonable bounds. Such tests of robustness are equivalent to sensitivity analyses commonly applied to statistical models.

Once verification and calibration have been performed, the final task of this phase is model validation. Validation asks whether the model has external validity—that is, does our synthetic system provide a sufficient analog to the real world given its intended purpose? It is important that we consider whether our models are valid, as this ultimately dictates what they can and cannot teach us about the systems they seek to mimic. The simplest means of validation is to assess if a model is capable of producing outcomes that mimic those observed in empirical research. The degree to which such equivalence is required is again is largely influenced by the type and intended use of the model (Axtell and Epstein 1994). Thus, where an abstract explanatory model might seek to understand the fundamental dynamics of a system, descriptive or distributional equivalence between empirical patterns and system outcomes may be appropriate. Here the greater the number of empirical signatures (and at various scales) the model is capable of generating, the more confidence one holds in its validity. Conversely, if a predictive model uses real-world calibration data concerning known individuals and their personal characteristics and situates them in a realistic environmental model with the hope of predicting their actions in order to inform practice or policy, the requirements for validity are likely considerably more stringent.

15.3.4.1 *SimRobbery*

Verification: Verification of SimRobbery involves unit tests that examine all key agent behaviors in both control and experimental configurations. Tests are first performed using one or two (in the case of interactive behaviors) agents and subsequently run with greater numbers of agents. At all stages of this process debug data are generated to allow inspection of internal behavioral logic of agents and ensure that behaviors operate as specified. To illustrate, we examine the spatial activity behavior by creating a single citizen agent, specifying that agent's home and routine activity nodes and highlighting them within the environment. Subsequently we modify the behavior code to output results of the pathfinding algorithm for inspection at each point the street network is traversed. In addition, we observe the overall spatial behavior of the agent to ensure that selected paths seem generally plausible. Similarly, testing the target selection behavior, we first generate a population of citizen agents with target suitability scores of zero (thus making them completely unattractive to offender agents) and ensure that no simulated crimes occur. Further unit tests are devised to examine the other key behaviors. In attempting to identify potential artifacts, we also run the model altering several ancillary assumptions, such as the order in which agents move and offend, to ensure that model outcomes are not affected by these development decisions beyond the purview of the theories to be examined.

Calibration: SimRobbery is largely abstract and exploratory in nature, so no empirical data are used for calibration.

Validation: Due to the explanatory nature of SimRobbery, validation of the model is largely also validation of the theoretical constructs it seeks to test. Accordingly, model validity is assessed by quantifying the degree to which simulated crime mimics characteristic regularities of empirical data concerning interpersonal victimization. The experiments that assess the presence of these regularities are discussed in the next phase.

15.3.4.2 *SimDespatch*

Verification: Verification of SimDespatch similarly follows a unit-testing approach with scrutiny of all key agent behaviors including navigation, incident prioritization, and patrol strategies. These are first performed with a single responder agent and call-for-service event and then multiple agents and events.

Calibration: Model calibration of SimDespatch is restricted to a calibration of simulation cycle length based on (*a*) the size of simulated grid cells in the environment, and (*b*) an estimation of responder vehicle speed. Here we assume that in an environment in which each cell is equivalent to an area of 1 km × 1 km and a responder vehicle traveling at an average speed of 60 kph can traverse a single cell in one cycle that is thus equivalent to one minute. By extension, in order to simulate a single 24-hour period we run the model for 1,440 (24 × 60) cycles. In addition, we set plausible bounds on the number call-for-service events occurring over a 24-hour period and the allocatable responders available to police an environment of similar size to that modeled. These estimations are derived from discussions with policing agencies. In the future we hope to generate call-for-service events using empirical data describing historical events.

Validation: In validating SimDespatch we primarily assess the distribution of simulated calls for service to ensure that they are both spatially and temporally concentrated like those observed in empirical research (Townsley, Homel, and Chaseling 2000). In addition, we may attempt to model currently implemented real-world response strategies in order to ensure that measures of effectiveness are compatible with empirical measures of current strategy effectiveness.

15.3.5 Phase 5: Conducting Simulated Experiments

The impetus behind constructing an ABM is more often than not associated with the experiments one can conduct on the simulated system. Mirroring the idealized empirical study, the simulation experiment typically manipulates some system component while holding all other constructs static and, in turn, observes the changes in outcomes that result from this manipulation. Manipulations might include global model configurations like the total number of agents in a particular class—for example, exploring simulated crime rates when twice as many police agents are created. Conversely, one may examine the impact of varying versions of a particular agent calculus. This approach allows researchers to observe multiple versions of a simulated world where actors act *this way* or *that way* and assess what impact that change might have. In explanatory models such manipulations can be used to test multiple competing hypotheses concerning a particular process, increasing confidence in the behavioral configuration that produces the most plausible outcome patterns. Predictive models that explore interventions might use manipulation to assess varying response strategy configurations and assess which is likely to produce the most fruitful range of outcomes.

An important point to note here is that ABMs are typically (but not necessarily) nondeterministic. This is the case because model constructs typically rely on probabilistic calculations that execute actions based on a draw from a random-number generator. In these cases multiple runs of the same model produce different outcomes (Axelrod 1997). Accordingly if a model is nondeterministic, it is impossible to assess if the results of a single run are in anyway typical of the underlying system. For this reason, when a nondeterministic model is used to carry out an experiment, multiple simulations must be conducted under each experimental configuration, with outcomes of these simulations aggregated and summarized. The number of simulations one should run is very much reliant on the model itself, but at the very least exploratory simulations should be performed to assess the variance in model outcomes over multiple model runs.

In concluding this section of the chapter, I now briefly discuss several illustrative experiments carried out using example models. As discussed previously, interested readers are directed to Birks, Townsley, and Stewart (2014) and Birks and Townsley (2018), where a series of simulation experiments using these models are described and analyzed in more detail than space permits in this chapter.

15.3.5.1 *SimRobbery*

Using SimRobbery, our primary goal remains to assess whether key mechanisms proposed by the routine activity approach, rational choice perspective, and crime pattern theory are sufficient to explain commonly observed patterns of interpersonal victimization: spatial clustering, repeat victimization, and journey-to-crime skewness. Employing the control and experimental conditions of each of the movement, target selection, and learning behaviors discussed above, we construct a traditional 2 × 2 × 2 experimental design that allows us to examine simulated crime patterns that result in each possible combination of the behaviors modeled. Given the probabilistic nature of the model, for each of these configurations we run 500 simulations. In order to maximize the generalizability of our findings in each simulation, we generate unique populations of offender and citizen agents and a unique environment for them to interact within. For each simulation we record data concerning simulated crime events and analyze them to quantify spatial clustering, repeat victimization, and the journey-to-crime distances. For each model configuration we then construct a distribution of our three outcome measures and compare these distributions to assess under which configurations simulated crime is most congruent with real-world crime patterns.

15.3.5.2 *SimDespatch*

SimDespatch seeks to assess the impact of varying response strategies on responder effectiveness. Here we are interested in the impact of three distinct response characteristics: (1) the number of responders; (2) the event prioritization strategy; and (3) the responder patrol strategy. Again following a traditional experimental approach, we construct a 5 × 2 × 4 experimental design and, due to the model's probabilistic nature, run 100 simulations in each of the 40 unique strategy configurations. Again, in each simulation we generate a unique distribution of calls for service and record data concerning the following outcome measures: (1) percentage of events responded to within a two-hour window; (2) average response time per event; (3) the total fuel consumed by responders; and (4) the percentage of time responders spend responding versus patrolling. Subsequently, we aggregate these measures by response strategy configuration and compare the effectiveness of each across all four metrics.

15.4 Ruminations on the Strengths and Limitations of ABM for Environmental Criminologists

Having summarized the key processes associated with the design, development, and use of an ABM, the remainder of this chapter discusses some broad observations concerning the potential strengths and limitations of the approach most pertinent to environmental criminologists.

Simulation as a thinking tool: For an environmental criminologist, designing and developing ABMs reinforces a constructive and objective way of thinking about crime, that is, as the generative property of a system—a set of interconnected entities that produce a particular outcome—in this case, crime events. We build a model of this system with the hope of better understanding it, and in order to do so we are forced to be explicit about our mental model of that system; how we believe it operates (formalization), which of its many pieces are most important in explaining the things it generates (abstraction), and how empirical insights support or undermine our mental model (calibration and validation). Here we cannot hide behind theoretical vagaries and must instead be precise in defining the mechanisms we propose are responsible for observed outcomes. Whether right or wrong, formalizing these hypotheses promotes precision in the way we think about crime and often highlights weaknesses in our mental models that are otherwise not easily identified. Subsequently, the ABM we construct provides a platform to formally assess the veracity of those hypotheses. Thus, simulation provides a distinct and useful thinking tool.

Acknowledging, accepting, and embracing complexity: A significant strength of the ABM approach is that it not only acknowledges, but also embraces, the complexity associated with crime events and patterns. While the opportunity theories that underlie environmental criminology provide intuitive individual-level descriptions of crime events, once considered as situated interacting processes operating among large numbers of heterogeneous individuals, their downstream impacts rapidly become overwhelmingly complex and, as a result, are difficult to estimate with any degree of certainty (Birks, Townsley, and Stewart 2012, 2014). This complexity is an inherent property of the empirical world. Yet traditional analytical techniques struggle to incorporate it and instead resort to abstractions that compromise description for the sake of mathematical tractability. ABMs provide a platform where this complexity can be explored, free from traditional constraints of empirical research. While engaging in ABM does not in isolation expose the causal engine that drives observed crime problems, it provides a unique vehicle to engage in new explorations of the considerable divide that exists between crime event theories and observed crime patterns.

Unification: Developing ABMs also serves to unify a range of dimensions within the field of environmental criminology. First, ABMs serve as a bridge between both micro and macro scales and theoretical and empirical efforts. Second, they provide an effective means to incorporate both qualitative and quantitative insight into a single unified analytical framework (Edmonds 2015). Third, they can, and often do, bring together experts from range of disparate backgrounds—criminology, computer science, cognitive science, economics, psychology, geography, and so on. Finally, the unit at which ABMs are specified provides a natural description of social systems accessible to a range of audiences, thus providing a collective platform for both academic and domain experts to discuss crime problems and the systems that give rise to them. Disseminating ABMs to practitioners can often generate considerable interest, which in turn supports better informed and criticized models—both desirable outcomes.

Theoretical-empirical-computational: While ABMs offer unique means to think about the complex systems that result in crime, they cannot, and should not purport to, replace empirical study. ABMs provide the means to explore whether proposed microspecifications are sufficient to generate known macro-outcomes (Epstein 1999). In doing so, some argue ABMs enable a new, third way of doing science (Axelrod 1997). Irrespective of their epistemological position, ABMs are another useful addition to the environmental criminologist's toolkit, and while crime problems remain hard to solve, expanding the approaches that might be brought to bear in understanding crime is undoubtedly a worthy endeavor. While these statements likely seem obvious to most readers, there does remain a small but vocal group of individuals who ardently oppose simulation studies, typically under the following rationale: the model is just based on assumptions. This assertion is undoubtedly true; of course the model is based on assumptions. It is a function of those assumptions, but so is any model—verbal, written, mathematical, or computational. To its advantage, the assumptions that underlie a computational model are often more explicit or accessible than those that make up other types of models. Moreover, the simulation provides means to think about those assumptions systematically, explore difficult to estimate impacts of their interactions, and, in favorable conditions, assess their plausibility as an approximation of the real world.

Sufficiency, not necessity: An obvious, but sometimes overlooked limitation associated with all ABMs is that any simulation we create can only demonstrate what *can* and *cannot* generate some observed real-world phenomena—not what *is* generating it. A simulation identifies candidate explanations (Epstein 1999) that are made up of *sufficient* but not *necessary* conditions. A consequence of the equifinality principle (Von Bertalanffy 1972), which states that the outcome of any open system can be brought about by any number of potential input states, this limitation applies to all theories, models, and analytical techniques at our disposal. There is no restriction on the number of potential alternative explanations that might be at play when we observe some real-world outcome. The ABM simply provides one method for assessing the viability of our proposed explanation, and when used appropriately, for falsifying those that are insufficient. Having identified one or more sufficient explanations, we then have the task of applying supporting methods to identify which of these candidate explanations is most compatible with existing knowledge. In this way the computational informs the empirical, and vice versa.

Similarly, predictive models aim to demonstrate what can and cannot happen under some particular configuration of a known system—not necessarily what *will* happen. In running a predictive model we seek to estimate a range of possible outcomes. This is perhaps easiest to understand if we acknowledge that the reality we observe today is undoubtedly only one of many potential realities that may have occurred since yesterday. To illustrate, today's range of possible futures likely contains the observation that the train was both late or on time. That the train instantaneously disappeared seems unlikely to feature. The significant implication here is that one should run a model many times from a range of informed initial conditions with the hope of best understanding the range of possible futures that might result, and, in turn, revealing how we might best steer the system to those that are most desirable.

15.5 The Future of Computational Criminology

The burgeoning field of computational criminology offers diverse possibilities for environmental criminologists. Yet throughout the history of criminological enquiry numerous methods have initially been touted as transformational, and subsequently only a few have produced significant impacts in the field. While computational criminology has yet to make such lofty claims, there remains a range of challenges that must be met in order to ensure the approach provides significant benefits above and beyond traditional enquiry.

Two interrelated areas in which progress is required concern the calibration and validation of ABMs of crime. Relative to traditional analytical models, ABMs typically require more, often less readily accessible, parameterization data. This is simply because modeling individual behavior requires researchers to make judgments about a whole series of moving parts that potentially influence individual crime event/response interactions. While simple explanatory and illustrative ABMs may rely on rudimentary assumptions, models should, where possible, be informed by suitable empirical data. This is particularly pertinent when we seek to transfer simulation outcomes to real-world settings, such as in the prototyping of crime prevention interventions.

To illustrate, a population-level model of the wide-scale uptake in home security might require estimation of the average reduction in crime risk resulting from a security upgrade. Conversely, an ABM devised to explore similar measures at the individual level might require parameters describing the deterrent effect of house alarms, upgraded door locks, CCTV cameras—and the context dependency of these measures relative to hour of day, state of home occupancy, offender experience, and so on. The granularity of these assumptions dictates the types of questions a model can answer, but also encumbers those involved in its construction with the task of identifying appropriate data to calibrate and validate it.

Significantly, the modeling of crime event interactions is somewhat of a special case with regard to obtaining suitable calibration data. As it stands, there are few disciplines where those engaging in the behavior of interest actively attempt to disguise their actions, and/or have a vested interest in portraying them in a less than accurate light. Moreover, data often sought to be representative of that behavior (reported, recorded, and subsequently detected crime, for instance) characterize cases where these processes of obfuscation ultimately fail. The important questions are, then, how do we construct models that most appropriately use the data we have? How do we go about finding new parameterization data where no immediate source exists? And what should we expect of our models relative to the data that we use to calibrate and validate them?

A growing body of research in the physical and, more recently, social sciences demonstrates the utility of employing small-scale empirical studies to inform calibration and validation of computational models. In these fields, empirical studies are devised from the ground up to incorporate measures that will subsequently be used to upscale "small-*n*" findings to large-scale models that enable insight beyond the reach of existing empirical methods. To illustrate, researchers in the field of computational economics have explored a range of economic decision-making experiments with human subjects that are subsequently used to inform agent-based modeling (see for instance Duffy 2006).

While the ease with which such approaches might reveal insight into the study of crime remains an open question, recent advances in offender location choice research (Lammers et al. 2015; Townsley et al. 2016) represent just one potential example of how empirical research might be used to calibrate realistic populations of offender agents for inclusion in an ABM of crime. Ultimately, there is likely much that environmental criminologists can learn from efforts in other disciplines that routinely couple empirical studies with computational models. While I am currently unaware of any existing criminological studies that have systemically incorporated measures for the specific purpose of informing ABMs, it stands to reason that in the coming years there will be greater collaboration between empirical and computational criminology.

While empirical research may inform the calibration of certain model parameters, for some model constructs it may be more appropriate to analytically derive appropriate values. This might be the case if the parameters in question define processes that are not easily accessible through expert knowledge, survey instruments, field observations, or experiments. Mimicking the mechanisms of biological selection, genetic algorithms (GA) provide one method to solve complex parameter search and optimization problems. The principles of GA are simple but profound. Given some problem, for which the solution can be encoded as a series of parameters, GA can be applied to identify optimal values. This process begins by generating a population of "candidate" solutions to the parameterization problem—each representing one potential permutation of parameters. For ABMs, these solutions might encode a unique combination of numeric model parameters, such as the mean propensity of simulated offenders and the variation of propensity throughout the population. Similarly, solutions might also encode behavioral preferences such that particular features of the environment are more or less important to simulated offenders in choosing where and when to commit crime (see Malleson et al. 2014).

Once a population of candidate solutions are generated, each is used to conduct simulations of the target system and the "fitness" of that solution assessed against some benchmark. This might entail assessing the plausibility of simulated crime patterns, or conversely in constructing ABMs of crime event responses, the configurations that produce the greatest reductions at the least cost, and so on. Subsequently, this initial generation of candidate solutions is ranked in terms of their fitness and "bred" to produce a subsequent generation of solutions. Breeding takes place by crossing over parameters from one good candidate to another to create a new unique candidate that represents the offspring of its parent solutions. Like the natural mechanism it seeks to mimic, crossover often includes a mutation process that probabilistically alters one or more parameters in order to maintain genetic diversity in the solution pool. This process is repeated over successive generations in order to evolve solutions that meet some criterion, such as a prescribed level of predictive accuracy or cost-benefit ratio. The key to success here is the design of an appropriate fitness function—that is, an objective classifier capable of assessing the utility associated with a particular solution.

It is here that appropriate validation data become paramount. In the case of models that seek to identify optimal strategies for responding to crime events, the key properties of a fitness function are relatively simple to envisage. To illustrate, GA could be applied to our example model SimDespatch to identify optimal response strategies encoded as, for instance, numbers of responders, response radius, event prioritization strategy, and a whole host of other response-related characteristics. For each candidate response strategy we run a series of simulation experiments that assess the effectiveness of that strategy with respect to our goals—costs, timeliness, etc. Over successive generations we seek to evolve the optimal response strategy configuration that best meets these requirements.

The challenge for more complex explanatory models that seek to model crime event processes and subsequently generate plausible crime patterns would be to devise an appropriate fitness function for simulated crime events—that is, how do we know if our simulated crime is sufficiently representative of real crime to the degree that it is useful? As discussed above, simulation models can be validated using a range of data and at varying ranges of granularity, from general qualitative distributional equivalence, to quantitative micro- and macroequivalence. In considering the validation process of increasingly complex models it is important to return to our discussion of the representativeness of data typically collected about crime.

The notion that all sources of data describing criminal activity are flawed is not new—only some crimes are reported to the police, only some of these are subsequently recorded, how they are recorded can differ based on numerous contextual factors—and importantly all of these biases are not randomly distributed. Similarly, ethnographic studies of crime event actor behavior are constrained by a number of well-acknowledged weaknesses. If we are to validate models using these data, the significance of these frailties is only amplified. This, in turn, may require the construction of more complex holistic models that seek to simulate not only the mechanisms that underlie crime events, but also the processes by which data describing those events are reported, recorded, and generally obfuscated (Eck 2006). This problem is ultimately circular in nature, in that poor and/or incomplete empirical data drive construction of the model, but also undermine its calibration and validation. Unfortunately, a definitive solution to this problem is not readily apparent.

What can be said is that models of some types of crime will likely be more easily validated against available data than others. This is simply a function of how indicative validation data are of the underlying behavior. Accordingly, models of residential burglary are likely easier to validate than models of domestic violence, because the former is well reported to (and recorded by) policing agencies relative to the latter. This observation also reinforces the requirement that those who apply ABM to study crime are not only adept in developing models, but also well versed in those factors that are likely to impact on the data they use to calibrate and validate them.

Ultimately, one might best assess the validity of a model through its ability to increase consideration of the system it seeks to mimic. In this way, the challenges faced in constructing the model and an understanding of the mechanisms responsible for them, in concert with both the model itself and the experiments performed using it, are of cumulative utility to the investigator.

15.6 Conclusion

Throughout this chapter I attempted to outline how the simulation method might be of use to scholars in the field of environmental criminology. In addition, I sought to provide an instructive overview of the key processes involved in engaging in ABM research, and discussed several associated strengths and weaknesses. Computational thinking and methods have the potential to offer new and unique insights to environmental criminologists. I, for one, am excited to see how they will be applied to better understand crime events, patterns, and the complex societal systems that give rise to them.

References

Axelrod, Robert. (1997). "Advancing the art of simulation in the social sciences." In R. Conte, R. Hegselmann, & P. Terna (Eds.), *Simulating Social Phenomena* (pp. 21–40). Berlin: Springer.

Axtell, Robert L., and Joshua M. Epstein. 1994. "Agent-based modeling: Understanding our creations." *Bulletin of the Santa Fe Institute* 9(2): 28–32.

Balke, Tina, and Nigel Gilbert. 2014. "How do agents make decisions? A survey." *Journal of Artificial Societies and Social Simulation* 17(4): 13.

Birks, Daniel J. 2017 "Formal models of the crime event: Agent-based modelling in support of crime prevention." In B. LeClerc and E. Savona (Eds.), *Crime Prevention in the 21st Century* (pp. 215–233). New York: Springer.

Birks, Daniel J., Susan Donkin, and Melanie Wellsmith. 2008. "Synthesis over analysis: Towards an ontology for volume crime simulation." In Lin Liu and John Eck (Eds.), *Artificial Crime Analysis Systems: Using Computer Simulations and Geographic Information Systems* (pp. 160–192). Hershey, PA: IGI Global.

Birks, Daniel J., and Henk Elffers. 2014. "Agent-based assessments of criminological theory." In Gerben J. N. Bruinsma and David Weisburd (Eds.), *Encyclopedia of Criminology and Criminal Justice* (pp. 19–32). New York: Springer.

Birks, Daniel J., and Michael Townsley. 2018. "Agent-based decision-support systems for crime scientists." In Richard Wortley, Aiden Sidebottom, Gloria K. Laycock, and Nick Tilley (Eds.), *Handbook of Crime Science*. New York: Routledge. Forthcoming.

Birks, Daniel J., Michael Townsley, and Anna Stewart. 2012. "Generative explanations of crime: Using simulation to test criminological theory." *Criminology* 50(1): 221–254.

Birks, Daniel J., Michael Townsley, and Anna Stewart. 2014. "Emergent regularities of interpersonal victimization: An agent-based investigation." *Journal of Research in Crime and Delinquency* 51(1): 119–140.

Block, Richard, and Sean Davis. 1996. "The environs of rapid transit stations: A focus for street crime or just another risky place?" In Ronald V. Clarke (Ed.), *Preventing Mass Transit Crime* (pp. 237–257), vol. 6 of *Crime Prevention Studies*. Monsey, NY: Criminal Justice Press.

Bonabeau, Eric. 2002. "Agent-based modeling: Methods and techniques for simulating human systems." *Proceedings of the National Academy of Sciences* 99 (suppl. 3): 7280–7287.

Bosse, Tibor, and Charlotte Gerritsen. 2010. "An agent-based framework to support crime prevention." In *Proceedings of the Ninth International Conference on Autonomous Agents and Multiagent Systems*, vol. 1: pp. 525–532. New York: ACM Press.

Braga, Anthony A., David M. Hureau, and Andrew V. Papachristos. 2011. "The relevance of micro places to citywide robbery trends: A longitudinal analysis of robbery incidents at street corners and block faces in Boston." *Journal of Research in Crime and Delinquency* 48(1): 7–32. doi: 0022427810384137.

Brantingham, Paul J., and Brantingham, Patricia L. (1991). "Introduction to the 1991 reissue: Notes on environmental criminology." In Paul J. Brantingham and Patricia L. Brantingham (Eds.), *Environmental Criminology* (pp. 1–6). Prospect Heights, IL: Waveland Press.

Brantingham, Paul J., and Patricia L. Brantingham. 2008. "Crime pattern theory." In Richard Wortley and Lorraine Mazerolle (Eds.), *Environmental Criminology and Crime Analysis* (pp. 78–94). Cullompton, Devon, UK: Willan Publishing.

Cornish, Derek B., and Ronald V. Clarke. 2008. "The rational choice perspective." In Richard Wortley and Lorraine Mazerolle (Eds.), *Environmental Criminology and Crime Analysis* (pp. 21–47). Cullompton, Devon, UK: Willan Publishing.

Davidsson, Paul. 2002. "Agent based social simulation: A computer science view." *Journal of Artificial Societies and Social Simulation* 5(1).

Dean, Jeffrey S., George J. Gumerman, Joshua M. Epstein, Robert L. Axtell, Alan C. Swedlund, Miles T. Parker, and Stephen McCarroll. 2000. "Understanding Anasazi culture change through agent-based modeling." In Timothy A. Kohler and George J. Kumerman (Eds.), *Dynamics in Human and Primate Societies: Agent-Based Modeling of Social and Spatial Processes* (pp. 179–205). New York: Oxford University Press.

Dibble, Catherine. 2006. "Computational laboratories for spatial agent-based models." In Leigh Tesfatsion and Kenneth L. Judd (Eds.), *Handbook of Computational Economics* (vol. 2, pp. 1511–1548).

Duffy, J. 2006. "Agent-based models and human subject experiments." In Leigh Tesfatsion and Kenneth L. Judd (Eds.), *Handbook of Computational Economics* (vol. 2, pp. 949–1011).

Eck, John E. 1995. "Examining routine activity theory: A review of two books", *Justice Quarterly* 12(4): 783–797

Eck, John E. 2006. "The devil's computer: A theory of crime patterns." Paper presented at the Environmental Criminology and Crime Analysis Annual Meeting, Chilliwack, BC, July 26–28.

Edmonds, Bruce. 2015. "Using qualitative evidence to inform the specification of agent-based models." *Journal of Artificial Societies and Social Simulation* 18(1): 18.

Edmonds, Bruce, and David Hales. 2003. "Replication, replication and replication: Some hard lessons from model alignment." *Journal of Artificial Societies and Social Simulation* 6(4).

Elffers, Henk, and Pieter Van Baal. 2008. "Realistic spatial backcloth is not that important in agent based simulation research: An illustration from simulating perceptual deterrence." In Lin Liu and John Eck (Eds.), *Artificial Crime Analysis Systems: Using Computer Simulations and Geographic Information Systems* (pp. 19–34). Hershey, PA: IGI Global.

Epstein, Joshua M. 1999. "Agent-based computational models and generative social science." *Complexity* 4(5): 41–60.

Epstein, Joshua M., and Robert Axtell. 1996. *Growing Artificial Societies: Social Science from the Bottom Up*. Washington, DC: Brookings Institution Press.

Farrell, Graham, and Adam C. Bouloukos. 2001. "International overview: A cross-national comparison of rates of repeat victimization." In Graham Farrell and Ken Pease (Eds.), *Repeat Victimization* (pp. 5–26), vol. 12 of *Crime Prevention Studies*. Monsey, NY: Criminal Justice Press.

Felson, Marcus. 2008. "Routine activity approach." In Richard Wortley and Lorraine Mazerolle (Eds.), *Environmental Criminology and Crime Analysis* (pp. 70–76). Cullompton, Devon, UK: Willan Publishing.

Galán, José Manuel, Luis R. Izquierdo, Segismundo S. Izquierdo, José Ignacio Santos, Ricardo Del Olmo, Adolfo López-Paredes, and Bruce Edmonds. 2009. "Errors and artefacts in agent-based modelling." *Journal of Artificial Societies and Social Simulation* 12(1): 1.

Gilbert, Nigel, and Pietro Terna. 2000. "How to build and use agent-based models in social science." *Mind and Society* 1(1): 57–72.

Gilbert, Nigel, and Klaus Troitzsch. 2005. *Simulation for the Social Scientist*. Buckingham: Open University Press.

Groff, Elizabeth R. 2007. "Simulation for theory testing and experimentation: An example using routine activity theory and street robbery." *Journal of Quantitative Criminology* 23(2): 75–103.

Groff, Elizabeth R. 2008. "Adding the temporal and spatial aspects of routine activities: A further test of routine activity theory." *Security Journal* 21(1): 95–116.

Groff, Elizabeth R., and Daniel Birks. 2008. "Simulating crime prevention strategies: A look at the possibilities." *Policing: A Journal of Policy and Practice* 2(2): 175–184.

Hedström, Peter. 2005. *Dissecting the Social: On the Principles of Analytical Sociology*. New York: Cambridge University Press.

Hill, Joanne F., Shane D. Johnson, and Herve Borrion. 2014. "Potential uses of computer agent-based simulation modelling in the evaluation of wildlife poaching." In Andrew M. Lemieux (Ed.), *Situational Prevention of Poaching* (pp. 120–153). New York: Routledge.

Lammers, Marre, Barbara Menting, Stijn Ruiter, and Wim Bernasco. 2015. "Biting once, twice: The influence of prior on current crime location choice." *Criminology* 53: 309–329.

LeBeau, James L. 1987. "Journey to rape-geographic distance and the rapist's method of approaching the victim." *Journal of Police Science and Administration* 15(2): 129–136.

Luke, Sean, Claudio Cioffi-Revilla, Liviu Panait, Keith Sullivan, and Gabriel Balan. 2005. "Mason: A multiagent simulation environment." *Simulation* 81(7): 517–527.

Malleson, Nicholas, and Patricia L. Brantingham. 2009. "Prototype burglary simulations for crime reduction and forecasting." *Crime Patterns and Analysis: The Journal of the International Symposium on Environmental Criminology and Crime Analysis* 2(1): 47–66.

Malleson, Nicholas, Linda See, Andrew Evans, and Alison Heppenstall. 2012. "Implementing comprehensive offender behaviour in a realistic agent-based model of burglary." *Simulation* 88(1): 50–71.

Malleson, Nicholas, Linda See, Andrew Evans, and Alison Heppenstall. 2014. "Optimising an agent-based model to explore the behaviour of simulated burglars." In Vahid Dabbaghian and Vijay Kumar Mago (Eds.), *Theories and Simulations of Complex Social Systems* (pp. 179–204). New York: Springer.

Marchione, Elio, Shane D. Johnson, and Alan Wilson. 2014. "Modelling maritime piracy: A spatial approach." *Journal of Artificial Societies and Social Simulation* 17(2): 9.

Minar, Nelson, Roger Burkhart, Chris Langton, and Manor Askenazi. 1996. "The swarm simulation system: A toolkit for building multi-agent simulations." Santa Fe Institute.

Moss, Scott, Bruce Edmonds, and Steve Wallis. 1997. "Validation and verification of computational models with multiple cognitive agents." CPM Report No. 97-25.

Mukherjee, Satyanshu Kumar, and Carlos Carcach. 1998. *Repeat Victimisation in Australia: Extent, Correlates and Implications for Crime Prevention*. Canberra: Australian Institute of Criminology.

North, Michael J., Thomas R. Howe, Nick T. Collier, and Jerry R. Vos. 2005. "The repast simphony runtime system." Agent 2005 Conference on Generative Social Processes, Models, and Mechanisms, Argonne National Laboratory, Argonne, Il.

Rao, Anand S., and Michael P. Georgeff. 1991. "Modeling rational agents within a BDI-architecture." *KR* 91: 473–484.

Schelling, Thomas C. 1971. "Dynamic models of segregation." *Journal of Mathematical Sociology* 1:143–186.

Segovia-Juarez, Jose L, Suman Ganguli, and Denise Kirschner. 2004. "Identifying control mechanisms of granuloma formation during M. tuberculosis infection using an agent-based model." *Journal of Theoretical Biology* 231(3): 357–376.

Tesfatsion, Leigh. 2002. "Agent-based computational economics: Growing economies from the bottom up." *Artificial life* 8(1): 55–82.

Townsley, Michael, and Daniel J. Birks. 2008. "Building better crime simulations: Systematic replication and the introduction of incremental complexity." *Journal of Experimental Criminology* 4(3): 309–333.

Townsley, Michael, Daniel J. Birks, Stijn Ruiter, Wim Bernasco, and Gentry White. 2016. "Target selection models with preference variation between offenders." *Journal of Quantitative Criminology* 32(2): 283–304. doi: 10.1007/s10940-015-9264-7.

Townsley, Michael, Ross Homel, and Janet Chaseling. 2000. "Repeat burglary victimisation: Spatial and temporal patterns." *Australian & New Zealand Journal of Criminology* 33(1): 37–63.

Valbuena, Diego, Peter H. Verburg, Arnold K. Bregt, and Arend Ligtenberg. 2010. "An agent-based approach to model land-use change at a regional scale." *Landscape Ecology* 25(2): 185–199.

Von Bertalanffy, Ludwig. 1972. "The meaning of general system theory." In *General System Theory: Foundations, Development, Applications* (pp. 30–53). New York: Braziller.

Wang, Xuguang, Lin Liu, and John Eck. 2008. "Crime simulation using GIS and artificial intelligent agents." In Lin Liu and John Eck (Eds.), *Artificial Crime Analysis Systems: Using Computer Simulations and Geographical Information Systems* (pp. 209–225). Hershey, PA: IGI Global.

Wilensky, U. (1999). NetLogo. Center for Connected Learning and Computer-Based Modeling, Northwestern University, Evanston, IL, http://ccl.northwestern.edu/netlogo/.

Wright, Richard T., and Scott H. Decker. 1997. *Armed Robbers in Action: Stickups and Street Culture*. Boston: Northeastern University Press.

PART III

EVERYDAY URBAN CRIME

Empirical Examples and Reviews of Research

Neighborhoods and Communities

CHAPTER 16

RESEARCH ON NEIGHBORHOODS IN EUROPEAN CITIES

LIEVEN J. R. PAUWELS, GERBEN J. N. BRUINSMA, FRANK M. WEERMAN, AND WIM HARDYNS

16.1 Introduction

This chapter provides an overview of European neighborhood studies of crime, victimization, and delinquency that were explicitly guided or inspired by social disorganization theory. Although the origin of social disorganization theory lies in the United States with a long-lasting tradition in urban research, considerable attention has also been given to this perspective in Europe, as well as in other parts of the world. In Europe, a long research tradition of studies on the effects of city or neighborhood characteristics on crime-related outcomes existed before the social disorganization perspective emerged in the United States. Recently, several studies have been conducted in European cities that report findings that differ from those usually found in an American context. Therefore, knowledge about these European studies is paramount for our insights on the role of the neighborhood in crime and criminal behavior.

It is important to realize that European cities differ substantially from US cities in many important features that may leave a mark on crime patterns—physically as well as socially. These differences are the result of historical processes, urban planning and other governmental policies, and important societal differences between the continents. For example, income inequality in the United States is much more pronounced than in Western Europe, and ethnic and cultural diversity is less pervasive in Western Europe than in the United States (Aaberge et al., 2002; Burkhauser & Poupore, 1997; Cutler, Glaeser, & Vigdor, 1999; Gangle, 2005; Gesthuizen, van der Meer, & Scheepers, 2008; Ihlanfeldt & Scafidi, 2004). Research has shown that these structural differences have a fundamental impact on the social fabric of societies (Putnam, 2007; Sampson, Raudenbush, & Earls, 1997; Wilson, 1987). In addition, expectations of, and proclivity toward, government are much stronger in Western Europe than in the United States. As a result of these societal differences, European and US neighborhoods may differ seriously in the role of informal control and social trust in crime and in the neighborhood dynamics that are taking place. As a consequence, US research results and conclusions cannot be applied directly to the (Western) European context.

In this chapter, we review several key European studies that were carried out within the scope of the social disorganization tradition. It would be virtually impossible to cover all European studies that have focused on the negative effects of structural disadvantage, poverty, inequality, and the processes of social (dis)organization. An enormous number of such studies have been conducted in Europe, from a wide array of disciplines (sociology, psychology, psychiatry, the life sciences, geography, cultural anthropology). Even if we restricted ourselves to studies of crime, victimization, and fear of crime (being the most typical criminological outcomes) completion of this task would be impeded by the fact that European studies are reported in a multitude of European languages. Until recently, it was the tradition in most European countries to write in their native language, which made accessibility of findings to the international audience problematic. Fortunately, over the past 15 years, European studies have increasingly been published in English, making them more visible to the international research community.

Against this background, this chapter aims to provide an abridged overview of the kind of research questions and results that have been found in key European studies from the perspective of social disorganization theory. European studies were selected by taking into account the following inclusion criteria:

(1) Studies that are oriented toward an international audience (i.e., English, German, French studies) as well as studies written in Dutch. The decision to concentrate on these languages may lead to some researcher bias, but we know from previous overviews of research in the social disorganization tradition (e.g., Oberwittler, Rabold, & Baier, 2013a) that our bias is situated toward countries that have a strong research tradition in social disorganization research.
(2) Studies that focus on neighborhoods within cities. More recently, European research in environmental criminology also focuses on smaller urban spaces like microplaces, but these are not taken into account in this chapter.
(3) Studies that focus on the most relevant outcomes for evaluating the social disorganization perspective. We decided to focus on neighborhood-level and differential contextual effects on offending, victimization, and fear of crime. Occasionally, when other outcomes are of relevance to the understanding of neighborhood effects on crime-related outcomes, we will briefly mention these studies. Studies of the effects of perceptions of ecological processes (perceptual disorder) are not taken into account, and cross-national studies (where the unit of analysis is the country) are omitted from this review.

This chapter begins with a description of particular characteristics of European cities, taking into account their historical development, their level of neighborhood (ethnic and social) segregation (as compared to US cities), and their typical urban physical structure of European cities. With this in mind, we discuss pioneering European studies that were conducted before the social disorganization perspective emerged in the United States. This is followed by more recent work within the social disorganization framework per region/country. We address studies that can be seen as representative of the kind of research that is guided or inspired by the social disorganization tradition. Finally, to provide the international audience with an idea of what contemporary research projects look like in the European context, we discuss three studies that can be seen as representative of contemporary research in the social disorganization tradition: The PADS+ in the UK, SPAN in the Netherlands, and SWING in Belgium. For each research project we pay attention to the design and methods that are used, the key questions that are dealt with, and the propositions that are tested. In the conclusion of this chapter we reflect on the significance for theory and models within the social disorganization perspective and on the methodological lessons that can be learned from the European studies.

16.2 European Cities

Cities in European countries have a long history, sometimes dating back to the beginning of the first century or even earlier, in the period of the Greeks and Romans (Bruinsma, 2007). Many cities originated in the early Middle Ages. Urbanization strongly accelerated in the nineteenth century as a consequence of the Industrial Revolution. New dwellings were built around the old centers of settlements. Uneducated rural workers moved from rural areas to the expanded cities to find jobs in newly established factories. New neighborhoods with cheap housing were planned by local governments in the late 1880s and 1890s to accommodate poorly educated and uneducated newcomers. Still today, in many European cities, blue-collar areas or belts are concentrated along the early European factories. Many cities were largely destroyed by World War II and had to be rebuilt: Dresden, Berlin, Warsaw, Rotterdam, to mention a few.

After World War II, a second acceleration in urbanization took place. As a result of economic growth and reduced need for agricultural workers, many rural residents moved to the cities, attracted by new jobs and prosperity. Many apartment buildings (big blocks of "flats") were hastily built in areas next to the older parts of the cities in the 1950s and the 1960s. Most neighborhoods in the expanding European cities were planned on the drawing tables of local government authorities. Housing in continental Europe was generally not ruled by the free market because most of the people could not afford a private house.

A third phase in urbanization took place from the 1970s to 1990s. Many people from Mediterranean countries (Algeria, Morocco, Turkey) and from former colonies in Africa, Asia, or South America came to Europe and settled in cities. Contemporary

European cities can be labeled as multicultural, with large minority groups and with hundreds of nationalities, especially in medium-sized and large cities (i.e., cities that have more than 500,000 inhabitants). Migrants often settle in poorer areas that were originally inhabited by native blue-collar workers. Slowly but steadily, neighborhoods became more heterogeneous, and the social and economic segregation took on an ethnic dimension. Non-Western immigrants, especially, settled in poor urban areas in European cities, resulting in Turkish or Moroccan enclaves in some cities. More recently, after the fall of communism, and with the extension of the European Union, Eastern Europeans (e.g., Polish, Bulgarian) entered the Western European labor market.

The infrastructures of European cities reflect these three phases of urbanization. The older neighborhoods in proximity to the ancient centers mostly originated in the late eighteenth and nineteenth centuries and were partially restored in the 1980s. In these neighborhoods, public housing is the most viable option for local government to accommodate people who cannot afford private housing. In the suburbs of cities, three types of neighborhoods emerged from the beginning of the 1960s. In some suburbs, single-family dwellings were built (with a mixture of public and private ownership). In others, large blocks of apartment buildings were built with few recreational facilities. Such buildings deteriorate quickly, with middle-class people leaving and less privileged residents moving in. A relatively recent phenomenon in European cities is that some older neighborhoods near the city centers are now "hot," and houses are bought up and renovated by well-to-do single-person households or by double-income couples without or with very young children. This process of gentrification is, however, an issue that has not been studied much in European criminological inquiries, while social workers and local policy workers often discuss the issue. A key question is, for example, what the tipping point is for gentrification to counter downward spirals of disorder and decline.

The city centers are pretty much the same in all European cities. They date from former times (mostly centuries ago) with a mixture of traditional and modern buildings. Streets have irregular forms and are full of shops, bars, and restaurants. Most of the centers are accessible to pedestrians, bicyclists, or public transport only, and ways through for cars are hard to find. In many continental cities (e.g., in Belgium, France, Germany, the Netherlands), traditional markets are held once or twice a week in or near the city center. In many cases, European city centers are not central business districts as in the United States: offices and small businesses are scattered around. Most of the larger business enterprises have moved to industrial and business areas outside the cities near highways. In other words, the zonal model of Burgess (1967 [1925]) does not apply to the development of most European cities.

Despite governmental efforts, most cities have deprived areas where all kinds of social problems converge. Differences between neighborhoods are not as extreme as in the United States or Asia, but borders between neighborhoods function as social barriers for interaction and for local networks: European cities still have a class structure (e.g., Reynald et al., 2008). People in general look for neighborhoods to settle where they can find people with a comparable lifestyle. The way neighbors dress, the kind of cars they drive, the language they speak, and the type of houses in the neighborhoods make people feel at home and comfortable in certain neighborhoods. All these factors constitute social barriers between neighborhoods.

16.3 The European Tradition of Social Disorganization

European studies on the effects of area characteristics on offending had already been carried out a long time before the emergence of the Chicago school. In the nineteenth century, Western Europe was rapidly transformed from a preindustrial agricultural society to a more urbanized and industrialized one. These developments resulted in radical changes and attracted the attention of scientists and policymakers. For the first time, researchers collected spatial data on convicted offenders and tried to map it systematically. Quételet (1796–1874) and Guerry (1802–1866) were the first to conduct systematic studies of convicts in French judicial districts (see more in chapter 1 of this volume). Their findings were innovative: they showed that crime was not distributed equally across differing districts. Guerry suggested that high levels of population density and poverty were the main causes of crime in these areas (Guerry, 1833). Quételet hypothesized that levels of violence would be higher in poor areas (this hypothesis reflects social disorganization theory in a preliminary version), while he thought that levels of property crime would be higher in more affluent areas (Quételet, 1847). Contrary to his hypotheses, Quételet found a strong correlation between all types of crime and literacy in areas. These geographical variations in crime patterns provided the first fuel for a discussion on the role of urban environments in the behavior of inhabitants.

Similar work was conducted at that time in the United Kingdom. Noteworthy in this respect are the studies of Mayhew (1812–1887) and Rawson (1812–1899) (see more in Bruinsma & Weisburd, 2014; Morris, 1957). Rawson's work was unique in the way he focused on different units of analysis, broader than political administrative units, to study the unequal distribution of crime (Rawson, 1839). Through Mayhew, London neighborhoods became the subject of thorough analysis (Mayhew, 1865). Mayhew was interested in, the specific characteristics of "criminal neighborhoods." His work concentrated on impoverished inner-city districts around the urban center. It is important to stress the attention of Mayhew on the social conditions in impoverished London neighborhoods. In this respect he was not a moral statistician, as some of his contemporaries were called, but a cultural anthropologist and a social reformer *avant la lettre*, who was effectively concerned about the social situation and conditions in these districts, just as Clifford Shaw was several decades after him in Chicago.

Joseph Fletcher (1848) continued the work of Guerry and other statisticians such as Rawson. For many years, he studied the relationship between education and crime by producing maps showing the levels of crime and illiteracy of England and Wales (Fletcher, 1850). His research can be seen as precursor of Emile Durkheim and the Chicago school's social disorganization theory. According to Fletcher, there were four causes of the level of "immorality" of populations (at that time, discussions about the level of morality across countries in Europe were popular. The country that was most successful in implementing the policy of reformism reached the "highest level of morality"): (1) population density, (2) the distribution of property across societies, (3) the number of people earning their own income, and (4) the level of illiteracy of the population (indicated by the number of crosses instead of signatures in the registers of marriage). He estimated the level of immorality of the population by the number and nature of crimes committed; the number of marriages with a man younger than 21 (indicating forced marriage because of pregnancy); the number of illegitimate children, and the number of bank accounts in the population (to measure the number of wealthy inhabitants).

Fletcher argued that not only were differences between regions important in the explanation of crime rates, but so was the *speed* with which these regions changed over time economically and demographically. These ideas preceded Emile Durkheim's famous concept of anomie, which was used to explain the impact of societal changes on people and society (Durkheim, 1964 [1893]). With this concept of "anomia", Durkheim (1858–1917) suggested that "*As a result of this fragmentation and atomization another serious condition arises in society—social isolation which brings about a decrease in social participation. People living in proximity but in a social vacuum*" (Lunden, 1960, p. 130). This sociological analysis of Durkheim provided "*a mechanismic explanation avant la letter*" for the observed geographical differences in crime rates: community differences in the density of social ties between residents and social isolation are key processes that were studied until this time. Central in the work of Durkheim is the relationship between the individual and the society when societal changes occur (Durkheim, 1964 [1893]). This relationship can be seen as a basis for social cohesion, the division of labor, religion, scientific knowledge, and morality. However, when speedy societal changes affect the division of labor, they can lead to more heterogeneity and more "organic" solidarity (with a focus on individuality), instead of "mechanical" solidarity (with a focus on equality of individuals).

When scholars attribute social disorganization theory to the Chicago school tradition, the previously described European studies are often neglected. Nevertheless, the Chicago school can be seen as the cradle from which contemporary urban criminology sprang by contributing to the development of the theory of social disorganization. In the next section we highlight the European contribution to the further development of the social disorganization theory by discussing some important and representative studies in different European contexts that are relevant to this perspective.

16.4 A Review of Previous European Social Disorganization Studies

16.4.1 United Kingdom

British studies played a major role in the understanding of the relationship between structural characteristics and neighborhood delinquency rates. It is important to mention the long-standing tradition of the Sheffield studies (Bottoms, Mawby, & Xanthos, 1981), which started blooming in the 1970s. British studies have been critical of the social disorganization perspective because of its assumption that neighborhoods develop as a consequence of the processes of competition (free market assumptions) (Baldwin, 1975; Morris, 1957). In the UK and other European countries, local and national policy have a strong influence on the housing market (Bottoms, Claytor, & Wiles, 1992; Bottoms & Wiles, 1986; Bottoms & Xanthos, 1981). For that reason, British studies developed a distinct research line that had an important added value to social disorganization theory. These studies highlighted the relationship between housing (real estate market) and crime and offender rates and the role the real estate market played in shaping the geographical distribution of offenders (Bottoms et al., 1992; Bottoms & Wiles, 2002; Herbert, 1982; Morris, 1957). The findings from this research were different from those reported in US studies using the Chicago approach. For example, Morris (1957) examined the offender rates in the county of Croydon (UK), but could not confirm the zone model of Burgess. Almost 15 years later, Morris's findings were replicated in the city of Sheffield (Baldwin, 1975; see also Bottoms & Wiles, 1986).

Besides the rich tradition of housing studies, British studies have also explored more traditional social disorganization / collective efficacy themes. More recently, multilevel models have been applied to reveal contextual effects in England and Wales, not only for delinquency but also for victimization (Tseloni, 2006). Tseloni examined household and area effects on the incidence of total property crimes, burglaries, and thefts. Both household and area characteristics, as well as selected interactions, explain a significant portion of the variation in property crimes. Personal criminal victimization is predicted by both individual and area characteristics. Using data collected for the British Crime Survey, Brunton-Smith and Sturges (2011) investigated the impact of neighborhoods on residents' fear of crimes. They demonstrated that neighborhoods exert independent influences on fear of crime through the incidence of reported crime of the neighborhood; the presence of visible signs of low-level disorder; weak social, economic, and structural characteristics; and lastly, moderators of individual-level causes of fear. Essentially their key conclusion was that neighborhoods play an important moderating role.

In Scotland, Suzan McVie (2006) found evidence for contextual effects of poverty on juvenile delinquency. Characteristics of the neighborhoods in which young people live appear to play a role in delinquent behavior, although their impact is relatively weak in comparison to the effect of individual characteristics, such as gender and personality.

A recent study by Sutherland, Brunton-Smith, and Jackson (2013) in the city of London is critical of the collective efficacy perspective (2013). Using data for 4,700 neighborhoods, they demonstrated that structural factors such as concentrated disadvantage, the extent of urbanization, and the presence of vacant properties were negatively related to collective efficacy. However, they did not find that collective efficacy mediated the relationship between disadvantage, residential instability, and recorded violent crime. Moreover, controlling for the aforementioned structural characteristics, collective efficacy was only very weakly related to the (log) recorded violent crime rate and unrelated to community violence as measured by ambulance data on reported injuries as the result of knife attacks. This finding is at odds with the comparative study by Sampson and Wikström, in which the effect of neighborhood disadvantage is seriously reduced. The authors raise an important concern for neighborhood studies of collective efficacy, namely the neighborhood definition. If only 9% of the variation in levels of collective efficacy can be explained by neighborhood structural characteristics derived from disorganization theory, this finding implies that 91% of this variation happens within neighborhoods. Therefore, neighborhoods may not be the appropriate unit of analysis to test social disorganization theory.

At best, evidence from the United Kingdom is mixed with regard to the effects of neighborhood characteristics on juvenile delinquency. Findings of the recently conducted PADS+ study may explain why research findings are mixed. The PADS+ study can be seen as a landmark study and will be addressed in more detail in the next section on contemporary studies.

16.4.2 Scandinavian Countries

The British studies partially inspired continental criminologists as well. In Sweden, Wikström examined through ecological structural equation models the aggregate relationship between characteristics derived from social disorganization theory, and included measures like the percentage of private versus public housing and the juvenile delinquency rate (Wikström, 1991). His path models demonstrated strong effects of housing policy on the neighborhood composition with regard to the key structural characteristics of social disorganization theory, just as British scholars argued (Bottoms et al., 1992; Bottoms & Wiles, 1986; Bottoms & Xanthos, 1981; Morris, 1957). Wikström pioneered the theoretical integration of ecological and individual-level (and developmental) traditions. In this early study, which served as an example for other European scholars, he linked several approaches in exploring urban crime in Sweden: (1) the offender and criminal career approach, (2) the contextual analysis of crime approach, (3) the victimological approach, and (4) the ecological/environmental approach. In another publication, Wikström and Dolmén (1990) integrated the disorganization perspective with the routine activities approach. Empirically, they found strong correlations between structural disadvantage and offender rates, and this result was replicated in comparative studies of Stockholm (Sweden) and Basel (Switzerland) (Eisner, 1997; Eisner & Wikström, 1999). The results of these Swedish studies suggested that offense rates were better predicted by opportunity characteristics than by social disorganization theory. Also, Dolmén (2002) found that opportunity characteristics were far better at explaining neighborhood differences in offenses, while structural demographic or population composition were better predictors of neighborhood offender rates. This result was previously also obtained in a Canadian study (Ouimet, 2000).

Further, Wikström and Dolmén (2001) showed that different neighborhood-level measures (social integration, informal social control, minor social disorder, victimization, and fear of crime) vary significantly with the degree of urbanization of a neighborhood (population density and number of residents). Key processes that came forward as an explanation for the effect of urbanization on neighborhood levels of victimization and fear of crime are neighborhood social integration, informal social control, and minor social disorder.

Sampson and Wikström (2008) conducted a comparative analysis between Stockholm and Chicago, and found substantively similar findings regarding neighborhood violence rates, despite the distinct structures of Chicago and Stockholm. In both cities, neighborhood inequality in social resources and collective efficacy came forward as the most important correlates of the unequal distribution of social order and violence. Nilsson and Estrada (2007) studied the effects of neighborhood structural characteristics on victimization and found particular support for selection effects. Selection effects lead to causal (contextual) interpretations observed of ecological correlations between indicators of disadvantage and delinquency/offender or victimization rates that have nothing to do with the causal impact of living or growing up in an area and juvenile delinquency, adolescent offending, or personal victimization. However, selection processes deserve more attention in social disorganization studies, because selection can in the long term have indirect causal effects on processes that are related to the development of crime propensities or choice processes. Mellgren, Pauwels, and Torstensson-Levander (2010) compared Malmö (Sweden) and Antwerp (Belgium) neighborhoods and found that a subdimension of collective efficacy (social trust) partially mediated the relationship between disadvantage and population density on the one hand and the crime rate on the other. Multilevel studies by Mellgren (2011) and by Mellgren, Pauwels, and Torstensson-Levander (2012) showed very small neighborhood contextual effects with regard to fear of crime. This also depended on the measure of the fear of crime. In a separate study, Mellgren, Pauwels, and Torstensson-Levander (see Mellgren, 2011) studied neighborhood-level variations in prevalence of preventive measures among residents, and no variation was found, once individual demographics were taken into account. Recently, Gerrell (2015) studied the problem of aggregation bias and concluded that neighborhoods are too heterogeneous. He argued that the microplace level deserves more attention.

In Iceland, a series of multilevel studies have shown neighborhood contextual effects on juvenile delinquency (Bernburg & Thorlindsson, 2005, 2007; Bernburg,

Thorlindsson, & Sigfusdottir, 2009a, 2009b) by using data on both community and individual adolescents' rates of delinquency. Besides the social disorganization perspective, the authors were also inspired by the perspectives of Durkheim and Parsons. They found that both community social instability (residential mobility, family disruption) and individual-level social control mechanisms (social ties linking parents and adolescents and normlessness) affect individual differences in offending, independent of demographic background characteristics.

16.4.3 The Netherlands

In the Netherlands, there is a thriving tradition with regard to neighborhood effects and spatial criminology. For the purpose of this chapter we restrict ourselves to social, ecological, and neighborhood contextual effects studies. Fiselier (1972) was one of the first studies in Europe that showed that the offender rate of neighborhoods in a Dutch city and the crime rate had a rather low correlation. He had revealed earlier that concentrations of offenders were in particular Nijmegen neighborhoods (Fiselier, 1968). Interestingly, 30 years later Van Wijngaarden and Boerman demonstrated that the same (old and deprived) neighborhoods in Nijmegen had the highest offender rates, despite population turnover (Van Wijngaarden & Boerman, 1997). In the 1990s, a test of social disorganization theory was conducted by Ben Rovers (1997). His study deserves special attention for several reasons. First, it was the first European multilevel test of social disorganization theory. Second, Rovers paid particular attention to theoretical elaboration by integrating social disorganization theory with an individual-level theory, strain theory, by focusing on personal and social resources. Third, Rovers combined different data collection methods (administrative data and self-reported delinquency data that were derived from a large-scale study of early adolescents). Unfortunately, no social processes were included in the analyses. The study was conducted in Rotterdam, one of the four biggest cities in the Netherlands. The findings showed that statistical effects of neighborhood disadvantage disappeared when individual-level characteristics were taken into account.

Kleemans (1996) showed that associations between key structural characteristics of social disorganization theory (disadvantage, immigrant concentration, and residential mobility) and neighborhood burglary rates disappeared in the city of Enschede once account was taken of the neighborhood offender rate. These results were interpreted from an opportunity perspective. Kleemans argued that his results suggested that local crime concentrations were by and large caused by the presence of high numbers of local offenders in particular neighborhoods (see also chapter 6 by Bottoms in this volume). However, the question of what caused neighborhood concentrations of offenders remained unanswered in that study.

Dutch research in the first decade of the twenty-first century was characterized by the use of multilevel modeling. Studies of victimization and fear of crime showed consistently the presence of small but significant neighborhood contextual effects, whereas contextual effects on juvenile delinquency were almost absent. A number of multilevel analyses have been conducted by Van Wilsem, Wittebrood, and De Graaf on victimization (Van Wilsem, De Graaf, & Wittebrood, 2003; Van Wilsem, Wittebrood, & De Graaf, 2006). These studies found neighborhood contextual effects of key structural variables from social disorganization theory. Weijters, Scheepers, and Gerris (2009) analyzed a three-level model in which structural neighborhood characteristics, city-level characteristics, and individual-level characteristics were taken into account, and they found no neighborhood effects but only small but substantial city-level effects. Steenbeek and Hipp (Steenbeek & Hipp, 2011) conducted both cross-sectional and longitudinal analyses of neighborhoods in the Dutch city of Utrecht. While the cross-sectional analyses replicate typical findings, the results of longitudinal cross-lagged models suggest that disorder has large consequences for subsequent levels of social control and residential instability, thus leading to more disorder. This is in contrast social disorganization theory, which assumes disorder to be a consequence of low collective efficacy rather than a cause. The work of Steenbeek underlines the importance of longitudinal data, allowing for simultaneously testing the causes and consequences of disorder.

16.4.4 Belgium

In Belgium, ecological studies of crime, victimization, and fear of crime were scarce during the twentieth century. Available studies focused on the individual relationship between urbanization, poverty, and fear of crime. Not all of these studies were published, and those that were appeared in native-language Belgian journals or research reports. Despite some small local initiatives that studied variations in neighborhood crime rates, the ecological research tradition in Belgium can be characterized by a rather late start due to poor data quality (Pauwels, 2002).

Vercaigne et al. (2000) conducted a study on self-reported juvenile delinquency in the urban context of Brussels. The study revealed no contextual effects of neighborhood disadvantage. However, the study did not measure and analyze any mediating variables. Puzzled by these findings, and inspired by Rovers's Dutch study on juvenile delinquency, Pauwels revived the ecological tradition in Belgium, using multilevel modeling and structural equation modeling to investigate the relationships between neighborhood characteristics and neighborhood concentrations of crime and juvenile delinquency.

Pauwels (2002, 2007) used a community survey of key informants instead of a survey of neighborhood residents to measure social disorganization (see also Pauwels & Hardyns, 2009). His findings demonstrated that the juvenile delinquency rate, the offender rate, and aggregated survey-based questions on serious offending (self-report) were related to the key structural characteristics of social disorganization theory. However, no contextual effects on juvenile delinquency were found, completely in line with Rovers's study.

Two studies that were published later showed some additional findings: (1) when school-level variation was taken into account in cross-classified modeling, school-level variation continues to exist (the school-level variance exceeds the neighborhood-level variances that was below 1%) (Pauwels, 2011), and (2) a cross-level interaction exists between neighborhood disadvantage and the effect of lifestyle risk on self-reported offending (Pauwels, Hardyns, & Van deVelde, 2010).

Pauwels and Hardyns (2010) built on the social disorganization tradition with regard to victimization and fear of crime (avoidance behavior). To test their hypotheses, they combined three waves of Belgium's national victim survey and merged these data with registered data on disadvantage, residential mobility, immigrant concentration, density, and disorder. Ecological concentrations of disorder had the strongest net effects on fear of crime and self-reported victimization (Hardyns, 2010; Pauwels et al., 2010).

Hardyns (2010) carried out in-depth analyses of the collective processes that are central to collective efficacy theory: informal social control and social trust. This study revealed no contextual effects of informal social control on individual differences in fear of crime (avoidance behavior), and small but significant contextual effects of social trust on individual differences in fear of crime. Hardyns used data from the Social Cohesion Indicators in Flanders (SCIF) project (Bircan, 2012; Hardyns, 2010). In this study, data that had been gathered for years by various administrative services were brought together systematically in a large coherent database, together with data from a representative population survey of 2009, linked to crime, victimization, and fear of crime.

More recent Belgian contextual studies changed focus to fear of crime and victimization at the municipality level (Hardyns, 2012; Hardyns, Pleysier, & Pauwels, 2010; Pauwels & Hardyns, 2009), the postal code area level (Hardyns & Pauwels, 2012; Pauwels & Hardyns, 2009), and the neighborhood (and neighborhood cluster) level (Hardyns & Pauwels, 2012; Pauwels & Hardyns, 2011). A recent new interdisciplinary study succeeded in gathering data on ecological processes for all Ghent neighborhoods (the SWING study). We address this empirical study in section 16.5 on contemporary neighborhood studies in Europe.

16.4.5 Germany

During the last decades, the issue of social segregation and disorganization has been a recurrent theme in German sociology and criminology (Friedrichs, 1998; Friedrichs & Blasius, 2000; Friedrichs & Oberwittler, 2007; Fuchs & Schmalz, 2010). In particular, the role of social cohesion and collective efficacy has been investigated in various articles by Dietrich Oberwittler, based on the Cologne-Freiburg Youth Survey. This youth survey (1999–2000), conducted at MPI Freiburg, has become a classic example of contemporary European research in the social disorganization tradition. The idea of this study was to include two different cities and a rural area to compare the impact of variations in different ecological settings. Oberwittler (2004a, 2007) found strong contextual effects of neighborhood disadvantage on a measure of self-reported serious juvenile delinquency, but only for juveniles who had strong local friendship circles. The moderating effects of local friendship circles suggest that the importance of processes of choice (self-selection of adolescents into urban activity fields). These findings additionally hint at the importance of (delinquent) peer relations as a social mechanism leading to delinquency. Further, the Cologne-Freiburg study found significant effects of intergenerational closure (a less-studied operational measure of collective efficacy for children in European studies). Intergenerational closure was measured in an independent residential survey on adolescent delinquency. Finally, cross-level interactions between individual propensity measures and social disorganization were unraveled. Oberwittler, Rabold, and Baier (2013b) summarize the state of the art of contextual effects studies on juvenile delinquency, including a number of German studies that demonstrate small but significant neighborhood effects on juvenile delinquency. This edited volume provides an overview of different contemporary studies on neighborhood disadvantage from different perspectives (not just social disorganization theory). Finally, it is worth noticing that different dimensions of fear of crime have also been studied from the perspective of social disorganization (Lüdemann, 2006), showing significant effects of population density and disadvantage.

16.4.6 Other European Countries

There is a lack of (multilevel) studies inspired by social disorganization theory in Eastern and Southern Europe. Different research traditions, a lack of valid data sources on crime or other relevant variables, lack of methodological expertise, and unavailable research funding are some of the key factors explaining this backlog. However, this situation is changing slowly, as a number of Eastern and Southern European countries currently participate in the International Self-Reported Delinquency Study, which includes perceptual measures of collective efficacy and neighborhood disorder. However, studies that focus on social disorganization at various levels of aggregation are still lacking. One exception to this rule is the Spanish study by Echazarra (2014) who studied the effects of neighborhood disadvantage, residential stability, ethnic diversity, family disruption, and urbanization on individual perceptions of crime. An interesting path for further analysis is the relationship between ethnic heterogeneity and perceptions of crime. A part of the study pays attention to factors that affect the crime-immigration relationship and the beliefs in the existence in such a relationship. Important for future inquiries, and in line with Sampson (2012), is the stigmatizing effect that some neighborhoods receive because of their ethnic composition. To achieve progress in our knowledge of contextual effects across European cities, it will be necessary for multilevel studies to be carried out in these countries.

16.5 Contemporary Research Examples in Europe

In this section we present three examples of contemporary, large-scale European research projects within the disorganization tradition; PADS+ in the UK, SPAN in the Netherlands, and SWING in Belgium. These studies were chosen because they reflect the tradition of combining structural data of social disorganization with data on social processes as measured by neighborhood resident or expert surveys, and individual data on self-reported offending, fear of crime, and/or victimization. Besides that, they focus on *small* spaces as well as on neighborhoods to connect traditional crime causation theories with environmental criminological research.

16.5.1 Peterborough Adolescent and Young Adult Development Study (PADS+)

16.5.1.1 *Design and Methods*

The PADS+ study is a longitudinal study of adolescent offending (Wikström et al., 2012). Its main objective is to identify the key individual and environmental factors that influence social behavior during the transition from child to adulthood. The PADS+ study is strongly inspired by situational action theory (Wikström et al., 2012). The PADS+ study focuses on causal mechanisms connecting ecological (setting) characteristics to individual propensities to explain individual differences and changes in rule-breaking. The interaction between individual and environmental factors is at the core of SAT. SAT argues that situations arise from person-environment interactions and that the person-environment interaction is responsible for an individual's perception of rule-breaking as a morally viable alternative and for the processes of choice (deliberatively or habitually).

PADS+ collects data covering three main topics:

(1) *Individuals.* PADS+ has been designed to explore how different individual characteristics and social experiences affect young people's social behavior. Individual-level data are collected through *interviewer-led questionnaires* and *psychometric exercises.* A Young Persons' Questionnaire is used to collect data on a number of topics, including a young person's family life, school experience, peer relations, moral values and emotions, generalized self-control, perception of risk and consequences, temptations, offending, and use of drugs and alcohol. The questionnaire contains measures derived from the PADS+ study, and some additional items to test hypotheses from other perspectives. An additional Parents' Questionnaire is used to collect data on their family life, childhood events, peer relationships, and school experience from the perspective of the parents.

(2) *Environmental settings.* PADS+ also aims to find out how the characteristics of different small-area environments of Peterborough affect the social activities (behavior) that take place in different parts of the city. Environmental-level data are collected through an *interviewer-led questionnaire* and a *community survey*. The Peterborough Community Survey (PCS) collected detailed data on the social-environmental characteristics of small, geographically identifiable areas spanning Peterborough and several surrounding villages. PCS data include information on formal and informal social control, social cohesion, general disorder, youth presence, youth problems, fear of crime, and intergenerational closure.

(3) *Exposure to criminogenic settings.* The staff of PADS+ are interested in how exposure to different environments in Peterborough affects different young people's social behavior. Data on exposure to settings are collected using a *space-time budget* interview (STB) that has been designed to collect data on individuals' exposure to different environments through a one-to-one interview. Participants are asked about their hourly activities over four days during the week prior to interview. This includes the last Friday and Saturday and the two other most recent school days. For each hour, participants provide data on the setting (e.g., home, school, shopping center), their companions (e.g., peers, parents, siblings), and their main activity (e.g., socializing, studying, playing football). For each hour, their geographic location is identified using geocoded maps. These geocoded data are then linked to data concerning the community survey.

When combined, the PADS+ data can be used to study the interaction between participants' individual characteristics and experiences and their exposure to different kinds of small physical environments (both cross-sectionally and longitudinally) in an advanced way. The STB data allow for an analysis of young people's offending and victimization at the situational level (number offenses per hour and environmental exposure with regard to the settings where people really are instead of focusing on the residential area).

Data were collected in the spring of each year from 2003 to 2008, and biannually since 2009. In 2005 and 2010, the Peterborough Community Survey (PCS) collected detailed social-environmental data on geographical areas covering Peterborough and several surrounding villages. In total, 716 young people took part in the first child sweep. PADS+ has maintained an impressive retention rate during the following years, losing less than 4% of its sample (mostly due to participants moving abroad).

16.5.1.2 *Results*

Based on the PADS+ data, Oberwittler and Wikström (2009) were able to show that small urban spaces yield better results in terms of ecological reliability and validity. The PADS+ study design makes it possible to distinguish between the context of development and the context of action. Regarding the social environment, PADS+ studies found that participants' exposure to criminogenic environments was related to adolescent offending. Neighborhood disadvantage (in the residential area) does not lead to offending, but the time spent in criminogenic environments (within and outside of one's neighborhood) is conditionally related to offending, among adolescents that have high scores on criminal propensity. Especially relevant is that PADS+ data reveal that the link between structural disadvantage (measured as individual and neighborhood disadvantage) is only very weakly related to offending (Wikström & Treiber, 2016). Aggregate-level analyses on the PADS+ data revealed that collective efficacy is significantly associated with the overall crime concentration (places of offenses), mediating most of structural effects (Wikström et al., 2012, p. 203). This finding is even more true for the adolescent crime concentration (Wikström et al., 2012, p. 220), but much less so for adolescent offenders' concentration (home address) (Wikström et al., 2012, p. 238). One implication of this finding is that collective efficacy is relevant as a mechanism that operates in contexts of actions (i.e., contributing in the person-environment-action process). It may therefore be that the role of collective efficacy as a developmental context, shaping propensities, is less important. This finding is strongly related to space-time budget data.

Indeed, the space-time budget methodology is more effective in capturing the effect of exposure to criminogenic (moral) settings (see also the chapter by Weerman, Hoeben, Bernasco, Pauwels, and Bruinsma in this volume on characteristics of settings). Up to now, only two other research projects have adopted the STB methodology: the MINDS study in Malmö and the SPAN study in the Netherlands. These will now be discussed.

16.5.2 The Study of Peers, Activities, and Neighborhoods (SPAN)

16.5.2.1 *Design and Methods*

The SPAN study is a two-wave (panel) study among adolescents in The Hague and its neighboring suburbs. The study instruments measure theoretical constructs at the individual, family, peer, school, and neighborhood levels. Different instruments have been used simultaneously:

(1) A *questionnaire* to measure self-reported adolescent offending, and several explanatory variables including morality, self-control, social bonds, and potential peer influences was administered.
(2) A face-to-face interview recorded the daily activities of participants using the *space-time budget method.*
(3) A *community survey* (2009) was administered in 110 small neighborhoods in The Hague area to measure social ecological processes such as disorder, social cohesion, and informal social control.
(4) *Systematic social observations* were conducted to measure disorder in the same area between September 2011 and June 2012. In total, 1,422 locations in The Hague were observed, classified on 61 indicators, and photographed every 100 meters.

(5) The collected data were complemented by *additional statistical data* on structural characteristics of the neighborhoods in the area of The Hague, including data on police-recorded offenses and residential offenders arrested by the police.

In total, 843 respondents participated fully in the first wave of the study (completing both the questionnaire and the space-time budget interview). A *community survey* was conducted in the same area (The Hague and its suburbs) and was completed in 2009 by 3,575 adult residents in 110 neighborhoods (the net response rate was 31%). The aim of the survey was to measure social ecological constructs derived from social disorganization theory (different versions of the Chicago school), broken window theory (Wilson & Kelling, 1982), and the collective efficacy perspective (Sampson, 2006; Sampson & Groves, 1989). *Systematic social observations* were carried out in numbered grids of 200 by 200 meters (0.04 square kilometers), which were also obtained to enrich the space-time budget data collection: the geographical unit of observation was the closest address to the centroid of the grid cell. From this address a street segment of 100 meters was observed using a checklist comprising 61 items to measure social and physical disorder. In addition, four photographs were made at each location with a GPS camera. Land use, physical disorder, social disorder, physical condition of buildings, evidence of defensible space, traffic, formal and informal surveillance, and guardianship were observed. Most of the *additional statistical data* on structural characteristics of neighborhoods are publicly available. They were collected from municipal databases on the World Wide Web (e.g., Denhaag.buurtmonitor.nl). The data include neighborhood measurements of population size, population density, ethnic composition, age composition, household composition (including percentage singles), mean income, average residential real estate value, residential mobility, residential stability, commercial land use, and percentage of high-rise residential property. Further, geocoded police records of offenses and residential offenders per neighborhood over the years 2009 were provided by the police force De Haaglanden (covering the greater area of The Hague). For more information on the SPAN study, we refer to the SPAN homepage (www.spanproject.nl).

16.5.2.2 *Results*

The SPAN project has several aims; one of its key aims was to test hypotheses derived from situational action theory. However, the data were used for other purposes too. Here, we only discuss results that are of direct relevance to social disorganization theory. Using spatial autoregressive error models, Bruinsma and colleagues tested six different models of disorganization/collective efficacy on the neighborhood offense and offender rates in The Hague, the Netherlands (Bruinsma, Pauwels, Weerman, & Bernasco, 2013) (Table 16.1). The six models under investigation were the classic model of social disorganization; the model of Shaw and McKay; Sampson's 1987 model, which included family disruption; the model tested by Sampson and Groves (1989); a community social capital model; and the collective efficacy model. The study revealed that none of the six models did a particularly

Table 16.1 Spatial Simultaneous Autogressive (SAR) Error Models of Offender Rates of Neighborhood for Six Social Disorganization Models ($N = 86$)

Offender rates	I Classic model	II Shaw and McKay	III Sampson 1987	IV Sampson and Groves	V Social capital	IV Collective efficacy
SES	-0.72^{***}	-0.73^{***}	-0.53^{***}	-0.73^{***}	-0.64^{***}	
Ethnic heterogeneity	-0.11^{ns}	-0.11^{ns}	-0.22^{ns}	-0.08^{ns}	-0.17^{ns}	
Residential mobility	0.29^{**}	0.29^{**}	0.41^{**}	0.39^{**}	0.30^{**}	
Concentrated disadvantage						0.66^{**}
Immigrant concentration						-0.12^{ns}
Residential stability				0.12^{ns}		-0.19^{*}
Heterogeneous tolerant value system		-0.01^{ns}				
Family disruption			0.32^{***}	0.08^{ns}		
Population density				-0.22^{**}		
Urbanization				-0.29^{***}		
Structural density				-0.20^{*}		
Local friendship networks				-0.14^{ns}	0.05^{ns}	
Organizational participation				-0.09^{ns}	0.00^{ns}	
Unsupervised peer groups				0.18^{ns}		
Neighborhood trust					-0.19^{ns}	
Collective efficacy						0.03^{ns}
Lambda	0.08^{ns}	0.08^{ns}	-0.16^{ns}	-0.18^{ns}	-0.00^{ns}	-0.05^{ns}

$^{***}p < .001$; $^{**}p < .01$; $^{*}p < .05$.

good job of explaining *offender rates*. Though SES (strong) and residential mobility (moderate) had empirical relationships with offender rates as predicted, residential mobility—one of the key concepts of disorganization—did not. Structural variables like population density and level of urbanization exhibited relations with offender rates that were in conflict with the theory. In addition, family disruption was only statistically significant when no other mediating variables were included in the regression equations.

For this sample, the classic model and the Shaw and McKay model did not explain *crime rates* very well (see Table 3 in Bruinsma et al., 2013). Sampson's extended model explained crime rates better: Both ethnic heterogeneity and higher numbers of single headed families had a positive relationship, as predicted. In the Sampson and Groves model (which basically extended the classic model with population density, female-headed households, and structural density as structural antecedents of the breakdown of social control) the impact of ethic heterogeneity became stronger, and that of single-headed families disappeared, while the level of organizational participation seemed to play its role as predicted. Population density had an effect opposite to what was predicted: higher density was associated with lower crime rates in neighborhoods. The social capital and collective efficacy models encounter problematic outcomes with the data as well. Only two of the mediating variables in the social capital model / collective efficacy model play a significant role as the theory predicted. In general, social disorganization models predict more variables will have an independent effect than the results presented in our study. Moreover, the empirical findings of SPAN indicate meaningful differences between the models when explaining crime rates or offender rates. First, the structural characteristics have opposing effects for crime rates compared to offender rates. Low SES and high residential mobility seemed to be stronger associated with high offender rates, but not to be related to crime rates. Lower levels of urbanization and population density were related to lower level of crime rates but not with higher levels of crime. Second, ethnic heterogeneity was not found to play a significant role in explaining offender rates. For crime rates, this neighborhood characteristic had an important statistical effect in three of the six models. Third, the data suggest that local friendship networks failed to explain offender rates in neighborhoods while the results for crime rates were ambiguous. These differences suggest that there may be distinct causal mechanisms responsible for crime rates and offender rates.

In another environmental criminological publication that used SPAN data, cross-classified modeling was used to investigate possible neighborhood and school contextual effects on individual juvenile delinquency (Pauwels et al., 2014). Again, with regard to juvenile delinquency all neighborhood variation was found to be related to the neighborhood composition with regard to demographic background variables (immigrant background, family structural background, SES). In technical terms this means that the intraclass coefficients in empty random intercept models were significant, but lost all significance when demographic controls were entered into the equation.

16.5.3 The Social Capital and Well-Being in Neighborhoods in Ghent Study (SWING)

16.5.3.1 *Design and Methods*

The data for this study were collected in the city of Ghent, in four successive cross-sectional waves of data collection (2011–2014). In 2015, an additional longitudinal data collection took place in 50 neighborhoods (SWING 5). Social capital is studied from different angles, and multiple definitions are used. At the individual level the concept refers to James Coleman's and Nan Lin's conceptualizations of social capital (i.e., people whom one can trust and are willing to help), while at the neighborhood level, social capital is defined in terms of collective efficacy. To measure collective efficacy, data were gathered at the individual level and then aggregated using the ecometric approach. The general objectives of the Belgium SWING study (2011–2015) were as follows:

(1) To develop a coherent multilevel data set of indicators on individual and neighborhood social capital and well-being that contains independent indicators of neighborhood social capital at a low level of aggregation.
(2) To measure social capital in line with the multidimensional nature of the concept.
(3) To test the collective efficacy theory for various crime related outcomes.

Multiple methods of data collection were used within each wave:

(1) At the individual level, 3,279 residents were interviewed by means of *face-to-face interviews*. This method was used for the measurement of individual social capital, and crime-related outcomes such as victimization, fear of crime, use of psychoactive substances, procedural justice, and trust in the police.
(2) At the neighborhood level, data were gathered using the *key informant technique* through a face-to-face standardized questionnaire. This method was used for the measurement of neighborhood social capital, and other neighborhood processes of social (dis)organization. Further, observations were completed by the interviewers to evaluate disorder, the facilities, and (green) space in the neighborhood by *observation checklists*, *photographs*, and *Google Street View pictures*.
(3) The data were complemented by (mainly) *administrative data* from existing, external databases from the City of Ghent and Ghent University on the social and economic structure of the neighborhoods. Additionally, police-recorded crime data on violence (intimidation), burglary, theft of/from cars, bicycle theft, robbery, vandalism, and drug use were gathered, together with data on disorder such as alcohol violations and noise nuisances.

In total, 3,279 neighborhood residents (the overall response rate was 48%) and 2,531 key informants were reached, 2,730 observation checklists were completed, and 4,222 photographs and 4,222 Google Street View pictures from 142 neighborhoods were taken.

Additional *administrative data* were made available by administrative agencies and comprised a multitude of social and structural indicators: demographic (gender, age, household size, residential mobility/turnover), structural (residential density, percentage of green zones), socioeconomic (ethnic minorities, mean income, income inequality, unemployment), and other (crime statistics, walkability) indicators. For more information on the research protocol of this study, we refer the reader to Hardyns et al. (2015).

16.5.3.2 *Results*

The SWING study has focused in particular on the fear of crime concept. Results suggest that individuals living in neighborhoods with lower levels of social trust and higher levels of disorder report more fear of crime. Individuals who experience more social support report lower levels of fear of crime. Another remarkable result from the SWING study is that social trust and informal social control do not correlate at the neighborhood level of analysis. In line with previous findings of Carpiano (2006), Hardyns (2012), and Pauwels and Hardyns (2010), this is another indication that it is difficult to combine both social trust and informal social control into one higher-order factor, that is, collective efficacy, in a European country like Belgium. Other researchers have suggested that the collective efficacy concept as developed in the United States cannot simply be transferred and applied to other countries and settings (Zhang et al., 2009), thus questioning its universal validity.

16.6 Conclusions and Discussion

16.6.1 Backgrounds

This chapter focused on the applications of social disorganization theory of the Chicago tradition in European criminological environmental studies and the results of these inquiries. Social disorganization theory continues to inspire European scholars to investigate the impact of neighborhoods (and smaller ecological units) on self-reported offending, fear of crime, and within-area victimization. A European tradition of empirical criminological research has, however, existed since the beginning of the nineteenth century, long before the social disorganization perspective emerged in Chicago in the first part of the twentieth century. Several European scholars suggested (partial) explanations of spatial urban crime concentrations (like population density, the unequal distribution of economic deprivation) or of individual criminal behavior that can be seen as modest precursors of the social disorganization theory of the Chicago school. With some notable exceptions, especially in the UK, in the twentieth century up until the 1970s and 1980s, these kinds of spatial criminological studies became marginalized in Europe, due to paradigm shifts toward the study of the societal reaction toward crime. The Sheffield studies were originally critical of the

US social disorganization perspective because of its free market assumption that cities and neighborhoods develop as a consequence of competition. In the UK and other European cities, local and national policy have historically had a strong impact on the housing market and decisions regarding who lives where. In the late 1990s, a shift toward the testing of contextual effects of area characteristics on individual differences in fear of crime, victimization in one's residential area, and juvenile delinquency was remarkable, this was especially so in Germany, the Netherlands, Belgium, the UK, and Sweden. The typical aggregated studies of offender or offense rates that were predominant in the twentieth century declined in European studies that were conducted on the basis of social disorganization theory.

16.6.2 Methods and Measurement

Most European studies of neighborhood effects were *cross-sectional* by design in the past and used survey questionnaires that were handed out to neighborhood inhabitants to measure ecological neighborhood mechanisms. These studies then aggregated individual-level responses of questions regarding the social climate in the neighborhoods to the neighborhood level. The typical design in European studies is a cross-sectional study that either asks for self-ratings on neighborhood problems in the residential area (the most common definition of a neighborhood is the "five-minute walking distance from someone's home"), or a cross-sectional study that combines individual-level data with aggregated secondary data on poverty, ethnic heterogeneity (or immigrant concentration), residential stability, and (structural) density at the neighborhood, area, or city level. While these studies provide interesting evidence regarding the magnitude of the associations between ecological characteristics and crime-related behavioral and attitudinal outcomes, they do not inform us about the causal relationship between ecological processes and crime-related behavioral and attitudinal outcomes.

The theoretical concepts used in disorganization research are seldom elaborated empirically by European researchers. Concepts were borrowed from American environmental research without consideration of whether these concepts were applicable in the same empirical sense in European cities (Bruinsma, 2007). Surprisingly few European studies have probed collective efficacy or other neighborhood processes of social capital, in comparison to the number of studies that have studied the (contextual) effects of "traditional" variables of social disorganization theory, that is, structural characteristics that are measured by governmental administrative data.

Few European studies are longitudinal by nature, enabling causal inferences from empirical research.

Contemporary research in the ecological tradition in Europe puts a stronger emphasis on different theories (integration), mechanisms, and an honest concern for the development of valid measurements of the key concepts of social disorganization theory (and its offspring like collective efficacy theory). At the same time, contemporary studies are exploring the possibilities of using innovative data collection methods (e.g., STB method, systematic social observations, Google Street View, photographs) used at the smallest possible spaces in neighborhoods.

European studies are increasingly following the US scholarly tradition that combines aggregates of scales to measure observations of social trust and informal control, and even observations of physical and social disorder. Before the 1990s, (spatial) multilevel modeling was not accessible for a broad audience and until the introduction of advanced software it was technically quite a problem to solve micro-macro questions and to avoid fallacies like the ecological fallacy and the contextual fallacy. Contemporary European studies primarily use (spatial) multilevel modeling to test contextual effects, at least when a person (home or place) can be assigned to a clearly defined area, such as a census tract, neighborhood, or municipality. Typically, the first studies used hierarchical linear modeling, while later studies have employed hierarchical logit models and negative binomial models. Unfortunately, not every study used multilevel modeling to statistically distinguish contextual effects from neighborhood compositional effects correctly. Hierarchical (multilevel) regression models were highly exceptional in the context of European criminology before 2000, while nonhierarchical multilevel models (cross-nested designs taking into account both neighborhoods and schools) and spatial multilevel models taking into account spatial autocorrelation were embraced in the twenty-first century.

Current cross-nested studies are restricted to the study of cross-level interaction between (1) neighborhood characteristics, municipality-level characteristics, and neighborhood crime rates, (2) neighborhood characteristics, individual-level characteristics, and individual offending.

Individual juvenile delinquency is no longer the only dependent variable used in criminological inquiries: studies on victimization and the fear of crime have flourished in Europe in particular. One of the reasons for the abundance of fear-of-crime and local victimization studies (in comparison to juvenile delinquency studies) is the fact that several countries only have national representative surveys on crime and victimization, which allow for the study of contextual effects at the municipality level and for contextual effects at the neighborhood levels in large cities (which are oversampled). This tradition was stimulated because there has been a number of government-initiated initiatives (mostly survey-based) that are used to evaluate (local) policies (e.g., the data gathered by the Home Office in the UK and its counterparts in other European countries). On some occasions, these studies have been used to test contextual effects on victimization and fear of crime. That has also been the case in the Netherlands, Belgium, the UK, and Sweden.

16.6.3 The Findings

Contextual European studies applying social disorganization theory has attempted to explain individual differences in offending, fear of crime, within-area victimization, and perceptions of collective efficacy. The general conclusion is that European empirical studies have produced mixed results with respect to social disorganization theory. Studies on neighborhood contextual effects on individual offending have demonstrated that neighborhood-level variables do not contribute much to the explanation of individual differences in offending; in most cases intraclass coefficients remain around or below 1%. Contextual studies of fear of crime reveal the strongest intraclass coefficients (+/− 8%). A majority of European self-report studies conclude that contextual effects of the residential area on adolescent offending are lacking within the European context. Only a few European studies report the existence of (very modest) contextual effects of neighborhood-level variables on self-reported delinquency. The study by Oberwittler (2007) is one of the exceptions, finding strong and conditional contextual neighborhood effects. These effects were found only for people who had lived in the same neighborhood for a long time and for whom the majority of their friends were living in the same residential area. But, it must also be concluded, when individual intervening mechanisms like delinquency tolerance or self-control are introduced in the regression models, in most cases the independent impact of social disorganization variables disappeared, with the exception of the study by Oberwittler (Oberwittler, 2004b). With regard to fear of crime and victimization, most of the studies we discussed reported small *contextual* effects on individual differences in local victimization and fear of crime.

Aggregated-level studies continue to exist with regard to a number of outcomes, mostly crime rates, offender rates, victimization rates, and aggregate levels of fear of crime. One of the central findings in European research is that crime rates are better explained by characteristics derived from opportunity theories than the key mechanisms of social disorganization theory. Another finding is that offender rates are strongly related to levels of poverty, but only moderately related to social disorganization variables. These aggregated studies have shown that collective efficacy levels are moderately related to neighborhood crime rate variations in a number of European studies, but not in all studies. At the moment, it is difficult to explain these differences. Therefore, we can only speculate at the moment. It is highly plausible that the city context may play a role. In particular, neighborhood levels of social cohesion seem to mediate the influences of neighborhood structural characteristics. When the effects of social cohesion and informal control are studied simultaneously, informal control performs badly as a predictor. It is difficult to explain this finding, but it may be that citizens in Europe are far less willing to personally intervene for the common good and rely much more than their US counterparts on the municipality and the police to solve neighborhood problems. Studies on neighborhoods with economic and housing improvements showed that social dynamics are an additional factor in causing higher crime rates (Bruinsma, 2007). It remains an important question why the relationship between collective efficacy (i.e., the dimension of social trust) and crime rates or offender rates holds in some neighborhood studies (e.g., Belgian and Swedish studies) and not in other studies (In Dutch and British studies). However, comparative studies of contextual effects are still rare.

A difficult-to-answer question is whether the lack of substantial empirical effects in European neighborhood studies is due to a theoretical problem (many environmental theories still overemphasize the role of residential areas and neglect the areas where crimes are committed or the individual offender or victim) or to empirical issues. Maybe cross-level interaction effects are responsible for the lack of effect in contextual studies. Perhaps European studies (e.g., Oberwittler, 2004a, p. 60; Pauwels, 2007, p. 42) are flawed because the number of neighborhoods used are limited compared to larger US cities (in the classic study by Sampson et al., 1997). European results point to the importance of differentiating between the context of development and the context of action. To get more in-depth knowledge, more longitudinal research is necessary. If context matters, but at a lower level, it is questionable to what extent multilevel modeling will remain the most adequate technique to solve the problem of contextual effects on actions. Publications based on the PADS+ project and the SPAN study reveal that environmental exposure is more action-relevant.

Another crucial theoretical issue that is not solved by social disorganization theory, is the question of what causes the segregation of individuals into neighborhoods. It is imperative that the processes of segregation be elucidated (Sampson, 2012). Why and how are individuals selectively segregated into ecological settings? Criminological inquiries in Europe have not yet unraveled this topic. It is for this reason that we advocate for explanatory studies on causal mechanisms in European cities before a discussion of context and the behavior and attitudes of individuals can begin.

16.6.4 Methodological Reflection

From a methodological point of view, some major criticisms remain unsolved. First, the accurate conceptual definition and measurement of ecological settings will continue to challenge (or plague) ecological and contextual studies, whether they be conducted for street blocks, neighborhoods, or larger units such as neighborhood clusters, postal code areas (zip code areas), and municipalities. The studies that were scrutinized used different operational measures of neighborhoods and used different ways to probe the respondents about their home address. These differences seem to be defended for pragmatic reasons. It is fair to assume that all of these measures have their shortcomings and their strengths, and such research is bound to find a balance between respecting the respondent's privacy and gathering sensitive data (such as the exact home address) and public reporting. Although it has been convincingly advocated and demonstrated (e.g., Oberwittler & Wikström, 2009) that small areas are theoretically much more important than large ones when the concentration of criminal events is studied, this does not mean that larger areas, such as cities, should be forgotten or omitted in ecological studies. Microplaces are situated in larger settings, and from a multilevel perspective it might be interesting to study the interaction between characteristics of microplaces and larger areas. In many countries municipalities have a degree of political independence, so that the municipality level represents a level that refers to a completely other type of mechanisms than the neighborhood mechanisms. Second, and strongly related to the conceptual definition and measurement of ecological settings, the measurement of actual exposure of an individual to particular ecological contexts is crucial. This is an important lesson to be drawn from the PADS+ and SPAN studies.

Additional methods are needed to measure the amount of time spent in an ecological setting. With regard to the study of adolescent offending, one such method is the space-time budget analysis, a new method that allows for collecting exact information on what adolescents have been doing, and more especially where. This is important for understanding activity patterns and daily routines of individuals, so that we can identify the kinds of settings that individuals are exposed to. Such information is of equal importance for the study of victimization and fear of crime. Regarding the measurement of ecological processes specifically, some progress has been made in the methodology used to capture the intervening ecological processes at work. At the same time, we must continue to question our restricted possibilities of using surveys to validly capture ecological processes such as social trust, informal control, and disorder. Belgian studies based on the SWING project have repeatedly found that social cohesion is significantly related to fear of crime, while informal control is not related to fear of crime.

The psychometric properties of both concepts (e.g., as measured by factor loadings and Cronbach's alpha) and ecometric properties of collective efficacy do well in most European studies. The *ecological reliability* of *measures of self-reported offending* (as measured by lambda and the intraclass coefficient, a measure ranging from 0% to 100% to describe how strongly units in the same group resemble each other) is extremely low in repeated empirical studies in different cities. It is at this stage impossible to provide a satisfactory explanation: it may be the unit of analysis (although the Belgian studies conducted at the municipality and neighborhood levels yield exactly the same poor results for informal control); it may be the conceptualization. Informal control may just not be a likely European response to social problems, and in that case, there is not enough variation to make a difference in a study. Another option would be to redirect the focus to alternative measures of informal control. An example can be found in Reynald's study of guardianship (Reynald, 2011).

Another neglected issue is the question of whether the effects of social cohesion, neighborhood social control, and disorder are cumulative and nonlinear. Most studies use traditional ways of analyzing the data: block-wise regression models are used because these express the idea that effects of neighborhood structural characteristics should decrease or vanish when account is taken of ecological processes. Of course, when effects are cumulative and nonlinear, these results are biased. Is a survey of neighborhood inhabitants the best way to capture these processes? Why do researchers continue to focus on processes of social control and ignore processes of the cultural transmission of norms that are conducive to crime, as in the early days of Shaw and McKay's research? In a typical contemporary social disorganization / collective efficacy study, survey responses of area inhabitants are aggregated to create measures of ecological processes. This procedure is not without flaws. There is a danger that the measurement of ecological processes, and thus the creation of ecological variables based on surveys that are also used to measure variables at the individual level, may create artificial results. It may be better to use other sources (different survey types and different structural data) when studying contextual effects and individual-level effects simultaneously (see Solymosi and Bowers in this volume). Ecological studies await new methodological challenges, like the use of new technologies, the use of Google Street View as a measurement instrument to validate neighborhood scores based on residents, and/or professional key informants.

Recently, Sutherland, Brunton-Smith, and Jackson (2013) have also pointed to the existence of endogeneity problems. Future research on collective efficacy will only be resolved through strong theorizing and better data that incorporate changes within and between neighborhoods over time and using methods that focus on change (such as fixed-effects longitudinal models). Such analysis has the potential to disentangle some of the complexity associated with how processes such as collective efficacy might operate (for an empirical example, see Hipp, Tita, & Greenbaum, 2009). It is therefore clear that research into survey measurement error should be seen as an integral part of the study of the social ecology of crime and insecurity. And because surveys play such a key role, it is important to understand the effects of method bias, response error, and questionnaire error in surveys that are applied in contextual studies.

16.6.5 Looking Back and Forward

A decade ago, Bruinsma (2007) offered ambitious suggestions for a future research agenda that are still valid today. One important task for European criminology is the establishment of a European-wide systematic research program on urbanization, collective integrative and disintegrative processes, and crime (e.g., Matsueda, 2006). Today, only scattered attention is paid to the causes of the unequal geographical distributions of crime, victimization, and feelings of insecurity. With such a program, fundamental scientific knowledge on urbanization can be built up in a more systematic way by answering a series of sequential research questions on the basis of reliable data.

Attention should also be paid to special topics such as the causes of variations in crime rates between rural areas (including smaller municipalities) and cities and across cities to newly troubled suburban areas of larger cities. The effects of law enforcement, especially policing, or of informal guardians can no longer be neglected. When the strengths of different universities and research institutes are joined in such an overarching research program, a theory-driven database can be established containing longitudinal data over longer periods and at several levels of aggregation. With such data, it will be possible to compare the effects of changes in European societies and in cities on crime rates. Good examples are the research programs of criminologists in Sheffield and Chicago who systematically and over a long period of time collected data to test traditional and new hypotheses on processes of social disorganization affecting crime rates across neighborhoods. Such a data set must contain not only statistical aggregates for areas or neighborhoods but also data especially collected for geographical and environmental research. European criminology needs essential, valid data on concepts such as social cohesion and informal control. We need to know more in depth about how and why residents live with each other and how they organize social cohesion and social control. In this program, systematic data should be included on how and why offenders observe and evaluate crime targets and what stimulates or prevents them from traveling to targets. Interviewing offenders is a high priority. Interviewing larger numbers of criminals in certain neighborhoods will enable us to gain more insight into the processes of how they influence each other in committing crimes or in establishing criminal infrastructures while others organize social control. In this respect, Shaw and McKay's (1942) concept of cultural transmission of values and Sutherland's concept of differential association (1947) can be inspiring and helpful (Bruinsma, 1999, 2000). New research can also critically assess the validity, and improve the applicability to European countries, of theoretical models developed in the United States.

References

Aaberge, R., Bjorklund, A., Jäntti, M., Palme, M., Pedersen, P. J., Smith, N., et al. (2002). Income inequality and income mobility in the Scandinavian countries compared to the United States. *Review of Income and Wealth 48*(4), 443–469.

Baldwin, J. (1975). British areal studies of crime: An assessment. *British Journal of Criminology 15*(3), 211–227.

Bernburg, J. G., & Thorlindsson, T. (2005). Violent values, conduct norms, and youth aggression: A multilevel study in Iceland. *Sociological Quarterly 46*(3), 457–478.

Bernburg, J. G., & Thorlindsson, T. (2007). Community Structure And Adolescent Offending In Iceland: A Contextual Analysis. *Criminology, 45*(2), 415–444.

Bernburg, J. G., Thorlindsson, T., & Sigfusdottir, I. D. (2009a). The neighborhood effects of disrupted family processes on adolescent substance use. *Social Science and Medicine 69*(1), 129–137.

Bernburg, J. G., Thorlindsson, T., & Sigfusdottir, I. D. (2009b). Relative deprivation and adolescent outcomes in Iceland: A multilevel test. *Social Forces 87*(3), 1223–1250.

Bircan, T. (2012). *Community Structure and Ethnocentrism. A Multilevel Approach: A Case Study of Flanders (Belgium)*. PhD diss., Catholic University of Leuven.

Bottoms, A. E., Claytor, A., & Wiles, P. (1992). Housing markets and residential community crime careers. In D. J. Evans, N. R. Fyfe, & D. T. Herbert (Eds.), *Crime, Policing, and Place: Essays in Environmental Criminology* (pp. 118–144). London: Routledge.

Bottoms, A. E., Mawby, R., & Xanthos, P. (1981). *Sheffield Study on Urban Social Structure and Crime, Part 3*. London: Home Office.

Bottoms, A. E., & Wiles, P. (1986). Housing tenure and residential crime careers in britain. In A. J. Reiss & M. Tonry (Eds.), *Communities and Crime: A Review of Research* (Vol. 8, pp. 101–163). Chicago: University of Chicago Press.

Bottoms, A. E., & Wiles, P. (2002). Environmental criminology. In M. Maguire, R. Morgan, & R. Reiner (Eds.), *The Oxford Handbook of Criminology* (pp. 620–656). Oxford: Oxford University Press.

Bottoms, A. E., & Xanthos, P. (1981). Housing policy and crime in the public sector. In P. J. Brantingham & P. L. Brantingham (Eds.), *Environmental Criminology* (pp. 203–226). Beverly Hills, CA: Sage.

Bruinsma, Gerben J. N. (1999). Stedelijke criminaliteit, sociale netwerken en differentiële-associatietheorie. *Tijdschrift voor Criminologie* 41, 138–140.
Bruinsma, Gerben J. N. (2000). *Geografische Mobiliteit en Misdaad (oratie UL)*. Leiden: Universiteit Leiden.
Bruinsma, Gerben J. N. (2007). Urbanisation and urban crime: Dutch geographical and environmental research. In M. Tonry & C. Bijleveld (Eds.), *Crime and Justice in the Netherlands* (Vol. 35, pp. 453–502). Chicago: University of Chicago Press.
Bruinsma, Gerben J. N., Pauwels, L., Weerman, F. M., & Bernasco, W. (2013). Social disorganization, social capital and collective efficacy and the distribution of crime and criminals: An empirical test of the relevance of six American neighborhood theories for a Dutch city. *British Journal of Criminology* 53(5), 942–963.
Bruinsma, Gerben J. N., & Weisburd, D. (2014). History of geographic criminology I: The 19th Century. In Gerben J. N. Bruinsma & David Weisburd (Eds.), *The Encyclopedia of Criminology and Criminal Justice* (pp. 2159–2163). New York: Springer.
Brunton-Smith, I., & Sturgis, P. (2011). Do neighborhoods generate fear of crime? An empirical test using the British Crime Survey. *Criminology* 49(2), 331–369.
Burgess, E. W. (1967 [1925]). The growth of the city: An introduction to a research project. In R. E. Park & E. W. Burgess (Eds.), *The City: Suggestions for the Investigation of Human Behaviour in the Urban Environment* (pp. 47–62). Chicago: University of Chicago Press.
Burkhauser, R. V., & Poupore, J. G. (1997). A cross-national comparison of permanent inequality in the United States and Germany. *Review of Economics and Statistics* 79(1), 10–17.
Carpiano, R. M. (2006). Toward a neighborhood resource-based theory of social capital for health: Can Bourdieu and sociology help? *Social Science and Medicine* 62(1), 165–175.
Cutler, D. M., Glaeser, E. L., & Vigdor, J. L. (1999). The rise and decline of the American ghetto. *Journal of Political Economy* 107(3), 455–506.
Dolmén, L. (2002). *Brottslighetens geografi: En analys av brottsligheten i Stockholms län*. Kriminologiska institutionen, Stockholm.
Durkheim, E. (1964 [1893]). *The Division of Labor in Society*. New York: Free Press.
Echazarra, A. (2014). La delincuencia en los barrios. Percepción y reacciones. *Colección Estudios Sociales*, 37.
Eisner, M. (1997). *Das Ende der Zivilisierten Stadt? Die Auswirkungen von Modernisierung und Urbaner Krise auf Gewaltdelinquenz*. Frankfurt am Main: Campus.
Eisner, M., & Wikström, P.-O. H. (1999). Violent crime in the urban community: A comparison of Stockholm and Basel. *European Journal on Criminal Policy and Research* 7(4), 427–442.
Fiselier, J. P. S. (1968). *Kriminaliteit van Nijmegen*. Nijmegen: Criminologisch Instituut.
Fiselier, J. P. S. (1972). Kriminaliteit en buurt. *Nederlands Tijdschrift voor Criminologie, 14*, 93–105.
Fletcher, J. (1848). Moral and educational statistics of England and Wales. *Journal of Statistical Society of London* 11, 344–366.
Fletcher, J. (1850). *Summary of the Moral Statistics of England and Wales*. London: Private distribution of the author.
Friedrichs, J. (1998). Do poor neighborhoods make their residents poorer? Context effects of poverty neighborhoods on residents. In H.-J. Andreß (Ed.), *Empirical Poverty Research in a Comparative Perspective* (pp. 77–98). Aldershot: Ashgate.
Friedrichs, J., & Blasius, J. (2000). *Leben in Benachteiligten Wohngebieten*. Opladen: Leske & Budrich.

Friedrichs, J., & Oberwittler, D. (2007). Soziales Kapital in Wohngebieten. In A. Franzen & M. Freitag (Eds.), *Sozialkapital* (pp. 450–486). Wiesbaden: VS Verlag für Sozialwissen schaften.

Fuchs, M., & Schmalz, S. (2010). Gewalt an Schulen: eine Mehrebenenanalyse zum Einfluss von Sozialisationsbedingungen und Klassenkomposition. *Zeitschrift für Soziologie der Erziehung und Sozialisation 30*(2), 134–148.

Gangle, M. (2005). Income inequality, permanent incomes, and income dynamics: Comparing Europe to the United States. *Work and Occupations 32*(2), 140–162.

Gerell, M. (2015). Collective efficacy, neighborhood and geographical units of analysis: Findings from a case study of Swedish residential neighborhoods. *European Journal on Criminal Policy and Research 21*(3), 385–406.

Gesthuizen, M., van der Meer, T., & Scheepers, P. (2008). Ethnic diversity and social capital in Europe: Tests of Putnam's thesis in European countries. *Scandinavian Political Studies 32*(2), 121–142.

Guerry, A.-M. (1833). *Essai sur la Statistique Morale de la France*. Paris: Crochard.

Hardyns, W. (2010). *Social Cohesion and Crime: A Multilevel Study of Collective Efficacy, Victimisation and Fear of Crime*. PhD diss., Ghent University.

Hardyns, W. (2012). Social cohesion and fear of crime in the Flemish region: Looking back on the results and a preview of additional research. In P. Ponsaers (Ed.), *Social Analysis of Security: Financial, Economic and Ecological Crime, (in)Security and (dis)Trust, Public and Private Policing* (pp. 167–202). The Hague: Eleven International Publishing.

Hardyns, W., & Pauwels, L. (2012). Collective efficacy, sociaal kapitaal en 'fear of crime': een evaluatie van contextuele effecten op drie aspecten van onveiligheidsbeleving. *Tijdschrift voor Criminologie, 54*(4), 306–321.

Hardyns, W., Pleysier, S., & Pauwels, L. (2010). Oorzaken van het mijden van onveilige situaties bij mannen en vrouwen: Een contextuele analyse op basis van de 'collective efficacy'-theorie. *Tijdschrift voor Criminologie 52*(4), 374–394.

Hardyns, W., Vyncke, V., Pauwels, L., & Willems, S. (2015). Study protocol: SWING–social capital and well-being in neighborhoods in Ghent. *International Journal for Equity in Health 14*(1), 36.

Herbert, D. T. (1982). *The Geography of Urban Crime*. New York: Longman.

Hipp, J. R., Tita, G. E., & Greenbaum, R. T. (2009). Drive-bys and trade-ups: Examining the directionality of the crime and residential instability relationship. *Social Forces 87*(4), 1777–1812.

Ihlanfeldt, K. R., & Scafidi, B. (2004). Whites' neighbourhood racial preferences and neighbourhood racial composition in the United States: Evidence from the multi-city study of urban inequality. *Housing Studies 19*(3), 325–359.

Kleemans, E. R. (1996). *Strategische misdaadanalyse en stedelijke criminaliteit: Een toepassing van de rationele keuzebenadering op stedelijke criminaliteitspatronen en het gedrag van daders, toegespitst op het delict woninginbraak*. PhD diss., Internationaal Politie Instituut Twente (IPIT), Enschede.

Lüdemann, C. (2006). Kriminalitätsfurcht im urbanen Raum: Eine Mehrebenenanalyse zu individuellen und sozialräumlichen Determinanten von Kriminalitätsfurcht im städtischen Raum. *Kölner Zeitschrift für Soziologie und Sozialpsychologie 58*(2), 285–306.

Lunden, W. A. (1960). *Emile Durkheim*. London: Stevens & Sons.

Matsueda, R. L. (2006). Differential social organization, collective action, and crime. *Crime, Law and Social Change 46*(1–2), 3–33.

Mayhew, H. (1865). *London labour and the London poor*. Vol 4: *Those that will not work*. London: Charles Griffin.

McVie, S., & Norris, P. (2006). *Neighbourhood Effects on Youth Delinquency and Drug Use*. Edinburgh: University of Edinburgh, Centre for Law and Society.

Mellgren, C. (2011). *What's Neighbourhood Got to Do with It? The Influence of Neighbourhood Context on Crime and Reactions to Crime*. PhD diss., Malmö University.

Mellgren, C., Pauwels, L., & Torstensson-Levander, M. (2010). Population density, disadvantage, disorder and crime: Testing competing neighbourhood level theories in two urban settings. In M. Cools, B. De Ruyver, & M. Easton (Eds.), *Safety, Societal Problems and Citizens' Perceptions: New Empirical Data, Theories and Analyses* (pp. 183–200). Antwerp: Maklu.

Mellgren, C., Pauwels, L., & Torstensson-Levander, M. (2012). Variance in avoidance behaviour between residential neighbourhoods: Context or composition? A multilevel approach. In M. Cools, B. De Ruyver, M. Easton, L. Pauwels, P. Ponsaers, T. Vander Beken, F. Vander Laenen, G. Vande Walle, A. Verhage, G. Vermeulen, & G. Vynckier (Eds.), *Social Conflicts, Citizens and Policing* (pp. 157–168). Antwerpen: Maklu.

Morris, T. (1957). *The Criminal Area: A Study in Social Ecology*. London: Routledge & Kegan Paul.

Nilsson, A., & Estrada, F. (2007). Risky neighbourhood or individuals at risk? The significance of neighbourhood conditions for violent victimization in residential areas. *Journal of Scandinavian Studies in Criminology and Crime Prevention 8*(1), 2–21.

Oberwittler, D. (2004a). A multilevel analysis of neighbourhood contextual effects on serious juvenile offending: The role of subcultural values and social disorganization. *European Journal of Criminology 1*(2), 201–235.

Oberwittler, D. (2004b). Stadtstruktur, Freundeskreise und Delinquenz: Eine Mehrebenenanalyse zu sozialökologischen Kontexteffekten auf schwere Jugenddelinquenz. In D. Oberwittler & S. Karstedt (Eds.), *Soziologie der Kriminalität* (pp. 135–170). Wiesbaden: VS Verlag für Sozialwissenschaften.

Oberwittler, D. (2007). The effects of ethnic and social segregation on children and adolescents: Recent research and results from a german multilevel study. Unpublished discussion paper, Social Science Research Center, Berlin.

Oberwittler, D., Rabold, S., & Baier, D. (Eds.). (2013a). *Städtische Armutsquartiere—Kriminelle Lebenswelten? Studien zu sozialräumlichen Kontexteffekten auf Jugendkriminalität und Kriminalitätswahrnehmungen*. New York: Springer.

Oberwittler, D., Rabold, S., & Baier, D. (Eds.). (2013b). *Städtische Armutsquartiere-Kriminelle Lebenswelten? Studien zu Sozialräumlichen Kontexteffekten auf Jugendkriminalität und Kriminalitätswahrnehmungen*. Wiesbaden: Springer Verlag.

Oberwittler, D., & Wikström, P.-O. H. (2009). Why small is better: Advancing the study of the role of behavioral contexts in crime causation. In D. Weisburd, W. Bernasco, & G. J. N. Bruinsma (Eds.), *Putting Crime in Its Place: Units of Analysis in Geographic Criminology* (pp. 35–59). New York: Springer.

Ouimet, M. (2000). Aggregation bias in ecological research: How social disorganization and criminal opportunities shape the spatial distribution of juvenile delinquency in Montreal. *Canadian Journal of Criminology and Criminal Justice 42*(2), 135–156.

Pauwels, L. (2002). *De Ene Buurt is De Andere Niet: Exploratie van Mogelijkheden tot Contextualisering van Geregistreerde Criminaliteit op Buurtniveau*. Brussels: VUBPress.

Pauwels, L. (2007). *Buurtinvloeden en Jeugddelinquentie: Een Toets van de Sociale Desorganisatietheorie*. The Hague: Boom Juridische uitgevers.

Pauwels, L. (2011). Adolescent offending and the segregation of poverty in urban neighbourhoods and schools: An assessment of contextual effects from the standpoint of situational action theory. *Urban Studies Research.* Article ID 659768.

Pauwels, L., & Hardyns, W. (2009). Measuring community (dis)organizational processes through key informant analysis. *European Journal of Criminology* 6(5), 401–417.

Pauwels, L., & Hardyns, W. (2010). Does it really have to be "an urban village"? A multi-level analysis of fear of crime. In L. Pauwels, W. Hardyns, & M. Van de Velde (Eds.), *Social Disorganisation, Offending, Fear and Victimisation: Findings from Belgian Studies on the Urban Context of Crime* (pp. 177–198). The Hague: Boom Juridische uitgevers.

Pauwels, L., & Hardyns, W. (2011). Jeugdcriminaliteit en grootstedelijke woonbuurten: een kwestie van sociale desorganisatie? *Handboek Politiediensten 98*, 29–38.

Pauwels, L., Hardyns, W., & Van deVelde, M. (2010). *Social Disorganisation, Offending, Fear and Victimisation.* The Hague: BJu Publishers.

Pauwels, L., Weerman, F. M., Bruinsma, Gerben J. N., & Bernasco, W. (2014). How much variance in offending, self-control and morality can be explained by neighbourhoods and schools? An exploratory cross-classified multi-level analysis. *European Journal of Criminal Policy and Research 21*(4), 523–537.

Putnam, R. D. (2007). E pluribus unum: Diversity and community in the twenty-first century. The 2006 Johan Skytte Prize Lecture. *Scandinavian Political Studies 30*(2), 137–174.

Quételet, A. (1847). Statistique morale de l'influence du libre arbiter de l'homme sur les faits sociaux, et particulierement sur le nombre des marriages. *Bulletin de la Commission Centrale de Statistique* 3, 135–155.

Rawson, R. W. (1839). An inquiry into the statistics of crime in England and Wales. *Journal of the Statistical Society of London* 2, 316–344.

Reynald, D. M. (2011). *Guarding against Crime: A Theoretical and Empirical Elaboration of the Routine Activity Concept.* London: Ashgate.

Reynald, D. M., Averdijk, M. D. E., Elffers, H., & Bernasco, W. (2008). Do social barriers affect urban crime trips? The effect of ethnic and economic neighbourhood compositions on the flow of crime in The Hague, the Netherlands. *Built Environment 34*, 21–31.

Rovers, B. (1997). *De buurt, een broeinest? Een onderzoek naar de invloed van de woonomgeving op jeugdcriminaliteit.* Nijmegen: Ars Aequi Libri.

Sampson, R. J. (2006). Collective efficacy theory: Lessons learned and directions for future inquiry. In F. T. Cullen, J. P. Wright, & K. R. Blevins (Eds.), *Taking Stock: The Status of Criminological Theory* (pp. 149–167). New Brunswick, NJ: Transaction Publishers.

Sampson, R. J. (2012). *Great American City: Chicago and the Enduring Neighborhood Effect.* Chicago: University of Chicago Press.

Sampson, R. J., & Groves, W. B. (1989). Community structure and crime: Testing social disorganization theory. *American Journal of Sociology 94*(4), 774–802.

Sampson, R. J., Raudenbush, S. W., & Earls, F. (1997). Neighbourhoods and violent crime: A multilevel study of collective efficacy. *Science 277*, 918–924.

Sampson, R. J., & Wikström, P.-O. H. (2008). The social order of violence in Chicago and Stockholm neighborhoods: A comparative inquiry. In I. Shapiro, S. Kalyvas, & T. Masoud (Eds.), *Order, Conflict, and Violence* (pp. 97–119). New York: Cambridge University Press.

Shaw, C. R., & McKay, H. D. (1942). *Juvenile Delinquency and Urban Areas.* Chicago: University of Chicago Press.

Steenbeek, W., & Hipp, J. R. (2011). A longitudinal test of social disorganization theory. *Criminology 49*(3), 833–871.

Sutherland, A., Brunton-Smith, I., & Jackson, J. (2013). Collective efficacy, deprivation, and violence in London. *British Journal of Criminology* 53(3), 1050–1073.

Sutherland, E. H. (1947). *Principles of Criminology*. Philadelphia: Lippincott.

Tseloni, A. (2006). Multilevel modelling of the number of property crimes: Household and area effects. *Journal of the Royal Statistical Society: Series A (Statistics in Society) 169*(2), 205–233.

Van Wijngaarden, J. J., & Boerman, F. A. (1997). *Criminaliteit in Nijmegen: Een beschrijving van aard, omvang en spreiding van criminaliteit, met speciale aandacht voor berovingen.* Amsterdam: Vrije Universiteit.

Van Wilsem, J. A., De Graaf, N. D., & Wittebrood, K. (2003). Cross-national differences in victimization: Disentangling the impact of composition and context. *European Sociological Review* 19(2), 125–142.

Van Wilsem, J. A., Wittebrood, K., & De Graaf, N. D. (2006). Socioeconomic dynamics of neighborhoods and the risk of crime victimization: A multilevel study of improving, declining, and stable areas in the Netherlands. *Social Problems* 53(2), 226–247.

Vercaigne, C., Walgrave, L., Mistiaen, P., & Kesteloot, C. (2000). *Verstedelijking, Sociale Uitsluiting van Jongeren en Straatcriminaliteit.* Leuven: (onderzoeksrapport DWTC).

Weijters, G. G. M., Scheepers, P., & Gerris, J. (2009). City and/or neighbourhood determinants? Studying contextual effects on youth delinquency. *European Journal of Criminology* 6(5), 439–455.

Wikström, P.-O. H. (1991). *Urban Crime, Criminals, and Victims: The Swedish Experience in an Anglo-American Comparative Perspective.* New York: Springer.

Wikström, P.-O. H., & Dolmén, L. (1990). Crime and crime trends in different urban environments. *Journal of Quantitative Criminology* 6(1), 7–30.

Wikström, P.-O. H., & Dolmén, L. (2001). Urbanisation, neighbourhood social integration, informal social control, minor disorder, victimisation and fear of crime. *International Review of Victimology* 8, 121–140.

Wikström, P.-O. H., Oberwittler, D., Treiber, K., & Hardie, B. (2012). *Breaking Rules: The Social and Situational Dynamics of Young People's Urban Crime.* Oxford: Oxford University Press.

Wikström, P.-O. H., & Treiber, K. (2016). Social disadvantage and crime: A criminological puzzle. *American Behavioral Scientist.* doi: 10.1177/0002764216643134.

Wilson, J. Q., & Kelling, G. (1982). Broken windows: The police and neighbourhood safety. *Atlantic Monthly* 249(3), 29–38.

Wilson, W. J. (1987). *The Truly Disadvantaged: The Inner City, the Underclass, and Public Policy.* Chicago: University of Chicago Press.

Zhang, L., Messner, S. F., Liu, J., & Zhuo, Y. A. (2009). Guanxi and fear of crime in contemporary urban China. *British Journal of Criminology* 49(4), 472–490.

CHAPTER 17

TESTING THEORIES OF SOCIAL DISORGANIZATION IN NIGERIA

FAISAL UMAR, SHANE D. JOHNSON, AND JAMES A. CHESHIRE

17.1 Introduction

As discussed in Chapters 1, 2, and 16, social disorganization theory evolved from the influential work of Clifford Shaw and Henry McKay in the city of Chicago, *Juvenile Delinquency and Urban Areas* (Shaw and McKay 1969). They argued that community social organization, seen as the ability of residents of a neighborhood to control and supervise teenage peer groups, is influenced by three structural factors—low socioeconomic status (SES), ethnic heterogeneity, and residential mobility—which, in turn, lead to higher rates of crime. The theoretical framework of this approach, particularly in the last three decades, has guided much criminological research. It is important, however, to note that existing research is predominantly based on the experiences of US cities (for example, Warner and Pierce 1993; Kawachi, Kennedy, and Wilkinson 1999; Sun, Triplett, and Gainey 2004) and other parts of the developed world (for example, Sampson and Grove 1989; Veysey and Messner 1999; Lowenkamp, Cullen, and Pratt 2003; Mazerolle, Wickes, and McBroom 2010; Bruinsma et al. 2013). Research concerning the developing world is scarce, partly due to the challenges associated with the availability (or rather lack) of appropriate and reliable data. The few studies that exist have focused on violent crime (e.g., Breetzke, 2010; Pereira, Mota, and Andresen 2016), and provide only partial support for theories of social disorganization. This means that little is known as to the applicability of theories of social disorganization in the context of the developing world, particularly sub-Saharan Africa.

As new and innovative methodologies for collecting data emerge (for examples, see Chapter 11), the empirical testing of such theories will become more practicable in other parts of the world. For now, such testing must rely on established methods of primary data collection. In the developed world, criminological theories are typically tested using either data recorded by the police, or from large-scale survey samples used to collect nationally representative data. As will be discussed in more detail below, in most developing countries, police-recorded crime data are either unavailable or lack the detail necessary for statistical analysis. Nationally representative surveys are sometimes conducted, and while there are clear advantages to this approach to sampling (see Chapter 14), what such surveys lack is detailed data at the micro level of place. Such detail is necessary for the testing of theories of environmental criminology, particularly those for which characteristics of the built environment are considered important. The research reported in this chapter is part of a larger study concerned with the testing of theories of environmental criminology in a developing country—Nigeria. In the absence of police-recorded crime data, and to address the need for micro-level data, a community-level survey and a block environmental inventory were conducted in a case study area to provide detailed data on those surveyed and the characteristics of the communities within which they live.

In this chapter, we focus on the social disorganization approach to understanding variation in area-level rates of crime. For context, the next section provides a brief description of the study area. Section 17.3 provides a review of the different components of social disorganization theory, the mechanisms through which they are believed to operate, how they have been estimated in previous studies, and whether they are meaningful in the context of Nigeria. In Section 17.4, we describe the data and survey methods employed followed by (Section 17.5) the geographical units of analysis used in this present study. The sixth section presents an empirical test of social disorganization theory using data for Nigeria. Finally, we discuss the findings and their implications for criminological understanding.

17.2 Our Focus: Kaduna Metropolis, Nigeria

In this section, we briefly describe the study site—Badarawa-Malali, which is an urban district in the city of Kaduna, Nigeria. Descriptive statistics and other details discussed are largely drawn from the work of Max-Lock Consultancy Nigeria (MLCN) (2010), an urban planning consortium commissioned by the government of Kaduna to map and review the master plan of the city. We begin with a brief description of Kaduna and the population of the city.

The city of Kaduna is strategically located at the center of Northern Nigeria—about 210 km north of Abuja, the seat of the federal government. It is the capital city of Kaduna state, the third largest state in the country. The city serves as an important regional transportation hub and is considered to be the symbolic political capital of

Northern Nigeria (Bununu, Luden, and Hosni 2015). Unlike the typical precolonial cities in the country that are characterized by conservative traditional urban settings, Kaduna exhibits influences of Western town planning (a map of the city is shown in Figure 17.1). It covers a geographical area of about 250 km^2 with an estimated population

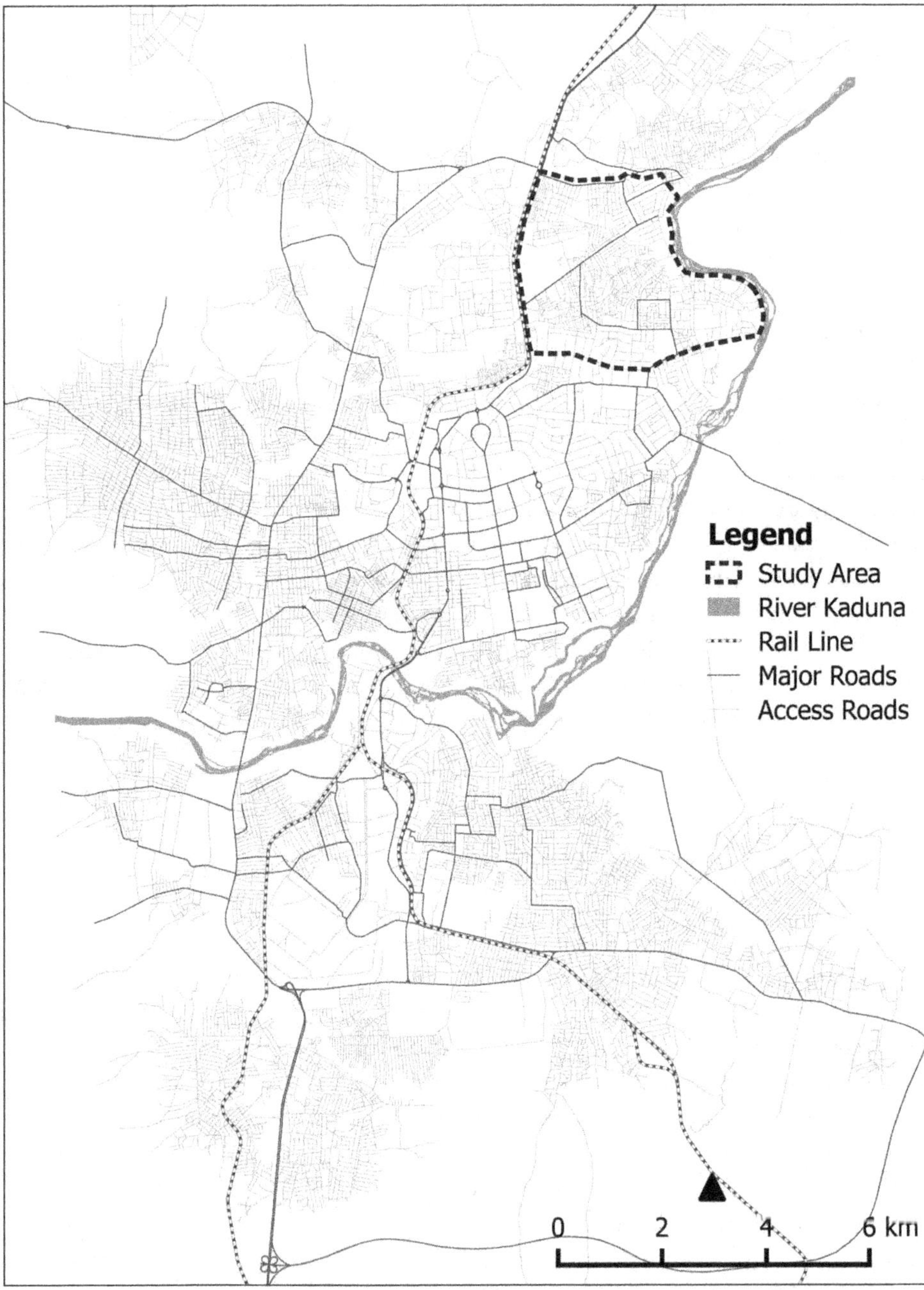

FIGURE 17.1 A map of Kaduna (Nigeria) metropolis

of 1.14 million (MLCN 2010) and, therefore, has a population density of about 4,560 persons/km^2. The population of the city is very diverse with Kaduna being home to almost all of the major ethnic groups in Nigeria, and some foreign nationals (Agbola 1986; Okpanachi 2010).

17.2.1 The Study Site: Badarawa-Malali Urban District

There are 65 "traditional"[1] districts in the city of Kaduna. These traditional districts are organized into 24 "urban" districts (wards)—the smallest administrative units in the city (MLCN 2010). Due to available resources, it was not practical to survey the entire city, and so the present study is limited to two urban districts—Badarawa-Malali (all four traditional districts in this urban district were sampled) and part of Kawo (four out of six traditional districts in this urban district were sampled), which are highlighted in Figure 17.1. The estimated population of the study area is 137,540, who reside in 13,865 households (MLCN 2010). This represents 12% of the total population of Kaduna and 13% of all households in the city. The average household size is about 9.91 persons per household, which is similar to the city average of 9.88. This study area was selected because the first author has a direct connection with a local partner, a university department in the state of Kaduna—which provided enumerators for the survey conducted—and also has good knowledge and understanding of both the physical and social settings of the area. This connection helped with the logistics of the fieldwork. Second, and perhaps most importantly, there is considerable variation in terms of both the physical and social settings between residential neighborhoods within these districts, making the district ideal for studying spatial patterns of urban crime. As will be discussed in Section 17.5, this provides an opportunity to study theories of social disorganization using spatial units that are closely based on Harvey Zoubargh's concept of the "natural area" (instead of administrative areas)—"a geographical area characterized both by a physical individuality and by the cultural characteristics of the people who live in it" (Zorbaugh [1926] in Lin and Mele 2005: p. 85).

There are broadly three distinct types of residential neighborhoods within the study area, these being high-, medium-, and low-density residential neighborhoods. The high-density residential areas, which MLCN (2010) refers to as urban villages, account for almost 50% of the total residential land use. These areas have no formal physical planning. They are characterized by irregular plot layouts with narrow streets that are mostly unpaved. Despite being the most deprived communities, these areas have the strongest traditional community identity, which encourages neighbors to care for each other. In contrast, the low- and the medium-density residential areas exhibit Western influences of physical planning. The streets are wide and mostly paved, with regular-sized plots aligned and well arranged on large street blocks. The most affluent groups in the population live in these areas—however, traditional community identity is weaker in these areas than in others (MLCN 2010).

17.3 Components of Social Disorganization Theory

As discussed elsewhere (e.g., Bruinsma et al. 2013; Chapters 1, 2, and 16 in this volume), the various components of social disorganization have been measured differently across different studies. In this section, we briefly discuss the various components that have been considered, the mechanism(s) through which they are assumed to impact crime, how they have been estimated, and whether they are meaningful in the context of Nigeria. To allow us to focus on conceptual issues, in this section, we avoid a detailed description of the data collected as part of the research reported here, leaving that discussion until Sections 17.4 and 17.6.

17.3.1 Socioeconomic Status (SES)

The association between SES, measured at the area level, and rates of crime is a dominant theme in ecological studies of urban crime. SES is one of the most important components of Shaw and McKay's (1969) social disorganization theory. As discussed in Chapter 1, in the original version of the theory, it was hypothesized that in 1940s Chicago residents of lower SES would have few housing options available to them—accordingly, they would tend to live in the less popular transitional zone of the city, but would aim to move out as soon as they had the resources to do so. This created transitory neighborhoods in which residents had little investment or the resources to change their surroundings—thus, the willingness of people to participate in local organizations would be weaker. This would impact on the ability of people to exert informal social control over the behavior of juveniles. These communities (the theory suggested) were accordingly characterized by high crime rates.

More recent research conducted in other cities has emphasized the latter structural characteristic of low-SES neighborhoods as a causal factor in neighborhood rates of crime, and this hypothesis has been empirically tested using different variables as an estimate of neighborhood SES. The average household income of those who live in an area has been the foremost indicator of SES—in some cases used as a single scale (see, for example, Cahill and Mulligan 2007; Markowitz et al. 2001), and in others as part of a composite measure that includes other dimensions of social class, such as educational attainment and employment level (see, for example, Sampson and Groves 1989; Veysey and Messner 1999; Lowenkamp, Cullen, and Pratt 2003). The data used in these studies were either obtained from national population censuses or household/crime surveys. In another study of social disorganization theory, Bruinsma et al. (2013) used data from a national census and a community survey to construct an index of SES that included the average household income variable together with unemployment rates, the average value of residential properties, and the percentage of residents receiving social benefits in a neighborhood.

In the context of the developing world, collecting data on such variables, particularly average household income, is difficult and rarely approached directly. Issues such as reporting-bias or nonresponse to questions relating to earnings or wealth have been a serious concern (Lindelow and Yazbeck 2004). Consequently, studies of SES have tended to use proxy measures, particularly those relating to housing characteristics and the possession of durable assets (Howe, Hargreaves, and Huttly 2008). This alternative approach reduces the problem of reporting-bias and nonresponse that is associated with conventional measures of income or wealth (Sahn and Stifel 2003)—data are typically collected using simple questions or less biased observational methods such as the block environmental inventory (Perkins, Meeks, and Taylor 1992), poverty scorecard (Schreiner 2010), or asset indices (Filmer and Pritchett 2001). This approach is adopted in the current study.

Our first hypothesis is that there will be a negative association between estimates of neighborhood SES (estimated using data collected as part of a block environmental inventory) and crime rates.

17.3.2 Ethnic Heterogeneity

From a social disorganization perspective, relative to those who live in homogeneous neighborhoods, residents of heterogeneous communities are considered less likely to be able to communicate effectively with one another, or to share common goals and normative values about what types of behavior are and are not appropriate. In turn, such communities are expected to be less cohesive, and to be less likely to act collectively to control crime (Sampson and Groves 1989; Kubrin 2000). Prior studies have measured heterogeneity as the proportion of the minority ethnic groups in the population, blacks, for instance (see Blau and Golden 1986; Messner and Golden 1992). However, as this fails to reflect the variety of racial groups in a neighborhood, other researchers have used (for example) the index of diversity (Simpson 1949) to calculate neighborhood heterogeneity.

However measured, the principle underlying the approach is that people from the same (different) ethnicity or race are likely to share similar (different) cultural beliefs and normative values. In many cities around the world, such an approach may make sense. However, in cities such as Kaduna, where almost all the population is of one race, it is less likely to provide a useful metric of neighborhood cohesion along these lines. An alternative interpretation of ethnicity in this context is captured by what some may refer to as "tribes". Nigeria is a multiethnic/cultural society—with over 300 different tribes (Otite 1990; Rakov 1992). Some share common values, and some form of trust, mutual assistance, and harmonious relations exists between some of these tribes (Otite 1990). Moreover, it is common to see intertribal marriages. However, it is also important to note that each tribe has its own unique language and culture. In the context of social disorganization theory (Shaw and McKay 1969), where a lack of effective communication between residents of a neighborhood is hypothesized to affect social cohesion, we argue that in Nigeria the notion of tribes better captures the spirit of the idea of "heterogeneity."

Our second hypothesis is that there will be a positive association between the ethnic heterogeneity (measured in terms of the diversity of tribes) of a neighborhood and rates of crime.

17.3.3 Residential Mobility/Stability

As alluded to above and discussed more explicitly in Chapter 10, residential stability and mobility are expected to have opposing effects on crime rates. On the one hand, residential mobility was hypothesized by Shaw and McKay (1969) to disrupt the social network of a community, which in turn may lead to higher rates of crime. On the other, Sampson and Groves (1989) suggest that residential stability has the opposite effect by allowing social ties to form in a community, which has an attendant effect on residents' investment in a community and their ability to "police" it.

While the two concepts (residential stability and mobility) are essentially reciprocal, the way they are measured means that they are not entirely interchangeable. Both are straightforward to calculate, and residential mobility is perhaps the most consistently computed variable employed in the social disorganization literature—typically measured as the percentage/ratio of new to total residents in a neighborhood. Those who have lived in an area for a period of less than one year are usually considered new residents (see, for example, Sampson and Groves 1989). In the case of residential stability, the numerator is the number of long-term residents—assumed to be those who have lived in an area for at least five years (Bruinsma et al. 2013) or those who were brought up in the neighborhood (Sampson and Groves 1989).

These measures are typically calculated using data collected for government censuses. In developed countries such as the United States and UK, such exercises are conducted every 10 years or so (every five years in Canada) and the data are readily available to researchers at different geographical scales of analysis. In the Netherlands, census data are essentially updated in real time, making them not just available for research purposes but also incredibly up to date. Although government population censuses in Nigeria are intended to take place every 10 years, in reality the National Population Commission (NPC) has only achieved this target on one occasion (the postindependence exercises were in 1963, 1973, 1991, and 2006). Furthermore, even when these censuses are conducted, the results have always been a subject of controversy—the consensus being that the census figures are skewed to favor a particular part of the country (Aluko 1965; Hollos 1992; Bamgbose 2009). Moreover, such population data are only available for large areal units—the smallest being local government areas, which have an average population of 230,000. This poses problems for estimating population stability at the local level and, consequently, in this study we collect such data locally.

Our third hypothesis is that there will be a positive association between the rate of residential mobility in a neighborhood and crime rates. Our fourth is that there will be a negative association between the rate of long-term residential stability in a neighborhood and crime rates.

17.3.4 Urbanization

In their extended model of social disorganization theory, Sampson and Groves (1989) included urbanization as an exogenous community characteristic that they hypothesized would influence area-level crime rates. The premise was that urban communities, when compared to suburban or rural areas, "have a decreased capacity for social control" (p. 782). The assumption is that the crowded nature of urban neighborhoods limits close personal interactions between residents. And, accordingly, this way of life is characterized by the depersonalization of relationships and a lack of identity, which tends to weaken the ability of residents of a neighborhood to form and maintain local friendship networks, which consequently affects their level of participation in local affairs (Hardyns and Pauwels 2009). In previous studies, the location of neighborhoods in relation to the center of the city—areas that are usually characterized by high population density, mixed land use, and intense activities (commonly referred to as inner-city neighborhoods)—has been used to measure urbanization (see, for example, Veysey and Messner 1999; Lowenkamp, Cullen, and Pratt 2003). Other studies have used population density derived from government population censuses (Cahill and Mulligan 2007), housing density, or a combination of the two (Bruinsma et al. 2013). These estimates of urbanization are not complex or unattainable in a setting of a developing country such as Nigeria. Identifying the inner-city neighborhoods—intense activity areas with different land uses—is fairly straightforward. In this chapter, we define urbanized neighborhoods as those areas that host business clusters (places such as markets or shopping areas).

Our fifth hypothesis is that there will be a positive association between urbanized neighborhood and crime rates.

17.3.5 Family Disruption

Another component of social disorganization measured in some studies (see Sampson 1987; Sampson and Groves 1989; Veysey and Messner 1999; Lowenkamp, Cullen, and Pratt 2003; Sun, Triplett, and Gainey 2004; Bruinsma et al. 2013) is family disruption. Sampson (1987) argued that informal social control is stronger in communities with less marital and family disruption, because such communities will have a greater capacity to supervise peer groups and delinquent youths. In the extended model of social disorganization theory (Sampson and Groves 1989), the level of family disruption in a neighborhood was measured using two variables—single-parent households (with children), and the ratio of divorced/separated adults to those who have ever married (see also Veysey and Messner 1999; Lowenkamp, Cullen, and Pratt 2003). Other studies have measured this component using only the percentage of divorced/separated (Sun, Triplett, and Gainey 2004) or the percentage of single-parent households in a neighborhood (Bruinsma et al. 2013).

While the components discussed, thus far, largely have some meaning in the context of a developing country such as Nigeria, family disruption—or estimates of it at least—are likely to be of limited utility. For instance, single parenting is not a common practice in Nigeria. In a recent study, Essien and Bassey (2012) revealed that single mothers faced enormous challenges in the Nigerian society, including discrimination and outright rejection from the community. The social norm dictates, for example, that a divorced woman move back to her parent's home, while a man is considered incapable of raising a child on his own. Also, premarital/out-of-wedlock childbearing is not common in many traditional societies such as Nigeria, and is in fact considered a taboo. Thus, single-parent households are likely uncommon in Nigeria, and it is unclear as to whether family homes that include single parents differ meaningfully in their ability to exert social control over those in their neighborhood. Consequently, despite the popularity of this measure in Western studies, in the current study we do not attempt to measure this indicator of social disorganization.

17.4 Data and Survey Method

Primary data were collected using three methods—(*a*) a field mapping exercise to create a base map of the study area; (*b*) a block environmental inventory (BEI) to obtain data on the condition of the built environment (see Perkins, Meeks, and Taylor 1992); and (*c*) a household and crime victimization survey to generate data on a range of demographic (independent) variables and to obtain data on the rate of crime victimization. The fieldwork and survey were conducted between April and May 2014.

17.4.1 Field Mapping

Prior to the BEI and survey, it was necessary to produce a base map of the study area. This was generated using high-resolution satellite images in the following way. For convenience, the study area was divided into 88 map sections, and a paper map (see Figure 17.2 for a sample of one map section) produced for each map section. Enumerators conducted site visits and used pencils to trace out the boundaries of all properties on the paper maps so as to best reflect the actual boundaries as observed in the field. A unique reference number (URN) was assigned to each property to allow the integration of all data sets in a geographical information system (GIS). The boundaries produced (and associated URNs) were subsequently digitized in QGIS 2.0 with the aid of the Google Satellite OpenLayers plugin.

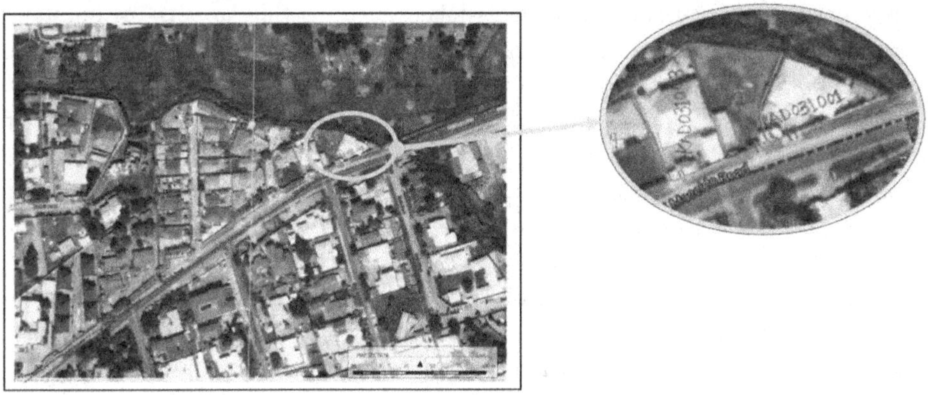

FIGURE 17.2 An example of a paper map showing one of the 88 sections of the study area

Note: all maps were printed on A3 paper.

17.4.2 Block Environmental Inventory (BEI)

A BEI is a procedure used to objectively assess the physical environment of properties and the street blocks on which they are located through independent observation. This method has previously been used in studies of crime to measure characteristics of the physical environment (see Perkins, Meeks, and Taylor 1992; Brown, Perkins, and Brown 2003; Perkins, Larsen, and Brown 2009). Informed by previous work, a structured BEI form was produced specifically for this study. To complete the current exercise, trained enumerators were sent to the field to observe and record the physical attributes associated with each property identified during the mapping exercise. The property URN was first entered on the BEI form and then a checklist concerned with all features of interest completed by an enumerator. The data recorded included the type of land use, type of property, the building material used for construction, and the presence of nonresidential activities such as petty trading. All records from the BEI exercise were entered into a spreadsheet and later "joined" to the spatial data generated from the mapping exercise.

17.4.3 Household and Crime Victimization Survey

A lack of accurate and reliable crime data has thwarted the progress of research in developing countries (Arthur and Marenin 1995). In Nigeria, for instance, official police incident report data are not readily available for public or research use (Alemika 2004)—and even if they were, underreporting would likely be a major issue (see, for example, Ebbe 1992; Gyong 2010; Ayodele and Aderinto 2014). For these reasons, a household and crime victimization survey was conducted.

A 44-item structured questionnaire interview was developed to collect data on (1) crime victimization and (2) demographic variables. The questionnaire was used as part of a larger study, and so in this section we describe only those items used here.

Where possible, the questions used were taken from existing surveys—11 questions related to demography such as ethnicity and household structure, and six questions concerned respondents' experience of the following types of victimization in the last 12 months: breaking and entering (B&E); domestic theft; damage to property; theft of automobile; theft from automobile; and damage to automobile. However, not all respondents answered questions relating to all crime types. For example, many did not have vehicles. Complete data were thus only available for B&E and domestic theft, and consequently, only those data relating to these two crime types were analyzed here.

To conduct the survey, houses were selected from within the study area using systematic random sampling, whereby one adult of every *k*th household was approached to participate in the survey. In contrast to most cities in the developed world, in Nigeria households may be home to 25 or more people, and several families (more than five) may live in the same housing unit. For each house selected, the household head (or any adult member where the head is not available) was surveyed.

A total of 3,294 households were interviewed, but only those data from 2,932 of the surveys were included in the analysis that follows—105 responses were rejected either because no URN was recorded, or because the URN duplicated an existing record. The remaining surveys were rejected because the respondent declined to respond to most (or all) questions during the interview. This means that there was a nonresponse rate of 7.8%, and of all those households approached, data were available for analysis for just under 90% of homes. With such limited attrition, we are confident that the data analyzed are representative of the local population from which the sample was drawn.

17.5 Geographic Units of Analysis and Social Disorganization Theory

The concept of Shaw and McKay's social disorganization is fundamentally "a group-level analog of control theory" (Bursik 1988: p. 521). However, in prior studies of social disorganization theory, the geographic definition of a group or, rather, a community, appears to be somewhat vague—there is no consistency throughout the literature on the standard areal unit of analysis. Even though the selection of any unit of analysis should be informed by theory, more often than not, researchers adopt area-level boundaries such as census blocks and tracts in the United States (for example, Sun, Triplett, and Gainey 2004), or electoral wards and polling districts in England and Wales (for example, Sampson and Grove 1989; Veysey and Messner 1999; Lowenkamp, Cullen, and Pratt 2003), for which data are readily available. In a recent study, Hart and Waller (2013: p. 16) suggested that "administrative proxies of neighborhoods are inconsistent with perceived neighborhood boundaries and that perceived neighborhood structural determinants of social disorganization are also inconsistent with official measures."

Moreover, it is important to note that these boundaries, while convenient, are usually constructed to serve purposes other than scientific research. Rengert and Lockwood

(2009) have highlighted some of the major problems that arise with this practice. For instance, little or no concern is given to bounding areas with similar populations or features when boundaries are drawn to serve political or administrative purposes. This undermines the objective of regionalizing space, which is principally to minimize internal (within-area) and maximize the external (between-area) variation. Even when such considerations are made at the time boundaries are initially defined, rarely are they adjusted to reflect any changes that may occur over time.

In addition to this, in contrast to the United States and elsewhere, in Nigeria the lowest areal unit for which data are available, such as from the government population census, is the local government level, for which the average population is over 230,000. Such areas are simply too large for studies concerned with environmental criminology, such as the one reported here. In this study, we are, hence, faced with a different challenge—not of dealing with inappropriate administrative boundaries, but that of not having any official small area units that could be used to represent a community or neighborhood.

We address this by constructing our own area-level boundaries. A variety of approaches could be taken to do this, but we adopted the following approach. First, the boundaries were defined with the intention of simultaneously minimizing the internal variance within neighborhoods and emphasizing the difference between them. We recognize that with any such exercise, we face what has become known in the literature as the modifiable areal unit problem (MAUP)—that changing a boundary set can lead to different conclusions (see Openshaw and Taylor 1979; Fotheringham and Wong 1991). Nevertheless, the approach we took had the following area demarcation rules:

Stage 1: Demarcation based on the type of residential area—with areas classified as high, medium, and low density based on the number of properties per unit of geographical area.

Stage 2: Following natural boundaries such as streams and rivers that would naturally divide a neighborhood.

Stage 3: Considering physical manmade features, specifically major roads, that would also physically divide a neighborhood.

This process was repeated until each neighborhood so defined contained a population of between 4,000 and 6,000 people.

Figure 17.3 shows the neighborhoods identified using the above approach. A total of 40 areas were delineated—36 met our definition of a residential neighborhood, but we only included 35 in this study (a survey in one neighborhood was abandoned for reasons of safety because a local chief—a traditional community leader—expressed strong disapproval of the exercise in the area). The remaining four areas, highlighted with dotted shading in the map, were not residential areas. For the purposes of what follows, all data collected from the household and crime victimization survey were aggregated to these neighborhood areas. A larger sample size would of course be preferred, but this was the largest possible given the available resources.

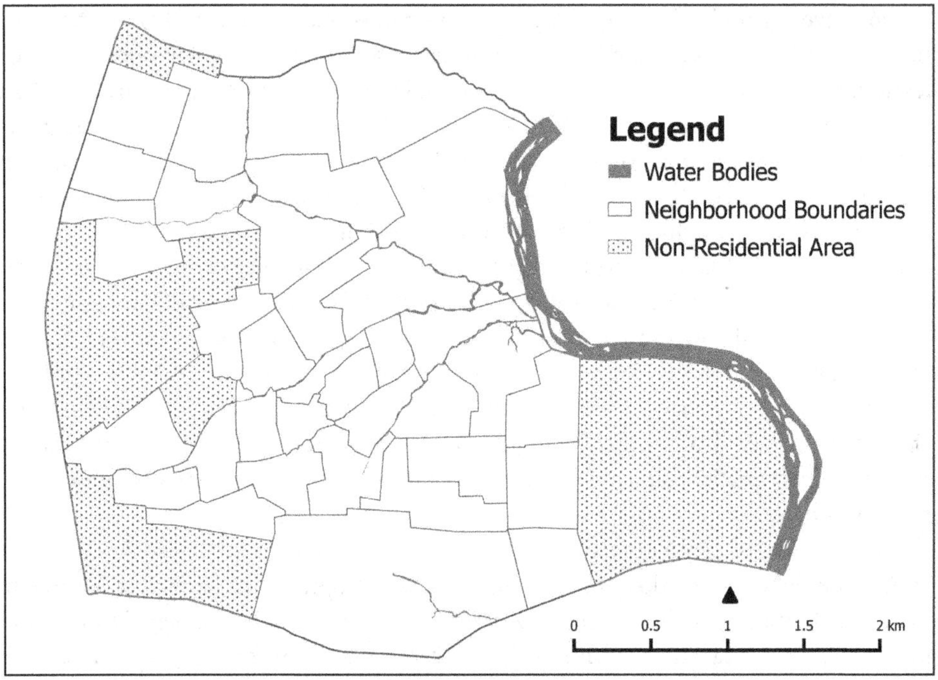

FIGURE 17.3 Neighborhoods boundaries

17.6 Analysis

17.6.1 Dependent Variables

We constructed our dependent variables from the household victimization data described earlier in this chapter. Rates per 100 households sampled were computed for breaking and entering, which is defined as an incident that involves breaking into a property with the intention to steal (B&E, n = 869), and theft, which is defined as an offense of stealing from a property without breaking in (n = 2,486).

17.6.2 Independent Variables

1. *Socioeconomic Status (SES)*: We constructed an index of neighborhood SES using three measures relating to housing characteristics (see below). The index of SES was derived by taking a composite (z) score of these three variables as described below:
   (a) Building construction material: Not all buildings are constructed using cement—the standard building construction material in Nigeria—some are constructed using mud. The concentration of mud houses in a neighborhood

is an indicator of a lack of resources, as the use of this material in construction is a matter of means rather than choice. Data for this variable were collected as part of the BEI, and we computed this variable as the percentage of properties within a neighborhood that were constructed using cement.

(b) Gate: Drive-in residential houses are usually more expensive to construct and to rent. They have facilities such as a private parking area that other houses lack. We calculate this index as the percentage of properties in a neighborhood with a gate.

(c) Road condition: As is the case in many developing countries, not all roads in urban areas are paved. Neighborhoods with good roads that have been paved will typically host the most valuable residential houses. This variable is measured as the percentage of properties in a neighborhood that could be accessed via a paved road.

For each dimension (a–c), a z-score was computed for each area. The mean z-score computed across the three indices was then used as a composite index of SES for each area.

2. *Ethnic heterogeneity*: A total of 65 different ethnic groups (or tribes, see above) were identified from the data collected as part of the household survey. However, for 50 such groups, these were represented by only one to five members in the whole sample. Based on the connectivity that exists between these ethnic groups (see above), we decided to reduce the number of groups used to produce a smaller set that would reflect the ideas that underpin social disorganization theory. To do this, we categorized the 65 ethnicities into five broader groups based on their region of origin and the sociocultural relationship that exists between them. The five categories were

(a) Northern Majority—comprising Hausa-Fulani, the largest indigenous ethnic group in the city and the Kanuri, a major tribe in the Northeast of Nigeria.

(b) Northern Minority—these are mainly minority ethnic groups of Northern Nigerian extraction.

(c) Middle Belt—the ethnic groups who originated from the Middle Belt region of Nigeria.

(d) Eastern—the Igbo and Niger Delta indigenes.

(e) Western—the Yoruba ethnic group from the Western region of Nigeria.

To measure neighborhood ethnic heterogeneity, we use Simpson's diversity index (Simpson 1949), which takes account of the number of groups and their relative sizes in the population. The formula used is expressed as

$$D = 1 - \left(\frac{\sum n(n-1)}{N(N-1)} \right),$$

where

N = Total sample size across groups

n = Sample size for a particular group

The level of diversity *D* is represented by a value between 0 and 1, where 0 indicates a perfectly homogeneous neighborhood, while 1 indicates a perfectly heterogeneous neighborhood.

3. *Residential Mobility*: We measure residential mobility as the percentage of households in the sample who have lived in a neighborhood for a period of less than one year. As part of the household survey described in this chapter, respondents were asked, *For how long have you lived at this address?* The response options were *Less than 1 year; Between 1–2 years, 3–5 years*, and *More than 5 years.*
4. *Residential Stability*: This was measured using the same data as for residential mobility. However, here we take the percentage of households in the sample that have lived at their address for a period of five years or more.
5. *Urbanization*: Urbanization is measured using a binary indicator. Neighborhoods with a business cluster such as a market or shopping area with 25 or more retail shops are identified as urbanized neighborhoods.

17.6.3 Results

Table 17.1 provides descriptive statistics for the dependent and independent variables. There is considerable variation in the rates of crime between neighborhoods—from a low of 2 and 9 to a high of 107 and 204 incidents per 100 households for B&E and theft, respectively. As for other contexts discussed in other chapters of this book, crime was clustered at the neighborhood level. There was also clear variation in the structural measures of social disorganization between neighborhoods—for instance, residential stability ranges from less than 17% to more than 89%, while residential mobility ranges from 0% to more than 20%.

To test hypotheses, we first use ordinary least square (OLS) regression models for each crime type. However, because one of the core assumptions of OLS regression—that

Table 17.1 Descriptive Statistics for the Dependent and Independent Variables

Variable	Minimum	Maximum	Mean	Std. Dev.
Dependent variables				
B&E per 100 HHOLDS	2.28	106.46	31.67	25.16
Theft per 100 HHOLDS	8.93	204.13	86.01	50.24
Independent variables				
SES	-1.28	1.42	0.00	0.62
Heterogeneity	0.10	0.63	0.34	0.13
Res. Mobility	0.00	20.51	5.60	4.43
Res. Stability	16.67	89.47	69.48	16.78
Urbanization	0.00	1.00	0.57	0.50

observations are independent—may be violated for data that have an explicitly spatial structure, we also compute the Moran's I test statistics (using a distance band contiguity weight) to assess whether this assumption was met. Where this assumption was not met, we used an appropriate spatial regression model, selecting from either a spatial lag or spatial error models, based on the values of the Lagrange multiplier (see Anselin 2005).

A further potential problem with regression models concerns multicollinearity—when two or more of the predictor variables in a regression model are correlated. To test for this, we estimated the extent to which multicollinearity was likely to be a problem by computing variance inflation factors (VIFs) for each variable. A VIF score of 10 or more is commonly regarded as indication of severe multicollinearity (Neter et al. 1996; O'Brien 2007), although the standard cutoff value can be as low as 4 (Fox 1991), while a value of less than 2 indicates highly independent variables (Judge et al. 1985). As can be seen in Table 17.2, none of the independent variables exceed either VIF threshold, indicating no serious problems with multicollinearity. The results of the OLS model are presented in Table 17.2. All the estimates, both the OLS and the spatial regression models, were computed using GeoDa 1.8.

17.6.3.1 *Theft*

In the case of theft, all coefficients were in the expected direction. However, only the coefficient for the SES variable[2] was statistically significant ($p = .01$)—neighborhoods with lower estimated SES tended to experience higher rates of theft than their counterparts. The Moran's I test for this dependent variable was nonsignificant ($p = .42$), suggesting no significant problem with spatial autocorrelation for this model, and no need for further analysis using a spatial regression model.

17.6.3.2. *Breaking and Entering*

For breaking and entering, a Moran's I test indicated positive spatial autocorrelation ($p < .002$) and, hence, it was necessary to analyze the data using a model that accounted for this. Based on diagnostic tests and advice provided in Anselin (2005), we analyzed the data using a spatial error model. The spatial error regression model is estimated by means of maximum likelihood, and unlike the traditional classic regression models,

Table 17.2 The Ordinary Least Squares (OLS) Regression Model for Theft

Variables	*B*	*t*	*Sig.*	VIF
SES	−36.949	−2.757	0.01	1.504
Heterogeneity	17.429	0.267	0.791	1.286
Res. Mobility	0.139	0.055	0.956	2.349
Res. Stability	−0.105	−0.149	0.883	2.826
Urbanization	32.253	1.876	0.071	1.438

$N = 2{,}932$. Adj. $R^2 = 0.29$. F-statistic = 3.795.

includes a spatial autoregressive error term (Anselin 1988). Formally, the regression model is expressed as

$$y = X\beta + \lambda W\varepsilon + u,$$

where
y is the dependent variable
X is a matrix of independent variables
β are associated parameters for the independent variables
λ is a parameter that measures spatial interaction
W is a spatial weights matrix
ε is vector of spatially autocorrelated error terms
u is an independent and identically distributed error term

The spatial weights matrix included in our spatial error regression model was based on a distance band—where a neighbor is defined based on the distance between the centroid of neighborhoods (see Anselin 2005). The results of the analysis are shown in Table 17.3.

With the exception of residential stability, the direction of all coefficients was consistent with expectation. However, only two of the coefficients were statistically significant, and one (residential stability) was in the wrong direction. Thus, for B&E the analysis provides little support for expectations derived from social disorganization theory.

17.7 Discussion

Both the social and physical settings of cities in the developing world, as discussed here, differ greatly from those in the developed world. Throughout this chapter we have highlighted these contextual differences and considered how social disorganization theory, which was developed to explain area-level crime rates in the developed countries (particularly the United States), might explain the distribution of crime in a developing

Table 17.3 Spatial (Error) Regression Model for Breaking and Entering

Variable	Coefficient	z-value	Significance
SES	−2.0123	−0.3288	0.7423
Heterogeneity	25.3718	0.9394	0.3475
Res. Mobility	3.2029	3.4091	0.0007
Res. Stability	0.6307	2.1224	0.0338
Urbanization	6.2004	0.8499	0.3953
LAMDA (spatial error term)	0.5288	3.3301	0.0009

country such as Nigeria. We have also discussed some of the challenges associated with testing hypotheses derived from such theories in the Nigerian context. Here we reflect on these issues, discuss how we addressed them and how future studies might do so, and consider how the findings inform the criminological enterprise.

Considering the challenges first, with respect to the dependent variable, in studies conducted in the United States and elsewhere, official police records are commonly used to estimate area-level rates of crime. Such data are rarely available for the purposes of research conducted in the developing world, ruling out the analysis of such secondary data sources. Even if such data were readily available, the scale of the underreporting of crime to the police in Nigeria is substantial—the overall rate of underreporting between 2006 and 2013 was over 80% (see Alemika 2013). As a result, it is likely that police data would represent a biased sample of offenses (Sherman, Gartin, and Buerger 1989), the analysis of which would likely lead to errors of statistical inference. While underreporting is a concern in most countries (Shaw, Van Dijk, and Rhomberg 2003; Sidebottom 2015), rates of reporting vary across crime types (see, for example, Skogan 1984; Tarling and Morris 2010). In their study of criminal victimization across the industrialized world, Van Dijk and Mayhew (1993) suggest that almost all burglary incidents (one of the crimes considered in this chapter) are reported to the police, minimizing reporting bias for analyses conducted in these countries. If underreporting is a particular problem in developing countries, however, care will need to be taken in future studies that involve the analysis of police recorded crime data.

Additionally, unlike the United States and other countries, in Nigeria police data are not available in digital form. While problematic in the here and now, the development of systems to capture such data in the future may provide opportunities to collect data, particularly spatial data, which are actually more accurate than data recorded in other countries. For example, in the UK and the United States, crimes reported to the police are (typically) initially recorded in a text format, and subsequently geocoded using geographical information systems. However, with the proliferation of GPS technology, which is now embedded into most mobile devices, it seems plausible to suggest that spatial data could be more directly captured either by the police or victims of crime (see Chapter 11).

In developed countries, large-scale sample surveys provide an alternative to police crime data. However, such data are not available in developing countries such as Nigeria. On a related note, nor are population data for units of analysis that would facilitate the types of analysis common in studies of environmental criminology. In the current study, we addressed the above issues by conducting a household and victimization survey and a BEI. Future research might use similar methods, perhaps taking advantage of the opportunities that mobile data capture devices provide (see Chapter 11).

With respect to the independent variables, various indicators of social disorganization have been used in previous studies. Our discussion of some of the most commonly used measures highlighted the fact that some are simply not appropriate in the context of Nigeria, or are too difficult to measure. For instance, SES, commonly estimated using data regarding average household income, is a sensitive issue that is difficult to measure in developing countries. For this reason, in the current study we used proxy measures, relating to housing characteristics, which are more easily collected and arguably more appropriate in studies of crime in developing countries. Future studies might consider other indicators that are sensitive to local context.

The measurement of neighborhood heterogeneity and indicators of family disruption also require consideration and sensitivity to the context and culture within which the research is conducted. For example, in Nigeria the population consists almost entirely of one race of people, making traditional estimates of ethnic heterogeneity of little value. An alternative measure of diversity, using tribal origin as the source of variation, was consequently used to better capture this component of neighborhood composition here.

Finally, an issue that is often acknowledged but rarely (if ever) addressed in studies of neighborhood crime rates concerns the boundaries used. Studies conducted in the UK and elsewhere generally employ boundaries derived to facilitate the collection of data for population censuses or administrative purposes. While effort may be expended to define areas that minimize within-area homogeneity and maximize between-area heterogeneity, such boundaries are not created for the purposes of studying crime, and do not necessarily represent what residents would consider "neighborhoods." In the current study, we faced a different problem—in the absence of existing administrative boundaries, which approach should be taken to define the areas used for analysis? In this chapter, the approach taken involved the systematic application of logical rules to delineate neighborhoods, a process also employed elsewhere (e.g., Sampson, Raudenbush, and Earls 1997). Future work might also explore the use of participatory mapping exercises (for example, see Hart and Waller 2013), whereby residents are consulted in an iterative fashion to ascertain their perceptions of neighborhood boundaries.

Having discussed key conceptual and practical differences between studies conducted in developed and developing countries, we turn to the question of what our findings tell us about the role that mechanisms of social disorganization might play in explaining area-level crime rates in Nigeria. In the case of theft, although all of the predictor variables were in the expected direction, the only coefficient that was statistically significant was our index of SES. For the crime of B&E, only two variables, residential mobility and residential stability, were reliable predictors of area-level rates of crime. However, while the finding for annual rates of residential mobility was in line with expectation (there was more crime in neighborhoods with high population turnover), that for residential stability was contrary to expectation—areas with more stable communities in the long term had more crime.

Our findings, thus, provide very limited support for social disorganization theory. For each model, of the five variables included, reliable associations were only observed for one variable. Perhaps this is not surprising because a number of studies in the United States and elsewhere have provided only partial support for theories of social disorganization (for example, Sun, Triplett, and Gainey 2004; Breetzke 2010; Bruinsma et al. 2013; Pereira, Mota, and Andresen 2016). What does this mean for such theory? One explanation is that the theoretical framework, originally developed to explain rates of crime in 1940s Chicago, simply does not apply universally and hence other explanations should be sought. Another possibility is that different local area conditions, other than (or in addition to) those originally conceived, would better explain the processes of social (dis)organization in other communities, and, thus, account for the between-area variations in the rates of crime. Understanding these local area conditions, therefore, is indispensable to contextualizing criminology theories such as that of social disorganization.

Other explanations are that our estimates of the various components of social organization failed to capture the constructs they sought to estimate, or that our sample size—which is admittedly modest—was insufficient to detect the kinds of associations reported in other studies (e.g. Sampson and Groves 1989). Which is the more likely explanation will be for future research to resolve, but for now what our study highlights is that caution should be exercised in studies that seek to explain rates of crime in one context using theories developed for another. We hope that future research will be informed by the issues discussed here, and encourage researchers to further test and develop theories of environmental criminology in new contexts.

Notes

1. Unlike the boundaries of urban districts, the geographic boundaries of "traditional districts are not defined by law. However, the local residents of the city will always refer to their traditional districts if asked where they live. Each district has a village head, usually an indigene of the area who is appointed by the emir (the head of the traditional institution).
2. When included in the model as stand-alone variables, all three coefficients were in the right direction, but were not statistically significant. One likely reason for this is that our sample size is not large and may lack the statistical power necessary to detect effects for a large number of coefficients.

References

Agbola, Tunde. 1986. "City profile: Kaduna." *Cities* 3(4): 283–352.

Alemika, Etannabi E. O. 2004. "Crime statistics and information management in Nigerian justice and security systems." In *Crime and Policing in Nigeria: Challenges and Options*, edited by Etannabi E. O. Alemika and Innocent C. Chukwuma. Lagos: Network on Police Reform in Nigeria (NOPRIN).

Alemika, Etannabi E. O. 2013. *Criminal Victimization, Policing and Governance in Nigeria.* CLEEN Monograph Series no. 18. Lagos: CLEEN Foundation.

Aluko, S. A. 1965. "How many Nigerians? An analysis of Nigeria's census problems, 1901–63." *Journal of Modern African Studies* 3(3): 371–92.

Anselin, Luc. 1988. *Spatial Econometrics: Methods and Models.* Dordrecht: Kluwer Academic.

Anselin, Luc. 2005. *Exploring Spatial Data with GeoDa: A Workbook.* Spatial Analysis Laboratory, Department of Geography, University of Illinois.

Arthur, John A., and Otwin Marenin. 1995. "Explaining crime in developing countries: The need for a case study approach." *Crime, Law and Social Change* 23(3): 191–214.

Ayodele, Johnson O., and Adeyinka A. Aderinto. 2014. "Nature of crime and crime reporting of victims in Lagos, Nigeria." *International Journal of Criminology and Sociological Theory* 7(1): 1–14.

Bamgbose, J. Adele. 2009. "Falsification of population census data in a heterogeneous Nigerian state: The Fourth Republic example." *African Journal of Political Science and International Relations* 3(8): 311–319.

Blau, Peter M., and Reid M. Golden. 1986. "Metropolitan structure and criminal violence." *Sociological Quarterly* 27(1): 15–26.

Breetzke, Gregory D. 2010. "Modeling violent crime rates: A test of social disorganization in the city of Tshwane, South Africa." *Journal of Criminal Justice* 38(4): 446–452.

Brown, Barbara, Douglas D. Perkins, and Graham Brown. 2003. "Place attachment in a revitalizing neighborhood: Individual and block levels of analysis." *Journal of Environmental Psychology* 23: 259–271.

Bruinsma, Gerben J. N., Lieven J. R. Pauwels, Frank M. Weerman, and Wim Bernasco. 2013. "Social disorganization, social capital, collective efficacy and the spatial distribution of crime and offences." *British Journal of Criminology* 53(5): 942–963.

Bununu, Y. A., A. N. M. Ludin, and Nafisa Hosni. 2015. "City profile: Kaduna." *Cities* 49:53–65.

Bursik, Robert J. 1988. "Social disorganization and theories of crime and delinquency: Problems and prospects." *Criminology* 26(4): 519–52.

Cahill, Meagan, and Gordon Mulligan. 2007. "Using geographically weighted regression to explore local crime patterns." *Social Science Computer Review* 25(2):174–193.

Ebbe, Obi N. I. 1992. "Juvenile delinquency in Nigeria: The problem of application of Western theories." *International Journal of Comparative and Applied Criminal Justice* 16(2): 53–370.

Essien, Anthonia M., and Agapetus A. Bassey. 2012. "The social and religious challenges of single mothers in Nigeria." *American Journal of Social Issues and Humanities* 2(4): 240–251.

Filmer, Deon, and Lant H. Pritchett. 2001. "Estimating wealth effects without expenditure data—or tears: An application to educational enrolments in states of India." *Demography* 38(1): 115–132.

Fotheringham, A. S., and D. W. S. Wong. 1991. "The modifiable areal unit problem in multivariate statistical analysis." *Environment and Planning A* 23(7) 1025–1044.

Fox, John. 1991. "Regression diagnostics: An introduction." Sage University Paper Series on Quantitative Applications in the Social Sciences No. 07–079.

Gyong, John E. 2010. "Criminal victimization and the reporting of crime in Kaduna State: Towards Integrating the victim of crime into criminological discourse." *Current Research Journal of Social Sciences* 2(5): 288–295.

Hardyns, Wim, and Lieven Pauwels. 2009. "The geography of social cohesion and crime at the municipality level." In *Contemporary Issues in the Empirical Study of Crime,* edited by Marc Cools, Sofie De Kimpe, Brice De Ruyver, Marleen Easton, Lieven Pauwels, Paul Ponsaers, Tom Vander Beken, Freya Vander Laenen, Gudrun Vande Walle, and Gert Vermeulen. Antwerp: Maklu.

Hart, Timothy C., and Jeremy Waller. 2013. "Neighborhood boundaries and structural determinants of social disorganization: Examining the validity of commonly used measures." *Western Criminology Review* 14(3): 16–33.

Hollos, Marida. 1992. "Why is it difficult to take a census in Nigeria? The problem of indigenous conceptions of households." *Journal of Quantitative and Interdisciplinary History* 25(1): 12–19.

Howe, Laura D., James R. Hargreaves, and Sharon R. A. Huttly. 2008. "Issues in the construction of wealth indices for the measurement of socio-economic position in low-income countries." *Emerging Themes in Epidemiology* 5(3): 1–14.

Judge, George G., William E. Griffiths, R. Carter Hill, Helmut Lütkepohl, and Tsoung-Chao Lee. 1985. *The Theory and Practice of Econometrics*. 2nd ed. New York: Wiley.

Kawachi, Ichiro, Bruce P. Kennedy, and Richard G. Wilkinson. 1999. "Crime: Social disorganization and relative deprivation." *Social Science and Medicine* 48(6): 719–731.

Kubrin, Charis E. 2000. "Racial heterogeneity and crime: Measuring static and dynamic effects." *Research in Community Sociology* 10:189–219.

Lindelow, Magnus, and Abdo Yazbeck. 2004. "Measuring Socioeconomic Status." Presentation to the World Bank conference "Reaching the Poor," Washington, DC, February 18–20.

Lowenkamp, Cristopher T., Francis T. Cullen, and Travis C. Pratt. 2003. "Replicating Sampson and Groves's test of social disorganization theory: Revisiting a criminological classic." *Journal of Research in Crime and Delinquency* 40(4): 351–373.

Markowitz, Fred E., Paul E. Bellair, Allen E. Liska, and Jianhong Liu. 2001. "Extending social disorganization theory: Modeling the relationships between cohesion, disorder, and fear." *Criminology* 39(2): 293–319.

Max-Lock Consultancy Nigeria (MLCN). 2010. Kaduna Master Plan: Draft Final Report, Max-Lock Centre, University of Westminster.

Mazerolle, Lorraine, Rebecca Wickes, and James McBroom. 2010. "Community variations in violence: The role of social ties and collective efficacy in comparative context." *Journal of Research in Crime and Delinquency* 47(1): 3–30.

Messner, Steven F., and Reid M. Golden. 1992. "Racial inequality and racially disaggregated homicide rates: An assessment of alternative theoretical explanations." *Criminology* 30(3): 421–448.

Neter, John, Michael H. Kutner, William Wasserman, and Christopher J. Nachtsheim. 1996. *Applied Linear Statistical Models*. 4th ed. New York: McGraw Hill / Irwin.

O'Brien, Robert M. 2007. "A caution regarding rules of thumb for variance inflation factors." *Quality and Quantity* 41(5): 673–690.

Okpanachi, E. 2010. "Ethno-religious identity and conflict in northern Nigeria: Understanding the dynamics of Sharia in Kaduna and Kebbi states." *IFRA-Nigeria e-Papers* 10(7): 1–51. http://www.cetri.be/IMG/pdf/Okpanachi_2010.pdf.

Openshaw, S., and P. Taylor. 1979. "A million or so correlation coefficients: Three experiments on the modifiable areal unit problem." In *Statistical Applications in the Spatial Sciences*, edited by Neil Wrigley. London: Pion.

Otite, Onigu. 1990. *Ethnic Pluralism, Ethnicity and Ethnic Conflict in Nigeria*. Ibadan: Safari Book.

Pereira, Debora V. S., Caroline M. M. Mota, and Martin A. Andresen. 2016. "Social disorganization and homicide in Recife, Brazil." *International Journal of Offender Therapy and Comparative Criminology*. In press.

Perkins, Douglas D., Courtney Larsen, and Barbara B. Brown. 2009. "Mapping urban revitalization: Using GIS spatial analysis to evaluate a new housing policy. *Journal of Prevention and Intervention in the Community* 37(1): 48–65.

Perkins, Douglas D., John W. Meeks, and Ralph B. Taylor. 1992. "The physical environment of street blocks and resident perceptions of crime and disorder: Implications for theory and measurement." *Journal of Environmental Psychology* 12: 21–34.

Rakov, Simon A. 1992. "Ethnicity in Nigeria." http://www.postcolonialweb.org /nigeria/ethnicity.html.

Rengert, George F., and Brian Lockwood. 2009. "Geographic units of analysis and the analysis of crime." In *Putting Crime in Its Place: Units of Analysis in Geographic Criminology*, edited by David L. Weisburd, Wim Bernasco, and Gerben J. N. Bruinsma. New York: Springer.

Sahn, David E., and David Stifel. 2003. "Exploring alternative measures of welfare in the absence of expenditure data." *Review of Income and Wealth* 49(4): 463–489.

Sampson, Robert J. 1987. "Urban black violence: The effect of male joblessness and family disruption." *American Journal of Sociology* 93:348–382.

Sampson, Robert J., and W. Byron Groves. 1989. "Community structure and crime: Testing social-disorganization theory." *American Journal of Sociology* 94:774–802.

Sampson, Robert J., Stephen W. Raudenbush, and Felton Earls. 1997. "Neighborhoods and violent crime: A multilevel study of collective efficacy." *Science* 277(5328): 918–924.

Schreiner, Mark. 2010. "A simple poverty scorecard for Pakistan." *Journal of Asian and African Studies* 45(3): 326–349.

Shaw, Clifford, and Henry McKay. 1969. *Juvenile Delinquency and Urban Areas*. Rev. ed. Chicago: University of Chicago Press.

Shaw, Mark, Jan van Dijk, and Wolfgang Rhomberg. 2003. "Determining trends in global crime and justice: An overview of results." *Forum on Crime and Society* 3(1–2): 35–63.

Sherman, Lawrence W., Patrick R. Gartin, and Michael E. Buerger. 1989. "Hot spots of predatory crime: Routine activities and the criminology of place." *Criminology* 27(1): 27–55.

Sidebottom, Aiden. 2015. "On the correlates of reporting assault to the police in Malawi." *British Journal of Criminology* 55(2): 381–398.

Simpson, E. H. 1949. "Measurement of diversity." *Nature* 163:688.

Skogan, Wesley G. 1984. "Reporting crimes to the police: The status of world research." *Journal of Research in Crime and Delinquency* 21(2): 113–37.

Sun, Ivan Y., Ruth Triplett, and Randy R. Gainey. 2004. "Neighborhood characteristics and crime: A test of Sampson and Groves' model of social disorganization." *Western Criminology Review* 5(1): 1–16.

Tarling, Roger, and Katie Morris. 2010. "Reporting crime to the police." *British Journal of Criminology* 50(3): 474–490.

Van Dijk, Jan J. M., and Pat Mayhew. 1993. "Criminal victimisation in the industrialized world: Key findings of the 1989 and 1992 International Crime Surveys." In *Understanding Crime: Experiences of Crime and Crime Control*, edited by Anna Alvazzi del Frate, Ugljesa Zvekic, and Jan J. M. van Dijk. Rome: United Nations Interregional Crime and Justice Research Institute.

Versey, Bonita, M., and Steven F. Messner. 1999. "Further testing of social disorganization theory: An elaboration of Sampson and Groves's community structure and crime." *Journal of Research in Crime and Delinquency* 36(2): 156–174.

Warner, Barbara D., and Glenn L. Pierce. 1993. "Re-examining social disorganization theory using calls to the police as a measure of crime." *Criminology* 31(4): 493–517.

Zorbaugh, Harvey. [1926] 2005. "The natural areas of the city—from Ernest W. Burgess (ed.)—*The Urban Community*." In *The Urban Sociology Reader*, edited by Jan Lin and Christopher Mele. New York: Routledge.

CHAPTER 18

GATED COMMUNITIES AND CRIME IN THE UNITED STATES

NICHOLAS BRANIC AND CHARIS E. KUBRIN

18.1 Introduction

The idea that neighborhoods and crime are intimately connected has a long history in the field of criminology. Dating back to the era of the Chicago School of sociology, and particularly the work of Clifford Shaw and Henry McKay, researchers have systematically studied neighborhoods in the United States for decades to understand how characteristics of areas within a city are correlated with crime and delinquency. This expansive literature reveals that scholars have learned a tremendous amount about crime rates across neighborhoods, the correlates of neighborhood crime, and the clustering of crime and other social ills in neighborhoods, yielding an important set of "neighborhood facts" (Sampson 2006: 34–35). A vibrant area of research, the investigation of how communities and crime are linked continues today.

Arguably, the theory most associated with the communities and crime literature is social disorganization theory. Social disorganization theory is a theory of places rather than people; it argues that the collective social ties, cohesion, and other characteristics of neighborhoods influence local levels of informal social control, and thus crime (Sampson & Groves 1989; Shaw & McKay 1942). Social disorganization theory has a long history of documenting how negative social conditions such as low socioeconomic status and residential instability differentially, and disproportionately, occur across neighborhoods within the metropolis, and what role they play in neighborhood crime rates. The theory has devoted less attention, however, to specifying how broader social trends shape and impact the structures and processes of communities themselves.

One such important trend is the rising prevalence of gated communities and the growing number of people who choose to live within these residential areas. Gated communities are private residential areas that use gates, walls, and fences to control who may enter the neighborhood. Since the 1980s, gated communities have become increasingly common across the United States and continue to attract large numbers of prospective residents (Blakely & Snyder 1997). Unfortunately, the precise extent of this trend is unknown. No comprehensive data set exists to document the exact number of gated communities in the United States, although prior research suggests some national-level estimates. In their seminal work on the subject, Blakely and Snyder (1997) estimated that in the 1990s, approximately 20,000 gated communities existed within the United States and that over three million households resided within their borders (see also Low 2003). Later, Sanchez and colleagues (2005) examined a nationally representative sample from the 2001 American Housing Survey (AHS) and reported over seven million "walled and fenced" communities (representing 5.9% of the sample) with over 16 million people living within such communities.[1] More recent estimates than these are difficult to obtain. Given strong consumer demand for homes in gated communities and the lucrative potential for residential developers (Blakely & Snyder 1997), however, there is little doubt that the current number of gated communities has increased considerably from earlier estimates.

Gated communities are found all across the United States, yet they are not distributed evenly across the spatial landscape. They are especially common in the American Sunbelt, which includes states such as Arizona, California, Florida, and Texas (Blakely & Snyder 1997; Romig 2005; Sanchez et al. 2005). Additionally, the growing prevalence of gated communities is not limited to the United States. Gated communities are emerging as a worldwide phenomenon with far-reaching social consequences. A growing literature and numerous researchers discuss the rise of these communities in nations across the world such as Ghana (Asiedu & Arku 2009), New Zealand (Dupuis & Thorns 2008), South Africa (Breetzke & Cohn 2013; Durington 2006), and the United Kingdom (Atkinson & Flint 2004).

Given the rapid expansion and growing pervasiveness of gated communities in recent decades, it is essential for researchers to consider the implications of this emerging trend on various facets of social life. For the most part, existing studies tend to discuss gated communities and their impact in more abstract terms—for example, how the rise of gated communities reflects the growth of a "risk society" more generally (Dupuis & Thorns 2008)—or focus on case studies of particular communities. Accordingly, there remains a need for "collecting systematic empirical evidence, which is central to understanding the full impact of these enclaves on any society" (Vesselinov 2010: 989). Many questions remain unanswered. In particular, very little is known about the relationship between gated communities and crime, and the handful of studies that do exist provide mixed evidence for this relationship (Addington & Rennison 2013; Blakely & Snyder 1997; Breetzke & Cohn 2013; Wilson-Doenges 2000). In this chapter, we seek to augment this body of literature by analyzing the relationship between gated communities and crime across neighborhoods in Orange County, California, a county with a large number of gated communities (Le Goix 2005; Wilson-Doenges 2000) and considerable diversity in terms of population demographics and crime rates. Given the lack of systematic data on gated communities, a key challenge for our analysis was developing a sample of gated communities. Drawing on professional real estate data, we identified home listings where the home was located within a gated community, geocoded the addresses, and identified all blocks containing at least one gated community home. We then analyzed the relationship between gated communities and both violent and property crime, respectively, while controlling for sociodemographic characteristics of the focal and nearby neighborhoods.

We begin by defining gated communities and situating the gated communities-crime relationship within existing scholarship and criminological theories. Next, we describe our data and methodological approach, and present findings from our analysis. We conclude by discussing the findings within the context of the study's limitations and by identifying some promising new directions for research on gated communities and crime.

18.2 Defining Gated Communities

The essence of what constitutes a gated community includes several core elements. From their early research, Blakely and Snyder (1997: 2) outline the main components that define gated communities:

> Residential areas with restricted access in which normally public spaces are privatized. They are security developments with designated perimeters, usually walls or fences, and controlled entrances that are intended to prevent penetration by nonresidents. They include new developments and older areas retrofitted with gates and fences, and they are found from the inner cities to the exurbs and from the richest neighborhoods to the poorest.

Definitions of gated communities, such as this one, tend to emphasize the physical characteristics of these distinctive neighborhood types, characterizing gated communities as (1) residential developments, that are (2) enclosed by barriers such as walls or fences, with (3) gating mechanisms at community entrances that restrict who may enter the neighborhood (Atkinson & Flint 2004; Low 2003; Romig 2005; Stark 1998; Vesselinov 2008). As their name suggests, an iconic feature of gated communities is the presence of gating mechanisms that control access into the community. In some developments, authorized individuals drive up to an exterior console, enter an access code or swipe a keycard, and retract the gate to open the way into the community (Low 2003). In other developments, private guardhouses are stationed at community entrances and security personnel individually authorize vehicles with legitimate purposes to pass through the gates. Regardless of the entry mechanism, the use of community gating creates a semipermeable entrance into the community where only certain individuals may enter the neighborhood and, by definition, the remaining population is excluded. These gated entryways are generally used to control vehicle access along roadways, although some gated communities feature even more selective barriers to entry by controlling pedestrian traffic as well. By erecting walls and fences around the development's exterior, gated communities can further limit opportunities for entry. Collectively, these physical barriers foster a sense of territoriality, establishing clearly defined boundaries that may dissuade nonresidents from entering the neighborhood (Felson & Boba 2010; Le Goix 2005).

The space within gated communities is *privatized* space, which includes the private status of features within the gates and walls (e.g., roadways, amenities) but also the internal governance and management of the community (Blakely & Snyder 1997; Vesselinov 2008). Gated communities fall within a larger designation of what are known as common interest developments (CIDs) (McKenzie 1994), where residents retain a communal interest and share in the collective neighborhood. As a safeguard for these shared community interests, CIDs establish internal governing bodies "where elected boards oversee the common property and establish covenants, conditions, and restrictions (CC&Rs) as part of the deed" (Vesselinov 2008: 539). These homeowners' associations (HOAs) fulfill a variety of roles. For example, HOAs often arrange for municipal services such as garbage collection, employ private security to monitor the neighborhood, and handle maintenance of the community. These organizations also perform other administrative roles such as determining common regulations and standards for community residents, enforcing residents' compliance with these regulations, and moderating disputes between residents. Thus, gated communities feature their own private systems of government that regulate what goes on in the neighborhood and require residents to follow contractual stipulations in order to remain a part of the community.

For many people, the phrase "gated community" connotes imagery of affluent, idyllic, and upper-class neighborhoods, although in truth there is greater variation across the demographic landscape of gated communities, as noted earlier in Blakely and Snyder's (1997) definition. Sanchez and colleagues (2005: 285) observe that gated communities may feature both owner-occupied and renter-occupied households, and find that "owners and renters have significantly different demographic profiles." Moreover, they find that socioeconomic status and income levels vary considerably across gated communities, a conclusion supported in other research (e.g. Blakely & Snyder 1997; Stark 1998; Wilson-Doenges 2000). Thus, the widely held belief that all gated communities are bastions of affluence is not accurate; rather, one might argue that affluent, high socioeconomic status gated communities represent a *type* of gated community. In turn, these varying conditions across gated communities suggest variation in the processes and outcomes often studied by neighborhood-level researchers, such as social organization and local crime rates, a point we return to later.

Building upon this discussion, we develop an operational definition of a gated community for the current study. First, a gated community is a residential area where gating mechanisms control who may enter the neighborhood and feature walls and fences along community borders. These exterior structures define the boundaries of the community and also distinguish the private space within from the public space without. Second, a gated community features private governance in the form of HOAs. As discussed earlier, HOAs create a private system of rules and conditions that residents must follow in order to live in the neighborhood. These regulations, in turn, help shape the social atmosphere within a gated community and the types of residents who live there. Third, a gated community consists of owner-occupied homes rather than rental units. This distinction is important for conceptual reasons. Gated communities with rental properties do not feature HOAs, making owner- and renter-occupied communities distinct from one another in a critical way (Sanchez et al. 2005). Restricting our definition to homeowner-only gated communities ensures that our definition is internally consistent.

18.3 Research on Gated Communities

Beyond just being a popular commodity, gated communities represent an important shift in how we conceptualize neighborhoods and subsequently understand neighborhood-level characteristics and processes. The growing number of gated communities challenges several important assumptions surrounding neighborhood-level research. Particularly important is the difference between public and private space. Research generally treats neighborhoods as public spaces with open access to anyone. From this perspective, a resident in one neighborhood could pass into an adjoining neighborhood without restriction, engage in social interaction, or commit a crime (or perform any number of other actions). Gated communities, however, consist of privatized spaces that create a certain discontinuity in the social landscape. In particular, the private space within gated communities necessarily restricts the mobility patterns of nearby nonresidents and shapes the social interactions and networks of gated and nongated residents alike (e.g., Asiedu & Arku 2009; Blakely & Snyder 1997; Low 2003). Considerations such as these have important ramifications for criminological theories.

In the context of social disorganization theory, there are several reasons why one might seek to characterize gated communities as ideal, prototypical socially organized neighborhoods. In theory, the presence of a homeowners' association should reinforce social solidarity and shared values within the community, as HOAs dictate the collective rules and expectations that community members agree to follow. HOAs also support and reinforce social homogeneity among residents (Le Goix & Vesselinov 2014), critical to developing internal consensus according to social disorganization theory. Moreover, one might expect that privatized spaces made available only to community members would foster cohesion and social interaction, reinforcing social ties between neighbors. In gated communities with lifestyle amenities such as private parks, golf courses, swimming pools, or playgrounds, residents may not need to leave the confines of the gates to participate in their preferred activities and, as a result, may spend yet more time engaging socially with community members (Blakely & Snyder 1997). Conversely, nonresidents may find themselves unable to partake in the activities located within a private community and instead must seek other activity hubs. The reduction of shared activity spaces between gated and nonresidents, then, may promote relations between community members but reduce the interactions and social ties between members and nonmembers residing within the same broader community (Lemanski 2006; Low 2003; Mantey 2017; but see Asiedu & Arku 2009).

At the same time, there are important reasons to question levels of social organization in gated communities. First, and despite their title, gated communities do not necessarily foster a sense of "community" among residents. Consistent with social disorganization theory, many neighbors within gated communities do interact and develop strong social ties through shared pastimes, activities, or participation in community-based organizations; yet research also finds that some residents remain consciously isolated from their gated peers (e.g., Blakely & Snyder 1997; Low 2003). Indeed, prior research supports the notion that gated communities are not inherently conducive toward a sense of community among residents. In her survey of gated and nongated community residents, Wilson-Doenges (2000) found that members of a high-income gated community reported a lower sense of community than residents of a comparable high-income nongated community, although sense of community was not significantly different between residents in low-income gated and nongated neighborhoods. Moreover, social interactions between residents may not be especially pronounced in all gated communities. As Blandy and Lister (2005: 294) find based on their qualitative research with gated community residents in the UK, "For the majority, a low level of informal associative contact with neighbours was both what they anticipated, and all that they wanted." While these points also apply to social life in nongated neighborhoods, it is important to dispel common stereotypes depicting gated communities as idealized social havens, or as perfectly socially organized neighborhoods.

In light of social disorganization theory, one might also expect that gated communities would exhibit greater levels of informal social control than nongated communities, thereby reducing crime in gated enclaves. Informal social control reflects the capacity of a community to regulate its residents according to mutually desired goals, such as the desire to live in a safe and crime-free environment. Indeed, the financial resources available in comparatively affluent gated communities allow some HOAs to hire private security personnel to guard entrances, patrol the community, or perhaps both. Private security personnel monitor the access of nonresidents into the neighborhood, dissuade deviant or criminal behavior from occurring, and may intervene when such events occur. Social disorganization theory suggests that homogeneity and an internal consensus among neighborhood residents on important norms and values should also lead to greater levels of informal social control (Kornhauser 1978) such as the formation of neighborhood watch associations, where volunteer residents actively patrol and monitor the neighborhood (Blakely & Snyder 1997). While not all gated communities demonstrate strong social ties and cohesion, as noted earlier, there are certainly many gated neighborhoods that do feature strong consensus and shared investment, which bolsters informal social control. Thus, concerned residents may group together and act to enforce the rules and standards within their community, which should result in less crime.

Many features of gated communities also lend themselves to theories of environmental criminology such as routine activities theory (Cohen & Felson 1979) and situational crime prevention (Clarke 1995). Indeed, some past studies on gated communities and crime have situated their research within these theoretical frameworks (Addington & Rennison 2013; Breetzke & Cohn 2013). As posited by Cohen and Felson (1979), routine activities theory consists of three central elements: (1) the presence of a suitable target, (2) the presence of a motivated offender, and (3) the absence of a capable guardian. When these elements converge in space and time, the likelihood of a crime occurring increases, whereas the lack of any of these elements may be sufficient to prevent a crime from occurring. Similarly, Clarke's (1995) theory of situational crime prevention enumerates various strategies, such as surveillance, target hardening, and controlled access, all of which focus on reducing opportunities for crime.

Of particular interest is the function of guardianship within gated communities and how the security implements located in these neighborhoods may impact local crime rates. Gated communities are designed to feature multiple layers of security, including gates, walls, and private security, which may dissuade potential offenders from entering and committing crimes (Branic, forthcoming; Cohen & Felson 1979; Felson & Boba 2010). It is likely, however, that the effectiveness of guardianship in gated communities depends on the level of securitization (i.e., the degree of *capable* guardianship discussed by Cohen and Felson (1979)). Luymes (1997: 198) describes how levels of physical security vary across gated communities, where increasingly sophisticated gating mechanisms (e.g., a 24-hour guarded gate vs. an unguarded electronic gate) improve controlled access into the neighborhood and more comprehensive community walls increase levels of "perimeter impermeability." Greater development of community gates and walls, Luymes argues, should correspond with greater levels of perceived security for the community. By extension, greater perceived security should translate to stronger, more efficacious guardianship against crime, although no research directly examines this hypothesis.

Gated communities may also play a role in shaping how neighborhoods relate to one another, an area of interest for communities and crime scholars. In their spatial analysis of southwestern US metropolitan areas, Le Goix and Vesselinov (2014) examined the social distance between gated and nongated communities in contiguous block groups, as reflected in levels of dissimilarity among neighborhood indicators of socioeconomic status, race/ethnicity, and age. The authors find that gated communities contribute to patterns of social segregation, noting that "the level of differentiation between gated enclaves and their vicinities is higher than the differentiation usually observed in the urban area between two adjacent neighbourhoods" (635). Thus, gated communities exert spatial influences critical for understanding the interdependence between neighborhoods.

18.4 Gated Communities and Inequality

Decades of research suggest that social segregation and inequality are central to the study of neighborhoods and crime (Hipp 2007; Massey & Denton 1993; Massey, Gross, &

Shibuya 1994; Squires & Kubrin 2006). Building upon this literature, emerging scholarship suggests how gated communities may reinforce or contribute to patterns of inequality and segregation (Atkinson & Flint 2004; Le Goix 2005; Le Goix & Vesselinov 2014; Low 2003; Vesselinov 2008; Vesselinov, Cazzesus, & Falk 2007), although the extent to which gated communities do this is likely dependent upon the area or region being studied. We focus our discussion on two types of inequality related to gated communities: (1) neighborhood selection and residential migration, and (2) social segregation.

As noted earlier, one of the key defining features of gated communities is the controlled access of nonresidents into the neighborhood; yet there are reasons to suspect that gated communities produce controlled access for *prospective* residents as well, unequally influencing who may move into the neighborhood. This issue relates more broadly to neighborhood selection—where individuals choose the types of neighborhoods that they would like to move into—and residential migration, the process by which individuals relocate to a new home. Research finds that not all individuals are equally able to move into particular neighborhoods (Sampson & Sharkey 2008; Squires & Kubrin 2006). A key limitation for potential in-movers to a neighborhood, gated or not, is a lack of necessary financial capital. For example, home mortgage loans, which individuals apply for to purchase a home, are important mechanisms influencing where potential residents may ultimately end up living, although access to these loans is not equal across the population (Squires & Kubrin 2006). Specifically, bias in the home mortgage lending industry precludes some, often lower-income individuals and minorities, from securing mortgage loans that would otherwise enable them to purchase homes (Ross & Turner 2005). Additionally, particular aspects of gated communities may further prevent some individuals from accessing the neighborhood. In addition to the high home values found in many gated communities, there are extra costs associated with living in these communities that might prevent some from establishing long-term residence. To fuel the services offered by HOAs, residents are required to pay regular financial dues that contribute to the broader community. These additional expenses exist in tandem with a system of contractual rules and regulations that all residents must follow in order to reside in the community. "These legal residential contracts," Vesselinov (2008) argues, "serve to exclude potential buyers based on income, race, or ethnic origin" (539; see also Low 2003), thus reinforcing inequality.

Many consider gated communities a modern form of social exclusivity and residential segregation, where certain groups within society seclude themselves from other groups (e.g., Atkinson & Flint 2004; Blakely & Snyder 1997; Durington 2006; Le Goix 2005; Le Goix & Vesselinov 2014; Low 2003; Vesselinov 2008; Vesselinov & Le Goix 2012; Vesselinov et al. 2007). In this respect, gated communities represent what have been termed contemporary "fortress-building" practices and mentalities (Blakely & Snyder 1997; Dupuis & Thorns 2008). A key driver behind the popularity of gated communities and subsequent residential segregation, Setha Low (2003) and others argue, is fear. Many seek out gated communities due to fear of crime and victimization, expecting that life within the gates will provide added security and safety. Moreover, prospective residents frequently elect to live in gated communities out of a fear of "others," for example, immigrants or those who contribute to "ethnic change" (Low 2003; see also Dupuis & Thorns 2008; Durington 2006). A common feature of gated communities is their homogeneity, where residents' demographic characteristics tend to be much more similar than different (e.g., Blakely & Snyder 1997; Low 2003; Romig 2005). In this way, then, gated communities can contribute to—and reinforce—larger patterns of social segregation and inequality. For example, in their spatial analysis of gated communities in three US metropolitan areas, Vesselinov and Le Goix (2012) find that the emergence of gated communities produces a "new layer of suburbanization" (218). In particular, they argue that both the growing prevalence of gated communities in the modern era and the mass suburbanization movement (e.g., "white flight") in past decades collectively create affluent, homogenous enclaves that seclude certain members of the population from others. Overall, then, the findings from the literature suggest that gated communities can contribute to social seclusion and segregation practices that reinforce divisions across different population groups, perpetuating social inequality. What are the implications of this for neighborhood crime rates? How do these broader patterns impact the neighborhood-crime relationship, both in and around gated communities?

18.5 Gated Communities and Crime

Despite the rapid growth of gated communities in recent decades, only very few studies examine the relationship between these residential areas and local crime rates, and the studies that do provide mixed findings. Analyzing National Crime Victimization Survey (NCVS) data for the years 2010 and 2011, Addington and Rennison (2013) find that homes in gated communities experience comparatively fewer burglaries. The authors report 33% lower odds of burglary victimization for gated community households compared to similar households in nongated communities. Breetzke and Cohn (2013) also examine the relationship between gated communities and burglary, yet they reach the opposite conclusion. Examining communities in South Africa, the authors find that gated neighborhoods have higher risks of both daytime and nighttime burglaries, respectively. Finally, some research suggests that there may be no significant relationship between gated communities and crime. In their national-level study of gated communities in the United States, Blakely and Snyder (1997) analyzed a series of communities across the nation and concluded that gated communities offer no particular protection against crime. Instead, the authors found that gated communities may actually inhibit first responders such as police because of the gates that restrict easy access into the community. Likewise, Wilson-Doenges (2000) found no significant differences in crime levels between gated and nongated communities. In her study, Wilson-Doenges randomly surveyed residents from four California neighborhoods: two gated and two nongated. She split these pairs of communities, respectively, in terms of income levels, with one being affluent and one being lower-income. After accounting for neighborhood socioeconomic status, Wilson-Doenges (2000) found that crime rates did not significantly differ across the gated and nongated communities in her sample. Given the limited number and mixed findings of these studies, clearly more research is warranted.

The present study analyzes the relationship between gated communities and crime in Orange County, California, an area known for its concentration of gated communities (Blakely & Snyder 1997; Le Goix 2005; Wilson-Doenges 2000). Our study makes several contributions to the current body of research. First, as just noted, findings on the relationship between gated communities and crime are both limited and inconclusive. Our study seeks to provide additional evidence and further the discussion surrounding these types of residential places. Second, we assess the relationship between gated communities and crime while including key control measures utilized in neighborhood-level research, adding to the robustness of our conclusions. Lastly, we incorporate spatial measures into the analysis, which allow us to examine the gated communities-crime relationship while accounting for the broader community context as well as address concerns related to spatial autocorrelation.

18.6 Data and Methods

Before conducting analyses, it was necessary to develop a sample of gated communities for the study. Because no comprehensive data set of gated communities exists for the United States, prior research has generally utilized national-level survey data (Addington & Rennison 2013; Sanchez et al. 2005; Vesselinov 2008; 2012) and small-sample case study data (e.g., McKenzie 2005; Romig 2005; Wilson-Doenges 2000). Le Goix (2005), however, suggests an alternative and innovative approach to identifying the spatial locations of gated communities, which involves creating "a database derived from the same sources as a prospective homebuyer would use" (325). Specifically, Le Goix (2005) constructed his sample of gated communities using Thomas Guides maps, real estate advertisements, and county assessor's maps. We draw from Le Goix's approach and develop our sample of gated communities using real estate listings for Orange County, California. In particular, we utilize data from the Multiple Listing Service (MLS)[2] to identify individual homes classified as being within a gated community. We compiled records between May 2014 and January 2015 and obtained specific addresses for individual homes located within gated communities. We then geocoded these addresses using ArcGIS v10.2 and used the coordinate data to identify all Orange County census blocks containing at least one home listed as being located within a gated community. Thus, we capture the presence of a gated community as a binary measure, where a value of 1 indicates at least one gated community home within a particular block and a value of 0 indicates no gated community homes present within the block.

As a check on our data, we assessed the temporal ordering of the gated communities in our sample relative to the 2010 census measures in order to ensure that the gated communities in the sample were built *before* 2010, the year measured by our census variables. Otherwise, our demographic data might predate the construction of a particular gated community and thus not necessarily represent the demographic characteristics therein. To make this assessment, we used the reported age of each gated community home, information that is included in the MLS listings, which served as a proxy for when the other homes in the neighborhood were constructed. We deemed this measure an effective proxy given that gated communities are often built as entire residential developments rather than individual homes. A tabulation of these data revealed that no gated community was developed later than 2010, suggesting that temporal ordering was not an issue for our analyses.

Drawing on annual, address-level crime incident data provided by police departments across Orange County, we constructed two dependent variables for our analyses: total property crimes and total violent crimes. For these measures, we averaged block-level counts of property (burglary, larceny, motor vehicle theft) and violent (aggravated assault, murder, robbery) crimes for the years 2009 to 2011, respectively. Taking a three-year average allowed us to control for idiosyncratic fluctuations in crime levels between years, which may distort any observed effects in our statistical models.[3]

We constructed several control variables to include in our statistical models by drawing on data from the 2010 census. Social disorganization theory informed the selection of these variables, which are commonly utilized in neighborhood-level research (Kubrin & Weitzer 2003; Sampson & Groves 1989). First, we accounted for the racial and ethnic composition of each neighborhood using a series of population percentage measures for Asian, black, Latino, and other race, respectively (percent white population is the reference category). Similarly, we included a measure of percent foreign-born within each neighborhood as a growing literature demonstrates that immigrant concentration is negatively associated with neighborhood crime rates (see Kubrin & Desmond (2015) for a review of this literature). We also controlled for neighborhood residential stability by including a measure of the percentage of residents who reported living within the same home five years ago. Lastly, we included a factor measure for concentrated disadvantage in the neighborhood, which included (1) average household income, (2) percentage of residents with a bachelor's degree, and (3) percentage living at or below 125% of the poverty level.[4] A principle components factor analysis on these variables revealed one factor with an eigenvalue greater than one and all factor loadings above 0.72.

In addition to these control variables, which represent the characteristics of each block in the sample, we also included spatially lagged versions of these variables in the models in order to account for the broader community context as well as potential spatial dependence between explanatory variables in adjacent blocks. The spatially lagged measures encompassed a half-mile buffer around each block; in other words, these variables captured the characteristics of all other blocks within a half-mile radius around the focal block. Thus, we were able to control for the characteristics of each particular block in the sample as well as the characteristics in adjacent blocks. There was no evidence of multicollinearity problems, as the variance inflation factor values (VIFs) were all below 5.9 (Kennedy 1998).

Prior to analysis, we imposed two restrictions on our sample. First, we dropped all blocks that contained zero population, as these blocks would have missing values for the control variables. Second, list-wise deletion from analyses dropped any additional cases with missing data (n = 2,921; these blocks were primarily [90%] missing data on violent and property crimes, due to the fact that not all police departments in Orange County provided access to crime data). Our final sample included 13,564 blocks in Orange County, of which 844 blocks identified as having at least one gated community located within. Because our dependent variables, property and violent crimes, measured counts within each block, we used Poisson-based regression models for the analyses. To account for overdispersion in our dependent variables, we estimated negative binomial regression models where appropriate (Osgood 2000). Following Osgood's suggestion, we included total block population as an exposure term in the models and constrained the coefficient to a value of one, which made our models comparable to examining per capita crime rates.

We estimated these models in three stages. First, we included only gated community status of the block as a predictor in the model. Next, we added demographic control variables for the focal block into the model. Finally, we added spatially lagged control variables into the model. This three-step approach allowed us to examine the effects of community gating while gradually controlling for the demographic context around each block, bolstering confidence in our findings. We begin our discussion of the findings by examining the spatial distribution of gated community blocks in Orange County. Next, we present descriptive statistics for the sample as a whole as well as split by gated and nongated neighborhoods. Lastly, we discuss the results from our regression models.

18.7 Findings

Figure 18.1 presents the distribution of gated communities across a subset of census blocks in Orange County, California.[5] Blocks shaded black reflect the presence of gated communities, whereas unshaded blocks indicate nongated neighborhoods. Figure 18.1 provides some useful insights about how gated communities are distributed across the county as well as their spatial relationships with other neighborhoods.

An important—but not surprising—observation is that gated communities are not equally distributed county-wide but rather are clustered. Two emergent patterns are the clustering of gated communities near both the southern edge and central area of the map, although the characteristics of these two clusters are notably different. The former includes cities such as Newport Beach and Huntington Beach, which occupy the Orange County coastline and are comparatively affluent. For example, the median household income across all Huntington Beach blocks was approximately $107,000, with a median poverty rate of just 6.5%. Moreover, 42% of residents, on average, held a bachelor's degree and the average length of residence in one's home was twelve and a half years. The latter, central cluster includes cities such as Garden Grove, Orange, and Santa Ana, which exhibit comparatively less affluence than those along the coast. For instance, the median household income in all Santa Ana blocks was approximately $42,000 and the

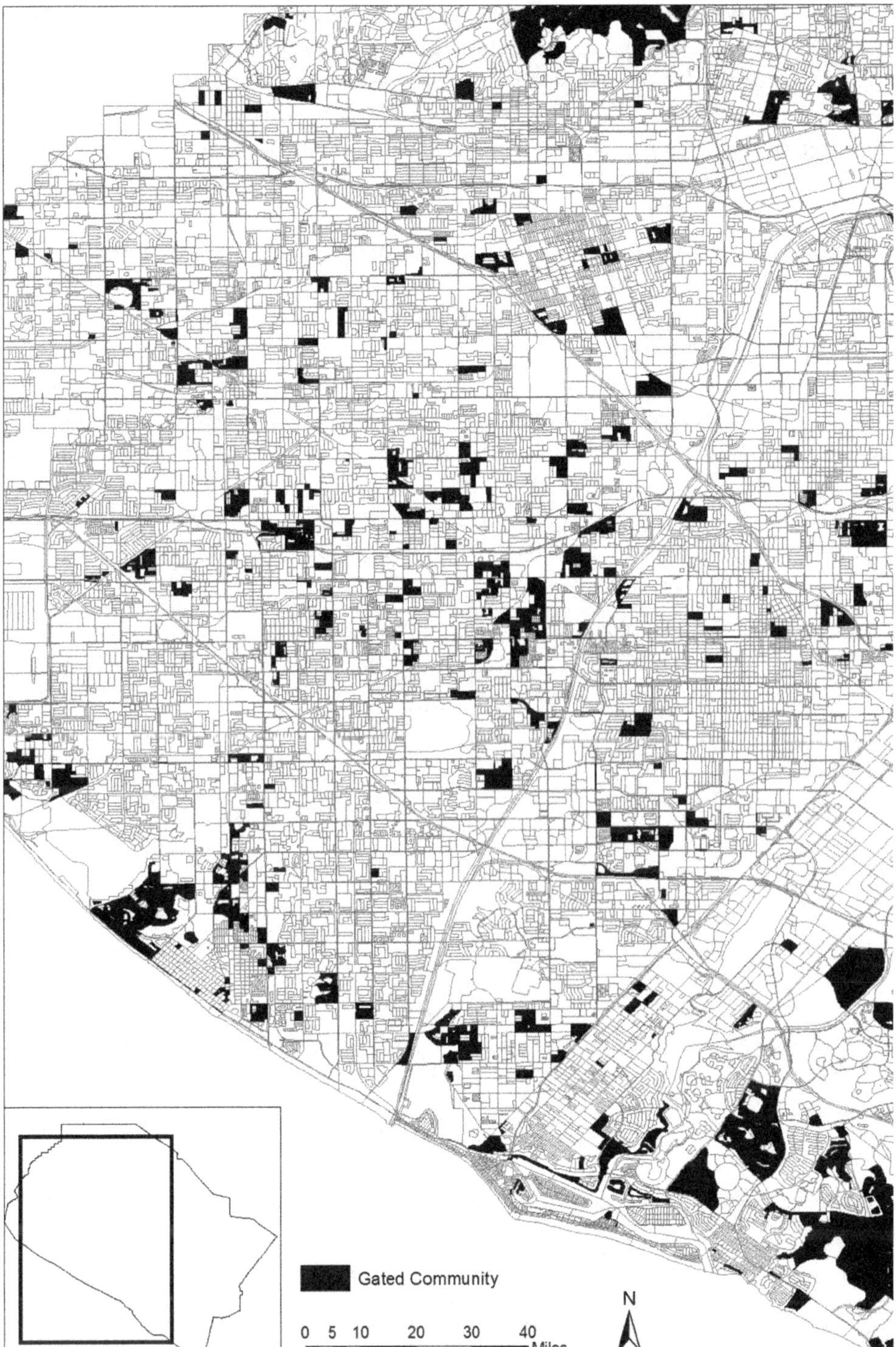

FIGURE 18.1 Gated communities in Orange County, California (U.S.), 2010

median poverty rate was about 20%, over three times that of Huntington Beach. While the percentage of residents with bachelor's degrees, on average, was lower in Santa Ana (31%), the average length of residence was also approximately 12 years. Thus, as suggested earlier, we find that gated communities cluster in cities with markedly different sociodemographic profiles, which may have implications for the relationship between gated communities and crime.

Table 18.1 presents a descriptive overview of the data in our sample. Overall, approximately 6% of the blocks in the sample contained at least one gated community home ($N = 844$). Descriptive statistics suggest some noteworthy differences between gated and nongated neighborhoods in Orange County. One salient difference is seen in the percentage of Latino residents, which was almost double in nongated communities. Moreover, the percentage of white residents in gated communities (63%) was higher, on average, than in nongated communities (51%). Differences between other characteristics, however, were less pronounced. While the percentage of Asian or "other" residents

Table 18.1 Descriptive Statistics for Gated, Nongated, and All Blocks in the Sample

	Gated Communities ($N = 844$)		Non-Gated Communities ($N = 12,720$)		Total ($N = 13,564$)	
	Mean	SD	Mean	SD	Mean	SD
Violent Crime	0.19	0.51	0.17	0.47	0.17	0.47
Property Crime	2.40	5.14	1.53	4.36	1.58	4.42
Gated Community					0.06	0.24
Pct. Asian	18.67	20.85	16.69	20.72	16.81	20.73
Pct. Black	1.03	2.06	1.19	3.99	1.18	3.90
Pct. Latino	14.60	19.30	28.20	29.53	27.36	29.19
Pct. Other	3.11	5.02	2.90	5.19	2.92	5.18
Pct. White	62.58	27.08	51.01	30.21	51.73	30.16
Pct. Foreign-Born	30.63	40.53	35.52	41.01	35.21	40.99
Residential Stability	64.97	37.17	68.79	35.50	68.55	35.61
Avg. Income	140,966.20	154,091.00	134,076.50	170,116.60	134,505.20	169,166.70
Pct. Bachelor's Degree	42.63	40.85	40.31	39.49	40.45	39.58
Pct. Poverty	11.06	15.17	15.28	18.46	15.02	18.30

were somewhat higher in gated communities, the percentage of black residents was only slightly higher in nongated communities. The percentage of foreign-born residents was higher on average in nongated than gated communities. Similarly, residential stability was slightly higher in nongated communities. The three variables comprising the concentrated disadvantage factor also indicated some slight differences within the sample. Namely, gated communities featured greater average household incomes, a higher percentage of residents with bachelor's degrees, and a lower percentage of residents living in poverty than nongated communities. Finally, the descriptive statistics presented here show that gated communities have, on average, slightly higher counts of violent and property crime, contrary to expectations. However, these crime measures do not account for the total population living within each neighborhood. Converting the crime measures into rates shows that gated communities in the sample averaged 0.26 violent crimes per 100 residents, whereas in nongated neighborhoods the average rate was 0.61 violent incidents per 100 people. Additionally, gated communities averaged 3.28 property crimes per 100 people, while non-gated neighborhoods averaged 6 incidents per 100 people.

We begin presenting our regression results by focusing on the violent crime models as displayed in Table 18.2. Model 1, which included only the binary gated community predictor, reveals a negative relationship between blocks classified as gated communities and levels of violent crime. Gated community blocks were associated with 42.4% fewer violent crimes [(exp(−0.551)—1) * 100] compared to blocks not designated as gated communities. As reflected in Model 2 of Table 18.2, this negative relationship between community gating and violent crime persisted after adding the control variables; controlling for important neighborhood demographic and socioeconomic characteristics, gated communities were still associated with 28.6% fewer violent crimes. Finally, the addition of spatially lagged variables in Model 3 only slightly reduced this effect, where the presence of gated communities corresponded with a 22.7% decrease in expected violent crimes. Overall, then, we find that gated community blocks were consistently and negatively related to counts of violent crimes even after controlling for neighborhood-level characteristics, in line with the findings of Addington and Rennison (2013).

The violent crime models reveal several significant relationships between neighborhood-level characteristics and crime. As shown in Model 3, higher levels of residential stability were associated with lower violent crime rates in the focal block, consistent with social disorganization theory. To contextualize this finding, we multiplied the coefficient by the average residential stability value for the sample (68.55%) and found that a neighborhood with an average level of stability corresponded with 47.8% fewer expected violent crimes, net of controls. At the same time, however, the model also indicated that greater stability in the area surrounding the block was associated with slightly higher levels of expected crime, a somewhat puzzling finding. The findings for concentrated disadvantage were similarly puzzling; whereas greater levels of disadvantage in the surrounding area were associated with greater levels of crime, consistent with the predictions of social disorganization theory, disadvantage in the focal block corresponded with fewer violent crimes. Previous research has identified similar

Table 18.2 Poisson and Negative Binomial Regression Models Predicting Violent Crime in Orange County, CA, Blocks (N = 13,564)

	Model 1[a]	Model 2[b]	Model 3[b]
Gated Community	–.551*** (0.086)	–.337*** (0.083)	–.258** (0.084)
Pct. Asian		.003 (0.002)	.005* (0.003)
Pct. Black		.048*** (0.005)	.033*** (0.007)
Pct. Latino		.020*** (0.001)	.007*** (0.002)
Pct. Other		.006 (0.010)	.022* (0.009)
Pct. Foreign-Born		.001 (0.001)	.000 (0.001)
Residential Stability		–.009*** (0.001)	–.007*** (0.001)
Concentrated Disadvantage		–.048** (0.016)	–.056*** (0.016)
Pct. Asian (0.5 mile)			–.007 (0.004)
Pct. Black (0.5 mile)			.106*** (0.020)
Pct. Latino (0.5 mile)			.001 (0.003)
Pct. Other (0.5 mile)			–.166*** (0.031)
Pct. Foreign-Born (0.5 mile)			–.014*** (0.004)
Residential Stability (0.5 mile)			.005 (0.003)
Concentrated Disadvantage (0.5 mile)			.071*** (0.006)
Constant	–6.613*** (0.022)	–7.131*** (0.093)	–6.282*** (0.304)
LR Chi^2	47.28***	1,252.51***	1,575.23***

Note: Results presented as logged odds coefficients and (standard errors).

[a] Negative binomial regression model.

[b] Poisson regression model.

* $p < .05$; ** $p < .01$; *** $p < .001$.

mixed findings regarding the impact of concentrated disadvantage (both in the focal and nearby areas) on crime at smaller units of analysis (Wo, Hipp, & Boessen 2016: 234).

Next, we discuss the results for the property crime models presented in Table 18.3. Similar to findings for violent crime, gated community blocks were associated with lower property crime rates. Model 4, or the baseline model, indicated that gated communities corresponded with a 22.8% reduction in expected property crimes compared to nongated blocks in the sample. This negative relationship persisted after including control variables for the focal block (Model 5), where the gated community indicator was associated with a 22.3% reduction in expected property crimes, and including spatially lagged control variables (Model 6) adjusted this effect to a 16.9% reduction in expected property crimes. Thus, the gated community variable demonstrated a robust negative relationship with property crime, consistent with findings from previous research (Addington & Rennison 2013).

Unlike in the violent crime models, we found that residential stability exerted a consistent negative effect on property crime at both the focal and surrounding levels, consistent with social disorganization theory. In other words, greater levels of stability in the focal tract as well as nearby were associated with fewer property crimes. Yet concentrated disadvantage continued to demonstrate a mixed relationship with crime rates. Each one-point increase in the disadvantage factor corresponded with an 8.4% decrease in expected property crimes, whereas a one-point increase in disadvantage in the surrounding area was associated with a 5.5% increase in property crimes, net of controls. Again, these mixed findings for concentrated disadvantage have been documented in similar block-level crime research (Wo et al. 2016).

18.8 Conclusion and Discussion

The study of neighborhoods and crime has a long history in the United States. Research in this vein typically has reflected the changing dynamics of America's urban centers. Consider, for example, the work of the Chicago School scholars, which developed during the first part of the 20th century—a period marked by rapid political, economic, and social change that affected virtually all aspects of life. Industrialization, urbanization, and immigration were central features of the American landscape during this time, and these changes paved the way for early research on how communities and crime may be linked (Shaw & McKay 1942). Following this foundational work, scholars have examined varying facets of the neighborhoods-crime nexus as US cities continue to evolve and undergo significant transformations such as deindustrialization (e.g., Sampson & Wilson 1995) and gentrification (e.g., Hwang & Sampson 2014), among others.

Arguably one of the most significant shifts in the American landscape over the last few decades is the rapid expansion of gated communities, especially in the Sunbelt states. As we detailed at the outset of the chapter, the number of gated communities in the United States has been steadily rising since the 1990s (Blakely & Snyder 1997). As community

Table 18.3 Negative Binomial Regression Models Predicting Property Crime in Orange County, CA, Blocks (N = 13,564)

	Model 4	Model 5	Model 6
Gated Community	−.259**	−.253***	−.185***
	(0.052)	(0.047)	(0.047)
Pct. Asian		.001	.005***
		(0.001)	(0.001)
Pct. Black		.026***	.022***
		(0.003)	(0.003)
Pct. Latino		−.000	−.002*
		(0.000)	(0.001)
Pct. Other		.017***	.019***
		(0.003)	(0.003)
Pct. Foreign-Born		.002***	.000
		(0.000)	(0.000)
Residential Stability		−.014***	−.012***
		(0.001)	(0.001)
Concentrated Disadvantage		−.065**	−.087***
		(0.015)	(0.015)
Pct. Asian (0.5 mile)			−.004*
			(0.002)
Pct. Black (0.5 mile)			.057***
			(0.014)
Pct. Latino (0.5 mile)			−.006***
			(0.002)
Pct. Other (0.5 mile)			−.042**
			(0.013)
Pct. Foreign-Born (0.5 mile)			−.012***
			(0.002)
Residential Stability (0.5 mile)			−.006**
			(0.002)
Concentrated Disadvantage (0.5 mile)			.054***
			(0.003)
Constant	−4.153***	−3.521***	−2.411***
	(0.014)	(0.044)	(0.003)
LR Chi^2	24.22**	1,984.97***	2,462.83***

Note: Results presented as logged odds coefficients and (standard errors).

* $p < .05$; ** $p < .01$; *** $p < .001$.

gating becomes increasingly prevalent, researchers have spent considerable time and energy examining the implications of this emerging trend on various facets of social life, including the interactions between residents (Asiedu & Arku 2009; Blandy & Lister 2005; Durington 2006) and patterns of social segregation and inequality (Atkinson & Flint 2004; Durington 2006; Le Goix 2005; Le Goix & Vesselinov 2014; Low 2003). Surprisingly, however, communities and crime scholars have been near silent on how the rise in gated communities may be impacting neighborhood crime rates. There are only a handful of studies on crime in and around gated communities, and to date they have produced mixed findings. For this reason, we know very little about gated communities and crime in the United States today.

The aim of this study has been to augment this small body of literature by analyzing the relationship between gated communities and crime across neighborhoods in Orange County, California. In doing so, we created a unique data set that draws on professional real estate data to identify where gated communities are located. Our findings show a consistent negative relationship between gated communities and crime. In particular, the presence of gated communities corresponded with a 22% decrease in expected violent crimes and a 17% decrease in expected property crimes in Orange County, after controlling for the standard neighborhood correlates of crime and taking into account broader spatial dynamics. These findings are consistent with Addington and Rennison (2013), although their study only examined the crime of burglary. Despite corroborating these earlier findings, it is premature to conclude that gated communities are simply safer than nongated communities, as much more research is necessary to fully tease out the nexus between gated communities and crime.

Findings from this study bear implications for contemporary theories of neighborhoods and neighborhood-level processes. For example, the findings from our study seem to support the arguments of social disorganization theory. Recall that this theory suggests that neighborhoods marked by high socioeconomic status, residential stability, and racial/ethnic homogeneity, among other factors, are likely to experience lower crime rates, in large part because they generate stronger social ties among residents, which activate informal social control and prevent crime. Gated communities share many of these characteristics; as presented in Table 18.1, they are generally places with high residential stability and high average incomes. Moreover, as previously discussed, research finds that gated communities are typically homogenous along demographic characteristics (Sanchez et al. 2005). Finally, gated communities often feature mechanisms of informal social control, such as neighborhood watch organizations and private security personnel, that can be important deterrents to local crime rates. Unfortunately, we do not have direct measures of these social processes, so at this point we are only able to speculate that the reason gated communities exhibit lower crime rates in our study is due to the mechanisms outlined in social disorganization theory.

Of course, our findings need to be interpreted within the context of the study's limitations. One important limitation is our operationalization of gated communities, which is somewhat rudimentary. In the current study, utilizing data from the Multiple Listing Service (MLS), we capture the presence of a gated community as a binary measure, where a value of 1 indicates at least one gated community home within a particular block and a value of 0 indicates no gated community homes present within the block. There are shortcomings to this approach. First, this coding method relies on home-listing data, which provide a useful avenue for identifying the locations of gated communities but may not be entirely exhaustive. We minimized this potential shortcoming by collecting realtor data over the course of several months, thus attempting to properly identify as many gated communities as possible, although we cannot determine the extent to which some communities may be missing from the sample. Second, using a binary measure of a gated community assumes homogeneity across gated communities rather than heterogeneity. In other words, treating all gated communities as conceptually similar (i.e., simply a value of 1) neglects important differences in design and organization that may impact crime rates, social processes, or other outcomes. Prior literature suggests some important ways that gated communities vary—for example, whether communities are designed to foster prestige, lifestyle, or security for residents (Blakely & Snyder 1997; see also Grant & Mittelsteadt 2004)—that our operationalization does not account for.

Yet this limitation is not unique to our study, and other researchers have faced similar challenges, owing largely to the fact that no comprehensive data set of gated communities exists for the United States. As we noted earlier, prior research typically utilizes national-level survey data (Addington & Rennison 2013; Sanchez et al. 2005; Vesselinov 2008; 2012) and small-sample case study data (McKenzie 2005; Romig 2005), both of which have their own limitations. Still, future researchers should attempt to more accurately and comprehensively capture the presence of gated communities beyond the binary measures we employed in the current study.

Another limitation of the current study is the fact that our data span a very short and specific time period, which raises questions both about whether the findings would be replicated in a different historical time period (for example, during the 2007–2008 housing market collapse) and whether a more dynamic methodological approach would yield similar findings. Concerning the latter point, our analysis reflects a cross-sectional analysis of the gated communities and crime relationship. Yet as we discussed earlier, there has been an exponential growth in the number of gated communities over time, and their rising prevalence has continued to shape the social landscape. Thus, longitudinal approaches to studying gated communities would help to bolster the findings of existing research.

A final limitation involves the generalizability of our findings. Because our study focused solely on neighborhoods in Orange County, California, our ability to extend these findings to other places—whether in the Sunbelt, across the United States, or in contrast to other nations—is limited. For example, while our study found a negative relationship between gated communities and crime, Breetzke and Cohn (2013) find a positive relationship in their analysis in South Africa. Important social, cultural, and historical differences between these two parts of the world may have influenced the difference in conclusions.

In sum, then, while the findings from the current study help to inform scholarship on gated communities, much work remains to be done. Future research should continue to analyze crime in and around gated communities, and build upon existing research—not in the least because gated communities are likely to remain popular for the foreseeable future.

Notes

1. Sanchez and colleagues' definition is more inclusive than that used by Blakely and Snyder, which limits our ability to make comparisons between the two studies. While gated communities are in fact "walled and fenced," the definition used by Sanchez et al. also includes places such as military housing, which fall outside of what most researchers consider a gated community (Addington & Rennison 2013; Vesselinov 2008).
2. The Multiple Listing Service (MLS) is a professional realtor database that records detailed information on all homes currently listed on the real estate market. These data provide many characteristics of the individual home and attributes of the broader community where it resides, including whether or not the home exists within a gated community. The professional nature of the data set bolsters our confidence in the quality and accuracy of these data.
3. We acknowledge a key limitation of our study, as with nearly all communities and crime studies, is an inability to identify certain attributes of offenders. In this particular case, we are unable to distinguish whether crime rates within gated communities reflect crimes committed by outsiders or gated community residents.
4. The census does not provide these variables at the block level, so we imputed the measures based on other variables available in the census data (see Boessen and Hipp 2015 for greater detail on this approach).
5. Due to the small spatial scale of census blocks, presenting an overview of the entire county would be difficult to interpret and less than intuitive compared to maps presenting data at, for example, the census tract level. Thus, we focus on a subset of blocks contained within the larger county.

References

Addington, Lynn A., and Callie Marie Rennison. 2013. "Keeping the Barbarians outside the Gate? Comparing Burglary Victimization in Gated and Non-gated Communities." *Justice Quarterly* 32(1): 168–192.

Asiedu, Alex Boakye, and Godwin Arku. 2009. "The Rise of Gated Housing Estates in Ghana: Empirical Insights from Three Communities in Metropolitan Accra." *Journal of Housing and the Built Environment* 24: 227–247.

Atkinson, Rowland, and John Flint. 2004. "Fortress UK? Gated Communities, the Spatial Revolt of the Elites and Time-Space Trajectories of Segregation." *Housing Studies* 19(6): 875–892.

Blakely, Edward J., and Mary Gail Snyder. 1997. *Fortress America: Gated Communities in the United States*. Washington, DC: Brookings Institute Press.

Blandy, Sarah, and Diane Lister. 2005. "Gated Communities: (Ne)gating Community Development?" *Housing Studies* 20(2): 287–301.

Boessen, Adam, and John R. Hipp. 2015. "Close-Ups and the Scale of Ecology: Land Uses and the Geography of Social Context and Crime." *Criminology* 53(3): 399–426.

Branic, Nicholas. Forthcoming. "Gated Communities." In Bruce A. Arrigo and Geoffrey Golson (Eds.), *The Sage Encyclopedia of Surveillance, Security, and Privacy*. Thousand Oaks: Sage.

Breetzke, Gregory D., and Ellen G. Cohn. 2013. "Burglary in Gated Communities: An Empirical Analysis Using Routine Activities Theory." *International Criminal Justice Review* 23(1): 56–74.

Clarke, Ronald V. 1995. "Situational Crime Prevention." *Crime and Justice* 19: 91–150.

Cohen, Lawrence E., and Marcus Felson. 1979. "Social Change and Crime Rate Trends: A Routine Activity Approach." *American Sociological Review* 44(4): 588–608.

Dupuis, Ann, and David Thorns. 2008. "Gated Communities as Exemplars of 'Forting Up' Practices in a Risk Society." *Urban Policy and Research* 26(2): 145–157.

Durington, Matthew. 2006. "Race, Space and Place in Suburban Durban: An Ethnographic Assessment of Gated Community Environments and Residents." *GeoJournal* 66: 147–160.

Felson, Marcus, and Rachel L. Boba. 2010. *Crime and Everyday Life*. Thousand Oaks, CA: Sage.

Grant, Jill, and Lyndsey Mittelsteadt. 2004. "Types of Gated Communities." *Environment and Planning B: Planning and Design* 31: 913–930.

Hipp, John R. 2007. "Income Inequality, Race, and Place: Does the Distribution of Race and Class within Neighborhoods Affect Crime Rates?" *Criminology* 45(3): 665–697.

Hwang, Jackelyn, and Robert J. Sampson. 2014. "Divergent Pathways of Gentrification: Racial Inequality and the Social Order of Renewal in Chicago Neighborhoods." *American Sociological Review* 79(4): 726–751.

Kennedy, Peter E. 1998. *A Guide to Econometrics*. Cambridge, MA: MIT Press.

Kornhauser, Ruth. 1978. *Social Sources of Delinquency*. Chicago: University of Chicago Press.

Kubrin, Charis E., and Scott A. Desmond. 2015. "The Power of Place Revisited: Why Immigrant Communities Have Lower Levels of Adolescent Violence." *Youth Violence and Juvenile Justice* 13:345–366.

Kubrin, Charis E., and Ronald Weitzer. 2003. "New Directions in Social Disorganization Theory." *Journal of Research in Crime and Delinquency* 40: 374–402.

Le Goix, Renaud. 2005. "Gated Communities: Sprawl and Social Segregation in Southern California." *Housing Studies* 20(2): 323–343.

Le Goix, Renaud, and Elena Vesselinov. 2014. "Inequality Shaping Processes and Gated Communities in US Western Metropolitan Areas." *Urban Studies* 52(4): 619–638.

Lemanski, Charlotte. 2006. "Spaces of Exclusivity or Connection? Linkages between a Gated Community and its Poorer Neighbour in a Cape Town Master Plan Development." *Urban Studies* 43(2): 397–420.

Low, Setha. 2003. *Behind the Gates: Life, Security, and the Pursuit of Happiness in Fortress America*. New York: Routledge.

Luymes, Don. 1997. "The Fortification of Suburbia: Investigating the Rise of Enclave Communities." *Landscape and Urban Planning* 39: 187–203.

Mantey, Dorota. 2017. "Social Consequences of Gated Communities: The Case of Suburban Warsaw." *Professional Geographer* 69(1): 151–161. doi: 10.1080/00330124.2016.1184986

Massey, Douglas S., and Nancy A. Denton. 1993. *American Apartheid: Segregation and the Making of the Underclass*. Cambridge, MA: Harvard University Press.

Massey, Douglas S., Andrew B. Gross, and Kumiko Shibuya. 1994. "Migration, Segregation, and the Geographic Concentration of Poverty." *American Sociological Review* 59(3): 425–445.

McKenzie, E. 1994. *Privatopia: Homeowner Associations and the Rise of Residential Private Government*. New Haven: Yale University Press.

McKenzie, E. 2005. "Constructing the *Pomerium* in Las Vegas: A Case Study of Emerging Trends in American Gated Communities." *Housing Studies* 20(2): 187–203.

Osgood, D. Wayne. 2000. "Poisson-Based Regression Analysis of Aggregate Crime Rates." *Journal of Quantitative Criminology* 16(1): 21–43.

Romig, Kevin. 2005. "The Upper Sonoran Lifestyle: Gated Communities in Scottsdale, Arizona." *City and Community* 4(1): 67–86.

Ross, Stephen L., and Margery Austin Turner. 2005. "Housing Discrimination in Metropolitan America: Explaining Changes between 1989 and 2000." *Social Problems* 52(2): 152–180.

Sampson, Robert J. 2006. "How Does Community Context Matter? Social Mechanisms and the Explanation of Crime." In *The Explanation of Crime: Context, Mechanisms, and Development*, edited by Per-Olof H. Wikström and Robert J. Sampson, pp. 31–60. New York and Cambridge: Cambridge University Press.

Sampson, Robert J., and W. Byron Groves. 1989. "Community Structure and Crime: Testing Social-Disorganization Theory." *American Journal of Sociology* 94(4): 774–802.

Sampson, Robert J., and Patrick Sharkey. 2008. "Neighborhood Selection and the Social Reproduction of Concentrated Inequality." *Demography* 45(1): 1–29.

Sampson, Robert J., and William Julius Wilson. 1995. "Toward a Theory of Race, Crime and Urban Inequality." In *Crime and Inequality*, edited by John Hagan and Ruth D. Peterson, pp. 37–54. Stanford, CA: Stanford University Press.

Sanchez, Thomas W., Robert E. Lang, and Dawn M. Dhavale. 2005. "Security versus Status? A First Look at the Census's Gated Community Data." *Journal of Planning Education and Research* 24: 281–291.

Shaw, Clifford R., and Henry D. McKay. 1942. *Juvenile Delinquency and Urban Areas: A Study of Rates of Delinquents in Relation to Differential Characteristics of Local Communities in American Cities*. Chicago: University of Chicago Press.

Squires, Gregory D., and Charis E. Kubrin. 2006. *Privileged Places: Race, Residence, and the Structure of Opportunity*. Boulder, CO: Lynne Rienner.

Stark, Andrew. 1998. "America, the Gated?" *Wilson Quarterly* 22(1): 58–79.

Vesselinov, Elena. 2008. "Members Only: Gated Communities and Residential Segregation in the Metropolitan United States." *Sociological Forum* 23(3): 536–555.

Vesselinov, Elena. 2010. "Gated Communities in the United States: From Case Studies to Systematic Evidence." *Sociology Compass* 4(11): 989–998.

Vesselinov, Elena. 2012. "Segregation by Design: Mechanisms of Selection of Latinos and Whites into Gated Communities." *Urban Affairs Review* 48(3): 417–454.

Vesselinov, Elena, Matthew Cazzesus, and William Falk. 2007. "Gated Communities and Spatial Inequality." *Journal of Urban Affairs* 29(2): 109–127.

Vesselinov, Elena, and Renaud Le Goix. 2012. "From Picket Fences to Iron Gates: Suburbanization and Gated Communities in Phoenix, Las Vegas, and Seattle." *GeoJournal* 77: 203–222.

Wilson-Doenges, Georjeanna. 2000. "An Exploration of Sense of Community and Fear of Crime in Gated Communities." *Environment and Behavior* 32(5): 597–611.

Wo, James C., John R. Hipp, and Adam Boessen. 2016. "Voluntary Organizations and Neighborhood Crime: A Dynamic Perspective." *Criminology* 54(2): 212–241.

CHAPTER 19

EGOHOODS

Capturing Change in Spatial Crime Patterns

JOHN R. HIPP AND CHRISTOPHER J. BATES

19.1 Introduction

Environmental criminology is rooted in the investigation of environmental design to reduce criminal opportunity at places (see Jeffery 1971; Newman 1972). The earliest geographic studies of the distribution of crime focused on macro ecological units and the social correlates of high crime concentration (Guerry 1833; Quételet 1842). Early 20th-century research sought to explain crime concentration in neighborhoods through concepts such as social disorganization (Park, Burgess, and McKenzie 1984 [1925]; Shaw and McKay 1942). However, in the late 20th century, Sherman, Gartin, and Buerger (1989) revealed that larger ecological units of space mask substantial variation in crime concentration across space. Crime concentrates not just in specific geographic areas, but in particular locations (Sherman, Gartin, and Buerger 1989). There is now burgeoning literature focused on crime concentration at places and microgeographic units, such as street segments (Weisburd et al. 2016). However, crime opportunities at a particular place cannot be separated from the surrounding ecological context of both the built and social environment (see Eck and Weisburd 1995). High crime does not just concentrate at a particular location, but spills over to nearby areas (Bernasco, Block, and Ruiter 2013; Roncek and Maier 1991). Similarly, efforts to reduce crime concentration have beneficial effects for surrounding blocks (Telep et al. 2014). Crime opportunities not only occur at places where people congregate, but also during the substantial time individuals spend in transit (Brantingham and Brantingham 1993). People not only form perceptions of, and attachment to, individual places, but also perceptions of their surrounding space (Aitken and Prosser 1990). Researchers need to carefully consider spatial units of analysis that capture both the importance of place and space. Furthermore, neighborhood boundaries remain elusive, because people contextualize space in terms of their own neighborhoods. A useful analysis of the crime event must consider three analytical levels of space: the micro, meso and macro (Brantingham and Brantingham 1981).

Virtually all research focusing on the ecological distribution of crime must start with determining an appropriate geographic unit (Brantingham and Brantingham 1981). Researchers have employed a wide range of possible units: ranging from macro units such as cities, counties, or even standard metropolitan statistical areas (SMSAs) in the 1980s (Messner and Blau 1987; Miethe, Stafford, and Sloane 1990) to meso-level units such as neighborhoods, census tracts, or zip codes (Hipp 2011; Rountree and Land 1996), to microgeographic units such as blocks, street segments, or facilities (Bernasco and Block 2011; Eck, Clarke, and Guerette 2007; Groff, Weisburd, and Yang 2010). Early research into the concentration of crime and space was constrained by technological and data limitations that dictated the geographic units of analysis (see Weisburd, Bruinsma, and Bernasco 2009 for a review). Recent advances in computing allow researchers to study environments at a more micro resolution over both time and space. Researchers can now account for spatial autocorrelation and address the modifiable areal unit problem (see Andresen in this volume; see Rengert and Lockwood 2009 for a review; Weisburd, Bruinsma, and Bernasco 2009). Despite many advances in understanding the distribution of crime in space, the concept of an ecological boundary has remained ever present in the neighborhood and place-based research. However, the insights of crime pattern theory actually caution against the use of absolute ecological units given that both offenders and victims cross multiple neighborhood boundaries during their daily activities (Brantingham and Brantingham 1993). For a crime event to occur, the activity space of both offenders and victims must overlap. Despite computational advances, it is currently infeasible to map the daily travel patterns of a population.

While the ecological unit in the study of environmental criminology has primarily shifted from meso administrative units to micro street segments, an essential feature of virtually all of these ecological units is that they are nonoverlapping. This is perhaps not surprising given that people often think of geographic units regarding their representation on a map in which we can draw boundaries between units. People typically think in terms of "their own" unit: their own neighborhood, their own city, their own county, or what is familiar to them.

In contrast to this vast body of research, Hipp and Boessen (2013) proposed a radically different conception of ecological space, which they termed *egohoods*. They argued that traditional, nonoverlapping units do not match the social and ecological processes they seek to explain. There is a spatial component to these processes that previous work using independent spatial units has not fully captured. Thus, their solution to this problem included constructing spatially dependent and overlapping units. Hipp and Boessen (2013) pointed out that residents do not conduct their daily activities only in their own "neighborhood" as defined by researchers, but rather most activity can be characterized by a distance decay function around a person's home (Block and Bernasco 2009; Koppen and Keijser 1997). Rather than measuring these activities using independent units, Hipp and Boessen (2013) recognized that a distance decay function around a person's home more closely captures the reality of daily routine activities and travel.

An egohood consists of a small unit at its center (e.g., a census block) and a buffer around it of a size defined by the researcher. The buffer distance around the block represents the distance decay function to approximate an individual's daily routine where they overlap and travel across neighborhood boundaries. The actual size of this area is an empirical question. For example, Hipp and Boessen (2013) test several different radii lengths: one mile, half mile, quarter mile, and so on. An example of egohoods is shown in Figure 19.1, which displays the half-mile egohoods of three census blocks. Thus, one egohood is constituted by the blue dot indicating the centroid of the block and the blue circle indicating the buffer with a half-mile radius around this block. Another egohood is the red dot indicating the centroid of an adjacent block, and the red circle indicates the half-mile buffer around this. The green dot and circle constitute yet another egohood. Note that these three egohoods overlap to varying extents. And blocks that are closer together overlap to a greater extent. Consequently, each block in the area will have a buffer around it that appears to provide its own unique egohood. But, importantly, each block is also contained in many other egohoods: for example, the block with the red dot is contained within its own egohood, as well as the blue and green egohoods (as well as the egohood of every other block in the red buffer). This is something that residents are typically not aware of, given our typical egocentric focus.

Egohoods account for both crime opportunities and ecological context simultaneously within microcommunities (e.g., a census block) and their surrounding neighborhood areas (e.g., buffer area). Compared to territorial neighborhoods, such as a census tract, ego-centered neighborhoods are more suitable for capturing exposure to environmental risk (Chaix et al. 2009). Therefore, rather than sharp delineation of administrative boundaries, egohoods represent the fuzzy delineation of neighborhoods as experienced through individual travel between places.

In this chapter, we motivate the use of egohoods regarding the three features of routine activities theory: suitable targets, motivated offenders, and capable guardians (Cohen and Felson 1979). We discuss the spatial patterns of these three concepts and how egohoods as a geographic unit are well suited to capture their dynamic processes. Further, we also extend the literature on egohoods by considering them in a longitudinal framework. That is, what are the consequences of sociodemographic and business pattern changes in egohoods for the distribution of crime? A longitudinal analysis of egohoods captures the shift in crime opportunities over time, as land use changes over time are not only dictated by a particular place but also the surrounding area. Given that offenders' awareness space may not change rapidly due to a changing environment, this allows us to assess whether these sociodemographic changes result in changing crime rates during the same decade. Does the change in egohoods have similar implications for crime as does the change in mesounits such as neighborhoods, or microunits such as street segments? We provide an empirical examination of these questions using data from the city of Los Angeles from 2000 to 2010 of robbery and burglary events.

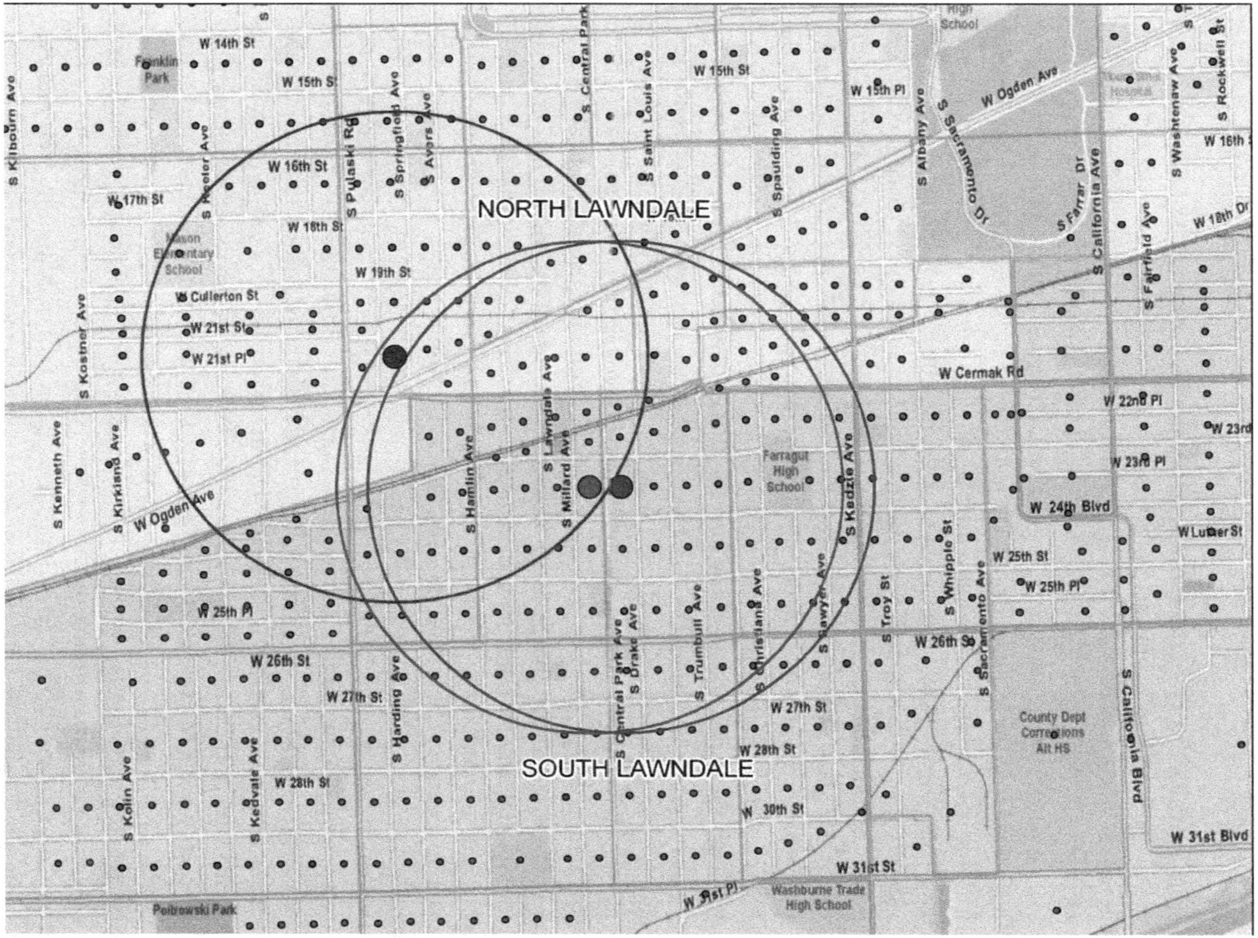

FIGURE 19.1 Map of three blocks and the half-mile buffer surrounding each that constitutes its egohood

19.2 Literature Review

19.2.1 Why Egohoods

Routine activities theory proposes that crime events are a function of the spatial and temporal confluence of a motivated offender, a suitable target, and the lack of capable guardians (Cohen and Felson 1979). This theory does not make specific predictions about who will offend, why some people or objects are more likely to be targeted, or why only some people might act as capable guardians. However, this theory is useful in providing insight into the ingredients that are necessary to observe a crime event. Routine activity theory examines how environmental changes over time affect the crime rate trends. Following the original work of Cohen and Felson (Cohen and Felson 1979) routine activity theory was expanded to explain crime concentration in space as offenders, guardians, and suitable targets converge. This theory has been used to explain the crime concentration at specific places, or "risky facilities," such as bars and motels (Eck, Clarke, and Guerette 2007; Sherman, Gartin, and Buerger 1989) while often de-emphasizing the surrounding ecological context of these sites.

Although these places may show how the three elements of crime converge, as a consequence of this focus on the crime event, empirical research often does not adequately consider the role of the surrounding context of the risky facility. The broader neighborhood of a place is fundamental for understanding the genesis of crime opportunities (Deryol et al. 2016). Environmental criminologists theoretically recognize that risk and protective factors for crime opportunity are conditional upon the environmental context (Wilcox, Gialopsos, and Land 2013). Thus, whereas a body of research focuses on nearby spatial spillover effects from nearby blocks, or how offenders can target adjacent blocks (Bernasco, Block, and Ruiter 2013), this approach does not ask whether the context of a risky facility impacts the level of crime. Thus, there are only occasional empirical exceptions that explore how the area surrounding the microgeographic unit might moderate the impact of crime attractors (Boessen and Hipp 2015; Groff and Lockwood 2014; Kubrin and Hipp 2016). The conjunctive analysis of place offers a description of the environmental context of a crime event, such as why the same facilities in different environmental contexts have different crime risks (Deryol et al. 2016; Miethe, Hart, and Regoeczi 2008; Newton and Hirschfield 2009). Nonetheless, these approaches differ in that they consider how the nearby area "acts upon" the unit at the center, whereas the egohood approach measures the buffer area as a unit rather than assuming the buffer affects the center unit. Although this may seem like an arcane distinction, Hipp and Boessen (2013) showed in their analyses that whereas distributional measures such as income inequality and racial/ethnic heterogeneity demonstrated robust positive relationships with crime within egohoods, no such relationship was detected in the approach assuming the buffer "acts upon" the unit at the center.

Furthermore, using insights from routine activities highlights that different ecological research traditions tend to focus on various components of this equation, while excluding other elements. For example, crime and place research of microgeographies such as facilities focuses primarily on capable guardians, such as place managers (Madensen and Eck 2008). On the other hand, the neighborhood and crime research at the meso level strongly focuses on the possible presence of capable guardians, through resident's perceptions of informal social control.

Similar to guardianship, ecological traditions on motivated offenders also differ. On the one hand, literature has addressed offender location choice in examining the features of suitable targets and lack of guardians that offenders consider when they commit crime (e.g., Bernasco and Block 2011). Nonetheless, although the theoretical importance of offenders is well known, the location and mobility of motivated offenders typically is not explicitly accounted for in most ecological research of crime rates at specific locations or neighborhoods. Earlier work has discussed the idea that certain characteristics of neighborhoods foster more offenders (Shaw and McKay 1942). Notably, some research highlighted how burglary rates in nearby neighborhoods are influenced by the number of offenders in neighborhoods (Bernasco and Luykx 2003). Some recent work has described an approach that attempts to explicitly account for the location and possible mobility of offenders given the insight that both residents and offenders tend to have activity spaces nearer rather than farther from their residences (Hipp 2016b). Here, egohoods are used as a proxy measure to capture the confluence of spatial patterns of offenders, guardians, and targets.

Considering motivated offenders may be particularly insightful, as their spatial patterns pose a significant challenge for existing research relying solely on micro and meso geographic units. We next consider the three elements, motivated offenders, suitable targets, and capable guardians of a crime event in the context of egohoods.

19.2.2 Motivated Offenders

The existence of offenders and their inherently spatial activity poses a particular challenge to existing research explaining neighborhood crime rates using nonoverlapping geographic units. For example, the concentration of potential offenders in geographic space could account for high-crime neighborhoods. However, a high-crime neighborhood does not require a large number of offenders, but only a few prolific offenders. This inherent spatiality of offenders poses a problem for microgeographic place-based research, as this research typically only focuses on the presence of attractive targets, and rarely focuses on the importance of nearby motivated offenders.

The spatial patterns of offenders pose a problem for meso-level neighborhood research that either implicitly ignores the location of offenders, or else assumes that offenders live in the neighborhood of interest. This latter assumption is problematic given the evidence of how offenders typically travel to crime events. Offenders may not travel far if opportunities are available (Bernasco and Luykx 2003), but this trip almost certainly takes them outside their own "neighborhood" quite frequently. The journey-to-crime literature has consistently shown that offender travel behavior exhibits a distance decay in which offenses are more likely to occur near the residence, but a smaller number of offenses occur at longer distances (Rossmo 1999; Wiles and Costello 2000; see Bernasco and Rossmo in this volume). The evidence shows that the average distance offenders travel is nontrivial, ranging up to averages of over three miles (Hodgkinsoi and Tilley 2007; Tita and Griffiths 2005). And offenders typically travel even farther to property crime events (Bichler, Christie-Merrall, and Sechrest 2011; Vandeviver 2013). White (1932) found the average distance to violent events was 0.83 miles but the average distance to property crimes was double that at 1.73 miles. The implication for many micro and meso ecological studies of crime is that the role of offenders is implicitly unaccounted for.

However, all individuals, including offenders, travel outside their home to conduct their routine activities, such as going to work, running errands, and leisure (Brantingham and Brantingham 2008). Offenders can increase their knowledge of criminal opportunities as they travel throughout their normal activity space and through interactions with other potential offenders (Brantingham and Brantingham 2008). Additionally, distance to crime is dependent on aggregate crime opportunities, as rural offenders travel further to crime events than urban and suburban offenders (O'Leary 2011). An advantage of egohoods is that they are explicitly spatial, and therefore, they are well suited to account for the activity space and travel patterns of offenders. Overlapping neighborhood boundaries account for the increases in motivated offenders as they coalesce toward a shared activity node and the decay in motivated offenders in the surrounding area where distribution around activity nodes are sparse. By not imposing specific boundaries on the measurement of the social world, the egohood approach sidesteps this potential problem. What is needed is a careful consideration of the potential area that offenders might typically travel to for crime. Then, measuring the number of offenders in a proper-sized egohood would capture this potential risk for crime in the area.

Offenders can also be attracted to locations because of crime opportunities in the neighborhood. "Crime attractors" are places that disproportionately attract offenders to take advantages of crime opportunities (Brantingham and Brantingham 1995). This is distinguished from crime generators, which are locations with offending opportunities simply because of the large confluence of offenders and targets, but do not disproportionately attract offenders. A crime attractor situated in a neighborhood with a high number of potential offenders should experience more crime events than a crime attractor located in a community with a small number of potential offenders. Whereas a liquor store may act as a crime attractor, there is little reason to assume that a liquor store surrounded by a middle-class neighborhood would attract the same amount of crime as one surrounded by disadvantaged neighborhoods (see Bottoms in this volume). Additionally, crime attractors near each other should have similar levels of crime, as offender population characteristics would be similar (Eck, Clarke, and Guerette 2007). However, potential crime attractors can experience varying numbers of crime events but can all be located in high-crime areas (Schmerler et al. 2009). Overlapping neighborhood boundaries account for the ways crime attractors are nested within neighborhoods and the travel patterns of the offender population.

19.2.3 Capable Guardians

Felson and Cohen (1980) describe guardianship as the supervision of people or property that prevents criminal action from occurring (see Felson in this volume). Guardianship is both spatial and temporal (Felson and Cohen 1980) and takes on many different forms. Guardianship includes informal agents (i.e., residents), semiformal agents (i.e., place managers), formal agents (i.e., police), or a combination of informal, semiformal, and formal (i.e., CCTV). Guardianship operates differently at different geographic scales and different characteristics of a place (i.e., residential versus commercial) (Hollis, Felson, and Welsh 2013). Whereas some "physical guardianship" research has focused on guardianship action at very micro scales such as a "risky facilities" (Eck, Clarke, and Guerette 2007), much of the social cohesion, neighborhoods, and crime research focuses on larger, meso-level units such as neighborhoods.

Physical guardianship at micro scale includes territorial boundaries, which delineate private space and public space, and accessibility that prevent access to private space (Taylor and Gottfredson 1986). For example, fences can prevent accessibility to a house, whereas manicured lawns are symbolic territorial boundaries that the property is occupied and maintained. Offenders assess territoriality at different units of space, including the neighborhood level, the street block level, and individual level (Brown and Altman 1983). Newman (1972) classified spaces as private, semiprivate, semipublic, and public, with management responsibilities varying for each classification. For example, a home is a private location and a vacant lot can be thought of semipublic space.

"Crime enablers" are locations where "place managers" have allowed crime to occur by not enhancing target protection (Eck, Clarke, and Guerette 2007). Place managers can play an important role in preventing crime concentration at place (Madensen and Eck 2008; see Madensen and Eck in this volume). However, this assumes place managers have an explicit commitment to a place, which may not be reasonable given that the surrounding area is almost certainly impactful for residents on a particular block (Rengert and Lockwood 2009). Additionally, employees serve as place managers that care for places and discourage crime (Eck 1994; Felson 1995). However, employees must be active place managers to overcome the potential number of crime opportunities (Eck 1994). There is much evidence that larger areas can impact residents' perceptions of cohesion beyond just their local block (Boessen et al. 2014; Forrest and Kearns 2001; Hipp and Perrin 2006).

Additionally, offenders target areas in which residential ties are weak and there is a lack of social cohesion (Baudains, Braithwaite, and Johnson 2013; Bernasco and Nieuwbeerta 2005; Johnson and Summers 2015; see Wilcox and Swartz in this volume). Research assessing whether the level of collective efficacy is associated with lower crime rates typically uses neighborhoods with a population of at least 4,000 (Bruinsma et al. 2013), or even 8,000 (Sampson, Raudenbush, and Earls 1997). A study on residents nested in neighborhoods found that residents with more social network ties in the neighborhood report higher perceptions of collective efficacy (Wickes et al. 2013). A study of residents in neighborhoods in the Netherlands tested the relationship between perceptions of responsibility for the neighborhood, and actual behavior, with changes in crime longitudinally (Steenbeek and Hipp 2011). A study of residents in Brisbane neighborhoods focused on the actual provision of informal social control behavior in response to observed problems and found that such behavior was most likely to occur in neighborhoods with a higher density of social ties (Wickes et al. 2013). A longitudinal study in rural North Carolina towns found that collective efficacy was only associated with lower disorder at the next time point when it was accompanied by high cohesion in the neighborhood in a multiplicative function (Hipp 2016a).

This literature often measures various structural characteristics of neighborhoods in hopes of capturing the capability for informal social control action, which can increase guardianship (Bellair 2000; Sampson and Groves 1989). But a challenge for this literature is the assumption that these larger nonoverlapping units are distinct units that are appropriate to measure. If, in fact, the area that captures residents' sense of cohesion and ability to provide guardianship does not match these units, then such studies will not appropriately capture this guardianship potential (Hipp 2007; Taylor 1997).

Furthermore, if the proper geographic unit at which guardianship potential is fostered is a much smaller microgeographic unit, then these meso-level measures will not capture guardianship, conducted by place managers. Places interact with their surrounding environment, and studies demonstrate that particular "risky" facilities can spill over crime to the nearby area. Informal social control, a neighborhood measure, could prevent places from becoming crime attractors, but one crime attractor also has the ability to break down informal social control in the area.

The physical design of places and neighborhoods may also hinder guardianship and contribute to residents' ability to generate informal social control. People are constrained in their ability to move throughout neighborhoods based on the street network and by physical barriers. There is evidence that neighborhoods, street segments (Johnson and Bowers 2010), and individual homes (Armitage 2007) that offer greater accessibility are at greater risk of victimization. The ability of social cohesion to deter crime may be less effective on certain types of streets (Reynald 2011; Weisburd, Groff, and Yang 2012).

19.2.4 Suitable Targets

Compared to motivated offenders and capable guardians, the distribution of suitable targets is more closely concentrated throughout space. Homes in a high-income neighborhood have more valuables than homes in low-income areas. Compared to residential neighborhoods, businesses districts have increased suitable targets for property crime, while also increasing likelihood of physical victimization through increased interactions of offenders and victims.

Even within neighborhoods, individual places can be suitable targets. Crime generators provide a concentration of times and places of gathering for offenders and targets that are not particularly motivated to commit a crime, but they provide opportunities for crime (Brantingham and Brantingham 1993). Neighborhood exposure to certain types of facilities, like a bar or liquor store, can increase the risk of crime at place (Groff 2013, 2014; Pridemore and Grubesic 2011; Snowden and Pridemore 2014). However, some businesses may reduce the risk to neighboring places of crime, while other types of businesses may increase the crime risk at neighboring businesses (Steenbeek and Hipp 2011). A central business district may have a vibrant nightlife scene with opportunity targets for robbery, yet both informal and formal guardianship through the large number of people (Wilcox, Madensen, and Tillyer 2007). However, the abundance of potential targets may not act as a major influence on the decision-making of the offender (Johnson and Summers 2015). Suitable targets are attractive to offenders not only because of their potential value, but must also offer low risk and high reward. Offenders' familiarity with the crime type and neighborhood alter the probability of discovering suitable targets. Their previous experiences with committing crime and their knowledge of specific neighborhoods affect the probability that they will discover crime opportunities, or suitable targets elsewhere. Most research on suitable targets focuses on the micro unit and excludes the broader context. Bernasco and Block (2011) demonstrated that census tracts with more crime attractors, crime generators, and illegal markets had more robberies than census tracts without them.

The awareness of suitable targets in space is dependent on the ecological context of opportunity areas with which the offender is familiar. Offenders choose to commit crime in areas that are similar to their home and activity space (Lammers et al. 2015). For example, burglars may be familiar with how to pick locks but not how to disarm alarm systems. Houses in high-income areas hardened by security alarms systems are not suitable targets, despite the potential valuables. Target hardening aims to increase the risk and lower the reward of the crime event. However, target hardening at individual units does not mean targets are hardened collectively throughout neighborhood (Wilcox, Madensen, and Tillyer 2007). This means that although one crime opportunity has been diminished, suitable targets throughout the neighborhood as a whole may attract motivated offenders.

Once a crime event is successfully carried out at a specific location, this location becomes a suitable target for a future crime event (Farrell, Phillips, and Pease 1995; Johnson and Bowers 2004). Research has shown that revictimization may be a result of both previous victimization and different levels of target attractiveness (Johnson, Lab, and Bowers 2008). High-crime and low-crime neighborhoods may have amounts of suitable targets that are similar to amounts in neighborhoods with no crime. However, suitable targets in high-crime neighborhoods frequently experience repeated victimization. Egohoods thus attempt to account for the nearby area, as nearby locations might also have attractive targets, which can reduce the frequency that any individual target within a specific neighborhood experiences crime events.

19.2.5 Specific Propositions

Environmental criminology theorizes the concentration of crime opportunities in microgeographies (e.g., facilities) and microcommnunities (e.g., street segments). However, places cannot be extracted from the contextual space from which they are located. Egohoods, a novel meso geographic conception, embeds places (e.g., census blocks) within their surrounding space with overlapping buffers. Overlapping neighborhood boundaries not only solve issues of edge effects commonly observed in administrative aerial units, but, additionally, egohoods also account for the space an individual moves through during daily routines. The present study will explore the extent to which egohoods can capture spatial shifts in offenders, guardians, and targets that lead to consequences for crime concentration.

Given the preceding discussion of how egohoods might proxy for the spatial patterning of offenders, targets, and guardians, we consider here four propositions of the consequences of sociodemographic change in egohoods for changes in crime. First, we expect that the change in crime attractors (measured here as bars, liquor stores, vacant units, and vacant lots) will have a short-term positive relationship with changes in crime. Second, we expect that the change in crime generators (measured here as retail employees and food employees) will have a short-term positive relationship with crime, but also a long-term positive relationship given that they presumably shape general activity patterns. Third, the presence of more guardians in an egohood (measured here as homeowners) will have a short-term and long-term negative relationship with changes in crime. Fourth, the hypothesized reduction in guardians due to mixing in an area (measured here as racial/ethnic heterogeneity and income inequality) will have a long-term positive relationship with crime, but not a short-term relationship given that the hypothesized impact on resident social networks arguably operates at a slower pace. We next describe the data.

19.3 Data and Methods

19.3.1 Data

For this study, we combined data from the Los Angeles Police Department, the US census in 2000, the American Community Survey five-year estimates in 2008–2012, the Longitudinal Employer Household Dynamics (LEHD) data set, business data from Reference USA (Infogroup 2015) and land use data from the Southern California Association of Governments (SCAG).

19.3.2 Constructing Egohoods

The process for constructing all egohoods variables is similar. Some of the measures we use are available for census block aggregations, the focal units used to construct egohoods. A "block" is the smallest aggregation of data from the US census, and is a small area typically surrounded by four street segments (in Southern California they have an average of about 70 residents). For measures that are in larger units (e.g., block groups) we used synthetic estimation for ecological inference to impute the larger unit values to the blocks within the larger unit (for an example of this approach, see Boessen and Hipp 2015). The Census Bureau defines "block groups" to have an average of about 1,400 residents. To construct our egohood measures, first, we determine the blocks that are within a particular egohood using ArcGIS 9.3 by drawing a radius of a particular distance around every set of block centroids (we used quarter-mile and half-mile buffers). Any census block that is within, or intersects with, the buffer is considered part of the egohood. We only include crime and census information from the blocks in Los Angeles; thus egohoods that extend across the city boundary will not include information from blocks outside the city. While this may introduce edge effects at the city boundary, Hipp and Boessen (2013) found that a similar decision did not impact their cross-sectional results. We then summed the information from the blocks within the buffer. For example, to compute the percent Latino in a egohood we summed up the number of Latinos in all blocks in the buffer and divided this by the sum of the population in all blocks in the buffer.

19.3.3 Dependent Variables

The outcome variables are changes in crime rates over the 2000 to 2010 decade. The data come from crime reports reported to the police department. We focused on two types of crime in this study: robberies and burglaries. We therefore classified crime events into these two Uniform Crime Report (UCR) crime types. We used crime data from three adjacent years at the beginning and end of the decade to minimize yearly fluctuations. Thus, we combined 2000–2002 data for the beginning time point, and 2009–2011 for the last time point. These are each divided by the population and multiplied by 10,000 to convert them to a rate per 10,000 persons, and then log transformed. The outcome variable then is the difference between these two measures.

19.3.4 Independent Variables

We constructed several sociodemographic measures based on data from the US Census Bureau that are aggregated to the egohood in 2000, and similar measures capturing the change in the egohood from 2000 to 2010. We measure the economic resources of the egohood with the *average household income*, and capture nonlinear effects with a quadratic version of this variable. To measure average income, we first assigned household incomes to the midpoint of their reported range (given that the Census Bureau only reports household incomes in particular ranges), and then computed the average income for residents in the egohood from this information. We captured *income inequality* by computing the standard deviation of the logged household income (Hipp and Boessen 2013). This again used the information on the number of households at the midpoints of the income bins, logged these values, multiplied them by the number of observations in each bin to get the logged incomes of these households, computed the mean logged income, and then computed the standard deviation of the incomes in an egohood based on these values.

We measured the racial/ethnic composition of the egohood with measures of *percent black*, *percent Latino*, and *percent Asian*. We constructed a measure of *racial/ethnic heterogeneity* as a Herfindahl index of five racial/ethnic groupings (white, African-American, Latino, Asian, and other races). To account for the presence of vacant units that might provide criminal opportunities, we computed the *percent vacant units*. Vacant units are structures that are not currently occupied by residents that represent loss of potential guardianship as well as an increase in potential criminal opportunity (Jones and Pridemore 2014; Spelman 1993). Given that homeowners may provide more guardianship, we computed a measure of the *percent owners*. Given that the presence of more residents nearby may impact the level of crime, we computed the *logged population* of the egohood; note that the constant areal size of egohoods implies that this is implicitly a population density measure.

Given that the presence of certain types of establishments might be attractive targets, we measured this by constructing measures of the number of employees in the area of certain types of firms. Violence in neighborhoods can increase based on shifts in business activity (Greenbaum and Tita 2004). We use employees rather than establishment counts, as a larger number of employees arguably acts as a proxy for more customers, and hence more people in the area. We constructed a measure of the number of *retail employees* in the area based on two-digit North American Industry Classification System (NAICS) codes (44-45) and data from the LEHD for 2002 and 2010. We also constructed a measure of the number of *food service employees* based on two-digit NAICS code (72) from the LEHD. For each of these measures of employees in the egohood we also constructed quadratic variables to account for nonlinearities, given that the presence of persons in these establishments is a complicated process that increases the number of targets, but also increases the number of potential guardians. Therefore, the impact on crime may be nonlinear. We also constructed a measure of the *total employees* in an area based on LEHD data, to capture the general daytime population in an area; note that total employees includes firms that do not attract customers, such as white-collar offices, industrial jobs, and so on. This also may show a nonlinear effect, so we also constructed a quadratic measure.

And certain types of establishments are posited to be unambiguously crime attractors; two such types of establishments are *liquor stores* and *bars* (Groff 2014; Roncek and Maier 1991). Alcohol establishments and crime cluster together, as they not only spatially attract both potential offenders and victims, they also can increase offender motivation and increase victim vulnerability (Gorman et al. 2001; Groff 2014; Newton and Hirschfield 2009; Pridemore and Grubesic 2013). On-premise (e.g., bars) or off-premise alcohol establishments (e.g., liquor stores) have differing effects on specific crime types

Table 19.1 Summary Statistics for Variables Used in Analyses

	2000 variables		Change 2000–2010	
	Mean	SD	Mean	SD
¼-mile egohoods				
Robbery rate, logged	3.16	1.46	−0.61	0.93
Burglary rate, logged	4.16	1.01	−0.34	0.75
½-mile egohoods				
Robbery rate, logged	3.33	1.09	−0.63	0.57
Burglary rate, logged	4.18	0.68	−0.36	0.51
¼-mile egohoods				
Percent vacant lots	3.42	11.11	0.09	18.33
Total employees (in 1,000s)	0.50	1.86	0.46	3.22
Retail employees (in 100s)	0.48	1.30	0.30	1.92
Food service employees (in 100s)	0.36	0.96	0.41	1.81
Bar employees (in 100s)	0.03	0.16	0.01	0.15
Liquor store employees (in 100s)	0.01	0.03	0.00	0.03
Average household income (logged)	3.52	0.68	0.26	0.56
Income inequality	0.89	0.16	0.01	0.16
Percent Asian	9.48	11.01	0.96	6.25
Percent black	10.73	17.76	−1.46	6.45
Percent Latino	39.77	29.48	2.21	10.84
Racial/ethnic heterogeneity	0.45	0.18	0.01	0.11
Percent owners	45.25	28.73	−0.57	13.78
Percent vacant units	4.73	4.99	1.79	7.71
Logged population	7.28	1.44	0.21	1.04
½-mile egohoods				
Percent vacant lots	4.99	12.17	−1.48	19.09
Total employees (in 1,000s)	2.02	4.20	2.11	8.85
Retail employees (in 100s)	1.99	3.28	1.39	4.45
Food service employees (in 100s)	1.48	2.45	1.72	4.84
Bar employees (in 100s)	0.11	0.39	0.03	0.33
Liquor store employees (in 100s)	0.05	0.08	0.00	0.07
Average household income (logged)	3.55	0.53	0.29	0.32
Income inequality	0.92	0.11	0.00	0.11
Percent Asian	9.66	9.67	1.09	3.93
Percent black	10.88	16.86	−1.59	4.35
Percent Latino	41.28	27.87	2.26	7.71
Racial/ethnic heterogeneity	0.48	0.16	0.01	0.08
Percent owners	43.98	25.17	−0.49	8.45
Percent vacant units	4.83	3.56	1.70	4.59
Logged population	8.81	1.10	0.23	0.85

$N = 29{,}972$ egohoods

(e.g., robbery versus aggravated assault) in the surrounding area (Toomey et al. 2012). We therefore included measures of the number of employees of each of these types of firms for 2000 and 2010 based on data from Reference-USA historical data.

Finally, given that some have posited that vacant parcels might affect the level of crime in a location (Garvin, Cannuscio, and Branas 2013), we computed the percentage of land in *vacant lots* based on parcel data from SCAG. Note that whereas a vacant *unit* is a household that is standing empty, a vacant *lot* is a land parcel that has no structure on it, which can have different impacts on crime (Raleigh and Galster 2015). Vacant lots lack active guardians (Kurtz, Koons, and Taylor 1998), and they can attract crime through encouraging drug sales or loitering. Vacant lots along with social disorganization characteristics were correlated with robbery on street block faces (Smith, Frazee, and Davison 2000). The summary statistics for the variables used in the analyses are presented in Table 19.1.

19.3.5 Analytic Strategy

The outcome variable is the difference in the crime rates between 2010 and 2000. Given that this is a continuous measure with a normal distribution, we used ordinary least squares regression. We included covariates that capture the amount of change in the egohoods: this allows us to assess the relationship between changes in the characteristics of egohoods and the change in levels of crime over the decade, or *short-term* impacts. In addition, we include measures of the level of these variables at the beginning of the decade: this allows us to assess the *long-term* impacts of these measures on change in crime over the decade. We thus estimated four models: two with robbery as the outcome (using quarter-mile egohoods, then half-mile egohoods), and two with burglary as the outcome (and the two different-sized egohoods).

19.4 Results

We begin by focusing on the measures capturing the change in the possible number of targets in an egohood. In Table 19.2, we find that an increase in the number of vacant lots in the egohood over the decade is associated with increasing levels of both robbery and burglary over the decade. We obtain this same result for both quarter-mile and half-mile egohoods, and in all cases the nonlinear effect when plotted shows a positive relationship that slows for the largest changes in the percentage of vacant lots. At the same time there is modest evidence that egohoods with more vacant lots at the beginning of the decade experience a slower crime appreciation than other egohoods. The size of this effect is similar to that of the change measure.[1] Thus, the egohood that will experience the largest increase in robberies or burglaries is one with relatively few vacant lots at the beginning of the decade but a large increase in vacant lots during the decade.

Table 19.2 Models Predicting Change in Robbery and Burglary Rate in Quarter-Mile and Half-Mile Egohoods in Los Angeles from 2000 to 2010

	Robbery		Burglary	
	1/4-mile egohoods	1/2-mile egohoods	1/4-mile egohoods	1/2-mile egohoods
Logged crime rate in 2000	−0.506** −(106.59)	−0.456** −(120.15)	−0.532** −(113.28)	−0.522** −(126.26)
Change variables				
Percent vacant lots	0.585** (7.78)	0.368** (9.52)	0.060 (1.14)	0.135** (4.69)
Percent vacant lots squared	−0.636** −(6.72)	−0.372** −(7.57)	−0.195** −(3.01)	−0.266** −(7.48)
Percent vacant units	0.941** (10.50)	0.708** (6.57)	0.718** (8.25)	0.715** (10.89)
Percent vacant units squared		2.108** (9.83)	0.750** (5.82)	
Bar employees	0.000 (0.00)	0.049** (3.95)	0.071* (2.09)	0.021* (2.09)
Liquor store employees	−1.010** −(5.38)	−0.442** −(8.45)	−0.055 −(0.39)	−0.243** −(5.81)
Retail employees	0.066** (15.82)	0.011** (9.81)	0.023** (7.37)	0.007** (8.32)
Retail employees squared	−0.002** −(6.68)	0.000** −(3.41)	−0.001** −(3.16)	0.000** −(4.92)
Food service employees	0.074** (14.14)	0.033** (23.79)	0.029** (7.33)	0.009** (8.05)
Food service employees squared	−0.003** −(11.96)	−0.001** −(21.03)	−0.002** −(11.12)	0.000** −(13.67)
Total employees	−0.020** −(6.93)	−0.010** −(11.85)	−0.019** −(8.73)	−0.006** −(9.73)
Total employees squared	0.000** (5.46)	0.000** (9.62)	0.000** (3.56)	0.000** (5.44)
Logged population	−0.033** −(5.90)	−0.032** −(7.53)	−0.008† −(1.94)	0.004 (1.53)
Logged population squared		0.010** (8.08)		

(continued)

Table 19.2 Continued

	Robbery		Burglary	
	1/4-mile egohoods	1/2-mile egohoods	1/4-mile egohoods	1/2-mile egohoods
Percent owners	−0.031 −(0.72)	−0.073† −(1.83)	0.454** (13.78)	0.021 (0.67)
Percent owners squared		−0.474** −(6.55)	−0.342** −(7.61)	
Average household income	−0.139** −(5.71)	−0.136** −(7.75)	0.107** (5.33)	0.277** (20.19)
Average household income squared		-0.036** −(5.81)	−0.038** −(5.57)	
Income inequality	0.158** (3.17)	0.017 (0.45)	0.202** (5.30)	−0.021 −(0.71)
Percent Asian	−0.760** −(6.96)	−0.938** −(9.66)	−0.905** −(10.88)	−0.903** −(11.60)
Percent black	−0.105 −(0.96)	0.021 (0.19)	0.716** (8.62)	0.140 (1.64)
Percent Latino	0.294** (4.82)	0.164** (3.41)	−0.222** −(4.77)	−0.667** −(17.36)
Racial/ethnic heterogeneity	2.392 (0.35)	−9.259† −(1.66)	18.051** (3.43)	−0.093 −(0.02)
Level variables in 2000				
Percent vacant lots	−1.225** −(9.03)	−1.005** −(14.34)	−0.781 −(8.59)	−0.463 −(9.36)
Percent vacant lots squared	1.914** (10.03)	1.813** (17.85)		
Percent vacant units	3.123** (15.54)	3.438** (21.17)	0.422 (3.16)	0.375 (4.09)
Percent vacant units squared	−2.064** −(7.33)	−4.903** −(12.83)		
Bar employees	0.073 (1.62)	0.003 (0.22)	0.041 (1.19)	0.015 (1.52)
Liquor store employees	1.564** (8.47)	0.558** (10.82)	0.322 (2.31)	0.461 (11.12)
Retail employees	0.107** (13.53)	0.025** (11.91)	0.025 (4.41)	0.000 (0.21)

Table 19.2 Continued

	Robbery		Burglary	
	1/4-mile egohoods	1/2-mile egohoods	1/4-mile egohoods	1/2-mile egohoods
Retail employees squared	−0.003** −(5.18)	−0.001** −(5.37)	−0.001 −(3.05)	
Food service employees	0.037** (5.82)	0.012** (7.44)	0.025 (5.24)	0.009 (7.67)
Total employees	−0.045** −(6.49)	−0.027** −(12.74)	−0.007 −(2.75)	−0.003 −(3.91)
Total employees squared	0.001* (2.25)	0.000** (6.48)		
Logged population	−0.122** −(19.94)	−0.036** −(8.33)	−0.529 −(24.41)	−0.661 −(44.92)
Logged population squared			0.027 (15.41)	0.032 (31.03)
Percent owners	−0.464** −(6.13)	−0.790** −(14.55)	1.084 (18.30)	0.740 (17.45)
Percent owners squared	0.229** (3.13)	0.884** (17.52)	−0.594 −(10.55)	−0.285 −(7.22)
Average household income	0.257** (4.16)	0.237** (4.20)	0.146 (2.46)	0.376 (9.73)
Average household income squared	−0.099** −(10.47)	−0.104** −(12.53)	−0.039 −(4.51)	−0.049 −(8.25)
Income inequality	−0.143* −(2.20)	0.240** (5.20)	0.176 (3.59)	0.031 (0.84)
Percent Asian	0.050 (0.90)	−0.216** −(5.72)	−0.962 −(22.91)	−0.939 −(31.04)
Percent black	1.117** (27.10)	0.872** (29.37)	0.680 (22.07)	0.721 (30.86)
Percent Latino	0.571** (17.29)	0.380** (16.87)	−0.324 −(13.10)	−0.283 −(15.84)
Racial/ethnic heterogeneity	5.292 (1.44)	5.131* (2.09)	45.493 (16.14)	35.054 (17.70)
Intercept	1.994** (16.38)	1.211** (11.43)	3.721 (30.67)	4.047 (57.82)
R-squared	0.315	0.418	0.399	0.522

Note: ** $p < 01$; * $p <05$; † $p < .10$. T-values in parentheses. $N = 30{,}478$ egohoods. Regression models

The effect of vacant *units* is somewhat different than that for vacant *lots*. An increase in the percentage of vacant units in a quarter-mile egohood is associated with greater increases in robbery and burglary during the decade. This effect is somewhat smaller than that for vacant lots. Instead, it appears the vacant units have a much stronger long-term effect than vacant lots: egohoods with more vacant units at the beginning of the decade experience a much sharper increase in crime over the decade, especially for robberies. Thus, the existence of many vacant units at the beginning appears to attract offenders and thus areas experience larger subsequent increases in crime.

The impact of liquor stores in egohoods also operates on longer-term scale, whereas the effect of bars appears quite weak. Although egohoods with more liquor stores at the beginning of the decade experience larger increases in robbery and burglary over the decade, egohoods that experience an *increase* in liquor store employees during the decade experience a counterintuitive drop in crime during the decade. This would suggest that it is not the immediate placement of a liquor store that results in crime increases, but rather the long-term placement of such establishments. Notably, both of these effects are stronger for robbery (compared to burglary) and for smaller egohoods compared to larger ones. The effect of bar employees was much weaker and present only for half-mile egohoods, as higher numbers of bar employees at the beginning of the decade, or increases in bar employees during the decade, are associated with larger robbery increases for half-mile egohoods. Thus, bar employees only appear to impact robbery for egohoods, and only in the larger egohoods, suggesting a somewhat broader spatial pattern.

We considered retail and food service employees as proxies for crime generators, given that they both attract large numbers of people to an area. Egohoods with increasing numbers of retail or food employees experience larger increases in robberies and burglaries. It is also the case that egohoods with more retail and food employees at the beginning of the decade experience larger increases in robbery and burglary over the decade—although the size of these effects is smaller than the decadal change effect—regardless of the size of the egohood.

We considered total employees to be a proxy for the daytime population in an egohood, whereas the residential population is a proxy for the nighttime population. Both have rather modest effects. Egohoods with more population or total employees at the beginning of the decade also experience a larger decrease in crime during the subsequent decade. This may be capturing the presence of more potential guardians in these egohoods, as discussed by Hipp and Roussell (2013).

Turning to the measures capturing characteristics of the residents living in egohoods, the measure of percent owners is attempting to capture the presence of more guardians. This is another measure that exhibits longer-term effects: egohoods with more owners at the beginning of the decade experience larger decreases in robberies during the subsequent decade. However, there is no such negative effect for burglaries: in fact, egohoods with more owners at the beginning of the decade experience a larger increase in burglaries over the subsequent decade. The short-term effect of egohoods in which the proportion of owners is increasing is similar to the long-term effects, as they result in lower robbery rates but higher burglary rates. This suggests that the presence of owners may be more effective for reducing a violent crime such as robberies than a property crime such as burglaries.

In viewing the economic resources of an egohood, the average income can represent both attractive targets at the high end, and more potential offenders at the low end. The results for average household income are similar to those for percent owners. Egohoods with higher average income, and those experiencing a larger increase in average income during the decade, experience larger decreases in robbery over the subsequent decade, regardless of the size of the egohood. These are very strong effects. However, egohoods with higher increasing average income actually experience modest increases in burglaries over the subsequent decade. Egohoods with higher average income at the beginning of the decade do experience modest decreases in burglaries during the subsequent decade.

Income inequality is positively associated with changes in crime. Egohoods with higher levels of inequality at the beginning of the decade experience larger increases in robberies in half-mile egohoods and burglaries in quarter-mile egohoods. And egohoods that experience an increase in income inequality during the decade simultaneously experience an increase in robberies and burglaries in smaller egohoods. A one-standard-deviation-greater increase in inequality during the decade results in about 3% greater robbery and burglary increases in quarter-mile egohoods.

Finally, we turn to the racial composition measures. The effects of racial/ethnic mixing are generally positive. Egohoods with higher levels of racial/ethnic heterogeneity at the beginning of the decade experience greater increases in burglary. Egohoods that experience a larger increase in racial/ethnic heterogeneity during the decade experience an increase in burglaries in quarter-mile egohoods. Egohoods with a higher percentage of black residents at the beginning of the decade experience larger increases in both robberies and burglaries, regardless of the size of the egohood. However, the presence of black residents appears to be more of a long-term effect, as egohoods with an increase in black residents during the decade only experience a modest simultaneous increase in burglaries. The relationship between Latinos and egohood crime is crime-specific. On the one hand, egohoods with one standard deviation more Latinos at the beginning of the decade experience a 11%–17% greater increase in robberies during the subsequent decade, and egohoods experiencing a large increase in Latinos (one standard deviation) experience a 1%–3% greater increase in robberies during the same decade. On the other hand, egohoods with more Latinos at the beginning of the decade experience an 8%–10% greater decrease in burglaries and those with an influx of Latinos experience a 2%–5% greater decrease in burglaries. Thus, egohoods with more Latinos experience a greater increase in robberies over the decade, but a greater decrease in burglaries, which could capture the possibility that Latinos who are undocumented immigrants may be particularly vulnerable as robbery victims given that they are typically constrained to the cash economy (Hipp, Tita, and Boggess 2009). Finally, the presence, or influx, of Asians is associated with decreases in crime rates.

19.5 Discussion

This chapter has explored the relationship between the changes in business patterns or sociodemographic characteristics—which represent the changes in potential targets, offenders, and guardians—of egohoods in Los Angeles from 2000 to 2010 and changes in robbery and burglary rates. Given the spatial patterning of offenders and, for some crimes, targets, we have suggested that egohoods are a useful unit of analysis for studying the spatial distribution of crime. We argue that egohoods provide results that likely differ from those of neighborhood analyses using more traditional nonoverlapping units (e.g., tracts) given that egohoods explicitly incorporate these spatial patterns. As evidence, Hipp and Boessen (2013) in cross-sectional analyses found that racial/heterogeneity and income inequality exhibited dramatically stronger relationships with crime than models aggregating to census tracts. Although it was outside our scope here to directly compare our egohood results to those using tracts, we believe there is considerable reason to expect substantial differences in such longitudinal models. The longitudinal analyses allowed us to disentangle short-term effects of changes in egohoods—how the change in sociodemographic characteristics during a decade is related to changes in crime rates during the simultaneous decade—and long-term effects of sociodemographic characteristics at the beginning of the decade on changes in crime rates during the subsequent decade. We order our discussion by focusing on measures that largely capture the presence of targets, offenders, or guardians.

We measured several characteristics that are likely crime attractors, and therefore likely to attract more offenders to the egohood. We found evidence consistent with our proposition that crime attractors would have a short-term positive relationship with burglaries and robberies for bars and vacant lots. It may be that motivated offenders are attracted to bars and vacant lots; however, over time these places may alter the density of targets and guardianship. For example, over time a vacant lot decreases potential suitable targets as residents' awareness of the vacant lot increases. On the other hand, an increase of patrons at a bar leads to an increase in potential guardianship over time. The changes in targets and guardianship from these establishments can lead to potential decreases in the motivated offender in the egohood. However, we did find that two types of crime attractors—vacant units and liquor stores—demonstrated long-term impacts on egohoods. Egohoods with more vacant units and liquor stores experienced larger increases in both robberies and burglaries over the subsequent decade. Previous studies have found that increases in neighborhood vacant units are associated with a rise in property crime, but not associated with a rise in violent crime (Jones and Pridemore 2014; Raleigh and Galster 2015; Williams, Galster, and Verma 2014). The longitudinal impact of the concentration of alcohol establishments and crime within neighborhoods is well documented (Hipp 2010; Livingston 2008; Wo 2014). However, the impact of these two attractors on egohood robberies and burglaries was weaker when measuring their simultaneous impact during the decade. This may suggest that these attractors change offenders' spatial patterns, but only in a very slow manner, as activity awareness areas are only slowly updated to account for these attractive crime locations.

We found evidence consistent with our proposition that crime generators—measured here as the presence of retail and food locations—would be positively related to changes in robberies and burglaries in both the short and long term. Nonetheless, the relationship was strongest in the short term, as increases in the number of retail or food employees in an egohood during the decade was simultaneously accompanied by substantial increases in robberies and burglaries. Given that retail and food establishments are typically sited in locations in which there are many other similar establishments, it may be that their placement is relatively easy for potential offenders to spot. A conjunctive analysis by Deryol et al. (2016) found specific risky establishments did not particularly increase crime unless the neighborhood context had a high density of commercial establishments. This would imply that awareness spaces are updated more quickly in response to the large change in activity patterns of potential targets. Nonetheless, these also showed long-term effects (albeit weaker than the short-term effects), as egohoods with more retail and food establishments at the beginning of the decade also experienced larger increases in robbery and burglary rates over the subsequent decade.

We included measures of total population and total employees in the egohood as proxies for the nighttime and daytime population, and both of these typically showed a negative relationship with robbery and burglary rates. This likely captures the fact that whereas the presence of more persons in an area will provide more targets, it also provides more potential guardians. Hipp and Roussell (2013) discussed how these countervailing predictions can lead to uncertainty in how crime rates may change, which is why we did not hypothesize here a specific relationship with changes in crime. They also suggested that it can lead to nonlinear relationships between crime and the population density in the microenvironment (e.g., an egohood) and the macroenvironment (the larger city). Such a possibility would be useful to explore with data using egohoods in a large number of cities.

Although we hypothesized that our measure of potential guardians—the presence of more homeowners in an egohood—would be negatively related to crime changes both in the short and in the long term, the results were crime-specific. One the one hand, more homeowners in an egohood led to both short-term and long-term decreases in the robbery rate, implying that they may indeed provide more effective guardians. On the other hand, such egohoods also experienced short-term and long-term increases in burglary rates, which was unexpected. If the presence of more homeowners implies more suitable targets for burglaries, then this could potentially explain this relationship. A possible explanation is that higher rates of homeowners participate in activities that take them further away from their home. The lack of guardianship during the day leaves these homes vulnerable to burglary. Analogous to our findings, Raleigh and Galster (2015) discovered that higher employment in blocks was associated with higher crime.

These crime-specific results for homeowners highlight that measures of sociodemographic characteristics of neighborhoods can sometimes simultaneously capture the presence of more targets or guardians, or even offenders. For example, we suggested that the average income of an egohood might represent more potential targets in high-income egohoods, or more guardians in high-income egohoods, but potentially more offenders in low-income egohoods. In fact, we found that higher-income egohoods experience long-term decreases in both robberies and burglaries. They also experienced short-term decreases in robberies, implying that it is only lower-income egohoods that experienced increases in robberies. Despite higher monetary rewards, higher-income neighborhoods may have greater resources to increase the risks of offending, through protective target hardening leading to a decrease in suitable targets. There was, however, evidence that egohoods experiencing increasing average income had simultaneously higher burglary rates during the decade, which is similar to the pattern detected for egohoods with increasing homeowners; this may again represent an increase in attractive targets in such egohoods. These considerations raise a general challenge for environmental criminologists, as there is a need to move beyond proxies and actually measure the number of offenders, targets, and guardians. Given the difficulty in distinguishing between these three types of persons—individuals can shift and overlap in their identities as potential offenders, guardians, or targets—this is certainly a challenge.

Finally, the results were consistent with our hypothesizing that the mixing implied by high levels of racial heterogeneity and income inequality in egohoods would result in less guardianship and hence greater long-term crime increases. Consistent with social disorganization theory's hypothesis that racial/ethnic heterogeneity reduces the ability of guardianship, egohoods with more heterogeneity at the beginning of the decade tended to experience long-term increases in burglaries. It was notable that the short-term impact of changing racial/ethnic heterogeneity was much more modest, perhaps suggesting that it is a slow process in which racial change impacts neighborhood social networks and then reduces guardianship ability. Income inequality demonstrated long-term positive relationships with burglaries and robberies, but unexpectedly also exhibited short-term positive relationships.

We acknowledge some limitations in our study. Further disaggregation of our independent variables would better account for the presences of suitable targets, offenders, and guardians. For example, future researchers could disaggregate employees by business types that serve customers on premise or off premise. The areas surrounding on-site and off-site businesses differ in risk for crime victimization (Yu and Maxfield 2014). Additionally, we could disaggregate the dependent variable of crime by time of day. Disaggregating crime by time of day and type could further explore the convergence of offenders, targets, and guardians in the egohood. There are additional facilities within egohoods, such as public transportation, that may contribute to convergence of offenders, guardians, and victims. Public transit accessibility is highly correlated with crimes near alcohol establishments (Deryol et al. 2016; Hart and Miethe 2015).

In conclusion, this chapter has demonstrated the utility of egohoods as a unit of analysis to proxy for the spatial patterning of offenders, targets, and guardians. Rather than using nonoverlapping boundaries, a strength of the egohood approach is that it allows for overlapping units. We have suggested that this approach is more consistent with the evidence in the literature that offenders tend to travel nontrivial distances to commit crime events. By measuring these larger spatial patterns, the egohood approach avoids the problem of ignoring the travel patterns of offenders—which is often characteristic of crime-and-place studies that focus on very small units—or assuming that offenders always commit their offenses within a specific neighborhood—which is often characteristic of the neighborhoods-and-crime literature. We have also highlighted that it is useful to distinguish between long-term and short-term effects of these structural characteristics for changes in robberies and burglaries.

Note

1. For example, whereas an increase from the 5th to 95th percentile in increasing vacant lots results in a predicted increase of 26% in robberies in quarter-mile egohoods, moving from the 95th to the 5th percentile in vacant lots at the beginning of the decade resulted in a predicted increase of 19% in robberies.

References

Aitken, Stuart C., and Rudy Prosser. 1990. "Residents' spatial knowledge of neighborhood continuity and form." *Geographical Analysis* 22: 301–325.

Armitage, Rachel. 2007. "Sustainability versus safety: Confusion, conflict and contradiction in designing out crime." Pp. 81–110 in *Imagination for Crime Prevention: Essays in Honour of Ken Pease*, edited by Graham Farrell, Kate J. Bowers, Shane D. Johnson, and Michael Townsley, vol. 21 of *Crime Prevention Studies*. Monsey, NY: Criminal Justice Press.

Baudains, Peter, Alex Braithwaite, and Shane D. Johnson. 2013. "Target choice during extreme events: A discrete spatial choice model of the 2011 London riots." *Criminology* 51: 251–285.

Bellair, Paul E. 2000. "Informal surveillance and street crime: A complex relationship." *Criminology* 38: 137–170.

Bernasco, Wim, and Richard Block. 2011. "Robberies in Chicago: a block-level analysis of the influence of crime generators, crime attractors, and offender anchor points." *Journal of Research in Crime and Delinquency* 48: 33–57.

Bernasco, Wim, Richard Block, and Stijn Ruiter. 2013. "Go where the money is: Modeling street robbers' location choices." *Journal of Economic Geography* 13: 119–143.

Bernasco, Wim, and Floor Luykx. 2003. "Effects of attractiveness, opportunity and accessibility to burglars on residential burglary rates of urban neighborhoods." *Criminology* 41: 981–1002.

Bernasco, Wim, and Paul Nieuwbeerta. 2005. "How do residential burglars select target areas? A new approach to the analysis of criminal location choice." *British Journal of Criminology* 45: 296–315.

Bichler, Gisela, Jill Christie-Merrall, and Dale Sechrest. 2011. "Examining juvenile delinquency within activity space: Building a context for offender travel patterns." *Journal of Research in Crime and Delinquency* 48: 472–506. doi: 0022427810393014.

Block, Richard, and Wim Bernasco. 2009. "Finding a serial burglar's home using distance decay and conditional origin-destination patterns: A test of empirical Bayes journey-to-crime estimation in The Hague." *Journal of Investigative Psychology and Offender Profiling* 6: 187–211.

Boessen, Adam, and John R. Hipp. 2015. "Close-ups and the scale of ecology: Land uses and the geography of social context and crime." *Criminology* 53: 399–426.

Boessen, Adam, John R. Hipp, Emily J. Smith, Carter T. Butts, Nicholas N. Nagle, and Zack Almquist. 2014. "Networks, space, and residents' perception of cohesion." *American Journal of Community Psychology* 53: 447–461.

Brantingham, Paul J., and Patricia L. Brantingham. 1981. "Introduction: The dimensions of crime." Pp. 7–26 in *Environmental Criminology*, edited by Paul J. Brantingham and Patricia L. Brantingham. Beverly Hills, CA: Sage.

Brantingham, Patricia L., and Paul J. Brantingham. 1993. "Nodes, paths and edges: Considerations on the complexity of crime and the physical environment." *Journal of Environmental Psychology* 13: 3–28.

Brantingham, Patricia L., and Paul J. Brantingham. 1995. "Criminality of place." *European Journal on Criminal Policy and Research* 3: 5–26.

Brantingham, Paul J., and Patricia L. Brantingham. 2008. "Crime pattern theory." Pp. 102–118 in *Environmental Criminology and Crime Analysis*, edited by Richard Wortley and Lorraine Mazerolle. New York: Routledge.

Brown, Barbara B., and Irwin Altman. 1983. "Territoriality, defensible space and residential burglary: An environmental analysis." *Journal of Environmental Psychology* 3: 203–220.

Bruinsma, Gerben J. N., Lieven J. R. Pauwels, Frank M. Weerman, and Wim Bernasco. 2013. "Social disorganization, social capital, collective efficacy and the spatial distribution of crime and offenders: An empirical test of six neighbourhood models for a Dutch city." *British Journal of Criminology*:53: 942–963.

Chaix, Basile, Juan Merlo, David Evans, Cinira Leal, and Sabrina Havard. 2009. "Neighbourhoods in eco-epidemiologic research: delimiting personal exposure areas. A response to Riva, Gauvin, Apparicio and Brodeur." *Social Science & Medicine* 69: 1306–1310.

Cohen, Lawrence E., and Marcus Felson. 1979. "Social change and crime rate trends: A routine activity approach." *American Sociological Review* 44: 588–608.

Deryol, Rustu, Pamela Wilcox, Matthew Logan, and John Wooldredge. 2016. "Crime places in context: An illustration of the multilevel nature of hot spot development." *Journal of Quantitative Criminology* 32: 1–21.

Eck, John E. 1994. "Drug markets and drug places: A case-control study of the spatial structure of illicit drug dealing." University of Maryland, Faculty of the Graduate School.

Eck, John E., Ronald V. Clarke, and Rob T. Guerette. 2007. "Risky facilities: Crime concentration in homogeneous sets of establishments and facilities." Pp. 225–264 in *Imagination for Crime Prevention: Essays in Honour of Ken Pease*, edited by Graham Farrell, Kate J. Bowers, Shane D. Johnson, and Michael Townsley, vol. 21 of *Crime Prevention Studies*. Monsey, NY: Criminal Justice Press.

Eck, John E., and David L. Weisburd. 1995. "Crime places in crime theory." Pp. 1–33 in *Crime and Place*, edited by John E. Eck and David Weisburd, vol. 4 of *Crime Prevention Studies*. Monsey, NY: Criminal Justice Press.

Farrell, Graham, Coretta Phillips, and Ken Pease. 1995. "Like taking candy: Why does repeat victimization occur?" *British Journal of Criminology* 35: 384–399.

Felson, Marcus. 1995. "Those who discourage crime." Pp. 53–66 in *Crime and Place*, edited by John E. Eck and David Weisburd, vol. 4 of *Crime Prevention Studies*. Monsey, NY: Criminal Justice Press.

Felson, Marcus, and Lawrence E. Cohen. 1980. "Human ecology and crime: A routine activity approach." *Human Ecology* 8: 389–406.

Forrest, Ray, and Ade Kearns. 2001. "Social cohesion, social capital and the neighbourhood." *Urban Studies* 38: 2125–2143.

Garvin, Eugenia C., Carolyn C. Cannuscio, and Charles C. Branas. 2013. "Greening vacant lots to reduce violent crime: A randomised controlled trial." *Injury Prevention* 19: 198–203.

Gorman, Dennis M., Paul W. Speer, Paul J. Gruenewald, and Erich W. Labouvie. 2001. "Spatial dynamics of alcohol availability, neighborhood structure and violent crime." *Journal of Studies on Alcohol* 62: 628–636.

Greenbaum, Robert T., and George E. Tita. 2004. "The impact of violence surges on neighbourhood business activity." *Urban Studies* 41: 2495–2514.

Groff, Elizabeth R. 2013. "Measuring a place's exposure to facilities using geoprocessing models: An illustration using drinking places and crime." Pp. 269–295 in *Crime Modeling and Mapping Using Geospatial Technologies*, edited by Michael Leitner. New York: Springer.

Groff, Elizabeth R. 2014. "Quantifying the exposure of street segments to drinking places nearby." *Journal of Quantitative Criminology* 30: 527–548.

Groff, Elizabeth R. and Brian Lockwood. 2014. "Criminogenic Facilities and Crime across Street Segments in Philadelphia: Uncovering Evidence about the Spatial Extent of Facility Influence." *Journal of Research in Crime and Delinquency* 51: 277–314.

Groff, Elizabeth R., David L. Weisburd, and Sue-Ming Yang. 2010. "Is it important to examine crime trends at a local 'micro' level? A longitudinal analysis of street to street variability in crime trajectories." *Journal of Quantitative Criminology* 26: 7–32.

Guerry, Andre-Michel. 1833. *Essai sur la Statistique Morale de la France: Precede d'un Rapport a l'Academie de Sciences*. Paris: Chez Crochard.

Hart, Timothy C., and Terance D. Miethe. 2015. "Configural behavior settings of crime event locations toward an alternative conceptualization of criminogenic microenvironments." *Journal of Research in Crime and Delinquency* 52: 373–402.

Hipp, John R. 2007. "Block, tract, and levels of aggregation: Neighborhood structure and crime and disorder as a case in point." *American Sociological Review* 72: 659–680.

Hipp, John R. 2010. "A dynamic view of neighborhoods: The reciprocal relationship between crime and neighborhood structural characteristics." *Social Problems* 57: 205–230.

Hipp, John R. 2011. "Spreading the wealth: The effect of the distribution of income and race/ethnicity across households and neighborhoods on city crime trajectories." *Criminology* 49: 631–665.

Hipp, John R. 2016a. "Collective efficacy: How is it conceptualized, how is it measured, and does it really matter for understanding perceived neighborhood crime and disorder?" *Journal of Criminal Justice* 46: 32–44.

Hipp, John R. 2016b. "General theory of spatial crime patterns." *Criminology* 54: 653–679.

Hipp, John R., and Adam Boessen. 2013. "Egohoods as waves washing across the city: a new measure of 'neighborhoods.'" *Criminology* 51: 287–327.

Hipp, John R., and Andrew Perrin. 2006. "Nested loyalties: Local networks' effects on neighbourhood and community cohesion." *Urban Studies* 43: 2503–2523.

Hipp, John R., and Aaron Roussell. 2013. "Micro- and macro-environment population and the consequences for crime rates." *Social Forces* 92: 563–595.

Hipp, John R., George E. Tita, and Lyndsay N. Boggess. 2009. "Inter- and intra-group violence: Is violent crime an expression of group conflict or social disorganization?" *Criminology* 47: 521–564.

Hodgkinsoi, Sarah, and Nick Tilley. 2007. "Travel-to-crime: Homing in on the victim." *International Review of Victimology* 14: 281–298.

Hollis, Meghan E., Marcus Felson, and Brandon C. Welsh. 2013. "The capable guardian in routine activities theory: A theoretical and conceptual reappraisal." *Crime Prevention and Community Safety* 15: 65–79.

Infogroup. 2015. "*Reference USA Historical Business Data*." edited by Infogroup. Papillion, NE: Reference USA.

Jeffery, Clarence Ray. 1971. *Crime Prevention through Environmental Design*. London: Sage.

Johnson, Shane D., and Kate J. Bowers. 2004. "The burglary as clue to the future the beginnings of prospective hot-spotting." *European Journal of Criminology* 1: 237–255.

Johnson, Shane D., and Kate J. Bowers. 2010. "Permeability and burglary risk: Are cul-de-sacs safer?" *Journal of Quantitative Criminology* 26: 89–111.

Johnson, Shane D., Steven P. Lab, and Kate J. Bowers. 2008. "Stable and fluid hotspots of crime: Differentiation and identification." *Built Environment* 34: 32–45.

Johnson, Shane D., and Lucia Summers. 2015. "Testing ecological theories of offender spatial decision making using a discrete choice model." *Crime and Delinquency* 61: 454–480.

Jones, Roderick W., and William Alex Pridemore. 2014. "A longitudinal study of the impact of home vacancy on robbery and burglary rates during the US housing crisis, 2005–2009." *Crime and Delinquency* 62: 1159–1179.

Koppen, Peter J., and Jan W. Keijser. 1997. "Desisting distance decay: On The aggregation of individual crime trips." *Criminology* 35: 505–515.

Kubrin, Charis E., and John R. Hipp. 2016. "Do fringe banks create fringe neighborhoods? Examining the spatial relationship between fringe banking and neighborhood crime rates." *Justice Quarterly* 33: 755–784.

Kurtz, Ellen M., Barbara A. Koons, and Ralph B. Taylor. 1998. "Land use, physical deterioration, resident-based control, and calls for service on urban streetblocks." *Justice Quarterly* 15: 121–149.

Lammers, Marre, Barbara Menting, Stijn Ruiter, and Wim Bernasco. 2015. "Biting once, twice: The influence of prior on subsequent crime location choice." *Criminology* 53: 309–329.

Livingston, Michael. 2008. "A longitudinal analysis of alcohol outlet density and assault." *Alcoholism: Clinical and Experimental Research* 32: 1074–1079.

Madensen, Tamara D., and John E. Eck. 2008. "Violence in bars: Exploring the impact of place manager decision-making." *Crime Prevention and Community Safety* 10: 111–125.

Messner, Steven F., and Judith R. Blau. 1987. "Routine leisure activities and rates of crime: A macro-level analysis." *Social Forces* 65: 1035–1052.

Miethe, Terance D., Timothy C. Hart, and Wendy C. Regoeczi. 2008. "The conjunctive analysis of case configurations: An exploratory method for discrete multivariate analyses of crime data." *Journal of Quantitative Criminology* 24: 227–241.

Miethe, Terance D., Mark C. Stafford, and Douglas Sloane. 1990. "Lifestyle changes and risks of criminal victimization." *Journal of Quantitative Criminology* 6: 357–376.

Newman, Oscar. 1972. *Defensible Space: Crime Prevention through Urban Design*. New York: Macmillan.

Newton, Andrew D., and Alex Hirschfield. 2009. "Measuring violence in and around licensed premises: The need for a better evidence base." *Crime Prevention and Community Safety* 11: 171–188.

O'Leary, Mike. 2011. "Modeling criminal distance decay." *Cityscape* 13: 161–198.

Park, Robert E., Ernest W. Burgess, and Roderick D. McKenzie. 1985 [1925]. *The City*. Chicago: University of Chicago Press.

Pridemore, William Alex, and Tony H. Grubesic. 2013. "Alcohol outlets and community levels of interpersonal violence: Spatial density, outlet type, and seriousness of assault." *Journal of Research in Crime and Delinquency* 50: 132–159.

Quételet, Adolphe. 1842. *A Treatise on Man*. Translated by R. Knox and T. Smibert. Edinburgh: Chambers.

Raleigh, Erica, and George Galster. 2015. "Neighborhood disinvestment, abandonment, and crime dynamics." *Journal of Urban Affairs* 37: 367–396.

Rengert, George F., and Brian Lockwood. 2009. "Geographical units of analysis and the analysis of crime." Pp. 109–122 in *Putting Crime in Its place: Units of Analysis in Geographic Criminology*, edited by David Weisburd, Wim Bernasco, and Gerben J. N. Bruinsma. New York: Springer.

Reynald, Danielle M. 2011. *Guarding against crime: Measuring guardianship within routine activity theory*: Ashgate Publishing, Ltd.

Roncek, Dennis W., and Pamela A. Maier. 1991. "Bars, blocks, and crimes revisited: Linking the theory of routine activities to the empiricism of "hot spots." *Criminology* 29: 725–753.

Rossmo, D. Kim. 1999. *Geographic profiling*: CRC press.

Rountree, Pamela Wilcox, and Kenneth C. Land. 1996. "Burglary victimization, perceptions of crime risk, and routine activities: A multilevel analysis across Seattle neighborhoods and census tracts." *Journal of research in crime and delinquency* 33: 147–180.

Sampson, Robert J., and W. Byron Groves. 1989. "Community structure and crime: Testing social-disorganization theory." *American Journal of Sociology*: 774–802.

Sampson, R. J., S. W. Raudenbush, and F. Earls. 1997. "Neighborhoods and violent crime: a multilevel study of collective efficacy." *Science* 277: 918–24.

Schmerler, K., D. Hunter, D. Eisenberg, and M. Jones. 2009. "Reducing crime and disorder at motels and hotels in Chula Vista, CA." *Submission for the Herman Goldstein Award for Excellence in Problem-Oriented Policing. Accessed on: March* 29: 2011.

Shaw, Clifford R., and Henry D. McKay. 1942. "Juvenile delinquency and urban areas." *Chicago, Ill.*

Sherman, Lawrence W., Patrick R. Gartin, and Michael E. Buerger. 1989. "Hot spots of predatory crime: Routine activities and the criminology of place*." *Criminology* 27: 27–56.

Smith, William R., Sharon Glave Frazee, and Elizabeth L. Davison. 2000. "Furthering the integration of routine activity and social disorganization theories: Small units of analysis and the study of street robbery as a diffusion process." *Criminology* 38: 489–524.

Snowden, Aleksandra J., and William Alex Pridemore. 2014. "Off-premise alcohol outlet characteristics and violence." *The American journal of drug and alcohol abuse* 40: 327–335.

Spelman, William. 1993. "Abandoned buildings: Magnets for crime?" *Journal of Criminal Justice* 21: 481–495.

Steenbeek, Wouter, and John R. Hipp. 2011. "A Longitudinal Test Of Social Disorganization Theory: Feedback Effects Among Cohesion, Social Control, And Disorder." *Criminology* 49: 833–871.

Taylor, Ralph B. 1997. "Social order and disorder of street blocks and neighborhoods: Ecology, microecology, and the systemic model of social disorganization." *Journal of Research in Crime and Delinquency* 34: 113–155.

Taylor, Ralph B., and Stephen Gottfredson. 1986. "Environmental design, crime, and prevention: An examination of community dynamics." *Crime and Justice* 8: 387–416.

Telep, Cody W., David Weisburd, Charlotte E. Gill, Zoe Vitter, and Doron Teichman. 2014. "Displacement of crime and diffusion of crime control benefits in large-scale geographic areas: A systematic review." *Journal of Experimental Criminology* 10: 515–548.

Tita, George, and Elizabeth Griffiths. 2005. "Traveling to violence: The case for a mobility-based spatial typology of homicide." *Journal of Research in Crime and Delinquency* 42: 275–308.

Toomey, Traci L., Darin J. Erickson, Bradley P. Carlin, Kathleen M. Lenk, Harrison S. Quick, Alexis M. Jones, and Eileen M. Harwood. 2012. "The association between density of alcohol establishments and violent crime within urban neighborhoods." *Alcoholism: Clinical and Experimental Research* 36: 1468–1473.

Vandeviver, Christophe. 2013. "Distance matters: A look at crime trip distances in Flanders." *Crime, violence, justice and social order: monitoring contemporary security issues* 1: 229–253.

Weisburd, David, Gerben J. N. Bruinsma, and Wim Bernasco. 2009. "Units of analysis in geographic criminology: Historical development, critical issues, and open questions." Pp. 3–31 in *Putting Crime in its Place: Units of Analysis in Geographic Criminology*, edited by David Weisburd, Wim Bernasco, and Gerben J. N. Bruinsma. New York: Springer.

Weisburd, David L., Elizabeth R. Groff, and Sue-Ming Yang. 2012. *The Criminology of Place: Street Segments and Our Understanding of the Crime Problem*. New York: Oxford University Press.

Weisburd, David, Cody W. Telep, Breanne Cave, Kate Bowers, John E. Eck, Gerben J. N. Bruinsma, Charlotte Gill, Elizabeth Groff, Julie Hibdon, and Joshua C. Hinkle. 2016. *Place Matters: Criminology for the Twenty-First Century*. New York: Cambridge University Press.

White, R. C. 1932. "The relation of felonies to environmental factors in indianapolis." *Social Forces* 10: 498–509.

Wickes, Rebecca, John R. Hipp, Elise Sargeant, and Ross Homel. 2013. "Collective efficacy as a task specific process: Examining the relationship between social ties, neighborhood cohesion and the capacity to respond to violence, delinquency and civic problems." *American Journal of Community Psychology* 52: 115–127.

Wilcox, P., B. M. Gialopsos, and K. C. Land. 2013. "Multilevel criminal opportunity." Pp. 579–601 in *The Oxford Handbook of Criminological Theory*, edited by Francis T. Cullen and Pamela Wilcox. New York: Oxford University Press.

Wilcox, Pamela, Tamara D. Madensen, and Marie Skubak Tillyer. 2007. "Guardianship in context: Implications for burglary victimization risk and prevention." *Criminology* 45: 771–803.

Wiles, Paul, and Andrew Costello. 2000. *The "Road to Nowhere": The Evidence for Travelling Criminals*. Home Office Research Studies No. 207. London: Research, Development and Statistics Directorate, Home Office.

Williams, Sonya, George Galster, and Nandita Verma. 2014. "Home foreclosures and neighborhood crime dynamics." *Housing Studies* 29: 380–406.

Wo, J. C. 2014. "Community context of crime: A longitudinal examination of the effects of local institutions on neighborhood crime." *Crime and Delinquency*.

Yu, Sung-suk Violet, and Michael G. Maxfield. 2014. "Ordinary business: Impacts on commercial and residential burglary." *British Journal of Criminology* 54: 298–320.

CHAPTER 20

SIGNAL CRIMES, SOCIAL REACTIONS, AND THE FUTURE OF ENVIRONMENTAL CRIMINOLOGY

MARTIN INNES AND HELEN INNES

20.1 Introduction

Some crimes and disorders clearly impact and influence how people interpret and make sense of their safety and security across different environments and social situations. There are myriad examples that both illuminate and validate this claim. Events such as the terrorist bombings of 9/11 in the United States, or 7/7 in London clearly conform to this pattern. Likewise, listing names like James Bulger, Rachel Nickell, Stephen Lawrence, and Milly Dowler invokes a small number of high-profile murders that were clearly consequential in terms of shaping how many people in the UK think about and understand crime as a social problem. Although somewhat harder to discern, analogous patterns of impact and influence attend to more "normal crimes" and everyday forms of urban disorder, in that at a local level, some incidents matter more than others in shaping people's situated perceptions of safety and security (Innes, 2014; Bottoms, 2006; Bottoms, 2012).

A key question for environmental criminology, then, is, "How and why do some crimes and disorders acquire these impacts?" This deceptively simple question has been relatively neglected due to a predominant focus on offender perceptions of risk and environmental opportunities for criminal behavior. But engaging with it has the potential to enrich future work in the environmental criminology tradition, and open up new pathways for understanding how the prevalence of crime, and reactions to crime, shift and alter across different spaces and places. Most notably, there is an opportunity to take processes of perception and attribution more seriously, in terms of both what crime and disorder actually means to the public in the context of a particular place, and how policing and community safety providers can understand this and use it to shape their interventions. Additionally, developing such an approach would help to orientate environmental criminology toward some profound contemporary challenges, such as, how will it adapt to and integrate the increasing importance that digital spaces have in shaping the etiology of crime and reactions to it?

The intent behind this chapter is to outline how the precepts associated with the signal crimes perspective (SCP) provide insights into and a new theoretical frame for engaging with and navigating some of these challenges. In developing and elaborating these ideas, the chapter starts by setting out that a signal is something that transmits messages to an audience. Thinking in terms of signals and "signaling" opens up new ways of seeing crime, disorder, and social control. In particular, it keys into an event-based unit of analysis, as opposed to measuring impacts in an aggregated form. Having laid out the conceptual apparatus of the signal crimes perspective, the discussion proceeds on to briefly consider how as an approach it compares with more established criminological frameworks for studying reactions to and consequences of crime, in particular, fear of crime, moral panics, and more recent attempts to measure harm.

The latter sections of the chapter focus in upon the ways that changes to the information environment, associated with an era of "big data" and proliferation of social media, are altering the incidents that signal and how their impacts travel across space and time. The encroachment of digital environments illuminates some key challenges for the future of a place-based environmental criminology, and the discussion considers how blending open-source communications data with a signal crimes-based approach might produce new insights about dimensions of social reaction processes that were hitherto imperceptible. Conceptually, it is argued that the signal crimes perspective can provide a meaningful addition and way forward to frame, process, and interpret data sets on reactions to crime.

20.2 On Signals and Signaling

Defined in its simplest terms, a signal is "a sign that has an effect" (Innes, 2004). Erving Goffman (1972) originally formulated the idea of signals to articulate how and why disturbances to "normal appearances" in a social situation can induce negative reactions. He emphasized that a signal is "a conventional sign, which, by prearrangement, has been arbitrarily established for this purpose—the purpose of announcing that there is something about which to be alarmed" (Goffman, 1972: 247). Elaborating this position, he differentiated between "signs of alarm" and "signs for alarm" as ways in which appearances of social order can be disrupted by the performance of incivilities and the physical traces of such acts, inducing sensations and perceptions of insecurity and risk.

A second conceptualization of signaling can be identified in Umberto Eco's (1976) pragmatist semiotics. For Eco, a signal is a sign that does something—it causes an effect. Although underpinned by different theoretical precepts with their respective emphases upon processes of signification, meaning attribution, and social reaction, there are compatible elements that can be identified between Goffman and Eco. Moreover, there is precedent for blending approaches from symbolic interactionist sociology with semiotic frameworks to be found in the work of Morris (1964) and Manning (1987), among others.

Applied to the task of understanding and interrogating how people individually and collectively interpret and make sense of crime, disorder, and social control, focusing upon signaling processes enables a conceptual accent upon how they function as forms of communicative action that send messages to a wider audience. Typically, but not exclusively, such messages speak to the distribution of risks and threats across social space, and the kinds of people, places, and events in the environment that are potentially dangerous and troublesome.

The development of these ideas about how crimes perform as signals has taken place along two principal tracks. One is more avowedly theoretical. The second has pivoted around applied empirical work associated with the policy development of reassurance policing and neighborhood policing (Fielding and Innes, 2006; Tuffin et al., 2006). It has been through an interaction and dialogue between the theoretical and empirical that the signal crimes perspective has developed. Casting it as a "perspective" is a way of conveying that it affords a new and different way of seeing the process via which people interpret, perceive, and make sense of crime, disorder, and social control. The principal constructs underpinning the perspective were originally set out in Innes and Fielding (2002) and Innes (2004). These papers defined three principal forms of "signal event," summarized in Figure 20.1: (1) signal crimes; (2) signal disorders; and (3) control signals. These notions were empirically elaborated and significantly developed in the series of studies published as Innes (2014).

The expression is the issue or problem responsible for causing some kind of effect. Devoid of any effect on perception, emotion, or behavior, the crime or disorder event is simply part of the background "noise" to everyday life. The remaining element of this conceptual triptych is the "content" that is used to capture the bearer of risk. The connections between these three component parts are exemplified in the following quotation from someone talking about a crime in the neighborhood:

> There had been a burglary, either it was that night or the night before . . . I was very anxious then . . . and it was the first time in eight years I actually did not feel one hundred per cent safe.

In this extract, "burglary" is the expression, and the effect is one of "fear." Because the interviewee locates this effect as affecting her, we can say that the content is one of "personal risk."

The important point here is that this woman was not the victim of the crime, but even so, it affected her. It is these more diffuse communicative properties that the SCP is particularly attuned to and concerned with. Through an extensive empirical research effort (summarized in Innes, 2004 and 2014), it has been demonstrated that this capacity to

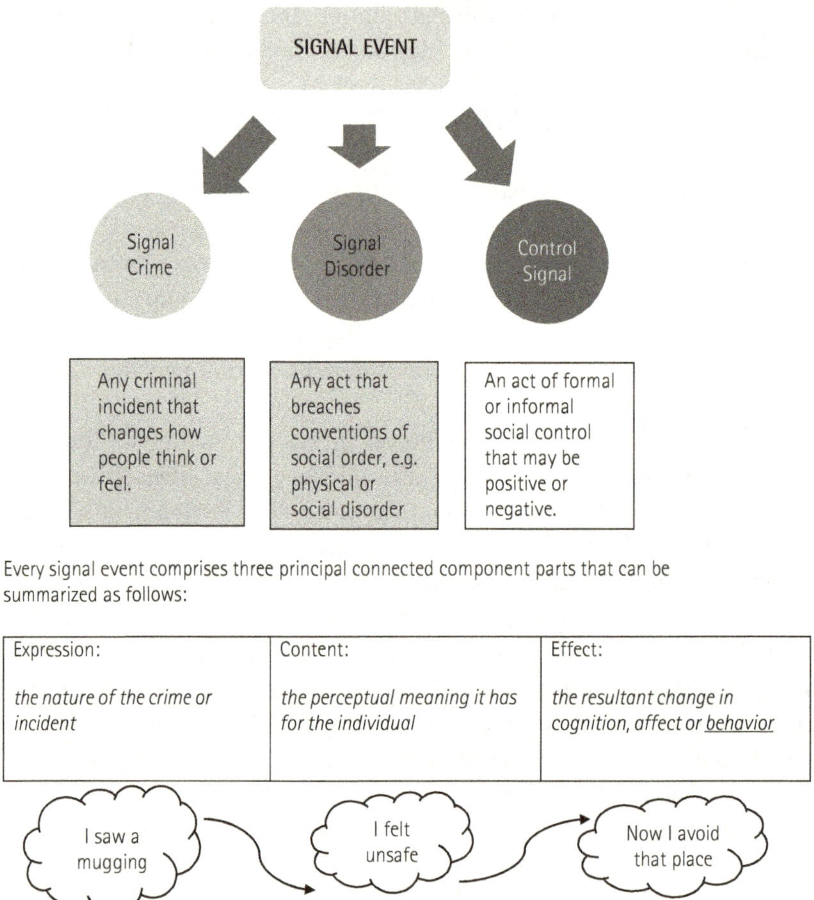

FIGURE 20.1 The three modal signal events in the signal crimes perspective

send messages can be detected in relation to all kinds of signal events: signal crimes and physical and social disorders, as well as the formal and informal control signal responses to these. As will be developed over the course of this chapter, a number of implications follow on from attending to the communicative properties of such signal events. Their capacities to function as signals of risk and threat are captured in the following fieldwork extract from a lady talking about her experiences in her neighborhood:

> Graffiti is the thing that sort of bothers me more because it is in my face every day. I mean obviously rape and murder are more horrendous crimes, but it is graffiti that I see.

Here the respondent conveys how repeated, local exposure to physical disorder sent a signal about the type of neighborhood in which she is residing. Even more significantly, this quotation articulates how the level of social harm associated with different acts may not automatically map onto their relative levels of harmfulness as they are conceptualized in law.

If acts of deviance, disorder, and criminality are understood to signal to people, we should also expect that acts and interventions taken in respect of these signals possess similar communicative qualities. This is set out in the next interview extract, where a London resident recalled observing an interaction between police and a member of the public, and that the way the police acted had a positive impact upon his confidence in the police institution more generally:

> I saw on Portobello Road, I saw them in action in a very good way, where a very big, a very aggressive black guy was . . . he was basically screaming abuse at two police officers who were remarkably calm and remarkably sort of together in dealing with him . . . so I think the police officers were very good in calming the situation, which I think in the area can become explosive quite quickly.

Of course, not all policing actions deliver positive effects; as Innes (2014) documents, there is an equal opportunity for "negative control signals" to be communicated.

The SCP approach to diagnosing how and why crime, disorder, and control events function as forms of communicative action was designed to provide a comprehensive, systematic, and structured method that could operate across different scales, ranging from micro-level interactions to institutional structures, identifying incidents and interventions that function to change how people think, feel, or act about their security. Compared with more orthodox and established positions in environmental criminology, adopting a signal crimes-inflected approach therefore brings forward a number of important innovations in thinking. The key elements can be summarized as follows:

- The majority disposition in environmental criminology research has been toward explaining and accounting for the prevalence and distribution of crime patterns in terms of causative factors. As a counterpoint, the signal crimes approach focuses upon processes of social reaction and, in particular, how and why some events generate more intense and profound reactions than do others. In so doing, it notes that these perceptual processes may recursively shape future crime patterns by inducing particular vulnerabilities and resilience.
- With its emphasis upon understanding and unpacking how crime, disorder, and social control are perceived, there are certain affinities with other ideas and concepts that have engaged with this issue, most notably fear-of-crime studies. However, and as developed below, a key difference is that the SCP seeks to far more precisely define, capture, and calibrate the range of different effects and impacts that crime, disorder, and social control can have, across the affective, cognitive, and behavioral registers.
- Focusing upon signal events is explicitly designed to establish an event-based unit of analysis that gauges how specific incidents influence people individually and collectively, and the ways they interpret the places and spaces that they pass through.

This responds directly to a limitation that Jacobs (1996) identified with much criminological scholarship, in that impacts and effects have tended to be measured at an aggregated level, rather than traced to specific and defined events.

- A fundamental difference is that the SCP places far more accent upon the meanings that are attributed to crime and disorder incidents, and responses to these. In this sense, it attends far more assiduously to matters of interpretation and the extent to which different contexts and settings exert a degree of situational influence over how particular occurrences are ascribed significance and salience.

As noted previously, the development of these theoretical tenets has been through an extensive empirical effort, much of which has been associated with reassurance policing and subsequently neighborhood policing. The National Reassurance Policing Program was a quasi-experimental police reform initiative that ran between 2003 and 2005 across 16 sites in eight police forces in England. Its primary interest was in testing the impacts upon levels of fear of crime and confidence in the police of a policing style designed to be more responsive to the local crime and disorder problems and concerns defined by communities. Positioned within a structured community policing model, the SCP provided a conceptual and empirical methodology for diagnosing neighborhood-level events and incidents that were exhibiting a disproportionate impact upon local communities' perceptions of safety and security. Through rigorous and detailed data collection and analysis framed by tents of the SCP, the local delivery of policing interventions was "tuned" to problem-solving the key signal crimes and disorders identified. A detailed account of this approach and its results is provided in Tuffin et al. (2006), but for the purposes of this chapter, it is sufficient to state that those areas where this methodology was implemented saw greater improvements in levels of fear and confidence compared with similar areas elsewhere.

Of course, the signal crimes perspective is not the only approach to studying social reactions to crime and disorder that has developed with reference to policing practices. Accordingly, in the next section we briefly review how some of the theoretical precepts traced in outline above articulate with the theory of broken windows and fear of crime, moral panics, and recent scholarship on harm.

20.3 Theories of Reacting to Crime and Disorder

In their original formulation of broken windows theory, Wilson and Kelling (1982) argued that the occurrence of untreated disorder has the potential to signal to onlookers that social control mechanisms in the area are weak and thereby set off a sequence of actions and reactions that can cause a low-crime area to tip into a high-crime area. In effect, they posit a basic developmental sequence whereby disorder and the failure to respond to it effectively induce fear. Fear then signals differently to two key audiences; for potential perpetrators, the lack of an efficacious response to the occurrence to disorder sends a message that it is a conducive environment for engaging in deviant actions, where sanction or censure is unlikely. At the same time, for a wider local audience, the presence of disorder functions as an indicator of insecurity, generating fear and a withdrawal from public spaces. In the process both create conditions more amenable to the further commission of disorder and crime.

Empirical support for a link between disorder and perceived crime problems in a neighborhood was provided by Skogan's (1990) survey analysis in American cities. More recently, an observational experiment conducted by Keizer et al. (2008) provided additional evidence to validate the pivotal claim that the occurrence of untreated disorder is criminogenic. However, it is the role attributed to broken windows in the crime drop in New York during the 1990s and 2000s that has garnered most attention, and also generated the most negative reaction (Zimring, 2011). Others have contested these claims. For example, Bowling (1999) has suggested that the reductions in crime in New York can be traced back more to changes in the dynamics of the city's drug markets, rather than any assertive policing strategies targeted at incivilities and antisocial behavior. Sampson and Raudenbush (1999) conclude, on the basis of their systematic observation of Chicago neighbourhoods, that both disorder and more serious crime possess similar structural roots. As such, rather than looking at disorder as a cause of crime, both disorder *and* crime should be interpreted as products of particular "neighbourhood effects".

In our view, it is not that broken windows is fundamentally wrong in terms of the causal sequence it advocates, as in certain circumstances and under particular conditions, disorder is criminogenic in the ways described. There is, however, a generalizability issue, in that the occurrence of disorder and incivilities does not intrinsically generate more crime. There are other pathways and possibilities that need to be accounted for. Taylor's (2000) detailed work in Baltimore, for instance, noted that the areas experiencing higher rates of crime and disorder, at the point in time he was assessing them, were those that had historically seen higher levels. In this broad vein, Sampson's (2012) theorization of the role of "neighborhood effects" suggests that at a neighborhood unit of analysis, experiences of crime and disorder are structured by wider socioeconomic and sociocultural conditions and that these persist quite strongly over extended periods of time. Over recent years, facilitated by the growing availability of small-area data, there has been a shift in focus toward microunits of analysis within neighborhoods, such as street segments, to show variation in disorder and the clustering of crime within neighborhoods (Welsh et al. 2015). However, Taylor (2015) points out that the nature of any association between spatial indicators and crime often remains indecipherable owing to difficulties inherent in establishing the theoretical meaning of ecological indictors and of matching geographical and temporal measures to the conceptual framework (see also, Taylor in this volume). Taylor also reminds us of nonrandom selection effects at the neighborhood level (e.g., outward migration) that have a bearing on crime and disorder.

There are, then, important limitations and concerns with the broken windows approach. However, what it does do is connect issues of perception and reaction to the occurrence of actual incidents, rather than seeing them as independent matters. In this sense, it affords a greater sense of the complexity and challenge for analysts seeking to study and understand the impacts and consequences of crime and disorder across different physical and social environments. It is not sufficient, as some have been wont to do, to either study incident rates or perceptual and attitudinal variables in isolation from each other. Rather, a comprehensive theory of the impacts of crime needs to encompass both the actual incidence of events, and the shape and form of public reactions to these. Sometimes actual levels of crime will track perceptions quite closely, but at other times they will display divergent patterns.

Where the SCP differs from broken windows is in its insight that meaning really matters. How local people interpret and make sense of any legal infraction or instance of antisocial behavior is profoundly important in shaping the scale and intensity of any resultant harm. Situated in some environments, some crimes and disorders matter very much, whereas in other settings, ostensibly similar occurrences are of far less significance.

20.3.1 Fear of Crime

Broken windows positions fear of crime as a pivotal mechanism in accounting for how and why areas tip into high crime. It is this affective reaction to the occurrence of disorder that creates the conditions whereby increases in crime result. This is, however, only one application of fear of crime, among many others, reflecting how, as a concept, fear of crime has come to dominate the ways criminologists have approached the issue of studying reactions to crime. As one might expect given this position, there are a plethora of formulations and accounts in the literature. Broadly speaking, these can be differentiated according to whether their principal causal accent is upon people, places or problems.

People-based accounts of fear of crime tend to focus upon how patterns in the distribution of fear track sociodemographic characteristics. This is exemplified by one of the most well-known and routinely cited findings, that rates of fear tend to be relatively high among older women compared to other groups, despite their risk of victimization being lower (see for example Hale, 1996). Contrastingly, place-based accounts of fear focus upon the ways certain localities and places evoke anxiety and concern. Several of the studies reviewed in the preceding section, notably Taylor (2001) and Sampson (2012), fall under this heading. The final group of studies identify the primary causal issue as being explaining the social mechanics of how and why some types of crime and disorder evoke profound and intense reactions. Elements of broken windows thinking, for instance, illustrate this tendency.

Cutting across these three different causal foci, what the literature on fear of crime has been especially good at is mapping the prevalence and distribution of reactions to crime and disorder, and evidencing that these are uneven (Hale, 1996). In part, this reflects the favored method of such studies, large-scale survey analysis. While there have been some important qualitative contributions to the fear of crime literature (e.g., Girling,

Loader, and Sparks, 2000), for the most part these have nuanced and introduced subtlety to themes derived from more quantitative approaches, as opposed to establishing new lines of academic enquiry.

There are though constraints and limitations that can be identified with the fear-of-crime approach. First, the predominance of quantitative analyses of large-scale surveys has meant that much of what has been written has tended to provide something of a "snapshot" of the conditions of perceptions and attitudes at a particular moment in time. What is not really captured and articulated are the temporal dynamics of reaction and the ways in which the impacts of incidents are amplified and then fade over time. A second area of concern relates to the label "fear of crime" itself. For what can be divined from reviewing the empirical literature is that much of what is categorized under this heading is not really "fear", nor is it just "of crime." Addressing the first point, Professor Jason Ditton and his colleagues undertook several careful studies that conclusively demonstrated that "anger" was a far more commonplace response to crime threats and risks than fear (Ditton et al., 1999; Ditton and Innes, 2005). Relatedly, many of the incidents triggering these kinds of responses did not actually involve an infraction of the criminal law (Bottoms, 2006). Collapsing these intricacies and differences under a broad label, such as fear of crime, is therefore misleading and inhibits developing analytically precise understandings of what is actually transpiring within and across different social environments.

20.3.2 Moral Panic

A rather different theoretical position in terms of reacting to crime is provided by moral panic theory. Since its initial introduction in the 1960s, moral panic theory has been applied to explaining how a range of private troubles were constructed as public problems. Originally pivoting off of Wilkins's (1964) ideas about deviancy amplification processes, Cohen's ([1966] 2002) formulation sought to explain how and why certain crime incidents trigger societal impacts disproportionate to the harm actually caused. He carefully mapped out a sequenced pattern in terms of how key authoritative institutions (including the police, judiciary, and mass media) collectively act to amplify the sense of threat to social order that is perceived to be posed, in the process encouraging widespread ramifications in terms of collective behavior and social values.

In the foreword to the third edition of his seminal text, Cohen ([1966] 2002) reflected upon the conceptual status of moral panic and its influence upon the study of social reactions to crime. According to his analysis, moral panic had become overextended and inappropriately applied in some cases. Clarifying his own position, he asserted that for a moral panic to be identified, it is vital that there be some consequences for the extant moral order. It is not just fear that is elicited by the occurrence, but rather deeper and more profound implications. Equally importantly, he emphasized that a panic implies an intense, debilitating period of reaction, but one that is not long-lasting or permanent.

Against this definitional backdrop, it is possible to delineate the boundaries between moral panic and signal crime. The latter covers the kinds of incidents that trigger effects in people, but not at the scale where this instigates reconfigurations to the moral order. However, what moral panic theory does provide to the study of social reactions is a temporal dimension. That is, the impacts and harms caused by crime and disorder events are not cast as static. Rather they are understood as something that evolve and adapt over time, increasing in their intensity and then after a while decaying in terms of their salience.

20.3.3 Social Harm

A more recent and emergent development in the study of social reactions to crime relates to how a number of scholars have appropriated the concept of harm. Sparrow (2008: 14) defines harm in a way that "covers the broadest set of bad things . . .. it can be understood to include 'potential harms' and 'patterns of harm,' as well as specific harms already done." He argues that the main purpose of governmental interventions should be preventing and minimizing the impacts of harmful events, rather than attempting to socially engineer perceived "social goods." Sparrow stresses that some harms are multi-dimensional; some are "high level"; while others are invisible or slow-acting.

Recently there have been several attempts to empirically operationalize the concept of harm, such as Greenfield and Paoli (2013) and Sherman et al. (2016), both of which set out alternative frameworks to enable the quantification of crime harms. The former study distinguishes between the severity of harm (graded according to whether it is catastrophic, grave, serious, moderate, or marginal) and its incidence (whether it occurs always, persistently, occasionally, seldom, rarely). This is to balance between grave harms that happen rarely, and less severe harms that arise with greater regularity. Developing this approach, the authors propose that it is also important to determine who bears the "harm"—whether it is an individual, private sector entity, government, or the environment. Sherman et al.'s (2016) Cambridge Crime Harm Index is somewhat different, appropriating instead the UK Sentencing Guideline tariffs associated with particular offenses as a proxy indicator for harm. The rationale is that this allows for the calculation of the aggregate harm associated with different crime hotspots, or area crime rates, thereby moving beyond the assumption that simply because an area experiences higher levels of crime, this necessarily translates into more intense and serious impacts. While providing a methodologically efficient way of estimating aggregated levels of harm at an area level, when compared with the empirical data on the impacts and consequences of signal events generated by the 10-year signal crimes research program, it appears limited in a number of key respects. Importantly, it neglects the role of antisocial behavior and physical disorder, which the SCP strongly suggests can be profoundly influential upon how people ascertain the levels of risk and threat associated with urban environments. Furthermore, a generic index cannot accommodate the extent to which certain situational features and factors amplify (or mitigate) the levels of harm that are experienced. As discussed subsequently, these are limitations that the SCP, with its accenting of the importance of local interpretations and meanings, has sought to overcome, in particular by bringing forward the notion of there being discernible "harm footprints."

Such tribulations notwithstanding, the potential value of harm as a conceptual resource connects to its willingness to attend to relative impacts. That is, rather than measuring the efficacy of criminal justice interventions in terms of detections or convictions, at least in principle, it shifts the focus to whether interventions reduced or ended the problem, and what were the economic, political, and environmental costs involved in doing so. At least that is the theory. For there are a number of trenchant and incisive critiques of how harm has been developed and deployed. Foremost among these is Harcourt's (1999) discussion of the "collapse" of the harm principle. He contends harm has become so ubiquitous in how it is used to justify and account for various forms of security intervention, that in effect it has lost any sense of precision of definition. Similarly, Kleinig (1978: 27) states that "harm is conceptually foggy, susceptible to fictional applications and subject to ideologizing."

According to Harcourt's analysis, a pivotal moment in this diffusion of the principle of harm was the publication of Wilson and Kelling's (1982) broken windows article. Prior to this, the notion of harm was carefully modulated so as to differentiate it from acts that caused, in Feinberg's (1987) terms, "offence" or mere "nuisance." In proposing a direct causal connection between incivilities and physical disorder, and more serious crimes, the boundaries between the merely annoying or offensive, and the harmful were eroded by Wilson and Kelling. In positing a causal relation between incivilities and serious crime they identified a particular form of what von Hirsch (1996: 263) labels "remote harms."

Positioned in this way, there is a certain affinity between focusing upon signal crimes and disorders, and the measurement of harm understood as a set of effects or outcomes. This is a relationship brought to the fore by Innes's (2014) empirical analysis of reactions to eight different criminal homicides. In the aftermath of these crimes, a research team conducted in-depth interviews with local residents living close to the crime scene in order to gauge their perceptions and interpretations of the incident. Importantly, the sampling of respondents incorporated a geographic element, in that interviews were conducted at increasing distances away from the crime scene to test how far the impacts were "traveling." To conceptualize the patterns in these empirical data, Innes (2014) appropriated Hunter's (1985) conceptual schema, where he differentiated between private, parochial, and public social orders. Applied to the task of tracking and tracing the impacts of criminal homicides, it is used to delineate three principal "harm footprints." Some crimes display a "private harm footprint" wherein any cognitive, affective, or behavioral consequences are confined to those directly connected to the crime in some way. Conversely, "public harm footprints" arise when the impacts transcend any one group, traveling widely. Positioned between these two extremes are crimes with a "parochial harm footprint" where the effects register across all members of a defined community. For example, murders involving homosexual victims quite often generate a parochial harm footprint. There is a clear conceptual bridge here between the literature on harm and signal crimes.

20.4 Signaling across Different Environments

If we review the preeminent accounts that have, in different ways, engaged with studying reactions to crime, it is clear they possess particular strengths and weaknesses, and consequently things that should be taken from them:

- Broken windows theory registers that the incidence of disorder and crime events needs to be connected to, and understood, as in some way related to public attitudes and perceptions.
- Fear of crime provides many insights into factors influencing the prevalence and distribution of public reactions, and the extent to which these can be influenced by a variety of people, place, and problem variables.
- Moral panic theory is important for its temporal dimension and recognizing that reactions are dynamic, evolving, and adaptive.
- Studies of harm nuance our understandings of the social impacts of crime, and the fact that not all crimes are equal in terms of their consequences.

These are dimensions of reaction that the signal crimes perspective seeks to integrate within its conceptual purview, and in so doing, establish a potential for expanding the interests of environmental criminology. Framed by the preceding discussion this trajectory of theoretical development could attend in particular to tracing and tracking the ways in which reactions to crime, disorder, and social control "travel" across social time and space. For these are significant issues that have arisen on several occasions in the previously mentioned empirical studies that have underpinned the inception of the SCP approach. During fieldwork conducted in Surrey (UK), for instance, as part of the interview process designed to encourage interviewees to talk about how certain crime and disorder events shape their local perceptions of safety, the participants were given maps of the local area and asked to draw upon these "any areas that you don't like to go to, or that you think are unsafe." Prompted in this way, several interviewees focused upon an area near to the local canal. When questioned in more detail about why they had drawn attention to this place in particular, several mentioned that there had been an infamous rape there some years previously. As a result of which, that area had acquired a stigmatized reputation as an unsafe area, best avoided.

Similarly, when this same methodology was applied in Cardiff, in an area to the east of the city, multiple local residents singled out a wooded area as an unsettling and troublesome location when presented with the local map. Intriguingly, many of those involved could not fully articulate or explain why this was an area to avoid. It took some time to establish that there had been a murder committed in the woods some 10–15 years previously. As a result, a collective memory had become embedded.

20.5 Digital Information Environments

The concepts and approaches reviewed above have, for the most part, focused upon crime and disorders in terrestrial and material settings. However, one of the principal challenges for contemporary scholarship in environmental criminology but also more widely, is to integrate an understanding of the disruptive effects of social media and new information communication technologies. Digital environments are changing the ordering of reality as events that occur in a physical space increasingly have, or acquire, a virtual component in terms of their causes and/or consequences. As a growing number of studies are cataloging, offline and online environments for social behavior are increasingly mutually interpolated in terms of their role in the interactional and institutional ordering of society (Lynch, 2016; Harcourt, 2015). This includes how crimes and disorders are being conducted, and the processes by which they are reacted to (Marx, 2016).

The key themes from studies providing sociological analyses of social media can be usefully summarized by Donald Mackenzie's (2006) linked notion of "engines" and "cameras." Seeking to distill how big-data processing algorithms have transformed the operations of financial trading markets, he argues that they simultaneously function as an "engine" and a "camera." By the former concept, he means the sense in which they propel processes of social change and development. The latter notion attends to how market mechanisms paint a picture, or representation, of a particular situation. This duality neatly encapsulates the workings and functions of "social media" more broadly in terms of how they afford new data sources to students of society (as cameras), while simultaneously propelling the events that they depict by changing the dynamics of public awareness and communications about these (Innes et al. 2016).

Set against this backdrop where these communications platforms and technologies are transforming the institutional and interactional ordering of society, there are a growing number of accounts that have sought to map and catalog their relevance for studying crime and disorder. In particular, these studies have sought to utilize the ways that social media provide real-time and high-resolution digital traces of the series of microevents and interactions that take place in the lead-up to, and following, high-profile crimes. Such approaches are clearly coherent with the theoretical precepts of the signal crimes perspective and its imperative to articulate the harms triggered by particular crimes. For the purposes of this chapter, these developments in virtual space are interesting in terms of how they (*a*) shape what events become signal crimes and disorders; (*b*) alter the reach and power of these signals; and (*c*) enable detailed empirical study of signal decay patterns that is more challenging in the physical environment.

To illuminate these issues and how the operations of digital environments are important for understanding how certain events are interpreted as signal crimes and signal disorders, we will focus upon the case of the terrorist murder of Lee Rigby in London in 2013. There have now been several studies of the Rigby case informed by social media analytics. These include a rapid content analysis of 20,000 Twitter messages to the Metropolitan Police Service in the wake of the killing of Fusilier Rigby performed by researchers at the think tank Demos. Demos used this analysis to conclude police organizations need to develop a "Socmint" (social media intelligence) capability (Bartlett and Miller, 2013). Quantitative analysis also underpins Williams and Burnap's (2015) modeling of "cyber-hate" that is conceptualized via aspects of Cohen's (1966) formulation of moral panics. A more qualitatively inspired approach is to found in McEnery et al.'s (2015) study, where they conclude mainstream media are influential in steering the social media conversation.

The most systematic and comprehensive study using social media data yet conducted of the Rigby killing is set out in Innes et al. (2016). Based upon a data set comprising 35 million data points, comprising Twitter traffic alongside other sources, spanning the first tweet from an eyewitness at the scene of the murder who reported this to his followers, through to the conclusion of the prosecution and conviction of the two suspects, the analysis provides a detailed exposition of how social media communications have important implications for both offline and online reactions to major crimes.

Figure 20.2 displays the overall volume of social media traffic relating to the Rigby case for a six-month period. Alongside the data lines are noted several key events that happened in the aftermath of the terrorist murder, including a number of public order conflicts in different parts of the country, helping to highlight that there is an association between social media traffic and key crime and public order events occurring in different communities.

Limitations on space prohibit developing a more detailed account of these time dynamics in this chapter. However, what has been presented is sufficient to indicate the ways such data could offer potential new insights into how the effects associated with signal crimes decay over time. With this in mind, Innes et al. (2016) distill "ten 'Rs' of social reaction" from their data on the Rigby killing: reporting, requesting, responding, recruiting, risking, retaliating, recruiting, rumoring, reheating, and resilencing. Several of these are worth highlighting because they are especially relevant to the agenda outlined in the preceding sections of this chapter in affording new insights into the social dynamics and mechanics of the situated community tensions and violence that can arise in the aftermath of major crimes.

The ubiquity of social media-enabled devices and platforms means that the ways in which crime occurrences are reported publicly has fundamentally changed. There is abundant evidence that social media platforms afford "fast data", outstripping conventional media in terms of making members of the public aware when significant events have occurred. This in turn results in the impacts and implications of such crimes arising

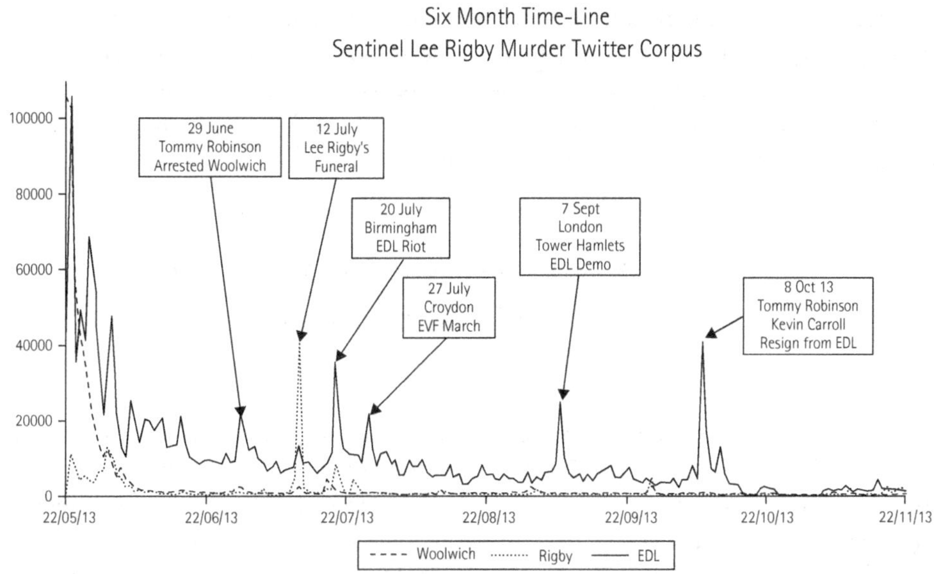

FIGURE 20.2 Data volumes for the Lee Rigby murder

more rapidly over larger geographic distances. Figure 20.2 denotes a major "spike" in social media traffic in the hours following the killing in the street of Lee Rigby as people shared reports across their social networks of the unfolding events. This included the following message from an eyewitness at the scene:

> Ohhhh myyy God! I just seen a man with his head chopped off right in front of my eyes! Woolwich (14.09, 22nd May 2013).

He then followed this up with a series of reports, including the fact that armed police had shot and arrested the two suspects. What is striking about the social media data collected and analyzed is not just the speed with which news of the killing reached around the world, but also how people locally in Woolwich were using these same platforms to inform and update one another as they encountered anomalous and unusual happenings locally—such as an air ambulance hovering overhead, large numbers of armed police officers and cars, and so forth.

Currently in the criminological literature, there exists a divide between studies of neighborhood effects of crime, and those that focus upon digital communications and the online transmission of information. They do not join up and connect in a convincing fashion to provide a comprehensive and compelling understanding of how the online affects the offline and vice versa following the occurrence of signal crimes. Indeed, this interaction is arguably one of the principal contemporary challenges for environmental criminology. Understanding how the new information environment influences behaviors, incidents, and interventions occurring in the physical world—the more orthodox fare of scholars working in this tradition—is a key undertaking for the future of this subdiscipline. Digital communications about crime and disorder are increasingly important in shaping levels of public awareness about particular events and occurrences. In effect, they are playing a key role in amplifying the impact of certain crimes so that they function as signal events, conveying messages and shaping perceptions about the distribution of risks, vulnerabilities, and threats.

20.6 Conclusions: From Fear to Public Understanding

The study of social reactions to problematic and troubling events has been an abiding concern of the social sciences. However, the discipline of criminology has not been especially well served by the way that its principal theoretical framings of the interactions between experiences and perceptions have developed. While concepts such as the fear of crime have provided compelling insights into how the occurrence of crime events have repercussions beyond those directly harmed, the key established positions attend to certain facets and vectors, rather than taking as their fundamental aim the intent to develop a comprehensive and holistic account of the causes and consequences of social reaction.

This situation can be contrasted with the approaches pertaining to other disciplines, such as the social studies of science, where the focus is upon detailing "public understanding" of reactions to innovations in scientific practice and technology (Yearley, 2005). Pivoting around a concept of "public understanding" provides the basis for a wider and more comprehensive intellectual agenda. The problems with the early formulations of public understanding of science and their adoption of a "knowledge deficit" model have been well rehearsed and dissected. Indeed, as a consequence of these early tribulations, thinking about and studying public reactions to scientific controversies has become manifestly more sophisticated and nuanced. Social scientific contributions to such debates routinely consider the interplay of how perceptions, values, knowledge, and expectations of different segments of the populace are segmented and alter over time in response to new developments in science.

There would seem to be considerable merit in criminology seeking to develop its own iteration of this kind of agenda, that is, shifting away from a focus upon fear of crime, and refocusing instead upon documenting the range of factors and influences that play into how individuals, groups, and institutions come to understand and perceive problems of crime and security. Environmental criminology's engagement with such matters should not be founded upon separating perceptions and experiences of crime, as some more established frameworks are inclined to do. Rather, perceptions and experiences are aspects of social reaction that need to be explained and accounted for on the grounds that, as W. I. Thomas opined nearly a century ago, "If men define situations as real, they are real in their consequences."

Framed in this way, the SCP has the potential to make an important contribution to such an effort. For what it affords is a conceptual apparatus via which it is possible to capture and articulate how and why some crime and disorder events exert more influence over how people perceive and interpret their situated sense of security than do others. Applied to the task of analyzing the new forms of data afforded by the proliferation and embedding of social media platforms, there is a clear potential in the SCP to generate and quantify innovative insights into processes of social reactions to crime and disorder. This aspect is important in keying into how events and their effects, in both online and offline environments, are now mutually and recursively shaping of each other. Getting to grips with these dynamics both empirically and theoretically is among the pre-eminent challenges for studies in the environmental criminology tradition.

References

Bartlett, J. and Miller, C. (2013) "@METPOLICEUK How Twitter is changing modern policing: The case of the Woolwich aftermath." Demos, London, June 19. https://www.demos.co.uk/files/_metpoliceuk.pdf?1371661838.

Bottoms, A. E. (2006) "Incivilities, offence and social order in residential communities." In A. von Hirsch and A. Simester (Eds.), *Incivilities: Regulating Offensive Behaviour*. Oxford: Hart, pp. 239–280.

Bottoms, A. E. (2012) "Developing socio-spatial criminology." In M. Maguire, R. Morgan, and R. Reiner (Eds.), *Oxford Handbook of Criminology*, 5th ed. Oxford: Oxford University Press, pp. 528–575.

Bowling, B. (1999) "The rise and fall of New York murder: Zero tolerance or crack's decline?" *British Journal of Criminology*, 39, 4: 531–554.

Cohen, S. ([1966] 2002) *Folk Devils and Moral Panics*. 3rd ed. London: Routledge.

Ditton, J., Bannister, J., Gilchrist, E., and Farrall, S. (1999) "Afraid or angry? Recalibrating the 'fear' of crime." *International Review of Victimology* 6(2): 83–99.

Ditton, J. and Innes M. (2005) "The role of perceptual intervention in the management of the fear of crime." In N. Tilley (Ed.), *The Handbook of Crime Prevention and Community Safety*. London: Willan, pp. 595–623.

Eco, U. (1976) *A Theory of Semiotics*. Bloomington: Indiana University Press.

Feinberg, J. (1987) *The Moral Limits of the Criminal Law*. Vol. 1: *Harm to Others*. Oxford: Oxford University Press.

Fielding, N. and Innes, M. (2006) "Reassurance policing, community policing and measuring police performance." *Policing and Society* 16(2): 127–145.

Girling, E., Loader, I., and Sparks, R. (2000) *Crime and Social Change in Middle England*. London: Routledge.

Goffman, E. (1972) "Normal appearances." In *Relations in Public: Microstudies of the Public Order*. New York: Harper & Row.

Greenfield, V. and Paoli, L. (2013) "A framework to assess the harms of crime." *British Journal of Criminology* 53(5): 864–865.

Hale, C. (1996) "Fear of crime: A review of the literature." *International Review of Victimology* 4(2): 79–150.

Harcourt, B. (1999) "The collapse of the harm principle." *Journal of Criminal Law and Criminology* 90(1): 109–194.

Harcourt, B. (2015) *Exposed: Desire and Disobedience in the Digital Age.* Cambridge, MA: Harvard University Press.

Hunter, A. (1985) "Private, parochial and public social orders: The problem of crime and incivility in urban communities." In G. F. Suttles and M. N. Zald (Eds.), *The Challenge of Social Control: Citizenship and Institution Building in Modern Society.* Norwood NJ: Ablex, pp. 230–242.

Innes M. (2004) "Signal crimes and signal disorders: Notes on deviance as communicative action." *British Journal of Sociology* 55(3): 335–355.

Innes, M. (2014) *Signal Crimes: Social Reactions to Crime, Disorder and Control.* Oxford: Oxford University Press.

Innes, M. and Fielding, N. (2002) "From community to communicative policing: 'Signal crimes' and the problem of public reassurance." *Sociological Research Online* 7(2). http://socresonline.org.uk/7/2/innes.html.

Innes, M., Roberts, C., Preece, A., and Rogers, D. (2016) "Ten 'Rs' of social reaction: Using social media to analyse the 'post-event' impacts of the murder of Lee Rigby." *Terrorism and Political Violence*, Epub July 7. doi.org/10.1080/09546553.2016.1180289.

Jacobs, Ronald N. (1996) "Civil Society and Crisis: Culture, Discourse, and the Rodney King Beating." *American Journal of Sociology* 101(5): 1238–1272.

Keizer, K., Lindenberg, S., and Steg, L. (2008) "The spreading of disorder." *Science* 322(5908): 1681–1685. Epub November 20. doi.org/10.1126/science.1161405.

Kleinig, J. (1978) "Crime and the concept of harm." *American Philosophical Quarterly* 15(1): 27–36.

Lynch, M. (2016) *The Internet of Us: Knowing More and Understanding Less in an Age of Big Data.* New York: Liveright.

Mackenzie, D. (2006) *An Engine Not a Camera: How Financial Models Shape Markets.* Cambridge, MA: MIT Press.

Manning, P. K. (1987) *Semiotics and Fieldwork.* Qualitative Research Methods No. 7. Thousand Oaks, CA: Sage.

Marx, G. (2016) *Windows into the Soul: Surveillance and Society in an Age of High Technology.* Chicago: University of Chicago Press.

McEnery, T., McGlashan, M., and Love, R. (2015) "Press and media reaction to ideologically inspired murder: The case of Lee Rigby." *Discourse and Communication* 9(2): 1–23.

Morris, C. W. (1964) *Signification and Significance: A Study of the Relation of Signs and Values.* Cambridge, MA: MIT Press.

Sampson, R. (2012) *Great American City.* Chicago: University of Chicago Press.

Sampson, R. and Raudenbush, S. (1999) "Systematic social observation of public spaces: A new look at disorder in urban neighbourhoods." *American Journal of Sociology* 105: 603–651.

Sherman, L., Neyroud, P., and Neyroud, E. (2016) "The Cambridge Crime Harm Index: Measuring total harm from crime based on sentencing guidelines." *Policing* 10(3): 171–183.

Skogan, W. (1990) *Disorder and Decline: Crime and the Spiral of Decay in American Cities.* Berkeley: University of California Press.

Sparrow, M. K. (2008) *The Character of Harms: Operational Challenges in Control.* Cambridge: Cambridge University Press.

Taylor, R. B. (2000) *Breaking Away from Broken Windows.* Boulder, CO: Westview Press.

Taylor, R. B. (2015) *Community Criminology: Fundamentals of Spatial and Temporal Scaling, Ecological Indicators, and Selectivity Bias.* New York: New York University Press.

Tuffin, R., Morris, J., and Poole, A. (2006) *An Evaluation of the Impact of the National Reassurance Policing Programme.* Home Office Research Study No. 296. London: Home Office.

Von Hirsch, A. (1996) "Extending the harm principle: 'Remote' harms and fair imputation." In A. P. Simester and A. T. H. Smith (Eds.), *Harm and Culpability.* Oxford: Clarendon Press, p. 259.

Welsh, B. C., Braga, A. A., and Bruinsma, G. J. N. (2015) "Re-imagining broken windows: From theory to policy." *Journal of Research in Crime and Delinquency* 52(4): 447–463.

Wilkins, L. T. (1964) *Social Deviance: Social Policy, Action and Research.* London: Tavistock.

Williams, M. L. and Burnap, P. (2015) "Cyberhate on social media in the aftermath of Woolwich: A case study in computational criminology and big data." *British Journal of Criminology* 56(2): 211–238.

Wilson, J. Q. and Kelling, G. L. (1982) "Broken windows: The police and neighborhood safety." *Atlantic Monthly,* March: 29–38.

Yearley, S. (2005) *Making Sense of Science.* London: Sage.

Zimring, F. (2011) *The City That Became Safe: New York's Lessons for Urban Crime and Its Control.* New York: Oxford University Press.

Built Environment

CHAPTER 21

BUILT ENVIRONMENT, LAND USE, AND CRIME

KATHRYN WUSCHKE AND J. BRYAN KINNEY

21.1 Introduction

The built urban environment plays an important role in shaping the movement patterns of residents. Individuals travel from their homes, to workplaces, schools, and shopping or entertainment areas as part of their daily routine movements. These movements occur at predictable times, using predictable routes, to predictable—and often shared—urban locations. The collective and patterned movements of urban residents lead to the convergence of both offenders and potential targets in time and space, and in doing so, shape the distribution of opportunities for crime. As a result, opportunities cluster in specific locations while being largely absent in other areas.

Grounded within environmental criminology, several theoretical frameworks have emphasized the important connection between land use and concentrations of urban crime, most notably Cohen and Felson's routine activities approach, and Brantingham and Brantingham's geometry of crime (Cohen and Felson 1979; Brantingham and Brantingham 1991, 1993). Guided by these approaches, this chapter provides an overview of existing research exploring the varied connections between urban land use and crime. These concepts are illustrated through the use of a multiscale research example centered on one Canadian municipality. The results from this research highlight the importance of locally based studies, and emphasize that the relationship between land use and crime varies according to both crime type and scale of analysis.

21.2 Land Use and Crime: Surveying the Field

The nonrandom nature of crime has been emphasized within and supported by environmental criminology theorists for decades. Cohen and Felson's routine activities approach explores criminal activity in the same lens as other everyday occurrences, resulting from the normal behavior patterns of urban residents (Cohen and Felson 1979). The urban population moves in predictable and patterned ways. These movement patterns facilitate the convergence of motivated offenders and suitable targets in time and space; if this interaction occurs in the absence of a capable guardian, this creates the opportunity for crime. This patterned movement occurs within the confines of the built urban environment—we travel from one specific place to another using the travel routes available.

At an individual level, daily travel patterns typically consist of movement between personal activity nodes: locations such as home, work or school, shopping, and entertainment areas are examples of such nodes. These locations are connected via pathways such as road networks. The Brantinghams' geometry of crime theory emphasizes that the network created by these routinely frequented nodes and pathways form an individual's activity space. This space, as well as the surrounding areas, forms a broader awareness space, within which individuals spend the majority of their time (Brantingham and Brantingham 1993). As such, offenders are most likely to search for and identify potential targets from within their personal awareness spaces (Brantingham and Brantingham 1991). Further, the majority of the specific nodes and pathways that form an individual awareness space are frequented by many people, and are therefore part of a broader, common awareness space. The common nodes and pathways that are shared by a greater proportion of the urban population, then, have the potential to attract more crime, as they form part of the awareness space of more offenders and potential targets alike (Brantingham and Brantingham 1993).

Common activity nodes and major pathways are, by definition, part of the legitimate awareness spaces of many people. Such features also tend to be spatially concentrated within urban areas: commercial businesses are often located in clusters along well-traveled streets, for example. Such areas may be bordered by higher-density residential areas, recreation centers, and other land use types that benefit from a large confluence of people. Areas where two or more land uses or environmental features converge form an edge within the urban environment. In these edges—the foci of change between one type of urban space and another—criminal events tend to concentrate. This may be associated with the increase in opportunities due to the convergence of activity nodes and pathways, as well as the decreased ability to identify insiders or outsiders within these areas (Brantingham and Brantingham 1993).

While such common spaces have the potential for more crime, in practice not all shared activity nodes and pathways are associated with equal amounts of criminal events. Recognizing this, the Brantinghams introduced the concepts of the crime generator and the crime attractor. Locations where large numbers of people travel to (or through) during daily routines can be crime generators (Brantingham and Brantingham 1995). With high volumes of people, concentrations of crime can emerge due to the increase in both offenders and potential targets. Criminal events that occur at generators are typically crimes of opportunity. Shopping centers and transit nodes are examples of common crime generators. In contrast, crime attractors are locations offenders specifically travel to for the purposes of committing crimes (Brantingham and Brantingham 1995). These locations may also have high volumes of routine visitors—though this is not necessary; rather, they tend to be well known as a "good" spot to commit specific types of crimes. Offenders will travel longer distances to reach crime attractors. As such, the types of offenses that concentrate at these sites are often specific to the location itself—they may be violent offenses at a particular bar, drug offenses at a specific park, or auto-related theft offenses at a suitable parking lot (Brantingham and Brantingham 1995).

These theoretical contributions have been tested and applied with increasing frequency in recent years. Such research has further emphasized the highly clustered nature of criminal activity, as well as the important connections between the physical urban environment, and local crime patterns. Land use, in particular, shapes the spatial distribution of urban crime: the land use of a specific area plays an important role in determining how and when that location is used, and by whom. Land use types that attract a large number of individuals, such as commercial areas, are also frequently found to be associated with higher concentrations of crime when compared to other land use types (Brantingham and Brantingham 1991; Hirschfield and Bowers 1997; Kinney et al. 2008; Song et al. 2013; Summers and Johnson 2017; Wang et al. 2017). Further concentration can be identified when exploring specific land use subtypes: schools, bars, parks, shopping malls, public housing, and transit nodes, to name just a few, are all regularly identified as higher-crime urban features (Roncek and LoBosco 1983; Brantingham and Brantingham 1995; Newton and Bowers 2007; McCord and Ratcliffe 2007, 2009; Kinney et al. 2008; Ratcliffe 2012; Groff 2011, 2014; Groff and Lockwood 2014; Newton et al. 2014). Crime does not concentrate uniformly across these facilities, however: micro-scale research has indicated that a small proportion of such crime attractors and generators tend to be associated with a large proportion of overall crime (Brantingham et al. 1976; Eck et al. 2007; Bowers 2013; Haberman et al. 2013; Weisburd, 2015). These findings also vary by urban setting, emphasizing the importance of a locally based understanding of the connections between crime and urban features (Rengert et al. 2000; Ackerman and Murray 2004; Charron et al. 2008; Song et al. 2017).

21.3 Research Example: Land Use and Crime within Coquitlam, British Columbia, Canada

Existing theoretical and empirical research exploring the connections between environmental features and urban crime have emphasized that crime concentrates within specific land use types and at specific facilities. To illustrate these patterns, the connections between land use and crime are explored in detail, within one Canadian municipality. Coquitlam, British Columbia, is a midsized suburb of Vancouver, which is the largest municipality in western Canada. With a population of just over 125,000, Coquitlam is predominantly a residential-based commuter suburb, although this trend is changing due to considerable local redevelopment and high population growth occurring within the locale (City of Coquitlam 2008; Statistics Canada 2012). The city center area has been the focus of particularly concentrated development, expanding to act as the regional downtown core for Coquitlam, as well as several other smaller surrounding suburbs (Metro Vancouver 2011). As a result, a dense urban mix of land uses have been approved for ongoing development within this neighborhood, including an expansion of the regional mall, a satellite campus of a large local college, and the development of a number of community centers and cultural facilities (City of Coquitlam 2008).

Given the rapid and concentrated redevelopment underway within Coquitlam, there is a pressing need for further insight into the local relationship between crime and land use. Guided by similarly structured research presented by Kinney and colleagues, this research explores the local connections between land use and two broad crime classifications: crimes against property, and crimes against persons (Kinney et al. 2008). Beginning with address-matched crime and land use data, we explore the relationship between the built environment and crime across multiple levels of aggregation.

21.3.1 Local Data Sources

Police services are provided in Coquitlam by a municipal detachment of the Royal Canadian Mounted Police (RCMP), which jointly serves several smaller neighboring communities. All records occurring within this detachment in 2008 (n = 41,881) were provided for this analysis. From this data set, all events classified as property crimes or crimes against persons were selected (12,033 events). This subset was geocoded according to the address recorded as the event location, with 98% of records resulting in a match. All events occurring outside of the municipal boundaries were excluded (accounting for 3,673 events that occurred outside of the city of Coquitlam), as were all events that were classified as unfounded (1,716 events) and all events recorded at the address of the detachment's main police station (56 events). The latter events were excluded based on reported inconsistencies with data-recording practices at such addresses (see, for example, Groff 2011). This initial data cleaning resulted in a data set including 5,363 property crimes and 989 founded crimes against persons occurring within the municipal boundaries of Coquitlam in 2008.

Land use data was provided for this analysis by the City of Coquitlam, and is collected by a provincial corporation that compiles actual use information about each property for taxation purposes. This detailed, address-level data classifies every taxable unit within the province into one of seven broad land use categories: residential; farm; commercial; stratified operational facilities areas (SOFA: common properties within stratified housing complexes); industrial, transportation, and utility (TCU); and civic, institutional, and recreational (CIR: a broad category including a variety of land use types, including park spaces, government buildings, schools, and hospitals). Each unit is further classified into a detailed subcategory, representing the actual use of land at the time of assessment. In 2008, there were 39,779 taxable property units listed within the Coquitlam data set. Each record was geocoded by address, with 99% of the data matching to a point location in the process.

While the detailed land use data provides a considerable amount of insight into the actual use of land within Coquitlam, there are some limitations associated with this source. As the data is collected for the purposes of taxation, each individually owned property is listed as a unique record. This results in different recording practices for some otherwise similar land use types: shopping complexes with one owner, and a number of tenanted stores, are listed as one record, while shopping complexes comprised of individually owned units result in separate records for each property. Likewise, residential condominiums typically include one record per unit, while rental apartments are listed as one record per complex. To maintain consistency across similar land use classifications, all data was merged according to address and land use category, resulting in one record for each land use at a given address. While this results in the loss of some data, it enabled consistency in comparison of similar property types. The final data set provided a list of 25,274 properties within Coquitlam in 2008, each represented by a spatial point. Figure 21.1 illustrates the land use data set and emphasizes the considerable amount of residential properties within the municipality.

21.3.2 Merging Data Sets

The crime and land use data sets form the basis of the analysis within this study. In order to explore the connections between local land use and crime, the two sources were joined based on address. The land use data set was joined to the crime records, enhancing each address-matched event with a detailed land use classification. While this match provided greater detail to the majority of the crime records, a number of events were recorded with uncertain address information and could not be directly matched. This included events recorded at intersections and those recorded at the 100 block, for example. These unmatched records form a sizable proportion of the data set: 17% of property crimes and 21% of crimes against persons could not be directly matched with a land use record.

Crime events with an address recorded at intersections and at the 100 block are naturally associated with a level of spatial uncertainty. Intersection events could be associated with any one of four (or more) contiguous properties; events recorded at the 100 block could be associated with any of the properties along either side of the block face on

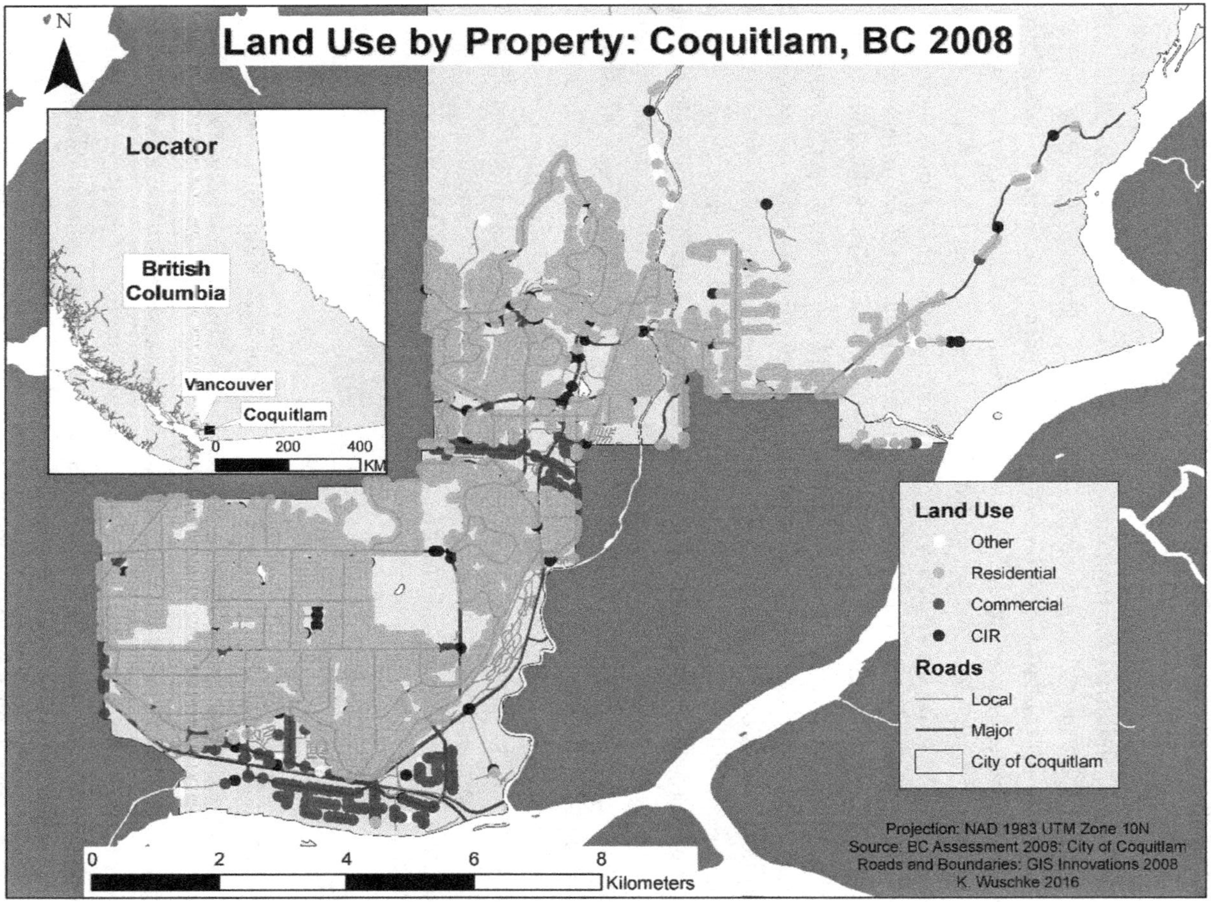

FIGURE 21.1 Spatial distribution of land use within Coquitlam, British Columbia, in 2008

which they were recorded. Further, these events may have occurred on the streets themselves, rather than at or on a nearby property. Several methods could be used to link these uncertain events to land use records, including spatially joining each crime event with the closest geocoded property, or allocating a proportion of each uncertain event to all neighboring properties (see, for example, Hibdon and Groff 2014). Further, events occurring on the road network could be analyzed separately, or could be removed from the analysis entirely (see, for examples, Braga et al. 2010; Andresen and Curman 2016; Weisburd et al. 2004, 2009). Given the focus of this particular analysis is to explore the relationship between specific land uses and crime, such events that could not be clearly linked to a direct property were removed from this analysis. This reduced the number of property crimes to 4,434 events, and the number of crimes against persons to 778.

The land use data set provides insight into the physical built environment, as well as the actual use of land within the study site. At the same time, the matched police records reveal the spatial distribution of recorded crime and disorder events in Coquitlam. Joining these data sets and analyzing the result at different levels of aggregation allows for a detailed understanding of the locally based connections between land use and crime within this midsized locale.

21.4 Results

21.4.1 Exploring Land Use at the Macro Level

As primarily a commuter-based suburb, Coquitlam is predominantly residential. As illustrated in Table 21.1, 96% of all lots within the municipality are classified as such. A considerably smaller proportion of the city properties are classified as commercial (2%) or CIR (1%). A nominal proportion of properties in the city fall into one of the remaining classifications: less than half of 1% of the total lots are industrial, TCU, farm, or SOFA. The overall count of both property crimes and crimes against persons follows a similar trend, with most events falling in residential areas, followed by commercial, then CIR; and very few events (if any at all) occurring on all other properties. When we consider the proportion of criminal events per property, a different picture begins to emerge. While 96% of the city is residential, only 55% of property crimes occur on residential lots. In comparison, a highly disproportionate amount of crimes fall on lots designated as commercial or CIR, with nearly three events per commercial lot, and just under one event per lot designated as CIR.

While crimes against persons occur much more infrequently than property crimes, the relative concentrations of such events per lot follow trends like those associated with more common property crimes. Within Coquitlam, 0.02 crimes against persons occur per residential lot, in comparison to 0.3 events per commercial lot, and 0.2 events per lot designated as CIR. While such violent crime is rare within Coquitlam as a whole, the rates are an order of magnitude greater on commercial and CIR land uses, than on residential properties. No violent offenses at all were recorded on any other property type in 2008.

Table 21.1 Macro-Level Analysis: Crimes against Property and Crimes against Persons by Broad Land Use Category

Land use	Lots	% of all lots	Crimes against property	% Crimes against property	Crimes against property / lot	Crimes against persons	% Crimes against persons	Crimes against persons / lot
Residential	24209	95.79	2428	54.76	0.10	517	66.45	0.02
Commercial	612	2.42	1664	37.53	2.72	180	23.14	0.29
CIR	353	1.40	322	7.26	0.91	81	10.41	0.23
Industrial	45	0.13	12	0.27	0.27	0	0.00	0.00
TCU	32	0.13	4	0.09	0.13	0	0.00	0.00
Farm	21	0.08	4	0.09	0.19	0	0.00	0.00
SOFA	2	0.01	0	0.00	0.00	0	0.00	0.00
Grand total	**25,274**	**100.00**	**4,434**	**100.00**	**0.18**	**778**	**100.00**	**0.03**

Considering the macro-level trends within Coquitlam, it is clear that over 99.5% of properties are identified as residential, commercial, and CIR, and over 99.5% of events fall on properties classified as such. However, crimes are not evenly distributed across these three categories: both commercial and CIR properties reveal disproportionate rates of events per lot. While there are considerably more property offenses than crimes against persons in the data set, the general proportion of crime events by land use category reveals similarities. These events are mapped in Figure 21.2 to explore whether

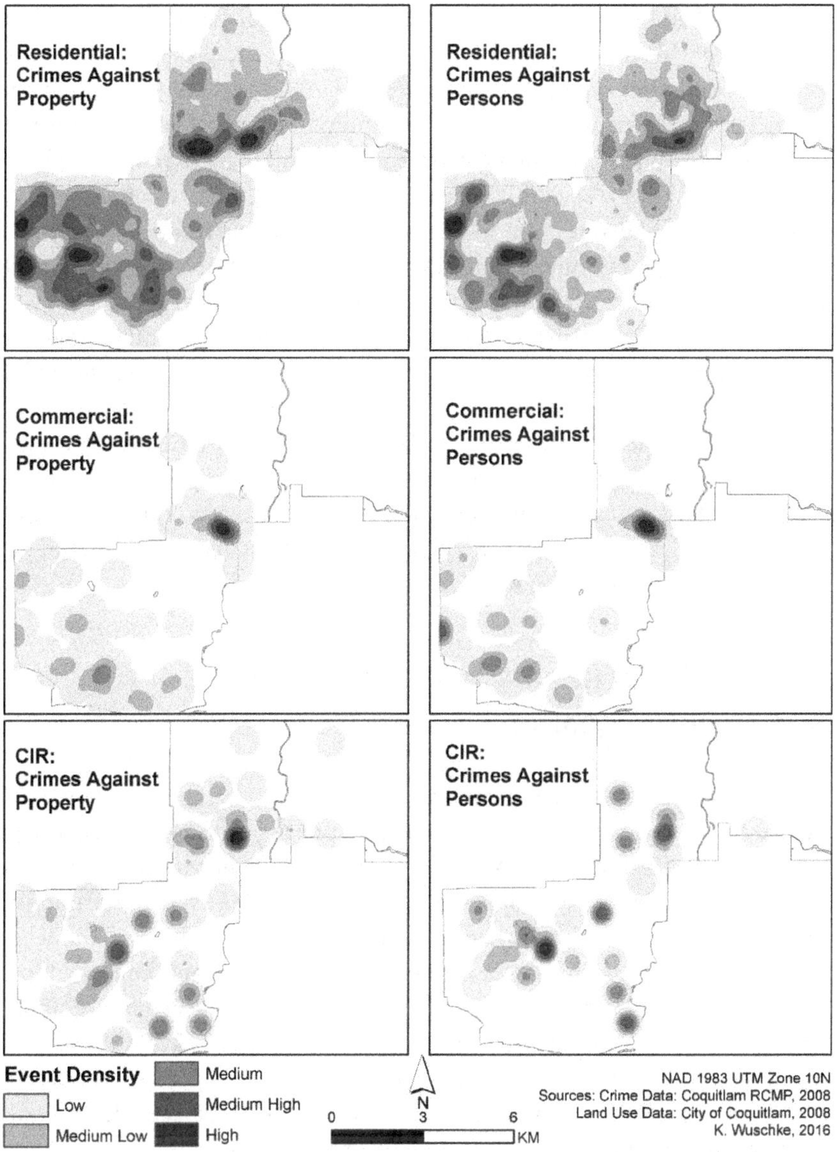

FIGURE 21.2 Spatial distribution of crimes against property and crimes against persons according to broad land use classification, Coquitlam, British Columbia, 2008

differences emerge when we consider the spatial distribution of these crime events according to land use category.

The maps displayed on the left side of Figure 21.2 reveal the spatial distribution of crimes against property, according to the land use on which the event occurred; those on the right side of the figure reveal the equivalent patterns for crimes against persons. When considered in connection with Figure 21.1, showing the spatial distribution of the land use types themselves, these maps emphasize the spatial concentration *within* land use categories. Further, this concentration within categories reveals some differences according to crime type. Andresen's spatial point pattern test (Andresen 2009) can be used to describe the difference between the distribution of crimes against persons and properties. With this test, point data for both crime types, classified according to the land use of the event address, is aggregated to small census areal units and compared for spatial similarity. The test produces an index of similarity, *S*, ranging between 0 (indicating no similarity) and 1 (representing perfect similarity). The results reveal that the spatial patterns of property crimes and crimes against persons are quite different when considering residential land use (with a global *S*-value of .25), but much more similar for both commercial properties (with a global *S*-value of .86) and CIR properties (with a global S-value of .77).

The tabular and mapped macro-level results emphasize that both crimes against property and crimes against persons cluster according to land use category, and across urban space. The results presented in Table 21.1 emphasize that the vast majority of events occur on lots designated as residential, commercial, or CIR, with the highest rates of events per lot associated with the latter two categories. Figure 21.2 illustrates that *within* these land use categories, further spatial clustering exists. These findings direct the subsequent analysis, which explores how crimes against both property and persons concentrate within land use categories.

21.4.2 Meso-Level Results: Exploring within Category Variation

While the connections between crime and land use are apparent at the macro level, such concentrations are further evident when exploring within land use categories. Tables 21.2, 21.3, and 21.4 illustrate a considerable variation in the rates of both crimes against property and crimes against persons, within each of the three key land use classifications. Each of these tables displays the top five land use subtypes with the highest rates of crime events per lot; first, for crimes against property, and followed by crimes against persons. These land use subclassifications represent the actual use of land for each property, as determined by the yearly taxation assessment. Table 21.2 emphasizes that not all residential properties exhibit the low rates of crime per lot portrayed by the macro-level analysis. Further, Tables 21.3 and 21.4 emphasize the considerable overrepresentation of specific commercial and CIR land use subtypes.

The residential land use category as a whole reveals a relatively high count of both crimes against property and crimes against persons. However, as the vast majority of

Table 21.2 Top Five Actual Land Uses, Sorted by Rate of Crime per Lot: Residential Properties

Crimes against property on residential properties

Actual use of land subcategory	Lots	% of residential lots (n = 24,209)	Crimes against property	% of crime on residential lots (n = 2428)	Crimes against property / lot
Mobile Home Park	4	0.02	16	0.66	4.00
Stratified Rental Apartments–Frame	7	0.03	26	1.07	3.71
Multi-Family Apartment Blocks	64	0.26	169	6.96	2.64
Strata Lot Residences (Condo)	174	0.72	384	15.82	2.21
Multi-Family–Conversions	18	0.07	38	1.57	2.11
Total, top 5 residential categories	**267**	**1.10**	**633**	**26.07**	**2.37**

Crimes against persons on residential properties

Actual use of land subcategory	Lots	% of residential lots (n = 24,209)	Crimes against persons	% of crime on residential lots (n = 517)	Crimes against persons / lot
Mobile Home Park	4	0.02	11	2.13	2.75
Multi-Family–Garden Apartments and Row Housing	18	0.07	26	5.03	1.44
Multi-Family Apartment Blocks	64	0.26	69	13.35	1.08
Multi-Family–Minimal Commercial	1	0.00	1	0.19	1.00
2 Acres or More–Manufactured Homes	2	0.01	2	0.39	1.00
Total, top 5 residential categories	**89**	**0.37**	**109**	**21.08**	**1.22**

Table 21.3 Top Five Actual Land Uses, Sorted by Rate of Crime per Lot: Commercial Properties

Crimes against property on commercial properties

Actual use of land subcategory	Lots	% of commercial lots ($n = 612$)	Crimes against property	% of crime on commercial lots ($n = 1,664$)	Crimes against property / lot
Regional Shopping Centres	1	0.16	293	17.61	293.00
Theatre Buildings	1	0.16	73	4.39	73.00
Community Shopping Centres	4	0.65	273	16.41	68.25
Food Markets	2	0.33	30	1.80	15.00
Hotels	4	0.65	57	3.43	14.25
Total, top 5 commercial categories	**12**	**1.96**	**726**	**43.63**	**60.50**

Crimes against persons on commercial properties

Actual use of land subcategory	Lots	% of commercial lots ($n = 612$)	Crimes against persons	% of crime on commercial lots ($n = 180$)	Crimes against persons / lot
Regional Shopping Centres	1	0.16	28	15.56	28.00
Theatre Buildings	1	0.16	7	3.89	7.00
Community Shopping Centres	4	0.65	21	11.67	5.25
Hotels	4	0.65	20	11.11	5.00
Motels and Auto Courts	1	0.16	3	1.67	3.00
Total, top 5 commercial categories	**11**	**1.80**	**79**	**43.89**	**7.18**

Table 21.4 Top Five Actual Land Uses, Sorted by Rate of Crime per Lot: Civic, Institutional, and Recreational (CIR) Properties

Crimes against property on CIR properties					
Actual use of land subcategory	Lots	% of CIR lots ($n = 353$)	Crimes against property	% of crime on CIR lots ($n = 322$)	Crimes against property / lot
Hospitals	2	0.57	26	8.07	13.00
Recreational and Cultural Buildings	13	3.68	78	24.22	6.00
Educational Institutions	48	13.60	174	54.04	3.63
Works Yards	2	0.57	3	0.93	1.50
Recreational Clubs	1	0.28	1	0.31	1.00
Total, top 5 CIR categories	**66**	**18.70**	**282**	**87.58**	**4.27**

Crimes against persons on CIR properties					
Actual use of land subcategory	Lots	% of CIR lots ($n = 353$)	Crimes against persons	% of crime on CIR lots ($n = 81$)	Crimes against persons / lot
Hospitals	2	0.57	11	13.58	5.50
Educational Institutions	48	13.60	51	62.96	1.06
Works Yards	2	0.557	2	2.47	1.00
Recreational and Cultural Buildings	13	3.68	7	8.64	0.54
Government Buildings	8	2.27	1	1.23	0.13
Total, top 5 CIR categories	**73**	**20.68**	**72**	**88.89**	**0.99**

Coquitlam is residential, the overall rate of crimes per residential property is minimal. When exploring the subcategories of residential land use, however, some additional concentrations emerge. Each of the top five residential land use subcategories with the highest rates of property crimes per lot is a multifamily unit. Further, four out of the top five residential categories with the highest rates of crimes against persons are multifamily. These results must be understood in context—each lot count represents the total number of properties, rather than the total number of units or residents. The rates of events per lot are therefore indicative of a high count of crimes per mobile home park or per apartment block, for example, rather than a high count of events per potential target. Accordingly, the rates for multifamily lots should be expected to be considerably higher than the corresponding rate per single family dwelling, and must be interpreted with care. Further, high crime rates generated by few events distributed across few lots provide little insight into local crime concerns. The fourth and fifth listings for crimes against persons per residential lot (Table 21.2) emphasize this pattern, and further highlight the low overall rates of this crime type within residential land use. While these results reflect the need for careful interpretation of results, these meso-level findings continue to emphasize considerable within-category concentration: 26% of all property crimes that occur on a residential lot fall on 1% of residential addresses; 21% of all crimes against persons occurring on a residential property occur on less than half of 1% of the total residential lots.

At an aggregate level, Coquitlam's commercial properties exhibit the highest rates of crimes per unit in comparison to other land use types within the locale. Looking within this land use category, the concentration of events is further apparent (see Table 21.3). When we consider only events occurring at commercial addresses, both crimes against properties and crimes against persons occur in highest counts at Coquitlam's regional shopping center. In fact, 34% of all property crimes and 27% of all crimes against persons recorded on commercial lots are concentrated at five shopping complexes (regional and community-level). As with the multifamily residential complexes, the count of commercial crimes per lot does not account for the increased availability of targets at such high-density commercial locations, so the associated events per lot can be expected to be considerably higher at a shopping mall, for example, than at a smaller commercial property. However, the considerable count of events attributed to the city's malls emphasizes the local importance of this land use subcategory in shaping the distribution of both property crimes and crimes against persons within Coquitlam. In addition to shopping centers, the city's large multiscreen movie theater complex and local hotels also reveal high rates of crime. Food markets reveal a high rate of property crime within the locale, while motels and auto courts round out the top five categories for crimes against persons—however, the rate of events per location at the latter location is inflated by a low number of events occurring at one address. Overall, 44% of both property crimes and crimes against persons occurring on commercial lots can be accounted for by just 2% of the total commercial lots.

Just as both the broad residential and commercial land use categories include subcategories with high concentrations of crime, the CIR category also reveals this within-category clustering. Table 21.4 emphasizes the concentration of crimes against property and persons occurring on land use designated within this broad category. The mixed-use CIR classification contains a large array of land use subcategories, encompassing a variety of actual uses. Coquitlam's two hospitals have the highest rate of both crimes against property and persons, with recreational buildings, schools, and works yards also making appearances among the top five categories for both crime types. However, Table 21.4 reveals a considerable variation in both the count of crimes and the count of units within the detailed CIR subcategories. When we consider the actual use subtypes with both high counts of crime and high rates of events per unit, the local hospitals, recreation centers, and schools appear to be important land use types when considering property crimes. Hospitals and schools alone appear to be the most relevant subtypes when considering crimes against persons. The overall concentration within the CIR category is illustrated in Table 21.4: nearly 90% of both property crimes and crimes against persons are concentrated on approximately 20% of the total CIR lots, and can be largely accounted for by the few, specific categories listed.

21.4.3 Micro-Level Results: High-Crime Addresses

Coquitlam's crimes concentrate in high rates on commercial and CIR properties; and in high counts (but very low rates) on residential land uses. When we explore the meso-level relationships between crime and land use, considerable within-category variation is present in each of these categories—some residential land use subcategories exhibit higher counts *and* rates of crime, and some commercial land use types emphasize even further concentration within this already high-crime category. Perhaps most interestingly, the CIR category further underscores the need for such within-category analysis: while the broad land use category reveals relatively high rates of both property crimes and crimes against persons, the meso-level analysis indicates that much of this concentration occurs on very specific land use subcategories—hospitals, schools, and, when we consider property crimes, at recreational and cultural buildings.

The concentrations noted at the meso-level naturally emphasize the need to consider a finer resolution of analysis. Are there further concentrations at the specific address? Tables 21.5 and 21.6 reveal the detailed land use of the top five addresses with the highest counts of crimes against property and crimes against persons in Coquitlam in 2008. The top single address location for both crime types is, as expected, the city's single regional shopping center. Nearly 7% of all property crime and 4% of all crimes against persons are concentrated within this target-rich address (see Tables 21.5 and 21.6). The remaining highest crime addresses, however, differ according to crime type. Each of the top five property crime locations is a commercial address, and four out of these five locations are shopping centers (see Table 21.5). In contrast, the addresses with the highest concentrations of crimes against persons display greater variability by land use type, with a hotel, a school, a single apartment block, and a mobile home park accounting for the top local

Table 21.5 Top Five Properties with Highest Crime Counts, reported by Actual Land Use Type: Crimes against Property

Actual land use description	Broad land use category	Crimes against property	% Crimes against property
Regional Shopping Centre (A)	Commercial	293	6.61
Community Shopping Centre (A)	Commercial	108	2.44
Community Shopping Centre (B)	Commercial	99	2.23
Theatre Building (A)	Commercial	73	1.65
Neighborhood Shopping Centre (A)	Commercial	45	1.01
Total, top 5 properties		**618**	**13.94**

Table 21.6 Top 5 Properties with Highest Crime Counts, Reported by Actual Land Use Type: Crimes against Persons

Actual land use description	Broad land use category	Crimes against persons	% Crimes against persons
Regional Shopping Centre (A)	Commercial	28	3.60
Hotel (A)	Commercial	14	1.80
Educational Institution (A)	CIR	11	1.41
Multi-Family Apartment Block (A)	Residential	10	1.29
Mobile Home Park (A)	Residential	9	1.16
Total, top 5 properties		**72**	**9.25**

crime spots in 2008 (see Table 21.6). It is worthy of note that all of the top crime locations reflect areas rich in targets, emphasizing the importance of contextualizing such findings according to the actual use of each address.

21.5 Discussion

Decades of research within environmental criminology and beyond have emphasized that crime concentrates within urban environments. Criminal events may cluster in areas that are part of the awareness spaces of many individuals, as these areas tend to be familiar to offenders, and rich in targets (Cohen and Felson 1979; Brantingham and Brantingham 1991). The land use of a given location has clear implications on the likelihood that it is part of a broader awareness space, and therefore, the likelihood that it could be associated with higher volumes of crime. These implications are apparent across a variety of spatial scales.

At the macro level, commercial areas are associated with a disproportionate rate of crime per address, when compared to other land use types in the study site. Such locations are naturally designed to attract residents and visitors. They are often located in easily accessible locations, and commercial properties themselves appear to concentrate in space. These local urban destinations may become hotspots of both property crimes and crimes against persons for these reasons. Likewise, properties designated under the broad civic, institutional, and recreational (CIR) category can also be frequent common destinations. Schools, hospitals, parks, and recreation centers all fall within this broad classification. While these types of locations exhibit less spatial concentration, they continue to act as local destinations, and it is not surprising that they are also associated with higher crime rates per address. Residential properties make up the vast majority of the suburban study site, and account for the largest proportion of overall crimes, but the overall rate of crimes per residential address is considerably lower than events falling on either commercial or CIR land uses.

There is little apparent difference in the overall patterning of different crime types according to land use at the aggregate, city-wide level: the highest rates of crime are identified on addresses classified as commercial, then CIR; relatively low rates are found on properties identified as residential, and a negligible amount is located on the very few properties falling into other land use classifications. However, when investigating the spatial distribution of these trends, some interesting disparities do emerge. The spatial distributions of both property crime and crimes against persons on residential properties are different; but quite similar spatial patterns emerge when considering the distribution of both crime categories on commercial and CIR properties. Distinct spatial crime clusters appear in all cases; however, both property crimes and crimes against persons appear to concentrate near the same commercial and CIR properties. This underscores the importance of exploring crime concentrations across different levels of aggregation. Further, such findings emphasize the importance of considering alternative crime categorizations: while a considerable difference between crime types was only illustrated within the predominant residential land use category, the two crime classifications considered are both highly aggregated categories. Recent research suggests that different spatial patterns are likely to emerge when considering more uniform crime classifications (Andresen and Linning 2012). Accordingly, more nuanced crime categories should be further explored within subsequent research.

Evidence of spatial clustering within land use categories fueled further explorations at the meso level. Results continue to emphasize clustering and reiterate the lack of within-category uniformity across each land use category of interest. Some residential land use classifications revealed considerably higher rates of crime per address. Multifamily properties reveal higher rates of both property crimes and crimes against persons per address; however, these findings underscore a limitation with the land use data incorporated into this analysis. With one record available for every address, these findings do not reflect the number of units, residents, or potential targets at a given address; rates are therefore expected to be considerably inflated at such multi-family properties. Accordingly, care must be taken to consider the actual use of each address when analyzing crime rates calculated at the property or lot level. While this is a shortcoming of the available data, this analysis nonetheless highlights specific locations with higher counts of crime within the broader, low-crime land use category as a whole.

A detailed analysis of commercial properties further emphasizes the within-category concentrations. Shopping centers, in particular, prove to be key crime generators within the study site, with the city's largest shopping mall associated with high counts (and disproportionate rates) of both property crime and crimes against persons. Smaller, community-level shopping centers, hotels, and theater buildings are also associated with disproportionate rates of crimes per address, further emphasizing the importance of considering the availability of targets at a given location. Keeping these data considerations in mind, we find that nearly 44% of all property crimes against property and persons attributable to commercial lots concentrate on less than 2% of commercial addresses. Commercial properties are importantly associated with the patterns of crime within Coquitlam; however, these patterns are disproportionately associated with a few very specific types of commercial properties.

This considerable concentration is perhaps most apparent when exploring the diverse CIR land use category. This aggregate category contains a variety of specific land use types; considered as a whole, it reveals a relatively high overall rate of both property crimes and crimes against persons per lot. However, underscoring the need for multi-level analysis, the subcategory breakdown reveals that very few land use subcategories display both high rates and high counts of crimes against property and persons: hospitals, schools, and (in the case of property crimes) recreation centers. This finding emphasizes the need to explore disaggregate land use categories for clearer understanding of the specific locales associated with high crimes—and leads to further, micro-level analysis.

Within Coquitlam, property crime and crimes against persons concentrate on properties classified as commercial, and within the broad civic, institutional, and recreational category. When we explore subcategories, shopping centers, theater buildings, hotels, hospitals, and schools—among several other categories—appear repeatedly as key land uses with both high rates and counts of crimes against property and persons. However, when we explore the single addresses with the highest counts of crime, further clarity into the local hotspots of crime can be gained. When considering property crime events, for example, shopping centers dominate the list of top addresses. Four out of the five locations represent a shopping mall, with the regional center attracting the highest counts, followed by two of the four community shopping malls. One smaller, neighborhood-level mall rounds out the top five addresses. These locations fit a classic description of crime generators, in that they are local destinations and are part of a broader awareness space. Such locations contain a variety of targets in the forms of individuals, individual stores, items, and parking lots.

While shopping centers on aggregate appear to be an important local feature within Coquitlam, it is important to emphasize the unequal distribution of crimes—particularly property crimes—across such local facilities. While a number of local malls reveal considerable levels of crime, not all malls follow this trend. Further, the introduction of a new classification of shopping center as a hot address—a neighborhood-level facility—raises additional interest. Neighborhood malls, as a category, did not appear at the meso level of analysis. There are 10 neighborhood shopping centers in Coquitlam, and, as an aggregate category, the rate of property crime attributed to this land use classification was not high enough to be recognized at the meso level. However, one single neighborhood mall housed enough property crimes in 2008 to rank as the fifth-highest single site of such crime within the municipality, re-emphasizing the importance of multiscale analysis.

Further variation is present when considering the addresses with the highest reported counts of crimes against persons. While the regional mall still appears as the address with the highest number of crimes against persons, a mix of land uses complete the top five rankings, including one hotel, one school, and two high-density residential properties. The variation in both broad land use categories and specific land use subcategories underscores the dynamic associations between land use and crime. Different crime types concentrate at different land uses. While property crimes concentrate predominantly on commercial lots, a far greater variation exists when considering crimes against persons. Further differences may be expected when considering more detailed subcategories as well.

21.6 Land Use and Crime: Concluding Remarks

Criminal events concentrate in space, clustering on a small proportion of specific locations. This concentration is apparent across a variety of levels of aggregation. Broadly, both property crimes and crimes against persons occur in highest numbers on residential properties, but in disproportionately highest rates on addresses classified as commercial and CIR. The criminal events concentrate differently within different land uses: while 91% of all properties within Coquitlam had no recorded property crimes in 2008, this was not consistent across land use categories. Among residential properties, 93% had no property crimes, as 80% of CIR properties; but only 49% of all commercial addresses were unaffected by such crime during the study year. Crimes against persons reveal further concentration: all events included within this analysis can be attributed to just 2% of the overall addresses; 98% of residential properties, 92% of CIR properties, and 88% of commercial properties have no recorded crimes against persons.

Criminal events concentrate both across land use categories and within land use categories, with some subtypes—residential, commercial, and CIR land uses—associated with far higher crime rates than others. Multifamily residential units, multistore commercial complexes (such as shopping malls), and common public locations such as hospitals, schools, and recreation centers have disproportionate rates of crime when compared to the average rates found within their more general land use classifications. The land use data set incorporated into this study is unable to account for the potential targets within each lot—including residents or units—resulting in an inflated rate at such locations; however, the overall counts of events per address continue to emphasize a disproportionate concentration of crime at the relatively few properties classified within each specific subcategory. This concentration is further apparent at the micro level of analysis, where single properties with the highest crime counts reveal another level of within-category concentration and identify single risky facilities.

Land use shapes the way that individuals move within urban space, providing both the starting point and destination of travel. In doing so, land use further shapes the patterns and concentrations of criminal activity. This analysis highlights the considerable concentrations of crime associated with a small and specific proportion of land uses and addresses within one midsized suburban location. These concentrations are best explored at a variety of spatial levels. With each subsequent level of disaggregation, a more nuanced understanding of the local connections between crime and land use can be identified. Future studies are needed to explore how these patterns change when considering disaggregate crime classifications. In addition, further studies must explore the compounding effects of proximity to multiple land use classifications, allowing for the incorporation of street-based events, or crimes associated with uncertain address locations.

References

Ackerman, W. V., and Murray, A. T. (2004). Assessing spatial patterns of crime in Lima, Ohio. *Cities*, 21(5): 423–437.

Andresen, M. A. (2009). Crime specialization across the Canadian provinces. *Canadian Journal of Criminology and Criminal Justice*, 51(1): 31–53.

Andresen, M. A., and Curman, A. S. (2016, February). The trajectories of crime at places: Understanding the patterns of disaggregated crime types. Paper presented at the meeting of the Western Society of Criminology, Vancouver, BC, February.

Andresen, M. A., and Linning, S. J. (2012). The (in) appropriateness of aggregating across crime types. *Applied Geography*, 35(1): 275–282.

Bowers, K. (2013). Risky facilities: Crime radiators or crime absorbers? A comparison of internal and external levels of theft. *Journal of Quantitative Criminology*, 30(3): 384–414.

Braga, A. A., Papachristos, A. V., and Hureau, D. M. (2010). The concentration and stability of gun violence at micro places in Boston, 1980–2008. *Journal of Quantitative Criminology*, 26(1): 33–53.

Brantingham, P. J., and Brantingham, P. L. (Eds.). (1991). *Environmental Criminology*. 2nd ed. Prospect Heights, IL: Waveland Press.

Brantingham, P. J., Dyreson, D. A., and Brantingham, P. L. (1976). Crime seen through a cone of resolution. *American Behavioral Scientist*, 20(2): 261–273.

Brantingham, P. L., and Brantingham, P. J. (1993). Nodes, paths and edges: Considerations on the complexity of crime and the physical environment. *Journal of Environmental Psychology*, 13: 3–28.

Brantingham, P. L., and Brantingham, P. J. (1995). Criminality of place: Crime generators and crime attractors. *European Journal on Criminal Policy and Research*, 3(3): 5–26.

Charron, M., Bédard, F., and Aston, C. (2008). Neighbourhood characteristics and the distribution of crime in Edmonton. In Savoie, J. (Ed.), *Neighbourhood Characteristics and the Distribution of Crime: Edmonton, Halifax and Thunder Bay*, 11–28. Ottawa: Statistics Canada.

City of Coquitlam. (2008). Citywide Official Community Plan: Area and Neighbourhood Plans (Updated in Bylaw No. 3960, 2008). Retrieved from the City of Coquitlam website http://www.coquitlam.ca.

Cohen, L. E., and Felson, M. (1979). Social change and crime rate trends: A routine activity approach. *American Sociological Review*, 44: 588–608.

Groff, E. R. (2011). Exploring 'near': Characterizing the spatial extent of drinking place influence on crime. *Australian and New Zealand Journal of Criminology*, 44(2): 156–179.

Groff, E. R. (2014). Quantifying the exposure of street segments to drinking places nearby. *Journal of Quantitative Criminology*, 30(3): 527–548.

Groff, E. R., and Lockwood, B. (2014). Criminogenic facilities and crime across street segments in Philadelphia: Uncovering evidence about the spatial extent of facility influence. *Journal of Research in Crime and Delinquency*, 51(3): 277–314.

Eck, J. E., Clarke, R. V., and Guerette, R. T. (2007). Risky facilities: Crime concentrations in homogeneous sets of establishments and facilities. In Farrell, G., Bowers, K. J., Johnson, S. D. and Townsley, M. (Eds.), *Imagination for Crime Prevention: Essays in Honour of Ken Pease*, 225–264, vol. 21 of *Crime Prevention Studies*. Monsey, NY: Criminal Justice Press.

Haberman, C. P., Groff, E. R., and Taylor, R. B. (2013). The variable impacts of public housing community proximity on nearby street robberies. *Journal of Research in Crime and Delinquency*, 50(2): 163–188.

Hibdon, J., and Groff, E. R. (2014). What you find depends on where you look: Using emergency medical services call data to target illicit drug use hot spots. *Journal of Contemporary Criminal Justice*, 30(2): 169–185.

Hirschfield, A., and Bowers, K. J. (1997). The development of a social, demographic and land use profiler for areas of high crime. *British Journal of Criminology*, 37(1): 103–120.

Kinney, J. B., Brantingham, P. L., Wuschke, K., Kirk, M. G., and Brantingham, P. J. (2008). Crime attractors, generators and detractors: Land use and urban crime opportunities. *Built Environment*, 34(1): 62–74.

McCord, E. S., and Ratcliffe, J. H. (2007). A micro-spatial analysis of the demographic and criminogenic environment of drug markets in Philadelphia. *Australian and New Zealand Journal of Criminology*, 40: 43–63.

McCord, E. S., and Ratcliffe, J. H. (2009). Intensity value analysis and the criminogenic effects of land use features on local crime patterns. *Crime Patterns and Analysis*, 2: 17–30.

Metro Vancouver. (2011). Regional Growth Strategy—Metro Vancouver 2040: Shaping our Future. Retrieved from the Metro Vancouver website: http://www.metrovancouver.org.

Newton, A., and Bowers, K. J. (2007). The geography of bus shelter damage: The influence of crime, neighbourhood characteristics and land-use. *Internet Journal of Criminology*. Retrieved from the Internet Journal of Criminology website: https://www.internetjournalofcriminology.com.

Newton, A. D., Partridge, H., and Gill, A. (2014). Above and below: Measuring crime risk in and around underground mass transit systems. *Crime Science*, 3(1): 1–14.

Ratcliffe, J. H. (2012). The spatial extent of criminogenic places: A changepoint regression of violence around bars. *Geographical Analysis*, 44(4): 302–320.

Rengert, G., Chakravorty, S., Bole, T., and Henderson, K. (2000). A geographic analysis of illegal drug markets. In Natarajan, M., and Hough, M. (Eds.), *Illegal Drug Markets: From Research to Prevention Policy*, 219–240, vol. 11 of *Crime Prevention Studies*. Monsey, NY: Criminal Justice Press.

Roncek, D. W., and LoBosco, A. (1983). The effects of high schools on crime in their neighborhoods. *Social Science Quarterly*, 64(3): 598–613.

Song, J., Andresen, M. A., Brantingham, P. L., and Spicer, V. (2017). Crime on the edges: Patterns of crime and land use change. *Cartography and Geographic Information Science*, 44(1): 51–61.

Song, J., Spicer, V., and Brantingham, P. L. (2013, June). The edge effect: Exploring high crime zones near residential neighborhoods. In *Intelligence and Security Informatics (ISI), 2013 IEEE International Conference*, pp. 245–250. IEEE.

Statistics Canada (2012). *Focus on Geography Series, 2011 Census: Census Metropolitan Area of Vancouver, British Columbia*. Retrieved from the Statistics Canada website: http://www12.statcan.gc.ca.

Summers, L., and Johnson, S. D. (2017). Does the configuration of the street network influence where outdoor serious violence takes place? Using space syntax to test crime pattern theory. *Journal of Quantitative Criminology*, 33(2): 397–420.

Wang, F., Hu, Y., Wang, S., and Li, X. (2017). Local indicator of colocation quotient with a statistical significance test: Examining spatial association of crime and facilities. *The Professional Geographer*, 69(1): 22–31.

Weisburd, D. (2015). The law of crime concentration and the criminology of place. *Criminology*, 53: 133–157.

Weisburd, D., Bushway, S., Lum, C., and Yang, S. M. (2004). Trajectories of crime at places: A longitudinal study of street segments in the city of Seattle. *Criminology*, 42(2): 283–322.

Weisburd, D., Morris, N. A., and Groff, E. R. (2009). Hot spots of juvenile crime: A longitudinal study of arrest incidents at street segments in Seattle, Washington. *Journal of Quantitative Criminology*, 25(4): 443–467.

CHAPTER 22

MACRO-LEVEL GENERATORS OF CRIME, INCLUDING PARKS, STADIUMS, AND TRANSIT STATIONS

ANDREW NEWTON

22.1 Introduction

This chapter examines the occurrence of crime at particular places that bring together lots of people in time and place, namely macro crime generators. Examples of these include hospitals, parks, large transit stations and interchanges, entertainment districts, and shopping malls. At these places, the spatiotemporal convergence of many people, including potential offenders and victims, generates multiple opportunities for crime to occur. However, crime is not necessarily a byproduct of the convergence of many people. First and foremost, these places should be considered macro activity generators, locations where and times when large numbers of people congregate. In the current literature the distinction between an "activity generator" and a "crime generator" is not well developed, but as a starting point: land use that encourages a convergence of people at a particular time, but without crime, could be considered an activity generator; and, an activity generator that experiences high levels of crime could be termed a crime generator.

This chapter begins by defining crime attractors and crime generators, and explores the subtle difference between them. It then examines why crime hotspots and crime generators tend to coexist, and considers the importance of scale in place-based studies of crime. Following this is a discussion of the "busyness" of crime generators, how the density of people, proximity of people, and interactions between people are all factors that influence crime opportunities at macro generators. It then explores how characteristics of place generators and attractors may vary between different crime types, for example, comparing two macro generators, one for pickpocketing and one for assault. Crime generators are further influenced by what is near to them, and this chapter then moves on to discuss how the surrounding environs of a generator may also influence crime opportunities. Finally, the chapter attempts to draw these ideas together by reviewing current evidence of three case studies of macro generators, namely parks, large stadiums, and large transit stations. It concludes with some suggestions for future research direction.

There are two key theoretical concepts that underpin crime generators, namely routine activities theory and crime pattern theory. Routine activities theory (Cohen and Felson, 1979) suggests crime is likely when three factors converge: a suitable target; a motivated offender; and, lack of capable guardianship. Crime pattern theory (Brantingham and Brantingham, 1993) brings together routine activity theory and rational choice perspective (Cornish and Clarke, 1986) to explain the spatial distribution of crime events (for more discussion of these, see Summers and Guerette in this volume; Brantingham et al. in this volume). Crime pattern theory contends that the spatial patterning of crime is nonrandom, clustered at particular places and times, often called crime hotspots. These concentrations are explained by the routine movement of people in their daily lives. They go to work, visit places of leisure and recreation, go to school, or go shopping, and in crime pattern theory these locations of activity space are termed nodes. Indeed, when large numbers of persons congregate at these nodes, they could be considered activity generators.

During journeys to and from nodes, offenders travel along paths, and this movement is bounded by edges. According to crime pattern theory, offenders develop awareness spaces, and encounter and learn more about potential places to offend during these journeys and through time spent at activity nodes. The research suggests most crime happens near to an offender's awareness spaces. Here potential offenders, suitable targets, and lack of guardians come together in situations favorable for offending. Using routine activity language, it is self-evident that generators bring many suitable targets into contact with one of more potential offenders. However, it is not clear why they do not encourage greater levels of suitable guardianship, whose presence discourages crime.

22.2 Defining and Distinguishing between Crime Generators and Attractors

A number of research studies have explored how places may act as a crime generator and/or crime attractor (Brantingham and Brantingham, 1995; McCord et al., 2007; Kinney et al., 2008; Kurland, Johnson, and Tilley 2014; Newton, 2014). At the outset their meaning appears relatively straightforward; crime generators are "places that are high in crime because they are exceptionally busy"; whereas, crime attractors are those known to offenders by reputation as "places that contain many suitable crime targets without adequate protection" (Eck, Clarke, and Guerette, 2007). However, when drilling down further, the distinction between the two is less clear. For example, a transit station is exceptionally busy, and pickpocketing may occur serendipitously under chance encounters, as many people are brought together in close proximity. However, an alternative possibility is that well-known opportunities exist for pickpockets near transit stations, and offenders go there specifically, in the knowledge that there will be lots of suitable targets without adequate protection. Therefore it is useful here to revisit the original definitions of crime attractors and crime generators:

> Crime generators are particular areas to which large numbers of people are attracted for reasons unrelated to any particular level of criminal motivation they might have or to any particular crime they might end up committing. Typical examples might include shopping precincts; entertainment districts; office concentrations; or sports stadiums . . .. Crime generators produce crime by creating particular times and places that provide appropriate concentrations of people and other targets . . . in settings that are conducive to particular types of criminal acts. Mixed into the people gathered at generator locations are some potential offenders with sufficient general levels of criminal motivation that although they did not come to the area with the explicit intent of doing a crime, they notice and exploit criminal opportunities. (Brantingham and Brantingham, 1995, p. 7)
>
> Crime attractors are particular places, areas, neighbourhoods, districts which create well-known criminal opportunities to which strongly motivated, intending criminal offenders are attracted because of the known opportunities for particular types of crime. Examples might include bar districts; prostitution areas; drug markets; large shopping malls, particularly those near major public transit exchanges; large, insecure parking lots in business or commercial areas . . .. Crimes in such locations are often committed by outsiders to the area . . .. Strongly motivated offenders will travel relatively long distances in search of a target. (When insiders commit crimes in such areas, they may have previously moved to those areas because of their crime attracting qualities; or, as in many cities, because poor areas are located near commercial areas thus creating many accessible targets near home.) The attraction is created by an ecological label . . . , often supplemented by the intending offender's personal past history, establishing that location as a known place to go for that kind of crime. As studies . . . have shown, such crime attracting areas can also generate other types of crime that are auxiliary or serendipitous by-products of the intending offender having been attracted to the area by the prospect of committing the primary crime. (Brantingham and Brantingham, 1995, p. 8)

Therefore, crime attractors and crime generators can both be conceived as small-level or micro places, for example, small to large individual facilities (see Madensen and Eck in this volume) such as a railway stations, bars and nightclubs, businesses, parks, or hospitals; or, alternatively, meso- to macro-level places such as groups of facilities, entertainment districts with a number of bars, central business districts, or neighborhoods. The shared characteristics of these places are they have an "appropriate" number of suitable targets for crime (persons or property) and one or more motivated offenders. However, the key distinction between the two is offender motivation; offenders who visit crime generators did not go to that place or facility purposely and for the explicit reason of committing a crime. The crime was generated by the presence of lots of suitable targets drawn together in close proximity. The offender also happened to be at that place at that time, and the volume of people present created a suitable opportunity for the offender to act upon.

In contrast, at crime attractor locations, offenders visit places due to their reputation, where chances of successful offending are expected to be high, and place management, guardianship, and other protective factors against crime are anticipated to be low. Crime attractors have an ecological label as being "bad" areas, perhaps identified by an offender directly; or, indirectly, perhaps the offender knows this place by reputation. Offenders are thus attracted to these places for the specific purpose of committing an intended crime.

While many of the factors necessary for a crime are present at both generator and attractor locations—a motivated offender, suitable target, lack of guardianship—the ultimate distinction between a crime attractor and crime generator is the offender's motivation for going there. Did the place generate offending opportunities the offender was not acutely aware of, or were the offender attracted to it in the knowledge of likely success? At this stage it is important to consider that offenders' awareness of crime opportunity may evolve in several stages, based on first and subsequent visits to a place as they develop their awareness space. These steps may include identifying a suitable location; spending time at that location and becoming more familiar with it; planning an offense, and finally committing a crime there. Thus it is entirely plausible that over time a macro generator of crime will evolve into a crime attractor.

Table 22.1 sets out some of the key examples of crime attractors and generators found in the existent literature on criminality of place. While this is not exhaustive, the fact that producing such a table was not as simple as expected at the outset demonstrates the difficulties in classing places as attractors or generators. The reasons victims, place managers, or capable guardians visit activity nodes is generally fairly transparent, for example, for leisure, tourism, recreation, or even work. However, the reason an offender travels to a crime attractor/generator is generally less well known. As Kurland, Johnson, and Tilley (2014) argue, attractor/generator "classification . . . is not unequivocal . . .. it is difficult to estimate the influence of particular facilities on crime patterns, as the facilities . . . are always present in the environment, which precludes the use of experimental methods to examine their impacts" (p. 7).

Bernasco and Block (2011) also suggest that one the distinguishing factors of crime attractors is that they have nearby cash economies, such as drug markets, betting shops, and pawnshops. This may impact on the ecological label placed on these by offenders, and indicate why they may have a reputation for having both suitable targets (with cash) and lower forms of guardianship and place management. Therefore an additional feature of attractors, one that is perhaps not present at crime generators, is they have cash economies associated with them. Again the distinction can become blurred, for example, when considering shopping precincts.

Table 22.1 Examples of Potential Crime Attractors and Generators

Crime generators	Crime attractors
Major transport nodes and interchanges	Transport exchanges and their surroundings
Large park and ride parking lots	Insecure parking lots
Shopping precincts/malls	Local shopping malls
Entertainment districts	Bar districts
Theater districts and casinos	Pawnshops/brokers
CBDs and business districts	Check-cashing stores
Universities, colleges, and schools	Prostitution areas
Recreation centers	Hotels and motels
Sports/music stadiums	Garage/petrol/gas store
Youth clubs	Drug markets and halfway houses
Parks	Homeless shelters
Hospitals	Pharmacies and drugstores

22.3 Crime Hotspots and Scale of Analysis

An important feature of crime attractors and generators is they often coexist with crime hotspots. While no common definition exists, crime hotspots can be considered areas that have a larger than average number of crime or disorder events, or where people have higher than average risks being a victim of crime (Eck et al., 2005). A defining feature of crime hotspots is that they are places that contain concentrations or spatial clusters of crimes. This spatial clustering is generally identified using crimes frequencies, so is based on a count of the total number of crimes. Hotspots are rarely based on crime rates; in other words they are not standardized by the number of people present (Malleson and Andresen, 2016). The significance of this will be explored in more detail later in this chapter. In simple terms crime generators bring lots of people together in one place, and it is not surprising this may result in several crimes being recorded at that locality. Thus crime hotspots (based on crime counts) emerge where many people congregate. Indeed crime generators and repeat victimization are cited as two of the key drivers of hotspots (Short et al., 2008).

It has been suggested when a crime hotspot is found it should be classified as a crime generator or crime attractor (Clarke and Eck, 2005). However, this perhaps causes confusion and ambiguity. Consider a hotspot classified as a crime generator. That crime hotspot may actually be the result of particular type of land use facility, such as a transit station. Yet this transit station itself can also be termed a crime generator. The choice of language here is unhelpful, as, ultimately, a crime generator (transit station) creates a crime generator (hotspot). There is perhaps a need to revisit these definitions when classifying places as activity generators, crime generators, crime attractors, and hotspots. Is a crime generator: an individual facility such as a transit station?; an individual location such as a street intersection where a hotspot has formed?; a group of facilities such as an entertainment district?; or a neighborhood crime hotspot? Furthermore, is there a specific difference between an activity generator, a crime generator, and a crime hotspot when they all occur conterminously?

A crucial factor in classifying places as attractors and/or generators is the unit of analysis, and here the use of the term "place" is often vague. Place-based crime analysis may be carried out at the micro level, a street segment or intersection; the meso level, an entertainment district or central business district (CBD); or the macro level, a neighborhood or district (Weisburd, Bernasco, and Bruinsma, 2009). A generator will have a high number of crimes and high number of persons present relative to surrounding or nearby areas (Clarke and Eck, 2005), and this relationship will be present at all three of these scales (micro to macro). Thus, this chapter is not prescriptive as to what definitions or categories of place should be considered crime generators; but it does urge more thought, at least when categorizing places. More consideration is required of context and scale. When a place is classed as a crime generator, a key step is to identify how this crime generator manifests itself in the context of the surrounding environment.

22.4 Density, Proximity, and Busyness

In the above discussion, a crime generator was noted as a place that is "exceptionally busy." In order for a place to be considered busy, it needs to bring lots of people together in a confined space. The size of a place is therefore a key factor in "busyness." However, size is only one of several important variables. A range of factors should be considered, including how many people are present (volume); the number of people relative to the size of the space, for example, how many people within a 10-square-meter radius (density); how close together these people are (proximity); and, perhaps most importantly, for how long they are in close proximity (level of proximate interaction). The latter two issues have been afforded limited attention in the literature, a gap perhaps best explained by difficulties in measuring these concepts (Solymosi, Borrion, and Fujiyana, 2015). However, there have been some attempts to measure the relationship between person density and crime.

Angel's (1968) study postulated that street robbery was more likely to occur at intermediate levels of pedestrian traffic, rather than places with low or high crowd densities. Translated into the language of routine activity theory, when pedestrian traffic is sparse, there are too few suitable targets to attract offenders; when it is high, many guardians are present to intervene. Angel postulated that a "critical intensity zone" existed at which street robbery was most likely. Clark, Belanger, and Eastman (1996) tested this relationship by examining daily ridership on subway stations, but, contrary to Angel's hypothesis, found station robbery inversely correlated to passenger density.

However, subway stations are perhaps a unique environment. Compared to above-ground situations, underground stations have limited entry and escape routes. For offenders, additional effort is required to visit underground stations that do not form part of their routine activities. The study found chances of robbery at subway stations increased when fewer people were present. This is perhaps reflective of the limited escape opportunities underground, compared to above-ground situations. Therefore density alone is not predictive of crime. Additional consideration should be given to the design and layout of a place, including how open and accessible it is, and levels of visibility and surveillance.

An additional hypothesis on the relationship between crowd density and crime is described by Loukaitou-Sideris (1999). This contends that beyond Angel's first critical intensity zone, as places get busier, serious robbery and violence offenses become less likely. However, as crowd density increases further, a new critical zone is reached. At this point, other offenses emerge, such as minor theft and pickpocketing in what is termed a "second critical intensity" zone. Thus, in high-density crowds, the presence of more people does not increase capable guardianship. Instead it acts as a barrier to detection, giving anonymity to offenders, reducing visibility, and limiting the likelihood of offenders being spotted or identified, thus increasing offenders' opportunities to commit theft undetected. This may explain in part why a crime generator, with lots of people present, does not necessarily equate to better guardianship.

The literature on macro generators of crime tends to focus on places that are fairly large in size. The general principle here is that as a place gets bigger, it can accommo date more people, which it could be argued will increase crime opportunities and in turn crime levels. However, the size and capacity of a place are not necessarily directly related to "busyness" and crime opportunity. Indeed, as discussed above, the proximity of people and the frequency and length of their interaction are key ingredients in opportunity for crime and in the extent to which potential guardians can intervene. The function of a place or facility is also critical here. For example, compare a transport interchange, shopping mall, and park. They have different opening hours, peak times, pedestrian flow management policies, and staffing levels, which may all impact on crime opportunity.

The opening hours of macro crime generators will impact on crime opportunity. Shopping centers are busier at holiday times and on Saturdays. Transport stops and stations have peak hours during the morning and late rush hour periods. Pickpocketing levels are higher during afternoon peak times than during morning peaks (Ceccato and Uittenbogaard, 2014; Newton, Partridge, and Gill, 2014a, 2014b). Around school closing time there is an early afternoon peak time, and then a secondary afternoon peak when people finish work. At weekends, different peak times emerge. Sports stadiums and music festivals have more sporadic opening hours, dictated by the events they host. Therefore it is important to think beyond how large, and indeed even how busy, a place is. A range of factors may impact on the density, availability, and concentration of targets for crime. These issues are explored later in this chapter for three different types of macro crime generators: transport interchanges, stadiums, and parks.

22.5 Crime Attractors, Crime Generators, and Crime Type

The above discussion also raises an additional question, namely when considering places as attractors and/or generators of crime, what types of crime are commissioned at these locations? Are some crime types more likely at crime attractors and others at crime generators? In Table 22.1 it is evident that it is difficult to classify places as crime generators or crime attractors. Transport interchanges and parking lots are good examples of this. A key feature of places often overlooked in the literature on crime attractors and generators is that, as stated in their original conception, places are rarely mutually exclusive to these categories. Indeed, they are "unlikely to be pure attractors or pure generators or purely neutral. Most areas will be mixed, in the sense that they may be crime attractors for some types of crime, crime generators for other types of crime, and neutral still with respect to other types of crime" (Brantingham and Brantingham, 1995, p. 9).

Consider three very different crime types, pickpocketing, assault, and criminal damage. The first is more likely in very crowded environments, the second in more intermediate crowd densities, and the latter when fewer people are present. Accepting the principle in the literature that busy places are indicative of crime generators, it could be argued that certain crime types more prominent at quieter times, such as those against property, do not occur at crime generators. However, what happens when criminal damage happens at a transit station around or just after closing time, when few guardians are present? Can crime generators only be considered so during busy periods? Are these places then crime attractors at off-peak times? These arguments do not hold if an offender happens to be at a crime generator by chance, at the end of the day under serendipitous circumstances. There are a number of possible scenarios here. First, a place may be a generator for different crime types at different times of the day. Conversely, it may be an attractor for different crime types at different times of the day. Third, it even be may be an attractor for one crime type at certain times and a generator for another crime type at different times of the day.

As an example, consider a bar or nightclub. At peak times, jostling and bumping, violent assault, and sexual groping may be problematic (intermediate to high densities of people), and toward the end of the evening, when there are lower densities of patrons, other offenses such as sexual assaults, attempted rape, and rape may be more likely. This may be an issue near to the premise rather than inside it. Offenders may attempt to intercept victims as they leave a bar and travel home. Thus, a bar or nightclub that at peak times is considered a crime generator for disorder and violence may become an attractor for other crime types such as sexual assault toward the end of the evening as people start to make their way home.

Alternatively, for crimes such as criminal damage, arson, and graffiti, the targets are property, not people. The presence of people as informal guardians may deter crime.

Table 22.2 Facilities, Densities of Persons, and Attractor/Generator Properties of Place

Crime type	Facility	Level of crowd density	Attractor or generator
Disorder	Park at quiet time	Low	Attractor
Disorder	Sports event or shopping mall	High	Generator
Sexual assault (rape)	Park at quiet time	Low	Attractor
Sexual assault (groping)	Station at peak time	High	Generator
Criminal damage and arson	Park at quiet time	Low	Attractor
Theft of/from car	Unsecured car park outside rail station	Low	Attractor
Assault	Train station late at night	Low	Generator
Assault	Nightclub	High	Generator or attractor
Robbery	Shopping center	Intermediate	Attractor
Theft from person	Bag snatch at shopping mall	Intermediate	Attractor or generator
Drug dealing	Park or open market	Intermediate	Attractor
Pickpocketing and petty theft	Train station	High	Generator

Therefore, crime against property rather than persons is perhaps more likely at crime attractors, or near to crime generators around or during closing times when fewer people are present. This could also be the case for theft from, and theft of, vehicles. At crime generators during peak times, a place may have many cars but also guardians. Thus opportunities to offend may increase nearer to closing time. This demonstrates that there are a number of interrelated factors that make distinguishing attractors and generators problematic. Table 22.2 provides further examples of how facility type, crime type, and person density all interact in the crime opportunity, and how this relates to the generator and attractor properties of place.

22.6 The Environs of Crime Attractors and Generators

Places and facilities such as those presented in Table 22.1 cannot be considered in isolation, they also interact with their surrounding environment. A number of studies have examined crime prevalence in the vicinity of crime attractors and generators, for example, near to bars (Ratcliffe, 2012), transport stations (Newton and Ceccato, 2015), and parks (Groff and McCord, 2011). One question is the extent to which macro generators of crime influence crime nearby. Several studies have found a distance decay effect; crime is greatest near to a facility, and as you move further away from it, the level of crime is generally reduced. This suggests macro crime generators have greatest influence on their nearby surroundings, and this impact reduces as you move further away from them.

However, this relationship is not always straightforward. Several studies have found a spatial lag, whereby crime reduces in the immediate vicinity of a facility. Then as you move slightly further away, crime increases. As you continue to move further away from the facility, crime reduces according to the expected distance decay function. Explanations are that immediately outside of these facilities several targets may be present, but these environments are also protected by place managers and capable guardians. Therefore, with the exception of perhaps pickpocketing and violent assaults in highly crowded environments, crime does not happen immediately outside these macro generators.

However, macro crime generators are unlikely to influence crime levels on their own. Other facilities and land uses surrounding macro generators will also impact on crime. Groff and McCord (2011) explored the effect of nearby land use on parks, comparing residential, commercial, and mixed land use. They found nearby mixed land use to moderate the impacts of crime generators by providing nearby eyes on the street and offering potential guardianship near parks. Bowers (2014) describes how facilities may act as radiators or absorbers, either pulling in (absorbing) offenders and victims in the surrounding area into that facility, or by radiating (pushing out) crime from that central locality to the surrounding environs. Her findings suggest risky facilities, which perhaps can be classed as a crime attractor rather than generator, tend to provide more of a crime radiator function. A question not yet explored in the literature is whether macro facilities, perhaps crime generators, serve to act as absorbers or radiators. Indeed, as a facility increases in size, does it become more of an absorber or a radiator?

An alternative scenario here is that places may contain more than one attractor or generator in close proximity; thus they may actually compete, both for offenders and for targets. One possibility is that a crime attractor actually takes offenders away from other nearby crime attractors. Alternatively, two attractors in close proximity may actually serve to bring more people to a place, thus increasing crime. In the spatial economics and marketing literature, these two opposing spatial effects are referred to as spatial agglomeration and spatial competition (Bernasco and Block, 2011). An entertainment district could have two or three bars classed as crime attractors. However, these may actually be part of the wider nighttime economy setting made up of several bars, which as a whole is categorized as a crime generator. Here crime attractors exist within a larger macro crime generator. Indeed, places may actually have a mix of both attractors and generators, resulting in highly complex interactions.

22.7 Macro Generators and Megafacilities

Very large macro crime generators perhaps cannot be considered a single facility. It may be more appropriate to consider them to be made up of several individual facilities. Good examples here are out-of-town shopping malls, large transit interchanges, or even university and college campuses. While each of these has a primary function, for example, retail at the shopping mall, and travel at the interchange, these "superfacilities" also contain a range of other businesses. Shopping malls may contain cinemas, restaurant and food areas, or even children's entertainment centers. Train stations often contain shops and other retail outlets, and restaurants and bars that serve alcohol. Should these macro generators be considered single facilities when they contain multiple premises? These megafacilities may offer multiple types of activity spaces and have multiple owners and place managers. Indeed it is plausible they even have their own internal activity nodes and paths. The accessibility of these sites may be multi-layered. For example, there may be one or more entrances to the main facility, such as the shopping center. Beyond this but within the main facility, there may then be secondary entrances and exits to individual facilities located inside these larger macrofacilities.

Parks are a good example of this. They may contain playing fields, children's play areas, restaurants or cafés, tennis courts, and basketball courts. Each of these could be classed as a facility within a larger superfacility, and the activities at each may conflict or even compete. The park may be a crime generator, bringing lots of people together. However, within the park itself there may be smaller subsets or components that actually have a reputation as a place to offend, such as an individual kiosk within a park. Thus there may be mini crime attractors present within a larger crime generator.

22.8 Measuring Crime Attractors and Generators

It was stated previously that the key distinguishing features between a crime generator and attractor is the offender's motivation for visiting it. However, the reason an offender travels to a particular location to commit crime is frequently unknown. Indeed, the offender's identity may never be established. As an alternative, Clarke and Eck (2005) suggest comparing crime numbers (frequencies or counts) with crime rates (per 100 persons, per 100 vehicles, for example) to distinguish between attractors and generators. They suggest generators have many crimes and also many people; thus they have a high crime count and a low crime rate. By comparison, crime attractors have many crimes

Table 22.3 Comparing Crime Numbers and Rates at Attractors and Generators

	Number	Rate
Crime generator	High	Low
Crime attractor	High	High

but, compared to crime generators, fewer targets; thus they have high crime numbers and high crime rates (Table 22.3).

While this is a useful starting point, there are some limitations to it. One of the key difficulties is calculating appropriate denominators to establish crime rates, for example, violence per 1,000 people, or theft from car per 100 cars. Crime rates are often based on residential census data, yet by their nature crime generators are not reflective of residential populations. They are dynamic activity spaces likely to contain more visitors than the number of people who live there. Indeed, offenders may travel considerable distances to visit crime attractors. Some studies have attempted to calculate alternative population denominators for crime rates, including the use of ambient population data (Malleson and Andresen 2015, 2016), alternative denominators of transport crime (Newton, Partridge, and Gill, 2014a), and sport stadium attendances (Kurland, Johnson, and Tilley, 2014). However, obtaining reliable information on crime rates using population denominators at crime generators is challenging.

It is also problematic to establish a measure of busyness of a place by time of day. Macro generators have peak times that vary by day of the week and hour of the day. For example, at transit stations during school days there is a morning peak time of work and school users combined, an afternoon school closing peak, and a secondary and slightly later end-of-workday peak time. Any calculation of crime rates needs to account for these temporal variations. However, despite the difficulties in establishing appropriate denominators, in the absence of information on offenders' motivations for traveling to a crime site, comparing crime counts and rates is a useful tool for distinguishing between attractors and generators.

This chapter has outlined the key distinctions between crime attractors and crime generators and demonstrated the difficulties in quantifying attractors and generators. It has shown how the relationship between a macro generator's size, density, busyness, and the interactions and proximity of people present there, influences levels of crime. It has also demonstrated the function of a facility, the time of day, and crime type all bring further complications to this interaction. The choice of unit of analysis was also shown to be of paramount importance when examining crime attractors and generators. Some of these complexities are now examined further through reviews of existing literature on three case studies of macro crime generators, namely parks, stadiums, and transit stations.

22.9 Parks, Stadiums, and Transit Stations as Macro Crime Generators

22.9.1 Example 1: Parks

The crime attractor/generator characteristics of neighborhood parks have been empirically examined in detail (McCord et al., 2007; Groff and McCord, 2011). They have a number of unique features. They are publicly owned and can be viewed as contested spaces. For example, they may contain several activity generators such as recreation centers, pools, playgrounds, and basketball courts that act as competing spaces. They can also contain low levels of natural guardianship. Indeed, as stated by Groff and McCord, they are "owned by all but controlled by none." A contrasting argument (Jacobs, 1961) is that parks can be viewed as neutral spaces. Whether they are classed by local residents as amenities or nuisances depends upon their design. For example, they could be considered "a well-used dynamic space" or "one that is neglected and dangerous."

Groff and McCord (2011) hypothesized that neighborhood parks act as crime generators, by bringing lots of people together and increasing crime in the area. Their findings support this hypothesis. They examined parks in Philadelphia and found them to have a higher crime rates than the rest of the city. They did not identify a straightforward distance decay effect. Crime actually reduced immediately near parks, then increased in subsequent buffers before gradually reducing again further away from the park. Groff and McCord suggest that parks serve as crime generators, and that this pattern is driven by more than just a few "bad" parks. However, they also found that the number of activity generators within a park to be important. Parks with higher numbers of activity generators tended to attract more legitimate users, and had less crime than those with fewer activity generators.

Moreover, the study found that the type of activities that occurred in parks, as measured by activity generators, further influenced crime rates. Those with a more diverse mix of activity generators had lower levels of crime. Some activity generators, for example, sports fields and courts used for organized sporting activities, tended to have lower crime levels. The authors suggest this is due to the presence of more legitimate users at the park. This supports the possibility that parks can be viewed as neutral areas, but the design of parks, and mix of activity generators, and characteristics of the surrounding environment will all influence levels of crime. Mixed land use around the park, measured by the activities available, appeared to moderate crime rates. The likely explanation offered is that of efficacy, the notion of there being more " 'eyes on the street." Therefore, lower levels of crime are associated with more people using the park legitimately throughout the day.

An issue not explored in this study is the difference between daytime use, when more legitimate users will be present, and nighttime use, when the park is effectively closed (no activity generators present). It was not clear in the study if access to parks was restricted at closing times. Furthermore, it did not consider actual crime rates at the parks. Indeed a possible limitation of this study is that activity generators were used as a proxy measure for park usage. The research found neighborhood parks act as a macro crime generator and, moreover, that this effect is moderated by park size, by the number and types of activity generators, and by the land use in environs near the park. All of these impacted differently on each crime type. Parks can be considered predominantly a daytime activity node. The opening hours of parks are substantially different from the next two crime generator types to be discussed, stadiums and transit stations.

22.9.2 Example 2: Stadiums

Two papers, Montolio and Planells (2015) and, in particular, Kurland, Johnson, and Tilley (2014) have tested whether stadiums act as crime generators. The first examined Barcelona Football Stadium in Spain, the second Wembley Stadium in London in the United Kingdom. Both found evidence to support the macro generator hypothesis. These facilities are very different from parks, as their usage is episodic. They open on a fraction of all days at specific times, during football matches and other events such as music concerts. For most of the week these facilities are closed, and, hypothetically, at this time they are crime neutral.

Both studies compared crime during event days with nonevent days. The first paper compared home football matches (in Barcelona), away football matches (not in Barcelona), and control days. The second compared match days (football matches) with comparable nonmatch days, and event days (concerts) with comparable nonevent days. Both examined two different crime types, broadly speaking theft and violence offenses. The first paper used residential population to devise crime rates, although a clear limitation is this is not reflective of populations generated at stadiums during football matches. The second used a measure of the ambient population combined with attendance figures to try to estimate more accurately street population on match days and event days and comparable days to calculate more accurately crime rates.

The Wembley study tested three possible hypotheses for stadiums: that they are mostly a crime attractor, mostly a crime generator, or simultaneously a crime generator and crime attractor. The study found that during match and events days, although the total number of crimes (volume) increased, the overall crime rates per person were lower. This suggests the overall risk to the population reduced during events and matches. This higher crime count but lower crime rate during events, in accordance with the Clarke and Eck's hypothesis, suggests stadiums are more likely to episodically generate crime than attract offenders. A range of possible reasons postulated to explain this include the use of appropriate place management and informal guardianship during match and event days, including increased presence of policing (both uniform and nonuniform), management of footfall and pinch points, public announcements, and other strategies.

Both studies found increases in theft rather than violence during match days. Thus, while the evidence supports the hypothesis that stadiums act as crime generators (high crime count, low crime rate), they also offer some backing for the "second critical density" hypothesis. Opportunities for pickpocketing in large crowds are much higher during match days and event days than are opportunities for violence, especially around match start and end times. In the Wembley study a greater proportion of theft offenses (80%) happened during the daytime on match days (before 6:00 p.m. on days when football matches were played, which typically occur mid-afternoon) than on nonmatch days (50%). While there are limitations in the spatial and temporal accuracy of the data available, both papers demonstrate that the capacity of a facility, its usage (as attendance varied, and on some match days this was considerably bigger than on others), the timing of the event, and type of event all influenced levels of crime and to some extent moderated the generator characteristics of stadiums.

The episodic nature of crime at stadiums can be summarized through a number of stages or sequences: early as crowds gather; just before an event as crowds get very busy; during the events peak, when crowds are at their maximum; later as crowds start to disperse and stragglers exist; and nonevent times when facilities are closed and few people are present. These levels of busyness influence crime rates, and indeed at each of these stages, opportunities for theft and violence will be different, as suggested by the notion of first and second critical density zones.

A different type of generator examined next is transit stations, which are open more regularly and less episodically than stadiums, and also have peak times different from those of neighborhood parks.

22.9.3 Example 3: Transit Stations

One type of facility to have been afforded perhaps the most attention around the idea of generators and attractors and crime is transit stations, stops, and interchanges (Newton, 2014; Newton and Ceccato, 2015). These are very different from parks and stadiums. Stations have rhythmic human activity, with passenger flows that systematically vary. For example, there are peak and off-peak periods during the daytime, and off-peak nighttime periods. Usage also varies on weekdays and weekends, on school days and non-school days, and during different seasons.

On Stockholm's Underground in Sweden, Ceccato and Uittenbogaard (2014) found the following:

Crime was more prevalent during winter months, when the Underground was used more intensely due to the cold weather outside.

During daily peak hours, stations with "hiding spots" were often targeted by offenders (possible attractors).

During off-peak hours, the more crowded stations generated or attracted more offenders.

During peak hours and holidays, stations with cash machines (ATMs) and dark corners tended to be associated with violence, whereas vandalism was concentrated at less populated stations.

While the above research did not separate the possible individual impacts of generators and attractors, there are two key papers that have. Newton and colleagues did so using data for pickpocketing on the London Underground (Newton, Partridge, and Gill, 2014a, 2014b) while Irvin-Erickson and La Vigne (2015) examined a range of crime types on the Washington, DC Metro.

The London study examined factors that might be associated with an increase or reduced risk of pickpocketing both inside a station and in its surrounding environment. It found a combination of factors together, and not in isolation, impacted on pickpocketing rates. Factors associated with an increased risk of theft included those that encouraged congestion of passengers (lifts and waiting rooms) and increased levels of accessibility and access: higher theft levels in surrounding environs; stations that were identified as crime attractors (high theft counts and high theft rates); and stations with high levels of tourist use. Factors associated with a reduced risk of pickpocketing included those likely to decrease anonymity and increase potential guardianship and offender detection. Examples here included higher levels of staffing, personal validators, shop rentals, and more domestic buildings nearby. Additionally, stations with more platforms enabled passengers to be dispersed more evenly throughout the station to avoid congestion. Terminus stations (end of line) were associated with lower levels of risk than those in the center of the network, which were better connected and more accessible. Better connected stations also experienced more crowded conditions during the afternoon rush hour (from work to home) than the morning rush hour (from home to work).

The authors developed an attractor-generator index to compare specific attractor and generator combinations by different times of the day, splitting this into six time periods across the day. Examples of the index include stations that had high theft counts but low theft rates for all time periods ("generator at all times"); high theft counts and high theft rates for all time periods ("attractor at all times"); intermittently high theft counts and rates (sometimes attractor); and low risk of theft counts and rates (neutral). The only significant variable found in the model to be associated with pickpocketing was "attractor at all time periods." This supports the hypothesis that stations with higher risk of pickpocketing are more likely to be a crime attractor than a crime generator.

In the United States, Irvin-Erickson and La Vigne modeled crime-generating and crime-attracting characteristics of stations on the Washington Metro for robbery, larceny, aggravated assault, and disorderly conduct. They examined time of day using the categories peak hours, off-peak day hours, and off-peak night hours. They proposed two variables as indicators of crime generators. The first was the connectedness of stations to the rest of the transit network, with highly connected stations more indicative of crime generators. The second was station accessibility; more accessible stations were considered representative of crime generators. Three variables were presented as indicative of crime attractors: the remoteness of a station from the CBD; the socioeconomic status (SES) of the surrounding area, and the prevalence of other crimes at the station (those not considered above).

The authors used a negative binomial regression analysis to model these attractor and generator principles. They found that, as with previous studies, "stations assume different nodal and place-based crime-generating and crime-attracting characteristics, but also these roles vary for different crimes and different times" (Irvin-Erickson and La Vigne, 2015, p. 11). More specifically, they found highly connected stations acted as a generator for larcenies and disorder at peak hours, and robberies at nonpeak times. Stations with high levels of accessibility were generators for robberies and larcenies at nonpeak night hours, and remote stations attracted larcenies during peak hours and disorderly conduct during off-peak night hours.

There are two important spatial and temporal influences here, between daytime and night-time off peak hours, and between stations at the center and edges of the network. Consistent with Newton, Partridge, and Gill (2014b) and Cecatto and Uittenbogaard (2014), larcenies were associated with peak hours at connected stations in the center of the network. At end of line, stations disorder was associated with off-peak night hours. At center stations at peak times, high levels of connectedness and accessibility are associated with generator characteristics of stations (Irvin-Erickson and La Vigne, 2015) for larcenies and other crimes. However, for the specific case of pickpocketing, Newton, Partridge, and Gill (2014b) argue that stations in the center of the network that are also popular with tourists have high levels of theft counts and theft rates and are likely to act as crime attractors. There may be discrepancies here between how offenders use the London Underground and Washington Metro that cannot be examined using the data available in these studies.

All three papers (Ceccato and Uittenbogaard, 2014; Newton, Partridge, and Gill, 2014b; and Irvin-Erickson and La Vigne, 2015) found that at subway stations crime is highly influenced by the accessibility of the stations, the characteristics of the station itself, and the features of the immediate environment surrounding the station. Moreover, on the transport network, crime generator and/or attractor characteristics are highly influenced by both type of crime and time of day.

22.10 Conclusions and Further Research

This chapter has attempted to clearly distinguish crime generators and crime attractors. The key difference identified is the offender's motivation for visiting a place. Crime attractors are places with a "bad" reputation, and the offender travels there explicitly for the purpose of committing a crime. Crime generators are places where lots of people congregate, and this convergence of people enables serendipitous opportunities for offenders who happen to also be at that place.

This chapter contends that more consideration should be afforded to the concept of places considered as attractors and generators, and, moreover, it is essential to consider the scale and context, in other words why a place is an attractor or generator relative to what is nearby. The use of terms such as "hotspot" and "activity generator" in conjunction with the "generator attractor" language needs further thought. Places where people converge that do not experience crime should perhaps be termed activity generators or even crime-neutral activity generators, and activity generators with high crime levels can then be considered crime generators. A hotspot may be driven by crime attractors and/or crime generators, but the phrases "hotspot attractor" or "hotspot generator" are perhaps less useful and complicate our understanding. It is the underlying land use that generates crime opportunity or attracts offenders, and subsequently crimes, which then create hotspots, rather than the other way around.

The environs of crime generators were also shown to be highly relevant to crime levels. Crime is influenced by both characteristics of crime generators themselves and features of the surrounding environment. Size is perhaps relevant here. Indeed, one question might be the following: as a generator becomes larger, does it have greater influence on its surrounding environs, and, vice versa, as it becomes smaller, do its environs have a greater influence? The length of opening hours may also be relevant to this question, both at generators and nearby. Do places with longer opening hours have more of an impact on crime than those that are open sporadically, and how does this interact with premise size and premise busyness?

There are specific challenges evident in quantifying attractors and generators. In the absence of specific knowledge as to why an offender visited a place, crime counts and crime rates in an area offer some insight; generators have high counts but low rates, and attractors have high counts and high rates. However, the challenge is gathering appropriate information on population denominators to calculate rates. It is also paramount to break this down by time of day, relating to the usage of places at different times of day. Indeed, the size, function, opening hours, density, proximity, and length and nature of interactions between people make such measures highly complex. Further, crime type and busyness interact, as conditions optimal for pickpocketing are very different from those for robbery, criminal damage, or violence. This in part explains why places are rarely pure attractors or pure generators, but often a mix or combination of the two. Indeed one offender may be attracted to a particular location to commit a crime, and another offender may commit a crime at the same place and time but be there by chance.

This begs the question, does it matter whether a place is identified as a crime attractor or crime generator? Perhaps the ultimate test should be the crime prevention implications. Should the prevention choices at attractors be any different from those at generators? This offers a potential avenue for further research. The Brantinghams contend that one possible important issue for prevention is spatial displacement (Guerette and Bowers, 2009). The Brantinghams hint that if a place is a pure crime generator, the introduction of situational crime prevention measures is unlikely to result in greater levels of crime displacement. If it is an attractor, crime-neutral site, or mixed attractor-generator, some displacement is possible. Here further research is clearly warranted.

This chapter has identified two theoretical issues to be explored further. At crime generators, why does the presence of more people not equate to greater levels of capable guardianship? This in part is answered by the idea of first- and second-level critical density. Thus criminal damage, robbery, and pickpocketing are more likely at very different crowd densities. Indeed, an interesting area for future studies is the extent to which the busyness of a place helps or hinders the role of capable guardianship (both informal and formal) for different types of crimes in different settings and environments.

A second question is the relationship between generators and an offender's awareness spaces. If it is accepted that offenders generally increase their familiarity of an area during their daily routines, then what happens when they are at a crime generator and meet an unforeseen opportunity for crime? How familiar with that area do they need to be in order to activate their criminal readiness, and to be confident of doing so without detection and with sufficient reward? This raises a further question. Over time, to what extent do crime generators transform to become crime attractors, as increased familiarity and perhaps a change in ecological labels results in a reputational change? One possible new research methodology that could be useful to examine this is agent-based modeling (Birks and Elfers, 2014). Indeed, many of the research questions posed in this chapter could be avenues for simulation models to examine offender choices, and how they interact with possible attractors and generators, and how these may change over time.

Future developments, especially societal and technological change, may also influence the formation of crime generators and attractors. For example, there have been some recent moves toward the notion of anticrowds at places. Places people visit may have optimal conditions for enjoyment; thus if a place is too quiet, there is no atmosphere and the social experience is reduced. If it is too busy, then this also impacts on levels of enjoyment, due to jostling, bumping, or long queues. Restaurants and bars are examples of this, as is shopping on Christmas Eve or during New Year sales. Indeed in Amsterdam a recent mobile phone app called Avoid the Shopping Crowds provides live information on when to avoid shops that are too busy, and optimal times to go. It even provides historical data on average store traffic. If there is a growth in the idea of "anti-crowd" establishments, then how will this impact on offending?

Technological advances may also impact on crime generators and attractors. For example, new technologies have introduced the possibility of cyber pickpocketing, whereby offenders use card readers to wirelessly steal cash from credit cards that have a "contactless" payment facility. While these are currently rare, this may add another modus operandi to a pickpocket's arsenal, but could also change the optimal crowd density for pickpocketing. Again this may alter the landscape of crime generators and attractors, as new attractor locations for cyber pickpocketing may develop, to steal not only cash but also valuable data such as people's identity information.

References

Angel, S. (1968). Discouraging Crime through City Planning. Working Paper No. 75, Center for Planning and Development Research, Berkeley, CA.

Bernasco, W., and Block, R. (2011). Robberies in Chicago: A Block-Level Analysis of the Influence of Crime Generators, Crime Attractors, and Offender Anchor Points. *Journal of Research in Crime and Delinquency* 48(1), 33–57.

Birks, D. J., and Elffers, H. (2014). Agent-Based Models for Exploring Criminological Theory. In Bruinsma, G. and Weisburd, D. (Eds.), *Encyclopedia of Criminology and Criminal Justice*. New York: Springer, 19–32.

Bowers, K. (2014). Risky Facilities: Crime Radiators or Crime Absorbers? A Comparison of Internal and External Levels of Theft. *Journal of Quantitative Criminology* 30(3), 389–414.

Brantingham, P. L., and Brantingham, P. J. (1993). Environment, Routine and Situation: Toward a Pattern Theory of Crime. In Clarke, R. and Felson, M. (Eds.), *Routine Activity and Rational Choice*, vol. 5 of *Advances in Criminological Theory*. New Brunswick, NJ: Transaction, 259–294.

Brantingham, P. L., and Brantingham, P. J. (1995). Criminality of Place: Crime Generators and Crime Attractors. *European Journal of Criminal Policy and Research* 3, 1–26.

Ceccato, V., and Uittenbogaard, A. (2014). Space-Time Dynamics of Crime in Transport Nodes. *Annals of the Association of the American Geographers* 105: 131–150.

Clarke, R., Belanger, M., and Eastman, J. (1996). Where Angel Fears to Tread: A Test in the New York City Subway of the Robbery/Density Hypothesis. In Clarke, R. (Ed.), *Preventing Mass Transit Crime*. Monsey, NY: Criminal Justice Press, 217–235.

Clarke, R., and Eck, J. (2005). *Crime Analysis for Problem Solvers in 60 Small Steps*. Washington, DC: US Department of Justice, Office of Community Oriented Policing Services.

Cohen, L., and Felson, M. (1979). Social Change and Crime Rate Trends: A Routine Activity Approach. *American Sociological Review* 44, 588–608.

Cornish, D., and Clarke, R. (1986). *The Reasoning Criminal*. New York: Springer.

Eck, J., Chainey, S., Cameron, J., and Wilson, R. (2005). *Mapping Crime: Understanding Hotspots*. Washington, DC: National Institute of Justice.

Eck, J., Clarke, R. V., and Guerette, R. (2007). Risky Facilities: Crime Concentration in Homogeneous Sets of Facilities. In Farrell, G., Bowers, K. J., Johnson, S. D., and Townsley, M. (Eds.), *Imagination for Crime Prevention: Essays in Honour of Ken Pease*, vol. 21 of *Crime Prevention Studies*. Monsey, NY Criminal Justice Press, 225–264.

Guerette, R., and Bowers, K. (2009). Assessing the Extent of Crime Displacement and Diffusion of Benefits: A Review of Situational Crime Prevention Evaluations. *Criminology* 47(4), 1331–1368.

Groff, E. R., and McCord, E. S. (2011). The Role of Neighborhood Parks as Crime Generators. *Security Journal* 25(1), 1–24.

Irvin-Erickson, Y., and La Vigne, N. (2015). A Spatio-temporal Analysis of Crime at Washington, DC Metro Rail: Stations' Crime-Generating and Crime-Attracting Characteristics as Transportation Nodes and Places. *Crime Science* 4, 14.

Jacobs, J. (1961). *The Death and Life of Great American Cities*. New York: Vintage.

Kinney, B., Brantingham, P. L., Wuschke, K., Kirk, M., and Brantingham, P. J. (2008). Crime Attractors, Generators and Detractors: Land Use and Urban Crime Opportunities. *Built Environment* 34(1), 62–74.

Kurland, J., Johnson, S., and Tilley, N. (2014). Offenses around Stadiums: A Natural Experiment on Crime Attraction and Generation. *Journal of Research in Crime and Delinquency* 51, 5–28.

Loukaitou-Sideris, A. (1999). Hot Spots of Bus Stop Crime: The Importance of Environmental Attributes. *Journal of the American Planning Association* 65(4), 395–411.

Malleson, N., and Andresen, M. (2015). Spatio-temporal Crime Hotspots and the Ambient Population. *Crime Science* 4(10). Available online: https://link.springer.com/article/10.1186/s40163-015-0023-8#citeas.

Malleson, N., and Andresen, M. (2016). Exploring the Impact of Ambient Population Measures on London Crime Hotspots. *Journal of Criminal Justice* 46(1), 52–63.

McCord, E. S., Ratcliffe, J. H., Garcia, R. M., and Taylor, R. B. (2007). Non-residential Crime Attractors and Generators Elevate Perceived Neighborhood Crime and Incivilities. *Journal of Research in Crime and Delinquency* 44(3), 295–320.

Montolio, D., and Planells, S. (2015). Measuring the Negative Externalities of a Private Leisure Activity: Hooligans and Pickpockets around the Stadium. IEB Working Paper No. 2015/15. Available online: http://ssrn.com/abstract=2606271.

Newton, A. (2014). Crime on Public Transport. In Bruinsma, G. and Weisburd, D. (Eds.), *Encyclopedia of Criminology and Criminal Justice*. London: Springer, 709–720.

Newton, A., and Ceccato, V. (2015). Theoretical Perspectives of Safety and Security in Transit Environments. In *Safety and Security in Transit Environments: An Interdisciplinary Approach*. London: Palgrave Macmillan, 23–39.

Newton, A., Partridge, H., and Gill, A. (2014a). Above and Below: Measuring Crime Risk in and around Underground Mass Transit Systems. *Crime Science* 3(1), 1–14.

Newton, A., Partridge, H., and Gill, A. (2014b). In and around: Identifying Predictors of Theft within and near to Major Mass Underground Transit Systems. *Security Journal* 27(2), 132–146.

Ratcliffe, J. H. (2012). The Spatial Extent of Criminogenic Places on the Surrounding Environment: A Change-Point Regression of Violence around Bars. *Geographical Analysis* 44(4), 302–332.

Short, M., D'Orsogna, M., Pasour, V., Tita, G., Brantingham, P. J., Bertozzi, A., and Chayes, L. (2008). A Statistical Model of Criminal Behaviour. *Mathematical Models and Methods in Applied Sciences* 18, 1249–1267.

Solymosi, R., Borrion, H., and Fujiyama, T. (2015). Crowd Spatial Patterns at Bus Stops: Security Implications and Effects of Warning Messages. In Ceccato, V. and Newton, A. (Eds.), *Safety and Security in Transit Environments: An Interdisciplinary Approach*. London: Palgrave Macmillan, 156–181.

Weisburd, D., Bernasco, W., and Bruinsma, G. J. N. (2009). *Putting Crime in Its Place: Units of Analysis in Spatial Crime Research*. New York: Springer.

CHAPTER 23

DOES CRIME IMPACT REAL ESTATE PRICES?

An Assessment of Accessibility and Location

VANIA CECCATO AND MATS WILHELMSSON

23.1 Introduction

Individuals regard safety as a key factor when looking for a home to buy or rent (Fransson, Rosenqvist, & Turner, 2002; Gibbons, 2004; Larsson, Landström, & Sandin, 2008). Although accessibility is also highly valued in the housing market, researchers and policymakers have acknowledged the negative aspects of transportation systems, such as crime, and their impact on housing markets (Boymal, Silva, & Liu, 2013; Ceccato, 2013; Ceccato, Cats, & Wang, 2015). Yet the interaction of accessibility and crime in determining housing preferences is still not well understood (Boymal et al., 2013; Ceccato & Wilhelmsson, 2011; Weisbrod, Ben-Akiva, & Lerman, 1980), because individuals make choices based on a series of housing characteristics, neighborhood features, job accessibility, and transportation trade-offs (Weisbrod et al., 1980).

In this study, we aim to contribute to this literature by assessing the impact of crime and accessibility on housing prices. Accessibility is expected to have a positive impact on housing prices, but good accessibility to a place may also mean more crime, because an accessible place allows more social interaction, more crime opportunities, and more crime, pulling housing prices down. Individuals make choices based on a trade-off between accessibility and criminality. Using hedonic modeling, we empirically assess this trade-off after controlling for other property and neighborhood characteristics.

In particular, we assess the effect of residential burglary on apartment prices in Stockholm, building on previous research (Ceccato & Wilhelmsson, 2011) that indicated residential burglary—not violence or vandalism—had the greatest effect on apartment prices in the Swedish capital. We assume that residential burglary has such an effect on housing prices because targets of this type of crime always include victims' most private property (their home and objects in it), so burglary can be perceived as more intrusive and more costly to victims than acts of property damage or violence that happen in their surroundings but often outside their private realm. We measured accessibility in two ways: a generalized monetary cost of travel to work (in Swedish crowns, SEK) and a centrality measure (distance to the city center). The analysis builds on previous research but is set apart by (1) extending the study area to all of Stockholm County (26 municipalities), encompassing 92,000 transactions of condominium apartments sold during 2012–2014, and (2) using an updated data set for police-recorded crime from 2013.

The chapter starts with a discussion in Section 23.2 of what influences buyers in their choice of home, especially in their attempt to avoid crime and fear of crime. We also discuss how the question has been addressed in previous research and summarize the results of earlier work. In Section 23.3, we present three hypotheses concerning the influence of burglary rates and accessibility on apartment prices. Section 23.4 describes the geographic area, data used, and the spatial hedonic models. This section includes a discussion of statistical problems and how they were solved. Section 23.5 presents the results from the models. Here we discuss the impact on apartment prices of a variety of factors, focusing on crime rates, accessibility, and distance from the central business district. Section 23.6 summarizes the study and discusses some of the limitations on using the results as a basis for general policymaking. Areas of future research are also suggested in this final section.

23.2 Theoretical Background

The decision to purchase a property is complex, because the price a person is willing to pay depends on the characteristics of the property as well as the surrounding neighborhood and how these characteristics relate to the city overall (Thaler, 1978). Hedonic regression is a preference method of estimating demand or value of an item, a product, or amenity. It decomposes the item into its constituent characteristics, and obtains estimates of the contributory value of each characteristic. Research in this area has long been applied to the concept of hedonic price to make inferences to a series of sales on the demand for certain housing characteristics (e.g., number of rooms) and characteristics of the location and neighborhood (e.g., accessibility to services). In reality, it is not easy to untangle these characteristics. Different land use and characteristics influence property values in different ways: some affect an area's attractiveness positively or negatively; some can have both effects simultaneously. What buyers pay for a property in a low-crime area is hypothetically more than in an area that is a crime hotspot, so safety (or the lack of it) is incorporated into different market prices.

More than three decades of research have been devoted to understanding the effects of crime and fear of crime on property prices (Table 23.1). Of the 31 studies written in English reviewed in Table 23.1, more than two-thirds show clear evidence that properties are discounted in areas with more crime or with poor perceived safety, while

Table 23.1 Crime, Accessibility Measures, and Real Estate Prices: A Review of the Literature

Author(s)	Study area	Method(s)	Safety indicators	Control for transport/ accessibility	Main results	Effect on prices
Vania Ceccato and Mats Wilhelmsson (2016)	Stockholm metropolitan area, Sweden	Hedonic price model	Residential burglary, car theft, vandalism, violence, and distance to a hotspot	Centrality measure, dummy for submarkets	Crime depresses property prices overall, but crime hotspots affect prices of single-family houses more than prices of apartments	Negative
Li et al. (2015)	Austin, Texas	Cliff-Ord spatial hedonic model	Violent crime rate within 1.6 km from the property	Network distance to nearest facilities, dummy for public transportation, walkability index	Violent crimes reduce property prices	Negative
Caudill, Affuso, and Yang (2015)	Memphis, Tennessee	Hedonic spatial error model	Locations of sex offenders	Distance to downtown, dummies for zip codes	Each additional sex offender in a one-mile radius results in a loss of about 2% of the property value	Negative
Iqbal and Ceccato (2015)	Stockholm municipality, Sweden	Hedonic quantile regression, spatial lag, spatial error	Rates of violence, property crime, and total crime in urban parks	Centrality measure, dummy based on distance to public transportation, main roads, submarkets	The price of apartments tends to be discounted in areas where parks have relatively high rates of violence and vandalism, but it depends on park type	Negative/No effect
Wilhelmsson and Ceccato (2015)	Middle-sized nonmetropolitan municipality, Sweden	Hedonic quantile regression, endogeneity dealt with two variables: young males and convenience stores	Residential burglary rates in 2005 and 2011	Centrality measure, dummy based on distance to main roads	Residential burglary reduced apartment prices in 2011 but not in 2005	Negative

Buonanno, Montolio, and Raya-Vílchez (2012)	City of Barcelona, Spain	Hedonic price model and quantile regressions, endogeneity dealt with past victimization index and percentage of youth	District-level data from Barcelona City Council victimization survey	Not declared	Homes in less safe districts have on average a valuation 1.27% lower than in the rest of the city	Negative
Congdon-Hohman (2013)	Summit County, Ohio, the city of Akron, Ohio,	Hedonic price model	Distance to methamphetamine laboratories	Zip code dummies, distance measures	Sale prices for houses decline 10%–19% in the year following discovery of a laboratory	Negative
D. G. Pope and Pope (2012)	3,000 urban zip codes in the United States	Hedonic model, endogeneity dealt with crime rate change that occurred over the same period for a "similar" zip code in a different area	Zip code's crime rate change, 1990–2000s, violent and property crimes	Distance measures, census tract dummies	Decreasing crime leads to increasing property values	Negative
Ceccato and Wilhelmsson (2012)	Stockholm municipality, Sweden	Hedonic model, spatial lag, and spatial error, endogeneity dealt with homicide rates	Rates of vandalism and/or fear of crime measures	Centrality measure, dummy based on distance to public transportation, main roads, submarkets	Fear of crime affects apartment prices even after signs of physical damage (vandalism) in an area are controlled for	Negative
Ceccato and Wilhelmsson (2011)	Stockholm municipality, Sweden	Hedonic model and spatial analysis, endogeneity dealt with homicide rates	Rates of total crime, robbery, vandalism, residential burglary, assault, theft	Centrality measure, dummy based on distance to public transportation, main roads, submarkets	Residential burglary shows a greater effect on prices, and the effect varies locally (neighborhoods) and regionally (submarkets)	Negative

(continued)

Table 23.1 Continued

Author(s)	Study area	Method(s)	Safety indicators	Control for transport/ accessibility	Main results	Effect on prices
Ihlanfeldt and Mayock (2010)	Miami-Dade County, Florida	Hedonic model, endogeneity dealt with difference in housing price index, crime measures, and other factors	Nine-year crime panel data, changes in crime densities	Not declared	Changes in crime density explain the greatest variation in changes in the price index, a 1% increase in crime is found to reduce housing prices .1%–.3%	Negative
Hwang and Thill (2009)	Buffalo–Niagara Falls region, New York	Market-wide stepwise hedonic regression	Rates of violent and property crimes	Job accessibility, submarkets	Violent crime has a negative impact and property crime a positive impact, depending on type of submarket	Inconclusive
Troy and Grove (2008)	Baltimore, Maryland	Hedonic price model	Crime index and crime rates		0.017% decrease in the values of the homes associated with a park	Negative
J. C. Pope (2008)	Hillsborough County, Florida	Hedonic price model	Fear of crime, locations of sex offenders	Census tract dummies	Housing prices fall 2.3% after a sex offender moves into a neighborhood, when the offender moves out, prices rebound	Negative
Linden and Rockoff (2008)	Mecklenburg County, North Carolina	Hedonic model polynomial regressions	Locations of sex offenders	Neighborhood fixed effects	Prices of properties fell 4% following the arrival of an offender	Negative
Munroe (2007)	Mecklenburg County, North Carolina	Hedonic model and spatial analysis	Total crimes per census block	Distance measures, e.g., distance to uptown (km)	Crime has a negative impact on prices	Negative

Tita, Petras, and Greenbaum (2006)	Columbus, Ohio	Hedonic price model, endogeneity dealt with murder rates	Changes in rates of total crime, property crime, violent crimes	Centrality measure	Crime impacts differently in different types of neighborhood and violence had the most significant impact	Negative/ Inconclusive
Gibbons (2004)	London area, UK	Hedonic price model, endogeneity dealt with spatially lagged dependent variables	Rates of criminal damage (vandalism, graffiti, arson), residential burglary, theft from shops	Diverse set of distance measures to facilities, centrality measure, dummies for local authorities	Crime damage has a negative impact on prices (1%), but residential burglary does not	Negative/ No effect
Bowes and Ihlanfeldt (2001)	Atlanta region, Dekalb County, Georgia	Hedonic price model	Density of total crimes in tract	Distance to CBD, several distance measures	Negative crime effects are found mainly close to downtown, effects vary regionally	Negative
Lynch and Rasmussen (2001)	Jacksonville, Florida	Hedonic price model	Crimes and the estimated cost of reported crime in the relevant police "beat"	Not declared	The cost of crime has virtually no impact on house prices overall, but homes are discounted (39% less) in high-crime areas	No effect / negative
Case and Mayer (1996)	Boston metropolitan area, Massachusetts	Hedonic price model, change in price, endogeneity dealt with lagged permits and amount of vacant land	Rates of total crime	Distance to Boston, centrality measure	House prices in towns with high crime rates appreciated faster in the boom but remained similar to other towns in the bust	Positive/ negative
Buck, Hakim, and Spiegel (1993)	64 communities, including Atlantic City, New Jersey	Hedonic price model, endogeneity dealt with lags of explanatory variables	Frequency of larceny, auto theft, burglary; crime rate of community	Centrality measure, accessibility, travel time in minutes	Highly mixed, with no consistent finding across model specifications; in the majority of models, the effect of crime was negative	Inconclusive/ negative

(continued)

Table 23.1 Continued

Author(s)	Study area	Method(s)	Safety indicators	Control for transport/ accessibility	Main results	Effect on prices
Buck, Hakim, and Spiegel (1991)	64 communities, including Atlantic City, New Jersey	Hedonic price model	Frequency of violent crimes (murder, assault, etc.) and property crimes (burglary, car thefts, etc.)	Centrality measure, travel time in minutes	Casinos and crime affect property values inversely as a function of distance; the impact of a casino and crime varies by location: accessibility and other localities	Negative
Clark and Cosgrove (1990)	Sample of public use microdata urban areas, US	Two-stage intercity hedonic model	Police expenditures / crime rate, homicide rates, input price of public safety	Dummy for property located in city center, commuting distances in miles	Police expenditures / Crime rates have a negative impact but are insignificant; public safety expenditures increase rental prices;	Negative
Burnell (1988)	Chicago suburban communities, Illinois	Hedonic price model, endogeneity dealt with community fiscal and demographic characteristics	Property crime rate, full-time police officers per thousand population	Distance from community to CBD, distance from the Loop	Property crime rate has negative and significant effect on housing prices	Negative
Dubin and Goodman (1982)	Baltimore metropolitan area, Maryland	Hedonic price model	Principal component analyses on property and violent crimes	Centrality measure	Both violent and property crimes have a significant reducing impact on housing prices	Negative

Weisbrod et al. (1980)	Minneapolis–St. Paul metropolitan area, Minnesota	Logit estimation of location	Crime rates for assaults and robberies	Work-trip access	5% reduction in automobile commute time results in a 4.1% decrease in the rate of assaults and robberies for the current location, or a 28% increase in the same crime rate for other locational alternatives	Negative in relation to accessibility
Naroff, Hellman, and Skinner (1980)	Boston, Massachusetts	Hedonic price model, endogeneity dealt with population density of tract	Rates of total crime and property crime	Travel costs, centrality measure	All crime variables have a negative and significant effect on housing prices	Negative
Rizzo (1979)	Chicago, Illinois	Hedonic price model	Rates of total crime, property crime, and violence	Centrality measure	All crime variables have a negative and significant effect on housing prices	Negative
Thaler (1978)	Rochester, New York	Hedonic price model	Rates of property crime	Average driving time, dummy for zones	Crime reduces 3% of the average price per home	Negative
Kain and Quigley (1970)	City of St. Louis, Missouri	Regression models	Number of major crimes	Miles from CBD, dummy for zones	Crime reduces prices but the effect is not significant	No effect

one-fifth of these studies show mixed results, and only two show no indication. The effect of crime is also corroborated in studies of cities of the global South; for a review see Ceccato (2016). Ceccato and Wilhelmsson (2011, p. 83) have shown that even if all demand factors do not vary in space, the implicit price may fluctuate as the supply of attributes may vary in space; for example, "the relative scarcity of *no crime areas* in the inner city would suggest the implicit price of *no crime* is high compared to the suburbs, where the attribute *no crime* might be more abundant. But even within the suburbs the pattern of interaction between place attributes and safety may be different: If the average income among the households is higher in one area, it could be expected that the implicit price of the attribute *no crime* is higher than in an area where income average is lower."

How crime affects housing prices is also related to the nature of crime itself. Most crimes depend on social interactions and human activities in places. They can only happen if individuals move around, meet each other, or become acquainted with crime opportunities. Most of these interactions are pleasant, but some turn into a fight, a theft, or an act of vandalism. Thus, accessibility to places is fundamental for crime, because crime occurs only when a potential victim (or target) and a motivated offender converge in place when there is nobody watching (Cohen & Felson, 1979). Modern public transportation systems not only *allow* people to meet one another; these systems themselves *generate* areas of social convergence that are more prone to crime. Moving between places also means that people are being exposed to unfamiliar environments where they may be at a higher risk of victimization by crime (Ceccato & Newton, 2015; Loukaitou-Sideris, 2012; Newton, Johnson, & Bowers, 2004). Even if transport systems may not generate more crime (e.g., Bowes & Ihlanfeldt, 2001), they make it possible for crime to occur in other places, as they shift people around and make places accessible.

Good accessibility often affects prices positively, but its impact depends on the types of transportation system (buses, subways, roads, railways) and what they represent in terms of urban landscape and their effects (noise, architectural disruptions). For instance, Ceccato and Wilhelmsson (2011) found that if apartments are within 300 meters of a subway station, the effect on prices is positive. It is clear that the negative externalities, for example noise and vibrations, do not outweigh the positive. In contrast, proximity to commuter train stations has a negative effect on apartment prices for the same distance range, while being located close to main streets seems to have a positive effect on price of the apartments.

One of the most interesting studies in this area *from a buyer's perspective* is from the early 1980s and assessed the trade-offs between accessibility and crime. Weisbrod et al. (1980, p. 7) found that the negative attributes of where people currently reside are at least as important as the positive attributes of locational alternatives in encouraging a decision to move. For example, for those using public transportation, "a 5% reduction in commute travel time was estimated to have an effect on locational attractiveness for the surveyed movers that is equivalent to 3.8% decrease in the rate of assaults and robberies per population." Their results suggest that households make significant trade-offs between transportation services and other factors, but that the role of both in determining where people choose to live is small compared with socioeconomic and demographic factors.

From a criminal's perspective, good accessibility means potential opportunities, such as for residential burglary. Yet any type of movement imposes travel costs. The farther criminals have to travel, the greater the travel costs (for the effect of street networks on crime and offenders' decision-making, see Beavon 1994; Johnson and Bowers 2010; Johnson and Summers 2015). As Burnell (1988, p. 187) suggested, if criminals are more likely to come from certain areas, the distance from these areas to the wealthier areas represents a cost to the criminal that must be weighed against the "potentially expected higher payoffs in these wealthier areas, [and] therefore a negative relationship between distance and crime is expected." Offenders' decision-making seems to be more complex than a cost-benefit analysis of distance and payoffs. Johnson and Summers (2015) examined how the characteristics of neighborhoods and their proximity to offender home locations affect offender spatial decision-making. Findings for adult offenders indicated that offenders' choices appear to be influenced by how accessible a neighborhood is via the street network. For younger offenders, results indicated that they favor areas that are low in social cohesion and closer to their home, or other age-related activity nodes.

How accessibility affects prices may also be a function of the way accessibility measures are incorporated into hedonic price models. Table 23.1 indicates at least three ways that can be summarised below:

(a) A global measure of centrality (e.g., distance decay from city center, Von Thunen model): The closer a property is to the inner city, the higher its price. This measure is often represented by a continuous variable from a central point in the city center.
(b) A local measure of accessibility (e.g., transport nodes, such as a station, distance to roads or schools, commuting time, travel costs): The closer to the transport node, the higher the property prices, though it may also be noisier, more polluted, and with a poorer quality of life with mixed land use. This measure is normally represented by dummy variables for locations, buffer distances to stations, or distance measures from properties to accessibility points.
(c) A measure of spatial arrangement of the data (e.g., boundary sharing with a zone with higher accessibility means that individuals living in these neighboring zones are more likely to experience higher accessibility). Despite not being completely homogeneous, housing submarkets[1] share a number of characteristics, including accessibility. These measures can vary, from simple dummy variables that flag differences between zones or neighborhoods, to measures of spatial autocorrelation for travel time or accessibility variables within a housing submarket.

However, it is remarkable that although both crime and accessibility normally are correlated with other neighborhood characteristics, such as deprivation, more than half of the studies summarized in Table 23.1 regard crime or accessibility as an *exogenous* variable. To find out "what causes what," instrumental variables are often used in these models. An appropriate instrumental variable must be highly correlated with the endogenous measure but, at the same time, be uncorrelated with the error term and correctly excluded from the estimated housing price equation. Of the 12 studies that do instrument crime, only a few tested the validity of the instruments. As suggested by Ihlanfeldt and Mayock (2010, p. 161), the endogeneity of crime has been overlooked because "it is extremely difficult to identify variables that satisfy the conditions required of a valid instrument." In this study, a set of instrumental variables is used (see 23.4.2, "Data and Methods)".

23.3 Hypotheses of the Study

This study builds on previous research in Stockholm (Ceccato & Wilhelmsson, 2011; Wilhelmsson & Ceccato, 2015) but represents a departure by testing the hypotheses articulated below.

First, we will test if *burglary rates have a negative impact on housing prices* (H1). We also test whether *accessibility increases property prices* (H2). At the same time, there is an expected link between crime and accessibility. Good accessibility is often positively related to higher crime rates and vice versa. Hence, a location further away from the city is often associated with lower housing prices because of poorer accessibility but higher prices because of lower criminality. Moreover, the distance to the central business district (CBD) and accessibility is positively related, of course, but not perfect, especially in a place like Stockholm that is an archipelago, which means that people live and routinely commute to and from the islands in a well-connected transportation network (for the effect of street network on crime, see Beavon 1994; Johnson and Bowers 2010). However, this also implies that any measure based on Euclidian distance is problematic in this context, as one cannot easily walk or drive from each location to every other even if they are physically close (therefore in this study two measures of accessibility are employed). Even in a more or less monocentric city such as Stockholm, smaller subcenters with shopping and good public transportation may increase the accessibility but not the distance to the CBD. Thus, we test *whether the impact of burglaries on apartment prices differ with accessibility and distance to the CBD* (H3).

23.4 Components of the Study

23.4.1 The Study Area

Stockholm County was chosen for the case study because it is one of the most accessible cities in Europe. This Scandinavian capital received the 2013 Access City award for disabled-friendly cities, in third place after Berlin and Nantes, France (European Commission, 2010). The area is served by an extensive public transportation system (three subway lines with more than 100 stations, 2,000 buses, 5,000 taxis, dozens of ferryboats, and several tram routes) as well as roads, so the islands that constitute the metropolitan area are well connected. However, the region is characterized by urban sprawl. It extends to a large area (6,519 square kilometers) with a relatively low population density (3.6 inhabitants/square kilometer, compared to 6.9 for Copenhagen, Denmark (Statistics Denmark, 2016). Moreover, accessibility is limited by the fact that the region is an archipelago, located on Sweden's south-central east coast, where Lake Mälaren, Sweden's third largest lake, flows into the Baltic Sea.

Stockholm's metropolitan area, or Stockholm County, is composed of the municipality of Stockholm and 25 other surrounding municipalities (Figure 23.1). It is the largest of the three metropolitan areas in Sweden, with about 2.2 million inhabitants in 2014, half of them residing in Stockholm municipality. Although other types of housing tenure can also be found, privately or cooperatively owned apartment buildings dominate the most central parts of the metropolitan area. Large sections of Stockholm's inner city have residential land use, where citizens enjoy a good quality of life with high housing standards. However, there are flats built in the 1960s and 1970s throughout the Stockholm region that do not command high prices in the housing market. Some more peripheral municipalities have areas associated with poor architecture, lack of amenities, and social problems, including crime.

The Swedish housing market has different forms of tenure: single-family, owner-occupied housing; cooperative multifamily housing; and multifamily rental housing. The multifamily rental housing market is subject to rent control, resulting, among other things, in a housing shortage in attractive locations. In the case of cooperative housing, the property is owned by a cooperative association. Each resident owns a share of the cooperative and occupies an apartment with tenancy rights nearly as strong as those of full ownership. Cooperatives are traded on an ordinary free housing market. Residents of cooperative apartments pay a monthly fee to the cooperative covering communal property expenses, such as maintenance, taxes, and other fees.

The geography of residential burglary has been changing since the early 1990s. Wikström (1991) showed that residential burglaries in Stockholm tend to occur mostly in outer-city wards with high socioeconomic status and especially in districts where there are high offender-rate areas nearby. For the latter, travel costs to targets are not too high because criminals do not need to travel long distances. Using data from the late 1990s, Ceccato, Haining, and Signoretta (2002) showed that high relative risks of residential burglary tended to occur both in the more affluent areas and in the more deprived areas. On the one hand, the higher the income, the higher the relative risk of residential burglary. Ten years later, Uittenbogaard and Ceccato (2012) found a similar geography for property crimes. What was striking at this time was that the geography of crime varied over space and time. This is because the risk of crime in a place varies as a function of the place's location, the characteristics of its built environment, and, most importantly, the human activities that the place generates at a particular time. These factors together determine different opportunities for burglary, even in areas with extensive use of housing safety measures (da Costa & Ceccato, 2015).

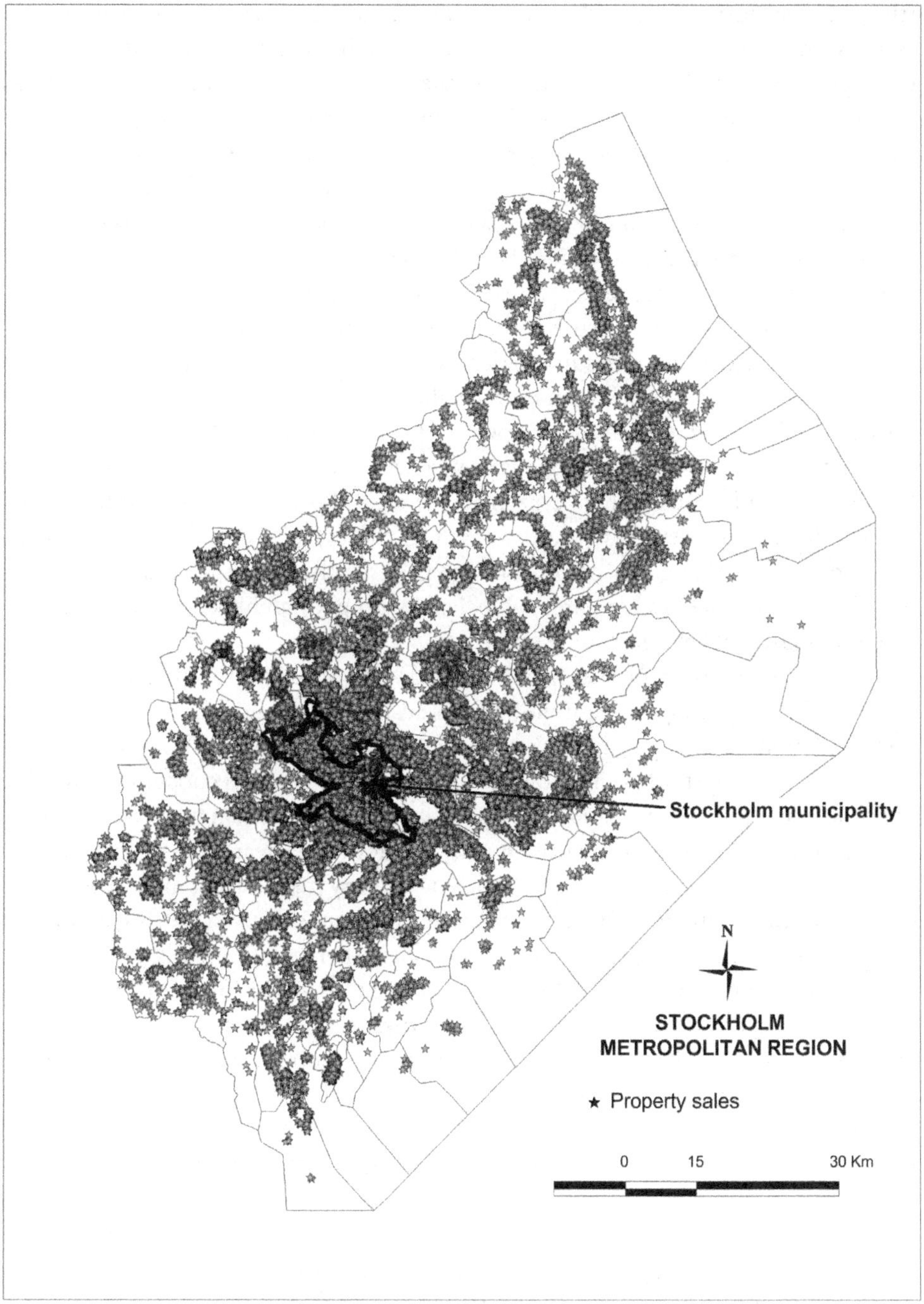

FIGURE 23.1 Stockholm metropolitan area: Study area

23.4.2. Data and Methods

23.4.2.1 *The Data Sets*

The data used comes from three sources. First, we used transactions of condominium apartments sold during 2012–2014 in Stockholm County (Figure 23.1), approximately 92,000 observations. Although the data covers three years, the x,y coordinates of each transaction are considered a cross-sectional database since a property cannot be sold every year, or multiple times (or rarely it is) in a short span of time. Each x,y coordinate is unique and illustrates a more robust picture of the housing market that would not be shown if only a year of data were used in the analysis.

The data comes from the company Valueguard, which gathers data on prices and property attributes. Only arm's-lengths transactions are included in the data set. The database contains property address, area code, parish code, selling price, living area, year of construction, presence of balcony and elevator, price per square meter, date of contract, monthly fee to the condominium association, number of rooms, date of disposal, number of the floor of the specific flat, total number of floors in building, postal code, and x,y coordinates. This vector of attributes at the x,y coordinate level of every single apartment sold was mapped using geographical information systems (GIS). There is also a second vector of attributes associated with the neighborhood context of the apartments (e.g., distance to CBD, crime rates, accessibility). Thus, if an apartment i is located in an area j, then all i are automatically associated in GIS with the attributes of j. Using GIS, area-level data was combined with x,y data using standard matching table procedures. Note that these areas, *basområde*, are the smallest geographical unit for which statistical data is available in Sweden, in a total of 1298 units. They vary in shape, size, and total population (mean population of 1,521 inhabitants with standard deviation of 1,508). The coverage of the data collected by Valueguard varies from 85% to 90% of all sales. Sales not included are transactions sold without a real estate broker.

The cross-sectional data was merged with land use data from the Stockholm metropolitan area's database and with police records from Stockholm Police headquarters. Police records were mapped using x,y coordinates for each offense in 2013. The data for accessibility and some of the control variables (e.g., indicators of urbanization) come from the company WSP (William Sale Partnership). The variable accessibility is measured as "generalized travel cost," the total cost a traveler experiences when taking a trip from one location to another relative to the location's attractiveness (here, number of jobs at the location). The costs include indirect costs for time and direct costs, such as for tickets. Here, travel cost is measured for public transportation (Ben-Akiva & Steven, 1985). The travel cost is not based on the distance between the transacted apartment and Stockholm CBD; instead it is the "average" travel cost to all other locations in the study area, weighted by number of jobs in that location. On the other hand, the variable distance to the CBD is the Euclidean distance between property addresses and the Stockholm CBD and has been estimated in GIS. Figure 23.2 exemplifies the accessibility measure and cases of residential burglary in Stockholm.

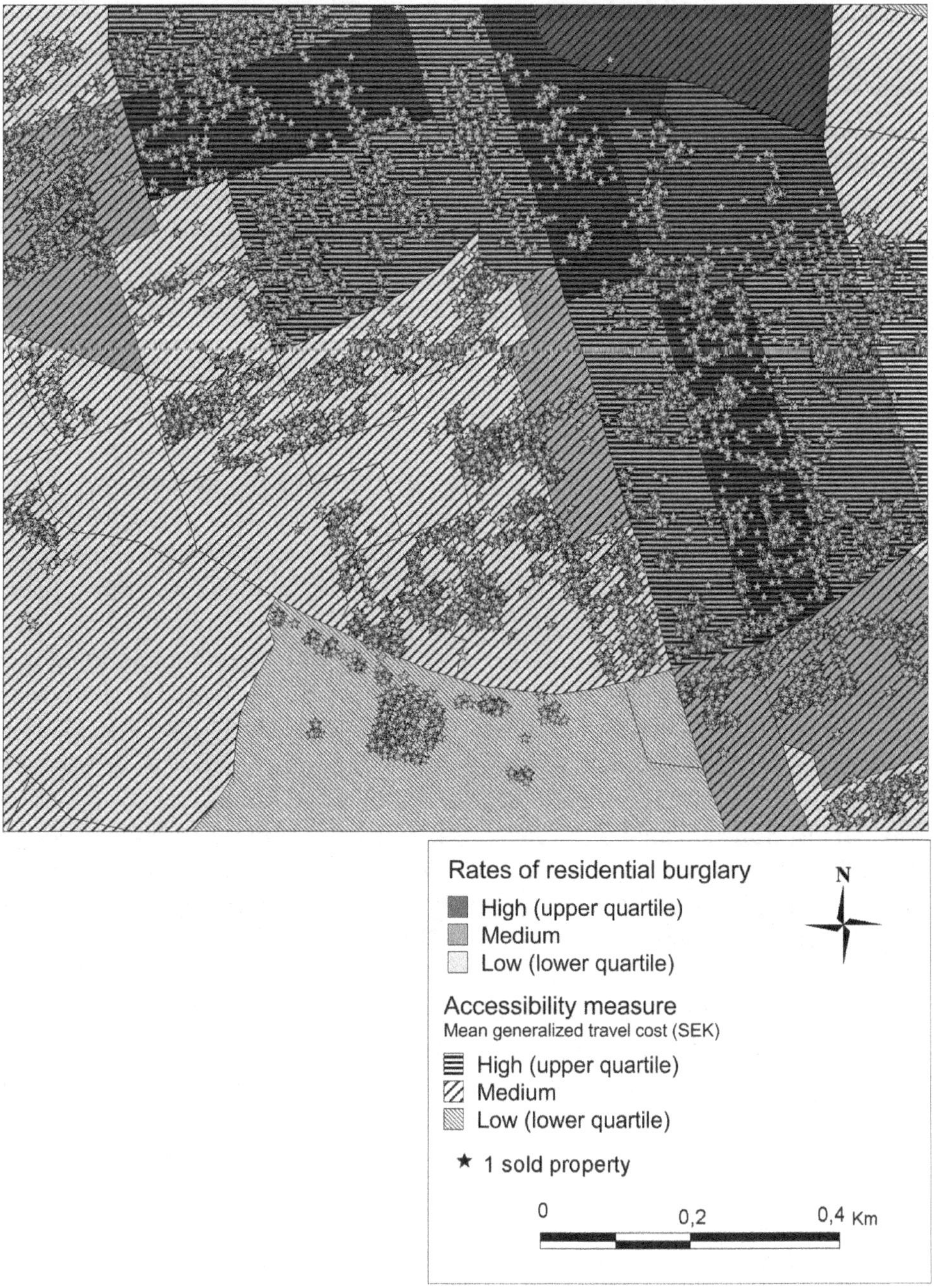

FIGURE 23.2 Overlaps in space of covariates "Accessibility" and "Residential burglary" in a snapshot of central Stockholm (Sweden)

Data source: Police headquarters, 2013 and WSP (William Sale Partnership).

Crime rates for residential burglary were calculated by using data for small unit areas (*basområde*). To link crime rates to the x,y coordinates of each property sale, the Stockholm metropolitan map with 1,298 units was layered over the properties' x,y coordinates. All sales within the boundaries of a small unit area would get that small unit area's crime rates. This procedure was performed using the standard table join function in GIS. For more details, see Ceccato and Wilhelmsson (2011). Note that these zones vary greatly in the total number of crimes, from no crime to 5,564 offences, with a standard deviation of 436,065 and a mean of 319,943 offences. For residential burglary, the mean was 7.6 per small unit areas, with a standard deviation of 11.14.

23.4.2.2 *The Models*

To test our hypotheses, we used spatial hedonic models (Wilhelmsson, 2002; but see also Ceccato & Wilhelmsson, 2011, 2012, 2016; Wilhelmsson & Ceccato, 2015). In spatial hedonic models, a commonly used model especially in real estate economics, the dependent variable equals price, and the independent variables are housing attributes, neighborhood characteristics, and time indicators if the sample is a combination of cross-section and time series (as in our case). The hedonic model is based upon the assumption that the value of a house or apartment is a function of its characteristics and that there exists an implicit price (or hedonic price or willingness to pay) for each characteristic. The characteristics could be attributes of the house or apartment (such as size, quality, and age), and/or the characteristics of the neighborhood (such as closeness to parks, sea view, and access to public transportation, as well as absence of traffic noise and crimes). Hedonic models are used in property valuation, estimation of willingness to pay, and construction of house price indexes. The term "hedonic" was introduced in an article by Court (1939). By estimating the so-called hedonic price equation, the implicit prices can be revealed. The stochastic version of the hedonic price equation takes the form

$$Y = X\beta + \varepsilon \quad (23.1),$$

where Y is a $1 \times n$ vector of observations of the dependent variable, and β is a $k \times 1$ vector of parameters associated with exogenous explanatory variables (X); X is an $n \times k$ matrix. The number of observations is equal to the number of transacted individual sales, that is, a cross-sectional data set. The stochastic term ε is assumed to have a constant variance and normal distribution. Usually the functional form is nonlinear but linear in parameters. The estimated parameters (a vector of β) can be interpreted as willingness to pay for the housing and neighborhood attributes (Rosen, 1974). In order to be able to interpret the coefficients as causal relationships, the explanatory variables must be exogenous. If the independent explanatory variable is endogenous, we need to utilize other methods such as the instrument variable approach discussed below.

The explanatory variables X can be divided into a number of different types of attributes. Here we used attributes controlling for structural differences such as size of apartment, age of property, and maintenance fees to the cooperative. But we also used neighborhood characteristics such as crime rate (here, burglary rates), distance to CBD, and accessibility via public transportation, as well as indicators of urbanization such as housing density.

A major concern in estimating Equation 23.1 is the problem of simultaneous causality (endogeneity); that is, we do not know whether it is burglaries that explain house prices or whether it is house prices that explain burglaries. Hence, the causality may go in both directions. If that is the case, the error and the independent variable "burglary" are correlated and the OLS estimates will be biased.

In addition to the simultaneity problem discussed above, there may also be a problem of spatial dependency, which is often the case in real estate models such as this (see, for example, Wilhelmsson, 2002). If spatial autocorrelation is not included when building the real estate model, OLS will be biased, and furthermore the estimated variance will be biased; that is, it will be difficult to make an inference (Anselin, 1988). To mitigate this problem, we estimated a spatial lag model, that is, spatial lagged house prices are included as an additional independent variable in the hedonic price equation. The spatial weight matrix that we are using is defined by the inverse distance between observations and is row-standardized. To reduce the problems of simultaneity and spatial dependency and to estimate unbiased, consistent, and efficient parameters, we adopted an instrument variable (IV) approach proposed by Kelejian and Prucha (1998) and refined in Drukker, Egger, and Prucha (2013). The instrument two-stage technique assumes the instrument to be uncorrelated with the error term but a good proxy for the endogenous variables. We use as instrument variables spatial lagged neighboring characteristics such as housing density and proportion of high-rise buildings as well as spatial lagged aggregated housing attributes such as size, maintenance fee, and number of rooms. Hence, the instrument variables are assumed to be correlated to our independent spatial and crime variables, but not correlated to our dependent variable housing price. This method, with the same type of instrument variables, has been used in previous research (Basile, 2008; Brasington, Flores-Lagunes, & Guci, 2016; Buettner, 2001; Buonanno, Prarolo, & Vanin, 2016; Gómez-Antonio, Hortas-Rico, & Li, 2016; Kügler & Weiss, 2016; Mandell & Wilhelmsson, 2015; Solé Ollé, 2003; Usai & Paci, 2003). The instrumental variables that we are using address the problem of endogenous independent variables (burglary and spatial lagged house prices) and were included in all five estimated models. If the instruments variables are good, it is possible to interpret the estimated parameters as causal relationships and not just correlations.

23.5 Results

23.5.1 Descriptive Analysis

Descriptive statistics for the variables used are shown in Table 23.2. Our dependent variable was transaction price, covering more than 90,000 apartment sales in Stockholm

Table 23.2 Descriptive Statistics

Variable	Definition	Mean	Standard deviation
Apartment data			
Price	Transaction price of apartments, SEK	2,756,114	1,833,382
Living area	Square meters	64.89	27.08
Fee	Maintenance fee to the cooperative, SEK	3,476.39	1,450.39
Rooms	Number of rooms	2.42	1.13
Year	Year of construction	1962.55	35.58
Neighborhood data			
Accessibility	Generalized travel cost to work, SEK	113.43	7.66
Distance to CBD	Distance to central business district, meters	9,701.13	10,190.25
Built area	Proportion of built area in the neighborhood	0.56	0.24
High-rise buildings	Proportion of high-rise buildings	0.48	0.40
Low buildings	Proportion of low-rise buildings	0.21	0.32
Single-family	Proportion of single-family houses	0.15	0.28
Criminality data			
Burglary rate		0.6089	1.49

County. Most of the sales were within the municipality of Stockholm. The apartments resemble condominiums in cooperative property associations. We used sales during the period 2012–2014. The average price was SEK 2.7 million, but the variation around the mean was large: SEK 1.8 million.

In our hedonic model, the variation in prices is modeled using our four independent variables (see above) after controlling for differences in the apartment (living area, maintenance fee, and number of rooms) and the year of construction of the property. On average, each apartment sold had an area of almost 65 square meters, allocated to 2.4 rooms. The standard deviation was around 27 square meters, that is, a slightly lower variation around the mean than for price. The maintenance fee was on average SEK 3,500, with a standard deviation of SEK 1,400. The typical apartment was located in a building built in 1962. Apartments in older buildings often command a higher price than apartments in newer buildings. The size of the fee has an impact on the user cost that is typically inversely correlated to price.

Besides apartment and property characteristics, neighborhood characteristics explain the value of an apartment. We used six different neighborhood variables to control for location. The first two measured how good the accessibility was and how far from the CBD the apartment was located. The accessibility measurement combined the cost of travel measured in SEK, such as direct cost of the trip and indirect cost of time, referred to as the generalized travel cost, relative to the attractiveness of the location. Here we used the generalized travel cost to work using public transportation; that is, we measured accessibility to work by public transportation, and we did that in more than 800 spatial units in Stockholm County. The accessibility was SEK 113, and the variation around this mean was low. Distance to CBD was measured by the Euclidian distance from each sold apartment to the CBD. On average, the apartments were located 9,700 meters from the CBD, and the variation was large. Besides the measurement of accessibility and distance, we used four different variables to measure the degree of urbanization: the proportion of built area in the neighborhood (that is, the inverse of the proportion of green area), the proportion of high-rise buildings and low-rise buildings, and the proportion of single-family houses. The expected impact on apartment prices was that accessibility and degree of urbanization increase the expected price.

Finally, we used burglary rates as one of the independent variables in the hedonic price equation. The average burglary rate was equal to 0.6, and the variation was very big, as the standard deviation was almost 1.5.

Table 23.3 shows the correlations between our main variables. Despite the fact that bivariate correlations can be misleading, as they ignore spatial structure and the influence of the other variables, some interesting results can be observed. Covariates "accessibility," "distance to CBD," and "burglary rate" are all only modestly correlated to price. The expectation is that location is very important, but the correlation between price and accessibility is only .48, and in absolute values the correlation is even lower between price and distance. However, what stands out is the very low correlation between burglary rates and apartment prices, only .03. Even more interesting is that the correlation is positive, which comes from the fact that burglary rates are often higher in locations with good accessibility. But again, burglary rates are not highly correlated with accessibility and distance, though the correlation coefficients may differ statistically from zero. Finally, it is interesting to observe that accessibility and distance to CBD are highly correlated but not perfectly correlated. Hence, there exist locations far from the CBD that have good accessibility, such as locations close to public transportation, and locations close to the CBD with bad accessibility, for instance, because they are disrupted by water between the islands.

Table 23.3 Selected Correlation Coefficients

	Price	Accessibility	Distance to CBD	Burglary rate
Price	1.00			
Accessibility	.48	1.00		
Distance to CBD	−.41	−.86	1.00	
Burglary rate	.03	.08	−.07	1.00

23.5.2 Modeling Results

Table 23.4 shows the results from the hedonic price equation. The model controls for spatial dependency and endogeneity by the instrument variable approach (a two-stage regression).

The overall effect using all data is presented in Model 1. Variables included in the hedonic price equation can explain about 70% of the variation in price. All apartment- and property-related attributes are statistically significant and have the expected sign and magnitude. The results also seem to suggest that spatial lagged apartment prices have a positive impact on apartment prices. Increased accessibility is expected to raise apartment prices, and distance from the CBD to decrease apartment prices. More urbanized areas are expected to increase house prices, while too many high-rise buildings lower apartment prices on average. Our results suggest that if the proportion of single-family houses increases, apartment prices increase. Hence, the conclusion that can be drawn is that urbanization has a positive effect on prices, but this effect only holds when there is a diversified supply of housing types in the neighborhood.

What about burglary and its effect on apartment prices? Here we can observe that higher burglary rates are associated with lower home prices. If burglary rates increase

Table 23.4 Two-Stage Least Square Regression Results (IV approach), Y = Log of Apartment Prices

	Hedonic price equation	
	Coefficient	*t*-value
Wprice[a]	.4971*	(28.14)
Burglary rate	−.0864*	(−7.40)
Living area	.0121*	(139.97)
Fee (10^2)	−.0081*	(−68.71)
Rooms	.0444*	(24.29)
Year (10^2)	−.0199*	(−6.35)
Accessibility	.0280*	(86.31)
Distance to CBD (10^2)	−.0011*	(−51.47)
Built area	.0812*	(17.17)
High-rise buildings	−.2188*	(−68.67)
Low buildings	−.2321*	(−42.06)
Single-family	.0728*	(11.02)
Constant	4.3079	(16.09)
R^2	0.7224	
No. of observations	88,979	

Note: Dependent variable: natural logarithm of transaction price.

[a] Wprice is equal to spatial lagged transaction prices.

* Statistically significant estimates on a 5% significance level.

by one unit, apartment prices are expected to fall by almost 0.09%. We have checked for multicollinearity by variance-of-inflation (VIF). The result indicates that we have no problem with multicollinearity. The VIF-value concerning variable "burglary" is below 2, that is, far from a rule-of-thumb value of 5. We have also corrected for the potential problem of heteroscedasticity. Hence, our interpretation is that our results indicate that there is a negative causal relationship between burglary rates and apartment prices.

To summarize, we can accept hypothesis 1, that burglaries have a negative impact on apartment prices. Moreover, there seems to be a variation in impact depending on where the apartment is located in respect of accessibility and distance from the CBD. The impact is higher in areas far away from the CBD or with poor accessibility to public transportation (or both), a finding that corroborates hypothesis 3. The impact is measured as a percentage of apartment prices. Of course, measured in absolute Swedish crowns, the impact can be higher because of higher prices.

What can we expect if the location has relatively good accessibility but is located far from the CBD, that is, if the apartment is located close to a public transportation hub? Table 23.5 presents the results from an analysis in which we split the data set into four subsamples: good accessibility close to CBD, good accessibility far from CBD, poor accessibility close to CBD, and bad accessibility far from CBD. Note that the regression model in Table 23.5 includes all of the other variables, but for simplicity here only the results of interest are presented.

For apartments located in areas with good accessibility near the CBD, burglaries have no statistically significant effect on prices. It appears that burglaries in the inner city are, in some sense, expected and therefore discounted less in the price (see also Ceccato & Wilhelmsson, 2011). However, in locations with poor accessibility, burglaries impact apartment prices negatively, pulling the prices down—and this effect is statistically significant. In locations far from the CBD, regardless of levels of accessibility, burglaries have a negative impact on apartment prices. However, the effect is much higher in locations with poor accessibility. Overall, the effect of burglaries on apartment prices seems to be of more importance far from the CBD than in the inner city.

In Stockholm County, if burglary rates increase 1%, apartment prices are expected to fall by almost 0.09%. For apartments in Stockholm municipality (note, not the County),

Table 23.5 The Impact of Burglaries on Apartment Prices

	Near CBD	Far from CBD
Good accessibility	.0121 (1.61)	−.1237* (−11.41)
Poor accessibility	−.0654* (−5.37)	−.4451* (−9.50)

Note: *t*-values within brackets. Dependent variable: natural logarithm of transaction price. Only coefficients concerning burglary rates are presented in the table.

Ceccato and Wilhelmsson (2011) found that the discounts were greater: If residential burglary increased by 1%, apartment prices were expected to fall by 0.21%, perhaps because apartments located in areas with lower burglary rates are more scarce the closer one gets to the central areas of the county. The impact of crime on housing prices in North American cities seems to be slightly greater than the impact found in Stockholm County or municipality (see, e.g., Lynch and Rasmussen, 2001 or Hellman and Naroff, 1979). For a discussion of potential reasons for this difference in prices see Ceccato and Wilhelmsson (2011). However, it is important to note that these results are not completely comparable because of differences in crime type and the methodology of these studies.

23.6 Conclusions and Implications of Results

This chapter sets out to assess the impact on apartment prices of residential burglary mediated by accessibility. A review of the literature on hedonic modeling covering more than three decades shows that, despite different modelling strategies, these studies consistently find evidence that crime affects housing prices. Two measures of accessibility are used: a "global" distance decay from Stockholm city center and a "local" measure of accessibility to work expressed as travel costs. Results for all of Stockholm County confirm previous findings once limited to Stockholm municipality only (Ceccato & Wilhelmsson, 2011), that residential burglary reduces apartment prices. However, such an effect varies across space and levels of accessibility. For instance, for apartments located in areas with relatively good accessibility near the CBD, burglary has no effect on prices; while for apartments in areas with poor accessibility, burglaries help reduce prices. In locations far from the CBD, regardless of levels of accessibility, residential burglary has a negative impact on apartment prices.

Results represented here estimate the trade-offs that buyers make in a single Swedish county at a single point in time when buying apartments. Therefore, there are obvious limitations to the policy-related conclusions that should be drawn or generalized for other urban centers, at any other moment in time, or for other types of housing. Note that despite being well connected by public transportation, the Stockholm region is an archipelago. New measures of accessibility as well as indications of safety should be tested in the future (for alternatives, see Table 23.1) Moreover, housing prices might be affected by regional factors, which suggests the existence of housing submarkets. Future research should test the effect of submarkets in Stockholm County, in other words, to check whether and how the implicit prices and/or the quantity of different housing attributes differ from one area to another within the same area of study.

Despite limitations, some issues can be highlighted on the basis of these findings. First, price-related policies (rent control, tax advantages, and mortgage ceilings) can potentially offset the impact of transportation on property prices. We agree with Weisbrod et al. (1980, pp. 7–8) that "a small change in housing costs may have an effect on residential location decisions equivalent to the effect of a larger proportional change in travel time." Thus, as far as the Swedish context is concerned, future research should also consider assessing differences in municipal taxes and other price-related policies that potentially make an area more (or less) attractive in the market. Second, investments to improve safety (in this case reduce burglary) and reduce travel time can contribute to increasing the attractiveness of some locations, especially in the more peripheral areas of Stockholm County, where both crime and poor accessibility decrease property prices.

Research of this kind also makes a direct contribution to environmental criminology. First, knowing how crime affects people's willing to pay for housing can help prevent its occurrence, as environmental criminology is about the study of crime and places (and the way crime reflects space-time activities of individuals and organizations). Areas that are highly discounted in the market are often associated with other environmental characteristics that pull prices down, including those that generate crime (e.g., "no-go areas"). These areas may decay even more if no intervention is made. Therefore, people's willing to pay for housing can be used as an indicator of an area's well-being. Second, crime can be place and time dependent, highly determined by the types of land uses (e.g., residential versus mixed land use) and activities that these areas may attract. This research can therefore be indicative to help criminologists to understand the nature of environments where crime takes place, but, more importantly, understand that crime opportunities are affected by a complex system of agents that go much beyond particular locations.

Note

1. Submarkets are typically defined as areas in which the implicit prices and/or the quantity of different housing attributes differ from those of another area. The challenge of dividing a large housing market into submarkets has been addressed in a number of papers, such as Goodman and Thibodeau (2003).

References

Anselin, L. (1988). *Spatial Econometrics: Method and Models*. Dordrecht: Kluwer Academic.

Basile, R. (2008). Regional economic growth in Europe: A semiparametric spatial dependence approach. *Papers in Regional Science, 87*(4), 527–544. doi:10.1111/j.1435-5957.2008.00175.x.

Beavon, D. J. K., Brantingham, P. L. & Brantingham, P. J. (1994). "The influence of street networks on the patterning of property offences." In R. Clarke (Ed.), *Crime Prevention Studies* (Vol. 2, pp. 115–48). Monsey, NY: Criminal Justice Press.

Ben-Akiva, M. E., & Steven, R. L. (1985). *Discrete choice analysis: Theory and application to travel demand*. Cambridge, MA: MIT Press.

Bowes, D. R., & Ihlanfeldt, K. R. (2001). Identifying the impacts of rail transit stations on residential property values. *Journal of Urban Economics*, 50(1), 1–25. doi:http://dx.doi.org/10.1006/juec.2001.2214.

Boymal, J., Silva, A., & Liu, S. (2013). Measuring the preference for dwelling characteristics of Melbourne: Railway stations and house prices. Paper presented at the 19th Annual Pacific Rim Real Estate Society Conference, Melbourne, Australia,

Brasington, D., Flores-Lagunes, A., & Guci, L. (2016). A spatial model of school district open enrollment choice. *Regional Science and Urban Economics*, *56*, 1–18. doi:http://dx.doi.org/10.1016/j.regsciurbeco.2015.10.005.

Buck, A. J., Hakim, S., & Spiegel, U. (1991). Casinos, Crime, and Real Estate Values: Do They Relate? *Journal of Research in Crime and Delinquency*, *28*(3), 288–303. doi:10.1177/0022427891028003003

Buck, A. J., Hakim, S., & Spiegel, U. (1993). Endogenous crime victimization, taxes, and property values. *Social Science Quarterly*, *74*(2), 334–348.

Buettner, T. (2001). Local business taxation and competition for capital: the choice of the tax rate. *Regional Science and Urban Economics*, *31*(2–3), 215–245. doi:http://dx.doi.org/10.1016/S0166-0462(00)00041-7

Buonanno, P., Montolio, D., & Raya-Vílchez, J. M. (2012). Housing prices and crime perception. *Empirical Economics*, *45*(1), 305–321. doi:10.1007/s00181-012-0624-y

Buonanno, P., Prarolo, G., & Vanin, P. (2016). Organized crime and electoral outcomes. Evidence from Sicily at the turn of the XXI century. *European Journal of Political Economy*, *41*, 61–74. doi:http://dx.doi.org/10.1016/j.ejpoleco.2015.11.002

Burnell, J. D. (1988). Crime and Racial Composition in Contiguous Communities as Negative Externalities: Prejudiced Households' Evaluation of Crime Rate and Segregation Nearby Reduces Housing Values and Tax Revenues. *The American Journal of Economics and Sociology*, *47*(2), 177–193.

Case, K. E., & Mayer, C. J. (1996). Housing price dynamics within a metropolitan area. *Regional Science and Urban Economics*, *26*(3–4), 387–407. doi:http://dx.doi.org/10.1016/0166-0462(95)02121-3

Caudill, S. B., Affuso, E., & Yang, M. (2015). Registered sex offenders and house prices: An hedonic analysis. *Urban Studies*, *52*(13), 2425–2440.

Ceccato, V. (2013). *Moving safely: crime and perceived safety in Stockholm's subway stations*. Plymouth: Lexington.

Ceccato, V. (2016). Segurança e mercado imobiliário urbano (Security and the housing market). In A. Vitte (Ed.), *Novas perspectivas analiticas e interprepativas da Ciencia geografica no atual contexto do sistema mundo* (p. 16). Sao Paulo, Brazil: Paco editorial.

Ceccato, V., Cats, O., & Wang, Q. (Eds.). (2015). The geography of pickpocketing at bus stops: An analysis of grid cells. In V. Ceccato & A. Newton (Eds.), *Safety and Security in Transit Environments: An Interdisciplinary Approach*, Basingstoke: Palgrave.

Ceccato, V., Haining, R., & Signoretta, P. (2002). Exploring crime statistics in Stockholm using spatial analysis tools. *Annals of the Association of American Geographers*, *22*, 29–51.

Ceccato, V., & Newton, A. (Eds.). (2015). *Safety and Security in Transit Environments: An Interdisciplinary Approach*. London: Palgrave.

Ceccato, V., & Wilhelmsson, M. (2016). Do crime hot spots affect housing prices? ERSA-conference, 2017, Groningen, Holland

Ceccato, V., & Wilhelmsson, M. (2011). The impact of crime on apartment prices: Evidence from Stockholm, Sweden. *Geografiska Annaler: Series B, Human Geography*, *93*(1), 81–103. doi:10.1111/j.1468-0467.2011.00362.x.

Ceccato, V., & Wilhelmsson, M. (2012). Acts of vandalism and fear in neighbourhoods: Do they affect housing prices? In V. Ceccato (Ed.), *The Urban Fabric of Crime and Fear* (pp. 191–213). New York: Springer.

Clark, D. E., & Cosgrove, J. C. (1990). Hedonic prices, identification and the demand for public safety. *Journal of Regional Science, 30*(1), 105–121. doi:10.1111/j.1467-9787.1990.tb00083.x.

Cohen, L. E., & Felson, M. (1979). Social change and crime rate trends: A routine activity approach. *American Sociological Review, 44*. doi:10.2307/2094589.

Congdon-Hohman, J. M. (2013). The lasting effects of crime: The relationship of discovered methamphetamine laboratories and home values. *Regional Science and Urban Economics, 43*(1), 31–41. doi:http://dx.doi.org/10.1016/j.regsciurbeco.2012.11.005.

da Costa, B., & Ceccato, V. (2015). Assessing the adoption of household safety protection (HSP) in Stockholm, Sweden. *Crime Science, 4*(1), 1–12. doi:10.1186/s40163-015-0027-4.

Drukker, D. M., Egger, P., & Prucha, I. R. (2013). On two-step estimation of a spatial autoregressive model with autoregressive disturbances and endogenous regressors. *Econometric Reviews, 32*(5–6), 686–733. doi:10.1080/07474938.2013.741020

Dubin, R. A., & Goodman, A. C. (1982). Valuation of education and crime neighborhood characteristics through hedonic housing prices. *Population and Environment, 5*(3), 166–181.

European Commission (2010). Stockholm—European green capital. Retrieved from http://ec.europa.eu/environment/europeangreencapital/winning-cities/2010-stockholm/index.html.

Fransson, U., Rosenqvist, G., & Turner, B. (2002). Hushållens värdering av egenskaper i bostäder och bostadsområden. Research report, Uppsala University.

Gibbons, S. (2004). The costs of urban property crime. *Economic Journal, 114*(499), F441–F463. doi:10.1111/j.1468-0297.2004.00254.x.

Gómez-Antonio, M., Hortas-Rico, M., & Li, L. (2016). The causes of urban sprawl in Spanish urban areas: A spatial approach. *Spatial Economic Analysis, 11*(2), 1–28. doi:10.1080/17421772.2016.1126674.

Goodman, A. C., & Thibodeau, T. G. (2003). Housing market segmentation and hedonic prediction accuracy. *Journal of Housing Economics, 12*, 181–201.

Hellman, D.A. & Naroff, J.L. (1979). The impact of crime on urban residential property values. *Urban Studies, 16*, 105–112.

Hwang, S., & Thill, J.-C. (2009). Delineating urban housing submarkets with fuzzy clustering. *Environment and Planning B: Planning and Design, 36*(5), 865–882.

Ihlanfeldt, K., & Mayock, T. (2010). Panel data estimates of the effects of different types of crime on housing prices. *Regional Science and Urban Economics, 40*(2–3), 161–172. doi:http://dx.doi.org/10.1016/j.regsciurbeco.2010.02.005.

Iqbal, A., & Ceccato, V. (2015). Does crime in parks affect apartment prices? *Journal of Scandinavian Studies in Criminology and Crime Prevention, 16*(1), 97–121. doi:10.1080/14043858.2015.1009674.

Johnson, S. D., & Bowers, K. J. (2010). Permeability and burglary risk: Are cul-de-sacs safer? *Journal of Quantitative Criminology, 26*(1), 89–111. doi:10.1007/s10940-009-9084-8.

Johnson, S. D., & Summers, L. (2015). Testing ecological theories of offender spatial decision making using a discrete choice model. *Crime and Delinquency, 61*(3), 454–480. doi:10.1177/0011128714540276.

Kain, J. F., & Quigley, J. M. (1970). Measuring the value of housing quality. *Journal of the American Statistical Association, 65*(330), 532–548. doi:10.1080/01621459.1970.10481102.

Kelejian, H. H., & Prucha, I. R. (1998). A generalized spatial two-stage least squares procedure for estimating a spatial autoregressive model with autoregressive disturbances. *Journal of Real Estate Finance and Economics, 17*(1), 99–121. doi:10.1023/a:1007707430416.

Kügler, A., & Weiss, C. (2016). Time as a strategic variable: Business hours in the gasoline market. *Applied Economics Letters, 23*(15), 1051–1056. doi:10.1080/13504851.2015.1133888.

Larsson, J., Landström, M., & Sandin, M. (2008). *Ombildning av hyresrätt: en studie av två fastigheter*. Mälardalens Högskola, Master thesis.

Li, W., Joh, K., Lee, C., Kim, J.-H., Park, H., & Woo, A. (2015). Assessing benefits of neighborhood walkability to single-family property values: A spatial hedonic study in Austin, Texas. *Journal of Planning Education and Research, 35*(4), 471–488. doi:10.1177/0739456x15591055.

Linden, L., & Rockoff, J. E. (2008). Estimates of the impact of crime risk on property values from Megan's laws. *American Economic Review, 98*(3), 1103–1127.

Loukaitou-Sideris, A. (2012). Safe on the move: The importance of the built environment. In V. Ceccato (Ed.), *The Urban Fabric of Crime and Fear* (pp. 85–110). New York: Springer.

Lynch, A. K., & Rasmussen, D. W. (2001). Measuring the impact of crime on house prices. *Applied Economics, 33*(15), 1981–1989. doi:10.1080/00036840110021735.

Mandell, S., & Wilhelmsson, M. (2015). Financial infrastructure and house prices. *Applied Economics, 47*(30), 3175–3188. doi:10.1080/00036846.2015.1013608.

Munroe, D. K. (2007). Exploring the determinants of spatial pattern in residential land markets: Amenities and disamenities in Charlotte, NC, USA. *Environment and Planning B: Planning and Design, 34*(2), 336–354. doi:10.1068/b32065.

Naroff, J. L., Hellman, D., & Skinner, D. (1980). Estimates of the impact of crime on property values. *Growth and Change, 11*(4), 24–30. doi:10.1111/j.1468-2257.1980.tb00878.x.

Newton, A. D., Johnson, S. D., & Bowers, K. J. (2004). Crime on bus routes: An evaluation of a safer travel initiative. *Policing, 27*(3), 302–319. doi:10.1108/13639510410553086.

Pope, D. G., & Pope, J. C. (2012). Crime and property values: Evidence from the 1990s crime drop. *Regional Science and Urban Economics, 42*(1–2), 177–188. doi:http://dx.doi.org/10.1016/j.regsciurbeco.2011.08.008.

Pope, J. C. (2008). Fear of crime and housing prices: Household reactions to sex offender registries. *Journal of Urban Economics, 64*(3), 601–614. doi:http://dx.doi.org/10.1016/j.jue.2008.07.001.

Rizzo, M. J. (1979). The effect of crime on residential rents and property values. *American Economist, 23*(1), 16–21.

Rosen, S. (1974). Hedonic prices and implicit markets: Product differentiation in pure competition. *Journal of Political Economy, 82*(1), 34–55.

Solé Ollé, A. (2003). Electoral accountability and tax mimicking: The effects of electoral margins, coalition government, and ideology. *European Journal of Political Economy, 19*(4), 685–713. doi:http://dx.doi.org/10.1016/S0176-2680(03)00023-5.

Statistics Denmark (2016) *Statistical Yearbook*. Copenhagen. Retrieved September 21, 2017, from http://www.dst.dk/en/Statistik/Publikationer/VisPub?cid=22256

Thaler, R. (1978). A note on the value of crime control: Evidence from the property market. *Journal of Urban Economics, 5*(1), 137–145. doi:http://dx.doi.org/10.1016/0094-1190(78)90042-6.

Tita, G., Petras, T., & Greenbaum, R. (2006). Crime and residential choice: A neighborhood level analysis of the impact of crime on housing prices. *Journal of Quantitative Criminology, 22*(4), 299–317. doi:10.1007/s10940-006-9013-z.

Troy, A., & Grove, J. M. (2008). Property values, parks, and crime: A hedonic analysis in Baltimore, MD. *Landscape and Urban Planning, 87*(3), 233–245. doi:http://dx.doi.org/10.1016/j.landurbplan.2008.06.005.

Uittenbogaard, A. C., & Ceccato, V. (2012). Space-time clusters of crime in Stockholm. *Review of European Studies, 4*, 148–156.

Usai, S., & Paci, R. (2003). Externalities and local economic growth in manufacturing industries. In B. Fingleton (Ed.), *European Regional Growth* (pp. 293–321). New York: Springer.

Weisbrod, G., Ben-Akiva, M., & Lerman, S. (1980). Tradeoffs in residential location decisions: Transportation versus other factors. *Transportation Policy and Decision-Making, 1*(1), 13–26

Wikström, P.-O. H. (1991). *Urban Crime, Criminals, and Victims: The Swedish Experience in an Anglo-American Comparative Perspective*. Stockholm: Springer.

Wilhelmsson, M. (2002). Spatial models in real estate economics. *Housing, Theory and Society, 19*(2), 92–101. doi:10.1080/140360902760385646.

Wilhelmsson, M., & Ceccato, V. (2015). Does burglary affect property prices in a nonmetropolitan municipality? *Journal of Rural Studies, 39*, 210–218. doi:http://dx.doi.org/10.1016/j.jrurstud.2015.03.014

CHAPTER 24

STREET NETWORKS AND CRIME

TOBY DAVIES AND KATE BOWERS

24.1 Introduction

In the context of crime, the term "environment" encompasses a wide range of features and concepts. The setting for a potential crime includes not only physical elements, but also the conditions in its vicinity: the people that are present, for example, and the activities taking place. It is well established—as can be seen elsewhere in this volume—that the presence or absence of factors of both these types can have a material effect on the potential for crime. It follows from this that, in order to understand the distribution of crime, it is necessary to examine how these elements are arranged in space. The questions of where places lie in relation to each other, and which places are encountered by which people, play a key role in behavioral theories of crime, and this suggests that patterns of crime are shaped by the configuration of urban form. A key determinant of this configuration is the street network, which not only provides a convenient representation of space but also affects behavior. In this chapter, we will examine the extent to which the criminal character of places can be reconciled with their position in the street network.

Street networks are the primary structures around which urban areas are arranged. This is most apparent from the perspective of morphology: buildings and other physical features are located at fixed positions on streets, and their arrangement is constrained by the shape of the network. Perhaps more significantly, though, the network acts as a substrate for movement, and defines the paths that can be taken between locations. It therefore determines, among other things, how far places are from each other, and the extent to which different features will be used in the course of movement activity. In this way, street networks play a key role in shaping interactions between people and the environment.

When the role of the street network is considered in this way, its relevance to the study of crime is clear to see. In practical terms, for example, it provides a meaningful representation of space for the purpose of analysis. The majority of crime occurs at some location on the network, and this, coupled with the fact that network features are generally small, coherent entities (e.g., street segments), means that network-based units are highly expedient. Indeed, the use of the street segment as the unit of analysis in empirical research is becoming more common, with a number of studies showing that they can display distinctive criminal character (Weisburd et al., 2012; Steenbeek & Weisburd, 2015). Recent research by Weisburd (2015) has demonstrated that not only is the street segment a unit of analysis at which significant concentration of crime within a small number of features can be observed, but also that the degree to which such concentration exists appears to be fairly stable over places and times. In his multiple-city analysis, he found that between 0.8% and 1.6% of segments consistently captured 25% of the crime problem.

In addition to their practical utility, however, street networks are also of theoretical importance. Much of the theory of environmental criminology, for example, is concerned at some level with the confluence of elements in space and time; in particular the targets, offenders, and guardians of routine activity theory (Cohen & Felson, 1979). Since the street network is such a crucial determinant of this convergence, via its role in shaping patterns of activity, it is natural that these theories should have implications concerning the distribution of crime on networks. Among these are questions concerning the relationship between crime risk and concepts such as centrality, accessibility, and permeability. In all cases, these arguments imply that network elements should not be considered independently, but in the context of their position within the wider structure.

Despite the potential significance of structural variation, however, in many cases it is far from clear how the concepts in question should be measured—or, indeed, defined. The notion of "accessibility," for example, while intuitively meaningful, is difficult to quantify on the basis of a map alone. This is problematic for criminological studies addressing network effects, which typically must rely on simple proxy measures of complex underlying principles. While such studies have shown promising results with respect to the quantification of network relationships, they are limited by the conceptual gap that exists between the principles as specified in criminological theory and those that are measured by the proxy measures employed.

In recent years, however, the emerging field of network science (see Newman, 2010) has provided a framework via which the analysis of network structure can be performed in a much more formal way. Network science builds on the mathematical field of graph theory, and is concerned with any system which can be modeled as a collection of links between discrete entities. Street networks are one such example of these, and their structural properties have been studied extensively within the physics and urban studies communities (Porta et al., 2006b; Louf & Barthelemy, 2014; Lagesse et al., 2015). Much of this involves the measurement of structural properties of networks, using an array of metrics designed to capture various aspects of their configuration. Some of these have been developed specifically for the street network context, and seek to measure properties that are relevant to human movement.

This explicit quantitative framework was applied in the context of crime by Davies and Johnson (2014), in a study of residential burglary in Birmingham, United Kingdom. Their analysis showed that a significant relationship exists between the risk of crime and several network properties; most notably the metric "betweenness." This measure corresponds closely to the notion of "awareness space" proposed by crime pattern theory (Brantingham & Brantingham, 1993), and the results therefore provide support for this, and other, environmental theories of crime. Nevertheless, the findings are subject to a number of caveats, most notably their restriction to residential burglary—a property crime against a fixed target—and their application in only one setting.

In this chapter, we seek to further advance the program of research in this area by applying a similar framework in the context of interpersonal crime. Using data from the city of London, we examine the relationship between the occurrence of common assault (hereafter referred to simply as "assault") and network centrality. This offense is distinct from burglary in a number of respects—it is not confined to residential locations, and occurs against a mobile, human target—and therefore poses a number of different theoretical considerations. The question of whether a relationship with network structure is also observed in this case has a number of potential implications from the perspectives of both policing and urban planning, while also representing a further test of criminological theory. Before presenting this empirical analysis, we will first review the theoretical background from the perspectives of both environmental criminology and network science.

24.2 Background

In this section, we provide some background information relating to both the spatial distribution of crime in general and the street network context in particular. In each case, we outline relevant theory and give an overview of past research.

24.2.1 Behavioral Theories

Much of the theory of environmental criminology, as it relates to the spatial dimension of crime, is derived ultimately from the routine activity framework introduced by Cohen and Felson (1979). Central to this is the fundamental observation that a crime that requires direct contact can only occur in a particular setting if three elements are simultaneously present: a motivated offender, a suitable target, and the absence of a capable guardian. From a spatial perspective, this implies that crime can only take place at locations where these conditions are met. Although it is of course far from certain that a crime will take place in these circumstances—the decision to offend will incorporate many other factors—it is reasonable to assume that, on average, locations in which this convergence occurs more often (i.e., the conditions for crime arise more frequently) will be subject to greater risk. It follows from this that understanding where these encounters take place is crucial to understanding the spatial distribution of crime.

In the case of interpersonal crime, the spatial distributions of offenders, victims, and potential guardians are likely to be influenced by the street network. As remarked earlier, the street network is a crucial determinant of movement patterns, and its structure governs the extent to which particular places will be used by people in the course of routine activities. This means that some places will contain more potential targets, and therefore more readily provide one of the elements necessary for crime, than others. Similarly, potential offenders (who are, of course, drawn from the same population as victims) will encounter opportunities for crime more often in places that they visit more frequently while traveling around the network. Furthermore, the supply of potential guardians at a place will depend on how it is used in the course of noncriminal movement. It is clear, therefore, that the network plays a key role in determining where the basic conditions for crime will be met.

The basic principles outlined above were developed further by Brantingham and Brantingham (1993), whose "crime pattern theory" offers a mechanistic explanation for why criminal interactions occur where they do in urban environments. The starting point for this theory is the idea that the majority of crimes are committed in locations that are known to the offender; that is, in places that the offender has encountered in the course of noncriminal activities. More specifically, it is suggested that offenders develop notional "awareness spaces" as they go about their daily lives, which represent those places with which they are familiar. The theory states that it is where suitable opportunities for crime arise within these awareness spaces that offending is likely to occur: put simply, offenders select targets from within places that they know. This implies that the question of how crime is distributed can be translated, to some extent, to the question of how awareness is distributed. Places of which more offenders are aware will, if all else is equal, experience greater risk simply because they will be more frequently considered as locations for crime. The task is therefore to find where awareness spaces overlap.

Since awareness spaces are formed during routine activities, their morphology can be understood by considering the movements that occur in the course of those activities. In crime pattern theory, it is argued that the activity patterns of individuals are centered around a small number of significant locations, such as homes, workplaces, and leisure facilities, referred to as "activity nodes." It follows straightforwardly from this that places that are activity nodes for a large number of people will display distinctive criminal character, since they give rise to a large volume of interactions that might lead to crime. Indeed, it has been shown that such locations—labeled "crime attractors" or "crime generators"—do indeed experience pronounced levels of risk, as shown in studies of drug markets (McCord & Ratcliffe, 2007) and liquor-buying facilities (Block & Block, 1995). This reasoning does not apply only to the activity nodes themselves, however: it is also to be expected that awareness will be built up on the routes between them, as people travel from one activity to another. This implies a secondary effect, by which locations that lie on the routes between the activity nodes of many people will be subject to greater exposure to crime. Such locations lie in the common activity spaces of many individuals and, therefore, will be more frequently considered as the settings for crime. It should also be noted that the crimes experienced within nodes and on the paths between them are not entirely independent. Facilities within which higher levels of incidents occur are more likely to be located on roads where more crime occurs in the external environment, again implying that travel patterns are an important element of the offender's activity landscape (Bowers, 2014).

The significance of routine movement in the formation of awareness spaces implies that street networks are likely to play a key role. Awareness spaces are typically conceptualized as amorphous regions, formed by placing a buffer around the areas through which an individual would be expected to travel. These regions represent some notion of ambient awareness, and it is where they overlap that risk would be expected to be highest. In reality, however, movements are much more specific: individuals travel down particular streets, along well-defined paths. Rather than overlapping regions, therefore, it may be more meaningful to view the issue of exposure as a question of how frequently particular streets feature in routine journeys. In these terms, it is those parts of the network that feature most often that will be most frequently considered as settings for crime.

The line of reasoning outlined above implies that both the provision of targets, and the exposure to potential offenders, are likely to be higher on streets that are used more frequently or are easier to access. While this suggests that such locations will experience greater levels of crime, there is a further effect, however—namely guardianship—that has the potential to counteract these factors. In this context, guardianship refers to the effect by which noncriminal actors prevent the commission of a crime by virtue of their presence, either by deterring it before it has taken place or interrupting it during its course. In most urban contexts, the majority of guardianship—at least by volume—is provided by informal guardians, such as passers-by, who have the potential to either intervene themselves or draw attention to an offense. Such behavior has the potential to nullify the risk posed by interaction between offenders and targets, by ensuring that opportunities are either not taken or are unsuccessful.

As might be expected, guardianship is also subject to the influence of the street network. Since the populations in question are essentially the same, all reasoning concerning the movement of targets can be applied equally well to guardians, and leads to a similar conclusion: that the supply of potential guardians will be greater on more central streets. This implies that the locations with greatest exposure to crime are also those with the greatest potential for guardianship, and this in turn raises the crucial question of whether the greater supply of guardians in such locations is sufficient to negate the increased risk due to exposure. In simple terms, the issue concerns whether more prominent places are safer (because there are more potential guardians) or more risky (because the supply of potential targets and offenders is greater).

In fact, this point is the subject of a long-running debate within the urban planning and design communities (see Mawby, 1977; Reynald & Elffers, 2009). On one hand, it is suggested that safety will be promoted when places are well used and open, and therefore frequently observed and encountered by members of the public. This effect is encapsulated in the notion of "eyes on the street" proposed by Jacobs (1961), which states that such passers-by act as informal guardians, maintaining a form of ambient surveillance and potentially intervening in offenses. The implication of this argument is that more central places will be safer, while more secluded ones—where offenders are less likely to be witnessed and victims more likely to be isolated—will experience more crime. In terms of urban planning, this suggests that designs which are well integrated and promote movement will be favorable from the perspective of crime prevention.

A counterpoint to this line of reasoning can be found in the "defensible space" theory promoted by the planner Oscar Newman (1972). The central principle of this is that a crucial aspect of community safety is territoriality: the sense in which places are subject to the ownership and authority of their residents. Places in which territoriality is high are thought to be intimidating to potential offenders, since they are likely to "stand out" or be challenged. Indeed, it is argued that guardianship may in fact be more powerful in such areas, since locals will have greater investment in the local community and therefore be more likely to intervene. This is supported by theories of "collective efficacy" (Sampson et al., 1997), which argue that more well-defined, cohesive communities have a greater willingness to take responsibility for the safety of their surroundings, either by challenging intruders or by suppressing criminal behavior within their own communities. Thus the question of guardianship may depend on which "eyes" are on which "streets."

Clearly a relationship exists between urban structure and the "defensibility" of space. Designs that encourage movement—and, in particular, throughput through areas—serve to decrease territoriality, since they introduce a transient population that cannot be monitored with the same level of familiarity. In direct contrast with Jacobs's argument, therefore, this argument implies that activity and accessibility foster crime: as well as introducing potential offenders and targets, they undermine the guardianship that would otherwise be present. It is clear, therefore, that a significant disparity exists between these theories of guardianship in terms of the expected relationship between network structure and crime.

A number of empirical studies are relevant to the issue of guardianship in this regard. Results from a number of studies (e.g., Sampson & Raudenbush, 1999) have suggested that collective efficacy is a significant effect at both the area level and for micro units such as street segments (Weisburd et al., 2012). In the case of burglary, this is supported by ethnographic studies (Cromwell et al., 1991; Ashton et al., 1998), which suggest that exploratory behavior is rare; that is, burglars are unwilling to travel to areas in which they will appear to be outsiders. Whether this is true for other offenses, in which targeting practices may differ, remains an open question, however. As for the question of guardianship itself, evidence (e.g., Reynald, 2010) suggests that the issue is a complex one, with the willingness to intervene highly dependent on context. Whether this uncertainty is manifested in the perceptions of offenders (i.e., whether the possibility of intervention is still sufficient to discourage them) is a key question when considering network effects.

24.2.2 Street Networks and Crime

There are a number of examples of research concerned with the relationship between network structure and crime in the environmental criminology literature. These have been published over a period of decades, and the approaches employed vary considerably, in terms of both the statistical methods employed and—perhaps more pertinently for this chapter—the way in which network centrality is conceptualized and quantified. It is also notable that the majority of work has concerned the crime of residential burglary, the reasons for which may be partly practical: burglary is a well-reported crime, for which the location is known with high accuracy. In addition, it is a crime for which theoretical arguments are relatively mature: it is a crime against a fixed target, and one to which arguments such as crime pattern theory apply straightforwardly. Other than the fact that there is one additional "moving part," however, there is no reason a priori why similar principles should not apply in the context of interpersonal crime.

The earliest attempt to examine street networks quantitatively is the study of Bevis and Nutter (1977), who examined residential burglary patterns in Minneapolis in the United States. The work is remarkable for its use of graph-theoretic terminology, and acts as a precursor to the formal analyses that follow. In empirical terms, it took two distinct approaches. The first was to identify a number of block types based on their connectivity (e.g., dead end, L-shape, through road) and explore the differences in crime rates between them. It was found that, in general, more connected segments, such as through roads and "T-shapes," displayed the greatest risk. A second, aggregate-level analysis was performed at census tract level, and examined the relationship between network density—defined as the ratio of segments to junctions—and crime. Although density is a coarse-grained measure, it does reflect the overall level of connectivity of a network: lower-density networks are tree-like, whereas higher values indicate that structures are more regular, with a greater plurality of route choices. In Minneapolis, it was found that, after controlling for demographic variables, higher-density tracts experienced greater crime, suggesting that additional connectivity of this type could have a criminogenic effect.

Other studies have also examined network connectivity at the area level, with a focus on the role of streets in facilitating access to particular areas. White (1990), for example, examined rates of burglary at the neighborhood level in Massachusetts in the United States. The analysis was motivated by the question of whether neighborhoods with more direct connections to major roads experienced elevated levels of offending, since such connections rendered them more accessible to external traffic. After controlling for other relevant factors, this was found to be the case, suggesting that these connections had the effect of exposing such neighborhoods to potential offenders. Much more recently, McCutcheon et al. (2016) examined a similar question in the context of robbery, analyzing the relationship between the number of interstate exits in the counties of Georgia in the United States, and their robbery rates. Again, it was found that the two were positively associated, which can be rationalized with the effect of interstate connectivity in both increasing the awareness of potential offenders and diminishing territoriality.

Although area-level analysis is sufficient to demonstrate the influence of overall network character, in order to understand how risk is affected at particular locations it is necessary to use micro-level units of analysis. The street segment is a natural choice for this, and was used by Beavon et al. (1994) in their analysis of property crime in Ridge Meadows in Canada. In a similar manner to Bevis and Nutter (1977), the authors measured the accessibility of segments in terms their direct connections to neighboring streets, finding that a higher number of connections was associated with greater crime (after controlling for other factors). Further analysis also explored differences across road classifications, which provide a broad indication of the importance of streets. In line with expectation, it was found that higher-ranked roads experienced greater risk in general.

Questions concerning urban configuration are, of course, also of interest to the planning community, and the issue of crime in particular has been addressed in a number of studies. Several of these employ an approach known as "space syntax" (Hillier, 1996), which is concerned with the configuration and organization of physical entities in urban areas. A central principle of the approach is the importance of lines of sight in determining the structure of space from the perspective of a user: In space syntax approaches, the intersections between these lines are used to produce a network representation of space; while this differs from the street network, the two are closely related. A number of metrics, such as "integration" and "closeness," can then be computed for these networks in order to quantify the accessibility or connectedness of particular locations. In all cases, it is emphasized that the properties of a particular location depend on its relationship with the remainder of the network, and cannot be viewed in isolation. Space syntax has been the subject of several criticisms (e.g., Ratti, 2004), but is one of the few approaches to focus explicitly on the way in which urban spaces are experienced by the public.

The results of space syntax studies of crime, however, conflict somewhat with what would be expected on the basis of criminological theory. Work by Hillier (2004), for example, examined a range of offense types in both London and an urban area in Australia. In both cases, it was found that risk was positively correlated with "connectivity" (the number of immediate neighbors a place has in the space syntax network) but negatively associated with "integration." Since integration measures how close a location is to all others in the network, this can be interpreted as suggesting that risk will be greatest in locations that are secluded or isolated. This supports Jacobs's assertion, to the extent that it implies that designs that promote accessibility should be encouraged. It should be noted, however, that the study emphasizes that local physical factors—such as the access points of properties and the presence of footpaths—can have a considerable effect in moderating the influence of network structure. This is a point supported by the work of Armitage (2007) in examining the physical designs of individual properties and the risks associated with them.

The issue of network structure was considered again by Johnson and Bowers (2010), who examined burglary data from Merseyside in the United Kingdom. This work was concerned with the concept of network "permeability"—the readiness with which people pass through a place—and its role in offender targeting. In fact, the network variables considered were similar to those examined by Beavon et al. (1994)—number of connections and administrative classification—and the primary innovation was in the statistical model employed. The authors used a Poisson-distributed hierarchical linear model (HLM), which accounts for spatial nesting in the data; that is, potential variation due to unobserved factors at the area level. Indeed, results indicated that such variation was present, and therefore controlled for in the measurement of network-related effects. These were found to be in agreement with pattern theory: street segments with more connections, and those of higher classification, were both found to be at greater risk after controlling for other contextual factors. The authors also considered the special case of cul-de-sacs: these were found to be the safest streets, on average, although those that were linear in shape were found to be significantly more risky than those with sinuous geometries. The study concluded that network permeability was positively associated with crime risk.

While the results of the Johnson and Bowers (2010) study and others show significant relationships, the extent to which they offer theoretical insight is limited somewhat by the way in which the properties of networks are measured. While the variables employed—connection count and road classification, for example—are indicative of some characteristics, they also have a number of crucial shortcomings. One of these is that they carry relatively little information: both have a limited number of possible values, and display substantial within-category variation. Perhaps more crucially, though, they correspond only loosely to the underlying concepts of interest from a theoretical point of view: it is far from clear, for example, that the number of neighbors a segment has corresponds to the extent to which it appears in activity spaces. This limits the extent to which the results of such studies can be interpreted with respect to specific behavioral theories.

Davies and Johnson (2014) sought to address these issues by adopting a more formal approach to the measurement of network properties. In their work, which examined residential burglary in the city of Birmingham in the United Kingdom, the network was analyzed using terminology and techniques from the field of network science. This involves the representation of networks as formal mathematical structures, known as *graphs*, for which a range of structural measures have been developed. The study in question concentrated on one of these—"betweenness"—which reflects the frequency with which parts of the network are expected to be used during travel through the network. Davies and Johnson calculated this metric for the street network of Birmingham and examined its influence on burglary risk, again using an HLM. After controlling for a number of other demographic variables, the estimated model showed a positive association between burglary risk and betweenness: that is, more central streets were found to experience greater victimization. Again, this was interpreted as providing support for crime pattern theory.

24.2.3 Measuring Network Properties

The review presented in the previous section reveals a relatively consistent view: that greater network connectivity is associated with higher levels of crime. Though notable exceptions to this do exist, this was found to be the case across a number of settings, and a range of spatial granularities. Nevertheless, what is also clear from the review is that there is a far from unified view within the literature concerning the precise sense in which centrality is measured and defined. There therefore remains a lack of clarity with respect to which aspects of network structure are most relevant to behavioral theory, and how these can be quantified most meaningfully. Since addressing these inconsistencies represents one of the primary motivations for this research, these issues bear some further reflection.

As is evident from the above, various terms are employed in discussions of the role of network structure in crime, with "permeability," "connectivity," and "accessibility" being among the most common. Rather than being defined formally, however, these terms are typically used in a broad sense, with the result that their meanings remain somewhat opaque. This can be problematic, particularly when seeking to reconcile these concepts with behavioral theory: the terms are sufficiently malleable that, by themselves, they refer to only the broadest structural principles.

A particularly clear example of this difficulty is the concept of "permeability," which is frequently invoked in studies of crime risk on networks. Most immediately, this refers to the ease with which traffic can flow through a place: a permeable location is one that can be readily accessed. While this can be understood intuitively, however, the question of how it can be quantified is far from clear-cut, as illustrated by the range of metrics employed in empirical studies. Most problematically, it is hard to argue that many of these measures—the number of direct connections, for example, or the density of the network—could not equally well be interpreted as measures of other notions, such as "accessibility."

Perhaps more problematic, however, is the extent to which these concepts correspond to the behavioral theories that motivate their study. The argument of crime pattern theory (outlined in Section 24.2.1) is relatively straightforward: that streets that are used more frequently will experience greater risk. Frequency of use does not necessarily correspond to permeability, however: just because streets *can* be accessed readily does not necessarily mean that they *will*. Conceptual misalignment such as this has the potential to lead to incorrect inferences or, otherwise, to suggest ambiguous conclusions.

In order to test principles such as crime pattern theory rigorously, therefore, it is necessary to measure network structure in a way that corresponds directly to the hypothesized mechanism. It was this argument that motivated the use of betweenness in the paper by Davies and Johnson described above: a measure explicitly designed to measure how frequently streets will be used during travel through the network. This was shown to be a significant predictor of burglary risk, in line with pattern theory. It should be noted that it cannot be claimed that betweenness actually counts the number of physical journeys that people take down streets; to do so would require spatiotemporal locational information for individuals. It does, however, more directly measure the likelihood of a journey using a particular street segment than the other measures typically employed.

The importance of using more accurate measures of street use is perhaps even more pertinent in the context of the present study, which seeks to extend the previous analytical approach to the case of interpersonal crime. From the perspective of the criminal event, two key distinctions separate this from the case of burglary. The first is the nonstatic nature of the victim: whereas burglaries take place at fixed locations, the potential targets for assault are also individuals moving around a network. As such, their movements are also influenced by the shape of the network, and it is these movements—along with those of offenders—that drive the confluence in space of the elements necessary for crime. Measuring network structure in a way that reflects the activity patterns of this population is therefore necessary in order to establish whether the distribution of interpersonal crime is consistent with this reasoning.

The second distinction that can be made in the case of interpersonal crime relates to the behavior of offenders themselves. The target selection processes involved are likely to differ from those of burglars, as are the relative contributions of opportunistic and exploratory behaviors. In particular, the role of awareness spaces in driving offending may be different. Burglary represents a natural application of crime pattern theory, since the targets are themselves a static part of the environment, but there is no guarantee that this will also apply for other crimes. If metrics similar to those used for burglary are also capable of predicting risk in these cases, this may represent evidence that opportunistic offending, shaped by awareness spaces, is also a dominant mechanism for assault.

24.3 Data

The setting for our study is the city of London, which is the capital city of the United Kingdom. London is the United Kingdom's largest city, with a population of approximately 8.5 million and an area of over 1,500 km^2. The city is highly diverse, with a large immigrant population, and also displays high levels of inequality. The city is divided into 32 administrative boroughs, which also form the basis for its policing: each borough represents an "operational command unit" of the Metropolitan Police Service (MPS), and many aspects of resourcing and crime recording are organized at this level.

Three primary forms of data are used in our analysis: geospatial data describing the structure of the street network; geo-referenced recorded crime data; and contextual sociodemographic data. We will describe each of these in turn, along with any preprocessing carried out prior to our analysis.

24.3.1 Street Network

The street network data used in this study was obtained from Ordnance Survey (OS)—the national mapping agency of the UK—via the Integrated Transport Network layer of its MasterMap product. The network data is provided as a single file for a defined geographical area, which is mappable using geographic information systems. In the United Kingdom, a certain volume of street network data can be downloaded free of charge through academic agreement between OS and universities. Similar, though less detailed, data can also be obtained from open sources, such as OpenStreetMap; this is available in a unified format for all countries.

The OS data set contains records for all streets that lie within London, including both vehicular and pedestrian thoroughfares. Each record represents a *street segment*: an uninterrupted portion of street that directly connects two junctions. For each of these, the geometry of the segment is provided, as well as a range of other information, including the name of the road and its classification ("A Road," "B Road," etc.). Figure 24.1a gives an indication of how this network data appears when it is mapped. In Section 24.4, we explain in detail the processing of the network and its analysis.

24.3.2 Recorded Crime

Our measurement of crime risk is based on recorded crime data provided by the MPS. In particular, we consider all cases of common assault that were recorded in London between January 2013 and October 2015, inclusive: a period of 34 months. In this period, a total of 273,669 incidents occurred. For each case, the location is provided as a British National Grid reference, with a resolution of 1 meter. In each case, the incident has previously been geocoded by police using a system of street center-points and prominent landmarks.

With the relationship of this work to previous studies concerned with burglary in mind, a couple of features of this data set are worthy of comment. One of these is the relative rate of reporting of the two crime types: evidence suggests that assault is typically reported at substantially lower rates than burglary (Tarling & Morris, 2010). While this does suggest that the completeness of data in this case will be lower, we have no reason to expect that this will be biased spatially. We cannot exclude the possibility that there may be specific places in which people are reluctant to admit to having been a victim of assault, though this possibility that would require further empirical analysis to confirm or falsify. In any case, the likely rarity of such cases suggests that any such bias is unlikely to substantially affect the substance of our results.

A further issue concerns the spatial accuracy of the data. Again, this is likely to be lower than in the case of burglary, for which incidents are associated with specific properties and therefore typically well geolocated. Nevertheless, the nature of assault is such that victims are likely to know their location with a relatively high degree of confidence: it is a discrete event that victims will certainly be aware of at the time of commission. Again, there are likely to be exceptions to this, as in the case of drunken and drugged victims who might not remember where a fight occurred. Indeed, in these cases it might also be unclear who should be classed as the victims and the offenders. From a geographic perspective, however, reporting victims in most cases will know their locations, while the police are likely to be aware of the locations of any disputes that they are involved in breaking up. Further, given that the required level of accuracy for our study is the street segment, we do not consider not knowing the precise location to be especially problematic.

Since our unit of analysis is the street segment, it is necessary to associate each recorded incident with a particular segment. We do this by identifying the closest street segment to the recorded location. In order to ensure reliability, we impose a maximum threshold of 50 m on this process: we consider that incidents that do not lie within this distance of any segment cannot reliably be associated, and omit them from the analysis. In the course of this process, 0.7% of incidents are removed, leaving a total of 271,767 for the analysis.

24.3.3 Sociodemographic Data

In order to control for a number of non network effects with the potential to influence crime, our analysis also requires sociodemographic data. For this, we use data from the 2011 UK census, which provides a range of data relating to economic, demographic, and housing attributes. The particular variables we use will be discussed in Section 24.7.2.

Again, some preprocessing is required in order to translate this data to the street segment level. The basic units in which census data is provided are Output Areas (OAs), which are polygonal areas constructed such that they contain approximately 150 households. In order to derive segment-level measures from this, we identify each segment with the OA that contains the largest portion of its length (i.e., the OA that it mostly falls within). The census attributes for this OA are then taken to apply to the segment in question.

24.4 Network Analysis

The central principle of our analytical approach is the use of formal and sophisticated metrics to capture relevant structural features of the street network. In order to apply these, it is first necessary to encode the network in mathematical terms. In particular, we represent the network as a *graph*: a well-studied mathematical object that provides the basis for network science.

Graphs provide a means of representing collections of entities and the relationships between them. A *graph*, $G = (V,E)$, is formed of a set of vertices, V, and a set of edges, E. The vertices are the basic entities that the graph represents: the number of vertices, N, is referred to as the *order* of the graph, and they are typically indexed by the integers $1, \ldots, N$. The edges of the graph encode connections between vertices: an edge $e \in E$ is an unordered pair (i,j) that denotes that vertices i and j are linked. Such vertices are said to be *adjacent*, and the total number of edges in a graph, M, is known as its *size*. A full introduction to formal graph theory can be found in the books by Bollobás (2002) and Diestel (2010).

There are a number of ways in which street networks can be represented as graphs. The most natural of these is known as the "primal" representation (Porta et al., 2006b), in which vertices represent junctions (i.e., points at which streets intersect) and edges correspond to street segments. The construction of this representation is shown in Figure 24.1: junctions are identified, and edges are placed between any pair that are directly connected by a street. This produces a spatially embedded graph that closely mirrors the map of the street network.

Alternative representations have been proposed for street networks (Jiang & Claramunt, 2004; Porta et al., 2006a; Lagesse et al., 2015) and have been explored in empirical studies. In general, these take a "dual" approach, in which the roles of vertices and edges are reversed: vertices denote streets, and edges represent their intersections. Furthermore, streets are typically defined in a more general sense: such approaches seek to unify groups of street segments into single entities, on the basis of either street

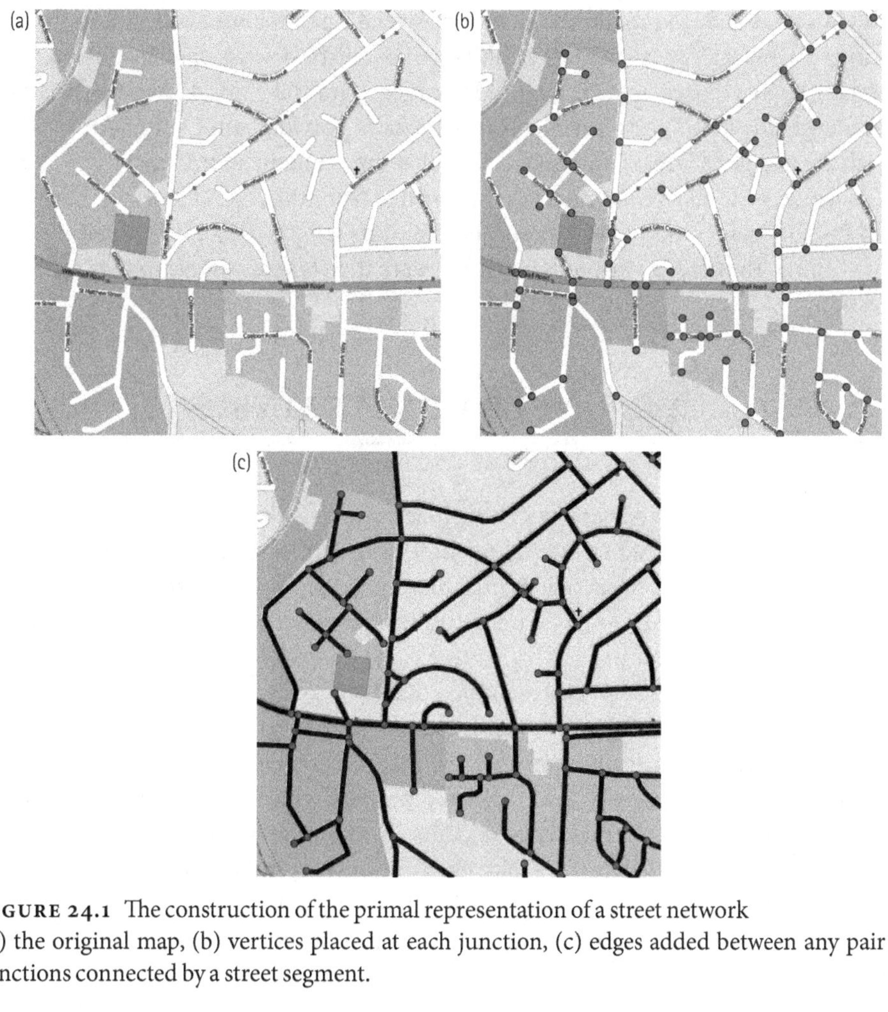

FIGURE 24.1 The construction of the primal representation of a street network
(a) the original map, (b) vertices placed at each junction, (c) edges added between any pair of junctions connected by a street segment.

naming or geometric continuity. While these approaches do have advantages, they also come at a cost, the most significant of which is spatial information: geometric distance is not well defined in such representations. This is our primary reason for using the primal representation here.

With the network expressed in these terms, its structural properties can be analyzed formally. Indeed, the quantification of graph structure is a central aspect of network science, in which a wide array of metrics have been developed (see Newman, 2010). Unfortunately, however, the nature of street networks—in particular, the fact that they are spatially embedded—means that many of the most common metrics are either inappropriate or simply uninformative in this context. An example of this is the analysis of vertex degree, which measures the number of neighbors that a node has (this is related closely to the measures used in several of the previous studies described in Section 24.2.2). Although this is often highly informative for other networks, its value is limited for spatial networks by the narrow range of value that it can take. Because of spatial constraints, almost all vertex degrees lie between 0 and 4 (it is rare to find more than five segments meeting at a single junction) and this—together with the fact that it relationship to road use is unclear—means that it offers little meaningful insight into road structure.

In order to define the metrics used in our study, it is necessary to introduce the concept of a network *path*. A path is a route through the network between two vertices; that is, a sequence of nodes that can be traversed by following edges. For networks in which the edges have an associated weight (e.g., geometric distance, as is the case for streets), the *length* of a path can be measured in two ways: metric and topological. In the metric case, the length is calculated on the basis of absolute physical distance, whereas the topological measure considers only the number of edges that must be traversed (i.e., it counts the number of "hops" from junction to junction). In this study, we focus on metric distance, which represents a more realistic measure of separation.

For any pair of vertices between which a path exists (for street networks, a path typically exists between all possible pairs), a *shortest path* is defined as a path of minimal length. There may be more than one of these for a given pair of vertices: if two distinct paths of equal length exist, then both are shortest paths. We can therefore define σ_{ij} as the total number of shortest paths between a given pair of vertices i and j. Furthermore, $\sigma_{ij}(e)$ can be defined for any edge e as the number of these shortest paths that pass through e (that is, the number of times that e occurs on shortest paths between i and j).

These terms allow us to define the network metric *betweenness*, which measures the regularity with which edges are used in travel through the network. For any edge e, the betweenness, B_e, is defined as

$$B_e = \sum_{\substack{i,j \in V \\ i \sim j}} \frac{\sigma_{ij}(e)}{\sigma_{ij}} \tag{24.1}$$

where $\sim$ represents the relation "there exists a path between i and j." The betweenness of an edge therefore measures the number of times that it features in paths through the network; indeed, its calculation can be expressed more intuitively as a sequence of steps:

1. For all edges, initialize $B_e = 0$.
2. Consider all pairs of vertices, i and j.
3. In each case, find the shortest path(s) through the network between i and j.
4. For each edge that appears on one of these paths, increment its B_e by $1/m$, where m is the number of shortest paths between i and j (m will only be greater than 1 when multiple distinct paths have exactly the same length).

Betweenness therefore represents an estimate of the frequency with which each edge in the network will be used, under the simple assumption that exactly one trip will take place between all pairs of junctions. It is a first-order heuristic for throughput, with the crucial property that it is a nonlocal measure: the centrality of an edge depends on its position and role within the wider network. Its relevance to criminal behavior—and pattern theory in particular—is immediate, since it reflects precisely the mechanism by which awareness spaces are hypothesized to be built up. Segments of higher betweenness are those that feature more regularly in travel routes, and will therefore be used by more people. In terms of the elements required for interpersonal crime, therefore, such segments: (*a*) are in the awareness spaces of more potential offenders; (*b*) are frequented by more potential targets; and (*c*) will have a higher supply of potential guardians. As an instrument, therefore, it corresponds closely to the argument outlined in Section 24.2.1.

The basic definition of betweenness is a broad one, and can be refined in order to capture more subtle effects. In particular, the range of journeys considered in its calculation can be modified by including only trips shorter than a given threshold. For a given radius, r, the local betweenness B_e^r is defined as

$$B_e^r = \sum_{\substack{i,j \in V \\ i \sim j}} \frac{\sigma_{ij}(e)}{\sigma_{ij}} \tag{24.2}$$

where the $\sim$ relation has been modified to "there exists a path of length at most r between i and j."

The value of betweenness as a network metric—particularly in comparison with alternative measures—can be illustrated by examining its distribution. Examining this at the aggregate level to start, it is immediately apparent that the distribution is long-tailed, and heavily skewed toward negative values; previous empirical studies have found this to be broadly exponential (Crucitti et al., 2006). For this reason, and with its eventual use as a regressor in mind, we take the logarithm of betweenness throughout our analysis. The distribution of these values across London is shown in Figure 24.2a.

A number of previous studies have used administrative road classification as a proxy measure for either the usage or permeability of streets. This has a number of

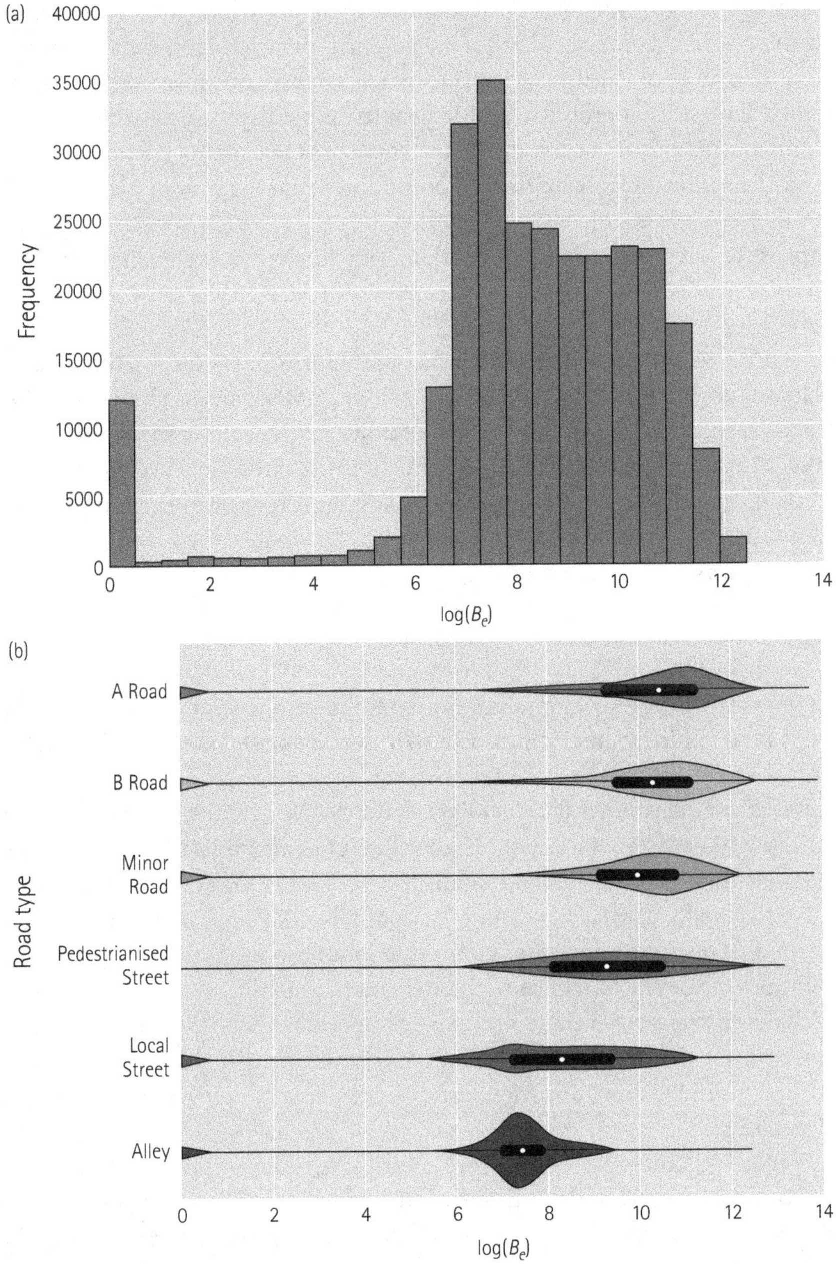

FIGURE 24.2 The distribution of betweenness
(a) overall distribution of the logarithm of betweenness, and (b) betweenness distributions for a range of administrative road classifications. In both cases, betweenness calculations are based on a radius of 2,500 m.

shortcomings, including the fact that classifications apply to long stretches of road, comprising many street segments. This has the potential to mask significant variation—and therefore risk an ecological fallacy—since streets can vary considerably in character along their length. This problem, and the ability of betweenness to address it, is illustrated in Figure 24.2b, in which the distribution of betweenness is plotted for a number of road classifications from the London data. While the overall hierarchy remains broadly intact, it is immediately apparent that the values exhibit extremely large within-category variation, and substantial overlap. This implies that classification is not an effective discriminant with respect to street usage (at least in the sense that is measured by betweenness).

In addition to betweenness, which has previously been shown to be positively associated with burglary risk, we also consider another network metric here. The *reach* of a vertex is defined as the number of other vertices that can be reached from it via paths. Since this is trivial in global terms (it is the same for all vertices), this value is also typically defined with a radial limit, so that it measures the number of other vertices with a given radius, r. In formal terms, the reach of a vertex, i, denoted R_i^r, can be defined as

$$R_i^r = \left|\{ j \in V : i \sim j \}\right| \tag{24.3}$$

where, as in the definition of betweenness, $\sim$ represents the relation "there exists a path between i and j." This can be easily translated to an edge-based measure: the reach of any edge is taken to be the mean reach of its two incident vertices.

Reach can be interpreted fairly straightforwardly as a local measure of the density of the network at any given location. High values of reach imply that a large number of intersections lie within the defined radius, which suggests that the built environment is relatively spatially dense. This density has a number of implications: in simple terms, it suggests that such locations are "close" to a lot of places, which may have implications for the likely levels of activity in the area in general. Indeed, it is plausible to expect that such density may reflect land use, since centers of activity are frequently dense and built-up. It is for this reason that we include this measure: it reflects the potential for activity in a given location, and therefore complements the movement-based measure of betweenness.

In order to illustrate the two network metrics introduced here, their distributions for network data from London are shown in Figure 24.3. For clarity of mapping, we show the network of the borough of Barnet, though the general patterns are replicated generally across all boroughs. The intuitive sense of betweenness can be seen: high-valued segments form an arterial system, identifying routes that would be primary conduits for traffic. The case of reach, on the other hand, shows how locations of high density are identified. High-reach areas appear to correspond to centers within the borough, and appear to show locations where the supply of people will be high. These images therefore illustrate the distinct but complementary effects captured by the two metrics used.

(a)

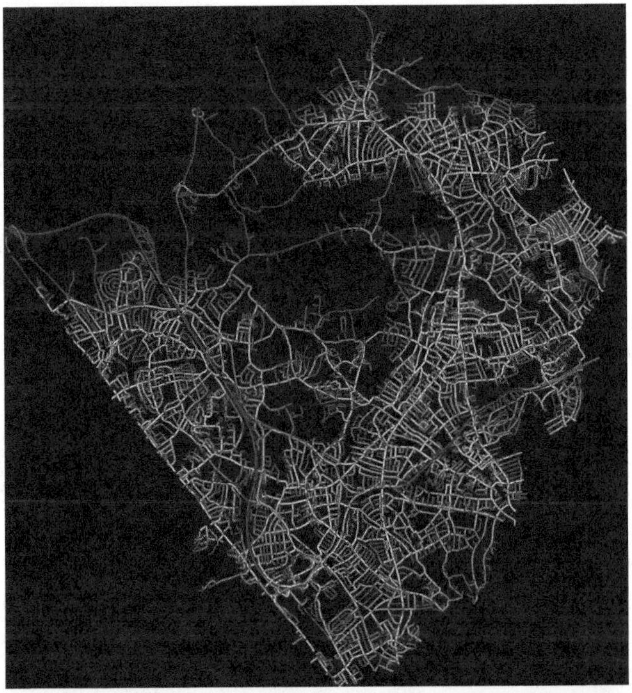

(b)

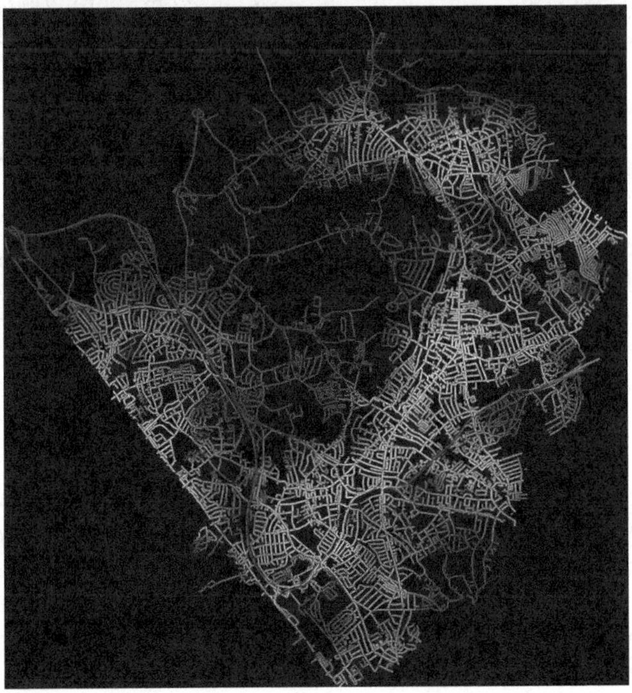

FIGURE 24.3 The London borough of Barnet (U.K.)
Segments colored according to (a) betweenness, and (b) reach. Both are calculated using a radius of 1,500 m.

24.5 Crime Clustering

Having introduced our analytical approach with respect to network structure, we now begin to examine the distribution of crime. As a first step in this direction, we first explore the simplest question: whether crime is distributed heterogeneously around the network. In a sense, that this should be the case represents a necessary prerequisite for the remainder of the analysis, since any relationship with network structure would imply that crime is distributed nonrandomly.

To address this issue, we replicate the analysis performed by both Johnson and Bowers (2010) and Davies and Johnson (2014), based on Monte Carlo simulation. Its purpose is to test for spatial clustering while ensuring that this is done in a way that controls for both random variation in crime location and the fact that levels of opportunity vary across segments. In those previous studies, which concerned burglary, this specifically sought to control for the number of potential targets (i.e., houses) on each segment. While this is no longer a meaningful unit for assault, it is still necessary to control for the variation in length between street segments, which will affect the opportunity for crime: if offending was completely random, longer streets would experience more offending.

The spatial clustering of incidents can be visualized by plotting a Lorenz curve for the accumulation of incidents over space. To do this, crime rates (incidents per meter) are calculated for each street segment, and the segments are then placed in descending order accordingly. The cumulative percentage of incidents is then plotted against the cumulative street length as we move through this ordering, thereby producing the Lorenz curve (see Figure 24.4a).

In order to compare the observed distribution of crime to that which would be expected if the location of incidents was random, we apply a Monte Carlo process. We take the total number of observed incidents and allocate them randomly to street segments, with probability proportional to the length of the segment. This is equivalent to an assumption that crime is uniformly distributed across the length of the network, and the process generates segment counts according to this hypothesis. We repeat this 99 times, and the mean Lorenz curve of these randomized data sets is also plotted on Figure 24.4a.

Clearly the disparity between the two curves suggests that crime is distributed more heterogeneously than would be expected. This can, however, be quantified by calculating the Gini (1921) coefficient. This is used to quantify inequality, and does so by comparing the area between the "observed" and "expected" curves to that above the "expected" curve. This generates values in the range [0,1], with 0 corresponding to perfect equality and 1 to perfect inequality.

The Gini coefficients across all 99 realizations of our randomization algorithm are plotted in Figure 24.4b. The values are tightly clustered around .575, suggesting that the observed distribution is highly heterogeneous. Indeed, it is notable that these values are

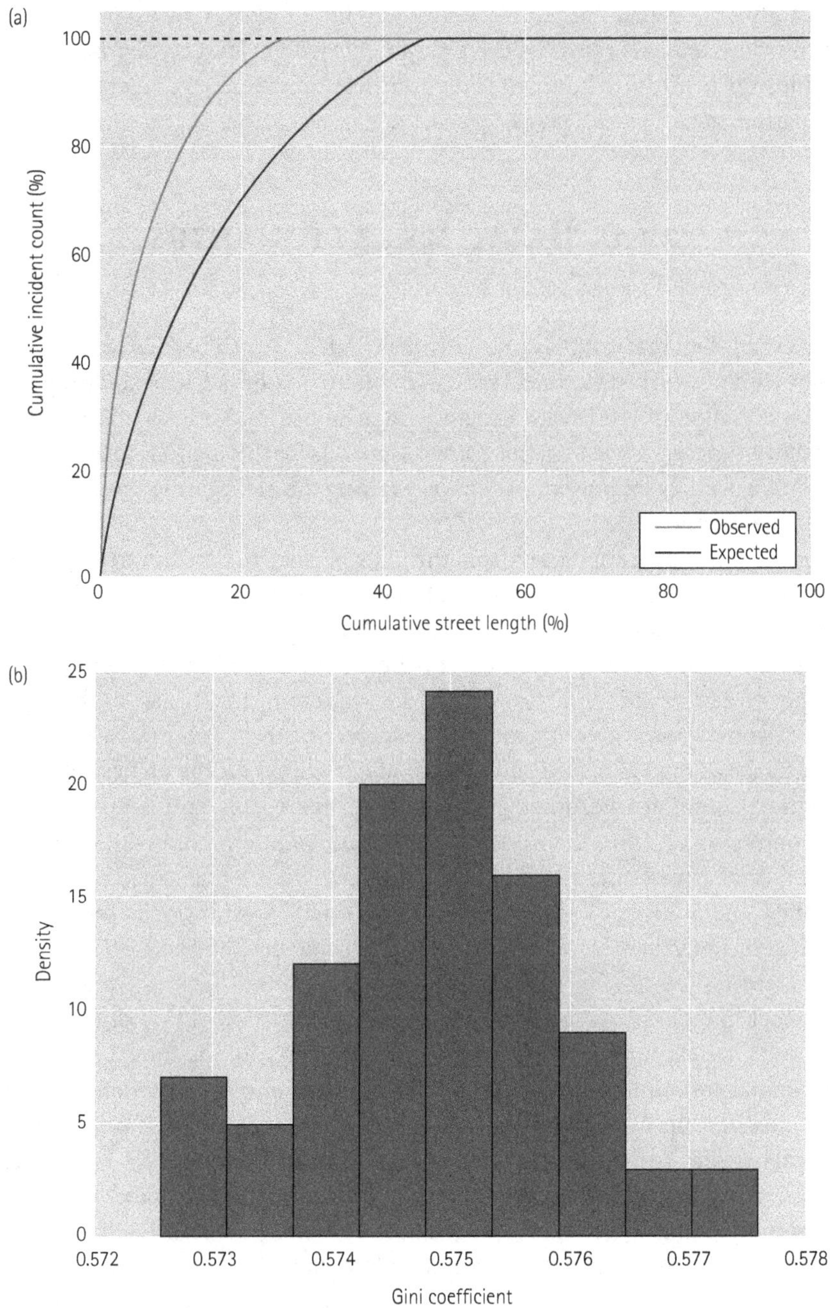

FIGURE 24.4 Heterogeneity in the distribution of crime
(a) Lorenz curves for observed and expected distributions, (b) distribution of Gini coefficient across 99 randomizations.

significantly higher than those previously found for burglary. One explanation for this is that previous analysis considered only segments with at least one house, whereas all segments were considered here, but this nevertheless implies that clustering of assault is particularly acute.

24.6 Basic Relationships

Having established that crime is unevenly distributed, we can begin to explore its relationship with network structure. This can be done in a broad sense by simply examining the variation in crime rate as betweenness increases. Since assault is a relatively rare event, it is necessary to aggregate street segments for this analysis to be meaningful, and so in Figure 24.5 we present bar charts showing the mean crime rates for a range of bands of betweenness.

A couple of trends are apparent from the plots presented. Most immediately, there is an overall positive trend between incident rate and betweenness, mirroring that which was previously found for residential burglary. This accords with crime pattern theory, and suggests that more central segments do indeed experience greater victimization.

The positive observed trend, however, is not monotonic in all cases, and notable variations exist between the various radii considered. In the 1,000 m case, for example, the rate peaks around .8 before falling away to a low level for the highest-betweenness segments. This pattern becomes gradually less apparent as radius increases, and is near-monotonic for 2,500 m. These results should be interpreted with caution, since the number of streets that fall into each category is not equal: since betweenness is long-tailed, the number of segments falling into the largest bands is relatively small. Nevertheless, the values for these cases do offer some insight into the levels of risk at these extremes.

The most likely explanation for the disparity across radii is that different notions of centrality are captured by the various radii: at low radii, the most between streets are those that are important to local travel, but as longer trips are taken into account, other routes become more important. The results have implications from this perspective: local betweenness is not sufficient to increase risk, whereas long-range betweenness is. A possible explanation for this, of course, involves guardianship: routes that are more important locally may experience a greater guardianship from the local (and perhaps more familiar) population. While empirically underexplored, such a phenomenon may be reconciled with notions of collective efficacy (Sampson et al., 1997), as well as Reynald's (2011) characterization of these effects in terms of an interplay between places being physically and psychologically accessible to offenders. In addition, such an effect could also be reconciled with the distances traveled by victims: journeys to entertainment districts tend to be longer than those involved in other regular activities.

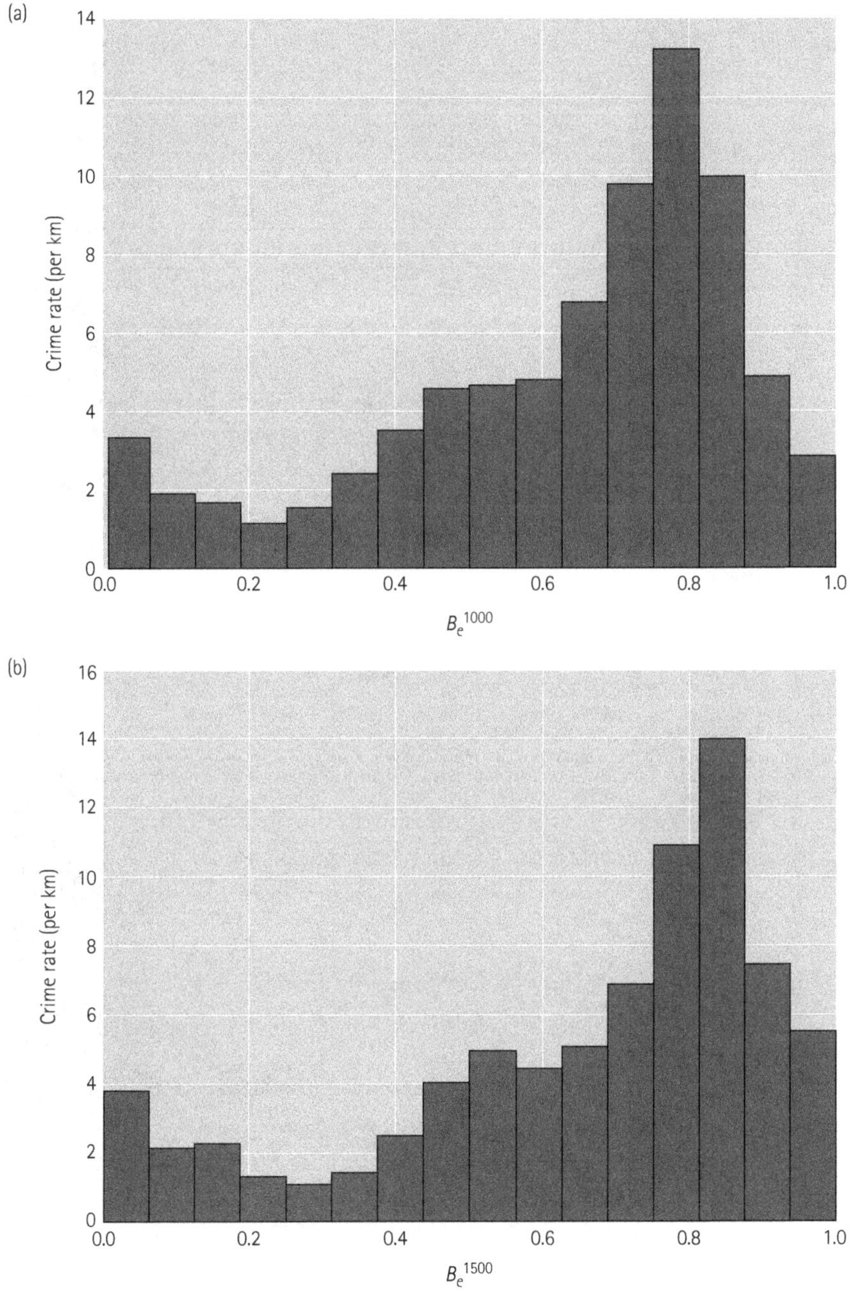

FIGURE 24.5 The relationship between crime rate and betweenness for a range of radii (a) 1,000 m, (b) 1,500 m, (c) 2,000 m, and (d) 2,500 m. In each case, the bar represents the aggregate incident rate per kilometer for segments falling within the corresponding betweenness band. Betweenness values have been normalized to lie in the range [0,1].

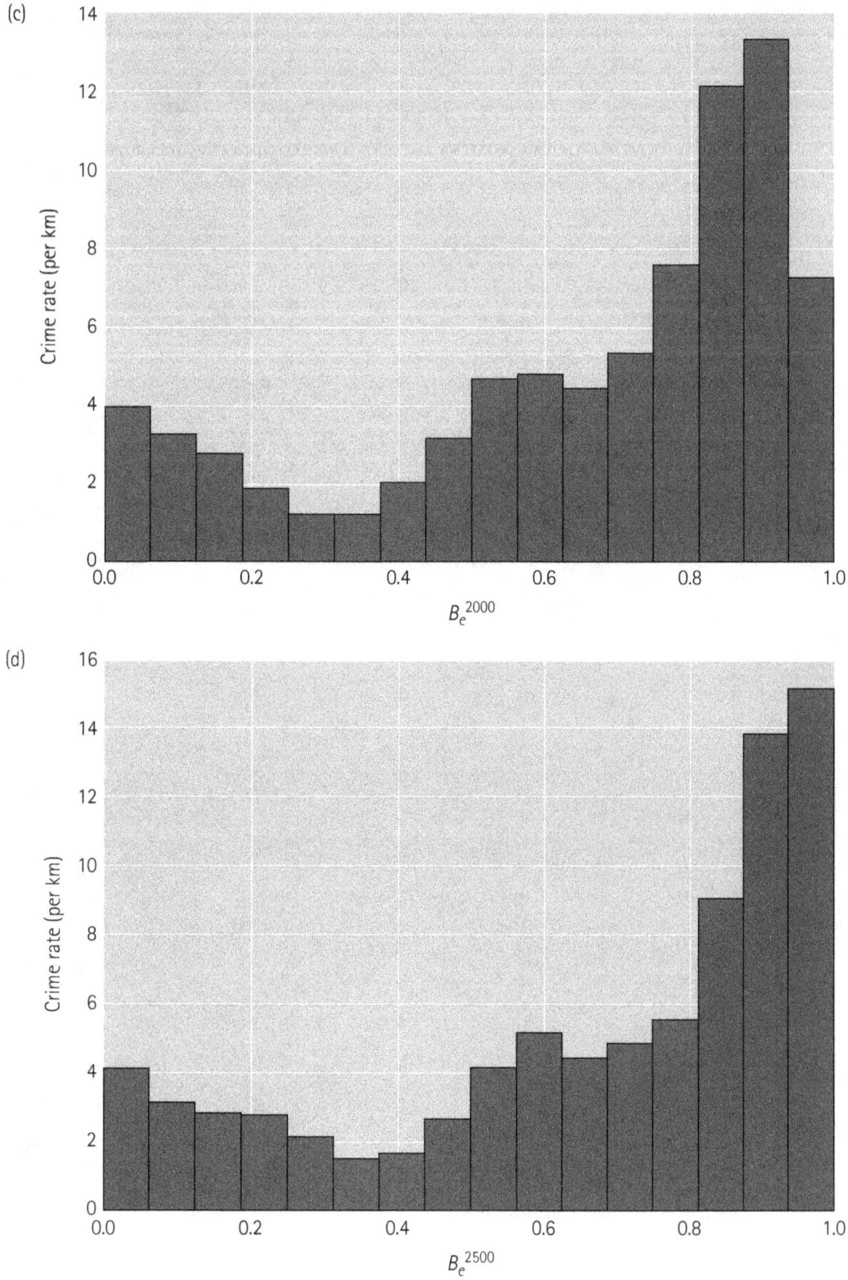

FIGURE 24.5 Continued

24.7 Statistical Model

The results of the previous section are broadly in agreement with those established previously for residential burglary, and we now proceed to more formal analysis of the relationships. In line with previous studies, we do this by applying a hierarchical linear model (HLM): a form of statistical model specifically designed to account for nested data (in this case in terms of spatial units). Using this model allows us to examine the effect of network structure while controlling for the effect of other relevant variables, including sociodemographic indicators.

The central principle of the HLM is to account for random effects in the model that vary across spatial units. These terms are intended to capture the effects of unobserved variables (i.e., effects that are not modeled explicitly), and are a common feature in regression models. The crucial innovation here is that these effects are allowed to vary—they are modelled as normally distributed constants—across areas. The rationale for this is that the unobserved effects are likely to vary from area to area, due to contextual factors (not least, in this case, the fact that different boroughs have different police forces).

In this analysis, we employ a three-level model. Our basic unit, and therefore lowest level, is the street segment. At the second level, we use Lower Super Output Areas (LSOAs), which are UK census units constructed so as to contain populations of approximately 1,500. This level can be taken to represent a notion of "neighborhood," and there are 4,827 covered in our data. Our third level is then the London borough, within which LSOAs are nested. As stated previously, London has 32 boroughs, each of which has a police division and a level of political autonomy. Boroughs vary substantially in character, and it is for this reason that we choose it as our highest hierarchical level.

24.7.1 Street Segment Metrics

The street segment measures we include in the model are precisely those introduced in Section 24.4: betweenness and reach. In both cases, we consider models with a number of different radii, corresponding to different levels of granularity. Furthermore, in each case we normalize values according to their maximum across the network as a whole: this is particularly important given the variation in radii, since both metrics scale with the radius used. In this way, comparison can meaningfully be made across scales.

The only other network variable included at the street segment level is segment length. This represents a coarse indicator of opportunity—there are more places for crime to occur on longer streets—and its inclusion therefore acts as a control for this. At a slightly more nuanced level, length may also relate to guardianship: if offenders are dissuaded by people anywhere on the same street, then guardianship effects may be amplified on longer streets.

24.7.2 Sociodemographic Variables

A number of sociodemographic variables, derived from the UK census, are also included in the model. Since evidence from developmental studies (Farrington, 1986; Lober et al., 2012) suggests that the peak age of offending is in the early teens, we include the percentage of residents aged between 10 and 15. For this crime type, and with the focus on guardianship in particular, it seems likely that social disorganization theory (Sampson & Raudenbush, 1999) is relevant here also. Following previous work, we use ethnic heterogeneity as a proxy indicator of this, and measure it using a standard index (Simpson, 1949; Blau, 1977). In addition to this, we also include variables for unemployment and the proportion of students.

24.7.3 Model Structure

The effects described above are incorporated into the HLM structure as independent variables. Since we are modeling count data (offense frequencies) we model the dependent variable as Poisson-distributed, and take a logarithmic link function. If we use an indexing system in which segments are indexed by *i*, LSOAs by *j*, and boroughs by *k*, then the model can be specified as follows:

$$\log \pi_{ijk} = \beta_0 + u_{jk} + v_k + \beta_1 x_{1ijk} + \ldots + \beta_m x_{mijk} + \beta_{m+1} x_{(m+1)jk} + \ldots + \beta_n x_{njk}$$

$$u_{jk} \sim N(0, \Omega_u) \quad v_k \sim N(0, \Omega_v) \tag{24.4}$$

where π_{ijk} is the incident count on segment *i* (in LSOA *j*, in borough *k*), and $x_1, \ldots, x_m$ are the explanatory variables defined at segment level. The terms u_{jk} and v_k are the "random intercepts" at LSOA and borough level respectively, both normally distributed.

24.7.4 Model Results

The results of fitting the model are presented in Table 24.1, with four different variations given (corresponding to four different radii used in the calculation of betweenness and reach).

In general, the results are strikingly similar across the four models, with few substantial differences for any variable. With respect to our primary topic of interest—the influence of network structure—the results provide clear evidence that both variables included in the model are positively associated with assault victimization.

For betweenness, results in all cases show a highly significant relationship with incident count. This is consistent with the findings of Davies and Johnson (2014) for burglary, albeit with a slightly smaller effect size in this case. This result implies that busier streets (in the sense that this is captured by betweenness) experience higher victimization, and the persistence of the effect suggests that this is true across a range of scales. Nevertheless, there is a clear downward trend in effect size as radius increases,

Table 24.1 Regression Coefficients for HLMs of Street Segment Risk for Common Assault

	Path length			
	1,000 m	1,500 m	2,000 m	2,500 m
Segment level				
Length (100 m)	1.58 (168.65)**	1.56 (170.08)**	1.55 (169.13)**	1.54 (168.31)**
log(betweenness)	2.13 (31.41)**	1.93 (29.85)**	1.75 (27.58)**	1.62 (25.32)**
Reach	4.41 (21.12)**	2.98 (21.1)**	2.8 (19.64)**	2.81 (18.89)**
% unemployment	1.04 (23.88)**	1.04 (24.59)**	1.04 (24.34)**	1.04 (24.26)**
% student	1.01 (7.82)**	1.01 (6.67)**	1.01 (6.65)**	1.01 (6.78)**
Ethnic heterogeneity	1.25 (41.68)**	1.25 (42.12)**	1.25 (42.12)**	1.25 (42.56)**
% Age 10–15	0.98 (−12.32)**	0.98 (−12.21)**	0.98 (−12.61)**	0.98 (−12.98)**
Random intercepts				
LSOA random variance	0.511	0.493	0.493	0.491
Borough random variance	0.100	0.096	0.094	0.094

Note: Estimated coefficients are given for several HLMs, in which the columns correspond to different definitions of betweenness and reach (in terms of the radius used in its calculation). The values given are exponentiated regression coefficients, and therefore represent the factor by which the mean count on a segment is estimated to change as a result of a one-unit change in the explanatory variable. *Z*-scores are given in brackets.

** Denotes significance at $p = .01$ level.

suggesting that more local variants of betweenness are more significant from the perspective of assault. This finding does, of course, conflict somewhat with the preliminary result shown in Figure 24.5. The most likely reason for this is that the influence of the small number of high-betweenness (low-risk) segments seen in Figure 24.5 is not strong enough to influence the overall statistical relationship found here: the trend is dominated by the overall positive relationship. Furthermore, the inclusion of additional independent variables may also have accounted for some of this variation.

The fact that reach is also found to be positively associated with risk justifies its inclusion in the model, and suggests that the property that it seeks to capture does play a role in shaping offending. Again, the size of the effect is greatest for lower radii, suggesting that particularly local representations of density offer greatest predictive value. In real-world terms, this implies that particularly concentrated areas of street network density—as might be found in areas of high commercial activity—represent the most risky places for this crime. Crucially, however, the inclusion of the reach statistic does not render the effect of betweenness insignificant. This signifies that the opportunity structure for assault—in terms of the confluence of many potential "victims" and "offenders" (noting that it is often difficult to separate one group from the other) in a suitable place setting—is not merely acting as a proxy measure for the likely land use of the street segments alone. Instead, it demonstrates the presence of an awareness space mechanism for assault that operates over and above that.

The sociodemographic variables included give results largely in line with what would be expected, and detailed discussion of these issues is away from the main scope of this chapter. The result for "Age 10–15" is notable, however, as it suggests that the presence of this group is, in fact, negatively associated with risk. The precise reasons for this will require further investigation, but one possibility is that assault is not a significant part of the offending of this group. If so, it is perhaps understandable that the places where such people are present, which are typically removed from risky areas for violence (e.g., entertainment premises), will be at lower risk.

24.8 Conclusion

In this chapter, we have shown that the distribution of assault incidents in London is strongly influenced by the structure of the street network. This extends previous work concerned with property crime (i.e., burglary) to the context of interpersonal crime, the nature of which differs in a number of ways. Despite these distinctions, however, our evidence suggests that similar factors play a role in shaping the distribution of the two crime types, suggesting in turn that common behavioral principles may apply in both cases.

In addition to these empirical findings, this chapter was also intended to demonstrate the utility of formal network analysis in the study of urban structure, particularly as it relates to crime. We have outlined the general framework by which networks can be rigorously studied and introduced two relevant metrics, both of which measure distinct structural properties. Their value has been demonstrated in a number of ways: aside from the fact that they give rise to significant results, the accompanying analysis shows that they offer substantially more richness in terms of the information they provide than the proxy measures used in previous studies. In addition to this, both metrics correspond directly to behavioral notions—their calculation mirrors the mechanism by which awareness spaces are hypothesized to develop, for example—meaning that they represent effective instruments for exploring the underlying behavioral principles of interest. It should be emphasized that the range of possible metrics is large, and that many others may be fruitfully employed in the study of crime: for most behavioral theories, a metric can be designed to measure precisely what is needed.

Returning to the implications of the results themselves, the fact that these results hold for interpersonal crime can be interpreted with respect to various aspects of the criminal event. Most immediately, the results provide support for crime pattern theory, and suggest that the notions of awareness space and encounter space are dominant drivers of crime. This is a finding of some consequence, since there is little reason a priori to expect that these will hold: in theory, the commission of assault relies less on prior knowledge of target locations than burglary. Furthermore, the results imply that these principles still hold when targets are mobile, and less directly associated with particular locations.

It is worth emphasizing that although this research finds similar relationships between levels of offending and accessibility for assault as prior studies have found for burglary, the contexts and drivers of these crimes are necessarily different. In research on burglary, reference is often made to the impact of awareness spaces on "target selection." We acknowledge that this language is not as readily applied to cases of assault; it is far from the case that all perpetrators of assault are out looking for a fight to get into. In many cases it is the mixture of provocations and intoxication that drive up levels of assault (e.g., Homel et al., 2001). However, even given the potential differences in mechanism of the crimes, the fact that both burglary and assault are more prevalent in busier places demonstrates the power of the network structure in shaping the physical locations of incidents.

The findings have further implications for guardianship. To an extent, the question of whether busy streets experience greater crime is a test of whether the increased guardianship in such places is sufficient to counteract their increased exposure to potential offenders. In this case, as with burglary, results suggest that this is not the case: the streets on which guardianship ought to be greatest experience the highest level of offending. Although clearly the issue of guardianship is a complex and context-specific one, this general finding does cast doubt on a number of prominent design principles, such as the fostering of natural surveillance via the encouragement of through traffic.

One further observation from the statistical results presented is their variation across radii. In our statistical model, both network measures display greater explanatory power at lower radii, in which only more local trips are considered. This mirrors what was found for burglary (see Davies & Johnson, 2014), and implies that this is the scale at which pattern theory can be applied most meaningfully. That local trips should be the most significant is perhaps unsurprising, since journey-to-crime literature suggests that offenders are biased toward short travel distances (Townsley & Sidebottom, 2010). However, it might also be speculated that the dominance of local trips suggests that pedestrian travel is the mode via which awareness is predominantly gained (since vehicular trips would typically be longer and favor different paths).

There are a number of implications for policy and practice arising from the findings presented here. A straightforward one concerns everyday policing: the relationship with network centrality provides a means via which police officers can profile the risk of streets, and deploy resources accordingly. The fact that the results are expressed in network terms is also convenient from this perspective, since it is the network on which patrol activity takes place. However, a counterpoint to this is provided by the apparent ineffectiveness of guardianship, and increased police presence on risky streets is not necessarily guaranteed to be effective in reducing crime. Further research is required on this point, and may require the development of alternative interventions.

A more long-term implication for crime policy relates to potential lessons for urban design. It seems natural that, if an environmental feature is known to be associated with crime, steps should be taken to remove it, but the manipulation of street networks is far from simple. Aside from the inherent engineering challenges associated with either building or blocking roads, such actions can lead to unintended consequences: traffic must still go somewhere, so will be rerouted down alternative paths and may (if the theory holds) cause a crime problem there.

A more realistic possibility with regard to the modification of street networks is the guidance of planning for future cities. Street networks can be designed in various different ways, leading to different centrality characteristics: grid-like cities, for example, give rise to balanced distributions of both betweenness and reach, whereas hierarchical structures are much more heterogeneous. To an extent, planning can be done with this in mind, with streets designed so that traffic flows are equitable, for example. Such practices could certainly lead to reduced overall betweenness, but it must also be borne in mind that this will not necessarily lead to an overall decrease in crime: the volume of incidents may remain the same, and merely be less concentrated on some streets.

The study of crime using this framework is at a preliminary stage, and there remain significant unanswered questions that might be addressed in a future program of research. As well as examining whether other aspects of network structure can be reconciled with other phenomena or theoretical issues, there are also more subtle questions that can be asked. In our present study, for example, we have not considered temporal effects and worked with aggregated data throughout. It is clear, however, that the relationship between centrality and activity will not be constant across time: the majority of streets see little activity overnight regardless of their centrality, for example. Indeed, many of the arguments presented here are highly time-dependent, with guardianship being a particularly stark example. Furthermore, recent research by Bernasco et al. (2013) has demonstrated that individual-level differences in behavioral patterns can be highly predictive of criminal activity: the *diversity* of settings encountered by individuals is a significant factor in determining their delinquency, for example. This highlights the fluidity of awareness spaces, and implies that the function and social context of places are important considerations when assessing their criminal character. Again, further research is needed to unpick—and, in many cases, disaggregate—many of the phenomena referred to here.

In summary, this chapter has sought to provide an example of research that can be done on the street network using a mathematical approach. Our empirical results extend previous findings, and offer insight into the (relatively understudied) relationship between urban form and interpersonal crime. Significant scope remains for research into what is a fundamental issue for urban development, and it is hoped that further developments on this topic will follow in the coming years.

Acknowledgments

The authors wish to thank the Metropolitan Police Service for providing the recorded crime data analyzed in this chapter. We also acknowledge the financial support of the Engineering and Physical Sciences Research Council (EPSRC) under the project "Crime, Policing and Citizenship: Space-Time Interactions of Dynamic Networks" (reference EP/J004197/1).

References

Armitage, R. (2007). Sustainability versus safety: Confusion, conflict and contradiction in designing out crime. In G. Farrell, K. J. Bowers, S. D. Johnson, & M. Townsley (eds.) *Imagination for Crime Prevention: Essays in Honour of Ken Pease*, vol. 21 of *Crime Prevention Studies*, pp. 81–110. Monsey, NY: Criminal Justice Press.

Ashton, J., Brown, I., Senior, B., & Pease, K. (1998). Repeat victimisation: Offender accounts. *International Journal of Risk Security and Crime Prevention, 3*(4), 269–280.

Beavon, D. J. K., Brantingham, P. L., & Brantingham, P. J. (1994). The influence of street networks on the patterning of property offences. In R. V. Clarke (ed.) *Crime Prevention Studies*, vol. 2, pp. 115–148. Monsey, NY: Criminal Justice Press.

Bernasco, W., Bruinsma, G. J. N., Pauwels, L. J. R., & Weerman, F. M. (2013). Adolescent delinquency and diversity in behavior settings. *Australian and New Zealand Journal of Criminology, 46*(3), 357–378.

Bevis, C., & Nutter, J. (1977). *Changing Street Layouts to Reduce Residential Burglary.* Minneapolis: Minnesota Crime Prevention Center.

Blau, P. M. (1977). *Inequality and Heterogeneity: A Primitive Theory of Social Structure.* New York: Free Press.

Block, R. L., & Block, C. R. (1995). Space, place, and crime: Hot spot areas and hot places of liquor-related crime. In J. E. Eck & D. Weisburd (eds.) *Crime and Place*, vol. 4 of *Crime Prevention Studies*, pp. 145–183. Monsey, NY: Criminal Justice Press.

Bollobás, B. (2002). *Modern Graph Theory.* 2nd ed. New York: Springer.

Bowers, K. (2014). Risky facilities: Crime radiators or crime absorbers? A comparison of internal and external levels of theft. *Journal of Quantitative Criminology, 30*(3), 389–414.

Brantingham, P. L., & Brantingham, P. J. (1993). Environment, routine and situation: Toward a pattern theory of crime. In R. V. Clarke & M. Felson (eds.) *Routine Activity and Rational Choice*, vol. 5 of *Advances in Criminological Theory*, pp. 259–294. New Brunswick, NJ: Transaction.

Cohen, L. E., & Felson, M. (1979). Social change and crime rate trends: A routine activity approach. *American Sociological Review, 44*(4), 588–608.

Cromwell, P. F., Olson, J. N., & Avary, D. W. (1991). *Breaking and Entering: An Ethnographic Analysis of Burglary*, vol. 8 of *Studies in Crime, Law and Justice.* Newbury Park, CA: Sage.

Crucitti, P., Latora, V., & Porta, S. (2006). Centrality measures in spatial networks of urban streets. *Physical Review E, 73*(3), 036125.

Davies, T., & Johnson, S. D. (2014). Examining the relationship between road structure and burglary risk via quantitative network analysis. *Journal of Quantitative Criminology, 31*(3), 481–507.

Diestel, R. (2010). *Graph Theory.* Graduate Texts in Mathematics No. 173. Heidelberg: Springer.

Farrington, D. P. (1986). Age and crime. *Crime and Justice, 7*, 189–250.

Gini, C. (1921). Measurement of inequality of incomes. *Economic Journal, 31*(121), 124–126.

Hillier, B. (1996). *Space Is the Machine.* Cambridge: Cambridge University Press.

Hillier, B. (2004). Can streets be made safe? *Urban Design International, 9*(1), 31–45.

Homel, R., McIlwain, G., & Carvolth, R. (2001). Creating safer drinking environments. In N. Heather, T. J. Peters, & T. Stockwell (eds.) *International Handbook of Alcohol Dependence and Problems*, pp. 721–740. Chichester: John Wiley & Sons.

Jacobs, J. (1961). *The Life and Death of Great American Cities.* New York: Random House.

Jiang, B., & Claramunt, C. (2004). A structural approach to the model generalization of an urban street network. *GeoInformatica, 8*(2), 157–171.

Johnson, S. D., & Bowers, K. J. (2010). Permeability and burglary risk: Are cul-de-sacs safer? *Journal of Quantitative Criminology, 26*(1), 89–111.

Lagesse, C., Bordin, P., & Douady, S. (2015). A spatial multi-scale object to analyze road networks. *Network Science, 3* (Special Issue 01), 156–181.

Loeber, R., Menting, B., Lynam, D. R., Moffitt, T. E., Stouthamer-Loeber, M., Stallings, R., Farrington, D. P., & Pardini, D. (2012). Findings from the Pittsburgh Youth Study: Cognitive impulsivity and intelligence as predictors of the age-crime curve. *Journal of the American Academy of Child and Adolescent Psychiatry, 51*(11), 1136–1149.

Louf, R., & Barthelemy, M. (2014). A typology of street patterns. *Journal of the Royal Society Interface, 11*(101), 20140924.

Mawby, R. I. (1977). Defensible space: A theoretical and empirical appraisal. *Urban Studies, 14*(2), 169–179.

McCord, E. S., & Ratcliffe, J. H. (2007). A micro-spatial analysis of the demographic and criminogenic environment of drug markets in Philadelphia. *Australian and New Zealand Journal of Criminology, 40*(1), 43–63.

McCutcheon, J. C., Weaver, G. S., Huff-Corzine, L., Corzine, J., & Burraston, B. (2016). Highway robbery: Testing the impact of interstate highways on robbery. *Justice Quarterly, 33*(7), 1292–1310.

Newman, M. (2010). *Networks: An Introduction*. Oxford: Oxford University Press.

Newman, O. (1972). *Defensible Space: Crime Prevention through Urban Design*. New York: Macmillan.

Porta, S., Crucitti, P., & Latora, V. (2006a). The network analysis of urban streets: A dual approach. *Physica A: Statistical Mechanics and its Applications, 369*(2), 853–866.

Porta, S., Crucitti, P., & Latora, V. (2006b). The network analysis of urban streets: A primal approach. *Environment and Planning B: Planning and Design, 33*(5), 705–725.

Ratti, C. (2004). Space syntax: Some inconsistencies. *Environment and Planning B: Planning and Design, 31*(4), 487–499.

Reynald, D. M. (2010). Guardians on guardianship: Factors affecting the willingness to supervise, the ability to detect potential offenders, and the willingness to intervene. *Journal of Research in Crime and Delinquency, 47*(3), 358–390.

Reynald, D. M. (2011) *Guarding against Crime: Measuring Guardianship Within Routine Activity Theory*. London: Routledge.

Reynald, D. M., & Elffers, H. (2009). The future of Newman's defensible space theory: Linking defensible space and the routine activities of place. *European Journal of Criminology, 6*(1), 25–46.

Sampson, R. J., & Raudenbush, S. W. (1999). Systematic social observation of public spaces: A new look at disorder in urban neighborhoods. *American Journal of Sociology, 105*(3), 603–651.

Sampson, R. J., Raudenbush, S. W., & Earls, F. (1997). Neighborhoods and violent crime: A multilevel study of collective efficacy. *Science, 277*(5328), 918–924.

Simpson, E. H. (1949). Measurement of diversity. *Nature, 163*, 688.

Steenbeek, W., & Weisburd, D. (2015). Where the action is in crime? An examination of variability of crime across different spatial units in The Hague, 2001–2009. *Journal of Quantitative Criminology, 32*(3), 449–469.

Tarling, R., & Morris, K. (2010). Reporting crime to the police. *British Journal of Criminology, 50*(3), 474–490.

Townsley, M., & Sidebottom, A. (2010). All offenders are equal, but some are more equal than others: Variation in journeys to crime between offenders. *Criminology, 48*(3), 897–917.

Weisburd, D. (2015). The law of crime concentration and the criminology of place. *Criminology, 53*(2), 133–157.

Weisburd, D., Groff, E. R., & Yang, S.-M. (2012). *The Criminology of Place*. Oxford: Oxford University Press.

White, G. F. (1990). Neighborhood permeability and burglary rates. *Justice Quarterly, 7*(1), 57–67.

Places

CHAPTER 25

CRIME CONCENTRATIONS AT PLACES

CODY W. TELEP AND DAVID WEISBURD

25.1 Introduction

Crime is not distributed geographically at random. The idea that crime concentrates is not a new one. As Eck and Weisburd (1995: 12) note in their chapter on theories of crime and place, "Crime events are not uniformly distributed, a fact known for over a century. At every level of aggregation, some geographic areas have less crime than others." This has been demonstrated historically at multiple levels of geography ranging from entire nations down to neighborhoods (Weisburd, Bernasco, and Bruinsma, 2009). Indeed, the idea that crime concentrates would not be surprising to the average citizen with no background in geography or criminology. Residents will often characterize some locations or neighborhoods as "good" and others as "bad," in part because of their level of criminal activity.

Our focus here, though, is not simply on the idea that crime concentrates. The past 30 years have seen major advances in environmental criminology and our understanding of the distribution of crime at place. A series of studies we review in this chapter suggest not only that crime is highly concentrated, but that crime is particularly concentrated at very small units of geography. Places in this "micro" context are specific locations within the larger social environments of communities and neighborhoods (Eck and Weisburd, 1995). They can range in size from addresses, to street segments (i.e., both sides of a street block between two intersections), to small groups of connected street blocks, but they are all much smaller than neighborhoods or communities that have traditionally been the focus of scholars interested in crime and place (Weisburd, Bernasco, and Bruinsma, 2009).

A focus on these small units of geography with high levels of criminal activity has a number of potential theoretical and practical benefits. While other chapters in this volume focus in particular on theory in environmental criminology, we discuss the importance of theory both in terms of guiding our understanding of why crime is so highly concentrated and in thinking about ways to apply what we know about the criminology of places to future theory building.

Practically, the strong concentration of crime at place has important implications for the distribution of police and other public safety resources. The places where crime is most highly concentrated are typically referred to as crime hotspots (Sherman and Weisburd, 1988; 1995). These small geographic areas with high levels of criminal activity (typically measured by crime incidents or emergency calls for service) relative to other places in the city have been the focus of a series of interventions to target police presence, enforcement, and activity. Hotspots policing has shown success in reducing crime in a number of rigorous trials (for a review see Braga, Papachristos, and Hureau, 2014).

The findings of remarkable concentration of crime at place raise a more general question about the dynamics of crime in cities. The consistent evidence that crime concentrates at very small units of geography has recently led Weisburd (2015) to propose a law of crime concentration at place (see also Weisburd, Groff, and Yang, 2012). Based on empirical knowledge to date, Weisburd (2015) argues it is reasonable to assume that levels of crime concentration will be fairly consistent across time and jurisdictions.

In the sections that follow, we discuss Weisburd's law of crime concentration in more detail before turning to a review of the studies offering support for this law. The evidence in this area dates to back to the late 1980s, but has grown exponentially in recent years with examples from across the United States and increasingly in international contexts as well. To reinforce the explosion of new research in this area, we completed a shorter recent review of the crime concentration literature (see Weisburd and Telep, 2014) that has quickly become outdated. We update that review here, drawing upon Weisburd's (2015) Sutherland Award address and a chapter on crime concentration in Weisburd et al.'s (2016) volume on the criminology of place. After reviewing the empirical evidence for the law of crime concentration, we address key questions in the criminology of places, focusing in particular on some of the reasons why crime is so highly concentrated, before concluding with calls for future research to further expand the scope of our knowledge about crime and microunits of geography.

25.2 The Law of Crime Concentration

Is there some general law that applies across cities that dictates the general concentration of crime? This is the question initially examined by Weisburd, Groff, and Yang (2012) and discussed more comprehensively by Weisburd (2015). The idea of a "law" related to crime, just like discussions of the distribution of crime, is not a new one. Emile Durkheim raised this possibility more than a century ago, when he suggested that crime was not indicative of pathology or illness in society, but at certain levels was simply evidence of the normal functioning of communities (Durkheim, 1893 [1964], 1895 [1964]).

For Durkheim, the idea of a normal level of crime reinforced his theoretical position that crime helped to define and solidify norms in society.

A normal level of crime would suggest year-to-year stability in crime rates within cities. The experience of most cities, particularly in the United States, over the last three decades offers little support for this proposition. Crime generally showed major upticks in the late 1980s and 1990s and then substantial declines in the mid-1990s with decreases (albeit of lesser magnitude) continuing in most cities through the first decade of the 2000s (see Baumer and Wolff, 2014; Zimring, 2007). While the absolute levels of crime in cities vary year to year, Weisburd et al. (2012) and Weisburd (2015) point to the similarity in levels of *crime concentration* both within and across jurisdictions.

Weisburd (2015: 138) argues that there is a law of crime concentration that states, "For a defined measure of crime at a specific microgeographic unit, the concentration of crime will fall within a narrow bandwidth of percentages for a defined cumulative proportion of crime." Thus, the law recognizes that the level of concentration might vary based on the measure of crime employed (e.g., all crime vs. violent crime) and the particular small geographic unit specified (e.g., addresses vs. street segments vs. small collections of street blocks). When comparing similar measures of crime and similar geographic units, the law of crime concentration predicts a narrow range in the percentage of units that contain a particular proportion of crime (e.g., 50%) across jurisdictions and contexts.

Weisburd (2015: 150) presents the law of crime concentration not simply to highlight its empirical novelty. Instead, he views the law as an important basis for moving theory and crime control policy forward, calling for a "turning point in the life course of criminology" and a refocus from the traditional criminological emphasis on individuals and larger units of geography to a greater concern with microunits of geography. This emphasis on the microcontext of crime and its control has also been the focus of environmental criminology. Much of the important theoretical and practical work in this area is reviewed in earlier chapters in this volume. Here, we discuss empirical support for the law of crime concentration, including evidence from the eight cities discussed by Weisburd (2015), before turning to a discussion of the law's potential impacts on theory and practice.

25.3 Empirical Examples

We have alluded to a growing body of empirical research from the last 30 years that provides strong support for the law of crime concentration. Here we review a series of studies offering evidence for the law across a variety of geographic contexts and crime types. There is some variability in how different studies have addressed the question of crime concentration. Some have focused on an aggregate measure of total crime (e.g., Weisburd et al., 2004), while others have looked at specific types of crime (e.g., Braga, Papachristos, and Hureau, 2010). There is also variation in the temporal scope of these studies with some using a single year of crime data (e.g., Sherman, 1987; Sherman, Gartin, and Buerger, 1989), and others amassing longitudinal data sets (e.g., Weisburd, Groff, and Yang, 2012; Wheeler, Worden, and McLean, 2016). We divide our discussion below based on geographic context by first examining work focusing on the concentration of crime in North American cities in the United States and Canada, before turning to similar examinations in a growing number of cities around the world.

25.3.1 Concentration of Crime in North American Cities

One of the most important early studies in this area was Sherman, Gartin, and Buerger's (1989) analysis of emergency calls for service to addresses over a single year (December 1985–December 1986; see also Sherman, 1987). Sherman et al. (1989) found that only 3.3% of the addresses in Minneapolis, Minnesota produced just over 50% of all emergency calls to the police. If crime were randomly distributed across the 115,000 addresses in Minneapolis, one would not expect any places to have 15 or more calls in a single year. Instead, Sherman and colleagues (1989) found 3,841 such addresses, indicating that crime is far more concentrated than would be expected by chance. Almost 40% of addresses did not experience a single call during the year. When examining particular types of crime, Sherman et al. found even stronger evidence of concentration. The 54 addresses (about 0.05% of the total addresses in the city) that had at least 10 calls for service for public predatory crime (a combination of robbery, auto theft, and rape) were responsible for over 7.5% of all such calls.

Pierce and colleagues (1988) found almost identical results when examining crime call concentrations in Boston, Massachusetts. In their analyses of data from 1977 to 1982, they found that the 3.6% of addresses averaging 20 or more calls per year were responsible for 50.1% of the total demand for police services. The 0.1% of street addresses that averaged 150 or more calls per year were responsible for 9.4% of total calls.

Weisburd, Maher, and Sherman (1992) examined the distribution of crime in Minneapolis when aggregating address-level data for a subsequent year (June 1987–June 1988) to crime hotspots of about one street block in length. Examining blocks with at least 20 hard-crime (i.e., serious violent and property crime) calls for service, they found 365 hotspots in the city, which represented about 2.5% of the street segments in Minneapolis. These streets accounted for 27.3% of all hard-crime calls for service in the city. These streets also accounted for 27.8% of soft crime (i.e., disorder) calls for service across the one-year period. Overall then, whether examining individual addresses or clusters of high-crime addresses, crime was highly concentrated at a small number of places.

Spelman (1995) was among the first to explicitly focus on longitudinal trends in crime. He examined calls for service at schools, public housing projects, subway stations, and parks and playgrounds longitudinally in Boston. He found evidence of a high degree of stability of crime at the "worst" of these places over a three-year period. While the top 10% of public places in terms of crime were responsible for about 30% of calls for service, he noted that "much of the concentration of crime among locations is due to random and temporary fluctuations that are beyond the power of the police and the public to control reliably" (Spelman, 1995: 142). Thus, even though many of the highest-crime places remained high crime, some of the change over time reflected random variation, an issue we revisit below in suggesting the importance of longitudinal approaches to the study of crime at place. Despite these cautions, Spelman (1995) still advocated for efforts such as community problem-solving to address underlying problems at persistent high-crime locations.

Two studies in Seattle, Washington, have examined the distribution of crime at street segments using a much longer time series than was available in earlier studies. Weisburd et al. (2004) not only confirmed the concentration of crime found in studies from the 1980s and 1990s, but also the stability of such concentrations across a long time span. Weisburd et al. (2004) examined crime incidents at street blocks from 1989 to 2002. They found that 50% of crime incidents over the 14-year period occurred at between 4% and 5% of the street segments each year, suggesting a remarkable degree of stability in overall concentration year to year.

Group-based trajectory models also suggested a generally stable trend in the majority of street segments over the 14-year time series. More than 80% of streets were in a trajectory group with generally stable trends longitudinally, while smaller percentages showed increasing trends (about 2%) and decreasing trends (about 14%). These findings suggested that not only is crime highly concentrated, but also low-crime places generally remain low crime, and high-crime street segments are typically repeatedly responsible for a disproportionate share of the city's crime problem. The streets with decreasing and increasing trajectories provide further evidence for thinking small when we consider the geography of crime. Between 1989 and 2002, the total number of incidents in Seattle declined about 24%. The trajectory analysis made clear that the citywide overall crime decline was not a result of uniform drops in crime across the city. Indeed, for the 2.1% of street segments with increasing trajectories, crime actually went up during this period of substantial decline at the city and national levels.

Weisburd, Groff, and Yang (2012) updated and expanded these analyses, examining crime incidents at street segments in Seattle from 1989 to 2004 using a more precise definition of street segments.[1] They again found that crime was highly concentrated, and these concentrations remained fairly stable across the 16-year study period. They found that each year 50% of crime incidents occurred on between 4.7% and 6.1% of street segments. All crime was found on around 60% of street segments each year, suggesting that about 40% of street segments recorded no crime each year in Seattle. The 247 highest-crime street segments, about 1% of the total in Seattle, were responsible for over 23% of crime incidents across the study year period. Weisburd et al.'s (2012) trajectory analyses tell a story similar to the Weisburd et al. (2004) findings. The majority of streets show relative stability in their year-to-year crime incident counts, providing further evidence of both the concentration of crime and its stability longitudinally.

Weisburd, Telep, and Lawton (2014) also found high rates of concentration when examining crime incidents in New York City in a two-year period (2009 and 2010).

About 77% of total incidents were geocoded to street segments. Approximately 52% of the incidents on street segments were found in the top 5% of street segments both years. Just under a quarter of crime incidents were found at 1% of the street segments. Similar concentrations were found when examining incidents geocoded to intersections. About half of incidents at intersections were found at the top 5% of the intersections, while slightly more than 20% were found at the top 1% of intersections. Between 55% and 60% of the street segments and intersections each year had no crime incidents.

Martin Andresen and colleagues have examined the concentration of crime in the Canadian context. Andresen and Malleson (2011) examined the distribution of calls for service for seven offense types in Vancouver, British Columbia, in 1991, 1996, and 2001. They found that for each crime type, 50% of calls were found on between about 1% and 8% of street segments. In examining stability over time, Andresen and Malleson (2011: 72) emphasize the importance of looking at the spatial dynamics of crime using small units of geography. As they note, "A *small* number of 'chronic' street segments dictate the results for the entire dissemination area or census tract much like a small number of chronic offenders can dictate the results for a larger set of individuals" (Andresen and Malleson, 2011: 72).

Andresen and Linning (2012) also report very high levels of concentration when examining one year of crime data from Ottawa, Canada. In examining all robberies, commercial and residential break-ins, and theft of vehicles, they found just 1.7% of street segments were responsible for 50% of crime. All of these offenses were found on only 9.5% of total street blocks. Using a year of data from Vancouver, all assaults, burglaries, robberies, sexual assaults, and thefts were found on 5.02% of street segments, suggesting less concentration than in Ottawa, but still evidence of crime being highly spatially concentrated.

More recently, Curman, Andresen, and Brantingham (2015) built on Andresen and Malleson's (2011) findings using 16 years of street-block level crime data on 22 index offenses in Vancouver. They found strong evidence of concentration, with only 7.8% of streets responsible for 50% of all criminal activity. Using trajectory analysis, they found a generally similar story to the Weisburd et al. (2012) analyses. More than 70% of streets were in largely stable trajectories that generally showed low levels of crime across the 16-year period. The remaining four trajectory groups all showed a decreasing trend and were largely responsible for the 40% crime decline during the study period. Each year, about 40% of street segments did not experience any index crime calls for service.

Further recent support for the law of crime concentration comes from Wheeler, Worden, and McLean (2016), who replicated the work of Weisburd et al. (2004) and Curman et al. (2015) in Albany, New York, using incident data from 2000 to 2013. About 44% of street units (segments or intersection) in the city experienced at least one crime during the 14-year period. Their findings add further support to the idea that microplace crime trends are generally stable over time. While they found a larger percentage of street units contributed to the crime drop in Albany than in Seattle, their trajectory analysis also suggested a great deal of year-to-year stability, particularly among the highest-crime street units. As Wheeler et al. (2016: 606) conclude: "That higher-crime micro places tend to remain higher-crime micro places in Albany, Seattle, and Vancouver supports the hypothesis that crime and place are tightly coupled together."

Gill, Wooditch, and Groff (2017) came to a similar conclusion using data from a suburban jurisdiction. Crime incidents were highly concentrated in Brooklyn Park, Minnesota, a city of approximately 78,000 people near Minneapolis. From 2000 to 2013, just 2% of street segments housed 50% of all crime incidents, suggesting even greater concentration than in larger cities. A quarter of all crime was found on just 0.4% of street segments. Trajectory analyses, as in other cities, suggested general year-to-year stability in crime across most street segments, with a small percentage of streets responsible for the citywide drop in crime.

Weisburd (2015) examined the extent of concentration in eight cities, using total crime incidents and the street segment as the unit of analysis for each. Across all eight jurisdictions, he found strong support for the idea that the percentage of street segments responsible for 50% of total incidents would fall into a fairly narrow bandwidth. He used the Seattle data described above, data from New York City spanning nine years, as well as crime incident data from three other large cities: Sacramento, California; Cincinnati, Ohio; and Tel Aviv–Yafo, Israel. In all five larger cities, 50% of crime was found on between 4.2% (Sacramento) and 6.0% (Cincinnati) of street segments. In Brooklyn Park and two other smaller cities (Redlands, California, and Ventura, California), there was evidence of even stronger concentration, with 50% of crime located on between 2.1% (Brooklyn Park and Redlands) and 3.5% (Ventura) of street blocks.

For half of these cities, Weisburd (2015) also had data to examine trends in concentration longitudinally. We have already discussed the consistency in crime concentration in Seattle and Brooklyn Park. The other cities where longitudinal data were available showed similar consistency in the year-to-year concentration of crime incidents. In New York City, for example, between 2004 and 2012, half of crime was found on between 4.7% and 6.0% of street segments annually.

A series of largely recent studies have also focused on the concentration of particular types of crime, generally finding even stronger evidence that crime is highly concentrated at a small number of microunits. Weisburd and Mazerolle (2000), for example, examined the number of calls for service in 56 drug hotspots in Jersey City, New Jersey, that made up about 4.4% of the street segments and intersection in the city. About half (47%) of both narcotics arrests and calls for service were found in these hotspots, suggesting the strong concentration of drug activity in Jersey City.

More recently, Hibdon and Groff (2014) examined the concentration of drug activity in Seattle in 2004 relying on both police incident data and drug-related emergency medical services calls (e.g., those related to drug overdoses). They found strong evidence of concentration in both data sets, with 50% of police drug incidents found on just 0.7% of streets and half of emergency medical service calls for drug-related activity on only 1.2% of Seattle streets. Hibdon and Groff (2014) did not, however, find strong evidence that these concentrations were colocated on the same street segments, suggesting the value of using multiple data sources to understand the concentration of drug activity.

Hibdon, Telep, and Groff (2017) expanded on these findings, examining five years of drug and alcohol data in Seattle from both police calls and emergency medical services calls. Like Hibdon and Groff (2014) they also found evidence of drug activity being highly concentrated, with a narrow band of concentration across the five-year period. Fifty percent of police drug-related calls, for example, were found on between 0.4% and 0.7% of street segments between 2009 and 2014.

Using group-based trajectory analysis, they found a great degree of year-to-year stability in drug activity in most Seattle street blocks, which is in line with Weisburd et al.'s (2012) findings about crime more generally. Hibdon et al. (2017) see evidence of some street segments with less consistent trends longitudinally, with small numbers showing sharp upticks or downturns in call volume. In comparing the year-to-year colocation of drug activity as identified by the police to drug activity from emergency medical services data, they found only limited evidence of spatial overlap between the two data sources.

This suggests the benefit of using multiple data sources to acquire a fuller picture of the scope of the drug problem. Police data provide important insights into the concentration of drug crime or crime more generally, but on its own may not provide a full picture of the extent and distribution of harm caused by drug use (see Ratcliffe, 2015). Particularly for crime types, such as drug activity, where concentrations may reflect both use/distribution patterns and police preferences and priorities in enforcement, additional sources of data could be useful in appropriately focusing governmental resources to reduce crime and harm.

Ariel, Weinborn, and Boyle (2015) similarly made use of alternative data sources in assessing the concentration of crime and related activity. They examined one year of data on assaults from both the police and ambulance emergency calls in Peterborough, England, finding evidence of concentration in both data sets. About 52% of police assault incidents were found in just 29 200-meter radius hotspots, which made up just 1.1% of the city. Similarly, 61.8% of ambulance calls related to assaults were found in just 28 200-meter radius hotspots. Interestingly though, these hotspots were not all colocated. They estimated an average overlap of 50% between police and ambulance hotspots, suggesting a substantial share of assault problem locations are not necessarily the focus of police activity.

In an effort to better understand the spatial dynamics of juvenile crime, Weisburd, Morris, and Groff (2009) examined the concentration of crime incidents in which a juvenile was arrested in Seattle. They relied on arrests largely because suspect age is not always reported in incident reports, especially for incidents in which a suspect is not identified. They found even stronger levels of concentration than for crime incidents more generally. Less than 1% of street segments were responsible for 50% of juvenile arrest incidents each year from 1989 to 2002. Only 86 street segments accounted for one-third of all official juvenile arrest incidents over the 14-year period.

Anthony Braga and colleagues also found strong evidence of concentration when examining longitudinal incident data for particular crime types in Boston. Braga,

Papachristos, and Hureau (2010) found that just 4.8% of the street segments were the site of 73.9% of all gun assaults over a 29-year period. Close to 89% of street segments and intersections never experienced a firearm assault between 1980 and 2008. In examining stability over time, they find that only about 3% of streets and intersections showed volatility over time, suggesting that the rise of gun violence in the late 1980s and 1990s and then subsequent downturn in later years was driven largely by a very small number of microplaces in the city.

Braga, Hureau, and Papachristos (2011) examined the concentration of robbery incidents at street segments and intersections in Boston from 1980 to 2008. Each year, about 2% of street units accounted for 50% of the robbery incidents in the city. The top 52 street units, which represented just 0.18% of total units in the city, were responsible for 10,886 of the 135,276 robberies (8.0%) over the 29-year period. Commercial robberies were even more highly concentrated than street robberies. From 1980 to 2008, just 1.3% of street segments were responsible for about half of commercial robberies.

Andresen and colleagues have also recently examined the distribution of particular crime types in Vancouver. Andresen, Curman, and Linning (2017) found strong evidence of concentration when examining specific property and violent crime types in Vancouver. Trajectory analyses by crime type suggested general stability longitudinally, but also some variability by crime type. In most cases, a very small number of microplaces drove citywide trends in a particular crime type. Andresen, Linning, and Malleson (2017) also found high levels of concentration when focusing specifically on property crime types. Overall, between 3.6% and 4.5% of street segments and intersections were responsible for 50% of total commercial burglary, theft from vehicle, theft of vehicle, and criminal mischief calls between 2003 and 2013 (see also Andresen and Malleson, 2011).

Vaughan and colleagues (2016) examined the spatial distribution of calls for service related to emotionally disturbed persons in an unnamed midsized Canadian city. They found that about 50% of total calls for service in a one-year period were concentrated at about 3.4% of street segments, again suggesting strong evidence of concentration. All calls were highly concentrated, with just 7.8% of streets having any calls. When they examined only those calls related to persons with emotional distress, 50% of such calls were found on only 1.2% of street blocks. Interestingly, the spatial patterning of calls involving an emotionally distressed person differed from all other calls, suggesting that calls related to mental health in particular may be concentrated in different locations than calls for criminal activity.

25.3.2 Concentration of Crime outside of North America

Recent place-based research from non–North American contexts is also supportive of the law of crime concentration. We noted earlier that Weisburd (2015) found a high degree of concentration when examining crime incidents over a 20-year period in Tel Aviv–Jaffa (see also Weisburd and Amram, 2014). More recently, de

Melo, Matias, and Andresen (2015) studied the concentration of crime at place in Campinas, Brazil, focusing in particular on robbery and theft. Using data from 2010–2013, they found evidence that crime is even more highly concentrated in Brazil than in most prior North American studies. As in many prior studies, 50% of all crime was found at 3.66% of the 49,173 total street segments. But 100% of total crime was found at just 28.69% of street blocks. All robberies were found on just 13.26% of streets.

Mazeika and Kumar (2017) examined the concentration of motor vehicle theft and burglary incidents in 2009 and 2010 in two stations in Jaipur, India. In a geographic context very different from most American cities, they still found evidence that these offenses are concentrated. Unlike most large American cities, Jaipur does not have a grid-style street pattern, making it infeasible to use street segments as the unit of analysis. The city also has few arterial roads. Additionally, the city's more informal zoning regulations than most American cities leads to less clearly defined residential versus commercial areas. Using 100- by 100-square-meter grid cells, they find strong evidence of clustering. About 43.5% of motor vehicle theft was concentrated at 1.89% of the land covered by these two stations. Burglary, which occurred less commonly, was even more concentrated, with 0.33% of land containing 21.1% of all burglaries. Using nearest neighborhood hierarchical clustering, Mazeika and Kumar (2017) identified hotspots for both burglary and motor vehicle theft that also demonstrated clustering. For example, just 0.09% of the land made up five motor vehicle theft hotspots that were responsible for 13.12% of all offenses.

Steenbeek and Weisburd (2016) assessed the extent to which the concentration of crime is a micro-level (i.e., street segment) phenomenon. Using crime data from 2001 to 2009 in The Hague, the Netherlands, they found evidence that crime is concentrated, although at the 50% level crime was somewhat less concentrated than in many US cities examined. In 2009, for example, 50% of all crime was found on 6.8% of street segments. Similar to other cities, close to half of street segments did not experience any crime incidents each year. They found further evidence for the importance of focusing on microplaces rather than exclusively larger units of geography when examining variability in crime. When partitioning the variance in crime across different-sized geographic units, differences in crime at the street-segment level were responsible for about 62% of the total variance. Neighborhoods, on average, were responsible for a small (6%) portion of the total variance, while about 32% of the variance could be attributed to districts (aggregations of a few nearby neighborhoods). This suggests that criminologists should not ignore larger units of geography in understanding crime distributions, but reinforces the amount of information on crime concentration that would be missed with a focus exclusively on neighborhoods or other more meso- or macro-level places. Very similar conclusions were reached by Gerell (2017) in an analysis of arson incidents in Malmö, Sweden. Schnell, Braga, and Piza (2017) similarly found the majority of variability in violent crime in Chicago, Illinois, between 2001 and 2014 was at the street segment level.

25.3.3 Summary

Overall, we find strong support for Weisburd's (2015) law of crime concentration at places across a range of outcomes, time periods, and geographic contexts. In Table 25.1, we provide a summary of the empirical evidence we reviewed above, focusing on studies that examined total crime and provided a measure of percentage of geographic units responsible for 50% of crime (or in some instances approximately 50% of crime). While we see variability across studies in Table 25.1, there is overall a narrow bandwidth for the percentage of streets or addresses responsible for 50% of crime.

Table 25.1 Summary of Crime Concentration Studies That Report on 50% Concentration for Total Crime

Study	Location	Microplace	Time	Outcome	50% concentration
Sherman (1987); Sherman et al. (1989)	Minneapolis, MN	Address	1986	Calls	3.3% (50.4%)
Pierce et al. (1988)	Boston, MA	Address	1977–1982	Calls	3.6% (50.1%)
Weisburd et al. (2004)	Seattle, WA	100 block	1989–2002	Incidents	4%–5%
Andresen and Linning (2012)	Ottawa, ON Vancouver, BC	Street segment Street segment	2006 2001	Incidents Calls	1.7% 5.0%
Weisburd et al. (2012)	Seattle, WA	Street segment	1989–2004	Incidents	4.7–6.1%
Weisburd and Amram (2014)	Tel Aviv–Yafo, Israel	Street segment	2010	Incident	4.5%
Weisburd et al. (2014)	New York, NY	Street segment/ intersection	2009–2010	Incidents	5% (50.8–52.6%)
Curman et al. (2015)	Vancouver, BC	Street segment	1991–2006	Index crime calls	7.8%
de Melo et al. (2015)	Campinas, Brazil	Street segment	2010–2013	Incidents	3.7%
Weisburd (2015)	5 large cities	Street segment	Varies (1989–2012)	Incidents	4.2%–6.0%
Weisburd (2015)	3 small cities	Street segment	Varies (2000–2013)	Incidents	2.1%–3.5%
Steenbeek and Weisburd (2016)	The Hague, Netherlands	Street segment	2001–2009	Incidents	6.3%–7.3%
Andresen et al. (2017)	Vancouver, BC	Street segment/ intersection	1991–2006	Index crime calls	3.3–4.4%
Gill et al. (2017)	Brooklyn Park, MN	Street segment	2000–2014	Incidents	2%

25.4 Key Questions for the Criminology of Places

In the sections that follow, we address some key questions related to the criminology of places and areas where future research is needed.

25.4.1 Are Small Units of Analysis Really Better?

An important question in examining the concentration of crime at microunits of geography is whether these concentrations simply reflect more macro-level trends. In other words, if the microunits where crime is highly concentrated are all located in particular neighborhoods or communities, then focusing on these larger units may be just as useful (and would allow for the integration of crime data with census data on sociodemographic characteristics that are not available at micro geographic units, at least in the United States). We have already reviewed some evidence suggesting that the concentration of microplaces reflects real differences at this unit of geography and not just larger-level trends (Steenbeek and Weisburd, 2016; Schnell et al., 2017).

In a series of analyses, Weisburd and colleagues (2012) also found that the microplace concentrations in Seattle were not just proxies for neighborhood-level effects (see also Groff, Weisburd, and Yang, 2010). While they did find some evidence of larger area effects in their analyses and some clustering of high-crime streets, particularly in the central business district, their overall conclusion was that there is a great deal of street-by-street heterogeneity in crime patterns. In other words, crime hotspots can be found throughout the city, and there is a great deal of variability street-to-street within both "good" and "bad" neighborhoods.

Thus, there is evidence that neighborhoods and larger units of geography play a role in the distribution of crime; the environmental backcloth matters in understanding why crime is concentrated in particular places (Deryol et al., 2016). An exclusive focus on larger geographic units, however, would miss much of the variability at the street or microplace level. Future research, though, should further examine the dynamics of crime at different levels of geography to further unpack the contribution of place-, neighborhood-, and jurisdiction-based factors to the concentration of crime.

25.4.2 What about Offenders?

Our focus here has been on the concentration of crime at particular places. This is not to suggest that people are not an important part of the crime equation. We discuss the concentration of targets and victims below as one explanation for the concentration of crime. Another question that can be raised about the criminology of places is its practical usefulness relative to a focus on high-rate offenders. Beginning with Wolfgang, Figlio, and Sellin's (1972) pioneering work, there is strong evidence that crime is also highly concentrated among a small number of offenders. Wolfgang and colleagues found that 6% of the individuals in a Philadelphia, Pennsylvania, birth cohort were responsible for 52% of the total offenses committed by the entire cohort by age 17. There is no doubt that offending (as well as victimization; see Farrell, 2015 and the volume edited by Farrell and Pease, 2001) is concentrated among a small group of individuals.

There are few direct comparisons of the extent to which crime is concentrated among offenders versus places. Sherman (1995: 36–37) argued that the clustering of crime at places is even greater than the concentration of crime among individuals. Comparing the concentration of calls in Minneapolis to the concentration of offending in the Philadelphia birth cohort study (see Wolfgang et al., 1972), he noted that future crime is "six times more predictable by the address of the occurrence than by the identity of the offender." Sherman (1995: 37) asked, "Why aren't we thinking more about wheredunit, rather than just whodunit?" Weisburd (2008: 5) argued similarly regarding longitudinal data in Seattle. He found that on average about 1,500 street segments accounted for 50% of the crime each year. During the same period about 6,108 offenders were responsible for 50% of the crime annually. Thus, the police would have to approach four times as many targets to identify the same level of overall crime when they focus on people as opposed to places.

This focus on places also aligns with the policing evaluation literature, which suggests police can be especially effective in reducing crime when they narrow their focus to hotspots (see Braga et al., 2014; Lum, Koper, and Telep, 2011). Place-based policing has proven to be an effective and efficient strategy for police, but also does not preclude a focus on chronic offenders. Recent hotspots policing work, for example, has also used intelligence to focus on high-rate offenders operating within hotspots, or in other words to target "hot" people offending in "hot" places (see Groff et al., 2015).

25.4.3 Why Is Crime So Concentrated?

Why is criminal activity so highly concentrated at a small number of places? We review a number of possible explanations below, recognizing that research on this question remains limited.

The concentration of crime follows patterns of concentration in many other areas of scientific inquiry (e.g., see Eck, Clarke, and Guerette, 2007; Koch, 1999; Sherman, 2007). Juran (1951) first noted this concentration in looking at economic activities, coining the phrase "the vital few and the trivial many." Juran sought to emphasize to managers that they should focus on the small number of events or cases that produce the majority of relevant business activities, for example, the small number of defects that cause most complaints about products, or the small number of clients that are responsible for the majority of revenue. Juran termed this phenomenon the "Pareto Principle" after Vilfredo Pareto (1909), who first brought attention to what is sometimes referred to as the 80-20 rule (see Koch, 1999). Pareto observed that a number of distributions seem to follow this specific pattern of concentration. For example, in studying landownership in Italy he found that 80% of the land was controlled by just 20% of the population. He also observed that 20% of the pea pods in his garden produced 80% of the peas.

The 80-20 rule is generally seen as only an approximation, but it applies fairly well to the crime concentrations we have reviewed above. In Seattle, for example, 80% of the crime incidents each year were found on between 19% and 23% of the street segments (Weisburd et al., 2012). Of course, this just provides evidence that the concentration of crime follows concentration in a number of arenas, but it does not offer insight into why crime is so highly concentrated.

One statistical issue concerns the number of offenses occurring at microplaces, particularly when examining specific crime types. Some offenses are fairly uncommon, even when looking at longer time spans, and so some degree of concentration is inevitable (Andresen and Linning, 2012). De Melo et al. (2015), for example, recognize that while total crime could theoretically appear on 100% of streets, most other crime types would show at least some level of concentration, because there were fewer offenses than street segments. Even so, they found evidence of greater concentration than would be expected from a random distribution of events. Vehicle theft was uncommon enough that at most 13.99% of street segments could be responsible for all vehicle theft incidents. The actual concentration was 8.56%, suggesting that vehicle theft showed evidence of concentration, but also reinforcing the importance of considering the inherent concentration that will occur when examining the distribution of rare events.

This relates to Spelman's (1995) explanations for the appearance of hotspots and their long-term sustainability. As Spelman (1995) argues, and recent research suggests (see Gorr and Lee, 2015), not all hotspots are chronic, and some represent more temporary spikes in crime as a result of seasonal trends or random variation. What is especially important for understanding the concentration of crime longitudinally is to better understand the factors that create persistent risks for high criminal activity in some areas or changes that increase (or decrease) the level of risk over time.

Eck, Clarke, and Guerette (2007) point to five potential reasons why crime might be concentrated at particular facilities, which are relevant to consider when understanding the concentration of crime at microplaces. The first was noted above; some portion of the concentration can be explained by random variation. That is, some hotspots of crime would likely cool off without any intervention. Random variation, however, is not the whole story, as Weisburd et al. (2012) demonstrated by showing that the hottest street segments in Seattle remained high crime throughout the 16-year study period. A second explanation is changes in reporting processes. If police changed their crime incident reporting protocols, for example, this could have some impact on the level and concentration of crime, although again this does not explain the stability of concentration in Seattle, which experienced no major change in reporting patterns from 1989 to 2004.

The last three potential explanations focus on the characteristics of particular facilities (or places). Eck and colleagues (2007) point to offenders, targets, and place management as potential reasons why some facilities may be riskier than others. Some places may be crime attractors if they tempt potential offenders with rampant opportunities for criminal activity. Places can also be rich in targets and be crime generators. Finally, poor place management (i.e., a lack of supervision and guardianship) can be a crime enabler.

Weisburd et al. (2012) examined the impact of a number of factors, drawing on both opportunity theories and social disorganization perspectives, to predict whether street segments in Seattle remained high crime over time relative to being crime free. The findings from a multinomial regression analysis overall suggested a high degree of statistical fit between theories of opportunity and social disorganization and crime at street segments, implying even in a fairly early stage of theorizing and empirical research that crime at place is very predictable.

Their results suggested a number of opportunity and social disorganization variables significantly predict whether a street segment is likely to be a crime hotspot instead of crime free. The two most important predictors of crime hotspots were drawn from the opportunity perspective (see Cohen and Felson, 1979). The larger the residential population of a street segment, the more likely it is to be a crime hotspot. Similarly, when there are more employees on a street segment, it is much more likely to become a hotspot of crime. When more people live on a block, there is more potential for crime because there are more potential victims (and perhaps higher numbers of motivated offenders as well). When more employees work on the block, they increase the amount of crime on that street, because they are likely to increase the volume of targets on the street. Another indicator of crime opportunities, arterial roads, also increased the risks of crime on street segments markedly. Arterial roads are more likely to bring together motivated offenders and suitable targets, because they are easily accessible.

Three variables that reflect the social disorganization perspective also had very large impacts on the likelihood of a street segment being a crime hotspot in Weisburd et al.'s (2012) analyses. The higher the level of physical disorder on a street segment, the greater the likelihood of it being a high-crime street segment. This is very much consistent with the idea that an inability of a street segment-level social system to control disorderly behavior will increase the risk of crime. High socioeconomic status, in contrast, acted as a protective factor for crime, with crime hotspots much less likely to be found at places with wealthier residents (as reflected in higher property values), who assumedly are able to cultivate both formal and informal social controls more effectively. Collective efficacy (see Sampson, Raudenbush, and Earls, 1997), measured by voter participation, also seemed to act as a strong protective factor for crime at place.

These findings demonstrate that crime opportunity and social disorganization factors both play a key role in explaining the concentration of crime in hotspots. These factors are important for understanding why some places become hotspots, but they do not necessarily explain why such a small number of hotspots are responsible for such a high percentage of crime citywide. This may be due in part to the concentration of other characteristics of places across the city. For example, Weisburd et al. (2012) noted that the concentration of bus stops or number of public facilities, like crime, stayed relatively stable over long periods. Perhaps the law of concentrations of crime is related to the overall distribution of social and environmental characteristics of places in cities.

Does the stability of patterns of business and employment in a city, for example, reflect more general patterns of concentration that are related to the growth and development of urban areas? Perhaps the normal concentrations of crime are simply a reflection of the normal concentrations of other social activities in the city. The law of concentrations of crime at place may simply be a reflection of a more general law of the stability of concentrations of specific aspects of social and economic life in the city, as discussed above with Juran's (1951) notion of the Pareto Principle. These are important areas for future research.

The relevance of concentration of other levels of social activity was explored by Johnson and Bowers (2010) in their examination of the link between street segment permeability (or accessibility) and burglary risk. In line with the Weisburd et al. (2012) findings, major roads were more likely to have burglaries, as were streets connected to these roads, suggesting the importance of the street network in understanding burglary risk. Burglary was less likely to occur on cul-de-sacs. Importantly, Johnson and Bowers examined burglary *risk*, rather than just burglary counts, by dividing the number of burglaries per street segment by the number of homes on each block (see also Davies and Johnson, 2015).

This emphasis on the appropriate denominator in place-based research has been more common at the jurisdiction level (e.g., standardizing crime counts by a city's population to create a crime rate comparable across cities) or the neighborhood level (e.g., standardizing crime counts by census tract population) (Ratcliffe, 2010). At the microunit, calculating risk is more challenging. For the crime of burglary, the number of households is a meaningful denominator, and one that can be calculated with governmental data. Calculating risk of robbery or other violent crime is more difficult, because of a lack of available data on population at risk per street block (see Telep and Hibdon, 2013).

Issues of microplace crime rates and risk are important to consider in future work on crime concentrations. While high-crime places may be important targets for police, regardless of their rate of crime, the highest-crime locations in a city may not be the "riskiest," if they also are the locations where the most activity is also concentrated. In other words, a street with 100 burglaries and 500 housing units would have a high count, but a much lower risk of burglary for each household relative to a street with 20 burglaries and 20 housing units.

An analysis of the Johnson and Bowers (2010) data reinforces this point.[2] The top 202 street segments in terms of burglary count in Merseyside, United Kingdom, data (streets with at least 10 burglaries) represent a sizable 23.3% of burglaries in just 2.0% of streets. But the per household risk is quite variable across even these high-burglary streets, ranging from 0.07 to 18.0 burglaries per house, with a median of 0.34. In contrast, the top 202 streets by rate represent a smaller percentage of burglaries (10.6%), but the median number of burglaries per house is 2.0. It may be more beneficial for police or other place-based interventions to focus on a balance between counts and rates. The 35 street segments that appeared among the highest burglary streets based on both counts and rates would seem especially useful to target.

25.5 Conclusions and Future Research

The evidence we have presented here offers strong support for the idea that crime is highly concentrated at microunits of geography. Research to date provides persuasive evidence for the law of crime concentration that Weisburd (2015) proposes. We have examined some of the key questions related to the criminology of places, but recognize, as Weisburd (2015) does, that much future research is needed to further our understanding of the dynamics of crime concentrations. We close with some important challenges and suggestions for future empirical and theoretical work in environmental criminology.

In particular, more research is needed on why crime concentrates to such a great extent. We have provided some explanations for the clustering of crime, but work to date still leaves many questions unanswered. What is the best way to measure key concepts from environmental criminology, opportunity theories, and social disorganization at the microgeographic level to help explain why crime concentrates at particular locations? Weisburd et al. (2012) collected data on a number of such indicators in Seattle, but recognized their retrospective measures were limited in scope (see Braga and Clarke, 2014). How, for example, can motivated offenders, suitable targets, and capable guardianship best be quantified at the street block level to test the impact of routine activity theory (Cohen and Felson, 1979) on crime concentrations? How do neighborhood- and jurisdiction-level factors affect crime concentrations? A small number of studies reviewed above suggest a great deal of the variability of crime is at the street segment, but how do neighborhood-level social and physical characteristics affect how crime is concentrated within and across communities? What other traditional criminological perspectives may be useful in explaining crime concentrations? For example, are individuals low in social control concentrated in particular areas? Mixed methods approaches incorporating official data, surveys, and qualitative observations, such as those currently being used in a large-scale prospective study of crime hotspots in Baltimore are promising for efforts to better understand why crime is concentrated at particular places and not others (see Weisburd, Lawton, and Ready, 2012).

Although existing empirical studies are supportive of the law, we suggest further replications of the studies we have reviewed in different geographic contexts, using different time spans, and multiple indicators of crime and disorderly behavior. How concentrated is crime in more rural areas? What are the levels of concentration using official data from nonpolice sources, such as emergency medical or public health agencies? How does concentration vary using alternative data sources like victimization surveys? Additionally, future research should further consider issues of risk at place by standardizing counts by population at risk. This will likely become more feasible with the increasing availability of alternative data sources, including measures of ambient population at smaller scales (see Andresen, 2011) and human mobility data from mobile phones (see

Palmer et al., 2013). We suspect that research on the criminology of places is only in its early stages and look forward to this review quickly becoming outdated as new literature improves our understanding of the concentration of crime at place.

Notes

1. Weisburd et al. (2004) followed the traditional approach of using 100 blocks to define street segments. As sometimes there are cases where 100 blocks may not accurately define street segments intersection to intersection, Weisburd et al. (2012) created a more precise street file based on the actual street grid of Seattle.
2. Thanks to Shane Johnson for providing these data.

References

Andresen, M. A. (2011). The ambient population and crime analysis. *Professional Geographer*, 63, 192–212.

Andresen, M. A., Curman, A. S., & Linning, S. J. (2017). The trajectories of crime at places: Understanding the patterns of disaggregated crime types. *Journal of Quantitative Criminology*, 32, 427–449.

Andresen, M. A., & Linning. S. J. (2012). The (in)appropriateness of aggregating across crime types. *Applied Geography*, 35, 275–282.

Andresen, M. A., Linning, S. J., & Malleson, N. (2017). Crime at places and spatial concentrations: Exploring the spatial stability of property crime in Vancouver BC, 2003–2013. *Journal of Quantitative Criminology*, 32, 255–275.

Andresen, M. A., & Malleson, N. (2011). Testing the stability of crime patterns: Implications for theory and practice. *Journal of Research in Crime and Delinquency*, 48, 58–82.

Ariel, B., Weinborn, C., & Boyle, A. (2015). Can routinely collected ambulance data about assaults contribute to reduction in community violence. *Emergency Medicine Journal*, 32, 308–313.

Baumer, E. P., & Wolff, K. T. (2014). Evaluating contemporary crime drop(s) in America, New York City, and many other places. *Justice Quarterly*, 31, 5–38.

Braga, A. A., & Clarke, R. V. (2014). Explaining high-risk concentrations of crime in the city: Social disorganization, crime opportunities, and important next steps. *Journal of Research in Crime and Delinquency*, 51, 480–498.

Braga, A. A., Hureau, D. M., & Papachristos, A. V. (2011). The relevance of micro places to citywide robbery trends: A longitudinal analysis of robbery incidents at street corners and block faces in Boston. *Journal of Research in Crime and Delinquency*, 48, 7–32.

Braga, A. A., Papachristos, A. V., & Hureau, D. M. (2010). The concentration and stability of gun violence at micro places in Boston, 1980–2008. *Journal of Quantitative Criminology*, 26, 33–53.

Braga, A. A., Papachristos, A. V., & Hureau, D. M. (2014). The effects of hot spots policing on crime: An updated systematic review and meta-analysis. *Justice Quarterly*, 31, 633–663.

Cohen, L. E., & Felson, M. (1979). Social change and crime rate trends: A routine activity approach. *American Sociological Review*, 44, 588–608.

Curman, A. S. N., Andresen, M. A., & Brantingham, P. J. (2015). Crime and place: A longitudinal examination of street segment patterns in Vancouver, BC. *Journal of Quantitative Criminology*, 31, 127–147.

Davies, T., & Johnson, S. D. (2015). Examining the relationship between road structure and burglary risk via quantitative network analysis. *Journal of Quantitative Criminology, 31*, 481–507.

de Melo, S. N., Matias, L. F., & Andresen, M. A. (2015). Crime concentrations and similarities in spatial crime patterns in a Brazilian context. *Applied Geography, 62*, 314–324.

Deryol, R., Wilcox, P., Logan, M., & Wooldredge, J. (2016). Crime places in context: An illustration of the multilevel nature of hot spot development. *Journal of Quantitative Criminology, 32*, 305–325.

Durkheim, E. (1893 [1964]). *The division of labour in society*. Translated by W. D. Halls. New York: Free Press.

Durkheim, E. (1895 [1964]). *The rules of sociological method*. Edited by G. E. G. Catlin. Translated by S. A. Solovay and J. H. Mueller. New York: Free Press.

Eck, J. E., Clarke, R. V., & Guerette, R. T. (2007). Risky facilities: Crime concentration in homogenous sets of establishments and facilities. In G. Farrell, K. J. Bowers, S. D. Johnson, & M. Townsley (eds.), *Imagination in crime prevention. Crime Prevention Studies*, vol. 21 (pp. 225–264). Monsey, NY: Criminal Justice Press.

Eck, J. E., & Weisburd, D. (1995). Crime places in crime theory. In J. E. Eck & D. Weisburd (eds.), *Crime and place. Crime Prevention Studies*, vol. 4 (pp. 1–33). Monsey, NY: Criminal Justice Press.

Farrell, G. (2015). Crime concentration theory. *Crime Prevention and Community Safety, 17*, 233–248.

Farrell, G., & Pease, K. (eds.). (2001). *Repeat victimization. Crime Prevention Studies*, vol. 12. Monsey, NY: Criminal Justice Press.

Gerell, M. (2017). Smallest is better? The spatial distribution of arson and the modifiable areal unit problem. *Journal of Quantitative Criminology, 32*, 293–318.

Gill, C., Wooditch, A., & Weisburd, D. (2017). Testing the "law of crime concentration at place" in a suburban setting: Implications for research and practice. *Journal of Quantitative Criminology, 32*, 519–545.

Gorr, W. L., & Lee, Y. (2015). Early warning system for temporary crime hot spots. *Journal of Quantitative Criminology, 31*, 25–47.

Groff, E. R., Ratcliffe, J. H., Haberman, C. P., Sorg, E. T., Joyce, N. M., & Taylor, R. B. (2015). Does what police do at hot spots matter? The Philadelphia policing tactics experiment. *Criminology, 53*, 23–53.

Groff, E. R., Weisburd, D., & Yang, S.-M. (2010). Is it important to examine crime trends at a local "micro" level? A longitudinal analysis of street to street variability in crime trajectories. *Journal of Quantitative Criminology, 26*, 7–32.

Hibdon, J., & Groff, E. R. (2014). What you find depends on where you look: Using emergency medical services call data to target illicit drug use hot spots. *Journal of Contemporary Criminal Justice, 30*, 169–185.

Hibdon, J., Telep, C. W., & Groff, E. R. (2017). The concentration and stability of drug activity in Seattle, Washington using police and emergency medical services data. *Journal of Quantitative Criminology, 32*, 497–517.

Johnson, S. D., & Bowers, K. J. (2010). Permeability and burglary risk: Are cul-de-sacs safer? *Journal of Quantitative Criminology, 26*, 89–111.

Juran, J. M. (1951). *Quality control handbook*. New York: McGraw-Hill.

Koch, R. (1999). *The 80/20 principle: The secret of achieving more with less*. Naperville, IL: Nicholas Brealey Publishing.

Lum, C., Koper, C., & Telep, C. W. (2011). The evidence-based policing matrix. *Journal of Experimental Criminology, 7*, 3–26.

Mazeika, D. M., & Kumar, S. (2017). Do crime hot spots exist in developing countries? Evidence from India. *Journal of Quantitative Criminology*, *32*, 45–61.

Palmer, J. R. B., Espenshade, T. J., Bartumeus, F., Chung, C. Y., Ozgencil, N. E., & Li., K. (2013). New approaches to human mobility: Using mobile phones for demographic research. *Demography*, *50*, 1105–1128.

Pareto, V. (1909). *Manuel d'économie politique*. Vol. 7 of *Oeuvres complètes*. Geneva: Droz.

Pierce, G., Spaar, S., & Briggs, L. R. (1988). *The character of police work: Strategic and tactical implications*. Boston: Center for Applied Social Research, Northeastern University.

Ratcliffe, J. H. (2010). Crime mapping: Spatial and temporal challenges. In D. Weisburd & A. R. Piquero (eds.), *Handbook of quantitative criminology* (pp. 5–24). New York: Springer.

Ratcliffe, J. H. (2015). *Harm-focused policing*. Ideas in American Policing. Washington, DC: Police Foundation.

Sampson, R. J., Raudenbush, S. W., & Earls, F. (1997). Neighborhoods and violent crime: A multilevel study of collective efficacy. *Science*, *277*, 918–924.

Schnell, C., Braga, A. A., & Piza, E. L. (2017). The influence of community areas, neighborhood clusters, and street segments on the spatial variability of violent crime in Chicago. *Journal of Quantitative Criminology*, 32, 469–496.

Sherman, L. W. (1987). *Repeat calls to the police in Minneapolis*. Washington, DC: Crime Control Institute.

Sherman, L. W. (1995). Hot spots of crime and criminal careers of places. In J. Eck & D. Weisburd (eds.), *Crime and place. Crime Prevention Studies*, vol. 4 (pp. 35–52). Monsey, NY: Criminal Justice Press.

Sherman, L. W. (2007). The power few: Experimental criminology and the reduction of harm. *Journal of Experimental Criminology*, 3, 299–321.

Sherman, L. W. & Weisburd, D. (1988). *Policing the hot spots of crime: A redesign of the Kansas City Preventive Patrol Experiment*. Research proposal submitted to the National Institute of Justice, Program on Research in Public Safety and Security.

Sherman, L. W., Gartin, P., & Buerger, M. E. (1989). Hot spots of predatory crime: Routine activities and the criminology of place. *Criminology*, *27*, 27–55.

Sherman, L. W., & Weisburd, D. (1995). General deterrent effects of police patrol in crime "hot spots": A randomized, controlled trial. *Justice Quarterly*, *12*, 625–648.

Spelman, W. (1995). Criminal careers of public places. In J. E. Eck & D. Weisburd (eds.), *Crime and place, Crime Prevention Studies*, vol. 4. (pp. 115–143). Monsey, NY: Criminal Justice Press.

Steenbeek, W., & Weisburd, D. (2016). Where the action is in crime? An examination of variability of crime across different spatial units in The Hague, 2001–2009. *Journal of Quantitative Criminology*, 32, 449–469.

Telep, C. W., & Hibdon, J. (2013). How unsafe are crime hot spots? An examination of the risk of victimization on high crime street blocks in Seattle, Washington. Presented at the American Society of Criminology Annual Meeting, Atlanta, GA.

Vaughan, A. D., Hewitt, A. N., Andresen, M. A., & Brantingham, P. L. (2016). Exploring the role of the environmental context in the spatial distribution of calls-for-service associated with emotionally disturbed persons. *Policing*, *10*, 121–133.

Weisburd, D. (2008). *Place-based policing*. Ideas in American Policing. Washington, DC: Police Foundation.

Weisburd, D. (2015). The law of crime concentration and the criminology of place. *Criminology*, *54*, 133–157.

Weisburd, D., & Amram, S. (2014). The law of crime concentrations at places: The case of Tel Aviv–Jaffa. *Police Practice and Research*, *15*, 101–114.

Weisburd, D., Bruinsma, G. J. N., & Bernasco, W. (2009). Units of analysis in geographic criminology: Historical development, critical issues, and open questions. In D. Weisburd, W. Bernasco, & G. J. N. Bruinsma (eds.), *Putting crime in its place: Units of analysis in geographic criminology* (pp. 3–31). New York: Springer.

Weisburd, D., Bushway, S., Lum, C., & Yang, S.-M. (2004). Trajectories of crime at places: A longitudinal study of street segments in the city of Seattle. *Criminology*, *42*, 283–321.

Weisburd, D., Eck, J. E, Braga, A. A., Telep, C. W., Cave, B., Bowers, K., Bruinsma, G., Gill, C., Groff, E. R., Hibdon, J., Hinkle, J. C., Johnson, S. D., Lawton, B., Lum, C., Ratcliffe, J. H., Rengert, G., Taniguchi, T., & Yang, S.-M. (2016). *Place matters: Criminology for the twenty-first century*. New York: Cambridge University Press.

Weisburd, D., Groff, E. R., & Yang, S.-M. (2012). *The criminology of place: Street segments and our understanding of the crime problem*. New York: Oxford University Press.

Weisburd, D., Lawton, B., & Ready, J. (2012). Staking out the next generation of studies of the criminology of place: Collective prospective longitudinal data at crime hot spots. In R. Loeber & B. Welsh (eds.), *The future of criminology* (pp. 236–243). New York: Oxford University Press.

Weisburd, D., Maher, L., & Sherman, L. (1992). Contrasting crime general and crime specific theory: The case of hot spots of crime. In F. Adler & W. Laufer (eds.), *New directions in criminological theory. Advances in Criminological Theory*, vol. 4 (pp. 45–69). New Brunswick, NJ: Transaction Press.

Weisburd, D., & Mazerolle, L. G. (2000). Crime and disorder in drug hot spots: Implications for theory and practice in policing. *Police Quarterly*, *3*, 331–349.

Weisburd, D., Morris, N. A., & Groff, E. R. (2009). Hot spots of juvenile crime: A longitudinal study of street segments in Seattle, Washington. *Journal of Quantitative Criminology*, *25*, 443–467.

Weisburd, D., & Telep, C. W. (2014). The law of crime concentrations at places. In G. Bruinsma & D. Weisburd (eds.), *Encyclopedia of criminology and criminal justice* (pp. 2827–2834). New York: Springer.

Weisburd, D., Telep, C. W., & Lawton, B. A. (2014). Could innovations in policing have contributed to the New York City crime drop even in a period of declining police strength? The case of stop, question and frisk as a hot spots policing strategy. *Justice Quarterly*, *31*, 129–154.

Wheeler, A. P., Worden, R. E., & McLean, S. J. (2016). Replicating group-based trajectory models of crime at micro-places in Albany, NY. *Journal of Quantitative Criminology*, *32*, 589–612.

Wolfgang, M. E., Figlio, R. M., & Sellin, T. (1972). *Delinquency in a birth cohort*. Chicago: University of Chicago Press.

Zimring, F. E. (2007). *The great American crime decline*. New York: Oxford University Press

CHAPTER 26

STUDYING SITUATIONAL EFFECTS OF SETTING CHARACTERISTICS

Research Examples from the Study of Peers, Activities, and Neighborhoods

FRANK M. WEERMAN, EVELIEN M. HOEBEN, WIM BERNASCO, LIEVEN J. R. PAUWELS, AND GERBEN J. N. BRUINSMA

26.1 Introduction

To examine the validity and value of situational explanations of crime, methods that are traditionally employed to test etiological and ecological theories of crime are limited. Individual-level etiological theories in criminology are usually investigated with data on characteristics of *individuals* and changes in these individual characteristics. Such data have been collected in large-scale cohort panel studies employing multiple-item scales (see for an overview of such studies, e.g., Thornberry and Krohn, 2003), or longitudinal life course studies based on administrative data (see, e.g., Blokland and Nieuwbeerta, 2010). Ecological theories in criminology have been traditionally investigated with data on *geographical areas* like neighborhoods or cities, employing municipal statistics, community surveys, or systematic social observations (see Sampson and Raudenbush, 1999). However, empirical tests of situational theories in criminology need to include more detailed information. Not only do situational mechanisms operate at much smaller geographical levels than have traditionally been studied in criminology (see, e.g., Oberwittler and Wikström, 2009; Weisburd et al., 2009), they also change over time much more quickly. For this reason, attempts have been made recently to collect detailed data on situational characteristics on different moments in time and on differential individual exposure to crime-prone contexts (see, e.g., Wikström et al., 2012a).

It is often argued that empirical investigation of situational influences on crime should focus on *(behavioral) settings*. In its basic form, a setting can be defined as that part of the social and physical environment which individuals can perceive with their senses (Wikström, 2006). This definition built upon a more complex conception of behavioral settings as slices in time and space, consisting of both physical elements (what is present) and social elements (who is present). Behavior settings have conceptually developed within human ecology and are theorized to have standing patterns of behavior that affect the behavior of individuals within the setting (Barker, 1963, 1968; Barker et al., 1978). Behavior settings are the contexts in which opportunities may arise that are necessary for a crime to be committed.

Neighborhoods or schools are not true settings, because they are too large. A street block and a classroom can be settings because they are small enough to perceive with the senses when activities are taking place, and because they can have standing patterns of behavior (think of a classroom with a teacher and students; Barker, 1968; Taylor, 1987). Settings are variable; every change in who is present or in the role people have generates a new setting. A classroom where an adolescent is alone is different from the same classroom where he or she is with peers, which is different from the same classroom with a teacher present.

The Study of Peers, Activities, and Neighborhoods (SPAN) in the Netherlands has been designed to study and test situational explanations of crime and offending behavior, specifically situational action theory (Wikström 2006; 2014), routine activity theory (Cohen and Felson, 1979), and the routine activity theory of general deviance, also referred to as the unstructured socializing perspective (Osgood et al., 1996). The SPAN study employed a combination of data collection methods that are particularly well suited to measure situational characteristics of behavioral settings. The most important method that was used in the SPAN study is the space-time budget (STB) interview.

The STB method was designed by Wikström and colleagues (Wikström and Butterworth, 2006; Wikström et al., 2012a; Wikström et al., 2012b) to capture the spatial activity patterns of young people and thereby to enable detailed operationalization of the behavior settings they are exposed to. The STB method offers a systematic way to question respondents about their hourly activities across four days prior to the interview; about the geographical and functional locations where these activities have taken place; about the people who were present; and about additional events that are relevant for criminological research (e.g., crime, victimization, and substance use). The STB method was modeled after the more commonly known time diaries, which have been applied to address research question in many different disciplines. For example, in sociology, time diaries have been applied to examine gender inequality in time spent on domestic work. In economics, time diaries have been used to make international comparisons of time spent on paid work relative to leisure (overviews of time diary applications are given by Fisher and Gershuny, 2013; Pentland et al., 1999). Within criminology, the application of (space)-time budget instruments is fairly new. Nevertheless, some scholars have incorporated similar methods to investigate crime or criminals. For example, Rengert and Wasilchick (1985) reconstructed "'journeys-to-crime" by asking burglars to describe their activities and whereabouts on the day of their offense. Rossmo et al. (2012) applied data recorded by an electronic monitoring corrections program to examine the journeys-to-crime of reoffending parolees. Riley (1987) related data on activity patterns of teenagers, collected with time budgets about the Saturday prior to the interview, to their self-reported involvement in delinquency. And Lemieux and Felson (2012) calculated activity based victimization risks by combining national-level time use data with data on victimization from the US National Crime Victimization Survey. The space-time budget method as developed by Wikström is the first time diary method in criminology to collect data on spatial *and* temporal activity patterns on a large scale. The method has been used within data collection projects in England (PYS; PADS+), Sweden (MINDS), Slovenia (SPMAD), and the Netherlands (SPAN).

In the SPAN project, the information from the STB interviews was combined with data from a more traditional survey among adolescents (including self-reports about offending) and with information on neighborhoods and small geographic areas derived from census data, community surveys, and systematic social observations. Census data were drawn from publicly available databases from the Internet, such as the "Neighborhood Map" from Statistics Netherlands and the "Neighborhood Monitor" from the city of The Hague. A community survey was conducted among residents of 110 neighborhoods in The Hague, to measure ecological constructs like informal control and social trust. Systematic social observations were conducted in over 1,400 small geographical areas of 200 by 200 meters, to capture in detail the social and physical disorder, traffic, land use, and other characteristics of these areas.

The combination of data collection methods (space-time budget interviews, census data, community surveys, and systematic social observations) enables precise measurement of what respondents do, with whom they undertake these activities, and in what kind of places (both the geographical area and the function of the location) they find themselves. Together, these data capture presence in and exposure to different kinds of settings during particular periods in time.

In this chapter we will provide an illustration of the usefulness of these methods for criminological research, by summarizing the results of three studies from the SPAN project that were particularly focused on situational questions. After this introduction, we first discuss the design of the SPAN data collection and the instruments that were used in it. In each of the three sections that follow, we separately review a sub-study by summarizing its theoretical motivation, data structure, and analytical strategy, and by describing the main findings it has generated. Table 26.1 presents an overview and comparison of these three studies. The first two studies focus on the relation between unstructured socializing and self-reported delinquency of adolescents over a longer period (one year). Both studies specify the situational characteristics that increase the criminogeneity of unstructured socializing. The first study (Hoeben and Weerman, 2014) focused on functional locations of unstructured socializing and the amount of social control (guardianship as well as control exerted by place managers) that is

Table 26.1 Key Features of the Three SPAN Studies Discussed in This Chapter

	Study 1	Study 2	Study 3
Unit of analysis	Individual ($N = 615$)	Individual ($N = 387$)	Situation/Hour (N = 4,949 hours, 76 individuals)
Dependent variable	12-month delinquency (self-report)	12-month delinquency (self-report)	96 × 1 hour delinquency (self-report)

Independent variables	Unstructured socializing in:
	Private space
	Semipublic space
	  Pub. entertainment
	  Pub. transportation
	  Other semipublic
	Public space
	  Street
	  Shopping center
	  Open space
		Unstructured socializing in neighborhoods characterized by high, medium, and low:
		Socioeconomic status
		Mobility
		Ethnic heterogeneity
		Family disruption
		Population density
		Structural density
		Collective efficacy
		Physical disorder
			Presence of peers
			Presence of adults
			Public space
			Unstructured activity
			Alcohol use
			Cannabis use
			Carrying weapon

Data sources	STB, questionnaire	STB, questionnaire, community survey, systematic social observations, administrative data	STB
Publication	Hoeben and Weerman (2014)	Hoeben (2016)	Bernasco et al. (2013)

connected to these locations; the second study (Hoeben, 2016) focused on the characteristics of the neighborhoods where adolescents spend time engaged in unstructured socializing. The third study (Bernasco et al., 2013) focused on situational features of time periods in which offenses occurred compared to situational features of time periods where no offenses occurred. We conclude this chapter with theoretical implications of our findings for understanding criminogenic behavior settings, with a summary of the gains and advantages of these methods to collect situational data, and we reflect on future possibilities to improve the measurement of situational characteristics.

26.2 The SPAN Study

The Study of Peers, Activities, and Neighborhoods is a longitudinal panel study, spanning two waves of data collection, among several hundreds of adolescents (843 in the first wave, 616 in the second) in the city of The Hague and its neighboring suburbs. The Hague is the third largest city of the Netherlands, with 486,000 inhabitants in 2009, when the first wave of the study was completed. The city is the residence of the central government of the Netherlands, is situated at the North Sea coast, and is ethnically mixed, with a large number of residents of Indonesian, Surinamese, Turkish, and Moroccan origin.

The first wave of the data collection with the questionnaire and space-time budget (STB) interviews took place between October 2008 and May 2009; the second wave took place between November 2010 and June 2011. Coordinators and research assistants supervised completion of the questionnaires and conducted space-time budget interviews during school hours in separate classrooms or in other undisturbed locations of the school (or, for one of the schools, in a room of a hotel nearby). After completion of both instruments, respondents received an incentive for their participation. Parents were informed about the study and could refuse participation in both waves. In general, participating adolescents were cooperative, and many of them indicated that they particularly liked the intensive STB interview because this really related to their personal, daily life.

26.2.1 Sample

Forty schools for secondary education were approached for the SPAN project, of which 10 schools (25%) agreed to participate. The main reasons to refuse participation were that schools already participated in other research, or that they had concerns about disturbing lessons.

The study was conducted among two cohorts of secondary school students. In the first wave of the data collection, all first graders (aged 12 and 13) and fourth graders (aged 15 and 16) of the participating schools were approached for interviews. In the second wave, most respondents of the younger cohort were in the third grade of secondary school (aged 14 and 15), while respondents from the older cohort were either in the sixth grade of the highest form of secondary education, in the first or second grade of follow-up education, were part time or full time working, or were jobless (aged 17 and 18).

In total, 843 respondents participated fully in the first wave of the study (completing both the questionnaire and the space-time budget interview). It was complicated to retrieve all respondents of the first wave two years later, because a substantial portion of the respondents had left the school they attended in the first wave. All schools were happy to participate again, and students who were still at the same school were contacted there. Respondents who left their original school were personally contacted by (mobile) phone, via Internet, or at their home address.

The total retrieval rate in the second wave is 73%; 616 respondents participated in the study for both waves. Analyses showed that boys and older respondents had relatively higher attrition rates between the waves; however, there was no significant difference in the average frequency of delinquency between those who exited the study and those who remained in the second wave. For many SPAN sub-studies (including the first two sub-studies in this chapter) only those respondents were incorporated who participated in both waves of the data collection. This sample of 616 respondents consists of 52.6% boys and 47.4% girls; 57.0% belong to the younger cohort (who were originally in the first grade), and 43.0% belong to the older cohort (originally fourth graders). The mean age was 14.4

years in the first wave and 16.5 years in the second. Although the majority are from native Dutch descent (55.0%), a relatively large portion come from ethnic minorities. The largest categories are adolescents from Turkish (9.2%), Moroccan (7.1%), and Surinamese descent (7.1%). Relatively many adolescents come from lower forms of secondary education: in the first wave of the study, 17.9% of the respondents were recruited in schools for "practice education," the lowest level of secondary education, and 47.7% of the respondents were following lower vocational education, the most common form of secondary education. The remaining respondents were recruited at medium-level schools (10.5%) and at the highest, pre-academic, level of secondary education (23.8%). As the sample was drawn from a nonrandom selection of schools in The Hague, it is not representative of Dutch youth, but it is highly varied in terms of ethnicity and education, with a focus on lower-educated youths from a highly urbanized region of the Netherlands. Due to this demographic variation, the sample is well suited to test situational theories of crime.

26.2.2 The Space-Time Budget Interview in SPAN

The space-time budget instrument that was employed in the SPAN study was developed by Wikström and other associated scholars of the Peterborough Adolescent Delinquency Study (PADS+; see Wikström et al., 2012a; Wikström et al., 2012b), building on a long tradition of time use measurement and travel research in geography and social sciences (see Hoeben et al., 2014 for an overview). The method consists of personal interviews in which a time diary approach is applied to collect data about the activities and whereabouts of adolescents. Such interviews are very detailed, and result in hourly data about *what* respondents did, *with whom* they were, and *where* the activity took place. Respondents were also asked to provide information about involvement in crime as an offender, witness, or victim during the exact hours that were covered by the space-time budget interview.

Respondents answered in their own words, and these answers were coded by the interviewer and immediately entered in a preformatted Excel file on a laptop. The Excel file consisted of four forms for each day, 24 rows for each hour of the day, and various columns for different dimensions of the activity and the setting. The first column in the STB form refers to *activity*, for example, "studying at school" or "playing soccer." If more than one activity took place in an hour, interviewers asked the respondent what the main activity was. The second column of the form refers to the *function of the location* where the activity took place, for example, "home," "at a friend's house," or "supermarket." The third column refers to the *geographical location*. The geographical location is coded by using detailed maps that show small units (200 by 200 meters) in the research area. The fourth, fifth, and sixth columns of the STB form address *the people present in the setting*, specified in terms of their relation with the respondent. "Family" members include parents, siblings, or other family members. "Peers" include friends, classmates, teammates, or a partner. Also specified is whether one peer is present or two or more peers, and whether they are male, female, or a mixed group. "Others" include teachers, trainers, or parents of friends. Finally, the "extra incidents" columns of the STB form leave room to register *truancy, substance use* (alcohol and drugs), witnessing or involvement in *risky situations* (e.g., fights, provocations, police contact), *victimization* (by theft, vandalism, or violence), involvement as an *offender* (in theft, vandalism, or violence), or *weapon carrying*. These incidents are unlikely to occur every hour; therefore the interviewer asked about them at the end of coding each day. To prevent coding mistakes or typing errors, all completed forms were cleaned according to a strict protocol.

Respondents participated in a single space-time budget interview per wave, that took approximately one hour on average. During the interview they were asked to reconstruct their activities and whereabouts during four recent days. These four days always needed to incorporate one Saturday, one Friday, and two weekdays (the most recent weekday before the interview and the most recent weekday before that). If respondents were on holiday or ill during that day, they were questioned about another "regular" day, with a maximum of seven days before the interview. If that was not possible, the days were recorded but a note was made that these days were "abnormal."

To help respondents recall their activities and whereabouts, various strategies were used. Respondents were allowed to check their schedule book or mobile phone, and interviewers made reference to activities that were already reported by the respondent, or made references to memorable events, such as television shows or the weather. As a last resort, interviewers could ask respondents what they would normally do "at such a day" or "at that time of day." For more particulars of the STB method, see Wikström et al. (2012b) and Hoeben et al. (2014).

26.2.3 Self-Report Questionnaires

The SPAN *questionnaire* included validated scales measuring self-reported delinquency and substance use, as well as constructs like bonds with parents and school, parental monitoring, shame and guilt feelings, self-control, and perceived peer delinquency. The questionnaire was self-administered in groups of four adolescents, supervised by one research assistant during a school hour of about 45–50 minutes. This relatively intensive procedure ensured that adolescents were closely monitored, supported, and stimulated, and that any questions or concerns that they had about the questionnaire were addressed immediately. The questionnaire was based on the questionnaire of the PADS+ study (Peterborough Adolescent and Young Adult Development Study) of Wikström and colleagues (Wikström and Butterworth, 2006, Wikström et al., 2010; Wikström et al., 2012a). The items were translated, extended with additional measurements, and, when necessary, adjusted to the Dutch situation.

26.2.4 Community Survey

For the *community survey*, questionnaires were sent out to adult residents in 110 neighborhoods. The neighborhoods needed to contain enough respondents to provide valid information about its social ecological characteristics. This meant that parks and industrial areas with few residents were excluded from the survey. In total, 11,505 questionnaires were sent out to residents; 3,696 questionnaires were returned, of which 3,545 remained useful for analysis (after thorough data-cleaning on item response tendencies and missing values). The net response rate is thus 31%. On average, about 36 residents per neighborhood completed the survey. The survey measured constructs derived from various ecological perspectives, including the social disorganization theory and broken windows theory, and measured constructs like collective efficacy, fear of crime, and (perceived) disorder and victimization. Respondents were asked to think of their "neighborhood" as an area within about five minutes walking distance from their home. The questionnaire closely followed the PADS+ community survey, with some items adjusted to the Dutch situation.

26.2.5 Systematic Social Observations

The systematic social observations were conducted by trained observers, who coded street segments within the small areas of 200 by 200 meters that were also used in the space-time budget interview. With the address closest to the centroid of the grid cell as starting point, a street segment of 100 meters in every third grid cell (1,422 of 4,561 grid cells) was observed and coded. The coding was aided with a structured observation list (partly based on the one from Sampson and Raudenbush, 1999) that took about ten minutes to complete. This observation form included 61 items concerning land use, physical disorder, social disorder, physical condition of buildings, signs of territoriality, traffic, formal and informal control, and guardianship.

26.2.5 Administrative Data

Additional statistical data on structural characteristics of neighborhoods were collected from publicly accessible online municipal databases and repositories. The data included neighborhood measurements of population density, ethnic composition, age composition, household composition (including percentage of single-parent families), mean income, average residential real estate value, residential mobility, and percentage of high-rise residential property.

26.3 Sub-study 1: Unstructured Socializing, Functional Locations, and Delinquency

The space-time budget method made it possible to investigate with greater detail than before how and where adolescents are spending their time. Several studies conducted with data from the SPAN study used these possibilities to test and specify the assumed association between delinquent behavior and spending time with peers (e.g., Hoeben and Weerman, 2014; 2016; Janssen et al., 2016; Janssen et al., 2017; McNeeley and Hoeben, 2017; Weerman et al., 2015). One sub-study from the SPAN study (Hoeben and Weerman, 2014) focused on the interplay between "unstructured socializing" (unstructured time with peers without the supervision of adults), and "functional locations" (the nature of the location, and whether it is public or private) in understanding adolescent involvement in delinquent behavior. The main research question of this sub-study was, in which type of locations is adolescents' involvement in unstructured socializing associated with their delinquency?

26.3.1 Theory

The sub-study combined two theoretical approaches: the unstructured socializing perspective of Osgood and colleagues (1996) and the classification of "responsibilities of places" of Felson (1995).

The term "unstructured socializing" was introduced by Osgood et al. (1996) in a paper that aimed to develop a situational perspective on individual delinquency, building on the routine activity theory (Cohen and Felson, 1979) and the lifestyle theory (Hindelang et al. 1978). They argued that deviant acts are not always the result of criminal dispositions and often not planned ahead. Rather, these acts occur in the spur of the moment, out of boredom, in search of excitement, or to express toughness in front of peers. Osgood et al. (1996) assumed that adolescent activities that can be characterized as "unstructured socializing" are particularly rich in opportunities and situational inducements for deviance. Unstructured socializing is characterized by three elements: (1) the presence of peers, (2) lack of structured activity, and (3) the absence of authority figures. According to Osgood et al., the *presence of peers* can make delinquency easier and more rewarding. Peers may serve as resources in delinquency: they can function as "backups" or "lookouts" when adolescents get into fights or commit theft. Peers may also serve as an audience, and this makes delinquency rewarding in terms of status and reputation. The *lack of structured activity* stimulates delinquency because it leaves time for deviant activity when opportunities for them are encountered, and because in unstructured activities it is less likely that responsibilities for social control are conferred on one or more of the individuals present. The *absence of authority figures* stimulates delinquency because it limits social control and reduces the chance of "getting caught." When combined, these three elements provide the most opportunities and situational inducements for deviance, which means that adolescents who spend a lot of time in "unstructured socializing" in their daily life are expected to be involved in relatively more acts of deviance and delinquency.

According to Felson (1995), an important situational characteristic determining the amount of deterrence against crime is the type of responsibility for a location, which can differ between very clear and outspoken to diffuse and implicit. The strongest form of responsibility (personal responsibility) is responsibility taken by those who own a place or live there. Their incentive for reacting to crime is to protect their own property. Other, weaker forms of responsibility are responsibilities taken by employees who are explicitly assigned to look after a place (assigned responsibility) or who work at a place, but were not explicitly assigned to look after it (diffuse job responsibility). The weakest form of responsibility is taken by incidental passers-by or bystanders whose presence discourages crime or who may respond to illegal behavior but are not obliged to do so (general responsibility). These categories of responsibility correspond with different categories of urban space (originally formulated by Newman, 1972). Felson argues that private places (like houses) are primarily looked over by people with personal responsibility. Semiprivate or semipublic places (e.g., shops, cinemas, bars) are mostly out of sight of the owners and usually monitored by both assigned and nonassigned employees and by people who have no particular relation to the place but happen to be there. Finally, public places (like streets and public parks) are mainly supervised by bystanders who do not have a particular incentive to intervene in acts of crime.

These two theoretical approaches led to the hypotheses that the extent to which adolescents spend time in unstructured socializing is associated with their involvement in delinquency, and that this relation is strongest for unstructured socializing in public places and least strong in private places.

26.3.2 Measurement and Analysis

The data that were collected with the space-time budget interviews were used to create very precise measurements of the number of hours that respondents had spent in *unstructured socializing* during four preceding days and specifically whether those hours were spent in private, semipublic, or public *locations*. For an hour to be counted as *unstructured socializing*, three conditions had to be met: one or more peers must have been present, no adult authority figure should have been around, and the respondent was involved in unstructured activity. The first two conditions were measured directly during the interview: for each hour respondents were asked whether peers and adults were around (and, with regard to the latter, whether these were parents, family members, or significant in other ways). The type of activity was measured in detail and later categorized as "unstructured" when these activities had no clear rules or agenda, for example, "hanging around" or "walking around without a destination." The *location* of the time that was spent unstructured socializing was established by categorizing the answers on the question about the type (or function) of the location where the activity took place (for example, a house, a schoolyard, a shop).

Unstructured socializing in private spaces was indicated by the total number of hours spent in unstructured socializing in locations that are primarily observed by those with personal responsibility for the space, such as owners, family, and friends; in particular the respondent's house or the houses of friends. *Unstructured socializing in public spaces* was indicated by the total number of hours spent in unstructured socializing in locations that are monitored solely by people with general responsibility, with three main subcategories: streets and squares, shopping centers, and open spaces. *Unstructured socializing in semipublic spaces* was indicated by the total number of hours spent in unstructured socializing in locations that are not private or public spaces, with three subcategories: public entertainment settings like bars and cinemas, public transportation settings like trains and trams, and other semipublic settings such as schools and clubs.

Involvement in delinquency was measured with an index composed of self-report questions from the SPAN questionnaire. The index comprised 20 items indicating how often the respondent committed various types of offenses in the preceding school year. The offenses ranged from minor offenses, like vandalism, kicking or hitting, stealing something small from a shop, to more serious offenses like injuring somebody, burglary, and robbery.

A multilevel analysis was employed to estimate *between person* as well as *within person* differences. The *between person* analyses investigate whether person A, who is more involved in unstructured socializing (in different locations) than person B, is also more involved in offending than person B. *Within person* analyses investigate whether an increase in involvement in unstructured socializing (in different locations) across the two waves for one person is associated with an increase in delinquency across the two waves for that same person, regardless of his or her initial participation in unstructured socializing or delinquency and regardless of other relevant differences in (stable) personal characteristics. In other words, within-person analyses result in a relatively conservative test that controls for selection effects (when relatively crime-prone individuals prefer unstructured socializing at certain locations). In the analysis, random intercept models were applied that included a between-person and a within-person parameter for each independent variable. The between-person parameter is computed by averaging the scores on the independent variables across both observations for each respondent. The within-person parameter is computed by subtracting the between-person score from the score on each observation. The random intercept models were executed in the form of negative binomial regressions, because the dependent variable of involvement in delinquency was highly and positively skewed (see Allison, 2009, and Hoeben and Weerman, 2014, for more details about the statistical analyses).

26.3.3 Results

First of all, it appeared that the general amount of hours individual respondents spent in unstructured socializing was positively associated with their involvement in delinquency, in line with the individualized situational approach of Osgood and colleagues (1996). This association was found for both between-person and within-person parameters (albeit somewhat stronger for the first). It also appeared that this association was not equally strong in all types of locations. For example, increased involvement in unstructured socializing in *private spaces* across the waves for a particular respondent was not significantly associated with his or her involvement in delinquency (within-person).

Also, the amount of unstructured socializing in shopping centers (a subcategory of public spaces) was not associated with delinquent behavior of individual adolescents. On the other hand, the strongest associations between individual involvement in unstructured socializing and delinquency were found for one subcategory of semipublic places, namely entertainment settings, and two subcategories of public places; in streets and in "open spaces" like parks and parking lots.

In general, these findings offered modest support for the hypotheses derived from Felson's classification of places (Felson, 1995). More importantly, it supported and specified the situational approach of Osgood and colleagues (1996). The amount of time that adolescents spend in unstructured socializing is not unconditionally related to their involvement in delinquency, but it depends strongly on the locations where they spend their time. In some, seemingly protective, locations, unstructured socializing does not increase the risks of becoming involved in delinquency. But there are also some quite specific types of locations where hanging out appears to be more risky. Spending a lot of time in unstructured socializing in these places is particularly related to relatively high levels of delinquency. This theory specification was only possible by using the kind of detailed data provided by the space-time budget interviews.

26.4 Sub-study 2: Unstructured Socializing, Neighborhood Characteristics, and Delinquency

Combining data from space-time budget interviews with data about neighborhoods and small areas makes it possible to determine the characteristics of the neighborhood where adolescents spend their time, and to investigate whether these neighborhood characteristics have an effect on delinquent behavior. The second sub-study from the SPAN study we address (Hoeben, 2016) used this combination of information. (See also Wikström et al., 2012a, for similar combinations of data). The main research goal was to examine whether characteristics of the neighborhoods where adolescents spend time engaged in unstructured socializing affected the relationship between unstructured socializing and delinquency.

26.4.1 Theory

This sub-study also combined several theoretical perspectives, in particular the unstructured socializing perspective described previously, social disorganization theory (e.g., Sampson et al., 1997; Shaw and McKay, 1942), broken windows theory (Wilson and Kelling, 1982), and the concept of "behavior settings" (Barker, 1968). According to the social disorganization perspective, rapid societal changes and urban population dynamics may lead to a "decay of existing social rules of behavior and institutions" (Thomas and Znaniecki, 1918–1920: 165), or an "inability of a community structure to realize the common values of its residents and maintain effective social controls" (Sampson and Groves, 1989: 777). Scholars within this perspective suggest that social disorganization processes occur frequently in neighborhoods with low socioeconomic status, high ethnic heterogeneity, high residential mobility (Shaw and McKay, 1942), high family disruption (Sampson, 1987), high population density, and structural density (Sampson and Groves, 1989). Contemporary perspectives within social disorganization theory emphasize "collective efficacy" as an indicator for processes of social disorganization (Sampson et al., 1997). Processes of social disorganization may lead to a "standing behavior pattern" (a concept from Barker's behavior settings perspective) in which residents will not interfere if someone violates rules, which is likely to result in relatively high crime levels. Additionally, disorganization also means less supervision and control over groups of adolescents who are hanging out in the neighborhoods. Adolescents who spend time in unstructured socializing in disorganized neighborhoods may feel that other behavior of them is expected than adolescents who hang out in organized neighborhoods, which makes it more likely that unstructured socializing in disorganized neighborhoods will result in delinquency.

According to broken windows theory, signs of disorder communicate to both residents of and visitors to a location that "no one cares" (Wilson and Kelling, 1982: 4). Signs like graffiti, broken bottles, or larger pieces of garbage that are spread out on the street show residents and visitors that littering and other inappropriate behavior is common in that area. These signs may be perceived as *cues* about standing behavior patterns for adolescents who are spending time in unstructured socializing in those areas, indicating that there is less need to conform to social norms and legal rules. Therefore, it can be expected that unstructured socializing is more strongly related to adolescent delinquency if it occurs in neighborhoods characterized by high levels of physical disorder than if it occurs in neighborhoods characterized by low levels of physical disorder.

26.4.2 Measurement and Analysis

The administrative neighborhood data, data derived from the community survey, and data from the systematic social observations were used to create measurements of characteristics of the neighborhoods where adolescents *spent their time* in unstructured socializing. The administrative neighborhood data were used to construct measures of socioeconomic status, neighborhood mobility, ethnic heterogeneity, family disruption, population density, and structural density (for more details about these measurements, see Hoeben, 2016, and Bruinsma et al, 2013). The *socioeconomic status* measure was a composite score based on factor analysis from standardized measures of the residential property value, the unemployment rate, the percentage of low-income households, and the percentage of households that received welfare benefits. *Neighborhood mobility* was measured by the number of residents that moved into the neighborhood in a year plus the number of residents that moved out of the neighborhood, divided by the total number of residents. The *ethnic heterogeneity* measure expressed the likelihood that two residents selected at random from the neighborhood would have a different ethnic origin (based on the five most prevalent ethnic categories). *Family disruption* was indicated by the percentage of single-parent households in the neighborhood. *Population density* was the number of residents per square kilometer in the neighborhood, and *structural density* was indicated by the percentage of residential properties in high-rise buildings.

Data from the community surveys were used to construct a measure of *collective efficacy* in each neighborhood. This measure consisted of a summation of two standardized multiple-item scales, one that measured social trust among the neighbors and one that measured informal control. Similar to the original construct as proposed by Sampson and colleagues (1997), the scale for social trust consisted of five items describing the quality of neighborhood bonds (e.g., "Neighbors are willing to help other neighbors," "The neighbors can be trusted"). The informal control scale consisted of six items indicating whether residents are willing and able to intervene in the neighborhood (e.g., "If a group of kids is skipping school and hanging around in the street, would your neighbors do something about it?" "Suppose your community center will be closed, would your neighbors organize something to keep it open?"). Both the alphas and lambdas of these scales were satisfactory, indicating that the scales had high internal reliability (coherence between items) and ecological reliability (coherence between neighborhood residents in answering).

The systematic social observation was used to obtain a measure of *physical disorder* in the neighborhood. Physical disorder was measured by trained observers using a checklist based on the instrument developed by Sampson and Raudenbush (1999; Raudenbush and Sampson, 1999). This checklist consisted of seven items about potential signs of physical disorder (e.g., dog feces, litter or broken glass, graffiti tags), using a dichotomous scale representing "observed" and "not observed." The level of physical disorder at the measured street segments was aggregated to the neighborhood level by applying a refined version of the ecometric method (Hoeben et al., 2016b).

These measures were combined with the data from the space-time budget interviews to derive measures of the amount of time spent in unstructured socializing in different kinds of neighborhoods. The space-time budget data indicated that the 387 respondents who were included in this study spent time engaged in unstructured socializing in 118 different neighborhoods across the four space-time budget days during the first wave of the data collection and in 135 neighborhoods during the second wave. Measures were created that expressed respondents' total number of hours spent in unstructured socializing in the 25% of neighborhoods with the highest score for each characteristic, in the 25% of neighborhoods with the lowest score, and in the 50% of neighborhoods with scores that were in between. Neighborhoods were classified as "disorganized" or "disordered" when they were in the least favorable quartile of scores on a relevant measure (the 25% of the neighborhoods with, for example, the lowest scores on socioeconomic status, or the highest scores on physical disorder), as "organized" or "ordered" when they were in the most favorable quartile (the 25% of the neighborhoods with, for example, the highest scores on socioeconomic status or the lowest scores on physical disorder), or as "average neighborhood" (the other 50% of the neighborhoods). This strategy was adopted for two reasons: (1) to avoid complicated nonhierarchical multilevel structures that arise because respondents spend time in more than one neighborhood and because respondents may overlap with other respondents in the neighborhoods they visit; (2) to enable comparison of the association between delinquency and the hours spent in unstructured socializing in disorganized and disordered neighborhoods with the association between delinquency and the hours spent in unstructured socializing in organized and ordered neighborhoods *for the same respondent*. The threshold of 25% was chosen arbitrarily; additional analyses with 10% measures showed substantially similar results.

Additionally, because it was assumed that neighborhood characteristics only affect unstructured socializing in the semipublic or public domain, hours were excluded if they took place in the respondents' homes or their friends' homes. Additional measures for *being outside of the residential neighborhood* were constructed that expressed the number of hours spent in unstructured socializing at locations more than one kilometer (0.62 miles) away from home (following Wiehe et al., 2008b).

In the analyses, negative binomial fixed effects panel models (time nested in persons) were estimated to examine the effects of the different measures about time spent engaged in unstructured socializing in particular neighborhoods on individual involvement in delinquency. Predictors were person-mean centered prior to analysis, and both person-means and deviations from person-means were entered into the models (as suggested by Allison, 2009). See Hoeben (2016), for more details about the statistical methods.

26.4.3 Results

A major descriptive result of this study was the finding that adolescents are often away from their residential neighborhood, in particular when they are spending their time in unstructured socializing. About half of the hours that the respondents from this study were awake were spent outside the residential neighborhood (as defined by Statistics Netherlands). Unstructured socializing occurred outside the residential neighborhood in 75% of the hours. More than half of the hours spent in unstructured socializing were spent further than one kilometer (0.62 miles) away from the home address of the respondents. This finding implies that it is important to look at the actual neighborhoods where respondents spent their time (in unstructured socializing) in addition to their residential neighborhood.

The results from the fixed effect models that estimated effects of neighborhood characteristics (disorganization indicators as well as observations of disorder) showed that the unstructured socializing-delinquency relationship is particularly affected by collective efficacy in the neighborhood. An increase of about one hour in unstructured socializing, outside of the residential neighborhood, in the 25% of neighborhoods with the lowest levels of collective efficacy was associated with an increase in delinquency of 6.8%. On the other hand, increases in time in unstructured socializing, outside of the residential neighborhood, in the 25% of neighborhoods with the highest levels of collective efficacy was not associated with delinquency at all. Other neighborhood characteristics associated with social disorganization (such as ethnic heterogeneity, family disruption, and population density) did not affect the relationship between unstructured socializing and delinquency. Neither did the amount of physical disorder in the neighborhoods where respondents spend their time in unstructured socializing.

In general, these findings are in line with recent elaborations of the social disorganization perspective (e.g., Sampson et al., 1997): That low levels of collective efficacy in a neighborhood condition the effect of unstructured socializing in that neighborhood on adolescents' delinquency may imply that residents exert control over visitors in their neighborhood. The findings did not offer support for the hypothesis derived from broken windows theory, nor did they confirm that structural neighborhood characteristics related to social disorganization are relevant for the unstructured socializing-delinquency relationship.

What is important to notice here is that the analyses of this study would not be possible without the combination of detailed data on time use (the space-time budget interviews) and detailed information about neighborhood characteristics (from the community surveys, administrative data, and systematic social observations). Moreover, using detailed geographical data about the whereabouts of adolescents revealed that an important part of their time is spent away from the residential neighborhood. This finding poses fundamental questions about the value of previous research within the ecological tradition in criminology that primarily focused on residential neighborhoods, and underscores the need for further empirical research on the situational causes of crime and delinquency.

26.5 Sub-study 3: Situational Causes of Offending

In sub-studies 1 and 2, situational variables (regarding the activities and whereabouts of adolescents) were related to a measure of delinquency *per year*. However, the space-time budget protocol also included a question about involvement in delinquency *per hour*. This measure makes it possible to investigate with even greater detail in which situations adolescents actually commit offenses and in which situations not. Again, this sub-study builds on the work of Wikström and colleagues, who used similar data in their analyses to test situational action theory (Wikström et al., 2010; Wikström et al., 2012a). In the third sub-study we address (Bernasco et al., 2013), the occurrence of an offense during a particular hour was related to the situational characteristics during that same hour, controlling for other situational characteristics and for offender characteristics.

26.5.1 Theory

This sub-study built on various theories and empirical studies about situational influences on offending. The theories include the group process perspective developed by Warr (2002), routine activity theory (Cohen and Felson, 1979), the previously addressed unstructured socializing approach of Osgood and colleagues (Osgood et al., 1996), and the classification of "responsibilities of places" of Felson (1995). The authors hypothesized that seven situational elements increase the probability of offending by adolescents at a particular moment in time: (1) presence of peers, (2) absence of adult handlers, (3) being in public space, (4) unstructured activities, (5) alcohol use, (6) cannabis use, and (7) carrying weapons.

The supposed situational effect of peer presence was based on various situational group mechanisms as described by Warr (2002), including fear of ridicule, display of loyalty, and status seeking. These mechanisms are rooted in the need to be accepted and respected by other group members, a need that is particularly salient during adolescence. Each of these mechanisms is strongly facilitated by the actual presence of peers in potential offending situations. Offending particularly disarms ridicule, proves loyalty, and confirms or produces status in the physical presence of peers who are aware of the act. Presence of peers may also makes offending easier and more rewarding (Osgood et al., 1996). The act of offending can be intrinsically rewarding when peers act as an audience, and the physical presence of peers may also facilitate offending because it provides access to potential co-offenders. Further, presence of peers may increase the likelihood of crime because peers may be potential competitors and provoke offenses, and thus become suitable targets of violent crime.

The supposed situational effects of absent adult handlers and being in public space were based on routine activity approaches (Cohen and Felson, 1979; Felson, 1995; Osgood et al., 1996). According to the theory, a necessary requirement for crime is the convergence in time and place of a motivated offender and a suitable target in the absence of a capable guardian, place manager, or handler. A handler is someone who knows the potential offender, who has been granted authority over him or her, who has been given responsibility for his or her conduct, and who has developed an emotional attachment to him or her (Felson, 1995). Parents, teachers, and sports coaches are examples of handlers of young people, and absence of such adult handlers can be regarded as a situational cause of adolescent offending.

A place manager is a person who has responsibility for managing the cleanliness, orderliness, and safety of a place (Eck 1994; Eck and Madensen, in this volume). Public places are open to the general public, and there are usually no specific place managers responsible for these places. These features of public places increase the probability that an adolescent will be engaged in offending when in such a place.

The hypothesized situational effect of unstructured activities was based on the perspective of Osgood and colleagues (1996), as discussed previously in this chapter.

The supposed situational effects of alcohol and cannabis use on offending were based on the immediate disinhibiting and psychopharmacological effects of these substances.

Alcohol use causes psychomotor and cognitive impairment, and it lowers self-control, which is theorized to be an inhibitor of crime. The temporary loss of self-control makes it more likely that small conflicts escalate into fights and that small opportunities for crime are reaped (Gottfredson and Hirschi, 1990). Cannabis distorts spatial and time perception and impairs cognitive and psychomotor performance, and might therefore be expected to facilitate offending. However, it is also possible that cannabis use reduces offending, because cannabis has a sedative effect as well.

Finally, the supposed effect of weapon carrying was simply based on empirical findings that carrying a weapon to school has been shown to be a risk factor for violence (DuRant et al., 1995; Resnick et al., 2004), which makes it a potential situational risk factor for offending. Carrying a weapon is likely an indicator of the willingness to use it if the need arises, and carrying a weapon may also create the opportunity to use it unpremeditatedly in unforeseen situations of conflict.

26.5.2 Measurement and Analysis

The units of analysis for this study were not the *respondents* who participated in the SPAN study, but the *hours* that were covered by the space-time budget interviews. Respondents reported on the 24 hours of four preceding days during this interview, and provided not only information about their main activities during these hours, their whereabouts, and their company, but also on whether they offended during those hours, whether they used alcohol or marijuana, and whether they carried a weapon. To analyze in which situations adolescents actually committed offenses, and in which situations they did not, the analysis focused on those respondents that self-reported that they offended at least once during the hours covered by the space-time budget interview. The analysis was limited to those hours that these 76 respondents were awake. This resulted in a total "sample size" of 4,949 hours.

The measure of *offending* during a particular hour was derived from the space-time budget interviews. Interviewers noted in a separate column of the space-time budget form in which hour respondents reported having committed an offense. The type of offense was also recorded. In total, 76 respondents reported 104 offenses; most of these were assaults (53 cases) and acts of vandalism (41 cases). A few of the offenses were property offenses (6 cases of thefts), traffic offenses, or other offenses (4 cases). Because of the relatively small number of offenses reported in the space-time budget interviews, all four offense-types were combined and analyzed as instances of generic offending.

The measures of the independent variables were also based on the space-time budget interviews. *Presence of peers* was derived from questions about the persons that were physically present in the setting during a particular hour. Persons that were personally known to the respondent and equal in status were counted as peers; this included friends and acquaintances (of both sexes), partners (girlfriend or boyfriend), and siblings (both sexes, only younger than 18 years of age). *Absence of adult handlers* was also derived from the indicators of who was present in a particular setting during a particular hour. Adult handlers included all family members who were 18 years old or older. These could be parents, stepparents, siblings, nephews, nieces, cousins, aunts, uncles, and grandparents. Adult handlers also included professional handlers and other adults who are personally known to the respondent: teachers, sports trainers, supervisors, peers' parents, adult neighbors, employers, adult colleagues, janitors, religious leaders, doctors, dentists, psychiatrists, barbers, professional caretakers, and homework counselors. The measure of *public space* was based on the question on the functional location in which respondents were present during one particular hour. Places were regarded as public when they were freely accessible to everyone. This included streets, squares, public parking places, bus stations, train stations, airports, parks, beaches, dunes, woodlands, public sports facilities, and recreation facilities, as well as malls and shopping strips. The presence in semipublic space was also measured, which included indoor and outdoor places that require some form of membership (e.g., school, sports club, and doctor's office) or payment for entry or service delivery (e.g., movie theater, football stadium, and restaurant). The measure of *unstructured activity* was based on the space-time budget question about what respondents were doing during a particular hour. Activities were counted as unstructured if they included socializing as their main activity, for example, hanging around, having a break/pause during school, walking or biking around, visiting someone, socializing, talking (face to face), talking on the phone, emailing/chatting/texting, attending a birthday party or other party, and going out to a bar or club. *Use of alcohol* (beer, wine, or liquor), *use of cannabis* (marijuana or hash), and *carrying weapons* (knife or other sharp object usable as a weapon or other blunt object usable as a weapon) were all measured by a separate question during the space-time budget interview, and entered in a separate column in the computer form. Further, two temporal control variables were included in the analysis: whether an hour was during the evening or night, and whether an hour was during a weekday or the weekend.

In the analysis, fixed effects logit models were estimated to compare situations in which offenders committed crimes with situations in which they did not. Fixed effects analyses can be regarded as a multivariate analysis of repeated measures within the same person (or other unit of analysis). This method rules out any measured and unmeasured differences between individuals as potential confounds. The data of the two waves were pooled in a single analysis. Next to the fixed effect analyses, descriptive analyses were carried out to provide basic information about the situational characteristics of the hours in which an offense was reported.

26.5.3 Results

The descriptive analysis indicated that most of the reported offenses were committed in the presence of peers. Only 8 of the 104 offenses were committed alone, and no less than 87 of 104 were committed with two or more peers. Further, most offenses were committed with no adult handlers around (78 cases) and in public or semipublic space (60 and 36 cases). Enhanced rates of offending were found for all situational conditions that were analyzed: adolescent committed relatively more offenses during times spent with peers, in the absence of adult handlers, in unstructured activities, in public space, when under the influence of alcohol or cannabis, and while carrying a weapon.

The findings of the fixed effects logit analysis showed that most of the situational conditions also increase the likelihood of offending independently from each other and from the temporal control variables. The strongest effect was for being in public space, with an odds ratio around 10. This means that the odds of offending (the probability of offending divided by the probability of nonoffending) increased by a factor of 10 when respondents were in this situation.

Substantial effects (odds ratios of 2 to 4) were also found for presence of peers, absence of adult handlers, unstructured activities, and alcohol use. No significant effects were found for carrying a weapon or for cannabis use.

Overall, these findings offer strong support for the situational hypotheses derived from various theoretical perspectives. The effects on actual offending were surprisingly large, and this suggests that situational conditions are fundamental in understanding time fluctuations in offending among offenders. Restricting the analyses to offenders ruled out between-individual differences in exposure to certain conditions.

26.6 Conclusion

The three sub-studies of the SPAN project described in this chapter demonstrate the possibilities and usefulness of the employed methods to test situational explanations of adolescent offending. The methods, therefore, allow for specification of which behavior settings are particularly criminogenic. Space-time budget interviews provided data about the routine activities of young people, and combined this information with data about the precise circumstances under which these activities occurred, the locations where the activities took place, and the people who were present. This made it possible to test and expand various situational theories, in particular the individualized routine activities approach of Osgood et al. (1996) that emphasizes unstructured socializing as an important influence on delinquent behavior. The detailed information from the space-time budget interviews importantly improved the measurement of unstructured socializing, providing much more precision than previously employed survey items and scales. Moreover, it made it possible to determine how much time was spent in unstructured socializing in different circumstances, such as in private, semipublic, or public locations. These measurements enabled the researchers of the first sub-study to test hypotheses derived from the situational classification of "responsibilities of places" in the routine activity approach of Felson (1995), and to use the results to expand and specify the unstructured socializing perspective. Such focused analyses and elaboration of situational theories would be impossible without detailed data on activity patterns and whereabouts collected by methods such as the space-time budget interview.

The combination of detailed data on time use (derived from the space-time budget interviews) with information on neighborhood characteristics (derived from administrative data, community surveys, and systematic social observations) further expanded the possibilities to empirically explore situational theories. It enabled tests of hypotheses grounded in the social disorganization perspective (e.g., Sampson et al., 1997; Shaw and McKay, 1942) and in the broken windows theory (Wilson and Kelling, 1982). Combining these methods made it possible to determine how much time adolescents spent in what kind of geographical settings. This also allowed the study to distinguish between residential neighborhoods and the neighborhoods to which individuals are exposed in their daily life. The use of situational data collection methods made it possible to discover that the majority of adolescents' unstructured socializing actually takes place away from the residential neighborhood, and that the type of neighborhood where this activity takes place is relevant for adolescents' involvement in delinquency.

Finally, the methods used in the SPAN study made it possible to investigate in which situations offenses are actually committed (or in which situations people actually become victimized; see Averdijk and Bernasco, 2015). Such data can be used to test hypotheses about direct facilitators of crime, independent from personal characteristics of the perpetrator or victim. It can also be used to analyze crime trips or activity sequences (e.g., which activities precede criminal activity and which activities follow substance use). In the third sub-study, the precise measurements of situations and behavior during short periods of time (in our case one hour covered by the space-time budget interviews) showed that there are various situational determinants of crime with substantial effects on the chance that an offender commits an offense at a particular time. These insights would have been impossible without such precise measurements of the settings during the hours in which crime actually occurs.

26.6.1 Toward Specification of Criminogenic Behavior Settings

Building on the theoretical legacy of Barker (1968; Barker et al., 1978), Wikström argued that "it is possible that some types of behavior settings are more likely than others to create situations in which individuals may act unlawfully" (Wikström and Sampson, 2003: 125) and proposed further investigation of such criminogenic behavior settings. The space-time budget method that we described in this chapter was developed by Wikström specifically to capture such criminogenic behavior settings. In applying the space-time budget method, the three studies that are described in this chapter provide insight into the situational conditions that are related to higher risks for delinquent behavior. Thereby their results offer clues to which elements in behavior settings are specifically criminogenic.

Integrating the results from the three discussed studies with insights from routine activity theory (Cohen and Felson, 1979), the unstructured socializing perspective (Osgood et al., 1996), and results from earlier studies, we can name three categories of social and physical "behavior objects" that (potentially) contribute to a criminogenic setting (i.e., a setting conducive of adolescent delinquent behavior). First, the *peers who are present* have an important impact on adolescents' behavior (sub-study 3; Bernasco et al., 2013; Weerman et al., 2015) and can provide immediate stimulation and facilitation of delinquency (as audience, instigators, reinforcers, provokers, and/or co-offenders). They can also contribute to deviance-conducive settings by shaping standing behavior patterns in which deviant talk and deviant acts are tolerated or even encouraged (Dishion et al., 1996; Osgood et al., 1996; Warr, 1996). Studies suggest that the gender composition of the group and the size of the group also affect individual delinquency, such that mixed-gender groups (Lam et al., 2014; Peterson et al., 2001) and larger groups (McGloin and Thomas, 2016) are more likely to contribute to criminogenic settings. Further, it appears that peers contribute to type-specific deviance conducive settings: unstructured socializing with vandalizing friends increases adolescents' risk for engaging in vandalism, and unstructured socializing with stealing, substance-using, and violent friends increase adolescents' risk for engaging in those respective behaviors (Hoeben et al., 2016a).

Second, the *people who are present but not actively participating* in the activity are potential sources of social control and supervision (e.g., Levine et al., 2011; for a literature review on guardianship see Hollis-Peel et al., 2011). Their effect on adolescents' delinquency is illustrated by the findings on functional location and neighborhood collective efficacy (first and second sub-study). Unstructured socializing is more strongly related to delinquency if it occurs in locations where other people generally do not feel responsible (Eck, 1994; Felson, 1995; Hoeben and Weerman, 2014) and in neighborhoods where residents feel unable or unwilling to interfere when rules are broken (Hoeben, 2016; Sampson et al., 1997). People who are present but not actively participating in the activity may also form targets or provokers of delinquency. One explanation for the finding that the unstructured socializing-delinquency relationship is amplified in public entertainment settings is that such locations are generally crowded with drunk and therefore inconsiderate people, which potentially evokes aggression (e.g., Graham et al., 2000).

Third, *attributes in the physical environment* have been theorized to offer targets for delinquent behavior (such as "hot products" in shopping centers, Clarke, 2002), to form cues that inappropriate behavior is tolerated (such as physical disorder; Keizer et al., 2008; Wilson and Kelling, 1982), or to facilitate delinquency in other ways (such as available alcoholic beverages in public entertainment settings that may evoke aggression and other inappropriate behaviors). Findings of the described SPAN studies do not indicate that physical disorder in the area strengthens the unstructured socializing-delinquency relationship (sub-study 2), nor do they indicate that unstructured socializing is particularly criminogenic in shopping centers (sub-study 1), nor that the presence of weapons increases risks for offending (sub-study 3). On the other hand, sub-study 3 (Bernasco et al., 2013) showed that alcohol use more than doubled the odds for delinquency, implying that alcoholic beverages are physical objects that, when available, can function as crime-conducive objects in settings. Given the central role that physical objects play in the behavior settings theory, as well as in the literature on situational crime prevention, future research is warranted to explore the criminogeneity of specific physical objects.

26.6.2 Recommendations for Further Research

Despite the promising potential of the concept of criminogenic behavior settings for theoretical development in criminology, research into situational conditions for crime and delinquency is still in its infancy. Much remains unclear about features that make behavior settings particularly criminogenic. For example, further research is necessary to determine why the presence of peers is a crime-conducive factor. Observational studies have suggested that provocation and "signifying" are important processes at play (Anderson, 1999; Short and Strodtbeck, 1965), quantitative studies have pointed at instigation (Warr, 1996; McGloin and Nguyen, 2012), and prior experimental research has established the presence of positive reinforcement (Dishion et al., 1996) and imitation (Bot et al., 2007; Larsen et al., 2010). Warr (2002) and emphasized the roles of status, loyalty, and fear of ridicule as important motives for adolescents to respond to pressure from peers to engage in delinquency and substance use. Future research needs to further scrutinize these, and perhaps other, group processes.

Also in need of further examination is the actual role of place managers. Despite persistent findings that crime concentrates in particular facilities (e.g., Eck et al., 2007; Felson, 1987), we do not know much about the role of place managers. It is possible that deterrent effects are not even explained with the presence of place managers, but that they are inherent to specific functional locations and standing behavior patterns at those locations.

Finally, research is needed to explore underlying processes in the relationship between criminogenic behavior settings and delinquency. Hoeben and Weerman (2016) attempted to disentangle such processes for the relationship between unstructured socializing and delinquency. Although exposure to opportunities for delinquency was of relevance, they found that long-term processes were important as well, in particular exposure to delinquent peers and adoption of attitudes favorable to delinquency. It would be interesting to examine underlying processes of the relationship between delinquency and more narrowly defined criminogenic behavior settings (e.g., unstructured socializing in low-collective-efficacy neighborhoods, or unstructured socializing in specific group settings), to see whether "opportunities" processes would gain in relative importance.

26.6.3 Limitations of the Methods

Of course, there are various limitations to the methods that were used in the SPAN study (see Hoeben et al., 2014 for a more expansive list regarding limitations to the space-time budget method). One important issue is that the four days that are covered in the space-time budget interviews represent a sample out of the lives of the respondents. It is uncertain to which extent these four days are representative, and various biases may occur. The most important one is seasonal influence and weather circumstances that can affect the activities of people in important ways.

Another limitation of the space-time budget interview is that crime is a rare event: not every person is involved in crime and for those who are, it is not a daily activity. This implies that data from these interviews may exclude much interpersonal variation, unless the sample is very large.

A third important limitation of the space-time budget interview is that the time unit of one hour may not be specific enough to establish the duration of activities that have a shorter time slot. Crimes usually unfold much more quickly than over the course of an hour, and the situations and settings in which they occur may also shift during one hour. The use of one-hour time slots may be less problematic if a researcher wants to get an overall indication of time use patterns of people. However, to really capture events and their situational determinants, these units are limited in precision.

Related limitations are relevant for the ecological measurements that can be combined with the space-time budget interviews. Seasonal and temporal influences may influence the neighborhood characteristics as reported by respondents of a community survey, and they may also bias data about social and physical disorder collected with systematic social observations. The neighborhood is probably a unit of analysis that is too large to really capture setting characteristics and situational influences on the behavior of adolescents (see also Weisburd et al., 2009). The areas of 200 by 200 meters, covered by the systematic social observations, seem to be more appropriate, but they may also represent a set of settings and locations that is too large. The exact spot where the observation was done within the grid cell of 200 by 200 meters may not be the setting that was relevant during a particular hour covered by the space-time budget interview. It is also possible that a condition that was relevant for the respondent during the hours that they spent their time in a certain setting was absent at the moment of observation.

26.6.4 Concluding Remarks

Despite these limitations, it is obvious that information from space-time budget interviews, combined with data on neighborhoods and small areas, strongly enhances the study of situational correlates of crime and criminal behavior. The current limitations of these methods might be mitigated in future research by zooming in on shorter time spans and even smaller areas and locations. Promising improvements in this regard are attempts to conduct time use research and space-time budget methodologies with the aid of smartphones and GPS tracking devices (e.g., Browning et al., 2014; Solymosi and Bowers, in this volume; Sonck and Fernee, 2013; Wiehe et al., 2008a). These and similar innovations may further improve the measurement of (criminogenic) behavior settings and thereby help us to capture the situational context of crime.

References

Allison, P. D. (2009). *Fixed Effects Regression Models* (Los Angeles: Sage).

Anderson, E. (1999). *Code of the Street: Decency, Violence, and the Moral Life of the Inner City* (New York: Norton).

Averdijk, M., and Bernasco, W. (2015). "Testing the Situational Explanation of Victimization among Adolescents." *Journal of Research in Crime and Delinquency* 52(2): 151–180.

Barker, R. G. (1963). *The Stream of Behaviour* (New York: Appleton-Century-Crofts).

Barker, R. G. (1968). *Ecological Psychology: Concepts and Methods for Studying the Environment of Human Behaviour* (Stanford, CA: Stanford University Press).

Barker, R. G., Barker, L. S., Fawl, C. L., Gump, P. V., Halstead, L. S., Johnson, A., Ragle, D. D. M., Schoggen, M. F., Schoggen, P., Wicker, A. W., Willems, E. P., and Wright, H. F. (1978). *Habitats, Environments, and Human Behaviour: Studies in Ecological Psychology and Eco-Behavioural Science from the Midwest Psychological Field Station, 1947–1972* (San Francisco: Jossey-Bass).

Bernasco, W., Ruiter, S., Bruinsma, G. J. N., Pauwels, L. J. R., and Weerman, F. M. (2013). "Situational Causes of Offending: A Fixed-Effects Analysis of Space-Time Budget Data." *Criminology* 51(4): 895–926.

Blokland, A. A., and Nieuwbeerta, P. (2010). "Life Course Criminology." In *International Handbook of Criminology*, edited by G. S. Shlomo, P. Knepper, and M. Kett, pp. 51–94 (Boca Raton, FL: CRC Press).

Bot, S. M., Engels, R. C. M. E., Knibbe, R. A., and Meeus, W. (2007). "Sociometric Status and Social Drinking: Observations of Modelling and Persuasion in Young Adult Peer Groups." *Journal of Abnormal Child Psychology* 35(6): 929–941.

Browning, C. R., Calder, C., Cooksey, E., and Kwan, M.-P. (2014). "Adolescent Health and Development in Context." http://sociology.osu.edu/browning-adolescent-health-and-development-context. Accessed 24 March 2014.

Bruinsma, G. J. N., Pauwels, L. J. R., Weerman, F. M., and Bernasco, W. (2013). "Social Disorganisation, Social Capital, Collective Efficacy and the Spatial Distribution of Crime and Offenders: An Empirical Test of Six Neighborhood Models for a Dutch City." *British Journal of Criminology* 53(5): 942–963.

Clarke, R. V. (2002). *Shoplifting* (Washington, DC: Community Oriented Policing Services, U.S. Department of Justice).

Cohen, L. E., and Felson, M. (1979). "Social Change and Crime Rate Trends: A Routine Activity Approach." *American Sociological Review* 44(4): 588–608.

Dishion, T. J., Spracklen, K. M., Andrews, D. W., and Patterson, G. R. (1996). "Deviancy Training in Male Adolescent Friendships." *Behavior Therapy* 27(3): 373–390.

DuRant, R. H., Getts, A. G., Cadenhead, C., and Woods, E. R. (1995). "The Association between Weapon Carrying and the Use of Violence among Adolescents Living in and around Public Housing." *Journal of Adolescent Health* 17:376–380.

Eck, J. E. (1994). *Drug Markets and Drug Places: A Case-Control Study of the Spatial Structure of Illicit Drug Dealing* (PhD Dissertation, University of Maryland, College Park).

Eck, J. E., Clarke, R. V., and Guerette, R. T. (2007). "Risky Facilities: Crime Concentration in Homogenous Sets of Establishments and Facilities." In *Imagination for Crime Prevention: Essays in Honour of Ken Pease*, ed. G. Farrell, K. J. Bowers, S. D. Johnson, and Michael Townsley, pp. 225–264, vol. 21 of *Crime Prevention Studies* Monsey, NY: Criminal Justice Press).

Felson, M. (1987). "Routine Activities and Crime Prevention in the Developing Metropolis." *Criminology* 25(4): 911–931.

Felson, M. (1995). "Those Who Discourage Crime." In *Crime and Place:*, edited by J. E. Eck and D. L. Weisburd, pp. 53–66, vol. 4 of *Crime Prevention Studies* (Monsey, NY: Criminal Justice Press).

Fisher, K., and Gershuny, J. (2013). "Time Use and Time Diary Research." In *Oxford Bibliographies in Sociology*, edited by J. Manza, pp. 1–23 (New York: Oxford University Press).

Gottfredson, M. R., and Hirschi, T. (1990). *A General Theory of Crime* (Stanford, CA: Stanford University Press).

Graham, K., West, P., and Wells, S. (2000). "Evaluating Theories of Alcohol-Related Aggression Using Observations of Young Adults in Bars." *Addiction* 96(6): 847–863.

Hindelang, M. J., Gottfredson, M. R., and Garofalo, J. (1978). *Victims of Personal Crime: An Empirical Foundation for a Theory of Personal Victimization* (Cambridge: Ballinger).

Hoeben, E. M. (2016). "Disadvantage in the Area." In *Hanging Out and Messing About: Elaborating on the Relationship between Unstructured Socializing and Adolescent Delinquency* (PhD Dissertation, Department of Criminal Law and Criminology, VU University Amsterdam).

Hoeben, E. M., Bernasco, W., Weerman, F. M., Pauwels, L. J. R., and Van Halem, S. (2014). "The Space-Time Budget Method in Criminological Research." *Crime Science* 3(12): 1–15.

Hoeben, E. M., Osgood, W., Siennick, S. E., and Weerman, F. M. (2016a). "Characteristics of the Present Peers." In *Hanging Out and Messing About: Elaborating on the Relationship between Unstructured Socializing and Adolescent Delinquency* (PhD Dissertation, Department of Criminal Law and Criminology, VU University Amsterdam).

Hoeben, E. M., Steenbeek, W., and Pauwels, L. J. R. (2016b). "Measuring Disorder: Observer Bias in Systematic Social Observation at Streets and Neighborhoods." *Journal of Quantitative Criminology*, online, doi: 10.1007/s10940-016-9333-6.

Hoeben, E. M., and Weerman, F. M. (2014). "Situational Conditions and Adolescent Offending: Does the Impact of Unstructured Socializing Depend on Its Location?" *European Journal of Criminology* 11(4): 481–499.

Hoeben, E. M., and Weerman, F. M. (2016). "Why Is Involvement in Unstructured Socializing Related to Adolescent Delinquency?" *Criminology* 54(2): 242–281.

Hollis-Peel, M. E., Reynald, D. M., Van Bavel, M., Elffers, H., and Welsh, B. C. (2011). "Guardianship for Crime Prevention: A Critical Review of the Literature." *Crime, Law, and Social Change* 56(1): 53–70.

Janssen, H. J., Bruinsma, G. J. N., Deković, M. and Eichelsheim, V. (2016). "A Between- and Within-Person Analysis of Parenting and Time Spent in Criminogenic Settings during Adolescence: The Role of Self-Control and Delinquent Attitudes." *Youth and Society*, online, doi: 10.1177/0044118X16636138.

Janssen, H. J., Weerman, F. M., and Eichelsheim, V. (2017). "Parenting as a Protective Factor against Criminogenic Settings? Interaction Effects between Three Aspects of Parenting and Unstructured Socializing in Disordered Areas." *Journal of Research in Crime and Delinquency* 54(2): 181–207.

Keizer, K., Lindenberg, S., and Steg, L. (2008). "The Spreading of Disorder." *Science* 322(5908): 1681–1685.

Lam, C. B., McHale, S. M., and Crouter, A. C. (2014). "Time with Peers from Middle Childhood to Late Adolescence: Developmental Course and Adjustment Correlates." *Child Development* 85(4): 1677–1693.

Larsen, H., Engels, R. C. M. E., Souren, P. M., Granic, I., and Overbeek, G. (2010). "Peer Influence in a Micro-perspective: Imitation of Alcoholic and Non-alcoholic Beverages." *Addictive Behaviors* 35(1): 49–52.

Lemieux, A. M., and Felson, M. (2012). "Risk of Violent Crime Victimization during Major Daily Activities." *Violence and Victims* 27(5): 635–655.

Levine, M., Taylor, P. J., and Best, R. (2011). "Third Parties, Violence, and Conflict Resolution: The Role of Group Size and Collective Acton in the Microregulation of Violence." *Psychological Science* 22(3): 406–412.

McGloin, J. M., and Nguyen, H. (2012). "It Was My Idea: Considering the Instigation of Co-offending." *Criminology* 50(2): 463–494.

McGloin, J. M., and Thomas, K. J. (2016). "Incentives for Collective Deviance: Group Size and Changes in Perceived Risk, Cost, and Reward." *Criminology* 54(3): 459–486.

McNeeley, S., and Hoeben, E. M. (2017). "Public Unstructured Socializing and the Code of the Street: Predicting Violence and Victimization." *Deviant Behavior* 38(6): 633–654.

Newman, O. (1972). *Defensible Space* (New York: Macmillan).

Oberwittler, D., and Wikström, P.-O. H. (2009). "Why Small Is Better: Advancing the Study of the Role of Behavioural Contexts in Crime Causation." In *Putting Crime in Its Place: Units of Analysis in Geographic Criminology*, edited by D. L. Weisburd, W. Bernasco, and G. J. N. Bruinsma, pp. 35–59 (New York: Springer).

Osgood, D. W., Wilson, J. K., O'Malley, P. M., Bachman, J. G., and Johnston, L. D. (1996). "Routine Activities and Individual Deviant Behaviour." *American Sociological Review* 61(4): 635–655.

Pentland, W. E., Harvey, A. S., Powell Lawton, M., and McColl, M. A. (1999). *Time Use Research in the Social Sciences* (New York: Kluwer Academic Publishers).

Peterson, D., Miller, J., and Esbensen, F.-A. (2001). "The Impact of Sex Composition on Gangs and Gang Member Delinquency." *Criminology* 39(2): 411–440.

Raudenbush, S. W., and Sampson, R. J. (1999). "Ecometrics: Toward a Science of Assessing Ecological Settings, with Application to the Systematic Social Observation of Neighborhoods." *Sociological Methodology* 29: 1–41.

Rengert, G. F., and Wasilchick, J. (1985). *Suburban Burglary: A Time and Place for Everything.* (Springfield, IL: Charles C. Thomas).

Resnick, M. D., Ireland, M., and Borowsky, I. (2004). "Youth Violence Perpetration: What Protects? What Predicts? Findings from the National Longitudinal Study of Adolescent Health." *Journal of Adolescent Health* 35:424.e1–10.

Riley, D. (1987). "Time and Crime: The Link between Teenager Lifestyle and Delinquency." *Journal of Quantitative Criminology* 3(4): 339–354.

Rossmo, D. K., Lu, Y., Fang, T. B. (2012). "Spatial-Temporal Crime Paths." In *Patterns, Prevention, and Geometry of Crime*, edited by M. A. Andresen and J. B. Kinney, pp. 16–42 (New York: Routledge).

Sampson, R. J. (1987). "Urban Black Violence: The Effect of Male Joblessness and Family Disruption." *American Journal of Sociology* 93(2): 348–382.

Sampson, R. J., and Groves, W. B. (1989). "Community Structure and Crime: Testing Social-Disorganization Theory." *American Journal of Sociology* 94(4): 774–802.

Sampson, R. J., and Raudenbush, S. W. (1999). "Systematic Social Observation of Public Spaces: A New Look at Disorder in Urban Neighbourhoods." *American Journal of Sociology* 105(3): 603–651.

Sampson, R. J., Raudenbush, S. W., and Earls, F. (1997). "Neighborhoods and Violent Crime: A Multilevel Study of Collective Efficacy." *Science* 277: 918–924.

Shaw, C. R., and McKay, H. D. (1942). *Juvenile Delinquency and Urban Areas* (Chicago: University of Chicago Press).

Short, J. F., Jr., and Strodtbeck, F. L. (1965). *Group Process and Gang Delinquency* (Chicago: University of Chicago Press).

Sonck, N., and Fernee, H. (2013). *Using Smartphones in Survey Research: A Multifunctional Tool. Implementation of a Time Use App; A Feasability Study* (The Hague: Netherlands Institute for Social Research, SCP).

Taylor, R. B. (1987). "Toward an Environmental Psychology of Disorder: Delinquency, Crime, and Fear of Crime." In *Handbook of Environmental Psychology*, edited by D. Stokols and I. Altman, pp. 951–986 (New York: John Wiley and Sons).

Thomas, W. I., and Znaniecki, F. (1918-1920). *The Polish Peasant in Europe and America: Organization and Disorganization in America* (Boston: Legacy reprint series).

Thornberry, T. P., and Krohn, M. D. (eds.) (2003). *Taking Stock of Delinquency: An Overview of Findings from Contemporary Longitudinal Studies* (Dordrecht: Kluwer).

Warr, M. (1996). "Organization and Instigation in Deliquent Groups." *Criminology* 34(1): 11–37.

Warr, M. (2002). *Companions in Crime: The Social Aspects of Criminal Conduct* (Cambridge: Cambridge University Press).

Weerman, F. M., Bernasco, W., Bruinsma, G. J. N., and Pauwels, L. J. R. (2015). "When Is Spending Time with Peers Related to Delinquency? The Importance of Where, What and with Whom." *Crime and Delinquency*, 61(10): 1386–1413.

Weisburd, D. L., Bernasco, W., and Bruinsma, G. J. N. (2009). "Units of Analysis in Geographic Criminology: Historical Development, Critical Issues, and Open Questions." In *Putting Crime in Its Place: Units of Analysis in Geographic Criminology*, edited by D. L. Weisburd, W. Bernasco, and G. J. N. Bruinsma, pp. 3–31 (New York: Springer).

Wiehe, S. E., Carroll, A. E., Liu, G. C., Haberkorn K. L., Hoch, S. C., Wilson, J. S., and Fortenberry, J. D. (2008a). "Using GPS-Enabled Cell Phones to Track the Travel Patterns of Adolescents." *International Journal of Health Geographics* 7(22): 1–11.

Wiehe, S. E., Hoch, S. C., Liu, G. C., Carroll, A. E., Wilson, J. S., and Fortenberry, J. D. (2008b). "Adolescent Travel Patterns: Pilot Data Indicating Distance from Home Varies by Time of Day and Day of Week." *Journal of Adolescent Health* 42(4): 418–420.

Wikström, P.-O. H. (2006). "Individuals, Settings, and Acts of Crime: Situational Mechanisms and the Explanation of Crime." In *The Explanation of Crime: Context, Mechanisms, and Development*, edited by P.-O. H. Wikström and R. J. Sampson, pp. 61–107 (Cambridge: Cambridge University Press).

Wikström, P.-O. H. (2014). "Why Crime Happens: A Situational Action Theory." In *Analytical Sociology: Actions and Networks*, edited by G. Manzo, pp. 74–96 (Hoboken, NJ: John Wiley and Sons).

Wikström, P.-O. H., and Butterworth, D. A. (2006). *Adolescent Crime: Individual Differences and Lifestyles* (Collumpton: Willan Publishing).

Wikström, P.-O. H., Ceccato, V., Hardie, B., and Treiber, K. (2010). "Activity Fields and the Dynamics of Crime: Advancing Knowledge about the Role of the Environment in Crime Causation." *Journal of Quantitative Criminology* 26(1): 55–87.

Wikström, P.-O. H., Oberwittler, D., Treiber, K., and Hardie, B. (2012a). *Breaking Rules: The Social and Situational Dynamics of Young People's Urban Crime* (Oxford: Oxford University Press).

Wikström, P.-O. H., and Sampson, S. J. (2003). "Social Mechanisms of Community Influences on Crime and Pathways in Criminality." In *Causes of Conduct Disorder and Juvenile Delinquency*, edited by B. B. Lahey, T. E. Moffitt, and A. Caspi, pp. 118–148 (New York: Guilford Press).

Wikström, P.-O. H., Treiber, K., and Hardie, B. (2012b). "Examining the Role of the Environment in Crime Causation: Small-Area Community Surveys and Space-Time Budgets." In *The Sage Handbook of Criminological Research Methods*, edited by D. Gadd, S. Karstedt, and S. F. Messner, pp. 111–127 (Los Angeles: Sage).

Wilson, J. Q., and Kelling, G. L. (1982). "Broken Windows: The Police and Neighborhood Safety." *Atlantic Monthly* 249(3): 29–38.

CHAPTER 27

PLACE MANAGEMENT

JOHN E. ECK AND TAMARA D. MADENSEN

27.1 Introduction

The theory of place management explains why some properties have a great deal of crime or disorder and most others have little or no crime or disorder. It is an extension of routine activity theory (Cohen and Felson, 1979). If place hotspots are viewed as dots on maps, then place management theory describes the processes inside the dots that make them hot, and how these processes connect to surrounding areas. Place management theory brings together, under a single explanation, a wide variety of alternative perspectives of why some places have more crime than others. Place management theory shifts the locus of crime control from outside policing to inside practices. It shows who will have to be engaged in prevention for crime to be reduced at places—the owner and any delegated managers of the property. Finally, place management theory provides an alternative foundation for understanding neighborhood-level crime concentration.

This chapter is divided into seven sections following this introduction. The first section provides a background necessary for understanding place management. It summarizes the research showing that places are fundamental to understanding crime. And it shows how different researchers have defined place, paying particular attention to proprietary places: the type of place relevant for place management theory. The second section describes the concept of place manager: who they are and how they differ from others involved in crime or its suppression. The third section describes what place managers do that is important for preventing or facilitating crime. The fourth section shows how place management theory embraces a wide variety of other explanations for crime at place. At least 10 different explanations have been proposed. With one exception, place management can describe each. In the fifth section, we look at the processes involved in place management. These operate over different time scales while linking actions within places to factors in the surrounding environment. The sixth section describes the empirical evidence that place management exists and can be manipulated. We divide the evidence into direct and indirect support. The final section shows that place management theory opens up several lines of enquiry that could give us a fuller explanation of crime patterns, and could lead to better ways to reduce crime.

27.2 Why Focus on Places?

It is difficult to imagine things we cannot see. The invention of the microscope allowed biologists to see organisms previously invisible and unimaginable, to develop theories of disease that were previously out of bounds, and eventually to help create interventions to treat these diseases. In a similar way, advances in computing and data management allowed researchers and practitioners to see important crime phenomena at subneighborhood scales. These new patterns required new explanations and suggested important new interventions to reduce crime. Before the advent of inexpensive, easy-to-use geographic information systems, the finest resolution of crime observable was at the area level. The easy availability of "neighborhood"-level data, and the difficulty of gathering data for smaller units, accounts for the continued popularity of neighborhood theories of crime within the criminological imagination.

Police pin maps predate the computer and have been used by police to show crime within neighborhoods (Buck et al., 1973). But pins and dots are hard for social scientists to analyze, so it was not until the late 1980s that two studies unveiled the hidden world of crime places to criminologists. In Boston, Glenn Pierce, Susan Spaar, and LeBaron Briggs (1988) showed that crime is highly concentrated at a relatively few addresses. Unfortunately, the authors did not publish their findings in an academic journal but printed them in a large research report. Consequently, this groundbreaking study received little attention. Far more attention was paid to Lawrence Sherman, Patrick Gartin, and Michael Buerger's (1989) paper on Minneapolis crime places, published in *Criminology*. Not only was their paper shorter and more accessible than the paper by Pierce, Spaar, and Briggs, but it also linked their empirical findings to a well-established theory: routine activity theory (Cohen and Felson, 1979).

The upper-left chart in Figure 27.1 shows the distribution of crime in Minneapolis across places, using Sherman and colleagues' data. In their study, places are addresses and street corners. If crime were randomly distributed, then the distribution should approximate a Poisson distribution, shown by the dashed line. The crime distribution most clearly does not look like a Poisson distribution, but follows a very different pattern. Most places have no crime and a few places have a great deal of crime. Sherman, Gartin and Buerger (1989) showed this was true even when they analyzed different crime types.

Since the late 1980s, over 60 studies of crime at place have been published showing that a few places have most crime and most places have no crime (Lee et al., 2015). As long as the crime is reasonably frequent, the type of crime does not matter. Further, it does not matter what type of places are examined. The first two studies looked at all places in two cities. But even when we isolate bars, or apartment buildings, or bus stops,

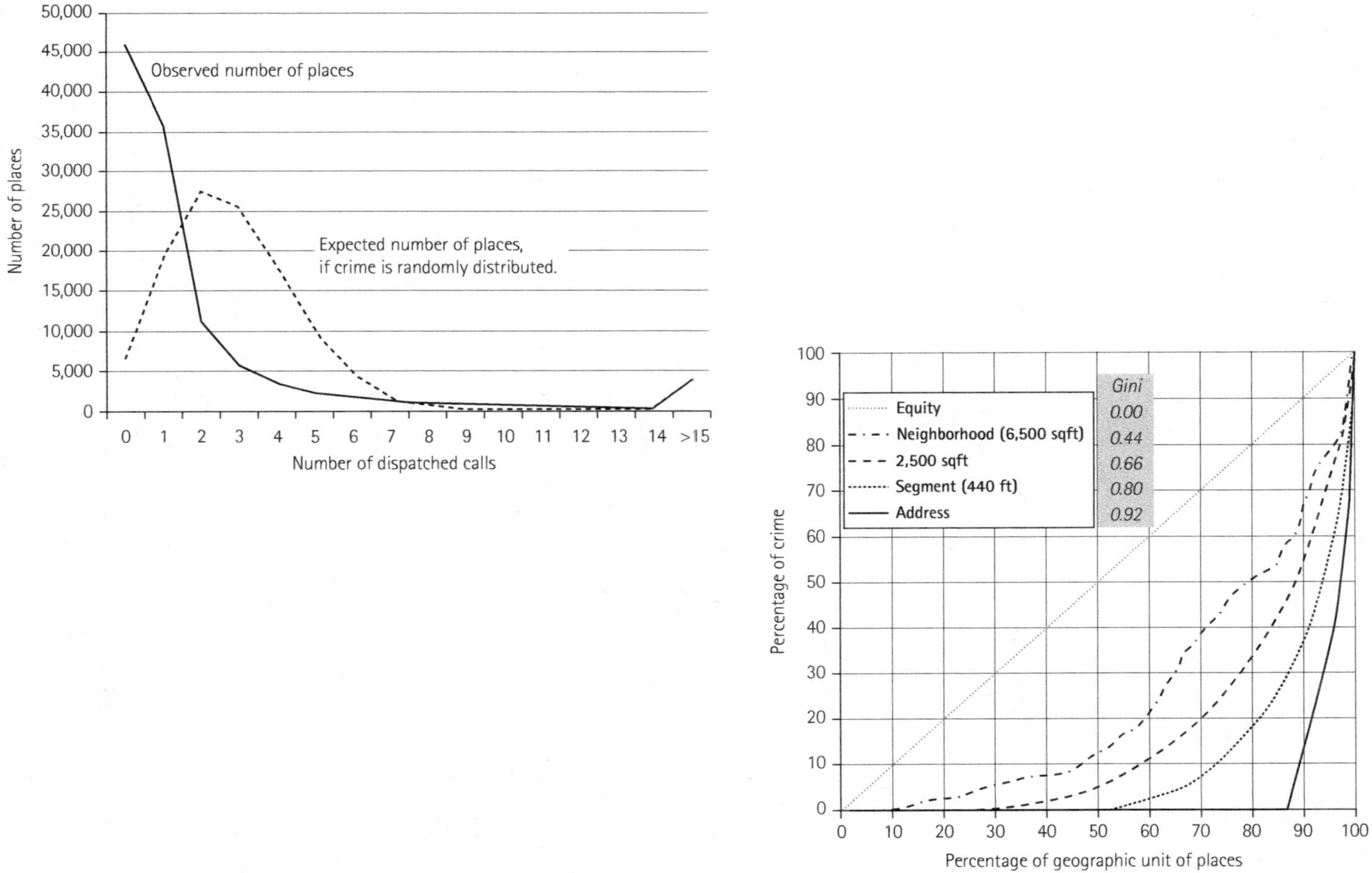

FIGURE 27.1 Concentration of crime at place

or any other type of place, this distribution shows up. John Eck, Ronald Clarke, and Rob Guerette (2007) call a homogeneous set of places facilities, and among any specific facility most are crime free, and a few are risky. Pam Wilcox and John Eck (2011) showed that there are no known studies of facilities that violate this rule, so they call this phenomenon "The Iron Law of Troublesome Places." David Weisburd has another, equally compelling name. He calls it the "Law of Crime Concentration" (Weisburd, 2015).

27.3 What Is a Place?

The meaning of "place" varies across studies, however. Sherman, Gartin, and Buerger (1989, p. 31) define a place as "a fixed physical environment that can be seen completely and simultaneously, at least on its surface, by one's naked eye." Street segments have been defined as places. David Weisburd and colleagues (2004, p. 290) state, "The geographic unit of interest for this study is the street segment (sometimes referred to as a street block or face block) defined as the two block faces on both sides of a street between two intersections" (see also Groff, Weisburd, and Yang, 2010, p. 12).

John Eck (1994, pp. 10–13) described five features that define places: location, boundaries, function, control, and size. We must be able to locate the place geographically: it does not require a fixed location (e.g., a bus), but we must be able to find it at any particular time. It must have a boundary, so we know what is within the place and what is without. The place must have a dominant function: for example, residence, entertainment, production of some good or service, and so forth. It must have a person, group, or organization that has legal authority to control how the site is used. This is a place manager and is an important concept we will describe in greater detail later. And it must be small: roughly no bigger than a block face, though probably no smaller than a one-room flat (or apartment).

Despite their specific differences, these researchers agreed that places are very small. Others, however, use the term "place" to refer to much larger units. Within the field of geography, for example, the term "place" can refer to geographic units over a wide range of sizes, and refer to concepts that are physically tangible and states of mind (Cresswell, 2015). But even within criminology, the term sometimes refers to larger entities. David Weisburd, Nancy Morris, and Justin Ready (2008) use the census block group. Todd Clear's (1996) "corrections of place" does not specifically define "place," but implies that it varies in size from an address to a neighborhood.

To address this variation, we distinguish among three different forms of places (Madensen and Eck, 2013). *Proprietary places* are usually small locations with a particular function and an owner. These generally correspond to addresses and are similar to the places described by Eck (1994). *Proximal places* are strings of proprietary places along streets, and correspond to the sorts of units described by Weisburd and colleagues (2004) and Groff, Weisburd, and Yang (2010). Usually, there are multiple owners (including local governments) involved in proximal places. Finally, *pooled places* are contiguous sets of proximal places. This is the category for neighborhoods, as well as census blocks, block groups, and tracts, and any larger area (Madensen and Eck, 2013). Theories of neighborhood crime and social disorganization describe pooled places.

There are two reasons to be careful how we define place. First, the concentration of crime varies considerably with the definition. This can be seen in the lower-right chart in Figure 27.1. The graph shows a set of Lorenz curves with accompanying Gini coefficients for places of different sizes in Cincinnati. The horizontal axis shows cumulative places ranked from least to most crime. The vertical axis shows the cumulative percentage of crime. The diagonal straight line indicates how crime would be distributed if it were evenly spread over the city: the least crime involved 10% of places would have about 10% of the crime, for example. The more bowed to the bottom right the Lorenz curve, the more concentrated the crime. The Gini coefficient measures concentration. The diagonal line has a Gini value of zero (no concentration). If all crime were concentrated at a single place, then the Gini would be 1.0, and the Lorenz curve would be flat along the horizontal axis, then zoom up vertically at the last place on the right.

The four curves in Figure 27.1 lay to the right of the diagonal line. They correspond to different definitions of place. There are around 70 areas that can be considered neighborhoods in Cincinnati. The Lorenz curve and Gini value show crime is modestly concentrated in these pooled places. However, these neighborhoods vary in size, so it is possible that we are measuring the concentration of land area or population within these neighborhoods, rather than crime.

To avoid this difficulty, and to demonstrate how concentration changes with the definition of place, a grid of square areas, 500 feet on a side, were laid over the city, and crime within each square was counted. The concentration of crime within these smaller pooled places is shown in the second curve. Crime is noticeably more concentrated than in the larger neighborhoods.

The third curve shows proximal places—street segments. Crime is even more concentrated among these places, as shown by the Lorenz curve and the Gini value. Finally, the concentration of crime at proprietary places—addresses—is shown. The concentration is even greater. Clearly, the smaller the area examined, the greater the concentration of crime observed. This negative association between place size and crime concentration also has been demonstrated by Martin Andresen and Nicholas Malleson (2010) for Vancouver, Canada.

The second reason for being careful about definition is that different concepts and theories apply at different scales. In particular, as will become clearer, place management makes sense for proprietary places; it makes less sense for proximal places as these involve multiple owners, and makes virtually no sense for pooled places. Traffic flow and street networks (Beavon, Brantingham, and Brantingham, 1994) might explain why some proximal places have more crime than others, but this cannot explain why some proprietary places on a street segment have more crime than their neighbors. Social disorganization theories and concepts have largely been applied to pooled places (Shaw and McKay, 1942; Sampson, Raudenbush, and Earls, 1997). David Weisburd, Elizabeth Groff, and Sue-Ming Yang (2012) have suggested such theories would be better applied to street segments. At proprietary places, this concept might not directly apply. However, later in this chapter we will show how it might be incorporated.

Because the theory of place management explains crime concentration in proprietary places, and is probably not applicable to proximal and pooled places, in the rest of this chapter we will set aside pooled and proximal places and focus our attention on proprietary places. In the last section of this chapter, we will ask if we can create an explanation of crime within proximal and pooled places by building on proximal places. This will require us to understand the diversity of proprietary crime places.

27.4 Types of Proprietary Places

Places with large numbers of crimes are *crime sites*. The discovery of crime sites in the late 1980s drew attention to the role of places, and these have received the most attention among researchers and police. There are, however, other types of crime involved proprietary places that have received less attention. *Convergent settings* (Felson, 2003) are locations where potential offenders meet, though they may not commit crimes at these places. These can include nightclubs, transit hubs, shopping centers, and other locations that draw people from a wide area (Bichler, Malm, and Enriquez, 2010). *Comfort spaces* are proprietary places where offenders stage crimes, stash their tools, drugs, or stolen goods, or where they hang out (Hammer, 2011). To protect these locations from police scrutiny, the offenders who use them avoid committing crimes at these sites. Madensen and Eck (2013) added a fourth type of place: the *corrupting spot*. These proprietary places directly foster crime at other locations. A metal recycling firm that buys stolen copper pipe, a pawnshop that resells stolen merchandise, and an automobile repair shop that uses stolen airbag units are all examples of corrupting spots. Because the crimes occurring at corrupting spots are largely consensual, the volume of reported crime at these locations is often low. Although crime sites can be observed by mapping crimes, these other three crime-involved places will be, mostly, invisible.

Place management theory can be applied to any proprietary place type to explain variation in crime involvement. So it is to place managers we turn next.

27.5 Who Are Place Managers?

There are two elements that define place managers. First, they must have the potential to exert control over a proprietary place. Second, they must have legal authority to exercise this control (Eck, 1994). Everyone who has legal authority to exercise control over a place is a place manager.

The most important place manager is the owner. The owner may be a person, a partnership, business, club, nongovernmental organization, religious group, college or university, or government entity. Owners often hire people to see to the functioning of the place: sell things, participate in the functioning of the place, keep it clean, assist place users, and carry out a host of other tasks. These people are also place managers. In a factory, a machine tool operator is a place manager. In a school, the principal, teachers, nurses, counselors, and janitors are all place managers. The sales clerk at a convenience store is a place manager, as is the lifeguard at the pool, and ticket taker at the ferry terminal. So are owners of a house, and the landlord of an apartment building. Some proprietary places are mobile—ferries and other boats and ships, planes, buses, trains, and trolleys. The people who operate these mobile places (e.g., bus drivers and flight attendants) are place managers, too.

27.5.1 Place Manager Characteristics

The central characteristic of a place manager is that this person's primary concern is the smooth functioning of the place. Place managers are one of three types of controllers within routine activity theory. The other two are guardians, whose primary concern is to protect targets from crime, and handlers, whose primary concern is to keep potential offenders out of trouble. A place manager may not be particularly concerned about crime, if it does not interfere with the way the place operates, or if the manager gains from the crime. An owner of an apartment building who ignores illegal activities in her building is an example of this. Another example is the owner of a metal recycling center that knowingly accepts stolen copper pipes and wire.

Place managers draw their authority from ownership and property rights. Ownership conveys rights and responsibilities. Within some limits, owners can restrict entry onto their property, use their property for a variety of purposes, alter the property's physical characteristics, promulgate rules of conduct, and promote other behaviors. They can even make a profit from the property. Owners can delegate their authority to employees, and in some cases volunteers. Delegation of authority over a place makes those who receive delegated powers, place managers. No other element of routine activity theory has this authority over places.

Owners of property can be held accountable, in civil court, for crimes at their places. This is usually done with premise liability suits brought by victims (or the estates of dead victims) (Eck, 1997). However, public prosecutors and local government attorneys can sue property owners who allow their places to be used for crime. These are usually called nuisance abatement suits (Mazerolle, Roehl, and Kadleck, 1998). Clearly, in the eyes of the law, owners have some ability to control crime on their property, and have some obligation to do so, though this varies from among countries, and even within countries, such as the United States.

Place managers have a larger role in crime control than the other two controllers: guardians and handlers. This is because they control the location. We will discuss this in more detail in the next section.

27.5.2 Place Management and Guardianship

Place management is not synonymous with guardianship. These two concepts do overlap in practice. A parent accompanying his child to school is exercising guardianship, but not place management, for example. A bar owner who decides to restrict sales of drinks to customers who appear drunk is exercising place management, but not guardianship. The homeowner who watches the street in front of her home and reports suspicious activities is exercising guardianship of the public place (street) and place management of her home. The store owner who hires a security guard is creating guardianship by exercising his place management function.

Although these two concepts do overlap, they are separate concepts. Consequently, it is important to itemize their differences (summarized in Table 27.1). We have already noted that place managers, by definition, have some legal authority over the property they manage. This is not always the case with guardians. A store patron, for example, has no property rights in the store, but can provide some level of guardianship relative to shoplifting. This might occur whether or not encouraged by the store owner or employees. A store clerk—a place manager—does have some legal authority delegated by the owner. The clerk might or might not act as a guardian, and this is in part dictated by the owner (or intermediate supervisors) through instructions, training, and job duties.

Table 27.1 Differences between Place Management and Guardianship

	Place manager	Guardian
Has legal authority over the place	Always	Variable
Principal concern	Functioning of place	Protection of people or assets
Can invoke the other	Yes	No
Situational prevention mechanisms able to influence	Effort Risk Reward Provocations Excuses	Risk
Sources	Legal authority	Legal authority Social convention
Scope of influence	Within place boundaries	Within offenders' perception

Another distinction between guardianship and place management has to do with their principal concerns. Guardianship is exclusively concerned with protection of possible crime targets. Place management is concerned with the functioning of the place. For the place manager, protecting targets is often a concern, but only in the context of promoting place functioning. Crimes that do not interfere with functioning are often ignored. Some stores, for example, have policies directing employees not to get involved in crimes occurring outside the store, but on store property (e.g., in the parking area).

This difference in concern suggests an important asymmetry. Place managers can create guardianship. They can hire security guards. They can train and encourage employees to surveil and intervene in suspicious activities. They can even promote informal guardianship among place users (e.g., the public address system announcements in US airports asking people to report suspicious people). The reverse is not true. A guardian, who is not a place manager, cannot promote place management. The store patron cannot rearrange the shelves in the store, or give orders to the clerks, or dictate what will and what will not be sold (all place management functions).

Place managers and guardians use mechanisms described in situational crime prevention (Clarke, 2009) to control crime. Place managers have access to all five situational mechanisms. They can increase effort for crime by altering the physical environment, for example. They can increase risk by installing surveillance equipment. They can reduce rewards by changing the types of possible targets inside the place, or by installing devices like ink tags. They can reduce provocations by altering the sound level, temperature, lighting, or other features of the place. They can reduce excuses by the use of signage. Guardians, on the other hand, only influence risk.

Although place management can trigger a greater range of prevention mechanisms than guardianship, guardianship has more sources than place management. As noted, place managements' source is in the legal authority conveyed by property rights. That is its sole source. Guardianship stems from several sources, including legal authority. Informal social control, however, comes from social convention rather than law. In short, place management is one way of invoking guardianship, but it is not the only way and might not even be the most common way.

Finally, place management might have a more restricted scope of influence. Managers can control the physical and social conditions within the place boundaries (see Table 27.1 and associated text). Beyond these boundaries, they have no authority. Guardianship can have a wider influence, as its effectiveness depends on the perceptions of potential offenders. A homeowner can provide guardianship to neighbors' residences, even though they are outside his property limits. And even if guardians are not present, do not detect suspicious behavior, or are unwilling to intervene (Reynald, 2009), if the potential offender believes they may be present, watching, and willing to intervene, then guardianship is working.

27.6 What Do Place Managers Do?

The description of place managers gives some idea of their activities, but it is important to be more specific. Tamara Madensen (2007) formalized their actions. She specified four basic elements of place management: the ORCA framework, from the first letter of the name of each element.

27.6.1 They Organize Space

Place managers control the physical setting of the place. This starts with the decision of where to put the place. The homeowner, for example, prior to renovating their house, first had to decide which house to buy. Similarly, an entrepreneur setting up a business has to decide where that business will be located. A local government, interested in creating park space, must first decide where to put the park. After that decision, place managers decide on the physical appearance and layout. The bar owner, for example, can put the drink-serving function at the front or back of her place, or upstairs or downstairs. All repair and upkeep decisions fall into this category.

The organization of space has a major influence on how the place is used by its users. And these decisions interact with other management elements.

27.6.2 They Regulate Conduct

Place managers set the rules for the uses of places—behaviors they encourage, activities they permit, and actions they prohibit. The owner of a sit-down restaurant implicitly sets the rule that guests will be shown to a table and the staff will take orders. The guest pays the waiter after the meal. The owner of a fast-food restaurant sets the rules that guests will come to the counter, order food, and then take it to a table or from the premises. The guest pays for the meal prior to receiving the food.

Clearly, the organization of space should work with the regulation of conduct. The physical layout of sit-down restaurants looks different than the layout of fast-food restaurants. This is what Barker (1968, p. 19) meant when he stated that the physical and behavioral elements of a behavioral setting are synomorphic.

Crime researchers typically think about regulation as restrictions designed to thwart crime. Place managers do use this form of regulation of conduct. However, they also promote particular behaviors, and this too has influence over the presence of absence of crime. Drinking establishments, for example, have different themes and encourage different forms of behavior: sitting quietly and conversing with friends; dancing; rooting for sports teams; and assorted competitive games (Madensen, 2007).

27.6.3 They Control Access

Place managers regulate who, when, and under what circumstances people can enter and use their places. Opening and closing times allow patrons into the place during some hours, and keep most people out at other times. This aspect of place management creates routines in place. An apartment manager may restrict 24-hour access to renters, require special actions for guests to gain access at other times of the day, and keep out everyone else. A bar that advertises "ladies' night" on Thursdays is attempting to encourage women to patronize the place. The owner of a clothing store that specializes in women's exercise apparel is not encouraging men to enter, and may even discourage older women, while she tries to attract younger women. The choice of music in a nightclub will influence who shows up, and who does not.

Control of access not only incorporates decisions about who is encouraged to enter and who is discouraged, it also includes decisions about whom to evict if they violate rules of conduct. Bar bouncers are obvious examples of this, as are provisions in leases, and vehicle parking rules.

27.6.4 They Acquire Resources

All places need resources to function. Commercial places need to generate revenue to pay for physical upkeep and staff, and they need to generate a profit to keep the owner interested in keeping the place open at its location. Acquisition of resources applies to noncommercial places, too. A city parks department needs to demonstrate to the mayor and council that its parks are used and deserving of some share of the city budget. If the department cannot do so, it will lose resources. A nongovernmental organization—say a homeless shelter or nonprofit theater—may need to raise money from donors. A college needs to attract students to get tuition revenue, please alumni to get donations, and appeal to foundations for grants. In all cases, the reputation of the place is critical to gaining resources. Without a reputation that appeals to customers, customers will not come, governments will not fund, and private donors will not donate.

The ability of a place to attract resources will influence each of the other three ORCA components. A well-funded place can renovate its space, but a poorly funded place cannot. A well-funded place can hire competent and honest staff and train them so they can regulate conduct, but a poorly funded place will have more trouble with this. And a well-funded place can afford to be more exclusive than a poorly funded place.

27.7 How Does Place Management Explain Crime Concentration?

It is one thing to conjure up the concept of place management, and quite another to demonstrate that it is viable explanation for why crime is highly concentrated at a relatively few places, relative to the many places without much crime. Even without invoking place management, there are at least 10 explanations for why some proprietary places have a great deal of crime while most places have little or no crime. All of them have some merit.

27.7.1 Random Variation

If a random process is at work, then every crime is independent of all other crimes, so knowing where one crime is gives us no ability whatsoever to determine where any subsequent crimes might occur. But even in such a circumstance, it is possible to observe crime concentration. There are three arguments against this as a general theory of crime places (Park and Eck, 2013). First, studies of crime have shown that even if there is some random variation, the concentration is inconsistent with what can be expected by chance (Sherman, Gartin, and Buerger, 1989; Spelman, 1995). Second, the stability of high- and low-crime places over time argues against this explanation (Andresen and Malleson, 2010; Braga, Papachristos, and Hureau, 2009; Spelman, 1995; Groff, Weisburd, and Yang, 2010). Finally, if crime were independent, then prevention programs that try to reduce crime at places where it is concentrated would not work. As we will see later, most of these interventions seem to work.

27.7.2 Physical Design

This is one of the oldest explanations of why some places have a great deal of crime, and can be traced back to Oscar Newman's (1972) ideas of "defensible space" as well C. Ray Jeffery's (1977) ideas about crime prevention through environmental design. Additionally, there is reasonably sound evidence that changing design can change crime (Eck and Guerette, 2012).

A good test of this would be to look at a set of franchise stores that use very similar designs—a fast-food restaurant chain, for example. If these stores have similar volumes of crime, then we would have evidence that design is critical, particularly if another chain selling similar products but having a different design had a very different average crime rate. We have no study so comprehensive. However, in the 1970s a study of a single chain of convenience stores revealed that some convenience stores in the same chain had many robberies and most had few or none (Crow and Bull, 1975). Further, a study of bus stops in Los Angeles also shows a pronounced concentration (Loukaitou-Sideris,

1999). Though hardly definitive, these studies indicate that even when designs are similar, crime levels can be very dissimilar. So whatever contribution physical design makes, it cannot be the full contribution.

27.7.3 Informal Social Control

This explanation has an even longer pedigree, though it has been mostly used to explain crime variation across neighborhoods. Recently, Weisburd, Groff, and Yang (2012) have suggested that social disorganization concepts can be used to explain crime variation across street segments, and they show that there is some evidence that measures of social disorganization are correlated with segment crime (however, see Braga and Clarke, 2014).

In principle, we could apply the same argument to proprietary places: for example, bars with a great deal of crime have less informal social control than other bars. However, this explanation has several limitations. First, there is an absence of evidence for this explanation at proprietary places (and only a limited amount of evidence at proximal places). Second, many places have low turnover of place users (mobility), do not cater to poor individuals (poverty), and do not serve a particularly heterogeneous clientele (heterogeneity), yet there is high variation in crime among these places. The concentration of bank robberies at a relatively few banks (Matthews, Pease, and Pease, 2001), for example, is a challenge to this idea. Finally, given that place managers can and do set and enforce rules for conduct, it is quite likely that whatever role social control plays at places, the process for creating it is probably different at proprietary places than on street segments or in the larger community.

27.7.4 Guardianship

Routine activity theory asserts that the absence of guardianship, when offenders and targets collide at the same place, is responsible for crime (Cohen and Felson, 1979). Indeed, studies that varied guardianship indicate that improving it reduces crime. So this is a very plausible hypothesis. However, routine activity theory clearly states that the absence of guardianship cannot be the single cause—the offender and target must also be together. Adding guardianship to places without targets or offenders is unlikely to do much but cost the place manager money. It is useful only when there is something or someone to guard, and someone to guard against. Further, there is a need to explain guardianship at places. Some of it may emerge, spontaneously, but place managers can also create it. Consequently, guardianship is another partial explanation.

27.7.5 Reporting Variation

It is theoretically possible that some places have a great deal of crime because they attract reports of crime, and others have little or no crime because crime reporting is suppressed. Sherman, Gartin, and Buerger (1989) give the example of the magnet phones: locations in a neighborhood where residents go to report crime that has occurred elsewhere. Drinking places, on the other hand, have an incentive to suppress crime reports, as having too many such reports puts their alcohol sales licenses at risk (Graham and Homel, 2008). Like random variation, this explanation cannot be rejected completely; some reporting variation seems likely. If this were a complete explanation, we would have to imagine a process that could completely suppresses crime reports at most places, but create overreporting at a few other places. Given the diversity of places showing concentration, this seems a poor candidate for a general explanation.

27.7.6 Repeat Victimization

This phenomenon has received considerable attention (Farrell and Pease, 2008), and may be responsible for high-crime places. First, however, we must dispense with a possible tautology. For some crimes and places, there is no useful distinction between high-crime places and repeat victimization. Repeat burglaries, for example, involve the same locations and often the same victims (who inhabit the places). Whether one calls this a place or victim phenomenon is a choice of terms, rather than a choice of explanations. On the other hand, someone who is repeatedly robbed in the parking area of his apartment building is a repeat victim (relative to other residents), and his misfortune is an explanation for why the apartment building might stand out as a hotspot of crime.

Unfortunately, we do not know how much repeat victimization overlaps with place concentration. It may be that it is common, or it could be infrequent. More than likely, it depends on circumstances. In apartment buildings, for example, a few tenants maybe repeatedly victimized due to their routines, or the location of their apartment in the building, or where they park their car, or for other reasons. And these few repeat victims are principally responsible for driving up the number of crimes for this facility. However, there are other types of facilities where this scenario is much less likely. Take hotels and motels, for example. Except for residential hotels, these facilities have a great deal of turnover in their occupants, and this happens quickly. It is far more likely that a high-crime motel has little repeat victimization (the one-time victims may not come back again).

27.7.7 Handling

This feature of routine activity theory (Felson, 1986) has received very little attention. Handlers are people who have an emotional connection to possible offenders, so potential offenders avoid misbehaving in their presence, or offending in ways that could lead to the handlers' discovery of the offenses. Perhaps places with little or no crime have many handlers, and those with many crimes never have handlers around. We cannot reject this explanation, though we are without any useful evidence by which to judge its validity. More critically, this explanation may be useful for some sorts of places and some types of offenses (perhaps for places and crimes dominated by juveniles), but it seems implausible as an explanation for all crimes at all types of places.

27.7.8 Offenders

In contrast, the presence of many offenders at the place seems like a very general explanation. Patricia and Paul Brantingham (1995) even have a name for this explanation: crime attractors. Clearly, if there were no offenders at a place, there could be no crime. A variant on this explanation is that there are a few, but highly active offenders at the place. However, the same is true of targets (see next explanation). It's not hard to imagine a place with many offenders (or a few active offenders), but in the absence of suitable targets, the offenders cannot offend. Though a useful and logical explanation, it cannot stand on its own. Could a crime attractor be maintained for long periods without potential targets leaving? It is possible to imagine particular circumstances—poverty or racism restricts the mobility of victims, so they cannot flee, for example—but more generally this seems implausible.

27.7.9 Targets

Patricia and Paul Brantingham (1995) suggest that some places have lots of crime because they have many targets. They call such places crime generators. Obviously, many targets alone cannot be the explanation: we need at least a few offenders who routinely attack these targets. Nevertheless, we would not be surprised to discover a large hotel has more crimes against patrons than a small hotel simply due to size (Sherman, 1998). This is one of the reasons we standardize crime measures by size: size being a proxy measure for the number of targets at risk (Brantingham and Brantingham, 1981–1982). As we have examples where the variation in crime persists after such standardization (Bichler, Schmerler, and Enriquez, 2013), this too fails as a useful general explanation.

27.7.10 Hot Products

An explanation related to the many targets thesis is the possibility that high-theft locations have products that are particularly attractive to thieves (Clarke, 1999). For some places, those suffering from product theft, this may be a useful explanation. But the concentration of crime at a few places applies to a wide variety of offenses, not just theft.

27.8 Place Management as a General Theory of High-Crime Places

To varying extents, place managers have influence over the mechanisms involved in each of these explanations, with the exception of the first, randomness. Each of the ORCA elements applies to place managers' actions that influence these explanations.

27.8.1 Organization of Space

The connection of physical design with this aspect of place management is obvious. Managers have the authority to create and alter the physical space of their places. If the physical design is the cause of crime at the place, then this suggests poor place management.

The organization of space can influence informal social control if physical features keep place users from controlling misbehavior or the design provokes bad behavior. The layout of bars, for example, can inhibit violence or promote it (Graham and Homel, 2008).

The organization of space can influence guardianship, by making it easier or harder for people in the place to see crime. Blind spots in stores created by high shelves, for example, make it easier for shoplifters to take things.

Perhaps the most important, and most easily overlooked, way place managers organize space are their decisions to open and close facilities. Someone made the decision to build a bowling alley at this corner, or to open a bank branch on another corner. Place managers select the environment of their places. Similarly, the manager can decide to close a place—the homeowner who owes more on her mortgage than she could ever get from reselling it may "walk away," default on the debt, and thus transfer ownership to the lending company. A bicycle store can close its doors in one neighborhood and reopen somewhere else. The used car dealership can go out of business.

27.8.2 Regulation of Conduct

Place managers have direct and indirect influence on the rules of their places. These rules can promote positive cooperative behavior that suppresses crime (informal social control, guardianship, and handling). Signs that encourage patrons to take care of their friends, for example, promote guardianship if the friends could be victims, or promote handling if their friends are likely to be offenders. In a business, rules of conduct can serve as guides for employees to regulate each other's behavior.

Place management can influence the reporting of crime to police by the rules and expectations that are set. A motel manager might tell employees to avoid calling the police, except in the most extreme circumstances. In contrast, a convenience store manager might demand that clerks call the police at the slightest provocation.

Repeat victimization may be partially under the control of place managers. Rules about noise and disruptive behavior in an apartment building could constrain some domestic violence. Policies governing how bartenders serve customers could influence how often some patrons become victims of theft, assault, or robbery (Graham and Homel, 2008).

Some shopping malls have established policies that prohibit juveniles unless accompanied by adults (Rawe, 2007). This is a clear example of place managers stimulating handling. Bars that encourage drinking by men unaccompanied by girlfriends and spouses may increase violence.

Enforced rules can also deter offenders, so they stay away from a place. The lack of rules may encourage offenders to come to the place. Landlords who do not use leases, or whose leases do not cover misbehavior on the property, may end up with more offenders who rent than landlords who use strong leases and enforce them (Campbell DeLong Resources, 2000).

Although most conduct at most places is probably handled by normal employees, there are employees who specialize in enforcement. Hiring security guards or contracting with a security company is a form of regulation of conduct that has direct bearing on crime.

27.8.3 Control Access

This element of place management overlaps with regulating conduct and acquiring resources. Requiring handlers be present is a rule that may be enforced by denying entry or by eviction from the place. Prohibiting known offenders from the place is a form of access control, as is evicting people who offend after they enter. Some bars are known to keep lists of patrons who have misbehaved and are therefore not to be served if they come in.

As noted earlier, access control is not merely screening people at the door or throwing out rowdy customers. Advertising and promotion make the place differentially attractive to people. The place attracts people who do not offend, or it attracts people who do offend.

This is true of targets as well. A casino that attracts thousands of people in a night is creating a potential victim pool, for example. Similarly, stadiums with their thousands of fans on game night create settings with many possible victims.

27.8.4 Acquire Resources

Commercial establishments sell goods and services. The more they sell, the greater the profit (as a general rule). So marketing decisions designed to increase volume, and therefore profit, have direct implications for the numbers of targets at the place. Place managers decide whether or not to sell merchandise that is very popular with customers, and to thieves.

Figure 27.2 illustrates the preceding discussion by showing how the ORCA elements connect to the explanations. The overlapping influences show how different sorts of management decisions can promote or suppress mechanisms that might create crime.

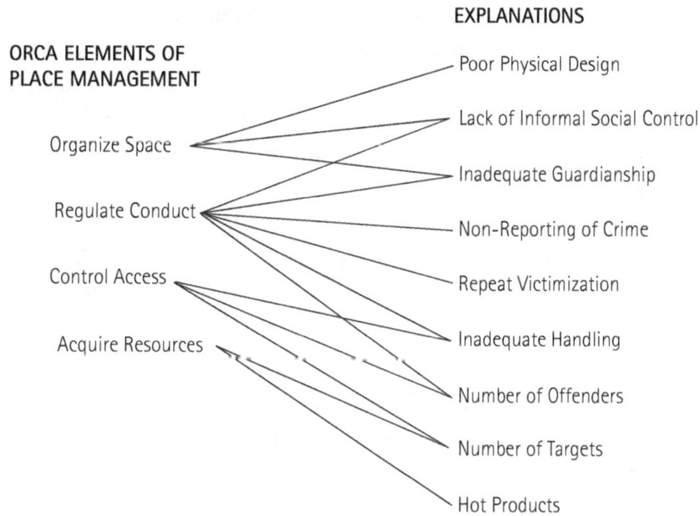

FIGURE 27.2 Place management and explanations for crime concentration at proprietary places

Place management many not be the only influence on these mechanisms: design can be altered by weather, time, and use; some guardianship may be created without place manager intent; and offenders might find ways of getting access despite place managers' actions, for example. Despite these limits on place management, the theory unifies an unruly collection of explanations and can be applied to all types of proprietary places and for any form of crime.

27.9 What Influences Place Management?

If place managers are responsible for much of the crime at their places, what explains variation in place management? Clearly, most place managers do not have serious crime problems—the Iron Law of Troublesome Places asserts this is true of all types of facilities. So why are most place managers doing well, but a few doing so poorly? Madensen addressed this question, too, in her dissertation.

We begin with Figure 27.3. It shows how events are created at a place in the immediate setting. Simply put, people in the place interact in the immediate setting and generate events. Most of the events will be legitimate, and even desirable. Dart playing in an English pub, buying clothing in a department store, fans cheering in a baseball stadium, children playing in a park are all examples of desirable events at different sorts of places. Crime events also occur through such interaction at the place.

The types of events influence the patrons. It may encourage the production of more of these events—cheering stimulates more cheering, for example, or a fight between two drunks in a bar can draw their friends into a general melee. Events can also suppress further

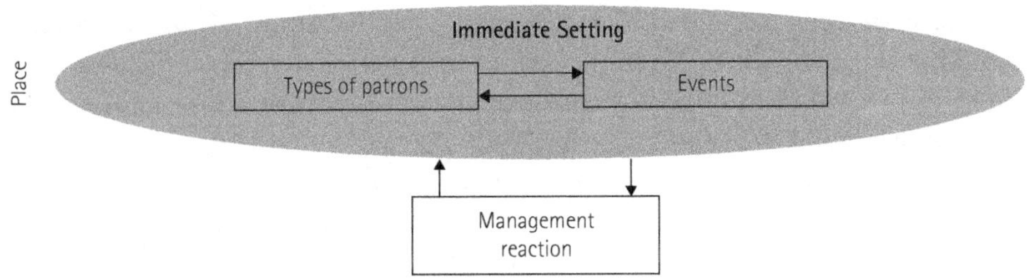

FIGURE 27.3 The theory of place management: Production of crime

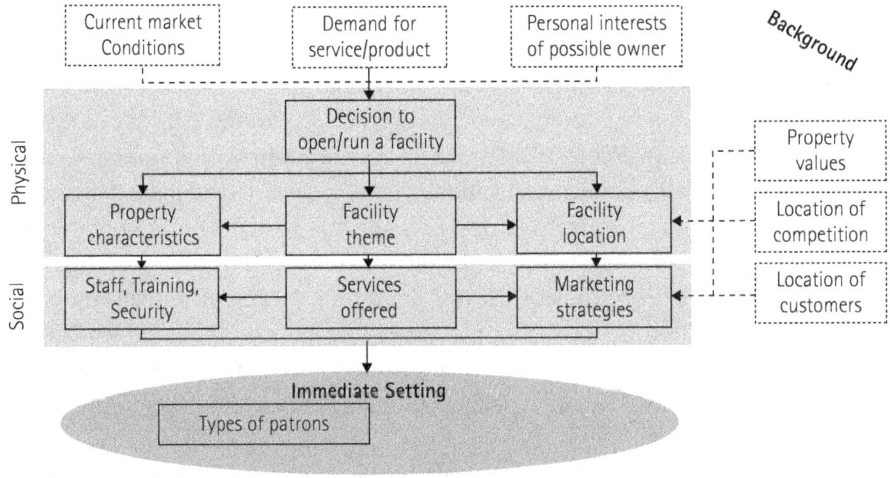

FIGURE 27.4 The theory of place management: Creation of the setting

such events—the announcement that a purse has been stolen may temporarily curb thievery until things get back to normal, for example. And events can simulate the place manager, who then promotes events he finds desirable at the place, or attempt to suppress events she finds unacceptable. These simple processes are at the center of Madensen's theory. Importantly, at this core, interactions can occur quickly, in seconds, minutes, or hours.

Figure 27.4 shows the creation of the immediate setting. Here processes take longer, and once a place manager has made a decision, things do not change fast. These strategic decisions create the setting. The manager's decisions about the physical and social aspects of the place produce the four elements of ORCA, and these define the physical setting and who comes to the place.

The place manager faces an operating environment over which she has very limited control. She makes strategic decisions to take advantage of this environment. The dotted boxes around the top and right in the figure represent salient environmental conditions: the market conditions including financing, expected demand for the goods or services from the place, and the personal interests of the owner.

An owner has to determine where to locate the place and how he wants the place to appear, property characteristics, and the theme for the place. Theme can be illustrated with bars: sports, gay, hip-hop, family-oriented, and other adjectives we use to describe drinking places illustrate themes. But many other places have themes—some parks cater to children, others to adults wanting exercise, and yet others to people who want quiet. Clothing stores select an appearance that announces not only what they are selling, but the kinds of customers they are trying to attract.

The physical setting should be congenial to the social atmosphere. This is set by staff selection, their training, and the types of security. The social atmosphere is also determined by what services the place provides and the marketing strategy the place manager uses (including the decision not to overtly market). Other background factors come into play here—property values, competition for similar services, and where customers are located.

Figure 27.4 shows long-term decisions that create the setting, and Figure 27.3 shows how patrons, events, and management interact within the setting. These quick management decisions depend upon a number of factors. These other factors are shown in Figure 27.5. How a manager reacts to events depends on what she knows. This is influenced by her social and professional network. The International Council of Shopping Centers is one of hundreds of professional organizations that serve a variety of place managers. All provide information on recommended practices and how to handle common problems.

How a place manager reacts will also depend on how much it costs to change things. The cost of change is probably less relevant in absolute terms. The manager is likely to judge this cost in terms of existing resources—if the resources are plentiful, then change is more likely, even if costly, than if resources are scarce, even if the changes are inexpensive. Included here are expectations of future revenues (appropriately discounted).

Also influencing the manager are the relative benefits of existing circumstances to the manager. He may feel comfortable with his management style and be reluctant to try something new and different. Customers, even if they often create trouble, may be friends. On the other hand, the current circumstances might pose a threat to the manager, and he might welcome some relief.

Finally, the manager will be influenced by external pressures: professional colleagues, neighbors, politicians, news media, and regulators. Some of these pressures may come from regulators with enforcement powers. Rana Sampson and colleagues (2009) call these super controllers.

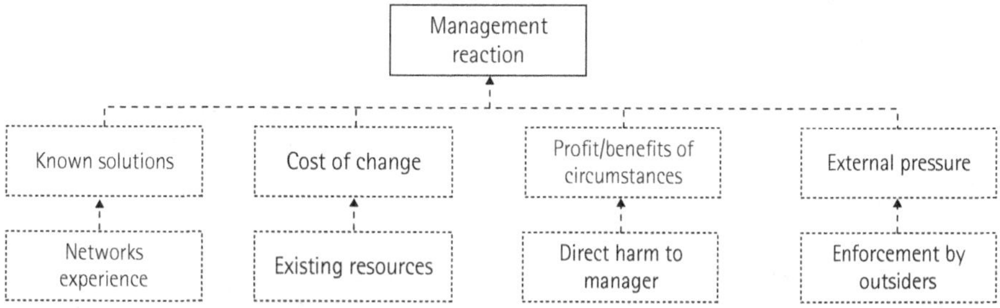

FIGURE 27.5 The theory of place management: Influences on management

The time scale the manager operates within for these decisions falls somewhere between the long-term decisions we saw in the previous figure, and the very short-term decisions in Figure 27.3.

Figure 27.6 assembles the pieces from the previous three figures in one illustration in order to highlight two forms of feedback. Managers can change the social and physical setting in response to events. Special events that generate positive events may be incorporated into the normal functioning of the place. Troublesome events may result in the manager altering the physical setting or social atmosphere—banning the general public from the restrooms, for example.

The events occurring in the immediate setting can also influence the four conditions along the bottom of the figure. Positive events can enhance the manager's position among her peers and increase the knowledge of the network. They can increase resources, and reduce harm to the manager. And they can improve relations with regulators, who might reduce their scrutiny. Negative events can have the opposite affects.

A place that begins to suffer negative events will have to expend resources to keep them from recurring, and to regain a positive reputation. Many places can do this successfully. However, if the actions—tactical and strategic—fail to curb the negative

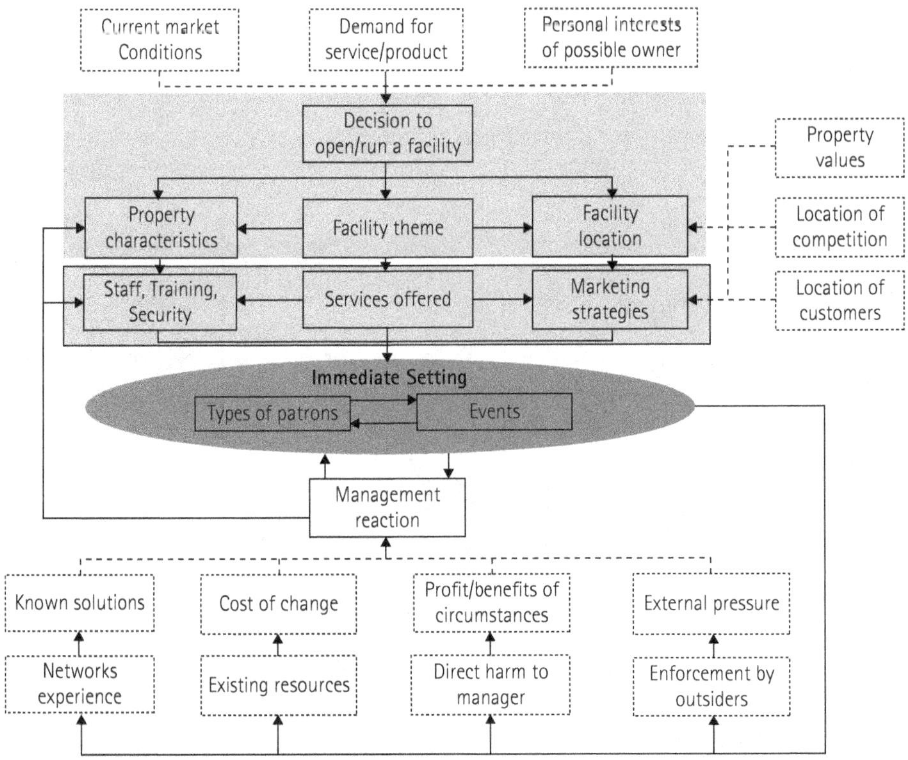

FIGURE 27.6 The full theory of place management

events, or the manager fails to take any action, then things can get worse and worse. Crimes are one form of negative events.

We have finished describing what place management entails. It is important to note that place management focuses on many things, only one of which is crime. It conveys the operating strategy or business plans of place managers. And it describes how place managers adapt their location's environment and processes to changing conditions, one of which is the threat of crime.

We summarize this in Figure 27.7. Many places have little or no crime threat. Crime does not accumulate at such locations. Some other places face a moderate to high threat. There are three options here. First, the place manager can close the place and leave (establishing a residence or business elsewhere). This removes crime opportunities and suppresses crime. The next place manager then is either confronted with no crime or modest crime, and if the second, the place manager has the same three options. Second, the place manager can stay and institute crime prevention measures. If these work, crime does not accumulate. If they do not, the place manager can reconsider which of the three options to take. Finally, the place manager can stay and acclimate to crime. By acclimate we mean that she can passively tolerate crime or she can actively facilitate crime, or she can do some of each. If the place manager acclimates, then crime accumulates. Offenders adapt to this, and crime continues to go up. Since most place managers do not stay and acclimate, many places have little crime.

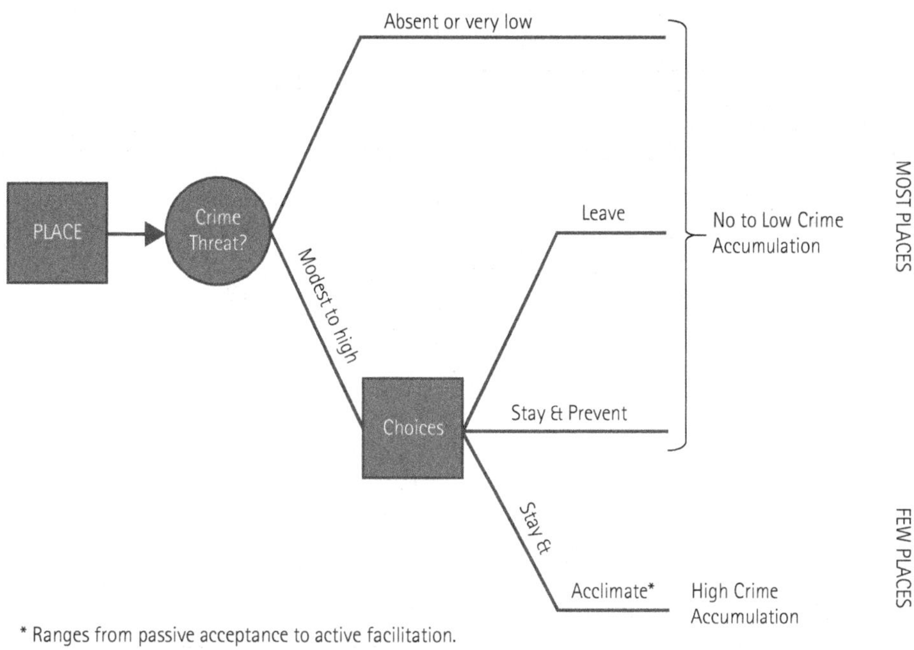

FIGURE 27.7 Place Management Responses to Crime

27.10 What Is the Evidence?

We do not have direct evidence for all the details of Madensen's theory of place management. It is too new to have been thoroughly tested. We have strong evidence that place managers can influence crime, however. There are numerous interventions at proprietary places that have been evaluated. In Western democracies, governments cannot alter the characteristics of places without the consent of the owner, the active cooperation of the owner, or a court order. Because all such interventions require some involvement of place managers, each evaluation is a partial test of the place management perspective.

27.10.1 Direct Evidence

In the very late 1990s, Eck (2002) identified over 100 studies and examined each of their conclusions. There were five studies that evaluated the impact of the use of civil sanctions to compel owners of apartment building with drug dealing to clean up their property. With one exception, these were relatively strong studies: two were randomized experiments, and three were moderately strong quasi-experiments. Four of the evaluations, including the two randomized experiments, showed that when landlords were compelled to address drug dealing, crime usually declined at their places. A fifth, contradictory, study did not collect data on crime before and after the intervention, but asked people following the intervention whether things had improved. Based on the results of these studies, it is clear that place managers have considerable control over crime in apartment buildings, and what was lacking in the crime-ridden places examined was a willingness to do something.

In addition to these evaluations, there were another four evaluations of interventions to reduce bar-related events, ranging from assaults to vehicle accidents. Here too, there was consistent evidence that interventions were successful in getting the place manager to change practices that reduced crime. Although these studies had weaker designs than used in the apartment evaluations, every study found place management could reduce crime. A more recent book that reviews the considerable research on bars—quantitative and qualitative, descriptive and evaluative—comes to very similar conclusions (Graham and Homel, 2008).

A very recent evaluation of a Chula Vista Police Department initiative to reduce calls to the police from motels also showed a positive impact from compelling owners to change management practices (Bichler, Schmerler, and Enriquez, 2013).

Ronald Clarke and Gisela Robertson-Bichler (1998) documented that for a set of high-crime apartment buildings, the places had become problems after ownership changes. Troy Payne (2010, p. 92) found that ownership changes of apartment buildings were associated with crime increases: "One ownership change increased the expected crime count by about 10%, net of other factors. This is most pronounced at apartments with high values for past crime and for apartments with more than 20 units."

In a later study, Payne examined the impact of charging property owners' fees for excessive calls to the police in two cities: Anchorage, Alaska, and Green Bay, Wisconsin. Overall, calls dropped by about 25% following notices from the police. This impact was spread across two-thirds of the properties (Payne, 2015).

This evidence demonstrates that place managers have the capacity to control crime. It does not explore the details that Madensen's theory lays out. More research is needed to nail this down.

27.10.2 Indirect Evidence

The studies just described involved some sort of direct manipulation of place management. They consistently show that altering place management can influence crime or disorder at high-crime/high-disorder proprietary places. There is an even larger body of research where the evaluator manipulated some place feature under the control of place managers. This literature was systematically reviewed at the beginning of the millennium (Eck, 2002) and again, a decade later (Eck and Guerette, 2012). Figure 27.8 summarizes the findings from the most recent systematic review.

In this review, studies were divided into groups depending on the type of place, using a typology described by John Eck and Ronald Clarke (2003). There were 39 evaluations of interventions at places where people sleep (single-family homes, apartments, and hotels).

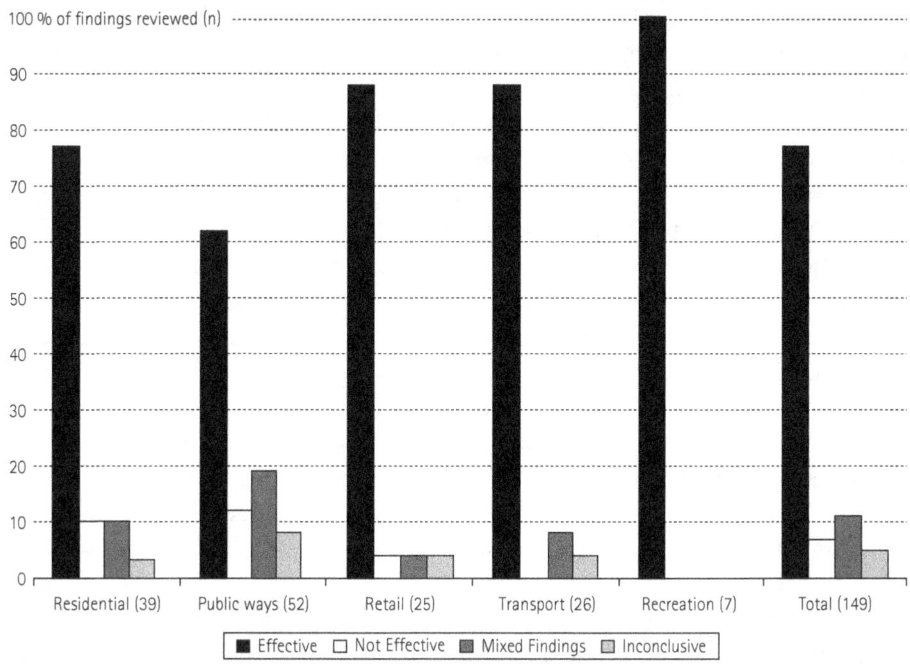

FIGURE 27.8 Effectiveness of situational techniques in different places

Another set of evaluations looked at interventions on streets and other public ways. For these places, a local government is the place manager rather than a private entity. Twenty-five evaluations looked at interventions at retail establishments (stores, for example). Public transport included buses, subway stations, and related facilities. Finally, a few studies were conducted at recreational facilities, primarily bars and taverns. The results are fairly obvious. Regardless of place type, most evaluations of place-based interventions show a reduction in crime, and very few show no impact. Overall, the interventions were more likely to be effective than otherwise. As the authors note, the evaluations varied considerably in the strength of their designs, so some of the findings are uncertain. Nevertheless, the consistency of these findings over different place types is important.

27.11 Where Does This Lead?

27.11.1 Place Management Theory: An Overview

The theory of place management is a theory of chronic crime places. It describes why a few proprietary places have much crime and most proprietary places have little or no crime. The short explanation is that poor management in the face of a crime threat creates a high-crime location and that most places are well managed or face little threat. When well-managed places have a crime, the managers adjust the physical or social environment of the place to block the crime opportunity. In poorly run places, no such adjustment occurs, or the adjustments are inadequate. External interventions, often by the police, can provoke improved management, as shown by the research literature. Until evidence arises falsifying this statement, we assert that this theory applies to all proprietary places and all crimes at such places.

The theory of place management was not created to explain crime at proximal or pooled places. The principal reason is that such places do not have a single owner. If one removed from street segments or neighborhoods all the crime at proprietary places, there may still be concentration at these higher levels of aggregation. Explaining this concentration probably requires other theories: street traffic (Brantingham and Brantingham, 1993) or social disorganization (Shaw and McKay, 1942; Weisburd, Groff, and Yang, 2012). As we note below, however, it is possible that crime spilling out of high-crime proprietary places also contributes to crime concentration at proximal and pooled places.

This theory has several notable features. First, it uses a simple and readily observable concept—people and institutions own property and often employ others to operate it. That such people and institutions exist is beyond dispute. The reverse of this coin is that the theory does not require new and difficult-to-observe concepts. Consequently, it meets the minimum requirement for a theory—it is plausible. Whether it is valid will depend on the outcomes of future research and evaluations of practices applying the theory.

Second, it provides a parsimonious framework for understanding why some places have a great deal of crime and most do not. This theory organizes nine partial explanations. The theory of place management does not contradict or compete with these other explanations. Rather, it organizes the nine within a larger conceptual structure. The very fact that we have nine loosely connected explanations suggests the need for some overarching structure.

Third, this theory is directly tied to a larger theoretical framework, routine activity theory. Place management theory expands upon one aspect of routine activity theory: the role of places. Place management theory, therefore, sits alongside other theories within routine activity theory: theories of victimization, theories of offending, and theories of routines.

Fourth, it is supported by numerous studies, including several with very strong research designs. Most of the evidence supporting place management theory comes from quasi-randomized or randomized experiments involving tests of interventions upon or by place managers. Compared to tests using statistical modeling without intentional manipulation of the intervention, these studies provide strong findings.

Fifth, the theory points to a class of prevention options directed at the people and institutions that own, control, and operate proprietary places with a great deal of crime. These options can supplement various offender-, victim-, or neighborhood resident-based crime prevention.

Finally, place management theory opens up interesting and useful questions for research that have been mostly overlooked. The following is a brief review some of the most notable questions.

27.11.2 When and Why Does Prevention Implementation Fail at Places?

Not all crime prevention efforts succeed. They can fail because the theories upon which they are based are faulty, or they can fail because the interventions were not carried out as planned. The ability to implement crime prevention at places depends on place managers, so these people and institutions have a great deal of influence over the success of place-based interventions. The study of the circumstances under which interventions succeed can be advanced by explicitly investigating the characteristics of place managers. Both the ORCA functions of place managers and Madensen's place management theory (Figure 27.6) provide frameworks for identifying the circumstances that drive successful implementation, and the development of countermeasures to achieve higher implementation success rates when these circumstances are not present.

27.11.3 Can Regulation Be an Effective and Fair Means for Controlling Crime at Places?

The crime place literature is closely associated with policing. In fact, it provides the empirical support for hotspots policing (Weisburd et al, 2016). Hotspots policing, however, does not address what is going on inside the spot that generates the crime. Therefore, it can only provide temporary relief and requires return visits by the police (Sherman, 1990). Place management looks within the spot and suggests that changing the internal workings of the place can have a longer-lasting impact on crime or disorder. This reduces the need for police, and potentially can reduce conflicts between police and the public arising from stop-and-frisk operations at hotspots.

Standard policing methods are not particularly useful for altering place managers' behaviors. In fact, because policing comes at no cost to place managers, place managers have no reason to alter conditions that give rise to crime. Eck and Eck (2012) suggest using regulatory incentives to do this. They show numerous examples of place regulation, much of it done by policing agencies. When done by the police, regulation is a form of third-party policing (Mazerolle and Ransley, 2005). However, there is no logical reason that other public entities could not carry out this function, and there are good reasons to be skeptical of the police officers' ability to consistently regulate place managers (Eck, 2015).

27.11.4 Are Crime Places Networked?

Research on crime places has tacitly assumed that these locations operate independently, even if they cluster spatially. Recent research based on police investigations suggests that there may be networks of crime places. That is, offenders move from place to place, and these places serve different functions in their crime processes. So convergent settings, corrupting spots, and comfort spaces provide a hidden infrastructure for some high-crime sites (Madensen and Sousa, 2016).

27.11.5 What Is the Relationship between Property Rights and Crime?

The standard ways to examine social control mechanisms in criminology are to either focus on the criminal justice system or upon emergent informal social control mechanisms that arise, seemingly spontaneously, from routine social interactions. Place management theory relies on neither. Instead, it asserts that the dominant social control process at proprietary places arises directly from the exercise of property rights by those who own property. Managers carry out the ORCA elements because they see that it is in their interests to do so. This often suppresses crime, but in some circumstances it does the opposite. In the process, place management theory breaks down the artificial distinctions between so-called street crime and white-collar crime, or business crime. This is because place management is often a business, but it strongly influences street crime.

27.11.6 Is Crime Concentrated among Place Managers?

Just as we can aggregate crime to addresses to detect high-crime locations, we can identify places owned by the same individual or organization. Not surprisingly, crime is even more concentrated at the owner level than the place level (Payne and Eck, 2007; Payne et al., 2013). That is, most owners of property have little or no crime at their places, but a few owners have many crimes across their places. The research here is limited and based on studies of apartment buildings. So this needs further investigation for other types of properties in many different cities and counties. If concentration of crime among owners proves to be as common as the concentration of crime among places, this has broad implications for policies: focusing on a few high-crime property owners might have larger crime reduction effects than focusing on a few high-crime places.

If a few place managers control most of the crime places in a neighborhood, then perhaps we should reconsider the standard forms of social disorganization theory. Rather than a breakdown in (or failure to establish) trust, social rules, and rule enforcement among residents, crime is largely due to the actions of a few owners of places who do not necessarily live in the neighborhood. In short, the problem is not with the residents, but with a particular set of outsiders who exploit the residents.

27.11.7 Do Chronic Crime Proprietary Places Radiate Crime into Their Surroundings?

There is good reason to believe that crime places export much crime, although the evidence is limited. Evaluations of situational crime prevention suggest that crime in the areas surrounding high-crime places drops. This is not inevitable, but it is common (Guerette and Bowers, 2009). This implies that many chronic places treated by the prevention were radiating crime prior to the interventions, and crime radiation may have dropped after the interventions. More directly, a pioneering study by Kate Bowers (2014) shows a strong relationship between crime inside places and crime outside places, and that the inside crime preceded the outside crime. Though place management influences crime inside of places, this new research implies it might influence crime outside. And if this is true, then place management may apply not only to proprietary places, but to proximal and pooled as well.

27.11.8 How Do Proximal and Pooled Places Influence Crime at Proprietary Places?

Although crime risk might radiate out from chronic proprietary places, the environmental context of proprietary places is likely to influence place management. Wilcox Roundtree, Land, and Hunt (2003) have proposed that crime opportunities are spread over multiple nested contexts, and this seems reasonable (Wilcox, Madensen, and Tillyer, 2007). That is, managed places are loosely coupled to their surroundings: neither completely at the mercy of their contexts, nor completely independent. This suggests that examining similar places, managed similarly, but in radically different street segments and neighborhoods would provide useful information.

27.11.9 How Is Crime Distributed across Proprietary Places That Are Unmanaged?

If management matters, then we should ask, how much does it matter? A risky facility study (Eck, Clarke, and Guerette, 2007) of low-management places could help answer this question. Old cemeteries are examples of such places, particularly in rural areas of the United States. Often, these places have no one in attendance, are abandoned, and the property rights for management are often obscure or conflicted. Abandoned buildings and vacant lots are also possible facilities for such studies. Discovering a uniform distribution of crime across such places suggests that place management matters a great deal. Discovering a highly skewed distribution, as noted in all risky facility studies to date (Wilcox and Eck, 2011) would indicate that management is an unlikely cause of much of the crime concentration. However, an impediment to such research is that crime reporting is likely to be very low due to the absence of management, thus biasing results in favor of a uniform distribution.

27.11.10 How Does Crime Vary across Proprietary Places with the Same Management?

Another way of testing the thesis that place management matters is to examine the distribution of crime across locations that have very similar management practices: chain restaurants, retail stores, motels, and other commercial enterprises. If crime is concentrated in the places owned by a single company that uses consistent management practices, then this suggests something other than management is responsible for the concentration. The most obvious alternative to place management would be the street or neighborhood context. However, one should not jump to premature conclusions, as it is possible that even subtle differences in management matter a great deal. Therefore, quantitative studies of this type should be supplemented with qualitative and mixed-methods studies to rule out this possibility.

27.11.11 Is Poor Place Management a Symptom of Poor Business Practices in General?

Place managers are concerned with a great deal that has little or nothing to do with crime. By definition, their function is to look after the well-being and operation of the place. So it is possible that place managers who are poor at preventing crime are poor at other things too. This is analogous to the point raised by Gottfredson and Hirschi (1990), that a person's self-control predicts crime involvement but also predicts her involvement in vehicle crashes, injuries, and numerous other unfortunate events. Conducting such research may require collaboration with researchers from business schools, as knowledge of business operations will be needed. Kennedy's (2014) study of employee theft illustrates the utility of drawing on insights from business. Further, it may be difficult to sort out the temporal order of outcomes: does bad management cause crime and other difficulties, or does crime undercut the ability of managers to operate profitably and efficiently?

27.12 Challenges to the Study of Place Management and Crime

In this chapter, we have described how place management theory explains the concentration of crime at very small places. We have also shown that this explanation easily incorporates other explanations. We have reviewed the empirical evidence for this theory. And we have shown how place management theory leads to other ideas and practices. We conclude this chapter with some challenges to the theory.

First, though highly plausible, and consistent with the evidence we have, the theory requires explicit testing. Such tests should be conducted to find contradictory evidence.

Second, studies using official data from hundreds, if not thousands, of places that are useful for finding crime patterns and identifying chronically crime ridden proprietary places, may not be as useful for testing the theory. The proposed studies of unmanaged and homogeneously managed facilities might be exceptions. Place management is not a simple concept that can be measured on a single scale. This means that any surveys will have to be quite complex. To test the mechanisms of place management will require mixed methods and qualitative studies, involving interviews with managers, site observations, and data from private businesses. This suggests that studies are likely to involve a relatively few cases, but each case is studied in great depth.

Third, the variety of types of places, the diversity of settings containing them, and range of crimes that can beset them suggest that a large number of studies will have to be conducted. It may turn out that for some types of places, crimes, or context, place management is not critical, but that for other types it is vital. Without numerous and diverse studies we cannot know the true scope of this theory.

Finally, and most important, it is not clear what types of tests are the most meaningful. Standard academic research tests hypotheses derived from a theory. Then from the results it draws implications about the theory's validity. Some of this may be useful, but we suggest a pragmatic perspective to theory testing, in addition. In a pragmatic approach we ask, "What practical difference will using this theory make in outcomes?" Here, evaluations of interventions based upon the theory are valuable and can often provide more rigorous findings due to their use of experimental and quasi-experimental designs.

In a pragmatic approach, we temporarily assume the theory is correct, derive an intervention from the theory, apply it, evaluate it with an experiment (randomized or quasi), and then observe the results. This is a stronger test, not only because of the nature of the study design, but because we can determine if the theory is useful. That is, standard testing might show it is valid, but experimental testing might show it is useless when applied. Or the results could be the opposite, tests using statistical modeling or mixed methods might show that the theory has serious flaws, but experimental manipulations of interventions based on the theory show that the theory has utility. If the theory is useful, then it serves a purpose. If it is not, then it should be abandoned.

Testing of interventions runs the risk of creating a black box if we follow a strict quasi-randomized or randomized experiment protocol. However, if we also use a realist's approach (Pawson and Tilley, 1997) we might be able to learn much about the mechanisms of the intervention. And this will tell us a great deal about the finer details of the theory.

References

Andresen, M. A., and Malleson, N. (2010). "Testing the Stability of Crime Patterns: Implications for Theory and Policy." *Journal of Research in Crime and Delinquency* 48(1): 58–82.

Barker, R. G. (1968). *Ecological Psychology: Concepts and Methods for Studying the Environment of Human Behavior* (Stanford, CA: Stanford University Press).

Beavon, D. J. K., Brantingham, P. L., and Brantingham, P. J. (1994). "The Influence of Street Networks on the Patterning of Property Offenses." In *Crime Prevention Studies*, vol. 2, edited by R. V. Clarke, pp. 115–148 (Monsey, NY: Criminal Justice Press).

Bichler, G., Malm, A., and Enriquez, J. (2010). "Magnetic Facilities: Identifying the Convergence Settings of Juvenile Delinquents." *Crime and Delinquency* 60(7): 971–998.

Bichler, G., Schmerler, K., and Enriquez, J. (2013). "Curbing Nuisance Motels: An Evaluation of Police as Place Regulators." *Policing* 36(2): 437–462.

Bowers, K. (2014) "Risky Facilities: Crime Radiators or Crime Absorbers? A Comparison of Internal and External Levels of Theft." *Journal of Quantitative Criminology* 30(3): 389–414.

Braga, A. A., and Clarke, R. V. (2014). "Explaining High-Risk Concentrations of Crime in the City: Social Disorganization, Crime Opportunities, and Important Next Steps." *Journal of Research in Crime and Delinquency* 51(4): 480–498.

Braga, A. A., Papachristos, A. V., and Hureau, D. M. (2009). "The Concentration and Stability of Gun Violence at Micro Places in Boston, 1980–2008." *Journal of Quantitative Criminology* 26(1): 33–53.

Brantingham, P. L., and Brantingham, P. J. (1981–1982). "Mobility, Notoriety and Crime: A Study of Crime Patterns in Urban Nodal Points." *Journal of Environmental System* 11(1): 89–99.

Brantingham, P. L., and Brantingham, P. J. (1993). "Environment, Routine, and Situation: Toward a Pattern Theory of Crime." In *Routine Activity and Rational Choice*, edited by M. Clarke and R. V. Felson, pp. 259–94, *Advances in Criminological Theory*, vol. 5 (New Brunswick, NJ: Transaction).

Brantingham, P. L., and Brantingham, P. J. (1995). "Criminality of Place: Crime Generators and Crime Attractors." *European Journal on Criminal Policy and Research* 3(1): 5–26.

Buck, G., Austin, R. Cooper, G., Gagnon, D., Hodges, J., Martensen, K., and O'Neal, M. (1973). *Police Crime Analysis Unit Handbook* (Washington, DC: US Department of Justice, Law Enforcement Assistance Administration, National Institute of Law Enforcement and Criminal Justice).

Campbell DeLong Resources, Inc. (2000). *Keeping Illegal Activity Out of Rental Property: A Police Guide for Establishing Landlord Training Programs*. NCJ 148656 (Washington, DC: US Department of Justice, Bureau of Justice Assistance).

Clarke, R. V. (1999). *Hot Products: Understanding, Anticipating and Reducing Demand for Stolen Goods* (London: Home Office, Policing and Reducing Crime Unit, Research Development and Statistics Directorate).

Clarke, R. V. (2009). "Situational Crime Prevention." In *Environmental Criminology and Crime Analysis*, edited by R. Wortley and L. Mazerolle, pp. 178–193 (Cullompton, Devon, UK: Willan Publishing).

Clarke, R. V., and Bichler-Robertson, G. (1998). "Place Managers, Slumlords and Crime in Low Rent Apartment Buildings." *Security Journal* 11(1): 11–19.

Clear, T. (1996) "Toward a Corrections of 'Place': The Challenge of 'Community' in Corrections." *NIJ Journal* August: 52–56. https://www.ncjrs.gov/pdffiles/nijjcomm.pdf.

Cohen, L., and Felson, M. (1979). "Social Change and Crime Rate Trends: A Routine Activity Approach." *American Sociological Review* 44(4): 588–605.

Cresswell, T. (2015). *Place: An Introduction*. 2nd edition (Chichester, UK: Wiley).

Crow, W. J., and Bull, J. L. (1975). *Robbery Deterrence: An Applied Behavioral Science Demonstration—Final Report* (La Jolla, CA: Western Behavior Sciences Institute).

Eck, J. E. (1994). "Drug Markets and Drug Places: A Case-control Study of the Spatial Structure of Illicit Drug Dealing." PhD dissertation (University of Maryland, College Park).

Eck, J. E. (1997). "Do Premises Liability Suits Promote Business Crime Prevention?" In *Business and Crime Prevention*, edited by R. V. Clarke and M. Felson, pp. 125–150 (Monsey, NY: Criminal Justice Press).

Eck, J. E. (2002). "Preventing Crime at Places." In *Evidence-Based Crime Prevention*, edited by L. W. Sherman, D. Farrington, B. Welsh, and D. L. MacKenzie, pp. 241–294 (New York: Routledge).

Eck, J. E. (2015). "Who Should Prevent Crime at Places? The Advantages of Regulating Place Managers and Challenges to Police Services." *Policing* 9(3): 223–233.

Eck, J. E., and Clarke, R. V. (2003). "Classifying Common Police Problems: A Routine Activity Approach." In *Theory for Practice in Situational Crime Prevention*, edited by M. J. Smith and D. B. Cornish, pp. 7–39 (Monsey, NY: Criminal Justice Press).

Eck, J. E., Clarke, R. V., and Guerette, R. T. (2007). "Risky Facilities: Crime Concentration in Homogeneous Sets of Establishments and Facilities." In *Imagination for Crime Prevention: Essays in Honour of Ken Pease*, edited by G. Farrell, K. J. Bowers, S. D. Johnson, and M. Townsley, pp. 225–264 (Monsey, NY: Criminal Justice Press).

Eck, J. E., and Eck, E. B. (2012). "Crime Place and Pollution: Expanding Crime Reduction Options through a Regulatory Approach." *Criminology and Public Policy* 11(2): 281–316.

Eck, J. E., and Guerette, R. T. (2012). "Place-Based Crime Prevention: Theory, Evidence, and Policy." In *The Oxford Handbook of Crime Prevention*, edited by B. Welsh and D. Farrington, pp. 354–383 (New York: Oxford University Press).

Farrell, G., and Pease, K. (2008). "Repeat Victimisation." In *Environmental Criminology and Crime Analysis*, edited by R. Wortley and L. Mazerolle, pp. 117–135 (Cullompton, Devon, UK: Willan Publishing).

Felson, M. (1986). "Linking Crime Choices, Routine Activities, Informal Control, and Criminal Outcomes." In *The Reasoning Criminal*, edited by D. B. Cornish and R. V. Clarke, pp. 119–128 (New York: Springer-Verlag).

Felson, M. (2003). "The Process of Co-offending." In *Theory for Practice in Situational Crime Prevention*, edited by M. J. Smith and D. B. Cornish, pp. 149–167 (Monsey, NY: Criminal Justice Press).

Gottfredson, M., and Hirschi, T. (1990). *A General Theory of Crime*. (Palo Alto, CA: Stanford University Press).

Graham, K., and Homel, R. (2008). *Raising the Bar: Preventing Aggression in and around Bars, Pubs and Clubs* (Cullompton, Devon, UK: Willan Publishing).

Groff, E. R., Weisburd, D., and Yang, S.-M. (2010). "Is it Important to Examine Crime Trends at a Local 'Micro' Level? A Longitudinal Analysis of Street to Street Variability in Crime Trajectories." *Journal of Quantitative Criminology* 26(1): 7–32.

Guerette, R. T., and Bowers, K. J. (2009). "Assessing the Extent of Crime Displacement and Diffusion of Benefits: A Review of Situational Crime Prevention Evaluations." *Criminology* 47(4): 1331–68.

Hammer, M. (2011). "Crime Places of Comfort." Unpublished paper. School of Criminal Justice, University of Cincinnati.

Jeffery, C. R. (1977). *Crime Prevention through Environmental Design* (Thousand Oaks, CA: Sage).

Kennedy, J. P. (2014). "A View from the Top: Managers' Perspectives on the Problem of Employee Theft in Small Businesses." PhD dissertation (School of Criminal Justice, University of Cincinnati).

Lee, Y., Eck, J. E., Soohyun, O., and Martinez, N. (2015). "Systematic Review of Place Concentration." Paper delivered at the American Society of Criminology Meeting, November 18–21 (Washington, DC).

Loukaitou-Sideris, A. (1999). "Hot Spots of Bus Stop Crime." *Journal of the American Planning Association* 65(4): 395–411.

Madensen, T. D. (2007). "Bar Management and Crime: Toward a Dynamic Theory of Place Management and Crime Hotspots." PhD dissertation (University of Cincinnati).

Madensen, T. D., and Eck, J. E. (2013). "Crime Places and Place Management." In *Oxford Handbook of Criminological Theory*, edited by F. T. Cullen and P. Wilcox, pp. 554–578 (New York: Oxford University Press).

Madensen, T. D., and Sousa, W. H. (2016). "Building Cases against Places: Crime Science and the Potential of Place-Based Investigations." Paper delivered at the Environmental Criminology and Crime Analysis Symposium, January 11–13 (Mahabalipuram, India).

Matthews, R., Pease, C., and Pease, K. (2001). "Repeated Bank Robbery: Theme and Variations." In *Repeat Victimization*, edited by G. Farrell and K. Pease, pp. 133–151, (Monsey, NY: Criminal Justice Press).

Mazerolle, L. G., and Ransley, J. (2005). *Third Party Policing* (New York: Cambridge University Press).

Mazerolle, L. G., Roehl, J., and Kadleck C. (1998). "Controlling Social Disorder Using Civil Remedies: Results from a Randomized Field Experiment in Oakland, California." In *Civil Remedies and Crime Prevention*, edited by L. Mazerolle and J. Roehl, pp. 141–159(Monsey, NY: Criminal Justice Press).

Newman, O. (1972). *Defensible Space: Crime Prevention through Urban Design* (New York: Macmillan).

Park, S. M., and Eck, J. E. (2013). "Understanding the Random Effect on Victimization Distributions: A Statistical Analysis of Random Repeat Victimizations." *Victims and Offenders* 8(4): 399–415.

Payne, T. C. (2010). "Does Change in Ownership Change Crime? An Analysis of Apartment Ownership and Crime in Cincinnati." PhD dissertation (University of Cincinnati).

Payne, T. C. (2015). "Reducing Excessive Police Incidents: Do Notices to Owners Work?" *Security Journal* 28(1): 1–18.

Payne, T. C., and Eck, J. E. (2007). "Who Owns Crime?" Paper delivered at the Annual Meeting of the American Society of Criminology, November 14–17 (Atlanta, GA).

Payne, T. C., Gallagher, K., Eck, J. E., and Frank, J. (2013). "Problem Framing in Problem Solving: A Case Study." *Policing* 36(4): 670–682.

Pawson, R., and Tilley, N. (1997). *Realistic Evaluation*. London: Sage.

Pierce, G. L., Spaar, S., and Briggs, L. (1988). *The Character of Police Work Strategic and Tactical Implications* (Boston: Northeastern University, Center for Applied Social Research).

Rawe, J. (2007). "Bye-Bye, Mall Rats." *Time*. June 28. Accessed March 14, 2016, http://content.time.com/time/magazine/article/0,9171,1638449,00.html.

Reynald, D. M. (2009). "Guardianship in Action: Developing a New Tool for Measurement." *Crime Prevention and Community Safety* 11(1): 1–20.

Sampson, R., Eck, J. E., and Dunham, J. (2009). "Super Controllers and Crime Prevention: A Routine Activity Explanation of Crime Prevention Success and Failure." *Security Journal* 23(1): 37–51.

Sampson, R. J., Raudenbush, S. W., and Earls, F. (1997). "Neighborhoods and Violent Crime: A Multilevel Study of Collective Efficacy." *Science* 277(5328): 918–24.

Shaw, C., and McKay, H. D. (1942). *Delinquency and Urban Areas* (Chicago: University of Chicago Press).

Sherman, L. W. (1990). "Police Crackdowns: Initial and Residual Deterrence." In *Crime and Justice: A Review of Research*, edited by M. Tonry and N. Morris, pp. 1–48 (Chicago: University of Chicago Press).

Sherman, L. W. (1998) "Violent Stranger Crime at a Large Hotel: A Case Study in Risk Assessment." *Security Journal* 1(1): 40–46.

Sherman, L. W., Gartin, P. R., and Buerger, M. E. (1989). "Hot Spots of Predatory Crime: Routine Activities and the Criminology of Place." *Criminology* 27(1): 27–55.

Spelman, W. (1995). "Criminal Careers of Public Places." In *Crime and Place*, edited by J. E. Eck and D. Weisburd, pp. 115–144 (Monsey, NY: Criminal Justice Press).

Weisburd, D. (2015). "The Law of Crime Concentration and the Criminology of Place." *Criminology* 53(2); 133–157.

Weisburd, D., Bushway, S., Lum, C., and Yang, S.-M. (2004). "Trajectories of Crime at Places: A Longitudinal Study of Street Segments in the City of Seattle." *Criminology* 42(2): 283–321.

Weisburd, D., Eck, J. E., Braga, A., Telep, C., Cave, B., Bowers, K., Bruinsma, G., Gill, C., Groff, E., Hinkle, J., Hibdon, J., Johnson, S., Lawton, B., Lum, C., Ratcliffe, J., Rengert, G., Taniguchi, T., and Yang, S.-M. 2016. *Place Matters: Criminology for the 21st Century* (New York: Cambridge University Press).

Weisburd, D., Groff, E. R., and Yang, S.-M. (2012). *The Criminology of Place: Street Segments and Our Understanding of the Crime Problem* (New York: Oxford University Press).

Weisburd, D., Morris, N., and Ready, J. (2008). "Risk-Focused Policing at Places: An Experimental Evaluation." *Justice Quarterly* 25(1): 163–200.

Wilcox, P., and Eck, J. E. (2011). "Criminology of the Unpopular: Implications for Policy Aimed at Payday Lending Facilities." *Criminology and Public Policy* 10(2): 473–482.

Wilcox, P., Madensen, T. D., and Tillyer, M. S. (2007). "Guardianship in Context: Implication for Burglary Victimization Risk and Prevention." *Criminology* 45(4):771–803.

Wilcox Roundtree, P., Land, K. C., and Hunt, S. A. (2003). *Criminal Circumstance: A Dynamic Multicontextual Criminal Opportunity Theory* (New York: Aldine de Gruyter).

CHAPTER 28

CRIME CONCENTRATIONS

Hot Dots, Hotspots, and Hot Flushes

DAINIS IGNATANS AND KEN PEASE

28.1 Introduction

Every research enterprise takes place in a context, political, economic, and technological. So it is with policing research. We begin by sketching out where we think the practice of policing is heading, and what we need to do differently so as to arrive at a roughly envisioned future ethically and in good order. A police presence at all places at all times being impossible, the practical issue is where and when to place officers or their technological surrogates. The chapter will consider optimized distribution of effort and resource, given the central aim of fairness in the distribution of crime harm. We will illustrate current levels of inequality of victimization, and claim that reducing the current concentration, at individual and area levels, should be an explicit underpinning vision for policing. We briefly review the relevant literature and its implications.

A decade hence, as regards policing the physical environment, we envisage a patrolling officer wearing an augmented reality headset on which will be displayed police-relevant events or circumstances: probability, time, and location of offenses of various types likely to be suffered by residents or visitors. The offense probabilities will be based upon prior victimizations at and near the location in view, weighted by recency of the events concerned and perhaps by the harm typically inflicted upon victims of offenses of the types in question. The information displayed would also include active criminal justice disposals against residents, thus (for example) providing full context to incidents of domestic abuse and driving while disqualified (driverless cars still being trialed). The equipment would incorporate the next generation of wearable camera.

While some officers patrol in physical space, others will be engaged in fundamentally similar estimation and oversight of risks in cyberspace (see the chapter by Miró Llionares and Johnson in this volume for a detailed discussion of this topic). There is as yet much less clarity about what counts as propinquity in cyberspace, where attacks come from anywhere on the planet, but the principle of deploying resources commensurate with risk or harm represents the same guiding principle. One-to-many communication, much easier in cyberspace, means that many potential victims may be contacted with one click, those responding thereby self-selecting as victims. Where offenders target victims, similarities among targets can be used as measures of vulnerability equivalent to location in physical space. Gullibility may be the cyberspace analogue of physical propinquity (see Titus and Dover 2001), and machine learning represents an emergent technology for identifying victim characteristics from massive data sources. Bear in mind that while understanding propinquity in cyberspace is an important issue for identifying cyber hotspots, it is not needed for repeated victimization of the same people or closely specified locations (the hot dots of the chapter title).

The information behind the headset display as described above is intentionally restricted to information that the police legitimately hold. There are other variables (such as age and poverty/wealth) that could enhance the precision of risk and harm estimates displayed on the headset. They are foregone here in anticipation of criticism that they are intrusive. However, if the majority of people accept Scott McNeally's advice, "You have zero privacy anyway. Get over it,"[1] the equipment could also weight hazards by resident characteristics empirically demonstrated to carry elevated or diminished crime risks. The headset may also make directional suggestions to police officers, based upon spatiotemporal patterns of recent crime or disorder, maximizing police presence (officers or drones) where the action is most likely to be found.

A future recognizable from the outline above is technically feasible and in our view on balance desirable, and the research program for the next decade should have that image clearly in mind as its likely scenario of application. Travel without a destination in mind is pointless (albeit fun at the weekend), and one can always change one's mind en route to the future. The envisaged research program should address both the content and ethics of the algorithms devised to underpin the envisaged future. Just as Darwinian evolution theory has progressed through the analysis of variation, so the aim of the research will be the fuller understanding of variation in crime risks across people, places, and times. At present, much fine research along these lines is already being conducted, albeit expressed with varying degrees of clarity as to the operational policing implications. In the writers' view, progress toward the vision outlined above will be expedited by keeping the following four injunctions in mind. The researcher will make most progress

1. By framing research questions as explicitly as possible in terms of their implications for police policy and deployment of resources; the operational importance of much applicable research is overlooked by dint of the way in which researchers frame the questions.
2. By examining *interactions* between time, place, and resident population. Subpopulations may be differentially vulnerable at certain times and locations. For instance, focusing exclusively on area-level risks precludes analysis of area-individual interactions in risk.

3. By complementing work on risk with intensive study of dose-response relationships linking police activity and risk consequences. There is little point in knowing how much someone is at risk without knowing the type and extent of intervention that would serve to reduce it.
4. By obtaining clearer evidence of how crime risk clusters in cyberspace. Crimes in physical space are locatable simply in two dimensions (three if height is included) but the variables defining propinquity in cyberspace are not. Particularly for near repeats (discussed later), we need to know what closer might mean in cyberspace.

28.2 Concentration and Fairness

Concentration is here used to indicate an association between presenting variation in presenting risk and variation in environmental circumstance or condition of people or places at risk. Attention here is restricted to those associations that are of clear and direct relevance to the crime control enterprise, such as the association between current and previous victimization on. The extent of a society's problem of victimization by crime may be expressed in three different ways, alone or in combination. These are most simply described by reference to people but can be applied to locations. *Crime incidence* is essentially the number of crimes suffered per head of the total population (or per location), so a town of 1,000 people suffering 200 crimes in a year has a crime incidence of 0.2 or 20%. *Crime prevalence* is the proportion of the population suffering a crime, regardless of how many times. Perhaps 100 people in the town suffered at least one crime, so the prevalence is 100/1000, or 0.1. The final measure, *concentration*, is the number of crimes per victim, that is, 200/100, or 2.0.

Most crime is unfair insofar as it deprives people of freedom of use of their bodies or possessions (indeed the criminalization of behaviors that do not do this should be questioned). The *concentration* of crime is arguably the central dimension in terms of which to think about fairness. In the light of this, it is surprising and regrettable that much early research has used prevalence as its key crime measure (e.g., Miethe and Meier 1990; Kennedy and Forde 1990). Crime concentration has been the Cinderella measure of crime until quite recently.

A crime-free society may be seen as utopia (no victimization) or dystopia (no freedom). For practical crime control, the relevant question concerns the equity of the current distribution of crime. Who (among people) and where (among locations) bears the burden of crime? To anticipate our conclusion, the distribution of victimization among people and places is so extreme that a laudable policy priority is to distribute the burden of crime more fairly.

Alfredo Pareto was a 19th-century polymath (see Femia 2006 for a sympathetic overview of Pareto's work), who is now remembered primarily for his eponymous principle, also known as the 80/20 rule, or the law of the vital few. The Pareto principle holds that, in general, roughly 80% of effects are attributable to roughly 20% of agents. For example, roughly 80% of wealth is held by roughly 20% of a population, and 80% of train journeys use 20% of the rail network. Someone Googling *Pareto principle* today would find the bulk of sites flagged to be concerned with how entrepreneurs can exploit the predominance of the "vital few" who account for most purchases, most wealth held, and most online usage. The 80/20 proportion is of course only a rough baseline; but a recognition, intuitive or data-based, of the existence of a "vital few" to whom attention must be paid in order to effect change is a prudent first step in any policy. In the crime context we think of prolific offenders or areas of high crime. Operational policing is substantially a question of applying the Pareto principle to the distribution of personnel and time appropriately, attending especially to the vital few. Policing and criminal justice should be concerned to stop the vital few from remaining vital, so distributing risks and harms more equitably. Criminology has historically been more concerned with retributive justice than distributive justice. Environmental criminology brings a change of emphasis, its point of departure being that a society's institutions and policies shape the distribution of benefits and burdens among its citizens. There is an extensive philosophical literature on distributive justice (see Allingham 2014). For present purposes two variants of the concept roughly reflect what police managers might accept as aspirations of the policing enterprise. These are strict egalitarianism and John Rawls's alternative distributive strategy, which he calls the difference principle. Strict egalitarianism is self-explanatory, though its practical implementation is not. It means that citizens should bear the burden of crime and disorder equally. The difference principle permits diverging from strict equality so long as the inequalities in question would make the least advantaged in society materially better off than they would be under strict equality. One thinks here of subsidy of security products or patrolling attention to those at highest risk.

At this point the distinction between crimes and crime harms should be noted briefly. Counting each crime as a single event contributing one to the crime count total neglects the wide range of impacts on victims of crime according to the particular crime suffered. The idea of weighting crimes according to the harm they inflict has recently excited interest (Sherman et al. 2014; Ignatans and Pease 2015). Weighting events by harm is possible as a refinement of all of the analyses described below, but doing so within this chapter would make it less focused and more tedious for the readership. The reader is asked simply to bear in mind that different victimization risks may be treated differently to achieve greater equality of harm, where different *risk* profiles are equal in anticipated *harm*. Equality of harm may (for instance) equate a small risk of wounding to a much higher risk of vandalism to one's car. If this route is taken, one must further decide whether individual vulnerabilities should be taken into account. The Rawls difference principle may propose that (for example) the elderly should expect more policing attention by dint of greater harm from objectively similar victimizations. These complexities are addressed by philosophers in an offshoot literature on what has come to be known as luck egalitarianism (see Lippert-Rasmussen 2015).

The last paragraph sounds academic, a world away from policing the streets now. It is not. All current dispositions of police strength and resources already make these kinds of decision. A police officer chooses to patrol in one place rather than another, to stop one person rather than another, or to have a special squad to address one or other crime type. In doing so, the officer is making the same kind of judgment as was discussed in the last paragraph, except that it is intuitive rather than reasoned and communicable. The last paragraph was essentially a plea for policing to be clear about the perfect (albeit never to be perfected) distribution of crime and harm toward which the profession is striving. All police officers have internal algorithms of which they are only partially aware. Explicit algorithms are better, but may turn, when unconsidered and left unchanged, into "weapons of math destruction" (O'Neil 2015). The preconscious heuristics of the patrolling officer are seldom if ever subject to the same scrutiny but are no less problematic.

28.3 A Few Vital Fews

Who or what are the "vital few" in policing? We may think of these in many ways, not mutually exclusive. Some of the most obvious vital fews include

1. The minority of perpetrators responsible for the bulk of crime or crime harm (prolific offenders)
2. The minority of *areas* hosting most crime (hotspots)
3. The episodic elevation of risk (hot flushes)
4. The minority of victims or microlocations suffering the bulk of crime events (hot dots)
5. The minority of attractive products being the most stolen (hot products)

The second, third, and fourth of these will be dealt with in this chapter. We attend in most detail to the fourth, for two reasons. First, the focus of the present volume is on environmental determination of crime events, thus de-emphasizing prolific offenders. Second, there is evidence that the inequality of "hotspots" is substantially a function of "hot dots" (Trickett et al. 1992; Johnson et al. 1997). Third, some hot dots are people rather than places (think of hate crime) who carry their risks around with them, which risks would not be evident from the analysis of spatial hotspots. A different emphasis would hold that some places, such as robbery hotspots, carry elevated risks for everyone who ventures there. The only prudent course of action is to look at both and, crucially, their interactions (Bowers et al. 2005). We start with hot dots. Hot products (see Bowers and Johnson 2013) are omitted from consideration because they can be regarded as mini-microlocations (the razor blade display in supermarkets, for example).

The term "hot dot" (Laycock and Pease 1999) was coined to emphasize the importance of the greatest possible disaggregation of units of count (usually people or microlocations) to maximize precision of intervention. In practical terms, in policing as in surgery, the more precise the focus the more targeted may be the intervention. What does a police officer put into a *hotspot* area do? What does a surgeon do knowing only that the problem is somewhere in the heart? Dealing with the hot dot of an individual or specific location, on the street or in the chest cavity, that question is easier to answer. There is also important empirical evidence bearing on the decision. Tseloni (2006) in a very substantial multilevel modeling exercise using census and victimization survey data demonstrated that "the current empirical evidence that area characteristics effect, albeit statistically significant, are lower than individual household effects implies that household victimization first and foremost relates to households' profile and lifestyle" (p. 228). The household is the most important hot dot, it appears. Tseloni's work, alongside the Trickett and Johnson work mentioned above, vindicates the choice of the hot dot rather than the hotspot as the preferred unit of analysis. The fact that it is more helpful operationally is a bonus.

28.4 Hot Dots: People

Returning to the world we currently inhabit, what is the level of inequality in victimization at the "hot dot" level? The person is here the unit of count, and the issue is how useful victimization of the individual is to estimating future risk. There are many ways in which the extent of repeat victimization is inadequately captured in any data you are likely to come across. (In what follows, *repeat, multiple*, and *chronic* victimization are synonyms, to avoid boring repetition of the same term.) Statistics of crime reported to and recorded by the police are flawed because only around a half of all crimes suffered are reported to and recorded by the police. This underestimation is especially large for multiple victims who become demoralized by authorities' lack of effort or lack of success in preventing the recurrence of their victimization. Such people often simply stop reporting what has happened. Relying on victimization surveys is better than police-recorded crime data, but there are two important ways in which underrepresentation of chronic victims is a problem with such surveys.

The first way in which victimization surveys understate the extent of multiple victimization is the capping of crime counts (Farrell and Pease 2007; Planty and Strom 2007; Lauritsen et al. 2012; Walby et al. 2016). It is currently almost ubiquitous among victimization surveys to limit in analysis the number of events that occur as part of a series, that is, with the same perpetrator in similar circumstances. The obvious example of such high levels of repetition is domestic violence. In such cases the Crime Survey for England and Wales (CSEW) caps the number of events in a series at five. So a victim tells the interviewer she has suffered a series of 50 assaults at the hands of the same perpetrator over the course of a year. This number will be capped at five events. The victim said 50; this appears in the published data as five. Please reread the last sentence. To the writers it represents the triumph of statistical convenience over human suffering. Long-overdue changes to this convention are at the time of writing being considered in both the United States and in England and Wales. Some academics have reanalyzed the data, placing the cap very much higher. A cap of 49 was applied for each crime type in the analyses presented below.

Ideally there would be no cap, but this would require supplementary interviews with chronic victims to establish the reliability of the numbers of events recounted. Failing that, the decision to cap at 49 was made after examining the frequencies of each offense type so that the exclusion of events was less than 0.1% in each case.

The second way in which victimization surveys understate the true extent of chronic victimization is the time window (Farrell, Sousa, and Weisel 2001). The underestimation occurs because with (say) a one-year recall period in victimization surveys, a crime described as having occurred in the January of the recall year may be a repetition of something that happened in the previous December, which is out of the survey's range. Similarly, an event recounted as having happened in the December of the recall year may be precursor of events after the recall year has ended. What sort of difference does this make? Table 28.1, modified from the Farrell et al. work, shows the extent of underestimation of repeat victimization involved.

Indexing the typical 12-month recall period to 100, it will be seen that a two-year recall period would capture around one-third more repeats. A three-year recall period would capture around 50% more repeats than the 12-month recall period. A six-month recall period would capture only around 70% of the one-year repeats. It is important not to confuse the time window effect with what is known as telescoping. The former refers to repeated events that occur across the boundary of the recall period. The latter refers to misremembering the date of an offense suffered.

Taken together, the capping of incidents and the time window effect are significant ways in which the extent of multiple victimization is understated.

Table 28.2 sets out the distribution of victimization events by respondent for the most recent sweep of CSEW (2014–2015). It includes cross-type repeats, so shows the inequality of distribution of crime events in general.

What is the reader to take from Table 28.2? The proportion of all crimes that are preventable in the sense that they are the second or subsequent events suffered during the one-year recall period is 47%. Capping would reduce that to 34%. The time window effect, and what happens behind the doors of households that refuse to respond to the

Table 28.1 Volume of Repeat Burglaries Using Different Time Windows, by City (Indexed to 100 at 12 months)

	Indexed to 100 at 12 months		
Time window (months)	Baltimore	Dallas	San Diego
6	69.6	72.7	69.0
12	100	100	100
18	119.0	117.7	122.6
24	133.2	127.3	140.6
30	149.6	137.3	152.3
36	161.5	146.1	163.2

Table 28.2 Victim Frequency by Number of Crimes Suffered: Crime Survey for England and Wales 2014–2015

	Total crimes	
Number of crimes	Frequency	Number of repeats
1	3,978	0
2	1,082	1,082
3	396	792
4	217	651
5	106	424
6	67	335
7	24	144
8	29	203
9	12	99
10	24	216
11	9	90
12	14	154
13	6	72
14	8	104
15	5	70
16	7	105
19	3	54
20	3	57
21	1	20
23	1	22
24	4	92
25	2	48
28	1	27
30	2	58
34	3	99
42	1	41
43	1	42
48	1	47
66	1	65
80	1	79
Total	6,009	5,292

survey (about which we confess to worrying greatly), will take the figure well beyond half of all crime experienced.

One approach to estimating the true extent of repeat burglaries on the basis of police-recorded crime data (Frank et al. 2012) looked at data from Vancouver. It concluded

> Whereas repeat burglaries constituted 20% of recorded burglaries, after adjustment they were half of burglaries. Moreover, households with five or more burglaries accounted for less than 1% of recorded incidents but, after adjustment, one in five actual burglaries (21%).

An adequate visual representation of the extent of inequality of victimization is difficult to come by. Figures 28.1, 28.2,. and 28.3 represent our attempt at such a representation. They show data for property, personal, and vehicle crime respectively from CSEW (2000–2012). They exclude cross-type repeats.[2] Please look at Figure 28.1. Respondents were ranked in terms of the number of victimizations they suffered. This ranking was expressed as percentiles on the abscissa. In Figure 28.1 the columns are shaded according to survey year shown in the key. Looking at the abscissa, nothing appears at the 80th percentile for any year. Thus 80% of respondents suffered no victimizations of the crime type depicted, whereas the rightmost cluster of columns shows that the most victimized 1% suffered an average of five property crimes each over the year (shown on the ordinate) in the most recent survey. Figures 28.2 and 28.3 are structured in the same manner, with Figure 28.2 showing that the top 1% of respondents suffered an average of seven crimes against their person in the most recent sweep of the survey. Figure 28.3 shows that the most victimized 1% of respondents with regard to vehicle crimes suffered around four such crimes each.

The data have been presented in this way to show the extreme inequality in victimization by each type but also so as not to hide the reduction in the absolute decline in the amount of victimization suffered in recent years, the quasi-global crime drop. Chronic victims have suffered progressively less crime over time. However, importantly, while the *number* of crimes suffered has thankfully dropped, the *proportion* of crime suffered by the "vital few" has *increased* both nationally (Ignatans and Pease 2015, 2016) and globally (Pease and Ignatans 2016). In line with our injunction to make

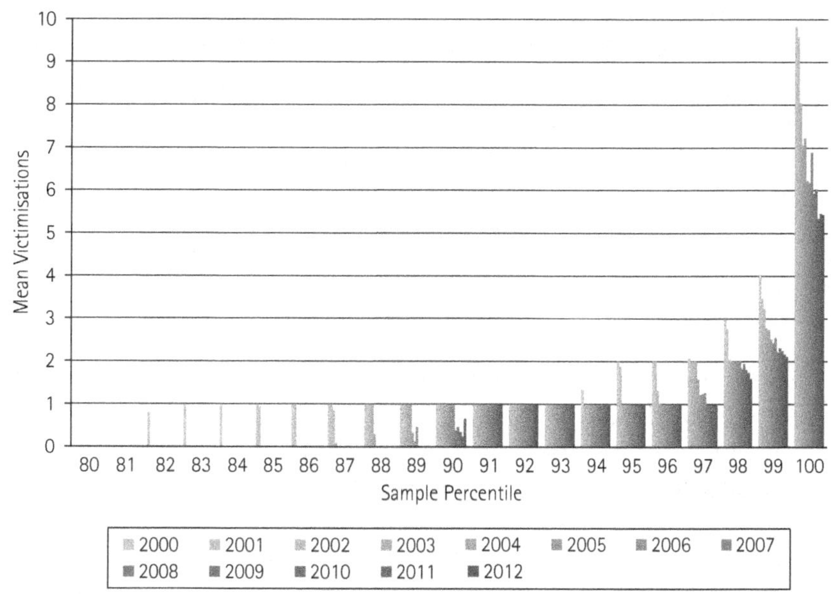

FIGURE 28.1 Average numbers of property victimizations per victim by percentile, CSEW sweeps 2000–2012

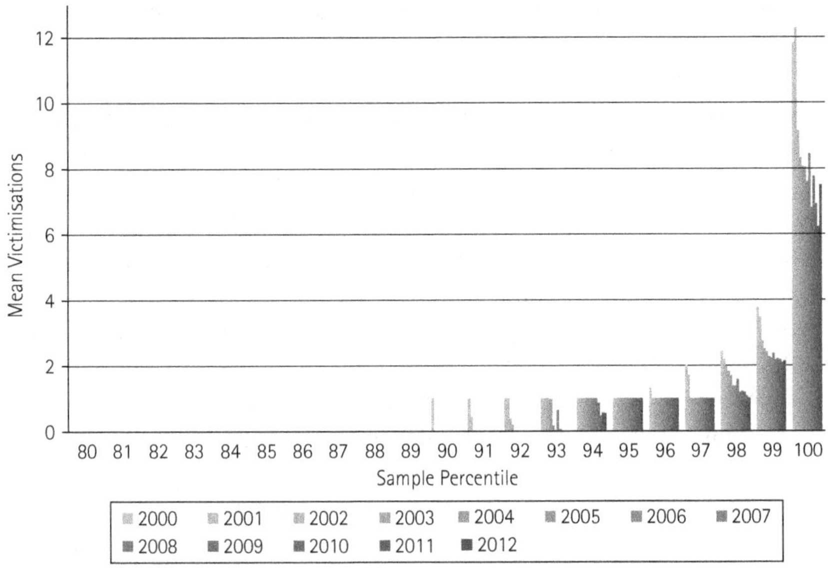

FIGURE 28.2 Average numbers of personal victimizations per victim by percentile, CSEW sweeps 2000–2012

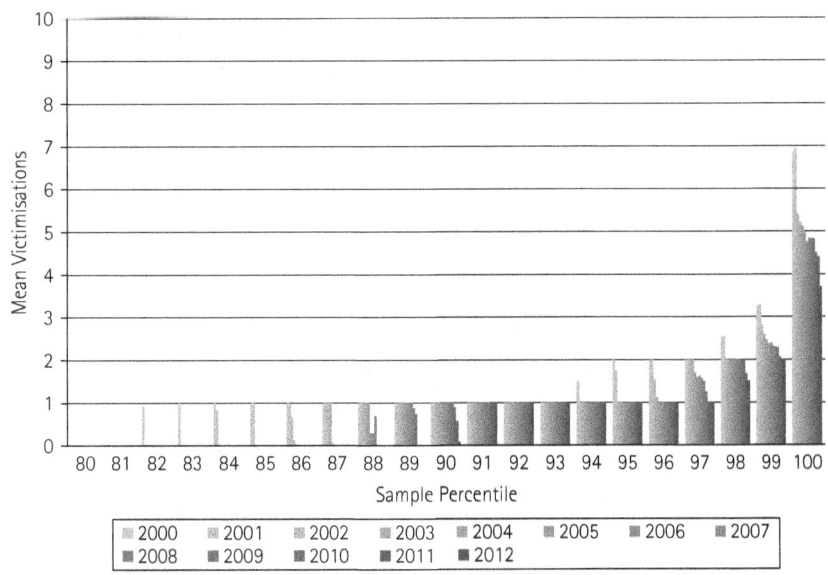

FIGURE 28.3 Average numbers of vehicle victimizations per victim by percentile, CSEW sweeps 2000–2012

explicit what we take to be operational implications of the research, we believe them to be as follows.

1. Crime control should concentrate on the prevention of repeat victimization, which, as the earlier text demonstrates, accounts for the bulk of all crime.
2. As crime declines, it is likely that the average travel distance between the locations of prior victimizations gets longer. This is not inevitably true, but is likely to be so, particularly if attention is given to hot dots. Look at a crime map, delete a few of the dots in the highest-crime zones, and you will readily see that the average distance between the remaining events is longer. This means that a patrolling officer will spend longer in transit between recent crime scenes. This is likely to mean that visible patrol is an ever less efficient means of prevention, making reliance on self-protection and neighbor cooperation increasingly important.

The importance of victimization concentration is demonstrated in a different way by Figures 28.4 and 28.5. The CSEW sweep of 2002–2003 was used in building these figures because this sweep of the survey was the last in which individual sampling points were identified. Up to and including that sweep, clusters of 60 addresses comprised the sample, so the cluster could be used as the unit of count. Screener questions (i.e., the initial questions asked of all respondents) were used and events reported capped at 49 per offense. We then have some 600 units of count (sampling points) and for each we can calculate *the number and proportion of responding households suffering one or more crimes* (prevalence), the number of *victimizations per household* (incidence), and the

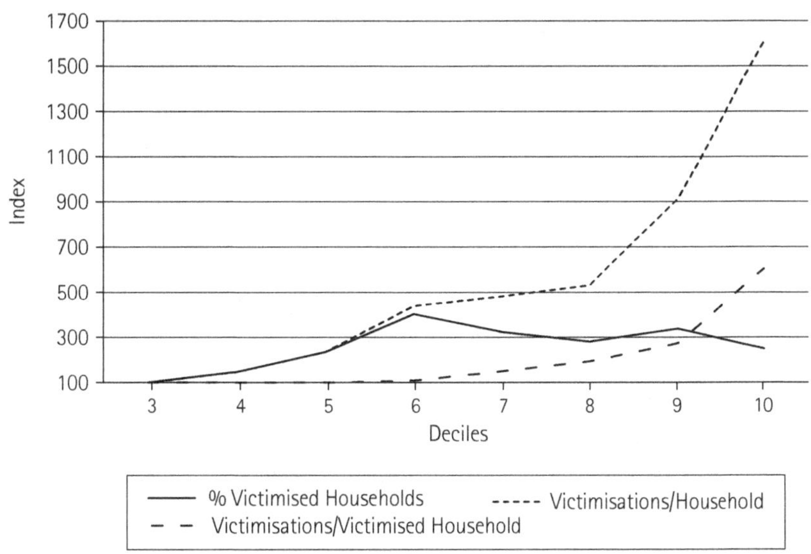

FIGURE 28.4 Proportion of victimized households, average victimization and victimization per victimized household experiencing personal crime, indexed to 100 and aligned by average victimization per victimized household, CSEW sweep 2002/2003

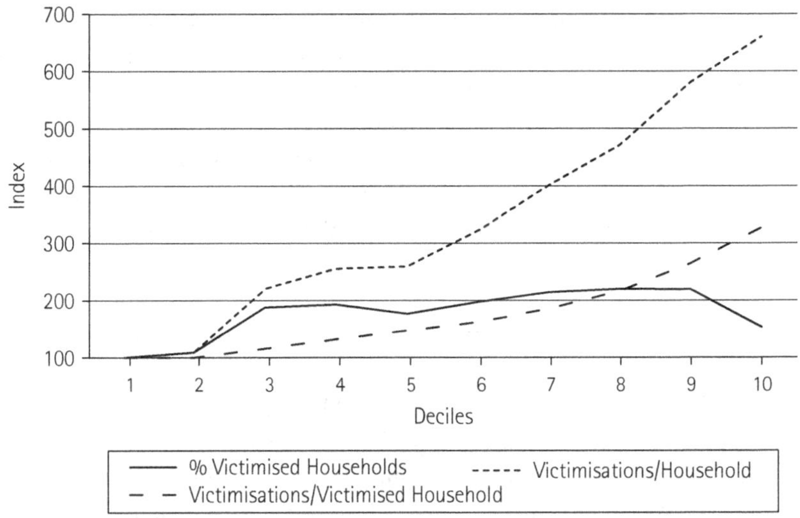

FIGURE 28.5 Proportion of victimized households, average victimization and victimization per victimized household experiencing property crime, indexed to 100 and aligned by average victimization per victimized household, CSEW Sweep 2002/2003

number of *victimizations per victimized household* (concentration). Sampling points were then ranked and the sampling points grouped into deciles. For violent crime the first two deciles were crime-free; therefore the third decile was indexed to 100. For property crimes, the first decile was indexed.

The pattern presented here further exemplifies the importance of inequality of victimization. These figures echo Trickett et al. (1992) and Johnson et al. (1997) perhaps even more dramatically than the earlier figures. To put it in practical terms, areas where repeats are more concentrated have fewer one-time targets; therefore, targeted prevention of repeats in the most victimized households in areas where crime is highest would further amplify effectiveness of the tactic of preventing repeats.

Figures 28.4 and 28.5 make the point that ranking areas by crime experienced shows that the top decile (10%) of areas suffers 17 times the violent crime and 6.5 times the property crime of the lowest decile. This is driven by concentration more than by prevalence.

So far this chapter seems parochial, with almost exclusive reliance on British data. This is simply because of confidence in and availability of that data. Many previous studies show the huge extent of hot-dot contribution to crime problems. In Minneapolis, Sherman showed that 64% of all calls for police service were from 5% of addresses. In Canada, Perreault, Sauve, and Burns (2004) showed that some 2% of adults suffered 60% of violent incidents. Sorensen (2004) showed the extent of repeat victimization in the "private Danish home." Using International Crime Survey sweeps of 1992 and 1996, Farrell and Bouloukous (2002) presented the proportion of incidents reported as repeats in Northern Ireland, Netherlands, Scotland, England and Wales, Switzerland, Belgium, France, Finland, Sweden, Italy, Austria, the United States, Canada, Australia, and New Zealand. A proportion of crimes was examined in a smaller number of countries (e.g., the 1992 sweep explored repeats of robbery only in Sweden). More detailed information is available in the original article, yet the presence of repeat victimization, its severity, and the necessity to address it reach all corners of the world.

We conducted analyses of more fragmentary data from other countries extracted from the International Crime Victimization Survey (Pease and Ignatans 2016). As demonstrated by Figure 28.6, repeated events are not merely an artifact of discourse in England and Wales. Essentially the picture is the same as that found by Farrell and Bouloukos (2002), Kleemans (2001), Morgan (2001), van Dijk (2001), and Mawby (2001). Australian data analyzed by Sagovsky and Johnson (2007) showed the probability of repetition to be some six times that of initial burglary victimization. The criticism may still be advanced that victimization surveys are exclusively conducted in the developed world, so repeat victimization may not be a global phenomenon. This makes a study conducted by Aiden Sidebottom in Malawi of special importance and interest (Sidebottom 2012). He demonstrated substantial rates of repeat burglary victimization, with some 2% of households suffering 28% of burglaries. This is an underestimate since the most victimized groups were asked only to specify "4 or more burglaries."

Another criticism may be that while multiple victimization has been amply demonstrated as regards domestic burglary, the evidence elsewhere is more sparse. This is true, but where it has been sought, such evidence has been found. It is self-evidently true for domestic violence (and all other series offenses captured in CSEW). It has been found to apply to racial attacks (Sampson and Phillips 1992), bank and building society robberies (Matthews et al. 2001), and bullying among children (Schwarz et al. 1993). Self-reports by offenders make clear the advantages of returning to offend against the same target (Shaw and Pease 2000).

The ubiquity of massive levels of hot dots tempts us to think in terms of a simple reward-based explanation for repeat victimization. If a bully beats up someone with no

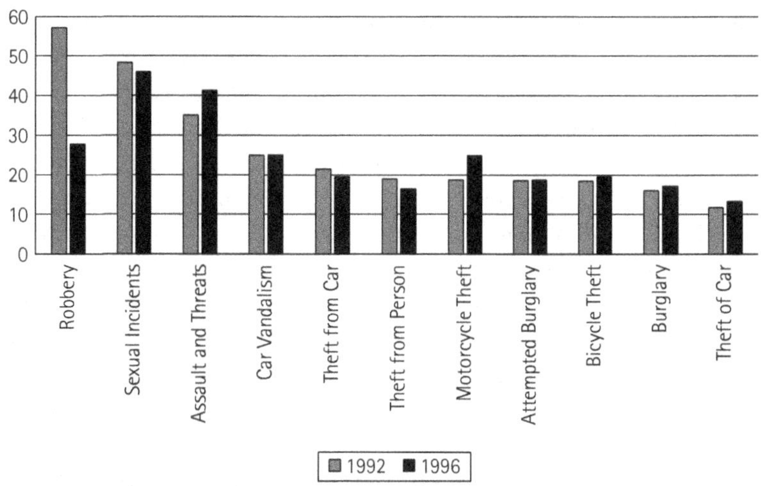

FIGURE 28.6 Reported repeats, ICVS sweeps 1992–1996

consequences, why would he or she not do it again? If domestic violence is inflicted and the victim stays in the relationship, what are the obstacles to its recurrence? The phrase "whipping boy" captures the idea that successful victimization fuels itself in a pan-human arguably pan-primate way given studies of chimpanzees (e.g., Wrangham and Wilson 2004).

Having dispensed with the charges of parochialism and burglary-centrism, let us now turn to the charge that we are neglecting the demographic and economic variables that make people vulnerable to crime, and that attention to repeat victimization allows an offender one "free go" at a vulnerable person. Responses to these will be made in turn. There are many studies demonstrating differences in vulnerability according to citizen age and household attributes (Budd 1999; Tseloni 2006; Tseloni et al. 2010; Tseloni and Pease 2014). As anticipated in the opening paragraphs of this chapter, a patrolling police officer will in the relatively short term come to have risk and harm information in real time. Privacy issues will arise insofar as information about individual households and businesses is included in the algorithm yielding risk and harm estimates. For that reason, such information is better excluded until and unless public demand for more precise harm estimation drives a change. Pragmatism also favors the use of prior victimization as a proxy for risk, including both measured and unmeasured variables that are risk relevant (Tseloni 2006). In other words, if there are things you haven't measured or things too subtle to measure but they contribute to victimization risk, just look at the victimizations themselves, to which these unmeasured factors contribute. In brief, cut to the chase and look at earlier crimes.

The argument that an exclusive attention to the prevention of repeat victimization gives offenders "one free go" is well made, though attention to "hot flushes" described later would mitigate the problem by police attention to places with what may be termed "referred risk." We also take it as a given that homes and cars should be built incorporating adequate security measures; that financial systems are designed to reduce money laundering, that facilities are available to keep perpetrators of domestic violence away from their victims, and so on, in short that prudent measures are taken to minimize crime by designing it out and deploying technology that protects (for example, pendant alarms to victims of domestic violence). The stress here is simply that the prevention of repeat victimization is a crucial and relatively neglected aspect of the crime control enterprise, not its totality.

Three closing points should be made about hot dots.

1 Generally, repeat crimes against the same target tend to happen swiftly. First demonstrated by Polvi et al. (1990), the finding seems ubiquitous. It is one of the bases for the near repeat phenomenon described later.
2 Diverse analyses, including offender self-report, establish that the bulk of repeats are committed by the same offenders (Bernasco 2008; Shaw and Pease 2000). The claim that repeat offenders against the same target tend to be more prolific remains contentious.
3 A systematic review of attempts to prevent domestic burglary through the prevention of repeat offenses against the same target indicates that they tend to be successful (Grove et al. 2012).

28.5 Hot Dots: Places

As described earlier, concentration at the most disaggregated level is important for crime control as providing the most focused attention for remedial action by police or other regulatory agencies. This is true for both people and locations. A typical pattern in any urban setting is that a small number of bars or clubs account for the bulk of crime and disorder problems. These have come to be termed "risky facilities" (Eck et al. 2007). In their words, "for any group of similar facilities (for example, taverns, parking lots, or bus shelters), a small proportion of the group accounts for the majority of crime experienced by the entire group" (p. 226).

Eck et al. provide examples from stores, bars, apartment complexes, and motels and reasons for the general pattern of extreme concentration of the few risky facilities. While this chapter is about patterns of concentration rather than what to do about them, there are many classic case studies in crime prevention that demonstrate what can be done by reducing risks in risky facilities. [34]

28.5.1 Hotspots and the Craft of Policing

The original usage of the term *hotspot* was in geology, referring to places of anomalous heat on the earth's surface above uprising plumes of magma. The hotspot is inferred by anomalous volcanic activity (i.e., not occurring at the edges of tectonic plates). Hotspots in this sense extend across time. While the term was borrowed by criminology from geology relatively recently, the existence and record of areas high in crime has a long history. Farrell and Sousa (2001) cite accounts of localities high in crime from the 18th century, but one suspects that there were such areas from the point at which people took to living in permanent settlements.

John Eck (Eck et al. 2005) defines the term *hotspot* so widely as to subsume the hot dot as described above:

> Researchers and police use the term in many different ways. Some refer to hot spot addresses . . . , others refer to hot spot blocks . . . and others examine clusters of blocks. . . . Though no common definition of the term hot spot of crime[1] exists, the common understanding is that a hot spot is an area that has a greater than average number of criminal or disorder events, or an area where people have a higher than average risk of victimization. (p. 2)

The literature of hotspots is often treated as coterminus with the criminology of place generally. David Weisburd, doyen of criminologists of place, proposed (Weisburd 2015) that "for a defined measure of crime at a specific micro geographic unit, the concentration of crime will fall within a narrow range of bandwidths of percentages for a defined cumulative proportion of crime" (p. 138). The unit of analysis he used was the street segment, and the degree of clustering was similar across four cities and years. The Weisburd law of crime concentration thus reflects the issues of clustering set out earlier in this chapter. Cory Haberman and colleagues (2016) sought to test Weisburd's law for street robberies across different "temporal scales," that is, clock time, date, and season. Their data supported the law. However, although the same small proportion of street segments hosts a large proportion of street robberies, they were not necessarily the same street segments. Their coincidence across times was slight. Put another way, the hotspots were slippery. They were not hot dots (place), stable over time. In the later section on hot flushes, we will describe how this slipperiness may be understood and put to use in predictive patrolling.

The common understanding described by John Eck is the one used here, which separates the hotspot from the hot dot (place). The default approach to the identification of hotspots is mapping, and thousands of maps are routinely prepared in police forces, where high-crime areas are defined by areas calculated to maximize the crime difference inside compared to outside the area identified. One way of distinguishing the hotspot from the hot dot (place) is that the latter is adequately represented by an old-fashioned pin map; the former is not. The question asked throughout this chapter is, what are the police operational implications of hotspotting? Locating areas with enduring high or low rates of crime, or having varied crime profiles by type, is useful for resourcing purposes. Beyond that its benefits depend on the links between the analytic approach and presumptions about reasons for the observed concentrations. In short, as argued by John Eck, you have to have ideas about what is happening "on the ground" for hotspot mapping to be useful. This point is developed in the following paragraph. Two clarifications are needed here. First, mapping that starts from an explicitly spatial base neglects those who carry their risks around with them, by dint of lifestyle or personal attributes (hot dots, people). It also neglects household-area interactions. For example, more expensive homes in deprived areas are more burglary prone than equivalent homes elsewhere (Tseloni 2006). This is important information for prevention-minded officers, but will not be evident in area maps.

Police analysis departments that produce maps with the same specification routinely are doing a useful job, but are missing an important trick. John Eck scrupulously identifies the link between how one frames questions to be addressed by mapping and presumptions about the reasons for the heat of hotspots. Clusters without theories as to the dynamics of crime are of marginal value in selecting patrolling routes, without knowing where precisely to go and what to do *within* the designated hotspot. One of us, in conversations with police officers, always asks what they would do first if they found themselves in an area designated a hotspot. Their answers typically take time to arrive and there is little consensus among them. The best response (in our view) is for the officer just to talk to people and see what they say. Sophisticated hotspot-mapping software exists, enabling clever analyses using techniques such as spatial autocorrelation and nearest-neighbor interpolation, but the many thousands of maps prepared for routine police use are, in our experience, more often than not unconnected with their policing implications. Gloria Laycock calls the mapping enterprise *as it currently exists* blobology, because of its lack of focus on operational policing decisions.

One of the most important shortcomings of the mapping of hotspots as it is currently practiced in policing is the way in which it sums events across time. The most obvious example of this is the production of maps depicting patterns across clock time. Crime profiles of an area vary shift by shift, but maps tend to show data aggregated across shifts, in areas with a thriving nighttime economy, averaging lively midnight with deserted 6:00 a.m. Perhaps the assumption of stability of crime hotspots is owed to the term's geological provenance. After all, the Old Faithful geyser in Yellowstone National Park has been erupting around 20 times a day since it was discovered in 1870. In 1870 no one had ever stolen a car, still less issued threats to kill on Facebook.

The above observations about the limitations of hotspotting must be qualified in one important way. Police officers are not pawns to be moved around the squares of a centrally managed chessboard. Any conscientious and experienced police officer placed in a designated hotspot would attempt to work out what the problem was. This is the basis of a rough-and-ready but practical approach developed by Alan Edmunds, a former officer in London's Metropolitan Police. His approach is most evident in Operation Cobra, whose report gained the Herman Goldstein Prize for Problem-Oriented Policing in 2004. The unit of count was the street rather than the individual person or home. The initial analysis showed that 1% of streets hosted 10% of vehicle crime, and 13% of streets accounted for half of all crime. The tactic was simply to talk to the people in the streets, analyze the crime data, and take remedial action. Streets with most vehicle crime applied customized warnings to victims, property marking, lighting and structure changes to the streets, and full forensic examination of crime scenes wherever possible. Streets with somewhat less vehicle crime omitted the forensic work, and those with still less crime excluded the structural changes. The crucial point, as seen by Alan Edmunds,[5] was making contact with local citizens who understood the problems and in one case remarked "What kept you?" to police officers responding to the concentrated problem. The obvious objection, that some streets are longer than others and hence will host more crime on a chance basis, is dismissed by Alan Edmunds. He notes that where a long street is included in Operation Cobra, the offenses are clustered at one or two places along it. In the first nine months of Operation Cobra, the number of vehicles stolen declined by 25%, and there was a 33% reduction in thefts from vehicles. This reduction was not experienced elsewhere in the force area. To demonstrate the agency of Cobra in the decline, greater declines were experienced in those streets that had previously hosted most crime, with reductions ranging from 37% to 58% in the previously most victimized streets. Alan Edmunds has since applied the same analytic approach to crimes of violence and criminal damage, which displayed similar inequality across streets.

The moral of the Edmunds approach is that hotspotting at the street or area level provides a rough focus for the craft of policing to come into play. One could almost characterize the craft of policing as the ability to convert hotspots into hot dots. This is also evident in some classic crime reduction success stories. Paul Ekblom (1986) identified that a high proportion of thefts from Oxford Street stores in London came from one store. A closer look showed that one single product sold in that store was responsible for the problem, and that a change in packaging practice saved the day (and much police time).

28.6 Hot Flushes

The anticipation of offense time and location is perhaps the least contentious type of prediction for the purposes of crime reduction. It simply seeks to locate effort where and when problems exist. The extent of crime fluctuates by season, day, and clock time (see, for instance, Johnson et al. 2012). Even modest crime "bursts" are useful for resource allocation, but this section is devoted to a particular type of episodic crime pattern, the near repeat. The clearest demonstration of the phenomenon lies with domestic burglary, the subject of most research on the topic. The phenomenon involves a temporary increase in rates of victimization following a burglary, extending over a matter of weeks and up to a distance of around 400 meters (Bowers et al. 2004; Johnson and Bowers 2004a, 2004b; Bowers and Johnson 2004). The same basic pattern exhibits itself in all the countries where it has been looked for (Johnson et al. 2007). The approach was later developed incorporating contextual variables (Johnson et al. 2009b).

An essentially similar approach and findings have been uncovered by George Mohler and colleagues (2011). Clustering in time and space has also shown itself in thefts from motor vehicles (Johnson et al. 2009a), insurgent activity in Iraq (Townsley et al. 2008), and patterns of shark predation (Martin et al. 2009). The scope of application of the near repeat approach is far from exhausted!

This space- and time-limited burglary risk elevation was interpreted as a reflection of optimal foraging, whereby homes near the initially burgled home are burgled up to the point where the rewards offered by the locale are exhausted and/or the risks involved are seen to have become unacceptable. The parallel of offender target choice with a foraging animal that exhausts one part of a habitat before moving off elsewhere is clear and simple. This is true both for academics (Eck 2014; Felson 2014; Johnson 2014; Pease 2014) and for operational police officers (fielding and Jones 2012; Rowley 2013). The optimal forager meme has proven extremely helpful to police and community safety practitioners as a means of communicating what this form of prediction is about. The process of local implementation of predicting crime based upon optimal forager thinking has been immensely aided by Jerry Ratcliffe's supply of a near repeat calculator and other useful free software. The near repeat calculator allows practitioners very easily to work out how many near repeats would occur by chance.[6] The ideal prediction device is simple to use and has useful predictive power and a "back office" that enables enhancement of the measure. An approach based simply on referred risk as a consequence of nearby victimization ticks all the relevant boxes.

The Rand Corporation published a substantial report on predictive policing (Perry et al. 2013). It was wide-ranging in its scope, going beyond prediction of time and place of crime but reached conclusions germane to the present discussion. It also has the virtue of being practitioner oriented. In the final chapter of their report, titled "Findings for Practitioners, Developers and Policymakers," the authors focus on dispelling some "commonly repeated myths" about the field. These myths are

The computer actually knows the future. "These techniques are useful to the extent that crime in the future will look similar to crime in the past" (p. 115). This is essentially a plea for iterative testing and flexibility.

The computer will do everything for you. "While it is common to promote software packages as end-to-end solutions for predictive policing, humans remain—by far—the most important elements in the process" (p. 117).

You need a high-powered (and expensive) model. "Most police departments do not need the most expensive software packages or computers to launch a predictive policing program" (p. 117). In the writers' view, this is the most pernicious of the myths identified.

Accurate predictions do not automatically lead to major crime reductions. "Achieving actual decreases in crime requires taking action based on . . . predictions" (p. 119). Shane Johnson and Toby Davies of University College London are currently undertaking an examination of dose response relationships, that is, how much police presence is necessary to effect reductions in crime, given the accuracy of their predictions. Prediction is potentially useful across the board, and good predictive power should not be discarded because of implementation failure or inadequate or excessive "treatment" dosage.

The advice is wise. One of the present writers has recognized this, having been involved in two impressive local initiatives (see Fielding and Jones 2012; Rowley 2013) based upon the Johnson and Bowers approach, namely to identify areas of radius 400 meters around prior burglaries. These were color coded according to time, with the first week after the event shown as red, with the color changing until it disappeared altogether after four weeks. Patrolling was mostly directed to red areas, and reverted to normal levels when the circle disappeared altogether. In one of the projects, the mapping was done in house; in the other it was contracted out. The former alternative proved much more satisfactory, primarily because of the greater closeness of the mapping analyst and police officers on the ground. In the event, both projects resulted in major reductions in domestic burglary, and the more successful one (because the analyst was the mapper) was able to show that the proportion of burglaries within targeted areas did not decline with the decreasing number of burglaries. In other words, the approach remained as successful at predicting burglary sites even as the total burglary count declined. This is important because it precludes the argument that burglars simply learn not to forage optimally. A common feature to both projects is that the crime decline was greatest the closer one came to the prior burglary event. We are almost at full circle now. There is much to be gained from the prevention of repeat victimization.

The hot-flush topic is currently fashionable and hence vulnerable to the merchandising of software that its users do not understand, formulaic implementation of projects imposed on unwilling front-line police officers, and in consequence inevitable failure. Yet the potential is great.

28.7 So What?

First let us think of the implications of the argument advanced for environmental criminology. The optimal forager approach opens a rich vein of possibilities for crime linkage analysis, geographic offender profiling, and crime forecasting (Johnson 2014). It has "heuristic value in suggesting new avenues for applicable research. Each of the current data shortcomings represents an opportunity for novel research approaches, and the optimum forager metaphor holds continuing appeal as an organizing principle helpful to operational policing" (Pease 2014, p. 221). The approach requires researchers to analyze their data with the fullest practicable spatial and temporal resolution. Insofar as we are correct in our perception of the technology that will be universally deployed within the decade, we do not have to put up with the fuzzy predictions of crime hotspots as hitherto envisaged. The limits to the full understanding of the risk terrain will be driven by ethical rather than empirical consideration. Interactions between personal, household, street segment, and design characteristics should take the foreground. Most of all, their research should have at its center an appreciation of the operational policing implications of their research. Failure to do that makes the discipline a practical irrelevance.

What should police practitioners who are interested in crime concentration do next? Suggestions have been extensively made throughout this chapter, so what is left must be pithy and general. Here goes.

The successful prevention of repeat victimization could prevent most crime, would most benefit high-crime areas, and carries little or no human rights baggage; that is, it is helping people who have asked for help. It requires no great analytic effort.

The more specific a point of concentration can be identified, the better: hot dots (places) and hot dots (people) are more useful than hotspots.

Hotspots are not useless. They are challenging, but the craft of policing does exist and can be used to turn hotspots into hot dots.

Predictive patrolling is possible, and simple locally grown software and expertise is generally to be preferred to commercial products because of the in-house learning and skills enhancement that it brings.

NOTES

1. https://www.youtube.com/watch?v=DaYn_PkrfvQ. Accessed November 5, 2016.
2. Sample sizes varied from 9,000 respondents in 2001 to 46,000 in 2012.
3. http://www.popcenter.org/library/awards/goldstein/1999/99-22(W).pdf. Accessed November 29, 2016.
4. http://www.popcenter.org/Responses/urban_parks/print/. Accessed November 29, 2016.
5. http://www.popcenter.org/library/awards/goldstein/2004/04-38(W).pdf. Accessed December 16, 2016.
6. http://www.jratcliffe.net/software/. Accessed December 1, 2016.

REFERENCES

Allingham M. (2014) *Distributive Justice*. London: Routledge.

Bernasco W. (2008) "Them Again: Same Offender Involvement in Repeat and Near Repeat Burglaries." *European Journal of Criminology*, 5, 411–431.

Bowers K. J. and Johnson S. D. (2004) "Domestic Burglary Repeats and Space-Time Clusters: The Dimensions of Risk." *European Journal of Criminology*, 1, 67–92.

Bowers K. and Johnson S. D. (2013) *Understanding Theft of "Hot Products"*. Washington, DC: US Department of Justice.

Bowers K. J., Johnson S. D., and Pease K. (2004) "Prospective Hotspotting: The Future of Crime Mapping?" *British Journal of Criminology*, 44, 641–658.

Bowers K. J., Johnson S. D., and Pease K. (2005) "Victimisation and Revictimisation Risk: Housing Type and Area, A Study of Interactions." *Crime Prevention and Community Safety*, 7, 7–17.

Budd T. (1999) *Burglary of Domestic Dwellings: Evidence from the British Crime Survey*. London: Home Office.

Eck J., Chainey S., Cameron J., Leitner M., and Wilson R. E. (2005) *Mapping Crime: Understanding Hot Spots*. Washington, DC: National Institute of Justice.

Eck J., Clarke R. V., and Guerette R. (2007) "Risky Facilities: Crime Concentration in Homogeneous Sets of Establishments and Facilities." In G. Farrell, K. J. Bowers, S. D. Johnson, and Michael Townsley, eds., *Imagination for Crime Prevention: Essays in Honour of Ken Pease*, vol. 21 of *Crime Prevention Studies*. Monsey, NY: Criminal Justice Press, 225–264.

Eck J. (2014) "If the Fox Knows Many Ways to Forage, the Modeler Cannot Be a Hedgehog: Reflections on the Use of Wildlife Foraging Models to Understand Criminal Target Search." *Legal and Criminological Psychology*, 19, 211–214.

Ekblom P. (1986) *The Prevention of Shop Theft: An Approach through Crime Analysis*. London: Home Office.

Farrell G. and Bouloukos A. (2002) "International Overview: A Cross-National Comparison of Rates of Repeat Victimisation." In G. Farrell and K. Pease, eds., *Repeat Victimisation*. Monsey, NY: Criminal Justice Press.

Farrell, G., & Pease, K. (2007). "The Sting in the Tail of the British Crime Survey: Multiple Victimisations." *Crime Prevention Studies*, 22, 33.

Farrell G. and Sousa W. (2002) "Repeat Victimisation and Hot Spots: The Overlap and Its Implications for Crime Control and Problem-Oriented Policing." In G. Farrell and K. Pease, eds., *Repeat Victimisation*. Monsey, NY: Criminal Justice Press, 221–241.

Farrell G., Sousa W., and Weisel D. (2001) "The Time Window Effect in the Measurement of Repeat Victimisation: A Methodology for Its Examination and an Empirical Study." In N. Tilley, ed. *Analysis for Crime Prevention*, vol. 13 of *Crime Prevention Studies*. Monsey, NY: Criminal Justice Press, 15–27.

Felson, M. (2014). "Eight Crime Foraging Contingencies: Comment on Johnson's Review." *Legal and Criminological Psychology*, 19, 215–217.

Femia, J. V. (2006) *Pareto and Political Theory*. London: Routledge.

Fielding M. and Jones V. (2012) "Disrupting the Optimal Forager." *International Journal of Police Science and Administration*, 14, 30–41.

Frank R., Brantingham P. L., and Farrell G. (2012) "Estimating the True Rate of Repeat Victimisation from Police Recorded Crime Data: A Study of Burglary in Metro Vancouver." *Revue Canadienne de Criminologie et de Justice Penale*, 48, 481–494.

Grove L. E., Farrell G., Farrington D. P., and Johnson S. D. (2012). *Systematic Review of Preventing Repeat Victimization*. Stockholm: Swedish National Council for Crime Prevention.

Haberman C. P., Song E. T., and Ratcliffe J. H. (2016) "Assessing the Validity of the Law of Crime Concentration across Different Temporal Scales." *Journal of Quantitative Criminology*, doi 10.1007/s10940-016-9327-4.

Ignatans D. and Pease K. (2015) "Distributive Justice and the Crime Drop." In M. Andresen and G. Farrell, eds., *The Criminal Act: Festschrift for Marcus Felson*. London: Palgrave Macmillan, 77–87.

Ignatans D. and Pease K. (2015) "Taking Crime Seriously: Playing the Weighting Game." *Policing*, 29, 1–10.

Ignatans D. and Pease, K. (2016) "On Whom Does the Burden of Crime Fall Now? Changes over Time in Counts and Concentration." *International Review of Victimology*, 22, 55–63.

Johnson S. D. (2014) "How Do Offenders Choose Where to Offend? Perspectives from Animal Foraging." *Legal and Criminological Psychology*, 19, 193–210.

Johnson S. D., Bernasco W., Bowers K. J., Eiffers H., Ratcliffe J., Rengert G., and Townsley M. (2007) "Space-Time Patterns of Risk: A Cross National Assessment of Residential Burglary Victimisation." *Journal of Quantitative Criminology*, 23, 201–219.

Johnson S. D. and Bowers K. J. (2004a) "The Burglary as Clue to the Future: The Beginnings of Prospective Hot Spotting." *European Journal of Criminology*, 1, 237–255.

Johnson S. D. and Bowers K. J. (2004b) "The Stability of Space-Time Clusters of Burglary." *British Journal of Criminology*, 44, 55–65.

Johnson S. D., Bowers K. J., Birks D. J., and Pease K. (2009b) Predictive Mapping of Crime by Promap: Accuracy, Units of Analysis, and the Environmental Backcloth." In D. Weisburd, W. Berneasco and G. J. N. Bruinsma, eds., *Putting Crime in Its Place*. New York: Springer, 171–198.

Johnson S. D., Bowers K. J., and Hirschfield A. (1997) "New Insights into the Temporal and Spatial Distribution of Repeat Victimisation." *British Journal of Criminology*, 37, 224–241.

Johnson S. D., Bowers K. J., and Pease K. (2012) "Towards the Modest Predictability of Daily Burglary Counts." *Policing*, 6, 167–176.

Johnson S. D., Summers L., and Pease K. (2009a) "Offender as Forager? A Direct Test of the Boost Account of Victimisation." *Journal of Quantitative Criminology*, 25, 181–200.

Kennedy L. W. and Forde D. R. (1990) "Routine Activities and Crime: An Analysis of Victimisation in Canada." *Criminology*, 28, 137, 152.

Kleemans E. (2001) "Repeat Burglary Victimisation: Results of Empirical Research in the Netherlands." In G. Farrell and K. Pease, eds., *Repeat Victimization*. Monsey, NY: Criminal Justice Press, 53–69.

Lauritsen, J., Owens, J. G., Planty, M., Rand, M. R., & Truman, J. L. (2012). "Methods for Counting High-frequency Repeat Victimizations in the National Crime Victimization Survey." *NCJ, 237308.*

Laycock G. and Pease K. (1999) "Revictimisation: Reducing the Heat on Hot Victims." In *Trends and Issues 128*. ACT: Australian Institute of Criminology.

Lippert-Rasmussen K. (2015) *Luck Egalitarianism*. London: Bloomsbury.

Martin R. A., Rossmo K., and Hammerschlag N. (2009) "Hunting Patterns and Geographic Profiling of White Shark Predation." *Journal of Zoology*, 279, 111–118.

Matthews R., Pease C., and Pease K. (2001) "Repeat Bank Robbery: Theme and Variations." In G. Farrell and K. Pease, eds., *Repeat Victimization.* Monsey, NY: Criminal Justice Press, 153–165.

Mawby R. (2001) "The Impact of Repeat Victimization on Burglary Victims in East and West Europe." In G. Farrell and K. Pease, eds., *Repeat Victimization.* Monsey, NY: Criminal Justice Press, 68–83.

Meithe T. and Meier R. (1990) "Opportunity, Choice and Criminal Victimisation." *Journal of Research in Crime and Delinquency*, 27, 243–266,

Mohler G., Short M. B., Brantingham J., Scjoenberg F., and Tita G. E. (2011) "Self Exciting Point Process Modeling of Crime." *Journal of the American Statistical Association*, 106, 100–108.

Morgan F. (2001) "Repeat Burglary in a Perth Suburb: Indicator of Short-Term or Long-Term Risk." In G. Farrell and K. Pease, eds., *Repeat Victimization.* Monsey, NY: Criminal Justice Press, 83–119.

O'Neil C. (2015) *Weapons of Math Destruction: How Big Data Increases Inequality and Threatens Democracy*. London: Penguin.

Pease K. (2014). "Voles Don't Take Taxis." *Legal and Criminological Psychology*, 19(2), 221–223.

Pease K. and Ignatans, D. (2016). "The Global Crime Drop and Changes in the Distribution of Victimisation." *Crime Science*, 5, 11–16.

Perreault S., Sauve J., and Burns M. (2004) *Multiple Victimisation in Canada 2004*. Ottawa: Public Safety Canada.

Perry W. L., McInnis B., Price C. C., Smith S. C., and Hollywood J. S. (2013) *Predictive Policing.* Santa Monica, CA: Rand.

Planty M. and Strom K. (2007) "Understanding the Role of Repeat Victims in the Production of Annual US Victimisation Rates." *Journal of Quantitative Criminology*, 23, 179–200.

Polvi N., Looman T., Humphries C., and Pease K. (1990) "Repeat Break and Enter Victimisation: Time Course and Crime Prevention Opportunity." *Journal of Police Science and Administration*, 17, 8–11.

Rowley C. (2013) *A Level 2 Outcome Evaluation of a Police Intervention Aimed at Reducing Future Burglary Dwellings in the Immediate Vicinity of a Burglary Dwelling*. Cambridge: Institute of Criminology.

Sagovsky, A., & Johnson, S. D. (2007). When does repeat burglary victimisation occur? *Australian & New Zealand Journal of Criminology*, *40*(1), 1–26.

Sampson A. and Phillips C. (1992) *Multiple Victimisation: Racial Attacks on an East London Estate*. Crime Prevention Unit Report 36. London: Home Office.

Schwartz, D., Dodge K., and Coie J. (1993). "The Emergence of Chronic Peer Victimization in Boys' Play Groups." *Child Development*, 64, 1755–1772.

Shaw M. and Pease K. (2000) *Research on Repeat Victimisation in Scotland: Final Report.* Edinburgh: Scottish Executive.

Sherman, L. W., Neyroud, P. W., and Neyroud, E. C. (2014). The Cambridge Crime Harm Index (CHI) Measuring Total Harm from Crime Based on Sentencing Guidelines, Version 3.0. Cambridge: Institute of Criminology.

Sidebottom A. (2012) "Repeat Burglary Victimisation in Malawi and the Influence of Housing Type and Area Level Affluence." *Security Journal*, 25, 265–281.

Sorensen D. (2004) *Repeat Victimisation in the Private Danish Home*. Faculty of Law: University of Copenhagen.

Titus R. and Dover A. (2001) "Personal Fraud: The Victims and the Scams." In G. Farrell and K. Pease, eds., *Repeat Victimization*. Monsey, NY: Criminal Justice Press, 133–153.

Townsley M., Johnson S. D., and Ratcliffe J. H. (2008) "Space Time Dynamics of Insurgent Activity in Iraq." *Security Journal*, 21, 139–146.

Trickett A., Osborn D. R., Seymour J., and Pease K. (1992) "What Is Different about High Crime Areas?" *British Journal of Criminology*, 32, 81–89.

Tseloni A. (2006) "Multilevel Modelling of the Number of Property Crimes: Household and Area Effects." *Journal of the Royal Statistical Society A*, 169, 205–233.

Tseloni A., Ntzoufras J., Nicolaou A., and Pease K. (2010) "Concentration of Personal and Household Crimes in England and Wales." *European Journal of Applied Mathematics*, 21, 325–348.

Tseloni A. and Pease K. (2014) *Modelling Crime to Predict and Prevent Victimisation*. New York: Springer.

van Dijk J. J. M. (2001) "Attitudes of Victims and Repeat Victims toward the Police: Results of the International Crime Victims Survey." In G. Farrell and K. Pease, eds., *Repeat Victimization*. Monsey, NY: Criminal Justice Press, 27–53.

Walby S., Towers J., and Francis B. (2016) "Is Violent Crime Increasing or Decreasing? A New Methodology to Measure Repeat Attacks Making Visible the Significance of Gender and Domestic Relations." *British Journal of Criminology*, 56, 1203–1234.

Weisburd D. (2015) "The Law of Crime Concentration and the Criminology of Place." *Criminology*, 53, 133–157.

Wrangham R. W. and Wilson M. L. (2004) "Collective Violence: Comparisons between Youths and Chimpanzees." *Annals of the New York Academy of Sciences*, 48, 365–390.

Routine Activity Convergence

CHAPTER 29

TIME AND OPPORTUNITY

LISA TOMPSON AND TIMOTHY COUPE

29.1 Introduction

Crime is a complex, dynamic, and often fleeting event; its occurrence is found to concentrate across many dimensions, including people, places, and products. The uneven temporal distribution of crime, however, is less well documented, even though time—as much as space—frames the routine activities of victims and offenders (Cohen and Felson 1979). Consequently, opportunities for crimes occur not only at particular places, but also at distinctive times. Work, schooling, leisure, and sleep activities result in opportunities to offend at particular times of the day and week, while seasonal changes in daylight-darkness, weather, and leaf cover modify target vulnerability and criminal behavior.

Despite this, few, if any, studies of crime concentration (Braga and Weisburd 2010; Weisburd, Groff, and Yang 2012) or "hotspot policing" (e.g. Braga, Papachristos, and Hureau 2012) measure *when* crimes occur, while Weisburd's (2015) "law of crime concentration" focuses on the stability of spatial incidence *over time*. Policing interventions directed at clusters of crimes require an understanding of the spatial and temporal dimensions of crime patterns to inform where and when resources should be deployed. After all, a police officer in a "hotspot" at a "cold time" has a tenuous crime control function.

The founding environmental criminology literature (Brantingham and Brantingham 1993; Cornish and Clarke 1986) thus accorded too little weight to the temporal incidence of crime, even though it is fundamental to understanding the relationships between victims, offenders, and the environments in which offending takes place. This chapter aims to address this shortcoming by providing insights into often-observed temporal regularities of different types of crime. We begin in section 29.2 by briefly appraising relevant theories that explain variations in time incidence. Section 29.3 then discusses methodological issues that are unique to temporal analysis. The bulk of section 29.4 presents temporal patterns from four years of crime data recorded by West Yorkshire Police, UK.

Several units of analysis are considered: years, months, weeks, and days, and a medley of theories are used to suggest putative explanations for the observed patterns. We focus first on crimes committed against property (predominantly theft and damage offenses), before considering crimes committed against people and, finally, Internet-enabled crimes against both people and their property. Our intention here is to illustrate a variety of empirical regularities for different crime types, and to posit plausible explanations for those patterns. We conclude by highlighting gaps in knowledge, methodologies, and aspects of theory, and point to the potential for additional research.

29.2 Theory

Routine activity (Cohen and Felson 1979), rational choice (Cornish and Clarke 1986), opportunity (Cohen, Kluegel, and Land 1981), and pattern theories (Brantingham and Brantingham 1993) all contribute when explaining temporal crime patterns, though alone each is insufficient. A more complete explanation requires appreciation of the climatic and weather factors that alter the physical environmental "backcloth," which subsequently modifies the crime risks faced by victims and offenders. A wider set of social processes may also contribute to the time incidence of different sorts of crime over the years. These include theories relating to the onset and desistance of offending, and security, technological, social, and economic changes that influence crime opportunities.

The daily cycle of sleep, work, schooling, and leisure shapes routine activities (Cohen and Felson 1979). This has the potential to reduce effective guardianship, by leaving empty homes vulnerable during the day and providing opportunities for crime en route to schools and workplaces and in car parks, where both vehicles and users are exposed to risk. Hence some routine activities weaken guardianship, creating opportunities for crimes against different sorts of victims and property in different places at different times (Cohen, Kluegel, and Land 1981).

Changes from served to self-service shops and the growth in attractive consumer goods have also been highlighted as inducements to offenders (Cohen and Felson 1979), who may exercise rational choices about crime, trading gain for risk of capture (Cornish and Clarke 1986). These factors can affect the timing of certain offenses across the day, as well as altering annual crime levels. The growth in female labor participation is particularly emphasized in explaining the steady increase of crime over time—especially property crime during the postwar years—making females and their homes more vulnerable and reducing pre- and postschool supervision of children (Cohen and Felson 1979). In a related vein, increases in leisure pursuits during weekend evenings over the second half of the twentieth century both increase the vulnerability of people's unguarded homes and enhance opportunities for violent, sexual, and personal-theft crimes in public spaces.

Temporal and geographical patterns of crimes reflect the intersection of opportunities for crime with offenders' *activity spaces* (Brantingham and Brantingham 1993). An activity space is the area in which an offender lives and undertakes his routine activities, so that accessible areas with crime opportunities are postulated to be prone to more crime. Activity spaces are likely to vary according to personal mobility, offending preferences, offense type, versatility, and prolificacy and may be extended by the activity areas of offenders' prior homes (Bernasco 2010) and those of co-offenders (Bernasco 2006). Within activity spaces, those routes, nodes, and neighborhoods most familiar and most frequently traveled are likely to experience more crime.

The outer limits of an activity space demarcates the farthest extent an offender will normally travel to commit crime (Brantingham and Brantingham 1981); the inner limits mark a "buffer zone" where elevated recognition risks may deter offending (Rengert, Piquero, and Jones 1999). In between, the supply of attractive targets hinges on victims' time-space activities and environmental factors that affect guardianship and sighting and arrest risks. Spatiotemporal patterns of crime are hence dependent on differences in access to crime opportunities, and the attendant varying gains and risks.

Cadences in routine activities mean that certain nodes, routes, and areas are likely to present different criminal opportunities at particular times of the day or week and attract criminals with different offending preferences. Equally, offenses occurring in certain areas at specific times may only match offenders with specific activity spaces and offending preferences. Offenders may shape their routines to take advantage of opportunities, while chance factors may also affect whether offenders encounter weakly guarded targets (Coupe and Fox 2012).

Research indicates that the quality of guardianship has important effects on the timing of crime opportunities. In their exploration of guardianship in action in the Netherlands, Reynald and Elffers (2015) show that levels of residential guardianship intensity (i.e., home availability, monitoring, and supervision activities from the home) vary considerably over different days of the week and times of the day. Such variations may reflect the dispositions of those residents to exercise effective guardianship, possibly meaning that more responsible citizens are available to prevent offenses at certain times of the day, as well as in certain areas.

If guardians are more willing to intervene in crimes against the person than against property (Gillis and Hagan 1982), this may affect the frequencies and relative importance of different crimes occurring at different times. The willingness of people to intervene should they see a crime may similarly be influenced by time-varying social and situational factors. For instance, at nighttime a lone woman may stay silent when witnessing a crime in progress, but may call out when she feels safer at the same spot in the daytime. Other times willingness to intervene might depend on who else is present, or the social rules of the setting.

Explanation of the timing of crime events needs to take account of contrasts and changes in the physical environment, as well as the social environment. These include the built and natural environments that modify visibility and guardianship, and affect the sightlines to properties and people. They also include climate, which underpins daily human activities (Figure 29.1). In warmer Mediterranean, subtropical, and tropical climates, there is traditionally a daily siesta period during the hottest midday and afternoon hours, with shops

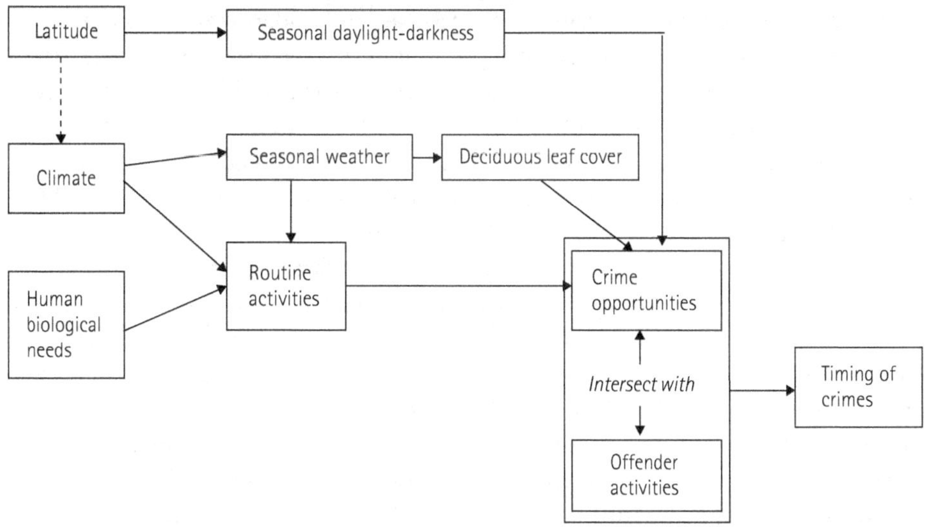

FIGURE 29.1 Theoretical influences on daily and monthly timing of crime

open in the evenings and dinner often eaten in the late evening, thus altering the timing of crime opportunities. The diurnal activities of people across different societies are thus influenced by cultural norms that are sensitive to the natural environment.

Monthly crime variation in middle and higher latitudes is likely to reflect seasonal weather changes, attributable to the specific microclimate and the same global motions that determine the diurnal day-night shifts that shape human routine activities (Figure 29.1). These natural forces modify deciduous vegetative cover and daylight and darkness hours, boosting effective guardianship for some types of crime as days lengthen. They change temperatures, with very low temperatures reducing pedestrian traffic and street crime opportunities (Cohn and Rotton 2000) and very hot or humid conditions affecting violent behavior (LeBeau 1994). Seasonal and monthly precipitation changes may also alter daily activities, which in turn affect the temporal opportunity structure for different crimes. The historic legacy of the summer harvest in temperate agricultural societies is still evident in European universities' long summer vacation and school holidays. This affects both offender availability and opportunities to offend against people and property. Even seemingly random weather abnormalities—that modify victim behavior and offending opportunities—tend to take place more during certain months or seasons, and consequently systematically affect the temporal incidence of crime. Hence, environmental forces modify the human activities that shape crime opportunities.

Crime changes across the years reflect varied factors that are difficult to tie to a specific set of theories. These include demographic shifts such as changing fertility rates and age-selective migration that affect youth populations (Fox 2000). Fluctuations in the value of stolen goods make some crimes more or less profitable over time (Sidebottom et al. 2011). Security changes render some crimes more or less risky (Farrell et al. 2011). Rising prosperity encourages more consumer goods to be carried on the person or in the home (Cohen and Felson 1979), while social and structural economic forces may predispose the onset of, and desistance from, offending (Eisner 1995). Values and habits, such as alcohol and drug use and socializing via the Internet rather than in person also contribute to shifting routine activities that may alter the composition of crime, with respect to the "on-street" compared with electronic crime, and property relative to personal offending.

29.3 Temporal Data and Methods

The veracity of findings from studies of temporal crime patterns depends on the accuracy of the data and the establishment of meaningful time intervals for the analysis. Where data collection is under the researchers' control, accuracy and the unit of analysis can be addressed early on. Yet much temporal crime analysis employs secondary data sources, which means that researchers need to be alert to the statistical consequences of time data aggregation choices.

29.3.1 Time Data Sources and Data Accuracy

There are three principal sources for data on the timing of crime events: surveys of crime victims and offenders, police crime records, and calls-for-service incident logs. All incur problems with knowing, or recalling, when offenses actually took place. Much crime is unreported to the authorities, and even that which is reported is not necessarily recorded (Maguire 2007). Victimization surveys better capture crime rates, although they suffer from sampling bias, which can be minimized, but not eliminated, by the careful weighting of the estimated rates. The upshot of this is that no data set provides a full picture for the purposes of space-time pattern detection. Triangulating across data sets (e.g., see Rock, Judd, and Hallmayer 2008 for an example with Accident and Emergency Department data) can help to corroborate (or not) temporal patterns in official statistics, although validating space-time patterns may prove more challenging.

Data from victims' accounts may suffer from memory lapses, and their knowledge of the timing and location of crime events may be imperfect. Unwitnessed crimes, such as noncontact property offenses like burglary or theft from vehicles, may only be discovered on the victim's return to their property. These result in wide *time spans* or *time windows* being recorded in the crime data—marking the earliest and latest times that events could have occurred. Even if the caller has reported a crime or suspicious behavior *in progress*, specialist police help is often needed to navigate and interrogate vast incident databases, and to identify which responses to calls for service resulted in recorded crimes. Investigators of serious crimes may spend considerable time eliciting victims' previous movements to generate estimates of the time and place of victimization, but this is not commonly done for more everyday volume crime.

For incidents with wide spans between the earliest and latest occurrence times, fixing an acceptable time for analysis can be intractable. When "time span" data straddle daylight and darkness periods, it is impossible to know the lighting conditions at the time of the crime. Other putative explanatory variables, such as the opening hours of a bar or other criminogenic facility, may also bisect a crime time span. Such records would typically be omitted from individual data analyses involving other variables, resulting in loss of data.

One solution that alleviates these data limitations is the use of *aoristic analysis*, a technique that can be applied to crime events with an indeterminate time stamp (Ratcliffe 2000). This uses the time span of crime records—that is, the earliest and latest possible time the event could have occurred—to compute a probability distribution of crime over the hours in the day. Doing so helps to mitigate the temporal imprecision in the data. It is superior to using the start, end, or midpoints of time spans for estimating the hourly distribution of bicycle thefts (Ashby and Bowers 2013).

Space-time budget methods can be used to generate primary data that combat poor memory recall and missing records (Wikström and Butterworth 2006). The space-time budget method involves a structured interview with participants to record their activities and offending/victimization experiences over microunits of time and space (hours and locations). Typically the activities and events of the past week are probed, thus maximizing memory recall. The data recorded through this instrument often have greater temporal precision than official data and reportedly have good correspondence with spatiotemporal patterns of youth crime recorded by the police (Wikström et al. 2012). Hence such space-time data enable the measurement of situational influences on offending (Bernasco et al. 2013; Wikström et al. 2010).

29.3.2 Unit of Time Analysis

As time is a continuous variable, crime events occurring at different times need to be aggregated into groups of time intervals for meaningful analysis. With precise time data for individual crime events, a myriad of time intervals might be defined. It is advisable to construct these time intervals with reference to the routine activities that underpin specific crime types, hence taking a *crime-specific* approach (Felson and Clarke 1998). Stranger violence, for instance, is associated with the convergence of victims and offenders in public places. Such convergences are more prevalent in the evenings, especially on weekends, and consequently, the timing of homicide concentrates in the same periods (Summers 2012).

Criminological research, however, frequently relies on secondary data that have not been collected with particular research objectives in mind. Consequently, independent variables cannot always be aggregated to the same time intervals as crime. Even when data collection and units of analyses can be tailored to individual research needs, studies with similar objectives can be at odds with regard to how units of time analysis are defined and measured. This can make comparisons between them difficult.

Due to the numerous ways in which humans define time, data can be sliced in various ways to elicit temporal patterns. Crime data are commonly categorized into hourly, daily, monthly, seasonal, or annual units of time, though many other time units have been used (see Tompson 2016 for an overview). A variety of subday time intervals have been used to measure dramatic variations in crime over the course of the day and days of the week. These have been based on daybreak, and on societal routine activities, such as the start and end of the working day or the onset of evening activities. The intervals vary from a rudimentary two-period division between 05:00–17:00 and 17:00–5:00 (Felson and Poulsen 2003), to empirically generated time periods that correspond to survey respondents' time use data: morning commuting (06.45–09.59), working or schooling time (10.00–16.29), evening commuting and leisure hours (16.30–21.14), and at home (21.15–06.44) (Haberman and Ratcliffe 2015). In other studies, the independent variable has been used to inform the boundaries of the time intervals. For instance, Tompson (2016) used Scottish sunrise and sunset times to create four intervals in the day, whereby dark conditions and light conditions were held as stable as possible throughout the year in two of those intervals (see Figure 29.2).

Time-series models, which examine changes over time, generally use annual or monthly counts of crime (Gorr, Olligschlaeger, and Thompson 2003). Putative explanatory variables are aggregated to the same time intervals to test for associations that might explain crime oscillations over long periods. Time-series models are suitable for investigating changes in societal routine activities over considerable timescales, such as those influenced by economic cycles or seasonal weather shifts. However, some scholars

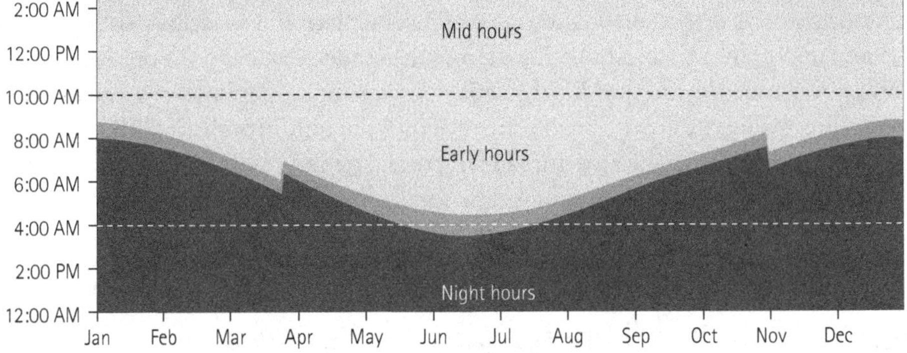

FIGURE 29.2 Variation in light levels over four six-hour intervals—based on sunrise, sunset, and twilight times for Glasgow, Scotland (56° north)

Source: reproduced from Tompson 2016.

claim that time-series models do not directly test causal relationships and consequently should be used only for ascertaining trends and for forecasting (O'Brien 2001; Shmueli 2010). This notwithstanding, time-series data may be used to draw theoretically feasible causal inferences.

29.3.3 Statistical Consequences of Time Data Aggregation

Aggregating crime data and influencing factors into meaningful time units can have implications for statistical analysis and interpretation. These include two aggregation bias issues: the boundaries of the time intervals affecting crime patterns, and the risk of ecologically fallacious inferences. Furthermore, the similarity of proximal observations can affect the interpretation of time-series data.

As with spatial boundaries in geographical analysis, temporal boundaries imposed on data are artificial. This can result in the "modifiable temporal unit" problem (Dorling and Openshaw 1992), whereby the observable patterns may be an artifact of the boundaries themselves. Hence crime patterns may be modified according to the timescale at which they are studied and the way the time interval is specified.

Ecologically fallacious inferences may be drawn about an individual (or collection of data points) from aggregated data for a time interval (Robinson 1950). For example, data defined in terms of daily intervals might show a Thursday peak in offenses that masks a public event on the last Thursday of each month that is when all the crime occurs. An inference that every Thursday has the same likelihood of high crime incidence would be false in such a scenario.

Another distinctive feature of temporally aggregated crime data is that proximal observations are likely to be more similar than those that are further apart. Hence, crime, like all social phenomenon, is related over time. This results in an underlying structure to the data, known as temporal autocorrelation. This is important because autocorrelation produces nonrandom residuals in regression models, which violate a key assumption in ordinary least squares (OLS) regression—namely that the residuals are independent. A systematic (i.e., nonrandom) pattern in the residuals suggests one or more important variables are omitted from the model. Critically, the presence of temporal autocorrelation may produce biased regression model parameter estimates, which can result in a type I error (incorrectly rejecting the null hypothesis). Thus failing to account for the underlying structure in temporal data can result in errors of inference. For this reason, modeling temporal data requires specialist statistical methods that account for the temporal autocorrelation.

29.3.4 Analysis and Interpretation Techniques

Sophisticated analytic techniques can produce visual outputs for advancing understanding of the timing patterns of crime events. *Trajectory analysis* has been used to study the developmental processes underpinning crime patterns over time at microplaces in Seattle (e.g., see Weisburd et al. 2012). These illustrate longitudinal crime trends over different geographical locations, enabling the interrogation of the space-time dimension of crime concentrations in a city. *Circular statistics* have similarly been used as a powerful visual aid to interpreting hourly patterns of crime (e.g., see Ashby and Bowers 2013; Brunsdon and Corcoran 2006).

Environmental criminologists, however, often rely on simple visualizations of temporal patterns of crime. Simple line charts of annual data have been used, for instance, to highlight the internationally observed crime drop (Farrell et al. 2011), and aoristic analysis charts portray concentrations of crime over the hours of the day. Exposing spatiotemporal crime clusters through these techniques is commonly the starting point of a research inquiry, acting as a potent hypothesis generator. Such patterns can expose where opportunities for crime exist and, coupled with knowledge of local routine activities, can supply clues as to the underlying situational factors driving the crime levels.

To summarize, various research methods are used to examine temporal patterns in crime. Each has its own strengths and weaknesses, and is best suited to answering particular questions, but all have to account for the special nature of temporal data. Typically there is no counterfactual in temporal analysis (i.e., you cannot investigate the times when crime did *not* occur), so most methods depend on correlation analyses to make inferences about probable causes. Despite having low internal validity, such methods can generate insight into the factors that might be responsible for temporal fluctuations in crime data over various scales of interest.

29.4 Crime Patterns in Time

Empirical evidence about the temporal incidence of crime is principally understood in terms of (1) the routine activities that shape human mobility patterns; (2) how victimization risk changes over time; and (3) the risks to offenders of sighting and apprehension. There is additional reliance on changes in climate and weather to account for monthly and seasonal variations on daily patterns. Annual changes not only require appreciation of routine activities and climatic-weather differences, but also a wider variety of factors and processes that alter the behavior of offenders, the routine activities of victims, the value of property, and the security of property and people.

29.4.1 Annual Trends

Long-term crime trends hold wide appeal to researchers, politicians, and the public alike. These can be studied over many different levels of aggregation: millennia, centuries, decades, and years. Violent offending, for instance, has fallen markedly since the Middle Ages in more developed countries as cities and nation-states developed the rule of law, values have changed, police services were more recently established, and communications improved so that controls could be exercised (Eisner 2001, 2002).

Following crime rises between the 1960s and the 1980s, an international "crime drop" has been observed since the mid-1990s (Tseloni et al. 2010; Farrell et al. 2011). A variety of theories have been proposed to explain such dramatic falls in many violent and property crimes in westernized democracies. These range from the legalization of abortion to the increase in police officer numbers, the strengthening of the economy, and many more besides (see Levitt 2004; Farrell 2013; Spelman 2000). Among the most persuasive evidence is in support of the *security hypothesis* (Farrell et al. 2011; Van Dijk 2006), which is that the "change in the quantity and quality of security was a key driver of the crime drop" (Farrell et al. 2011, p. 147), as well as explaining the sharp rise in cybercrime and mobile phone theft in the twenty-first century.

The accurate estimation of crime rates over time is, though, plagued with the familiar limitations of official crime data. Much modern crime is not reported to the police. For instance, many banks deal with fraud against customers without involving the police, so that cases are underreported and undercounted (Barnard 2015; Clarke 2015). Incidents like "sexting" and "revenge porn," now rife among young people, are similarly underrepresented in official figures. The scale of the crime decline may, therefore, be overestimated. Modern crime is often said to be "borderless" insofar that perpetrators of Internet-enabled crime can be anywhere in the world. Other age-old offenses—such as human trafficking involving slavery—occur across many borders over protracted periods. Consequently, long-term temporal analyses using crime data for individual countries are likely to be flawed.

Undoubtedly, the prevalence of security strategies, tactics, and devices over the past quarter of a century has changed the landscape of opportunities for crime (Clarke and Newman 2006). Societal changes in routine activities, which might plausibly impact the frequency and timing of crime incidents, have coincided with securitization. These include recreational trends, such as the decline in drug and alcohol use by youths, the proliferation of social media, and the opportunities afforded by technology, such as home working and shifts to online rather than outdoors evening socialization. These trends are also thought to have helped lower crime in the last decade. At a broad level of abstraction, the routine activities approach and other crime event theories facilitate theorizing on how these changes might be causally related to temporal patterns in crime. In what follows, these trends are illustrated for specific crimes at different temporal scales for the case study area of West Yorkshire in the UK. Similarities and dissimilarities to the temporal incidence of specific crime types found in other contexts are discussed.

29.4.2 Seasonality/Monthly Trends

The seasonality of criminal behavior has been a topic of interest since the inception of criminology, although it is important to note the relationship between the two has eluded universal theorizing. A thorough summary of studies on crime seasonality, up to the mid-1990s, is provided by Baumer and Wright (1996). Recent studies typically employ the routine activity approach framework to explain seasonal oscillations in crime rates, since routine activities are manifestly dissimilar across the seasons. To name a few examples: school and university calendars are aligned to particular seasons; holiday periods typically fall within summer or winter months; certain industries, such as tourism or agriculture, have predictable seasonal rhythms in activity; and the timing of the financial year dictates business processes that can potentially affect some types of crime. Seasonal changes also alter the physical environment in which daily routine activities take place. Changes in weather, deciduous leaf cover, and daylight-darkness hours modify opportunities for crime through changes in guardians' ability to see or hear crimes in progress (Coupe and Fox 2012).

Generally speaking, in most temperate climates, summertime promotes outdoor activities, whereas in winter people stay indoors more often. Two natural conditions are believed to influence these social patterns: temperature and the presence or absence of daylight. Both conditions support the greater use of public space in summer months for legitimate activities (Böcker, Dijst, and Prillwitz 2013), which has differential consequences for specific crime types and their opportunity structures. To elaborate, residents spending more time at home during the winter months enhance the potential for guardianship at their homes and consequently reduce opportunities for residential burglary (although see Coupe and Blake 2006). In contrast, people spending more time outside in summer months increases the likelihood of social contact with others, a small proportion of which may result in interpersonal crimes such as assault (e.g., see Andresen and Malleson 2013) and homicide (Summers 2012). The distinction between crimes that occur *indoors* and those that occur *outdoors* can therefore be important. The winter cold of continental high-latitude countries, such as Sweden, for example, drastically lowers outdoor sexual offense levels, compared with the opportunities provided by hot summers: the incidence of outdoor rape and indecent exposure in Stockholm is two-thirds higher between May and October than between November and April (BRÅ 2012–2014).

Seasons, however, should be viewed as aggregations of monthly crime patterns, and monthly peaks may exist within the calendar-defined seasons. To take one prominent example, Halloween—and to a lesser extent, the UK public holiday "Bonfire Night"—are associated with higher frequencies of crime and disorder and attendant police activity (Ashby and Tompson 2015). Other US public holidays have similarly been found to increase the demand on police response to crime, with crimes of expressive violence significantly more likely to occur on major holidays, and property crime less likely to occur on these same days (Cohn and Rotton 2003).

Figure 29.3 illustrates the monthly distribution of arson[1] in West Yorkshire, UK. From this we see that November has the highest frequency of arson for the fall months. This can be explained by 75 arson events recorded on Bonfire Night (a festival of fireworks held on 5 November), which is well above the mean daily crime rate for the month (17.0) and season (15.7). In a similar vein, the total of all crimes on Halloween across the four years (2,159) is notably higher than the mean daily crime rate for the month (1,914.9) and season (1,810.6). Other public holidays and large-scale events, such as sports events and

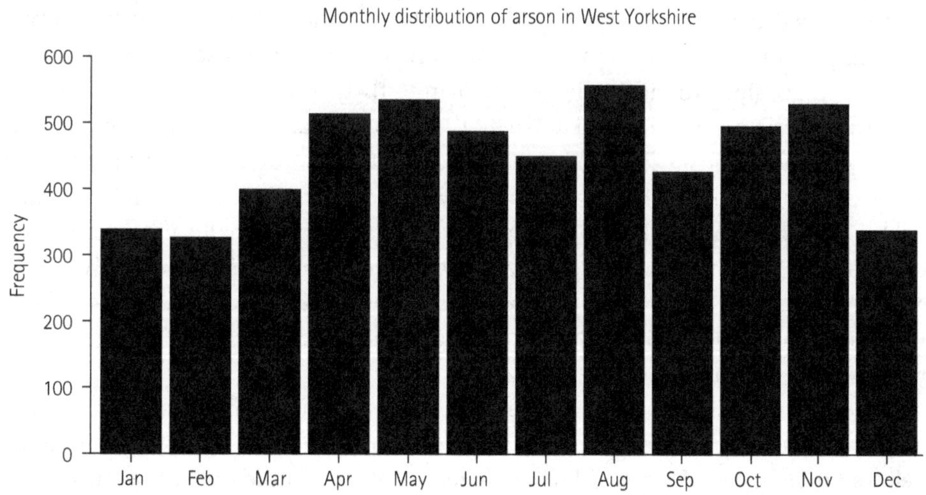

FIGURE 29.3 Monthly distribution of arson, West Yorkshire (U.K.)

music concerts, may result in similar offending "spikes." These are masked when aggregated to coarser units of analysis and pose risks of ecologically fallacious interpretation.

The August peak in arson in West Yorkshire (Figure 29.3) mirrors previous UK and US seasonal trend analysis (Hird and Ruparel 2007; US Fire Administration 2005). Elsewhere, in the fire-prone continent of Australia, seasonal patterns vary across states and depend upon seasonal vegetation growth and how dry the organic fuel is (AIC 2009). Given this, one might speculate that August is the month when vegetation is driest, and plentiful in the UK and United States, and therefore prone to successful fire setting. August is also the month when school pupils are customarily on vacation, when their routine activities are less structured, and the potential for guardianship is weaker.

Bicycle theft is another crime that peaks notably in summer months in the United States and UK (Johnson, Sidebottom, and Thorpe 2008), and likely other mid- and high-latitude countries with continental or temperate climates. This is linked to increased bicycle use in warmer months, making them more plentiful to steal. The opportunity structure for bicycle theft varies at the local level, however. For example, in the UK city of Cambridge low frequencies of bicycle theft in summer are followed by a large October peak, which corresponds to the start of the academic year at Cambridge University (Hird and Ruparel 2007). European cities such as Amsterdam, where cycling is highly popular, may experience other trends that are synchronous with the habits of the cycling community. Temporal distributions of crime cannot, therefore, be divorced from spatial distributions and local context, as seasonal patterns of crime vary over space (Andresen and Malleson 2013; Sorg and Taylor 2011).

Residential burglaries also vary according to season in temperate climates and higher latitudes, in part due to changes in daylight hours. More residential burglary occurs outside of the summer months, whereas commercial burglary peaks during summer in temperate climates in the northern hemisphere (Farrell and Pease 1994; Gorr, Olligschlaeger, and Thompson 2003). These patterns may reflect school and industrial holidays, coupled with warmer weather, resulting in more people, and therefore more potential guardians, being near residential premises (Blake 2006), as opposed to commercial premises. Compounding this, there is greater visibility in residential areas on long summer days, so that sheds and outbuildings there are less risky targets in the evenings than commercial premises situated in nonresidential areas, where guardianship is poorer (Coupe and Fox 2012).

The seasonal patterns in residential burglary potentially correspond to the risks to offenders of being seen. Burglaries committed in darkness decline steadily from spring (see Figure 29.4), reflecting the decrease in the early evening hours of darkness during which dwellings are likely to be unoccupied. A similar pattern is seen for monthly incidences of UK robbery (Tompson and Bowers 2013), whereby robberies committed in dark conditions peak in winter, while those committed in daylight rise precipitously after daylight saving time begins. As with commercial robbery in Holland (van Koppen and Jansen 1999), street robbery levels are significantly associated with higher levels of darkness, even when temperature is controlled for (Tompson 2016).

It would appear from this that darkness is an important environmental condition that alters the opportunity structure of different crime types. Darkness impairs visibility and increases reliance on audibility (Coupe and Fox 2012), which can weaken the potential for guardianship, consequently elevating victim vulnerability. This effect may be compounded by fewer guardians being available, and those that are might be more reluctant to intervene after dark (Reynald 2009).

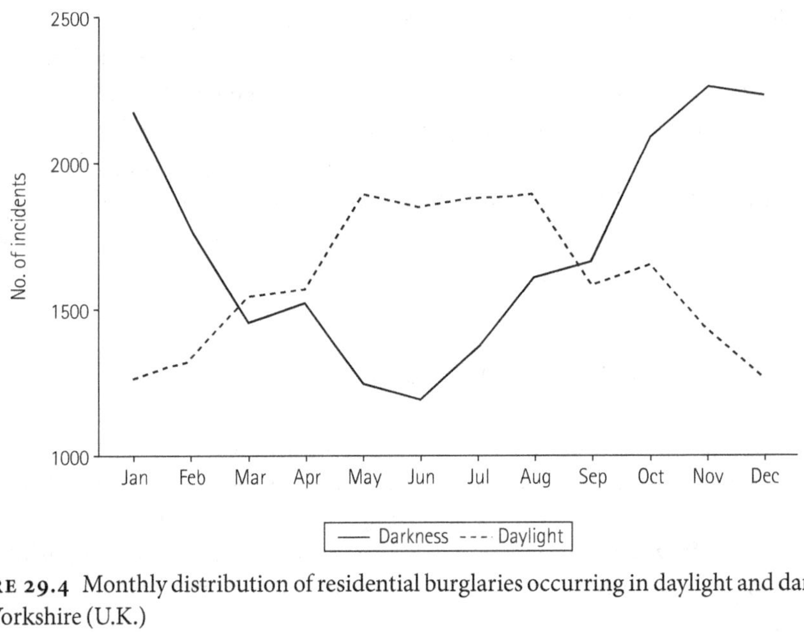

FIGURE 29.4 Monthly distribution of residential burglaries occurring in daylight and darkness, West Yorkshire (U.K.)

FIGURE 29.5 Monthly distribution of violent crime, West Yorkshire (U.K.)

Note: the scale on the y-axis has been modified.

Temperature, and other elements of weather such as precipitation, can also affect crime seasonality. Few universal trends emerge from the large corpus of literature on this topic, possibly because of the variety of ways used to aggregate data to define meaningful spatial and temporal units of analysis (Andresen and Malleson 2013). One of the only certainties is that Adolphe Quételet's (1842) "thermic law"—whereby crimes against people are most prevalent in summer and crimes against property are most prevalent in winter—does not hold across all regions in the world (see, for example, Cohn and Rotton 2000 and Yan 2004). Nevertheless, a large number of studies have found that violent crime increases in summer months in Israel (Landau and Fridman 1993), Brazil (Ceccato 2005), the United States (Hipp et al. 2004), and Canada (Andresen and Malleson 2013), to name a few examples. Confirming this general trend, violent crime in the West Yorkshire area of the UK was seen to increase in the summer months, with this most pronounced for violence that resulted in injury (see Figure 29.5). Some scholars attribute this consistent finding to the effect temperature has on the body (and temper) (see Anderson et al. 2000 for a good summary). Others have attributed warmer weather to socialization patterns, bringing people together (Felson 1987).

29.4.3 Hour of Day / Day of Week

Humans are generally diurnal creatures who undertake formal obligatory activities during the daytime and discretionary activities in the evenings and at weekends (LeBeau 1994). The biological need to sleep places temporal constraints on mobility patterns (Ratcliffe 2006) and provides home guardianship and limits opportunity for crime outside the home during sleep periods. Daily activity, evening-weekend leisure, and nighttime rest also govern social behavior and the environment built to support it. When in structured obligatory activities, such as school and work, people are less vulnerable to certain personal crimes, though commuting, parked cars and bicycles, and unguarded homes create weekday property crime opportunities. Lunch breaks allow for mobility and particular crime opportunities. Truants and unemployed people may create daytime opportunities for crimes by becoming offenders and/or victims.

For property crimes such as burglary the patterns are complicated, since this category reflects a multitude of heterogeneous scenarios. For example, rather more domestic burglaries occur in daylight (Budd 1999) and have been found to peak during weekday mornings and afternoons in Victoria, Australia (Sagovsky and Johnson 2007). In comparison, more nonresidential burglaries have been found to take place after dark and outside the working week in the UK and Canberra, Australia (Coupe and Kaur 2005; Ratcliffe 2001), reflecting times when many premises are routinely unoccupied.

Incidence at dwellings in the UK differs between weekends, when many offenses occur in evening darkness (Maguire and Bennett 1982), and weekdays, when, apart from low incidence during the early morning hours, a more constant level is maintained all day (Blake 2006). With more people out at work, and low occupancy on weekdays at residential targets and neighboring properties, burglars commit daylight burglary, whereas at weekends, there are daytime risks due to higher occupancy at targets and neighboring dwellings but evening opportunities relating to low occupancy and darkness (Blake 2006).

The timing of domestic burglaries similarly varies by residential property environment. This relates to vegetative cover and to the location being either on arterial or residential streets (Blake 2006). Detached properties, which have better vegetative cover, are targeted in daylight in the UK with burglars breaking in via the front of properties. In contrast, terraced dwellings—with limited vegetative cover and a higher number of neighbors to act as guardians—are burgled in darkness, with burglars entering via the rear of premises (Coupe and Blake 2006). Residential environments with more retired or unemployed households have superior daytime neighbor and occupant guardianship that deters daylight burglars in various states in the United States (D'Alessio, Eitle, and Stolzenberg 2012).

Easier access to premises and reduced target visibility elevates opportunities for burglary in certain places at certain times of the day. Domestic properties on main or nearby roads can be less risky for burglars during the working day than those on residential estates (Blake 2006), whereas nonresidential premises close to main roads are riskier than those on industrial estates, especially outside the working week (Rengert and Wasilchick 1985). In daylight, the semidetached dwellings targeted in daylight on main roads have strikingly lower occupancy rates than terraced dwellings in residential streets (Blake 2006), and burglars may find the relative anonymity of main roads, where strangers look less suspicious, an advantage (Bowers and Johnson 2015). In contrast burglars seem to appreciate less well-lit and quieter residential roads and industrial estates at night (Coupe and Fox 2012; Blake 2006).

Other types of property crime are restricted to particular hours, since offenders can steal only from targets that are available. Shoplifting, for instance, occurs when shops are open and goods are accessible to employees as well as customers, peaking during the daytime (Figure 29.6). The temporal peak of offending seen in police recorded data may, though, be indicative of the working hours of security guards or the offending patterns of prolific shoplifters.

Street robbery is an offense that involves violence or the threat of violence to steal property from a person; it has been found to occur in the nighttime at weekends in the United States and elsewhere (Cohn and Rotton 2000; Tompson 2016). Due to the universal finding from victimization surveys across westernized countries that the frequency of socializing outside the home is correlated with victimization risk (Sampson and Wooldredge 1987), discretionary activities are postulated as playing an important role in robbery and other violent crime occurrence. Moreover, discretionary activities often take place in darkness, in environments hosting leisure pursuits, which have been found to be associated with spatial concentrations in robbery (Felson et al. 2013; Smith 2003). Given this, weekend evenings plausibly bring suitable victims into contact with motivated offenders, in environments where capable guardians are absent or ineffective, and many people may be intoxicated. This explanation is likely relevant to other, more general, forms of violent crimes too.

For violent crimes like street robbery, which require both victim and offender to interact, weather can determine whether people are present in an outdoor environment to provide the opportunity for crime occurrence. Since obligatory activities have to be performed in all but extreme weather conditions, weather is likely to have a stronger effect on robbery at times when discretionary, recreational activities are pursued (LeBeau and Corcoran 1990). Pleasant weather increases the likelihood of street robbery and adverse weather decreases it during night hours and

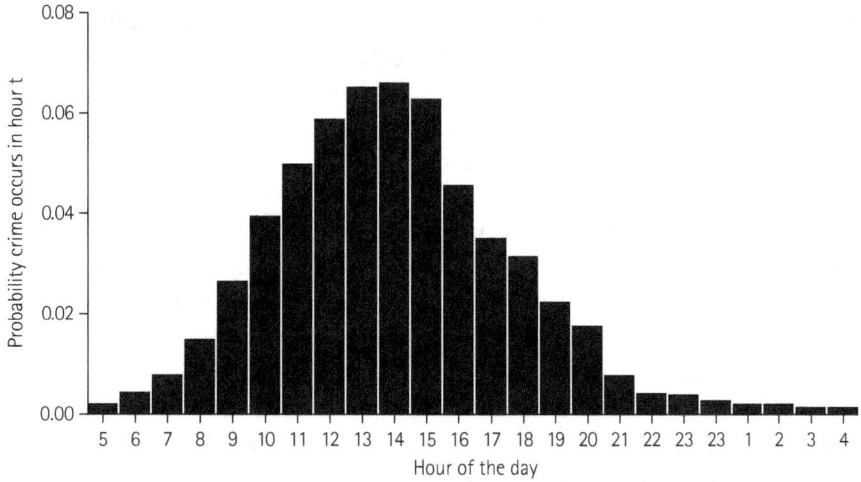

FIGURE 29.6 Aoristic analysis of the hourly distribution of shoplifting, West Yorkshire (U.K.)

weekends, when people are commonly free from obligatory activities (Tompson and Bowers 2015).

A broader range of violent crime appears to conform to these temporal social patterns. Violence acutely peaks in evening and weekend hours across a range of settings, when greater social interaction increases the likelihood of violence (Uittenbogaard and Ceccato 2012; Newton and Hirschfield 2009). Domestic violence commonly occurs in the evenings (LeBeau 1994), perhaps when family members are at home, while violent crime outside the home is also typically more prevalent in the evening and late-evening hours (Figure 29.7), particularly at weekends. Weekend evenings also have the highest frequencies of homicides (Summers 2012).

The rise of cybercrime and its incidence may, at first glance, evade such neat spatiotemporal categorization. Yet, when the timings are examined, the emerging patterns provide glimpses of the opportunity structures for different variants of Internet-enabled crime. These include the initiation of sex crimes via grooming, illegal pornography, extortion, stalking, bullying, and fraud. Fraud may be committed against businesses or individuals, and while attempted attacks are seemingly directed to electronic devices at all times of the day and days of the week, the temporal distribution of attacks can show a more nuanced profile. For instance, many victims of vehicle and bogus holiday villa fraud make the critical decision that results in money being sent in the late evenings when they log on to electronic devices when they are tired (Barnard 2015). The incidence of Internet-enabled fraud may, therefore, vary more temporally than spatially, since offenders may take account of victims' routine online behaviors when timing their offenses.

Telephone fraud against businesses can involve hacking into Internet-enabled phones and then automatically calling costly phone numbers owned by criminals, often in countries with high call prices (Duffy 2016). Charges incurred by the victim and paid

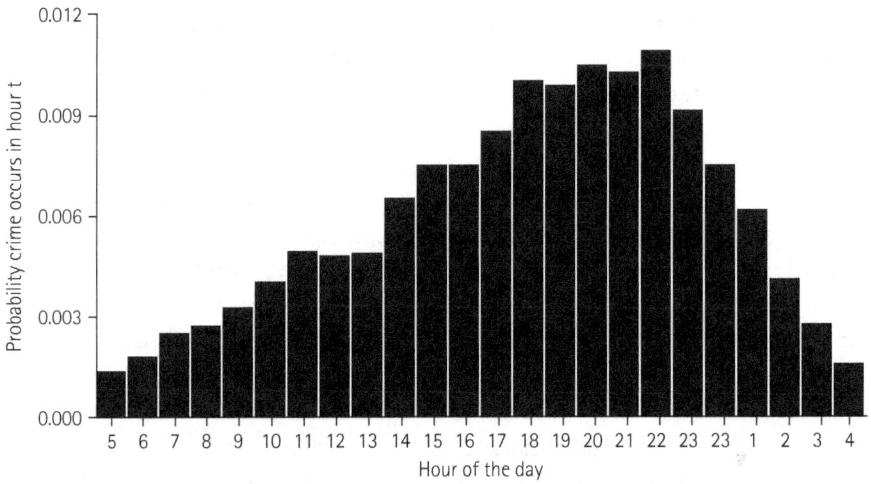

FIGURE 29.7 Aoristic analysis of the hourly distribution of violence, West Yorkshire (U.K.)

to the phone company must, by international agreement, be paid and in many cases such charges may be sizable. It is often difficult to trace the eventual recipients. Whereas most normal calls are made during weekday business hours, fraudulent calls particularly occur between 20:00 and 08:00, and during weekends (Duffy 2016). This is when premises are empty and phones are not being used, and the telephone system owner is unlikely to be able to intervene. "Phone hacks," therefore, are timed to avoid office workers' availability through predicting their daily and weekly working hours.

In contrast, other calls involving card fraud occur during business hours (Duffy 2016). These involve a new phone system customer using a stolen bank card to make calls to criminals' costly phone numbers before the phone company realizes a stolen card is being used. This form of fraud is timed to match normal business hours, since the offender wishes to appear to be a genuine customer (Duffy 2016). Therefore, some cybercrime opportunities fit routine activities, albeit in different ways. Telephone fraud mirrors office employees' working day, while telephone "hacking" avoids it.

29.5 Conclusions

The temporal incidence of crime is principally understood in terms of the routine activities that shape human mobility patterns, vulnerability to victimization, and risks of sighting and apprehension for offenders. Daily routines of work, schooling, leisure, and sleep structure opportunities for different crimes at different times. Guardianship of property and people ebbs and flows over time and, when absent or ineffective, attracts motivated offenders. With crime opportunities reflecting aggregate societal routines, activities, and mobility, crime rises through the day, peaking during the evenings, with violent crime particularly weighted toward the end of the day. There is far less crime during sleeping hours, which occur during the middle of the day as well as at night in hot countries. Crime pattern theory (Brantingham and Brantingham 1993) offers the most complete explanation of hourly spatiotemporal crime patterns, though seasonal climate shifts and short-term weather events modify victims' mobility and crime opportunities during the day.

Monthly and seasonal changes in crime appear to be associated with weather variations that, in turn, depend on climate regime and on changes in amounts of daylight and darkness, as well as routine activities. These modify the physical environment, particularly darkness-daylight, temperature, rainfall, and deciduous leaf cover, and alter opportunities for effective guardianship and crime. Seasonal contrasts in weather result in adjustments to mobility patterns, altering the monthly incidence of different sorts of crimes. Seasonal shifts in daily and monthly crime opportunities are more pronounced in middle and high latitudes, where differences in temperature, precipitation, and ambient light are often more marked than in some low-latitude equatorial climates. There are few studies that systematically compare the seasonal patterns of crimes in different climatic and cultural regimes (see Yan 2004 for an exception), meaning that our understanding of comparative patterns is superficial and incomplete. It is in this spirit that we caution readers that the case study area we have used to illustrate temporal patterns may not be representative of temporal patterns in other regions or cultural contexts.

Annual changes in crime require explanations grounded not only in routine activity theory and climate-weather theory, but also in a variety of other theories tied to social, demographic, economic, and security changes, particularly if the epoch under study encompasses swift social and technological changes. A variety of factors and processes have been implicated that alter the behavior of offenders, the routine activities and social norms of victims, the value of goods to steal, and the security of property and people. Whereas daily, weekly, and monthly crime patterns often show repeating cyclic patterns, annual trends are rather more iterant. The relative importance of different explanations of annual changes in crime has proved difficult to resolve, given inductive methodologies that involve drawing inferences from correlations between time incidence and large numbers of putative causal variables. Statistical issues relating to the time lapse of some causal processes, and substantive matters like increasing globalization and crime perpetrated electronically or through travel, with offenders resident in different countries than victims, provide additional analytic complications. In sum, a larger variety of theories is needed to account for annual crime trends over time.

Studies of temporal crime patterns incur problems that future research would do well to address. First is that there is little consensus on which time intervals should guide the aggregation of data, so that differences in findings may reflect unit-of-analysis differences as much as real differences in temporal patterns. Time distributions in this chapter have been described principally in terms of hourly, weekly, monthly, seasonal, and annual time units. Research that examines possible causal influences can involve a far wider variety of time category definitions, and this can compound difficulties in establishing the reasons for the timing of crime, defeating attempts at coherent systematic reviews.

A second issue is that the absence of fine-grained "ambient" or street population data is a serious impediment to spatiotemporal research. Street populations and temporal variations in pedestrian traffic are exceptionally difficult to estimate. They are, however, the bases of spatiotemporal differences in victim and guardian densities and, thereby, opportunities for offending and the risks and gains of doing so. These influence offender decision-making and help shape the spatiotemporal incidence of many outdoor crimes and some indoor offenses such as burglary. Estimating web traffic at different times of the day, for different types of websites, would similarly assist in understanding why certain sites are vulnerable at particular times.

Explanations of temporal crime patterns by opportunity theories deliberately deemphasize the offender's motivation, preferring to leave this aspect of criminality to other criminological disciplines. This means that the prevailing theories neglect to account for the effects of offender characteristics such as mobility, prolificacy, versatility, and co-offending status on spatiotemporal patterns of crime. Despite the importance of offenders' activity spaces, they have rarely, if ever, been measured in time-crime studies. Full "tests" of the opportunity model that link space-time offense data with the known activities of offenders and overlay these onto a crime opportunity "surface" are rare, if indeed they exist at all. Furthermore, little is known about offenders' routines and mobility for crimes with low detection rates, so that the model of overlapping victim and offender activity spaces has never been convincingly examined. Addressing this third issue requires a combination of data about the timing of crime events, their spatial incidence, and offender activities over a considerable period of time. Their inclusion in temporal crime research and crime event theory, though complex, offers promise for additional insights into the situational influences on the patterning of crime.

This chapter has been focused on temporal patterns of crimes, but it is only by simultaneously examining spatial and temporal characteristics that crime incidence, and the factors that influence this, can be properly understood. The routine behavior of crime victims differs as much in terms of time characteristics as of spatial ones, but the two cannot be divorced from each other. The tendency of scholarly enquiry to focus on one dimension at the neglect of the other reflects the complex nature of analyzing spatio-temporal patterns in crime. This is, though, changing as data and sophisticated analytic techniques are developed and promulgated.

Considering both time and space patterns also has important implications for criminal justice policy, enabling demand to be identified more precisely. This means security and policing resources may be targeted more accurately and frugally by identifying more specific, concentrated time-space units (Braga, Papachristos, and Hureau 2012). Crimes that occur in daylight, for instance, are often easier to solve (Coupe 2016), while the higher warm-weather incidence of violent crimes, which attract heavier custodial sentences than property crimes, elevates remand prisoner demand during the summer months.

Despite its importance for scholarship and for criminal justice system resourcing and effectiveness, crime-time information remains scattered and less well appreciated than its spatial cousin. This chapter has aimed to help redress this by drawing together material to give an illustrated overview, albeit necessarily selective, of the principal features of temporal crime patterns and the processes and theories that shape them. It is clear that considerably more research is needed that takes account of the methodological pitfalls of working with temporal data, to fill knowledge gaps and address misconceptions, particularly with regard to the influences on the timing of crime. Such a task requires data to match across appropriate time intervals so that, for instance, understanding of hourly crime incidence for every day of the calendar year is informed with data on offenders, victims, climate-weather, ambient light, and the physical-built-social environments. Only then may the relative importance of the factors influencing temporal crime patterns be properly understood.

Note

1. It should be noted that in the UK arson is recorded as a form of criminal damage, and can relate to any property, street furniture, or natural resources being set alight.

References

Anderson, C. A., K. B. Anderson, N. Dorr, K. M. DeNeve, and M. Flanagan. 2000. "Temperature and aggression." *Advances in Experimental Social Psychology* 32: 141–144.

Andresen, Martin A., and Nicolas Malleson. 2013. "Crime seasonality and its variations across space." *Applied Geography* 43: 25–35.

Ashby, Matthew P. J., and Kate J. Bowers. 2013. "A comparison of methods for temporal analysis of aoristic crime." *Crime Science* 2(1): 1–16.

Ashby, Matthew P. J., and Lisa Tompson. 2015. "Routine activities and proactive police activity: A macro-scale analysis of police searches in London and New York City." *Justice Quarterly*, doi: 10.1080/07418825.2015.1103380.

Australian Institute of Criminology (AIC). 2009. *Patterns in Bushfire Arson*. No. 58. Available at http://www.aic.gov.au/media_library/publications/bfab/bfab058.pdf.

Barnard, Paul. 2015. "Online vehicle sales fraud: Can police target prevention messages more efficiently and effectively?" MSt thesis, University of Cambridge.

Baumer, Eric, and Richard Wright. 1996. "Crime seasonality and serious scholarship: A comment on Farrell and Pease." *British Journal of Criminology* 36(4): 579–581.

Bernasco, Wim. 2006. "Co-offending and the choice of target areas in burglary." *Journal of Investigative Psychology and Offender Profiling* 3: 139–155.

Bernasco, Wim. 2010. "A sentimental journey to crime: Effects of residential history on crime location choice." *Criminology* 48(2): 389–416.

Bernasco, Wim, Stijn Ruiter, Gerben Bruinsma, Lieven Pauwels, and Frank Weerman. 2013. "Situational causes of offending: A fixed-effects analysis of space-time budget data." *Criminology* 51(4): 895–926.

Blake, Laurence. 2006. "Catching residential burglars in the act." PhD diss., University of Birmingham.

Böcker, Lars, Martin Dijst, and Jan Prillwitz. 2013. "Impact of everyday weather on individual daily travel behaviours in perspective: A literature review." *Transport Reviews* 33(1): 71–91.

Bowers, Kate J., and Shane D. Johnson. 2015. "Poetry in motion: The case of insider and outsider offenders." In *The Criminal Act: The Role and Influence of Routine Activity Theory*, edited by Martin A. Andresen and Graham Farrell. New York: Palgrave Macmillan.

Braga, Anthony A., Andrew W. Papachristos, and David M. Hureau. 2012. *Hot Spots Policing Effects on Crime*. Campbell Systematic Reviews No. 8. Cambridge, MA: Campbell Collaboration.

Braga, Anthony A., and David Weisburd. 2010. *Policing Problem Places: Crime Hot Spots and Effective Prevention*. Studies in Crime and Public Policy. New York: Oxford University Press.

Brantingham, Patricia L., and Paul J. Brantingham. 1993. "Environment, routine and situation: Toward a pattern theory of crime." In *Routine Activity and Rational Choice*, vol. 5 of *Advances in Criminological Theory*, edited by Ronald V. Clarke and Marcus Felson. New Brunswick, NJ: Transaction.

Brantingham, Paul J., and Patricia L. Brantingham. 1981. *Environmental Criminology*. Beverly Hills, CA: Sage.

Brottsförebyggande rådet (BRÅ). 2012–2014. Anmälda brott.

Brunsdon, C., & Corcoran, J. (2006). "Using circular statistics to analyse time patterns in crime incidence." *Computers, Environment and Urban Systems* 30(3): 300–319. Available at http://doi.org/10.1016/j.compenvurbsys.2005.11.001.

Budd, Tracey. 1999. *Burglary of Domestic Dwellings: Findings from the British Crime Survey*. Issue 4/99. London: Home Office.

Ceccato, Vania. 2005. "Homicide in São Paulo, Brazil: Assessing spatial-temporal and weather variations." *Journal of Environmental Psychology* 25(3): 307–321.

Clarke, David. 2015. "Tracking the victims of boiler-room fraud: Citizens at risk! MSt thesis, University of Cambridge.

Clarke, Ronald V., and Graeme R. Newman. 2006. *Outsmarting the Terrorists*. Westport, CT: Praeger.

Cohen, Lawrence E., and Marcus Felson. 1979. "Social change and crime rate trends: A routine activities approach." *American Sociological Review* 44: 588–608.

Cohen, Lawrence E., James R. Kluegel, and Kenneth C. Land. 1981. "Social inequality and predatory criminal victimization: An exposition and test of a formal theory." *American Sociological Review* 46: 505–524.

Cohn, Ellen G., and James Rotton. 1997. "Assault as a function of time and temperature: A moderator-variable time-series analysis." *Journal of Personality and Social Psychology* 72(6): 1322–1334.

Cohn, Ellen G., and James Rotton. 2000. "Weather, seasonal trends and property crimes in Minneapolis, 1987–1988: A moderator-variable time-series analysis of routine activities." *Journal of Environmental Psychology* 20(3): 257–272.

Cohn, Ellen G., and James Rotton. 2003. "Even criminals take a holiday: Instrumental and expressive crimes on major and minor holidays." *Journal of Criminal Justice* 31(4): 351–360.

Cornish Derek B., and Ronald V. Clarke. 1986. *The Reasoning Criminal: Rational Choice Perspectives on Offending*. New York: Springer.

Coupe, Richard Timothy. 2016. "Evaluating the effects of resources and solvability on burglary detection." *Policing and Society* 26(5): 563–587.

Coupe, Timothy, and Laurence Blake. 2006. "Daylight and darkness targeting strategies and the risks of being seen at residential burglaries." *Criminology* 44(2): 431–464.

Coupe, Timothy, and Bryanna H. Fox. 2012. "A risky business: How do access, exposure and guardians affect the chances of non-residential burglars being seen?" *Security Journal* 28: 71–92.

Coupe, Timothy, and Satverg Kaur. 2005. "The role of alarms and CCTV in detecting non-residential burglary." *Security Journal* 18(2): 53–72.

D'Alessio, Stewart J., David Eitle, and Lisa Stolzenberg. 2012. "Unemployment, guardianship and weekday residential burglary." *Justice Quarterly* 29(6): 919–932.

Dorling, Danny, and Stan Openshaw. 1992. "Using computer animation to visualize space-time patterns." *Environment and Planning, Series B: Planning and Design* 19: 639–650.

Duffy, Colin. 2016. "Does opportunity also make the cyberthief? An investigation into Internet telephony fraud." MSt thesis, University of Cambridge.

Eisner, Manuel. 1995. "The effects of economic structures and phases of development on crime." In *Crime and Economy* 32, *Criminological Research*, edited by Council of Europe. Strasbourg: Council of Europe.

Eisner, Manuel. 2001. "Modernization, self-control and lethal violence: The long-term dynamics of European homicide rates in theoretical perspective." *British Journal of Criminology* 41: 618–638.

Eisner, Manuel. 2002. "Long-term trends in violence: Empirical research and theoretical approaches." In *Handbook of Violence Research*, edited by John Hagan and Wilhelm Heitmeyer. New York: Westview.

Farrell, Graham. 2013. "Five tests for a theory of the crime drop." *Crime Science* 2(1): 1–8.

Farrell, Graham, and Ken Pease. 1994. "Crime seasonality: Domestic disputes and residential burglary in Merseyside 1988–90." *British Journal of Criminology* 34(4): 487–497.

Farrell, Graham, Andromachi Tseloni, Jen Mailley, and Nick Tilley. 2011. "The crime drop and the security hypothesis." *Journal of Research in Crime and Delinquency* 48(2): 147–175.

Felson, Marcus. 1987. "Routine activities and crime prevention in the developing metropolis." *Criminology* 25(4), 911–931.

Felson, Marcus, and Ronald V. Clarke. 1998. "Opportunity makes the thief: Practical theory for crime prevention." Police Research Series Paper No. 98. Policing and Reducing Crime Unit, Research, Development and Statistics Directorate, Home Office, London.

Felson, Marcus, and Erica Poulsen. 2003. "Simple indicators of crime by time of day." *International Journal of Forecasting* 19: 595–601.

Felson, Richard B., Jukka Savolainen, Mark T. Berg, and Noora Ellonen. 2013. "Does spending time in public settings contribute to the adolescent risk of violent victimization?" *Journal of Quantitative Criminology* 29: 273–293.

Fox, James A. 2000. "Demographics and U.S. homicide." In *The Crime Drop in America*, edited by Alfred Blumstein and Joel Wallman. Cambridge: Cambridge University Press.

Gillis, A. R., and John Hagan. 1982. "Bystander apathy and the territorial imperative." *Sociological Inquiry* 53: 449–460.

Gorr, Wilpen, Andreas Olligschlaeger, and Yvonne Thompson. 2003. "Short-term forecasting of crime." *International Journal of Forecasting* 19: 579–594.

Haberman, Cory P., and Jerry H. Ratcliffe. 2015. "Testing for temporally nuanced relationships among potentially criminogenic places and census block street robbery counts." *Criminology* 53 (3): 457–483.

Hipp, J. R., D. J. Bauer, P. Curran, and K. A. Bollen. 2004. "Crimes of opportunity or crimes of emotion? Testing two explanations of seasonal change in crime." *Social Forces* 82(4): 1333–1372.

Hird, Celia, and Chandni Kuparel. 2007. *Seasonality in Recorded Crime: Preliminary Findings*. Home Office Online Report 02/07.

Johnson, Shane D., Aiden Sidebottom, and Adam Thorpe. 2008. *Bicycle Theft*. Washington, DC: US Department of Justice, Office of Community Oriented Policing Services.

Landau, S. F., and D. Fridman. 1993. "The seasonality of violent crime: The case of robbery and homicide in Israel." *Journal of Research in Crime and Delinquency* 30(2): 163–191.

LeBeau, James L. 1994. "The oscillation of police calls to domestic disputes with time and the temperature humidity index." *Journal of Crime and Justice* 17(1), 149–161.

LeBeau, James L., and William T. Corcoran. 1990. "Changes in calls for police service with changes in routine activities and the arrival and passage of weather fronts." *Journal of Quantitative Criminology* 6(3): 269–291.

Levitt, Steven D. 2004. "Understanding why crime fell in the 1990s: Four factors that explain the decline and six that do not." *Journal of Economic Perspectives* 18(1): 163–190.

Maguire, Michael. 2007. "Crime data and statistics." In *The Oxford Handbook of Criminology*, 4th ed., edited by Michael Maguire, Robert Reiner, and Rod Morgan. Oxford: Oxford University Press.

Maguire, Michael, and Trevor Bennett. 1982. *Burglary in a Dwelling: The Offence, the Offender and the Victim*. London: Heinemann.

Newton, A., and A. Hirschfield. 2009. "Measuring violence in and around licensed premises: The need for a better evidence base." *Crime Prevention and Community Safety* 11(3): 171–188.

O'Brien, Robert M. 2001. "Theory, operationalization, identification, and the interpretation of different differences in time series models." *Journal of Quantitative Criminology* 17(4): 359–375.

Quételet, Alphonse. 1842. *A Treatise on Man*. Edinburgh: William and Robert Chambers.

Ratcliffe, Jerry H. 2000. "Aoristic analysis: The spatial interpretation of unspecific temporal events." *International Journal of Geographical Information Science* 14(7): 669–679.

Ratcliffe, Jerry H. 2001. *Policing Urban Burglary*. Trends and Issues in Crime and Criminal Justice No. 213. Canberra: Australian Institute of Criminology.

Ratcliffe, Jerry H. 2006. "A temporal constraint theory to explain opportunity-based spatial offending patterns." *Journal of Research in Crime and Delinquency* 43(3): 261–291.

Rengert, George F., Alex R. Piquero, and P. R. Jones. 1999. "Distance decay re-examined." *Criminology* 37: 427–445.

Rengert, George, and John Wasilchick. 1985. *Suburban Burglary: A Time and a Place for Everything*. Springfield, IL: CC Thomas.

Reynald, Danielle M. 2009. "Guardianship in action: Developing a new tool for measurement." *Crime Prevention and Community Safety* 11(1): 1–20.

Reynald, Danielle M., and Henk Elffers. 2015. "The routine activity of guardianship: Comparing self-reports of guardianship intensity patterns with proxy measures." *Crime Prevention and Community Safety* 17(4): 211–232.

Robinson, W. S. 1950. "Ecological correlations and the behavior of individuals." *American Sociological Review* 15: 351–357.

Rock, D. J., Judd, K., & Hallmayer, J. F. (2008). "The seasonal relationship between assault and homicide in England and Wales." *Injury, International Journal of the Care of the Injured* 39(9): 1047–1053.

Sagovsky, Alex, and Shane D. Johnson. 2007. "When does repeat victimization occur?" *Australian and New Zealand Journal of Criminology* 40: 1–26.

Sampson, Robert J., and John D. Wooldredge. 1987. "Linking the micro- and macro-level dimensions of lifestyle-routine activity and opportunity models of predatory victimization." *Journal of Quantitative Criminology* 3(4): 371–393.

Shmueli, Galit. 2010. "To explain or to predict?" *Statistical Science* 25(3): 289–310.

Sidebottom, Aiden, Jyoti Belur, Kate Bowers, Lisa Tompson, and Shane D. Johnson. 2011. "Theft in price-volatile markets: On the relationship between copper price and copper theft." *Journal of Research in Crime and Delinquency* 48: 396–418.

Smith, Jonathan. 2003. *The Nature of Personal Robbery*. London: Home Office.

Sorg, Evan T., and Ralph B. Taylor. 2011. "Community-level impacts of temperature on urban street robbery." *Journal of Criminal Justice* 39(6): 463–470.

Spelman, William. 2000. "The limited importance of prison expansion." In *The Crime Drop in America*, edited by Alfred Blumstein and Joel Wallman. Cambridge: Cambridge University Press.

Summers, Lucia. 2012. "The role of place in outdoor serious violence." PhD diss., University College London.

Tompson, Lisa A. 2016. "Explaining temporal patterns in street robbery." PhD diss., University College London.

Tompson, Lisa A., and Kate J. Bowers. 2013. "A stab in the dark? A research note on temporal patterns of street robbery." *Journal of Research in Crime and Delinquency* 50(4): 616–631.

Tompson, Lisa A., and Kate J. Bowers. 2015. "Testing time-sensitive influences of weather on street robbery." *Crime Science* 4(8).

Tseloni, Andromachi, Jen Mailley, Graham Farrell, and Nick Tilley. 2010. "The international crime drop: Trends and variations." *European Journal of Criminology* 7: 375–394.

US Fire Administration. 2005. "The seasonal nature of fires." Federal Emergency Management Agency. Available at www.usfa.fema.gov/downloads/pdf/publications/fa-236.pdf.

Uittenbogaard, U., and V. Ceccato. 2012. "Space-time clusters of crime in Stockholm, Sweden." *Review of European Studies* 4(5): 148–156.

Van Dijk, Jan. 2006. "What goes up, comes down: Explaining the falling crime rates." *Criminology in Europe* (newsletter of the European Society of Criminology), 5(3): 3 and 17–18.

Van Koppen, Peter J., and Robert W. J. Jansen. 1999. "The road to the robbery: Travel patterns in commercial robberies." *British Journal of Criminology* 38: 230–246.

Weisburd, David L. 2015. "The law of crime concentration and the criminology of place." *Criminology* 53(2): 133–157.

Weisburd, David L., Elizabeth R. Groff, and Sue-Ming Yang. 2012. *The Criminology of Place: Street Segments and Our Understanding of the Crime Problem.* New York: Oxford University Press.

Wikström, Per-Olaf, and David A. Butterworth. 2006. *Adolescent Crime: Individual Differences and Lifestyles.* Cullompton, Devon, UK: Willan Publishing.

Wikström, Per-Olaf, Vania Ceccato, Beth Hardie, and Kyle Treiber. 2010. "Activity fields and the dynamics of crime." *Journal of Quantitative Criminology* 26(1): 55–87.

Wikström, Per-Olaf, Dietrich Oberwittler, Kyle Treiber, and Beth Hardie. 2012. *Breaking Rules: The Social and Situational Dynamics of Young People's Urban Crime.* Oxford: Oxford University Press.

Yan, Y. Y. (2004). "Seasonality of Property Crime in Hong Kong." *British Journal of Criminology* 44(2): 276–283. Available at http://doi.org/10.1093/bjc/44.2.276.

CHAPTER 30

GUARDIANSHIP

DANIELLE M. REYNALD

30.1 Introduction

First introduced in the routine activity approach (Cohen & Felson, 1979), guardianship was defined as "any spatio-temporally specific supervision of people or property by other people which may prevent criminal violations from occurring" (Felson & Cohen, 1980: 392). Research on guardianship has revealed that, as a key process of crime prevention and control by informal citizens, it is negatively associated with crime, suggesting its importance as an effective crime control strategy. Empirical evidence supports the perspective that guardianship intensity is a function of place, as it is critically determined by the opportunities available for supervision that are generated by the spatio-physical and sociodemographic context. With this in mind, this chapter will provide an overview of the theoretical origins of the guardianship concept, and will review key empirical studies that have contributed to the development of criminological understanding of how guardianship functions to control crime. This chapter will conclude with a discussion of current research and the new directions currently being charted for continued insights into the processes and mechanisms that facilitate effective guardianship for crime prevention.

30.2 Guardians and Guardianship

Cohen and Felson's (1979) routine activity approach explains that crime is the product of the convergence of three fundamental elements: a likely offender, a suitable target (defined as a person, object, or place), and the absence of a capable guardian. The absence of capable guardians, as the ultimate informal protectors and defenders of people and property against criminal violations, makes crime more likely. According to the routine activity approach, a capable guardian can be any person or thing that discourages crime from taking place (Cohen & Felson, 1979). Because guardians serve the function of keeping an eye on potential crime targets, their mere presence can discourage crime, while their absence makes crime more likely (Felson, 1995). Felson (1995) explains how this works by giving the example of those who work away from home during the day, leaving their property unattended and more vulnerable through their absence. By the same token, retired persons at home may discourage burglary at their own property and neighboring properties simply by their presence.

Who fulfills the role of a guardian in a given situation is therefore dependent on who is present within the context of the crime opportunity. Felson (1995) contends that his conceptualization of the guardian within the routine activity approach is not a formal policeman or security guard but an informal person or ordinary citizen whose daily routines determine his or her availability to provide security to potential targets/victims of crime. Guardians can be household residents (who can act as guardians over their own as well as nearby properties) and/or passers-by (who may act as guardians over others in their presence), as they are more likely to be present to discourage crime than formal guardians like police officers and security guards. In spite of the central role that capable guardians play in discouraging criminal victimization, research on guardians and guardianship has lagged significantly behind research on victimization and offending.

30.2.1 Crime Controllers, Guardians, and Informal Social Control

Recent developments in the routine activity approach extend the roles assumed by crime controllers or actors who are responsible for crime control. While guardians were highlighted as crime controllers who supervise and protect targets against victimization in the original conceptualization of the routine activity approach, this crime controller role has since been expanded to include handlers who supervise potential offenders (Felson, 1995) and managers who supervise places (Eck, 1994). Linking the routine activity approach and Hirschi's control theory, Felson (1995) introduced the concept of handlers to explain how parents and others in a community who are in close proximity to and know a likely offender can serve as "intimate handlers" who have the capability to exert control over them when they see them rule-breaking. Eck (1994) introduced another group of controllers—place managers—who have the power to discourage crime at places through the effective supervision and management of those places.

These three groups of controllers or supervisors highlight the fact that crime can be prevented by exercising control over potential targets, crime sites, or offenders through supervision. Thus the concept of guardianship is subsumed under the umbrella of informal social control, where supervision by the guardian over the target, the handler over the offender, and the place manager over the place is enhanced by social bonds and informed by social norms that lead ultimately to crime control (Reynald, 2014). Felson and Cohen's (1980) definition of guardianship as spatiotemporally specific supervision of potential crime targets emphasizes the importance of looking out for, keeping an eye on, or monitoring people or property, as these behaviors increase the likelihood of preventing victimization. This definition also highlights that guardianship is place and time specific, and therefore highly situation dependent.

30.2.2 Guardian Availability

Since citizens' capability to guard against crime is defined by their routine activities that determine their availability to guard, early research on guardianship focused exclusively on testing guardianship in neighborhood contexts by estimating the availability or presence of household residents as potential guardians. Results confirmed that household occupancy or frequency of time people spend at home is negatively associated with burglary victimization. For instance, Miethe, Stafford, and Sloane (1990) operationalized guardianship in terms of household occupancy, using the number of persons in a household over the age of 12 as its measure. They found that individuals with a decreased level of guardianship over time showed an increased risk of victimization. These results suggest that while time spent away from home decreases property guardianship by leaving properties unattended, it simultaneously increases individual exposure to the risk of personal victimization. Garofalo and Clark (1992) surveyed residents about their availability by asking household members how often they were at home, as well as indicators such as the presence of a dog, an alarm system, a timer for lights or radio, informal arrangements with neighbors, and other security measures. They reported that this combination of guardianship measures reduce the likelihood of residential burglaries, with the strongest effect observed when they are used in concert.

The majority of this early empirical research on guardianship used proxy measures for home occupancy to measure guardianship. In lieu of direct measures of guardianship, indicators such as the number of owner-occupied households, percentage labor-force participation, and number of household members have traditionally been used to approximate availability as a means of estimating the level of guardianship at places. Exceptions include the British Crime Survey (BCS) and Garofalo and Clark (1992), which use self-report survey items to measure the amount of time people spend at home as an indicator of guardianship at the property level. Nevertheless, all the aforementioned measures of guardianship were aimed at estimating the availability of potential guardians. The rationale for this is that the concept of guardianship for crime prevention is based on the core idea that any individual can serve as a guardian against crime by being present at the scene of a potential crime event (Felson, 1995). Routine activities that involve a higher proportion of time spent at or around the home rather than away from home increase the likelihood that guardians will be available to guard in this context. The mere presence of a guardian has the potential to discourage offenders who are in search of low-risk opportunities to commit crime (Reynald, 2014). Availability therefore can be viewed as the most fundamental dimension of guardianship.

Availability, however, is just one dimension of guardianship. It is important to recall that the guardianship concept is defined in the routine activity approach as "spatiotemporally specific supervision" that prevents crime. Availability conveys very little about actual supervision by the guardian who is present, or about the likelihood that a guardian who is present would take action to stop a crime in progress (Reynald, 2011b, 2014). This highlights issues related to the inadequacy of some commonly used proxy measures of guardianship (see Miethe & Meier, 1994 for discussion). While availability is a necessary condition for guardianship, the presence of guardians is merely the starting point of the spectrum of capability that citizens can draw upon to guard against crime (Reynald, 2011b, 2014).

30.2.3 Guardianship in Action, Including Supervision and Intervention

While presence/availability is arguably its most fundamental dimension, Reynald (2009, 2010, 2011a) advanced guardianship research by demonstrating that given availability, capable guardianship can be enhanced by actual supervision or monitoring of residential space and property, and by intervention when necessary. Felson (2006) notes that the absence of supervision explains when and where crime occurs since offenders primarily seek to escape supervision by choosing places and targets that are not well attended to. However, Brown and Bentley (1993) explain that the risk of being seen is not always sufficient to deter a burglar since "burglars also need to know whether potential onlookers would care about their presence . . .. Burglars also may decide that some neighbours will intervene and others will not" (Brown & Bentley, 1993: 52). The power to guard against crime can therefore be further intensified when guardians take action to intervene when they witness crime or related activity in their surroundings. Intervention is any action taken to disrupt or prevent a crime or related event. This can include a range of actions including shouting out to perpetrators, calling the police, or physically intervening to stop a crime.

Reynald (2009, 2011a) elaborated on this multidimensional conceptualization of guardianship, arguing that these action components of supervision and intervention are directly observable and provide a more ecologically valid measure of guardianship than traditionally used proxy measures. These new observational measures revealed that guardianship intensity is strongest and is significantly associated with lower property crime rates when guardians are (1) available, (2) engage in supervision/monitoring/surveillance over targets in their surroundings, and (3) take action by intervening when necessary in order to prevent or disrupt crime or related violations. These findings were replicated by Hollis-Peel and Welsh (2014). Together, availability, monitoring/supervision and intervention form a reliable and valid integrated measure of guardianship.

30.2.4 Decision-Making by Available Guardians: Willingness to Supervise and Intervene

Research on the multidimensional concept of guardianship was furthered by extending the observational research on the most visible, action-oriented dimensions of guardianship by conducting interviews with available guardians to uncover what motivated their guardianship decisions and behaviors. Based on the basic premise that guardianship encompasses more than availability of guardians, Reynald's (2010) study was the first interview study with available residential guardians. It revealed that supervision and/or intervention when necessary were not automatic consequences of availability. Of a sample of 255 available guardians, 15% admitted to choosing not to supervise or even pay attention to what happened in their surroundings. Results revealed that supervision enhanced guardianship capabilities, as residents explained that monitoring heightened their contextual awareness by improving their ability to recognize people and situations that were suspicious and out of the ordinary in their particular residential context. These findings support the results from the observational guardianship in action (GIA) studies that highlight the importance of monitoring/supervision in increasing the intensity of guardianship at places.

Only 16% of 217 residents that reported witnessing crime or related events in their surroundings reported their willingness to intervene directly, regardless of the type of crime event they witnessed. These results are consistent with findings about low rates of bystander intervention in crime events from social psychology. Moreover, 20% of this subsample admitted they would not take any (direct or indirect) action to intervene when they observed suspicious, crime-related activity. The majority of the sample reported they would opt for indirect intervention by calling the police for help, with many residents explaining that their choice of direct or indirect intervention would depend on the severity of the crime event in progress.

These data about the various types of responses guardians have when they observe crime-related events in their home environments revealed fundamental stages involved in guardian decision-making. Results showed that once a crime or related event is observed by available guardians, their response is based on a series of rational assessments of the costs and benefits associated with the interaction of both individual and situational factors. These were broadly categorized as (1) perceived risk to personal safety, (2) perceived capability to respond, and (3) perceived responsibility to respond. Available guardians were more likely to express a willingness to intervene when their perceived risk to safety was low and their perceived capability and responsibility was high. These results support Clarke's (1992) suggestion that guarding against crime within the situational crime prevention context is about encouraging guardians and place managers to take responsibility for supervising and protecting the places they inhabit. For residents this translates into taking responsibility for public areas around residences, while for place managers it means taking responsibility for monitoring their workplaces (Clarke, 1992). Felson (1995) extended this idea by highlighting various levels of responsibility that guardians take for guarding against crime, and these are influenced by factors including social distance in terms of familiarity and attachment, and physical distance to potential targets/victims (see Reynald, 2011b). The interviews with available guardians also revealed distinct decision-making stages that determine residents' willingness to supervise and intervene, which are affected by interrelated individual, contextual, and situational factors (see Reynald, 2010). Guardianship decision-making is one critical aspect of guardianship research that requires additional attention to further elucidate the relationship among the mechanisms that facilitate supervision and intervention by guardians, as well as those that hinder these guardianship processes (Reynald, 2014).

30.2.5 Environmental Factors Related to Guardianship

Alongside these behaviors required to effectively guard against crime, the local environment or the characteristics of a place play a critical role in supporting efforts by local citizens to guard against crime (Reynald, 2011b, 2014). Wilcox et al. (2007) argued that contextual factors that affect the various dimensions of guardianship have not been given adequate consideration by previous research. Physical, spatial, social, and demographic factors all comprise what is holistically perceived as the residential environment. In turn, each of these groups of factors affects the (visible) availability of residents, their monitoring capabilities, and whether or not they are willing to intervene to disrupt or prevent crime events (Reynald, 2011b, 2014). Opportunities generated by the environment can therefore aid in empowering residents to act as capable guardians against crime.

Previous research has revealed several environmental factors that clearly influence residents' capabilities to guard against crime in their home environments. These factors and the underlying mechanisms that facilitate their relationship with guardianship will be discussed, along with relevant theoretical explanations and empirical evidence to support the relationship between the environment and the dimensions of active guardianship.

30.3 Guardianship Opportunities and the Spatio-Physical Context

30.3.1 Defensible Space: Natural Surveillance

The design and layout of the built environment provide opportunities for surveillance that determine residents' physical capability to monitor their surroundings, and affect the likelihood that residents are perceived as being visibly available to guard. Newman's (1972) defensible space theory explains how the spatio-physical environment affects residents' capability to act as guardians by either facilitating or blocking opportunities for natural surveillance. Newman argues that residents can maximize their ability to be seen and their monitoring capability if windows and doors of properties are oriented toward public space and designed to face each other along a street, and by creating clear, unobstructed lines of sight between private residences and public space. This enables residents to oversee their property, neighboring properties, and public space immediately surrounding them. With the support of these environmental design and layout features, residents can supervise their surroundings purposely or inadvertently while carrying out routine household activities (Newman, 1972). This is reinforced by Felson (2006), who explains that supervision is maximized when guardians can see as much of their residential space as possible. These natural surveillance opportunities facilitate crime prevention by increasing the observability of residential areas as well as the visibility of residents who are at home, which in turn increases the risk that potential offenders will be seen (Reynald, 2014).

30.3.2 Defensible Space: Image/Maintenance and Territoriality

Newman's (1972) defensible space theory also explains how the level of guardianship available at a place can be expressed through territoriality. Territoriality reflects the level of territorial control and care that residents have for their properties. Symbols of control and ownership include the use of property signs and decorations as well as property landscaping. These indicators are conceptualized by Newman (1972) as *symbolic barriers*, as they communicate to outsiders and potential offenders that a property is well cared for and controlled by its owners, and therefore discourage territorial breaches. Alongside symbolic barriers, Newman (1972) argues that territorial control can also be expressed through the use of actual *physical barriers* that clearly demarcate the boundary between public and private property and restrict access to outsiders. According to Newman (1972), the better the territorial definition of the property in terms of the use of territorial markers through physical and symbolic barriers, the less likely territorial borders will be breached.

Similar to territoriality, the image of a residential environment reflects the extent to which it is controlled, maintained, and well cared for by its residents. Image cues provide information about the management of a residential place and whether or not its residents are likely to be effective guardians of their property. According to defensible space theory (Newman, 1972), therefore, image reflects the extent to which residents take responsibility for keeping a place clean and well maintained. Broken windows theory (Wilson & Kelling, 1982) supports this perspective that residents can help guard against crime through the regular upkeep of properties and surroundings. This theory explains that cues like broken windows and graffiti reflect poor management and maintenance, consequently promoting an image of vulnerability and encouraging crime. Empirical evidence corroborates this perspective, as it shows how physical incivilities like broken windows, litter, graffiti, and general disrepair encourage social incivilities and lead to increases in crime, fear of crime, and community withdrawal (see Skogan, 1990; Welsh et al., 2015). The image of a place can thus have a significant impact on guardianship as it can affect the frequency with which residents are present in their home environment, as well as their willingness to monitor their surroundings and intervene when necessary.

30.3.3 Accessibility, Land Use, and the Routine Activities of Place

While the image of a place is affected by residents' maintenance of their properties, it is also affected by the routine activities of that place. The routine activities of a place can be viewed as a function of the social organization of behavior at a place, which is determined by the level of activity and the type of activity encouraged therein. Place accessibility and land-use patterns in turn contribute to the level and type of activity that is routine at a place. Accessibility and land use can generate or inhibit opportunities for effective monitoring and direct intervention by guardians when necessary. By altering the ratio of outsiders to regulars on a block, nonresidential land-use at places can reduce the extent to which residents are familiar with the users of space on their block (Taylor et al., 1995), resulting in reduced capability to effectively guard their residential environment against crime. Exacerbating this issue is the fact that nonresidential land-uses on a residential block create "holes" in the residential fabric that residents do not take responsibility for (Taylor et al., 1995: 122).

A similar mechanism seems to be at work for areas that are highly accessible. Accessible places tend to attract a higher proportion of outsiders. This affects residents' monitoring capabilities by reducing the likelihood that they will be able to detect suspicious activity or individuals who are in search of illegitimate opportunities. Empirical research shows that crime tends to be higher in more accessible, highly utilized areas of the street network. High accessibility and activity levels at a place also generate increased opportunities for crime by encouraging opportunities for physical and social incivilities (Taylor et al., 1995). The high usage of space and the number of external users that are attracted to it can have a negative effect on residents' place attachment, participation, and territorial behavior (Taylor et al., 1995). This withdrawal by residents restricts opportunities for capable guardianship and reinforces the negative place image.

Some debate persists, however, over the effect of accessibility and mixed land use on residents' guardianship capabilities and on crime in general. Jacobs (1961) argued that mixed land usage and the regular flow of people this attracts at different times of the day actually encourage, rather than discourage, opportunities to guard against crime. This argument is based on the rationale that more people translates into more available guardians. Based on Jacobs' (1961) theories, new urbanism promotes residential developments comprised of mixed land use including public transportation stops and other amenities.

30.4 Guardianship and the Sociodemographic Context

30.4.1 The Density of Acquaintanceship and the Social Context

Citizens' willingness to guard against crime is also influenced by their sociodemographic context. Freudenburg (1986) argues that supervision by residents and the effect this has on crime are mediated by the social context and the degree to which residents know each other. He argues that the *density of acquaintanceship*, or the degree to which residents in a community know each other, is a critical factor in determining the extent to which residents keep an eye out in areas with stable populations (Freudenburg, 1986). Sampson et al. (1997) also found evidence to suggest that residents' willingness to intervene is linked to social cohesion among neighbors, and is negatively associated with variations in violent victimization in neighborhoods. These studies emphasize the importance of the social environment in encouraging residents' willingness to guard against crime.

30.4.2 Residential Mobility, Ethnic Heterogeneity, Income, and Social Ties

Residents' immediate social environment is fundamentally shaped by demographic characteristics of the broader neighborhood context (Reynald, 2014). The demographic characteristics of certain neighborhoods, such as ethnic heterogeneity, low income, and high residential mobility, contribute to high crime and delinquency rates by weakening informal social control and disrupting social organizations and networks within neighborhoods (Sampson & Groves, 1989). This has been corroborated by empirical studies both at the street and at the property level. Xie and McDowall (2008), for example, reported that residential turnover independently increases the risk of property victimization as a result of constrained capabilities for guardianship by residents, ultimately changing the opportunity structure for crime. They explain that high residential turnover on streets tends to increase the vulnerability of households to crime through the convergence of several mechanisms involving the interaction between the sociodemographic environment and the guardianship dimensions of monitoring and intervention. According to Xie and McDowall (2008), when residents move, this weakens local ties and social control. They go on to explain that "newcomers tend to have fewer friends in the neighborhood who might act as guardians of their homes . . .. Long-term neighbors are more likely to recognize unusual patterns and unfamiliar people that may be signs of criminal activity. They will also be more likely to intervene, ask questions, and notify the police of clear indications of unusual activities" (Xie & McDowall, 2008: 543). High rates of resident mobility mean high numbers of new residents whose lack of contextual awareness and knowledge about their residential area has a negative effect on their supervision capabilities and likely on their confidence and willingness to intervene. Xie and McDowall (2008) suggest that these vulnerabilities of newcomers, including their diminished capacity to distinguish those who belong to the area from those that do not, are likely to be perceived by offenders, thereby encouraging opportunities to offend.

30.4.3 Guardianship, the Environment, and Situational Crime Prevention

Based on this premise that specific situational characteristics help generate opportunities for offenders to commit crime, Clarke (1992) builds on Newman's defensible space thesis by arguing that crime can be prevented by systematically manipulating situational elements to block these opportunities by using a range of situational crime prevention strategies and techniques. Clarke (1992) highlights the importance of increasing guardianship as one of the core 25 situational crime prevention techniques. Situational crime prevention is designed to affect the offender's decision-making process by manipulating the perceived costs and benefits associated with particular crime opportunities. The main focus therefore is to manipulate situations so that the costs of committing crime outweigh the benefits, thereby increasing the likelihood that the offender is discouraged from committing the criminal act. In the same overarching vein as Newman's defensible space theory, Clarke (1997) explains that the ultimate goal is to create unfavorable circumstances for the offender through "discrete managerial and environmental change" (1997: 2) in order to reduce opportunities for crime and prevent its occurrence.

With this core objective in mind, we see that one of the key situational crime prevention strategies is to *increase the risks* that offenders will be caught. One of the main techniques associated with this strategy is extending or increasing guardianship and providing assistance or tools for guardians that help facilitate natural and other forms of surveillance, including improved street lighting, use of CCTV, and so on. According to Clarke, the implementation of these guardianship techniques is fundamental to crime prevention, as it heightens the offender's perception that he will be detected, and is therefore likely to discourage offending in that situation. This lends credence to the notion that guardians can discourage crime and protect targets through their presence and through supervision.

Burglars in the Bennett and Wright (1984) study provided evidence to support this, explaining that household occupancy and the risk of being seen or detected by others played a significant role in the targets selected for burglary. Offenders expressed concern over the presence and proximity of guardians in the form of neighbors, and also about the capability of guardians in terms of whether neighbors would spot them, and whether they would take action upon noticing them and their suspicious activity.

30.5 Alternative Applications and Extensions of the Guardianship Concept

30.5.1 Mechanical Surveillance

Cohen and Felson (1979) explain that while capable guardians are usually people, the guardianship function can also be served to some extent by mechanical objects. CCTV cameras are increasingly being used as technological/mechanical replacements for, or extensions of, the supervision and control provided by human guardians. CCTV cameras are said to create the perception that someone is watching, whether they are manned or not. This type of mechanical surveillance is therefore meant to have a similar effect to supervision by guardians, as it discourages offenders in search of crime opportunities by elevating the risk of detection (see Clarke & Eck, 2003. This highlights the value of multidimensional guardianship, as it suggests that the effectiveness of guardianship is likely to be enhanced when different forms of guardianship are used in combination (see Wilcox et al., 2007). When guardians are not able or available to provide constant supervision over targets, people, and places, CCTV cameras can be an effective form of surveillance under certain circumstances. Welsh and Farrington (2009) found that CCTV is more effective in reducing property crime than violent crime, and is most effective in reducing vehicle crime and crime in car parks where camera coverage is high and when coupled with other interventions (e.g., security guards and improved lighting). On the other hand, CCTV programs introduced in city/town centers, public housing, and public transport were not shown to have a significant effect on crime (Welsh & Farrington, 2009).

30.5.2 Target Hardening

Physical guardianship or the protection of targets through physical control has been defined as "routine activities that provide physical protection of homes" (Wilcox et al., 2007: 774) or other property targets. According to Wilcox et al. (2007) physical guardianship includes target-hardening measures that are consistent with situational crime prevention and overlap with guardianship, such as the use of alarm systems and locks. Target hardening can be used to discourage offenders by increasing the effort required to commit crime. Several studies have characterized these types of target hardening measures as a specific form of guardianship (e.g., Miethe & Meier, 1994; Garofalo & Clark, 1992). It is important to note, however, that this is not in keeping with the routine activity conceptualization and definition of guardianship, and even within the situational crime prevention literature, target hardening and guardianship are considered separate techniques for crime prevention (Reynald, 2011b, 2014). While increasing guardianship is categorized as a crime prevention technique that increases the risk that offenders will be identified or caught, target hardening is a separate technique designed to increase the effort required by offenders to illegally acquire or access a target (Clarke, 1997). Though related, these are viewed and conceptualized as distinct techniques that operate successfully both independently and in concert to prevent crime via distinct strategies and mechanisms.

30.5.3 Self-Protection Measures

A new branch in the conceptualization of guardianship was born out of the fusion of the routine activities approach with the lifestyle-exposure perspective of Hindelang et al. (1978). Studies by Mustaine and Tewksbury (Mustaine & Tewksbury, 1998; Tewksbury & Mustaine, 2003) conceptualize guardianship in terms of specific behaviors aimed at self- or target protection, thereby moving away from the routine activity conceptualization of guardianship as an expression of social control. Based on the idea that individual lifestyle and routine activities determine variations in exposure to dangerous places, times, and others (Miethe & Meier, 1994), Mustaine and Tewksbury (1998: 834) define guardianship as "*the degree of protection afforded to property or persons*." With this definition in mind, we can operationalize guardianship as the use of self-protective behaviors by individuals, including weapon possession (e.g., carrying a knife or gun) and possession of body alarms or Mace (Tewksbury & Mustaine, 2003). There remains, however, a great deal of debate about the extent to which personal protection measures are consistent with the original concept of guardianship and reduced risk of victimization (see Wilcox et al., 2007; Reynald, 2009).

30.6 Current and Future Directions in Guardianship Research

One of the most obvious conclusions to be drawn from reviewing the development of the routine activity concept of guardianship is that this area of research is dominated by testing focused on guardianship by one type of guardian, against a particular type of crime. Research on guardianship has tended to concentrate predominantly on residents as guardians, and on guardianship against property crime. More recent scholarship on guardianship has extended this body of research by examining how guardianship functions in the context of other types of crime, including sexual offenses and cybercrime. Cook and Reynald (2016) discuss research on the role of guardians in preventing, disrupting, and reducing the severity of sexual offenses against adult women. They explain that existing research shows that the likelihood and type of intervention by available guardians vary across situational contexts. Moreover, trends in the characteristics of available and active guardians in these crime situations point to the importance of individual characteristics such as age, and most significantly gender, in the willingness to intervene. These individual factors also affect guardians' perceptions of their capability to intervene in different situational contexts.

Beauregard and Leclerc (2007) found that one of the key factors identified by their Canadian sample of incarcerated serial sex offenders in assessing the risk of apprehension was the presence/absence of capable guardians who were near the crime scene and could interfere with the completion of the offense. In another study that focused specifically on the effect of guardianship on the severity of child sexual abuse, Leclerc, Smallbone, and Wortley (2013) reported that the presence of a guardian reduced the risk of sexual penetration of victims by 86%. These data were acquired from a survey completed by 87 adult male offenders in Queensland, Australia, who were incarcerated for committing a sexual offense against a child under the age of 16. The aforementioned studies are examples of a small but growing body of research that examines the effectiveness of guardianship as a prevention technique against sexual offending.

Like research on sexual offenses, research on cybercrime has recently begun to explore how guardianship functions in the cybercontext. In the first empirical analysis of guardianship in cyberspace against cyberabuse, Vakhitova and Reynald (2014) found that cyberguardianship against cyberabuse functions similarly to guardianship against property crime in the terrestrial context. Akin to the results found in Reynald's (2010) interview study with available guardians, Vakhitova and Reynald's (2014) survey of 650 Australian Internet and social media users revealed that contextual awareness of cyberspace was predictive of reported witnessing and intervening to disrupt cyberabuse events. Moreover, the results of this study revealed that prior victimization was the strongest predictor of witnessing and intervening to disrupt cyberabuse incidents. This is the first empirical study to establish an association between prior victimization and guardianship behavior.

In addition to examining guardianship against different types of crime, emerging guardianship research has also employed new ways of measuring guardianship that will aid in further developing the theoretical foundations of the concept through triangulation of findings using a range of different measurement methods. Results from the observational and interview GIA studies (Reynald 2009, 2010, 2011a) revealed patterns in when, where, and under what circumstances available guardians are likely to exercise guardianship behaviors to prevent crime or disrupt a crime in progress. The results from these studies also highlight the value of available guardians as units of analysis, as they hold vital information about the processes involved in active guardianship.

The new guardianship survey method was designed to access self-reports of guardianship behavior patterns from residents themselves. This is the first survey that asks residents about how often they are available at home at four different time periods across seven days of the week, and about crime-related events they witnessed as third parties on their street and how they responded to these events. Additionally, the survey measures factors that previous research has shown to be associated with guardianship, including questions about residents' sense of responsibility for guardians, their relationship with their neighbors, and their perceptions of police (see Reynald, 2011c, 2012; Reynald & Elffers, 2015; Reynald & Moir, in preparation). Thus far, the survey has been fielded in the Netherlands and Australia. The advantages of using the survey to supplement the GIA measures are that a much larger sample of potential guardians were accessed, and these samples were representative of the general population in the countries in which they were fielded. Most importantly, these survey findings help to fortify the knowledge base we have about how guardianship functions in residential places (Reynald & Elffers, 2015). Reynald and Elffers (2015), for instance, compared self-report guardianship measures of availability and supervision habits with traditionally used proxy measures of guardianship, including homeownership, number of household members, and so on. They found that availability and supervision are not well approximated by these proxy measures. Reynald and Moir (in preparation) turned their attention to the underexplored role of individual factors in explaining supervision behavior by guardians, and they found that factors like residents' perceptions of crime, sense of responsibility for guarding, security training, and national security values positively predict supervision intensity.

Taken together, these new avenues of guardianship research promise to address some of the major gaps that exist in this body of literature by exploring the role of individual factors in supplementing the traditional focus on environmental factors, as well as exploring how guardianship functions in different domains and contexts. Further research is still required to elucidate the role that individual factors play in explaining guardianship behavior, with a view to clarifying our knowledge about how the interaction between the individual and the situation determines guardianship outcomes as they relate to crime control.

References

Beauregard, E., & Leclerc, B. (2007). An application of the rational choice approach to the offending process of sex offenders: A closer look at the decision making. *Sex Abuse*, 19: 115–133.

Bennett, T., & Wright, R. (1984). *Burglars on Burglary: Prevention and the Offender*. Aldershot: Gower.

Brown, B. B., & Bentley, D. L. (1993). Residential burglars judge risk: The role of territoriality. *Journal of Environmental Psychology*, 13, 51–61.

Clarke, R. V. (1992). *Situational Crime Prevention: Successful Case Studies*. Albany, NY: Harrow and Heston.

Clarke, R. V. (1997). *Situational Crime Prevention: Successful Case Studies*, 2nd ed. Albany, NY: Harrow and Heston.

Clarke, R. V., & Eck, J. (2003). *Become a Problem-Solving Crime Analyst: In 55 Small Steps*. London: Jill Dando Institute of Crime Science, University College London.

Cohen, L. E., & Felson, M. (1979). Social change and crime rate trends: A routine activity approach. *American Sociological Review*, 44(4), 588–608.

Cook, A., & Reynald, D. M. (2016). Guardianship against sexual offences: Exploring the role of gender in intervention. *Journal of Contemporary Criminal Justice*, 26(2), 98–114.

Eck, J. E. (1994). *Drug Markets and Drug Places: A Case-Control Study of the Spatial Structure of Illicit Drug Dealing*. PhD dissertation, University of Maryland, College Park.

Felson, M. (1995). "Those Who Discourage Crime." In J. E. Eck & D. Weisburd (Eds.), *Crime and Place*, 53–66, vol. 4 of *Crime Prevention Studies*. Monsey, NY: Criminal Justice Press.

Felson, M. (2006). *Crime and Nature*. Thousand Oaks, CA: Sage.

Felson, M., & Cohen, L. E. (1980). Human ecology and crime: A routine activity approach. *Human Ecology*, 8(4), 389–406.

Freudenburg, W. R. (1986). The density of acquaintanceship: An overlooked variable in community research? *American Journal of Sociology*, 92(1), 27–63.

Garofalo, J., & Clark, D. (1992). Guardianship and residential burglary. *Justice Quarterly*, 9(3), 443–463.

Hindelang, M. J., Gottfredson, M. R., & Garofalo, J. (1978). *Victims of Personal Crime: An Empirical Foundation for a Theory of Personal Victimization*. Cambridge, MA: Ballinger.

Hollis-Peel, M. E., & Welsh, B. C. (2014). What makes a guardian capable? A test of guardianship in action. *Security Journal*, 27(3), 320–337.

Jacobs, J. (1961). *The Death and Life of Great American Cities*. New York: Random House.

Leclerc, B., Smallbone, S., & Wortley, R. (2013). Prevention nearby: The influence of the presence of a potential guardian on the severity of child sexual abuse. *Sexual Abuse*. doi: 10.1177/1079063213504594.

Miethe, T. D., & Meier, R. F. (1994). *Crime and Its Social Context: Toward an Integrated Theory of Offenders, Victims and Situations*. Albany: State University of New York Press.

Miethe, T. D., Stafford, M. C., & Sloane, D. (1990). Lifestyle changes and risks of criminal victimization. *Journal of Quantitative Criminology* 6(4), 357–376.

Mustaine, E. E., & Tewksbury, R. (1998). Predicting risks of larceny theft victimization: A routine activity analysis using refined lifestyle measures. *Criminology*, 36, 829–858.

Newman, O. (1972). *Defensible Space: Crime Prevention through Urban Design*. New York: Macmillan.

Reynald, D. M. (2009). Guardianship in action: Developing a new tool for measurement. *Crime Prevention and Community Safety*, 11(1), 1–20.

Reynald, D. M. (2010). Guardians on guardianship: Factors affecting the willingness to monitor, the ability to detect potential offenders & the willingness to intervene. *Journal of Research in Crime and Delinquency*, 47(3), 358–390.

Reynald, D. M. (2011a). Factors associated with the guardianship of places: Assessing the relative importance of the spatio-physical and socio-demographic contexts in generating opportunities for capable guardianship. *Journal of Research in Crime and Delinquency*, 48(1), 110–142.

Reynald, D. M. (2011b). *Guarding against Crime: Measuring Guardianship within Routine Activity Theory*. Surrey: Ashgate.

Reynald, D. M. (2011c). The International Guardianship Survey: First results from the Netherlands. Paper presented at the 67th Annual American Society of Criminology Meeting, Washington, DC, 16–19 November.

Reynald, D. M. (2012). The Guardianship Survey: Exploring the differences between silent versus active crime witnesses. Paper presented at the 68th Annual American Society of Criminology Meeting, Chicago, IL, 14–17 November.

Reynald, D. M. (2014). Informal guardianship. In G. J. N Bruinsma & D. L. Weisburd (Eds.), *Encyclopedia of Criminology and Criminal Justice*. New York: Springer.

Reynald, D. M., & Elffers, H. (2015). The routine activity of guardianship. *Crime Prevention and Community Safety*, 17, 211–232.

Reynald, D. M., & Moir, E. C. (in preparation). Who is watching: Exploring individual factors that explain supervision patterns among residential guardians.

Sampson, R. J., & Groves, B. W. (1989). Community structure and crime: testing social-disorganization theory. *American Journal of Sociology*, 94(4), 774–802.

Sampson, R. J., Raudenbush, S. W., & Earls, F. (1997). Neighbourhoods and violent crime: A multilevel study of collective efficacy. *Science*, 277(5328), 918–924.

Skogan, W. G. (1990). *Disorder and Decline*. New York: Free Press.

Taylor, R. B., Koons, B., Kurtz, E., Greene, J., & Perkins, D. (1995). Street blocks with more nonresidential land use have more physical deterioration: Evidence from Baltimore and Philadelphia. *Urban Affairs Review*, 30, 120–136.

Tewksbury, R. A., & Mustaine, E. E. (2003). College students' lifestyles and self-protective behaviors: Further consideration of the guardianship concept in routine activity theory. *Criminal Justice and Behavior*, 30(3): 302–327.

Vakhitova, Z. I., & Reynald, D. M. (2014). Cyberguardians: An empirical study of guardianship against cyber abuse. *International Journal of Cyber Criminology*, 8(2), 156–171.

Welsh, B. C., Braga, A. A., & Bruinsma, G. J. N. (2015). Reimagining broken windows: From theory to policy. *Journal of Research in Crime and Delinquency*, 52(4), 447–463.

Welsh, B. C., & Farrington, D. P. (2009). *Making Public Places Safer: Surveillance and Prevention.* Oxford: Oxford University Press.

Wilcox, P., Madensen, T. D., & Tillyer, M. S. (2007). Guardianship in context: Implications for burglary victimization risk & prevention. *Criminology* 45(4), 771–803.

Wilson, J. Q., & Kelling, G. (1982). Broken windows: The police and neighborhood safety. *Atlantic Monthly*, 249, 29–38.

Xie, Min, & McDowall, David. (2008). The effects of residential turnover on household victimization. *Criminology*, 46(3), 539–575.

CHAPTER 31

MOBILITY AND LOCATION CHOICE OF OFFENDERS

WIM BERNASCO

31.1 Introduction

Environmental criminology tends to focus on things—the built environment, neighborhoods, crimes, disorder—more than on people. This chapter is about where crime takes place, but its focus will not be on places but on people. It takes an offender perspective not by relying on the personal accounts of offenders, but by analyzing the main topics and questions about offender mobility and crime location choice in terms of individual motivations, resources, constraints, and decisions.

The chapter sets out with a brief overview of the four main frameworks that have been used to theorize offender mobility and crime location choice. This overview is followed by a characterization of general human mobility as a series of cyclical movements between a limited set of anchor points, and a review of two research initiatives that collected detailed spatial and temporal information on offender mobility. The subsequent section addresses the extent to which offenders plan and prepare their crimes. The two sections that follow discuss empirical findings on two essential elements of mobility in general and criminal mobility in particular: distance and direction. The chapter subsequently discusses two core elements in crime pattern theory, namely the facilities that attract offenders and offenses (crime generators and attractors) and awareness space. These two elements come together in the section on crime location choice, which is followed by a section on the role of offenders' previous crime locations in subsequent crime locations choices. The last section discusses the spatial unit of analysis in offender mobility and location choice.

Inevitably, the present text overlaps to some extent with recent reviews that cover many of the same materials. Bernasco (2014) reviews theories, data, and methods used in the study of crime journeys. He applies the vocabulary of transportation research to characterize the mobility of offenders in relation to the crimes they commit. Crime location choice is addressed in three recent reviews (Bernasco and Ruiter 2014; Ruiter 2017; Townsley 2017). Ruiter (2017) specifically covers temporal variability in crime, whereas Townsley (2017) includes a comprehensive review of the journey-to-crime literature. Compared to these prior texts, the present chapter covers a more diverse array of topics but is more concise about each of them.

31.2 Theories

The four theoretical approaches most relevant for understanding offender mobility and crime location choice are *rational choice, time geography, routine activity*, and *crime pattern theory*. Rational choice has been applied to virtually all human behavior, including habitual and subconscious forms of behavior. Time geography addresses human spatial behavior, including individual and collective patterns of movement, concentration, and dispersion. Routine activity and crime pattern theory have been developed to specifically explain aspects of criminal behavior. The common feature of these four theories is that their explanations focus on how opportunities and constraints shape human behavior, while they are silent on how motivations and preferences emerge and develop. Motivation is considered given and not a target of explanation. A brief sketch of the main features of each of the four theories follows.

Rational choice theory is a microeconomic theory that claims that human choices are purposeful and that they are best understood by assuming that given the constraints they face, individuals make decisions that maximize their utility. Utility is a concept that includes not only material incentives, like money and physical comfort, but also immaterial incentives like social status. Becker (1968) introduced the economic approach to the analysis of crime and law enforcement, and applied it to the effects of sanction severity and certainty on crime. Rational choice accounts of criminal *location choice* suggest that in general, offenders choose targets and target locations that maximize benefits and minimize costs and risks (Bernasco and Nieuwbeerta 2005; Cornish and Clarke 1986). For example, burglars would be expected to prefer properties that suggests affluence, but only if they are unoccupied and easy to enter. Street robbers would be expected to prefer wealthy-looking victims but only those that do not carry a weapon or would be expected to resist a robbery attempt for other reasons. According to rational choice theory, offenders perpetrate crimes near their homes instead of further away, because it minimizes travel costs. Optimal foraging theory, a theory from behavioral ecology, is essentially a rational choice theory of foraging, and has also been applied to the mobility and crime location choice of offenders (Bernasco 2009; Felson 2006; Johnson 2014).

Time geography (Hägerstrand 1970; Miller 2005) is a perspective on human geography that emphasizes the capability, coupling, and authority constraints humans face when they engage in activities across time and space. *Capability constraints* include biological constraints (e.g., need to sleep), but also technological constraints such as a lack of transportation tools. For example, young people cannot drive a car or motorbike, and some lack financial resources for public transport. *Coupling constraints* require people to be at specific places at specific times because of the social roles they fulfill. For example, most people have fixed school hours or work schedules. *Authority constraints* are limits to accessibility because place owners do not allow access. The freedom of individuals to be where and when they want is restricted by these three types of constraints. These constraints also apply to humans in their roles as offenders and victims of crime, and can therefore be used to help understand crime patterns (Ratcliffe 2006).

The geometry of crime is an element of *crime pattern theory* (Brantingham and Brantingham 1991, 2008), and deals specifically with the issue of where crimes are committed. It states that for a crime to be perpetrated at a certain location, two conditions are necessary: the place must provide an opportunity for crime, and the prospective offender must be aware of the existence of the place and the opportunity. Thus, where spatial awareness and criminal opportunities overlap, crime becomes a possibility. An offender's awareness space is developed through repeated experience. It has been demonstrated empirically that when they commit crimes, offenders have a tendency to select their current or prior neighborhoods of residence and areas where they previously offended (Lammers, Menting, Ruiter, et al. 2015).

Routine activity theory is based on the premise that a necessary and sufficient condition for (predatory) crime to take place is the convergence in time and space of a motivated offender and a suitable and unguarded victim. The theory was originally developed to explain macro-level phenomena (Cohen and Felson 1979), but it has mostly been applied at meso level (e.g., analyzing crime rate variations between streets) and micro level (e.g., analyzing victimization rate variability between individuals). Its premises correspond to those of crime pattern theory, but it does not address offender cognitions.

Three of these four theories—space-time geography, routine activity, and crime pattern theory—go hand in hand and are complementary rather than incompatible. Often rational choice theory is also seen as compatible with the other three. This leads to a polite but somewhat unproductive silence. An important difference between rational choice theory and the other three theories is that in rational choice theory the individual has an important role in shaping outcomes, whereas the other theories suggest that their choices are determined by their exposure to external forces (capable guardianship, capability constraints, criminal opportunities) outside their sphere of control.

31.3 Human Mobility

Mobility—movement across space—is usually motivated by the wish to be elsewhere. People do not normally derive intrinsic pleasure from travel but from reaching their destination (Bhat and Koppelman 1999). Admittedly hikers and bikers move around for pleasure or exercise, truck drivers and flight attendants travel as part of their work, and dog owners walk their dog because they have to. But most of the time people travel because it allows them to perform activities (e.g., work, sleep, leisure, or perpetrate a crime) that require them to relocate because these activities are distributed in space.

Most species in the animal kingdom have no homes. Some have nests while breeding and nursing offspring, but most species spend their lives wandering. Their movements, like those of humans, are also driven by needs that are distributed in space (e.g., escape danger, find food), but because they have no homes their whereabouts are difficult to predict, and are best described by mathematical models of random walks, such as Brownian motion and Lévy flights (Humphries, Queiroz, Dyer, et al. 2010). We humans do have homes, and this is reflected in our spatial behavior. Because we return to our homes at least once per day to sleep, our homes are the spatial centers of our activities.

The central role of home in human mobility is confirmed by the results of recent studies that utilized large volumes of detailed data from mobile phones. Of particular interest are studies that tracked the movements of individual mobile phones (and thus people) repeatedly or semicontinuously over multiple days or weeks, allowing researchers to explore patterns in human mobility (Gonzalez, Hidalgo, and Barabasi 2008; Hidalgo and Rodriguez-Sickert 2008; Julián, Marta, Pu, et al. 2008; Padgham 2012; Simini, Gonzalez, Maritan, et al. 2012; Song, Qu, Blumm, et al. 2010). This body of literature has concluded that the spatial behavior of human individuals is regular and thus predictable. The reason is that humans tend to travel between a limited number of highly frequented nodes such as home, work, and school, and because these patterns of recurrent mobility follow daily and weekly rhythms. Knowing that I was at work today at 9:00 makes it likely that I will also be at work at 9:00 tomorrow and next week. The fact that human activity patterns are governed by daily and weekly time cycles had been observed already in prior transportation research (Gärling and Axhausen 2003; Hanson and Huff 1988).

31.4 Offender Mobility

Although the studies discussed in the previous section provide insights in general human mobility, they do not inform us about the mobility of offenders specifically. They tell us neither about offenders' mobility during legal activities, nor about their whereabouts immediately before, during, and after offending. Data on offender mobility are typically restricted to where they live and where they offend. A few ethnographic studies on burglary recorded interesting and useful information on the journey to crime (e.g., Rengert and Wasilchick 2000), but their results have not been extensively and systematically analyzed.

As more detailed data on offender mobility are very rare, two recent research initiatives are worth discussion here. They both collected data on the mobility of offenders at detailed spatial and temporal resolutions.

Rossmo, Lu, and Fang (2012) used data of 17 parolees who committed an offense while participating in an electronic monitoring and global positioning system (GPS) program that continuously tracked their whereabouts 24/7 (obviously with the aim of recidivism prevention). The parolees' travel over a period of at least eight days was recorded, and allowed the authors to analyze the movement patterns of offenders before, during, and after offending. It also allowed them to assess whether these patterns were different from movement patterns on nonoffending days. The authors describe these movements using three-dimensional space-time maps that display the movement tracks of individual parolees. Some offenders perpetrated the crime on days that, as far as their travel behavior was concerned, appeared the same as any other day. But for others, their travel behaviors during the days preceding the crime clearly suggest that they were preparing it. One sexual offender, for example, appeared to hang around the location where he would commit the crime the next days. Although this study is technically and conceptually innovative, its results are only descriptive because of the small convenience sample it draws on.

As part of an ongoing panel study among a random sample of adolescents in Peterborough (United Kingdom), Wikström and colleagues (Wikström and Butterworth 2006; Wikström, Ceccato, Hardie, et al. 2010; Wikström, Oberwittler, Treiber, et al. 2012; see also Weerman, Hoeben, Bernasco, et al., Chapter 26 in this volume) developed a space-time budget instrument that was used to retrospectively reconstruct and record the whereabouts of the respondents during four recent days. The instrument consisted of an interview protocol with supporting materials. During the personal interview, activities of the respondent during four recent days (4 times 24 hours, including a Friday, a Saturday, and two other weekdays) were recorded. Detailed information was collected about the main activities of the adolescents for each hour of the day. The information recorded for every hour included the nature of the main activity (e.g., sports, learning, sleeping), the geographic location where it took place (using small spatial units of analysis known as output areas in the UK Census Geography), the function of the place where the activity was performed (e.g., home, school, shop, friend's home, bar), and any persons present in the setting (e.g., teacher, parent, peers). Examples of the simple questions that respondents were asked are "Where did that happen?"; "Who else was there?"; "What were you doing?" In addition, the interviewers always specifically asked whether at any time during that day the respondent had been involved in offending, whether she or he had used alcohol or used drugs, and whether she or he had carried a weapon. In sum, the space-time budget interview recorded detailed information about *where, when*, and *what* respondents were doing *with whom*, during four days of the week before the interview. The study also included a self-administered questionnaire with items measuring involvement in a variety of offense types during a period of 12 months, which allows researchers to distinguish offenders from nonoffenders. The space-time budget data make it possible both to analyze spatial behavior of offenders on routine nonoffending days and (for those reporting offending in the space-time budget interview) to analyze spatial behavior before and after offending, that is, their journey before and after crime. Space-time budget data have thus far been used in a limited number of studies.

Wikström et al. (2010) used space-time budget data from five sweeps of the Peterborough Adolescent and Young Adult Development Study (PADS+), a panel study among a cohort of young persons who were 11 years old when the study started. They noted that of the time spent awake, young people spend nearly half of their time in and in around their homes and just over a quarter of their time in and around their schools. They also found that delinquent and nondelinquent youth differed with respect to the time spent in criminogenic settings. Adolescents who spent more time unsupervised with peers reported significantly more delinquent behaviors.

A series of studies in The Hague, the Netherlands, used the space-time budget instrument to relate the content and the variability of adolescents' activities to a 20-item scale of delinquency measured in a self-report questionnaire. One study (Weerman et al. 2015) used the space-time budget instrument to investigate the specific conditions under which spending time with peers is conducive to delinquent behavior. The results demonstrated that the association between time with peers and delinquency varies strongly between conditions. Delinquency was positively related to time with peers when it was spent in public, without supervision, just socializing and with two or more peers. The relation was weak or nonsignificant, however, for time with peers "online" or by phone, supervised by adults, in nonpublic places, doing activities, and with only a single peer.

Another study (Bernasco, Bruinsma, Pauwels, et al. 2013) investigated the relation between adolescents' delinquency and the geographic, functional, and social diversity of the adolescents' activities, that is, whether their activities were at different locations, in different types of places, and with different people. The results demonstrated that diversity was positively related to delinquency. For geographic and functional setting diversity, but not social diversity, a substantial part of the positive association was independent of gender, age, and other potentially confounding variables.

Two other studies (Hoeben and Weerman 2014, 2016) used the space-time budget instrument to investigate in detail the relation between delinquency and adolescents' amount of time spent unstructured socializing with peers.

The space-time budget interview also registers offending behavior during the four days during which activities are recorded hour by hour. The offenses reported by the respondents can therefore be linked directly to particular days, locations, times, and situations. Two studies used this feature to more precisely explore the situational correlates of offending, that is, the specific conditions that facilitate or inhibit offending behavior.

Bernasco, Ruiter, Bruinsma, et al. (2013) used a fixed effect regression model to compare characteristics of 104 offending situations with characteristics of nonoffending situations of the same respondents. They demonstrated that presence of peers, absence of adults, unstructured activity, presence in public space, and alcohol use were highly predictive of offending.

Wikström et al. (2010) considered the modifying role of the individual's criminal propensity, which was defined as a combination of crime-prone moral attitudes and weak self-control. They demonstrated that a low crime propensity (crime-averse morality and strong ability to exercise self-control) makes adolescents almost immune to the situational influence of criminogenic settings, whereas a having a high criminal propensity makes them extra vulnerable.

31.5 Premeditation, Search, Serendipity, and Coincidence

There are many different ways to find a crime target. An important dimension for differentiation is the level of premeditation involved (Figure 31.1). This dimension not only divides theories but is also relevant for crime prevention.

In a sample of burglars, Bennett and Wright (1984) distinguish three categories, based on the amount of premeditation that would typically be involved in their burglaries. One category, "planners," consists of offenders who would plan and prepare a burglary for a period of time, possibly weeks. Their planning would involve information collection and a comparison of alternative targets. The way they select targets is best described by rational choice theory.

At the other extreme are "opportunists," who find a target without searching one. For them, the decision to offend is spontaneous and triggered by noticing a suitable target. Their choice of target is unprepared and has a large random component. This process of selecting targets is best described by routine activity theory.

In terms of premeditation, a middle category is "searchers," who are motivated for crime and looking for an opportunity, but have not yet selected a suitable target. These three categories distinguished by Bennett and Wright (1984) are very similar to the "planning offender," "wandering offender," and "haphazard offender" described by Elffers (2004).

Based on interviews with active robbers, Jacobs (2010) describes a range of situations between opportunistic target selection (labeled "pure serendipity") and situations where offenders create situations where crime opportunities are likely to arise ("manufactured serendipity").

The level of premeditation has implications for how offenders relate to the place of the crime. Planners and searchers are at the crime site to commit a crime because that is where they found their chosen target. The planned crime is why they are there. For opportunists and those who encounter a target through manufactured serendipity, the crime was not the main reason for being at the crime site. Rather, they were involved in legal activities when they encountered a seduction or a provocation that made them perpetrate the crime.

There are a few empirical studies on burglars and robbers that inform us about what offenders were after when they ended up committing a crime. Fernandez, Clare, and

FIGURE 31.1 Levels of premeditation in target search

Morgan (2006) asked a sample of 243 incarcerated Australian burglars why they were in the area when they committed the burglary. Only 47% answered they were there with the purpose of perpetrating a burglary. The others answered they were there to visit friends, to shop, by chance, or because the place was near their home.

Feeney (1986) found that of the 30% of 113 robbers who committed a robbery in a town other than where they lived, only half had gone there with the intention of committing a robbery. The other half were there to visit friends or relatives, or were just passing by. Other research on robbery confirms that many robberies feature minimal planning (Lindegaard, Bernasco, and Jacques 2015; Wright and Decker 1997; Wright, Brookman, and Bennett 2006).

Given that burglary and robbery are usually considered to involve more deliberation and planning than many other types of crime (Rhodes and Conly 1981: 178), it is reasonable to assume that most crime-related mobility is initiated with an intention other than committing a crime. Pure or manufactured serendipity is more common than search and premeditation. As is discussed in the next section, this observation may require some revisions to common interpretations of the empirical phenomenon of distance decay.

31.6 Distance

Since White (1932), many dozens of studies on the home-crime distance have consistently demonstrated that most offenders commit crimes within a short distance from where they live, and that the frequency of crimes decreases as the distance from home increases. The latter finding is labeled "distance decay." Reviews of this literature include Wiles and Costello (2000) on property crime and Beauregard, Proulx, and Rossmo (2005) on sexual offending. Adolescents travel shorter distances (Levine and Lee 2013), although a recent large-scale study established the relation between age and distance to be inversely U-shaped (Andresen, Frank, and Felson 2014). Distances to property crimes are generally larger than distances to violent crimes (Baldwin and Bottoms 1976; Hesseling 1992). A handful of studies have challenged the distance decay finding by pointing to possible geographic selection effects overrepresenting local offenders (Siegel 2014; Van Daele, Vander Beken, and Bruinsma 2012). Another study has challenged the distance decay finding on methodological grounds, arguing that the finding only applies to a minority of persistent offenders when the analysis takes into account that in the data structure crime trips are nested in offenders (Townsley and Sidebottom 2010).

Studies that document the home-crime distance are often labeled "journey-to-crime studies," which is a somewhat misleading label because it suggests that all crimes are premeditated, and that all crime locations have been deliberately chosen.

The distance decay phenomenon can be observed in numerous phenomena related to mobility. The interpretation of the distance decay pattern is that distance is a friction or a barrier between two places, because costs are involved in moving persons and objects from one place to the other. When selecting a place to pursue an activity, and having available two equally attractive alternatives, people would generally prefer the one that takes least time and effort to arrive at. This argument of energy conservation is embodied in Zipf's law, which states that any organism will take the path of least effort to reach a given goal (Zipf 1949). It can be interpreted to mean that when offenders decide to commit a crime, they will consider the distances to each of the alternative crime sites and choose the site that is most easy to reach. One underlying assumption of linking Zipf's law to distance decay is that offenders are at home when they decide to commit a crime.

If we accept the conclusion of the previous section that many journeys during which a crime is committed were not initiated with that intention, the interpretation that "offenders prefer nearby targets over distant targets" may not correctly describe the cause of the distance decay phenomenon. Rather, according to Zipf's law, people prefer nearby locations over distant ones for performing any given activity, not only for perpetrating crime. The distance decay pattern in crime may thus often be simply the logical consequence of the presence of a distance decay pattern in all human activity (Gonzalez et al. 2008; Pappalardo, Simini, Rinzivillo, et al. 2015).

An activity-corrected *criminal* distance decay would exist if the distance to crime were smaller than the offenders' average distance to their homes over a full day. It would suggest that individuals are more likely to offend when they are near home than when they are far away from home, and vice versa. This hypothesis could be tested, but has not been tested, with the space-time path data of offending parolees (Rossmo et al. 2012) and those of the space-time budget instrument (Wikström et al. 2012).

It has been suggested that the distance decay pattern in crime includes a "buffer zone," an area around the offender's residence where offenders are less likely to commit crimes for fear of being recognized (Rossmo 2000). There is, however, little empirical evidence to support this claim (Canter and Gregory 1994; Kent, Leitner, and Curtis 2006; LeBeau 1987).

The limiting role of distance in crime is also explored in studies of criminal location choice (see later in this chapter), where distance is one among multiple independent variables, and the location of the crime is the dependent variable. This design reflects the possibility that in choosing a location for a planned activity, people weight multiple criteria rather than focus on a single characteristic like distance. Without exception the location choice studies demonstrate that the probability of committing a crime at a certain location decreases with the distance of that location from the offender's home.

31.7 Directionality

While the distance of crime journeys has been extensively studied, their direction has received much less attention. Although arguably less relevant than crime trip destinations or distances, directions may inform us about offenders' spatial behavior in two ways.

First, we can assess to what extent serial offenders tend to travel in the same or similar directions each time they commit a crime. A directionally consistent offender always moves in the same direction, whereas a directionally inconsistent offender takes a different direction each time. Several studies have been devoted to defining a measure of directional consistency, assessing directional consistency, and linking it to other offender characteristics (Constanzo, Halperin, and Gale 1996; Frank, Andresen, and Brantingham 2013; Frank, Andresen, and Brantingham 2012; Iwanski, Frank, Dabbaghian, et al. 2011; Kocsis, Cooksey, Irwin, et al. 2002; Van Daele and Bernasco 2012).

A more complicated point is made in the work by Frank and colleagues (Frank, Dabbaghian, Singh, et al. 2011; Frank, Andresen, Cheng, et al. 2011; Frank et al. 2012). In a series of papers based on the geometry of crime (Brantingham and Brantingham 1991), they develop the Directionality-based Activity Space Creator (DASC), which is a method to establish areas within a city where offenders routinely go as part of their legal activities.

The DASC method is based on the assumption that when an offender commits a crime, the location of the crime lies on the path that she or he is taking from home toward some destination that is also visited by many other people (including other offenders). Thus, if we extend the path from home to the crime location, we should expect to cross at some point the planned destination of the offender's journey. Next, if we extend the path of all offenders in a city, we should expect to find crime attractors and crime generators at the points of intersection of these paths. At the core of the method is the idea that where people live and where they commit crime may tell us something about where they were heading when the crime took place, especially if we combine this information with the same information from other offenders.

31.8 Crime Attractors and Generators

What distinguishes routine activity theory and crime pattern theory most from other criminological theories is their emphasis on the ways in which criminal behavior is similar to and connected to ordinary human activities. Both stipulate that crime is most likely to take place where and when people congregate in large numbers, which in turn is a function of aggregated patterns of individual human movements between the locations where they sleep, eat, work, learn, exercise, and socialize (their activity nodes).

Crime pattern theory stipulates that certain activity nodes, *crime generators* and *crime attractors*, are characterized by elevated crime rates. The category of crime generators is the most generic one:

> Crime generators are particular nodal areas to which large numbers of people are attracted for reasons unrelated to any particular level of criminal motivation they might have or the particular crime they might end up committing . . .. Crime

> generators produce crime by creating particular times and places that provide appropriate concentrations of people and other targets in settings that are conducive to particular types of criminal acts. Mixed into the people gathered at generator locations are some potential offenders with sufficient general levels of criminal readiness that although they did not come to the area with the explicit intent of doing a crime, they notice and exploit criminal opportunities as presented (either immediately or on a subsequent occasion). (Brantingham and Brantingham 1995: 8)

Crime generators are thus conducive both to opportunistic and to premeditated crime. If individuals immediately reap the coincidental opportunities they are exposed to during their legal activities at the crime generator, their crimes are opportunistic. However, their crime is planned or premediated if they return to the crime generator at a later occasion, in order to commit a crime after having spotted the criminal opportunity during a prior visit. This implies that the crime-generating effects of crime generators are not necessarily limited to the times that they are open to the public. The findings of recent research on temporal variations in crime near crime generators show that many generators attract crime when they are closed (Haberman and Ratcliffe 2015), suggesting that this attraction is caused by offenders who return to exploit opportunities observed during the opening hours of the facilities.

Crime attractors are a more specific category of nodes with elevated levels of crime:

> Crime attractors are particular places, areas, neighborhoods, districts which create well-known criminal opportunities to which strongly motivated, intending criminal offenders are attracted because of the known opportunities for particular types of crime. Examples might include bar districts; prostitution areas; drug markets; large shopping malls, particularly those near major public transit exchanges; large, insecure parking lots in business or commercial areas. (Brantingham and Brantingham 1995: 7)

The evidence demonstrating that certain places and facilities have elevated crime levels is massive. Facilities that have been associated with increased crime levels are, to mention a few, schools (Roncek and LoBosco 1983; Roncek and Faggiani 1985), retail businesses (Bernasco and Block 2011), bars and other alcohol outlets (Groff 2011; McCord and Ratcliffe 2007; Ratcliffe 2012), and transit stations (Block and Block 1999; Ceccato and Uittenbogaard 2014; Irvin-Erickson and La Vigne 2015). Flows of movement toward and away from these businesses and facilities typically results in concentrations of activity in the immediate vicinity, and part of the literature explores the extent to which elevated crime levels of facilities spill over to nearby areas (Bernasco and Block 2011; Groff 2011; Ratcliffe 2012).

31.9 Awareness Space

Based on the work of Lynch (1960), crime pattern theory assumes that offenders, like everybody else, learn about their environment in going about their normal legitimate everyday activities. An *activity node* is a place where an individual normally performs activities for more than a trivial amount of time. Common activity nodes are a home, a workplace, a shopping area, places for structured leisure activities, and the homes of family and friends. *Paths* are the routes that people take when they move from one node to the other. Nodes and paths together form an individual's *activity space*. The *awareness space* is the slightly larger area that includes places that are within visual range of the activity space (Brantingham and Brantingham 2008).

The empirical finding that much crime takes place in the proximity of the offender's home has been explained by the principle of least effort (see section on distance). Another possible explanation is that offenders are more familiar with the area around their home, which makes it easier to assess vulnerability and profitability of targets, risk of apprehension, and other strategically important information about committing crimes. Still another explanation—one that does not depend on any premeditation or other cognitive activity on the offenders' part—is that offenders just spend more time in the proximity of their home environments.

31.10 Crime Location Choice

Crime generators and crime attractors can help us understand and predict aggregate spatial crime patterns, but their role is more limited when it comes to explaining where specific individuals offend. The purpose of studying where specific individuals commit crimes is that it allows more targeted tests of one of the basic propositions of crime pattern theory, the proposition that offenders commit crimes at the places where their awareness space overlaps with criminal opportunities.

This dual explanatory structure of crime pattern theory (criminal opportunity and awareness space) is reflected in the combination of generic and personal location characteristics included in crime location studies. First, location choice studies include location characteristics that reflect criminal opportunities for every potential offender. Typically, these generic opportunities are measured by the presence of crime attractors and crime generators. For example, Bernasco, Block, and Ruiter (2013) demonstrated that offenders are more likely to commit street robberies near businesses and facilities where cash transfers are common (including both businesses like bars and pawnshops and illegal businesses like drug-dealing and prostitution areas) and near transit stations.

Location choice studies typically also include locations that are specific to individual offenders because these locations are (proxy) measures of their activity space. All location choice studies have included offenders' home addresses, and all have shown that the farther a potential crime location is from the offender's home, the less likely it will be selected as a target (e.g., Baudains, Braithwaite, and Johnson 2013; Bernasco and Block 2009; Clare, Fernandez, and Morgan 2009). Bernasco (2010) collected data on the residential histories of burglars in The Hague, the Netherlands, and demonstrated that offenders not only commit burglaries near their current residence, but also have a tendency to commit them near their former homes, in particular if they lived more than two years in the former residence and if they have recently left. Nearly identical results were reported by Bernasco and Kooistra (2010) in a study on commercial robbers in the Netherlands.

In addition, offenders tend to select targets that are relatively easy to access from where they live, so that major obstacles function as barriers to criminal mobility. For example, offenders are less likely to target areas that are separated by a river from their own area of residence (Baudains et al. 2013; Clare et al. 2009). In a similar vein, train and street networks can function as connectors or bridges that facilitate criminal mobility. Clare et al. (2009) showed that burglars in Perth were more likely to target areas that were connected by a train line to their own area of residence, and Johnson and Summers (2015) demonstrated that theft from vehicles in the county of Dorset (UK) was most likely in neighborhoods that were easily accessible via the street network from the offenders' home areas. These findings on barriers and connectors do not necessarily mean that the infrastructures directly restrict or facilitate the journey to crime. As Clare et al. (2009) note, few burglars travel by train to their target. Barriers and connectors can also have an effect because over the long term they affect the offenders' routine travel and thus their awareness space.

The residences of family members are possibly also part of the offenders' awareness spaces. After accounting for confounding factors (including the offenders' own current and former residences), it has indeed been shown that a location is more likely to be selected by an offender if his or her parents, siblings, or children live or previously lived at the location (Menting, Lammers, Ruiter, et al. 2016). Finally, offenders' prior crime locations have arguably also become part of their awareness spaces. Two studies (Bernasco, Johnson, and Ruiter 2015; Lammers et al. 2015) that are discussed in more detail in the next section find support for the claim that offenders are more likely to select locations where they have previously offended.

The results of crime location choice studies have generally demonstrated that the explanatory power of the (individual) awareness space measures is much greater than the explanatory power of the generic measures (Ruiter 2017).

Crime location choice studies apply the economic theory of random utility maximization (RUM) to explain and predict at which locations offenders perpetrate crimes. The "locations" can be as large as neighborhoods (e.g., Bernasco and Block 2009), but can also be census blocks (Bernasco, Ruiter, Bruinsma et al. 2013) or even individual properties (Vandeviver, Neutens, van Daele, et al. 2015). The RUM theory assumes that offenders have complete knowledge of the existence and attributes of all alternatives, and that they offend at the location that maximizes their expected benefits. A stylized example is an offender's choice between areas that vary with respect to numbers of crime attractors, numbers of crime generators, and distance from the offender's home. The utility that the individual will derive from targeting area j is a linear function of its attributes:

$$U_{ij} = \alpha A_j + \gamma G_j + \delta D_{ij},$$

where U_{ij} is the utility that individual i will derive from committing a crime at location j, A_j and G_j measure the presence of crime attractors and crime generators respectively at location j, and D_{ij} is the distance between the residence of offender i and location j. The parameters α, γ, and δ are estimated on the basis of empirical data, and can be interpreted as the weights that offenders assign to the characteristics when deciding about their most preferred crime location. Note that crime attractor and generator characteristics A and G are generic because they only have a "location" subscript j, whereas the distance D is a location-specific individual characteristic because it includes both subscripts i and j.

Although crime location choice models are based on an econometric framework, their statistical implementation is strongly related to more common approaches in environmental criminology. Most importantly, any crime location choice model that only includes generic characteristics (the single-index crime attractors and crime generators in the above equation) is numerically completely equivalent with a Poisson model of aggregated crime counts of the same data (Guimaraes, Figueirdo, and Woodward 2003), although the interpretations of the two models are different (Schmidheiny and Brülhart 2011): in the location choice framework the total volume of crime is fixed, and any changes in attributes will at most relocate crimes. In the Poisson framework the total volume of crime is not fixed, and changes in attributes may affect crime volumes.

31.11 Repeat Location Choice

Offenders need not only learn how to commit crimes, they must also learn where to do it. As is the case for most human behaviors, successful choices are likely to be repeated. It has been empirically demonstrated that when offenders commit crimes, they often do so at and near locations where they previously committed crimes. Furthermore, the effect of prior crimes is stronger the more crimes they committed near the location, is stronger the more recent the previous crime, and is also stronger if the previous crime was a similar type of crime (Bernasco et al. 2015; Lammers et al. 2015). These findings provide a mechanism that can explain the massive evidence for the phenomenon of repeat victimization (Pease 1998; see also Ignatans and Pease, in this volume) and the related phenomenon labeled "near repeat victimization" (Bowers and Johnson 2004; Townsley, Homel, and Chaseling 2003), "communicability of risk" (Johnson and Bowers 2004), "self-exiting point process" (Mohler, Short, Brantingham, et al. 2011), and "spatio-temporal interaction" (Grubesic and Mack 2008). Repeat victimization refers to the fact that in the wake of a crime, the target's risk of victimization is temporally elevated. Near repeat victimization refers to the extension of this elevated risk to targets nearby the original target. The risk decays over time, and in the case of near repeats also over space (Johnson, Bernasco, Bowers, et al. 2007). Empirical research on detected burglary cases has revealed that the same offenders are often involved in both initial and "near repeat" burglaries (Bernasco 2008; Everson and Pease 2001; Johnson, Summers, and Pease 2009).

31.12 Spatial Units of Analysis

During the past decades, the increasing availability of high-resolution spatial data on crime and other urban phenomena has boosted the use of small spatial units in theory and research. Since the classic works of Shaw and McKay ([1942] 1969) most ecological studies of crime and of criminal involvement have used the neighborhood as the main spatial unit of analysis. Neighborhoods are typically large-scale spatial entities where 3,000–10,000 people live. In the US context, neighborhoods correspond roughly to census tracts in urban environments.

Environmental criminologists have recognized that the choice of appropriate spatial units of analysis is important, but also that the choice should consider the theoretical perspective that guides the analysis, rather than only the availability of data or statistical models (Weisburd, Bruinsma, and Bernasco 2009).

Although the four theories that inspire environmental criminology do not strictly prescribe any particular spatial unit of analysis, the causal mechanisms proposed in crime pattern theory and routine activity theory generally seem to advocate the use of small spatial units of analysis, such as street blocks (Taylor 1997, 1998) or street segments (Weisburd, Bushway, Lum, et al. 2004) and "output areas" (comprising 300 residents on average) in the United Kingdom (Oberwittler and Wikström 2009).

Street segments come close to what environmental psychologists call a behavior setting: the part of the social and physical environment that individuals can perceive with their senses (Wikström 2006). Behavior settings are small because by definition they can be overseen and overheard with the senses. They will generally also be more homogeneous than larger spatial entities, such as census block groups or neighborhoods. Weisburd and colleagues have demonstrated in a number of studies (Steenbeek and Weisburd 2015; Weisburd, Groff, and Yang 2012; Weisburd 2015) that the concentration of crime in street segments or other microplaces is much stronger than at higher levels of aggregation such as neighborhoods. In the United Kingdom, the focus on street segments not only emphasizes small spatial units, but, inspired by space syntax theory (Hillier 2007), also stresses the role of street segments as the building blocks of street networks. Street networks channel human mobility and are therefore seen as important in the mobility and awareness space of offenders (Davies and Johnson 2015). A good example is the finding that cul-de-sacs have consistently lower burglary rates than other street segments (Johnson and Bowers 2010): because cul-de-sacs are almost exclusively used by those who live there, they and the properties located on them do not become part of the awareness space of other people, including many potential offenders.

31.13 Conclusion

Mobility and location choices of offenders have been analyzed theoretically and empirically with generic theories and methods that apply to all human mobility and all location choice. Obtaining reliable and valid information on these topics is difficult because many offenders are unwilling to share the details of their criminal actions with researchers, and also because police information systems often contain no information on the travel habits of offenders. A promising new development is the design and application of innovative data collection instruments (notably the space-time budget interview; apps with similar functions and with automated geo-tracking are currently being developed for smartphones).

A major conceptual difficulty for all research on criminal mobility and location choice appears to lie in the presumed motivation for mobility. Assumptions about why offenders travel seem to function as a watershed, both theoretically and empirically. They divide rational choice theory and crime location choice research on the one hand and crime pattern theory, routine activity theory, space-time geography, and empirical research on situational correlates of crime on the other hand. Rational choice theory as it is applied in location choice research assumes that crime is a planned action and that it forms the explicit motivation for travel (i.e., the term "journey to crime" underlines this assumption). The other theories do not exclude this possibility, but they stress that offenders mostly travel to perform daily routines that are unrelated to crime (e.g., school, work, friends, shops, or entertainment facilities). Both approaches agree that certain locations and areas are conducive to crime because they provide criminal opportunities, but rational choice theory assumes that offenders seek these opportunities, whereas the others assume they encounter them inadvertently and commit crimes impulsively in response to situational seductions or provocations.

The distinction seems to be reflected in an empirical division of labor as well. The large majority of crime location choice studies have focused on burglary and robbery, two high-impact acquisitive crimes that are likely to involve at least some premeditation and preparation. Research on situational correlates of crime that use the space-time budget instrument covers all types of crime, but in practice mostly records cases of interpersonal violence and vandalism, crimes that may indeed often take place without much premeditation and preparation.

For many other types of crime (e.g., rape, arson, theft) and in fact also for the types of crime already mentioned, the amount of premeditation may vary from case to case between pure premeditation and pure serendipity. Like many other types of behavior, offender mobility and crime location choice may be driven by a mix of reflexive and impulsive determinants (for an authorative account on multiple types of cognitive processes, see Kahneman 2011), and the field may need models that can integrate both modes of decision-making.

References

Andresen, Martin A, Richard Frank, and Marcus Felson. 2014. "Age and the Distance to Crime." *Criminology and Criminal Justice* 14:314–333.

Baldwin, John and Anthony E. Bottoms. 1976. *The Urban Criminal: A Study in Sheffield.* London: Tavistock Publications.

Baudains, Peter, Alex Braithwaite, and Shane D. Johnson. 2013. "Target Choice during Extreme Events: A Discrete Spatial Choice Model of the 2011 London Riots." *Criminology* 51:251–285.

Beauregard, Eric, Jean Proulx, and Kim Rossmo. 2005. "Spatial Patterns of Sex Offenders: Theoretical, Empirical, and Practical Issues." *Aggression and Violent Behavior* 10:579–603.

Becker, Gary S. 1968. "Crime and Punishment: An Economic Approach." *Journal of Political Economy* 76:169–217.

Bennett, Trevor and Richard T. Wright. 1984. *Burglars on Burglary: Prevention and the Offender.* Aldershot: Gower.

Bernasco, Wim. 2008. "Them Again? Same Offender Involvement in Repeat and near Repeat Burglaries." *European Journal of Criminology* 5:411–431.

Bernasco, Wim. 2009. "Foraging Strategies of Homo Criminalis: Lessons from Behavioral Ecology." *Crime Patterns and Analysis* 2:5–16.

Bernasco, Wim. 2010. "A Sentimental Journey to Crime: Effects of Residential History on Crime Location Choice." *Criminology* 48:389–416.

Bernasco, Wim. 2014. "Crime Journeys: Patterns of Offender Mobility." Pp. 1–19 in *Oxford Handbooks Online in Criminology and Criminal Justice*, edited by M. Tonry. Oxford: Oxford University Press.

Bernasco, Wim and Richard Block. 2009. "Where Offenders Choose to Attack: A Discrete Choice Model of Robberies in Chicago." *Criminology* 47:93–130.

Bernasco, Wim and Richard Block. 2011. "Robberies in Chicago: A Block-Level Analysis of the Influence of Crime Generators, Crime Attractors and Offender Anchor Points." *Journal of Research in Crime and Delinquency* 48:33–57.

Bernasco, Wim, Richard Block, and Stijn Ruiter. 2013. "Go Where the Money Is: Modeling Street Robbers' Location Choices." *Journal of Economic Geography* 13:119–143.

Bernasco, Wim, Gerben J.N. Bruinsma, Lieven J.R. Pauwels, and Frank M. Weerman. 2013. "Adolescent Delinquency and Diversity in Behavior Settings." *Australian and New Zealand Journal of Criminology* 46:357–378.

Bernasco, Wim, Shane D. Johnson, and Stijn Ruiter. 2015. "Learning Where to Offend: Effects of Past on Future Burglary Locations." *Applied Geography* 60:120–129.

Bernasco, Wim and Thessa Kooistra. 2010. "Effects of Residential History on Commercial Robbers' Crime Location Choices." *European Journal of Criminology* 7:251–265.

Bernasco, Wim and Paul Nieuwbeerta. 2005. "How Do Residential Burglars Select Target Areas? A New Approach to the Analysis of Criminal Location Choice." *British Journal of Criminology* 45:296–315.

Bernasco, Wim and Stijn Ruiter. 2014. "Crime Location Choice." Pp. 691–699 in *Encyclopedia of Criminology and Criminal Justice*, edited by G. J. N. Bruinsma and D. Weisburd. New York: Springer.

Bernasco, Wim, Stijn Ruiter, Gerben J. N. Bruinsma, Lieven J. R. Pauwels, and Frank M. Weerman. 2013. "Situational Causes of Offending: A Fixed-Effects Analysis of Space-Time Budget Data." *Criminology* 51:895–926.

Bhat, Chandra R. and Frank S. Koppelman. 1999. "A Retrospective and Prospective Survey of Time-Use Research." *Transportation* 26:119–139.

Block, Richard and Carolyn Rebecca Block. 1999. "Risky Places: A Comparison of the Environs of Rapid Transit Stations in Chicago and the Bronx." Pp. 137–152 in *Analyzing Crime Patterns: Frontiers of Practice*, edited by J. B. Mollenkopf. Thousand Oaks, CA: Sage.

Bowers, Kate J. and Shane D. Johnson. 2004. "Who Commits Near Repeats? A Test of the Boost Explanation." *Western Criminology Review* 5:12–24.

Brantingham, Patricia L. and Paul J. Brantingham. 1991. "Notes on the Geometry of Crime." Pp. 27–54 in *Environmental Criminology*, edited by P. J. Brantingham and P. L. Brantingham. Prospect Heights, IL: Waveland Press.

Brantingham, Paul J. and Patricia L. Brantingham. 1995. "Criminality of Place: Crime Generators and Crime Attractors." *European Journal of Criminal Policy and Research* 3: 5–26.

Brantingham, Paul J. and Patricia L. Brantingham. 2008. "Crime Pattern Theory." Pp. 78–93 in *Environmental Criminology and Crime Analysis*, edited by R. Wortley, L. Mazerolle, and S. Rombouts. Cullompton, Devon, UK: Willan Publishing.

Canter, David V. and A. Gregory. 1994. "Identifying the Residential Location of Rapists." *Journal of the Forensic Science Society* 34:169–175.

Ceccato, V. and A. C. Uittenbogaard. 2014. "Space-Time Dynamics of Crime in Transport Nodes." *Annals of the Association of the American Geographers* 105:131–150.

Clare, Joseph, John Fernandez, and Frank Morgan. 2009. "Formal Evaluation of the Impact of Barriers and Connectors on Residential Burglars' Macro-Level Offending Location Choices." *Australian and New Zealand Journal of Criminology* 42:139–158.

Cohen, Lawrence E. and Marcus Felson. 1979. "Social Change and Crime Rate Trends: A Routine Activity Approach." *American Sociological Review* 44:588–608.

Constanzo, C. Michael, William C. Halperin, and Nathan Gale. 1996. "Criminal Mobility and the Directional Component in Journeys to Crime." Pp. 73–95 in *Metropolitan Crime Patterns*, edited by R. M. Figlio, S. Hakim, and G. F. Rengert. Monsey, NY: Criminal Justice Press.

Cornish, Derek B. and Ronald V. Clarke, eds. 1986. *The Reasoning Criminal: Rational Choice Perspectives on Offending*. New York: Springer.

Davies, Toby and Shane D. Johnson. 2015. "Examining the Relationship between Road Structure and Burglary Risk via Quantitative Network Analysis." *Journal of Quantitative Criminology* 31:481–507.

Elffers, Henk. 2004. "Decision Models Underlying the Journey to Crime." Pp. 182–197 in *Punishment, Places and Perpetrators: Developments in Criminology and Criminal Justice Research.*, edited by G. Bruinsma, H. Elffers, and J. W. De Keijser. Cullompton, Devon, UK: Willan Publishing.

Everson, Steve and Ken Pease. 2001. "Crime against the Same Person and Place: Detection Opportunity and Offender Targeting." Pp. 199–220 in *Repeat Victimization*, edited by G. Farrell and K. Pease, vol. 12 of *Crime Prevention Studies*. Monsey, NY: Criminal Justice Press.

Feeney, Floyd. 1986. "Robbers as Decision Makers." Pp. 53–71 in *The Reasoning Criminal: Rational Choice Perspectives on Offending, Research in Criminology*, edited by D. B. Cornish and R. V. Clarke. New York: Springer.

Felson, Marcus. 2006. *Crime and Nature*. Thousand Oaks, CA: Sage.

Fernandez, John, Joe Clare, and Frank Morgan. 2006. "Suburban Travel Patterns in Burglary." Crime Research Centre, University of Western Australia, Perth.

Frank, Richard, Martin A. Andresen, and Patricia L. Brantingham. 2012. "Criminal Directionality and the Structure of Urban Form." *Journal of Environmental Psychology* 32:37–42.

Frank, Richard, Martin A. Andresen, and Patricia L. Brantingham. 2013. "Visualizing the Directional Bias in Property Crime Incidents for Five Canadian Municipalities." *Canadian Geographer / Le Géographe Canadien* 57:31–42.

Frank, Richard, Martin A. Andresen, Connie Cheng, and Patricia L. Brantingham. 2011. "Finding Criminal Attractors Based on Offenders' Directionality of Crimes." Pp. 86–93 in European Intelligence and Security Informatics Conference (EISIC), Athens, Greece.

Frank, Richard, V. Dabbaghian, S. Singh, A. Reid, J. Cinnamon, and Patricia J. Brantingham. 2011. "Power of Criminal Attractors: Modeling the Pull of Activity Nodes." *Journal of Artificial Society and Social Simulation* 14:6.

Gärling, Tommy and Kay Axhausen. 2003. "Introduction: Habitual Travel Choice." *Transportation* 30:1–11.

Gonzalez, Marta C., Cesar A. Hidalgo, and Albert-Laszlo Barabasi. 2008. "Understanding Individual Human Mobility Patterns." *Nature* 453:779–782.

Groff, Elizabeth. 2011. "Exploring 'Near': Characterizing the Spatial Extent of Drinking Place Influence on Crime." *Australian and New Zealand Journal of Criminology* 44:156–179.

Grubesic, Tony and Elizabeth Mack. 2008. "Spatio-Temporal Interaction of Urban Crime." *Journal of Quantitative Criminology* 24:285–306.

Guimarães, Paulo, Octávio Figueirdo, and Douglas Woodward. 2003. "A Tractable Approach to the Firm Location Decision Problem." *Review of Economics and Statistics* 85:201–204.

Haberman, Cory P. and Jerry H. Ratcliffe. 2015. "Testing for Temporally Differentiated Relationships among Potentially Criminogenic Places and Census Block Street Robbery Counts." *Criminology* 53:457–483.

Hägerstrand, Torsten. 1970. "What about People in Regional Science?" *Papers of the Regional Science Association* 24:7–21.

Hanson, Susan and O. James Huff. 1988. "Systematic Variability in Repetitious Travel." *Transportation* 15:111–135.

Hesseling, René B.P. 1992. "Using Data on Offender Mobility in Ecological Research." *Journal of Quantitative Criminology* 34:95–112.

Hidalgo, Cesar A. and C. Rodriguez-Sickert. 2008. "The Dynamics of a Mobile Phone Network." *Physica A: Statistical Mechanics and its Applications* 387:3017–3024.

Hillier, Bill. 2007. *Space Is the Machine*. London: Space Syntax.

Hoeben, Evelien and Frank Weerman. 2014. "Situational Conditions and Adolescent Offending: Does the Impact of Unstructured Socializing Depend on Its Location?" *European Journal of Criminology* 11:481–499.

Hoeben, Evelien M. and Frank M. Weerman. 2016. "Why Is Involvement in Unstructured Socializing Related to Adolescent Delinquency?" *Criminology* 54:242–281.

Humphries, Nicolas E., Nuno Queiroz, Jennifer R. M. Dyer, Nicolas G. Pade, Michael K. Musyl, Kurt M. Schaefer, Daniel W. Fuller, Juerg M. Brunnschweiler, Thomas K. Doyle, and Jonathan D. R. Houghton. 2010. "Environmental Context Explains Lévy and Brownian Movement Patterns of Marine Predators." *Nature* 465:1066–1069.

Irvin-Erickson, Yasemin and Nancy La Vigne. 2015. "A Spatio-Temporal Analysis of Crime at Washington, DC Metro Rail Stations' Crime-Generating and Crime-Attracting Characteristics as Transportation Nodes and Places." *Crime Science* 4:1–13.

Iwanski, Natalia, Richard Frank, Vahid Dabbaghian, Andrew Reid, and Patricia L. Brantingham. 2011. "Analyzing an Offender's Journey to Crime: A Criminal Movement Model (CriMM)." Pp. 70–77 in European Intelligence and Security Informatics Conference (EISIC), Athens, Greece.

Jacobs, Bruce A. 2010. "Serendipity in Robbery Target Selection." *British Journal of Criminology* 50:514–529.

Johnson, Shane D. 2014. "How Do Offenders Choose Where to Offend? Perspectives from Animal Foraging." *Legal and Criminological Psychology* 19:193–210.

Johnson, Shane D., Wim Bernasco, Kate Bowers, Henk Elffers, Jerry H. Ratcliffe, George F. Rengert, and Michael T. Townsley. 2007. "Space-Time Patterns of Risk: A Cross National Assessment of Residential Burglary Victimization." *Journal of Quantitative Criminology* 23:201–219.

Johnson, Shane D. and Kate J. Bowers. 2004. "The Burglary as Clue to the Future: The Beginnings of Prospective Hot-Spotting." *European Journal of Criminology* 1:237–255.

Johnson, Shane D. and Kate J. Bowers. 2010. "Permeability and Burglary Risk: Are Cul-De-Sacs Safer?" *Journal of Quantitative Criminology* 26:89–111.

Johnson, Shane D. and Lucia Summers. 2015. "Testing Ecological Theories of Offender Spatial Decision Making Using a Discrete Choice Model." *Crime and Delinquency* 61:454–480.

Johnson, Shane D., Lucia Summers, and Ken Pease. 2009. "Offender as Forager? A Direct Test of the Boost Account of Victimization." *Journal of Quantitative Criminology* 25:181–200.

Julián, Candia, C. González Marta, Wang Pu, Schoenharl Timothy, Madey Greg, and Barabási Albert-László. 2008. "Uncovering Individual and Collective Human Dynamics from Mobile Phone Records." *Journal of Physics A: Mathematical and Theoretical* 41:224015.

Kahneman, Daniel. 2011. *Thinking, Fast and Slow*. New York: Farrar, Straus and Giroux.

Kent, Josh, Michael Leitner, and Andrew Curtis. 2006. "Evaluating the Usefulness of Functional Distance Measures When Calibrating Journey-to-Crime Distance Decay Functions." *Computers, Environment and Urban Systems* 30:181–200.

Kocsis, R. N., R. W. Cooksey, H. J. Irwin, and G. Allen. 2002. "A Further Assessment of 'Circle Theory' for Geographic Psychological Profiling." *Australian and New Zealand Journal of Criminology* 35:43–62.

Lammers, Marre, Barbara Menting, Stijn Ruiter, and Wim Bernasco. 2015. "Biting Once, Twice: The Influence of Prior on Subsequent Crime Location Choice." *Criminology* 53:309–329.

LeBeau, James L. 1987. "The Methods and Measures of Centrography and the Spatial Dynamics of Rape." *Journal of Quantitative Criminology* 3:125–141.

Levine, Ned and Patsy Lee. 2013. "Journey-to-Crime by Gender and Age Group in Manchester, England." Pp. 145–178 in *Crime Modeling and Mapping Using Geospatial Technologies*, edited by Michael Leitner. Springer Netherlands.

Lindegaard, Marie Rosenkrantz, Wim Bernasco, and Scott Jacques. 2015. "Consequences of Expected and Observed Victim Resistance for Offender Violence during Robbery Events." *Journal of Research in Crime and Delinquency* 52:32–61.

Lynch, Kevin A. 1960. *The Image of the City*. Cambridge, MA: MIT Press.

McCord, Eric S. and Jerry H. Ratcliffe. 2007. "A Micro-spatial Analysis of the Demographic and Criminogenic Environment of Drug Markets in Philadelphia." *Australian and New Zealand Journal of Criminology* 40:43–63.

Menting, Barbara, Marre Lammers, Stijn Ruiter, and Wim Bernasco. "Family Matters: Effects of Family Members' Residential Areas on Crime Location Choice." *Criminology* 54:413–433.

Miller, Harvey J. 2005. "A Measurement Theory for Time Geography." *Geographical Analysis* 37:17–45.

Mohler, George O., Martin B. Short, P. Jeffrey Brantingham, Frederic P. Schoenberg, and George E. Tita. 2011. "Self-Exciting Point Process Modeling of Crime." *Journal of the American Statistical Association* 106:100–108.

Oberwittler, Dietrich and Per-Olof H. Wikström. 2009. "Why Small Is Better: Advancing the Study of the Role of Behavioral Contexts in Crime Causation." Pp. 35–59 in *Putting Crime in Its Place: Units of Analysis in Geographic Criminology*, edited by D. Weisburd, W. Bernasco, and G. J. N. Bruinsma. New York: Springer.

Padgham, Mark. 2012. "Human Movement Is Both Diffusive and Directed." *PLoS ONE* 7:e37754.

Pappalardo, Luca, Filippo Simini, Salvatore Rinzivillo, Dino Pedreschi, Fosca Giannotti, and Albert-Laszlo Barabasi. 2015. "Returners and Explorers Dichotomy in Human Mobility." *Nature Communications* 6.

Pease, Ken. 1998. *Repeat Victimisation: Taking Stock*. London: Police Research Group, Home Office.

Ratcliffe, Jerry H. 2006. "A Temporal Constraint Theory to Explain Opportunity-Based Spatial Offending Patterns." *Journal of Research in Crime and Delinquency* 43:261–291.

Ratcliffe, Jerry H. 2012. "The Spatial Extent of Criminogenic Places: A Changepoint Regression of Violence around Bars." *Geographical Analysis* 44:302–320.

Rengert, George F. and John Wasilchick. 2000. *Suburban Burglary: A Tale of Two Suburbs*. Springfield, IL: Charles C. Thomas.

Rhodes, William M. and Catherine Conly. 1981. "Crime and Mobility: An Empirical Study." Pp. 167–188 in *Environmental Criminology*, edited by P. L. Brantingham and P. J. Brantingham. Beverly Hills, CA: Sage.

Roncek, Dennis W. and Donald Faggiani. 1985. "High Schools and Crime: A Replication." *Sociological Quarterly* 26:491–505.

Roncek, Dennis W. and Antoinette LoBosco. 1983. "The Effect of High Schools on Crime in the Neighborhood." *Social Science Quarterly* 64:598–613.

Rossmo, D. Kim. 2000. *Geographic Profiling*. Boca Raton, FL: CRC Press.

Rossmo, D. Kim, Yongmei Lu, and T. Bernie Fang. 2012. "Spatial-Temporal Crime Paths." Pp. 16–42 in *Patterns, Prevention, and Geometry of Crime*, edited by M. A. Andresen and J. B. Kinney. New York: Routledge.

Ruiter, Stijn. 2017. "Crime Location Choice: State-of-the-Art and Avenues for Future Research." Pp. 398–420 in *Oxford Handbook of Offender Decision Making*, edited by W. Bernasco, J.- L. Van Gelder and H. Elffers. Oxford: Oxford University Press.

Schmidheiny, Kurt and Marius Brülhart. 2011. "On the Equivalence of Location Choice Models: Conditional Logit, Nested Logit and Poisson." *Journal of Urban Economics* 69:214–222.

Shaw, Clifford R. and Henry D. McKay. [1942] 1969. *Juvenile Delinquency and Urban Areas*. Chicago: University of Chicago Press.

Siegel, Dina. 2014. *Mobile Banditry: East and Central European Itinerant Criminal Groups in the Netherlands*. Meppel: Boom-Lemma.

Simini, Filippo, Marta C. Gonzalez, Amos Maritan, and Albert-Laszlo Barabasi. 2012. "A Universal Model for Mobility and Migration Patterns." *Nature* 484:96–100.

Song, Chaoming, Zehui Qu, Nicholas Blumm, and Albert-Laszlo Barabasi. 2010. "Limits of Predictability in Human Mobility." *Science* 327:1018–1021.

Steenbeek, Wouter and David Weisburd. 2015. "Where the Action Is in Crime? An Examination of Variability of Crime across Different Spatial Units in the Hague, 2001–2009." *Journal of Quantitative Criminology* 32:449–469.

Taylor, Ralph B. 1997. "Social Order and Disorder of Street Blocks and Neighborhoods: Ecology, Microecology, and the Systemic Model of Social Disorganization." *Journal of Research in Crime and Delinquency* 34:113–155.

Taylor, Ralph B. 1998. "Crime and Small-Scale Places: What We Know, What We Can Prevent, and What Else We Need to Know." Paper presented at Crime and Place: Plenary Papers of the 1997 Conference on Criminal Justice and Evaluation, Philadelphia.

Townsley, Michael. 2017. "Offender Mobility." Pp. 142–161 in *Environmental Criminology and Crime Analysis; Situating the Theory, Analytic Approach and Application*, edited by R. Wortley and M. Townsley. Abingdon: Routledge.

Townsley, Michael T., Ross Homel, and Janet Chaseling. 2003. "Infectious Burglaries: A Test of the near Repeat Hypothesis." *British Journal of Criminology* 43:615–633.

Townsley, Michael T. and Aiden Sidebottom. 2010. "All Offenders Are Equal, but Some Are More Equal Than Others: Variation in Journeys to Crime between Offenders." *Criminology* 48:897–917.

Van Daele, Stijn and Wim Bernasco. 2012. "Exploring Directional Consistency in Offending: The Case of Residential Burglary in the Hague." *Journal of Investigative Psychology and Offender Profiling* 9:135–148.

Van Daele, Stijn, Tom Vander Beken, and Gerben J. N. Bruinsma. 2012. "Does the Mobility of Foreign Offenders Fit the General Pattern of Mobility?" *European Journal of Criminology* 9:290–308.

Vandeviver, Christophe, Tijs Neutens, Stijn van Daele, Dirk Geurts, and Tom Vander Beken. 2015. "A Discrete Spatial Choice Model of Burglary Target Selection at the House-Level." *Applied Geography* 64:24–34.

Weerman, Frank M., Wim Bernasco, Gerben J. N. Bruinsma, and Lieven J. R. Pauwels. 2015. "When Is Spending Time with Peers Related to Delinquency? The Importance of Where, What, and with Whom." *Crime & Delinquency* 61:1386–1413.

Weisburd, David. 2015. "The Law of Crime Concentration and the Criminology of Place." *Criminology* 53:133–157.

Weisburd, David, Gerben J.N. Bruinsma, and Wim Bernasco. 2009. "Units of Analysis in Geographic Criminology: Historical Development, Critical Issues, and Open Questions." Pp. 3–31 in *Putting Crime in Its Place: Units of Analysis in Geographic Criminology*, edited by D. Weisburd, W. Bernasco and G. J. N. Bruinsma. New York: Springer.

Weisburd, David, Shawn Bushway, Cynthia Lum, and Sue-Ming Yang. 2004. "Trajectories of Crime at Places: A Longitudinal Study of Street Segments in the City of Seattle." *Criminology* 42:283–322.

Weisburd, David, Elizabeth R. Groff, and Sue-Ming Yang. 2012. *The Criminology of Place: Street Segments and Our Understanding of the Crime Problem*. Oxford: Oxford University Press.

Wikström, Per-Olof H. 2006. "Individuals, Settings, and Acts of Crime: Situational Mechanisms and the Explanation of Crime." Pp. 61–107 in *The Explanation of Crime: Context, Mechanisms, and Development*, edited by P.-O. H. Wikström and R. J. Sampson. Cambridge: Cambridge University Press.

Wikström, Per-Olof H. and David A. Butterworth. 2006. *Adolescent Crime: Individual Differences and Lifestyles*. Cullompton, Devon, UK: Willan Publishing.

Wikström, Per-Olof H., Vania Ceccato, Beth Hardie, and Kyle Treiber. 2010. "Activity Fields and the Dynamics of Crime." *Journal of Quantitative Criminology* 26:55–87.

Wikström, Per-Olof H., Dietrich Oberwittler, Kyle Treiber, and Beth Hardie. 2012. *Breaking Rules: The Social and Situational Dynamics of Young People's Urban Crime* Oxford: Oxford University Press.

Wiles, Paul and Andrew Costello. 2000. *The "Road to Nowhere": The Evidence for Traveling Criminals.* Home Office Research Study (HORS) No. 207. London: Home Office, Research, Development and Statistics Directorate.

Wright, Richard T., Fiona Brookman, and Trevor Bennett. 2006. "The Foreground Dynamics of Street Robbery in Britain." *British Journal of Criminology* 46:1–15.

Wright, Richard T. and Scott H. Decker. 1997. *Armed Robbers in Action.* Boston: Northeastern University Press.

Zipf, George Kingsley. 1949. *Human Behavior and the Principle of Least Effort: An Introduction to Human Ecology.* Cambridge, MA: Addison-Wesley.

Crime Prevention

CHAPTER 32

WHAT HAVE WE LEARNED FROM ENVIRONMENTAL CRIMINOLOGY FOR THE PREVENTION OF CRIME?

BRANDON C. WELSH AND SEMA A. TAHERI

32.1 Introduction

It is not an exaggeration to say that the contribution of environmental criminology to the prevention of crime has been and continues to be highly significant. This holds true in both absolute and relative terms. A wealth of scholarship and programmatic, policy, and legislative developments attest to its contributions across a wide range of public and private life. A recent study of the role of theory in modern-day crime prevention makes the case that situational crime prevention (SCP), compared to the two other major crime prevention strategies of developmental and community prevention, has had a greater influence on practice (Welsh, Zimmerman, and Zane 2017). Indeed, one would need to write a separate handbook to cover the full scope and richness of this body of work. Come to think of it, this is not such an outlandish idea. It is high time we had a third edition of Ron Clarke's important book *Situational Crime Prevention: Successful Case Studies* (1997).

The main aim of this chapter is to survey environmental criminology's contribution to the prevention of crime. It does so through the lens of SCP and its highly influential classification system (Smith and Clarke 2012). As one of the major crime prevention strategies, SCP is an organizing concept for a wide range of theories that contribute to practices focused on "reducing opportunities for highly specific forms of crime" (Clarke 1992, p. 4). For a host of reasons, this chapter is not meant to be an exhaustive review of the literature. To ensure its coverage has some breadth and depth, it draws upon leading empirical and narrative reviews of the effectiveness of SCP (e.g., Eck 2006; Eck and Guerette 2012; Ekblom 2012) as well as more recent studies in the published literature.

The organization of this chapter is as follows. Section 32.2 provides some background on SCP. Sections 32.3, 32.4, and 32.5 report on the effectiveness of various SCP techniques targeted on the major crime types of property, violent, and fraud, respectively. Section 32.6 offers some concluding comments.

32.2 Background

Situational crime prevention has been defined as "a preventive approach that relies, not upon improving society or its institutions, but simply upon reducing opportunities for crime" (Clarke 1992, p. 3). Reducing opportunities for crime is achieved essentially through some modification or manipulation of the physical environment in order to directly affect offenders' perceptions of increased risks and effort and decreased rewards, provocations, and excuses (Cornish and Clarke 2003). These different approaches serve as the basis of the highly detailed classification system of SCP, which can be divided into 25 separate techniques within these five categories (essentially a 5 × 5 table; Cornish and Clarke 2003).

The theoretical origins of SCP are wide-ranging (see Newman et al. 1997; Garland 2000), but it is largely informed by opportunity theory. This theory holds that the offender is "heavily influenced by environmental inducements and opportunities and [is] highly adaptable to changes in the situation" (Clarke 1995a, p. 57). Opportunity theory includes several more specific theories. One of these is the rational choice perspective. This perspective appears to have had the greatest influence on the pragmatic orientation of SCP, as articulated by its chief architect, Ron Clarke (1995a, 1995b, 1997).

Three main components make up the rational choice perspective: (1) the image of a reasoning offender; (2) a crime-specific focus; and (3) the development of separate models for the decision to commit a crime and the choice of the target (Cornish and Clarke 1986, p. 7). The image of a reasoning offender is understood to mean that crime is purposive behavior designed to meet the offender's commonplace needs for such things as money, status, sex, and excitement, and that meeting these needs involves the making of (sometimes quite rudimentary) decisions and choices, constrained as these are by limits of time and ability and the availability of relevant information (Clarke 1995b, p. 98).

On the basis of this view, it is assumed that rationality is not limited to offending behavior of a less serious nature (e.g., property crime), but is also present in violent offending. However, Trasler (1986, 1993) argued that opportunity-reducing prevention is effective only with "instrumental" offenses (i.e., property, including robbery), not with "expressive" offenses. The examples given by Trasler (1993, p. 318) for expressive crimes were homicide or wounding where, in his words, "the notion of a rational calculus was unconvincing." Building on Clarke's work, Wortley (1997, 2001) highlighted the ways in which the person interacts with his or her environment, such that property, as well as violent, crimes were also the result of multiple frustrations placed upon an individual in a given situation. He suggested that opportunity-reduction would be complemented by a prevention technique of reducing provocations to an individual. The empirical literature on the subject would suggest that SCP can indeed be effective in reducing violent crimes (see Eck and Guerette 2012).

The crime-specific focus of the rational choice perspective is driven by its concern with environmental influences and criminal events. The adoption of a crime-specific focus is important to take account of the different decision processes and information used for the many different offenses (Clarke 1995b). This focus ensures that the scope of intervention is not limited to the commonplace distinctions between crimes (e.g., residential or commercial burglary), but takes into account even the smallest variations.

In contrast, most other criminological theories assume that offenders are versatile and that it is unnecessary to propose a different theory for every different type of crime. For example, developmental and life-course theories aim to explain why offenders develop rather than why offenses occur. Put another way, they aim to explain the development of a potential for offending rather than how the potential becomes the actuality in any given situation. However, theories have been proposed that include both approaches and address both questions (Farrington 2005). A crime-specific focus seems more necessary in explaining immediate situational influences on criminal acts than in explaining the development of a more general tendency to commit offenses.

The final main component of the rational choice perspective on criminal behavior is the view that the decision processes involved in choosing the criminal event (the target) are equally important to the decision processes surrounding criminal involvement (deciding to offend). However, SCP concentrates on the event, because decisions are easier to influence at this stage. Event decisions take place in the present and depend on immediate circumstances and situations (Clarke 1995b; Cornish and Clarke 1986).

The situational approach is further supported by theories, such as routine activities theory (Cohen and Felson 1979), that emphasize natural, informal surveillance as a key to crime prevention. For example, Jacobs (1961) drew attention to the role of good visibility combined with natural surveillance as deterrents to crime. She emphasized the association between levels of crime and public street use, suggesting that less crime would be committed in areas with an abundance of potential witnesses. These witnesses act as natural guardians of the public space, reducing the opportunities for and increasing the risks associated with any wrongdoing (see Reynald in this volume).

32.3 Prevention of Property Crime

Property crime seems to hold special relevance to SCP techniques. Drawing on routine activities theory and rational choice perspective, situational crime prevention techniques are useful in making property less accessible or less attractive to offenders.

Routine activities theory and rational choice perspective allow for techniques that are centered on minimizing the benefit of theft or vandalism, and increasing the risks of such behaviors. Where changes are made to property itself, interventions can affect the "deliberate choices" made by offenders to engage in crime (Clarke 1983, p. 227). Property, compared to persons, is easier to protect through SCP interventions meant to harden a target and prevent it from falling victim to criminal behavior. SCP techniques such as opportunity blocking (Clarke 1992) can be as simple as installing anti-theft devices in cars or as complex as designing a new apartment complex with security and SCP in mind. SCP techniques such as CCTV and lighting improvements are particularly suited for reducing property crimes by increasing risks to offenders. In some contexts, almost anyone can make use of SCP to prevent damage to or theft of property with minimal cost.

This section surveys the effectiveness of key situational crime prevention techniques targeted on property crimes, including burglary, theft, vehicle theft, and vandalism. We focus on two of SCP's main approaches: increasing the effort and increasing the risks.

32.3.1 Assessing Effects

As a means of increasing the effort involved in committing a crime, the target-hardening approach aims to make it more difficult for an offender to access and use property to achieve a criminal purpose (Clarke 1983; Smith and Clarke 2012), and has been widely successful in the prevention of property crime. In residential and public places, this might be achieved through the use of gates, locks, secure window installations, or alarms (e.g., Bowers, Johnson, and Hirschfield 2004; Casey et al. 2004). In retail stores, managers might attach ink tags to clothing items (e.g., DiLonardo and Clarke 1996), and individuals might invest in electronic vehicular immobilizers to prevent vehicular theft (Brown 2013). These techniques limit an offenders' access to property, and reduce opportunities for criminal activity through the protection of the property itself.

Another method of increasing the effort required of offenders to commit property crimes includes making alterations to the broader environment. The most common strategy to achieve this end is crime prevention through environmental design (CPTED), which restricts access and movement of individuals so as to deflect offenders from target-rich environments (Smith and Clarke 2012) and alters patterns of movement. Based on the concept of "defensible space" (Newman 1972; Ekblom 2013), CPTED techniques structure the environment in a way that creates easily observable space and increases monitoring of the built environment. By locking access to places that provide opportunities for crime using physical barriers and controlling the flow of movement to targets (Reynald 2015), and by taking into consideration the community context (Ekblom 2013), CPTED strategies can be effective in reducing theft and burglary. Interventions have included street closures, barricades, and traffic modifications (e.g., Wagner 1997; Lasley 1998), as well as public housing designs aimed at protecting residents, such as "Secured by Design" in the United Kingdom (Armitage 2000).

Most recently, there has been renewed interest in the relationship between environmental design and the risk of property crimes such as burglary (e.g., Ha, Oh, and Park 2014; Davies and Johnson 2015; Addington and Rennison 2015). These designs make alterations to the surrounding environment to develop settings that are more conducive to guardianship and provide fewer opportunities for crime. The Dutch "Police Label Secure Housing" program (Jongejan and Woldendorp 2013), which is highlighted at the end of this section, is an example of a successful intervention that relies on CPTED principles. While they are increasingly popular, the evidence to date of the effectiveness of CPTED and other defensible space techniques is limited by the small number of high-quality evaluations, and by the extensive variability in design and contexts in which the interventions are implemented (Cozens, Saville, and Hillier 2005).

In addition to making access to property more difficult, SCP also supports the adoption of measures that increase the risks involved in criminal behavior. Extending guardianship over property targets increases the likelihood that an offender will be seen and prevented from taking or damaging the property. Guardians, such as security guards, store employees, or neighbors, will witness criminal actions, and even if they cannot stop the crime from occurring, will be able to identify features of offenders so as to improve the chances of catching and prosecuting the offender (Welsh, Farrington, and Taheri 2015).

Security guards exercise formal guardianship over a public space, providing visible forms of surveillance and increasing the possibility of apprehension of offenders. Three high-quality studies examined security guards in parking lots, yielding two desirable effects (Laycock and Austin 1992; Barclay et al. 1996) and one null effect on the theft of motor vehicles. In Vancouver, Canada, an intervention in commuter parking lots found that the program and one month of security patrols reduced vehicle thefts in the experimental lots, compared to an increase in vehicle thefts in the surrounding areas (Barclay et al. 1996).

Unlike security guards, place managers are an informal method of surveillance, such that the main function of managers is not necessarily to prevent crime. They can do so, however, as a secondary function of their job, simply by being present. Unfortunately, our knowledge of the effects of place managers is also limited to a small number of studies, all of which are several years old. One evaluation from the United Kingdom found a desirable effect for reducing vandalism in public housing complexes (Skilton 1988) and another resulted in no measurable effects when using parking lot attendants to prevent vehicle crimes (Poyner 1991). These results provide no clear conclusion on the effectiveness of place managers in preventing property crime. There is, however, a burgeoning empirical literature on place managers that may help expand the current knowledge base on the effects of this method of prevention, particularly as it relates to the work of law enforcement and regulatory agencies (Eck 2015).

Similar to place manager surveillance, technologies that alert managers to shoplifting are also common in retail locations. These technologies include electronic article surveillance tags attached to property in retail stores, thus hardening the targeted property and increasing the risks to the offender. If an article of clothing or another product is taken from the store without first having the tag removed, an alarm will sound and the manager can recover the stolen item. In reviewing five evaluations of this tag technology, Eck (2006) finds that shoplifting is preventable, but the magnitude of the effect could not be discerned.

While training place managers to respond appropriately to potential criminal behavior can be important in reducing property crime, the most common way of increasing guardianship is surveillance, including CCTV cameras and improved street lighting (Welsh and Farrington 2014; see also Welsh and Farrington 2009). CCTV enhances the ability of a guardian to watch over pedestrians and potential offenders in an area and to call for police intervention—or intervene themselves—if trouble is detected. In a systematic review and meta-analysis of CCTV, a pooled effect size using 22 evaluations showed a desirable effect of CCTV cameras, reducing vehicle crimes by 26%. These effects were particularly strong for cameras used in public transportation systems and in parking lots (Welsh and Farrington 2014).

In a review of place-based crime prevention techniques, Eck and Guerette (2012) also outline the effectiveness of SCP interventions in preventing multiple types of crimes. Most of the 25 evaluations of interventions in retail locations considered in their review were concerned with the effects of interventions on burglary and theft ($n = 17$). Burglary and theft were also the most common crime types measured in evaluations of residential interventions (24 of 39 evaluations) and public transportation (7 of 26 evaluations), and the second most common single crime type measured in public place interventions (6 of 52 evaluations). CCTV was used in all four settings, and the authors' review suggests that it was most likely to be effective in preventing property crimes in retail locations and on public transportation. Its effects in public and residential places were much less clear.

However, a recent randomized controlled experiment of CCTV camera implementation in commuter parking facilities for patrons of the Washington, DC, commuter train services found cameras to have little to no effect on property crime, especially vehicle theft or theft from vehicles (La Vigne and Lawry 2011). No clear explanation was given for this result. Two additional studies were concerned with the effectiveness of cameras used by police departments in multiple sites, and both studies showed mixed effects of cameras on crime more broadly (Cameron et al. 2008; Ratcliffe, Taniguchi, and Taylor 2009).

A final approach to improving guardianship is through encouraging natural surveillance. Programs such as Neighborhood Watch and community involvement can encourage people to provide protection and guardianship over one another's property and therefore reduce opportunities and increase risks for potential offenders (Bennett, Holloway, and Farrington 2006). Natural surveillance can also involve changing the physical appearance of a place, such as trimming bushes in front of homes to increase visibility or installing additional street lighting to increase feelings of safety and encourage more foot traffic (Ekblom 2013). The overall effect of improved lighting interventions on property crime was significant and desirable in a systematic review and meta-analysis (Welsh and Farrington 2008), echoing findings from a decade earlier that cities that made strategic improvements to neighborhood lighting had decreases in crime rates (Pease 1999). In pooling effects across 13 evaluations from the United Kingdom and the United States, it was found that improved lighting resulted in an approximately 17% reduction in property crime. The desirable effect varied across settings, from parking garages to residential neighborhoods to public market centers, with little difference between the effects on day and night crime. The tendency for effective studies to measure both daytime and nighttime crimes, and for ineffective studies to measure only nighttime crimes, suggests that a theory of street lighting focusing on its role in increasing community pride and informal social control may be more plausible than a theory focusing on increased surveillance and deterrence. Unfortunately, the findings are based on studies carried out in the 1970s in the United States and the 1990s in the United Kingdom. There is a need for newer evaluations that also take account of changes in lighting technology.

32.3.2 Program Profile

An example of the effective use of CPTED principles to prevent property crime is the Dutch Police Label Secure Housing (PLSH) standard for building new homes and estates. The program was developed following the United Kingdom's Secured by Design program, and has been implemented nationwide in the Netherlands since 1996. Focused on urban planning and landscaping, the design aims to prevent a range of property crimes (e.g., burglary, car theft, vandalism) by improving physical security of buildings (Jongejan and Woldendorp 2013).

The goal of developing new homes and buildings that can act as barriers to criminal activity is achieved when security measures are incorporated, and communication is improved among planners, architects, and residents. Once built, the dwelling undergoes a number of tests against potential burglary, theft, vandalism, as well as inclement weather. This process of target hardening helps reduce the vulnerability of the home, and increases the efforts involved for offenders who may want to burglarize a home or take property.

The program requires that 30 basic and 18 additional standards be met in the process of building a new home. This requires that architects and developers must begin thinking about the security of the building from the first stage of planning, and identifying the performance requirements such as the amount of illumination considered "good lighting," and whether or not parking facilities are capable of providing adequate supervision of parked cars. Developers and managers are encouraged to also adopt additional elements such as a "plan for the management and supervision of public areas," outlining the procedures for dealing with vandalism or theft if it occurs, and who is responsible for repair or cleaning.

From 1994 to 1998, the Dutch government and police departments developed the program further to design manuals and standard practices for dwellings across the country. Today, the manuals for new estates specify requirements to obtain certificates of Secure

Housing. Due to its success, the Netherlands has adopted the manuals as part of the Dutch building regulations. Similar to buildings in the United States, new estates in the Netherlands have to undergo inspections. If they meet all criteria outlined in the manuals, they can receive a certificate for the PLSH program. If a new estate does not meet the criteria on first review, the building architects and urban planners are encouraged to find a new solution to meet the needs of residents and to reapply. If the developers can meet the same preventive effect required using a different method than outlined in the manual, it can be accepted and count toward certification. By 2011, approximately 600,000 estates had been granted the PLSH certification. Insurance companies have also been providing rebates to companies that certify their dwellings. One study showed that the risk of a home being burgled dropped significantly in new and existing estates, as did the chance of being a victim of burglary (Nauta 2004).

32.4 Prevention of Violent Crime

SCP is no longer viewed as irrelevant or inconsequential to addressing violent crime. In the last 20 years, the literature on SCP's applicability to and effectiveness in reducing violent crime has grown considerably (see, e.g., Eck and Guerette 2012). This has also come with a much greater appreciation of the depth and breadth of SCP as it relates to different types of violent crime and in different contexts.

This section surveys the effectiveness of key SCP techniques targeted on violent crimes, with a special focus on different types of robbery, as well as facilitators of violence like alcohol. We focus on three of SCP's main approaches: increasing the effort, increasing the risks, and decreasing the rewards.

32.4.1 Assessing Effects

Where the prevention of property crime benefits from the hardening of property targets and making it increasingly difficult for offenders to come into contact with the property, the prevention of violent crimes is heavily informed by the altering of opportunities for crime and the surrounding areas in which individuals may interact with one another. Modifications to the environment have the potential to make violent criminal behavior riskier, more difficult, and less rewarding.

Violent crime, like property crime, responds to cues from the physical environment. Clarke (1992) outlined ways in which removing the opportunities to offend could be conceptualized. SCP is focused on highly specific forms of crime, and may benefit from interventions such as making changes to an environment or a target of crime, rather than attempting to change the individual. The prevention of violent crimes may also be achieved through the installation of CCTV cameras and improved lighting. However, the few evaluations which include violent crime outcomes have shown effects that are mixed over time and across contexts, including retail locations and public places (Welsh and Farrington 2009; Eck and Guerette 2012).

SCP may be effective in reducing violent crimes, such as robbery, more specifically, by opting to make changes to the environment or setting in which interactions may facilitate robberies. For instance, taxi drivers are high-risk targets for robbery because they have increased contact with a large number of strangers, may work very late hours into the night, and often carry a large amount of cash with them (Smith 2005). In a guide created to address concerns about robberies of taxi drivers, the Center for Problem Oriented Policing suggests a range of measures, including separating drivers from passengers to increase the effort and recording activity with security cameras to increase the risk associated with committing a robbery (Stone and Stevens 2000). Unfortunately, the effect of these measures remains unclear. Suggestions about the large sums of money that taxi drivers collect center around somehow reducing the amount kept in the cab and available to be taken (Smith 2005) in order to reduce the benefits to the offender and make the taxi driver a less attractive target. Hired services such as Uber or Lyft use phone applications that handle payment electronically and do not allow cash tips to be given, thereby removing the opportunity for cash exchange entirely. Future investigation as to how well these strategies reduce crime is needed.

Limiting the amount of cash on hand is also a recommendation for the prevention of convenience store robberies and robberies in general. Doing so makes the driver, store, or individual a less attractive target for the offender and reduces the benefits that can be achieved. However, convenience stores may also benefit from additional measures informed by SCP (Exum et al. 2010). Specifically, convenience stores that draw on CPTED principles and manage their access to the register and do not provide access to cash machines are less likely to be robbed. CPTED and surveillance measures that reduce the opportunities for crime, but also increase the risks involved, such as improving interior and exterior lighting, installing cameras, and maintaining low-display units to allow clearer customer observation, may also reduce robberies in convenience stores (Altizio and York 2007). However, the knowledge of intervention effectiveness continues to vary by business location and type, suggesting once again that place and context remains significant in the application of SCP (Eck 2006).

Alcohol plays a large role in the occurrence of violence and the provocation of offenders. Managing the environments in which alcohol is consumed may limit the opportunities for intoxicated individuals to interact with one another. In Australia, a number of studies have been carried out to evaluate the effects of policies in entertainment districts on violence and crime more generally. Districts with policies that provide incentives to reduce binge drinking, lower the cost of nonalcoholic drinks, use smaller glasses, and provide training to staff security experience substantial reductions in drunkenness and violence around their institutions (Homel et al. 1997). Reducing binge drinking, encouraging the purchase of nonalcoholic drinks, and training security staff in appropriate responses to disruptive individuals also reduce provocations for potential offenders. Training for staff and security might include refusal of overserved individuals and proper identification policies, with increased responsibilities for staff (Homel and Clark 1994). These policies reduce opportunities for violence, increasing the offenders' risk of being caught, and reduce the provocation of intoxicated patrons. When staff members are able to keep more control over their reactions, they may reduce their likelihood of escalated violence from intoxicated patrons (Scott and Dedel 2006). Importantly, findings did not show any significant displacement. "Regulars" were still patronizing the same establishments, but were "better behaved" (Homel et al. 1997, p. 75).

Policies that attempt to prevent the overconsumption of alcohol may also affect violent crimes such as accidents due to drunk driving. While the current literature has not systematically evaluated these policies, focused efforts in Australia and Europe suggest that increasing the risk of apprehension (e.g., highway breathalyzer stops) and reducing opportunities (e.g., preventing overconsumption, providing transportation) may be effective in reducing violent outcomes of alcohol consumption (Scott et al. 2006). Increasing the risks may take the form of improving detection of alcohol impairment when stopped by law enforcement, or by increasing the perception of offenders of the likelihood of being apprehended, such as setting up sobriety checkpoints and increasing enforcement during high-risk time frames (Loebmann 2002).

32.4.2 Program Profile

Burnley, in the northwest of England, was the setting for one of the most effective CCTV schemes targeted at violent crime. In the mid-1990s, cameras were installed in the town center to address a steady increase in violent crime and crime rates in general. The local police department spearheaded the initiative, and an evaluation was carried out by Armitage, Smyth, and Pease (1999).

The authors used a rigorous quasi-experimental evaluation design (with pre- and post-CCTV measures of crime in experimental and control areas) to investigate the effects of the CCTV scheme. The experimental area consisted of three police beats in the town center with CCTV coverage. (No information was provided on camera coverage or type of monitoring.) Two control areas were established. The first comprised police beats that shared a common boundary with the beats covered by CCTV. The second control area consisted of other police beats in the police division. It was determined that the first control area was more comparable to the experimental area.

After 12 months of the CCTV scheme's operation, the experimental area, compared with the two control areas, showed substantial reductions for violent crime, a number of property crimes (i.e., burglary, criminal damage, theft of and from vehicles), and total crime. For example, total incidents of crime fell by 28% in the experimental area compared with a slight decline of 1% in the first control area and an increase of 9% in the second control area. Incidents of violent crime were down by 35% in the experimental area, compared with a 20% decline in the first control area and no change in the second control area. Importantly, the authors also investigated for any displacement of crime and diffusion of crime prevention benefits. They found evidence of diffusion of benefits for the categories of total crime, violent crime, and vehicle crime, and evidence of territorial displacement for burglary.

32.5 Prevention of Fraud and Related Crimes

SCP techniques may also be applicable to offenses other than violent and property crimes. Yet, while systematic reviews and meta-analyses of SCP techniques have included many evaluations with violent and property crime outcomes, evaluations with outcomes of fraud and white-collar crimes have been far less common. In this section, we draw upon the few reviews that have included evaluations measuring fraud.

Fraud is generally understood to be a white-collar crime, where an offender gains financial advantage or causes financial loss through deception (for a more detailed definition, see Levi and Burrows 2008). Although there are a number of different types of fraud, the most targeted in the SCP literature are credit card fraud, fair evasion, and identity theft. As with property crime, the interventions that have been used also fall under the approaches of increasing the effort of offending and increasing the risks to fraudulent behavior. It may be that the targets of fraud offenses can be hardened or made less attractive to offenders in the same way that physical property can be. However, Pratt et al. (2010) suggest that many of the correlates of fraud offenses differ from street crime more generally, such that the victims of fraud are younger and better educated than those targeted for property or violent offenses. Thus, it is important to evaluate the relevance of SCP theory and the effectiveness of SCP techniques in the prevention of fraud and related crimes.

White-collar crimes, such as fraud and identity theft, may arise out of the opportunity that is granted through access to particular occupations and positions (Benson and Madensen 2007). SCP assumes that potential offenders decide whether or not to engage in crime based on the availability and suitability of targets, and they weigh the costs and benefits of their options.

32.5.1 Assessing Effects

In a cross-case analysis of 25 different environmental crimes, Huisman and van Earp (2013) suggest that white-collar offenders may be more sensitive to changes in the opportunities for fraud, and the costs and benefits of their offenses, than street criminals. The authors draw on routine activities theory and suggest that better law enforcement, detection strategies, and environmental awareness can reduce the benefits and increase the costs of fraud and white-collar crimes. Applying SCP to fraud crimes against individuals and companies may be increasingly beneficial, as the number of victims and costs of fraud to society may exceed the figures of those victimized by serious street crime, with just over 25 million US adults having been the victims of fraud during 2011 alone (Pratt, Holtfreter, and Reisig 2010; Anderson 2013).

One way to increase the effort of offending involves target hardening, or making the desired property or information more difficult to access. In their review of place-based crime prevention, Eck and Guerette (2012) identified eight studies since 1990 that examined interventions aimed at preventing fraud. Four of the eight studies fit under the theme of target hardening, such as making retail refund policies more restrictive and requiring proof of purchase for every return (Challinger 1996), and installing high-wheel turnstiles to make fare evasion more difficult in train stations (Weidner 1996). Also included in their review were two evaluations of interventions that reduced access to available targets. In the London train system, automated gates and ticketing systems were installed to reduce fair evasion, allowing access only to those with appropriate tickets (Clarke 1993). In another study, Bichler and Clarke (1996) found that by reducing the number of pay phones and removing international dialing capacities of the phones, the Manhattan Port Authority was able to prevent fraudulent calls through the terminal's phone lines, and potentially improve the atmosphere for patrons.

The remaining four studies identified by Eck and Guerette (2012) were of interventions that focused on increasing the risks associated with fraudulent behavior. In three of these studies, retail managers trained their employees to recognize fraudulent behavior, to profile potential offenders, and to use identification recognition technology (Masuda 1992). The increased supervision provided by the employees made it more likely that offenders would be caught and prosecuted. As in the prevention of property crimes, these interventions are built on the premise that offenders are deterred from committing fraud when supervision is visible and effective.

Perpetrators of fraud are also taking advantage of the increased use of technology and online business, but the difficulty in regulating Internet transactions makes the prevention and prosecution of online fraud offenses challenging (Barker, D'Amato, and Sheridon 2008; Hartel, Junger, and Wieringa 2011). Routine activity theory predicts that more time away from home results in greater victimization, but as victims are increasingly targeted online, their risk may be just as high while they are "safe" at home (Reyns, Henson, and Fisher 2011). Therefore, SCP may work best by increasing the effort required of offenders through online safety measures and educating Internet users on how to limit the availability of their personal information online (Pratt et al. 2010).

Unfortunately, the current reviews of SCP in this area have not yet included evaluations of techniques used to prevent cyber-fraud or identity theft. However, drawing on the information securities literature, Hartel and colleagues (2011) suggest that the use of computer firewalls, stronger passwords, and encryption software could increase the effort required of offenders to gain access to and misuse others' information. Though there has been some dialogue in the scholarly literature (Hinduja and Kooi 2013) on applying SCP techniques to cybercrimes, the empirical literature is sorely lacking in evaluations.

32.5.2 Program Profile

Developed during a 2009 software programming competition, a fraud detection model was proposed that uses a customer's own credit card history to identify fraudulent behavior. While not yet implemented commercially, FraudMiner represents an innovative analytical program that can be used by companies and individuals to prevent credit card fraud on the Internet or in retail locations. Programs like FraudMiner are "taught" to identify fraudulent behavior on credit cards based on an individual's charge history and location. Using the information provided, the program identifies patterns in valid spending, is tested with additional charges and information, and then must decide whether or not the new charges are fraudulent. The analysis measures how similar each new case is to the individual's legitimate spending behavior and how similar each new case is to fraudulent patterns. Through mathematical calculations and projections, the program then alerts the company to either the legitimacy or the fraudulent nature of the credit card charge (Seeja and Zareapoor 2014).

The program was tested using real-world data from e-commerce transactions maintained by the University of California, San Diego, with a focus on its fraud detection rate, false alarm rate, and ability to classify transactions correctly. Compared to established measures of fraud detection, the FraudMiner program detected fraud just as accurately as, and in some cases better than, established classification methods (Seeja and Zareapoor 2014). This program has the potential to influence significantly the decision-making process of potential fraud offenders by increasing the risks of apprehension and reducing the rewards of any information or credit cards obtained. These innovative interventions and policies used to combat fraud, cybercrime, and other white-collar crimes, fit well within the immediate and narrow focus of SCP. Programs similar to FraudMiner are improving the methods by which companies and individuals can maintain a comfortable level of guardianship over their own credit and identity.

32.6 Discussion and Conclusions

In its most basic terms, SCP aims to reduce opportunities for crime. Under this directive, preventing crimes, such as burglary, robbery, and fraud, is made possible by increasing risks and effort and decreasing rewards, provocations, and excuses. The theoretical underpinnings of SCP are highlighted in programs such as the Dutch Police Label Secure Housing, CCTV use in the United Kingdom, and new software programs to prevent fraudulent behavior, such as FraudMiner. Routine activities theory informs the effectiveness of CCTV and lighting programs that provide much-needed guardianship to remove the opportunities for criminal behavior. Furthermore, interventions that alter the design of the environment through CPTED principles, and increase the effort required of offenders through improved locks or barriers, are driven by components of the rational choice perspective, adding to the costs in the decision-making process of a potential offender.

The research summarized and highlighted in this chapter points to the variability of program effects across crime types, contexts, and time. It seems safe to say that SCP has been far more effective in the prevention of property crime, but there is no questioning the strength of the research evidence on its effectiveness in preventing violent crime. The views about SCP being incapable of effecting change with violent crimes have long been put to rest. Research on the application of SCP to some types of fraudulent crimes and the rapidly expanding world of white-collar crimes shows many promising developments.

SCP's focus on opportunity and the specific target of crime makes SCP more versatile than other prevention strategies, but it also comes with its own limitations and criticisms. One reason for community resistance to the implementation of SCP techniques might be the fear of displacement of crime. Displacement can take a number of different forms, including offenders changing location, changing the times of offending, changing the target of their criminal behavior, or adopting new behavior to attack the same target. SCP does not tend to cause major displacement effects. In fact, often crime prevention benefits are diffused through neighboring areas, and when displacement does occur, the effect is less pronounced than the overall effect on the targeted crime (Eck 2006; Guerette and Bowers 2009). Additionally, crime prevention may not be the only benefit to the use of environmental interventions. Strategies to prevent crime may have the added benefit of reducing fear of crime in certain contexts (Lorenc et al. 2013).

There may also be concerns over the generalizability of CPTED techniques. This is particularly true when designers fail to take into consideration the context of the community and the needs of its residents (Ekblom 2013). Additional research is necessary to understand the effects of CPTED and the sustainability of designs over time. Furthermore, CCTV cameras and other means of surveillance come with their own trade-offs with respect to social inclusion and individual rights to privacy. Where these concerns threaten the effectiveness of surveillance measures, additional research could prove beneficial (Welsh, Farrington, and Taheri 2015).

Recent research concerning CCTV indicates that scholars and policymakers must consider the contexts in which surveillance and other SCP techniques are being implemented. For instance, cameras may be most effective when highly concentrated in high-crime areas, actively monitored, and used often by law enforcement. These systems may also be more effective if potential offenders are aware of the presence of cameras (La Vigne and Lowry 2011).

References

Addington, Lynn A., and Callie Marie Rennison. 2015. "Keeping the Barbarians outside the Gate? Comparing Burglary Victimization in Gated and Non-gated Communities." *Justice Quarterly* 32:168–192.

Altizio, Alicia, and Diana York. 2007. *Robbery of Convenience Stores*. Problem-Oriented Guides for Police: Problem-Specific Guides Series No. 49. Washington, DC: US Department of Justice, Office of Community Oriented Policing Services.

Anderson, Keith B. 2013. *Consumer Fraud in the United States, 2011: The Third FTC Survey*. Staff Report of the Bureau of Economics Federal Trade Commission. Washington, DC: Federal Trade Commission.

Armitage, Rachel. 2000. "An Evaluation of Secured by Design Housing within West Yorkshire." Briefing Note by the Policing Reduction Crime Unit. London: Home Office.

Armitage, Rachel, Graham Smyth, and Ken Pease. 1999. "Burnley CCTV Evaluation." In *Surveillance of Public Space: CCTV, Street Lighting and Crime Prevention. Crime Prevention Studies*, vol. 10, edited by Kate Painter and Nick Tilley. Monsey, NY: Criminal Justice Press.

Barclay, Paul, Jennifer Buckley, Paul J. Brantingham, Patricia L. Brantingham, and Terry Whinn-Yates. 1996. "Preventing Auto Theft in Suburban Vancouver Commuter Lots: Effects of a Bike Patrol." In *Preventing Mass Transit Crime. Crime Prevention Studies*, vol. 6, edited by Ronald V. Clarke. Monsey, NY: Criminal Justice Press.

Barker, Katherine J., Jackie D'Amato, and Paul Sheridon. 2008. "Credit Card Fraud: Awareness and Prevention. *Journal of Financial Crime* 15:398–410.

Bennett, Trevor, Katy Holloway, and David P. Farrington. 2006. "Does Neighborhood Watch Reduce Crime? A Systematic Review and Meta-analysis." *Journal of Experimental Criminology* 2:437–458.

Benson, Michael L., and Tamara D. Madensen. 2007. "Situational Crime Prevention and White-Collar Crime." In *International Handbook of Corporate and White Collar Crime*, edited by Henry Pontell and Gilbert Geis. New York: Springer.

Bichler, Gisela, and Ronald V. Clarke. 1996. "Eliminating Pay Phone Toll Fraud at the Port Authority Bus Terminal in Manhattan." In *Preventing Mass Transit Crime. Crime Prevention Studies*, vol. 6, edited by Ronald V. Clarke. Monsey, NY: Criminal Justice Press.

Bowers, Kate, Shane D. Johnson, and Alex Hirschfield. 2004. "Closing Off Opportunities for Crime: An Evaluation of Alley-Gating." *European Journal on Criminal Policy and Research* 10:285–308.

Brown, Rick. 2013. "Regulating Crime Prevention Design into Consumer Products: Learning the Lessons from Electronic Vehicle Immobilization." *Trends and Issues* 453:1–8.

Cameron, Aundreia, Elke Kolodinski, Heather May, and Nicholas Williams. 2008. "Measuring the Effects of Video Surveillance on Crime in Los Angeles." Technical Report by the California Research Bureau. Los Angeles: School of Policy Planning and Development, University of Southern California.

Casey, Cathy, Bhavani PaulRaj, Susie Jacka, and Tanya Segessenmann. 2004. *Evaluation of the Target Hardening Pilot Programme*. Wellington, New Zealand: Ministry of Justice.

Challinger, Dennis. 1996. "Refund Fraud in Retail Stores." *Security Journal* 7:27–35.

Clarke, Ronald V. 1983. "Situational Crime Prevention: Its Theoretical Basis and Practical Scope." *Crime and Justice: A Review of Research*, vol. 4, edited by Michael Tonry. Chicago: University of Chicago Press.

Clarke, Ronald V. 1992. "Introduction." In *Situational Crime Prevention: Successful Case Studies*, edited by Ronald V. Clarke. Albany, NY: Harrow and Heston.

Clarke, Ronald V. 1993. "Fare Evasion and Automatic Ticket Collection on the London Underground." In *Crime Prevention Studies*, vol. 1, edited by Ronald V. Clarke. Monsey, NY: Criminal Justice Press.

Clarke, Ronald V. 1995a. "Opportunity-Reducing Crime Prevention Strategies and the Role of Motivation." In *Integrating Crime Prevention Strategies: Propensity and Opportunity*, edited by Per-Olof H. Wikström, Ronald V. Clarke, and Joan McCord. Stockholm: National Council for Crime Prevention.

Clarke, Ronald V. 1995b. "Situational Crime Prevention." In *Building a Safer Society: Strategic Approaches to Crime Prevention. Crime and Justice: A Review of Research*, vol. 19, edited by Michael Tonry and David P. Farrington. Chicago: University of Chicago Press.

Clarke, Ronald V. 1997. "Introduction." In *Situational Crime Prevention: Successful Case Studies*, 2nd ed., edited by Ronald V. Clarke. Guilderland, NY: Harrow and Heston.

Cohen, Lawrence E., and Marcus Felson. 1979. "Social Change and Crime Rate Trends: A Routine Activity Approach." *American Sociological Review* 44:588–608.

Cornish, Derek B., and Ronald V. Clarke. 1986. "Introduction." In *The Reasoning Criminal: Rational Choice Perspectives on Offending*, edited by Derek B. Cornish and Ronald V. Clarke. New York: Springer.

Cornish, Derek B., and Ronald V. Clarke. 2003. "Opportunities, Precipitators and Criminal Decisions: A Reply to Wortley's Critique of Situational Crime Prevention." In *Theory for Practice in Situational Crime Prevention. Crime Prevention Studies*, vol. 16, edited by Martha J. Smith and Derek B. Cornish. Monsey, NY: Criminal Justice Press.

Cozens, Paul, Greg Saville, and David Hillier. 2005. "Crime Prevention through Environmental Design (CPTED): A Review and Modern Bibliography." *Property Management* 23:328–356.

Davies, Toby, and Shane D. Johnson. 2015. "Examining the Relationship between Road Structure and Burglary Risk via Quantitative Network Analysis." *Journal of Quantitative Criminology* 31:481–507.

DiLonardo, Robert L., and Ronald V. Clarke. 1996. "Reducing the Rewards of Shoplifting: An Evaluation of Ink Tags." *Security Journal* 7:11–14.

Eck, John E. 2006. "Preventing Crime at Places." In *Evidence-Based Crime Prevention*, rev. ed., edited by Lawrence W. Sherman, David P. Farrington, Brandon C. Welsh, and Doris Layton MacKenzie. New York: Routledge.

Eck, John E. 2015. "Who Should Prevent Crime at Places? The Advantages of Regulating Place Managers and Challenges to Police Services." *Policing* 9:223–233.

Eck, John E., and Rob T. Guerette. 2012. "Place-Based Crime Prevention: Theory, Evidence, and Policy." In *The Oxford Handbook of Crime Prevention*, edited by Brandon C. Welsh and David P. Farrington. New York: Oxford University Press.

Ekblom, Paul. 2012. "The Private Sector and Designing Products against Crime." In *The Oxford Handbook of Crime Prevention*, edited by Brandon C. Welsh and David P. Farrington. New York: Oxford University Press.

Ekblom, Paul. 2013. "Redesigning the Language and Concepts of Crime Prevention through Environmental Design." Paper presented at the Sixth Ajman International Urban Planning Conference: City and Security. Ajman, United Arab Emirates.

Exum, M. Lyn, Joseph B. Kuhns, Brad Koch, and Chuck Johnson. 2010. "An Examination of Situational Crime Prevention Strategies across Convenience Stores and Fast-Food Restaurants." *Criminal Justice Policy Review* 21:269–295.

Farrington, David P., ed. 2005. *Integrated Developmental and Life-Course Theories of Offending. Advances in Criminological Theory*, vol. 14. New Brunswick, NJ: Transaction.

Garland, David. 2000. "Ideas, Institutions and Situational Crime Prevention." In *Ethical and Social Perspectives on Situational Crime Prevention*, edited by Andrew von Hirsch, David Garland, and Alison Wakefield. Oxford: Hart.

Guerette, Rob T., and Kate J. Bowers. 2009. "Assessing the Extent of Crime Displacement and Diffusion of Benefits: A Review of Situational Crime Prevention Evaluations." *Criminology* 47:1331–1361.

Ha, Taehoon, Gyeong-Seok Oh, and Hyeon-Ho Park. 2014. "Comparative Analysis of Defensible Space in CPTED Housing and non-CPTED Housing." *International Journal of Law, Crime and Justice* 43:496–511.

Hartel, Pieter, Marianne Junger, and Roel Wieringa. 2011. "Cyber-crime Science = Crime Science + Information Security." Technical Report by the Centre for Telematics and Information Technology, University of Twente.

Hinduja, Sameer, and Brandon Kooi. 2013. "Curtailing Cyber and Information Security Vulnerabilities through Situational Crime Prevention." *Security Journal* 26:383–402.

Homel, Ross, and Jeff Clark. 1994. "The Prediction and Prevention of Violence in Pubs and Clubs." In *Crime Prevention Studies*, vol. 3, edited by Ronald V. Clarke. Monsey, NY: Criminal Justice Press.

Homel, Ross, Marg Hauritz, Richard Wortley, Gillian McIlwain, and Russell Carvolth. 1997. "Preventing Alcohol-Related Crime through Community Action: The Surfer's Paradise Safety Action Project." In *Policing for Prevention: Reducing Crime, Public Intoxication and Injury*, edited by Ross Homel. Monsey, NY: Criminal Justice Press.

Huisman, Wim, and Judith van Erp. 2013. "Opportunities for Environmental Crime: A Test of Situational Crime Prevention Theory." *British Journal of Criminology* 53:1178–1200.

Jacobs, Jane. 1961. *The Death and Life of Great American Cities*. New York: Random House.

Jongejan, A., and T. Woldendorp. 2013. "A Successful CPTED Approach: The Dutch 'Police Label Secure Housing.'" *Built Environment* 39:31–49.

Lasley, James. 1998. "'Designing out' Gang Homicides and Street Assaults." Research in Brief. Washington, DC: National Institute of Justice.

La Vigne, Nancy G., and Samantha S. Lowry. 2011. *Evaluation of Camera Use to Prevent Crime in Commuter Parking Facilities: A Randomized Controlled Trial.* Washington, DC: Urban Institute.

Laycock, Gloria, and Claire Austin. 1992. "Crime Prevention in Parking Facilities." *Security Journal* 3:154–160.

Levi, Michael, and John Burrows. 2008. "Measuring the Impact of Fraud in the UK: A Conceptual and Empirical Journey." *British Journal of Criminology* 48:293–318.

Loebmann, Rebecca. 2002. "Drunk Driving: Probability of Detection and Its Perception." *Policing* 25:770–788.

Lorenc, Theo, Mark Petticrew, Margaret Whitehead, David Neary, Stephen Clayton, Kath Wright, et al. 2013. "Environmental Interventions to Reduce Fear of Crime: Systematic Review of Effectiveness." *Systematic Reviews Journal* 2:1–30.

Masuda, Barry. 1992. "Credit Card Fraud Prevention: A Successful Retail Strategy." In *Crime Prevention Studies*, vol. 1, edited by Ronald V. Clarke. Monsey, NY: Criminal Justice Press.

Nauta, Oberon. 2004. *De Effectiviteit van het Politie Keurmerk Veilig Wonen*. Amsterdam: DSP-group.

Newman, Graeme, Ronald V. Clarke, and Shlomo Giora Shoham, eds. 1997. *Rational Choice and Situational Crime Prevention: Theoretical Foundations*. Aldershot, UK: Ashgate/Dartmouth.

Newman, Oscar. 1972. *Defensible Space: Crime Prevention through Urban Design*. New York: Macmillan.

Pease, Ken. 1999. "A Review of Street Lighting Evaluations: Crime Reduction Effects." In *Surveillance of Public Space: CCTV, Street Lighting and Crime Prevention. Crime Prevention Studies*, vol. 10, edited by Kate Painter and Nick Tilley. Monsey, NY: Criminal Justice Press.

Poyner, Barry. 1991. "Situational Crime Prevention in Two Parking Facilities." *Security Journal* 2:96–101.

Pratt, Travis C., Kristy Holtfreter, and Michael D. Reisig. 2010. "Routine Online Activity and Internet Fraud Targeting: Extending the Generality of Routine Activity Theory." *Journal of Research in Crime and Delinquency* 47: 267–296.

Ratcliffe, Jerry H., Travis Taniguchi, and Ralph B. Taylor. 2009. "The Crime Reduction Effects of Public CCTV Cameras: A Multi-method Spatial Approach." *Justice Quarterly* 26:746–770.

Reynald, Danielle M. 2015. "Environmental Design and Crime Events." *Journal of Contemporary Criminal Justice* 31:71–89.

Reyns, Bradford W., Billy Henson, and Bonnie S. Fisher. 2011. "Being Pursued Online: Applying Cyber Lifestyle Routine Activities Theory to Cyberstalking Victimization." *Criminal Justice and Behavior* 38:1149–1169.

Scott, Michael S. and Kelly Dedel. 2006. *Assaults in and around Bars*. 2nd ed. Problem-Oriented Guides for Police: Problem-Specific Guides Series No. 1. Washington, DC: U.S. Department of Justice, Office of Community Oriented Policing Services.

Scott, Michael S., Nina J. Emerson, Louis B. Antonacci, and Joel B. Plant. 2006. *Drunk Driving*. Problem-Oriented Guides for Police: Problem-Specific Guides Series No. 36. Washington, DC: US Department of Justice, Office of Community Oriented Policing Services.

Seeja, K. R., and M. Zareapoor. 2014. "FraudMiner: A Novel Credit Card Fraud Detection Model Based on Frequent Itemset Mining." *Scientific World Journal*. DOI: 10.1155/2014/252797.

Skilton, Mike. 1988. *A Better Reception: The Development of Concierge Schemes*. London: Estate Action and Department of the Environment.

Smith, Martha J. 2005. *Robbery of Taxi Drivers*. Problem-Oriented Guides for Police: Problem-Specific Guides Series No. 34. Washington, DC: US Department of Justice, Office of Community Oriented Policing Services.

Smith, Martha J., and Ronald V. Clarke. 2012. "Situational Crime Prevention: Classifying Techniques Using 'Good Enough' Theory." In *The Oxford Handbook of Crime Prevention*, edited by Brandon C. Welsh and David P. Farrington. New York: Oxford University Press.

Stone, John, and Daniel Stevens. 2000. "Effectiveness of Taxi Partitions." *Transportation Research Record* 1731:731–78.

Trasler, Gordon. 1986. "Situational Crime Control and Rational Choice: A Critique." In *Situational Crime Prevention: From Theory into Practice*, edited by Kenneth Heal and Gloria Laycock. London: Her Majesty's Stationery Office.

Trasler, Gordon. 1993. "Conscience, Opportunity, Rational Choice, and Crime." In *Routine Activity and Rational Choice. Advances in Criminological Theory*, vol. 5, edited by Ronald V. Clarke and Marcus Felson. New Brunswick, NJ: Transaction.

Wagner, Allen E. 1997. "A Study of Traffic Pattern Modifications in an Urban Crime Prevention Program." *Journal of Criminal Justice* 25:19–30.

Weidner, Robert R. 1996. "Target-Hardening at the New York City Subway Station: Decreased Fare Evasion—at What Price?" In *Preventing Mass Transit Crime. Crime Prevention Studies*, vol. 6, edited by Ronald V. Clarke. Monsey, NY: Criminal Justice Press.

Welsh, Brandon C., and David P. Farrington. 2008. "Effects of Improved Street Lighting on Crime: A Systematic Review." *Campbell Systematic Reviews* 4:1–43. DOI: 10.4073/csr.2008.13.

Welsh, Brandon C., and David P. Farrington. 2009. "Public Area CCTV and Crime Prevention: An Updated Systematic Review and Meta-analysis." *Justice Quarterly* 26:716–745.

Welsh, Brandon C., and David P. Farrington. 2014. "CCTV and Crime Prevention." In *Encyclopedia of Criminology and Criminal Justice*, edited by Gerben J. N. Bruinsma and David L. Weisburd. New York: Springer.

Welsh, Brandon C., David P. Farrington, and Sema A. Taheri. 2015. "Effectiveness and Social Costs of Public Area Surveillance for Crime Prevention." *Annual Review of Law and Social Science* 11:111–130.

Welsh, Brandon C., Gregory M. Zimmerman, and Steven N. Zane. 2017. "The Centrality of Theory in Modern Day Crime Prevention: Developments, Challenges, and Opportunities." *Justice Quarterly*. DOI: 10.1080/07418825.2017.1300312.

Wortley, Richard. 1997. "Reconsidering the Role of Opportunity in Situational Crime Prevention." In *Rational Choice and Situational Crime Prevention: Theoretical Foundations*, edited by Graeme Newman, Ronald V. Clarke, and Shlomo Giora Shoham. Aldershot, UK: Ashgate/Dartmouth.

Wortley, Richard. 2001. "A Classification of Techniques for Controlling Situational Precipitators of Crime." *Security Journal* 14:63–82.

PART IV

SPECIAL CRIMES AND CIRCUMSTANCES

CHAPTER 33

RIOTS, SPACE, AND PLACE

PETER BAUDAINS AND SHANE D. JOHNSON

33.1 Introduction

Riots are extreme events that, at first glance, may appear completely random with offenders acting entirely irrationally. As such, one might expect theories of environmental criminology to offer little insight into such events. However, recent research demonstrates that, just like everyday urban crime, there are clear regularities in when and where incidents of disorder associated with riots take place (Baudains, Braithwaite, and Johnson 2013a, 2013b) and, moreover, that the spatial decision-making of rioters can, at least in part, be explained by theories of environmental criminology. This previous work, and that reported in this chapter, takes a rational choice perspective (Cornish and Clarke 1986) as its starting point. That is, in accordance with perspectives which argue that, in fact, there is a certain amount of logic exhibited in the behavior of rioters (e.g., Berk 1974; Mason 1984), we assume that, instead of being random, offender behavior is subject to constraints and that when deciding when and where to engage in disorder, offenders consider (however briefly) the costs, effort, and benefits associated with available choices. In Baudains, Braithwaite, and Johnson (2013a), we examined the spatial decision-making of rioters detected by the police during the 2011 riots in Greater London, and found evidence to support hypotheses motivated by routine activity, crime pattern, and social disorganization theory regarding where rioters chose to offend.

The current chapter extends our earlier study in four ways. First, we use new and up-to-date data sources to operationalize variables included in the model, which, at the time of the earlier study, were unavailable. This improves the validity of the inferences made and allows us to test how robust our model was. Second, we extend our testing of crime pattern theory by including additional routine activity nodes that were not considered in our earlier model. In particular, we examine the influence of activity nodes that offenders might visit for the purposes of entertainment and recreation, most likely during the evening, a time during which the majority of riot offenses took place. These types of nodes are often referred to as risky facilities (see Eck and Madensen in this volume). Third, in this chapter, we perform the analysis at a much finer scale of spatial resolution, using UK census output areas in Greater London as our unit of analysis. This enables us to be more precise about the influence of crime attractors in an area (and those nearby) and follows the aspiration discussed in other chapters of this book (e.g., Andresen in this volume) to use smaller units of analysis when analyzing spatial patterns of crime. However, the use of smaller units of analysis brings with it methodological complications associated with the estimation of factors that influence offender spatial decision-making. In what follows, we describe these complications and how we overcame them—the fourth extension to our earlier work.

This chapter is organized as follows. We first provide some theoretical motivation for the present study, explaining the findings of Baudains, Braithwaite, and Johnson (2013a). We also explain in more detail why the presence of risky facilities might have influenced rioter decision-making and consider how this study builds upon prior research in this area. We then provide an overview of our modeling framework, before outlining the analytical procedures adopted when working with a large number of small spatial units of analysis. We give an overview of the variables used to populate our model, and include the results of two principal components analyses, which were undertaken to reduce the number of independent variables modeled. Finally, we present our results and offer some concluding remarks.

33.2 Theoretical Motivation

One of the key differences between rioting and more regular types of crime is that riots require a number of individuals engaging in some form of violent behavior (or the threat of such behavior) at the same time and place. Because of this, much existing research on riots stems from academic traditions considering the behavior of crowds. We begin by discussing this perspective.

Early accounts of riots (e.g., Le Bon 1960) portrayed offenders as irrational actors whose actions could only be understood from the perspective of the crowd, whose collective decision-making was animal-like and random. Later work (e.g., Berk 1974; Mason 1984), however, suggested that rather than being irrational, rioters decide whether to engage in riots and where to do so based on available information and some form of internal cost-benefit calculation. For instance, research (e.g., Berk 1974) suggests that certain types of facilities are more likely to be targeted at a higher rate (per opportunity) during riots than are others, and that the spatial and temporal distribution of riots is far from random (e.g., Baudains, Braithwaite, and Johnson 2013a).

This is not to say that the behavior of crowds has no influence on rioter decision-making, just that this can be understood from a rational choice perspective. For example, crowds can influence the individual decision-making of offenders at nearby locations, increasing the likelihood that those who observe the disorder directly will engage in it either by prompting this behavior, provoking it, or (since others are doing it) making them perceive that it is permissible (Wortley 2008; see also Wortley in this volume). In line with this perspective (which comes from environmental criminology), a more traditional approach to understanding riots that a number of studies have emphasized is that the decision to engage in rioting is likely affected by the number of people already involved in the disorder (Granovetter 1978). Accordingly, in our recent studies (Baudains, Braithwaite, and Johnson 2013a, 2013b; Baudains, Johnson, and Braithwaite 2013) we have examined how the location of rioting activity in one time period affects that in the next, and find evidence to suggest that rioting does tend to escalate in affected areas, as expected (see also Epstein 2002; Davies et al. 2013). We also found (see Baudains, Johnson, and Braithwaite 2013) that incidents of disorder tended to spill over into nearby areas more than would be expected on a chance basis, suggesting a process of contagion. In contrast, we found little evidence of a systematic process of relocation whereby activity simply moved (or was displaced) from one area to those nearby. Our interpretation of this is that the characteristics of an area matter and have an effect on offender decision-making, a point to which we will return below.

Of course, the activity of crowds can also influence offender decision-making over larger spatial scales, since reports may travel via the popular press or online social media. In the case of the 2011 London riots in particular, it is thought that social media activity (largely the Blackberry messaging service) caused a number of individuals to engage in the disorder who may have otherwise not have offended (Lewis et al. 2012). An individual who becomes motivated to engage in rioting as a result of such communication has to make an important decision regarding where and when to offend. Such individuals might decide to travel to areas already experiencing disorder that are some distance away. However, doing so may incur travel costs, and the locations may be unfamiliar, increasing the offender's uncertainty as to the risks, effort, and rewards involved. Accordingly, unless areas that are farther away are near to or contain other activity nodes offenders routinely visit—and which are therefore in their awareness spaces—just like everyday offenders (see Rossmo 2017; Bernasco in this volume), and in line with crime pattern theory (Brantingham and Brantingham 1993; see also Summers and Guerette in this volume), we would expect rioters to be less likely to select them. In support of this, in Baudains, Braithwaite, and Johnson (2013a), we find clear evidence that, all else equal, offenders not only tend to select those areas in which riots are already ongoing but those that are near to their home location.

As discussed in other chapters of this book, theories of environmental criminology suggest that, in addition to propinquity, the characteristics of a neighborhood influence where offenders choose to offend, at least for everyday urban crime. In Baudains, Braithwaite, and Johnson (2013a) we examine whether expectations based on such theories apply in the extreme conditions of a riot and find support for both crime pattern and social disorganization theories. As discussed in the chapter by Wilcox and Swartz in this volume (for example), social disorganization theory (Shaw and McKay 1969) considers how the social fabric of a community can influence the likelihood of crime occurrence. In the context of riots, variation in social disorganization may influence the spatial patterning of riots in (at least) two ways. First, high levels of neighborhood social cohesion may lead to visual cues that discourage rioters from selecting a particular area. Second, in neighborhoods with high levels of social organization, the theory would suggest that neighbors would be more likely to exert informal social control over those who live in the area, reducing the likelihood that they would engage in the disorder.[1] In a recent study, and using data for the 2011 London riots, Kawalerowicz and Biggs (2015) investigated the latter explanation, finding support for it. In this chapter, our focus is on the former.

In Baudains, Braithwaite, and Johnson (2013a) we examined whether offenders were more likely to offend in areas that had those characteristics commonly associated with socially disorganized neighborhoods: high levels of neighborhood deprivation, ethnic heterogeneity, and population turnover (see Wilcox and Swartz in this volume). While our findings were not unequivocal (the patterns varied across different days of the disorder), support was found for theories of social disorganization, with the likelihood of offenders selecting an area generally increasing in those locations with higher rates of deprivation, ethnic diversity, and population churn. A weakness of the previous study, however, was that data from the 2001 UK census were used to estimate levels of social disorganization. Leaving aside the fact that these are indirect measures of social disorganization, the estimates were rather out of date (albeit that they were the best available data at the time of that study). In the present study, we take the opportunity to use data from the 2011 UK census, which were made available after the publication of our earlier work. We also make use of data for much smaller areal units, allowing us to re-examine our hypotheses using more up-to-date data at a finer scale of geographical resolution (for a discussion of why this is important, see Andresen; Lawton in this volume).

As discussed in the chapters by Summers and Guerette (also see the chapter by Brantingham et al. in this volume), crime pattern theory emphasizes the role that offenders' routine activity patterns play in shaping their awareness of criminal opportunities and the types of places they are most likely to offend. Motivated by this perspective, in Baudains, Braithwaite, and Johnson (2013a), we examined whether, all else being equal, offenders were more likely to target those areas that were close to their place of residence and hence that they would likely be familiar with. We also examined whether, after controlling for the effects of distance, they would be more likely to offend in those areas that contained routine activity nodes that they would be likely to visit during their routine activities, in this case, retail centers, London Underground stations, and schools. Our findings confirmed that, like other offenders (see Bernasco in this volume), rioters typically committed offenses closer to their home and were more likely to select those areas that contained the types of routine activity nodes considered.

With respect to crime pattern theory, the principal theoretical contribution of this chapter is to examine whether the presence of routine activity nodes not considered in our earlier research help to explain some of the variation in rioter target choice. In particular, we examine the influence of activity nodes associated with the nighttime economy such as bars, betting shops, and restaurants. There are a number of reasons for expecting such facilities to influence rioter spatial decision-making. First, just like other activity nodes that people visit, their presence will increase collective awareness of the areas within which they are located. Some people who visit them will be those motivated to engage in the riots and, as such, they will be more familiar with these areas and, according to crime pattern theory, more likely to offend in them. Second, the majority of offenses that occurred during the 2011 London riots took place at night (see Baudains, Braithwaite, and Johnson 2013b). Consequently, we might expect facilities that are frequented by people at night to have a particular influence on where offenses took place during the riots, either because they routinely attract people to them at night, which may help to create a convergence in space and time of those motivated, or subsequently provoked (see above), to engage in the disorder, or because they shape people's awareness of what an area looks like at that particular time of day. Third, as discussed by Eck, Clarke, and Guerette (2007) and in the chapter by Eck and Madensen (in this volume), some "risky" facilities of this type can be described as "crime enablers," where weak place management does little to discourage crime or may even encourage it. In the context of the riots, the convergence of people at or near to such facilities coupled with weak or nonexistent place management may have contributed to the outbreak of disorder at these locations. Accordingly, we hypothesize that (all else equal) the presence of risky facilities in an area will increase the likelihood that such an area will be targeted.

33.3 Model Framework

In our earlier study and the research reported here, we use a discrete choice framework to model offender spatial decision-making. This approach has a long econometric tradition (Luce 1959; McFadden 1974, 2001) and has more recently been considered in the context of a number of spatial choice problems (i.e., where the alternatives consist of a particular location or geographic area in space). With respect to problems in the study of crime (see Bernasco in this volume), it has been used recently to investigate the target choice of offenders for a wide range of different crime types including burglary (Townsley et al. 2015; Bernasco and Nieuwbeerta 2005), robbery (Bernasco, Block, and Ruiter 2013; Bernasco and Block 2009), and theft from vehicles (Johnson and Summers 2014).

The simplest discrete choice model—the conditional logit—is particularly well suited to testing hypotheses in a criminological context for two reasons: first, it explicitly compares characteristics of areas that were selected by offenders to those that were not. This moves beyond simply observing the correlates of crime targets, by considering more precisely why locations stand out in comparison to similar locations that could have been chosen but were not. Second, the model enables the inclusion of variables that depend on both the target area (the alternative) and the offender (the decision-maker). Consequently, the approach makes it possible to control for certain attributes of offenders (such as where they live) in identifying the targets that they were more likely to select.

The conditional logit model is predicated upon the theory of rational choice and, more specifically, the axiom that a decision-maker will select the alternative that provides the most utility. The conditional logit model is then constructed through the perspective of random utility, by supposing that the utility decision-maker *i* obtains by selecting alternative *j* is given by

$$U_{ij} = V_{ij} + \varepsilon_{ij}, \tag{33.1}$$

where V_{ij} is the portion of utility that can be observed by the researcher and that reflects the utility representative of the population. This part of the utility function can be estimated via sample data from the population. The error term, given by ε_{ij}, is the portion that reflects individual idiosyncrasies that cannot be expected to be captured explicitly in a model. Assuming that this error component is distributed in a certain way (specifically, that the errors are independent and identically distributed according to an extreme value type I distribution), then the probability that decision-maker *i* selects alternative *j* is given by

$$\Pr(Z_i = j) = \frac{\exp(V_{ij})}{\sum_{k=1}^{J} \exp(V_{ik})}, \tag{33.2}$$

where *J* is the total number of alternatives available to decision-maker *i*. Thus the probability that a decision-maker selects a particular option *j* is calculated as a ratio of the exponentiated observed component of utilities between option *j* and all other options *k*. The model then reduces to finding appropriate specifications of the observed utility function V_{ij}. This is usually taken to be a linear function of variables that capture characteristics of those choices, which are hypothesized to influence the decision-making at the population level.

The conditional logit model is encumbered with the independence of irrelevant alternatives (IIA) property. This property states that the ratio of probabilities for selecting two possible alternatives does not depend on the other alternatives that might be available. It arises due to the assumption of independence of the error terms and is problematic in many practical applications, including those where choices are situated in space. In particular, it implies that a choice is made purely as a function of the characteristics of each alternative, independently of others that might be available. In a spatial context, this means that characteristics of nearby areas play no role in the decision-making of the offender. In many cases, this assumption is violated. For instance, spillover effects may exist by which individuals who were originally attracted to a particular area due to features of that area (e.g., the presence of risky facilities) then decide to commit their offense nearby.

A number of different models have been proposed to account for the interdependence between alternatives, which alleviate the restrictions associated with the IIA property (see, for instance, Train 2009). Many of these incorporate such dependence in the error term of equation (33.1). However, as Bernasco, Block, and Ruiter (2013) point out, this method of dealing with the IIA property may mask substantive effects that might otherwise be incorporated within the observed component of utility. They argue that a suitable model that circumvents the IIA property is the universal logit model, which is equivalent to equation (33.2) but where Vij is not just a function of attributes of area *j* but also a function of attributes in neighboring areas. The universal logit model enables the identification of spillover effects and interdependencies between possible targets. We employ this model in what follows to test whether attributes of certain areas encourage the spillover of riot offenses to nearby locations.

33.4 Spatial Units of Analysis

A trend within environmental criminology, particularly when examining crime concentration, has been a focus on smaller spatial units of analysis. This includes census output areas, city blocks, street segments, and even individual addresses. This study continues this trend. In Baudains, Braithwaite, and Johnson (2013a), the geographic unit of analysis was the Lower Super Output Area, a geographic partition of the UK where each unit contains, on average, 1,500 residents. In this study, we use census output areas, the smallest level of geography for which UK census data is released. In Greater London, these areas contain an average of 326 residents. For the 2011 UK Census there are 25,053 output areas contained within the boundaries of Greater London. We take these output areas as the set of alternatives for each rioter when deciding where to participate in the rioting.

Dealing with this many units of analysis is problematic when it comes to estimating the conditional logit and universal logit models. This is because, for each offender, it is necessary to compare the choice that he or she actually made with the choices that were not made. With so many alternatives in the choice set, this can mean that, even for a relatively modest number of offenses, the computational requirements necessary to calibrate the model can become prohibitive. To circumvent this issue, we randomly sample 99 alternatives from the choice set as alternatives that were not chosen for each rioter. This enables us to compare the alternative chosen by the rioter with a sample of alternatives that were not. It has been shown that this approach to sampling from alternatives provides model estimates that are consistent with estimates calculated from the full choice set (McFadden 1978; Train 2009).

A question that might be asked is whether 99 alternatives are enough. Two different random selections of 99 alternatives from a choice set of 25,053 are likely to contain very different choices, which may alter the conclusions resulting from the model. To account for this, we employed a bootstrap procedure by randomly sampling the data set used in this study 10 times. That is, for each rioter, 10 randomly selected choice sets of 99 alternatives are included in the calibration procedure. Following Bernasco, Block, and Ruiter (2013), we report the pooled parameter estimates and standard errors from these 10 iterations using Rubin's (1987) formulae. This accounts for any variation that might be observed due to random sampling of alternatives.

33.5 Data

In this section, we describe the data used to populate our model of rioter target choice. We begin by describing the dependent variable: riot-related offenses detected by the police that occurred during the 2011 riots in Greater London. We then outline each independent variable, including, where appropriate, justification for its inclusion.

33.5.1 Offender Data

Riots occurred across the UK between August 6 and August 10, 2011, but were most concentrated in the cities of London, Manchester, and Birmingham. The Metropolitan Police Service provided data on 2,229 riot-related offenses that occurred in London and for which a suspect had been apprehended. The data for each included an identifier for the output area in which the offense took place (within Greater London), the output area of the offender's residential address (also within Greater London), and the time and date of the offense. All of these offenses were used in the analysis that follows.

As with any empirical studies that use police-recorded data, there exists the possibility of selection bias in that we only analyze data for offenders who *were* arrested. If those offenders who were not detected behaved differently than those that were, then this has the potential to bias our study and its conclusions. However, during the London riots, a substantial and unprecedented effort went into detecting offenders and prosecuting them quickly. Extensive use was made of CCTV footage and courts' hours were extended to enable swift prosecutions (Metropolitan Police Service 2012). Thus, while many offenses will have gone undetected, we have good reason to believe that detection bias of the kind described will be lower in the current study than in other similar work, which has considered crimes such as burglary (e.g., Bernasco and Nieuwbeerta 2005). Furthermore, recent work that has examined the influence of detection bias in the analysis of spatial patterns of crime suggests that any effects may be small or nonexistent (Johnson et al. 2009; Lammers 2014).

33.5.2 Crime Pattern Theory Variables

Following Baudains, Braithwaite, and Johnson (2013a), we counted the number of schools and the number of London Underground and regional train stations in each output area. We also calculated the number of retail sites per 100 m squared (i.e., retail site density) in each output area. These three variables were obtained from Ordnance Survey (OS) points of interest data (Points of Interest 2015).

To test our (novel) hypotheses concerning the influence of "risky" facilities on offender spatial decision-making, we also used the OS points of interest data (Points of Interest 2015) to count the number of facilities associated with the nighttime economy located within each output area. The facilities included were bars, betting shops, casinos, cinemas, fast-food outlets, nightclubs, and restaurants.

Having derived these counts, we found a substantial amount of collinearity between them. Output areas that tended to contain more (less) of one type of facility also tended to contain more (less) of another. Because high levels of collinearity in multivariate models can cause problems for statistical inference, a principal components analysis was used to reduce the dimension of the data. Using the Kaiser criterion (Kaiser 1960), two principal components were retained, whose factor loadings are shown in Table 33.1.

Table 33.1 PCA Factor Loadings for Entertainment Variables

	Spontaneous	Purposeful
Bars	0.47	−0.17
Betting shops	0.39	−0.30
Casinos	0.18	0.56
Cinemas	0.22	0.57
Fast food	0.46	−0.33
Nightclubs	0.29	0.37
Restaurants	0.49	0.02

The first component emphasized facilities that are often found on the UK high street: bars, betting shops, fast-food outlets, and restaurants. These are locations that might encourage serendipitous or spontaneous trips to an area. Offenders may not have to go out of their way or to plan a trip to attend these sorts of facilities. In contrast, the second component placed an emphasis on casinos, cinemas, and nightclubs, which are not necessarily as prominent on the typical high street in the UK. Accordingly, these facilities often require a planned and specific trip to attend them. These types of facilities also tend to be larger in size and to employ more people. Consequently, such facilities may also provide more (in)formal guardianship and have more formal place management strategies (see Eck and Madensen in this volume) than the (typically) smaller high-street facilities discussed above. In addition to helping address the problem of collinearity, this distinction between the two components (or kinds of facilities) offers an opportunity to conduct a further substantive test with regards to the particular type of facilities that are most likely to influence the decision-making of rioters.

As discussed above, our earlier work showed that, like other offenders and consistent with expectations from crime pattern theory, rioters tended to commit offenses close to their home location. To examine this influence, for each offense we computed the Euclidian distance between the centroid of the output area within which rioters lived, the output area in which they offended, and all alternative output areas considered in the model (see above).

33.5.3 Contagion Variables

To measure the influence of prior activity in an area on rioter spatial decision-making, as in Baudains, Braithwaite, and Johnson (2013a), we computed the number of offenses that occurred in each output area in the previous 24 hours before an offender engaged in the disorder. As rioters took part in the disorder at different times and on different dates, this variable was calculated separately for every offense analyzed.

In including the number of prior offenses in the area, it is possible that, rather than capturing the effect of crowds, this variable instead captures unobserved heterogeneity in the characteristics of the areas. That is, there may be time-stable area-level attributes that attracted rioters that were important but that (in the interests of parsimony) were not included in the model. To check for this possibility, we run a test similar to that in Baudains, Braithwaite, and Johnson (2013a). This test calibrates the model with just three variables: the origin-destination distance between the residence of the offender and the alternative, the number of offenses that occurred in each alternative in the previous 24 hours, and the number of offenses that occurred in each alternative over the entire time period minus the number in the previous 24 hours. We found that all variables were significant in the expected direction. While this does not rule out the possibility that unobserved heterogeneity is present, the significance of the number of offenses in the previous 24 hours highlights that this variable is capturing at least some of the precipitating influence of prior events (for more details, see Baudains, Braithwaite, and Johnson 2013a).

33.5.4 Social Disorganization Variables

As in Baudains, Braithwaite, and Johnson (2013a), variables were also included in the model to capture estimates of social disorganization. In contrast to our earlier work, we make use of data from the 2011 UK census, which has only recently been made available at the census output area level. These data are particularly useful, as they were captured on March 27, 2011, just a few months prior to the 2011 riots in London. This means that the variables used in this chapter more accurately capture the neighborhood measures of interest than the data used in our previous work.

We use four different variables to estimate the social disorganization of neighborhoods. As discussed in other chapters of this book, social disorganization theory states that the inability for residents in an area to identify common goals and to mobilize themselves for the purposes of joint community action can result in a lack of informal social control, and, therefore can increase the level of delinquency. As outlined above, when it comes to the choice of targets of would-be rioters, we hypothesize that those areas with a lack of social organization will be unable to repel rioters from selecting that area in which to riot (regardless of whether those rioters come from within or outside the neighborhood).

The first variable intended to capture social disorganization is a measure of deprivation, derived at the output area level. In line with social disorganization theory, we hypothesize that neighborhoods with a higher level of deprivation will lack the resources to be able to exert informal social control and, therefore, make attractive locations in which to riot.[2] This variable considers four indicators of household deprivation. These are

(i) whether any member of the household, who is not a full-time student, is either unemployed or long-term sick;
(ii) whether no person in the household has at least level 2 education (roughly corresponding to good grades obtained from exams taken at 16) and no person aged 16–18 is a full-time student;

(iii) whether any person in the household made a self-assessment of their health as either "bad" or "very bad" or has a long-term health problem or disability that limits day to day activities; and
(iv) whether the household's accommodation is either overcrowded, in a shared dwelling, or has no central heating.

The percentage of households meeting at least two of these deprivation criteria are calculated, and this is the variable used in the analysis.

The second variable we use is a measure of population churn. It is supposed that a high rate of population churn prevents neighbors from forming social ties, which, in turn, impedes the development of collective efficacy and informal social control in a neighborhood (see Wilcox and Swartz in this volume). A measure of population churn, as described in Dennett and Stillwell (2008), was derived for each output area in Greater London. This measure sums the number of people who have moved into the area in the last year, the number of people who have moved out of the area in the last year, and the number who have moved within that area within the last year and divides this by the population of the area.

A third variable to capture social disorganization is ethnic diversity, computed using the index of qualitative variation (Agresti and Agresti 1978). This measure calculates the probability that two randomly selected individuals within the same neighborhood will be of different ethnicity. The ethnic categories used to calculate this index were obtained from the UK census definition.[3]

Our final variable to capture the level of social disorganization in an area is the percentage of households in the output area with a single parent. Following Sampson and Groves (1989), this variable is used since a neighborhood with a large number of single-parent households influences that neighborhood's ability to exert social control among younger people.

As with our indices of risky facilities, a significant amount of collinearity was present for our estimates of social disorganization. Consequently, we conducted a principal components analysis. Using the Kaiser criterion for component selection, two components were retained and included in the analysis. The factor loadings for these four variables are shown in Table 33.2.

The first component, with high loadings on deprivation and the percentage of single parents, might be thought of as the level of disadvantage in the neighborhood,

Table 33.2 PCA Factor Loadings for Social Disorganization Variables

	Disadvantage	Lack of social ties
Deprivation	0.63	−0.09
Churn	−0.13	0.83
Ethnic diversity	0.48	0.53
Single parent	0.60	−0.16

whereas the second component, with higher levels of churn and ethnic diversity, might be thought of as capturing an estimate of barriers to the formation of social ties in a neighborhood.

33.5.5 Spillover Effects

As explained above, variables with neighboring areas are also included in our model to investigate the importance of potential spillover effects. These variables are calculated by taking the average value of each variable in output areas that share a border with the focal area. Table 33.3 shows the correlations between the destination variables included in the model and their corresponding neighboring variable. For the variables relating to social disorganization, the correlations are very high, indicative of a substantial amount of spatial autocorrelation. For this reason, we do not include these particular variables in the analysis. All other neighboring variables are included. In some cases, the correlation is still quite high. For this reason, we present the results of both the conditional logit model (which does not estimate spillover effects) and the universal logit model (which does estimate spillover effects) to determine whether the inferences for the focal areas are consistent across models.

To further model potential contagion (see above), we also include an additional spillover variable, calculated as the average number of offenses that occurred in the previous 24 hours in the neighboring output areas. This enables us to capture the potential for the riots to spread geographically over time (see Baudains, Johnson, and Braithwaite 2013).

Prior to analysis, we examined whether there were issues of collinearity for all destination specific variables. Table 33.4 shows that the variable associated with spontaneous risky facilities is the only one to exhibit any potential collinearity issues. Unsurprisingly, it has a relatively high level of correlation with the density of retail stores and the number of Underground and railway stations. We retain these variables in our analysis, as they speak to different theoretical aspects within the model (retail stores may be more

Table 33.3 Correlations between Alternative Specific Variables and the Average Value of the Same Variable in Neighboring Areas

Spontaneous venues	.50
Purposeful venues	.27
Neighborhood disadvantage	.80
Lack of social ties	.76
Retail density	.48
Schools	.09
Underground and rail stations	.05

Table 33.4 Correlation Matrix for the Alternative Specific Variables

	Spontaneous venues	Purposeful venues	Disadvantage	Lack of social ties	Retail density	Schools	Underground and rail stations
Spontaneous venues	1						
Purposeful venues	.00	1					
Disadvantage	−.03	−.03	1				
Lack of social ties	.21	−.04	.00	1			
Retail density	.42	−.07	−.01	.24	1		
Schools	.10	−.01	−.04	.07	.04	1	
Underground and rail stations	.32	−.12	−.02	.09	.10	.07	1

targeted due to looting, while railway stations speak to the accessibility of a particular area), but keep this in mind when interpreting coefficient estimates.

33.6 Results and Discussion

Table 33.5 shows the odds ratios associated with the variables tested for both the conditional logit model and the universal logit model (the latter estimating spillover effects). Odds ratios are given by the exponentiated value of each coefficient in the linear observed utility. The odds ratio thus gives an estimate of the multiplicative effect on the odds of a one-unit increase in a variable for a particular area (all else equal). Thus, an odds ratio equal to one demonstrates no effect between the independent variable and the odds that an area is chosen. Values greater than one suggest a positive relationship, such that areas with higher values will be more likely to be chosen, while values less than one suggest a negative relationship, whereby targets with higher values are less likely to be chosen. In this section, we discuss each variable in turn and consider its importance in explaining rioter target choice.

Considering the patterns observed for the focal areas first, in line with crime pattern theory, and consistent with our previous analysis (conducted using larger areal units), the density of retail facilities, the presence of schools, and the proximity to an offender's residential location were all associated with an increase in the odds of being chosen as

Table 33.5 Odds Ratios and Standard Errors (in Parentheses) for Each Variable as Obtained from the Conditional Logit Model and the Universal Logit Model (I.e. including spillover effects)

		Conditional logit	Universal logit
Crime pattern theory	Retail density	1.143**	1.120**
		(0.013)	(0.012)
	Underground and rail stations	0.543**	0.583**
		(0.091)	(0.089)
	Schools	1.408*	1.540**
		(0.164)	(0.167)
	Origin-destination distance	0.604**	0.604**
		(0.007)	(0.007)
	Spontaneous venues	1.108**	1.122**
		(0.018)	(0.025)
	Purposeful venues	0.940*	0.931*
		(0.021)	(0.025)
Contagion	Previous 24 hours offenses	1.200**	1.173**
		(0.040)	(0.035)
Social disorganization	Disadvantage	1.324**	1.310**
		(0.033)	(0.032)
	Lack of social ties	1.560**	1.522**
		(0.050)	(0.051)
Spillover effects	Neighboring retail density		1.147**
			(0.022)
	Neighboring Underground and rail stations		3.943**
			(1.063)
	Neighboring schools		0.417**
			(0.100)
	Neighboring offenses in previous 24 hours		1.314**
			(0.034)
	Neighboring spontaneous venues		0.878**
			(0.020)
	Neighboring purposeful venues		1.055
			(0.033)

**$p < 0.001$; *$p < 0.01$.

a target. That is, all else equal, areas containing these routine activity nodes or that were closer to the offender's home location were more likely to be selected. In contrast, the variable for the number of Underground and rail stations was associated with a reduction in the odds that an area was selected. That is, for every additional Underground or rail station in the target area, the odds of selecting the area are reduced by nearly half.

Considered in isolation, this finding is inconsistent with expectation and our previous findings. We return to this point below.

Considering the role of "risky" facilities, in both models we observe effects in different directions for the two components included in the model. Specifically, the presence of places associated with the first type of facility was associated with an increase in the odds that a particular area was selected for rioting; while the presence of those associated with the second type of facility was associated with a decrease in the odds that a particular area was selected for rioting. Put differently, areas containing facilities whose business relies predominantly on the nighttime economy and whose locations might facilitate spontaneous trips were more likely to be selected by rioters. In contrast, areas containing similar nighttime-focused facilities that tend to require a more purposeful trip, were less likely to be selected.

The presence of recent rioting in each area was also a significant determinant of target choice, with each additional detected offense in the previous 24 hours being associated with an increase of an area being selected by around 20%. Our estimates of social disorganization were also positively associated with the odds of an area being selected. That is, those neighborhoods that were characterized by socioeconomic disadvantage, and in which proxy data suggest there would be barriers to the formation of strong social ties, were more likely to be selected by rioters, as expected.

Moving on to spillover effects, with the exception of the purposeful facilities variable, the relationship between target choice and variables for neighboring areas (estimated in the universal logit specification) were all significantly associated with target choice. This suggests that these variables play some role in explaining the variation in rioter target choice. Consistent with theory, the spillover variables for retail density, Underground and rail stations, and detected offenses in the previous 24 hours were positively associated with the odds of offenders selecting an area.

Interestingly, the effect of the presence of Underground and rail stations was particularly strong, with each additional station in a neighboring area causing a nearly fourfold increase in the odds of a neighborhood being selected. This finding, combined with the negative relationship for stations in the focal area of interest, suggests that, overall, rioters may not have targeted those areas that contained transport links, but, instead, in many instances, chose those nearby. An explanation consistent with this pattern of findings would be that rioters traveled to or met in areas containing transport facilities, but decided to offend in nearby locations, perhaps due to the fear of being detected near the station due to the presence of CCTV or station staff, or other place management practices implemented at Underground stations (for a discussion of place management, see Eck and Madensen in this volume).

The presence of spontaneous nighttime facilities in neighboring areas was associated with a reduction in the odds that an area was selected. Thus, although the presence of these facilities in an area increased the likelihood of that area being selected, it appears that rioters did not view areas that were simply near to them as suitable alternatives. The same goes for the presence of schools.

33.7 Conclusion

In this chapter, we have reanalyzed data concerning the 2011 riots in Greater London. We have extended prior work in a number of directions, using variables more representative of the areas in which rioting took place, using smaller geographical units of analysis, and extending the analysis to examine the role of risky facilities. Our conclusions both support our previous work and extend it (Baudains, Braithwaite, and Johnson 2013a). That is, using a random utility framework, we find support for crime pattern and social disorganization theories, as well as the precipitating influence of crowds, in explaining rioter decision-making. In addition, we find that different types of facilities appear to have different influences on the spatial decision-making of those engaged in the riots. In explaining these differences, we have drawn attention to the fact that some facilities are more common on the high street and visited more spontaneously, while others require a more purposeful visit, are likely to provide more guardianship, and are more likely to have formal place management practices. Future research might explore these issues more directly than was possible here.

There are, of course, a number of limitations to this study. Chief among these is that the data used to estimate levels of social disorganization come from a secondary data source (the UK census), rather than being collected through methods of systematic social observational (see Brunton-Smith in this volume). This is typical for studies of the kind reported here but should nevertheless be borne in mind. A further issue is that the data analyzed here are (naturally) only for those offenders who were detected by the police. The concern is that the spatial decision-making of those offenders who went undetected may have been quite different from that of those who were detected. However, as discussed above, the use of CCTV footage to detect offenders after the riots is likely to have minimized such effects.

Our findings are powerful, as they suggest that theories of environmental criminology apply to types of offending more extreme than those that they were developed to explain. As far as we are aware, the use of a random utility framework to study rioter decision-making, or the decision-making of offenders engaged in other extreme events, is limited to our earlier work and that reported here. Accordingly, we would encourage others to use this approach (and others) to test theories of environmental criminology in other contexts and for other types of (extreme) events.

Notes

1. An alternative expectation, not examined here, is that rioting that is the outcome of a social protest that most people support may be more likely to originate from cohesive neighborhoods, since it is in such neighborhoods that residents are most likely to share common views and to act collectively to protest. As discussed by Kawalerowicz and Biggs (2015), while such an explanation may apply to other riots, it does not apply here, as the majority

of the public did not support the 2011 London riots, and the activity of the rioters largely involved looting and destructive behavior in or near to their own neighborhoods, which impacted negatively on their neighbors.

2. A different explanation for why more deprived areas might coincide with more rioting is that (*a*) deprived members of the population have more incentive to riot in the hope that, by doing so, their situation will improve; and (*b*) deprived members of the population will lack the resources to be able to travel and so riot in their own neighborhoods. The inclusion of the distance between residential location and offence location controls for distance traveled and therefore goes some way to discount this explanation.
3. These are white British; white Irish; white Gypsy or Irish traveler; other white; mixed Caribbean; mixed African; mixed Asian; other mixed; Indian; Pakistani; Bangladeshi; Chinese; other Asian; black African; black Caribbean; other black; Arab; other ethnic group.

References

Agresti, A. and Agresti, B. F. 1978. Statistical analysis of qualitative variation. In Schuessler, K. F. (ed.), *Sociological Methodology*, 204–237. San Francisco, CA: Jossey-Bass.

Baudains, P., Braithwaite, A., and Johnson, S. D. 2013a. Target choice during extreme events: A discrete spatial choice model of the 2011 London riots. *Criminology* 51(2): 251–286.

Baudains, P., Braithwaite, A., and Johnson, S. D. 2013b. Spatial patterns in the 2011 London riots. *Policing* 7(1): 21–31.

Baudains, P., Johnson, S. D., and Braithwaite, A. 2013. Geographic patterns of diffusion in the 2011 London riots. *Applied Geography* 7(1): 21–31.

Berk, R. A. 1974. A gaming approach to crowd behavior. *American Sociological Review* 39(3): 355–373.

Bernasco, W. and Block, R. 2009. Where offenders choose to attack: A discrete choice model of robberies in Chicago. *Criminology* 47(1): 93–130.

Bernasco, W., Block, R., and Ruiter, S. 2013. Go where the money is: Modeling street robbers' location choices. *Journal of Economic Geography* 13: 119–143.

Bernasco, W. and Nieuwbeerta, P. 2005. How do residential burglars select target areas? A new approach to the analysis of criminal location choice. *British Journal of Criminology* 44(3): 296–315.

Brantingham, P. J. and Brantingham, P. L. 1993. Environment, routine, and situation: Toward a pattern theory of crime. In Clarke, R. V. and Felson, F. (eds.), *Routine Activity and Rational Choice*, vol. 5 of *Advances in Criminological Theory*, 259–294. New Brunswick, NJ: Transaction.

Cornish, D. B. and Clarke, R. V. 1986. *The Reasoning Criminal: Rational Choice Perspectives on Offending*. New York: Springer.

Davies, T. P., Fry, H. M., Wilson, A. G., and Bishop, S. R. 2013. A mathematical model of the London riots and their policing. *Scientific Reports* 3: 1303.

Dennett, A. and Stillwell, J. 2008. Population turnover and churn: Enhancing understanding of internal migration in Britain through measures of stability. *Population Trends* 134: 24–41.

Eck, John E., Clarke, Ronald V., and Guerette, Rob, T. 2007. Risky facilities: Crime concentration in homogeneous sets of establishments and facilities. In Farrell, G., Bowers, K. J., Johnson, S. D., and Townsley, M. (eds.), *Imagination for Crime Prevention: Essays in Honour of Ken Pease*, vol. 21 of *Crime Prevention Studies*, 225–264. Monsey, NY: Criminal Justice Press.

Epstein, J. M. 2002. Modeling civil violence: An agent-based computational approach. *Proceedings of the National Academy of Sciences of the USA* 99, Suppl. 3(2): 7243–7250.

Granovetter, M. 1978. Threshold models of collective behavior. *American Journal of Sociology* 83(6):1420–1443.

Johnson, S. D. and Summers, L. 2015. Testing ecological theories of offender spatial decision making using a discrete choice model. *Crime and Delinquency* 61(3): 454–480.

Johnson, S. D., Summers, L., and Pease, K. (2009). Offender as forager? A direct test of the boost account of victimization. *Journal of Quantitative Criminology* 25: 181–200.

Kaiser, H. F. 1960. The application of electronic computers to factor analysis. *Educational and Psychological Measurement* 20: 141–151.

Kawalerowicz, J. and Biggs, M. 2015. Anarchy in the UK: Economic deprivation, social disorganisation, and political grievances in the London riot of 2011. *Social Forces* 94(2): 673–698.

Lammers, M. 2014. Are arrested and non-arrested serial offenders different? A test of spatial offending patterns using DNA found at crime scenes. *Journal of Research in Crime and Delinquency* 51(2): 143–167.

Le Bon, G. 1960. *The Crowd: A Study of the Popular Mind.* New York: Viking Press.

Lewis, P., Newburn, T., Taylor, M., Mcgillivary, C., et al. 2012. *Reading the Riots: Investigating England's Summer of Disorder*. The Guardian and LSE.

Luce, R. D. 1959. *Individual Choice Behavior: A Theoretical Analysis.* New York: Wiley.

Mason, T. D. 1984. Individual participation in collective racial violence: A rational choice synthesis. *American Political Science Review* 78: 1040–1056.

Metropolitan Police Service. 2012. *4 Days in August: Strategic Review into the Disorder of August 2011.* Final Report. London: Metropolitan Police Service.

McFadden, D. 1974. Conditional logit analysis of qualitative choice behavior. In Zarembka, P. (ed.), *Frontiers in Econometrics*, 105–142. New York: Academic Press.

McFadden, D. 1978. Modeling the choice of residential location. In Karlkvist, K., Lundkvist, F., Snikars, F., and Weibull, J. (eds.), *Spatial Interaction Theory and Planning Models*, 75–96. Amsterdam: North-Holland.

McFadden, D. 2001. Economic choices. *American Economic Review* 91(3): 351–378.

Points of Interest [CSV geospatial data] 2015. Scale 1:1250, Items: 451099, Updated 10 December 2015, Ordnance Survey (GB), using EDINA Digimap Ordnance Survey Service, <http://digimap.edina.ac.uk>, Downloaded 27 January 2016.

Rubin, D. B. 1987. *Multiple Imputation for Nonresponse in Surveys*. New York: Wiley & Sons.

Sampson R. J. and Groves, W. B. 1989. Community structure and crime: Testing social-disorganization theory. *American Journal of Sociology* 94(4): 774–802.

Shaw, C. R. and McKay, H. D. 1969. *Juvenile Delinquency and Urban Areas*. Chicago: University of Chicago Press.

Townsley, M., Birks, D., Bernasco, W., Ruiter, S., Johnson, S. D., White, G., and Baum, S. 2015. Burglar target selection: A cross-national comparison. *Journal of Research in Crime and Delinquency* 52: 3–31.

Train, K. E. 2009. *Discrete Choice Methods with Simulation*. New York: Cambridge University Press.

Wortley, R. 2008. Situational precipitators of crime. In Wortley, R. and Mazerolle, L. G. (eds.), *Environmental Criminology and Crime Analysis*, 48–69. Portland, OR: Willan.

CHAPTER 34

GEOPROFILING TERRORISM

D. KIM ROSSMO

34.1 Introduction

Research in the field of environmental criminology has demonstrated clear regularities in the spatial behavior of offenders. Drawing upon crime pattern theory, the geographic profiling of serial criminals exploits these regularities to produce estimates of their probable anchor points. The technique has been used successfully by police to investigate serial crimes in countries around the world, demonstrating its utility in an operational setting. A recent advance, and the focus of this chapter, is the application of geographic profiling to counterterrorism.

Geoprofiling is an investigative methodology that uses the locations of a connected series of crimes to determine the most probable area of offender residence. It provides an information management strategy to focus criminal investigations by prioritizing suspects and tips. Counterterrorism investigations commonly suffer from information overload problems that can make relevant patterns difficult to discover.

Environmental approaches in criminology seek to understand how criminals make use of space and the physical and social environments where they offend. Crime locations are, in effect, spatial clues, and their geography has an underlying pattern and logic. To understand criminal target patterns and hunting behavior—how they search for, find, and attack victims—it is necessary to examine the micro-level dimensions of offender, target, crime, and environment.

A number of recent research projects have explored applications of geographic profiling to counterterrorism and counterinsurgency. These efforts have analyzed geospatial patterns of terrorist cells (e.g., the spatial relationship between safe houses and weapon storage sites), tested the ability of these techniques to locate terrorist bases from minor crimes and seditious graffiti, and examined the utility of geoprofiling for locating preparation sites used by insurgents for IED (improvised explosive devices) and rocket attacks. In appropriate cases, geoprofiling models have utility for prioritizing geointelligence and identifying logistic bases of terrorist operations.

This chapter is organized as follows. Section 34.2 discusses environmental criminology and the geography of crime. Section 34.3 covers the basics of geographic profiling and its various applications. The role of geospatial intelligence and crime pattern theory in counterterrorism are explained in Section 34.4. In the final section, the geospatial and temporal patterns of terrorism are examined to show how geoprofiling can be used to analyze seditious graffiti, insurgency attacks, cyberterrorism, and bioterrorism.

34.2 Environmental Criminology

Terrorism has been explored through political, religious, economic, and sociological perspectives. More recently, researchers have used environmental criminology to analyze the actions and decision-making of terrorists. This multidisciplinary approach, influenced by human ecology, environmental psychology, behavioral geography, and the cognitive sciences, focuses on how criminals make use of their physical and social environments (Brantingham and Brantingham 1981).

Locations serve specific functions in terms of criminal requirements. As a result, the geography of crime, and of terrorism, is not random but rather structured with underlying patterns and logic. Environmental criminologists use three central theories to explain the spatial and temporal patterns of crime (see Summers and Guerette's chapter in this volume for more detail on these theories).

The rational choice perspective adopts a decision-making approach in explaining crime (Cornish and Clarke 1986). Crime and criminal behavior are seen as the products of choices. These, in turn, are influenced by a rational consideration of the efforts, rewards, and costs involved in alternative courses of action. Researchers have noted the utility of terrorist behavior and the importance of the broader environmental context (Clarke and Newman 2006). In a study in Northern Ireland, for example, the majority (80%) of even low-level terrorist incidents were found to exhibit some degree of structure and planning (Taylor 1993).

Routine activity theory states that for a direct contact predatory crime to occur, the paths of the offender and victim/target have to intersect in time and space within an environment appropriate for criminal activity. Specifically, there needs to be the convergence of motivated offenders, suitable targets, and the absence of capable guardians (Cohen and Felson 1979). This perspective studies the processes and patterns associated with these requirements by examining how illegal acts depend upon regular legal activities. Hamm (2007) converts the approach to a tactical tool by asking the question, what routine activities surrounding a target are jihadists likely to exploit during their attack planning?

Crime pattern theory suggests criminal acts are most likely to occur in areas where the awareness space of an offender intersects with perceived suitable targets (Brantingham and Brantingham 1993). Crime pattern theory combines rational choice, routine activity theory, and environmental principles to explain the spatial and temporal distribution of crimes. Even so-called random crimes like serial murder (Rossmo 2000) and senseless violence like terrorism have underlying patterns.

Guided by crime pattern theory, Tench, Fry, and Gill (2016) modeled the locations and dates of IED incidents during the Northern Ireland conflict. Using a Hawkes process, they found the spatial-temporal patterns of IED attacks were influenced by organizational changes within the Provisional Irish Republican Army (PIRA) and by retaliations in response to British Security Forces interventions. Townsley, Johnson, and Ratcliffe (2008) discovered nonrandom patterns in the space-time dependency of insurgent activity in Iraq that suggested risk communication in space and time. Johnson, Johnson, and Restrepo (2016) were able to explain both the timing and severity of insurgent and terrorist attacks using dynamic mathematical models.

34.2.1 The Geography of Crime

Three specific areas in the geography of crime literature provide a basis for analyzing the spatial behavior of terrorists: (*a*) distance and crime journeys; (*b*) the psychology of place and land use; and (*c*) the nature of neighborhoods and their human interactions.

Perhaps the most basic concept in geography is the nearness principle, known in psychology as the principle of least effort (Zipf 1949). In general, when multiple destinations of equal desirability are available, these principles indicate the closest one will be chosen. However, the subjective psychological perception of distance is just as critical as objective physical space. An individual's perception of distance is influenced by several factors, including relative attractiveness of origins, routes, and destinations, number and types of barriers, familiarity with routes, and actual physical distance (Stea 1969). Income and socioeconomic status are also important spatial influences, as limited financial resources constrain options and choices.

The journey to crime—the distance between a crime site and the offender's residence—has long been of interest to criminologists (Baldwin and Bottoms 1976; McIver 1981; Wiles and Costello 2000; for more information, see Bernasco's chapter in this volume). While the distances between terrorism incidents and associated terrorist cell sites are the equivalent of journeys to crime, the actual crime trip for a terrorist is only one part of a much larger process. Distances between cell sites (e.g., safe houses, weapons storage, communication points, etc.) are likely to be equally, if not more, important. Nearness and least-effort principles also influence terrorist cell planning activities.

Ecological psychology studies how places "work" and the manner in which they organize people's lives. Behavior settings, or places, are freestanding natural units of the everyday environment with recurring patterns of activities and a surrounding and supporting physical milieu. Examples include schools, churches/mosques, public transit stops, bars, parking lots, playgrounds, markets, parks, and welfare offices. Terrorists must plan and operate within the physical environment, exposing them to the same influences of time and place as other people.

The ability to model terrorists' spatial behavior is an underlying assumption in geographic profiling (Cutter, Richardson, and Wilbanks 2003). This rests on the premise that their actions are both endogenously and exogenously motivated. Endogenously motivated behaviors are those controlled by the individual, such as the choice of residence, school, recreation, shopping, or social activities; these fall under the rubric of "routine activities" (Felson 2002, 2006). Exogenously motivated behaviors are those beyond the control of the individual, such as the selection of suitable flight schools or other agencies instrumental in the planning or act of terrorism. Both types of behavior are nonrandom, resulting in some degree of channeling of movement and clustering of settlement.

Clustering occurs in both terrorist and social networks. Terrorist networks involve associations between persons with similar objectives in terms of an operation, and bring together individuals who need to communicate in order to be briefed and trained on their duties. Clustering may be physical or virtual. In a physical cluster, individuals live and work in relatively close proximity to each other in order to facilitate cooperation and communication. In a virtual cluster, communications are maintained between group members by telephone, email, texting, or other electronic means, and physical interactions may occur seldom or not at all.

Social networks place terrorism-prone persons in those communities where they feel comfortable in terms of language, religion, and culture. While terrorist and social networks may intertwine, clarification of the geographic relationships involved in social networks can help us understand the terrorism-planning process. There is a demonstrated relationship between who people are, what they do, and where they live.

34.3 Geographic Profiling

Geographic profiling is an investigative methodology for determining the most probable area of offender residence by analyzing the locations of a connected crime series (Rossmo 2000). Its major functions are suspect prioritization and information management. Geographic profiling is based on the theories, concepts, and principles of environmental criminology, and the observation that individuals, including criminals, do not move randomly through their environment (Harries 1999). Any understanding of the target patterns and hunting behavior of criminal predators—how they search for, find, and attack victims—must include the micro-level dimensions of offender, target, crime, and environment. Crime pattern theory, routine activity theory, and the rational choice perspective provide the foundation for understanding the target patterns and hunting behavior of criminal predators.

These theories provide a method for describing the mathematical relationship between offender travel and likelihood of offending. This relationship can be described by a buffered distance-decay function that looks in cross-section rather like a volcano with a caldera. The function is encoded in a computer algorithm. Specialized crime-mapping software based on this algorithm analyzes the point patterns of the crime sites and generates a three-dimensional probability surface—known as a jeopardy surface—outlining the most likely area of offender residence (see Figure 34.1). Positions higher on the jeopardy surface are more likely to contain the offender's residence; those lower, less likely. Investigators can prioritize suspect addresses and other locations by their position on this probability surface, typically displayed as a two-dimensional geoprofile (see Figure 34.2).

A number of investigative strategies can be based on a geoprofile, including suspect and tip prioritization, police record searches, patrol saturation, surveillance deployment, neighborhood canvasses, department of motor vehicle searches, postal/zip code prioritization, and information mail-outs. Geographic profiling does not solve cases, but rather provides a method for managing the large volume of information typically generated in a major crime investigation.

Geographic profiling is a robust and versatile methodology. Originally developed for analyzing serial murder cases, it has now been used for rape, arson, robbery, bombing, kidnapping, burglary, auto theft, and credit card fraud investigations (Rossmo 2012). More recently, a number of innovative operational applications in areas beyond law enforcement have emerged, including homeland security (Rossmo et al. 2008), intelligence analysis (Rossmo 2008), and military operations (Brown et al. 2005).

The technique has also been applied in biology (Le Comber et al. 2006; Stevenson and Le Comber 2013), ecology (Le Comber and Stevenson 2012; Stevenson et al. 2012),

FIGURE 34.1 Berlin Hampel jeopardy surface (top 8%)

FIGURE 34.2 Berlin Hampel geoprofile (top 2%) with family residences

zoology (Martin, Rossmo, and Hammerschlag 2009), epidemiology (Le Comber et al. 2011), and archaeology research (Rossmo 2013). The adoption of geographic profiling by other scholarly disciplines makes it a rare example of a method from the social sciences gaining traction in the natural sciences.

34.4 Counterterrorism

As terrorists are a covert threat, counterterrorism efforts typically suffer from information overload problems. Investigators must search through large quantities of data, such as tips and reports, cellular telephone intercepts, photographs, electronic intelligence, and official records. For example, the FBI received 260,000 tips in the weeks following 9/11 (Shenon and Johnston 2001). As of December 2012, the US government's terrorist watch list contained the names of over 875,000 distinct individuals (National Counterterrorism Center 2013).

Identifying suspicious patterns is difficult under such circumstances. Large volumes of data can be a challenge in major police investigations and intelligence assessments (Doney 1990; Montgomery 1993; Rossmo 2000). Because of the prevalence of spatial information, however, geographic prioritization models can be useful tools in the management of information overload situations. A better understanding of the geography, movements, planning processes, and targets of terrorist groups can help agencies decode and interpret their underlying spatial patterns.

34.4.1 Geospatial Intelligence

A Director of National Intelligence (DNI) Open Source Center (OSC) study of terrorism in Afghanistan illustrates the sophistication of geointelligence and its potential to reveal significant patterns in terrorist activity. The OSC study identified the spatial distributions, means, and hotspots of terrorist incidents, and examined temporal changes in activity levels and location patterns. Geostatistical analyses of population density, ethnicity, and district/province were also conducted. The major correlates of terrorism were population, access, and proximity to Pakistan's northwest tribal regions. Most incidents occurred in population centers on or near the main national highway and adjacent connecting roads in south Afghanistan. OSC used these associations to build a predictive model that has demonstrated some ability to forecast the locations of future terrorist attacks (Open Source Center 2009).

Before Osama bin Laden was killed, attempts were made to outline probable locations for his hiding place using biogeographic theories and remote-sensing data (Gillespie and Agnew 2009). The biogeographic theories involved distance decay, island biogeography, and bin Laden's life history characteristics. The remote-sensing data included various types of satellite imagery for landscapes, topography, urban areas, and buildings. The analysis suffered from key omissions (the authors lacked access to confidential information) and was only roughly accurate, but it did demonstrate how different approaches and methods applied over various spatial scales (global, regional, and local) could be creatively combined to focus counterterrorism search efforts.

The hypothesis that terrorists have geographic patterns has been questioned by some. Terrorism is a global problem and many fanatically religious and political organizations are now transnational in structure and function. Some jihadist groups, like al-Qaeda, are virtual decentralized networks, their members communicating using cellular telephones and the Internet. Does this mean that geography has no role in the study and control of terrorism?

Despite this decentralization, personal interactions are still necessary for many terrorist functions. For example, the assassination of Mehmet Topaç, a former Turkish minister of justice, while originated in and controlled from Western Europe, required the physical presence of operatives in Ankara (see Subsection 34.5.2 below). The necessity of human contact in decentralized terrorist networks was observed in an analysis of jihadist terrorism in Spain (Jordán and Horsburgh 2005). Interpersonal relationships, meetings, recruitment using jihad videos, propaganda distribution, theft, credit card fraud, and robbery were all important aspects of the al-Qaeda-inspired Madrid 11-M train bombing operation.

Crime pattern theory proposes that crime locations are the product of a search influenced by the offender's activity space and home base:

residence → activity space → mental map → hunting/search process → crime location

Many low-level terrorist actions are ordinary crimes such as robbery, theft, fraud, vandalism, and graffiti. In such cases, traditional crime pattern theory would apply.

The locations of certain terrorist attacks, however, do not follow this process, as they are a function of target-intrinsic factors. Central to such cases is symbolism—a target's political, military, or economic features. This influence can work in both directions, as the specific strategies and tactics adopted by a terrorist group may also influence target choice (Drake 1998b).

Actual and prospective terrorist targets within the United States have included airplanes and airports, office buildings, theaters, embassies, the United Nations, world leaders, subways, churches, federal buildings, pipelines, tunnels, and landmarks (McGee 2001). "When a group takes the decision to use violence, an early step is to decide who or what will be attacked" (Drake 1998a, p. 56). While available resources and security levels influence target selection, ideology is particularly important, as terrorists use it to justify their actions and choice of victims. Terrorist groups operating in the same region may develop different target patterns (e.g., civilians vs. public officials) depending on their ideology and their particular judgment of who or what is a "legitimate" victim or target. Different targets represent different symbols. Police in Germany, for example, concluded: "banks stand for capitalism, department stores for consumism [*sic*], military installations for imperialism, and multi-national businesses for colonialism in the Third World" (Segaller 1987, p. 295).

Terrorist cells are sometimes established in a given city for the specific purpose of committing a significant act of terrorism against such a symbolic target—perhaps their only operation in the region. The target/residence relationship in these instances is the inverse of the process outlined by traditional crime pattern theory (Rossmo and Harries 2011):

target → planning/logistic requirements → cell establishment → residence locations

In either situation,[1] whether the target of a major attack determines the locations of the terrorist cell sites, or the terrorist cell sites determine the target of a minor attack, a geographic relationship exists.

Geographic profiling can therefore be employed in counterterrorism in two different ways. First, it can help identify terrorist bases from low-level crimes such as theft, robbery, and credit card fraud, similar to how the technique is used in most serial crime investigations; this includes the analysis of seditious graffiti, banners, and similar incidents. Second, it can be used to spatially relate known locations of a terrorist cell to both unknown locations and to future terrorist attacks.

34.5 Geoprofiling Terrorism

34.5.1 Place and Space

By its very nature, terrorism is shrouded in secrecy. The information available in the literature on the routine activities of terrorists reveals a careful consideration for security and concealment. Automobiles, easy to obtain by theft or cash purchase, are the preferred mode of transportation because of their availability, privacy, and security (Segaller 1987). Weapons and other contraband are readily transported by vehicle and, unlike in train or air travel, drivers can circumvent known security checks. An al-Qaeda jihad training manual seized by police in England warns operatives to avoid travel modes "subject to frequent checking along the way" (al-Qaeda, n.d.). Unsurprisingly, terrorists have been known to travel long distances by automobile.

Many of the factors considered by terrorist groups in establishing operational bases resonate with the theories and concepts of environmental criminology discussed here and elsewhere in this volume. The al-Qaeda manual directs operatives to select an apartment adequate for their mission in terms of location, size, storage capacity, and security. Ground floor apartments are recommended to facilitate escape, but they should not be viewable from higher apartments. Places near police stations, government offices, problem complexes known to authorities, or buildings in isolated areas should be avoided. New developments where neighbors are less likely to know one another are recommended. Operatives are instructed to arrange planning meetings at street intersections "to facilitate entry, exit, and escape" and to avoid crowded places that allow "security personnel to hide and monitor those who meet."

In the 1970s, the German federal police, the Bundeskriminalamt (BKA), analyzed Red Army Faction (RAF) preferences and observed specific geographic features and travel patterns (Johnson 2001). For example, RAF terrorists preferred high-rise apartments with underground parking where they could hide the stolen cars they drove. They selected buildings near autobahn interchanges for quick getaways. Rent was paid by cash. Knowing the RAF's residential preferences and "movement pictures," and the types of automobiles they typically stole, allowed police to establish optimal investigative search patterns. The same approach is still used today; terrorist "sleepers" are identified through indicators such as age, proximity to technical universities, and nearby radical mosques.

Cothren et al. (2008) analyzed the spatial and temporal patterns of preparatory acts in US terrorism cases. "[T]here is a tendency to think of terrorists as operating from afar . . . [but] most terrorism on American soil has been conducted by persons who have resided in or near the community where the target is located" (pp. 32–33). They found approximately half of the terrorists they studied prepared for their attacks within a 30-mile radius of the target. This distance varied by group—international terrorists resided nearer their targets, while right-wing domestic terrorists lived further away, often in rural areas, during their preparations for attacks on urban targets. "Funding crimes" (robberies, burglaries, and thefts) were committed at significant distances from both terrorist homes and their targets, while other preparatory crimes and planning occurred closer to the target. International terrorists spent more time planning than domestic terrorists. Preparatory acts shifted closer to the target location as the incident date approached.

Berrebi and Lakdawalla (2007) found the main drivers of attack risk in Israel to be ease of access and proximity to a terrorist home base. Border locations suffered almost twice as many terrorist attacks as interior locations. The median distance from target locations to the nearest terrorist home base was 8 miles. A 10-mile increase in distance from a terrorist base cut the probability of attack almost in half. This proximity could be explained either by terrorists attacking nearby sites or by terrorists setting up bases near high-value targets (a point also made by Cothren et al. 2008). In either case, proximity lowers the cost of a terrorist attack. "In principle, the authorities could exploit such a systematic basing strategy, and use it to discover terrorist groups. In practice, however, terrorists often situate their homebases in densely populated areas, where detection and removal is much more difficult even if the authorities are aware of a general location" (note 16, p. 123).

Where, when, and how attacks occur can be influenced by the goals and strategies of a terrorist organization. In 1978, the Basque separatist group Euskadi Ta Askatasuna (ETA) changed its strategy from territorial control to a prolonged war of territorial attrition (LaFree et al. 2012). Territorial control required contagious diffusion (future operations in adjacent areas), while territorial attrition resulted in hierarchical diffusion (future operations in distant, nonadjacent regions) that produced a dispersed incident pattern. This shift in geography also altered ETA's temporal patterns and decreased the frequency of their attacks, most likely because of the planning and resources needed to target distant locations.

34.5.2 Geospatial Patterns of Terrorist Cells

Major terrorist attacks involve significant planning and preparation, activities typically conducted by a group of operatives functioning in a cell structure. A terrorist cell can involve safe houses, communication sites, weapons storage, cell houses, and other logistical sites. The locations, arrangements, and distances of these different places can be measured and spatially analyzed.

Employing an environmental criminology perspective, Rossmo and Harries (2011) examined terrorist cells in urban Turkey to determine their geospatial structure. Turkey has been victimized by terrorist attacks for more than three decades, resulting in over

37,000 deaths and $100 billion in lost economic opportunity. These attacks have originated from a wide variety of terrorist organizations, including separatist, left-wing, and religiously inspired groups. The principal separatist terrorist organization in Turkey is the Kurdistan Workers' Party (PKK), responsible for attacks against both civilians and police.

Their study identified and geocoded locations from Turkish National Police (TNP) terrorism files of Marxist-Leninist, Maoist, or radical Islamic terrorist groups.[2] About half (49%) of the cases were bombings, assassinations, or police shootings/attacks; all of the incidents occurred in Ankara or Istanbul. They adopted an analytic framework in which locations were grouped into terrorist cell (logistical) sites and terrorism target (incident) sites. The former included cell houses, safe houses, storage, communication points, residences, and other planning or preparation sites. The latter included terrorism attacks (e.g., bombings, assassinations) and terrorism-related acts (e.g., robberies, seditious graffiti, banners). Distances between cell sites, and from cell sites to targets, were then measured. These measurements showed that the terrorist cells possessed a nonrandom geospatial structure.

A political assassination committed by the DHKP/C illustrates a typical TNP case and the various cell locations involved in an act of terrorism. The DHKP/C (Devrimci Halk Kurtuluş Partisi/Cephesi, Revolutionary People's Liberation Party/Front), an anti-American/NATO, Marxist-Leninist terrorist group in Turkey, sent two elite, militant "revolutionary propaganda teams" from Istanbul to Ankara to assassinate the former Turkish minister of justice, Mehmet Topaç. The two teams of three members spent months planning the attack. On September 29, 1994, they shot and killed Topaç in his law office in central Ankara, leaving a red DHKP/C banner behind at the scene.

Key locations associated with the terrorist cell included two cell houses, two safe houses, a street where firearms were delivered in a vehicle, a telephone booth, a work site, and a warehouse, among other locations. One of the cell houses was situated just over a mile from Topaç's office building. Both cell houses were located in high-density and anonymous urban areas. By contrast, the preexisting safe houses (used after the assassination) were in neighborhoods known for leftist antigovernment sentiments, areas where police and strangers stood out. Most of the cell locations were between 1 and 3.5 miles from the incident site (median 2.6 miles); none was closer than 1 mile.

Geographically, terrorists behave rationally and choose areas that work for them. The cell sites in the Turkish study were clustered, and situated near—but not too near—their targets. The median nearest-neighbor distance (the distance from a cell site to its closest neighboring cell site) was 0.63 miles; the median inter-cell distance (the distance from each cell site to every other cell site in that case) was 4.0 miles. Targets were similarly grouped, with a median nearest-neighbor distance of 0.42 miles and a median inter-target distance of 2.50 miles. A strong and statistically significant correlation was found between target trip and cell site neighbor distances, suggesting that knowledge of one could be used to estimate the other.

The median target trip distance was 3.67 miles. However, a terrorist operation requires a mixture of places that serve different functional purposes. For example, one of the DHKP/C revolutionary propaganda teams lived in an apartment close to Topaç's office building to facilitate target surveillance; following the assassination, the team members retreated to a distant safe house. A more useful measure, therefore, is the distance between a target and the closest cell site. The median target-to-nearest cell site distance was 0.62 miles (mean 1.16 miles), comparable to typical journey-to-crime distances for violent crime (see Rossmo 2000, Table 7.1, pp. 105–110).

Similar patterns were found in the planning of the Madrid 11-M train bombings (Rossmo et al. 2012), the Lashkar-e-Tayyiba Mumbai attack, the 9/11 hijackings, and Shabaab-associated plots in Australia (Sisak 2016). These spatial probability distributions can be used to prioritize searches for potential targets near known cell sites, and for cell sites from terrorist attacks. They can also be used to reevaluate intelligence regarding possible cell sites in proximity to each other (in other words, two suspicious locations should be considered more suspicious if they are close to each other). Geography remains a ubiquitous and importance source of intelligence.

34.5.3 Seditious Graffiti

Although much attention is focused on major attacks—bombings, kidnappings, hijackings—many terrorist or insurgent organizations also engage in low-level seditious activities such as antigovernment graffiti, leaflet distribution, banner posting, or vandalism. The creation of geospatial databases of terrorism-related graffiti may help police locate terrorist support bases before the occurrence of more serious incidents (Rossmo and Harries 2011).

During the Second World War, the Gestapo employed the basic ideas of geographic profiling in their search for two dissidents, Otto and Elise Hampel, who had distributed hundreds of anti-Nazi postcards throughout Berlin.[3] The postcard and letter drop sites in the Hampel case, obtained and translated from Gestapo records, were analyzed using modern geographic profiling to test and illustrate its applicability in these types of situations (though our sympathies lie with the dissidents here). The technique prioritized the Hampel's Berlin apartment in less than 0.5% of the area of interest after just 35 of the 214 (16%) recorded incidents (Rossmo et al. 2014). This geographic focus would have been possible as early as spring 1941, a full 18 months before the arrest of the Hampels in the fall of 1942. Figure 34.1 shows the top 8% of the jeopardy surface (based on all incidents) for the case. Figure 34.2 shows the locations of the Hampel's apartment (middle square), along with the homes of Otto's parents (left square) and sister (right square), situated in the top 2% of the geoprofile.

Beyond its historical interest, the analysis of the Hampel case demonstrates the potential of geographic profiling in similar situations today. Modern counterterrorism investigations and counterinsurgency efforts also deal with information overload. This is exactly the problem geographic profiling is designed to address by prioritizing large lists of suspects in a meaningful way. The Hampel case provides empirical evidence that analysis of subversive postings, such as antigovernment graffiti, can help locate terrorists. Further research illustrating how geographic profiling can be used to identify the origins of anonymous art graffiti provides additional support for this proposition (Hauge et al. 2016).

34.5.4 Demographics

It has been suggested that demographics could play a role in geoprofiling terrorism by prioritizing neighborhoods through measures of poverty, depression, and underdevelopment. Ehrlich and Liu (2002) noted that "demographic and socioeconomic factors, especially poverty, inequality and large numbers of young men facing dim economic prospects, also are likely contributors to such terrorism" (p. 185). Terrorist conflicts have been linked to depressed economic conditions (Azam and Mesnard 2003), and to underdevelopment and certain GDP components, in particular government services and agriculture (Feridun and Sezgin 2008).

However, the notion of poverty and terrorism as cause and effect is far from universally accepted. In a macro-level study of 96 countries involving an array of social, economic, and political indicators, Piazza (2006, p. 159) found that "contrary to popular opinion, no significant relationship between any of the measures of economic development and terrorism can be determined." Krueger (2007) resoundingly rejects the hypothesis that "economic deprivation and lack of education cause people to adopt extreme views and turn to terrorism" (p. 1).

While the ambiguity in the literature creates a confusing picture, the use of demographics in geoprofiling faces three specific challenges. First, demographic research is usually based on large areas, while geographic profiling has a local focus. Generalizations from the macro to the micro level can create an ecological fallacy by ignoring intraunit variation (Langbein and Lichtman 1978).

Second, terrorist attack locations have no functional connection to the socioeconomic environment with respect to a possible causal relationship to the terrorism process. Other incident locations, while somewhat more relevant to the living environments of terrorists, are still unreliable guides to their home neighborhoods.

Third, the international nature of some terrorist attacks undermines local influences. An analysis of the 2004 Madrid 11-M train bombings using the Synthetic Global Index and an Index of Core Vulnerability failed to find support for the "poverty causes terrorism" hypothesis (Harries 2012). Given that the attacks were the responsibility of al-Qaeda-inspired Moroccan, Syrian, and Algerian Muslims, it is not unreasonable to surmise that the ultimate causes lay in other countries, and had no direct connection to ambient conditions in Spain.

Despite these challenges, demographic information may still have a role in geoprofiling terrorism. However, more research, using neighborhood-level census data, is needed to better understand the influence of local areas on terrorist operations and the conditions under which these influences affect their geography.

34.5.5 Counterinsurgency

While terrorism and insurgency are not equivalent, they can sometimes overlap, and jihadist terrorist groups have been known to operate in theaters of war. Previous research has demonstrated the nonrandom nature of insurgent attacks. Townsley et al. (2008) discovered patterns in IED incidents in Iraq, noting that "insurgents are constrained in space and time and select targets in a rational fashion" (p. 145). Johnson and Braithwaite (2009) found spatial-temporal clustering in the locations of insurgent targets, with the specific nature of the patterning varying by attack type. They suggest this variation is the product of different insurgent strategies, and therefore requires customized counterinsurgent tactics. Common mathematical patterns underlying the timing and severity of insurgent attacks have also been observed (Johnson, Johnson, and Restrepo 2016).

Braithwaite and Johnson (2012) noticed a spatial-temporal interrelationship between insurgency and counterinsurgency in Iraq; of particular interest was the finding that indiscriminate Coalition operations increased the likelihood of subsequent insurgency actions. They later (Braithwaite and Johnson 2015) demonstrated that risk heterogeneity—specifically, greater population levels, high road densities, and the presence of military garrisons—provided the most compelling explanation for the location of insurgency in Baghdad.

Geographic profiling has been applied in theater in Iraq and Afghanistan for counterinsurgency (COIN) operations (Brown et al. 2005; Brueckner 2009; Grau 2004; Kucera 2005; The Economist 2016). Specifically, the technique has been used to prioritize possible bomb makers/workshops from IED incidents in cities, and rocket assembly/storage locations from launch sites, determined by counterbattery radar, in rural village areas. Informal reports on the accuracy and utility of the method have been quite positive; however, information on COIN activities is classified, precluding formal evaluation research outside military circles. Personnel from various military branches and intelligence agencies in several different countries have now been trained in military applications of geographic profiling.

34.5.6 Cyberterrorism and Bioterrorism

Geographic profiling may have further applications to other forms of terrorism, including cyberterrorism and bioterrorism. Environmental Criminology Research Inc. (ECRI), Scientific Research Corporation (SRC), and Texas State University conducted a security exercise involving simulated cyberattacks in which wireless Internet sites, accessed by anonymous "hackers," were geoprofiled and used to locate their home, work, and hotel bases (Laverty and Rossmo 2012). The accuracy rates of the analyses in the study were similar to those for serial criminals. While the "hackers" involved in the project were given specific instructions to behave realistically and to try to protect their identities, it is unknown how closely their spatial choices reflect those of real cyberterrorists.

Finally, the ability of geographic profiling to identify the sources of certain diseases, such as mosquito breeding pools for malaria and contaminated water wells for cholera (Le Comber et al. 2011; Stevenson and Le Comber 2012), suggests the technique may have potential value in identifying origin points of bioterrorism attacks. However, this particular application has never been tested, and the conditions under which the method might work, and how well, have not been fully delineated.

34.6 Conclusion

An understanding of the geography of terrorism allows law enforcement and intelligence agencies to detect suspicious patterns and identify terrorist acts in their planning stages. Geographic profiling can be used to prioritize suspects, tips, and other geointelligence and help police manage major investigations. The method is not a stand-alone system; rather, its results should be combined with other forms of intelligence to produce a comprehensive analysis for optimal investigative decision-making.

Minor terrorism incidents that involve little planning and expertise and that are directed toward general and low-value targets (e.g., theft, seditious graffiti, etc.) can be explained by traditional crime pattern theory. Major terrorism incidents that involve significant planning and specialized skills and that are directed toward specific and high-value targets (e.g., assassinations, bombings, etc.) can be explained by an inverted crime pattern theory. In either situation, geography plays a role. The relationship between target selection and terrorist planning, logistics, operations, and attacks is intriguing, and hopefully one future studies will continue to explore.

The operational intelligence capabilities of geographic profiling in counterterrorism and counterinsurgency could be enhanced by more research and testing, and certain areas appear to hold particular promise (see also Flint 2003). Bennell and Corey (2007) used geographic profiling techniques to analyze four building bombings in Paris, France, by the communist group Action Directe, and seven vehicle and building bombings in Athens, Greece, by the leftist Revolutionary People's Struggle (ELA). They concluded that accurate geographic profiles are possible when the appropriate assumptions are met, cautioning that further research is necessary to determine the specific conditions under which the method can be useful in counterterrorism.

Interdiction possibilities might be increased if we better understood the spatial-temporal functioning of terrorist cells and the movement patterns of terrorists during the planning and preparation phases of an attack. Any demographic relationships underlying terrorist cell formation and operation might be revealed though research in countries that have comprehensive census data at the neighborhood level. Finally, the development of local geospatial databases of terrorism-related graffiti could prove to have significant operational utility.

Every location targeted or used by terrorists provides a geographic clue. Environmental criminology offers a framework for analyzing these clues and connecting the dots. In appropriate situations, geographic profiling can be used to analyze spatial data and help law enforcement and intelligence agencies prioritize and manage information in large-scale investigations. Combating terrorism effectively requires a multidisciplinary response.

Acknowledgments

I wish to acknowledge the assistance and support of Dr. Keith Harries, Professor Emeritus, Geography and Environmental Systems, University of Maryland, Baltimore County, and members of the Anti-Terrorism Department of the Turkish National Police.

Notes

1. This is not a clear dichotomy—local terrorists may be directed through a global network, local sympathizers can support foreign terrorists, and major attacks might involve a number of minor incidents.
2. The information in these files reflects only what is known to the police. While this is an issue for all analyses of official crime data, it is particularly problematic for terrorism studies because of the covert nature of such operations. A further complication for researchers is the number of different law enforcement, intelligence, and military departments monitoring and collecting data on terrorist threats; the Intelligence Community in the United States involves 16 separate federal agencies, each with different but often overlapping mandates (and rivalries). There are also various state and local organizations, some of considerable size, such as the New York Police Department (NYPD) Intelligence Division & Counterterrorism Bureau.
3. This investigation formed the basis of Hans Fallada's classic 1947 novel, *Alone in Berlin*, originally published in German as *Jeder Stirbt für Sich Allein* (*Every Man Dies Alone*).

References

al-Qaeda. n.d. "The Military Series Related to the Declaration of Jihad: Training Manual." https://www.justice.gov/sites/default/files/ag/legacy/2002/10/08/manualpart1_1.pdf.

Azam, Jean-Paul, and Alice Mesnard. 2003. "Civil War and the Social Contract." *Public Choice* 115:455–475.

Baldwin, John, and Anthony E. Bottoms. 1976. *The Urban Criminal: A Study in Sheffield.* London: Tavistock Publications.

Bennell, Craig, and Shevaun Corey. 2007. "Geographic Profiling of Terrorist Attacks." In *Criminal Profiling: International Theory, Research, and Practice*, edited by Richard N. Kocsis. Totowa, NJ: Humana Press.

Berrebi, Claude, and Darius Lakdawalla. 2007. "How Does Terrorism Risk Vary across Space and Time? An Analysis Based on the Israeli Experience." *Defense and Peace Economics* 18:113–131.

Braithwaite, Alex, and Shane D. Johnson. 2012. "Space-Time Modeling of Insurgency and Counterinsurgency in Iraq." *Journal of Quantitative Criminology* 28:31–48.

Braithwaite, Alex, and Shane D. Johnson. 2015. "The Battle for Baghdad: Testing Hypotheses about Insurgency from Risk Heterogeneity, Repeat Victimization, and Denial Policing Approaches." *Terrorism and Political Violence* 27:112–132.

Brantingham, Patricia L., and Paul J. Brantingham. 1993. "Environment, Routine and Situation: Toward a Pattern Theory of Crime." In *Routine Activity and Rational Choice, Advances in Criminological Theory*, vol. 5, edited by Ronald V. Clarke and Marcus Felson. New Brunswick, NJ: Transaction.

Brantingham, Paul J., and Patricia L. Brantingham, eds. 1981. *Environmental Criminology*. Beverly Hills, CA: Sage.

Brown, Roger O., D. Kim Rossmo, Tom J. Sisak, Rhonda Trahern, Joni Jarret, and Jennifer Hanson. 2005. "Geographic Profiling Military Capabilities." Final report submitted to the Topographic Engineering Center, Department of the Army, Fort Belvoir, VA.

Brueckner, Sven A. 2009. "Swarming Geographic Event Profiling, Link Analysis, and Prediction." Paper presented at the Third International Conference on Self-Adaptive and Self-Organizing Systems, San Francisco, CA, September.

Clarke, Ronald V., and Graeme R. Newman. 2006. *Outsmarting the Terrorists*. Westport, CT: Praeger Security International.

Cohen, Lawrence E., and Marcus Felson. 1979. "Social Change and Crime Rate Trends: A Routine Activity Approach." *American Sociological Review* 44:588–608.

Cornish, Derek B., and Ronald V. Clarke, eds. 1986. *The Reasoning Criminal: Rational Choice Perspectives on Offending*. New York: Springer.

Cothren, Jackson, Brent L. Smith, Paxton Roberts, and Kelly R. Damphousse. 2008. "Geospatial and Temporal Patterns of Preparatory Conduct among American Terrorists." *International Journal of Comparative and Applied Criminal Justice* 32:23–41.

Cutter, Susan L., Douglas B. Richardson, and Thomas J. Wilbanks, eds. 2003. *The Geographical Dimensions of Terrorism*. New York: Routledge.

Doney, Richard H. 1990. "The Aftermath of the Yorkshire Ripper: The Response of the United Kingdom Police Service." In *Serial Murder: An Elusive Phenomenon*, edited by Steven A. Egger. New York: Praeger.

Drake, C. J. M. 1998a. "The Role of Ideology in Terrorists' Target Selection." *Terrorism and Political Violence* 10:53–85.

Drake, C. J. M. 1998b. *Terrorists' Target Selection*. Houndmills, UK: Macmillan.

The Economist. 2016. "Shrinking the Haystack." January 16–22.

Ehrlich, Paul R., and Jianguo G. Liu. 2002. "Some Roots of Terrorism." *Population and Environment* 24:183–192.

Felson, Marcus. 2002. *Crime and Everyday Life*. 3rd ed. Thousand Oaks, CA: Sage.

Felson, Marcus. 2006. *Crime and Nature*. Thousand Oaks, CA: Sage.

Feridun, Mete, and Selami Sezgin. 2008. "Regional Underdevelopment and Terrorism: The Case of Southeastern Turkey." *Defence and Peace Economics* 3:225–233.

Flint, Colin. 2003. "Terrorism and Counterterrorism: Geographic Research Questions and Agendas." *Professional Geographer* 55:161–169.

Gillespie, Thomas W., and John A. Agnew. 2009. "Finding Osama bin Laden: An Application of Biogeographic Theories and Satellite Imagery." *MIT International Review* (February 17). http://web.mit.edu/mitir/2009/online/finding-bin-laden.pdf.

Grau, Lester W. 2004. "Something Old, Something New: Guerrillas, Terrorists, and Intelligence Analysis." *Military Review* (July–August).

Hamm, Mark S. 2007. *Terrorism as Crime: From Oklahoma City to al-Qaeda and Beyond.* New York: New York University Press.

Harries, Keith D. 1999. *Mapping Crime: Principle and Practice* (NCJ 178919). Washington, DC: National Institute of Justice.

Harries, Keith D. 2012. "Geoprofiling of Terrorist Cell Structures: Madrid 11-M Bombings—Socioeconomic Context." Final report submitted to the Space and Naval Warfare Systems Command, North Charleston, SC.

Hauge, Michelle V., Mark D. Stevenson, D. Kim Rossmo, and Steven C. Le Comber. 2016. "Tagging Banksy: Using Geographic Profiling to Investigate a Modern Art Mystery." *Journal of Spatial Science* 61:185–190.

Johnson, Ian. 2001. "Another Autumn." *Wall Street Journal* (December 10).

Johnson, Neil F., Daniela E. Johnson, and Elvira M. Restrepo. 2016. "Modelling Insurgent Attack Dynamics across Geographic Scales and in Cyberspace." *European Journal of Applied Mathematics* 27:357–376.

Johnson, Shane D., and Alex Braithwaite. 2009. "Spatio-Temporal Modeling of Insurgency in Iraq." In *Reducing Terrorism through Situational Crime Prevention, Crime Prevention Studies*, vol. 25, edited by Joshua D. Freilich and Graeme R. Newman. Monsey, NY: Criminal Justice Press.

Jordán, Javier, and Nicola Horsburgh. 2005. "Mapping Jihadist Terrorism in Spain." *Studies in Conflict and Terrorism* 28:169–191.

Krueger, Alan B. 2007. *What Makes a Terrorist?* Princeton, NJ: Princeton University Press.

Kucera, Henry. 2005. Hunting Insurgents: Geographic Profiling Adds a New Weapon. *GeoWorld* (October).

LaFree, Gary, Laura Dugan, Min Xie, and Piyusha Singh. 2012. "Spatial and Temporal Patterns of Terrorist Attacks by ETA 1970 to 2007." *Journal of Quantitative Criminology* 28:7–29.

Langbein, Laura Irwin, and Allan J. Lichtman. 1978. "Ecological Inference." Sage University Paper Series on Quantitative Applications in the Social Sciences No. 10.

Laverty, Ian, and D. Kim Rossmo. 2012. "Cyber-security Exercise Results." Final report submitted to Scientific Research Corporation, North Charleston, SC.

Le Comber, Steven C., Barry Nicholls, D. Kim Rossmo, and Paul A. Racey. 2006. "Geographic Profiling and Animal Foraging." *Journal of Theoretical Biology* 240:233–240.

Le Comber, Steven C., D. Kim Rossmo, Ali N. Hassan, Douglas O. Fuller, and John C. Beier. 2011. "Geographic Profiling as a Novel Spatial Tool for Targeting Infectious Disease Control." *International Journal of Health Geographics* 10:35–42.

Le Comber, Steven C., and Mark D. Stevenson. 2012. "From Jack the Ripper to Epidemiology and Ecology." *Trends in Ecology and Evolution* 27:307–308.

Martin, R. Aidan, D. Kim Rossmo, and Neil Hammerschlag. 2009. "Hunting Patterns and Geographic Profiling of White Shark Predation." *Journal of Zoology* 279: 111–118.

McGee, Jim. 2001. "Ex-FBI Officials Criticize Tactics on Terrorism: Detention of Suspects Not Effective, They Say." *Washington Post* (November 28).

McIver, John P. 1981. "Criminal Mobility: A Review of Empirical Studies." In *Crime Spillover*, edited by Simon Hakim and George F. Rengert. Beverly Hills, CA: Sage.

Montgomery, James E. 1993. "Organizational Survival: Continuity or Crisis?" In *Policing in the Global Community: The Challenge of Leadership*, edited by Monique Layton. Burnaby, BC: Simon Fraser University.

National Counterterrorism Center. 2013. "Terrorist Identities Datamart Environment (TIDE)." www.nctc.gov/docs/Tide_Fact_Sheet.pdf.

Open Source Center. 2009. "Afghanistan: Geospatial Analysis Reveal Patterns in Terrorist Incidents 2004–2008" (April 30). http://fas.org/irp/dni/osc/afghan-geospat.pdf.

Piazza, James A. 2006. "Rooted in Poverty? Terrorism, Poor Economic Development, and Social Cleavages." *Terrorism and Political Violence* 18:59–177.

Rossmo, D. Kim. 2000. *Geographic Profiling*. Boca Raton, FL: CRC Press.

Rossmo, D. Kim. 2008. *Geographic Profiling in Counterterrorism: Data and Feasibility Study*. Final report submitted to the Intelligence Advanced Research Projects Activity, Washington, DC.

Rossmo, D. Kim. 2012. "Recent Developments in Geographic Profiling." *Policing* 6:144–150.

Rossmo, D. Kim. 2013. "Geographic Profiling." In *Encyclopedia of Criminology and Criminal Justice*, edited by Gerben Bruinsma and David L. Weisburd. New York: Springer.

Rossmo, D. Kim, and Keith D. Harries. 2011. "The Geospatial Structure of Terrorist Cells." *Justice Quarterly* 28:221–248.

Rossmo, D. Kim, Keith D. Harries, Jonathan Allen, and Patricia A. Hom. 2012. "Geoprofiling of Terrorist Cell Structures: Madrid 11-M Bombings—Geography." Final report submitted to the Space and Naval Warfare Systems Command, North Charleston, SC.

Rossmo, D. Kim, Heike Lutermann, Mark D. Stevenson, and Steven C. Le Comber. 2014. "Geographic Profiling in Nazi Berlin: Fact and Fiction." *Geospatial Intelligence Review* 12(2): 44–57.

Rossmo, D. Kim, Quint C. Thurman, Jay D. Jamieson, and Kristine Egan. 2008. "Geographic Patterns and Profiling of Illegal Crossings of the Southern U.S. Border." *Security Journal* 21: 29–57.

Segaller, Stephen. 1987. *Invisible Armies: Terrorism into the 1990's*. San Diego: Harcourt Brace Jovanovich.

Shenon, Philip, and David Johnston. 2001. "A Nation Challenged: The Investigation; Preventive Steps." *New York Times* (October 9).

Sisak, Tom J. 2016. *Patterns in Geospatial Behavior During the Preparatory Phase of Terrorist Attacks*. Doctoral dissertation, Henley-Putnam University, San Jose, CA.

Stea, David. 1969. "The Measurement of Mental Maps: An Experimental Model for Studying Conceptual Spaces." In *Behavioral Problems in Geography*, edited by Kevin R. Cox and Reginald G. Golledge. Evanston, IL: Northwestern University Press.

Stevenson, Mark D., and Steven C. Le Comber. 2013. "Biological Geographical Profiling." In *Encyclopedia of Criminology and Criminal Justice*, edited by Gerben Bruinsma and David L. Weisburd. New York: Springer.

Stevenson, Mark D., D. Kim Rossmo, Robert J. Knell, and Steven C. Le Comber. 2012. "Geographic Profiling as a Novel Spatial Tool for Targeting the Control of Invasive Species." *Ecography* 35:704–715.

Taylor, Max. 1993. "Rational Choice, Behavior Analysis, and Political Violence." In *Routine Activity and Rational Choice*, edited by Ronald V. Clarke and Marcus Felson. New Brunswick, NJ: Transaction.

Tench, Stephen, Hannah Fry, and Paul Gill. 2016. "Spatio-Temporal Patterns of IED Usage by the Provisional Irish Republican Army." *European Journal of Applied Mathematics* 27:377–402.

Townsley, Michael, Shane D. Johnson, and Jerry H. Ratcliffe. 2008. "Space Time Dynamics of Insurgent Activity in Iraq." *Security Journal* 21:139–146.

Wiles, Paul, and Andrew Costello. 2000. *The "Road to Nowhere": The Evidence for Travelling Criminals*. Home Office Research Study No. 207. London: Research, Development and Statistics Directorate, Home Office.

Zipf, George K. 1949. *Human Behavior and the Principle of Least Effort: An Introduction to Human Ecology*. Cambridge, MA: Addison-Wesley.

CHAPTER 35

CHILD SEXUAL ABUSE AND OPPORTUNITY

RICHARD WORTLEY

35.1 Introduction

THE role of opportunity in crime, for many years considered a trivial consideration by the majority of criminologists, is increasingly becoming accepted as a crucial component of the offending dynamic. Clarke (2012) identifies Sutherland's (1947) declaration in *Principles of Criminology* that "the situation operates in many ways, of which perhaps the least important is the provision of an opportunity for a criminal act" (p. 5) as setting the tone for the dispositional bias in criminology for the next 50 years or so. Clarke himself moved gingerly in the claims made for opportunity. In the seminal *Crime as Opportunity* (Mayhew, Clarke, Sturman, and Hough, 1976) the issue of causation was avoided altogether and it was not until *Opportunity Makes the Thief* (Felson and Clarke, 1998) that opportunity was claimed as a cause of crime. A symbolic breakthrough in the acceptance of opportunity as valid criminological variable came when Frank Cullen (2011)—ironically in his American Society of Criminology 2010 Sutherland Address—urged criminologists to "put out the welcome mat to crime scientists and to understand that the future of criminology will be advanced by exploring systematically the nexus between propensity and opportunity" (p. 315).

But the battle for the recognition of the role of opportunity in crime is not yet won. The preparedness to accord a meaningful role to opportunity can vary according to the crime in question, with a distinction typically made between so-called prudent and expressive crimes. For the former category, involving crimes such as burglary that involve tangible rewards, it may be conceded that offenders proceed of the basis of their assessment of the crime opportunities offered in the immediate environment. For crimes in the latter category, those involving violent and sexual motivations, the default remains to frame the action in terms of the offenders' entrenched dispositions (e.g., aggressive personality, sexual deviance) and/or immediate psychological states (e.g., anger, sexual arousal). The view expressed by Hayward (2007) below is typical of the stubborn resistance to seeing beyond a person-centered perspective in these cases:

> Set against the mass of acquisitive/property crimes that are the stock-in-trade of RC theorists are the growing number of crimes containing a high emotional or "expressive" element—what I have referred to elsewhere as the world of the "irrational" actor. . . . While undeniably useful as a means of reducing certain forms of "shallow end" or "volume" crime, the situational/RC approach may be a less effective tool against the chaotic, violent or so-called "expressive crimes" that cause most public distress and community disharmony. . . . Consider the inherent problems RC theorists might encounter when trying to devise initiatives to stem offences such as gang-related crime, hoax emergency service call-outs, hedonistic drug use, child molestation, rape, or drunken assault. (p. 237)

In this chapter I examine the role of opportunity and other situational variables in child sexual abuse. I challenge the notion that child sex offenders are irresistibly driven to offend and that situational conditions are irrelevant to them. I argue that many child sex offenders lack strong deviant sexual motivations, and that even those who do possess such motivations do not act on them in every circumstance. I examine the evidence supporting the role of opportunity in child sexual abuse and show that observed patterns in child sexual abuse can only be explained in terms of variations in situational conditions. Finally, I address the "So what?" question and examine the implications of taking a situational perspective on child sexual abuse for prevention.

35.2 The Pathologization of Child Sexual Abuse

There are surely no offenders so reviled as those who sexually abuse children. The thought of a child being sexually exploited is for most of us repellent and we wonder how any normal person could perpetrate such acts. Both popularly and in the clinical literature, those who sexually abuse children are widely considered to be psychologically "sick," literally suffering the mental disorder of pedophilia. From this perspective, the cause of child sexual abuse is framed squarely in intrapsychic terms, with the deviant behavior driven by the offenders' "recurrent, intense sexually arousing fantasies (and) sexual urges" (American Psychiatric Association, 2013).

And yet this pathologization of sexual contact between adults and children is relatively recent, and even today there is wide variation across cultures in the legal age at which people can engage in sexual conduct (Wortley and Smallbone, 2012). The treatment of children as sexual beings was apparently common in ancient Greek, Roman, Chinese, and Indian societies (Bullough, 2004). In medieval Europe there are documented cases of brides as young as seven, while Shakespeare's Juliet was just 13, a matter that seemed to cause little consternation among other characters in the play. At the beginning of the nineteenth century in England the age of consent for girls was still just 10 years, not raised to sixteen until 1885. It was a year later in 1886 that sexual attraction to children was first formally classed as a psychological disorder when psychiatrist Krafft-Ebing introduced the concept of pedophilia. In fact, even Krafft-Ebing did not view all child sexual abusers as pedophiles. He believed that most child sexual abuse was a vice or "perversity," the result of moral weakness, and he reserved the diagnosis of pedophilia for a relatively small number of individuals whom he considered to have a "mental weakness" caused some physical or psychological infirmity. Despite Krafft-Ebing's qualifications concerning the prevalence of "true" pedophilia, the portrayal of sexual attraction to children as psychopathology has come to now dominate the way the problem is understood both by experts and by the general public (Angelides, 2005).

The blanket pathologization of child sexual offenders is problematic on two counts. First, it suggests that the population can be neatly divided into pedophiles and nonpedophiles. This is a comforting position to take, conveniently confining the problem of child sexual abuse to a small and deviant subsection of the community—the "other." More challenging is to take the view that, like most human psychological attributes, sexual attraction to children falls on a continuum with no clear dividing line between pedophiles and nonpedophiles. While there is a relatively small core of individuals who are strongly predisposed to sexually abuse children, the potential to be sexually aroused by a child extends further back into the normal curve than we might care to acknowledge. There is empirical support for this assertion. Experiments using plethysmography to measure penile volume have shown that many normal (i.e., non-sex offender) participants are sexually aroused by pictures of naked children, albeit typically less so than is the case for diagnosed pedophiles (Freund, 1971; Marshall and Barbaree, 1988; Wormith, 1986). Similarly, self-report studies have shown that up to a quarter of male college students admit to having experienced sexual attraction toward a child (Briere and Runtz, 1989; Smiljanich and Briere, 1996), while Finkelhor and Lewis (1988) found that between 13% and 21% of males in a general population sample admitted having actually molested a child. On the other side of the coin, Wortley and Smallbone (2014b) found that 60% of respondents in a sample of convicted child sex offenders denied having a dispositional sexual attraction to children, suggesting that activation of their deviant sexual arousal was situationally dependent.

The second problematic consequence of pathologizing child sexual offenders is that it encourages the view that they are psychologically compelled to offend and are unable to exercise control over their behavior (Jahnke, Imhoff, and Hoyer, 2015). In this regard, we are inclined to see child sexual abuse as a special case governed by rules different from those that apply to other crimes. We conflate the desire to carry out a particular behavior with the willingness to do so. In the case of property crime, for example, we understand that most people can desire wealth without ever seriously considering perpetrating theft, fraud, or robbery. We are less willing to make a similar concession for child sexual abuse. However, there is evidence that many child sexual offenders are less driven in their behavior than is often assumed. People can experience sexual attraction to children without physically acting on those feelings. For example, while there is debate about the extent of the overlap, most research indicates that the majority of individuals who access child sexual exploitation imagery online do not commit contact child sexual abuse (Seto, Hanson, and Babchishin, 2011).[1] There is also evidence that many individuals who are sexually attracted to children find their feelings disturbing and self-estranging, and actively fight any desire to offend. For example, over half (54%) of calls made to the child sexual abuse hotline Stop It Now in the UK are made by individuals seeking help with their own thoughts, feelings, and behavior (Denis and Whitehead, 2013). Finally, the persistence of many child sex offenders would seem to be less than one would expect for compulsive behavior. Smallbone and Wortley (2000) found that almost half (49%) of convicted child sex offenders report having had sexual contact with just one victim. Further, the reconviction rates for child sex offenders are surprisingly low. The meta-analysis carried out by Hanson and Bussière (1998) found that just 13% of child sex offenders were convicted for a further sexual offense after five years' release.

Taken together, the research suggests that for many child sex offenders a control perspective on behavior may provide a better explanation of their offending than a sexual deviance model. According to the control perspective, the essential question is not how some individuals acquire deviant characteristics but rather why is it that most individuals act in prosocial ways. The control perspective on crime begins with the assumption that the tendency to act impulsively and selfishly is the natural human condition and does not need to be explained. What needs to be explained is the process by which these natural impulses are brought under control. Extending this concept to child sexual abuse, a control perspective suggests that the potential to become sexually attracted to an underage person is inherent and does not need to be learned. In fact, most people have had the experience of being sexually attracted to someone underage—when they themselves were underage. Some researchers see latent sexual attraction to young people in evolutionary terms. According to this argument, males have been evolutionarily designed to prefer young female sex partners because youthfulness is associated with fertility (Thornhill and Thornhill, 1987). This does not mean, of course, that all men are at risk of becoming child sex offenders. The extent to which any latent potential is realized, if at all, depends upon a range of biological, developmental, social, and situational factors. Most men will not develop a sexual attraction to children and will happily fulfill their sexual desires with appropriately aged partners. It also does not mean that sexual contact with children should be accepted as appropriate behavior or that those men who do sexually abuse children should not be held accountable for their actions. As a society we have decided that child sexual abuse is abhorrent and we make laws precisely for the purpose of stopping people doing things that they might want to do that we collectively agree they should not.

In short, much of what we think we know about child sex offenders is based on stereotypical assumptions. The moral outrage we feel toward child sex offenders can get in the way of a more objective, dispassionate analysis of their behavior (Wortley, 2015). If many child sex offenders are not peculiarly compelled to offend by internal psychological forces, then their crimes can be subjected to the same sorts of criminological analyses as any other crime. We can start thinking, therefore, about how their offending might be initiated and patterned by opportunity structures and other situational factors.

35.3 Child Sexual Abuse as a Person-Situation Interaction

As I have tried to make clear in the preceding section, it is not my contention that the sexual abuse of children is purely a matter of opportunity and that the offenders' disposition does not matter. Common sense alone tells us that not everyone is at equal risk of engaging in child sexual abuse. Child sexual abuse is the product of an interaction between the psychological characteristics of the individual and the circumstances in which the offense occurs (Wortley, 2012). There are undoubtedly individuals who are strongly predisposed to sexually abuse children and require little in the way of encouragement to offend. Moving backward along the normal curve, the risk of an individual sexually abusing children reduces, although some may be tempted to engage in sexually exploitative behavior in a moment of weakness and given the "right" situational conditions.

Cornish and Clarke (2003) proposed a general offender typology that sought to capture the interaction between disposition and situation. They proposed three categories of offender—the antisocial predator, the mundane offender, and the provoked offender—based on the respective strengths of the offender's criminal propensity and the criminogenic nature of the immediate environment. This typology has been adapted for child sexual abuse, with the three categories relabeled committed, opportunist, and reactive, and was found to do a good job of accounting for the offending patterns observed (Smallbone, Marshall, and Wortley, 2008; Wortley and Smallbone, 2006; Wortley and Smallbone, 2014a).

Committed offenders are stereotypic predatory child molesters. They possess a preferential sexual attraction to children and are likely to be high-frequency, chronic offenders. This does not mean the situational considerations are unimportant to them—on the contrary. Committed offenders are calculating in their offending, and their offenses involve premeditation and at least some rudimentary planning, utilizing situational data to maximize anticipated benefits and to reduce costs. They actively seek out and groom victims for abuse and will have developed a repertoire of skills and techniques to allow them to carry out their task. They are likely to be adept at identifying vulnerable children who will present the fewest risks of apprehension.

Opportunistic offenders are ambivalent in their sexual attraction to children and sporadic in their child sexual offending. Often, they may have an isolated child sex offense within a wider criminal career that includes a variety of nonsex offenses. The criminal versatility of these offenders suggests a generalized failure to inhibit self-gratifying urges rather than active pedophilia. Often they will commit crime more or less on the spur of the moment with minimal forethought. They are opportunity takers who will exploit the chance to sexually abuse a child when temptations present and personal and situational constraints on their behavior weaken.

Reactive offenders will generally not possess an entrenched sexual attraction to children, or if they do, they will have been largely successful in keeping it under control. Their offending occurs as a response to some specific triggering event that activates a sexual attraction to a child. Such events include situations that induce emotional arousal and weaken usual restraints—for example, giving the child a bath while alone babysitting. Reactive offenders will typically have no other criminal involvement, and their sexual offending may represent an aberration that would not have occurred if it were not for the precipitating events.

It is important to note that the typology outlined above extends the notion of opportunity beyond the everyday meaning of the word. Opportunity implies only that favorable circumstances exist to enable someone to achieve a desired outcome. When applied to crime generally and child sexual abuse in particular, opportunity theory assumes that the offender comes to the situation already motivated to offend and that circumstances merely permit the crime to proceed. With the description of reactive offenders we see the immediate environment playing a more active role in *precipitating* offending (Wortley, 2001; Wortley and Smallbone, 2006). Wortley (2017, p. 63) defines a situational crime precipitator as "any aspect of the immediate environment that creates, triggers or intensifies the motivation to commit crime." Precipitators induce individuals to commit crimes that they might not have otherwise considered carrying out at that time and place. Including precipitators as a component of the situation better captures the dynamic nature of the readiness to offend. While the concept of precipitators has been discussed above with respect to reactive offenders, the principle that specific instances of offending may be triggered by the immediate environment applies to all three offender categories. Indeed, following the logic of offending as the outcome of a person-situation interaction, crime is most likely to occur when an individual strongly predisposed to offend encounters an environment that actively encourages offending. Thus, if anything, committed child sex offenders are likely to more susceptible to precipitating influences than are reactive offenders.

35.4 Evidence for the Role of Situations

If opportunity and other situational factors play a role in child sexual abuse, then we should see evidence of this in the offending patterns we observe. In accordance with situational crime theories—the routine activity approach, rational choice perspective, and the concept of crime precipitators—we would expect offending to cluster at times and in places where potential offenders and victims come together in circumstances where the temptations are strong and where personal, social, situational, and legal controls are weak. However, researching child sexual abuse throws up a number of methodological challenges. Police-recorded crime data are of limited value for two reasons. First, such data do not contain the sort of detailed information about the offense required to draw conclusions about the role of immediate environments. Second, underreporting, an issue for virtually all crime types, is especially problematic for child sexual abuse, with official reporting rates estimated to be between 3% (Finkelhor and Dziuba-Leatherman, 1994) and 15% (Kilpatrick and Saunders, 1997). Most research, therefore, relies on offender and victim self-report data. These strategies in turn have different strengths and weaknesses. There are a few offender self-report studies carried out on general population samples (e.g., Finkelhor and Lewis (1988). These can provide offending prevalence estimates, but they rarely go into much detail about the actual offending behavior. More common are studies that survey convicted offenders (e.g., Smallbone and Wortley, 2000) that can provide detailed information about where, when, how, and against whom the abuse was perpetrated, including for those crimes for which the offender was not arrested. However, this strategy remains limited by the fact that the samples comprise only convicted offenders and it is uncertain just what sorts of biases this might introduce. Plausibly, for example, prison samples will comprise the most serious and persistent offenders. Self-serving bias may also be an issue with this sample, although reliability checks (e.g., test retest, the inclusion of "lie" scales) can help address this problem (e.g., Smallbone and Wortley, 2000). Finally, victimization surveys can provide good estimates of victimization prevalence, but with questions about child sexual abuse experiences typically tacked onto a broader victimization survey (e.g., Office for National Statistics, 2016), there is little room for more detailed questioning. However, on selected items these surveys provide the opportunity to check for consistency between offender and victim accounts.

The role of environmental influences on child sex offending is a relatively new topic of research, and evidence must be drawn from across number of different research strands that examine the circumstances in which offenses occur. Relevant research includes that examining the victim-offender relationship, the psychosocial backgrounds of offenders, their modus operandi, and the times and locations that offending occurs. All of these research areas bear on the crucial role of the person-situation interaction in child sex offending. Based on this research, the following predictions will be examined in this section:

1. Offenders will target children with whom they have a preexisting relationship in line with the least-effort principle.
2. Sexual offending onset will coincide with a time in the offender's life or career when opportunities to access children increase.
3. Sexual abuse will occur in places and at times that that are consistent with the routine activities of offenders and victims.
4. There will be particular increases in Internet-related child sexual abuse, reflecting the increased opportunities for offending offered by the Internet.
5. The incidence of child sexual abuse will be high in environments characterized by a breakdown of social and personal constraints on behavior.

35.4.1 Offender-Victim Relationship

The image of the predatory stranger is the dominant child sex offender stereotype. It is every parents' nightmare that their child may be sexually abused while engaging in some outside activity such as walking to school, running an errand, or playing in the park. Such events do of course occur, sometimes with especially tragic outcomes, but research has shown consistently that most child sexual abuse occurs between perpetrators and victims who have a preexisting relationship (Kaufman, Homberg, Orts, et al. 1998; Office for National Statistics, 2016; Simon and Zgoba, 2006; Smallbone, Marshall and Wortley, 2008; Smallbone and Wortley, 2000). For example, according to victimization data from the Crime Survey for England and Wales (Office for National Statistics, 2016), of respondents who said they were sexually assaulted as a child 50% nominated a family member as the perpetrator, 30% a friend or acquaintance, 6% a person in authority, and 14% a stranger. Examining offender self-report data from 189 convicted child sex offenders, Smallbone and Wortley (2000), found a broadly similar pattern; in 57% of cases the offender reported living with the child, in 37% knowing the child outside the home, and in 7% not previously knowing the child. Overall, in 73% of cases the offender had known to victim for more than a month before the abuse occurred, and in over a half of cases (51%) for more than a year.

The observed relationship patterns between offenders and victims are consistent with the principle of least effort (Zipf, 1949) and the routine activities approach (Cohen and Felson, 1979). All things being equal, offenders will expend the minimal amount of effort necessary to access victims. Locating and grooming a previously unknown child for the purpose of sexual contact may be time consuming and require a degree of planning and commitment. Those offenders who are strongly motivated to sexually abuse children will be prepared to commit this time and effort if necessary. However, as a general rule, offenders are more likely to exploit the immediate opportunities offered by the preexisting relationships that they have with children they encounter routinely in the course of their daily activities.

35.4.2 Offending Onset

The traditional view of child sex offenders presented in the clinical literature is that early onset of offending is the norm (Abel, Becker, Mittleman, et al., 1987; Abel and Osborn, 1992). Most offenders were believed to begin offending in adolescence and to continue offending into adulthood. More recent analysis of the evidence challenges this view. While it is estimated that adolescents are responsible for between 30% and 50% of child sex abuse cases (Bourke and Donohue, 1996; Finkelhor and Dziuba-Leatherman, 1994), adolescent sexual recidivism is around just 10%; that is, relatively few adolescents progress to sexual offending as adults. Instead, another peak in offending onset occurs in early middle age comprising a distinct population of offenders. In their research, for example, Smallbone and Wortley (2000, 2004) found that the mean age of adult offenders at the time of their first sexual contact with a child was 32.4 years and the modal age bracket (accounting for 37.2% of the sample) was 31 to 40 years.

The offending pattern displayed by the early onset group of child sex offenders is broadly consistent with what would be expected for crime generally. Criminal involvement for most crimes peaks in late adolescence, but the majority of offenders age out of crime by early adulthood; those who continue offending tend to posses an underlying antisocial disposition and become persistent high-volume offenders (Moffitt, 1993). The emergence of the late-onset group of child sex offenders, however, is at variance with the usual criminal careers model of offending and, more particularly, challenges the interpretation of child sexual abuse as pathology-driven behavior. That many offenders were able to resist sexually abusing children for so long suggests the absence in many of strong sexually deviant motivations. Moreover, it suggests that something changed in the offenders' circumstances to trigger the onset of offending. The most plausible explanation is that access to potential victims increases significantly in early middle age. It is at this stage of life where potential offenders are most likely to have young children, to have friends who have young children, and to be in careers (e.g., teaching) or be involved in community activities (e.g., coaching) that give them greater access to young children.

A study by Terry (2008) on child sexual abuse in the Catholic Church helps illustrate the point. Terry examined US records between 1950 and 2002 of sexual abuse allegations involving nearly 14,000 victims and over 4,000 priests. She found that the onset of offending occurred on average 11 years after the ordination of the priest. This, she argued, coincided with the progression of priests to parish residences, a move that was accompanied by greater levels of autonomy and more direct engagement with children (Terry and Ackerman, 2008).

35.4.3 Place and Timing of Abuse

So far in this chapter the intersection of the routine activities of offenders and victims has been examined at a macro level of analysis. There is some research that allows us to drill down further to examine at a more micro level where and when offenders gain access to victims and how they set up or exploit opportunities to carry out sexual abuse. In their study of adult child-sex offenders, Smallbone and Wortley (Smallbone and Wortley, 2000; Wortley and Smallbone, 2006) asked offenders where they located victims for abuse, how they came to be alone with the child, and where the abuse took place. Intrafamilial offenders by definition located their victims in the home. Looking just at extrafamilial offenders, most located victims in domestic or work-related contexts—for example, at a friend's home (40%), while babysitting (21%), through and organized activity (20%), and at the offenders' place of employment (17%) (multiple responses permitted). In contrast, relatively few offenders located victims in public places—for example, in a public toilet (13%), in a shopping mall (12%), in a playground (5%), and hitchhiking (5%). When all offenders (intrafamilial and extrafamilial) were asked what they were doing with the child immediately prior to the abuse, the most frequent responses revolved around domestic, and often caregiving, activities—for example, watching TV with the child (42%), letting the child sleep in the offender's bed (36%), tucking the child into bed (30%), and giving the child a bath (18%). Overwhelmingly, the abuse itself occurred in the offenders' home (69%), with almost three-quarters (72%) of offenders moving victims less than 60 meters from where they first located them.

Leclerc and Felson (2016) replicated the Smallbone and Wortley (2000) study with a sample of 116 convicted sex offenders who were adolescents and reported strikingly similar patterns. The main differences were that adolescent offenders were more likely than adult offenders to locate victims in their local neighborhood and to carry out the abuse in their own home, and were correspondingly less likely to find victims through an organized activity or place of employment. These findings make sense from a routine activity perspective, reflecting the more restricted opportunities available to adolescents.

McKillop, Brown, Wortley, and Smallbone (2015) examined the time of day sexual abuse occurred as reported by a sample of 100 convicted adult child-sex offenders. In this group, 48% of cases occurred between 6:00 a.m. and 3:00 p.m., 34% between 3:00 pm and 9:00 p.m., and 18% between 9:00 p.m. and 6:00 a.m. There were significant differences among these time bands in the mean ages of victims. Younger children were more likely to be abused during the day (mean age 8.8 years), "middle-aged" children were more likely to be abused in the evening (mean age 10.8 years), and older children were more likely to be abused at night (mean age 12.6 years). In addition, it was found that younger children were more likely than older children to be abused by a family member, while older children were more likely than younger children to be abused by a nonfamily member. Taken together, these findings would seem to reflect the differing routine activities of children at different ages. Young children are more likely to be at home and interacting with family members during the day, while as children get older they are more likely to become involved in out-of-home activities (visiting friends, playing outside unsupervised) and to interact with nonfamily members.

35.4.4 Internet-Related Child Sexual Abuse

In 1980 the rates of online sexual harassment, unwanted exposure to online sexual material, unwanted online sexual solicitations, and the production, distribution and downloading of Internet child abuse material were precisely 0%; today each of these activities is a significant social and criminal problem (Jones, Mitchell, and Finkelhor, 2013; Mitchell, Jones, Finkelhor, and Wolak, 2014; Wolak and Finkelhor, 2013). At one level, of course, this is a banal statistic—there was no Internet in 1980. However, the fact that these behaviors have so quickly become problematic reveals something fundamental about the role of opportunity in sex offending.

I will focus on the example of child abuse material. In 1980—three years before the first standardized Internet protocols were signed in January 1983—the largest-selling child pornography magazine in the United States was reckoned to sell about 800 copies (Jenkins, 2001). Twenty years later, the Internet child pornography company Landslide Productions was shut down and found to have over 250,000 subscribers worldwide (Krone, 2005). Today, the number of offenders regularly accessing child abuse material online is estimated in the millions, and individual offenders have been caught with in excess of a million abuse images (see Wortley and Smallbone, 2012). What has changed between 1980 and today to cause this escalation? Are we to conclude that in the 30 years or so that the Internet has existed the number of pedophiles in the world has for some reason exponentially increased? If this is so, it has not been reflected in an increase in contact child sexual abuse over that period. Victimization surveys indicate that, in line with crime more generally, rates of contact child sexual abuse have dropped significantly since the early 1990s (Dunne, Purdie, Cook, et al., 2003; Finkelhor, 2008; Jones and Finkelhor, 2010; Office for National Statistics, 2016). The proposition that offenders have simply moved from contact offending to online offending also does not withstand scrutiny. While, as noted earlier, the exact relationship between contact and online offending is a matter for debate, the two groups of offenders generally have different psychological and sociodemographic profiles (Babchishin, Hanson, and Van Zuylen, 2015; Wolak, Finkelhor, and Mitchell, 2011). Compared with contact sexual offenders, online offenders tend to have less pronounced clinical features, including fewer problems with victim empathy, cognitive distortions, and emotional identification with children. Online offenders also have more conventional sociodemographic features, such as having a higher level of education and being more likely to be in employment. Perhaps the most interesting difference between the two groups is that online offenders are less likely to be in a relationship and to have children, suggesting that they may have less access to potential offline victims.

The most plausible reason that child abuse material has become such a serious problem is the increased opportunity offered by the Internet. Before the Internet, child pornography was a highly restricted activity, and law enforcement could claim considerable success in keeping the problem under control (Ahart, 1982). Images were generally locally produced, of poor quality, expensive, and difficult to obtain, traded furtively in hard-copy form among small, closely-knit networks of dedicated consumers. The Internet has dramatically increased the amount of child abuse material available, the efficiency of its distribution, and the ease by which it can be accessed. In doing so, it has created a new pool of offenders, allowing many individuals, who in earlier times would have been deterred by the difficulty of obtaining child pornography, to explore their perhaps casual and vaguely formed sexual attraction to children. Vast quantities of technically high-quality images are now instantly available, at any time, and with (apparent) anonymity. Alone and in the comfort of their own homes, individuals are able to satisfy their secret curiosities and desires conveniently, cheaply, and relatively risk free.

35.4.5 The Breakdown of Constraints

Some environments—those that induce high levels of emotional arousal, enhanced in-group identification, and feelings of anonymity—can engender a breakdown in the usual social and personal constraints on behavior, allowing individuals to engage in deviant activities that in other circumstances they would successfully inhibit. Among the forms of deviant behavior, these conditions may produce sexual violence including, where children are present, endemic child sexual abuse (Rayment-McHugh, Smallbone, and Tilley, 2015). Taking a control theory perspective, a breakdown in the constraints on behavior does not positively create a sexual attraction to children; rather it frees the individual to act on preexisting latent desires. Environments that may induce a breakdown in constraint include total institutions, remote communities under stress, and war zones.

35.4.5.1 Total Institutions

Total institution is a term coined by Erving Goffman (1961) to describe "a place of work and residence where a great number of similarly situated people, cut off from the wider community for a considerable time, together lead an enclosed, formally administered round of life" (p. 17). Total institutions include prisons, army barracks, monasteries, and, of particular relevance to the current analysis, institutions that cater to children, such as children's homes, boarding schools, and youth detention centers. Goffman argued that the inherent power imbalance in such institutions—the all-controlling staff and the dependent, depersonalized residents—inevitably results in abuses of power. The capacity for institutions to bring out the worst in human nature was famously demonstrated by the Stanford Prison Experiment (Haney, Banks, and Zimbardo, 1973). Male college students randomly allocated to the role of guards in a mock prison quickly became brutal and authoritarian toward those allocated to prisoner roles. The researchers argued that the guards deindividuated—submerged their identities within the group—allowing them to carry out what they would in other circumstances regard as reprehensible behavior.

In the case of the Stanford Prison Experiment, the environmentally induced deviance largely involved acts of physical and psychological abuse. However, deindividuation can allow all manner of latent impulses, including sexual ones, to find expression. Zimbardo (2007), for example, drew on the experiment to explain the highly sexualized acts of brutality carried out by American guards on Iraqi prisoners at Abu Ghraib prison. Similarly, the concept of total institutions and the process of deindividuation can help explain the high incidence of child sexual abuse reported in child-centered institutions. The seriousness of the problem is evidenced by the plethora of major public inquiries that has been carried out around the world in recent years. These include in the UK, the Tribunal of Inquiry Into the Abuse of Children in Care in the Former County Council Areas of Gwynedd and Clwyd Since 1974 (2000), and the Independent Inquiry into Child Sexual Abuse (2015); in Ireland, the Commission to Inquire into Child Abuse (2009); in Australia, the Royal Commission into Institutional Responses to Child Sexual Abuse (2014); and in Canada, Restoring Dignity: Responding to Child Abuse in Canadian Institutions (Law Commission of Canada, 2000). Each of these inquiries details systemic sexual abuse of child residents by staff, often extending over many years. Within these institutions children become viewed as things and staff develop a sense of immunity from any consequences for their behaviors. As these inquiries typically conclude, the incidence and nature of child sexual abuse in institutions cannot be explained in terms of the deviance of individual staff members. It is the pathological nature of the institutions that creates the conditions in which sexual abuse flourishes. As Zimbardo (2007) puts it, it is not so much a case of rotten apples as of rotten barrels.

35.4.5.2 Remote Communities

A breakdown of constraint can also occur in isolated and deprived communities. One such example is the case of remote indigenous communities in Australia. As with many colonized lands, since the settlement of Australia by Europeans in 1788, there has been a steady process of dispossession, marginalization, and impoverishment of the original population. Few Australian Aborigines now lead a traditional nomadic life, but over a quarter (27%) still live in discrete and often very remote communities that may be a day's drive along a rough, dirt road from the nearest other settlement (Human Rights and Equal Opportunity Commission, 2006; Memmott and Moran, 2001). Most Aboriginal communities are severely disadvantaged on a range of socioeconomic indices (Memmott and Moran, 2001; Northern Territory Law Reform Committee, 2003). While larger settlements (300–600 inhabitants) generally have a school (although often only to primary level), health clinic, and access to essential services such as water and electricity, there are generally no permanent police or doctors. Of these settlements, 14% do not have permanent dwellings, and 29% of houses are in a substantial state of disrepair. These physical deprivations are frequently accompanied by a serious breakdown in social order. Most communities have a limited economic base, and, leaving aside work schemes, unemployment is as high as 85% (Northern Territory Law Reform Committee, 2003). In the absence of meaningful work and with the loss of traditional ways of life, chronic alcohol abuse and associated high levels of public and family violence have become major social problems in many communities (Aboriginal and Torres Strait Islander Women's Taskforce on Violence, 1999).

Set against this background of chronic economic, physical, and social disadvantage, a series of inquiries and reports has detailed disturbing levels of child sexual abuse within many Aboriginal communities (Aboriginal and Torres Strait Islander Women's Taskforce on Violence, 1999; Crime Prevention Committee, Parliament of Victoria, 1995; Gordon, Hallahan, and Henry, 2002; NSW Aboriginal Child Sexual Assault Taskforce, 2006; Northern Territory Board of Inquiry into the Protection of Aboriginal Children from Sexual Abuse, 2007; Smallbone, McHugh-Rayment, and Smith, 2013).

These reports indicate that Aboriginal children are three times more likely to be sexually abused than non-Aboriginal children. Various patterns of child sexual abuse were found. In some cases, the abuse was perpetrated by individuals who exploited positions of power and trust in the community. Other cases involved perpetrators who were affected by alcohol or drugs and offended on the spur of the moment after encountering an unattended child. Sexual activity among young people was also highlighted in many reports. In some cases, juveniles were the perpetrators of sexual abuse, assaulting or coercing younger and more vulnerable children. In other cases, children as young as 10 or 12 years of age routinely engaged in consensual sex with one another. In some communities the practice had arisen for teenage girls to willingly engage in sex with men or older boys in exchange for money, alcohol, or other goods. The reports stress that sexual activity with or among children is not part of Aboriginal culture, and on the contrary, that there were traditionally strict taboos governing sexual contact between individuals and severe punishments for those who broke the customary law. What is occurring in remote Aboriginal communities is not an Aboriginal problem; it is a problem that can occur in any community that experiences similar levels of isolation, deprivation, and cultural disintegration (Rayment-McHugh et al. 2015).

35.4.5.3 War Zones

The final example of environments that can induce a breakdown of constraint relates to the chaotic conditions that occur in war and conflict zones. The history of sexual violence perpetrated by soldiers against civilians caught up in armed conflicts goes back to ancient times, and there is a depressing litany of examples from more recent years (Bastick, Grimm, and Kunz, 2007; Ward and Marsh, 2006; Wood, 2006). In many of these cases, there seems to have been little discrimination exercised by soldiers between adult and child victims. During the Japanese Rape of Nanking in 1937, as many as 80,000 women and girls were reported raped, with particularly harrowing accounts of young children being cut open to enable penetration to occur (Chang, 1997). The notorious mass rapes committed by Soviet troops as they moved into German territories toward the end of World War II was reported often to include "every female over the age of twelve or thirteen" (Naimark cited in Wood, 2006, p. 309). In an infamous case from the Vietnam War in 1968, around 20 women and girls as young as 10 years old were raped by US troops before being executed along with 500 or so fellow villagers at My Lai (Cookman, 2007; Olson and Roberts, 1998). During the breakup of Yugoslavia in the early 1990s, more than 20,000 Muslim women and girls from Bosnia-Herzegovina were systematically raped by Bosnian Serb forces, with young girls and virgins a particular target (Wood, 2006). Conflicts in Bangladesh in 1971 (Neill, 2000), Rwanda in 1994 (Bijleveld, Morssinkhof, and Smeulers, 2009), the Democratic Republic of Congo in 1998 (Baaz and Stern, 2009), and Sudan in 2003 (Arieff, 2010), among many others, can be added to this list.

As the list of conflict zones indicates, atrocities against civilians are not limited to the soldiers of any particular country or culture. Nor is rape in conflict zones inevitable: Cohen (2013) analyzed 86 conflicts and estimated that for 53 (62%) there was evidence of widespread or elevated sexual violence. Wood (2006) suggests that variations in the prevalence of rape in war can depend upon factors such as the implicit and explicit expectations of military leaders, the socialization process undergone by soldiers, cultural norms, and the nature of group dynamics. The underlying reasons for the occurrence of sexual violence in war zones are complex and matters for debate, and it is beyond the scope of this chapter to explore them in detail. For the current argument it is enough to conclude that the incidence of child sexual abuse dramatically escalates in conflict zones and is perpetrated by individuals who would most likely not contemplate carrying out such acts in their everyday life.

35.5 Implications and Conclusions

The ultimate purpose of conducting research on child sexual abuse is, or should be, to gain insights that can be used to devise effective strategies for protecting children from sexual victimization. To date the overwhelming bulk of research has been directed at understanding the psychology of offenders. In turn, the task of preventing child sexual abuse is typically framed in terms of identifying, catching, and treating individuals who pose a risk to children. Many jurisdictions now have mandatory police checks before allowing people to work with children in professional and voluntary roles (Jacobs and Blitsa, 2012) and sex offender registers for those convicted of child sex offenses (Thomas, 2013). A great deal of research has gone into the development of risk assessment instruments that might be used to assist sentencing and prison release decisions (Barberee, Seto, Langton, and Peacock, 2001; Hanson and Bussière, 1998), while sentences for child sex offenders are generally getting tougher (Cohen and Jeglic, 2007) and the introduction of "dangerous offender" legislation in some jurisdictions has allowed child sex offenders to be kept in prison after the expiry of their original sentence (Mercado and Ogloff, 2007; Smallbone and Ransley, 2005). And in an era where the investment in rehabilitation has generally diminished (Cullen and Gilbert, 2013), prison sex offender treatment programs are flourishing (Marshall, Fernandez, Hudson, and Ward, 2013).

It is not my argument that there should be no attention paid to the role of offender characteristics in child sexual abuse or that sensible strategies to deflect, catch, and treat offenders do not have a place in prevention efforts. But the limitations of an offender-focused approach need to be understood. Screening potential employees and volunteers for child-related organizations will not detect offenders who have not previously come to the attention of authorities nor those individuals who are yet to offend. When it comes to sentencing and release decisions, popular risk prediction instruments have reported correlations with sexual recidivism of between just .06 and .26 (Barbaree, Seto, Langton, and Peacock, 2001), raising serious questions about our ability to reliably distinguish between those offenders who pose a continuing risk and those who do not. As for rehabilitation programs, research indicates that treatment can produce significant reductions in recidivism. For example, Marshall, Marshall, Serran, and Fernandez (2006) reported recidivism rates after five years for treated the child sex offenders was 3.2% and for non-treated offenders 16.8%. While such findings are encouraging, the overall impact of reductions in recidivism needs to be assessed against the heavy attrition from offending to treatment. As noted earlier in this chapter, at best just 15% (Kilpatrick and Saunders, 1997) of cases are reported to authorities. The criminal justice process further thins the pool of offenders. In an Australian study of 3,351 cases substantiated by child protection authorities, 2,143 were reported to police, 630 accused were charged, and 404 (12% of substantiated cases) were found guilty of at least one charge (Gallagher, Hickey, and Ash 1997). Finally, not all convicted offenders will be sent to prison, and only a proportion of those who do go to prison will receive treatment. Thus, offenders who benefit from treatment are the proverbial tip of the iceberg. Moreover, rehabilitation programs—as with most of the strategies discussed above—are concerned with stopping *re*offending; they do nothing to prevent the sexual abuse occurring in the first place.

It has been argued in this chapter that greater attention needs to be given to the situational dynamics of child sex offending. A shift in thinking is required from conceptualizing child sexual abuse purely in terms of the deviant dispositions of offenders to an understanding that offending occurs as an interaction between the characteristics of a potential offender and the nature of the immediate circumstances in which the abuse may occur. From a research perspective, we need to know more about the child sexual abuse event—where and when the abuse occurs, how victims and offenders come together at those places and times, how offenders go about creating or exploiting offending opportunities, what facilitates their offending, and what might have deterred them. From a prevention perspective, taking a situational perspective provides us with an array of new interventions. Rather than trying to create safer individuals, the goal of situational prevention is to create safer environments for children that reduce their exposure to the risk of sexual abuse. If child sex offenders are not a special case, then we can turn our attention to devising situational prevention strategies to thwart potential offenders before they carry out their abuse (Smallbone et al. 2008; Wortley and Smallbone, 2006).

Note

1. Of course, accessing child sexual exploitation material is itself a crime and is an example of individuals acting on their sexual desires. There is no suggestion that accessing child exploitation material is not a serious problem in its own right. The point being made here is simply that online offenders do not necessarily physically offend.

References

Abel, G. G., Becker, J. V., Mittelman, M., Cunningham-Rathner, J., Rouleau, J., and Murphy, W. (1987). "Self-Reported Sex Crimes of Nonincarcerated Paraphilics." *Journal of Interpersonal Violence*, 2(1): 3–25.

Abel, G. G., and Osborn, C. (1992). "The Paraphilias: The Extent and Nature of Sexually Deviant and Criminal Behavior." *Clinical Forensic Psychiatry*, 15(3): 675–687.

Aboriginal and Torres Strait Island Task Force on Violence. (1999). *The Aboriginal and Torres Strait Island Task Force on Violence Report*. Brisbane: Queensland Government.

Ahart, G. J. (1982). *Sexual Exploitation of Children: A Problem of Unknown Magnitude*. Report to the Chairman, Subcommittee on Select Education, House Committee on Education and Labor. Gaithersburg, MD: US General Accounting Office.

American Psychiatric Association. (2013). *Diagnostic and Statistical Manual of Mental Disorders*. 5th ed. Arlington, VA: American Psychiatric Association.

Angelides, S. (2005). "The Emergence of the Paedophile in the Late Twentieth Century." *Australian Historical Studies*, 36(126): 272–295.

Arieff, A. (2010). *Sexual Violence in African Conflicts*. CRS Report for Congress. Washington, DC: Congressional Research Service.

Baaz, M. E., and Stern, M. (2009). "Why Do Soldiers Rape? Masculinity, Violence, and Sexuality in the Armed Forces in the Congo (DRC)." *International Studies Quarterly*, 53(2): 495–518.

Babchishin, K. M., Hanson, R. K., and Van Zuylen, H. (2015). "Online Child Pornography Offenders Are Different: A Meta-analysis of the Characteristics of Online and Offline Sex Offenders against Children." *Archives of Sexual Behavior*, 44(1): 45–66.

Barbaree, H. E., Seto, M. C., Langton, C. M., and Peacock, E. J. (2001). "Evaluating the Predictive Accuracy of Six Risk Assessment Instruments for Adult Sex Offenders." *Criminal Justice and Behavior*, 28(4): 490–521.

Bastick, M., Grimm, K., and Kunz, R. (2007). *Sexual Violence in Armed Conflict: Global Overview and Implications*. Geneva: Geneva Centre for the Democratic Control of Armed Forces. Available online at http://www.essex.ac.uk/armedcon/story_id/sexualviolence_conflict_full%5B1%5D.pdf.

Bijleveld C., Morssinkhof, A., and Smeulers, A. (2009). "Counting the Countless: Rape Victimization during the Rwandan Genocide." *International Criminal Justice Review*, 19(2): 208–224.

Bourke, M. L., and Donohue, B. (1996). "Assessment and Treatment of Juvenile Sex Offenders: An Empirical Review." *Journal of Child Sexual Abuse*, 5(1): 47–71.

Briere, J., and Runtz, M. (1989). "University Males' Sexual Interest in Children: Predicting Potential Indices of 'Pedophilia' in a Nonforensic Sample." *Child Abuse and Neglect*, 13(1): 65–75.

Bullough, V. L. (2004). "Children and Adolescents as Sexual Beings: A Historical Over-view." *Child and Adolescent Psychiatric Clinics of North America*, 13: 447–459.

Chang, I. (1997). *The Rape of Nanking: The Forgotten Holocaust of World War II*. New York: Basic Books.

Clarke, R. V. (2012). "Opportunity Makes the Thief. Really? And So What?" *Crime Science*, 1:3.

Cohen, D. K. (2013). "Explaining Rape during Civil War: Cross-national Evidence (1980–2009)." *American Political Science Review*, 107(3): 461–477.

Cohen, L. E., and Felson, M. (1979) "Social Change and Crime Rate Trends: A Routine Activity Approach." *American Sociological Review*, 44(4): 588–608.

Cohen, M., and Jeglic, E. L. (2007). "Sex Offender Legislation in the United States: What Do We Know?" *International Journal of Offender Therapy and Comparative Criminology*, 51(4): 369–383.

Commission to Inquire into Child Abuse. (2009). *Final report.* Available online a: http://www.childabusecommission.ie/rpt/pdfs/.

Cookman, C. (2007). "An American Atrocity: The My Lai Massacre Concretized in a Victim's Face." *Journal of American History*, 94(1): 154–162.

Cornish, D. B., and Clarke, R. V. (2003). "Opportunities, Precipitators and Criminal Decisions: A Reply to Wortley's Critique of Situational Crime Prevention." In M. Smith and D. Cornish (eds.), *Theory for Practice in Situational Crime Prevention*, vol. 6 of *Crime Prevention Studies.* Monsey, NY: Criminal Justice Press.

Crime Prevention Committee, Parliament of Victoria. (1995). *Combating Child Sexual Assault: An Integrated Model. First Report.* Melbourne: Government Printer.

Cullen, F. T. (2011). "Beyond Adolescence-Limited Criminology: Choosing Our Future. The American Society of Criminology 2010 Sutherland Address." *Criminology*, 49(2):287–330.

Cullen, F. T., and Gilbert, K. E. (2013). *Reaffirming Rehabilitation*. Waltham, MA: Elsevier.

Denis, D., and Whitehead, H. (2013). *Stop It Now: Helpline and Campaign Report, 2002–2012.* Available online at http://www.lucyfaithfull.org.uk/files/stop_it_now_helpline_campaign_10_year_report_2013.pdf.

Dunne, M. P., Purdie, D. M., Cook, M. D., Boyle, F. M., and Najman, J. M. (2003). "Is Child Sexual Abuse Declining? Evidence from a Population-Based Survey of Men and Women in Australia." *Child Abuse and Neglect*, 27(2): 141–152.

Felson, M., and Clarke, R. V. (1998). "Opportunity Makes the Thief: Practical Theory for Crime Prevention." Police Research Series Paper No. 98. London: Home Office.

Finkelhor, D. (2008). *Childhood Victimization: Violence, Crime, and Abuse in the Lives of Young People.* New York: Oxford University Press.

Finkelhor, D., and Dziuba-Leatherman, J. (1994). "Children as Victims of Violence: A National Survey." *Pediatrics*, 94(4): 413–420.

Finkelhor, D., and Lewis, I. A. (1988). "An Epidemiologic Approach to the Study of Child Molestation." *Annals of the New York Academy of Sciences*, 528(1): 64–78.

Freund, K. (1971). "A Note on the Use of the Phallometric Method of Measuring Mild Sexual Arousal in the Male." *Behavior Therapy*, 2(2): 223–228.

Gallagher, P., Hickey, J., and Ash, D. (1997). *Child Sexual Assault: An Analysis of Matters Determined in the District Court of New South Wales during 1994.* Sydney: Judicial Commission of NSW.

Goffman, E. (1961). *Asylums.* Garden City, NY: Anchor Books.

Gordon, S., Hallahan, K., and Henry, D. (2002). *Putting the Picture Together: Inquiry into Response by Government Agencies into Complaints of Family Violence and Child Abuse in Aboriginal Communities.* Perth: WA Department of Premier and Cabinet.

Haney, C., Banks, C., and Zimbardo, P. (1973). "Interpersonal Dynamics in a Simulated Prison." *International Journal of Criminology and Penology*, 1: 69–97.

Hanson, R. K., and Bussière, M. T. (1998) "Predicting Relapse: A Meta-analysis of Sexual Offender Recidivism Studies." *Journal of Consulting and Clinical Psychology*, 66(2): 348–362.

Hayward, K. (2007). "Situational Crime Prevention and Its Discontents: Rational Choice Theory versus the 'Culture of Now.' " *Social Policy and Administration*, 41: 232–250.

Human Rights and Equal Opportunity Commission. (2006). *A Statistical Overview of Aboriginal and Torres Strait Islander Peoples in Australia.* Canberra: Human Rights and Equal Opportunity Commission. Available online at http://www.hreoc.gov.au/Social_Justice/statistics/index.html.

Independent Inquiry into Child Sexual Abuse. (2015). *Opening Statement*. Available online at https://www.iicsa.org.uk/.

Jacobs, J. B., and Blitsa, D. (2012). "US, EU and UK Employment Vetting as Strategy for Preventing Convicted Sex Offenders from Gaining Access to Children." *European Journal of Crime, Criminal Law and Criminal Justice*, 20: 265–296.

Jahnke, S., Imhoff, R., and Hoyer, J. (2015). "Stigmatization of People with Pedophilia: Two Comparative Surveys." *Archives of Sexual Behavior*, 44(1): 21–34.

Jenkins, P. (2001). *Beyond Tolerance: Child Pornography on the Internet*. New York: New York University Press.

Jones, L. M., and Finkelhor, D. (2010). *Updated Trends in Child Maltreatment, 2007*. Durham, NH: Crimes Against Children Research Center.

Jones, L. M., Mitchell, K. J., and Finkelhor, D. (2013). "Online Harassment in Context: Trends from Three Youth Internet Safety Surveys (2000, 2005, 2010)." *Psychology of Violence*, 3(1): 53–69.

Kaufman, K. L., Holmberg, J. K., Orts, K. A., McCrady, F. E., Rotzien, A. L., Daleiden, E. L., and Hilliker, D. R. (1998). "Factors Influencing Sexual Offenders' Modus Operandi: An Examination of Victim-Offender Relatedness and Age." *Child Maltreatment*, 3(4): 349–361.

Kilpatrick, D., and Saunders, B. (1997). *Prevalence and Consequences of Child Victimization: Results from the National Survey of Adolescents, Final Report*. Washington, DC: US Department of Justice, Office of Justice Programs, National Institute of Justice.

Krone, T. (2005). *International Police Operations against online Child Pornography*. Trends and Issues in Crime and Criminal Justice No. 296. Canberra: Australian Institute of Criminology.

Law Commission of Canada. (2000). *Restoring Dignity: Responding to Child Abuse in Canadian Institutions*. Minister of Public Works and Government Services. Available online at http://www.attorneygeneral.jus.gov.on.ca/inquiries/cornwall/en/hearings/exhibits/Peter_Jaffe/pdf/Restoring_Dignity.pdf.

Leclerc, B., and Felson, M. (2016). "Routine Activities Preceding Adolescent Sexual Abuse of Younger Children." *Sexual Abuse*, 28(2): 116–131.

Marshall, W. L., and Barbaree, H. E. (1988). "The Long-Term Evaluation of a Behavioral Treatment Program for Child Molesters." *Behaviour Research and Therapy*, 26(6), 499–511.

Marshall, W. L., Fernandez, Y. M., Hudson, S. M., and Ward, T., eds. (2013). *Sourcebook of Treatment Programs for Sexual Offenders*. New York: Springer Science and Business Media.

Marshall, W. L., Marshall, L. E., Serran, G. A., and Fernandez, Y. M. (2006). *Treating Sexual Offenders: An Integrated Approach*. New York: Routledge.

Mayhew, P. M., Clarke, R. V. G., Sturman, A., and Hough, J. M. (1976). *Crime as Opportunity*. Home Office Research Study No. 34. London: HMSO.

McKillop, N., Brown, S. J., Wortley, R., and Smallbone, S. (2015). "How Victim Age Affects the Context and Timing of Child Sexual Abuse: Applying Routine Activities Approach to the First Sexual Incident." *Crime Science*, 4:17

Memmott, P., and Moran, M. (2001). *Indigenous Settlements of Australia*. State of the Environment Second Technical Paper Series (Human Settlements) Series 2. Canberra: Department of the Environment and Heritage. Available online at http://www.environment.gov.au/soe/2001/publications/technical/indigenous/settlement.html.

Mercado, C. C., and Ogloff, J. R. (2007). "Risk and the Preventive Detention of Sex Offenders in Australia and the United States." *International Journal of Law and Psychiatry*, 30(1): 49–59.

Mitchell, K. J., Jones, L. M., Finkelhor, D., and Wolak, J. (2014). *Trends in Unwanted Online Experiences and Sexting: Final Report*. Durham, NH: Crime Against Children Research Center.

Moffitt, T. E. (1993). "Adolescence-Limited and Life-Course-Persistent Antisocial Behavior: A Developmental Taxonomy." *Psychological Review*, 100(4): 674–701.

Neill, K. G. (2013). "Duty, Honor, Rape: Sexual Assault against Women during War." *Journal of International Women's Studies*, 2(1): 43–51.

Northern Territory Board of Inquiry into the Protection of Aboriginal Children from Sexual Abuse. (2007). *Little Children Are Sacred: Report of the Northern Territory Board of Inquiry into the Protection of Aboriginal Children from Sexual Abuse*. Darwin: Northern Territory Government.

Northern Territory Law Reform Committee. (2003). *Aboriginal Communities and Aboriginal Law in the Northern Territory*. Background Paper 1 for the Committee of Inquiry Talking about Aboriginal Customary Law in the Northern Territory. Darwin: Northern Territory Law Reform Committee. Available online at http://www.nt.gov.au/justice/docs/lawmake/ntlrc_final_bckgrd_paper_01.pdf.

NSW Aboriginal Child Sexual Assault Taskforce. (2006). *Breaking the Silence: Creating the Future. Addressing Child Sexual Assault in Aboriginal Communities in New South Wales*. Sydney: NSW Attorney General's Department.

Office for National Statistics. (2016). "Abuse during Childhood: Findings from the Crime Survey for England and Wales, Year Ending March 2016." Available online at https://www.ons.gov.uk/releases/abuseduringchildhoodfindingsfromtheyearendingmarch2016crimesurveyforenglandandwales.

Olson, J. S., and Roberts, R. (1998). *My Lai: A Brief History with Documents*. Boston: Bedford Books.

Rayment-McHugh, S., Smallbone, S., and Tilley, N. (2015). "Endemic Sexual Violence and Abuse: Contexts and Dispositions." *International Journal for Crime, Justice and Social Democracy*, 4(2): 111–124.

Royal Commission into Institutional Responses to Child Sexual Abuse. (2014). *Interim Report*. 2 vols. Available online at https://www.childabuseroyalcommission.gov.au/about-us/our-reports.

Seto, M. C., Hanson, R. K., and Babchishin, K. M. (2011). "Contact Sexual Offending by Men with Online Sexual Offenses." *Sexual Abuse*, 23(1): 124–145.

Simon, L. M. J., and Zgoba, K. (2006). "Sex Crimes against Children: Legislation, Prevention and Investigation." In R. K. Wortley and S. W. Smallbone (eds.), *Situational Prevention of Child Sexual Abuse*, vol. 19 of *Crime Prevention Studies*. Monsey, NY: Criminal Justice Press.

Smallbone, S., Marshall, W. L., and Wortley, R. (2008). *Preventing Child Sexual Abuse: Evidence, Policy and Practice*. Cullompton, Devon, UK: Willan Publishing.

Smallbone, S., and Ransley, J. (2005). "Legal and Psychological Controversies in the Preventive Incapacitation of Sexual Offenders." *University of New South Wales Law Journal*, 28(1): 299–305.

Smallbone, S., Rayment-McHugh, S., and Smith, D. (2013). *Preventing Youth Sexual Violence and Abuse in Western Cairns and Aurukun: Establishing the Scope, Dimensions and Dynamics of the Problem*. Brisbane: Griffith University. Available online at https://www.datsip.qld.gov.au/resources/datsima/programs/ysv-report.pdf.

Smallbone, S. W., and Wortley, R. (2000). *Child Sexual Abuse in Queensland: Offender Characteristics and Modus Operandi*. Vol. 2 of Project Axis. Brisbane: Queensland Crime

Commission. Available online at http://www.childtrafficking.com/Docs/child_sexual_abuse_2000_in_queensland_offender_characteristi_1.pdf.

Smallbone, S. W., and Wortley, R. K. (2004). "Onset, Persistence and Versatility of Offending among Adult Males Convicted of Sexual Offenses against Children." *Sexual Abuse*, 16: 285–298.

Smiljanich, K., and Briere, J. (1996). "Self-Reported Sexual Interest in Children: Sex Differences and Psychosocial Correlates in a University Sample." *Violence and Victims*, 11: 39–50.

Sutherland, E. H. (1947). *Principles of Criminology*. 3rd ed. New York: Lippincott.

Terry, K. J. (2008). "Stained Glass: The Nature and Scope of Child Sexual Abuse in the Catholic Church." *Criminal Justice and Behavior*, 35(5): 549–569.

Terry, K. J., and Ackerman, A. (2008). "Child Sexual Abuse in the Catholic Church: How Situational Crime Prevention Strategies Can Help Create Safe Environments." *Criminal Justice and Behavior*, 35(5): 643–657.

Thomas, T. (2013). "Sex Offender Registration in the United States and the United Kingdom." In K. Harrison and B. Rainey (eds.), *The Wiley-Blackwell Handbook of Legal and Ethical Aspects of Sex Offender Treatment and Management*. Hoboken, NJ: Wiley-Blackwell.

Thornhill, R., and Thornhill, N. W. (1987). "Human Rape: The Strengths of the Evolutionary Perspective." In C. B. Crawford, M. Smith, and D. L. Krebbs (eds.), *Sociobiology and Psychology: Ideas, Issues, and Applications*. Hillsdale, NJ: Lawrence Erlbaum.

Tribunal of Inquiry Into the Abuse of Children in Care in the Former County Council Areas of Gwynedd and Clwyd Since 1974. (2000). *Lost in Care: Report of the Summary of Report with Conclusions and Recommendations in Full*. Stationery Office. Available online at http://tna.europarchive.org/20040216040105/http:/www.doh.gov.uk/lostincare/20102a.htm.

Ward, J., and Marsh, M. (2006). "Sexual Violence against Women and Girls in War and Its Aftermath: Realities, Responses and Required Resources." In *Symposium on Sexual Violence in Conflict and Beyond*, vol. 21. Available online at http://www.svri.org/sites/default/files/attachments/2016-01-15/CCEF504C15AB277E852571AB0071F7CE-UNFPA.pdf.

Wolak, J., and Finkelhor, D. (2013). "Are Crimes by Online Predators Different from Crimes by Sex Offenders Who Know Youth In-Person?" *Journal of Adolescent Health*, 53(6): 736–741.

Wolak, J., Finkelhor, D., and Mitchell, K. (2011). "Child Pornography Possessors: Trends in Offender and Case Characteristics." *Sexual Abuse*, 23(1): 22–42.

Wood, E. J. (2006). "Variation in Sexual Violence during War. *Politics and Society*, 34(3): 307–342.

Wormith, J. S. (1986). "Assessing Deviant Sexual Arousal: Physiological and Cognitive Aspects." *Advances in Behaviour Research and Therapy*, 8(3): 101–137.

Wortley, R. (2001). "A Classification of Techniques for Controlling Situational Precipitators of Crime." *Security Journal*, 14(4): 63–82

Wortley, R. (2012). "Exploring the Person-Situation Interaction in Situational Crime Prevention." In N. Tilley and G. Farrell (eds.), *The Reasoning Criminologist: Essays in Honour of Ronald V. Clarke*. London: Routledge.

Wortley, R. (2015). "Science and Child Sexual Abuse: Navigating the Pathway between Emotion and Objectivity." *Crime Science*, 4:18.

Wortley, R. (2017). "Situational Precipitators of Crime." In R. Wortley and M. Townsley (eds.), *Environmental Criminology and Crime Analysis*. 2nd ed. London: Routledge.

Wortley, R., and Smallbone, S. (2006). "Applying Situational Principles to Sexual Offending Against Children." In R. Wortley and S. Smallbone (eds.), *Situational Prevention of Child Sexual Abuse*, vol. 19 of *Crime Prevention Studies*. Monsey, NY: Criminal Justice Press.

Wortley, R., and Smallbone, S. (2012). *Internet Child Pornography: Causes, Investigation and Prevention*. Santa Barbara, CA: Praeger.

Wortley, R., and Smallbone, S. (2014a). "A Criminal Careers Typology for Child Sexual Abusers." *Sexual Abuse*, 26: 569–585.

Wortley, R., and Smallbone, S. (2014b). "Emotional Arousal and Child Sex Offending: A Situational Perspective." In J.-L. van Gelder, H. Elffers, D. Nagin, and D. Reynald (eds.), *Affect and Cognition Affect and Cognition in Criminal Decision Making: Between Rational Choices and Lapses of Self-Control*. London: Routledge.

Zimbardo, P. (2007) *The Lucifer Effect*. New York: Random House.

Zipf, G. K. (1949). *Human Behavior and the Principle of Least Effort*. Cambridge, MA: Addison-Wesley.

CHAPTER 36

GANGS AND SPACE

MATTHEW VALASIK AND GEORGE E. TITA

36.1 Introduction

THE relationship between urban street gangs and the built environment has been a topic of interest since Thrasher's (1927) seminal work. Understanding how gangs emerge and interact with the local geography has provided important insight into both the general sociological understanding of place (Anderson, 1976; Liebow, 1967; Suttles, 1968; Whyte, 1943) as well as the broader community and crime literature (Blasko, Roman, & Taylor, 2015; Brantingham & Brantingham, 1995; Miller, 1966/2011; Simon & Burns, 1997; Sullivan, 1989; Tita & Ridgeway, 2007). The social relationships binding the members of a gang to the broader community are complex and sometimes competing. From the romanticized notion of the gang as the protector and provider of the community (Jankowski, 1991; Yablonsky, 1962) to the realization that gang members are someone's son/daughter, father/mom, brother/sister within the community (Decker & Van Winkle, 1996; Durán, 2013; Moore, 1991; Pattillo-McCoy, 1999), a gang member is much more than an antagonist seeking to prey upon the local community.

In this chapter we explore the ways in which space shapes the territoriality of urban street gang members as well as the ways in which a gang exploits the local landscape. We begin by providing a brief overview of the classic works on the emergence of gangs, paying particular attention both to the literature on human terrain/territoriality and to the ecological studies of place, especially the Chicago school. Then we look at the criminal enterprises of gangs as they relate to space. Next we investigate how residency, technology, and territoriality may be influencing the relationship modern street gangs have with space. Finally, we conclude with a look at the use of geographically targeted policing to curtail gang activity, especially intergang violence.

36.2 Territoriality and Gang Locations

Generally defined, territoriality is a spatial strategy employed by a group or an individual in order to control a specific space(s) and the resources within its boundaries (Lyman & Scott, 1967; Sack, 1983). Oscar Newman's (1972) theory of defensible space, a sociophysical phenomenon requiring both social and physical elements, asserts that crime is diminished in an area when residents take responsibility and ownership over common spaces in combination with environmental design. Territoriality, one component of defensible space theory, is usually considered the practice of a group or individuals protecting their inhabited space (Newman, 1972). Defending a claimed space is thought of as a process to assert dominance, control the local population and resources, and reify power relationships (Dyson-Hudson & Smith, 1978; Sack, 1983; Taylor, 1988; Van Valkenburg & Osborne, 2013). These goals are particularly salient with the territorial behaviors of urban street gangs, who attempt to affect the actions and interactions of individuals (e.g., local residents, rival gang members) within the area they preside over (Padilla, 1992; Popkin et al., 2000; Venkatesh, 1997).

An emerging gang demarcates a public location (e.g., street corner, park, alley, etc.) and establishes a "home territory" where members can have a sense of security and be unrestrained in their actions, thereby turning a space into a place (Lyman & Scott, 1967, p. 240). Using both the built environment (i.e., roads, highways, railways, buildings, etc.) and symbolic barriers (i.e., spaces demarcated with graffiti) a gang constructs an unmistakable and defendable area, forming a discrete zone of influence (Adamson, 2000; Ley & Cybriwsky, 1974; Newman, 1972; Phillips, 1999; Schneider, 1999; Taylor, 1988; Wolseth, 2011). In these claimed spaces "gang leaders hold sway like barons of old, watchful of invaders and ready to swoop down upon the lands of rivals and carry off booty or prisoners or to inflict punishment upon their enemies" (Thrasher, 1927, p. 6). In order to objectify these spaces, their territorial boundaries must be reified by the gang through the use of rituals, maps (i.e., physical and/or cognitive), and competition against rivals to create what Lefebvre (1974/1991, p. 33) refers to as "representations of space." Thus, gang territoriality is a form of "learned behavior with intergenerational adherence to historical boundaries and rules of engagement" (Pickering, Kintrea, & Bannister, 2012).

As an additional means of declaring ownership over a particular space, a gang will regularly name itself after streets, features, or neighborhoods from where members emerge (Moore, 1991; Monod, 1967; Salagaev & Safin, 2014; Thrasher, 1927). For instance, the Avenues gang in Los Angeles formed in a region of the city where all of the streets begin with the word "Avenue" followed by the number of that particular avenue. The Avenues gang and its cliques (e.g., Avenues 43) have expropriated these street markers in creating their group's moniker (Leap, 2012; Rafael, 2007). Likewise, the Rollin' 90s refers to just one particular clique of the Crip faction of gangs occupying a series of streets between 90th Street and 100th Street in South Los Angeles (Alonso, 2004; Brown, Vigil, & Taylor, 2012).

36.3 The Ecology of Gang Territories

36.3.1 Gang Territoriality and the Chicago School

Frederic Thrasher's (1927) foundational study on the emergence of street gangs in Chicago helped define the Chicago school of sociology. The study focused specifically on the relationship between ecology and ethnicity on gang formation. The emergence of gangs and "Gangland" occurred in the interstitial areas where the central business district gave way to the neighborhoods of the working class. With an abundance of affordable (though crowded and poorly maintained) housing and its geographic proximity to an ample supply of jobs in the central business district, these *zones in transition* (Park & Burgess, 1925/1967) experienced a constant churning of impoverished immigrants from Europe seeking to better their lot in life. It was observed that these areas, regardless of the racial/ethnic composition of the inhabitants, maintained consistently high levels of delinquency and crime over time. Shaw and McKay (1942) argued the crime and delinquency were the result of three structural characteristics that differentiated these communities from those places with lower levels of crime: residential instability, ethnic heterogeneity, and low economic status (see Wilcox & Swartz in this volume). These three elements interacted to impede the development of social ties among residents, a necessity for building cohesion and trust, needed to combat crime and disorder (Sampson & Groves, 1989; Sampson, Raudenbush, & Earls, 1997).

Just as one might expect in any community, playgroups developed in these interstitial spaces, but because the structural/ecological conditions prevented the development of informal social control, the playgroups evolved into urban street gangs (Thrasher, 1927). Research over the years has reinforced Thrasher's findings, noting that local socioeconomic conditions continue to play an important role in where gangs form (Cartwright & Howard, 1966; Tita et al., 2005) and that a gang's presence often seeks to fulfill multiple voids such as offering protection to the neighborhood (Decker & Van Winkle, 1996; Jankowski, 1991; Patillo-McCoy, 1999; Yablonsky, 1962), providing economic support/opportunities (Hagedorn, 1988; Padilla, 1992; Sullivan, 1989; Valdez & Sifaneck, 2004; Venkatesh, 1997, 2000), or supplying a collective social identity (Decker & Van Winkle, 1996; Hennigan & Spanovic, 2012; Vigil, 1983, 1988.

36.3.2 Gang Hangouts and Set Space

The idea of "turf" or the attachment to a particular space is one of the defining features of urban street gangs. Cartwright and Howard (1966) examined the kinds of places that street gangs formed and concluded that communities with low-quality housing units, fewer owner-occupied housing units, a higher percentage of low-income residents, and a lower ratio of adults to children were unique features to neighborhoods where gang members hang out. Classic ethnographic studies of youth gang members in low-income neighborhoods regularly highlighted the importance of particular street corners serving as a preferred activity space (Liebow, 1967; Miller, 1966/2011; Suttles, 1968; Whyte, 1943). A particular street corner might be particularly appealing because of certain physical benefits such as clear sight lines and visibility. The importance of street corners as an activity space is still observed in contemporary studies (Simon & Burns, 1997; Rodgers, 2006; Taniguchi, Ratcliffe, & Taylor, 2011). Routine activities theory suggests that street corners may lack the capable guardians necessary for informal social control to function (Cohen & Felson, 1979; Felson, 1987). Public spaces, such as a park, alley, street corners, or other subareas within the larger neighborhood become the "group's life space" (Klein, 1995a, p. 79) providing the gang a refuge from the outside world (Thrasher, 1927). It is within this sanctuary that members feel protected and routinely "hang around, brag a lot, eat again, drink, hang around some more," spending the majority of their daily activity in these hangouts (Klein, 1995a, p. 11). Over time, habitually congregating in the same area, the gang "becomes fairly attached to a definite locality and wanders only occasionally beyond its frontiers" (Thrasher, 1927, p. 166). These hangouts become so established within the community that residents, specifically youth, learn how to navigate through their neighborhood becoming adept at avoiding encounters with local gang members or their rivals in these dangerous areas (Garot, 2010; Tita et al., 2005).

Investigating the gang formation process in the city of Pittsburgh, Tita and colleagues (2005) introduced the concept of gang *set space*, defined generally as a localized, geographically distinct area where gang members congregate within their territory. A consistent and compelling characteristic about the location of a gang's set space is the lack of social control, either formal or informal. Without the presence of social control agents these spaces lack an overall ability to prevent the predatory or inappropriate behaviors of gang members, thereby exempting these individuals from their actions (Eck, 1995).

Research has also demonstrated that the activity spaces of a gang are likely to be located in places with greater criminogenic properties (Block, 2000; Tita, et al., 2005). For instance, the percentage of vacant housing units in an area remains a powerful indicator for the presence of set space (Sullivan, 1989; Tita, 1999). Vacant properties are indicative of the physical and psychological abandonment of an area by local residents, and serve as a visible signal of the community's limited ability to surveil, supervise, and sanction gang behavior in these spaces. Blasko and colleagues (2015) further find that residents that live closer to a greater number of street gang set spaces are more likely to perceive incivilities of youth groups in their neighborhood as problematic. Furthermore, Lane and Meeker (2003) indicate that residents' fear of gangs is linked to a perception of incivility by youth groups, which could dissuade residents from censuring inappropriate behaviors, such as aggression or violence, and could contribute to a maturation process of youth playgroups into street gangs.

Research has also suggested that police are less attentive to areas where vacant buildings are prevalent, which in turn increases local residents' fear of crime and gangs (Lane, 2002; Mills, 1990). Anecdotal evidence further suggests that gang members are drawn to vacant buildings because they provide "cuts" to escape police detection or evade rival gang members (Tita, 1999). Yet, it is not only in areas plagued with abandoned properties where social control is deficient. Areas characterized by high levels of population density are also susceptible to insufficient social control (Cohen & Felson, 1979; Felson, 1987). For instance, Tita (1999) finds that a gang's set space is also likely to be in densely populated areas. It may seem contradictory at first that vacant properties attract gangs but high population density increases the probability of gang set space being present. However, more vacant properties in an area do not necessarily mean that a "ghost town" exists. Instead, it could be that the units remaining occupied have a large number of individuals residing in them, such as in a public housing high-rise, and are surrounded by derelict properties (Popkin, Gwiasda, Olson, Rosenbaum, & Buron, 2000; Simon & Burns, 1997; Venkatesh, 2000). Additionally, an area that has high population density with people milling around outside can actually be a desirable feature, allowing loitering gang members to camouflage their activities from the police. Venkatesh (2000) argues that high-volume pedestrian traffic is a valuable tool that can aid in concealing a gang's drug-dealing activities. Vacant properties also afford gang members escape routes to either evade the police or avoid attacks from rival gangs (Popkin et al., 2000; Sullivan, 1989; Tita, 1999).

36.3.3 Other Approaches to Understanding of Gang Territories

Borrowing from the ecology/biology literature, Brantingham and colleagues (2012) use Lotka-Volterra models to explore the formation of gang territory. Competition models, like Lotka-Volterra, have been used to model predator-prey distributions (Gilpin, 1973; Jost, Devulder, Vucetich, Peterson, & Arditi, 2005; Sabelis, Diekman, & Jansen, 1991) along with the territories of other various competing species, including ant colonies, birds, and lion prides (Heinsohn & Packer, 1995; MacArthur, 1958; Ryti & Case, 1992). In summary, this ecological approach considers the formation of gang turf as the end result of a process driven exclusively through violent social interactions occurring between a gang and its rivals. With activity patterns of gang members being tethered to their gang's set space, Brantingham et al. (2012) use these known geographic locations as the point of origin from where a gang's territory emanates. Their models reveal that gang violence is concentrated around a predicted boundary between the gang of the offender and the victim's gang. Therefore, the creation of a stable boundary around one's territory is a byproduct of a gang's aggressive competition for resources (i.e., turf, reputation).

The results from the theoretical Lotka-Volterra model are consistent with several observational studies. Tita (1999) noted that buffers existed between the set space of rival gangs and cautiously conjectured that these observed patterns represented a gang's preference of wanting a safety zone between the set space of a rival. This perceived preference is revealed by Curtis and colleagues' (2014) spatial analysis of gang members' environmental perception of fear, finding that gang members feel less safe near the borders of their rival's turf. Taniguchi and colleagues (2011) reveal that more violence occurs on street corners deemed favorable for the distribution of drugs when multiple gangs are competing over control than similar street corners controlled by only one gang.

36.4 Gangs, Crime, and Space

36.4.1 Gangs and the Spatial Distribution of Violence

The role that space/territory play in shaping the spatial distribution of crime and violence has been a central topic of study in criminology, especially with the emergence of desktop geographic information system (GIS) software in the early 1990s (Anselin, Cohen, Cook, Gorr, & Tita, 2000; Block, 2000). GIS permits one to easily map the distribution of various crimes, overlay gang territories, and explore spatial relationships. The rise of GIS coincided with the homicide epidemic of the early 1990s. Coupled with the spread of gangs both within "chronic" gang cities and to "emergent" gang cities (Howell, Egley, Tita, & Griffiths, 2011; Howell & Griffiths, 2016; Spergel & Curry, 1993), researchers began to investigate the role that gangs played in the diffusion of violence, especially homicide (Cohen & Tita, 1999; Rosenfeld, Bray, & Egley, 1999; Morenoff & Sampson, 1997; Tita & Cohen, 2004). As noted by Tita and Radil (2011), there are two defining features of gangs that make them especially germane to the study of the diffusion of violence: the retaliatory nature of gang violence and the importance of turf.

Though controlling for both the spatial dependence and temporal dependence is necessary to identify true diffusion, presenting enormous methodological challenges, the extant literature has time and again argued that controlling for the presence of gangs is important in understanding the concentration of gang violence as well as its spread. This has been demonstrated in a variety of cities throughout the United States including Boston (Braga, Hureau & Papachristos, 2014; Kennedy, Braga, & Piehl, 1997; Kennedy, Piehl, & Braga, 1996; Papachristos, Hureau, & Braga, 2013); Chicago (Block & Block, 1993; Griffiths & Chavez, 2004; Mares, 2010; Mears & Bhati, 2006; Morenoff & Sampson, 1997; Papachristos & Kirk, 2006; Papachristos, Hureau, & Braga, 2013); St. Louis (Curry & Decker, 1996; Huebner, Martin, Moule, Pyrooz, & Decker, 2016; Kubrin & Weitzer, 2003; Rosenfeld et al. 1999); Newark (Zeoli, Pizarro, Grady & Melde, 2014; Zeoli, Grady, Pizarro, & Melde, 2015) Pittsburgh (Cohen & Tita, 1999; Tita & Cohen, 2004; Tita & Greenbaum, 2009); and Los Angeles (Brantingham et al., 2012; Radil, Flint, & Tita, 2010; Tita & Radil, 2011; Valasik, Barton, Reid & Tita, 2017).

To explain why crime/violence is concentrated in particular kinds of neighborhoods, researchers often invoke the presence of gangs without directly measuring them (e.g., Valasik et al., 2017). That is, they argue that rivalries among different gangs in the city could be responsible for the spillover or diffusion of violence from one community into a neighboring community over some temporal time frame. Tita and colleagues (Tita & Greenbaum, 2009; Tita & Radil, 2011) have attempted to make the presence of gangs and the process of diffusion across space more explicit. In Pittsburgh and the Hollenbeck Community Policing Area of Los Angeles, respectively, the authors mapped the set spaces of the street gangs and gathered social network data on the rivalries among gangs. They exploited this information to construct a spatial weights matrix (a central component in any type of spatial analysis) that links geographic units of analysis (neighborhoods, census tracts, etc.) if and only if the pair of places possess the turf of a rival gang. Though true that some gang rivals do occupy geographically neighboring spaces, other rivalries can span large differences. Thus, the influence that gang rivalries and their retaliatory nature have on the diffusion of violence is more complex than can be captured by simply invoking the principle of geographic nearness.

Isolating the causal relationship of the presence of gangs in an area is difficult on two fronts. First, the same factors that give rise to urban street gangs are also shown to be important covariates of crime and violence. This has been true since the time of Thrasher (1927) and persists to this day. The second challenge is that nearly all community-level studies of gangs and crime are conducted after gangs have long been established, therefore making it difficult to construct a counterfactual of what local crime patterns would look like in the same (similar) neighborhood had gangs not been present. In an ecological study of gangs and crime to include both pregang and postgang formation periods, Tita (1999) was able to demonstrate that, unsurprisingly, gangs formed in high-crime areas and that these high-crime areas where characterized by a litany of social ills (e.g., concentrated poverty, dense population, single-parent households, etc.) that we have come to associate with highly impacted urban communities. Tita and Ridgeway (2007) demonstrated that the impact of gang presence differed by crime type. Consistent with the notion of gangs as protectors of the community, their presence seemed to marginally reduce the amount of property crimes in an area. Drug market activity was also reduced. An alternative explanation to these findings, however, is that the presence of the gang dramatically decreased the reporting of crime. The most robust findings relate to violence: the number of assaults fell; the level of activity involving guns increased dramatically. This is consistent with a sort of substitution effect: with the proliferation of firearms during this period, individuals rarely got into fistfights, instead trading their knuckles or knives for guns (see Blumstein & Cork, 1996).

Reinforcing the results of prior research on gang violence, Papachristos and colleagues (2013) find that when gangs have turf boundaries adjacent to each other, there is a greater likelihood that violence between these gangs will occur. However, in addition to the important role that geography plays in predicting intergang conflict, their research suggests that "social distance" also matters. Much as in the work of Tita and colleagues (see Tita & Greenbaum, 2009; Radil et al., 2010), prior conflicts among gangs that lack a common border strongly predicts violence (Papachristos et al., 2013). Gang members are not socially or criminally disentangled from their local communities. "The lives of gang members are woven into the larger social fabric of the neighborhoods, social networks, families, and friends" (Papachristos, Braga, Piza, & Grossman, 2015, p. 627). Thus, gang violence does not stay contained within static spatial boundaries of a gang's turf but instead is connected across ties in an individual's social network

(Papachristos et al., 2012, 2013, 2015). That being said, there appears to be an interactive effect between the reciprocity of intergang conflicts and spatial adjacency, revealing that intergang violence is amplified by the combination of social interaction and spatial proximity (Papachristos et al., 2013).

Therefore, to fully understand the dynamic nature of gang violence it becomes necessary to investigate both the social and spatial characteristics associated with gangs and their members (Brantingham et al., 2012; Papachristos, 2009; Papachristos et al., 2015; Tita & Radil, 2011). Geographic space clearly matters, but with the adoption of social network analysis, researchers are also demonstrating that the social spaces linking places are another important predictor of violence.

36.4.2 Gangs and Drug Markets

The role of gangs in the establishment and control of local drug markets differs across place and is influenced by whether the market is controlled by the gang as a collective or by individuals who happen to be gang members (Bellair & McNulty, 2010; Bergmann, 2008; Bjerregaard, 2010; Fader, 2016; Fagan, 1989; Hagedorn, 1994; Taylor, 1993; Valdez & Sifaneck, 2004). The literature is full of thick descriptions of gang members' involvement in local drug markets. Sullivan (1989) demonstrates that the level and duration of involvement is dependent upon larger macro-scale forces in the community, chiefly the access to legitimate employment opportunities. Jankowski (1991) argues that drugs play an even greater role in the emergence of gangs, stating that they emerge "as one organizational response . . . seeking to improve the competitive advantage of its members in obtaining an increase in material resources" (p. 22). Even though gangs engage in a variety of economic activities, "the biggest money-maker and the one product nearly every gang tries to market is drugs" (p. 120).

Over time it is possible for a group to "corporatize," transforming into an entrepreneurial gang and focusing its energy entirely on the drug trade (Densley, 2013; Levitt & Venkatesh, 2000; Skolnick, 1990; Taylor, 1990; Valdez & Sifaneck, 2004; Venkatesh, 1997). It has been suggested that the attraction of untapped markets influences gang members to travel beyond the borders of their gang's claimed turf in the hope of turning a quick profit (Fagan, 1989; Klein & Maxson, 1985). Teasing out the true impact that expanding drug markets have on the spread of gangs is difficult. Research has primarily found that the expansion or migration of gangs into new neighborhoods or distant cities is the result of residential mobility (often the relocation of a parent) and not a calculated organizational decision (Hagedorn, 1988; Huff, 1989; Maxson, 1998; Tapia, 2012).

Despite not reaching a consensus on the primacy of gangs as an entity controlling the drug market, gang members clearly participate in the market and can benefit greatly from their gang's territorial control of a marketplace (Densley, 2013; Padilla, 1992; Skolnick, 1990; Taniguchi et al., 2011; Tita & Ridgeway, 2007). Specifically, within their gang's claimed turf, a gang member is provided protection against two issues. First, drug-dealing gang members are protected against competition, as their gang will not tolerate the sales of narcotics within their turf by anyone but their own gang members (Levitt & Venkatesh, 2000; Phillips, 2012; Skolnick, 1990; Stephenson, 2015). Second, the gang provides some level of security and protection against attempted drug robbery. Perhaps more reminiscent of popular culture's romanticized version of the Italian Mafia making the streets safe for local residents, some do argue that urban street gangs can provide informal social control with regards to regulating the activities in their turf (Calderoni, Berlusconi, & Garofalo, 2016; Densley, 2013; Gambetta, 1996; Jankowski,1991; Stephenson, 2015; Varese, 2011).

Whatever protections a gang might provide through the control of its turf, drug markets are dangerous places (Contreras, 2013; Simon and Burns, 1997; Vargas, 2016). Again, teasing apart the influence a drug market, versus the existing rivalries between gangs, has on the levels and patterns of violence is challenging at best (Bellair & McNulty, 2010; Bjerregaard, 2010). "Conflicts over drug territory are only one of many circumstances that may lead to collective gang violence" (Fagan, 1989, p. 661). However, a few studies suggest how the duality of drug markets and turf might influence violence. For example, Levitt and Venkatesh (2000) argue that, "as an explicit strategy for shifting demand," a drug sale may initiate violent acts in a rival's turf, producing a hostile environment, disrupting this competing drug market. Taniguchi and colleagues (2011) note a similar pattern of escalating violence around drug corners where multiple gangs compete for control. While Taniguchi et al. (2011) are unable to explicitly articulate the causes for the increased levels of violence over gang set space locations (e.g., competition, intimidation, desirable location), it is clear that street corners with multiple gangs vying to distribute drugs experience greater levels of violence than a set space location dominated by only one gang.

36.5 Gangs and Patterns of Territoriality

The dominant ecological perspective guiding research on the relationship between neighborhoods and gangs remains the Chicago school (Huebner, Martin, Moule, Pyrooz, & Decker, 2016; Katz & Schnebly, 2011; Pyrooz & Mitchell, 2015). In this model of gang formation and territoriality, the gang comprises youth who reside in the neighborhood in which the gang forms and stakes its claim to a certain territory. The key here is the overlap between where gang members live and where their gang is rooted. Yet gangs are a dynamic phenomenon, adapting and responding to the conditions of their local environment (Densley, 2013; Klein, 1995b). Bursik and Grasmick (1993, p. 132) contend that "contemporary urban dynamics necessitate several important modifications of traditional systemic analyses of neighborhoods and gangs" and also attest that "the nature of neighborhood territoriality has changed significantly." While a gang may emerge as a fixed group, tied to a particular place or neighborhood, greater accessibility to public transportation and widespread use of automobiles afford gang members greater territorial flexibility (Chambliss, 1973; Huff & McBride, 1993; Miller, 1966/2011). Empirical studies report that greater levels of residential mobility and increased flexibility in school choices have also diminished the strong relationship between one's place of residence and the location of one's turf (Brunson & Miller, 2009; Fagan, 1996; Hagedorn, 2008; Spergel, 1995; Watkins & Moule, 2014). Furthermore, when parents decide to move the household it is not unprecedented for a youth gang member to live in a neighborhood claimed by a rival (Flores, 2014; Fremon, 2008; Ley & Cybriwsky, 1974; Lien, 2005). The youth often has to decide whether to continue commuting to his or her original turf, disavow gang membership altogether, or join the new local gang (Garot, 2010).

Technology is also playing a role in diminishing the importance of space as it relates to the relationship between place of residence and location of gang turf. There is no denying that advances in cellular technology, the use of social media services (e.g., Facebook, Myspace, Periscope, Twitter), computer-mediated communication, and the Internet more broadly is impacting the ecology of these groups (Décary-Hétu & Morselli, 2011; Densely, 2013, King, Walpole, & Lamon, 2007; Morselli & Décary-Hétu, 2013; Moule, Pyrooz, & Decker, 2014; Patton, Eschman & Butler, 2013; Patton, Eschman, Elsaesser, & Bocanegra, 2016; Patton, Lane, Leonard, Macbeth, & Smith-Lee, 2016; Pyrooz, Decker, & Moule, 2015; Sela-Shayovitz, 2012; Sela-Shayovitz, Pyrooz, & Decker, 2016; Storrod & Densley, 2017; Womer & Bunker, 2010). In fact, Pyrooz and colleagues (2015) find that gang members spend more time online than both former members and nongang individuals.

The ability to connect with others in the online world is not dependent upon spatial nearness, and connecting online further diminishes the frequency of face-to-face interactions. In the mid-1990s, the availability of relatively inexpensive mobile phones reshaped the illicit drug market as open-air drug markets that defined the gang-involved crack market of the early 1990s receded into public and private space (Johnson, Golub, & Dunlap, 2000; May & Hough, 2004; Reuter, 2009). The Internet, online gaming, and social networking sites today facilitate young people's spending less time on the street and more time indoors and online (Aldridge et al., 2012; Moule, Pyrooz, & Decker, 2014). Gang members do not need to come together in a central location in order to engage friends and rivals on social media, text their friends, or scour the Internet for news or entertainment. Researchers have coined terms like "cyber-banging" to capture the online presence and various activities of gang members, including the promotion of gang activities through posting videos or pictures of violent acts, tagging social media sites, or questioning the street credibility/reputations of rivals (Densley, 2013; Morselli & Décary-Hétu, 2013; Patton et al., 2013, 2016; Sela-Shayovitz, 2012; Storrod & Densley, 2017).

But even in the virtual world of "cyber-banging," geographic space still matters. For example, take collective criminal actions such as *flash robs* or *swarming*. Densley (2013) describes a flash rob occurring when a group of gang members target a retailer and simultaneously steal merchandise or victimize individuals in a targeted area. Swarming is when gang members are notified by a text or social media post to gather and participate in a fight with another street gang (White, 2006). Social media and the Internet may facilitate gang members' engaging and planning crime actions in the virtual realm, but, eventually, the crimes are committed in the real world.

To better understand the activity spaces of gang members, Valasik and colleagues (2016) create a spatial typology using data from field interviews (FI), a particular type of police investigatory stop used to chronicle gang members and their associates (Katz & Webb, 2006; Papachristos et al., 2012, 2015; Rios, 2011; Valasik, Reid, & Philips, 2016). Valasik, Gravel and Tita (2016) use the distribution of the following geographical indicators to build their typology: *the location of a gang member's residence, the location of his gang's turf, the location of where the FI took place*. Five mutually exclusive spatial types are constructed from the unique combination of the indicators: *attached, commuting to turf, detached, directed action*, and *mobile*. *Attached* territoriality is defined as a gang member living and hanging out within his gang's claimed turf. The category *commuting to turf* is when a gang member lives outside of his gang's claimed territory but returns to hang out inside his gang's claimed turf. A gang member who lives outside of his gang's territory and hangs out near his residence is engaging in *detached* territoriality. *Directed action* territorial behavior is when a gang member resides within his gang's claimed territory but is observed outside of his gang's turf. Lastly, *mobile* territoriality occurs only when a gang member's residence, his gang's turf, and where he encounters a law enforcement officer are each in a unique space (for more detail see Valasik, Gravel, & Tita, 2016).

According to the traditional gang literature, gang members would adhere to the attached spatial category with members residing and hanging out in their gang's territory. In fact, it is not uncommon for modern gang studies to still rely upon gang members' residences as a proxy for their activity space (Huebner et al., 2016; Katz & Schnebly, 2011). Yet Valasik and colleagues (2016) find that where a gang member lives and where a gang member hangs out are rarely the same, finding that 59% of gang members reside outside the boundaries of their gang's claimed turf. That said, of all the encounters between gang members and local law enforcement, nearly 64% of encounters occur within the boundary of their gang's turf. This latter observation is consistent with existing literature (Klein, 1995a; Thrasher, 1927; Tita et al., 2005) indicating that gang members spend an overwhelming amount of their time in and around their gang's set space.

36.5.1 Nontraditional Relationships between Gang Members' Residence and Gang Turf

Not all gang research supports the inference that a gang's turf does not necessarily correspond with the location of a gang member's residence (Ong, 2003; Vigil, 2002). Scholars have documented several groups in the United States that refrain from the traditional perspective of attached territorial behavior. Mexican American or Chicano gang members have been identified as routinely practicing commuting-to-turf territoriality (Moore, 1978, 1991; Moore et al., 1983; Vigil, 1988, 2007). Surfer gangs are another unique group utilizing the territorial pattern of commuting to turf (Kaffine, 2009; Comley, 2011). Under the Eurogang definition,[1] surfer gangs are considered to be street gangs

(Weerman et al., 2009). Lastly, Vietnamese gangs are very fluid groups and extremely mobile in their criminal behaviors (Du Phuoc Long, 1996; Lam, 2015; Ong, 2003; Vigil, 2002; Vigil & Yun, 2002).

Moore and colleagues (1983) argue that the continuous arrival of Mexican immigrants into the barrios of East Los Angeles (e.g., regular waves of Mexican migrants outpacing the succession of ethnic migrations) contributed to ecological patterns of gang behavior differing from those observed in Chicago. Over time, the cultural continuity and durability of these neighborhoods reduced the necessity for members to reside within their gang's claimed turf (Adamson, 1998; Aldridge et al., 2011, 2012; Durán, 2013; Philips, 1999). Accordingly, Mexican-American gangs are more likely to participate in commuting-to-turf territorial behavior. The ubiquity of automobiles has also allowed gang members to reside elsewhere in the city but regularly return to their claimed barrio, thereby maintaining the gang's heritage, reputation, and norms (Gerber, 2014; Leap, 2012; Moore et al., 1983).

Groups of surfers can also be extremely territorial over a particular surfing spot and have exhibited behaviors similar to urban street gangs, using intimidation and fighting to aggressively maintain territorial control over their "turf" (Comley, 2011; Kaffine, 2009; Usher & Kerstetter, 2015). Members of these surf gangs often do not reside in the adjacent shoreline communities of where their claimed surf break is located but instead regularly commute to their turf to hang out or "hang ten" (Kaffine, 2009). This behavior has been widely documented by the Bay Boys, a surf gang near Los Angeles that is currently composed of affluent, middle-age, white men (Carroll & Smith, 2015; Shaw, 2016). The Bay Boys have a decades-long history of intimidation, vandalism, and assault to keep outsiders from accessing their surf break (Carroll & Smith, 2015; Perry, 1995; Therolf, 2015; Waters, 1991). While this cafeteria style of criminal acts is analogous to the offending patterns of typical street gangs, members of the Bay Boys have generally escaped prosecution (Harper, 2015). However, a lawsuit for the enjoinment of the Bay Boys with a civil gang injunction, inhibiting them from congregating as a group around their claimed surf break, is pending (Kandel & Crouch, 2016; Shaw, 2016).

Vietnamese gang members have never held the importance of place/space in high regard (Vigil & Yun, 2002). As noted by Vigil (2002, p. 113), "Vietnamese gangs are certainly street gangs but their street is often an interstate highway." Vietnamese gang members are unconcerned about controlling a turf. "For us, [the] most [important thing is] we try to make money. We don't fight for a little neighborhood 'cause that's stupid" (Vigil & Yun, 2002, p. 133). Finances are procured almost entirely through home invasion robberies, typically targeting the Vietnamese individuals across the country who do not trust, and refrain from using, banks or other financial institutions, hoarding large amounts of currency (Ong, 2003; Vigil, 2002).

36.5.2 Global Perspectives on Gang Member Territoriality

As emphasized in Table 36.1, gang members in urban centers across the globe have been observed practicing a variety of the territorial behaviors described by Valasik,

Table 36.1 Gang Member Territorial Behaviors Documented throughout the World

Type of territoriality	Country	Study
Commuting to turf		
	Australia	Perrone & White, 2000; Polk, 1994, 1995; White, 2006, 2008, 2013; White, et al., 1999
	Finland	Gatz & Klein, 1993; Klein, 1995a
	Germany	Gatz & Klein, 1993; Klein, 1995a
	England	Aldridge et al., 2011
	Guatemala	Levenson, 2013; Winton, 2004, 2005
	Mexico	Loyola, 2013
	Netherlands	Gatz & Klein, 1993; Klein, 1995a
	New Zealand	Hazlehurst, 2007
	Nicaragua	Rocha, 2011; Rodgers & Jones, 2009
	Russia/Soviet Union	Salagaev & Safin, 2014; Stephenson, 2015
	Sweden	Lien, 2001, 2005, 2013
	Switzerland	Sarnecki, 2001
Directed action		
	Russia/Soviet Union	Salagaev & Safin, 2014; Stephenson, 2015
	Norway	Bjørgo, Carlson, & Haaland, 2004
	Sweden	Rostami et al., 2012
Mobile		
	Bangladesh	Atkinson-Sheppard, 2016
	Brazil	Hecht, 1998; Rizzini & Butler, 2003
	Columbia	Aptekar, 1988
	Dem. Rep. of Congo	Geenen, 2009
	Dominican Republic	Wolseth, 2009
	El Salvador	Rodgers & Baird, 2015; Rodgers & Jones, 2009; Wolf, 2012; Zilberg, 2004
	Ethiopia	Heinonen, 2011
	Guatemala	Levenson, 2013; Winton, 2004, 2005
	Honduras	Mateo, 2011
	India	Smith, 2016

Gravel and Tita (2016). Commuting-to-turf territoriality is common throughout cities in Europe, Russia, Australia, and New Zealand. Robust public transportation systems are routinely used and allow gang members to not be restricted by municipal borders or "geographically fixed areas" and to scatter their movements openly, moving all around a city, tagging places with gang graffiti, and confronting rival groups (Lien, 2001, p. 169; Loyola, 2013; Perrone & White, 2000; Polk, 1995). Vehicles also permit gang members' set space to be a good distance from their residence (Hazlehurst, 2007;

Lien, 2005). Aldridge and colleagues (2011, p. 72) also indicate that these "residential outsiders" could be produced by the voluntary or involuntary rehousing of gang members, youths' transitory progression between school grades, specifically from local primary schools to wider catchments of secondary schools, or the preservation of kinship ties with fellow gang members who continue to reside within their gang's territory.

Economic restructuring has influenced the territoriality of gang members in many regions throughout the world. Developing nations are particularly impacted, where a strong public infrastructure is lacking and high levels of unemployment, poverty, and disorder govern daily life (Katz, Maguire, & Choate, 2011). Greater levels of residential instability contribute to a lack of turf stability among gangs, producing conditions where territorial claims are constantly under dispute (Geenen, 2009; Heinonen, 2011; Winton, 2014). The flexibility of mobile territorial behavior benefits these gangs and facilitates their survival. Many gang members know where their natural families reside but put greater value in being autonomous from parents, living on the street in makeshift accommodations that frequently change on nightly basis (Atkinson-Sheppard, 2016; Geenen, 2009; Smith, 2016). Where gang members loiter also varies, with no particular boundary or claim to a specific set space. This high degree of mobility results in gangs being dispersed throughout the city and having limited contact with opposing gangs (Heinonen, 2011). It is also common for transnational gangs, or *maras*, in Latin America (Rodgers & Baird, 2015; Rodgers & Jones, 2009; Winton, 2004; Wolf, 2012; Zilberg, 2004) to exhibit patterns of mobile territoriality. For instance, gangs originating in many Honduran neighborhoods have members routinely traveling back-and-forth through Guatemala, El Salvador, and parts of Mexico (Mateo, 2011).

Members of gangs in Norway, Sweden, and Russia have also been documented engaging in directed action territoriality, going on excursions to raid nearby cities (Stephenson, 2015). For instance, ethnic gangs in Norway display directed action territorial behavior, rapidly mobilizing members from their turf and hunting for rival neo-Nazi gang members throughout the city center when rumors arise that there were "Nazis in town" (Bjørgo, Carlson, & Haaland, 2004, p. 570). Also, Rostami and colleagues (2012, pp. 438–439) find the majority of Swedish gang members' crimes are "committed outside of their own residential area" and do not "have a clear pattern regarding living in a specific residential area."

Overall, more empirical research examining how territoriality, mobility, and residential transience and relocation influence the behaviors of gang members, including patterns for violence, is needed. Future studies should further investigate the complex relationship between space and its utilization by gang members in the modern age.

36.6 Responding to Gangs with Geographically Targeted Interventions

Ecological theories of crime, such as routine activities theory (Cohen & Felson, 1979; Felson, 1987; Felson & Boba, 2010) and crime pattern theory (Brantingham &

Brantingham, 1984), examine the production of criminal opportunities in particular spatial locations by focusing on the interaction between the activity patterns of an individual and the context of the criminal event. That is, the social, natural, and built environments impact individuals' activity patterns, bringing together a motivated offender with a suitable target that lacks the protection of a capable guardian. This suggests that utilizing situational crime prevention strategies can disrupt the recurring day-to-day activity patterns of an individual, thereby curbing opportunities for crime to occur (Clarke, 1997). Coupled with the use of problem-oriented policing strategies, spatially targeted policing, in general, rarely has resulted in crime displacement but instead produced crime control benefits that diffuse beyond the targeted area (Grogger, 2002; Ratcliffe & Breen, 2011; Weisburd, Wyckoff, Ready, Eck, Hinkle, & Gajewski, 2006).

The role that space plays in shaping the activities of gangs also has enormous implications for policies aimed at controlling gang-related crime and has generated a number of placed-based policing strategies (Braga et al., 2014; Groff, Ratcliffe, Haberman, Sorg, Joyce, & Taylor, 2015; Lasley, 1998; Papachristos, Meares, & Fagan, 2007; Ratcliffe & Breen, 2011; Tita et al., 2003; Valasik, 2014). The geography of an area, both natural and built, influences a gang's claimed territorial space, either facilitating or impeding social interactions among street gangs (Grannis, 2009). Therefore, before any form of intervention strategy targeting gang violence gets employed, it is essential to account for the activity patterns of a gang and how space is utilized (Kennedy et al., 1996; Radil et al., 2010).

36.6.1 Altering the Built Environment

An approach favored by policymakers to influence criminal opportunities is altering the built environment (MacDonald, 2015), what is generally referred to as CPTED, or crime prevention through environmental design (Crowe & Zahm, 1994; Jeffery, 1971; Moffat, 1983; Newman, 1972; Taylor & Gottfredson, 1986). An example of using CPTED to directly affect gang crime and violence is Operation Cul de Sac (OCDS). A situational crime prevention strategy, OCDS was deployed by the Los Angeles Police Department, placing traffic barriers (i.e., K-rails) at the end of targeted streets to restrict traffic flow in areas impacted by gang violence. The basic premise was that by restricting vehicle access, the opportunities available for gang violence to occur, specifically drive-by shootings, would also be reduced. Lasley's (1998) evaluation found homicides and assaults decreased, especially those involving gangs. However, once the program was discontinued, restoring normal traffic patterns, increases in gang-related violence returned to the targeted area (see also Vargas, 2016).

36.6.2 Civil Gang Injunctions

A civil gang injunction (CGI) can be thought of as a restraining order wherein gang members are restricted from congregating within a defined geographical region, called a "safety zone." CGIs have become one of the most popular antigang strategies in the United States, United Kingdom and Australia in the last decade (Lansdell, Eriksson, Saunders, & Brown, 2012; Rosen & Venkatesh, 2007; Treadwell & Gooch, 2015), and the allure of CGIs or similar dispersal orders does not appear to be abating as an anti-gang strategy (Aldridge, Ralphs & Medina, 2011; Ayling, 2011; Barajas, 2007; Branson-Potts, 2013; Crawford, 2009; Crofts, 2011; Harling, 2008; Home Office, 2015; O'Deane, 2012; Palomo, 2002; Rossi, 2005; Swan & Bates, 2017; Walsh, 2002, 2003). As discussed above, members regularly hang out in their gang's set space, which tend to be public locations, such as a park or street corner (Tita et al., 2005). However, if a CGI is effective at influencing the daily behaviors of enjoined gang members, then gang members would refrain from loitering in these known set space locations. Valasik (2014) investigated the influence that a CGI has on the patterns of association among members of a gang before and after the group was enjoined with a CGI. Results showed that enjoined gang members were less likely to be observed hanging out in their gang's set space following the enactment of a CGI (Valasik, 2014). However, the CGI did not displace the activities of enjoined gang members into the adjacent regions outside of a CGI's safety zone. Instead, the CGI actually constrained the mobility of enjoined gang members, decreasing the likelihood that these individuals ventured outside of their gang's territory. The lack of gang member displacement into neighboring communities also parallels Grogger's (2002) findings that CGIs do not move crime around the corner. Valasik (2014) did reveal that enjoined gang members shifted where they associated with other members from public spaces to private spaces (i.e., private residences, driveways, front or back yards, etc.), a finding consistent with the research of Hennigan and Sloane (2013).

36.7 Conclusions

We have attempted to present the importance of geographic space in terms of how gangs exploit as well as react to the local built environment. We know that gangs are more likely to form in neighborhoods where local levels of informal social control are lacking and levels of social disorganization are high. When choosing a suitable turf or set space, gang members are also likely to consider the accessibility and particular protective factors offered by the built environment (i.e., vacant buildings, street corners, alleys, etc.). High levels of crime often predate the arrival of a gang (Tita, 1999). We have also shown that exploiting the local geography is an important component of gang-specific crime control policies.

Perhaps the primacy of place of residence in terms of which gang one joins and the location of a gang's turf has diminished; however, we have no doubt that the local built environment will continue to play an important role in providing a life-space for gangs, especially the traditional urban street gang (Klein & Maxson, 2006). Just as the crack market of the early 1990s retreated from the streets into spaces more immune to criminal justice surveillance, the classic "street corner boys" of the mid-twentieth century may also be taking their daily routine activities into more private spaces. Certain criminal justice practices may also alter the importance of street corners and set space in terms of where gang members associate. Curfews, CGIs, and other forms of surveillance may cause gang members to shift from associating in public to gathering in a private setting instead (Aldridge et al., 2012; Hennigan & Sloane, 2013; Smith, S. 2014; Valasik, 2014). That being said, when gang-related crime or violence does occur, it does not remain in private or restricted to the virtual world but transpires outside on the streets (Densely, 2013; Patton et al., 2013, 2016; White, 2006).

Though we might be witnessing the declining significance of space, it is unimaginable that the importance of the local environment will completely disappear. Street gangs remain a localized phenomenon that is dependent upon the trust between individuals, requiring a medium for face-to-face interactions (Densley, 2013). As long as trust remains an important part of gang life, place will play an important role in the formation and maintenance of street gangs.

Note

1. The Eurogang definition identifies a street gang as "any durable, street-oriented youth group whose involvement in illegal activity is part of their group identity."

References

Adamson, C. (1998). "Tribute, turf, honor and the American street gang: Patterns of continuity and change since 1820." *Theoretical Criminology*, 2(1): 57–84.

Adamson, C. (2000). "Defensive localism in white and black: A comparative history of European-American and African-American youth gangs." *Ethnic and Racial Studies*, 23(2), 272–298.

Aldridge, J., Medina-Ariz, J., & Ralphs, R. (2012). "Counting gangs: Conceptual and validity problems with the Eurogang definition." In F. Esbensen & C. L. Maxson (eds.), *Youth Gangs in International Perspective: Research from the Eurogang Program of Research* (pp. 35–51). New York, NY: Springer.

Aldridge, J., Ralphs, R., & Medina, J. (2011). "Collateral damage: Territory and policing in an English gang city." In B. Goldson (ed.), *Youth in Crisis? "Gangs", Territoriality and Violence* (pp. 72–88). New York, NY: Routledge.

Alonso, A. A. (2004). "Racialized identities and the formation of black gangs in Los Angeles." *Urban Geography*, 25(7), 658–674.

Anderson, E. (1976). *A Place on the Corner*. Chicago, IL: The Univeristy of Chicago Press.

Anselin, L., Cohen, J., Cook, D., Gorr, W., & Tita, G. E. (2000). "Spatial analyses of crime." *Crime Justice*, 4, 213–262.

Aptekar, L. (1988). *Street Children of Cali*. Durham, NC: Duke University Press.

Atkinson-Sheppard, S. (2016). "The gangs of Bangladesh: Exploring organized crime, street gangs and 'illicit child labourers' in Dhaka." *Criminology and Criminal Justice*, 16(2), 233–249.

Ayling, J. (2011). "Pre-emptive strike: How Australia is tackling outlaw motorcycle gangs." *American Journal of Criminal Justice*, 36(3), 250–264.

Barajas, F. P. (2007). "An invading army: A civil gang injunction in a Southern California Chicana/o community." *Latino Studies*, 5, 393–417.

Bellair, P. E., & McNulty, T. L. (2010). "Gang membership, drug selling, and violence in neighborhood context." *Justice Quarterly*, 26(4), 644–669.

Bergmann, L. (2008). *Getting Ghost: Two Young Lives and the Struggle for the Soul of an American City*. Ann Arbor: University of Michigan Press.

Bjerregaard, B. (2010). "Gang membership and drug involvement untangling the complex relationship." *Crime and Delinquency*, 56(1), 3–34.

Bjørgo, T., Carlsson, Y., & Haaland, T. (2004). "Hate crime or gang conflict? Violence between youth groups in a Norwegian city." In G. Mesko, M. Pagon, & B. Dobovsek (eds.), *Policing in Central and Eastern Europe: Dilemmas of Contemporary Criminal Justice* (pp. 1–19). Maribor, Slovenia: Faculty of Criminal Justice, University of Maribor.

Blasko, B. L., Roman, C. G., & Taylor, R. B. (2015). "Local gangs and residents' perceptions of unsupervised teen groups: Implications for the incivilities thesis and neighborhood effects." *Journal of Criminal Justice*, 43(1), 20–28.

Block, C. R. & Block, R. L. (1993). *Street Gang Crime in Chicago*. Washington, DC: National Institute of Justice.

Block, R. L. (2000). "Gang activity and overall levels of crime: A new mapping tool for defining areas of gang activity using police records." *Journal of Quantitative Criminology*, 16(3), 369–383.

Blumstein, A., & Cork, D. (1996). "Linking gun availability to youth gun violence." *Law and Contemporary Problems*, 59(1), 5–24.

Braga, A. A., Hureau, D. M., & Papachristos, A. V. (2014). "Deterring gang-involved gun violence: Measuring the impact of Boston's Operation Ceasefire on street gang behavior." *Journal of Quantitative Criminology*, 30(1), 113–139.

Branson-Potts, H. (2013, September 26). "Gang injunction granted in Echo Park." *Los Angeles Times*. http://www.latimes.com/local/lanow/la-me-ln-gang-injunction-granted-in-echo-park-20130926,0,7807855.story#axzz2tutWglxo.

Brantingham, P. J., & Brantingham, P. L. (1984). *Patterns in Crime*. New York, NY: Macmillan.

Brantingham, P. J., & Brantingham, P. L. (1995). "Criminality of place: Crime generators and crime attractors." *European Journal of Criminal Policy and Research*, 3(3), 5–26.

Brantingham, P. J., Tita, G. E., Short, M., & Reid, S. E. (2012). "The social ecology of gang territorial boundaries." *Criminology*, 50(3), 851–885.

Brown, G. C., Vigil, J. D., & Taylor, E. R. (2012). "The ghettoization of blacks in Los Angeles: The emergence of street gangs." *Journal of African American Studies*, 16(2), 209–225.

Brunson, R. K., & Miller, J. (2009). "Schools, neighborhoods, and adolescent conflicts: A situational examination of reciprocal dynamics." *Justice Quarterly*, 26(2), 183–210.

Bursik, R. J., Jr., & Grasmick, H. G. (1993). *Neighborhoods and Crime: The Dimensions of Effective Community Control*. Lanham, MD: Lexington Books.

Calderoni, F., Berlusconi, G., Garofalo, L., Giommoni, L., & Sarno, F. (2016). "The Italian mafias in the world: A systematic assessment of the mobility of criminal groups." *European Journal of Criminology*, 13(4), 413–433.

Carroll, R., & Smith, N. (2015, May 18). "California's surf wars: Wave 'warlords' go to extreme lengths to defend their turf." *Guardian*. http://gu.com/p/492af/sbl.

Cartwright, D. S., & Howard, K. I. (1966). "Multivariate analysis of gang delinquency: I. Ecologic influences." *Multivariate Behavioral Research*, 1(3), 321–371.

Chambliss, W. J. (1973). "The saints and the roughnecks." *Society*, 11(1), 24–31.

Clarke, R. V. (1997). *Situational Crime Prevention: Successful Case Studies*. New York, NY: Harrow & Heston.

Cohen, J., & Tita, G. E. (1999). "Diffusion in homicide: Exploring a general method for detecting spatial diffusion processes." *Journal of Quantitative Criminology*, 15(4), 451–493.

Cohen, L. E., & Felson, M. (1979). "Social change and crime rate trends: A routine activity approach." *American Sociological Review*, 44 (August), 588–608.

Comley, C. (2011). "Fall in line: How surfers' perceptions of localism, territoriality and waves as limited resources influence surf-related aggression." *McNair Scholars Research Journal*, 15, 15–29.

Contreras, R. (2013). *The Stickup Kids: Race, Drugs, Violence, and the American Dream*. Berkeley: University of California Press.

Crawford, A. (2009). "Criminalizing sociability through anti-social behavior legislation: Dispersal powers, young people and the police." *Youth Justice* 9(5), 5–26.

Crofts, T. (2011). "The law and (anti-social behaviour) order campaign in western Australia." *Current Issues in Criminal Justice* 22(3), 399–414

Crowe, T., & Zahm, D. (1994). "Crime prevention through environmental design." *NAHB Land Development*, 1994(Fall), 22–27.

Curry, G. D., & Decker, S. H. (1996). "Understanding and responding to gangs in an emerging gang problem context." *Valparaiso University Law Review*, 31(2), 523–533.

Curtis, J. W., Shiau, E., Lowery, B., Sloane, D., Hennigan, K., & Curtis, A. (2014). "The prospects and problems of integrating sketch maps with geographic information systems to understand environmental perception: A case study of mapping youth fear in Los Angeles gang neighborhoods." *Environment and Planning B: Planning and Design*, 41(2), 251–271.

Décary-Hétu, D., & Morselli, C. (2011). "Gang presence in social network sites." *International Journal of Cyber Criminology*, 5(2), 876–890.

Decker, S. H., & Van Winkle, B. (1996). *Life in the Gang: Family, Friends and Violence*. New York, NY: Cambridge University Press.

Densley, J. A. (2013). *How Gangs Work: An Ethnography of Youth Violence*. New York, NY: Palgrave Macmillan.

Du Phuoc Long, P. (1996). *The Dream Shattered: Vietnamese Gangs in America*. Boston, MA: Northeastern University Press.

Durán, R. J. (2013). *Gang Life in Two Cities: An Insider's Journey*. New York, NY: Columbia University Press.

Dyson-Hudson, R., & Smith, E. A. (1978). "Human territoriality: An ecological reassessment." *American Anthropologist*, 80(1), 21–41.

Eck, J. E. (1995). "A general model of the geography of illicit market places." In J. E. Eck & D. Weisburd (eds.), *Crime and Place*. Monsey, NY: Criminal Justice Press.

Fader, J. J. (2016). "Criminal family networks: Criminal capital and cost avoidance among urban drug sellers." *Deviant Behavior*, 1–16. DOI:10.1080/01639625.2016.1177388.

Fagan, J. A. (1989). "The social organization of drug use and drug dealing among urban gangs." *Criminology*, 27(4), 633–669.

Fagan, J. A. (1996). "Gangs, drugs and neighborhood change." In C. R. Huff (ed.), *Gangs in America*, 2nd ed. (pp. 39–74). Thousand Oaks, CA: Sage.

Felson, M. (1987). "Routine activities and crime prevention in the developing metropolis." *Criminology*, 25(4), 911–931.

Felson, M., & Boba, R. (2010). *Crime and Everyday Life*. Thousand Oaks, CA: Sage.

Flores, E. O. (2014). *God's Gangs: Barrio Ministry, Masculinity, and Gang Recovery*. New York, NY: New York University Press.

Fremon, C. (2008). *G-Dog and the Homeboys: Father Greg Boyle and the Gangs of East Los Angeles*. Albuquerque: University of New Mexico Press.

Gambetta, D. (1996). *The Sicilian Mafia: The Business of Private Protection*. Cambridge, MA: Harvard University Press.

Garot, R. (2010). *Who You Claim: Performing Gang Identity in School and on the Streets*. New York, NY: New York University Press.

Gatz, M., & Klein, M. W. (1993). "Europe's new gangs break American pattern by crossing ethnic lines, commuting to turf." *Psychology International* 4(2), 1, 10–11.

Geenen, K. (2009). "'Sleep occupies no space': The use of public space by street gangs in Kinshasa." *Africa: Journal of the International African Institute*, 79(3), 347–368.

Gerber, M. (2014, February 3). "With gentrification, Echo Park gang members move outside their turf." *Los Angeles Times*. http://articles.latimes.com/2014/feb/03/local/la-me-echo-park-gang-20140126.

Gilpin, M. E. (1973). "Do hares eat lynx?" *American Naturalist*, 107(957), 727–730.

Grannis, R. (2009). *From the Ground Up: Translating Geography into Community through Neighbor Networks*. Princeton, NJ: Princeton University Press.

Griffiths, E., & Chavez, J. M. (2004). "Communities, street guns and homicide trajectories in Chicago, 1980–1995: Merging methods for examining homicide trends across space and time." *Criminology*, 42, 941–978.

Groff, E. R., Ratcliffe, J. H., Haberman, C. P., Sorg, E. T., Joyce, N. M., & Taylor, R. B. (2015). "Does what police do at hot spots matter? The Philadelphia policing tactics experiment." *Criminology*, 53(1), 23–53.

Grogger, J. (2002). "The effects of civil gang injunctions on reported violent crime: Evidence from Los Angeles County." *Journal of Law and Economics*, 45, 69–90.

Hagedorn, J. M. (1988). *People and Folks: Gangs, Crime, and the underclass in a Rustbelt City*. Chicago, IL: Lakeview Press.

Hagedorn, J. M. (1994). "Neighborhoods, markets, and gang drug organization." *Journal of Research in Crime and Delinquency*, 31(3), 264–294.

Hagedorn, J. M. (2008). *A World of Gangs: Armed Young Men and Gangsta Culture*. Minneapolis: University of Minnesota Press.

Harling, N. (2008). "A review of Charleston, South Carolina's anti-loitering ordinance and its likelihood of surviving constitutional scrutiny." *Charleston Law Review*, 4, 775–806.

Harper, J. (2015, August 4). "A gang of rich, white surfer dudes is terrorizing a California beach town." *VICE News*. https://www.vice.com/en_us/article/nn9eed/a-gang-of-rich-white-surfer-dudes-is-terrorizing-a-california-beach-town-721

Hazlehurst, C. (2007). "Observing New Zealand 'gangs,' 1950–2000: Learning from a small country." In J. M. Hagedorn (ed.), *Gangs in the Global City: Alternatives to Traditional Criminology* (pp. 120–151). Urbana: University of Illinois Press.

Hecht, T. (1998). *At Home in the Street: Street Children of Northeast Brazil*. Cambridge: Cambridge University Press.

Heinonen, P. (2011). *Youth Gangs and Street Children: Culture, Nurture and Masculinity in Ethiopia*. New York, NY: Berghahn Books.

Heinsohn, R., & Packer, C. (1995). “Complex cooperative strategies in group-territorial African lions.” *Science*, 269(5228), 1260–1262.

Hennigan, K. M., & Sloane, D. (2013). “Improving civil gang injunctions: How implementation can affect dynamics, crime, and violence.” *Criminology and Public Policy* 12(1), 7–41.

Hennigan, K. M., & Spanovic, M. (2012). “Gang dynamics through the lens of social identity theory.” In F. Esbensen & C. L. Maxson (eds.), *Youth Gangs in International Perspective* (pp. 127–149). New York, NY: Springer.

Home Office (2015, July 16). “Injunctions to prevent gang-related violence and drug dealing: Statutory guidance.” https://www.gov.uk/government/publications/statutory-guidance-injunctions- to-prevent-gang-related-violence--2.

Howell, J. C., Egley, A., Jr., Tita, G. E., & Griffiths, E. (2011). “U.S. gang problem trends and seriousness, 1996–2009.” US Department of Justice: Office of Juvenile Justice and Delinquency Prevention. National Youth Gang Center Bulletin, May (no. 6).

Howell, J. C., & Griffiths, E. (2015). *Gangs in America's Communities*. Thousand Oaks, CA: Sage.

Huebner, B. M., Martin, K., Moule, R. K., Jr., Pyrooz, D., & Decker, S. H. (2016). “Dangerous places: Gang members and neighborhood levels of gun assault.” *Justice Quarterly*, 33(5), 836–862.

Huff, C. R. (1989). “Youth gangs and public policy.” *Crime and Delinquency*, 35(4), 524–537.

Huff, C. R., & McBride, W. D. (1993). “Gangs and the police.” In A. P. Goldstein & C. R. Huff (eds.), *The Gang Intervention Handbook* (pp. 401–416). Champaign, IL: Research Press.

Jankowski, M. S. (1991). *Islands in the Street: Gangs and American Urban Society*. Berkeley: University of California Press.

Jeffery, C. R. (1971). *Crime Prevention through Environmental Design*. Beverly Hills, CA: Sage.

Johnson, B., Golub, A., & Dunlap, E. (2000). “The rise and decline of hard drugs, drug markets, and violence in inner-city New York.” In A. Blumstein, & J. Wallman (eds.), *The Crime Drop in America* (pp. 164–206). New York, NY: Cambridge University Press.

Jost, C., Devulder, G., Vucetich, J. A., Peterson, R. O., & Arditi, R. (2005). “The wolves of Isle Royale display scale-invariant satiation and ratio-dependent predation on moose.” *Journal of Animal Ecology*, 74(5), 809–816.

Kandel, J., & Crouch, A. (2016, April 5). “Planned class-action lawsuit targets Bay Boys ‘surfer gang.’” NBC Los Angeles. http://www.nbclosangeles.com/news/local/Planned-Class-Action-Lawsuit-Targets-Lunada-Bay-Boys-Surfer-Gang-374019821.html.

Kaffine, D. T. (2009). “Quality and the commons: The surf gangs of California.” *Journal of Law and Economics*, 52(4), 727–743.

Katz, C. M., Maguire, E. R., & Choate, D. (2011). “A cross-national comparison of gangs in the United States and Trinidad and Tobago.” *International Criminal Justice Review*, 21(3), 243–262.

Katz, C. M., & Schnebly, S. M. (2011). “Neighborhood variation in gang member concentrations.” *Crime and Delinquency*, 57(3), 377–407.

Katz, C. M., & Webb, V. J. (2006). *Policing Gangs in America*. Cambridge: Cambridge University Press.

Kennedy, D. M., Braga, A. A., & Piehl, A. M. (1997). “The (un)known universe: Mapping gangs and gang violence in Boston.” In D. L. Weisburd & J. T. McEwen (eds.), *Crime Mapping and Crime Prevention* (pp. 219–262). Monsey, NY: Criminal Justice Press.

Kennedy, D. M., Piehl, A. M., & Braga, A. A. (1996). “Youth violence in Boston: Gun markets, serious youth offenders, and a use-reduction strategy.” *Law and Contemporary Problems*, 59(1), 147–196.

King, J. E., Walpole, C. E., & Lamon, K. (2007). "Surf and turf wars online: Growing implications of Internet gang violence." *Journal of Adolescent Health*, 41(6), S66-S68.

Klein, M. W. (1995a). *The American Street Gang*. New York, NY: Oxford University Press.

Klein, M. W. (1995b). "Street gang cycles." In J. Q. Wilson and J. Petersilia (eds.), *Crime* (pp. 217–236). San Francisco, CA: Institute for Contemporary Studies Press.

Klein, M. W., & Maxson, C. L. (1985). "'Rock' sales in South Los Angeles." *Sociology and Social Research*, 69(4), 561–565.

Klein, M. W., & Maxson, C. L. (2006). *Street Gang Patterns and Policies*. Oxford: Oxford University Press.

Kubrin, C. E., & Weitzer, R. (2003). "Retaliatory homicide: Concentrated disadvantage and neighborhood culture." *Social Problems*, 50(2), 157–180.

Lam, K. D. (2015). *Youth Gangs, Racism, and Schooling: Vietnamese American Youth in a Postcolonial Context*. New York, NY: Palgrave Macmillan.

Lane, J. (2002). "Fear of gang crime: A qualitative examination of the four perspectives." *Journal of Research in Crime and Delinquency*, 39(4), 437–471.

Lane, J., & J. W. Meeker. (2003). "Fear of gang crime: A look at three theoretical models." *Law and Society Review* 37(2), 425–456.

Lansdell, G., Eriksson, A., Saunders, B., and Brown, M. (2012). "Infringement systems in Australia: A precarious blurring of civil and criminal sanctions?" *Alternative Law Journal* 37(1), 41–45.

Lasley, J. (1998). "'Designing out' gang homicides and street assaults." Washington, DC: U.S. Department of Justice, Office of Justice Programs, National Institute of Justice.

Leap, J. (2012). *Jumped In: What Gangs Taught Me about Violence, Drugs, Love, and Redemption*. Boston, MA: Beacon Press.

Lefebvre, H. (1974/1991). *The Production of Space*. D. Nicholson-Smith (trans.). Oxford: Blackwell.

Levitt, S. D., & Venkatesh, S. A. (2000). "An economic analysis of a drug-selling gang's finances." *Quarterly Journal of Economics*, 115(3), 755–789.

Levenson, D. T. (2013). *Adiós Niño: The Gangs of Guatemala City and the Politics of Death*. Durham, NC: Duke University Press.

Ley, D., & Cybriwsky, R. (1974). "Urban graffiti as territorial markers." *Annals of the Association of American Geographers*, 64(4), 491–505.

Liebow, E. (1967). *Tally's Corner: A Study of Negro Streetcorner Men*. New York, NY: Little, Brown.

Lien, I. (2001). "The concept of honor, conflict, and violent behavior among youths in Oslo." In M. W. Klein, H. Kerner, C. L. Maxson, & E. G. M. Weitekamp (eds.), *The Eurogang Paradox: Street Gangs and Youth Groups in the U.S. and Europe* (pp. 165–174). Dordrecht, NL: Kluwer Academic Publishers.

Lien, I. (2005). "Criminal gangs and their connections: Metaphors, definitions, and structures." In S. H. Decker & F. M. Weerman (eds.), *European Street Gangs and Troublesome Youth Groups* (pp. 31–50). New York, NY: AltaMira Press.

Loyola, B. (2013, November 27). "The subterranean scene: On the rails with Mexico City's reggaeton-loving subway gangs." VICE News. http://www.vice.com/video/the-subway-gangs-of-mexico-city.

Lyman, S. M., & Scott, M. B. (1967). "Territoriality: A neglected sociological dimension." *Social Problems*, 15(20), 236–249.

MacArthur, R. H. (1958). "Ecology of some warblers of northeastern coniferous forests." *Ecology* 39(4), 599–619.

MacDonald, J. (2015). "Community design and crime: The impact of housing and the built environment." *Crime and Justice* 44(1), 333–383.

Mares, D. (2010). "Social disorganization and gang homicides in Chicago, IL: A neighborhood level comparison of disaggregated homicides." *Youth Violence and Juvenile Justice*, 8(1), 38–57.

Mateo, J. (2011). "Street gangs of Honduras." In T. Bruneau, L. Dammer, & E. Skinner (eds.), *Maras: Gang Violence and Security in Central America* (p 87–104). Austin: University of Texas Press.

Maxson, C. L. (1998). *Gang Members on the Move*. Washington, DC: US Department of Justice, Office of Justice Programs, Office of Juvenile Justice and Delinquency Prevention.

May, T., & Hough, M. (2004). "Drug markets and distribution systems." *Addiction Research and Theory*, 12(6), 549–563.

Mears, D. P., & Bhati, A. S. (2006). "No community is an island: The effects of resource deprivation on urban violence in spatially and socially proximate communities." *Criminology*, 44(3), 509–548.

Miller, W. B. (1966/2011). *City Gangs*. S. H. Decker (ed.). Phoenix: Arizona State University.

Mills, E. S. (1990). Housing economics: A synthesis. In M. Chetterji & R. E. Kuenne (eds.), *New Frontiers in Regional Science: Essays in Honor of Walter Isard*, vol. 1 (pp. 257–274). New York: New York University Press.

Moffatt, R. E. (1983). "Crime prevention through environmental design: A management perspective." *Canadian Journal of Criminology*, 25, 19–31.

Monod, J. (1967). "Juvenile gangs in Paris: Toward a structural analysis." *Journal of Research in Crime and Delinquency*, 4(1), 142–165.

Moore, J. W. (1978). *Homeboys: Gangs, Drugs, and Prison in the Barrios of Los Angeles*. Philadelphia, PA: Temple University Press.

Moore, J. W. (1991). *Going Down to the Barrio: Homeboys and Homegirls in Change*. Philadelphia, PA: Temple University Press.

Moore, J. W., Vigil, J. D., & Garcia, R. (1983). "Residence and territoriality in Chicano gangs." *Social Problems*, 31(2), 182–194.

Moule, R. K., Jr., Pyrooz, D. C., & Decker, S. H. (2014). "Internet adoption and online behaviour among American street gangs: Integrating gangs and organizational theory." *British Journal of Criminology*, 54(6), 1186–1206.

Morenoff, J. D., & Sampson, R. J. (1997). "Violent crime and the spatial dynamics of neighborhood transition: Chicago, 1970–1990." *Social Forces*, 76(1), 31–64.

Morselli, C., & Décary-Hétu, D. (2013). "Crime facilitation purposes of social networking sites: A review and analysis of the 'cyberbanging' phenomenon." *Small Wars and Insurgencies* 24(1), 152–170.

Newman, O. (1972). *Defensible Space: Crime Prevention through Urban Design*. New York, NY: Random House.

O'Deane, M. D. (2012). *Gang Injunctions and Abatement: Using Civil Remedies to Curb Gang-Related Crimes*. Boca Raton, FL: CRC Press.

Ong, A. (2003). *Buddha Is Hiding: Refugees, Citizenship, the New America*. Berkeley: University of California Press.

Padilla, F. M. (1992). *The Gang as an American Enterprise*. New Brunswick, NJ: Rutgers University Press.

Palomo, E. (2002). "'The sheriff knows who the trouble makers are. Just Let him round them up': Chicago's new gang loitering ordinance." *University of Illinois Law Review*, 3, 729–760.

Papachristos, A. V. (2009). "Murder by structure: Dominance relations and the social structure of gang homicide." *American Journal of Sociology*, 115(1), 74–128.

Papachristos, A. V., Braga, A. A., & Hureau, D. M. (2012). "Social networks and the risk of gunshot injury." *Journal of Urban Health*, 89(6), 992–1003.

Papachristos, A. V., Braga, A. A., Piza, E., & Grossman, L. S. (2015). "The company you keep? The spillover effects of gang membership on individual gunshot victimization in a co-offending network." *Criminology*, 53(4), 624–649.

Papachristos, A. V., Hureau, D. M., & Braga, A. A. (2013). "The corner and the crew: The influence of geography and social networks on gang violence." *American Sociological Review*, 78(3), 417–447.

Papachristos, A. V., & Kirk, D. S. (2006). "Neighborhood effects on street gang behavior." In J. F. Short Jr. & L. A. Hughes (eds.), *Studying Youth Gangs* (pp. 63–84). Lanham, MD: AltaMira Press.

Papachristos, A. V., Meares, T. L., & Fagan, J. (2007). "Attention felons: Evaluating project safe neighborhoods in Chicago." *Journal of Empirical Legal Studies*, 4(2), 223–272.

Park, R. E., & Burgess, E. W. (1925/1967). *The City*. Chicago, IL: University of Chicago Press.

Pattillo-McCoy, M. E. (1999). *Black Picket Fences: Privilege and Peril among the Black Middle Class*. Chicago, IL: University of Chicago Press.

Patton, D. U., Eschmann, R. D., & Butler, D. A. (2013). "Internet banging: New trends in social media, gang violence, masculinity and hip hop." *Computers in Human Behavior*, 29(5), A54-A59.

Patton, D. U., Eschmann, R. D., Elsaesser, C., & Bocanegra, E. (2016). "Sticks, stones and Facebook accounts: What violence outreach workers know about social media and urban-based gang violence in Chicago." *Computers in Human Behavior*, pp. 1–10, DOI:10.1016/j.chb.2016.05.052.

Patton, D. U., Lane, J., Leonard, P., Macbeth, J., & Smith-Lee, J. R. (2016). "Gang violence on the digital street: Case study of a South Side Chicago gang member's Twitter communication." *New Media & Society*, pp. 1–19, DOI:10.1177/1461444815625949.

Perrone, S. & White, R. (2000). "Young people and gangs." Trends and Issues in Crime and Criminal Justice No. 167. Canberra: Australian Institute of Criminology.

Perry, T. (1995, May 8). "Turf wars spoil sanctity of Southland surf beaches." *Los Angeles Times*. http://articles.latimes.com/1995-05-08/news/mn-63795_1_lunada-bay.

Phillips, S. A. (1999). *Wallbangin': Graffiti and Gangs in L.A.* Chicago, IL: University of Chicago Press.

Phillips, S. A. (2012). *Operation Fly Trap: L.A. Gangs, Drugs, and the Law*. Chicago, IL: University of Chicago Press.

Pickering, J., Kintrea, K., & Bannister, J. (2012). "Invisible walls and visible youth: Territoriality among young people in British cities." *Urban Studies*, 49(5), 945–960.

Polk, K. (1994). "Youth violence: Myth and reality." In D. Chappell & S. Egger (eds.), *Australian Violence: Contemporary Perspectives II*. (pp. 51–70). Canberra: Australian Institute of Criminology.

Polk, K. (1995). "Masculinity, honour, and confrontational homicide." In T. Newburn & E. A. Stank (eds.), *Just Boys Doing Business? Men, Masculinities and Crime* (pp. 166–188). New York, NY: Routledge.

Popkin, S. J., Gwiasda, V. E., Olson, L. M., Rosenbaum, Dennis P., & Buron, L. (2000). *The Hidden War: Crime and Tragedy of Public Housing in Chicago*. New Brunswick, NJ: Rutgers University Press.

Pyrooz, D. C., Decker, S. H., & Moule, R. K., Jr. (2015). "Criminal and routine activities in online settings: Gangs, offenders, and the Internet." *Justice Quarterly*, 32(3), 471–499.

Pyrooz, D. C., & Mitchell, M. M. (2015). "Little gang research, big gang research." In S. H. Decker & D. C. Pyrooz (eds.), *The Handbook of Gangs* (pp. 28–58). New York, NY: Wiley.

Radil, S. M., Flint, C., & Tita, G. E. (2010). "Spatializing social networks: Using social network analysis to investigate geographies of gang rivalry, territoriality, and violence in Los Angeles." *Annals of the Association of American Geographers*, 100(2), 307–326.

Rafael, T. (2007). *The Mexican Mafia*. Jackson, TN: Encounter Books.

Ratcliffe, J. H., & Breen, C. (2011). "Crime diffusion and displacement: Measuring the side effects of police operations." *Professional Geographer*, 63(2), 230–243.

Reuter, P. (2009). "Systemic violence in drug markets." *Crime, Law and Social Change*, 52(3), 275–284.

Rios, V. M. (2011). *Punished: Policing the Lives of Black and Latino Boys*. New York, NY: New York University Press.

Rizzini, I., & Butler, U. M. (2003). "Life trajectories of children and adolescents living on the streets of Rio de Janeiro." *Children, Youth and Environments*, 13(1), 182–201.

Rocha, J. L. (2011). "Street gangs of Nicaragua." In T. Bruneau, L. Dammer, & E. Skinner (eds.), *Maras: Gang Violence and Security in Central America* (pp. 105–120). Austin: University of Texas Press.

Rodgers, D. (2006). "Living in the shadow of death: Gangs, violence and social order in urban Nicaragua, 1996–2002." *Journal of Latin American Studies*, 38(2), 267–292.

Rodgers, D., & Baird, A. (2015). "Understanding gangs in contemporary Latin America." In S. H. Decker & D. C. Pyrooz (eds.), *Handbook of Gangs and Gang Responses* (pp. 478–502). New York, NY: Wiley.

Rodgers, D., & Jones, G. A. (2009). "Youth violence in Latin America: An overview and agenda for research." In G. A. Jones & D. Rodgers (eds.), *Youth Violence in Latin America: Gangs and Juvenile Justice in Perspective* (pp. 1–24). New York, NY: Palgrave Macmillan.

Rosen, E., & Venkatesh, S. A. (2007). "Legal innovation and the control of gang behavior." *Annual Review of Law and Social Science*, 3, 255–270.

Rosenfeld, R., Bray, T. M., & Egley, A. (1999). "Facilitating violence: A comparison of gang-motivated, gang-affiliated, and nongang youth homicides." *Journal of Quantitative Criminology*, 15(4), 495–516.

Rossi, M. J. (2005). "Striking a balance: The efforts of one Massachusetts city to draft and effective anti-loitering law within the bounds of the Constitution." *Suffolk University Law Review*, 4, 1069–1088.

Rostami, A., Leinfelt, F., & Holgersson, S. (2012). "An exploratory analysis of Swedish street gangs applying the Maxson and Klein Typology to a Swedish gang dataset." *Journal of Contemporary Criminal Justice*, 28(4), 426–445.

Ryti, R. T., & Case, T. J. (1992). "The role of neighborhood competition in the spacing and diversity of ant communities." *American Naturalist*, 139(2), 355–374.

Sabelis, M. W., Diekmann, O., & Jansen, V. A. A. (1991). "Metapopulation persistence despite local extinction: Predator-prey patch models of the Lotka-Volterra type." *Biological Journal of the Linnaean Society*, 42(1–2), 267–283.

Sack, R. D. (1983). "Human territoriality: A theory." *Annals of the Association of American Geographers*, 73(1), 55–74.

Salagaev, A. L., & Safin, R. R. (2014). "Capitalizing on crime: Gangs, ideology, and the transition to a liberal economy in the Russian Federation." In J. M. Hazen & D. Rodgers (eds.),

Global Gangs: Street Violence across the World (pp. 65–83). Minneapolis: University of Minnesota Press.

Sampson, R. J., & Groves, B. W. (1989). "Community structure and crime: Testing social-disorganization theory." *American Journal of Sociology*, 94(4), 774–802.

Sampson, R. J., Raudenbush, S. W., & Earls, F. (1997). "Neighborhoods and violent crime: A multilevel study of collective efficacy." *Science*, 277(5328), 918–924.

Sarnecki, J. (2001). *Delinquent Networks: Youth Co-offending in Stockholm.* Cambridge: Cambridge University Press.

Schneider, E. C. (1999). *Vampires, Dragons, and Egyptian Kings: Youth Gangs in Postwar New York.* Princeton, NJ: Princeton University Press.

Sela-Shayovitz, R. (2012). "Gangs and the web: Gang members' online behavior." *Journal of Contemporary Criminal Justice*, 28(2), 389–405.

Sela-Shayovitz, R., Pyrooz, D. C., & Decker, S. H. (2016). "Israeli and US gangs in the virtual world: The sociocultural context of gang members' online activity." In C. L. Maxson & F. Esbensen (eds.), *Gang Transitions and Transformations in an International Context* (pp. 115–138). New York, NY: Springer.

Shaw, C. R., & McKay, H. D. (1942). *Juvenile Delinquency in Urban Areas.* Chicago, IL: University of Chicago Press.

Shaw, M. B. (2016, April 1). "Sad days at Lunada Bay: Class action suit has L.A. surf 'gang' in hot water." *Surfer*. http://www.surfermag.com/features/sad-days-at-lunada-bay/.

Simon, D., & Burns, E. (1997). *The Corner: A Year in the Life of an Inner-City Neighborhood.* New York, NY: Broadway Books.

Skolnick, J. H. (1990). *Gang Organization and Migration: Drugs, Gangs, and Law Enforcement.* [Sacramento:] Office of the Attorney General, California Department of Justice.

Smith, C. M. (2014). "The influence of gentrification on gang homicides in Chicago neighborhoods, 1994 to 2005." *Crime and Delinquency*, 60(4), 569–591.

Smith, S. (Creator). (2014, June 13). "Surveillance City." Episode 12. In B. Maher (executive producer), *VICE*. New York, NY: Home Box Office.

Smith, S. (Creator). (2016, August 29). "City of Lost Children." Episode 11. In B. Maher (executive producer), *VICE*. New York, NY: Home Box Office.

Spergel, I. A. (1995). *The Youth Gang Problem: A Community Approach.* New York, NY: Oxford University Press.

Spergel, I. A., & Curry, G. D. (1993). "The national youth gang survey: A research and development process." In A. P. Goldstein & C. R. Huff (eds.), *The Gang Intervention Handbook* (pp. 359–400). Champaign, IL: Research Press.

Stephenson, S. (2015). *Gangs of Russia: From the Streets to the Corridors of Power.* Ithaca, NY: Cornell University Press.

Storrod, M. L., & Densley, J. A. (2017). "'Going viral' and 'Going country': the expressive and instrumental activities of street gangs on social media." *Journal of Youth Studies* 20(6), 677–696.

Sullivan, M. (1989). *Getting Paid: Youth Crime and Unemployment in Three Urban Neighborhoods.* Ithaca, NY: Cornell University Press.

Suttles, G. D. (1968). *The Social Order of the Slum: Ethnicity and Territory in the Inner City.* Chicago, IL: University of Chicago Press.

Swan, R. S., & Bates, K. A. (2017). "Loosening the ties that bind: the hidden harms of civil injunctions in San Diego County." *Contemporary Justice Review* 20(1), 132–153.

Taniguchi, T. A., Radcliffe, J. H., & Taylor, R. B. (2011). "Gang set space, drug markets, and crime around drug corners in Camden." *Journal of Research in Crime and Delinquency*, 48(3), 327–363.

Tapia, M. (2014). "Latino street gang emergence in the Midwest: Strategic franchising or natural migration?" *Crime and Delinquency*, 60(4), 592–618.

Taylor, C. S. (1990). *Dangerous Society*. East Lansing: Michigan State University Press.

Taylor, C. S. (1993). *Girls, Gangs, Women and Drugs*. East Lansing: Michigan State University Press.

Taylor, R. B. (1988). *Human Territorial Functioning: An Empirical, Evolutionary Perspective on Individual and Small Group Territorial Cognitions, Behaviors, and Consequences*. Cambridge: Cambridge University Press.

Taylor, R. B., & Gottfredson, S. D. (1986). "Environmental design, crime, and prevention: An examination of community dynamics." *Crime and Justice*, 8(1986), 387–416.

Therolf, G. (2015, December 30). "Palos Verdes police chief promises to take on the 'Bay Boys' of Lunada." *Los Angeles Times*. http://www.latimes.com/local/crime/la-me-lunada-bay-20151230-story.html.

Thrasher, F. M. (1927). *The Gang: A Study of 131 Gangs in Chicago*. Chicago, IL: University of Chicago Press.

Tita, G. E. (1999). *An Ecological Study of Violent Urban Street Gangs and Their Crime*. PhD dissertation, Carnegie Mellon University.

Tita, G. E., & Cohen, J. (2004). "Measuring spatial diffusion of shots fired activity across city neighborhoods." In M. F. Goodchild & D. G. Janelle (eds.), *Spatially Integrated Social Science* (pp. 171–204). New York, NY: Oxford University Press.

Tita, G. E., Cohen, J., & Engberg, J. (2005). "An ecological study of the location of gang 'set space.'" *Social Problems*, 52(2), 272–299.

Tita, G. E., & Greenbaum, R. T. (2009). "Crime, neighborhoods, and units of analysis: Putting space in its place." In D. Weisburd, W. Bernasco, & G. J. N. Bruinsma (eds.), *Putting Crime in Its Place: Units of Analysis in Geographic Criminology* (pp. 145–170). New York, NY: Springer.

Tita, G. E., & Radil, S. M. (2011). "Spatializing the social networks of gangs to explore patterns of violence." *Journal of Quantitative Criminology*, 27(4), 521–545.

Tita, G. E., & Ridgeway, G. (2007). "The impact of gang formation on local crime patterns." *Journal of Research in Crime and Delinquency*, 44(2), 208–237.

Tita, G. E., Riley, K. J., Ridgeway, G., Grammich, C. A., Abrahamse, A., & Greenwood, P. W. (2003). *Reducing Gun Violence: Results from an Intervention in East Los Angeles*. Santa Monica, CA: RAND.

Treadwell, J., & Gooch, K. (2015). "An ASBO for violent gangsters or just continuing criminalisation of young people? Thinking about the value of 'Gangbo.'" *Papers from the British Criminology Conference*, 15, 60–76.

Usher, L. E., & Kerstetter, D. (2015). "Re-defining localism: An ethnography of human territoriality in the surf." *International Journal of Tourism Anthropology*, 4(3), 286–302

Valasik, M. (2014). *"Saving the World, One Neighborhood at a Time": The Role of Civil Gang Injunctions at Influencing Gang Behavior*. PhD dissertation, University of California, Irvine.

Valasik, M., Barton, M.S., Reid, S. E., & Tita, G. E. (2017). "Barriocide: Investigating the temporal and spatial influence of neighborhood structural characteristics on gang and non-gang homicides in East Los Angeles." *Homicide Studies*, 21(4), 287–311.

Valasik, M., Reid, S. E., & Phillips, M. D. (2016). "CRASH and burn: Abatement of a specialised gang unit." *Journal of Criminological Research, Policy and Practice*, 2(2), 95–106.

Valasik, M., Gravel, J. & Tita, G. E. (2016). "Gangland it is a territorial thing: The influence of residency and mobility on the territoriality patterns of gang members." Unpublished manuscript.

Valdez, A., & Sifaneck, S. J. (2004). "'Getting high and getting by': Dimensions of drug selling behaviors among American Mexican gang members in South Texas." *Journal of Research in Crime and Delinquency*, 41(1), 82–105.

Van Valkenburg, P., & Osborne, J. F. (2013). "Home turf: Archaeology, territoriality, and politics." *Archaeological Papers of the American Anthropological Association*, 22(1), 1–27.

Varese, F. (2011). *Mafias on the Move: How organized Crime Conquers New Territories*. Princeton, NJ: Princeton University Press.

Vargas, R. (2016). *Wounded City: Violent Turf Wars in a Chicago Barrio*. New York, NY: Oxford University Press.

Venkatesh, S. A. (1997). "The social organization of street gang activity in an urban ghetto." *American Journal of Sociology*, 103(1), 82–111.

Venkatesh, S. A. (2000). *American Project: The Rise and Fall of a Modern Ghetto*. Cambridge, MA: Harvard University Press.

Vigil, J. D. (1983). "Chicano gangs: One response to Mexican urban adaptation in the Los Angeles area." *Urban Anthropology*, 12(1), 45–75

Vigil, J. D. (1988). *Barrio Gangs: Street Life and Identity in Southern California*. Austin: University of Texas Press.

Vigil, J. D. (2002). *A Rainbow of Gangs: Street Cultures in the Mega-city*. Austin: University of Texas Press.

Vigil, J. D. (2007). *The Projects: Gang and Non-gang Families in East Los Angeles*. Austin: University of Texas Press.

Vigil, J. D., & Yun, S. C. (2002). "A cross-cultural framework to understand gangs: Multiple marginality and Los Angeles." In C. R. Huff (ed.), *Gangs in America III* (pp. 161–167). Thousand Oaks, CA: Sage.

Walsh, C. (2002). "Curfews: No more hanging around." *Youth Justice*, 2(2), 70–81.

Walsh, C. (2003). "Dispersal of rights: A critical comment on specified provision of the anti-social behaviour bill." *Youth Justice*, 3(2), 104–111.

Waters, T. (1991, July 5). "The hazards of surfing Lunada Bay peninsula." *Los Angeles Times*. http://articles.latimes.com/1991-07-05/local/me-1657_1_lunada-bay.

Watkins, A. M., & Moule, R. K., Jr. (2014). "Older, wiser, and a bit more badass? Exploring Differences in juvenile and adult gang members' gang-related attitudes and behaviors." *Youth Violence and Juvenile Justice*, 12(2), 121–136.

Weerman, F. M., Maxson, C. L., Esbensen, F., Aldridge, J., Medina, J., & van Gemert, F. (2009). "Eurogang programme manual background, development, and use of the Eurogang instruments in multi-site, multi-method comparative research." https://www.umsl.edu/ccj/Eurogang/EurogangManual.pdf.

Weisburd, D., Wyckoff, L. A., Ready, J., Eck, J. E., Hinkle, J. C., & Gajewski, F. (2006). "Does crime just move around the corner? A controlled study of spatial displacement and diffusion of crime control benefits." *Criminology*, 44(3), 549–592.

White, R. (2006). "Swarming and the social dynamics of group violence." *Trends & Issues in Crime & Criminal Justice*, 326, 1–6.

Whyte, W. F. (1943). *Street Corner Society*. Chicago, IL: University of Chicago Press.

Winton, A. (2004). "Young people's views on how to tackle gang violence in 'post-conflict' Guatemala." *Environment and Urbanization*, 16(2), 83–99.

Winton, A. (2005). "Youth, gangs and violence: Analysing the social and spatial mobility of young people in Guatemala City." *Children's Geographies* 3(2), 167–184.

Winton, A. (2014). "Gangs in global perspective." *Environment and Urbanization*, 26(2), 401–416.

Wolf, S. (2012). "Mara Salvatrucha: The most dangerous street gang in the Americas?" *Latin American Politics and Society*, 54(1), 65–99.

Wolseth, J. (2009). "Good times and bad blood: Violence, solidarity, and social organization on Dominican streets." In G. A. Jones & D. Rodgers (eds.), *Youth Violence in Latin America: Gangs and Juvenile Justice in Perspective* (pp. 63–82). New York, NY: Palgrave Macmillan.

Wolseth, J. (2011). *Jesus and the Gang: Youth Violence and Christianity in Urban Honduras*. Tucson: University of Arizona Press.

Womer, S., & Bunker, R. J. (2010), "Sureños gangs and Mexican cartel use of social networking sites." *Small Wars and Insurgencies*, 21(1), 81–94.

Yablonsky, L. (1962). *The Violent Gang*. New York, NY: MacMillan.

Zeoli, A. M., Grady, S., Pizarro, J. M., & Melde, C. (2015). "Modeling the movement of homicide by type to inform public health prevention efforts." *American Journal of Public Health*, 105(10), 2035–2041.

Zeoli, A. M., Pizarro, J. M., Grady, S. C., & Melde, C. (2014). "Homicide as infectious disease: Using public health methods to investigate the diffusion of homicide." *Justice Quarterly*, 31(3), 609–632.

Zilberg, E. (2004). "Fools banished from the kingdom: Remapping geographies of gang violence between the Americas (Los Angeles and San Salvador)." *American Quarterly*, 56(3), 759–779.

CHAPTER 37

ORGANIZED CRIME AND PLACES

EDWARD R. KLEEMANS

37.1 Introduction

Environmental criminology has produced major theoretical and empirical progress regarding the explanation and prevention of specific types of crime, particularly opportunistic street-level crime. The primary focus on these types of crime can be explained by the fact that the emergence of environmental criminology in the 1970s and 1980s coincided with pressing urban crime problems, including car crime, robbery, and burglary, in many Western, industrialized countries. Only later on, ideas from environmental criminology and situational crime prevention theory were transplanted to other, more serious types of "organized crimes," often requiring a higher degree of social organization (e.g., Cornish and Clarke 2002; Van de Bunt and Van der Schoot 2003; Levi and Maguire 2004; Van der Schoot 2006; Bouloukos, Farrell, and Laycock 2003; Bullock, Clarke, and Tilley 2010; Von Lampe 2011; Kleemans, Soudijn, and Weenink 2012; Kleemans and Soudijn 2017).

Organized crime, however, is a highly contested concept (see Paoli and Vander Beken 2014). In an overview of theoretical perspectives on organized crime, Kleemans (2014) made a distinction between three types of organized crime and three lines of research: racketeering, transit crime, and the local provision of illegal goods and services. The following sections (37.2, 37.3, and 37.4) go briefly into these three types of organized crime and the significance of place. Furthermore, the role of places and the (built) environment for organized crime is discussed (Section 37.5). The main message is that place has a different meaning for these three types of organized crime and raises several theoretical challenges. As these types of organized crime often require a higher degree of social organization than opportunistic street-level crime, Section 37.6 elaborates on two theoretical concepts that should be included in the study of organized crime and place: social opportunity structure and offender convergence settings.

Without including these concepts, researchers run the risk of missing the main driving mechanisms behind the emergence and activities of criminal networks at specific places. Furthermore, the full potential of environmental criminology can only be realized if "place" is conceptualized in a different way and on a higher level than a specific point in space where an offender meets a target.

37.2 Racketeering

Absence of the state and/or state legitimacy is an important condition for certain forms of organized crime. Before the emergence of the major transnational drug markets that are so salient for organized crime groups today, organized crime groups already made profits in peasant societies such as Sicily in the late nineteenth century, by controlling the territory and acting as an "alternative government." Other historical examples include the Hong Kong triads, the Russian mafia, and the Japanese yakuza (for a review, see Varese 2011; Kleemans 2015). Forms of "racketeering," illicit activities on legal markets, can also be distinguished by focusing on Italian-American Mafia families in New York, exploiting dominant positions in the building sector, the waste disposal industry, the Fulton fish market, the labor unions, the harbor, et cetera (e.g., Jacobs 1999). The basic idea is that organized crime groups gain control over certain regions or economic sectors and act as "alternative government." Traditionally, the state is supposed to protect citizens, businesses, property rights, and business transactions through enforcement and is able to collect taxes for this common goal. If strong and legitimate state control is absent, organized crime groups are able to make profits by taking over these two traditional state monopolies (the monopoly of violence and taxation). Basically, control is exercised through (threats of) violence, and local productive activities are "taxed" by asking for protection money, putting people on the paying list, asking higher prices, or forcing buyers to accept and pay for certain goods and services. These profits, from "organizing" competition and cartel formation to outright extortion, are made possible through a power structure related to people, businesses, and politics (see, for a review, Varese 2014).

If we focus on the concept of place, for these types of criminal activities (racketeering), place actually means "territory," including the control over people, activities, and resources. This control is based on social relations and economic and political power relationships. Therefore, theoretical explanations for the emergence and endurance of organized crime groups engaged in these activities often relate to state formation and borrow from theories from political science (e.g., public choice) and economics (monopoly, cartel formation) (for a review, see, e.g., Von Lampe 2006). In modern Western societies, we are used to the idea that the control over territories is in the hands of "strong states," but these historical examples show that in many other countries and other periods of history, organized crime phenomena are often accompanied by the absence of a strong and/or legitimate state, "failed states," or evaporating state control, such as in the case of the sudden collapse of the Soviet Union in the 1980s and 1990s.

Protection theory is often used to explain the emergence and endurance of criminal organizations, such as Mafia control in Sicily (Varese 2014). A specific interpretation by Gambetta (1993) is that organized crime groups actually render a "service" by selling private protection that the state cannot guarantee. Gambetta argues that Mafia groups respond to a demand for private protection: the Mafia actually is a specific economic enterprise that produces, promotes, and sells private protection and protects property rights and economic transactions, both legal and illegal. Paoli (2003) does not agree with this interpretation and views Mafia groups as multifunctional organizations, founded on premodern status and fraternization contracts. Mafia groups, in her opinion, have been used for a variety of goals and to accomplish a variety of functions. Both authors agree, however, on the "political" dimension of these organized crime groups: the power structure of these groups facilitates a variety of illicit activities on legal markets. Furthermore, they draw attention to the tacit or explicit support of the population and important economic and political actors. Whereas Gambetta favors a more "benevolent" interpretation (Mafia groups providing a service), Paoli traces Mafia power positions back to culture, history, and politics, and clearly interprets Mafia control as a "social bad" (yet hard to get rid of, as it also serves powerful interests).

In my view, one of the strong aspects of protection theory is that it interprets place on a higher level: as control over a territory, normally in the hands of a strong, legitimate state. This means that in the absence of a strong, legitimate state, organized crime groups can take over the control of territories and sectors and neutralize formal and informal social control. Or even worse: refocus informal social control and guardianship from preventing to promoting illicit activities. Organized crime research shows that Mafia control can relate to regions and business sectors or to smaller villages or neighborhoods, but varies and is not evenly spread (for examples, see, e.g., Varese 2014; Bruinsma 2015). In all cases, however, formal and informal social control serves the power structure promoting illicit activities instead of preventing them.

An interesting recent example relates to worldwide opium production. Unlike producing coca leaves (which requires quite specific conditions), opium can be produced in many areas all over the world. Nevertheless, opium production is geographically highly concentrated in only a few countries, characterized to a large extent by weak states and "lax law enforcement" (Paoli, Greenfield, and Reuter 2009). Being left alone by the government and by law enforcement, therefore, is an important prerequisite for the emergence and endurance of organized crime groups and related activities. In some cases, organized crime groups take over state control and serve as an "alternative government," but also in other cases a focus on power structures (and "governance") in territories and economic sectors might help explain the opportunities for organized crime groups and the limitations of formal and informal control and guardianship.

Compared to the discussion about opportunistic street-level crime, the dominant focus of contemporary environmental criminology, three things are different. First, place is interpreted as "territory" and goes beyond a specific point in space where an offender meets a target. Second, control by Mafia groups and the absence of government control and law enforcement are the main issues. Third, the idea of guardianship and informal and formal control is reversed: the power structure facilitates illicit activities instead of preventing them.

37.3 Transit Crime

Mafia control is an interesting theoretical topic, and there are clear empirical examples of Mafia control in particular countries in particular periods in history (see for a review, e.g., Varese 2014). However, the empirical reality in many modern Western industrialized countries is that organized crime as Mafia control is the exception rather than the rule.[1] In terms of economic profits, "transit crime" gives a much better description of the activities of organized crime groups in many Western European countries: criminal groups are primarily involved in illegal international trade, using the same opportunity structure that facilitates legal activities (Kleemans 2007, p. 176). In a review of organized crime in the Netherlands, a prime example of a transit economy, Kleemans (2007) argues that the major business of organized crime groups boils down to international smuggling activities: drug trafficking, smuggling illegal immigrants, human trafficking for sexual exploitation, arms trafficking, trafficking in stolen vehicles, and other transnational illegal activities, such as money laundering and evasion of taxes (e.g., cigarette smuggling, value-added tax fraud, and European Community fraud).

The concept of "transit crime," as opposed to racketeering and Mafia control, is very relevant to the study of organized crime and environmental criminology. It refocuses attention from "place" to "borders": links between places as well as between people living in different countries. It is not the coca farmer in Colombia who earns most of the illicit profits, but the highest profits are made by the people who are able to import cocaine into the major consumer markets in the United States and Western Europe (Reuter 2014). An important finding of organized crime research relates to brokerage. Because transnational trafficking activities often involve high potential financial gains as well as high risks (due to seizures, arrests, and rip-offs), social ties play a crucial role in the functioning of criminal networks (Kleemans and Van de Bunt 1999). However, social ties are clustered and related to social and geographical proximity. This means that social networks contain "structural holes" (Burt 2005), particularly between different countries, different ethnic groups, and the underworld and the licit world. As few people can bridge these structural holes and transnational criminal activities require a high level of trust, offenders who can bridge these structural holes have all kinds of strategic opportunities to make a profit: They are the ones who make the connections between networks that would otherwise have remained apart. Because trust is so important, these connections are often based on family ties or other strong social bonds (Kleemans 2007, pp. 179–180).

Due to the importance of trust and the relatively high level of social organization that is required for transnational criminal activities, the study of organized crime cannot neglect the structure of social ties facilitating these activities. A good example is the prime position of the Netherlands as a transit country for drugs in Europe. On the one hand, this can be explained by the transit character of the Dutch economy and its excellent facilities, including harbors in Rotterdam and Antwerp (Belgium) and a large transit airport (see below). On the other hand, an important explanatory factor relates to social ties created by migration: the major immigrant groups in the 1960s and 1970s originated from drug-producing or exporting countries such as Suriname, the former Netherlands Antilles, Morocco, and Turkey (Fijnaut et al. 1998, pp. 83–87). This created social and economic links to cocaine-exporting countries (Southern America), cannabis-exporting countries (Morocco), and transit countries for heroin (Turkey). This "social" aspect of a country's opportunity structure for transnational illegal activities is also visible in migrant smuggling. Human smugglers have often been smuggled themselves and have relationships with destination countries as well as with countries of origin, whereas smuggled migrants want to migrate to countries where family and/or larger communities are present.

Opportunities for transit crime, therefore, have both social and more physical aspects. The social opportunity structure relates to links between people: criminal organizations or criminal networks linking specific persons in different countries. Without such links and such social organization, the transnational criminal activities are difficult to execute, whereas existing links may foster new streams of illegal goods and people. When researchers fail to take into account existing social ties and existing criminal networks, explanations for transnational criminal activities run the risk of only highlighting comparative advantages and opportunities that are never fully realized, because the social ties between people who would have to realize this potential have never been there in the first place.

Research on "borders" and "border crossing" (instead of place and the journey to crime) may also focus on the licit opportunity structure. An interesting early example is the comparison of drug prices in several European countries by Farrell (1998), concluding that (low) drug prices are closely related to licit transportation flows through certain logistical nodes in Europe.

This brings us also to the point that crossing borders and evading customs and other controlling agencies have physical, social, and economic aspects. Some people are allowed to cross borders without restrictions, whereas other people are more intensively checked when crossing borders. The same applies to particular economic goods being transited from one country to another. The modus operandi of smugglers, regardless of whether we are talking about people, drugs, or other goods, is closely related to the legal possibilities of crossing borders, including loopholes. Drugs are often smuggled alongside licit cargo (without being noticed) or in cargo that is difficult to check, or where checks are very labor intensive or economically infeasible (e.g., fresh goods that have to be moved quickly such as fruit, meat, fish, flowers, et cetera). Similarly, people smuggling often involves "regular channels": entering as a legal citizen (using false documents), (fake) marriage, visas for students, scholars, or tourists, business invitations, and so on (for a review, see, e.g., Zhang 2007).

The parallel with routine activity theory stands out, as illicit activity feeds off licit activities and the opportunity structure that is created by licit activities and licit actors.

Empirical research could take into account findings from environmental criminology and focus on transnational flows and the connections between particular countries. Furthermore, particular techniques (such as graph theory) could also be used when analyzing these new issues (similar to the analysis of street networks by using graph theory). In this respect, an important missing link is empirical research into central logistical nodes such as airports and harbors. Street segments and "pockets of crime" have been investigated in great detail, but important logistical nodes such as airports and harbors have largely been neglected by criminologists. This is problematic, as border crossing takes on many forms: at airports, passengers, luggage, cargo, catering, waste, and facilitating personnel goes into and out of "landside" and "airside" zones on a massive scale and on a daily basis, but empirical criminological research into these processes and accompanying security problems is largely nonexistent. Furthermore, government agencies such as customs and border police are relatively small players in a field consisting of many private companies and private security companies. This makes central logistical nodes such as airports and harbors very interesting new empirical themes for environmental criminology.

For situational crime prevention, transit crime creates three types of problems (Kleemans, Soudijn, and Weenink 2010, pp. 31–32). First many transit crime problems are "hidden" problems: If flows of passengers, luggage, or cargo are not checked systematically, smuggling flows go unnoticed or may be disregarded as a minor problem. Second, there is often a difference between the countries that would have to take security measures and the countries suffering the consequences. Exporting countries and transit countries typically are well positioned to play a crucial role in preventing smuggling, but often have a much smaller interest in preventing these activities than the receiving countries (of, e.g., smuggled passengers and illegal goods). The very nature of illegal cross-border activities thus creates political tensions between different countries with different interests. Finally, there is the difficult trade-off between security interests and economic interests. A free flow of goods and people serves economic interests, and balancing these interests with adequate border controls is a very real problem for open Western economies. At airports and in harbors, this difficult trade-off is aggravated by the fact that private companies and private security companies reign supreme in these logistical nodes, creating problems of collective action, coordination, or outright defection (as strict controls, except for, e.g., explosives, involve high costs and low benefits for some private partners).

37.4 Local Markets of Illegal Goods and Services

Local markets of illegal goods and services have been studied intensively by various scholars, as access to these types of markets is easier than getting access to detailed information on transnational criminal activities. A landmark study is Reuter's analysis of specific local illegal markets such as gambling, numbers, and loansharking (Reuter 1983). In his book *Disorganized Crime*, Reuter argues that most criminal enterprises will be small and ephemeral, as offenders have to deal with various constraints of illegality: illegal activities have to be concealed, people can be arrested, and assets can be seized at any time.

Later studies often focused on local drug markets (for recent examples see, e.g., Bernasco and Jacques 2015; Piza and Sytsma 2016),[2] with a strong focus on "open air" drug markets. In many Western European countries, specific recent ethnic immigrant groups dominate the trade in open-air drug markets, whereas native offenders are more prevalent in other major sectors of the drugs market, most notably those for cannabis and synthetic drugs, including production, importation, and exportation, and indoor drug markets (Paoli and Reuter 2008). However, the major focus of criminological research is on visible and accessible open-air drug markets and street dealing.

Seminal work on the geographic analysis of illegal drug markets has been done by Eck (1995), Rengert et al. (2000), and Rengert, Ratcliffe, and Chakravorty (2005). Many studies reflect theoretical notions spelled out by John Eck (1995) in his general model of the geography of illicit retail marketplaces. The basic idea is that sellers and buyers of illicit goods and services have to find ways to meet each other. One strategy is to use social networks, by selling only to people you know or to related people being introduced through social networks. This is relatively safe but restricts the number of potential customers. A different, more risky strategy is to sell to strangers, but meeting and trading in a safe way with strangers is a complicated task. Eck (1995, pp. 74–76) describes three problems. First, sellers and buyers cannot rely on a network for communication, so they have to use routine activities and meet in places in which both already conduct licit routine activities. Therefore, these places

> will be located along major thoroughfares and at nodes of major activities, such as shopping centers, places of employment, recreation areas or schools. In short, illicit retail market areas where stranger-to-stranger selling takes place are likely to be near where people naturally concentrate. (Eck 1995, p. 75)

Second, security is a major problem, as strangers have to identify each other as potential buyers and sellers and face difficulties identifying and locating each other. Third, they often need the help of place managers to turn a blind eye, tolerate, or facilitate their behavior. According to Eck, this leads to four geographical characteristics: high place attachment, the involvement of place managers, distribution along arterial routes and near nodes of high licit activities, and high density of the illicit marketplace (as they can serve many people).

In a recent study, Bernasco and Jacques (2015) add two important concepts from recent literature on retail geography: multipurpose shopping and comparison shopping. Multipurpose shopping means that customers' trips often serve multiple purposes. Comparison shopping refers to the finding that customers often want to compare multiple retailers, which means that retailers often locate in the proximity of competitors. The empirical study provides evidence that dealers go to places where the likelihood of successfully soliciting customers is high, but no evidence is found that they avoid places with informal and formal social control.

Piza and Sytsma (2016, pp. 40–42) explore the defensive actions of drug sellers in open-air markets: the use of partners in drug transactions (co-offenders, lookouts, or stashers of drugs or money), particular transactional mediation schemes (to obscure the occurrence of the transaction), conducting different phases of the transaction at different places, the use of stash spots (for drugs, guns, or money), and raising or slowing down the speed at which transactions occur. In the empirical study, dealers mainly turn out to work alone (90% of all transactions) and only involve partners (mostly runners) during the evening. Many defensive actions are related to geographic settings (commercial versus mixed residential settings) and time of day (daytime versus evening), but transactions were most often observed to occur immediately and lacked any mobility by the participants. Virtually no transactional schemes and stashes were used: sellers often held the drugs in an easily accessible place on their person (particularly when operating in a commercial setting) and in a minority of transactions they used an off-person stash (particularly in mixed residential settings).

All in all, the empirical study, similar to other studies, largely focuses on transactions on the spot between a seller and a buyer. It is important to note that such lower-level drug distribution by drug sellers is often studied, but in many countries falls outside of the official definitions of organized crime (see for a review, e.g., Paoli and Vander Beken 2014). Many definitions require cooperation between two, three, or more offenders over a prolonged period as well as criminal activities with substantial social harm (often meaning transnational drug trafficking and medium-level distribution of drugs instead of retail distribution by individual sellers). That means that most of the empirical work that has been done by researchers from the field of environmental criminology (i.e., on the geography of drug dealing) would not qualify in many countries as research into organized crime. However, a lot can be learned from these studies regarding criminal activities (rather than criminal cooperation).

37.5 Places and the Role of the (Built) Environment

MacDonald (2015) reviews the literature on the impact of housing and the built environment on crime. It is striking that the reviewed studies mainly focus on predatory crime and public nuisance and that organized crime is largely absent, except for lower-level drug dealing. This is not because organized crime activities do not depend on the built environment. For cannabis cultivation, for example, offenders need property (attics, cellars, sheds, [rented] commercial properties) to grow, harvest, dry, and parcel out cannabis; sellers of cuttings; wholesale cannabis buyers; and service providers such as electricians or "grow room builders" (Spapens, Van de Bunt, and Rastovac 2007; Decorte, Potter, and Bouchard 2011). The physical and social environment is critical for the successful operation of these illicit activities.

In a review of the importance of the environment for organized crime activities such as drug trafficking, human smuggling, human trafficking, money laundering, and various forms of organized fraud, Kruisbergen, Van de Bunt, and Kleemans (2012, pp. 81–228) describe extensively how the environment facilitates organized crime and how offenders depend on facilitating environments. For each type of criminal activity, logistical requirements can be formulated, and how the environment enables criminal collaboration and criminal activities can be described.

Two things stand out compared to more traditional topics in environmental criminology. First, the facilitating environment comprises physical, social, economic, and even political factors. All these factors go beyond the individual rational actor. Social relationships with other persons are very important for access to co-offenders, lawyers, notaries public, financial advisors, employees of airports, harbors, or government agencies. Furthermore, legal entities and companies are important for combining legal and illegal activities or for getting access to other companies. Offender behavior in organized crime does not only naturally involve co-offending, but also combines social relationships with the opportunities created by institutional arrangements (legal entities and companies). Finally, whole subcultural or ethnic communities or economic sectors may be more or less supportive for carrying out certain illicit activities. This is important, as organized crime activities often involve prolonged co-operation in criminal activities that can be noticed by law enforcement and the immediate social environment. Shielding activities from formal and informal social control, therefore, is the heart of the matter. In environmental criminology, the wider social, economic, and sometimes political aspects of the physical environment are often disregarded.[3] When studying organized crime, it is unwise to disregard these salient factors.

Second, many organized crime activities have a "glocal" character (Hobbs 1998). Illicit activities are both transnational in character and locally rooted in cities, neighborhoods, and economic sectors. Offenders are located in neighborhoods and economic sectors, search for suitable co-offenders, organize their activities, and invest their illicit proceeds in specific locations and economic activities. It is striking that Italian Mafia groups do not invest in sectors with the highest economic profitability. On the contrary, control of the territory seems to explain their investment behavior better than economic factors (Savona 2015). Furthermore, offenders in Dutch organized crime cases primarily invest in their countries of origin and economic sectors familiar to them: proximity explains their investment behavior better than power or profit motives (Kruisbergen, Kleemans, and Kouwenberg 2015). Although the "glocal" character of organized crime is straightforward, research often focuses either on the transnational aspects of organized crime (disregarding the concentration of co-offenders and illegal activities in particular places) or on the lower end of local distribution markets of illegal goods and services.

37.6 Theoretical Progress on Organized Crime and Places

Environmental criminology has a lot to offer for the study of organized crime and places. However, the full potential of environmental criminology can only be realized if "place" is conceptualized in a different way and on a higher level than a specific point in space where an offender meets a target. Also for predatory crime, much progress has been made by including empirical research into offender behavior (e.g., the journey to crime and offender decision-making processes), the distribution in space of potential offenders (including the influence of housing), and routine activities of offenders and victims (influencing the interactions of motivated offenders and suitable targets in space and time in the absence of capable guardians). For organized crime, we need to go one step further and take co-offending seriously. As organized crime often requires a higher degree of social organization than opportunistic street-level crime, I will elaborate on two theoretical concepts that should be included in the study of organized crime and place: social opportunity structure and offender convergence settings. Without including these concepts, researchers run the risk of missing the main driving mechanisms behind the emergence and activities of criminal networks at specific places.

37.6.1 Social Opportunity Structure

For certain types of predatory crime, such as burglary, robbery, or theft, opportunities are ubiquitous and open to everyone. For organized crime, and particularly transnational criminal activities, opportunities are only there for individuals with the right connections who are able to organize successful cooperation—often over a longer period of time—to seize these opportunities. For explaining organized crime, therefore, it is important to focus not only on the physical opportunity structure, but also on the social opportunity structure, a concept coined by Kleemans and De Poot (2008) and defined as "social ties providing access to profitable criminal activities" (p. 75). Social opportunity structure can not only explain the development of individual criminal careers but also be combined with topics such as crime script analysis and the connection between crime and place. The fact that people operate within criminal networks means that the continuity and flexibility in the execution of criminal activities are enhanced. Depending on their criminal network contacts, offenders have access to co-offenders and alternative ways to organize specific criminal activities. Morselli and Roy (2008) combine this idea with crime script analysis and point out that nodes in networks create permutations to crime scripts, which means that there are alternative ways of carrying out specific criminal activities. Conversely, isolated offenders will never be able to organize these criminal activities.

For crime and place, regardless whether we are talking about racketeering, transit crime, or local markets of illegal goods and services, it is important to focus also on *the geographical structure of criminal networks and criminal ties*. For racketeering, it is important that a strong, geographically isolated social network is already there and that legitimate government and law enforcement are absent, creating the opportunity for criminals to build a power structure, based on social contacts, economic interests, and political interests. The best situation to achieve this is relative isolation, in a social, economic, and political sense. In his book *Mafias on the Move*, Varese (2011) describes situations conducive to Mafia control, for example, a small, isolated village with a relatively isolated and monoculture economy, versus situations in which Mafia control fails, for example, a much larger city in which various economic actors operate on interregional or international markets (having no interest in "protection" as well as many possibilities to evade Mafia control).

For transit crime, the social and economic links between particular countries are important, as criminal networks are built upon existing social relationships and criminal activities are facilitated by licit flows of goods and people between countries. It explains why most cocaine to Europe is shipped through Spain (with its historical social and economic links to South America) and the Netherlands (with its links to Suriname and the former Dutch Antilles as well as the ports of Rotterdam and Antwerp [Belgium]). It also explains human smuggling routes, as states with social and economic bonds often ease travel and trade restrictions and create more opportunities for licit and illicit flows of goods and people. Important examples are travel options between (former) Communist countries such as China, Russia, and Eastern European countries, and changes in human smuggling and heroin-trafficking routes after the end of the Cold War and the new membership of former Communist countries of the European Union.

Finally, for local markets of illegal goods and services, social ties are also important, if we focus on the connections between transnational criminal activities and the local infrastructure or distribution through social networks. For open-air drug markets, it seems less relevant or perhaps only for shielding activities from law enforcement, through good contacts with other dealers and place managers. However, for more elaborate structures, such as local cannabis cultivation and distribution, it is clear that social ties are also important for getting access to co-offenders, enablers, and different locations that are necessary for carrying out these criminal activities.

37.6.2 Offender Convergence Settings

For organized crime, existing social ties are very important, but not all necessary capabilities can be found in existing relationships, and for successful criminal activities, networks need to be expanded. Therefore, introductions by existing contacts to third parties are vital, and this draws attention to the places where offenders spend their social and professional life. Felson (2006) coined the term "offender convergence setting" and explained it with the example of the tough bar where offenders can meet potential co-offenders and which allows criminal cooperation to persist even when the particular persons vary. Such offender convergence settings enhance the durability of offender networks and create a source for new potential recruits (Felson 2006, pp. 97–99; Kleemans and Van de Bunt 2008).

For organized crime, we have to look beyond the tough bar and include several aspects of social life: meeting places in neighborhoods, nightlife, entertainment districts, and leisure activities (e.g., shooting and motorcycle clubs). However, the idea of offender convergence settings can also be extended to professional life and work settings.

There are different ways in which occupations may present opportunities for committing organized crime: first, through international contacts and travel movements. Contacts with other countries and other social groups provide ample opportunity to discover and act on certain opportunities for (transit) crime. Examples are occupations involving mobility, transport, and logistics. Second, individual freedom of movement and/or discretion is important. This explains the involvement of directors of (small) businesses, independent professionals, and, in some cases, individuals with relative autonomy in larger organizations, such as companies and banks. More trust and autonomy means more opportunity for abuse as well. Third, the social nature of certain occupations is important. Occupations in which people often meet with different people also present many opportunities for encounters with potential co-offenders (Kleemans and Van de Bunt 2008, p. 195).

Due to the thin line between licit and illicit activities, the concept of offender convergence settings should be extended from the tough bar (in which known criminals meet) to salient offender convergence settings in social and professional life. It is important to note that these settings need not only be "place based," as they follow the logic of social relationships and shared activities. For transnational crime, it means that these settings often transcend borders (e.g., transnational licit activities and connected professional settings) or are connected to international logistical nodes such as airports and harbors. For more local aspects of organized crime, offender convergence settings may be "place based" and typically lack formal guardianship or even reverse the mechanisms of guardianship when criminal activities are protected rather than prevented. Examples described by Huisman and Jansen (2012) include trailer camp communities and outlaw motorcycle gangs. In such areas and/or communities, it is easy to find co-offenders, use the "criminal infrastructure," and shield criminal activities from the authorities.

37.7 Conclusion

This chapter described the connection between organized crime and places for three types of organized crime: racketeering, transit crime, and the local provision of illegal goods and services. Place turns out to have a different meaning for these three types of organized crime and raises several theoretical challenges. As these types of organized crime often require a higher degree of social organization than opportunistic street-level crime, two theoretical concepts should be included in the study of organized crime and place: social opportunity structure and offender convergence settings. Without including these concepts, researchers run the risk of missing the main driving mechanisms behind the emergence and activities of criminal networks at specific places. Furthermore, the full potential of environmental criminology can only be realized if "place" is conceptualized in a different way and on a higher level than a specific point in space where an offender meets a target.

Notes

1. Campana (2011) describes how Mafia groups may change their modus operandi across territories and different contexts: being involved in protection rackets in their territory of origin, while behaving just like any other actor in other places.
2. Because of space limits, I do not go into the study of street and window prostitution. For a review of research into e.g., the social ecology of Red-Light Districts, see Weitzer (2014), and for a review of criminogenic aspects and relationships with organized crime, see Kleemans and Huisman (2015).
3. For certain types of crime and offender behavior this is not problematic. Furthermore, studies on criminogenic environments and 'gentrification' often include these aspects.

References

Bernasco, Wim, and Jacques, Scott. 2015. "Where Do Dealers Solicit Customers and Sell Them Drugs? A Micro-level Multiple Method Study." *Journal of Contemporary Criminal Justice* 31(4): 376–408.

Bouloukos, Adam C., Farrell, Graham, and Laycock, Gloria. 2003. "Transnational Organised Crime in Europe and North America: The Need for Situational Crime Prevention Efforts." In *Crime and Criminal Justice in Europe and North America 1995–1997: Report on the Sixth United Nations Survey on Crime Trends and Criminal Justice Systems*, edited by K. Aromaa, S. Leppä, S. Nevala, and N. Ollus, 176–192. Helsinki: HEUNI.

Bruinsma, Gerben J. N. 2015. *Histories of Transnational Crime*. Springer: New York.

Bullock, Karen, Clarke, Ron V., and Tilley, Nick (eds.). 2010. *Situational Prevention of Organised Crimes*. Cullompton, Devon, UK: Willan Publishing.

Burt, Ronald S. 2005. *Brokerage and Closure: An Introduction to Social Capital*. Oxford: Oxford University Press.

Campana, Paolo. 2011. "Eavesdropping on the Mob: The Functional Diversification of Mafia Activities across Territories." *European Journal of Criminology* 8(3): 213–228.

Cornish, Derek B., and Clarke, Ronald V. 2002. "Analyzing Organized Crimes." In *Rational Choice and Criminal Behavior: Recent Research and Future Challenges*, edited by A. R. Piquero and S. G. Tibbetts, 41–64. New York: Garland.

Decorte, Tom, Potter, Gary, and Bouchard, Martin (eds.). 2011. *World Wide Weed: Global Trends in Cannabis Cultivation and Its Control*. Farnham, UK: Ashgate.

Eck, John E. 1995. "A General Model of the Geography of Illicit Retail Marketplaces." In *Crime and Place*, edited by J. Eck and D. Weisburd, 67–93. Monsey, NY: Criminal Justice Press.

Farrell, Graham. 1998. "Routine Activities and Drug Trafficking: The Case of the Netherlands." *International Journal of Drug Policy* 9: 21–32.

Felson, Marcus. 2006. *Crime and Nature*. Thousand Oaks, CA: Sage.

Fijnaut, Cyrille, Bovenkerk, Frank, Bruinsma, Gerben J. N., and Van de Bunt, Henk. 1998. *Organized Crime in the Netherlands*. Boston: Kluwer Law International.

Gàmbetta, Diego. 1993. *The Sicilian Mafia*. Cambridge, MA: Harvard University Press.

Hobbs, Dick. 1998. "Going Down the Glocal: The Local Context of Organized Crime." *Howard Journal of Crime and Justice* 37(4): 407–422.

Huisman, Sander, and Jansen, Floor. 2012. "Willing Offenders Outwitting Capable Guardians." *Trends in Organized Crime* 15(2–3): 93–110.

Jacobs, Jacob B. 1999. *Gotham Unbound: How New York City Was Liberated from the Grip of Organized Crime*. New York: New York University Press.

Kleemans, Edward R. 2007. "Organized Crime, Transit Crime, and Racketeering." In *Crime and Justice in the Netherlands. Crime and Justice*, vol. 35, edited by M. Tonry and C. Bijleveld, 163–215. Chicago: University of Chicago Press.

Kleemans, Edward R. 2014. "Theoretical Perspectives on Organized Crime." In *Oxford Handbook of Organized Crime*, edited by L. Paoli, 32–52. Oxford: Oxford University Press.

Kleemans, Edward R. 2015. "Criminal Organization and Transnational Crime." In *Histories of Transnational Crime*, edited by G. J. N. Bruinsma, 171–185. Springer: New York.

Kleemans, Edward R., and De Poot, Christianne J. 2008. "Criminal Careers and Social Opportunity Structure." *European Journal of Criminology* 5(1): 69–98.

Kleemans, Edward R., and Huisman, Wim. 2015. "Multi-agency Approaches in 'Criminogenic' Settings: The Case of the Amsterdam Red Light District." *Crime, Law and Social Change* 64 (4–5): 247–261.

Kleemans, Edward R., and Soudijn, Melvin R. J. 2017. "Organised Crime." In *Handbook of Crime Prevention and Community Safety*, edited by N. Tilley and A. Sidebottom, 394–406. Cullompton, Devon, UK: Willan Publishing.

Kleemans, Edward R., Soudijn, Melvin R. J., and Weenink, Anton. 2010. "Situational Crime Prevention and Cross-Border Crime." In *Situational Prevention of Organised Crimes*, edited by K. Bullock, R. V. Clarke, and N. Tilley, 17–32. Cullompton, Devon, UK: Willan Publishing.

Kleemans, Edward R., Soudijn, Melvin R. J., and Weenink, Anton W. 2012. "Organized Crime, Situational Crime Prevention and Routine Activity Theory." *Trends in Organized Crime* 15(2–3): 87–92.

Kleemans, Edward R., and Van de Bunt, Henk G. 1999. "The Social Embeddedness of Organized Crime." *Transnational Organized Crime* 5(1): 19–36.

Kleemans, Edward R., and Van de Bunt, Henk G. 2008. "Organised Crime, Occupations and Opportunity." *Global Crime* 9(3): 185–197.

Kruisbergen, Edwin W., Kleemans, Edward R., and Kouwenberg, Ruud F. 2015. "Profitability, Power, or Proximity? Organized Crime Offenders Investing Their Money in Legal Economy." *European Journal on Criminal Policy and Research* 21(2): 237–256.

Kruisbergen, Edwin W., Van de Bunt, Henk G., and Kleemans, Edward R. 2012. *Georganiseerde criminaliteit in Nederland: Vierde rapportage op basis van de Monitor Georganiseerde Criminaliteit*. The Hague: Boom Lemma Uitgevers.

Levi, Michael, and Maguire, Mike. 2004. "Reducing and Preventing Organized Crime: An Evidence-Based Critique." *Crime, Law and Social Change* 41(5): 397–469.

MacDonald, John. 2015. "Community Design and Crime: The Impact of Housing and the Built Environment." *Crime and Justice* 44: 333–383.

Morselli, Carlo, and Roy, Julie. 2008. "Brokerage Qualifications in Ringing Operations." *Criminology* 46(1): 71–98.

Paoli, Letizia. 2003. *Mafia Brotherhoods: Organized Crime, Italian Style*. New York: Oxford University Press.

Paoli, Letizia, Greenfield, Victoria A., and Reuter, Peter. 2009. *The World Heroin Market: Can Supply Be Cut?* Oxford: Oxford University Press.

Paoli, Letizia, and Reuter, Peter. 2008. "Drug Trafficking and Ethnic Minorities in Western Europe." *European Journal of Criminology* 5(1): 13–37.

Paoli, Letizia, and Vander Beken, Tom. 2014. "Organized Crime: A Contested Concept." In *Oxford Handbook of Organized Crime*, edited by L. Paoli, 13–31. Oxford: Oxford University Press.

Piza, Eric L., and Sytsma, Victoria A. 2016. "Exploring the Defensive Actions of Drug Sellers in Open-Air Markets: A Systematic Social Observation." *Journal of Research in Crime and Delinquency* 53(1): 36–65.

Rengert, George F., Chakravorty, Sanjoy, Bole, Tom, and Henderson, Kristin. 2000. "A Geographic Analysis of Illegal Drug Markets." In *Illegal Drug Markets: From Research to Prevention Policy*, edited by M. Natarajan and M. Hough, 219–239, vol. 11 of *Crime Prevention Studies*. Monsey, NY: Criminal Justice Press.

Rengert, George F., Ratcliffe, Jerry, and Chakravorty, Sanjoy. 2005. *Policing Illegal Drug Markets: Geographic Approaches to Crime Reduction*. Monsey, NY: Criminal Justice Press.

Reuter, Peter. 1983. *Disorganized Crime: Illegal Markets and the Mafia*. Cambridge, MA: MIT Press.

Reuter, Peter. 2014. "Drug Markets and Organized Crime." In *Oxford Handbook of Organized Crime*, edited by L. Paoli, 359–380. Oxford: Oxford University Press.

Savona, Ernesto U. 2015. "The Businesses of Italian Mafias." *European Journal on Criminal Policy and Research* 21(2): 217–236.

Spapens, A. C. M., Van de Bunt, H. G., and Rastovac, L. 2007. *De wereld achter de wietteelt*. The Hague: Boom Juridische Uitgevers.

Van de Bunt, Henk G., and Van der Schoot, Cathelijne R. A. 2003. *Prevention of Organised Crime: A Situational Approach*. Onderzoek en Beleid No. 215. The Hague: WODC.

Van der Schoot, Cathelijne R. A. 2006. *Organised Crime Prevention in the Netherlands: Exposing the Effectiveness of Preventive Measures*. PhD dissertation, Erasmus Universiteit Rotterdam.

Varese, Federico. 2011. *Mafias on the Move*. Princeton, NJ: Princeton University Press.

Varese, Federico. 2014. "Protection and Extortion." In *Oxford Handbook of Organized Crime*, edited by L. Paoli, 343–358. Oxford: Oxford University Press.

Von Lampe, Klaus. 2006. "The Interdisciplinary Dimensions of the Study of Organized Crime." *Trends in Organized Crime* 9(3): 77–95.

Von Lampe, Klaus. 2011. "The Application of the Framework of Situational Crime Prevention to 'Organized Crime.'" *Criminology and Criminal Justice* 11(2): 145–163.

Weitzer, Ronald. 2014. "The Social Ecology of Red-Light Districts: A Comparison of Antwerp and Brussels." *Urban Affairs Review* 50(5): 702–730.

Zhang, Sheldon X. 2007. *Smuggling and Trafficking in Human Beings: All Roads Lead to America*. Westport, CT: Praeger.

CHAPTER 38

CYBERCRIME AND PLACE

Applying Environmental Criminology to Crimes in Cyberspace

FERNANDO MIRÓ LLINARES
AND SHANE D. JOHNSON

38.1 Introduction: "Crime and Place" Meets Cybercrime

In terms of technology and our interaction with it, we are in a period of rapid change. In fact, so many technological changes have occurred recently that social scientists are practically required to analyze and understand their impact on society on-the-go. We are only really just beginning to understand how information technologies (ITs) are changing society, but already we have to attempt to identify and understand (among other things) the opportunities for offending they may create. When researching new forms of offending it is important to embrace different perspectives and what they might offer in terms of explaining the phenomenon of interest. Equally important, however, is the need to exercise appropriate caution when applying to one form of offending the concepts and ideas developed to explain a different form. This chapter focuses on crime facilitated by the Internet and how theories of environmental criminology might inform our understanding of these types of crimes.

Cybercriminality has received some but only limited attention from environmental criminologists (e.g., Newman and Clarke 2003; Reyns 2010; Miró 2011). This could be due to the relative recency of this type of offending, which is constantly evolving, or it may be due to difficulties (real or perceived) associated with obtaining the data necessary to study it. Alternatively, it may be due to hastily formed perceptions that an approach centered, as it is, on crime at places would have limited utility in explaining cybercrime or informing solutions intended to prevent it. Consequently, the aim of this chapter is to discuss how environmental criminology can be applied to this form of crime. The intention is to provide a balanced view that identifies the ways in which the environmental criminology perspective is compatible with cybercrime, and where—as currently conceived at least—it is not. A key point of compatibility to raise from the outset is that theories of environmental criminology tend not to focus on criminals—or at least not what motivates them to offend—but on the criminal event, and how characteristics of the environment (settings or places) can make crime more or less likely. As will be discussed in more detail below, cyberspace can be conceptualized as just another space, the configuration of which affects how people (or computers) interact, and how likely it is that the necessary ingredients for a crime to occur will converge. From such a perspective, it seems sensible to suggest that advantage can be taken of what has been learned about how physical spaces shape the likelihood for these convergences when attempting to understand cybercrime.

The chapter is organized as follows. In Section 38.2, we discuss the concept of cybercrime and how—like crime in urban environments—there are different types of offending and opportunities. The aim is to delineate what is considered cybercrime in what follows. Section 38.3 considers the architecture of cyberspace and how it differs from physical spaces. In particular, thought is given to how concepts of time and space differ across the two environments, and why it is necessary to rethink or adapt models of environmental criminology to understand crimes in cyberspace. In Section 38.4, attention is given to some of the criminal opportunities afforded by the configuration of the Internet and how it is used. Finally, in Section 38.5 conclusions are drawn, and (some) policy implications that follow from an environmental criminology approach to cybercrime are discussed.

38.2 What Do We Mean by Cybercrime?

To assess the potential contribution that environmental criminologists might make to our understanding of cybercrime, it is first necessary to define the types and classes of events to which we are referring when we speak of cybercrimes. As with many phenomena, there is no universally accepted definition of what cybercrime is. However, disagreements about the definition of cybercrime are, in truth, disagreements about the extent of what is included in the category (Miró 2011). Some authors prefer to use the term "Internet-related crimes" or "e-crimes," allowing for the inclusion of any crime in which information technologies (ITs) are used, even though those crimes may be perpetrated in physical space. Arguably, such a definition is so extensive that it becomes dysfunctional. For example, it would include offenses where a burglar searches for a specific home address using the Internet, or when an offender sends a message to an accomplice using a messaging service. The term *cybercrime* (used hereafter) itself has a more narrow definition and refers to criminal events that, while they may be initiated in the real world, could not take place in the absence of cyberspace. As such, cybercrime covers all crimes committed through the social intercommunication media that is the Internet (Miró 2012). For example, while crimes such as cyber harassment, the spreading of malware, or the sale of illicit drugs on the Dark Web (see below) may be initiated by an offender at one physical location and affect a victim located at another, the convergence setting in which the offender and victim interact is not a physical location, but a digital environment created by ITs.

Just like urban crime, cybercrime is not homogeneous, but instead encompasses many distinct crime types (Wall 2007). A core tenet of situational crime prevention (e.g., Felson and Boba 2010) and environmental criminology more broadly is that different mechanisms and facilitating conditions are at play for different types of crime, and that studying these is essential for understanding a particular type of crime and preventing it. Ignoring heterogeneity in the different forms cybercrime can take would thus be misleading and would limit understanding of such offenses. On a related note, the failure to recognize this, or to be explicit about it, can encourage another fallacy—that cybercrime is always a complicated and technical form of delinquency—as complex in its execution as in its prevention (Miró 2015). In truth, while some forms of cybercrime (e.g., computer hacking) are very sophisticated and may require access to specific forms of IT, much offending (e.g., cyberbullying) is not. Instead, many forms of cybercrime can be committed using smartphones or other commonly available devices, and can require technical knowledge no more complicated than being able to communicate using IT.[1]

It is not the intention of the chapter to describe every form of cybercrime, or to present a typology, but it is important to provide some indication of the variety in both broad and more specific terms. Economic crimes include fraud, which may be committed through various means, such as phishing and pharming, as well as cyber money laundering or cyber extortion. Social cybercriminality encompasses criminal acts that traditionally have been perpetrated in physical space, that can now be committed through social networks online and other spaces of personal communication on the Internet. Specific offenses of this kind include cyberbullying (e.g., Hinduja and Patchin 2014), cyberstalking (e.g., Bocij 2004), and Internet sexual crimes (e.g., Miró 2013). Other crimes may be committed to achieve ideological objectives, for example, criminal cyber activism (e.g., Illia 2002; Hampson 2012) and cyberterrorism (e.g., Macdonald, Jarvis, and Chen 2013).

A key point then is that just like urban crime, there are many varieties of cybercrime. In what follows, the intention is to provide a broad conceptual vision of how the environmental criminology perspective can inform understanding of cybercrime, focusing mostly on forms of cybercrime that affect regular citizens (as opposed to denial-of-service attacks, for example, which are more spectacular in their effect and reach). In doing so, it will be necessary to talk about cybercrime in general terms, but it is important for the reader to remember that the empirical investigation of specific types of cybercrime is likely to yield more insight than is a general investigation of this type of offending.

38.3 The Architecture of Cyberspace as a New Environment Where Cybercrime Happens

When considering the contribution that environmental criminology might make to understanding cybercrime, it is important to recognize that cyberspace and physical spaces differ in a number of important ways. As a consequence, it may be necessary to rethink some of the concepts and paradigms of environmental criminology to understand crime in this space. Some of these differences are discussed in this section.

ITs, particularly the Internet as a global network, are technological tools that facilitate communication between people and computers. Their increasing popularity, the development of online social networks, and the ability to trade in goods and services have brought about the emergence of a new place of transnational social communication that is in constant technological evolution—cyberspace. Cyberspace is a virtual space in that physical distances are (essentially) irrelevant and the possibilities of communication greatly expanded. But it is also a real space in the sense that people use the Internet to communicate or interact with each other and establish relationships in it (Kellerman 2016). Similarly, crimes perpetrated on the Internet have consequences in the real world (Newman 2009) and occur at discrete (albeit not geographic) locations. As with physical spaces, cyberspace provides the backcloth on which social (and other) interactions occur and criminal opportunities present themselves (for a discussion of the dimensions of crime, see Brantingham and Brantingham 1981). As such, environmental criminology provides a lens through which (at least some of) the opportunities for crime that cyberspace can facilitate or generate might be understood.

In contrast to geographic space, cyberspace is a relational one in which (digital) interaction is not subject to the same constraints that shape activity in the real world (Graham 2002). Like any network, cyberspace is constructed of nodes and links that connect them.[2] Places in the real world can and have been described in network terms too, with nodes representing places of (routine) activity and streets the links that connect them (see the chapter by Davies and Bowers in this volume). However, unlike movement in the real world, the transmission of data through the Internet is essentially instantaneous, and hence in cyberspace physical distance does not determine or limit interaction between people (see Figure 38.1). Instead, ITs essentially contract space (the space of geography), increasing opportunities for contact and communication (Miró 2011). Moreover, in contrast to physical space, nodes in the network of cyberspace can be occupied by many entities at the same time (Graham 2002), even if those involved are located at different geographical locations. This decoupling of geographic and cyberspace further expands the opportunity for and the nature of online interaction (Green 2002), including crime.

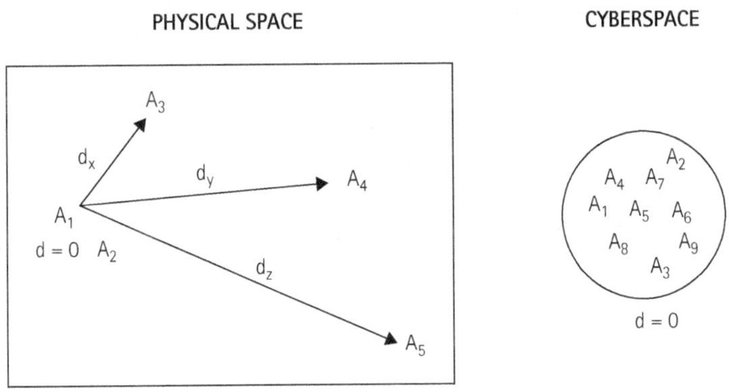

FIGURE 38.1 Contraction of distance in cyberspace and expansion of the communication capacity

Source: Miró 2011.

The contraction of distance also influences the range and extent over which an event occurs. In physical spaces, an agent chooses exactly when and where to act, and the laws of physics constrain the range over which these actions have an impact. In cyberspace, some actions may be directed against a single user (one-to-one attacks), others against a collective (one-to-many attacks), others still against a particular institution. In this context, it is more difficult to determine the precise environment in which the actions of an actor will manifest, who will be affected and where.

In urban environments, contiguity has traditionally influenced social networks and social interaction. Much of this has been dominated either by familial association or by proximity at the neighborhood, or other local levels. However, cyberspace has made possible the formation of virtual communities of people separated by physical space but united by interests and concerns. At the same time, ITs have also made it easier for people who are not part of virtual communities to interact in a way that would have been physically impossible in offline environments. As a consequence, daily activities and social interaction are to a lesser degree determined by physical closeness than by cultural or other forms of closeness. Again, this provides opportunities for people to interact—which may provide opportunities for offending—that would otherwise be unlikely.

The Internet also affects how time influences activity (Lee and Liebenau 2000). It is not that events necessarily happen more rapidly (Wellman 2001), but the contraction of space described above reduces the amount of time needed for social communication and interaction (Kitchin 1998), which creates "an acceleration of the subjective experience of time" (Green 2002) (Figure 38.2).

Furthermore, the types of communication made possible by cyberspace (e.g., Twitter, Facebook) can make communicative expressions that would otherwise be fleeting more persistent. Examples exist in physical space (e.g., offensive graffiti), but cyberspace increases our capacity to control how long communications or actions persist.

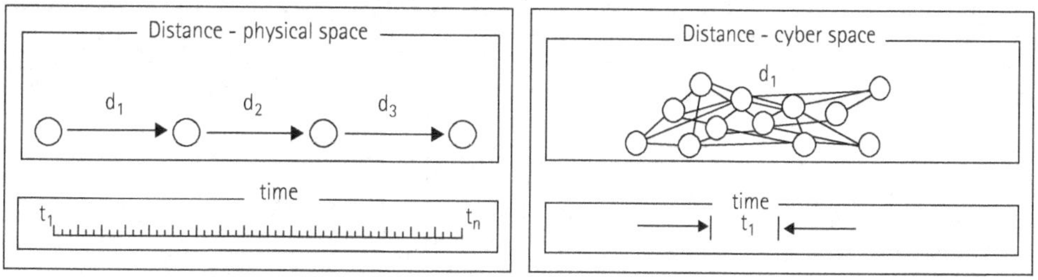

FIGURE 38.2 Contraction of time in cyberspace

Source: Miró 2011.

The transnational character of cyberspace is also important to discuss. The absence of borders, and of a centralized authority, means that activity is not subjected to the national laws of a single country (but, in truth, many countries can exercise authority upon a specific cyberplace). Accordingly, for some behaviors it can be difficult to determine if they are socially acceptable or oven legal (Goodman and Brenner 2002). This is exacerbated by the fact that as an environment, cyberspace is subject to constant changes that are, in many cases, initiated by users. Such change can make what is considered normative behavior in cyberspace unclear and subject to change.

Lastly, in cyberspace contact between people is often indirect, occurring through some virtual representation or extension of those involved. Consequently, relative to physical space, cyberspace affords the anonymity of those involved. This can change how people interact, the (perceived or actual) risks associated with offending and getting caught, and the likely effectiveness of the actions of guardians who might attempt to make crime less likely (see below).

38.4 Criminal Opportunity in Cyberspace

As noted above, theories of environmental criminology shift the focus of criminological enquiry from what explains criminal motivation to how people's routine activity shapes opportunities for crime (e.g., see chapters by Brantingham and colleagues and by Summers and Guerette in this volume). While this approach has traditionally been applied to crimes perpetrated in physical space, there is general agreement in the literature that it should also be useful for cybercrime (Capeller 2001; Grabosky 2001; Pease 2001). However, as discussed in the previous section (see also Yar 2005; Leukfeldt and Yar 2016), there exist differences in how people interact in physical and cyberspace, which has implications for understanding cybercrime (Miró 2012). In this section, further consideration is first given to these differences and the extent to which they are consistent with key concepts from environmental criminology. Research findings are also reviewed to assess how well expectations from environmental criminology align with the empirical record.

38.4.1 Offenders, Targets, and Guardians in Cyberspace

Just like crime in physical space, cybercrime can only occur if the basic premise of the routine activity theory (Cohen and Felson 1979) is met. That is, cybercrime can only happen when, through IT, an offender—or the outcome of his or her actions (e.g., when malware is opened)—converge at a certain place in cyberspace at a given moment with a suitable target in the absence of a guardian capable of preventing the event. However, differences in the dynamics of physical and cyberspace (see above) require that we consider IT's impact on the likely convergence of these essential elements.

If, as discussed, cyberspace increases the ease with which people can interact and the number who can do so simultaneously, this suggests that it provides additional opportunities for offending to those available in physical space (Grabosky 2001; Hutchings and Hayes 2009). Because of the ease of interaction, Clough (2010) goes so far as to say that cyberspace has a "potential" multiplying effect on criminal opportunity that has no precedent in history. Why is this so?

To explain, first consider the contraction of distance in cyberspace. As discussed in chapters by Bernasco and Rossmo in this volume, in the case of urban crime, most crime trips are short, with criminals committing offenses near to their home location or other routine activity nodes (see also Brantingham and Brantingham 1984). One of the reasons commonly invoked to explain this pattern is the principle of least effort (Zipf 1949)—offenders (as rational actors) can be expected to seek to minimize the cost of travel associated with their offending. In addition, offenders are more likely to become aware of and exploit opportunities for crime in their local area, since constraints to movement mean that it is this locale with which they are most likely to be familiar, and to spend much of their time in. In contrast, in cyberspace, geographic distance incurs no physical cost and hence does not influence the generation of crime opportunities or the choices available to offenders, at least not as directly as it does for urban crime (Brenner and Clarke 2005; Jones 2007; McQuade 2009; Miró 2012). As discussed below, other factors such as language barriers or cultural similarities can constrain activity, but distance in and of itself does not.

The contraction of distance in cyberspace also reduces, and in some cases eliminates, the cost of "travel" from one suitable target to another, thereby multiplying the damaging potential of criminal behavior. For example, absent the constraint of being able to occupy only one physical space at any one time, on the Internet, an offender can select from among many potential victims, and attack several (or thousands) of them simultaneously (a one-to-many attack), wherever they happen to be geographically (Hartel, Junger, and Wieringa 2011). Targeting many victims simultaneously with little effort can also mean that only a few need to be successfully victimized to justify the effort involved. Furthermore, the effects of one crime can be more easily multiplied through a process of diffusion in cyberspace. For instance, a victim of a virus attack may become the vector of a new attack, in a chain reaction that need not require further effort by the instigator of the initial crime (Nazario 2004). In physical spaces, diffusion processes—such as the spread of many diseases—are dependent upon proximity since physical contact is an essential part of the process. This is not the case in cyberspace due to the interconnectivity of IT and the speed with which data can be transmitted.

Turning to the dimension of time, in urban environments, a crime event typically occurs when an offender acts. For example, a burglary occurs when an offender breaks into a home, an assault occurs when one person attacks another. However, in cyberspace the timing of crime events can be independent from the time an offender takes action. For example, in the case of malware infections, the crime event is not realized until the victim interacts with the malicious content.

Thus, differences in "mobility" and the impact of time in physical and cyberspace have clear implications that need to be considered when attempting to understand cybercrime. The convergence necessary for a crime to occur still exists, but is subject to different constraints than for crimes committed in physical spaces.

The anonymity afforded by cyberspace can also directly affect offender decision-making. For example, it can provide offenders with a feeling of safety by decreasing their fear of apprehension (Pittaro 2007). It can allow them to reinvent themselves, adopting new virtual personalities through which they may commit crimes (Yar 2005). Multiple personas may be used consecutively, or in parallel. In the case of the latter this can allow criminals to engage in large-scale activity without law enforcement (or others) detecting that the activity of multiple personas is actually the work of a single individual.[3] Moreover, as victims may also be anonymous, this can depersonalize them, making their victimization by the offender easier to reconcile psychologically (Montoya, Junger, and Hartel 2013).

Switching perspectives from the offender to suitable targets, we note that from a macro perspective, the number of potential victims an offender may target in cyberspace will be greater than in physical space, because there is no need for their paths to cross in space. At the micro level, this suggests that a wider field of suitable targets will be available for an offender to choose from. This makes the analysis of what renders a target suitable for cybercrimes of particular importance.

In the case of urban acquisitive crime, scholars have sought to identify those elements of targets that make them particularly attractive to offenders. Cohen and Felson (1979) introduced the acronym VIVA, suggesting that the key parameters that define attractive targets are their Value, Inertia (the ease with which they can be removed), Visibility, and Accessibility. Recently, researchers (Yar 2005; Miró 2012, 2015; Leukfeldt and Yar 2016) have examined the applicability of such frameworks in the context of cybercrime. As would be expected, some elements (such as inertia) do not translate so well, but others such as value, visibility, and accessibility represent useful dimensions for thinking about cybercrime, particularly after some adaptation of their meaning (Miró 2012).

Take accessibility. In the physical world, this refers to the ease with which an offender can approach a suitable target and remove it (Felson 1998). In cyberspace, given the contraction of distance, all suitable targets present are theoretically accessible to others (Yar 2005), unless systems are in place to protect them. Accordingly, an association may be expected between the volume of objects of personal worth introduced online and the likelihood of victimization. Consistent with this, researchers (Wolak et al. 2008; Marcum 2011) have found that for crimes such as cyberbullying and the sexual stalking of minors at least, there is a positive association between the amount of personal information people introduce online and their risk of victimization (see also Miró 2013).

As hinted at, for some threats (e.g., viruses), accessibility can be reduced through the use of automated protections systems, such as antivirus software, antispyware, and firewalls. Restricting access to IT in such a way has been shown to be effective in reducing some forms of victimization online (Choi 2008; Holt and Bossler 2009), although it is difficult to determine the precise level of protection such systems provide (Leukfeldt and Yar 2016).

A second element of the VIVA formula that seems to be particularly relevant with some revision (Leukfeldt and Yar 2016) is the visibility of users. As in physical space, cybercriminals can only attack the suitable targets of which they are aware. Yar (2005) suggests that this is a particular problem in cyberspace, since everything is visible worldwide. However, this is not entirely true. While everything may be visible theoretically, the sheer volume of connections means that only a fraction of online content will be perceived by offenders in reality. Visibility in cyberspace depends on the interaction between the user (and, therefore, his or her system), other users and other services. The greater the interaction with these, the greater the possibility of being perceived by others (Choi 2008; Leukfeldt and Yar 2016).

In support of the expected association between visibility and victimization risk, empirical studies find (for example) that the habitual use of chat rooms online (including Internet Relay Chat and Instant Messenger) is related to nonsexual cyber harassment and sexual requests online (Holt and Bossler 2009; Ngo and Paternoster 2011; Bossler, Holt, and May 2012); the acquisition of goods through sale and bidding online is associated with greater levels of fraud online (Pratt, Holtfreter, and Reisig 2010; Conradt 2012); behaviors like "pirating media," "hacking," or "unauthorized access to the Internet" bring with them a greater risk of malware infection (e.g., Bossler and Holt 2009); while the use of online banking correlates with the risk of victimization by phishing (Hutchings and Hayes 2009).[4] Victimization by phishing seems also to be positively related to greater utilization of email, social networks, and online contact with unknown persons (Miró 2015). As is the case in the real world (e.g., Sampson and Lauritsen 1990), a person's own deviant behavior online too has been found to accentuate the risk of cyber harassment, the reception of unwanted pornography, and phishing (e.g., Ngo and Paternoster 2011, p. 783; Reyns, Henson, and Fisher 2011, p. 1163). Thus, the routine activities of potential targets and the extent to which this makes them visible appear to be associated with victimization risk.

Finally, as stated above, in urban settings the third requisite for a crime to occur is that those capable of guarding against it are absent. In relation to cybercrime, the concept of guardianship is complicated (Farrell and Pease 2006). The factors discussed—the contraction of space-time, the ease of anonymity, and the transnational nature of cyberspace, together with the hermetic or almost private nature of most interactions between offenders and victims—create difficulties for formal guardians capable of protecting potential victims. While the contraction of space means that guardians do not need to travel to accomplish their task, the places where many interactions take place are not public or easily visible and the number of suitable targets to be guarded is large. The absence of a central system of management and normative regulatory mechanisms make impossible the idea of "centralized managers" that guard cyberspace and protect potential victims (Yar 2005). It is not that there is no policing of the Internet, but that the space is enormous. Perhaps more promising is the role that the managers (discussed further below) of specific cyber places can take. However, relative to urban settings (see the chapter by Eck and Madensen in this volume) place management may be more challenging in cyberspace. Of course parents, neighbors, and friends can also act as capable guardians and we will discuss their roles in a little more detail below.

38.4.2 The Places of Cybercrime

Having discussed what might make some targets more suitable than others, and how cyberspace might influence the "mobility" of offenders, in this section we consider the places of convergence where cybercrimes are most likely to occur, reviewing some of the empirical evidence on this issue.

38.4.2.1 *Physical and Virtual Places for the Convergence of Offenders and Targets*

For urban crime, physical space plays a key role in whether crime events take place, since an offender has to encounter a suitable target somewhere for a crime to occur. As discussed, this physical convergence is not a requirement of cybercrime. However, as will become apparent, geographic space is not irrelevant. At the macro level, cyberspace allows offenders to operate in different countries without moving physically. To take an example, Klausen (2012) find that while jihadist groups used to use European servers to host their materials, as their content would now be deemed illegal on the continent, they instead register their domain names on US platforms to take advantage of the greater provision for freedom of expression in that country. In this example, physical space does not constrain the activity of cybercriminals, but differences in regulations across countries make some more attractive than others. Consequently, geography can be seen to play a role, albeit an indirect one.

It also seems clear that there will be variation in the number of potential suitable targets across countries, or even territories. For instance, the volume of suitable targets with economic worth is likely to vary across countries and regions, thereby influencing the potential for particular types of cyberattacks at those locations. Furthermore, while space may not constrain the activity of cybercriminals, habitual schedules and cultural similarities, especially linguistic ones, may do so. Consistent with this, in their research,

Maimon et al. (2015) find that some forms of attacks against systems in one country tend to be more likely to originate from that country or those nearby.

At the micro level, the role that physical space might have on cybercrime seems less obvious. However, for some types of offending there are clear reasons for expecting physical propinquity to matter. For example, some malware infections are spread through a chain of emails, whereby a message is first sent to one set of addresses, and once the virus has been received, it is forwarded to those whose email addresses that are to be found on the infected computer. These will often be friends and coworkers of the initial victims, many of whom will generally live nearby. Moreover, for some forms of offending, there will be many cases in which physical closeness between the offender and victim plays an important role. Classic examples include cyberbullying among classmates (Kwan and Skoric 2013) or other social groups, and "sexting" between people who have been in a relationship (García Guilabert 2014). Thus, for some types of cybercrimes, physical space may constrain who is likely to be involved, be they an offender or a suitable target.

While the concepts of place and space have traditionally been used to refer to specific locations in physical space, they can also be used to refer to discrete nodes or areas of activity on the Internet where one is not physically located but can nevertheless act. Cyberspace is not uniform and allows for the interaction between people, and between people and information, in many different modalities. Each can be thought of as different types of digital spaces. Moreover, while a web page and a social network are semantically (Hartel, Junger, and Wieringa 2011) cyber places, as is communication through email accounts, they are different. Email accounts allow for contact between people who are geographically distant; web pages are sites that are visited, and for which people leave behind only a digital footprint; social networks are specific places in which the subject, or his or her representation, can stay a certain amount of time and interact with others (see Figure 38.3).

These and other spaces can be configured in many different ways and may include many different places. For example, Facebook includes private places in which only known contacts can interact, but it also includes places in which anyone can communicate. One way of differentiating different types of cyberspaces is to consider the different forms in which communication, or contact, take place at them. Interaction with a web page is clearly different from that which takes place in a social network because of the way in which contact occurs. This difference will affect the specific form that criminal events can take and how they are committed. One set of factors that influence whether an offender will encounter a suitable target in the absence of capable guardianship in cyber places is (*a*) the modality of contact facilitated by the IT used; (*b*) the potential for external observation and place management, and hence guardianship; and (*c*) the type of activity (Brantingham and Brantingham 1993) that is usual for the digital place in question. Depending on their configuration in these terms, different digital spaces will influence the likelihood that offenders, victims, and potential guardians will interact and how they will do so. In what follows, each of these factors will be discussed in a little more detail.

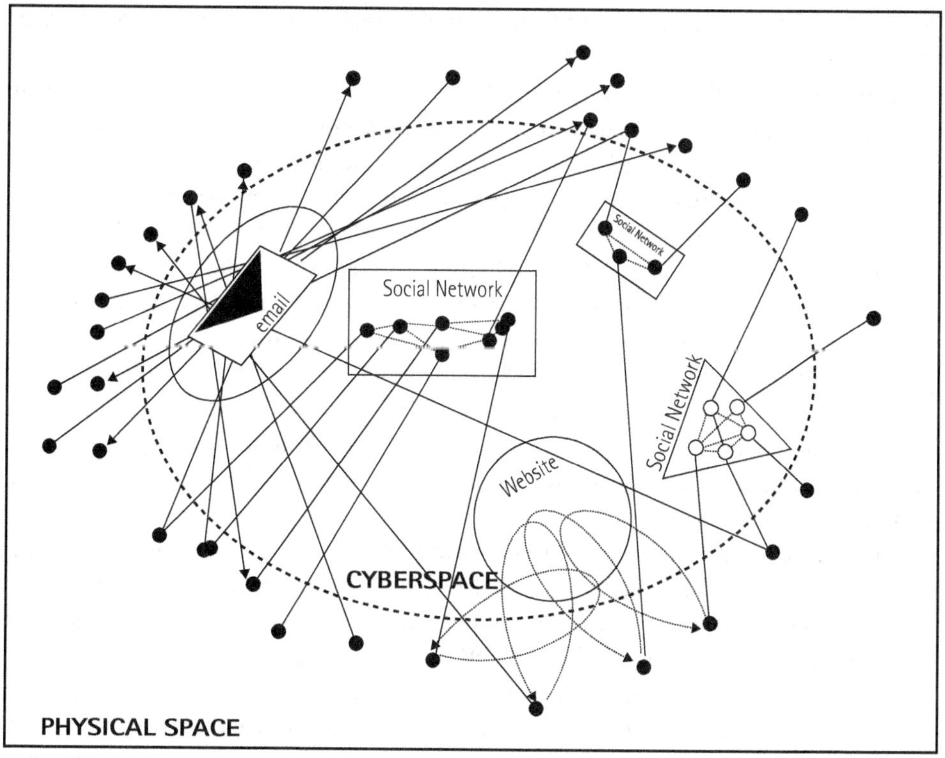

FIGURE 38.3 Examples of cyberspaces

38.4.2.1.1 *Modality of Contact*

Beginning with the type of contact, in cyberspace interaction can be more or less direct depending on whether communication is synchronous or whether there is a delay between the transmission and receipt of information. In the first case, communication is in real time and involves live streaming. Places that facilitate such communication include platforms such as Skype, Google Hangouts, or online games that facilitate video chatting. The second type of communication is described as store-and-forward contact, and in this case, messages are sent but not received immediately (Long and Baecker 1997). This type of communication is used on web pages, electronic mail, some chat rooms, and some forums. In some instances, such as chat rooms, communication comes close to being a streaming service since there is only a slight delay between the transmission and receipt of information, but the time difference will vary. In other cases, such as electronic mail and forums, the way in which they are used necessarily results in a delay in communication. There are, however, cyber places that allow both types of spaces. For example, Twitter is a social network in which contact is store-and-forward, but it has an application, Periscope, that facilitates streaming communication. Some cybercrimes will be committed at places for which contact is store-and-forward, such as the transmission of viruses through email. In this case, a message is sent containing a malicious attachment, but this is not activated until and unless the victim opens the attachment. In contrast, other cybercrimes will happen when there is contact in real time, as is the case for some forms of online grooming for which advantage is taken of the streaming contact in order to request the performance of sexual acts (for example) from a minor. Nevertheless, even if the majority of cybercrimes of a particular type are committed using one form of contact or another, some forms of offenses may involve both modalities. For example, a cyber fraud scam can materialize thanks to a Skype conversation, but most offenses involve electronic mail. The same is true for other types of offending such as radicalization online and cyberbullying.

Among the places in which the contact is store-and-forward, it is necessary to differentiate between those spaces in which communication remains indefinitely (e.g., Facebook or Twitter) and those in which it is temporary, as is the case for social network sites like Snapchat or 4chan, or in chat rooms to which access is restricted.

38.4.2.1.2 *Guardianship and Natural Surveillance*

Places on the Internet are also differentiated in terms of how the identity of different people is represented. This may include a personal image, data that characterize their identity, the IP address of the system from which they access the Internet, and so on. Social networks such as LinkedIn require users to provide a high level of representation of their real identity. This is increasingly encouraged for networks such as Twitter, Instagram, and Facebook, and while users can partially or completely conceal their identity by (for example) using nicknames, in the event of an infraction, users are easily identifiable. At the other end of the spectrum, there are other social networks and interactive cyberspaces, such as 4chan or Snapchat, that promote anonymity. In these cases, access to a user's IP address is only possible through a central server. Other places include dating sites such as Ashley Madison that "guarantee"[5] anonymity, and other types of specialized forums in which users do not know each other's identities even if they treat each other with familiarity. Of course, the greatest level of anonymity is found outside of social networks, on the World Wide Web (WWW). When individuals navigate and access a web page only their IP address is registered. And even this can be concealed using a browser such as *the onion router* (Tor), which is used to increase anonymity by hiding a user's identity and/or location, or services that mask users' details by routing their activity through an intermediate network.

The level of anonymity afforded by particular cyber places and the way in which they are configured will affect the extent to which guardianship (formal or informal) will be effective and the level of "natural surveillance" (Gleason and Wilson 1989), whereby users can "keep an eye on both their own spaces and semipublic and public areas" (p. 23), that is possible. The Internet is a public space, but that does not mean that the possibilities for natural surveillance are high. As with urban environments, elements of cyber places both facilitate and limit opportunities for effective natural surveillance which can have attendant effects on criminal opportunity (Katyal 2003). There are (at least) three factors associated with the configuration of digital spaces that affect the potential for natural surveillance: (*a*) access restrictions to cyber places, which can vary from open entry to all users (public), to highly restricted access (private); (*b*) the level of traffic at each place—some spaces will have substantial traffic while others may experience little; and (*c*) the configuration of the network in question. Specifically, some networks (such as onion routers) have complex structures and routing protocols that are intended to facilitate anonymous communication and to conceal the user's identity.

To take an example, a private chat room for which access is difficult is likely to have light traffic. In such places, natural surveillance by others will be limited and guardianship difficult. This can and is exploited. For example, terrorist organizations are known to take advantage of this when attempting to recruit suitable targets (Mahmood 2012). In contrast, on social network sites like Facebook, a minor (for example) may create a profile that incorporates her friends, parents, and acquaintances, all of whom can provide active surveillance that may deter or prevent victimization. Similarly, the comments of someone using Twitter or YouTube can be seen by many more people than those made in a specialized forum. Such platforms thus provide more opportunities for external observation and "natural surveillance," and therefore more guardianship potential.

38.4.2.1.3 *Types of Activity Spaces*

The last element that configures different spaces or digital places is the activity performed at them and when this occurs. From the perspective of environmental criminology, people's routine activity patterns and their activity spaces (Brantingham and Brantingham 1993; see also Brantingham et al. in this volume) are seen as pivotal in explaining when and where crime events take place, since they influence where and when motivated offenders encounter suitable targets, and whether they do so in the absence of capable guardians. Given some of the above discussion, it is tempting to assume that activity patterns and people's routine activity spaces have little relevance to cybercrime. However, this is not the case since people engage in particular activities at particular cyber "places" at particular times. Consequently, the types of victims or suitable targets sought by an offender may more likely be found at specific cyber places and at particular times. These types of places may also influence the technique an offender must use, and temporal patterns of victimization.

To elaborate, in cyberspace there are places for leisure, such as social networks and online games. The Internet is also a place for consumption, for the buying and selling of goods and services, and for online banking. It is also a place of work, which is used for communication via platforms such as email or through virtual meetings using some form of video streaming.

In addition, like activity in the real world, the type of activity undertaken in cyberspace has a rhythm. For example, it has been found that user patterns of Twitter and other social networks tend to peak outside of school and work hours (Li, Goodchild, and Xu 2013). These rhythms influence the mix and volume of users at particular cyber places at particular times and hence the opportunities for offending.

38.4.2.1.4 *Place Management*

As with places in the real world, cyber places are managed by someone. And those responsible for a particular cyber place can pay more or less attention to making those places secure. In the real world, management policies that might affect whether crime occurs at a facility such as a bar will include the physical design of the facility, the number of security staff employed, and the door policy enforced (for a detailed discussion, see the chapter by Eck and Madensen in this volume). In cyberspace, similar management issues exist. To take an example, consider websites. Many include online advertising, since this a source of substantial income generation online ($59.6 billion in 2015 [IAB 2015]). While most advertising may be legitimate, some is not. Website owners can manage the security of such content in a number of ways. Advertising is delivered by *ad exchanges*, and website owners might choose to work exclusively with those known to employ sufficiently sophisticated means of detecting malicious content. Web page owners might take advantage of the security features of modern browsers, such as the "sandbox" feature, which is used to execute content independently from other running programs or system resources so as to reduce the risk of infection or other malicious activity (e.g., automatically redirecting the browser to a malicious website). Such management practices are known to vary considerably (e.g., Zarras et al. 2014) and can make users more or less vulnerable to attack.

Taken together, the above features define the environmental characteristics of different cyberspaces and (it is argued that) their composition will influence the space of criminal opportunity and activity associated with them.

38.4.2.2 Crime Patterns and Cyber Places

Having conceptualized digital sites as cyber places/spaces in which the convergence of offenders and suitable targets is possible, and differentiated and categorized them, we can explore the relation between cyber places and crime using many of the approaches common to studies of environmental criminology. For example, as other chapters in this book demonstrate, crime is not randomly distributed in space, but instead forms "hotspots" of crime (Sherman, Gartin, and Buerger 1989). Moreover, it appears that certain types of crime are more likely at certain types of facilities (e.g., bars) than others. Following the above discussion, there are good reasons to expect crime also to concentrate in particular ways in cyberspace, and research suggests it does. For example, malware infections and incidents of phishing appear more common on email (Miró 2015), although pharming—a variation of phishing whereby an attempt is made to redirect legitimate website traffic to a fake one—appears more common on Facebook (Vishwanath 2014). Even though there is not enough empirical evidence yet, some authors argue that cyberbullying appears to be more common on social networks characterized by little vigilance (Kwan and Skoric 2013). Crimes such as child grooming are more common in chat rooms than other forms of cyberspaces (Hartel, Junger, and Wieringa 2011). In contrast, sexting is more likely on forums such as Snapchat—where images are only stored for a limited time and then removed (Poltash 2013)—than WhatsApp, where all information may be stored without limits (although this platform is also used). In short, some cyberspaces will be more susceptible to host certain types of cybercrimes because of the type of activity that occurs in that space. The Dark Web deserves a special mention. It is part of the "Deep Web," which is not indexed by standard search engines. The Dark net is hosted on servers using particular encryption algorithms, and access to it requires the use of a special browser such as "The Onion Router" (Tor) which uses the same encryption.[6] While the "Deep Web" refers to all spaces that search engines cannot access (some of which are innocuous), the Dark Web comprises those sections of inaccessible cyberspaces that have been intentionally hidden through encryption. Access to the Dark Web is thus restricted, making guardianship difficult. Not surprisingly then, the majority of offers of child pornography, drugs, and other illicit commercial goods are to be found on the Dark Web (Moore and Rid 2016) to the extent that more than half of what is offered on the Dark Web is illicit.

In urban environments, crime also clusters at the micro level of place (e.g., Eck and Weisburd 1995), so that a small fraction of street segments account for a large proportion of violence (Sherman, Gartin, and Buerger 1989), a small fraction of bars account for a large proportion of crime in bars (Scott and Dedel 2006), and so on. Such findings have informed a number of successful crime prevention approaches (see the chapter by Welsh and Taheri in this volume). A natural question then is whether the same patterns of concentration exist in cyberspace and whether they do so for the same reasons. While the research to date concerning cyber places is limited, there is some evidence of this. For example, Zarras et al. (2014) found that 82% of malicious advertising was observed on 23% of the websites they sampled ($N = 43{,}000$). In this case, the rate of malicious advertising observed was correlated with the volume of advertisements overall, suggesting that offenders had targeted those websites that were most likely to generate the most throughput (the websites that generated 82% of the problem also hosted 77% of all advertisements), rather than those that had specific features. However, for other forms of offending, the sites targeted may differ in specific ways. For example, fake sites used for phishing might have domain name system (DNS) patterns that make them visible to victims but not vigilantes (Berger et al. 2016). In the case of Facebook or online games, threats and insults may be more common via private direct messages than public or semipublic fora. And for Twitter, hate and radicalization may be more likely to be sent from false accounts.

Considering the formation of "hotspots" of crime, in urban settings Brantingham and Brantingham (1995) differentiate between those that emerge because the volume of people that visit or pass through them increases the (serendipitous) opportunity for criminal opportunity (crime generators), and those that attract offenders to them for the sole purpose of committing crime (crime attractors). In the case of the Zarras study discussed above, the concentration observed would appear to be a consequence of crime generation. Other studies (see above) too have shown that the use of particular cyberspaces increases the risk of victimization within them (Holt and Bossler 2009; Hutchings and Hayes 2009; Ngo and Paternoster 2011; Bossler, Holt, and May 2012).

However, it remains to be determined concretely the way in which the use of cyber places determines one's risk of victimization, and if and how different spaces influence an offender's decision to perpetrate crimes there.

As discussed in the chapter by Ignatans and Pease in this volume, another empirical regularity observed in studies of environmental criminology is that victims are at a temporarily elevated risk of crime following their victimization (e.g., Farrell and Pease 1993). So too are those nearby (e.g., Johnson and Bowers 2004). At the time of writing, there have been few studies of repeat cyber-victimization (Pereira, Spitzberg, and Matos 2016) and none have examined repeat victimization at cyber places. Nevertheless, the very functioning of malware, based as it is on the construction of software that seeks vulnerabilities in systems, and the theoretical and empirical robustness on which such ideas are based, we are led to think that repeat victimization is a likely reality in relation to cybercrime (Hartel, Junger, and Wieringa 2011; Farrell and Pease 2014). In relation to this, data from the Crime Survey for England and Wales 2016 show that 18% of online fraud and computer virus victims have been victimized two or more times. Further research is necessary to explore such patterns systematically, but this pattern is line with expectations from the urban crime literature.

In physical spaces, it is apparent that environmental cues (e.g., in the case of burglary this may include signs of occupancy, or the extent to which neighboring homes overlook a property) are used by offenders to assess whether a potential victim or object is a suitable target (Brantingham and Brantingham 1981). Over time, offenders develop templates or schema that inform how they commit a particular crime or for the types of targets they prefer. The cybernetic environment also provides signals, or indicators, that can be used to identify suitable targets or victims. A cybercriminal that places a weblink that will cause an infection with a virus in a certain place in cyberspace selects the site taking into consideration the number and typology of potential suitable targets, their potential interests, the manner in which they interact, and so on. This also happens with social cybercrimes, to identify the most vulnerable subjects and to configure attacks with a specific target in mind (Wolak et al. 2008; Miró and García 2014).

As discussed, in physical space, criminals travel from certain nodes of activity to others, moving along the pathways that connect them. In doing so, they develop awareness of the locations they visit and those in between, including the criminal opportunities they offer (Brantingham and Brantingham 1984). Relative to locations about which little or nothing is known, the reduced uncertainty associated with the criminal opportunities within an offender's awareness space makes them more likely targets for victimization. As noted, and in contrast to urban environments, in cyberspace there are no paths (at least that could be considered equivalent to those traveled in urban environments) that must be traversed to travel from one place to another, and hence offenders are unlikely to develop their awareness of cyberspace in exactly the same way that they likely do in the real world. However, this is not to say that they do not develop awareness spaces. Indeed, it is reasonable to suggest—but we still need empirical evidence—that in cyberspace individuals will also feel more comfortable acting in those cyber zones about which they possess the most knowledge. Nonetheless, as we have seen, in cyberspace the level of anonymity and the visibility afforded to users will influence the decision to engage in certain types of activities in particular cyberspaces. Accordingly, further research is necessary to understand how offenders become aware of and perceive opportunities for crime and the risk of offending at particular cyber places.

38.5 Some Conclusions: Cyber Places and Crime Prevention

A central aim of this chapter was to reflect on whether theories of environmental criminology, and the approaches taken, might offer insight into crimes committed in digital spaces, to understand better how those cybercrimes are perpetrated, how they are influenced by the mode (or place) in which the offender and the victim (or object) interact, and how they might be prevented. While it is clear that cybercrime occurs in a very different "space" than the urban crimes theories of environmental criminology were originally developed to explain, it is evident that a number of frameworks associated with environmental criminology provide a useful lens through which to understand cybercrime. One reason for this is that theories of environmental criminology focus on the crime event and how human ecological processes (such as patterns of people's routine activities) influence the likelihood of crime occurrence. This contrasts with other approaches for which distal explanations of why someone might engage in crime are the focus of enquiry.

Furthermore, the objective of environmental criminology is not limited to just "better understanding" crime, but also to preventing it. There are reasons to suggest that the environmental criminology approach can be especially useful in this respect. To explain, consider that much is still unknown about cyberspace, and that it is a changing environment in which new tools of social communication emerge that can modify and influence people's online behavior. For this reason, an approach based on how the current and changing configuration of cyberspace affects how people use it might help to better understand how opportunities for cybercrime emerge. On a related point, despite the fact that the Internet is now a ubiquitous tool for social communication, we can say that its architecture, or urban planning, is still to be defined and seems modifiable from both technical and normative perspectives. This presents an opportunity for preventing crime in cyberspace. That is, understanding how the defining elements of cyber places—such as the typology of contacts between people, the representation of their identity, and possibilities for natural surveillance—affect crime risk might inform how cyberspaces can be constructed to reduce crime.

While perspectives from environmental criminology can contribute to the prevention of cybercrime in many ways, three aspects will be discussed in this closing section: (*a*) improving the education of potential victims in digital spaces; (*b*) modifying cyber places to transform them into defensible spaces; and (*c*) improving the efficiency of cybersecurity tools, and specifically, increasing the efficiency of law enforcement in digital spaces.

In relation to the first point, the information we currently have suggests that cybercrimes, as events, are heavily influenced by the decisions and activity that victims routinely engage in, and the fact that their perception of risk is often unrealistically low (Holt and Bossler 2009; Hutchings and Hayes 2009; Miró 2011; Ngo and Paternoster 2011; Bossler, Holt, and May 2012). The education of victims regarding informatics security, awareness of the need to employ protective software and safe routines in their daily online activities, and the provision of realistic information about the risk of crime in cyberspace, would represent initial steps that might be adopted for the prevention of cybercrime. For that, and to provide more than generic advice, it will be essential to identify those factors associated with the risk of cybercrime in different types of cyber places, and how risk varies across cyber places (Vakhitova et al. 2015).

On the second point, environmental criminology can inform understanding of how virtual spaces might be better configured to reduce crime opportunity. In the 1960s Jeffery (1969) noted that "we are not yet planning our cities for personal and property securities." This point is currently applicable to cyber places, and it is an issue that sooner or later we will have to confront. On the one hand, we might attempt to apply systems of informal community prevention in cyberspace, such as the vigilant neighborhood or other forms of informal control or "natural surveillance" that might make crime less likely. For that, it may be necessary to change cyber places to limit some of their functions and characteristics (type of contact, expression of identity, and so on), or at least to make explicit the risks of certain types of places in which surveillance and guardianship are limited. Furthermore, more attention could be given to the application of the situational crime prevention approach (see the chapter by Welsh and Taheri in this volume) in relation to the security policies used in the information society and in the configuration of social networks (Hartel, Junger, and Wieringa 2011).

Finally, the prevention of cybercrime requires more efficient formal guardianship in the different spaces of cyberspace. If, as it seems, there are crime-producing places in which some cybercrimes are concentrated, then better place management (see the chapter by Eck and Madensen in this volume) of those spaces by those responsible for them may represent one solution to prevention. Moreover, if there are places in which criminals contact each other and exchange information (Soudijn and Zegers 2012), if we are capable of identifying them, and if we can improve our knowledge of the patterns of crime in such cyber places, law enforcement resources could be focused on those places to make crime more difficult, or detection easier. A better understanding of the places in which such contacts occurs could improve the targeting of online surveillance. We might better understand what attracts criminals through the use of honeypots—which are essentially false websites used to detect and observe illicit activity—created to attract criminals to them. Such an approach is currently being applied in relation to cyberterrorism to integrate undercover agents in the different cyberspaces frequented by terrorist organizations (Barfar, Zolfaghar, and Mohammadi 2011). The possibilities of enforcement and crime prevention are many and will improve in effectiveness and efficiency if we understand the manner in which the offender and victim interact in different cyber places.

Notes

1. For a recent extreme example at the time of writing, the source code (named "Mirai") for the distributed denial of service (DDOS) attack that caused unprecedented disruptions to websites on the Internet on 21 October 2016 has been publicly released, making it easier for others to launch such attacks.
2. Locations on the Internet are addressed through IP (*Internet Protocol*) addresses. These are numeric codes assigned to every computer (but also other electronic devices) included in a computer network. The interlinked nature of cyberspace allows IP addresses to connect and interact within several cyberspaces with different nature.
3. For example, so-called crypto-currencies such as Bitcoin allow people to trade using as many pseudonames as they like. Accordingly, a single individual can make large numbers of trades without anyone realizing that this is the case. The implications for money laundering are substantial (for a discussion, see Meiklejohn et al. 2013).
4. Phishing occurs where an attacker obtains sensitive information (e.g., passwords) about individuals when they respond to a deceptive communication that appears to be from a reputable source.
5. In this case, anonymity was, of course, not guaranteed, as a cyberattack led to the release of users' information; see https://www.theguardian.com/technology/2016/feb/28/what-happened-after-ashley-madison-was-hacked (last accessed 11 September 2016).
6. It is important to note that while it may be used for criminal activity, the dark web is also used for more positive purposes. In fact, Tor was developed by the US military to allow operatives to communicate anonymously. To ensure the anonymity of their operatives, it was necessary to conceal their activity among that of (many) others, and consequently Tor was released into the public domain.

References

Barfar, Arash, Kiyana Zolfaghar, and Shahriar Mhammadi. 2011. "A Framework for Cyber War against International Terrorism." *International Journal of Internet Technology and Secured Transactions* 3(1): 29–39.

Berger, Andreas, Alessandro D'Alconzo, Wilfried N. Gansterer, and Antonio Pescapé. 2016. "Mining Agile DNS Traffic Using Graph Analysis for Cybercrime Detection." *Computer Networks* 18: 1–17.

Bocij, P. (2004). Cyberstalking: *Harassment in the Internet Age and How to Protect Your Family.* Westport, CT: Greenwood Publishing Group.

Bossler, Adam M., and Thomas J. Holt. 2009. "On-line Activities, Guardianship, and Malware Infection: An Examination of Routine Activities Theory." *International Journal of Cyber Criminology* 3(1): 400–420.

Bossler, Adam M., Thomas J. Holt, and David C. May. 2012. "Predicting Online Harassment Victimization among a Juvenile Population." *Youth and Society* 44(4): 500–523.

Brantingham, Patricia L., and Paul J. Brantingham. 1993. "Environment, Routine, and Situation: Toward a Pattern Theory of Crime." In *Routine Activity and Rational Choice, Advances in Criminological Theory*, vol. 5, edited by Ronald V. Clarke and Marcus Felson. New Brunswick, NJ: Transaction.

Brantingham, Patricia L., and Paul J. Brantingham. 1995. "Criminality of Place: Crime Generators and Crime Attractors." *European Journal of Criminal Policy and Research* 3(3): 5–26.

Brantingham, Paul J., and Patricia L. Brantingham, eds. 1981. *Environmental Criminology*. Beverly Hills, CA: Sage Publications.

Brantingham, Paul J., and Patricia L. Brantingham. 1984. *Patterns in Crime*. New York, NY: Macmillan.

Brenner, Susan W., and Leo L. Clarke. 2005. "Distributed Security: Preventing Cybercrime." *John Marshall Journal of Information Technology and Piracy Law* 23(4): 659–710.

Capeller, Wanda. 2001. "Not Such a Neat Net: Some Comments on Virtual Criminality." *Social and Legal Studies* 10(2): 229–242.

Choi, Kyung-Shick. 2008. "Computer Crime Victimization and Integrated Theory: An Empirical Assessment." *International Journal of Cyber Criminology* 2(1): 308–333.

Clarke, Ronald V. 1999. "Hot Products: Understanding, Anticipating and Reducing Demand for Stolen Good." Police Research Series Paper No. 112. London.

Clough, Jonathan. 2010. *Principles of Cybercrime*. Cambridge: Cambridge University Press.

Cohen, Lawrence E., and Marcus Felson. 1979. "Social Change and Crime Trends: A Routine Activity Approach." *American Sociological Review* 44(4): 588–608.

Conradt, Christine. 2012. "Online Auction Fraud and Criminological Theories: The Adrian Ghighina Case." *International Journal of Cyber Criminology* 6(1): 912–923.

Eck, John E., and David Weisburd. 1995. "Crime Places in Crime Theory." In *Crime and Place*, edited by John E. Eck and David Weisburd. Monsey, NY: Criminal Justice Press.

Farrell, Graham, and Ken Pease. 1993. "Once Bitten, Twice Bitten: Repeat Victimisation and Its Implications for Crime Prevention." Crime Prevention Unit Series Paper No. 46. London: Home Office Police Department.

Farrell, Graham, and Ken Pease. 2006. "Criminology and Security." In *The Handbook of Security*, edited by Martin Gill. Basingstoke, UK: Palgrave Macmillan.

Farrell, Graham., & Pease, Ken. (2014). "Repeat Victimization." In *Encyclopedia of Criminology and Criminal Justice* 4371–4381. New York: Springer.

Felson, Marcus. 1998. *Crime and Everyday Life*. 2nd ed. Thousand Oaks, CA: Sage.

Felson, Marcus, and Rachel Boba. 2010. *Crime and Everyday Life*. 4th ed. Thousand Oaks, CA: Sage.

García-Guilabert, Natalia. 2014. "Victimización de Menores por Actos de Ciberacoso Continuado y Actividades Cotidianas en el Ciberespacio." PhD dissertation, Universidad de Murcia.

Geason, Susan, and Paul R. Wilson. 1989. *Design Out Crime: Crime Prevention through Environmental Design*. Crime Prevention Series. Canberra, AU: Australian Institute of Criminology.

Goodman, Marc D., and Susan W. Brenner. 2002. "The Emerging Consensus on Criminal Conduct in Cyberspace." *International Journal of Law and Information Technology* 10(2): 139–223.

Grabosky, Peter N. 2001. "Virtual Criminality: Old Wine in New Bottles?" *Social Legal Studies* 10(2): 243–249.

Graham, Phil. 2002. "Space and Cyberspace: On the Enclosure of Consciousness." In *Living with Cyberspace: Technology and Society in the 21st Century*, edited by John Armitage and Joanne Roberts. New York: Continuum.

Green, Nicola. 2002. "On the Move: Technology, Mobility, and the Mediation of Social Time and Space." *Information Society* 18: 281–292.

Hampson, Noah C. N. 2012. "Hacktivism: A New Breed of Protest in a Networked World." *Boston College International and Comparative Law Review* 35(2): 511–542.

Hartel, Pieter, Marianne Junger, and Roel Wieringa. 2011. *Cyber-Crime Science = Crime Science + Information Security*. Technical Report TR-CTIT-10-34, University of Twente.

Hinduja, Sameer, and Justin W. Patchin. 2014. *Cyberbullying: Identification, Prevention, and Response*. Cyberbullying Research Center.

Holt, Thomas J., and Adam M. Bossler. 2009. "Examining the Applicability of Lifestyle-Routine Activities Theory for Cybercrime Victimization." *Deviant Behavior* 30(1): 1–25.

Hutchings, Alice, and Hennessey Hayes. 2009. "Routine Activity Theory and Phishing Victimisation: Who Gets Caught in the 'Net'?" *Current Issues in Criminal Justice* 20(3): 1–20.

Illia, Laura. 2002. "Passage to Cyberactivism: How Dynamics of Activism Change." *Journal of Public Affairs* 3(4): 326–337.

Interactive Advertising Bureau (IAB). 2015. Internet Advertising Revenue Report 2015. https://www.iab.com/wp-content/uploads/2016/04/IAB-Internet-Advertising-Revenue-Report-FY-2015.pdf.

Jeffery, C. Ray. 1969. "Crime Prevention and Control through Environmental Engineering." *Criminologica* 7: 35–58.

Johnson, Shane. D., & Bowers, Kate. J. (2004). "The Stability of Space-Time Clusters of Burglary." British Journal of Criminology 44(1): 55–65.

Jones, Benjamin R. 2007. "Virtual Neighborhood Watch." *Journal of Criminal Law and Criminology* 97(2): 601–630.

Katyal, Neal K. 2003. "Digital Architecture as Crime Control." *Yale Law Journal* 112: 2261–2289.

Kellerman, Aharon. 2016. "Image Spaces and the Geography of Internet Scree-Space." *GeoJournal* 81(4): 503–517

Kitchin, Robert M. 1998. "Towards Geographies of Cyberspace." *Progress in Human Geography* 22(3): 385–406.

Klausen, Jytte, Eliane Tschaen Barbieri, Aaron Reichlin-Melnick, and Aaron Y. Zelin. 2012. "The YouTube Jihadists." *Perspectives on Terrorism* 6(1), 36-53.

Kwan, Grace Chi En, and Marko M. Skoric. 2013. "Facebook Bullying: An Extension of Battles in School." *Computers in Human Behavior* 29(1): 16–25.

Lee, Heejin, and Jonathan Liebenau. 2000. "Time and the Internet at the Turn of the Millennium." *Time Society* 9(1): 43–56.

Leukfeldt, Eric Rutger, and Mijad Yar. 2016. "Applying Routine Activity Theory to Cybercrime: A Theoretical and Empirical Analysis." *Deviant Behavior* 37(3): 263–280.

Li, L., M. F. Goodchild, and B. Xu. 2013. "Spatial, Temporal, and Socioeconomic Patterns in the Use of Twitter and Flickr." *Cartography and Geographic Information Science* 40(2): 61–77.

Long, Byron, and Ronald Baecker. 1997. "A Taxonomy of Internet Communication Tools." In *WebNet97: World Conference of the WWW, Internet, & Intranet*, edited by Suave Lobodzinski and Ivan Tomek. Charlottesville, VA: AACE.

Macdonald, Thomas, Lee Jarvis, and Thomas Chen. 2013. *A Multidisciplinary Conference on Cyberterrorism: Final Report.* Cyberterrorism Project Research Report. Swansea, UK: Swansea University.

Mahmood, Shah. 2012. "Online Social Networks: The Overt and Covert Communication Channels for Terrorists and Beyond." In *Homeland Security (HST), 2012 IEEE Conference on Technologies*, 574–579, IEEE.

Maimon, David, Theodore Wilson, Wuling Ren, and Tamar Berenglum. 2015. "On the Relevance of Spatial and Temporal Dimensions in Assessing Computer Susceptibility to System Trespassing Incidents." *British Journal of Criminology* 55: 615–634.

Marcum, Catherine D. 2011. "Adolescent Online Victimization and Constructs of Routine Activities Theory." In *Cyber Criminology: Exploring Internet Crimes and Criminal Behavior*, edited by Karuppannan Jaishankar. Boca Raton, FL: CRC Press.

McQuade, Samuel C., III. 2011. "Cybercrime." In *The Oxford Handbook of Crime and Public Policy*, edited by Michael Tonry. New York, NY: Oxford University Press.

Meiklejohn, S., M. Pomarole, G. Jordan, K. Levchenko, D. McCoy, G. M. Voelker, and S. Savage. 2013. "A Fistful of Bitcoins: Characterizing Payments among Men with No Names." *Proceedings of the 2013 Conference on Internet Measurement Conference*, 127–140. New York: ACM.

Miró, Fernando. 2011. "La Oportunidad Criminal en el Ciberespacio: Aplicación y Desarrollo de la Teoría de las Actividades Cotidianas para la Prevención del Cibercrimen." *Revista Electrónica de Ciencia Penal y Criminología* 13(7), 1–55.

Miró, Fernando. 2012. *El Cibercrimen: Fenomenología y Criminología de la Delincuencia en el Ciberespacio*. Madrid: Parcial Pons.

Miró, Fernando. 2013. "La Victimización por Cibercriminalidad Social. Un Estudio a partir de la Teoría de las Actividades Cotidianas en el Ciberespacio." *Revista Española de Investigación Criminológica* 11(5): 1–35.

Miró, Fernando. 2015. "That Cyber Routine, That Cyber Victimization: Profiling Victims of Cybercrime." In *Cybercrime Risks and Responses: Eastern and Western Perspectives*, edited by Russell G. Smith, Ray Chak-Chung Cheung, and Laurie Yiu-Chung Lau. London: Palgrave Macmillan.

Miró, Fernando, and Natalia García. 2014. *CiberApp: Aprender, Prevenir, Proteger. Estudio Sobre el Alcance de la Cibercriminalidad contra Menores de la Provincia de Alicante*. Elche, Spain: Centro Crímina.

Montoya, A. Lorena, Marianne Junger, and Pieter H. Hartel. 2013. "How 'Digital' Is Traditional Crime?" Paper presented at EISIC 2013, Uppsala, Sweden, August.

Moore, Daniel, and Thomas Rid. 2016. "Cryptopolitik and the Darknet." *Survival* 58(1): 7–38.

Nazario, Jose. 2004. *Defense and Detection Strategies against Internet Worms*. Boston, MA: Artech House.

Newman, Graeme R. 2009. "Cybercrime." In *Handbook on Crime and Deviance*, edited by Marvin D. Krohn, Alan J. Lizotte, and Gina Penly Hall. New York: Springer.

Newman, Graeme R., and Ronald V. Clarke. 2003. *Superhighway Robbery: Preventing E-Commerce Crime*. New York: Routledge.

Ngo, Fawn T., and Raymond Paternoster. 2011. "Cybercrime Victimization: An Examination of Individual and Situational Level Factors." *International Journal of Cyber Criminology* 5(1): 773–793.

Pease, Ken. 2001. "Crime Futures and Foresight Challenging Criminal Behaviour in the Information Age." In *Crime and the Internet*, edited by David S. Wall. London: Routledge.

Pereira, Filipa, Brian H. Spitzberg, and Marlene Matos. 2016. "Cyber-harassment Victimization in Portugal: Prevalence, Fear and Help-Seeking among Adolescents." *Computers in Human Behavior* 62: 136–146.

Pittaro, Michael L. 2007. "Cyber Stalking: An Analysis of Online Harassment and Intimidation." *International Journal of Cyber Criminology* 1(2): 180–197.

Poltash, Nicole A. 2013. "Snapchat and Sexting: A Snapshot of Baring Your Bare Essentials." *Richmond Journal of Law and Technology* 19(4): 1–24.

Pratt, Travis C., Kristy Holtfreter, and Michael D. Reisig. 2010. "Routine Online Activity and Internet Fraud Targeting: Expanding the Generality of Routine Activity Theory." *Journal of Research in Crime and Delinquency* 47(3): 267–296.

Reyns, Bradford W. 2010. "A Situational Crime Prevention Approach to Cyberstalking Victimization: Preventive Tactics for Internet Users and Online Place Managers." *Crime Prevention and Community Safety* 12(2): 99–118.

Reyns, Bradford W., Billy Henson, and Bonnie S. Fisher. 2011. "Being Pursued Online: Applying Cyberlifestyle-Routine Activities Theory to Cyberstalking Victimization." *Criminal Justice and Behavior* 38(1): 1149–1169.

Sampson, R. J., and J. L. Lauritsen. 1990. "Deviant Lifestyles, Proximity to Crime, and the Offender-Victim Link in Personal Violence." *Journal of Research in Crime and Delinquency* 27(2): 110–139.

Scott, Michael S., and Kelly Dedel. 2006. *Assaults in and around Bars.* 2nd ed. Problem-Oriented Guides for Police: Problem-Specific Guides Series No. 1. New York: Center for Problem-Oriented Policing.

Sherman, Lawrence W., Patrick G. Gartin, and Michael E. Buerger. 1989. "Hot Spots of Predatory Crime: Routine Activities and the Criminology of Place." *Criminology* 27(1): 27–56.

Soudijn, Melvin R. J., and Birgit C. H. T. Zegers. 2012. "Cybercrime and Virtual Offender Convergence Settings." *Trends in Organized Crime* 15: 111–129.

Vakhitova, Zarina I., Danielle M. Reynald, and Michael Townsley. 2015. "Toward an Adaptation of Routine Activity and Lifestyle Exposure Theories to Account for Cyber Abuse Victimization." *Journal of Contemporary Criminal Justice* 32(2): 169–188.

Vishwanath, Arun. 2014. "Habitual Facebook Use and Its Impact on Getting Deceived on Social Media." *Journal of Computer-Mediated Communication* 20(1): 83–98.

Wall, David S. 2007. *Cybercrime: The Transformation of Crime in the Information Age.* Cambridge: Polity Press.

Wellman, Barry. 2001. "Computer Network as Social Network." *Science* 293(5537): 2031–2034.

Wolak, Janis, David Finkelhor, Kimberly J. Mitchell, and Michele L. Ybarra. 2008. "Online 'Predators' and Their Victims: Myths, Realities, and Implications for Prevention and Treatment." *American Psychologist* 63(2): 111–128.

Yar, Majid. 2005. "The Novelty of 'Cybercrime': An Assessment in Light of Routine Activity Theory." *European Journal of Criminology* 2(4): 407–427.

Zarras, Apostolis, Alexandros Kapravelos, Gianluca Stringhini, Thorsten Holz, Christopher Kruegel, and Gionavanna Vigna. 2014. "The Dark Alleys of Madison Avenue: Understanding Malicious Advertisements." In *Proceedings of the 2014 Conference on Internet Measurement Conference*, 373–380. New York: ACM.

Zipf, George K. 1949. *Human Behavior and the Principle of Least Effort: An Introduction to Human Ecology.* Cambridge, MA: Addison-Wesley.

CHAPTER 39

MARITIME PIRACY

MICHAEL TOWNSLEY

39.1 Introduction

The word "pirate" evokes images from popular entertainment that, for many, are inextricably linked to childhood stories of adventure and daring. The practices, style, fashion, colorful vernacular, and personalities most people associate with piracy comes from the so-called golden age of piracy, the late 17th and early 18th centuries. It is surprising for many to learn that today's shipping industry has been tackling a piracy problem for the past 20 years. The Strait of Malacca (Southeast Asia) was the global piracy hotspot from 1998 to 2006, and the Gulf of Aden (east coast of Africa) became the epicenter of a new piracy hotspot in 2006.

The problem of piracy has attracted a diverse range of research disciplines. Economists (Bowden 2010; Carney 2009; Hallwood and Miceli 2013; Leeson 2009, 2010), criminologists (Marchione and Johnson 2013; Rengelink 2012; Shane and Lieberman 2009; Shane et al. 2015; Townsley and Oliveira 2015; Worrall 2000), security specialists (Brown 2012; Carafano and Rodeback 2011; Chalk 2012; Chalk et al. 2009; Hastings 2009; Ho 2009; Kraska and Wilson 2009; Liss 2007; Nakamura 2009; Struwe 2012; Tsilis 2011; Warner 2010; West et al. 2010; Wheeler 2012), transport researchers (Min 2011; Sullivan 2010; Van der Meijden 2008), lawyers (Forbes 2011; Geiss and Petrig 2011; Guilfoyle 2010; Hallwood and Miceli 2012; Kontorovich 2012; Kontorovich and Art 2010; Lubberts 2011; Ramsey 2011; Scott 2014), and historians (Anderson 1995; De Souza 2002; Elleman 2015; Murphy 2012) have all attempted to explain the contributing factors for existence and/or rise of maritime piracy or the reasons why efforts to curb piracy have floundered.

This chapter will outline how theories of environmental criminology can inform our understanding of maritime piracy and assess empirically how the incidence of maritime piracy is influenced by opportunities created by a maritime setting. The chapter is organized into three sections. The first discusses different periods of piracy, spanning ancient times, the Middle Ages, and up to present day. While the factors contributing to piracy in each age vary, I argue there is a common explanation for how piracy has been quashed: establishing effective place management in the maritime realm. The second section focuses on some key constructs in environmental criminology and illustrates how they operate in a maritime setting. The concluding section deals with patterns that have been observed in maritime piracy in recent times. Thanks to the recording and reporting practices of maritime intelligence agencies, we are able to study the dynamics of modern maritime piracy in ways not possible for pirates of the past. These patterns help to illustrate the role that environmental criminology and situational crime prevention can play in preventing pirate attacks.

39.2 A Short History of Piracy

Maritime piracy is an old problem, dating back as far as maritime transport itself. Historical records indicate pirates operating in ancient Greece and in Roman times (De Souza 2002). Pirates operated freely in the Middle Ages right up until the start of the 18th century (Elleman 2015). In more modern times outbreaks of piratical activity have been observed in Southeast Asia and the east coast of Africa.

These different pirate epochs share characteristics. They each caused a degree of consternation among dominant and aspirant nation states, pirate groups were often permitted to undertake attacks under the authority of a polity, and each pirate era ended once the dominant naval power decided to take the problem seriously.

Prior to the rise of the Romans, there was little to distinguish warfare from piracy; both involved the use of violence to plunder and pillage third parties (Elleman 2015). In the latter days of the Roman Republic (100 B.C.) nearly every country touching the Mediterranean Sea was under Roman rule. While piracy was a perennial source of irritation for Romans, it ceased to be tolerated once Rome established its dominance. Cicero (n.d.) first labeled pirates "the common enemy of all (*communis hostis omnium*)" and their hostilities made them enemies not only of Rome but of all nations. Murphy (2012) explains that, while acknowledging the public consternation over piracy, the pirate label was used for political as much as criminal purposes. Groups deemed pirates were, in fact, individuals who defied Roman rule or did not recognize Roman authority. One man's pirate is another man's freedom fighter, if you will.

It was only at the point that the Republic achieved wholesale dominance of the Mediterranean it treated piracy as a threat. Until that point pirate attacks might usefully weaken Rome's adversaries, but now they could only hurt Rome and its allies. Initial efforts at piracy suppression were entirely reactive—a fleet would be sent out in response to a report of pirate activity. But these efforts did nothing to curb pirate enterprises. The trigger event that crystallized Roman efforts and attention was Cillian pirates cutting Rome's supply line to North Africa, which created the potential for famine in the capital (De Souza 2002). The ensuing response re-established the grain supply, and Roman forces resettled captured pirates. The latter tactic proved ineffective in the long term, with many returning to piracy. The later conquest of Cyprus and Crete destabilized pirate powerbases, leading to their dissolution.

Murphy (2012) suggests two lessons from the Roman experience. First, counterpiracy needs to occur on land as well as at sea. Without ports and trading opportunities, piracy is not a viable enterprise. Second, due to the mobile nature of piracy, naval hegemony is a prerequisite. In the Roman case, there was strong resistance to establishing a standing navy. A naval presence throughout the Mediterranean Sea would necessitate the largest concentration of military power under a single individual, a state of affairs that Roman senators were justifiably reluctant to allow.

The Middle Ages witnessed the rise of the Barbary pirates, which reached the zenith of activity and influence in the 16th and 17th centuries. Operating from the coast of North Africa, they concentrated largely on the western Mediterranean, but operated near the West African coast and the North Atlantic (Elleman 2015).

Two factors explain the rise of the Barbary pirate reach and activity—they also explain their downfall. First, a number of fledgling ports in North America capitalized on the increased trading and goods realized by piracy. In addition Morocco, Algeria, Tunisia, and Turkey hosted "safe harbor" ports, representing operating bases, supply lines, and trading markets for the pirates that were located close to merchant shipping.

The second factor was the intense competition between European mercantile nation states. Spain was the most advanced naval power in the 16th century and its richest thanks to establishing and exploiting key colonies. Aspirant nations—Britain, the Netherlands, Portugal, and France—began to embrace mercantilism. In a bid to avoid outright war, a likely outcome if everyone adopts a mercantile economy, countries granted licenses for private groups to attack foreign ships. This practice, known as privateering or corsairing, frustrated trade without resorting to direct hostilities (and provided plausible deniability to rulers).

Once Britain gained worldwide naval dominance in the 17th century, its mercantile economic policy no longer required privateering.[1] At this time the sun never set on the British Empire, with colonies and trade interests and routes across the globe. Coupled with true global naval strength, this was probably the first time in recorded history that a single nation had both the means and motives to tackle maritime piracy.

Ports that previously welcomed pirates' trade transitioned to more legitimate markets. In the North American ports, trade routes had stabilized, and merchants, who had become increasingly wealthy, no longer *had* to trade with pirates; they now had viable, that is, legitimate, trading options. The political climate had also become intolerant of piracy. In 1830 France occupied Algeria, closing down a major pirate stronghold. British strength at sea, coupled with shrinking access to markets, meant that pirate operations became severely curtailed and then withered.

In recent times there have been two significant outbreaks of maritime piracy, in the 1990s the Strait of Malacca in Southeast Asia and in the last half of the 2000s in the Gulf of Aden (East Africa). I will provide a detailed treatment of the latter outbreak in the second half of this chapter but deal briefly with Malacca here.

The Strait of Malacca is a body of water that connects the Pacific Ocean with the Indian Ocean and is one of the busiest and most important shipping lanes in the world (accounting for 24% of *all* world trade according to Twyman-Ghoshal 2014). Piracy in the region, which started to rise sharply in 1998,[2] was a contentious issue for the nations affected. Singapore wished help from the international community, but Indonesia and Malaysia steadfastly refused foreign intervention. The political standoff lasted for nearly a decade. In 2005 Lloyd's of London declared the Strait of Malacca an "area of increased war risk," resulting in dramatically increased insurance premiums for ships using this strategic passage and a potentially disastrous economic impact on local maritime interests. The defense forces of all three countries drew up a multinational response to address pirates and permitted assistance from other nations' navies. Lloyd's of London removed its declaration in 2006.

These brief history lessons illustrate a core observation about piracy, and crime, in general. Piracy has historically been permitted to operate, tacitly or not, by whoever governs the sea. Pirates operated in Roman times because the Roman Empire did not exert its authority. The Barbary pirates attacked with impunity because of rivalries between nation states. Once naval hegemony was achieved, pirates ceased to be useful to the British and so their operating environment was made much less feasible. And pirates operated in the Strait of Malacca because there was no effective law enforcement.

This observation would not surprise crime prevention researchers. Whenever a place has no or little effective place management, there is a good chance that crime will flourish. Indeed, any location with high crime almost invariably has ineffective place management.

39.3 Defining Piracy

As is common in crime problems, much effort and ink has been devoted to teasing out the contradictions and inconsistencies in the definition of piracy. The legal definition of piracy often cited comes from Article 101 of the United Nations Convention on the Law of the Sea (1982, p. 61):

(a) any illegal acts of violence or detention, or any act of depredation, committed for private ends by the crew or the passengers of a private ship or a private aircraft, and directed:
   (i) on the high seas, against another ship or aircraft, or against persons or property on board such ship or aircraft;
   (ii) against a ship, aircraft, persons or property in a place outside the jurisdiction of any State;
(b) any act of voluntary participation in the operation of a ship or of an aircraft with knowledge of facts making it a pirate ship or aircraft;
(c) any act of inciting or of intentionally facilitating an act described in subparagraph (a) or (b).

This definition explicitly restricts piracy to international waters. Attacks in territorial waters come under the jurisdiction of the corresponding nation state. But there are considerable inconsistencies about how piracy is defined in domestic legislation. Some countries have specific offenses for piracy, whereas others view piracy as a particular case of existing offenses, such as assault, robbery, or theft.

A more practical definition of piracy is provided by the International Maritime Bureau (ICC International Maritime Bureau 2006, p. 3):

> An act of boarding or attempting to board any ship with the apparent intent to commit theft or any other crime and with the apparent intent or capability to use force in the furtherance of that act.

The IMB definition is more liberal about what can be considered piracy. Location is not important; however, piracy does include ships that might be berthed in a dock or harbor. In addition, this definition includes theft as piratical activity. This is problematic because theft is normally distinguished from robbery by an absence of violence. In this case, a theft from a ship shares more characteristics with burglary than with robbery. In most people's imagination a pirate attack features one party forcing its way onto a vessel using violence or the threat of it.

From a practical perspective, being comprehensive gets us only so far. Jurisdiction is only important with respect to criminal justice approaches. As we shall see in the case of Somali-based piracy, there is no difference between territorial and international waters. In the interests of avoiding unnecessary complexity, the remainder of the chapter will focus on the use of force, at sea, to rob ships for private economic gain. I exclude military, terrorist, insurgent, or ostensibly political acts from consideration.

39.4 How Opportunity Shapes Maritime Piracy

This section articulates the main factors that shape the opportunities for (modern) maritime piracy. As other chapters in this volume attest, environmental criminology stresses the role that opportunities play in crime. Where crime is easier to commit, there should be more crime; crimes can be suppressed and offenders disrupted by making crime harder to commit. This is brought about by some combination of increasing the risks of being caught, increasing the effort of successfully exploiting criminal opportunities, and reducing the rewards of criminal opportunities (Clarke 1997, 1995, 2017).

Environmental criminology is a collection of three distinct theoretical approaches: the rational choice perspective (Cornish and Clarke 2017), the routine activity approach (Felson 2017), and crime pattern theory (Brantingham et al. 2017). Each aims to explain a distinct aspect of where and when crime occurs and how the crime commission process operates. The rational choice perspective explains how individual offenders weigh up criminal opportunities, underpinned by a bounded version of utility maximization. The routine activity approach posits the minimum ingredients for a crime event to take place; motivated offenders converge with suitable targets in the absence of capable guardians. Finally, crime pattern theory explains the spatial patterning of crimes and explains how offenders' awareness of criminal opportunities is bound by their everyday routines and how the search patterns for offending are partly bound by their activity space, the set of places where they spend the majority of the time (home, work, school, etc.), and the paths between them.

To understand why piracy may be subject to the same influences as terrestrial crimes it is useful to consider one of the fundamental constructs articulated by Patricia and Paul Brantingham that comprise crime pattern theory. The *environmental backcloth* is the culmination of the social, economic, political, and physical aspects of our society. It explains why and how individuals can move through society, constrains where and when we can move, and, most importantly, sets the baseline potential for crime.

Local government regulations on land use determine clusters of residential housing and housing density. These also, in turn, determine retail sectors, nighttime entertainment precincts, education, public health, and light and heavy industrial areas in a community. Layered on top of this is the transport infrastructure in the form of street networks and various forms of public transportation. These last two features determine the ambient population throughout a community, a core component of the opportunity surface for crime.

Of course, one of the limitations is that both land use and transport infrastructure need to observe the terrain of the environment. Rail is unlikely to be used for public transport in a hilly location, so buses will be preferred. Some cities have such steep inclines that funiculars[3] are used to move people. The point here is that the terrain and landscape shape much of the opportunity surface for crimes.

So much for terrestrial crimes. How does the environmental backcloth apply to maritime settings? Remarkably well, it turns out. Due to globalization, different nation states have specialized in manufacturing and extractive industries. Raw materials from Africa, South America, and Australia are transported to China, where they are transformed into all manner of consumer goods. These are transported around the world to consumers. This supply chain is designed to be an efficient distribution mechanism. And just like the network on land, merchant shipping uses shipping lanes. Figure 39.1 shows major shipping routes used by merchant shipping. Solid lines show routes that have high levels of traffic.

The importance of the sea lines of communication (SLOC) is they largely determine the potential for maritime piracy. Outside shipping lanes, there is an incredibly small chance that one would encounter a seafaring vessel, and even then it would almost certainly be a private one. So we would expect pirates to focus on shipping lanes, as they would be the most reliable place to find suitable targets. Car thieves focus on the street network and car parks to scan for suitable targets, and so pirates, we assume, do the same.

Transport infrastructure on land is constrained by the physical and legal dimensions that comprise the environmental backcloth; so too do these dimensions influence the

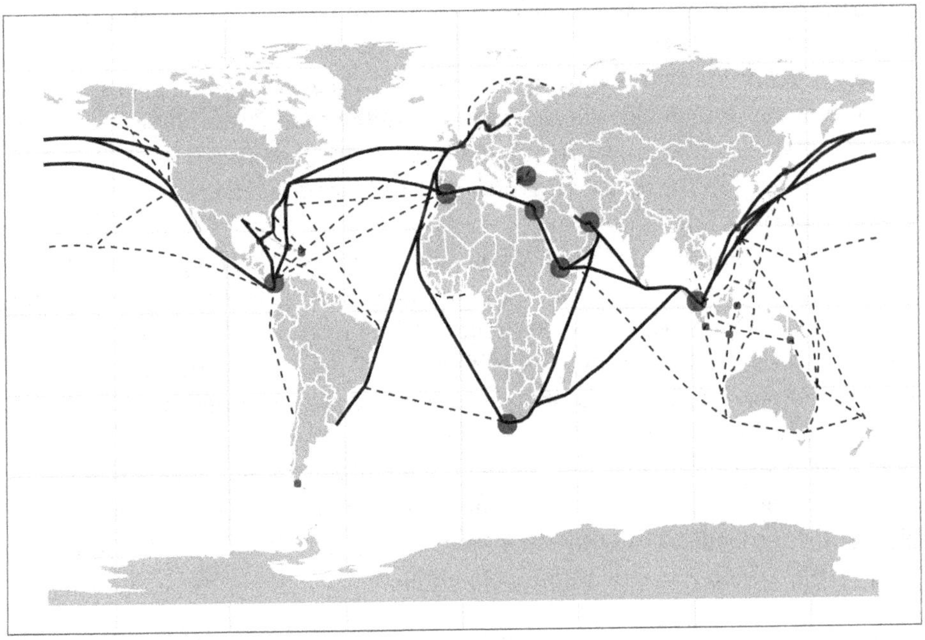

FIGURE 39.1 Worldwide merchant shipping lanes and strategic passages

maritime transport network. Physical barriers such as coastlines, capes, straits and reefs, ocean depth, wind, and currents all play a role in shaping the optimal route between two points worldwide. Legal constraints take the form of territorial waters for each nation state, within which passing vessels are bound to comply with the corresponding legislation and regulations.

Of these elements of the backcloth, one worth spending time considering is so-called *strategic passages* (depicted in Figure 39.1 by shaded circles). These are usually represented in the form of a naturally occurring strait (Malacca) or man-made passage (Suez Canal). Strategic passages are often referred to as choke points or bottlenecks by the maritime industry, for two reasons: (1) they are physically constrained in capacity, resulting in ships moving much slower through the body of water or being scheduled for transit; and (2) the volume of traffic moving through these nodes means that even modest disruptions have ramifications for the global supply chain of consumer goods and impact economies of many countries if not the world (Rodrigue et al. 2009). Well-known examples of strategic passages include the Suez Canal, the Panama Canal, the Strait of Malacca, and the Strait of Hormuz.

Thus, strategic passages are a necessary part of the maritime transport infrastructure, as they are part of the optimal route for shipping. Yet, because they are so critical, a net effect of high patronage is congestion. The very nature of these nodes is that capacity cannot be increased, and so merchant ships, replete with attractive and desirable cargoes, face the risk of being targeted by pirates around strategic passages. Not only are strategic passages located near landmasses (making it easy to launch pirate attacks) but merchant vessels move more slowly or are stationary around these locations, making them easier to overwhelm.

The two maritime factors informing the environmental backcloth considered thus far relate to physical and logistical constraints, in the form of the physical geography of oceans and seas. The final factor that informs the opportunity surface of piracy is the legal dimension. Unlike terrestrial problems, legality and sovereignty in the maritime realm are often unclear or disputed.

The UN Convention on the Law of the Sea (1982) defines a range of jurisdictions that set out sovereignty, responsibilities, and rights. Every nation state with a coastline has defined territorial waters up to 12 nautical miles from its coast. Within this space, that state's laws and conventions apply. Ships of all nations are granted the right of innocent passage into territorial waters. Between 12 and 24 nautical miles offshore is the contiguous zone, where states can exert limited control of their laws (e.g., customs, immigration, and environmental protections). Up to 200 nautical miles offshore is the exclusive economic zone, where states have full exploitation rights of the resources within the zone. States, however, cannot forbid passage or loitering in the contiguous or exclusive economic zones. Beyond the exclusive economic zone are international waters.

The UN Convention of the Law of the Sea applies in international waters. While it does define piracy (see earlier), Twyman-Ghoshal (2014) explains that the primary focus of UNCLOS was not criminal matters, but legitimizing territories for new (i.e., postcolonial) nations and enshrining passage rights for established nations. Of the 320 articles listed in the Convention, a mere seven relate to piracy.

Jurisdictional issues aside, a further inhibiting factor is that policing of the maritime realm is logistically infeasible. Murphy (2012) states that in 1945 global maritime dominance shifted from Britain to the United States. Britain (and other major players) continued to protect their interests into the 1970s, but their gradual reduction in influence has left a power vacuum. The major ramification of this change is the United States never saw national security as intertwined with trade to the extent that Britain did and so has not felt compelled to serve as the globe's maritime policeman.

The UNCLOS grants all states "the duty to cooperate in the repression of piracy" (Article 100), but even if pirates are apprehended, the prospects of going to trial and being found guilty and then sentenced are incredibly small. One study suggested that the vast bulk of arrests of pirates are "catch and release exercises" (Kraska and Wilson 2009). Unless a ship is able to defend itself or evade capture or seek help from a nearby vessel or naval ship, there is almost nothing to prevent a pirate from attacking. The size of the bodies of water that need patrolling and the number of units available to provide a deterrent are so misplaced that maintenance of order is an impossible task.

In summary, a range of constraints shape the spatial distribution and direction of the maritime transport industry worldwide. These constraints inevitably create locations and situations that are more advantageous for pirates than other locations. Consequently, we would expect a greater incidence of pirate attacks in particular situations, all other things being equal.

The final section of this chapter will focus on piracy in recent times. Highly detailed pirate attack data are available for the last 20 years, which permit an exploration of the factors underpinning pirate operations as well as piracy prevention activities.

39.5 Recent Piracy Patterns

There are two main sources of data on piracy, the International Maritime Bureau (IMB) and the Anti-Shipping Alert Message (ASAM) databases. The IMB database is used widely in academic research and has the advantage of focusing solely on piracy. Reports are collected from ships, so it can be thought of as a type of victimization survey. The weaknesses of these data are that incidents can include attacks at ports and the self-report nature of the information may underreport certain types of incidents.

The ASAM database is a composite of IMB data, naval, and coast guard reports, and newspaper reports. It seeks to capture threats in a maritime context, and thus is really designed to be a tool for naval intelligence. In this regard the incidents it captures are broader than piracy and can include incidents of a military or political nature. In addition, there is much less cleaning of this database—some incidents are duplicated, for instance. For a fuller treatment of the advantages and disadvantages of both data sets see Twyman-Ghoshal (2014) and Twyman-Ghoshal and Pierce (2014).

Unless otherwise indicated all of the data used in this section come from the ASAM database. It provides an additional 30% incidents over the IMB database, once duplicates and nonpiracy incidents are removed. In addition, all incidents occurring in ports have been removed. See Townsley et al. (2015) for a full description of the data processing used, which was based heavily on the procedure used by Twyman-Ghoshal and Pierce (2014) to establish a comprehensive piracy database.

39.6 Where Piracy Occurs

Figure 39.2 shows the spatial distribution of reported pirate attacks worldwide between 2005 and 2014 (this depicts a subset of the maritime realm but does capture both recent piracy hotspots). Pirate attacks cluster around the shipping lanes, which is entirely to be expected. Merchant vessels will only be found in shipping lanes and ports. What is noteworthy is the extent of concentration around a small number of locations around the world. This degree of concentration is remarkably similar to the sorts of spatial crime patterns observed on land. A small number of places account for a disproportionate amount of crime.

So what explains the degree of concentration and the location of pirate hotspots? Caplan et al. (2011) applied risk terrain modeling to maritime piracy to demonstrate that high-risk environments are the result of the spatial distribution of *the conditions suitable*

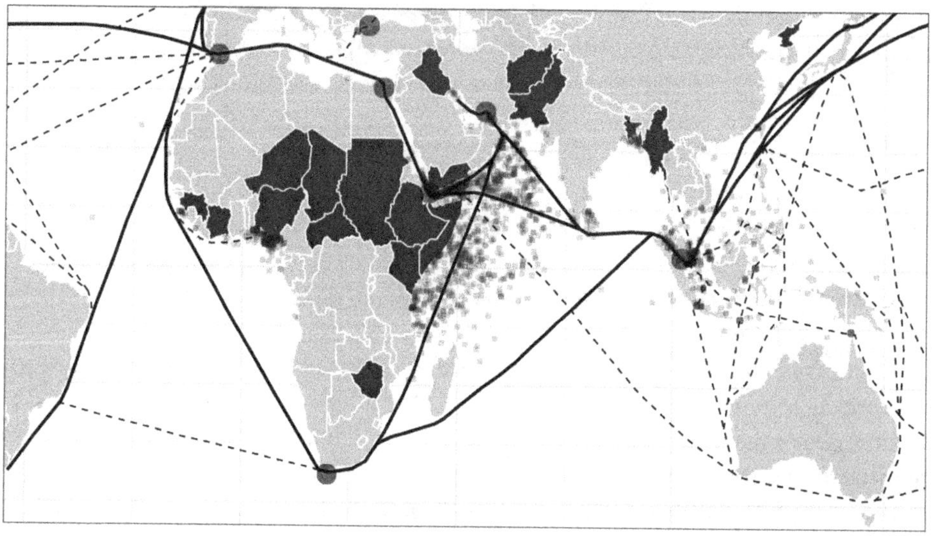

FIGURE 39.2 Spatial concentration of pirate attacks

for piracy. Risk terrain modeling creates a series of maps from disparate, spatially referenced risk factors and combines these into a "composite risk terrain" map. I want to unpack their results slightly to understand what the context is for maritime piracy and how well aligned it is to environmental criminology. The risk factors they used were national stability, maritime shipping routes, and locations of maritime choke points. Let us look at each of these in turn.

It is possible that piracy hotspots are located near countries that host or are unable to suppress pirates. Countries with this characteristic are likely to have disputed authority about the governance of the country (e.g., civil war), have a weak criminal justice system, or be unable to police their territorial waters.

Caplan et al. (2011) used the Fragile States Index (http://www.fundforpeace.morg/global/?q=fsi) as a measure of the stability of countries worldwide. It provides annual assessments of the stability and capacity of every country using 12 indicators across social, political, economic, and military dimensions. For the analysis here, for 2005–2014 (each year of pirate activity data) the countries in the highest-risk category were included.

Another factor that might influence the creation of pirate hotspots is strategic passages. Chalk (2008, p. xi) highlights "narrow and congested maritime chokepoints" that "require ships to significantly reduce speed to ensure safe passage, which dramatically heightens their exposure to mid-sea interception and attack" (see also Nincic 2002). In other words, locations near strategic passages will have a supply of targets that will be vulnerable with restricted capacity to evade attackers. This would seem, on the surface, to be ideal place for pirates to find suitable targets.

Figure 39.2 also depicts the strategic passages of the world (depicted as circles) as well as "fragile" states (shaded dark gray). Judging by eye, it seems there is a degree of spatial clustering between pirates' attacks and fragile states and strategic passages. An empirical question remains as to whether both conditions are necessary for piracy hotspot generation, specifically whether pirate activity concentrates around fragile nation states *or* strategic passages or both. This is a nontrivial question as state stability is something that can conceivably be alleviated through nation-building efforts, but strategic passages are a "hard" feature of the environmental backcloth. Their very existence is testament to the fact they are permanent and immovable on the sea lanes of communication.

To investigate this further, the distance in nautical miles to the border of the closest fragile state and the closest strategic passage was computed for every pirate attack in the data set. The minimum of both these distances was used to create a third distance measure. Gini coefficients were calculated for these three distances. The Gini coefficient is a common statistic used to quantify inequality in frequencies, most common in measuring income inequality (Milanovic 2011). A score of zero indicates perfect equality within the group; a score of one indicates extreme inequality (one person has all the income). To illustrate, income inequality in Sweden has been located somewhere between .25 and .35, and most large developed nations have scores about .4.

Our data revealed a Gini coefficient of .45 for strategic passages, .58 for fragile states, and .58 for both, indicating quite unequal distributions for all three distance measures. Figure 39.3 contains a graphical depiction of the Gini coefficient that is more revealing. It shows the cumulative proportion of pirate attacks (y-axis) taking place within cumulative distances of either strategic passages or fragile states (x-axis). The straight line at 45 degrees indicates an equal distribution.

For all three distances there is a skew toward shorter distances that is consistent with the aggregate Gini coefficient statistics. In other words pirate activity tends to be closer

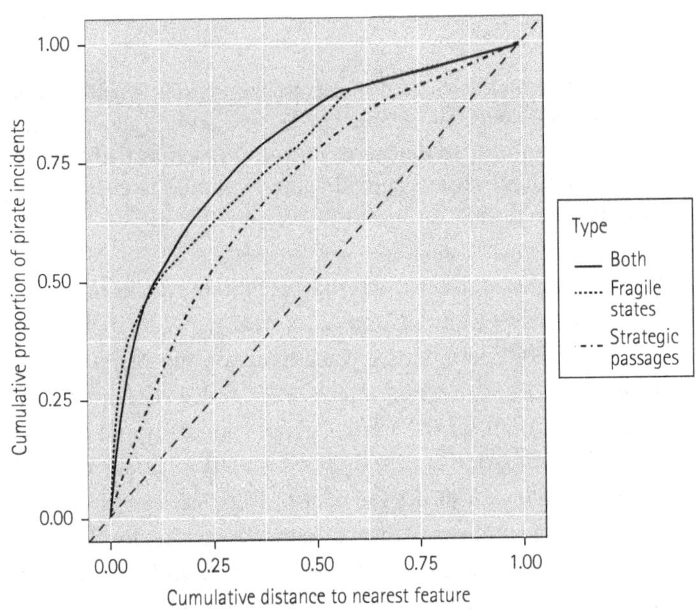

FIGURE 39.3 Concentration of pirate attacks around fragile states and strategic passages

to these features than not. Strategic passages had the lowest Gini coefficient, and the curve is the closest to the line representing equality. About 40% of pirate attacks occur in the closest 20% of distances from strategic passages (32 nautical miles, or 60 km), but the rate levels out after this point. The curve for fragile states is more extreme; nearly 40% of pirate attacks occur very close to the border of fragile states, around the fifth percentile (1.74 nautical miles, or 3.2 km). The smallest 20% of distances from fragile states (29 nautical miles, or 53 km) account for nearly 60% of pirate activity.

When the smallest distance between strategic passages *and* fragile states is considered, a very interesting pattern emerges. The initial trajectory is close to identical to the fragile states curve, but deviates from it and continues to display a higher level of skewness than the other two distance measures. This is illuminating because it suggests that pirate activity locations are a product of the spatial distribution of both fragile states *and* strategic passages. If the curve for the combined distances merely traced the fragile states curve, then we could infer that the primary factor for determining piracy locations was proximity to fragile states. But this result suggests that, consistent with the results of the Caplan et al. (2011) analysis, suitable environments for piracy are created by multiple factors.

39.7 What Ships Do Pirates Target?

Like other types of acquisitive crime, pirates evaluate potential targets and aim to select ships that are valuable or are easy to overpower or both. For instance, pirate gangs select targets to attack

> according to their size and calculated vulnerability, including low free board (the distance from the upper deck to the waterline); slow speed (generally less than 15 knots); the absence of on-board defensive measures (such as barbed wire and fire hoses); and medium to large tonnage (which are presumed to elicit higher ransom demands). (Chalk 2010, p. 92)

Mejia et al. (2009) examined the characteristics of pirate attacks taking place between 1996 and 2005. Their analysis went beyond most treatments by including information of the worldwide merchant fleet (ships greater than 300 gigatons). Many studies that associate ship characteristics with piracy attack risk simply use frequencies of attacks by ship type. This fails to account for the relative proportions of types of ships and can be misleading. If the ship population is included in calculation, attack rates by ship can be directly comparable. Figure 39.4 shows the relationship between pirate attack rates and the underlying proportion comprising the world merchant fleet for the major ship types.

The straight line represents equivalence of attack rate and ship type prevalence. If ships get attacked at relatively the same rate as their fleet proportion, they will be located close to the line. Those ships located above the line get attacked more than expected

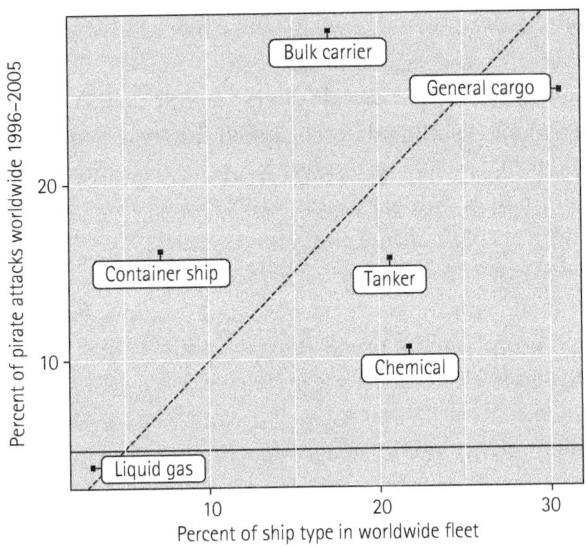

FIGURE 39.4 Container ships and bulk carriers attacked at higher rates than random chance

based on chance, and those under get attacked less than chance expectation. Only container ships and bulk carriers get attacked more than expected (liquid gas tankers are above the line but only marginally).

Cimpanu (2016) describes an extreme case of the targeting of valuable ships. A pirate group hired a hacker to access a shipping company's database and retrieved bills of lading, shipment schedules, and routes that were accessible because of insecure data practices. With this information the pirates could plan attacks more effectively and identify shipments with the most valuable cargo. During attacks the pirates used barcode readers to more efficiently locate high-worth cargo.

39.8 How to Prevent Piracy

In the first decade of the 21st century, the Horn of Africa became the global piracy hotspot, with headlines detailing multi-million-dollar ransoms, rescue operations, and violence (Charter 2011; Gaskell 2009; Guardian 2012). The response to Somali-based piracy was to put in place a series of initiatives to tackle piracy on land and at sea and to implement ship protection measures. Since their introduction, Somali-based piracy has all but disappeared.

The factors leading to the rise of Somali-based piracy are a mix of long-standing social and governance issues and relatively recent changes to the opportunity surface. The overthrow of the Saeed regime in Somalia in 1991 left the country without a government, and by extension no functioning criminal justice system and law enforcement capacity. The subsequent two decades saw continual civil war. This environment, punctuated by a number of droughts and famines, has produced a generation of young men without viable employment but with ready access to weaponry.

During this time Somalia's territorial waters were not policed, which attracted the attention of international fishing interests. Somali fishermen claim international companies illegally overfished in their waters. Without effective enforcement a group of fishermen took matters in their own hands and boarded several vessels, demanding tribute. So began the modern era of maritime piracy in Somalia.

Attacking fishing vessels was never going to lead to riches, however. The Gulf of Aden, the body of water that forms the northern border of Ethiopia, happens to have the second busiest shipping route in the world running straight through it. Nearly all of the goods out of China aimed for the European market (estimated at some 70%) as well as gas and petroleum transit the Gulf of Aden. It did not take long for the Somali warlords to realize this could be a lucrative business opportunity. Why simply mug a vessel when you could steal it? A typical merchant vessel is worth in excess of US$100 million, putting aside the value of the cargo and the crew.[4] Shipping companies lose money every day their vessels are not at sea, so owners often agree to ransom demands. Estimates of the economic impact of Somali-based piracy are difficult to calculate with precision, but Oceans Beyond Piracy (2014) claims the figure is as much as US$2.3 billion annually, excluding human costs.

In late 2008 and early 2009 the UN Security Council passed three resolutions (1816, 1846, and 1851) expressly permitting states to deploy tactics designed to suppress Somali-based piracy, thereby providing explicit grounds for international navies to intervene. UN Security Council Resolution 1851 established the Contact Group on Piracy off the Coast of Somalia (CGPCS), a broad coalition of states, organizations, and industry groups seeking to coordinate political, military, and other entities to abolish piracy in the region. It consists of five working groups, each concentrating on a discrete dimension of the piracy problem in Somalia:

- Working Group 1 focuses on military, operational, and capacity building (chaired by the United Kingdom).
- Working Group 2 focuses on deterring piracy through judicial mechanisms (chaired by Denmark).
- Working Group 3 collaborates with the commercial shipping industry to raise awareness and increase capabilities (chaired by the Republic of Korea).
- Working Group 4 raises awareness to the general public, especially Somalia, with respect to the impact of piracy (chaired by Egypt).
- Working Group 5 examines financial transactions with a view to disruption (chaired by Italy).

The CGPCS's substantive achievements include the coordination of joint naval operations off the coast of Somalia, the development and dissemination of best management practices (BMPs) for ship protection measures, and the establishment of the IMO Djibouti Code of Conduct Trust Fund.

39.9 Tackling Pirates at Sea

The CGPCS introduced two significant interventions to disrupt Somali pirates at sea. The first was joint naval patrols, comprising over 40 vessels (Bowden 2010), with the running costs estimated to exceed US$2 billion annually (Chalk 2012). The second change was establishing the Internationally Recommended Transit Corridor (IRTC). Vessels enter the IRTC at scheduled times, determined by ship speed, in order to travel in groups. These "group transits" are timed so that vessels traverse the area of highest risk at nighttime, which has the lowest piracy success rate (Tsilis 2011). Naval assets are focused throughout the IRTC in such a way as to provide the quickest response times to transiting vessels.

The twin impact of the IRTC and joint naval patrols was to generate a saturation patrol in the areas most associated with pirate activity. As a result, the favorable conditions sought by pirates in which to launch attacks occurred far less frequently. This meant that pirates would need to tolerate either more risky attacks or undertake greater preparations if they wished to continue operating. Analysis by Townsley et al. (2015) suggests a form of tactical displacement took place. While patrolling the IRTC did suppress pirate activity initially, pirates started attacking ships further out to sea, well into the Indian Ocean. This was only possible through the use of "motherships," larger ships that acted as sea-based operational bases. This facility greatly increased the pirates' operating range, which undermined the rationale of the saturation patrol tactic. Figure 39.5 shows the annual counts of pirate attacks at different locations (constructed as buffer regions around the IRTC).[5] It shows decreasing pirate activity inside the IRTC and its immediate vicinity every year since its inception in 2009. But there was a corresponding increase in piracy in other parts of the high-risk area, most notably the 10°–20° buffer region.

39.10 Tackling Pirates on Land

Bueger (2012) describes two classes of land-based initiatives implemented to disrupt Somali-based piracy. The first focused on bolstering criminal justice and law enforcement capabilities in Somalia and neighboring nations. Such programs include training and capacity building of the respective criminal justice systems. The second type of initiative is less centralized and is aimed at the clan or village level. These are typically community-based interventions, such as awareness raising or diversionary programs. The majority of land-based interventions fell in the former class. Townsley et al. (2015) examined their impact on pirate suppression and found no effect. Bueger (2012) reviewed the community-based interventions and concluded they were too small, vague, and unfocused to have any serious impact on Somali piracy.

Shortland and Varese (2014) do provide some optimism with respect to land-based approaches. Somalia is a clan-based society and, accordingly, clan elders play a critical

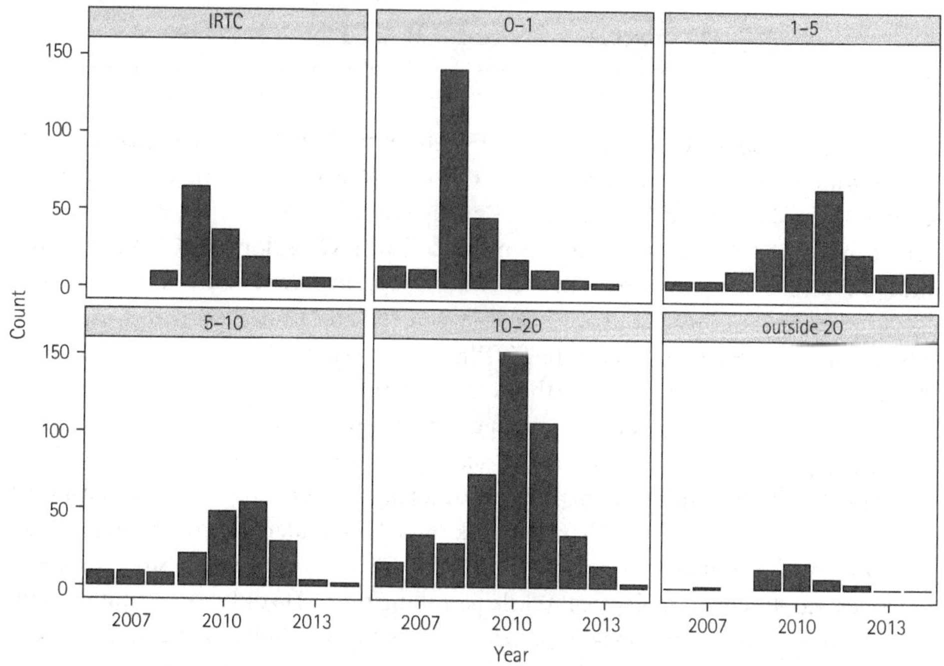

FIGURE 39.5 Annual counts of pirate activity in buffers around the IRT

role in condoning or condemning piracy. This is what Shortland and Varese define as the *protector's choice*. Clans that cooperate with pirate groups receive income (for protection, safe harbor, supplies, etc.). Thus, clans that have few or no legitimate sources of income are more likely to condone piracy, whereas those that do have alternative sources of income are much less likely to protect pirates. For instance, Shortland and Varese describe how politicians in the town of Eyl protected pirate enterprises as a means to fund a political campaign during 2008–2009. Once in power, local politicians abandoned piracy in favor of building infrastructure to connect with the transport network, greatly increasing the capacity for trade and legitimate income. Shortland and Varese (2014) suggest trade (or its taxation) is the most immediate, lucrative, and legitimate income source for clans. However, some clans are located far away from regional trading hubs, and the quality of roads is highly variable; during Somalia's monsoon season many roads are not usable. A clear role, then, for central government is to remove obstacles to free trade and other sources of legitimate income.

39.11 Target-Hardening Ships

Prior to CGPCS establishment there existed no crime prevention guidance for preventing pirate attacks, nor were there standard operating procedures in navigating known pirate hotspots (Hansen 2012). This has changed in two important respects. First, CGPCS Working Group 3 developed a guidance, known as best management practices (BMPs), detailing the most effective actions and precautions shipowners and masters can take to prevent pirate attacks. The first version (BMP1) was based on what worked for piracy during the 1990s and early 2000s in Southeast Asia, the South China Sea, and the Indian Ocean. Because Somali-based pirates operate differently than Asian pirates, BMP2 (August 2009) contained more specific and practical advice. BMP3 (June 2010) was even more specific (e.g., stipulating a minimum speed while transiting the Gulf of Aden) with a greater focus on "target-hardening" the ship. The current protocol is BMP4 (August 2011). The main difference between BMP3 and BMP4 was the inclusion of private military security contractors (PMSCs), both armed and unarmed, as stated ship protection measures. Throughout 2011 nearly all nations with significant maritime industries publically recommended the use of armed guards as a piracy countermeasure, a major reversal of position (Brown 2012).

There are 13 BMP4 situational measures that can be grouped into two categories: pre- and postboarding measures. Preboarding antipirate measures are designed to prevent boarding or securing physical access to the ship. These include (1) watch keeping and enhanced vigilance, (2) physical barriers; (3) water spray and foam monitors, (4) alarms, (5) evasive maneuvering, and (6) guards. Postboarding antipirate measures are aimed at delaying or stopping pirates from seizing the ship or crew once boarded. These include (1) enhanced bridge protection, (2) control of access to bridge, accommodation, and machinery spaces, (3) closed circuit television (CCTV), (4) upper-deck lighting, (5) denial of use of the ship's tools and equipment, (6) protection of equipment stored on the upper deck, (7) safe muster points/citadels, and (8) guards. Please refer to UK Maritime Trade Operations (2011) full details of each measure.

Several studies have attempted to evaluate the collective and individual efficacy of ship protection measures (Psarros et al. 2011; Shane and Magnuson 2014; Shane et al. 2015), but each has particular methodological problems. Individual measures are rarely used in isolation, so estimating the effectiveness of individual measures runs a risk of multicollinearity. In addition, regression-type techniques are limited to "all things being equal" caveats, which are highly impractical in the real world.

Bryant et al. (2014) took a different approach and used conjunctive analysis. This technique (see Miethe et al. 2008) partitions records into groups based on the presence or absence of the independent variables and computes a success/failure rate for the dependent variable for all cases within that group. This provides much more realistic findings because the collinearity of independent variables becomes a feature of the data, not a methodological problem. Bryant et al. (2014) found the combined use of watch keeping and enhanced vigilance (preboarding tactic 1) and a minimum of two other protective measures increased the chances of preventing pirate attacks to well over 90%.

Townsley et al. (2015) analyzed the collective impact of the CGPCS's activities. Situated in the routine activity approach, they argued the CGPCS was a type of *supercontroller*, an actor who can either help or hinder those in position to prevent

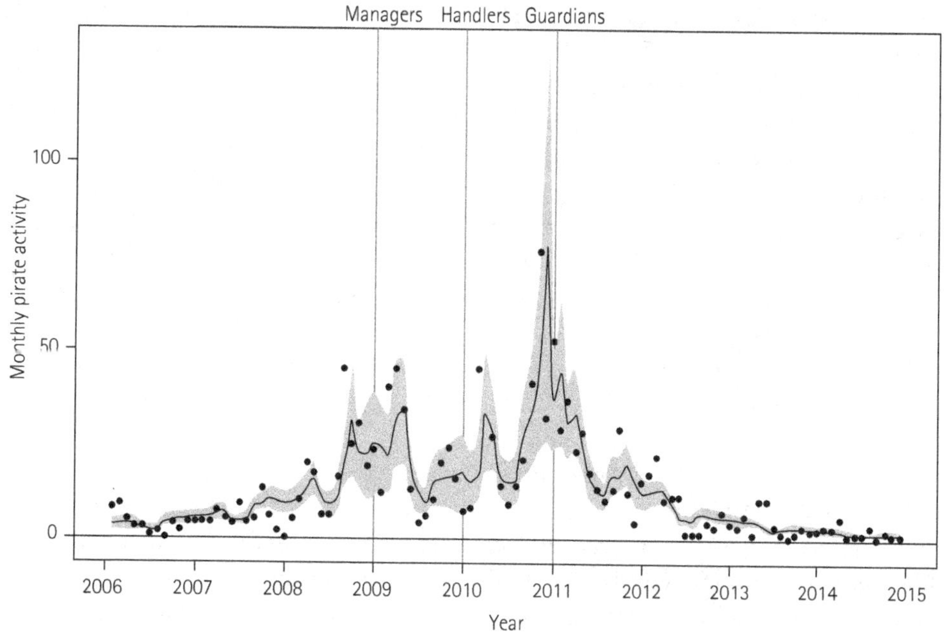

FIGURE 39.6 Time-series model of three major interventions

crime (Sampson et al. 2009). At an abstract level, the CGPCS *increased place management* (by joint naval operations and establishing the IRTC), *increased handlers* (establish pirate courts and prisons), and *increased guardianship* (developing BMPs). Figure 39.6 contains the time-series analysis evaluating the three types of interventions introduced by the CGPCS. The timing of the interventions is depicted with the solid vertical lines. The observed pirate activity is depicted by the filled circles, and time-series model is the solid dark line. A 95% confidence interval is indicated by the dark gray polygon.

Townsley et al. (2015) concluded that place management was effective, but did lead to spatial and tactical displacement. The criminal justice system changes had no impact, for reasons most likely related to obvious challenges in establishing effective deterrence. The ship protection measures appeared to be the most effective, with pirate activity effectively suppressed shortly after their introduction.

39.12 Conclusion

This chapter set out to explore how theories of environmental criminology can be used to provide insight into maritime piracy and its prevention. This was done in three ways. First, three different historical periods associated with piracy were briefly outlined and the means by which the piracy problem in each era was successively tackled described.

Second, several core environmental criminological concepts were defined and their relevance in a maritime setting was illustrated. Third, recent detailed incident level data on maritime piracy were analyzed to illustrate important patterns in pirate attacks. The emphatic suppression of Somali-based piracy was briefly explored.

It is intriguing to imagine what the future might hold for maritime piracy. Merchant shipping has taken considerable steps toward minimizing labor costs, with "skeleton crewing" now a widespread practice. The transportation industry has been tipped to be substantially disrupted with advances in automation, robotics, and autonomous vehicles, so one can only imagine a scenario where for, at least the majority of ship transits, container ships have no humans onboard. How this changes the opportunity structure is uncertain. The most effective ship protection measures (enhanced watch keeping, armed guards, and evasive maneuvering) require some form of active human intervention. It is likely that ships would be more vulnerable to attack as only passive ship protection measures would be in place and the ship and its cargo still remain valuable. On the other hand if much of the operation of the ship can be managed remotely, it may be possible that more active ship protection measures could be triggered remotely as well. Instead of armed guards, ships may carry drones, which could be deployed if onboard sensors detect suspicious activity from nearby ships.

Piracy, like many acquisitive crimes, exists because we allow it. Piracy appears to require three conditions to exist: access to suitable targets, a land base (i.e., port) for supplies and disposal of plunder, and a lack of enforcement at sea. It is this final aspect that is critical. Either through omission or commission, pirates have never been able to operate in an environment with effective place management.

Acknowledgement

I would like to thank Dr. J.-P. Rodrigue of Hofstra University in New York for kindly providing a digital map of maritime shipping lanes and strategic passages.

Notes

1. In addition, at the turn of the 17th century one of the Great Mughal's ships was attacked by pirates and he blamed Britain for the attack. Murphy (2012) argues that this provided the context for the English to get serious about piracy suppression.
2. While this region is associated with modern piracy, Elleman (2015) describes piracy existing in the waters of western India across to Indonesia for centuries.
3. Tram-like carriages that are moved up steep hills via cables.
4. Although these costs can be astronomical too. Bendall (2010) estimated that the *Sirius Star*, a very large crude carrier, was carrying $110 million worth of oil when it was overpowered by pirates.
5. Latitude degree is the spatial unit of the buffers. For locations close to the equator, 1° latitude is roughly 111 kilometers. The buffers we used were 0° to 1°, 1° to 55°, 5° to 10°, and 10° to 20°.

References

Anderson, J. L. (1995). Piracy and World History: An Economic Perspective on Maritime Predation. *Journal of World History*, *6*(2), 175–199.

Bendall, H. (2010). Cost of Piracy: A Comparative Voyage Approach. *Maritime Economics and Logistics*, *12*(2), 178–195.

Bowden, A. (2010). The Economic Costs of Maritime Piracy. Working paper, One Earth Future Foundation, Broomfield, CO.

Brantingham, P. J., Brantingham, P. L., & Andresen, M. A. (2017). The Geometry of Crime and the Rules of Crime Pattern Theory. In R. Wortley & M. Townsley (Eds.), *Environmental Criminology and Crime Analysis*. 2nd ed. New York: Routledge.

Brown, J. (2012). *Pirates and Privateers: Managing the Indian Ocean's Private Security Boom*. Sydney: Lowy Institute for International Policy.

Bryant, W., Townsley, M., & Leclerc, B. (2014). Preventing Maritime Pirate Attacks: A Conjunctive Analysis of the Effectiveness of Ship Protection Measures Recommended by the International Maritime Organisation. *Journal of Transportation Security*, *7*, 69–82.

Bueger, C. (2012). Drops in the Bucket? A Review of Onshore Responses to Somali Piracy. *WMU Journal of Maritime Affairs*, *11*(1), 15–31.

Caplan, J. M., Moreto, W., & Kennedy, L. W. (2011). Forecasting Global Maritime Piracy Utilizing the Risk Terrain Modeling (RTM) Approach to Spatial Risk Assessment. In L. W. Kennedy & E. F. McGarrell (Eds.), *Crime and Terrorism Risk: Studies in Criminology and Criminal Justice*. New York: Routledge.

Carafano, J. J., & Rodeback, J. (2011). *Taking the Fight to the Pirates: Applying Counterterrorist Methods to the Threat of Piracy*. Backgrounder No. 2524. Washington, DC: Heritage Foundation.

Carney, S. (2009, July 7). Cutthroat Capitalism: An Economic Analysis of the Somali Pirate Business Model. *Wired*, http://www.wired.com/politics/security/magazine/17-07/ff_somali_pirates.

Chalk, P. (2008). *The Maritime Dimension of International Security: Terrorism, Piracy, and Challenges for the United States*. Vol. 697. Santa Monica, CA: Rand Corp.

Chalk, P. (2010). Piracy off the Horn of Africa: Scope, Dimensions, Causes and Responses. *Brown Journal of World Affairs*, *16*(2), 89–108.

Chalk, P. (2012). Assessing the Utility of Current Counterpiracy Initiatives Off the Horn of Africa. *Studies in Conflict an Terrorism*, *35*(7–8), 553–561.

Chalk, P., Smallman, L., & Burger, N. (2009). *Countering Piracy in the Modern Era: Notes from a Rand Workshop to Discuss the Best Approaches for Dealing with Piracy in the 21st Century*. Vol. 269. Santa Monica, CA: Rand Corp.

Charter, D. (2011, September 8). Airdrop of $2.8m End Pirate Ordeal of Sailing Family. *The Australian*.

Cimpanu, C. (2016, March 2). Sea Pirates Hacked Shipping Company to Plan Attacks, Find Valuable Cargo. *Softpedia*, http://news.softpedia.com/news/sea-pirates-hacked-shipping-company-to-find-valuable-cargo-501268.shtml.

Clarke, R. (Ed.). (1997). *Situational Crime Prevention: Successful Case Studies*. 2nd ed. Monsey, NY: Criminal Justice Press.

Clarke, R. V. (1995). Situational Crime Prevention. In M. Tonry & D. P. Farrington (Eds.), *Crime and Justice: A review of research* (vol. 19, pp. 91–150). Chicago: University of Chicago Press.

Clarke, R. V. (2017). Situational Crime Prevention. In R. Wortley & M. Townsley (Eds.), *Environmental Criminology and Crime Analysis* (pp. 286–303). 2nd ed. New York: Routledge.

Cornish, D. B., & Clarke, R. V. (2017). The Rational Choice Perspective. In R. Wortley & M. Townsley (Eds.), *Environmental Criminology and Crime Analysis* (pp. 29–61). 2nd ed. New York: Routledge.

De Souza, P. (2002). *Piracy in the Graeco-Roman World*. Cambridge: Cambridge University Press.

Elleman, B. (2015). Historical Piracy and Its Impact. In G. J. N. Bruinsma (Ed.), *Histories of Transnational Crime* (pp. 9–40). New York: Springer.

Felson, M. (2017). Routine Activity Approach. In R. Wortley & M. Townsley (Eds.), *Environmental Criminology and Crime Analysis* (pp. 87–97). 2nd ed. New York: Routledge.

Forbes, A. (Ed.). (2011). *Australia's Response to Piracy: A Legal Perspective*. Canberra: Department of Defence Sea Power Centre.

Gaskell, S. (2009, April 14). Three Navy Seals Freed Capt. Phillips from Pirates with Simultaneous Shots from 100 Feet Away. *Daily News*, http://www.nydailynews.com/news/world/navy-seals-freed-capt-phillips-pirates-simultaneous-shots-100-feet-article-1.360392.

Geiss, R., & Petrig, A. (2011). *Piracy and Armed Robbery at Sea: The Legal Framework for Counter-piracy Operations in Somalia and the Gulf of Aden*. Vol. 1. New York: Oxford University Press.

Guardian. (2012, February 16). Italian Ship Fires on Indian Fishing Boat, 2 Dead. *Guardian*, http://www.guardian.co.uk/world/feedarticle/10096441.

Guilfoyle, D. (2010). The Laws of War and the Fight against Somali Piracy: Combatants or Criminals? *Melbourne Journal of International Law*, *11*(1), 141–153.

Hallwood, P., & Miceli, T. J. (2012). The Economics of International Cooperation in the Apprehension and Prosecution of Maritime Pirates. *Ocean Development and International Law*, *43*(2), 188–200.

Hallwood, P., & Miceli, T. J. (2013). An Economic Analysis of Maritime Piracy and Its Control. *Scottish Journal of Political Economy*, *60*(4), 343–359.

Hansen, S. J. (2012). The Evolution of Best Management Practices in the Civil Maritime Sector. *Studies in Conflict and Terrorism*, *35*(7–8), 562–569.

Hastings, J. V. (2009). Geographies of State Failure and Sophistication in Maritime Piracy Hijackings. *Political Geography*, *28*(4), 213–223.

Ho, J. (2009). Combating Piracy and Armed Robbery in Asia: The ReCAAP Information Sharing Centre (ISC). *Marine Policy*, *33*(2), 432–434.

ICC International Maritime Bureau. (2006). *Piracy and Armed Robbery against Ships: Annual Report*. Essex, UK: International Chamber of Commerce.

Kontorovich, E. (2012). The Penalties for Piracy: An Empirical Study of National Prosecution of International Crime. Faculty Working Papers 211, Northwestern University School of Law Scholarly Commons, Evanston, IL.

Kontorovich, E., & Art, S. (2010). An Empirical Examination of Universal Jurisdiction for Piracy. *American Journal of International Law*, *104*(3), 436–453.

Kraska, J., & Wilson, B. (2009). The Pirates of the Gulf of Aden: The Coalition Is the Strategy. *Stanford Journal International Law*, *45*(2), 243–287.

Leeson, P. T. (2009). *The Invisible Hook: The Hidden Economics of Pirates*. Princeton, NJ: Princeton University Press.

Leeson, P. T. (2010). Pirational Choice: The Economics of Infamous Pirate Practices. *Journal of Economic Behavior and Organization*, *76*(3), 497–510.

Liss, C. (2007). *Maritime Piracy in Southeast Asia and Bangladesh, 1992–2006: A Prismatic Interpretation of Security*. PhD dissertation, Murdoch University.

Lubberts, D. (2011). *Prosecuting Somali Pirates: Analyzing the Impact of EUNAVFOR's efforts*. Master's thesis, University of Twente.

Marchione, E., & Johnson, S. D. (2013). Spatial, Temporal and Spatio-Temporal Patterns of Maritime Piracy. *Journal of Research in Crime and Delinquency*, *50*(4), 504–524.

Marcus Tullius Cicero. (n.d.). *De officiis (on duties)*. Translated by Walter Miller. London: Loeb Classical Library.

Mejia, M. Q., Jr., Cariou, P., & Wolff, F.-C. (2009). Is Maritime Piracy Random? *Applied Economics Letters*, *16*(9), 891–895.

Miethe, T., Hart, T., & Regoeczi, W. (2008). The Conjunctive Analysis of Case Configurations: An Exploratory Method for Discrete Multivariate Analyses of Crime Data. *Journal of Quantitative Criminology*, *24*(2), 227–241.

Milanovic, B. (2011). More or Less. *Finance and Development*, *48*(3), 6–11.

Min, H. (2011). Modern Maritime Piracy in Supply Chain Risk Management. *International Journal of Logistics Systems and Management*, *10*(1), 122–138.

Murphy, M. (2012). Counterpiracy in Historical Context: Paradox, Policy, And Rhetoric. *Studies in Conflict and Terrorism*, *35*(7–8), 507–522.

Nakamura, M. (2009). *Piracy Off the Horn of Africa: What Is the Most Effective Method of Repression*. Technical report. Defense Technical Information Center, Naval War College, Newport RI, http://www.dtic.mil/get-tr-doc/pdf?AD=ADA503032.

Nincic, D. J. (2002). Sea Lane Security and US Maritime Trade: Chokepoints as Scarce Resources. In S. J. Tangredi (Ed.), *Globalization and Maritime Power* (pp. 143–170). Washington, DC: National Defense University, Institute for National Strategic Studies.

Oceans Beyond Piracy. (2014). *The State of Maritime Piracy 2014: Assessing the Human and Economic Cost Report*. Denver, CO: One Earth Future Foundation.

Psarros, G. A., Christiansen, A. F., Skjong, R., & Gravir, G. (2011). On the Success Rates of Maritime Piracy Attacks. *Journal of Transportation Security*, *4*, 309–335.

Ramsey, A. (2011). *Barriers to Prosecution: The Problem of Piracy*. Thematic Report. Civil-Military Fusion Centre.

Rengelink, H. (2012). Tackling Somali Piracy. *Trends in Organized Crime*, *15*(2–3), 180–197.

Rodrigue, J., Comtois, C., & Slack, B. (2009). *The Geography of Transport Systems*. 2nd ed. New York: Routledge.

Sampson, R., Eck, J. E., & Dunham, J. (2009). Super Controllers and Crime Prevention: A Routine Activity Explanation of Crime Prevention Success and Failure. *Security Journal*, *23*(1), 37–51.

Scott, K. (2014). *Prosecuting Pirates: Lessons Learn and Continuing Challenges*. Broomfield, CO: One Earth Future Foundation.

Shane, J. M., & Lieberman, C. A. (2009). Criminological Theories and the Problems of Modern Piracy. In M. R. Haberfeld, A. von Hassell, & A. Brown (Eds.), *Maritime Piracy and Maritime Terrorism: The Challenge of Piracy for the 21st Century*. Dubuque, IA: Kendall Hunt Publishing Company.

Shane, J. M., & Magnuson, S. (2014). Successful and Unsuccessful Pirate Attacks Worldwide: A Situational Analysis. *Justice Quarterly*, (ahead of print), 1–26. doi:10.1080/07418825.2014.958187.

Shane, J. M., Piza, E. L., & Mandala, M. (2015). Situational Crime Prevention and Worldwide Piracy: A Cross-Continent Analysis. *Crime Science*, *4*(1), 1–13.

Shortland, A., & Varese, F. (2014). The Protector's Choice: An Application of Protection Theory to Somali Piracy. *British Journal of Criminology*, *54*(4), 741–764. doi:10.1093/bjc/azu046.

Struwe, L. B. (2012). Private Security Companies (PSCs) as a Piracy Countermeasure. *Studies in Conflict and Terrorism*, 35(7–8), 588–596.

Sullivan, A. (2010). Piracy in the Horn of Africa and Its Effects on the Global Supply Chain. *Journal of Transportation Security*, 3(2), 231–243.

Townsley, M., Leclerc, B., & Tatham, P. (2015). How Super Controllers Prevent Crimes: Learning from Modern Maritime Piracy. *British Journal of Criminology*. doi:10.1093/bjc/azv071.

Townsley, M., & Oliveira, A. (2015). Space-Time Dynamics of Maritime Piracy. *Security Journal*, 28, 217–229, doi:10.1057/sj.2012.45.

Tsilis, T. (2011, June). *Counter-Piracy Escort Operations in the Gulf of Aden*. Master's thesis, Naval Postgraduate School, Monterey, CA.

Twyman-Ghoshal, A. A. (2014). Contemporary Piracy Research in Criminology: A Review Essay with Directions for Future Research. *International Journal of Comparative and Applied Criminal Justice*, 38(3), 281–303.

Twyman-Ghoshal, A. A., & Pierce, G. (2014). The Changing Nature of Contemporary Maritime Piracy Results from the Contemporary Maritime Piracy Database 2001–10. *British Journal of Criminology*, 54(4), 652–672. doi:10.1093/bjc/azu019.

UK Maritime Trade Operations. (2011). *Best Management Practices for Protection against Somalia Based Piracy: Suggested Planning and Operational Practices for Ship Operators, and Masters of Ships Transiting the High Risk Area*. Edinburgh: Witherby Publishing Group.

United Nations. (1982). United Nations Convention on the Law of the Sea. New York: United Nations.

Van der Meijden, L. R. (2008). *The Influence of Modern Piracy on Maritime Commercial Transport*. PhD dissertation, Erasmus University, Rotterdam.

Warner, L. A. (2010). Pieces of Eight: An Appraisal of US Counterpiracy Options in the Horn of Africa. *Naval War College Review*, 63(2), 61–87.

West, M., Cooper, T., & Kachoyan, B. (2010). AIS Analysis in Support of Counter-piracy Operations. *Australian Journal of Maritime and Ocean Affairs*, 2(4), 110.

Wheeler, J. (2012). The Importance of Privately Contracted Armed Security Personnel in a Multi-layered Defense. In N. Block and others (Eds.), *The Challenge of Piracy off the Horn of Africa: U.S. Policy in Dealing with Criminal Elements and Dangerous Non-state Actors*. Seattle: Henry M. Jackson School of International Studies, University of Washington.

Worrall, J. L. (2000). The Routine Activities of Maritime Piracy. *Security Journal*, 13(4), 35–52.

INDEX